קִצּוּר דִּקְדּוּק לְשׁוֹן עִבְרִי

A

COMPENDIOUS

HEBREW GRAMMAR.

BY

M. H. BRESSLAU.

PROFESSOR OF HEBREW, ETC.

LONDON:
JOHN WEALE, 59, HIGH HOLBORN.

M.DCCC.LV.

LONDON:
PRINTED BY J. WERTHEIMER AND CO.,
CIRCUS PLACE, FINSBURY CIRCUS.

CONTENTS.

SYNTAX.

HEBREW GRAMMAR.

CHAPTER I.

On the Consonants, Vowels, and Pronunciation of the Hebrew Language.

1.—The Hebrew, like most Oriental Languages, is read from right to left, and the alphabet consists of twenty-two letters, all consonants. Five of these, when used at the end of a word, take a different form, and are called finals; these are technically termed מנצפך *menatzphach.*

Those letters having a dot in the centre, called *dagesh*, have a harder pronunciation than when it is omitted.

Particular attention should be paid to those letters resembling ach other, as also to the difference between the שׁ and שׂ.

Hebrew Alphabet, etc., etc.

Biblical Characters.	Rabbinical.	Name.	Sound.	Numerical Value.
א	א	Aleph	A, feeble aspirat.	1
בּ ב	ב	Beth *or* Veth	B, V	2
גּ ג	ג	Gimel	G, as in *go*	3
דּ ד	ד	Daleth	D	4
ה	ה	He	H, aspirated	5
ו	ו	Vau	V	6
ז	ז	Zain	Z	7
ח	ח	Cheth	German *ch* in *auch*	8
ט	ט	Teth	T	9
י	י	Yod	Y, in *yes*	10
Finals. ך כּ כ	ך כ	Caph, Chaph	C, as in *call*, Germ. *ch* in *auch*	20
ל	ל	Lamed	L	30
ם מ	ם מ	Mem	M	40
ן נ	ן נ	Nun	N	50
ס	ס	Samech	S	60
ע	ע	Ain	*ng*, as in the French word *bon*	70
ף פּ פ	ף פ	Pe, Phe	P, Ph	80
ץ צ	ץ צ	Tsadik	Ts	90
ק	ק	Koph	K	100
ר	ר	Resh	R	200
שׂ שׁ	ש	Shin, Sin	Sh, S	300
תּ ת	ת	Tau, Thau	T, Th	400

2.—The six letters בְּגַד כְּפַת (technically called *Begad chephat*) as appears in the table of alphabet, have a dot in the centre. called *dagesh*, which when used, is placed in the above-mentioned etters to regulate the pronunciation; but every other letter (except the letters אהחעשר) also admits of a *dagesh*, though this does not effect any change in the pronunciation, denoting in general, different powers and significations in Prosody and Grammar, for which see Chap. IX.

3.—The letter ה when used as a possessive pronoun in the feminine gender, will be found likewise to have a dot in the centre, which is called *mappik* (מַפִּיק) and has thence a stronger aspiration than the common ה; as שְׁמָהּ her name, לָהּ to her.

CHAPTER II.

On the Division and Interchanging of Letters, etc.

4.—Letters are divided into five classes, according to the organs by which they are pronounced.

א ה ח ע Gutturals.
ג י כ ק Palatals.
ד ט ל נ ת Linguals.
ז ס ש ר ץ Dentals.
ב ו מ ף Labials.

Those letters which proceed from the same organ are frequently nterchanged with each other; as, מְתָאֵב for מְתָעֵב (Amos vi. 8); פְּסִחִים for פְּסָעִים (1 Kings xviii. 21); הַרְמוֹן for אַרְמוֹן (Amos iv. 3); קוֹבַע for כּוֹבַע (1 Sam. xvii. 38); יִסָּכֵר for יִסָּגֵר (Ps. lxiii. 12); חוֹמֵץ for חוֹמֵס (Ps. lxxi. 4); נִשְׁכָּה for לִשְׁכָּה (Neh. xiii. 7); זָעַק for צָעַק; גֵּז for פֵּזֵר; צָחַק for שָׂחַק, etc.

The letters ם and ן although not of the same organic sound, are ubstituted one for another: as, הַיָּמִין for הַיָּמִים (Dan. xii. 13); עֶשְׂתֹּנֹתָיו for עֶשְׁתֹּנֹת.

The letters ד and ר being nearly alike in form, are also frequently changed one for another: as, רִיפַת for דִּיפַת (Gen. x. 3); רַקּוֹת for דַּקּוֹת (*Ibid.* xli. 6, 19).

consonant is unaccompanied by any other vowel: as מֹשֶׁה *mo-sheh*: and when the ש has a point both right and left thus שׁ, without any other vowel-point to the right, it is characteristic of *sheen*, and that to the left is its accompanying vowel cholem: thus שֹׁנֶה *sho-neh;* but when that letter is accompanied by a vowel, then the point to the right is the cholem belonging to the preceding consonant, and that to the left the characteristic of *seen*: as נֹשֵׂא *no-sēh*. The characteristic point of *seen* serves likewise as its own vowel *cholem* when the latter is unaccompanied by any other vowel: as שׂנֵא *so-neh*,

8.—The י following the long chirik (as represented in the table of vowel points) is also omitted sometimes, but not often.

9.—The long shurek is always placed in ו, and is considered as the vowel belonging to the preceding consonant: as הוּ *hoo*, יוּ *yoo*, etc., excepting וּ at the beginning of a word; as וּקְשַׁרְתֶּם *oo-kee-shar-tem*, etc.

10.—(ַ) Patach under ע ח ה at the end of a word, is pronounced before its consonant: as אֱלֹהַּ *e-lo-ah*, God; רוּחַ *ru-ach*, wind; מַדּוּעַ *mad-du-ang*, why. But, according to Kimchi, these words are pronounced *Elo-wah*, *ru-wach*, *madu-wang*, as if the vowels were placed under the ו.

11.—When any one of the vowels ָ, ַ, or וּ is followed by י at the end of a word, a kind of diphthong is formed: as אֲדֹנָי *adonai*, the last syllable of which is pronounced as *ai* in Greek דַּי *dai*, as *y* in my; גּוֹי *goi*, as *oi* in moiety; גָּלוּי *galui*, as *oui* in French; but when followed by any other vowel, the preceding is only lengthened thereby, as עֲנִיִּים, גּוֹיִם, גְּלוּיִם. This remark applies likewise to the letters ו ה א, as קָרָא, בָּנָה, and תֹּהוּ.

CHAPTER IV.

On the Milrang, Milel, Metheg, and Makkaph.

12.—Besides the points aforesaid, there are other marks of different forms and powers, called *tonic accents* נְגִינוֹת טַעַם, which are placed above or below the letters; such accents when place on the last syllable are called מִלְּרַע : as שְׁמַע יִשְׂרָאֵל ; but when this accent is placed on the *penultima* it is called מִלְּעֵיל : as מֶלֶךְ, יֹשְׁבֵי, חֶסֶד.

13.—There is another accent, called *metheg*, which is a short perpendicular line: it is placed under the letters thus (אֽ), has but half the power of the accent called נְגִינָה, and may be considered among the accents, what the *sheva* is amongst the vowels. The metheg is generally placed, either on the third syllable before the accent: as אָֽנֹכִי, or before a sheva: as קָֽרְבָה.

14.—Makkaph is a small stroke, thus ־, between words joining them together, and generally follows words of one syllable; but in some instances it succeeds words of more than one syllable, which will be treated of in a future chapter, with the power and value of the accents.

CHAPTER V.

On the General Rules of Nouns and Pronouns.

15.—There are three forms of noun substantives:—1st. Radical nouns, i. e. such nouns as are composed of the same letters as the verb, without any addition; as דָּבָר *a word,* from דִּבֵּר *to speak.* 2nd. Formative or *Hemantiv* nouns, that is, such as are formed by having one or more of these letters האמנתיו, added to the root, or part thereof: as מָגֵן *a shield,* from גָּנַן *to shield*: מ is here the preformative letter. 3rd. Participial nouns; as רֹדֵף *a pursuer,* or *pursuing;* שׁוֹמֵר *a keeper,* or *keeping.*

16.—There are two genders in nouns, viz. masculine and feminine: as אִישׁ *a man,* אִשָּׁה *a woman.* When a noun without any variation is used for both genders, it is said to be common: as אֵשׁ *fire,* רוּחַ *wind,* שֶׁמֶשׁ *the sun.*

17.—The genders of nouns are known by their terminations, a noun masculine may have any termination except ָה, ַת, ִית, וּת, which are generally feminine: as נְקֵבָה *female,* גְּבֶרֶת *a mistress,* מִצְרִית *an Egyptian woman,* מַלְכוּת *a kingdom.*

18.—The numbers of nouns are generally but two, namely,

singular and plural, yet a dual number is met with in nouns which relate to things that are double by nature or art: as יָד *hand*, יָדַיִם *two hands;* רֶגֶל *a foot*, רַגְלַיִם *feet;* נַעַל *a shoe*, נַעֲלַיִם *shoes.*

19.—To form a noun plural from a noun singular, add, when the noun is of the masculine gender, the termination ־ִים to the noun singular: as שׁוֹר *an ox*, שׁוֹרִים *oxen.* But in nouns feminine, if the singular ends in ־ָה or ־ֶת change that termination into וֹת: as נְקֵבָה *a female*, נְקֵבוֹת *females;* עֲטֶרֶת *a crown*, עֲטָרוֹת *crowns.* If the noun singular terminate in ־ִית, change the termination into ־ִיּוֹת: as עִבְרִית *a Hebrew woman*, עִבְרִיּוֹת *Hebrew women;* and if the singular end in וּת, change it into ־ֻיּוֹת: as מַלְכוּת *a kingdom*, מַלְכֻיּוֹת *kingdoms.* The dual in nouns of either gender is formed by adding to the nouns singular the termination ־ַיִם (as noticed in the preceding rule); but if the feminine singular should end in ה, change it first into ת, and then add the dual termination: as שָׂפָה *a lip*, שְׂפָתַיִם *the lips;* שָׁנָה *a year*, שְׁנָתַיִם *two years.*

NOTE.—Some nouns, however, are irregular, having the masculine termination in the singular, and the feminine or both in the plural: as אָב *a father*, אָבוֹת *fathers;* צָבָא *a host*, צְבָאִים or צְבָאוֹת *hosts.* Others have the feminine termination in the singular, and the masculine in the plural: as אִשָּׁה *a woman*, נָשִׁים *women.*

20.—ה is sometimes prefixed to the noun, with the vowel kamets (ָ), or patach (ַ), and also, though but seldom, with segol (ֶ), is called the definite article הֵא הַיְדִיעָה.

21.—Nouns have no distinguishing marks of cases in themselves, that is, the form of the noun remains the same throughout with the exception of some nouns when in the possessive case but the cases are known by certain letters or particles respectively prefixed to the noun: as—

Nom.	סֵפֶר	a book
Gen.	שֶׁל־סֵפֶר	of a book
Dat.	אֶל־סֵפֶר or לְ	to a book
Accus.	אֶת־סֵפֶר	a book
Voc.	הַסֵּפֶר	O book!
Abl.	בְּ־מְ־מִן־סֵפֶר	from a book.

NOTE.—The signs of the genitive and vocative are generally omitted; the former is sometimes supplied by ה or has the sign of the regimen, which will be hereafter explained. The other prefixes are also used, at times, one for another, and either of them may be omitted or retained.

CHAPTER VI.

PRONOUNS, ADJECTIVES, ETC.

22.—The pronouns are divided into two general classes, namely, Separable and Inseparable; by the former is understood those which are separate and distinct words, and by the latter, syllables affixed to other words, either to nouns, verbs, or particles. To the first class belongs (I.) the nominative case of the three persons of the personal pronoun; (II.) the demonstrative; (III.) the relative; and (IV.) the interrogative. To the second class belong (I.) the rest of the cases of the personal pronouns; (II.) the possessive pronouns; and (III.) the pronouns affixed to verbs and particles.

TABLE OF SEPARABLE & INSEPARABLE PRONOUNS.

SEPARABLE.

Nominative Case.

I. Singular.

אֲנִי or אָנֹכִי	I, *com.*
אַתָּה	thou, *mas.*
אַתְּ	thou, *fem.*
הוּא	he
הִיא or הִוא	she

II. Plural.

אָנוּ אֲנַחְנוּ נַחְנוּ	we, *com.*
אַתֶּם	you, *mas.*
אַתֵּן or אַתֵּנָה	you, *fem.*
הֵם or הֵמָּה	they, *mas.*
הֵן or הֵנָּה	they, *fem.*

INSEPARABLE.

Affixes Singular to Nouns Singular.			Affixes Plural to Nouns Singular.		
—ִי	1st pers.	com.	—ֵנוּ	1st pers.	com.
—ֶךָ or —ָךְ —ְךָ	2nd	mas.	—ְכֶם	2nd	mas.
—ִיךְ —ֵךְ	2nd	fem.	—ְכֶן	2nd	fem.
וֹ—הֹ —ֵהוּ —ִיו —מוֹ	3rd	mas.	—ָם מוֹ	3rd	mas.
—ָהּ	3rd	fem.	—ָן	3rd	fem.
—ַי —ָי	1st	com.	—ֵינוּ	1st	com.
—ֶיךָ	2nd	mas.	—ֵיכֶם	2nd	mas.
—ִיךְ	2nd	fem.	—ֵיכֶן	2nd	fem.
—ָיו	3rd	mas.	—ֵיהֶם	3rd	mas.
—ֶיהָ	3rd	fem.	—ֵיהֶן	3rd	fem.

TABLE OF A NOUN SUBSTANTIVE WITH THE POSSESSIVE PRONOUN AFFIXED.

A word דָּבָר, a noun, sing., m.		*Law* תּוֹרָה, a noun, sing., f.
דְּבָרִי	my, *com.*	תּוֹרָתִי*
דְּבָרְךָ	thy, *mas.*	תּוֹרָתְךָ
דְּבָרֵךְ	thy, *fem.*	תּוֹרָתֵךְ
דְּבָרוֹ	his,	תּוֹרָתוֹ
דְּבָרָהּ	her,	תּוֹרָתָהּ
דְּבָרֵנוּ	our, *com.*	תּוֹרָתֵנוּ
דִּבְרְכֶם	your, *mas.*	תּוֹרַתְכֶם
דִּבְרְכֶן	your, *fem.*	תּוֹרַתְכֶן
דְּבָרָם	their, *mas.*	תּוֹרָתָם
דְּבָרָן	their, *fem.*	תּוֹרָתָן

†דְּבָרִים *Words*, a noun, m., pl.		תּוֹרוֹת *Laws*, a noun, f., pl.
דְּבָרַי	my, *com.*	תּוֹרֹתַי
דְּבָרֶיךָ	thy, *mas.*	תּוֹרֹתֶיךָ
דְּבָרַיִךְ	thy, *fem.*	תּוֹרֹתַיִךְ

---

* The termination ה in nouns fem. must be changed into ת before th possessive pronouns are affixed.

† The termination ם in nouns mas. pl. is rejected before the pronoun affixed, but the י is retained.

דְּבָרִים *Words*, a noun, m., pl.		תּוֹרוֹת *Laws*, a noun, f. pl.
דְּבָרָיו	his,	תּוֹרֹתָיו
דְּבָרֶיהָ	her,	תּוֹרֹתֶיהָ
דְּבָרֵינוּ	our, *com.*	תּוֹרֹתֵינוּ
דִּבְרֵיכֶם	your, *mas.*	תּוֹרֹתֵיכֶם
דִּבְרֵיכֶן	your, *fem.*	תּוֹרֹתֵיכֶן
דִּבְרֵיהֶם	their, *mas.*	תּוֹרֹתֵיהֶם
דִּבְרֵיהֶן	their, *fem.*	תּוֹרֹתֵיהֶן

Table of Personal Pronouns, Declined.

		First Person Singular.	First Person Plural.
Nom.	*com.*	אֲנִי I	אָנוּ *or* אֲנַחְנוּ we
Gen. & Dat.		לִי of, *or* to me	לָנוּ of, *or* to us
Accus.		אֹתִי me	אֹתָנוּ us
Ablat.		מִמֶּנִּי from me	מִמֶּנּוּ from us
		בִּי in me	בָּנוּ in us

		Second Person Singular.	Second Person Plural.
Nom.	*mas.*	אַתָּה thou	אַתֶּם you
	fem.	אַתְּ thou	אַתֵּנָה, אַתֶּן you
Gen. & Dat.	*mas.*	לְךָ, לְכָה, לָךְ of, *or* to thee	לָכֶם of, *or* to you
	fem.	לָךְ of, *or* to thee	לָכֶן of, *or* to you
Accus.	*mas.*	אֹתְךָ thee	אֶתְכֶם you
	fem.	אֹתָךְ thee	אֶתְכֶן you
Abl.	*mas.*	מִמְּךָ, מִמֶּךָּ from thee	מִכֶּם, מִמְּכֶם from you
	fem.	מִמֵּךְ from thee	מִכֶּן, מִמְּכֶן from you
	mas.	בְּךָ, בָּךְ in thee	בָּכֶם in you
	fem.	בָּךְ in thee	בָּכֶן in you

		Third Person Singular.	Third Person Plural.
Nom.	*mas.*	הוּא he	הֵם they
	fem.	הִיא she	הֵן they
Gen. & Dat.	*mas.*	לוֹ of, *or* to him	לָהֶם of, *or* to them
	fem.	לָהּ of, *or* to her	לָהֶן of, *or* to them

PERSONAL PRONOUNS (*continued*)

	Third Person Singular.		Third Person Plural.
Accus.	*mas.* אתו him		אֶתְהֶם *or* אֹתָם them
	fem. אֹתָהּ her		אֶתְהֶן *or* אֹתָן them
Ablat.	*mas.* מִמֶּנּוּ from him		מֵהֶם from them
	fem. מִמֶּנָּה from her		מֵהֶן from them
	mas. בּוֹ in him		בָּהֶם in them
	fem. בָּהּ in her		בָּהֶן in them

23.—The Relative Pronouns are אֲשֶׁר, שֶׁ, and ה, signifying *who*, and *which*, and are of the common gender: the two latter are used as prefixes; as to the first, although undeclinable like other pronouns, its cases are nevertheless defined in the same way as the personal pronouns: as—

Nom.	אֲשֶׁר	who
Gen. / Dat.	אֲשֶׁר לוֹ	whose / to whom
Accus.	אֲשֶׁר	whom
Abl.	אֲשֶׁר בּוֹ	in whom
	אֲשֶׁר מִמֶּנּוּ	from whom

24.—The Demonstrative Pronouns are:—

זֶה, הַלָּזֶה this *or* that, *mas.*
הַלֵּזוּ, זוֹ, זֹה, זאת „ „ *fem.*
זוּ and הַלָּז „ „ *com.*
אֵל and אֵלֶּה these, those, *com.*

25.—The Interrogative Pronouns are:—

מִי who, *or* what person, *com.*
מָה, מַה,* מֶה

ADJECTIVES.

26.—Adjectives agree with their nouns in gender and number: thus, אִישׁ טוֹב *a good man*, אִשָּׁה טוֹבָה *a good woman*, אֲנָשִׁים טוֹבִים *good men*, נָשִׁים טוֹבוֹת *good women*; and are either epithets or pre-

* מָה is used before the letters ר, ה, א, and מֶה before ע, ח.

dicates: they are generally placed after their respective nouns as qualifying words: as אִישׁ טוֹב *a good man*, not טוֹב אִישׁ, and take the article ה when the noun is in the definite state, or has any of the pronominal affixes, otherwise the attribute ceases to be the qualifying word, and becomes the predicate of the noun: as, הָאִישׁ הַטּוֹב *the good man*, הָאִישׁ טוֹב *the man is good*; בְּנִי הַקָּטָן *my little son*, בְּנִי קָטוֹן *my son is little*; אֶבֶן גְּדוֹלָה *a great stone*, הָאֶבֶן גְּדוֹלָה *the stone is great*.

Comparison of Adjectives.

27.—The degrees of comparison are expressed in Hebrew by prefixing to the nouns the letter מ or מִן as forming the comparative, or the letter בְּ for the superlative: thus, Positive גָּדוֹל *great*; Comparative גָּדוֹל מִמֶּנּוּ *greater than he is*; Superlative הַגָּדוֹל בְּכֻלָּם *the greatest of all*. The superlative is, however, often formed by the repetition of the adjective: as, עָמֹק עָמֹק *very deep*, or by the word מְאֹד *very much*; as, גָּדוֹל מְאֹד *very great*, כָּבֵד מְאֹד *very heavy*, etc.

CHAPTER VII.

On The Verbs.

28.—A verb in Hebrew is either perfect, defective, or quiescent; the first is called a regular verb, and the two latter irregular verbs. Verbs are regular when the root consists of three letters, which are commonly called radicals, each of which is distinctly sounded; in other words, when none of the letters א ה ו י נ form part of the root, and when the two last letters are not alike, e. g. לָמַד *lâmăd*, the verbs are called *perfect* (שְׁלֵמִים); where one of the above five letters forms part of the root they are *irregular*; if א ה ו י form part of the theme, they are called *quiescent* (נָחִים); if the נ be the first radical they are termed *defective* (חֲסֵרִים); and when the second and third radical letters are alike, receive the name of *doubles* (כְּפוּלִים).

29.—A verb has two numbers, two genders, and three persons, all of which with the exception of the third person masc. pret (which is considered the participle), are expressed by prefixes a suffixes, i. e. by a letter or syllable added to the verb, either the beginning or end of a word: as, לָמַד *he learned*, לָמְדָה *learned*, where the feminine gender is expressed by the additio ־ָה, לָמְדוּ *they learned*, where the third person plural is express by ו. In order to assist the memory of the student to retain t several letters, commonly called *serviles*, which are added to t verb to denote number, person, and gender, we will present th to his view in words instead of separate letters: thus, those us in the preterite tense as suffixes, form the word תְּהִימוּן; those the future tense form אֵיתָן; and the suffixes to the same יוֹנָה; tl latter word answers likewise to the suffixes of the imperati mood; but the future tense has, in addition to the affixes נָה one of the letters אֵיתָן also prefixed to the different persons; t participles have the same terminations as nouns, i. e. the femini singular ends in ־ָה or ־ֶת, and the plural in וֹת; the masculi singular may have any termination except the two mentioned, a its plural ends in ־ִים.

30.—A verb active has seven conjugations, or rather variatio and in each conjugation the verb expresses the same action various lights; thus the first conjugation (which on account of simple form, without any additional characteristic, except what required to denote the number, gender, and person, is called *light, unburdened*) expresses the action done, and is simply acti as פָּקַד: the second conjugation, which has נ prefixed to its ro is passive, and is called נִפְעַל; as נִפְקַד: the third conjugati which is characterised by *dagesh forte* (see Chap. IX.) in the seco radical, and a change in the original vowels, is likewise acti but denotes that the action is performed energetically, and called פִּעֵל, as פִּקֵּד: the fourth conjugation, which is likew known by *dagesh forte* in the second radical, and differs from t third in vowels only, is passive in the same sense as the third active, and is called פֻּעַל, as פֻּקַּד: the fifth conjugation, kno by ה prefixed, is active, and called הִפְעִיל, as הִפְקִיד, and whi is either causative, i. e. causing a person to act, or permitting h to act: the sixth conjugation, known likewise by ה prefixed, but pointed with *kamets* (ָ), is passive in the same as the fifth is active, and is called הָפְעַל, as הָפְקַד; the seventh conjugation, distinguished by הִתְ prefixed, and the *dagesh forte* in the second radical, is commonly used specifically or reciprocally, sometimes is passive like the second conjugation, and in a few instances denotes acting under pretence or disguise, and is called הִתְפַּעֵל, as הִתְפַּקֵּד.

31.—The tenses in the Hebrew are but two, viz. past and future, and even these two are not always used with the same precision as they are in the Western languages, for at times the past tense is used, where, according to the context, the future ought to be used, and the future instead of the past; so that reader or hearer must determine the time spoken of by the context and connection.

32.—Instead of the present tense, the participle active is sometimes used, but more frequently both the past and future tenses are used for the present.

There are two participles in the first conjugation, namely, active and passive, or, as some grammarians have designated them, present and past participles; but by the Jewish grammarians they are called בֵּינוֹנִי and בֵּינוֹנִי פָּעוּל; the former name is derived from בֵּין *between*, not expressing, as some grammarians have erroneously supposed, a time between the past and the future, but from its being between the noun and the verb; פָּעוּל is so called from its passive form, as will be seen in the paradigm.

33.—There are three moods: Indicative, Infinitive, and Imperative, in every conjugation, except פֻּעַל and הָפְעַל which have no imperative mood.

34.—In the imperative mood we have only the second person and two genders; namely, masculine and feminine. Instead of the third person in the imperative mood used in the Western languages, the Hebrews use the third person of the future tense

35.—In verbs whose radical is one of the letters שׂ, שׁ, צ, ס, I we find either that one of these letters is transposed with ת, th characteristic of the Hithpael conjugation, or sometimes that I thus transposed is again changed into ד or ט: as from זִמֵּן *to ap point time,* Hithpael הִזְדַּמֵּן: the letter ד is here instead of ת fo הִתְזַמֵּן, and however the example is found in the Chaldaic Boo of Daniel, there is no doubt that euphony would require the sam change in Hebrew. From סָתַר *to conceal,* Hith. הִסְתַּתֵּר; here th ת and ס are transposed: from צָדַק *to justify,* Hith. הִצְטַדֵּק fo הִתְצַדֵּק: from שָׁמַר *to keep,* Hith. הִשְׁתַּמֵּר: from שָׂרַר *to be maste* Hith. הִשְׂתָּרֵר for הִתְשָׂרֵר.

36.—The foregoing paradigm will serve as an example for a regular verbs, and the import of the several conjugations, is a given in Rule 30.

37.—In some verbs, the second radical in the root is (ֵ), o (cholem ֹ), instead of (ַ): as חָפֵץ *to be willing,* מָלֵא *to be full* קָטֹן *to be little,* יָכֹל *to be able,* most of such verbs are intransitive.

38.—A verb has no participle passive, where the first, or ק conjugation is intransitive; and some intransitive verbs hav neither participle active nor passive in קַל; but the adjective i used instead of both: as, קָרוֹב *near,* רָחוֹק *distant,* קָטוֹן *little,* from קָרַב *to approach,* רָחַק *to be at a distance,* קָטֹן *to be small.*

39.—When the קַל conjugation is intransitive, the פִּעֵל or הִפְעִיל is used transitively: as עָמַד *he stood,* הֶעֱמִיד *he placed*; in a few instances only we find that even פִּעֵל and הִפְעִיל remain intransitive and their power is merely emphatic: as צָמַח and צִמֵּחַ *to grow* there are likewise some verbs where קַל is used intransitively i one verb, and for the transitive sense of it, the הִפְעִיל of anothe verb is used: as from שָׁתָה *he drank,* הִשְׁתָּה is not used, bu הִשְׁקָה *he gave to drink,* or *watered,* from the root שָׁקָה.

40.—The second conjugation, which is generally passive, an the patient of קַל the agent, is, in a few instances, the patient o פִּעֵל or הִפְעִיל: as from הָיָה *he was,* is formed נִהְיָה, which canno be the patient of קַל, but must be that of הִפְעִיל, although the verb is not found in הִתְפַּעֵל: and so נָגַשׁ, קָרַב, and the like verbs.

41.—One of the letters בְּכְלַם is frequently prefixed to an infinitive; the infinitive is then used as a gerund, and the signification of these prefixes is the same as when prefixed to nouns.

42.—When the future tense is intended for the preterite, it is known by the vowel point under the ו prefixed to the future, which is then (ָ) or (ַ): namely, (ָ) if the following letter is א, וָאֹמַר *I said:* but (ַ) if the following letter be either נ, ת, or י, in which case, the letters נ, ת, י, have also *dagesh forte:* as וַיִּתֵּן *he gave,* וַתֵּלֶךְ *she went,* וַנֹּאמֶר *we said,* except before a *yod* י with (ְ) sheva: as וַיְהִי.

43.—It will be observed from the foregoing paradigm, that the first radical י is changed into ו, in נִפְעַל, הִפְעִיל, and הָפְעַל; and in the future of קַל the deficiency of י is compensated by ֵ under the letters אֵיתָן instead of short chirik (ִ) or segol (ֶ), which those letters have in the regular verbs, for the vowel (ֵ) implies י although this letter is not always expressed: for example, we find וַיַּבְדֵּל *he separated,* Gen. i. 4, instead of יַבְדִּיל third person future, Hiphil.

44.—Some verbs, however, of the form נחי פי retain י radical in the future of קַל: as from יָבֵשׁ *to dry up,* the future tense is formed as follows:—

אִיבַשׁ	תִּיבְשִׁי	תִּיבַשׁ	תִּיבַשׁ	יִיבַשׁ
נִיבַשׁ	תִּיבַשְׁנָה	תִּיבְשׁוּ	תִּיבַשְׁנָה	יִיבְשׁוּ

45.—In the two verbs ירה and יחל, the first radical י is retained in the future נִפְעַל: as יִיָּרֶה for יִוָּרֶה *he shall be shot,* Exod. xix. 13; and וַיִּיָּחֶל for וַיִּוָּחֶל *he waited,* Gen. viii. 12.

46.—In the following eight verbs, when the first י is omitted, compensation is made by *dagesh forte* in the second radical, as in the defective verbs: as from יָנַח *to permit,* הִנִּיחַ; from יָצַר *to form,* אֶצֹּר; from יָצַק *to pour out,* אַצִּיק; from יָצַע *to spread,* אַצִּיעַ; from יָצַג *to place,* הַצֵּג; from יָצַב *to stand,* הִצִּיב; from יָקַף *to encompass,* הַקֵּף; and from יָצַת *to kindle,* הַצֵּת.

CHAPTER VIII.

On the Changes of the Vowels.

47.—The student must have observed in Chap. III. that (ָ is sometimes a long vowel, and corresponding to *a* in *parlou* whilst at other times it is a short *o*. To distinguish one from th other, regard must be had to the subsequent letter ana points thus, (ָ) is short and pronounced as *o*, whenever it is without *metheg* (ֽ), and followed by a (ְ); or without an accent an followed by a dageshed letter; or followed by a consonant with out a vowel at the end of a word, when at the same time th accent is upon the penultima, or before the (ֳ): as חָכְמַת *th wisdom of,* חָגָּא *terror,* וַיָּקָם *he arose,* אָהֳלוֹ *his tent*; IN EVER OTHER CASE THE (ָ) IS LONG.

48.—It has been said (in Rule 6) that the three compoun vowels (ֳ ֲ ֱ) occur under gutturals, where another lett would only take (ְ), and the student must now remark, th whenever gutturals have one of these compounds, the precedin short vowel is changed into the same vowel as that under th guttural, but unaccompanied with (ְ): as יַעֲמֹד *he shall stan* for יִעְמֹד, which ought to be the vowels, according to the paradig לְמֹד; but (ְ) under ע is changed into (ֲ), which causes (ִ under the *yod* to be changed into (ַ).

(ְ) is sometimes dropped, and the vowels (ָ ַ ֶ) remai and yet the preceding vowel must be the same as if followe by a compound: as יַעַשׂ third person, future tense, Kal, fro עָשָׂה; here, in consequence of ה being dropped, which deprives of its vowel, and unites it in the same syllable with ע, it is require that the letter ע should have (ַ) instead of (ֲ), else neither nor ע could be properly pronounced.

But as the gutturals, in some instances, like every other lette have (ְ) alone, it is necessary to point out when they ought t have one or the other. In cases where (ְ) would be pr nounced if the consonant were no guttural, there the guttura must invariably have a compound vowel, the variation will consequently only occur where the single (ְ) would remain quiescent under a letter not guttural, and hence the following Rules must be observed:—

(1)—Single (ְ) under a guttural takes place when the following letter is the pronominal affix, and the accent precedes it; as, יָדַעְתִּי *I know*, שְׁלַחְנוּ *we have sent;* but if the accent follow in the next syllable, the gutturals have the compound vowel; as, וְהוֹקַעֲנוּם *and we will hang them up*, נְגַעֲנוּךָ *we touched thee.*

(2)—Single (ְ) also finds a place when י accompanied by a vowel follows the guttural; as, מַעְיָן *a fountain*, מִחְיָה *sustenance*, etc., except in the following instances, לֶחֱיָהּ *her cheek*, as well as the Hiphil of חָיָה *to live*, הֶחֱיָה *he revived.*

49.—As two (ְ), or compound (ֲ), and simple (ְ) under the first two letters of a word or syllable cannot be pronounced, the first (ְ) is changed commonly into a short vowel; thus, if a compound (ֲ) follow one of the prefixed וכלב, which prefixes would, according to Rule 48, require (ְ), the (ְ) is changed into the same vowel as the compound following; as, וַאֲכַלְתֶּם *and ye shall eat*, כַּאֲשֶׁר *according as*, לֶחֳדָשָׁיו *to his new moons*, except where the compound occurs in any part of the verb הָיָה and חָיָה, for in these the compound is changed into single (ְ), and the prefixes take (ִ) or (ֶ); as, בִּהְיוֹת *in being*, לִהְיוֹת *to be*, וִחְיִיתֶם *and ye lived*, וֶחְיֵה *and live*. In most cases, where the gutturals have (ֱ) and, consequently, the prefix ought to have (ֶ), the points are changed into (ֵ), which is placed under the prefix, and the guttural has no vowel, but remains quiescent; as, לֵאמֹר *to say*, for לֶאֱמֹר; בֵּאלֹהִים *by God*, for בֶּאֱלֹהִים; some of those which have (ֲ) likewise reject it, and the prefix retains (ַ): בַּאדֹנָי *in the Lord*, for בַּאֲדֹנָי, and in one instance, וְאַעַנֶּה *and I will afflict*, 1 Kings 11: 39, for וַאֲעַנֶּה; but if those prefixes which ought to have (ְ) are followed by any letter not guttural, which has (ְ), in that case, the prefixes כלב generally change their (ְ) into (ִ); as, בִּרְנַּת *over the fishes of*—, לִזְכּוֹר *to remember;* but וְ is changed into וּ; as, וּשְׁמַע *and hear*, and before (ְ) when י remains without any vowel; as וִיהִי *and shall be*, for וְיְהִי.

CHAPTER IX.

On the Dagesh.

50.—Having already mentioned that a dot placed in the letter בגד כפת is sometimes called *dagesh lene*, and causes those letter to be pronounced differently from what they are when they hav no dagesh; but that a dagesh will sometimes be placed in ar other letter, as well as in these six, for other purposes, and called *dagesh forte*; we come now to point out when they a *dageshed*, and when they are not so; and when the dagesh is t be considered as *lene* or *forte*.

בגד כפת have *dagesh lene*—

1.—When they are placed at the beginning of a word, ex cept where the last letter is one of the quiescent letter אהוי, and without a pause accent; as, בָּרַךְ *blesse* הָיְתָה תֹהוּ *was formless*, etc. The ת in תֹהוּ is n *dageshed*, because the preceding word terminates in quiescent ה. The הּ with the dot in it, called *mapp* at the end of a word, is not considered a quiesce letter.

2.—In the middle and end of a word, after a quiescent (ְ as נִלְבְּנָה *we will make bricks*, לָמַדְתְּ *thou didst learn*, b in every other case they have no dagesh lene, whil they may have a dagesh forte, like every other lett אהחער excepted.

51.—The use of dagesh forte is said to be either necessa or euphonic. Necessary, when it is to supply the deficiency some other letter; as, יִגַּשׁ *he shall approach*, from the root נָגַשׁ; where the dagesh in גּ (by which means that letter is doubled pronunciation, and the word is pronounced *yig-gash*) denotes th the first radical is rejected. And also where it is characteristic of the conjugations, such as Piel, Pual, and Hithpael, where the second radical is dageshed, to denote the respective conjugations. It is euphonic after a short vowel; as, קְטַנִּים *little*, after the prefixes הַ, the article, and וַ conversive, and after a long vowel with an accent; as, לָמָּה *wherefore*, שָׁמָּה *there*.

CHAPTER X.

On the Classification of Nouns.

52.—As a general rule (stated in R. 19, p. 8) the genders of nouns are known by their terminations, namely, nouns feminine end in ָה or ת (the cardinal numbers are an exception to that rule), and the nouns of the masculine gender, in any other terminations; but as there are several exceptions to this general rule, both in proper names and others, as well in substantives as in adjectives, we think it necessary to notice some other characteristics by which the genders of nouns may be known with more certainty.

Masculine nouns are:—

1.—The proper names of men, whatever their termination may be; as, שְׁמוּאֵל, מֹשֶׁה, etc.

2.—Offices filled by men; as, מֶלֶךְ *a king*, שַׂר *a ruler*, etc.

3.—Names of nations; as, יִשְׂרָאֵל, יְהוּדָה, etc.

4.—Names of rivers; as, יַרְדֵּן, חִדֶּקֶל, פְּרָת, etc.

5.—The months; as, זִיו, אֲדָר etc.

6.—Mountains; as, סִינַי, כַּרְמֶל, etc.

7.—Nouns which terminate either in a radical letter, or in one of the serviles אנם; as, מִבְטָא *pronunciation*, from בָּטָא; פִּדְיוֹן *ransom;* from פָּדָה, etc. The exceptions are the following, which are feminine: אֶבֶן, אָוֶן, אַמָּה, אֲשׁוּר, בְּאֵר, גֹּרֶן, חֶרֶב, יָתֵד, כַּר, כּוֹס, כִּכָּר, נָוֶה, צָב, עַיִשׁ, עֶרֶשׂ, פַּת, צָפוֹן, שְׁלָו, תֵּבֵל, and those nouns which have a dual number.

Feminine nouns are :—

1.—Proper names of women ; as, רִבְקָה, רָחֵל, etc.

2.—Most members of the human body ; as, לְחִי, בֶּטֶן, etc.

3.—Names of cities ; as, חֶבְרוֹן, יְרוּשָׁלַיִם, etc.

4.—Names of countries ; as, מָדַי, פָּרַס.

Nouns of common gender are : גַּן, שָׁמִיר, בֶּגֶד, אָרוֹן, אֹרַח, אֳנִי, שֵׁבֶט, חֶבֶל, הָמוֹן, שֶׁמֶשׁ, רֹתֶם, רִצְפָּה, סִיר, מַטֶּה, מַחֲנֶה, יָצִיעַ, חַלּוֹן, גֶּפֶן; the three last-mentioned nouns are, however, for the most part used as masculine; the following are generally feminine : אֶרֶץ, שַׁבָּת, רְחוֹב, רוּחַ, קֶשֶׁת, עֵת, נֶפֶשׁ, יוֹבֵל, חָצֵר, דֶּרֶךְ, דֶּלֶת, גֶּדֶר, אֵשׁ, אוֹת, שְׁאֹל, תְּהוֹם, תַּעַר. Some names of animals are found in the masculine gender only ; as, עַיִט, שָׁפָן, נֶשֶׁר, עוֹף, עַכְבָּר, חֲזִיר, כֶּלֶב, בָּקָר: and others feminine only ; as, יַעֲנָה, דַּיָּה, חֲסִידָה, יוֹנָה, אַרְנֶבֶת.

CHAPTER XI.

53.—With regard to the numbers of nouns, which have been noticed in Rule 18, we now observe, that some nouns are used in the singular, some in the dual, and others in the plural only.

Those used in the singular number are proper names; as, מֹשֶׁה, דָּוִד, אַהֲרֹן. The names of metals and minerals; as, בַּרְזֶל, זָהָב, כֶּסֶף, מֶלַח, גָּפְרִית, עֹפֶרֶת, נְחֹשֶׁת, בְּדִיל; we find, however, כַּסְפֵּיהֶם, which is in the form of a noun plural, with the possessive pronoun, but it may be said to refer to silver coin, as בְּדִילָיִךְ refers to the dross mixed with the metal.

The names of liquids; as, דְּבַשׁ, יִצְהָר, תִּירוֹשׁ, יַיִן; those used in the dual are : אַפְסַיִם, פַּחֲדַיִם, עַפְעַפַּיִם, מָתְנַיִם, מֵעַיִם, מַיִם, צָהֳרַיִם, שָׁמַיִם, מִכְנָסַיִם, מֹאזְנַיִם, רֵחַיִם, כִּירַיִם, כִּלְאַיִם, אָבְנַיִם, יְרוּשָׁלַיִם, מִצְרַיִם, חָפְנַיִם, מִשְׁפְּתַיִם, שְׁפָתַיִם.

Those which have the plural only are : זְקוּנִים, נְעוּרִים, עֲלוּמִים, בְּתוּלִים, מְתִים, חַיִּים, פָּנִים, טְנִים, טוּחוֹת, יָעִים.

Those that are used in the singular and dual number are : אַף, עַיִן, אֹזֶן, שֵׁן, יָד, רֶגֶל, בֶּרֶךְ, יָרֵךְ, צִפֹּרֶן, קַרְסֹל, שׁוֹק, שַׁד, some of these nouns have also a plural, but then they do not refer to parts of the body; as, עֵינוֹת, which is the plural of עַיִן, signifies in the plural number, *wells*, not *eyes*.

Those which have three numbers, singular, dual, and plural, are: בֶּרֶךְ, אֶלֶף, מֵאָה, פַּעַם, נַחַל, מַחֲנֶה, שָׁנָה, יוֹם, שָׂפָה, קֶרֶן, כַּף, כָּנָף.

54.—The exceptions to Rule 19, where it has been stated that a noun masculine becomes plural by adding ־ִים, and a noun feminine by changing ־ָה into וֹת, are in the following nouns, where the singular masculine has the termination וֹת in the plural number; אָב sing., אָבוֹת pl.; דָּרְבָן, גּוֹרָל, גַּג, בּוֹר, אַרְמוֹן, אֶשְׁכֹּל, אוֹצָר, אוֹב, מֵסַב, מָטָר, מַזְלֵג, מִזְבֵּחַ, לַיִל, לוּחַ, כִּסֵּא, טֶפַח, חֶשְׁבּוֹן, חֲלוֹם, חָזֶה, זָנָב, קִיר, קוֹל, צְרוֹר, צָבָא, עֵשֶׂב, עָפָר, עוֹר, נֵר, נָוֶה, נֹאד, מַקֵּל, מָקוֹם, מַעֲשֵׂר, תְּהוֹם, שֵׁת, שֶׁמֶשׁ, שֵׁם, שֻׁלְחָן, שׁוֹפָר, שׁוֹר, רַתּוֹק, רוּחַ, קָרְבָּן, קֶרֶב. The following nouns feminine have in the plural number a masculine termination, אֵלָה sing., אֵלִים plural:—בֵּיצָה, דְּבֵלָה, דְּבוֹרָה, זְמֹרָה, פִּלֶּגֶשׁ, עִיר, סְאָה, נְמָלָה, מִלָּה, לְבֵנָה, כֻּסֶּמֶת, כַּד, יַאֲנָה, יוֹנָה, חֲשֵׁכָה, חִטָּה, תְּאֵנָה, שִׁפְחָה, פַּת, שְׂעֹרָה, שִׁבֹּלֶת, שְׁבוּעַת, שְׁבִית.

Some nouns masculine have in the plural both a masculine and feminine form; as, אֲרִי singular, אֲרָיִם and אֲרָיוֹת plural: הֵיכָל, גַּב, מִזְרָק, מִגְדָּל, מִבְצָר, מָגֵן, לֵבָב, מָבוֹא, מָאוֹר, כִּיּוֹר, יַעַר, יוֹם, זִכָּרוֹן, זֶבַח, שֶׁבֶר, פֶּרֶץ, פֶּלֶא, עָקֵב, עָוֹן, עֲבוֹת, סַף, מִשְׁכָּן, מִשְׁכָּב, מַעְיָן, מַכְאוֹב, מַטְּעַם, קַרְדֹּם, שָׂדֶה, שׁוֹפָר, תַּנִּין and תַּנִּים singular, תַּנִּינִים and תַּנּוֹת plural, and some nouns feminine have both the masc. and fem. form in the plural; as, אֵימָה singular, אֵימִים and אֵימוֹת plural: אֲלֻמָּה, אֲשֵׁרָה, בְּכוֹרָה, חֲנִית, כָּתֵף, כִּכָּר, עָב, עֲרֵמָה, שָׁנָה.

A few instances are found where the nouns in the plural number are derived from a root wholly different from the singular; as, אִישׁ *a man*, אֲנָשִׁים *men*, from אֱנָשׁ (the regular form would be אִישִׁים); אִשָּׁה *a woman*, נָשִׁים *women*. Nor is the noun in the feminine gender always formed by adding ־ָה to the masculine; as, עֶבֶד *a man-servant*, אָמָה or שִׁפְחָה *a maid-servant*, אָדוֹן *a master*, גְּבִירָה and גְּבֶרֶת, *a mistress*.

CHAPTER XII.

On the Changes of Vowels.

55.—The change of the vowels is caused by an increase of the letters, for the purpose of preserving, when it is possible, the same number of syllables, and the increase of letters is required for the following reasons, which are technically called סָרְכָּן; the letters of which that term is composed being the initials of the words סְמִיכוּת *construction*, רִבּוּי *plural*, כִּנּוּי *suffixes*, and נְקֵבָה *feminine gender*.

56.—סְמִיכוּת *constructive.* When nouns are in *construction*, that which stands first commonly undergoes a change in its vowels except where ל is prefixed to the second noun as a sign of the genitive case; and not only substantives but likewise participles and adjectives preceding a substantive, are subject to the same change when in construction; as, גְּדֹל הָעֵצָה *the great of counsel* i. e. *great counsellor*, מַחְכִּימַת פֶּתִי *making the simple wise*; we have indeed some instances of a participial noun being in construction when followed by a pronoun; as, חוֹסֵי בוֹ *trusting in him.*

57.—Nouns which have two (ָ) in the absolute form, singular masculine, change the first (ָ) into (ְ), and the second, if not followed by quiescent א, into (ַ): as, דָּבָר *a word*, דְּבַר *a word of;* עָשָׁן *smoke*, עֲשַׁן *smoke of;* but when א third radical follows (ָ) it remains unchanged; as, מִקְרָא *a convocation*, מִקְרָא קֹדֶשׁ *a convocation of holiness*, i. e. *an holy convocation.* (Exceptions.) The following two nouns, חָלָב, לָבָן, absolute, in construction are חֲלֵב לְבֶן; and in the following nouns the last (ָ) is retained אוּלָם פִּתְאֹם, and once מַתָּן. Nouns after the form פְּעָל have both vowels changed when in regimen into וֹ; as, אָוֶן, תָּוֶךְ, מָוֶת into אוֹן, תּוֹךְ, מוֹת; עָוֶל into construction, from עָוֶל absolute, but if the last letter of the noun be ה third radical, as, שָׂדֶה, it becomes in construction שְׂדֵה. Some few nouns after the form פְּעָל do not change; as, כְּתָב, שְׁאָר.

58.—A noun with (ֶ) in the absolute form, retains the same

likewise when in construction, except (ֶ) precedes or follows: as from יֶתֶר–יֶתֶר, זָקֵן–זְקַן; the following three nouns excepted, אָבֵל, מֵיטַב, יָבֵן; the two following יָרֵךְ and כָּתֵף have in construction (ֶֶ).

59.—(ֶ) never changes in singular construction; thus, מֶלֶךְ, מֶלֶךְ יְהוּדָה; except ה quiescent follows, then (ֶ) is changed into (ֵ); as, מִקְנֶה abs., מִקְנֵה const.

60.—(ַיִ) is changed into (ֵי); as, בַּיִת, בֵּית.

61.—When a noun consists of a monosyllable, the (ָ) in its absolute form is changed, when in construction, into (ַ) דָּם, דַּם, except in יָם, עָב, which sometimes retain (ָ) in construction; and these three אָב, אָח, חָם change, sometimes, when in construction into אֲבִי, אֲחִי, חֲמִי.

62.—A monosyllabic noun changes its long vowel into a short one; viz., (ֵ) generally into (ֶ); (ָ) into (ַ); and וֹ into (ָ) chateph; as, בֶּן הָאָדָם from בֵּן; יַד יְיָ from יָד; כָּל הָאָדָם from כֹּל. But (ֵ) often changes into (ִ), and וֹ into (ֻ) when followed by a dagesh forte; as, אִמִּי from אֵם; חֻקָּה from חֹק; with this exception, that if the accent be on the syllable, it then remains unchanged: שַׁמָּה, הֵמָּה

63.—Both the dual and the plural masculine in construction drop ם final, and change the dual and plural forms of (ַ) and (ִ) into (ֵ); and when (ָ) precedes the plural termination, it is changed into (ְ), and the preceding (ָ) into (ַ); as, דְּבָרִים absolute plural, דִּבְרֵי in construction. Exceptions: the following nouns retain (ָ) עָרִים, עָרֵי; מְגִנִּים, מָגִנֵּי; הָרִים, הָרֵי; רָאשִׁים, רָאשֵׁי; אִפְרִים, אֶפְרֵי; חַטָּאִים, חַטָּאֵי.

64.—(ֵ) before the plural termination is changed into (ְ), and the preceding (ָ) into (ִ); as זְקֵנִים plural absolute, זִקְנֵי in construction. The exceptions in which (ֵ) is retained are: אֲבֵלִים, אֲבֵלֵי; חֲפֵצִים, חֲפֵצֵי; שְׂמֵחִי, שְׂמֵחֵי; זֵיתֵי, עֵינֵי.

65.—Nouns plural formed from a singular of two (ֶ), change the second (ֶ) when in construction into (ְ), and the first sometimes into (ַ), and sometimes into (ִ); but if the first consonan' be guttural, it is changed into (ַ); as, from מֶלֶךְ sing., מַלְכֵי plura in construction: נֶדֶר, נִדְרֵי; רֶגֶל, רַגְלֵי; הֶבֶל, הַבְלֵי.

66.—Those of (ֵ ֶ) in the singular, change in the plural whe in construction the (ֵ) into (ִ): as שֵׁבֶט, שִׁבְטֵי; but when th consonant is a guttural, it changes (ֵ) into (ֶ): as חֵלֶק, חֶלְקֵי.

67.—The feminine singular termination ָה is changed into ַת when in construction; as, יִרְאָה, יִרְאַת. Nouns after the form בְּרָכָה, צְדָקָה undergo the additional change of the first two vowel (ְ) and (ָ) into (ִ); as צְדָקָה, צִדְקַת; בְּרָכָה, בִּרְכַּת, and som nouns ending ָה change into ֶ ֶת; as מִלְחָמָה abs., מִלְחֶמֶת const. but when the letter preceding the feminine termination is a guttural, the changes are into ַ ַת; as, אַמְתַּחָה, אַמְתַּחַת; and althoug we find a few instances in which the termination ֶ ֶת is used i the absolute form, yet for the most part, the termination is th *status constructus*. The same is the case with the participles activ of קַל, נִפְעַל and הִפְעִיל, where the absolute form ends in ָה.

68.—Nouns derived from verbs quiescent in ו or defective i the second radical, retain (ָ) in the second regimen: as, קָמָה קָמַת; צָרָה, צָרַת; and so likewise nouns whose first (ָ) is instea of (ַ): as, בַּקָּשָׁה, בֶּהָלָה, תְּעָלָה, and those that end in ָת: a מְנָת, זִמְרָת, מִקְצָת.

69.—In feminine nouns plural with (ָ) penultimate, and (ְ antepenultimate, (ָ) is changed into (ְ), and (ְ) into (ִ): a צְדָקוֹת, צִדְקוֹת; but when the first letter is a guttural with a com pound vowel, (ָ) is dropped: as, חֲרָבוֹת, חָרְבוֹת.

70.—רִבּוּי plural. (ָ), (ֵ) or (ֶ), under the first letter of a nou sing. mas. are changed into (ְ) when the noun is in the plur number: as, from דָּבָר, דְּבָרִים; סֵפֶר, סְפָרִים; מֶלֶךְ, מְלָכִים; th same change takes place when the first vowel is (ַ), before guttural: as, נַעַר, נְעָרִים; except, 1.—in חָרָשׁ, חָרָשִׁים; for the (ָ under ח is a change for (ַ), and the subsequent dagesh (aft the form גַּנָּב, גַּנָּבִים), on account of ר in חָרָשׁ being incapable having dagesh. 2.—In שָׁלִישׁ, שָׁלִישִׁים *captains*; here (ָ) is n changed in the plural, that it may not be confounded with שְׁלִישִׁים

the third part. 3.—In שָׁבוּעַ, from which say שָׁבֻעוֹת *weeks;* for here (ָ) remains to distinguish it from the word שְׁבֻעוֹת *oaths.* Yet in a few instances those nouns which have (ֶֶ) in the singular, do change (ָ) into וֹ: as מָוֶת, מוֹתִים; אָוֶן, אוֹנִים.

71.—If the first vowel be וֹ followed by (ֶ) or by (ֵ) when its accompanying consonant is a guttural, it is changed in the plural number into (ְ), (ֳ) and (ָ): as קֹמֶץ, קְמָצִים; פֹּעַל, פְּעָלִים; but if the first consonant be a guttural, וֹ is changed to (ֳ) and in a few instances the same change takes place without a guttural; as קֹדֶשׁ, קֳדָשִׁים; and sometimes into (ָ) only: as שֹׁרֶשׁ, שָׁרָשִׁים; but if the second vowel be not (ֶ) the וֹ remains unchanged: as כּוֹכָב, כּוֹכָבִים.

72.—When the vowels are (ַ) and (ִ), (ַ) is changed into (ְ) and (ִ) into (ָ): as תַּיִשׁ, תְּיָשִׁים, or both vowels together are contracted into (ֵ): as זַיִת, זֵיתִים; except in בַּיִת, בָּתִּים.

73.—If the last vowel be (ָ), a change seldom takes place: as אֵבֶר, אֲבָרִים; yet sometimes (ָ) is changed into (ַ), and is followed by a dagesh: as אוֹפָן, אוֹפַנִּים; קָטָן, קְטַנִּים.

74.—The last vowel (ֵ) if not preceded by (ָ), is changed into (ְ): as שׁוֹמֵם, שׁוֹמְמִים; עִוֵּר, עִוְרִים; a few nouns excepted, in which (ֵ) remains: as זְאֵב, זְאֵבִים; פַּרְדֵּס, פַּרְדֵּסִים; but (ֵ) preceded by (ָ) is not changed: as כָּבֵד, כְּבֵדִים; except in such nouns as are derived from verbs, the two last radicals of which are alike, when (ֵ) is changed into (ַ), and is followed by a dagesh: as מָגֵן, מְגִנִּים.

75.—When (ֶ) is the last vowel and is followed by ה, it is dropped in the plural, and changed into (ִ): as יָפֶה, יָפִים; רֵעֶה, רֵעִים; but if not followed by ה, or both vowels are (ֶ), the latter (ֶ) is changed into (ָ): as מֶלֶךְ, מְלָכִים; עֵגֶל, עֲגָלִים.

76.—The last וֹ is seldom changed, but when changed, it is into (ֻ) followed by a dagesh, for the sake of euphony: as אָדוֹם, אֲדֻמִּים; the following nouns excepted, צִפּוֹר, צִפֳּרִים; מָדוֹן, מְדָנִים; שָׁפוֹט, שְׁפָטִים and שְׁפוּטִים; אַרְמוֹן, אַרְמְנוֹת.

77.—The last vowel (ֵ) does not change, but the subsequent

consonant receives the dagesh in the plural: as אֹגֶם, אֲגַמִּים מְעַם, מְעַטִּים; but if the following letter be one of the אהחער which are incapable of the dagesh, (ַ) is changed into (ָ).

78.—The last syllable ִי undergoes no change of vowels i the plural: as עִבְרִי, עִבְרִים; except in נָקִי, נְקִיִּם.

79.—The latter vowel וּ seldom changes, but whenever an change takes place, it is into (ֻ) followed by a dagesh: as גְּדוּד גְּדוּדִים.

80.—Monosyllabic nouns come commonly under the abov several rules of the changes in the last vowels; nevertheless, w observe here and there some deviations caused by the variou derivations from the several roots: as דָּג, דָּגִים; and all thos derived from quiescent verbs in ו. In יָם, יַמִּים; the change made to denote that the root is ימם (see Rule 55): חֵץ, חִצִּים root חָצַץ; לֵב, לִבּוֹת and לְבָבוֹת, root לָבַב. When the vowel is and the noun is derived from a verb with the two last radica alike, which is mostly the case, ו is changed into (ֻ) followed b a dagesh: as חֹק, חֻקִּים; but the few nouns of that kind which a derived from the quiescent verbs in ו are changed into short (ָ as יוֹם, יָמִים; רֹאשׁ, רָאשִׁים. Nouns with (ַ) are likewise for th most part derived from the geminated verbs, and therefore th (ַ) either remains unchanged (the following letter only takin dagesh: as דַּל, דַּלִּים), or is changed into (ִ), and dagesh follow as פַּת, פִּתִּים; and when the following letter is guttural, (ַ) changed into (ָ). Those which have וּ and ִי are all deriv from the quiescent verbs which have ו or י in the second radic and undergo no change.

81.—The changes of vowels in the feminine plural are t same as the masculine plural. It is only in the last syllable th they differ from the nouns masculine, and for which see Rule 1

82.—Nouns after the form of פְּעָלָה, פְּעֻלָּה, and פִּעְלָה, form th plurals like צְדָקָה, צְדָקוֹת as אִמְרָה, אֲמָרוֹת; חֶרְפָּה, חֲרָפוֹת; שִׂמְ עֲלָמוֹת; and some undergo no other change, except in the l syllable, in order to denote the plural number: as מִצְוָה, מִצְוֹת; מַרְאֶה, מַרְאוֹת; מַחְתָּה, מַחְתּוֹת.

83.—כִּנּוּי suffixes.—The changes of nouns masculine of (ֶ ֶ) will already appear clear from the tables exhibited, Rule 22, we have therefore only to mention here some few deviations, such as instead of דַּרְכְּךָ we find some end in ךְ: as שָׂדְךָ, עֶבְדְּךָ; the change is occasioned by the accent. Instead of ִי in the first singular, we have sometimes נִי: as בַּעֲדֵנִי, תַּחְתֵּנִי. The first plural נוּ is sometimes changed into (ְ) mobile, when another (ְ) or long vowel precedes it: as עַבְדְּכֶם, כֻּלְּכֶם. ָם is sometimes changed into ָמוֹ, and sometimes into הֶם; as פָּנֵימוֹ, פִּיהֶם, בְּנֵיהֶם.

84.—Nouns which have (ָ ֵ), change (ָ) into (ְ), and (ֵ) is retained: as חָצֵר, חַצְרִי, חֲצֵרֵינוּ; זָקֵן, זְקֵנָיו, זִקְנֵיכֶם; יָרֵךְ, יְרֵכִי, יְרֵכוֹ.

85.—(ֶ ֶ) are for the most part changed into וֹ: as תָּוֶךְ, תּוֹכוֹ; but in some few instances (ֶ) is changed into (ַ), and (ֶ) into (ְ): as עָוֶל, עַוְלוֹ.

86.—In וֹ (ָ) is changed into (ְ), but וֹ is retained: as אָדוֹן, אֲדֹנִי; גָּדוֹל, גְּדוֹלְךָ; קָרוֹב, קְרֹבוֹ; שָׁלוֹם, שְׁלֹמִי; except קָטוֹן, קְטַנִּי; קָטוֹב, קְטָבְךָ; קָבוֹל, קְבָלוֹ; and also רַתּוּק, פִּתּוֹן, for (ַ) with dagesh following is equal to (ָ).

87.—In וּ (ָ) is likewise changed into (ְ) but וּ is retained: as פָּעוּל, פְּעוּלוֹ; חָרוּל, חֲרוּלִי: except in שָׁבוּעַ, שְׁבֻעוֹתֵיכֶם, *week*: here (ָ) is retained, in order not to confound it with the word שְׁבֻעוֹתֵיכֶם, *oath*. The following nouns take the same form: מַבּוּר, תַּגּוּר, רַחוּם, חַנּוּן; although ח takes no dagesh, (ַ) still remains, it being usually the case as to that guttural, that the preceding short vowel is not changed into a long one, to compensate for the omitted dagesh, as is the case with regard to the *other* gutturals.

88.—In (ָ ִ), (ָ) is changed into (ְ), but (ִ) is retained; as, בָּצִיר, בְּצִירוֹ; נָזִיר, נְזִירְךָ; except in שָׁלִישׁ, שָׁלִישׁוֹ, שָׁלִישָׁיו and סָרִים, סָרִיסֶיהָ, nor do those with (ַ ִ) or when (ָ) is used instead of (ַ) and dagesh, undergo any change.

89.—In (ֵ ָ), (ֵ) is changed into (ְ), but (ָ) remains; as in נֵכָר, לֵבָב, לְבָבִי, עֵנָב, עֲנָבָיו; but with the suffixes כֶם, כֶן, הֶם, הֶן

(which are called by Jewish grammarians, the heavy suffixes) (◌ֶ is likewise changed; as לִבְבֵיהֶן, עֲנָבְכֶם.

90.—(◌ֶ◌ֶ) and (◌ֵ◌ֶ) are subject to nearly the same changes indeed some nouns have both forms, sometimes (◌ֶ◌ֶ), and other (◌ֵ◌ֶ); as שֶׁכֶל and שֵׁכֶל, נֶדֶר and נֵדֶר, נֶבֶל and נֵבֶל; (◌ֵ) and (◌ֶ with a pause accent are sometimes changed into (◌ָ). The change of the vowels in the plural of those nouns are universally the same, and follow the same rule as nouns with (◌ָ◌ָ); as, סֵפֶר, סְפָרָיו סְפָרֵינוּ; כֶּרֶם, כְּרָמָיו, כְּרָמֵינוּ. In the singular regimen there is some difference; those of (◌ֶ◌ֶ) change the (◌ֶ) into (◌ַ), but if followed by a guttural, always into (◌ִ), and the second into (◌ְ); as, נֶדֶר נִדְרִי, מֶלֶךְ מַלְכִּי, כֶּרֶם כַּרְמִי; but those of (◌ֵ◌ֶ), change (◌ֵ) into (◌ִ), and (◌ֶ) into (◌ְ), and when the first letter is guttural, (◌ֵ) is changed into (◌ֶ); as עֵגֶל, עֶגְלִי, חֵלֶב, חֶלְבִּי. Nouns of (◌ֵ◌ֵ) undergo the same changes as (◌ֵ◌ֶ) and (◌ֶ◌ֶ).

91.—(◌ָ וֹ) undergo no change in the singular, but only in the plural; as, אוֹצָר, אוֹצָרְךָ, אוֹצְרוֹתֶיךָ.

92.—Neither (◌ִ וֹ) nor (וֹ◌ָ) change, except in צִפּוֹר, צִפֳּרָיו.

93.—In (◌ֵ וֹ), (◌ֵ) is changed into (◌ְ); as, יוֹנֵק, יוֹנְקָיו, אֹיֵב אֹיִבְךָ; but אֹיִבְךָ has (◌ִ) instead of (◌ְ) before another (◌ְ) in conformity with the general rule.

94.—In (◌ֶ וֹ), the first is changed into its corresponding shor vowel (◌ֳ chataph), and the second into (◌ְ); as, חֹדֶשׁ, חָדְשׁוֹ שֹׁרֶשׁ, שָׁרְשׁוֹ; but sometimes וֹ is changed into a compound vowe under the guttural; וֹ is then sometimes retained: תֹּאַר, תָּאֳרוֹ, פֹּעַל, פָּעֳלוֹ Nouns of that form whose second letter is ה, have (◌ַ) instead c (◌ֶ); as, צֹהַר, בֹּהַק, except אֹהֶל, בֹּהֶן.

95.—(◌ָ◌ְ) do not change; as, כְּתָב, כְּתָבְךָ; יְקָר, יְקָרִי, except i זְמָן, זְמַנִּי, which is the usual form of nouns with (◌ָ); as, מְעַט מְעַטִּים.

96.—(◌ָ◌ְ) do not change; as, נְגָב, נְגָבָיו.

97.—(◌ִ◌ַ) are changed into (◌ֵ); as, בַּיִת, בֵּיתִי; זַיִת, זֵיתְךָ, except in מַיִם, which has a peculiar form, as in מֵימֵי by doubling but when the second letter of the noun is not י, the vowels are retained; as, אַבִּיר, אַבִּירָיו. This is likewise the case with nouns which have (ֵ), (וֹ), and (וּ); but in (ֵ), the latter is changed into (ָ); as, מַקֵּל, מַקְלוֹ.

98.—Nouns of one syllable, if they are derived from a quiescent verb in the second radical, do not change, whether the vowel be (ָ), (ֵ), (ָ), (וֹ) or (וּ), except יוֹם and דָּג: as דְּגָתָם, יְמֵיהֶם, יְמֵיכֶם; but in those that are derived from the quiescent in the third radical, the vowel (ָ) is changed into (ָ) when the heavy suffixes are added; except in אָב, אָח, חָם, which have a particular form: as אָבִיךָ, אָבִיו, אֲבִיהוּ, אָחִיו, אֲחִיהוּ, אֲחִיכֶם. Those with (ֵ) do not change, except in בֵּן; as בְּנִי, בִּנְךָ, בְּנוֹ, בָּנֵינוּ, בְּנֵיכֶם.

Those derived from verbs defective in the second radical, and whose vowel is וֹ, change וֹ into (ֻ): as תֹּם, תֻּמִּי; עֹל, עֻלִּי; חֹק, חֻקִּי; כֹּל, כֻּלּוֹ; and in some nouns וֹ is changed into short (ָ): as עֹז, עָזִּי. Those which have (ֵ) generally retain it with the suffixes: as עַם, עַמִּי. In some few nouns it is changed into (ִ): as פַּת, פִּתִּי: such as have (ֵ) change it into (ִ): as לֵב, לִבִּי, etc.

99.—Nouns feminine singular which end in ה, change the ה into ת when affixes are to be added, as has been already shown, but some retain the same vowels: as אִמְרָה, אִמְרָתִי; מִשְׁפָּחָה, מִשְׁפַּחְתִּי; חִטָּה, אַהֲבָה, פַּחְדָּה, חֶרְפָּה, עֶרְוָה, חָכְמָה, עָרְלָה, טֻמְאָה, חֶמְצָה, except פִּשְׁתָּה, פִּשְׁתִּים.

100.—Nouns which take the form of צְדָקָה, בְּרָכָה, קְעָרָה, are changed into צִדְקָתִי, בִּרְכָתִי, קַעֲרָתִי; and in the plural into צִדְקוֹתֵינוּ, בִּרְכוֹתֶיךָ, קַעֲרֹתֵינוּ, after which form are the nouns חָרָבָה, קְעָרָה.

101.—Nouns which have two forms, that of ָה and ֶת, take, when suffixes are added, the form of ֶת: as מִלְחָמָה, מִלְחֶמֶת. מִלְחַמְתּוֹ is derived from the latter form ֶת, because no noun singular ending in ָה changes vowels by the addition of suffixes, except those of the form of צְדָקָה. But whenever we find a noun singular feminine, with suffixes in which there is change of vowels, it must have been derived from ָה or ֶת. בְּהֶמְתּוֹ is not derived from בְּהֵמָה, but from בְּהֶמֶת, nor is נִבְלָתוֹ derived from נְבֵלָה, b-from נְבָלָה, although that absolute form is not found in scripture. So likewise in the plural feminine with suffixes, no change of of vowels takes place in that form.

102.—In nouns feminine with ֶ ֶת or ֵ ֶת, the first (ֶ) or (ֵ) is changed into (ִ) or (ַ), and the second (ֶ) into (ְ), the same as in the noun masculine.

103.—Nouns feminine with (ֶ) and ֹ in the last syllables change ֹ into short (ָ), and (ֶ) into (ְ): as כֻּתֹּנֶת, כָּתָּנְתִּי, plura כָּתְּנוֹת; but nouns ending in וּת and ִית never change by the ad- dition of suffixes.

104.—נְקֵבָה Feminine. Nouns whose first vowel is (ָ) in the masculine gender, change it into (ְ) in the feminine: as גָּדוֹל masc., גְּדוֹלָה fem., except in בָּגוֹד masc., בָּגוֹדָה fem.; and in al those nouns which end in ָה, when the second vowel is (ָ), it i retained in the feminine, except in קָטָן: as קְטַנָּה.

105.—If the second vowel be (ֵ) it is changed into (ָ): a עִוֵּר, עִוְרָה (except אֹכְלָה, סֹרֵרָה, נוֹטֵרָה); but not if preceded by (ָ) as כָּבֵד, in construction כְּבֵדָה. If however ֶת is at the end of word to denote the fem. gender, then (ֵ) is changed into (ֶ) as אַחֵר, אַחֶרֶת; פֹּקֵד, פֹּקֶדֶת.

106.—When two (ֶ) are in the masculine, the first is change into (ִ) or (ַ), and the second into (ְ): as כֶּבֶשׂ, כִּבְשָׂה, כַּבְשָׂה the same changes take place when the vowels are (ֶ ֶ).

107.—(ֶ ֵ) are changed into (ֶ ְ): as אֵבֶר, אֶבְרָה.

108.—When the last syllable is ִי it is retained in the feminin with ת: as תַּחְתִּי, תַּחְתִּית; if followed by ה pronounce the י as i תַּחְתִּיָּה.

CHAPTER XIII.

On the Numerals.

109.—It has already been observed that in the numer adjectives, the genders are known by terminations exact opposed to those of other nouns, namely, that those of the ma culine end in ָה from 3 to 10. We have now to remark th from 11 to 19 in the feminine, the word denoting 10, terminates in ה, but the units remain as before. The terms for 20 to 90 inclusive, have a masculine termination, ִים, but 100 has a feminine termination, and 1000 a masculine termination. From 20 and upwards, the units may either precede or follow the word denoting *ten.*

110.—The noun which accompanies the numeral adjective from 2 to 9 is in the plural number, but from 10 to 1000 in the singular, and from 1000 and upwards in the plural.

111.—In the ordinal numbers, the terminations are, from 1 to 10 inclusive, in conformity with the general rule of nouns, as the following table will show; but from 11 and upwards the cardinals are used for ordinals, by repeating the noun, or the number following the noun: as חֲמֵשׁ עֶשְׂרֵה שָׁנָה *fifteen*, but שְׁנַת הַחֲמֵשׁ עֶשְׂרֵה or שְׁנַת הַחֲמֵשׁ עֶשְׂרֵה שָׁנָה means *the fifteenth year.*

The fractions are expressed by ordinals: as שְׁלִישִׁית הַהִין *the third part of a hin*, etc., except that *a half* is expressed by חֲצִי, masculine, מֶחֱצָה feminine.

Ordinal Numbers.

Feminine.		Masculine.
רִאשׁוֹנָה	First	רִאשׁוֹן
שֵׁנִית & שְׁנִיָּה	Second	שֵׁנִי
שְׁלִישִׁית	Third	שְׁלִישִׁי
רְבִיעִית	Fourth	רְבִיעִי
חֲמִישִׁית	Fifth	חֲמִישִׁי
שִׁשִּׁית	Sixth	שִׁשִּׁי
שְׁבִיעִית	Seventh	שְׁבִיעִי
שְׁמִינִית	Eighth	שְׁמִינִי
תְּשִׁיעִית	Ninth	תְּשִׁיעִי
עֲשִׂירִית	Tenth	עֲשִׂירִי

Cardinal Numbers.

Feminine. Const.	Feminine. Absol.		Masculine. Const.	Masculine. Absol.
——	אַחַת	1	אַחַד	אֶחָד *
שְׁתֵּי	שְׁתַּיִם	2	שְׁנֵי	שְׁנַיִם
שְׁלֹשׁ	שָׁלֹשׁ	3	שְׁלֹשֶׁת	שְׁלֹשָׁה
——	אַרְבַּע	4	אַרְבַּעַת	אַרְבָּעָה
חֲמֵשׁ	חָמֵשׁ	5	חֲמֵשֶׁת	חֲמִשָּׁה
——	שֵׁשׁ	6	שֵׁשֶׁת	שִׁשָּׁה
שְׁבַע	שֶׁבַע	7	שִׁבְעַת	שִׁבְעָה
——	שְׁמוֹנֶה	8	שְׁמוֹנַת	שְׁמוֹנָה
תְּשַׁע	תֵּשַׁע	9	——	תִּשְׁעָה
——	עֶשֶׂר	10	——	עֲשָׂרָה
——	אַחַת עֶשְׂרֵה עַשְׁתֵּי עֶשְׂרֵה	11	——	אַחַד עָשָׂר עַשְׁתֵּי עָשָׂר
——	שְׁתַּיִם עֶשְׂרֵה שְׁתֵּי עֶשְׂרֵה	12	——	שְׁנַיִם עָשָׂר שְׁנֵי עָשָׂר
——	שְׁלֹשׁ עֶשְׂרֵה	13	——	שְׁלֹשָׁה עָשָׂר
——	אַרְבַּע עֶשְׂרֵה	14	——	אַרְבָּעָה עָשָׂר
——	חֲמֵשׁ עֶשְׂרֵה	15	——	חֲמִשָּׁה עָשָׂר
——	שֵׁשׁ עֶשְׂרֵה	16	——	שִׁשָּׁה עָשָׂר
——	שְׁבַע עֶשְׂרֵה	17	——	שִׁבְעָה עָשָׂר
——	שְׁמֹנֶה עֶשְׂרֵה	18	——	שְׁמֹנָה עָשָׂר
——	תְּשַׁע עֶשְׂרֵה	19	——	תִּשְׁעָה עָשָׂר
——	עֶשְׂרִים	20	——	עֶשְׂרִים
——	אַחַת וְעֶשְׂרִים	21	——	אֶחָד וְעֶשְׂרִים
——	שְׁתַּיִם וְעֶשְׂרִים	22	——	שְׁנַיִם וְעֶשְׂרִים
——	עֶשְׂרִים וְשָׁלֹשׁ	23	——	עֶשְׂרִים וּשְׁלֹשָׁה
——	——	30	——	שְׁלֹשִׁים
——	——	40	——	אַרְבָּעִים
——	——	50	——	חֲמִשִּׁים
——	——	60	——	שִׁשִּׁים
——	——	70	——	שִׁבְעִים

* אֶחָד and עֲשָׂרָה admit of a plural: as אֲחָדִים *units*, עֲשָׂרוֹת *tens*.

Cardinal Numbers (continued).

Feminine.			Masculine.	
Const.	*Absol.*		*Const.*	*Absol.*
—	—	80	—	שְׁמֹנִים
—	—	90	—	תִּשְׁעִים
—	—	100	מְאַת	מֵאָה
—	—	200	—	מָאתַיִם
—	—	Hundreds	—	מֵאוֹת
—	—	300	—	שְׁלֹשׁ מֵאוֹת
—	—	400	—	אַרְבַּע מֵאוֹת
—	—	1000	—	אֶלֶף
—	—	2000	—	אַלְפַּיִם
—	—	Thousands	—	אֲלָפִים
—	—	3000	—	שְׁלֹשֶׁת אֲלָפִים
—	—	10000	—	רִבּוֹא & רְבָבָה
—	—	20000	—	רִבֹּתַיִם

CHAPTER XIV.

On the Particles.

112.—Under this name we comprehend conjunctions, prepositions, some adverbs, and even some few nouns; which, whilst they are generally used as nouns, yet in some instances occur as prepositions. To some of the particles the suffixes are added, as in nouns, which are called declinable. They are divided into three classes: 1) the separable and declinable; 2) the separable and indeclinable; 3) the inseparable.

Separable and Declinable Particles.

אַחַר *behind, after;* the suffixes which are added to אַחַר are those of a noun in the plural number: as אַחֲרַי *after me,* or *behind me,* אַחֲרֶיךָ, אַחֲרַיִךְ, אַחֲרָיו, אַחֲרֶיהָ, אַחֲרֵינוּ, אַחֲרֵיכֶם, אַחֲרֵיכֶן, אַחֲרֵיהֶם, אַחֲרֵיהֶן.

אַיֵּה, in construction אֵי, *where?* By adding the suffixes, ה i-dropped, and (ֵ) is changed: as אֵיוֹ *where is he?* אַיָּם *where are they?* Joined to the adverbs: as אֵיפֹה or אֵפוֹא, from פֹּה *here, hither*.

אַיִן, and in construction אֵין, *there is not*, or *none;* with the suffixes, אֵינֶנִּי, אֵינְךָ, אֵינֶנּוּ, אֵינָם. It is likewise found with the prefixes בכלם: as in בְּאֵין, כְּאֵין, לְאֵין, מֵאַיִן. With מ prefixed it has a two-fold signification, namely *from whence* (Josh. 9:8), and *from*, or *of nothing* (Isa. 41:24).

אֶל and אֱלֵי *to*, from which is derived the prefix לְ. It is likewise declined with the suffixes added to a noun plural: as אֵלַי *to me*, אֵלֶיךָ, אֵלַיִךְ, אֵלָיו, אֵלֶיהָ, אֵלֵינוּ, אֲלֵיכֶם, אֲלֵיכֶן, אֲלֵיהֶם, אֲלֵיהֶן.

אֶפֶס *nothing;* in most instances it is used substantively: as *nothingness*, and *end*.

אֵצֶל *by*, with suffixes, אֶצְלִי, אֶצְלוֹ, אֶצְלְכֶם.

אֵת has a two-fold signification: 1st. when it follows a verb active, it denotes that the noun which follows is in the accusative case: as בָּרָא אֵת הַשָּׁמַיִם *he created the heaven;* but with the verb passive, it is sometimes found before a nominative: as בְּגוֹרָל יֵחָלֵק אֶת־הָאָרֶץ *by lot shall the land be divided* (Numb. 26:55); and by adding suffixes, (ֵ) is changed into וֹ: as אוֹתִי, etc., except in the second person plural, when (ֵ) is for the most part retained, as is shewn in the table of the declension of personal pronouns; and 2ndly, it signifies *with:* as אֶת יְשָׁרִים סוֹדוֹ *his counsel is with the upright;* and when it is used in that sense, (ֵ) is changed into (ִ) followed by dagesh: as אִתָּהּ, אִתּוֹ, אִתְּךָ, אִתִּי, אִתָּם, אִתְּכֶם, אִתָּנוּ; except (2 Kings 1:15) רֵד אוֹתוֹ *go down with him*, and וַיֵּרֶד אוֹתוֹ *and he went with him;* and (Ezek. 3:24) וַיְדַבֵּר אֹתִי *he spoke with me;* some suppose that מֵאוֹתִי (Isa. 45:15) is likewise included in the above exception, but it is more likely used in this instance for מִפָּנָי.

בֵּין and בֵּינוֹת, dual בֵּינַיִם, *between, betwixt;* with suffixes, בֵּינִי, בֵּינְךָ, בֵּינוֹ, בֵּינָהּ, בֵּינֵינוּ, בֵּינֹתֵיכֶם, and בֵּינוֹתֵינוּ. This preposition is repeated before each noun: as בֵּינְךָ וּבֵין הָאִשָּׁה *between thee and between the woman*, בֵּינִי וּבֵינֶךָ *between me and between thee;* except when לְ is prefixed to the second noun; בֵּין מַיִם לָמָיִם *between water and water*, בֵּין מַיִם וּבֵין מַיִם.

בִּלְעֲדֵי *except*, is only used in the form of a noun masc. plur. in construction, the affixes added to it are therefore those which belong to a plural noun: as בִּלְעָדַי, בִּלְעָדֶיךָ, בִּלְעָדָיו, בִּלְעָדֵינוּ; with מִ prepos. the (ְ) under בּ is then changed into (ַ): as מִבַּלְעֲדֵי.

בִּלְתִּי *except, without*; י is paragogic, which is dropped whenever an affix is added: as בִּלְתִּי *except me*, בִּלְתְּךָ *except thee*; sometimes the prepositions ל, מ, are prefixed to it without undergoing any change.

בַּעֲבוּר *on account of*, is formed from עֲבוּר and ב preposition, it never occurs in the bible without the preposition ב, but not so in the rabbinical writings; but it is likewise found with ל prefixed: as לְבַעֲבוּר.

בְּעַד *about, for*, is formed from עַד and בְּ preposition: it is likewise declinable: בַּעֲדִי *about*, or *for me*, בַּעַדְךָ, בַּעֲדֵךְ, בַּעֲדוֹ, בַּעֲדֵינוּ, בַּעֲדֵיכֶן, בַּעַדְכֶם, etc.; it has also מִ preposition prefixed, as in מִבַּעַד.

הֵן, and with paragogic ה, הִנֵּה *behold*, is declined with suffixes הִנְנִי or הִנֵּנִי, and הִנְּנִי, הִנְּךָ, הִנּוֹ, הִנֵּנוּ, and הִנְנוּ, הִנְּכֶם, הִנָּם.

זוּלָתִי *besides*: י is paragogic, and by adding the suffixes, י is dropped: as זוּלָתִי, זוּלָתְךָ, זוּלָתוֹ.

לְמַעַן *for the sake of, in order to*, declines thus: לְמַעֲנִי, לְמַעַנְךָ, לְמַעֲנוֹ, and לְמַעֲנֵהוּ, לְמַעֲנֵנוּ, לְמַעַנְכֶם. לְמַעֲנָם is never used without ל.

עֻמַּת, לְעֻמַּת, once used in the plural, לְעֻמּוֹת *before, over against*, declinable: as לְעֻמָּתוֹ, לְעֻמָּתָם.

לְפָנִים *formerly, before*, in construction לִפְנֵי, and declined thus: לְפָנַי, לְפָנֶיךָ, לְפָנֵינוּ, לִפְנֵיכֶם, לִפְנֵיכֶן, לִפְנֵיהֶם, לִפְנֵיהֶן.

מִן, מִ, מֵ; when ן is dropped, and מ prefixed to a noun or infinitive, it is pointed מִ, and followed by a dagesh; but if the following letter be guttural, it is pointed מֵ. In a few instances we find מִנִּי and מִנֵּי instead of מִן. With the addition of the suffixes, it mostly occurs with a reduplication: as מִמֶּנִּי, מִמְּךָ, מִמֵּךְ, מִמֶּנּוּ, and sometimes מֶנְהוּ and מִנְּהוּ, etc.

נֶגֶד *opposite to*, declined thus נֶגְדִּי, נֶגְדְּךָ, נֶגְדּוֹ; and with the prepositions כלם prefixed; thus, כְּנֶגֶד, לְנֶגֶד, מִנֶּגֶד.

עַד, עֲדֵי *unto, to, till, until;* referring both to place and time declined with suffixes like a noun plural mas.; עָדַי, עָדֶיךָ, עֲדֵיכֶם.

עוֹד *yet, again, still;* עוֹדִי and עוֹדֶנִּי, עוֹדְךָ, עוֹדֶךָ, עוֹדֶנּוּ, עוֹדֶנָּה עוֹדָם. בְּ is sometimes prefixed; as, בְּעוֹד.

עַל, עֲלֵי, *upon, over,* declined like a noun plural masculine; as עָלַי, עָלֶיךָ, עָלַיִךְ, עָלָיו, עָלֶיהָ, עָלֵינוּ, עֲלֵיכֶם, עֲלֵיהֶם.

עִם *with,* declines thus: עִמִּי and עִמָּדִי, עִמְּךָ, עִמָּךְ, עִמּוֹ, עִמָּהּ, עִמָּנוּ עִמָּכֶם, עִמָּכֶן, עִמָּהֶם, עִמָּהֶן.

תַּחַת *beneath, underneath, below, instead of,* declined like a plural as, תַּחְתַּי, תַּחְתֶּיךָ, תַּחְתֵּינוּ, תַּחְתֵּיכֶם, and also with מ prefixed.

CHAPTER XV.

Separable and Undeclinable Particles.

112.—כֵּן, הֵן *yes, yea,* from whence is formed לָכֵן, עַל־כֵּן *therefore,* אַחַר כֵּן and אַחֲרֵי־כֵן *afterward.*

אָמְנָה, אָמְנָם *truly, verily,* אָכֵן *indeed,* אֲבָל *but truly,* אוּלָם *of truth,* רַק, אַךְ *only.*

אִלּוּ, כִּי, אִם *if,* לוּלֵא and לוּלֵי *if not;* אִם is likewise used interrogatively; sometimes כִּי אִם is used together, signifying, *but only.* כִּי signifies likewise *when, but, for.* לוּ, אוּלַי *perhaps.*

Negatives.—אַל, לֹא, בַּל, בְּלִי. לֹא is used in forbidding a thing as, לֹא יִהְיֶה לְךָ אֵל זָר *thou shalt not have a strange God.* But אַל is generally, though not always, used in prayer; as, רוּחַ קָדְשְׁךָ אַל תִּקַּח מִמֶּנִּי *do not take thy Holy Spirit from me.* בַּל and בְּלִי *without.*

אַף־גַּם *even more,* עוֹד *again,* יוֹתֵר *more,* רַב *greatly,* מְאֹד *very* מְאֹד מְאֹד *exceedingly,* הַרְבֵּה *greatly,* אַף־כִּי *how much more, how much less.*

אָז, אֲזַי *then,* כְּבָר *already,* קֶדֶם and מִקֶּדֶם *time past, of old,* טֶרֶם טֶרֶם *before,*

מָתַי *when?* עַד אָן and עַד אָנָה *until when?*

עַתָּה, נָא *now,* רֶגַע *momentary,* פֶּתַע, פִּתְאֹם *suddenly,* בְּכֵן *hence.*

פֹּה *here,* אָנָה *whither,* אֵיפֹה, *where,* חוּץ *abroad, without the house outwardly,* מוּל *opposite,* עֵבֶר *beyond,* סָבִיב *round about,* נֹכַח *o against*, פְּנִימָה *within, inwardly*, אָחוֹר *backward*. Of nonentity: רֵיקָם *vainly, emptily*, חִנָּם *freely*, יַחַד and יַחְדָּו *together*.

כֹּה *thus*, and כָּכָה; כֵּן *so*, כְּמוֹ־כֵן *such like*.

Intercession: נָא, אָנָּא, אַחֲלַי, בִּי *O! I pray*,—אוֹי and אוֹיָה, אַלְלַי *woe*, הָהּ, אֲהָהּ, הוֹי, אָח *alas!*

Of joy: הֶאָח *ah!*

Inseparable Particles; משה וכלב.

113.—מִ denotes generally the ablative case; sometimes, likewise, a part of any thing,—*some*.—It is derived from מִן, its usual accompanying vowel is therefore (ִ), and is followed by a dageshed letter, to compensate for the dropped ן; as, מִשָּׁם, מִסִּפְרִי, מִכֹּהֵן; but if the subsequent letter be a guttural, and consequently incapable of having a dagesh, מ or ר has then (ֵ); as, מֵעָפָר, מֵחוֹל, מֵהָהֵל, מֵרִיב, except in מִחוּט and מִחוּץ, and as well as in some instances when מ is followed by (ְ); as, מִבְּצִיר, מִרְדוֹף, מִקְצֵיהֶם, מִקְצָה, מִלְּאֹם, מִהְיוֹת. The same is the case when מ is followed by י; as, מִיְנִיעַ, מִימֵי; מִיְּשֵׁנֵי and מִירוּשָׁתְךָ: מ is in some instances accompanied by (ַ) instead of (ִ); as, מַחְמָאוֹת, לְמַדַּי, לְמִבָּרִאשֹׁנָה. מִן and מִ are likewise used to express the comparative degree; as, טוֹבִים שְׁנַיִם מִן הָאֶחָד *two are better than one*, טוֹב שֵׁם מִשֶּׁמֶן *fame is better than oil*.

114.—שֶׁ derived from אֲשֶׁר, relative pronoun. It is for the most part, accompanied by (ֶ), and followed by dagesh; but (ֶ) remains unchanged even if the following letter be guttural; as, שֶׁאַהֲבָה, שֶׁיֹּרֵד, שֶׁשָּׁכְבָה, שֶׁתַּחְפֹּץ, שֶׁאַתָּה; it occasionally has the vowel (ַ); as, שַׁקַּמְתִּי, שַׁלָּמָה. In two places שׁ is acompanied by (ָ); as, שָׁהוּ and שָׁהֵם.

115. ה is used, first, as the definite article, and is perhaps derived from הוּא personal pronoun. The article ה is never prefixed to a proper name, nor to a noun in construction, neither to a noun to which the suffixes are added; except in הֶעֶרְכְּךָ, וְהֶחָצְיוֹ, and לַמְאַהֲבַי (which is instead of לְהַמְאַהֲבַי) also in הָאָהֳלִי and הַחִרוֹתֶיהָ, in בְּעֶבְרֵינוּ, which stands for בְּהָעֶבְרֵינוּ, and in כַּנֶּבְרְתָּה, used for כְּהַגְּבִרְתָּה.

As to those few proper names which have the article prefixed, it is the opinion of Kimchi that some of them are used adjectivel as national or family names; as, הַמְנַשֶּׁה (Deut. 3:18) for הַמְנַשִּׁי *the Menassites*, אֶרֶץ הַמָּגוֹת for הַמָּגוֹנִי; and in some cases in regimen, a noun is to be supplied; as, הָעָם יִשְׂרָאֵל for הָעָם עַם יִשְׂרָאֵל *the nation, the people of Isra·l*, הַיַּיִן הַחֵימָה for הַיַּיִן יֵין הַחֵימָה, *th wine*, namely, *the heating wine* (Jer. 25:23), &c.

Secondly, as a relative pronoun, which sense it bears in mos cases when prefixed to a participle; as, הַבָּאִים *who are coming* for אֲשֶׁר בָּאוּ *who came*, הַנּוֹלָד לוֹ *who was born unto him*. When ה is used as a relative pron., the participle then used as the presen tense, may have the pronominal pronouns affixed; as, הַמְאַזְּרֵנִי *wh is girding me*, הַמַּעַלְךָ *who is bringing thee up:* in that sense it i likewise prefixed to a prep.; as, וְהֶעָלֶיהָ *and that which is upon it.*

Thirdly, ה denotes sometimes the vocative case; as, הַדּוֹר *(generation!* הָאוֹיֵב *O enemy!* הַיַּרְדֵּן *O Jordan!* In that sense it i prefixed to a noun in regimen, as, הַבַּת יְרוּשָׁלָםִ *O daughter (Jerusalem!*

Fourthly, ה localis is used for אֶל and לְ; as, אַרְצָה שֵׂעִיר fc לְאֶרֶץ שֵׂעִיר *to the land of Seir*. In that sense it is suffixed, an according to the general opinion of Grammarians ה mobile neve occurs as a prefix; from which opinion some differ, and conside that ה in הַפְּלִשְׁתִּים (1 Sam. 13:20) is used instead of אֶל or לְ, an supplies אֶרֶץ; and so the Chaldaic paraphrase has אַרַע פְּלִשְׁתָּאֵי *to the land of the Philistines.*

116.—The vowel which accompanies ה, namely (ַ) is the san whatever sense it may bear, and the following consonant dageshed, as has been shown by the above examples, except the following instances, where dagesh is omitted: first, before participle whose first letter is מ with (ְ); as, הַמְלַמֵּד, הַמְבַשְּׂרוֹת. Secondly, the dagesh is omitted in י; as, הַיְאֹר, הַיְלָדִים, unless יְ followed by ה, ח, ע; as in הַיְּהוּדִים, הַיְּעָפִים. Thirdly, the dage

* In these four participles, however, מ has Dagesh, הַמְּשֻׁגָּע, מְּעֻנָּה, הַמְּבַשְּׁלִים, הַמְּנָאֶפֶת.

is omitted in לְ of the noun הַלְוִיִּם, and in צ of the word הַצְפַרְדְּעִים; likewise in its singular form, one instance excepted, וַתַּעַל הַצְּפַרְדֵּעַ (Exod. 8:2).

117.—ה before one of the letters אהחעׄר, which are incapable of having a dagesh, has sometimes (ָ) or (ֶ), and in a few instances (ַ) is retained; thus, before אשר it has (ָ), except in הַעֲרֻכִים* (Is. 65:11), הַעֲזֻבִים (Prov. 2:16), and before most nouns which have ה or ח for their first letter; as in הַהִלָּכֶת, הַהִין, הַחַיָּה; but when הע and א, which sometimes follow the article have (ָ), and the word consists of polysyllables, the article ה has (ֶ); as, הֶהָרִים, הֶעָרִים, הָאֹמֵר; but if the noun be a monosyllable, ה has (ָ); as, הָעָם, הָהָר; before חָ in monosyllables, and חֳ in polysyllables, ה has (ֶ); as, הֶחָי, הֶחֳרָבוֹת.

118.—ה likewise is interrogative, and as such its usual vowel is (ֲ); as הֲבַת? הֲמִן? but if followed by (ְ) ה interrogative has (ַ); as, הַכְּתֹנֶת? הַבְרָכָה; once it is found even without (ְ) following, and yet has (ַ), and dagesh follows; as in הַיִּטַב? If followed by a guttural it has either (ַ) or (ֶ); as הַעֵינַיִם, הַאֹרַח, הַחִיִּתֶם, הֶאָנֹכִי, הֶחָזָק: in two instances it has (ָ) before a guttural, as in הָאַתֶּם (Judg. 6:31) and הָאֶפְרָתִי (Ibid. 12:5): we, however, find instances of ה interrogative being omitted while the context still requires it to be understood interrogatively; as in אַף כִּי אָמַר אֱלֹהִים *has then God said?* תִּמְשֹׁךְ לִוְיָתָן *canst thou draw Leviathan, &c.*

119.—ו is sometimes used conjunctively; as in רְאוּבֵן וְשִׁמְעוֹן *Reuben and Simeon*: but sometimes it is idiomatic, like ﻭ in Arabic; as in וְאַיָּה וַעֲנָה, for אַיָּה וַעֲנָה *Ayah and Anah;* and again on the commencement of a narrative; as in וַיְהִי בִּימֵי אֲחַשְׁוֵרוֹשׁ instead of הָיָה בִּימֵי אֲחַשְׁוֵרוֹשׁ *it happened in the days of Ahasverosh;* again בַּיּוֹם הַשְּׁלִישִׁי וַיִּשָּׂא אַבְרָהָם אֶת־עֵינָיו, for נָשָׂא אַבְרָהָם אֶת־עֵינָיו *on the third day Abraham lifted up his eyes.* It is likewise used disjunctively: as, מַכֵּה אָבִיו וְאִמּוֹ *he who smiteth his father or his*

---

* Some editions of the Hebrew Bible read הָעֲרֻכִים.

mother: likewise adverbially: as, אִם בְּחֻקֹּתַי תֵּלֵכוּ וְנָתַתִּי *if you walk in my statutes, then will I give, &c.*

120.—When ו is prefixed to the future tense accompanied by the vowel (ַ) and followed by a dagesh, or when before א it has (ָ), it denotes that the future tense is to be understood as a past tense, and frequently the preterpluperfect is to be understood; thus, וַיֹּאמֶר *and he said,* וַתּוֹצֵא הָאָרֶץ *and the earth brought forth,* וַנֹּאמֶר *and we said,* וָאֹכַל *and I ate,* וַיְכַל אֱלֹהִים *and God had finished:* but with any other vowel in the future tense, it is not conversive.

121.—ו prefixed to the preterite tense, may likewise be conversive; but there is no distinction in its vowels to point out when it is conversive or when conjunctive, etc., thus in וְשָׁמְרוּ בְנֵי יִשְׂרָאֵל אֶת־הַשַּׁבָּת *and the children of Israel* shall keep *the sabbath day,* אָכַל וְשָׁתָה *he ate and* drank, ו is conjunctive in the latter example; yet the difference is easily detected by the context; and we may lay it down as a rule, that whenever a preterite tense with ו follows another preterite, ו is conjunctive: otherwise it is conversive.

122.—ו conjunctive or conversive in the preterite tense, has for its usual points (ְ), but before another (ְ) it has וּ, as in וּלְמַדְתֶּם, וּקְשַׁרְתֶּם; except before יְ, when it has (ִ) and י drops (ְ); as in וִיהִי for וְיְהִי. It has likewise shurek before the labials בומף; as in וּפָקַד, וּמִלְאוּ. Before a guttural with a compound vowel, ו takes the same vowel uncompounded with (ְ); as in וַאֲסַפְתּוֹ, וַאֲמַרְתֶּם; except before (ֱ), in אֱלֹהִים, when it takes (ֵ) and א drops its (ֱ); and this is likewise the case with (ֲ) in אֲדֹנָי, whence ו takes (ַ). This rule is common to the serviles וכלב.

123.—ו conjunctive has (ָ) when only two nouns are coupled, and the accent placed on the antepenultimate; as in רֶכֶב וָסוּס, שַׁחַל וָפֶתֶן; but if the accent be on the ultima, ו has (ְ); as in עֹשֶׁר וְכָבוֹד; when more than two nouns are joined, the first ו takes (ְ), and the following takes (ָ); as in עַם גָּדוֹל וְרַב וָרָם: likewise before the labials in nouns it has (ָ) instead of וּ; as in תֹהוּ וָבֹהוּ, גָּפְרִית וָמֶלַח: and it has (ָ) likewise in verbs when both are in the same tense and mood, and the last has its accent on the antepenultimate, or is prefixed to a monosyllable; as in חָלוֹךְ וָשׁוֹב, תּוֹקְרִי וָבֹשֶׁת, קָחֶנָּה וָבֹאָה, קַח וָלֵךְ. The same is the case when it is prefixed to the particles; as in מִשָּׁם, מִי וָמִי, אֲנִי וָאַתָּה, הוּא וָהִיא, וָהָלְאָה, except in the following, וְכָל־הָעֶרֶב וכו׳, אִישׁ וְאִישׁ. ו both conjunctive and conversive has likewise (ָ) when a pause accent immediately follows; as in מִמְּךָ וָהֵנָּה, וַמִּתְנוּ, וַמָּתוּ, וָקָם; ו is also sometimes affixed like ה, and is paragogic; as in בְּנוֹ בְעֹר for בֶּן־בְּעוֹר: חַיְתוֹ־אֶרֶץ for חַיַּת־אֶרֶץ.

124.—כ is commonly used for comparing two things, and then is called Caph of similitude; sometimes both things about to be compared have כ prefixed to each, by way of brevity; as כָּמוֹךָ כְּפַרְעֹה instead of פַּרְעֹה כָּמוֹךָ וְאַתָּה כְּפַרְעֹה *Pharaoh is like thee, and thou art like Pharaoh.* Sometimes כ is omitted; as in גּוּר אַרְיֵה יְהוּדָה, for כְּגוּר, *Judah is like a lion's whelp.* It is likewise used as the preposition *about;* as in כְּאַלְפַּיִם אִישׁ *about two thousand men,* כַּחֲצוֹת הַלַּיְלָה *about midnight:* the usual points of כּ are (ְ); before another (ְ) it has (ִ); as in כִּלְשׁוֹן: before a guttural with a compound vowel, it has the same vowel uncompounded; as in כַּעֲשֶׂרֶת, כַּאֲשֶׁר; except before אֱלֹהִים and אֲדֹנָי, as mentioned before. It has (ָ) before a monosyllable, or when the accent is on the penultimate; as in כָּאֵלֶּה, כָּהֵנָּה, כָּזֶה, כָּזֹה; likewise before the pronominal suffixes; as in כָּמוֹךָ, except before the plural; as in כְּמוֹהֶם, כְּמוֹכֶם: yet in Judges 8:18, we read כְּמוֹהֶם. When prefixed to a noun which ought to have the article ה, the article is dropped, and כ takes the vowel which would have been under ה; as in כַּכֹּהֵן for כְּהַכֹּהֵן, כָּעָם for כְּהָעָם, כָּאֲרִי for כְּהָאֲרִי. There are found, however, a few exceptions. The same rule holds good in כּ prefixed to the infinitive Hiphil; as כַּגְלוֹתְךָ *when leading thee,* for כְּהַגְלוֹתְךָ. This rule is common to the serviles בלכ.

125.—ל is generally used to denote the noun to be in the dative case; as וַיֹּאמֶר לְנֹחַ *and he said to Noah,* נָתַתִּי לָכֶם *I gave to you.* It is nevertheless used instead of בַּעֲבוּר *on account of, concerning;* as in Gen. 20:13, אִמְרִי לִי אָחִי הוּא *say concerning me, he is my brother,* and 23:8, וּפִגְעוּ לִי *and intercede for me.* It is likewise used for ב; as לְכָל־דְּרָכָיו מַשְׂכִּיל instead of בְּכָל־ *he was pros-*

perous in all his ways. It is sometimes used as in Chaldaic* and Syriac to denote the accusative case, for אֵת; as in הָרְגוּ לְאַבְנֵר for הָרְגוּ אֶת־אַבְנֵר *they slew Abner.* It denotes likewise the genitive case; as in מִזְמוֹר לְדָוִד *a psalm of David.* It is sometimes idiomatic; as in שְׁלַח לְךָ *send thou,* לֶךְ לְךָ *go thou,* or *get thee out.*

Its usual points are (ְ); but before another (ְ) it has (ִ); as in לִזְנוּת: and before a compound vowel it has the same as כּ. When prefixed to an infinitive which consists of a monosyllable, it has (ָ); as in לָמוּת; and before any other infinitive which has the accent on the penultimate, as in לָקַחַת: but all those terms where ל has (ְ), as לְצֵאת, לְשֶׁבֶת, לְבוֹא, are to be considered as nouns, and not as infinitives, although they are both of the same form. There are, however, some nouns to which לָ is prefixed, particularly when a pause accent follows, as לָשֹׂבַע, לָמַיִם; and before עַד, as לָעַד. In any other case it is subject to the same rule as כּ. See 124.

126.—בּ denotes the ablative case: sometimes בּ is omitted; as in שֵׁשֶׁת יָמִים עָשָׂה for בְּשֵׁשֶׁת *in six days.*§ It is likewise used in the sense of בַּעֲבוּר *on account of;* as וַיַּעֲבֹד יִשְׂרָאֵל בְּאִשָּׁה *Israel served for the sake of a wife.* It likewise has the signification of עִם *with,* as in בְּחַרְבִּי וּבְקַשְׁתִּי *with my sword and bow.* The vowels are the same as under ל, as stated above.

CHAPTER XVI.

On Construing and Parsing.

127.—After the learner has gained some familiarity with the verbs, and which acquisition is easily made by only transcribing the paradigm of the regular verb several times, he may im

* That part of Chaldaic found in the Bible. But in the Chaldaic paraphrases, commonly called the Targum, יָת for the Hebrew אֵת is used to denote the accusative case.

§ Some commentators assign a reason for the omission of בּ in this passage. It is to signify that the Lord is not only the creator of heaven and earth, but even of the six days; God being the creator of time.

mediately begin to construe some easy part of the Bible, with the assistance of a Hebrew Lexicon, and refer to the several subsequent rules as occasion requires; but as in most Hebrew Lexicons, the roots only are arranged alphabetically, so that the derivatives cannot be traced till the root is ascertained, the following general rules will be necessary to find out the root in each word, which root, with very few exceptions, must consist of three letters, as has been already mentioned.

128.—If the word, the root of which is to be ascertained, consist of more than three letters, some of those letters must necessarily be serviles, and if after separating the serviles, there remain three letters, these will form the root; as, תִּפְקֹדְנָה *ye or they shall visit*, consisting of six letters, reject ת as being one of the letters א י ת ן used in the future tense, the three following letters must all be radical, and נָה as the feminine plural termi- in the future tense; consequently the root is פָּקַד *he visited*, which is a regular verb.

129.—But if there remain two letters, or only one, the word must be derived from an irregular verb, and the omitted letter or letters must be supplied either by נ, י, or ל, as being the first radical; י or ו as the second radical: ה, ן, ת, as a third radical; or by doubling the last radical. To ascertain which of those letters are to be supplied, we must have recourse to the following rules:—

If two radicals remain and the first of them have a dagesh, supply נ as the first radical; as, מַסָּע *a journey;* מ is formative, and the root נָסַע *to travel,* except the word is derived from one of the eight verbs enumerated in Rule 46, in that case י must be supplied instead of נ; if the word be derived from לָקַח then ל must be supplied; as, מִקַּח (2 Chron. 19:7), root לָקַח *to take.* If one radical only remain, prefix נ and affix ה, as הַטִּי, root נָטָה, *incline*, but if the last of the two remaining radicals have dagesh, double that same radical; as, סֻכָּה *a hut,* from סָכַךְ *to cover over,* except the following terms: אַפַּיִם *face, anger,* חִטָּה *wheat,* בָּתֵּי *m-*

daughter, תִּתִּי *my giving*, שְׁתַּיִם *two*, and אַתָּה *thou*, where dagesh forte supplies נ medial, and they are derived from אָנַף, חָנַט, בָּנָה, נָתַן, שָׁנָה and אָנַת. If two radicals remain without either of these having dagesh forte, and a prefix is accompanied by וֹ, or ו or (ֵ) supply י as first radical, as תּוֹכֵחָה *a reproof*. ָה shows the noun to be feminine, the prefixed ת is an Heemantive or formative letter, and וֹ denotes the deficiency of י the first radical. Quiescent letters in ו or י as second radicals, and ה last radical, if omitted, are not supplied by any characteristic; but as those verbs with ה last radical, are by far most in number, the student will save time when such a doubtful case occurs, to look first in his Lexicon to the נחי ל׳ ה, and if not successful, it will be found amongst the נחי ע׳ ו׳, as גָּלוּת *captivity;* the termination וּת denotes the feminine gender;—then remain two radicals ג ל; the third radical might be י or ו medial, or ה final, look under the root גָּלָה; again רַע *evil*, insert ו the root being רוּעַ. We will now proceed to construe and parse the following lines (Ex. 9:1—7):—

and thou shalt speak Pharaoh to come Moses to the Eternal said
וַיֹּאמֶר יְהוָה אֶל מֹשֶׁה בֹּא אֶל־פַּרְעֹה וְדִבַּרְתָּ

my people send the Hebrews God [of] the Eternal said thus to him
אֵלָיו כֹּה אָמַר יְהוָה אֱלֹהֵי הָעִבְרִים שַׁלַּח אֶת־עַמִּי

and yet to send thou refusest if for and they shall serve me.
וְיַעַבְדֻנִי׃ כִּי אִם־מָאֵן אַתָּה לְשַׁלֵּחַ וְעוֹדְךָ

on thy cattle being the Eternal the hand of behold them. holdest thou
מַחֲזִיק בָּם׃ הִנֵּה יַד־ יְהוָה הוֹיָה בְּמִקְנְךָ

on the camels on the asses on the horses in the field which is
אֲשֶׁר בַּשָּׂדֶה בַּסּוּסִים בַּחֲמֹרִים בַּגְּמַלִּים

and will divide very. grievous a pest and on sheep on horned cattle
בַּבָּקָר וּבַצֹּאן דֶּבֶר כָּבֵד מְאֹד׃ וְהִפְלָה

the cattle of and between Israel the cattle of between the Eternal
יְהוָה בֵּין מִקְנֵה יִשְׂרָאֵל וּבֵין מִקְנֵה

Israel (which is) to the sons of of all shall die and not the Egyptians
מִצְרָיִם וְלֹא יָמוּת מִכָּל־ לִבְנֵי יִשְׂרָאֵל׃

to-morrow saying an appointed time the Eternal and made anything.
דָּבָר׃ וַיָּשֶׂם יְהוָה מוֹעֵד לֵאמֹר מָחָר

the Eternal   and did   in the land.   that   thing   the Eternal   will do

יַעֲשֶׂה יְהוָֹה הַדָּבָר הַזֶּה בָּאָרֶץ׃ וַיַּעַשׂ יְהוָֹה

the cattle of   all   and died of   in the morrow   that   thing

אֶת־הַדָּבָר הַזֶּה מִמָּחֳרָת וַיָּמָת כֹּל מִקְנֵה

died   not   Israel   the sons of   but of the cattle of   the Egyptians

מִצְרָיִם וּמִמִּקְנֵה בְּנֵי יִשְׂרָאֵל לֹא מֵת

from the cattle of   had died   not   and behold   Pharoah   and sent   one.

אֶחָד׃ וַיִּשְׁלַח פַּרְעֹה וְהִנֵּה לֹא מֵת מִמִּקְנֵה

and not   Pharoah   the heart of   and was hardened   one   even   Israel

יִשְׂרָאֵל עַד אֶחָד וַיִּכְבַּד לֵב פַּרְעֹה וְלֹא

the people.   did send

שִׁלַּח אֶת־הָעָם׃

וַיֹּאמֶר ו with its accompanying (ַ), and following dagesh, shows that the future tense is used for the preterite, see Rule 42; י is one of the letters אית̇ן forming the third person singular masculine. Root אָמַר *he said.*

יְהוָֹה a proper name of the Deity, and is derived from the root, הָיָה or הָוָה *to be.**

אֶל *to*, a preposition.

פַּרְעֹה a title given to Egyptian kings.

וְדִבַּרְתָּ ו conversive, prefixed to the preterite tense of Piel conjugation, and must therefore be rendered like the future.

אֵלָיו *to him*, from אֶל preposition, and the suffix ָיו used instead of ו (see the Particles).

כֹּה *thus*, is probably a compound of כ *as, like*, the particle of comparison, and ה derivative, from הוּא, *he, it, hence, like it, thus.*

אָמַר the root.

אֱלֹהֵי a noun masculine plural in regimen, from the absolute

---

* Some Jewish writers assign as a reason why the Deity has the name of יְהוָֹה, because that term expresses his eternity, immutability, and omnipresence, inasmuch as the four letters are the component parts of the past, present, and future tenses: הָיָה or הָוָה *he was*, הוֶֹה *he is*, and יִהְיֶה *he will be.*

form אֱלֹהִים, after the form of אֲדֹנִים; from the root אלה *to be mighty*.

הָעִבְרִים, הָ article, and has (ָ) before a guttural on account of its incapability of taking a dagesh; ִים a plural masc. termination; sing. עִבְרִי, the termination ִי denotes nationality, from עֵבֶר, a proper name, or עָבַר *to pass over*.

שַׁלַּח imperative Piel, like לַמֵּד, only that the vowel (ֵ) in the latter case is here changed into (ַ), because the last radical is ח, which requires either an accompanying or preceding (ַ).

אֶת denotes the accusative case of the following noun, עַמִּי, ִי is the sign of the first person singular common of the possessive pronoun; the last of the two remaining radicals having dagesh shows that another ם is to be supplied; root עָמַם.

וְיַעַבְדֻנִי, ו is conjunctive, and נִי affixed, denotes the first person of the personal pronoun, accusative case, instead of אֹתִי. עַבְדוּ third person masculine plural of the future tense, Kal, and ו is here changed into (ֻ), its corresponding short vowel, because of the increase נִי, according to the general rule,—"when a word increases in letters, it must decrease in vowels."

כִּי אִם are both particles. אַתָּה personal pronoun, second person masculine singular, dagesh forte in ת supplies the place of the rejected נ; root אנת.

לְשַׁלֵּחַ infinitive mood in Piel, which with ל prefixed becomes a gerund.

וְעוֹדְךָ, ו conjunctive, עוֹד adv. and root, but is used like a noun with the pronoun ךָ affixed, which affix is here used for אַתָּה, which ought to precede the participle. See Rule 32.

מַחֲזִיק participle Hiphil, from the root חָזַק like מַלְמִיד, only that (ְ) is here changed into (ֲ) because of its accompanying consonant being a guttural.

בָּם ablative of the personal pronoun, third person plural.

הִנֵּה interjection, with ה paragogic, from הֵן of the same import.

יַד a noun in regimen, from יָד absolute; the change from (ָ) to (ַ) denotes regimen, because a noun governing another considered as if both were united: hence it comes within th limits of the rule before stated, that if a noun increase in letters, it must decrease in its vowel points.

הוֹיָה a participle fem. singular, Kal, like גּוֹלָה; root הָיָה.

בְּמִקְנְךָ, בְּ ablative case; מִ formative, ךָ possessive pronoun; root קָנָה *to possess.*

אֲשֶׁר relative pronoun, indeclinable.

בַּשָּׂדֶה, בּ as before; by the accompanying (ַ) and subsequent dagesh, הַ the article is supplied according to rule; for article הַ is rejected before a noun which has one of the letters ב כ ל prefixed.

בַּסּוּסִים, בַּ as before; ־ִים plural masculine termination, from סוּס singular, which is the root.

בַּחֲמֹרִים and בַּגְּמַלִּים, the same remarks apply to their prefixes and terminations.

וּבַצֹּאן, וּ conjunctive, instead of וְ, because it stands before a labial; root צֹאן collective noun.

דֶּבֶר כָּבֵד מְאֹד radical nouns; for although מְאֹד is rendered adverbially, it has nevertheless all the properties of a noun.

וְהִפְלָה, ו as before; the Hiphil conjugation, third person singular masculine, from פלה of the נחי ל׳ ה׳.

בֵּין preposition.

מִקְנֵה a noun Heemantive in regimen, absolute מִקְנָה, rule,—a noun ending in ־ָה is changed into ־ֵה when in regimen; root קָנָה.

יִשְׂרָאֵל, a proper name, compounded of שַׂר *a Prince,* and אֵל *God,* and formative יִ.

וּבֵין as before.

מִצְרָיִם, properly the name of the country, Egypt, but is frequently used for the people,—the Egyptians.

וְלֹא, ו conjunction, prefixed to the negative particle.

יָמוּת third person singular masculine Kal, from מוּת, of the נחי ע׳ ו.

מִכָּל, מ a derivative from מִן, from which ן is here supplied by the dagesh in כּ; both מִן and מ denote the ablative case. כָּל a-adjective; it is pointed with (ָ) before makkaph or hyphen, otherwise it would have cholem over it; the mark (־), called makkaph causes the same changes in the preceding points as a noun in regimen, root כָּלַל; the ל omitted in כל ought to be supplied by a dagesh in the remaining ל, but is omitted whenever that radical is the final letter of a word.

לִבְנֵי a noun plural masculine in regimen with ל prefixed absolute בָּנִים, singular בֵּן, root בָּנָה *to build.*

דָּבָר a radical noun.

וַיָּשֶׂם, ו as before; יָשֶׂם for יָשִׂים third person masculine, future tense, in Hiphil; root שׂוּם:—see note in Paradigm קוּם.

מוֹעֵד, מ formative having for its vowel וֹ denotes that י first radical is rejected; root יָעַד *to appoint.*

לֵאמֹר infinitive, which ought, agreeably to the Paradigm, to be לֶאֱמֹר, and as according to rule (see the Chapter on the change of vowels), the vowel preceding the compound vowels (ֲ), (ֱ), (ֳ) is changed into the same, uncompounded with (ְ), the prefixed ל ought to have (ֶ), but for the sake of euphony, the vowels (ֶ) and (ֱ) are changed into (ֵ); therefore instead of לֶאֱמֹר we read לֵאמֹר.

מָחָר radical noun.

יַעֲשֶׂה third person singular masculine, future, in Kal, from עָשָׂה according to the Paradigm גָּלָה, it ought to be pointed יִעְשֶׂה, like יִגְלֶה, but ע being a guttural, requires the compound (ֲ), which by the rule above-mentioned, changes the preceding (ִ) into (ַ)

הַדָּבָר הַזֶּה both the noun and the demonstrative pronoun have the article prefixed, in conformity with the general rule "when the article is prefixed to the noun, the adjective agreeing with it requires the same."

בָּאָרֶץ, בָּ preposition having (ָ) instead of (ְ) denotes that the article is rejected on account of ב prefix, but (ָ) remains, which is the regular vowel under ה article before a guttural, as the guttural letters are incapable of having dagesh.

וַיַּעַשׂ, ו conversive prefixed to the future יַעֲשֶׂה; the last radical is dropped, which leaves ש without any vowel, and changes preceding (ָ) which ought to have been under ע, as before, into (ַ).

וַיָּמָת for וַיָּמוּת, see note in paradigm קוּם; מֵת third person singular masculine, preterite tense of Kal, root מוּת; the first radical מ has here (ֵ) instead of (ָ) which is a deviation from the common rule.

וַיֵּלֶךְ future tense with ו conversive prefixed.

עַד preposition, and adverb.

אֶחָד numeral adjective.

וַיִּכְבַּד; root כָּבֵד *to be heavy*, intransitive.

SYNTAX.

CHAPTER XVII.

Before we consider the rules of Syntax, it is proper to remark, that several rules which have already been treated upon, as well as many others which will be given in the General Remarks, have by modern Grammarians, from the great scholar, the elder Buxtorf, down to our own times, been usually allotted to this division o the Grammar. The arrangement herein chosen is partly tha of Rabbi David Kimchi.

There are two agreements in Syntax: first, between the nomi native and the verb; second, between the noun and the adjective

130.—A verb, for the most part, agrees with its nominative i person, number, and gender;* as, וַיֹּאמֶר יַעֲקוֹב *Jacob said,* יִשְׁתַּחֲווּ לְךָ בְּנֵי אִמֶּךָ *the sons of thy mother shall bow to thee,* הוּא אָמַר לִי *h*

---

* The proof of the doctrine of a plurality of persons in the Divine Bein deduced from the grammatical construction of the first verse of the Boo of Genesis, viz. בְּרֵאשִׁית בָּרָא אֱלֹהִים, where the verb singular בָּרָא has plural nominative אֱלֹהִים, cannot, we think, be fully sustained, because v find that בַּעַל, אָדוֹן and אֱלֹהַ, when applied to man, are in the plur number, and the verb is singular; as, אִם אֲדֹנָיו יִתֶּן לוֹ אִשָּׁה *if his mast should give him a wife* (Exod. xxi. 4); for here likewise is a nominati plural אֲדֹנָיו, to a verb singular. וְלָקַח בְּעָלָיו *and his master shall ta* (Exod. xxii. 10), also has a nominative plural, בְּעָלָיו, with a verb singul וְלָקַח. Further we may notice וְהִגִּישׁוֹ אֲדֹנָיו אֶל הָאֱלֹהִים וְהִגִּישׁוֹ אֶל הַדֶּלֶת אוֹ אֶל הַמְּזוּזָה וְרָצַע אֲדֹנָיו אֶת־אָזְנוֹ (Exod. xxi. 6). And it may be r marked here, that we think this passage ought not to be rendered as t Septuagint and the English versions have it; for the nominative to t second verb וְהִגִּישׁוֹ is אֱלֹהִים, else there could not be אֲדֹנָיו repeated aft וְרָצַע, but that it should be read thus, *his master shall make him come befo the* אֱלֹהִים *Judge, and he* (namely, the Judge), *shall make him draw nigh the door, and there his master shall pierce his ear.*

said to me.—Exceptions: (1 Sam, 25:27) אֲשֶׁר הֵבִיא שִׁפְחָתְךָ *which thy handmaid has brought*, a verb mas. with a nominative fem. and so
כִּי חָזַק מִמֶּנּוּ הַמִּלְחָמָה, וְהָיָה הָעַלְמָה, וְהָיָה הַנַּעֲרָה, וְהָיָה הָעִיר הַקְּרֹבָה,
וּבָא אֵלֶּה, וַיְהִי בִּרְכַּת יְהוָה, כִּי יִהְיֶה נַעֲרָה בְתוּלָה, אֶחְבְּשָׁה לִּי הַחֲמוֹר
וְאֶרְכַּב עָלֶיהָ, פִּלֶּגֶשׁ כָּלֵב מַעֲכָה יָלַד, וְעַוְלָה לֹא נִמְצָא, וּבָא בִּשְׁנָה הַשְּׁמוּעָה,
וּבָא עָלֶיךָ רָעָה, וּתְבוּאָתִי מִכֶּסֶף נִבְחָר, תַּחַת הַשְּׁאֵלָה אֲשֶׁר שָׁאַל,
וּזְעָקָה בָנִים נִשְׁמַע, תִּפְלַצְתְּךָ הִשִּׁיא, וְדַעַת מֵחָרוּץ נִבְחָר, יֵעָשֶׂה מְלָאכָה,
כָּמוֹהוּ לֹא נִהְיָתָה, וִיאַבֵּד אֶת־לֵב מַתָּנָה, הָעֲבוֹדָה הַקָּשָׁה אֲשֶׁר עֻבַּד,
הַמִּנְחָה אֲשֶׁר יֵעָשֶׂה, וַתַּעַשׂ הָרָעוֹת וַתּוּכַל, תַּחְתֶּיךָ יֻצַּע רִמָּה וּמְכַסֶּךָ תּוֹלֵעָה,
וְתִכָּרֵת לְךָ מֵהֶם, הַמְּדַבֵּר אֵלֶיךָ וַהֲבֵאתוֹ אֵלַי, עַד מָתַי תָּלִין בְּקִרְבֵּךְ
מַחְשְׁבוֹת אוֹנֵךְ, תְּהִי נֶעְלָמָה,

131.—The nominative case of the personal pronoun is seldom expressed before a verb, except by way of emphasis; as in וְאַתְּ תְּדַבֵּר אֵלֵינוּ *and thou (alone) shalt speak to us;* in that case the nominative generally precedes the verb, with the exception of the imperative mood; otherwise the verb precedes its nominative case.

132.—When a participle is used as the present tense, the separable pronoun must be expressed; as, אֶת־חֲטָאַי אֲנִי מַזְכִּיר *I mention my faults*, אָנֹכִי נֹגֵף *I do smite.*

133.—A noun of multitude in the singular number may be preceded either by a verb plural or singular; as, פֶּן יִנָּחֵם הָעָם *lest the people may repent;* וַתִּשָּׂא כָּל־הָעֵדָה וַיִּתְּנוּ אֶת־קוֹלָם *and the whole congregation lifted up and uttered their voices.*

134.—The vocative case of nouns agrees with the imperative mood of the verb in person, number, and gender; as, שִׁמְעוּ שָׁמַיִם וְהַאֲזִינִי אֶרֶץ *Hear, O ye heavens, and incline thine ear, O earth!* שִׁמְעוּ נָא הַמֹּרִים *Hearken ye, I pray, O rebellious!*

135.—When two or more nominatives of various genders precede the verb, the verb is generally put in the plural number and masculine gender, though each nominative be in the singular number; as, הַצֹּאן וְהַבָּקָר אַל יִרְעוּ *the flock and the horned cattle shall not feed;* but if they follow the verb, the verb is then put in the singular number; as, וַיָּמָת נָדָב וַאֲבִיהוּא *and Nadab and Abihu died*, אָז יָשִׁיר מֹשֶׁה וּבְנֵי יִשְׂרָאֵל *then sang Moses and the children of Israel.*

CHAPTER XVIII.

136.—Adjectives and participles agree with their substantives in gender, number and case; as, דָּבָר טוֹב *a good thing*, זֶבַח גָּדוֹל *a great sacrifice*, הַבְּהֵמָה הַטְּהוֹרָה *the clean cattle*, מְלָכִים וְשָׂרִים יֹשְׁבִים *kings and princes sitting*, אֶת־הַתְּשׁוּעָה הַגְּדוֹלָה הַזֹּאת *this great salvation.*

137.—Adjectives and participles are frequently used as substantives, or in other words, the substantive is understood; as, פִּי צַדִּיק יָנוּב חָכְמָה *the mouth of the just* (*man*) *produces wisdom*, טוֹב נִקְלֶה וְעֶבֶד לוֹ מִמִּתְכַּבֵּד וַחֲסַר לָחֶם *the* (*man that is*) *despised and has a servant, is better than* (*the man*) *that honoureth himself and lacketh bread*; כְּדַבֵּר אַחַת הַנְּבָלוֹת תְּדַבֵּרִי *like the speaking of one of the foolish* (*women*) *thou speakest.*

138.—Adjectives are sometimes put in the feminine gender, when in English the noun which is to be supplied is of the neuter gender; as, דִּבֶּר אִתָּנוּ קָשׁוֹת *he spoke with us hard* (*things*), אֵין בְּפִיהוּ נְכוֹנָה *there is not a right* (*utterance*) *in his mouth.*

139.—Adjectives and participles following several substantives of various genders, are put in the plural number and masculine gender: as, אַבְרָהָם וְשָׂרָה זְקֵנִים בָּאִים בַּיָּמִים *Abraham and Sarah were old, advancing in years*; but sometimes they agree in gender with the proximate noun; as, וּפְנֵיהֶם וְכַנְפֵיהֶם פְּרֻדוֹת *their faces and wings were separated;* פְּרֻדוֹת, feminine plural, agreeing with כָּנָף a noun feminine.

140.—As two nouns in construction must follow each other without any intervention, it sometimes happens that the adjective which belongs to the first of the two nouns, does yet agree in gender and number with the latter, being its proximate; as צַפַּחַת הַשֶּׁמֶן לֹא חָסֵר *and the bottle of the oil faileth not*: חָסֵר agrees with שֶׁמֶן, although according to the sense it belongs to צַפַּחַת.

CHAPTER XIX.

141.—When two nouns follow each other signifying different ideas, the first is to be considered in construction; as, סֵפֶר זִכְרוֹנוֹת *the book of memorials.* As it has been shown in Rule 73, &c., that every noun does not change its vowels when in construction, and indeed sometimes a noun having the form as if in construction, is yet in its sense absolute; as, מַכַּת בִּלְתִּי סָרָה for מַכָּה: the above rule is particularly worthy the attention of the student. But when two nouns of the same idea follow each other, they are in apposition; therefore some grammarians do not consider יְהוָֹה צְבָאוֹת *the Lord of hosts,* to be in construction, as it has been usually rendered; it being considered contrary to rule for יְהוָֹה a proper noun cannot be put in construction; but rather in apposition, for in Jehovah all hosts are comprised: He is all in all. He is denominated by Rabbinical writers מָקוֹם as being the *place* of every thing. And thus likewise may be understood לְמשֶׁה וּלְיִשְׂרָאֵל עַמּוֹ Moses being considered equal or superior to the whole people, as we read in Exod. 18:1.

142.—Adjectives are sometimes put in construction with a noun; as, גְּדוֹל הָעֵצָה *the great of counsel,* i.e. *great in counsel.*

143.—The adjective כֹּל *all, every, the whole, any,* may be followed by a verb singular or plural; as, כָּל־אִשָּׁה חַכְמַת לֵב בְּיָדֶיהָ טָווּ *every woman of an ingenious mind (they) did spin with her hands,* כָּל־אִישׁ וְאִשָּׁה אֲשֶׁר יָבוֹא *every man and woman who comes.*

144.—A repetition of nouns denotes distribution, increase, and fervency; as, אִישׁ אִישׁ *any one,* or *every one, each,* שֵׁשׁ כְּנָפַיִם שֵׁשׁ כְּנָפַיִם לְאֶחָד *every one had six wings;* מְאֹד מְאֹד *exceedingly great,* אֶרֶץ אֶרֶץ אֶרֶץ *earth, earth, earth,* such like repetition is not only found in nouns, but also in verbs, where it has a similar force; as, שׁוּבוּ שׁוּבוּ מִדַּרְכֵיכֶם *return, return from your ways.* In a similar way an infinitive is used with an imperative mood, with the preterite and future tenses; as, שִׁמְעוּ שָׁמוֹעַ *hear ye hearing*, i.e. *hear ye attentively*, טָרֹף טֹרַף יוֹסֵף *Joseph was indeed torn*, אָח לֹא פָּדֹה יִפְדֶּה אִישׁ *indeed no man will redeem a brother*, מוֹת תְּמוּתוּן *ye shall surely die.*

CHAPTER XX.

On the Accents, called נְגִינוֹת or טְעָמִים.

Accents are conjunctive and disjunctive. The former are pointed by placing (-) after them: those that occur over a word are placed thus -°, and those which occur under a word thus -°, the two principal pause or disjunctive accents are distinguished by (**), the minor pauses by (*).

The following Table exhibits the forms, names, and powers of the accents.

Forms.	Names.	Forms.	Names.
-	.... קַדְמָא	-	.... זַרְקָא
	.... אַזְלָא		.... סֶגוֹל
	.... גֵּרֵשׁ		.... מוּנַח |
	.... גֵּרְשַׁיִם	-	.... מוּנַח
-	.... דַּרְגָּא	*	.... רְבִיעַ
	.... תְּבִיר	-	.... מַהְפַּךְ
	.... יְתִיב		.... פַּשְׁטָא
|	.... פְּסִיק |	*	.... זָקֵף קָטֹן
** : *	.... סִלּוּק :	*	.... זָקֵף גָּדוֹל
	.... שַׁלְשֶׁלֶת	-	.... מֵרְכָא
	.... קַרְנֵי פָרָה		.... טִפְחָא
-	.... יֶרַח	**	.... אֶתְנַחְתָּא
	Euphonic Accents.		.... פָּזֵר
	.... מֶתֶג		...... תְּלִישָׁא גְדוֹלָה
-	.... מַקַּף	-	.... תְּלִישָׁא קְטַנָּה

---

* The סִלּוּק (:) is of a modern date.

145.—In every book of the Hebrew bible, with the exception of the books of Psalms, Proverbs, and Job,* each word not followed by (־) has at least one of those accents, over or under it; but when the word consists of three syllables, or sometimes even of two syllables, it may have two accents; as, מִשְׁבְּתֵיכֶם, מַ֫יִם; but where both are alike, the stress lies upon the first, and the vowel preceding the accent is always accompanied by Metheg, the euphonic accent; but when words have two dissimilar accents, the first is considered as Metheg, and the second is then the principal accent.

146.—It has been stated, Chapter IX, that when a word ends in one of the quiescent letters אהוי, and is unaccompanied by a pause accent, then the letters בגד כפת at the beginning of the following word have no dagesh; as, נִשְׁכְּבָה בְבָשְׁתֵּנוּ: (֣) being a conjunctive accent, ב remains without dagesh, being preceded by a quiescent letter; but in וְהַמֶּלֶךְ שְׁלֹמֹה בָּרוּךְ ה״, (֔) being a disjunctive accent, בּ is dageshed, although the preceding word ends in ה quiescent.

147.—The two principal pauses are (֑) and (֑), the latter is always followed by (׃), they not only possess the same power as the other disjunctive accents, but they moreover effect a change of that vowel which accompanies them; thus (ַ) is changed into (ָ), (ֵ), or (ֹ); as, טוֹב הַדָּבָר שָׁמָעְתִּי for שָׁמַעְתִּי; נָזֹלוּ, חָדֵלּוּ: (ְ) into (ָ) and sometimes into (ֹ); as, וְהֵשִׁיב יְהוָה אֶת־רָעָתְךָ בְּרֹאשֶׁךָ for בְּרֹאשְׁךָ; וְלֹא יָכֹלוּ for יָכְלוּ: (ֶ) into (ָ); as, הָאָרֶץ for הָאֶרֶץ; the change, however, in the latter noun, occurs likewise with the minor pauses.

148.—A word which terminates in (ֵ) or (ֹ) followed by Makkaph generally changes (ֵ) into (ֶ), and (ֹ) into a short (ָ) as, כָּל־ כֹּל, בֶּן־ בֵּן, אֶת־ אֵת, except the same ends in a quiescent letter; as, כֹּה־. זֶה and מַה followed by (־) respectively require the dagesh for the sake of euphony; as, מַה־טּוֹב, מַה־לָּכֶם, וְזֶה־לָּכֶם הָאוֹת.

---

* _ _ _ _ occur only in the Psalms, Proverbs, and Job.

Position of the Accents.

149.—In Hebrew, as in Greek, every word, monosyllables included, receives an accent, and this is usually placed on that syllable which is elevated above the general tone of discourse, except when two or more words are connected together by Makkaph; which, being considered as forming a single word, take but one accent between them. Now as no Hebrew word has in its simplest or radical form more than three consonants,* making but two syllables, the accent can be placed only either on the ultimate or penultimate. When accented on the ultimate syllable, the word is termed *Milrang* (מִלְּרַע *from below*), and when on the penult, *Mil'hêl* (מִלְּעֵיל *from above*); and even when the word is lengthened, the chief accent can never be placed farther back than the penult. When, as occasionally happens, an accent appears on the antepenult, it is only a secondary one, supplying the place of Metheg.

150.—The following letters and syllables can in no case receive an accent:

1. A letter accompanied by (ְ); because this does not constitute a syllable, except when taking a pause accent, which changes the Sheva into a vowel, e.g. דִּבֶּ֑רְךָ for דִּבַּרְךָ.

2. A consonant enunciated by means of one of the extremely short vowels which has arisen from Sheva; as such a syllable is too brief to allow of its being made the prominent one.

3. A syllable consisting of ה paragogic, or mobile, and its vowel of union; which, as regards the accent, are not considered as forming an integral part of the word.

General Rules of Position.

151.—The following will serve as general rules for the position of the accent:

1. A long vowel, when, contrary to its nature, it makes a mixed syllable, must take an accent to increase its quantity; and

---

* A very small number of quadriliterals excepted.

it is by means of this addition that the final consonant of the syllable is pronounced: for example, in the word קֹל, the ק is expressed by the help of its own vowel Cholem, and ל by means of the addition made to the same vowel, in consequence of its taking the accent, which may be represented thus—*kōᵒl*. Hence arises the rule, that *an accent enables a long vowel to make a mixed syllable.*

2. A short vowel, when, contrary to its nature, it makes a simple syllable, must be accompanied by an accent; by which its quantity is increased, and made equivalent to that of a long one; thus in the word מֶ֫לֶךְ *mélech*, the first syllable takes the accent. Whence the rule, that *an accent enables a short vowel to make a simple syllable.*

3. In Hebrew, as in other languages, a *long* vowel always has the preference over a *short* one in receiving the accent; except when, as in the instance just given, it is absolutely necessary, that the latter should take it, in order to form a simple syllable.

4. *Cæteris paribus*, an accent will be placed on the *ultimate* syllable rather than on the *penult.*

Position on Nouns.

152.—1. As a general rule, every noun whose ultimate is a long syllable, whether simple or mixed, will take the accent on that syllable. If the ultimate be a simple syllable, it will receive the accent on account of the preference which it has in that respect over the penult, e.g. הַיַּבָּשָׁה Gen. 1:9, וּנְקֵבָה Ibid 1:27; and if a mixed one, the accent is indispensably necessary to its completion, e.g. בְּרֵאשִׁית. But if this long vowel be one which has arisen in consequence of the addition of a paragogic ה, the accent will be on the penult, e g. יְשׁוּעָתָה Ps 3:3, for יְשׁוּעָה; לַ֫יְלָה Gen. 1:5, for לַיִל; and the same is the case with nouns receiving ה mobile, e.g. סֻכֹּ֫תָה Gen. 33:17, אַ֫רְצָה Ibid 37:10, בַּ֫יְתָה Ibid 43:17. In a few instances also we find the paragogic syllable ִי without the accent, e g. רַבָּתִי, שָׂרָתִי Lam. 1:1.

2. Every noun whose ultimate is a short mixed syllable, pre-

ceded either by a long vowel or by a short simple syllable, is Milhel, i. e. has the accent on the penult, e. g. בֹּקֶר Gen. 1:5, עֶרֶב Ibid, הַשָּׁמַיִם Ibid 1:1; for if the penult is a long vowel, it has the preference in taking the accent; and if it be a short one not succeeded by a vowelless consonant, it must have the accent, as otherwise it could not make a simple syllable. In the case, however, of an ultimate short vowel taking the place of a long one, as for instance, the termination of the fem. construct, the accent retains its former position on that syllable, e. g. חַיָּה, constr. חַיַּת Gen. 2:19; רָעָה, constr. רָעַת Ibid 6:5; and the same is the case with a short vowel which has arisen from the coalescence of a long vowel with Patach furtive, e. g. רֹגַע Is. 51:15, for רֹגֵעַ; רֹקַע Ps. 136:6, for רֹקֵעַ. And if the penult. and ultimate are both short mixed syllables, the accent will be placed on the latter, e. g. בַּרְזֶל 2 Kings 6:5, גַּרְזֶן Is. 10:15.

3. Since all vowels are considered long in which one of the אהוי letters quiesces, the masc. termination ־ֶה likewise takes the accent, e. g. בְּקָנֶה Gen. 41:5, הַמִּשְׁנֶה Ibid 41:43; unless the consonant bearing (ֶ) be immediately preceded by a short vowel, when the accent must be placed on the penult, e. g. הֶגֶה Ezek. 2:10. Of course this rule applies also to ־ֶא, e. g. פֶּלֶא Ps. 77:15.

Participles are considered as verbal nouns, and are accordingly subjected to the foregoing rules.

Position on Verbs.

153.—The place of the accent on the verb, when without a suffix, is to be decided as follows:

1. Every verb whose root consists of three perfect consonants, will take the accent on the second, in all the persons of the preterite, future, and imperative, and in both states of the infinitive, viz. absolute and construct., whenever such radical has a vowel of its own, as this vowel is the principal one of the root: e. g. קָטַל, קָטַלְתָּ &c.; יִקְטֹל, תִּקְטֹל, &c.; קְטֹל, קְטֹלְנָה; קָטוֹל, קְטֹל. But in those persons where the second radical has (ְ) the accent is placed on the third, e. g. קָטְלָה, תִּקְטְלִי, קִטְלִי, &c.

2. In the following cases, however, the accent is on the ultimate syllable, although the second radical has a vowel: viz. in the second person plural masc. and fem. preterite, e.g. קְטַלְתֶּם, קְטַלְתֶּן; and in the first and second person masc. preterite, when taking ו conversive, to distinguish it from the same person and tense with ו conjunctive, e.g. וְדִבַּרְתִּי, וְשָׁמַרְתָּ.

3. The verbs ע״ו and ע״ע in those persons of the preterite where the third radical has (ְ) after the rejection of the second, will take the accent on the first, e.g. קַמְתָּ, קָמָה; but in those where the third radical receives an epenthetic vowel, it also takes the accent, which, were it suffered to remain on the first, would be carried back, against the rule, to the antepenult., e.g. סַבּוֹתָ.

4. The persons of the future tense which when standing alone have the accent on the ultimate, will invariably shift it to the penult., if a simple syllable, on receiving ו conversive: thus, in Piel of verbs ע״ gutt., as וַיְבָרֶךְ; in Kal of verbs פ״א, as וַיֹּאמֶר; פ״י, as וַיֵּשֶׁב, וַיֹּסֶף; ע״ע, as וַיָּגֶל; and ל״ה, as וַיִּפֶן; unless the penult. is a mixed syllable, when the accent remains on the ultimate, e.g. וַיִּקְטֹל, וַיְקַטֵּל, וַיִּגַּשׁ.

Position on Nouns and Verbs with Suffixes.

154.—1. The suffixes ־ִי, ־ַי, ־ָהּ, ו, ־ָם, ־ָן, כֶם, כֶן, הֶם, הֶן, as a general rule receive the accent; so that all words to which they are appended are Milrah; e.g. דְּבָרִי, דְּבָרַי, דְּבָרַי, קְטָלוֹ, קְטָלָהּ, שְׁבָרָם, קְטַלְכֶם, ־כֶן, יְדֵיהֶם, ־הֶן, ־הֶן.

2. The following are preceded by the accent: ־ָם, ־ָהּ, הוּ, נוּ, נִי, ־ֶן, מוֹ; hence words receiving them are Milhel; e.g. קְטָלַנִי, זְכָרָנוּ, קְטָלוּהָ, יָדֶיהָ, קְטַלְתַּם, קְטָלְתַן, מוֹסְרוֹתֵימוֹ Ps. 2:3.

3. When the suffix of the second person masc. sing. ךָ is preceded by (ְ), the word is accented Milrah, e.g. דְּבָרְךָ; when preceded by a vowel, Milhel, e.g. דְּבָרֶיךָ, אֵלֶיךָ.

Further Use of Accents.

155.—Since we sometimes meet with words entirely alike in their letters and vowel-points, and differing only in the position of their accents, an acquaintance with the principles by which this position is regulated is not only useful, but is absolutely necessary to the perfect understanding of many passages of the Hebrew Scriptures. For it frequently so happens that the accentuation is the only means whereby we can determine with precision whether a given word is a noun or a verb, and, if a verb, whether it is derived from this or that root, or belongs to this or that mood or tense; thus, for instance, in the following passage, כִּי־מָ֫רָה נֶפֶשׁ כָּל־הָעָם 1 Sam. 30:6, as the word מָ֫רָה is accented Milhel, it must be the third person fem. sing. pret. of the ע"ע verb מָרַר *to be bitter*, of the form סַ֫בָּה from סָבַב; while the accent on the last syllable of the same word in the phrase מָרָה אֶת־פִּי 1 Kings 13:26, shows it to be the third person masc. pret. of the ל"ה verb מָרָה *to be rebellious*, like גָּלָה. The word שָׂמֵ֫חָה, which occurs Esth. 8:15, is shown by the accent on its penultimate to be the third person fem. sing. pret. of the verb שָׂמַח *to rejoice*; but the accent on the ultimate—thus שְׂמֵחָה Ps. 113:9—points it out as the fem. part. of the same verb employed as a noun. So likewise סָבָה, בָּאָה, שָׁבָה, are preterites when the accent is Milhel, and participles when Milrah. In the command קוּמִי אוֹרִי *arise, shine*, Is. 60:1, the imperative is designated by the accent on the penult., but in the expression לְיוֹם קוּמִי *till the day of my rising up*, Zeph. 3:8, the accent on the ultimate syllable of קוּמִי shows it to be a noun with the pron. suffix ִי, etc., etc.

Recession of the Accent.

156.—On account of the difficulty of enunciating two tone-syllables in immediate succession, any two accents, whether placed on the same word, or on two different words in juxtaposition, require a vowel, or at least a Sheva mobile, between them. So that if of two concurrent words the accent of the first is on its last syllable, and that of the second on its first, the accent of the first word will be removed to the penult. This was called by the old grammarians נָסוֹג אָחוֹר *turned back*.

Thus a word may have two accents, the first a conjunctive,

and the second a disjunctive, with either a vowel or Sheva between them, e. g. הַכּוֹכָבִים Gen. 15:5, מְבָרְכֶיךָ Ibid 12:3; in which case the first accent has merely the power of a Metheg, for which it is the substitute. But if two words come together, the first accented Milrah, and the second—a dissyllable—Milhel, so that one accent follows the other without either a vowel or Sheva mobile between them, the accent of the first word must be thrown back one degree, in order to separate them: thus the preterite קָרָא is to be accented Milrah, and the noun לַיְלָה Milhel, but when the two concur, as in Gen. 1:5, instead of קָרָא לַיְלָה, the accent of the first word is thrown back, and we have קָרָא לָיְלָה; so יִמָּלֵא מָיִם 2 Kings 3:17. Of course this recession of the accent on the ultimate regularly takes place when the following word is a monosyllable, e. g. וְעָשָׂה לוֹ Gen. 37:3, for וְעָשָׂה לוֹ.

157:—To the above rule, there are the following exceptions:

1. If the first accent is a disjunctive, it may remain on the ultimate, although immediately followed by another; as the words are somewhat separated by the pause, e. g. שָׁמַע עֶבֶד Gen. 24:52, הוֹאֵל קַח 2 Kings 5:23.

2. If both accents are conjunctive, no change in the position of either takes place; for the situation of the words bearing them is somewhat analogous to that of words followed by Makkaph; i. e. as in the latter case the accent entirely disappears, so in the former it loses so much of its force as no longer to cause offence to the ear, or difficulty in the enunciation, when two of them occur together, e. g. מֵעַל זֶבַח Lev. 4:31.

3. If a dissyllable accented Milrah is immediately preceded by an accent, it will not be altered to Milhel even though another accent should directly follow; for the object of such change from the normal position would remain unaccomplished, as two accented syllables would still concur, e. g. לֹא שֹׂנֵא הוּא Deut. 19:6.

4. An ultimate syllable having a long vowel, followed by a perfect consonant must necessarily receive an accent, which consequently retains its position, although immediately followed by another accent, e. g. יוֹבֵל הִיא Lev. 25:12.

5. Words taking the grave suffixes כֶם, כֶן, הֶם, הֶן, and the second pers. plur. of the pret. of verbs, ending in תֶּם and תֶּן, invariably retain the accent on the ultimate.

6. When the penultimate is a short mixed syllable, the accent is not thrown back, as such a syllable avoids the reception of an accent; e. g. וְנִסְלַח לוֹ Lev. 5:13, וַיַּכּוּ אִישׁ 2 Kings 3:23.

Keri and Ketib

158.—In the current editions of the Hebrew Bible, we meet with a number of notes in the margin which contain directions as to the proper method of reading and writing many words, and concerning which the following brief remarks may suffice. In the course of the laborious revision of the biblical text undertaken by a celebrated body of Jewish critics, called Masorets (מוֹסְרִים *handers-down*, from מְסַר Talm. *to deliver*), who lived in the beginning of the sixth century, a multitude of passages were found, which, according tc received opinion, were in some respect defective; still the high degree of veneration in which these scholars held the sacred text, prevented their rejecting readings however faulty, in which the manuscripts concurred. They accordingly suffered all such passages to remain; but when they came to a word which seemed erroneously written, they left th text undisturbed, and placed the emendation in the margin, wit the accompanying remark קְרֵי וּכְתִיב (Chald. part. pass.) *read an written:* thus in Job 13:15, the word *written* (i. e. occurring i the text) לֹא is to be *read* לוֹ. When a word was considere superfluous, they left it unpointed, and placed in the margin th observation כְּתִיב וְלֹא קְרֵי *written but not read*, e. g. the word א 2 Kings 5:18. And when, on the contrary, a word was though wanting to complete the sense, the vowels alone were inserted i the text, and the word itself placed in the margin, with the no קְרֵי וְלֹא כְתִיב *read but not written*, e. g. the word יָמִים Jer. 31:3 The number of these critical remarks varies in different edition thus Elias Levita reckons them at 848, while Capel, in t second edition printed at Venice, found 1171. Among the Keri and Ketib may be reckoned the word יהוה, which, as the complete and most holy name of God (שֵׁם הַמְּפֹרָשׁ), was forbidden to be uttered by any except the high priest, and by him but once a year in the Holy of Holies. On all other occasions it was to be read אֲדֹנָי *Lord*, and hence the Masora (מָסוֹרָה *tradition*) has given it the points of that word, thus יְהֹוָה; except in those cases where יהוה is immediately preceded by the word אֲדֹנָי, when, to avoid repetition, it was read אֱלֹהִים *God*, and pointed accordingly; thus אֲדֹנָי יֱהֹוִה. Various other marks are to be found in the Bible, which, in modern editions, are generally explained either in the prolegomena or at the end.

GENERAL REMARKS.

The following are general remarks upon the anomalies of Verbs, which will be best understood by a reference to the paradigm in this Grammar.

Preterite of KAL.

1. In לָמְדָה we find ־ָה sometimes changed into ־ַת; as in אָזְלַת יָד (Deut. 32:36).

2. לָמַדְתָּ is found with paragogic ה; as in בָּגַדְתָּה (Mal. 2:14), הִסְכַּנְתָּה (Ps. 139:3).

3. In לָמַדְתְּ with a guttural for the third radical, the first (־ְ) is changed into (־ַ); as in שָׁמַעַתְּ (Ruth 2:8).

4. In לְמַדְתֶּם (־ֶ) is sometimes changed into (־ָ); as in וִרְשְׁתָּם and into (־ֻ); as in וּשְׁאֶלְתֻּם.

Participle.

In לוֹמֵד, if the last radical be ע or ח, that letter will have (־ַ) as in נוֹטֵעַ, פּוֹתֵחַ; it, however, sometimes happens that (־ֵ) i changed into (־ַ) without being followed by a guttural; as in אֹבַד but this is rarely the case. In the two verbs תָּמַךְ and יָסַף, (־ֵ) i the participle is changed into ־ִי; as in תּוֹמִיךְ, יוֹסִיף. In th poetical parts of scripture we sometimes find the י paragogi affixed to the particle; as, מְקִימִי, מוֹשִׁיבִי, הַמַּגְבִּיהִי, שֹׁכְנִי, אֹסְרִי.

לֹמֶדֶת.—With ע or ח as the third radical, we find (־ַ־ַ) instea of (־ֶ־ֶ); as in יוֹדַעַת, בֹּרַחַת: sometimes we have likewise י parа gogic added; as, אֹהַבְתִּי, אֵיבְתִּי.

לָמוּד.—Sometimes וּ is changed into (־ֻ); as in ־ֻשׁ; and th is found likewise, although seldom, with י paragogic; as in גְּנֻבְתִּי

Infinitive Mood.

לְמוֹד.—Absolute. Sometimes וֹ is changed into (ֹ), as in וְגָדֹל, וּבְשׁ.

When לְמוֹד is in construction, and followed by makkaph, וֹ is changed into short (ָ); as in אֱמָר־לְךָ (Prov. 25:7); it is also found with ה paragogic; as in לְחֶמְלָה, לְאַהֲבָה, לְדָבְקָה. In verbs intransitive, and sometimes in verbs transitive, וֹ is changed into (ַ), as in שְׁאַל: the same is the case when the last radical is ח; as in שְׁלַח.

Imperative Mood.

לְמוֹד.—With makkaph, as לְמָד־, and with ה paragogic it is formed like זָכְרָה from זְכֹר, and in some instances it takes the form of שִׁכְבָה from שְׁכַב, that of שִׁלְחָה from שְׁלַח, נִצְרָה from נְצוֹר, מִכְרָה from מְכוֹר, &c. When the first radical letter is a guttural, and ה is suffixed, then the guttural letter has a (ָ), as in אָסְפָה (Num. 11:16). We have likewise the form of לְמָדָה as רְפָאָה, שְׁמָעָה, סְלָחָה.

Observation.—It is asserted by some Grammarians, that the infinitive is sometimes used for the imperative mood; as, זָכוֹר אֶת יוֹם הַשַּׁבָּת לְקַדְּשׁוֹ *remember the Sabbath day to keep it holy*; because they consider זָכוֹר to be the infinitive mood; but as that would be an extraordinary anomaly, it is more likely, that the imperative has sometimes (ָ) for (ְ).

לִמְדוּ.—Sometimes (ִ) is changed into short (ָ); as in חָרְבוּ, מָשְׁכוּ; and when the second radical is a guttural with a compound vowel (ֲ) is then, according to the common rule, changed into the simple vowel of the guttural; as in שַׁחֲטוּ, אֶהֱבוּ. Yet in some instances (ִ) is retained, as in שִׁחְרוּ.

לִמְדִי.—(ִ) is likewise changed into short (ָ); as in מָלְכִי (Judg. 9:10), and at other times into (ֶ); as in חֶשְׂפִּי (Is. 47:2).

לְמוֹדְנָה.—וֹ is sometimes changed into (ֶ); as in צְעַקְנָה (Jer. 49:3): sometimes ה is dropped; as in שְׁמַעַן, קְרָאן and קְרָאֶן.

אֶלְמוֹד.—It has been already observed, that the future ten-is formed from the imperative mood, hence, whatever irregularity is found in the latter, will likewise be met with in the former.

תִּלְמְדוּ.—With the accent מִלְעֵיל, the second (ְ), is changed into וֹ or (ְ); as in תְּנוֹבוּ, תִּשְׁמָעוּ.

תִּלְמוֹדְנָה.—Irregularly, וַתִּגְבְּהֶינָה for וַתִּגְבַּהְנָה (Ez. 16:50) in the verb שָׁכַן we find נ feminine omitted; as in תִּשְׁכֹּנָּה, and in one case ת feminine is changed for י masculine; as יַעֲמֹדְנָה (Dan. 8:22).

Preterite of NIPHAL.

נִלְמְדָה.—With a pause accent מִלְעֵיל (penultima) נִלְמָדָה. The placing of the accent distinguishes the preterite from the participle feminine of this verb, which is likewise נִלְמָדָה, where the accent is placed מִלְרַע (ultima).

נִלְמְדוּ, irregularly with נְגֹאֲלוּ (Is. 59:3).

Participle.

נִלְמָד.—(ֵ) for (ָ); as in נוֹקֵשׁ. In Exod. 15:6, נֶאְדָּרִי is probably used for נֶאְדֶּרֶת fem., the nominative being יְמִינְךָ fem.

נִלְמָדִים.—Some few instances are found where (ָ) is changed into (ְ); as in נִטְמְאִים, הַנִּמְצְאִים.

Infinitive.

הִלָּמֵד.—Irregularly נִשְׁאֹל (I Sam. 20:28), נִכְסֹף (Gen. 31:30) and הִנָּתֹן. א for ה (Ezek. 14:3), הַאִדָּרֵשׁ to avoid the reduplication of ה for the sake of euphony. נִגּוֹף for נִנְגּוֹף, sometime dagesh is omitted; as in כְּהִנְדֹף (Ps. 68:3).

Imperative Mood.

הִלָּמֵד.—But with the accent מִלְעֵיל (ֵ) is changed into (ֶ); a הִשָּׁמֶר.

Future Tense.

אֶלָּמֵד—(ָ) is somtimes changed into (ְ); as, אִשָּׁבֵעַ, וּמָּלְטָה. Instead of (ֵ) we likewise find (ֶ); as, וַיִּנָּפֵשׁ, וַתֵּעָצֵר.

תִּלָּמַדְנָה.—(ֵ) is changed into (ַ); as, תִּרָמַסְנָה, תִּשָּׁאַרְנָה.

PIEL.

לִמֵּד, לִמַּד and שִׁבֵּר.—The following have (ֶ) instead of (ֵ)— דִּבֶּר, כִּבֶּס. With a guttural second radical letter (ֵ) is changed into (ֶ); as in מֵאֵן, בֵּרֵךְ, with some few exceptions; such as נִאֵץ, לִהֵט and זֵרְמוּ.

PARTICIPLE.

מְלַמֵּד.—With a second radical guttural (ַ) is changed into (ָ); as in מְבָרֵךְ, מְתָאֵב, except in מְנַהֵל and מְנַחֵם. With א for the first radical, that letter is omitted in the participle; as, מַלְּפֵנוּ for מְאַלְּפֵנוּ (Job 35:11).

מְלַמֶּדֶת.—Irregularly מְשָׁרַת for מְשָׁרֶתֶת (1 Kings i. 15).

INFINITIVE MOOD.

לַמֵּד.—Sometimes with (ֵ) for (ַ); as, נָאֵץ, נַאֶצְתָּ, likewise with (ֶ); as, לְחֶנְנָה, and sometimes (ֵ) is changed into (ָ); as, לְצַחֵק.

IMPERATIVE MOOD.

לַמֵּד.—With Makkaph following, (ֵ) is changed into (ֶ), as in the infinitive mood; thus קַדֶּשׁ־לִי imp., וְדַבֶּר־אָוֶן inf. Sometimes into (ַ); as in פַּתַּר, פַּלַּג.

PRETERITE OF PUAL.

לֻמַּד.—With a guttural second radical (ֻ) is changed into וֹ; as in דּוֹחוּ, וּמֹרָק, נֹאַץ; except, however, in רֻחַץ, and a few more instances where (ֻ) is retained before ח.

PRETERITE OF HIPHIL.

הִלְמַדְתָּ.—(ִ) is once changed into (ֵ); as in הֵעֲבַרְתָּ (Jos. 7:7), and also into (ֶ); as in הֶכְלַמְנוּם (1 Sam. 25:7).

הִלְמַדְתִּי.—(ִ) is in one instance changed into (ֵ): viz. in הִשְׁאִלְתִּיהוּ (1 Sam. 1:28), and according to some Grammarians ה is changed into ת; as in תִּרְגַּלְתִּי (Hos. 11:3) for הִרְגַּלְתִּי, although others take this word to be a noun from the absolute תִּרְגֹּלֶת. Various other changes occur in the Hiphil conjugation; as in אֶגְאָלְתִּי (Is. 53:3) for הִגְאַלְתִּי, where the א is used instead of ה, ain the Chaldaic. In וְהֶאֶזְנִיחוּ (Is. 19:6), however, the Hebrew הֶ, as characteristic of Hiphil, is joined to א, the characteristic of the same conjugation in the Chaldaic.

Participle.

מַלְמִיד for מְהַלְמִיד, and מֵזִין (Prov. 17:4) for מַאֲזִין.—In the adjectives derived from the participle in Hiphil, (ִ) is changed into (ַ); as, מַשְׁחִת, מַרְשַׁעַת.

מַלְמִידִים, irregularly, מְעֻזָּרִים for מַעֲזִירִים, and so in מְחַלְּמִים, מְחַצְּרִים, מְהַלְּכִים: this last is either from a quadriliteral root, or is similar to the 12th conjugation in the Arabic language.

מַלְמִידוֹת.—Once (Lev. 26:16) מְדִיבֹת for מַדְאִיבֹת.

Infinitive Mood.

הַלְמִיד.—Very frequently ִי is changed into (ֵ), particularly when the word is without the letters בכלם: in a few instances י is retained after (ֵ); as in הַשְׁמִיד, הַעֲנִיק. Sometimes (ִ) is changed into (ָ); as in וְהִמְלִיט (Is. 31:5), לַאֲדִיב (1 Sam. 2:33), for לְדְאִיב. The Chaldaic characteristic א is likewise used for ה; as in אַשְׁכֵּים (Jer. 24:4) for הַשְׁכֵּם, and אַבְרֵךְ (Gen. 41:43) for הַבְרֵךְ.

Future Tense.

יַלְמִידוּ.—Sometimes (ָ) for ִי; as in יַדְרִכוּ, יַדְבִּקוּ.

Preterite of HOPHAL.

הָלְמַד and הֻלְמַד.

Infinitive.

הָלְמֵד, הָלְמַד and הִכַּבֵּס (Lev. 13:55): this last is perhaps a compound of הָקְטַל and הִתְקַטֵּל, or the dagesh in כ may be euphonic.

Preterite of HITHPAEL.

הִתְלַמֵּד and הִתְלַמַּד.—Sometimes ת is omitted, and compensation made by a dagesh in the subsequent letter; as, מִדַּבֵּר for

מִתְדַּבֵּר, מִטַּהֵר for מִתְטַהֵר, הִזַּכּוּ for הִתְזַכּוּ, which last, becomes הִזָּכּוּ. When the second radical letter is a guttural or ר, the preceding (ַ) is changed into (ָ); as in וְהִתְבָּרֵךְ: except before ח, when (ַ) is retained; as in הִתְנַחֵם.

הִתְלָמְּדוּ.—In one instance (ָ) is used instead of (ַ), which may be compounded of this and the Hophal conjugation. וְהִתְגֹּעֲשׁוּ (Jer. 25:16) is likewise supposed to be a compound of this and Piel conjugation.

תִּתְלַמֵּד.—Irregularly וַתֵּתַצַּב, from the root יָצַב, for וַתִּתְיַצֵּב.

Verbs Defective in the First Radical נ י, and One Defective Verb in ל.

Infinitive of KAL.

גֶּשֶׁת.—Some verbs have (ֶ ֶ), as לָטַעַת, בְּגַעַת, etc., and from נָשָׂא, שְׂאֵת and שֵׂאת; from לָקַח, קַחַת—once קְחַת, and also in the regular form; as לִקוֹחַ, from נָתַן, תֵּת. See Paradigm. In general it may be observed, that most of the defective verbs in the first radical, are found occasionally to have the same form as regular verbs; as, נְגוֹחַ, נְפוֹל, תִּנְדּוֹף, תִּנְחַל, תִּנְחַת, וְאֶנְחֵהוּ, יִנְקְפוּ, יִנְצְרוּ, נִלְקַח, מִנְעִילוּם, הִנָּתְּקוּ, and so forth. *In the preterite* they are always like regular verbs, except in קַח and תַּתָּה.

Future Tense.

יִגַּשׁ.—Sometimes with ו; as, יִבּוֹל, and with second radical guttural, like יִנְחַת, and even without a guttural, it is in some few places found with (ַ) instead of (ֵ); as in יִשַּׁל.

NIPHAL.

נִגַּשׁ, and once נִפּוֹל.—Some grammarians maintain that נִתָּעוּ (Job 4:10) in the Niphal, is from the root נָתַע; but Kimchi and others, derive it from תָּעָה, and consider it a compound of נִפְעַל and הִתְפַּעֵל.

Verbs Defective in the Second Radical, that is, having the Second and Third Radical Alike.

Observation.—The verbs כָּהָה and לָהָה should not be classed amongst the above; since the first ה is pronounced, and the last is quiescent: the following are conjugated like a regular verb, זָמַם, בָּלַל, עָשַׁשׁ; and there are others, which although frequently defective, are nevertheless sometimes used as regular verbs.

Preterite of KAL.

סַבּוּ.—Sometimes with וֹ; as in שֹׁמּוּ, רֹמּוּ, וְרֹבּוּ, בָּזְאוּ for בָּזְזוּ (Is. 18:2), and according to some Grammarians, תַּמְנוּ (Lam. 3:22) is used for תַּמּוּ and תָּמְמוּ, and so likewise מָעֻזְּנֶיהָ (Is. 23:4) for מָעֻזֶּיהָ.

Infinitive Mood.

סוֹב.—When followed by makkaph, וֹ is changed into short (ָ); as in בְּרָן־יַחַד (Job 38:7). Sometimes וֹ is changed into (ֻ): as in לָרֹד (Isa. 45:1), and sometimes into וּ; as in וְלָבוּר (Ecc. 9:1) לָעוּת (Isa. 50:4).

Imperative Mood.

סֹב.—Sometimes with (ַ); as in גַּל (Ps. 119:18). סֹבּוּ—sometimes וֹ is changed into short (ָ); as in רָנּוּ.

Future Tense.

אָסֹב.—We find אָקֹב; אָבוֹת, יָשׁוֹם with ו conversive like וַיָּחָם. In some instances וֹ is changed וּ; as in יָרוֹן; and sometimes וּ is again changed into its corresponding short vowel (ֻ); as in וַיָּרָם תְּסֻבֶּינָה, and irregularly תְּצִלֶּינָה and תְּצִלְּנָה.

Preterite of NIPHAL.

נָסַב.—Before ח (ָ) is changed into (ֵ); as in נִחַר, נִחַת, נִחַל; sometimes into (ֵ); as in נָקַל, וְנָמֵם.

נָסַבּוּ.—We have in somes cases (ַ) changed into וֹ; as in נוֹזוּ, נָגֹלּוּ, נָקֹשׁוּ; and before ח we have (ֵ), as in the singular number נְסַבָּה and נָסֵבָה. Also the form of וְנָקַבָּה, וְנָסַבָּה.

Participle.

נָסֵב.—(ֵ) instead of (ָ); as in נָמֵס, נְסַבִּים, and with (ֵ) under the first letter, as in נֵאָרִים, נֵחָמִים and נְסַבָּה.

Infinitive.

הִסּוֹב, הִסֵּב and הָסֵב, and hence לְהֵחַלּוֹ.

Future Tense.

אָסֵב.—And with (ַ), as in אִכֹּף; and sometimes with אֵ; as in אֵיתַם, וָאֵקַל and וָאֵחַל.

תְּסֻבִּי.—And with וֹ; as, תְּדוֹמִּי.

תִּסַּב.—Sometimes with (ֵ) like יִמַּר, and with (ָ); as in תִּתַּם.

Preterite of HIPHIL.

הֵסֵב.—And often after the form of הִסֵּב, as in הֵשַׁח, הֵדַק, הֵתַז.

הֵסֵבָּה.—And without dagesh הֵעֵזָה (Prov. 7:13).

הֲסִבּוֹתָ.—With first radical guttural הֲ; as in הַחִתּוֹתָ and sometimes וֹ is changed into (ִ); as in הֲפִתִּיהָ.

הֵסֵבּוּ and הֵסַבּוּ, הֵשַׁמּוּ, הֵתַמּוּ.

Future Tense.

וַיָּסֵב, יַשִּׁים, תָּסִיב, תָּסֵב—before makkaph, and with ו conversive (ֵ) is changed into (ֶ); as in וַיָּגֶל, יָסֶף־לְךָ.

נִסֵּב.—Likewise in the form of וַנַּשִּׁים (Num. 21:30).

Verbs Quiescent having י for their First Radical.

Infinitive Mood.

שֶׁבֶת, דֵּעַת, and דֵּעָה, from יָדַע; but when an infinitive is used together with any of the tenses, it has the form similar to that derived from a regular verb: as in יָשׁוֹב אֵשֵׁב, יָרֹד יָרַדְנוּ, except the following: וְלִיסוֹד, לִישׁוֹן, בִּיבוֹשׁ. Sometimes the first radical י is dropped without ת being suffixed; as in שׁוֹב תָּשְׁבוּ. In one instance the first and third radicals are dropped, as in לָלֶת for לָלֶדֶת (1 Sam. 4:19).

Imperative Mood.

שֵׁב.—If followed by makkaph, (ֵ) is changed into (ֶ); as in לֶךְ־, sometimes into (ַ); as in הַב, צַק, דַּע: some retain י as in the regular verbs; and in Ps. 34:10, we find יְראוּ (root יָרֵא *to fear*) for יְראוּ, in order to distinguish it from יִרְאוּ (third person plur. future tense) from רָאָה *to see.*

Future Tense.

אֵשֵׁב.—י is sometimes retained, as in אֵילְכָה, וַיִּישַׁר, but in most cases where י is retained, the letters אֵיתָן are accompanied by (ִ), and the last vowel is (ַ); as in אִיצַק, אִיבַשׁ, yet (ַ) is found even in some instances where י is dropped; as in וָאֵלֵךְ: once with וֹ in וַיֵּבוֹשׁ (Hos. 13:15).

תֵּשַׁבְנָה,—Some verbs have (ַ) under the second radical; as in תֵּלַכְנָה, וַתֵּלַדְנָה: in two instances the prefix י, masculine gender, is put instead of ת fem., as in וַיֵּחַמְנָה and וַיִּשַּׁרְנָה.

The verb יָכֹל *to be able*, is found only in the preterite of Kal, and the future of Hophal.

Future Tense of NIPHAL.

אִוָּלֵד, אִוָּרֵשׁ.—But וַיִּיָּחֶל and יִיָּרֶה are formed like regular verbs.

Preterite of HIPHIL.

הוֹשִׁיב.—Irregularly וְהֵילִיל, and in 1 Sam. 21:3, יוֹדַעְתִּי for הוֹדַעְתִּי.

Future Tense.

אוֹשִׁיב.—In the following instances ה characteristic is retained as in the Chaldaic, יְהֵילִילוּ, יְהוֹשִׁיעַ, יְהוֹדֶה, אֲהוֹדֶנּוּ.

Verbs Quiescent having ו and י as their Second Radicals.

Preterite of KAL.

קָם.—With (ֵ), as in מֵת and וֹ, as in אוֹר. Sometimes ו is supplied by א, as in וְקָאם (Hos. 10:14), and in וְרָאֲמָה from רוּם (Zech. 14:10): twice it is found with (ַ) in בַּז (Zech. 4:10), and in מַח (Isa. 44:18).

קָמָה, מֵתָה, בּוֹשָׁה, and after the Chaldaic form וְשָׁבַת (Ezek. 46:17), and once we have (ֶ) for (ָ) in וְלָנָה (Zech. 5:4).

קָמְתָּם. Once (ָ) is changed for (ִ) in וּפִשְׁתֶּם Mal. 3:20.

Participle Active.

קָם.—There is no distinction as to form between the preterite and participle singular, masculine and feminine, except that in the singular feminine, the accent is put מִלְעֵיל in the preterite, but מִלְרַע in the participle.

Infinitive.

קוּם and קוֹם.—The same is the case in the imperative mood.

אָקוּם.—And from בּוֹשׁ, אֵבוֹשׁ. This is the only verb amongst the נָחֵי ע״ו in which the letters איתן have (ֵ). We have sometimes וֹ instead of וּ; as in וְיָרֹם.

Preterite of NIPHAL.

נָקוֹם.—Once with (ֵ) for (ָ) in נֵעוֹר (Zech. 2:17), נְקוֹמָה; irregularly נְקָמָה, from קוּם.

Participle.

נְקוֹמִים.—Once (ָ) for וֹ in נְבֻכִים (Ex. 14:3).

PIEL and PUAL.

As the second radical in these conjugations regularly requires a dagesh, which cannot take place in a quiescent ו and י, the deficiency thereof is compensated by doubling the last radical; as from כּוּל, כִּלְכֵּל, and from פּוּץ, וַיְפַצְפְּצֵנִי: this latter form is called by some grammarians *Pilpel.*

Future Tense.

יְקוֹמְמוּ.—And from עוּר, irregularly יְעֹשֵׁרוּ, for יְעֹרְרוּ, and so likewise from לוּעַ, יְעַלְעוּ, for יְלַעְלְעוּ.

HIPHIL.

הֵקִים.—Throughout this conjugation we find that י is sometimes changed for (ֵ); as in הֲרֵעֹתִי, and in a few instances into (ִ), as in הַעִדֹתִי; and sometimes, though rarely, into (ֶ); as in הֶבִינוּ from בִּין.

Infinitive Mood.

הָקֵם.—And with בכלם prefixed הָקִים. The following terms שִׁית, עִיר, דִּין, גִּיל, בִּין, are considered by some grammarians to be of the Hiphil conjugation, ה being irregularly dropped, whilst others maintain that they belong to the conjugation of Kal. In the Hithpael conjugation, ת is in one instance omitted and compensated by a long vowel under the prefix; as in אֵרוֹמָם (Isa. 33:10) for אֶתְרוֹמָם.

Quiescent Verbs having א for their Last Radical.

Various verbs of this class sometimes assume the form of those quiescent in ה, as מָלֵתִי, מָלוּ, כָּלָאתִי, רִפֵּאתִי, and indeed א is itself in the root already changed into ה; as from רָפָא *he healed*, we find רָפָה (Ps. 60:4), we also find יֵרָפוּ for נִרְפְּתָה; וְצָמִית for צָמֵאת; חֹטֶא for חֹטְאִים, חֹטֵא; צֹבְאֶיהָ for צֹבֶיהָ, and וְהִתְנַבֵּית for מֵהִתְנַבּוֹת.

Preterite of KAL.

מָצָא.—Some verbs in א have (ֵ) under the second radical instead of (ָ); as, שָׂנֵא, מָלֵא, יָרֵא.

מָצָאתִי.—Once מָצָתִי (Numb. 11:11) without א.

Infinitive Mood.

מְצוֹא.—But (1 Sam. 18:29) לְרֹא for לִירֹא or לְיִרְאָה.

Future Tense.

תִּמְצֶאנָה.—(Jer. 9:17) וְתִשֶּׂנָה from נָשָׂא.

Verbs Quiescent having ה for their Last Radical.

Preterite of KAL.

גָּלָה.—The verb חָיָה is sometimes conjugated like those of the נחי ע״ו, as קוּם, which has קָם in the preterite third person singular masculine, and קָמָה for the feminine gender. Thus we read in (Gen. 5:5) אֲשֶׁר חַי, and (Exod. 1:16) וְאִם בַּת הִיא וָחָיָה *and if it be a daughter she shall live*, for וְחָיְתָה. Kimchi, however, contends that the root is חיי. In the verb קָרָה *to happen*, we find that ה is sometimes changed into א, as in פַּחַד קְרָאַנִי *terror happened to me* (Job 4:14).

גָּלְתָה.—ה radical is changed into ת, as in nouns in the feminine gender when suffixes are subjoined, where ה is changed into ת. See Table of nouns and possessive pronouns. In some places ה is dropped; as in וְעָשְׂת for וְעָשְׂתָה, and in קָרָאת (Deut. 20:10). ה third radical is likewise in a few verbs changed into י; as in חָסָיָה for חָסְתָה; and ה is changed for א in וַגְבְהָא קוֹמָתוֹ (Ezek. 31:5) *his height is exalted.*

גָּלִיתָ.—Here ה is changed into י; but we have instances where י is omitted; as in בָּנִתָה (1 Kings 9:3), and in one passage instead of י we have א, רְצָאתִי for רְצִיתִי (Ezek. 43:27), and in Job 3:26, י is changed into ו, and its form is, as if derived from a verb regular, שָׁלַוְתִּי for שָׁלִיתִי.

גָּלוּ.—ה which is here dropped, is in some verbs changed into י; as in חָסָיוּ, נָטָיוּ; and in Is. 38:12, א is irregularly added in the word אָבוּא. In 2 Sam. 21:12, ה is changed into א in תְּלָאוּם from תָּלָה *to suspend*, but some copies read תְּלוּם.

גָּלִינוּ.—(Jer. 3:22) אָתָנוּ from אָתָה, after the form of מָצָאנוּ.

Participles.

גּוֹלֶה.—In Is. 38:12, י is found instead of ה, רֹעִי for רֹעֶה; and in some verbs א is used instead of ה, as in נֹשֵׂא, נֹשְׂאִים; and some have י inserted for ה, as in כְּעֹטְיָה from עָטָה, in בֹּכִיָּה, הֹמִיָּה, פֹּרִיָּה, צֹפִיָּה, and in אֹתִיּוֹת from אָתָה *to come*.

גָּלוּי.—And without י, as in וְצָפוּ and הֶעָשׂוּ (Job 15:22, and 41:25). Some have א, as in גְּלוּאִים, תְּלוּאִים.

Infinitive Mood.

גְּלוֹת and גְּלֹה.—Sometimes ת is dropped, as in וְהוֹנוּ, בְּכוּ, רָאוּ, הוֹו; and in a few instances we have א instead of ה, as in רְצֹא, נְצֹא.

Imperative Mood.

גְּלֵה.—And under first radical guttural we have a compound

vowel, as in הָיָה, עָלוּ; irregularly אֶפוּ (Exod. 16:28); sometimes with י inserted, as in בְּעָיוּ, אֶתָיוּ and חָתָיוּ.

Future Tense.

אֶגְלֶה.—Sometimes the last (ֶ) is changed into (ֵ); as, וְאֶשְׁעֵה, אֶהֱמָיֵה. It is sometimes, though rarely, found with (ַ), as in תַּעֲשָׂה (Gen. 26:29) but some copies read תַּעֲשֶׂה. Verbs of this class are the only ones which are used apocopated in the future tenses of every conjugation, Pual and Hophal excepted, and sometimes in the imperative mood. When ה is dropped the letters אִיתָן have regularly (ִ) (except before אהער), and (ֶ) is removed from the second to the first radical; as, יֶגֶל, יֶקֶן, יֶקֶשׁ, יֶרֶב, תֶּבֶן; but before a guttural, those four letters have for the most part (ַ), and the gutturals themselves have likewise (ַ); as, וַאַעַן, תַּעַשׂ; and with ח also; as, יַחַר, וַיִּחַן. Sometimes we have (ֵ) for (ִ); as in וָאֵפֶן, וָאֵרֶד, יֵרֶא, תֵּחַת, תֵּרַע (Deut. 33:21), וַיֵּתֵא for וַיֶּאֱת, which is a transposition. When the second radical is one of the letters בגד כפת, the letters איתן have either (ִ) or (ֵ), and both the two following radicals have (ְ); as וַיֵּשְׁבְּ, וַתֵּבְךְּ, וַיֵּרְדְּ, וַיִּחַדְּ, וַתֵּשְׁתְּ, and in the last case (ַ) is put for the sake of euphony, the consonant being ח.—יֵשְׁתְּ and וַיַּשְׁקְ assume an irregular form, and וַיִּיף and וַיֵּרְא (Ezek. 31:7) are also anomalies. The verbs הָיָה and חָיָה, when used in apocopatum in the future tense, differ from the above; as, אֱהִי, תְּהִי, יְהִי, נְהִי, תְּחִי, יְחִי, and once (Ecc. 11:3) יְהוּא.

Preterite of HITHPAEL.

נִגְלֵית.—With (ִ), as in וְנִקֵּית. נִגְלוּ, and with י for radical ה, as in נִטְיוּ; and א instead of ה, as in נִבְּאוּ for נִבּוּ.

Participle.

נִגְלֶה.—If the first radical be guttural, it takes the form of נַעֲנֶה, and in the feminine is like נַחְלָה or נֶחְפָּה.

נִגְלוֹת.—And from ינה, נוגות.

Future Tense.

יִגָּלֶה.—Before the gutturals, the letters איתן have (ֵ) instead of (ֵ); as in יַעֲשֶׂה, אֶעֱנֶה: we find likewise (ַ) under the first radical instead of (ֵ); as in יַרְחוּ. The future tense in apocopated is the same, with the exception, that with the rejection of ה the preceding (ֶ) is likewise omitted; as in תְּגַל, וָאֵרֶא, וָאֵפְתְּ, יִפַּח, וַתַּעַשׂ.

Preterite of PIEL.

גִּלָּה.—ה is changed for א, as in שִׂנֵּא and שִׂנֵּאתִיךָ.—גִּלִּיתָ and גִּרִּיתָ.

Participle.

מְגַלֶּה.—And in construction (ֵ), as in מְזָרֵה, מְחַכֵּה. ה is changed for א, as in מְרַפֵּא. ה is also changed into ו, as in מְטַחֲוֵי.

Infinitive Mood.

גַּלּוֹת.—From whence the form חַלּוֹתִי (Ps. 77:11). גַּלֵּה, ה is changed for י, as in וּכְחַכֵּי (Hos. 6:9).

גַּלֵּה.—And (ֵ), as in רַבֵּה (Judg. 9:29); sometimes ה is dropped, as in צַו, גַּל, הַם. ה is once changed for י; viz. in דַּלְיוּ.

Future Tense.

אֲגַלֶּה.—Irregularly אֲרַיֶּךְ from רָוָה; so וָאֲעַנֶּה; and הֵנָּה from ינה.

תְּגַלּוּ.—Sometimes with (ֵ) and no Dagesh following, as in תְּתָאוּ: and ה radical is changed into י, as in תְּרַמְּיוּנִי.

יְגַלּוּ.—Irregularly וַיְּדוּ for וַיְּיַדּוּ; ה is changed into א, as in יְחַפְּאוּ from חָפָה; and into י, as in יְכַסְיֻמוּ from כָּסָה; and apocopated, וַיְגַל, וַיְצַו, יְקַו, תְּשַׁר, וַיְתָו.

Preterite of PUAL.

גֻּלָּה.—Where the dagesh is omitted in the second radical, the preceding vowel is וֹ; as in הֹרָה, הֹגָה; and once we find וּ, viz. in זוּנָּה (Ezek. 16:34). This omission is sometimes compensated by a preceding long vowel; as in דֹּחוּ; but not in every case; as for instance רֻאוּ (Job 33:22). We find in some copies א is dageshed in this text, contrary to rule, and likewise the (ֻ) is changed into (ֻ), as in כָּלּוּ (Ps. 72:20) and כָּסּוּ (Ibid 80:11).

Participle.

מְגַלֶּה and מְזוֹרֶה.—These words take this form owing to ר being incapable of dagesh, and so in the future יְזוֹרֶה; and in Ecc. 8:1, we have ה, the last radical, changed for א; as יְשֻׁנֶּא from שָׁנָה.

Preterite of HIPHIL.

הִגְלָה.—Before a guttural letter הֶ, as in הֶעֱרָה, הֶחֱלִי. In the latter case י is substituted for ה, and therefore the preceding vowel is (ִ); in some instances we have (ֳ) for (ֱ), as in הֶעֱלָה, הֶעֱבַרְתָּ. In some few cases we even have הָ without being followed by a guttural, as in הָגְלָה (Est. 2:6).

הִגְלְתָה.—And irregularly הֶלְאֵת, הִרְצֵת, הִגְלֵיתָ and הִגְלִיתָ. הִגְלוּ, and after the Chaldaic form הִמְסִיו.

Infinitive Mood

הַגְלוֹת.—With ל prefixed ה is dropped, as לַצְּבוֹת, for לְהַצְּבוֹת.

Imperative Mood.

הַגְלֵה.—The last radical is sometimes dropped when the vowels are (ֶ ֶ), or when with a guttural they are (ֲ ֶ), as הֶרֶב, הֶרֶף, הַעַל. הָשַׁע occurs (Ps. 39:14), but irregularly, from שָׁעָה.

Future Tense.

יַגְלֶה.—In this tense we find likewise several verbs in which the last radical ה is changed for א; as in יַפְלִא (Lev. 27:2), יַשִּׁיא (Ps. 89:23), and יַשִּׁי (Ps. 45:16), and apocopated יֶפֶר, וַתֶּמֶם, וַיֶּגֶל, וַיֶּפֶן; and with a guttural for the first radical, וַתַּעַל, וַיַּעַל.

Preterite of HOPHAL.

הָגְלָה.—When a guttural is the first radical, הָ is changed into הֹ, as in הֹעֲלָה, הֹעֲלָתָה.

Preterite of HITHPAEL.

הִתְגַּלָּה.—But from ידה the Hithpael is הִתְוַדָּה, and in the participle מִתְוַדֶּה. From שָׁחָה, ו is inserted; as in הִשְׁתַּחֲוָה, and so in the participle מִשְׁתַּחֲוִים; and מִשְׁתַּחֲוִיתֶם (Ezek. 8:16) has the pronominal suffix like the participle Piel in Chaldee; and נִשְׁתָּוָה

(Prov. 27:15) is a compound of Niphal and Hithpael:—This form is very frequently found in rabbinical writings.

Infinitive Mood.

הִתְגַּלֵּה, הִתְגַּלּוֹת. And without ה, as in הִתְחַל. Sometimes the characteristic ת is dropped, and compensated by dagesh in the first radical; as in הִזַּכּוּ for הִתְזַכּוּ or rather הִזַּכּוּ.

Future Tense.

אֶתְגַּלֶּה—And by rejecting ת, like אֲדַדֶּה, אֲדַמֶּה. נִתְגַּלֶּה—sometimes (ֶ) is changed into (ֵ); as in נִשְׁתָּעָה.

From שָׁחָה we have once וַיִּשְׁתַּחוּ (Gen. 27:29). The following verbs are apocopated: תִּשְׁתַּע, וַיִּתְגַּל, תֵּתָאו, יִשְׁתַּחוּ.

Observations on Verbs Doubly Defective.

In the Paradigm a scale of one class of doubly defective verbs has already been given, namely, נָתַן having נ at the beginning and at the end. As to the defective verbs in the first and second radical, which have נ for the first radical, and the last two radicals are the same, they occur but rarely, and are נָדַד, נָסַס, נָצַץ. All that is necessary to be remarked is, that both defects never occur at the same time; for in יִדּוֹד future of Kal the נ is rejected, but the ד is retained. In יְנִדֻהוּ (Job 17:18) future of Hiphil, ד is rejected, but נ is retained; and so in וַיֻּדַּד in Hophal. נ only is rejected.

נָשָׂא which is defective in the first radical and quiescent in the last, is consequently conjugated like נָגַשׁ and מָצָא. Pret. נָשָׂאתָ, נָשָׂא, נָשָׂאָה. Imp. שָׂא, שְׂאִי, שְׂאוּ, שְׂאֶנָה (Ps. 10:12), נְשָׂא for שָׂא. Future tense תִּשֶּׂנָה or תִּשֶּׂאינָה and תִּשֶּׂאנָה, תִּשָּׂא, אֶשָּׂא. Inf. שְׂאֵת, שֵׂאת and נְשׂוֹא. Participle act. נוֹשֵׂא and pass. נָשׂוּא. Pret. of Niphal נִשָּׂא, נִשֵּׂאתָ. Imp. and inf. הִנָּשֵׂא. Pret. of Hiph. הִשִּׂיא. Inf. הַשִּׂא. Hoph. הֻשָּׂא.

נָטָה is conjugated like גָּלָה and נָגַשׁ except in the inf. and imp. moods, which are formed like the Pret. of Kal in regular verbs, (Ps. 73:2) נָטָיוּ for נָטוּ, נָטִיתָ, נָטְתָה, נָטָה. Imp. נְטֵה. Fut. תִּטֶּה, אֶטֶּה. We find likewise a future apocopated, as in וַיֵּט, תֵּט, יֵט

and נְוֵי from נָוָה. Pret. of Niph. נִשָּׁה, נִמְתָה, נְשֵׁיתָ, plural נִשּׁוּ for נִשְּׁיוּ. Imp. הִנָּשֶׁה. Fut. אֶנָּשֶׁה. Inf. הִנָּשׁוֹת. Participle נִשָּׁה. Pret. of Hiph. הִשָּׁה, הִשְׁתָה. Imp. הַשֵּׁה and הַשׁ. Fut. אַשֶּׁה and אַשׁ. Participle מַשֶּׁה. Inf. הַשּׁוֹת. Hoph. הֻשָּׁה and ו for (ֻ), הוּכָּה (Ps. 102:4).

אָבָה and the like verbs which are quiescent in the first radical א, and in the last radical ה, are conjugated in Kal like גָּלָה, except that the letters אֵיתָן have cholem, as in יֹאבֶה; and in the first person sing. א radical is dropped. In Prov. 1:10, we have תֹּבֵה for תֹּאבֶה, and 1 Sam. 28:24, וַתֹּפֵהוּ. From אָתָה, תֵּאתֶה and by apocopatum וַיֵּאת.

יָרֵא or יָצָא may serve as examples to all verbs quiescent in י first and א last radical.

Pret. Kal יָרֵא, יָרְאָה, יָרֵאתָ, יְרֵאתֶם or יְרֵאתֶם. Imp. mood, &c. יְרָא, יִרְאוּ. Fut. יִירָא, תִּירָא. Inf. יְרוֹא, and with ל prefixed לִירוֹא. Participle יָרֵא, יְרֵאִים. Pret. of Niph. נוֹרָא; the same in the Part., Imp., and Inf. moods, הִוָּרֵא: none of the other conjugations are used.

Pret. Kal, יָצָתִי, (Job 1:2), יָצָא, יָצָאתָ, יָצָאתִי. Imp. mood, צְאִי, צֵא. Fut. אֵצֵא, תֵּצֵא. Inf. צֵאת, and when accompanied by a verb, יָצוֹא. Part. יוֹצֵא. Pret. of Hiph. הוֹצִיא, הוֹצֵאתָ. Imp. הַיְצֵא. Fut. אוֹצִיא. Pret. of Hoph. הוּצָא. Participle, מוּצֵאת.

יָרָה and all those verbs which are quiescent in י first, and ה last radical, take the form of יָשַׁב and גָּלָה.

בּוֹא. Pret. Kal, בָּא, בָּאָה, בָּאתָ, בָּאת, בָּאתֶם, בָּאתֶן, בָּאנוּ, בָּאוּ. Imp. בּוֹא, בֹּאִי, בֹּאוּ, בֹּאנָה. Fut. תָּבוֹא, אָבוֹא and with ה paragogic תְּבוֹאתָה fem. Inf. mood בּוֹא. Part. בָּא, בָּאָה, בָּאִים, בָּאוֹת. Pret. of Hiph. הֵבִיא, הֵבִיאָה, הֵבֵאתָ and הֵבֵיאתָ. Imp. הָבֵא, הָבִיאִי. Fut. תָּבִיא, אָבִיא and with ו conversive וַיָּבֵא. Inf. הָבִיא. Part. מֵבִיא. Pret. of Hoph. אוּבָא, הוּבָאָה, הוּבָאתָ. Part. מוּבָא.

Verbs of four radicals are few in number, and are seldom used. The following are the forms in which they occur: פַּרְשֵׁז (Job 26:9) usually פָּרַשׂ *to expand ;* רֻטֲפַשׁ (Ibid 33:25), usually רָטֹב *to be fresh* מְתַחֲרֶה (Jer. 22:15) and תְּתַחֲרֶה (Jer. 12:5), from תָּחוֹר *to cover over ;* כִּרְסֵם and יְכַרְסְמֶנָּה (Ps. 80:14) from כָּרַם *to waste ;* יְדַבְּלְתְהוֹן

Dan. 3:21) and מְכֻרְבָּל (1 Chron. 15:27), from כַּרְבֵּל to cloak; lso שַׁאֲנַן and שַׁאֲנַנּוּ to be quiet; and a few others.

In the following verbs the first and second radical letters are loubled, namely, שַׁעֲשַׁע, הִשְׁתַּעַשְׁעוּ (Is. 29:9), from שָׁעָה to delight; הִתְעַרְעֵר, עַרְעֵר (Ps. 102:18), from עָרָה to lay waste; תְּשַׂגְשֵׂגִי Is. 17:11), from שָׂגָה to increase; כִּמְתַעְתֵּעַ (Gen. 27:12), from תָּעָה to err; לְהִתְמַהְמֵהַּ (Exod. 12:39), from מָהָה to tarry; מִתְלַהְלֵהַּ (Prov. 26:18), from לָהָה to be mad; יָפְיָפִיתָ (Ps. 45:3), from יָפֶה handsome, fair. The conjugation is called in this case, Pilpel for Piel), and Hithpalpel (for Hithpael): some derived from uiescent ו and י second radical take the same form; as from כּוּל) maintain, כִּלְכֵּל (Zec. 11:16); from סוּךְ to confound, סִכְסַךְ (Is. :10); from כִּיר to dance, מְכַרְכֵּר (2 Sam. 6:16); from פּוּר to reak, וַיְפַרְפְּרֵנִי (Job 16:12); from פּוּץ to shake, וַיְפַצְפְּצֵנִי (Ibid); rom צִיף to peep, הַמְצַפְצְפִים (Is. 8:20); from קִיר to demolish, מְקַרְקַר Ibid 22:5); from שׁוּק to justle, יִשְׁתַּקְשְׁקוּן (Nahum 2:5). Some f the defective verbs called כְּפוּלִים have the first radical doubled, hus, from חרר—חַרְחֻר, from גלל—גִּלְגֵּל, from סלל—סִלְסֵל; and a few f the regular verbs double the second radical; thus, from חמר—חֳמַרְמַר, from סחר—סְחַרְחַר.

Upon verbs with pronouns affixed, we have to observe—

I.—That sometimes the pronoun thus affixed is redundant, as 1 the Syriac; thus וַיְשַׁנּוֹ אֶת־טַעְמוֹ (I Sam. 21:13) he changed it, amely, his behaviour; עֲוֹנוֹתָיו יִלְכְּדֻנוֹ אֶת־הָרָשָׁע his iniquities will atch him, the ungodly; וַיַּכּוּ הָאֶחָד אֶת־הָאֶחָד and one smote one, he other; וְזִהֲמַתּוּ חַיָּתוֹ לָחֶם his life abhorreth it, the bread; אֲשֶׁר לֹא יַעַבְדוּ אֹתוֹ אֶת־נְבוּכַדְנֶאצַּר who shall not serve him, Nebuchadnezzar; nd so forth.

II.—Sometimes the noun is used where in English a pronoun vould be used; as in, וַיֹּאמֶר לֶמֶךְ לְנָשָׁיו—נְשֵׁי לֶמֶךְ (Gen. 4:23) Lemech said to his wives—O wives of Lemech! instead of נָשַׁי my wives; וְאֶל־מֹשֶׁה אָמַר עֲלֵה אֶל יְהוָה (Exod. 24:1) and to Moses He aid, Ascend to the Lord, for אֵלַי to me.

III.—When pronouns are affixed to verbs, they generally express the accusative case of the persons, as stated above, yet in

a few instances, they stand for the dative case לִי *to me*, for
ablative and comparative degree, and for עִם *with*; as i
נְתַתָּנִי *thou hast given (to) me a dry land*, for נָתַתָּ לִי (.
יְכָלְתִּיו *I have prevailed over him* (Ps. 13:5), for תִּי לוֹ.
וַאֲנִי עֲשִׂיתִנִי *the river is mine, and I have made it for m*
29:3) for עָשִׂיתִי לִי;—חֲזַקְתַּנִי וַתּוּכָל *thou wast stronger t*.
didst prevail (Jer. 20:7) for חָזַקְתָּ מִמֶּנִּי;—בָּנַי יְצָאֻנִי (Ib
for יָצְאוּ מִמֶּנִּי *they are gone away from me*; בִּשְּׁלָם הַבָּשָׂר —
the meat for them (1 Kings 19:21) for בִּשֵּׁל לָהֶם;—רָע דְּ
does not dwell with thee (Ps. 5:5) for יָגוּר עִמְּךָ;—וַיִּלָּחֲמוּנִי
109:3) for וַיִּלָּחֲמוּ בִּי *they fought against me*.

FINIS.

J. Wertheimer and Co., Printers, Circus Place, Finsbury Circus.

An

Paragr. of Letters.	הִתְפַּעֵל Hithpael.	הָפְעַל Hophal.		קַל Kal.
ה	הִתְלַמֵּד הִתְלַמְּדָה הִתְלַמַּדְתְּ	הָ or מַר מְדָה מַדְתְּ		לָמַד לָמְדָה* לָמַדְתְּ

אוצר לשון עברי וכשדי

HEBREW AND ENGLISH DICTIONARY,

BIBLICAL AND RABBINICAL:

CONTAINING

THE HEBREW AND CHALDEE ROOTS OF THE OLD TESTAMENT POST-BIBLICAL WRITINGS.

BY

M. H. BRESSLAU,

PROFESSOR OF HEBREW, ETC.

LONDON:
JOHN WEALE, 59, HIGH HOLBORN.

M.DCCC.LV.

PREFACE.

Although there are several Hebrew Lexicons extant, some large and some small, some original and some translations or adaptations, it may be stated, without detracting in the least from the respective merits of the works which have hitherto appeared, that, as far as regards the Hebrew-English Dictionaries, the old ones are incompatible with the present approved system of modern study, whilst the modern, which were published with a view to cheapness, are incomplete and deficient. Some of them pretend to be translations from the best German works; but the originals have been, either from doctrinal motives or those of economy, shorn and cut down to that extent, that the term "mutilated" may be appropriated to them more fairly than "abridged."

In no language are found words and roots with so various, and not unfrequently opposite significations, as in the Hebrew, besides the peculiarities in that remarkable tongue arising from the various paradigms. It ought also to be remembered, that the great standard by which the principle of the language is judged rests upon the twenty-four books of the Old Testament Scriptures; by them we are guided in our estimate, valuatior and classification of roots, and from them we derive our information as to the primitive and adopted significations of these roots. Hence the sense of several roots or words which occur once in Scripture, and for which we can find no analogous passage to guide us, must be rendered according to the context; and since this rendering is liable to different versions, the commentators and translators of the Bible differ in the interpretation. It is therefore the duty of the compiler of a Hebrew Lexicon to have his thoughts continually directed to the Sacred Scriptures, they being the fountain-head from whence all post-biblical works in the Hebrew language flow, and on the basis of which new words and terms have been formed to convey ideas and sentiments necessarily occurring in the large number of scientific, metaphysical and rabbinical works, with which the post-biblical literature of the Jews abounds. These latter works constituting by far the greatest portion of the Hebrew literature, it is no less the duty of a writer of a Lexicon to supply the words and terms of the derivatives from the original Hebrew, and to furnish their various graduations, developments, and significations. Both duties the compiler of the present Lexicon has made it his task, scrupulously and faithfully, to discharge, taking care, at the same time, to point out the primitive words, as well as those of later introduction, and carefully distinguishing the adopted offsprings from the mother-tongue.

Among all the Hebrew Lexicons published, both in England and on the Continent, there are none that can be compared for compactness, completeness, and cheapness, to the Hebrew and Chaldee Lexicon by Dr. Julius Fürst, the eminent Hebrew teacher of the University of Leipzig, which, therefore, has been selected as a model for this Dictionary. Meanwhile due regard has been had to the Authorised English Translation of the Bible, and its rendering of those scriptural passages in which it was found necessary to deviate therefrom. In the numerous quotations from Scripture given in this Lexicon, which will prove of incalculable advantage to the Biblical student, the Authorised English Version has been given, as well as the rendering adopted in this Lexicon, based on well-matured philological grounds.

It is only left now for the compiler to give a list of the abbreviations and an explanation of certain terms which are met with throughout this Work.

The term "Aram." signifies the Chaldee language, in which part of the Book of Daniel is composed, and which is interspersed with the Hebrew in both Talmuds, the Jerusalem as well as the Babylonian, the Book Zoar, the Medrashim, and many other post-biblical works.

The terms "later," "new Hebrew," and "modern," are applied to those words which have been introduced either subsequent to the Pentateuch or Prophets, or all post-biblical writings.

The term "not used" is applied in respect to the form of the word, such form not occurring in the Scriptures, but being found requisite to shew the root, from which branch out the different forms in use, accompanied by their various significations and modifications.

LONDON, *January*, 1855.

LIST OF ABBREVIATIONS.

Accus. or acc. accusative
adj. adjective
adv. adverb
Aph. or Af. Aphal, Afal
apoc. apocopated
appell. appellative
Aram. Aramaic
author. vers. authorised version

c. *or* const. state of construction
caus. causative
coll. collective
com. common
comp. compare
conc. concrete
constr. construed
contr. in contrast

dat. dative
def. definite
dem. demonstrative
denom. denominative
dim. diminutive

equiv. to *or* = equivalent to

f. *or* fem. feminine
fig. *or* figur. figuratively
fut. future

gen. genitive
gent. gentile
Gr. Greek

Heb. Hebrew
Hiph. Hiphil
Hith. *or* Hithp. Hithpael
Hoph. Hophal

imp. imperative
indef. indefinite
inf. or infin. infinitive
inter. interrogative
intrans. intransitive

Ithp. Ithpael

m. *or* masc. masculine

neut. neuter
Niph. Niphal
Nith. Nithpael

origin. originally, original

Pa. Pael
part. particle
part. *or* particip. participle
pass. passive
patron. patronymic
pers. person
Pers. Persian *or* Persiac
Pi. Piel
pl. *or* plur. plural
p. n. proper noun
p. n. f. proper noun feminine
p. n. m. proper noun mascu-[line
poet. poetically
pref. prefix
prep. preposition
pron. *or* pr. pronoun
pronom. pronominal
Pu. Pual

Rab. Rabbinical
reflec. reflective
relat. relative

sing. singular
signif. signification
subs. substantive
suff. suffix
syn. synonymous

Tal. Talmud
Targ. Targum
transf. or trans. transferred
trans. transitive

HEBREW DICTIONARY,

Biblical and Rabbinical.

א called אָלֶף (pl. אַלְפִין) signifies as the name of a letter, either bull, and hence the old Phœnician figure of a bull's head of the mark of Alef; or (=אַלּוּף) chief or leader of the entire letter-group. As a numerical figure it signifies 1; but א֞ 1000. The interchange of א with ה and ע is fully explained in the grammar.

אֲ serves as a preformative to several substantives and adverbs whose first consonant is a fixed one, e.g. אֲבַטִּיחַ (בַּטִּיחַ), אֶגֶּף (גַּף) אֲדַרְכּוֹן (דַּרְכּוֹן); but such first syllables may be dropped, e.g. נַחְנוּ from אֲנַחְנוּ.

אַ, אָ 1) a customary prefix to the formation of an adjective to express an intense and persevering qualification: e. g. אַכְזָב very deceiving. 2) the performative like אֲ to words beginning with the semi-vowel (*sheva*), e. g. אֶפְרֹחַ young brood, hatch; אַרְנֶבֶת hare. In many particles the preformative changes אַ into אֶ: as אֶבֶן.

אָב (c. אֲבִי in Gen. 17: 5, אַב; in p. n. אַב, אֲבִי; with suff. אָבִי, אֲבִיכֶם; pl. אָבוֹת c. (אֲבוֹת) m. father, the physical, or the spiritual, i.e. God. The following sub-significations have developed themselves from the above, retaining the characteristic of FATHER: 1) benefactor, provider, supporter; representing paternity, in external relation: 2) teacher, instructor, father in intellectual relations; therefore addressed to national teachers, old men, prophets, priests, viziers, kings; father of the king, i. e. vizier, שִׂים לְאָב to confer on one the dignity of vizier. In reference to paternal rights, expresses the idea of lord, possessor, (proprietor,) almost like בַּעַל; this signification appears especially in compound proper nouns, and in other Semitic dialects. As founder of a family, a generation, or a tribe, אָב signifies: 1) the head of a family, tribe, (syn. רֹאשׁ בֵּית אָבוֹת, אַלּוּף, רֹאשׁ הַמַּטֶּה, נָשִׂיא, שַׂר), hence בֵּית אָב family-circle, family of the head of a tribe; 2) ancestor, forefather; אָב הָרִאשׁוֹן Adam; 3) ancestor of a guild, i.e. creator, inventor, the first composer or former. This noun is primitive, although it follows the analogy of the derivatives from ל"ה.

אַב (c. אֲב, with suff. אֲבוּ, אָבוּ, def. אַבָּא, pl. אֲבָהָן, def. אֲבָהָתָא) Aram. the same.

אֵב (with suff. אִבּוֹ, pl. אִבִּים, c. אִבֵּי) m. properly the shining of bloom; hence 1) time of blooming, age of blooming, also the bright verdure; 2) fruit, from which אֵב Aram. month of fruit, i. e. August, and in Targum אֵב often for תְּבוּאָה, פְּרִי. Root אָבַב.

אֵב (Talm. אִנְב def. אִבָּא, with suff. אִבֵּיהּ or with the נ interpolated אִנְבָּא, אִנְבֵּהּ) Aram. the same, but often fruit, hence:

אַבֵּב to yield fruit.

אָבַב (not used) to shine; next, to bloom, after a usual rendering: as פָּרַח, נָצַץ, זָהָה etc., derivatives אֵב, אָבִיב.

אֲבַגְתָא (Persian) p. n. m. one beautifully formed, from *bag*, Pers. *beh*, beautiful, and *ta* = *tan*; Pers. *ten* body.

אָבַד fut. יֹאבַד and יֹאבֵד (intrans.) originally, to be estranged, forsaken, (see בָּד); hence 1) to err about, to go astray in the desert, or in solitude, שֶׂה אֹבֵד Ps. 119: 176, a sheep wandering about in abandonment. The unstable life of the Nomades; as אֲרַמִּי אֹבֵד a wandering Aramite, Deut. 26: 5; of the wandering about in a foreign country, Isa. 27: 13. 2) to lose oneself, to disppear, e. g. to lose courage (לֵב); to lose all hope (תִּקְוָה); part. אֹבַד עֵצוֹת (seldom c. אֹבֵד) being a want of counsel, transferred to the sense of uselessness, in vain: e. g. refuge is vain (מָנוֹס), the vision (חָזוֹן) with לְ, מִן the person for whom something is in vain and useless; 3) to cease, to perish, of man, animals, etc., therefore אֹבֵד, an unhappy one, here sometimes the addition of מֵעַל הָאָרֶץ. Piel אִבֵּד; 1) to dismember, to scatter, to disperse; הוֹן to squander property; 2) to destroy (things), to murder (human beings), deprive: e. g. לֵב the understanding. Hiphil, to cause to be ruined, destroyed, annihilate, with the addition of מִתַּחַת הַשָּׁמַיִם, מִקֶּרֶב הָעָם, for 1 pers. fut., also stands the form אֹבִידָה with a quiescent Alef which is subsequently dropped.

אֲבַד fut. יֵאבַד Aram. the same, affirm. הוֹבֵד like Hiphil. Hophal after a Hebraism, passive of Hiphil.

אֹבֵד m. 1) equiv. to אָבַד annihilation, destruction; 2) part. n. an unfortunate man.

אֲבֵדָה f. 1) abyss, precipice, (as inf. n.); 2) a lost thing, (part. n.)

אֲבַדּוֹ m. in Ketib for אֲבַדּוֹן; the affix ה־, changes often with וֹן־, probably read in Ketib אֲבַדָּה.

אֲבַדּוֹן m. 1) annihilation; 2) place of destruction, the region of the dead.

אַבְדָן also אָבְדַן (c. אָבְדַן) m. destruction, Est. 8: 6, 9: 5.

אָבָה fut. יֹאבֶה (in relation with יָאַב, תָּאַב, with the same root), to be fond of, to incline to; hence 1) to consent, to obey, with לְ of the person; 2) the more active inclination, to incline, to be willing: with לֹא not willing, (unwilling), (like מֵאֵן) with the accusative of the noun or of the infinitive, but always from readiness of inclination; 3) to will violently, to be anxious, to be eager, to lust after, to desire.

אֵבֶה only in Job 9: 26, probably a foreign word. According to some, a reed, rush, suitable to an Arabic analogy.

אֲבוֹי m. according to Abulwalid Ibn Ganah, from אָבָה, also a lust, eagerness or distress, like אֶבְיוֹן. But more correct with Kimchi equiv. to אוֹי, wo, according to an Aram. analogy.

אֵבוּס (for אֵבוּם pl. אֲבוּסִים) m. originally satisfying, feeding, hence crib, grate for the use of feeding; see אָבַס.

אבות see אוֹבוֹת.

אָבַח (not used) equiv. to זָבַח σφαγ to slaughter, σ spiritus, changes into ! like אָחַר (of אֲחֵרוֹן) with זָחַר.

אִבְחָה (poetical. טִבְחָה) f. slaughter, murder, Ezek. 21: 20, LXX. σφάγια.

אֲבַטִּיחַ only pl. אֲבַטִּיחִים m. melon, Targ. מְלַפְּפוֹן i. e. μηλοπέπων, see בָּטַח II.

אֲבִי p. n. f. strong desire, longing, 2 Chr. 29: 1, for which also אֲבִיָּה.

אֲבִי עַלְבוֹן p. n. m. (father of shame, a shamed one, a modest one); see עָלַב 1 Chron. 11: 32.

אֲבִיאֵל p. n. m. one who possesses godliness, a pious one.

אֲבִיאָסָף p. n. m. father of an assembly, a gatherer.

אָבִיב m. (from אָבַב time of bloom, (as קָצִיר, חָרִישׁ), hence time of ripe ears; חֹדֶשׁ הָאָבִיב month of ripe ears (like נִיסָן); next transferred to ear, fruit of ears.

אֲבִיגַיִל p. n. f. (head of the group of dancers). See גּוּל.

אֲבִינַל p. n. f. the same.

אֲבִידָן p. n. m. (father of judgment, judge). See דִּין.

אֲבִידָע p. n. m. (father of knowledge, one that knows). See יָדַע.

אֲבִיָּה 1) p. n. m. (God is provider); 2) p. n. f., see אֲבִי.

אֲבִיָּהוּ p. n. m. the same.

אֲבִיהוּ p. n. m. (He, i. e. God is the father).

אֲבִיהוּד p. n. m. (possesser of fame) Πάτροκλος. See הוֹד.

אֲבִיחַיִל 1) p. n. f. (the head of the singers), a songstress. See חוּל=חָלַל; 2) p. n. m. (a variation of אֲבִיחַיִל).

אֶבְיוֹן (from אָבָה) adj. asking, begging, poor, needy; from which the subst. the poor one, the sufferer. בְּנֵי אֶבְיוֹן the poor.

אֲבִיּוֹנָה f. desire, longing, lust, Ecc. 12: 5, according to others, the means of desiring, specially scranberry. (אֲבִיּוֹנִין berries.)

אֲבִיחַיִל p. n. f. (father of valour, the valourous one.)

אֲבִיטוּב p. n. m. (father of goodness, the good one.)

אֲבִיטַל p. n. f. (father of dew, the freshness of life.)

אֲבִיָּם p. n. m. (father of the sea, navigator.)

אֲבִימָאֵל p. n. m. (belonging to the tribe of Mahil.)

אֲבִימֶלֶךְ p. n. m. (father-king) kingly titles of the Philistines; as also אָגָג, פַּרְעֹה.

אֲבִינָדָב p.n.m. (father of noble-mindedness, the noble-minded one.)

אֲבִינֹעַם p. n. m. (possessor of loviness, grace.)

אֲבִינֵר p. n. m. (possessor of light, luminary.)

אֶבְיָסָף p. n. m.=אֶבְיָאסָף contracted from אֲבִיאָסָף, which see.

אֲבִיעֶזֶר p. n. m. (father of help); helper, patron. אֲבִי הָעֶזְרִי.

אָבִיר adj. and subst. m. helper, protector, hero, (from אָבַר), only applied to God.

אַבִּיר adj. m. very valorous, manly; hence the subst.: 1) a valiant one, courageous one, with the addition of לֵב; poetically, the daring bull, the bold horse; 2) the distinguished, the worthy, אַבִּיר הָרֹעִים the most distinguished of the shepherds, לֶחֶם אַבִּירִים bread of the superior (manna); 3) inflexible, hardened, stubborn, with לֵב (=קְשֵׁה לֵב).

אֲבִירָם p. n. m. (father of pride, the proud one).

אֲבִישַׁג p. n. f. (female professor of agility, the agile one). See שָׁגַג.

אֲבִישׁוּעַ p. n. m. (father of luck, the fortunate one.) See שׁוּעַ.

אֲבִישׁוּר p. n. m. (the father of melody, singer). See שׁוּר.

אֲבִישַׁי p. n. m. (the father of will, one who is strong in will). See שָׁוָה.

אֲבִישָׁלוֹם p. n. m. (father of friendship; friend, probably father of peace).

אֶבְיָתָר p. n. m. (father of preference, the preferred one).

אָבַךְ (poetically) only Hithp. to rise as in a column, applied to smoke which curls in rising. Isa. 9 : 17.

אָבַל fut. יֶאֱבַל (poetic.), originally to sink oneself, to fall together, to perish; hence 1) to wither, to parch, to mourn, used of grass, (related to אָמַל); 2) mourning, of man, originally the sinking of the head, (the bowing down). Hiph. caus. of Kal. Hith. (pros.) as Kal, with אֶל, עַל, of the person for whom one is mourning.

אָבַל (not used) to dampen, related בָּלַל to irrigate.

אָבֵל (c. אֲבֵל, pl. אֲבֵלֵי) adj. m. mourning, (syn. חָרֵב, שָׁמֵם). Root אָבַל.

אָבֵל p. n. f. (fresh, verdant place, meadow, common, from אָבַל), name of a town, hence אָ׳ הַגְּדוֹלָה, and with ה mobile אָבֵלָה; more frequently in compound pp. nn. as:

אָבֵל בֵּית מַעֲכָה, p. n. f. (meadow of Bet Maacha) city adjacent to מַעֲכָה (which see) below Lebanon, also אָבֵל and אָ׳ מַיִם.

אָבֵל הַשִּׁטִּים p. n. f. (Accacia-place) a city in the plains of Moab.

אָבֵל כְּרָמִים p. n. f. (vineyard) an Amonite village.

אָבֵל מְחוֹלָה p. n. f. (place of the national dancers); town in the dominion of Issachar.

אָבֵל מַיִם p. n. f. (meadow of water), city beneath Lebanon.

אָבֵל מִצְרַיִם p. n. f. (meadow of the Egyptians), a place near Jordan.

אֵבֶל (with suff. אֶבְלִי) m. mourning, עָשָׂה אָ׳ to institute a funeral procession; with לְ of the person, of whose honor, etc.; 2) (poet.) voice of mourning, hence אָ׳ יָחִיד mourning for the single branch.

אֲבָל adj. and conj. 1) certainly, indeed, decidedly, in the golden age of the language; 2) (later) decidedly opposite, but, however; see בַּל.

אֻבָל or אוּבָל (אוּבַל in the latter period of the language, and rare), m. shore of the river, river-district, used for the shore of the Caspian Sea (אוּלַי). Root אָבַל.

אָבַן (not used) equivalent to אָמַן to be firm, to be hard. Hence:—

אֶבֶן f. (m. only 1 Sam. 17: 40), stone-rock, אַבְנֵי־בָרָד hail-stone, אֶ׳ יְקָרָה precious stone; figuratively weight. אֶ׳ הָעֹפֶרֶת weight of lead, lead for measurement; אֶ׳ הַבְּדִיל the leof sounding (plummet); ־בֹּהוּ lead of devastation; root אָבַן.

אֶבֶן בֹּחַן; see בֹּחַן.

אֶבֶן הָאֶזֶל p. n. f. (stone of separation) name of a place.

אֶבֶן הָעֶזֶר p. n. f. (stone of victory), name of a monument near Mispa.

אֲבָנָה p. n. f. (firm foundation) name of a river. See אֲמָנָה.

אֹבֶן (=אֹפֶן) m. only dual אָבְנַיִם (double mill-stones); 1) stool of delivery (labour), which consisted of two stones; 2) stool of the potter, the potter's mould, in the East consisting of two stones; however, a correcter view of אָבְנַיִם is taking it for אָפְנַיִם, viz. a tool consisting of two wheels, a pair of wheels or moulds, from אֹבֶן=אֹפֶן in the signification of mould, wheel.

אַבְנֵט m. girdle of a priest, girdle of office, originally a tie, girding. Aram. פּוּנְדָּא see בָּנַט.

אַבְנֵר p. n. m. See אֲבִינֵר.

אָבַס to nourish, to feed, of cattle, but only part. pass. אָבוּס fed, fattened.

אֲבַעְבֻּעָה f. blister of the skin, a swelling boil. Root בּוּעַ which see.

אָבַץ (not used) to glitter, to shine.

אֶבֶץ p. n. f. (glimmering) name of a town in the dominion of the tribe of Issachar.

אִבְצָן p. n. m. full of brilliancy.

I. אָבַק (not used) to swerve, vacillate, (Lat. *vacillare*) to move to and fro.

II. אָבַק a lighter form of the Root חָבַק, to fold one in another, but only in Niph. נֶאֱבַק to embrace; and hence to struggle, to wrestle, therefore weaker than נִלְחַם to destroy one another, and synonymous with נִפְתַּל.

אָבָק a thin dust flying about. See שַׁחַק, דַּק.

אֲבָקָה (only const. אַבְקַת) f. dust (of spices), רוֹכֵל spice-dust of grocers. Root אָבַק I.

אָבַר (not used) 1) to cover, to clothe, to veil, wrap round; 2) to protect, to defend, to resist: hence to act vigorously on the principle of protecting, shielding. The stronger form is כָּבַר, חָבַר.

אֵבֶר m. pinion, wing, from אָבַר, likewise כָּנָף wing, from כָּנַף to cover, עוֹף from עוּף to veil.

אֶבְרָה (poetic.) f. wing, pinion.

אַבְרָהָם p. n. m. father of many nations as explained in Scripture. רָהָם from רָהַם=רָעַם, רָגַם equivalent to הָמָה, applied to the roaring multitude, equivalent to אַב הָמוֹן which is also etymologically correct.

אַבְרֵךְ m. form of salutation of the Egyptians to Joseph (Gen. 41:

43); probably a noun like בְּרָכָה, viz. from בָּרַךְ to wish joy, to congratulate, to bless: hence blessing, hail! The form is like אַבְנֵט; see בָּרַךְ.

אַבְרָם p. n. m. (a contraction of אַב אֲרָם, father of Aramea, or patriarch of Aram), the former name subsequently called Abraham. The patriarch of Aram became, after the promise, the father of many nations.

אַבְשַׁי the same as אֲבִישַׁי which see.

אַבְשָׁלוֹם the same as אֲבִישָׁלוֹם for which see.

אָגָא (not used) after the Arabic, to flee, to run away.

אָגֵא p. n. m. (fugitive).

אֲגַג p. n. m. (with עוֹג etymologically combined) the sovereign title of Amalekite princes, as פַּרְעֹה and אֲבִימֶלֶךְ from which nouns gent.: אֲגָגִי of Haman, hence the tradition of his Amalekite descent.

אָגַד (not used) to bind, combine, synonym. with it is עָקַד, אָבַד.

אֲגֻדָּה (formed from אָגַד) f. 1) something bound together, a bundle, e.g. אֲגֻדַּת אֵזוֹב a hyssop-bunch; 2) band, troop; 3) a joining together, chained together, bound together: hence vaulted arch, more particularly, the horizonal arch, the sky.

אֱגוֹז (poetical, seldom used) m. nut. גִּנַּת א׳ nut-garden. It seems that etymologically אֱגוֹז is derived from אֱגוֹז = אֶגְנוֹז, where נ is added.

אָגוּר p. n. m. (the accepted among the wise), the name of the author of the 30th chapter of Proverbs. Root אָגַר.

אֲגוֹרָה f. berry, grain, bean, as the smallest weight of coin; hence small coin, originally something round that turns and rolls about, from אָגַר 3 = גָּרַר.

אָגַל (not used) to roll (of water), to whirl, to swell, to spring, to be in form of waves, syn. with גָּלַל.

אֵגֶל (only c. pl. אֶגְלֵי) m. drops, on account of the round form. Root אָגַל.

אֶגְלַיִם p. n. of a city (double-fountain) in the territory of Moab, 24 miles from Arepolis.

אָגַם (not used), a lighter form of עָגַם, crooked, bent, to be mournful, hence אָגֵם, אַגְמוֹן.

אָגֵם adj. dejected, bowed down; אַגְמֵי נֶפֶשׁ 'bent down in mind,' Isa. 19: 16.

אָגַם (not used), to gather, to flow together, (root גַּם which see,) but not be rendered burn, or to be spoiled, or to have an aversion for anything. From which comes אֲגַם and אַגְמוֹן.

אֲגַם (c. אֲגַם, also Isa. 35: 7, where מַיִם is omitted, pl. אֲגַמִּים c. hoever אֲגַמֵּי the same as דִּבְרֵי), m. 1) place of the collecting of waters, pond, that which refreshes, Isa. 35: 7, therefore never rendered a ditch, root אָגַם; 2) rush, a reed that bends; root אָגַם. The rush in ponds which prevented the crossing of enemies was frequently set on fire by the latter, Jer. 51: 32.

אַגְמוֹן m. 1) equivalent to אָגָם pond, (therefore cannot be rendered 'a kettle,') אַגְמוֹן נָפוּחַ a seething pot, Job 41: 12, root אָגַם; 2) hook, from being bent or crooked, Job 40: 26. Hence reed, rush, as אָגָם, hence a symbol of the humble, root אָגַם.

אָגַן (not used,) to hollow out, to excavate; hence the Aram. אִגָּנָא a tub, אֲגָנְיָא a pit.

אַגָּן (c. אַגַּן, pl. אַגָּנוֹת) m. a basin, a bowl, a dish, from its being deepened out. אַ' הַסַּהַר a basin of roundness, a round bowl.

אָגַף (a branch; from גַּף), only in pl. אֲגַפִּים m. wings. See גַּף.

אָגַר fut. יֶאֱגֹר 1) to gather, to collect, gather fruits, (syn. with אָסַף); 2) to gather, to receive in, (see אָגוּר); 3) the same as אָגַל to form into waves, to be undulating, (see אֲגוּרָה) hence to roll, to roll together; root אָגַר = גָּרַר, גָּלַל.

אִגְּרָא (c. אִגֶּרֶת, def. אִגַּרְתָּא, pl. אִגְּרִין def. אִגְּרָתָא) Aram. f. roll, scroll, letter, (comp.) מְגִלָּה. Root אָגַר 3.

אֲגַרְטָל (later, c. pl. אֲגַרְטְלֵי) m. basin, a vessel for sprinkling. Alef is prosthetic, and ל ־ַ is a very old affix of nouns. Root גָּרַט, which see.

אֶגְרֹף m. a clinched hand, fist; root גָּרַף.

אִגֶּרֶת (later, pl. אִגְּרוֹת) f. roll, a roll of manuscript, (as מְגִלָּה); hence a written letter, ban, edict, document. Root אָגַר. 3.

אֵד (after the form of מֵת) m. wrapt up in a vapour or cloud, properly the covering, from אוּד covering, wrapping, which see.

אָדַב (only the inf. Hiphil לַאֲדִיב for לְהַאֲדִיב) is transferred from דָּאַב to faint, pine away. Hiphil, to trouble, afflict.

אַדְבְּאֵל p. n. m. (= אֶדְבַּעְאֵל finger of God, sign of Omnipotence; Aram. אֶצְבַּע=אֶדְבַּע).

אָדַד (not used) to endure, last, continue.

אֲדַד (for which is also הֲדַד) p. n. m. era, space, duration, long-living.

אִדּוֹ p. n. m.

אָדוֹן (c. אֲדוֹן, pl. אֲדֹנִים m. 1) a governor, lord, husband, God, etc.; particularly in addressing where the person addressed, if masc. calls himself עֶבֶד, if fem. אָמָה; 2) steward, possessor. Peculiarities of this noun are: 1) that הָאָדוֹן (seldom אָדוֹן) is always used of God, as well as the superlative form אֲדֹנֵי הָאֲדֹנִים only implies God; 2) that the plural is often only used as singular in signification and construction; root אָדַן or דִּין.

אֲדֹנָי m. the reigning one, governing one, only used of Jehovah, who calls himself so, and is so addressed. The affix ־ָי is the ancient adjective form equiv. to the modern ־ִי, hence אֲ׳ is to be taken as a denominative from אָדוֹן. Compare the adjective שַׁדַּי from שַׁד, which see.

אֲדוֹרַיִם p. n. f. (double habitation), a city in the dominion of the tribe of Judah.

אֲדוֹרָם p. n. m. abbrev. of אֲדֹנִירָם.

אדוה see אוֹרוֹת.

אֱדַיִן Aram. adv. properly *ibi*, in the same place, related to אַיִן *ubi?* from which its application to time, *tunc;* joined to a preposition the usual contraction takes place, as בֵּאדַיִן.

אַדִּיר adj. m. properly, splendid, magnificent, from אָדַר to beam, radiate, to glitter: hence 1) shining afar, celebrated, *illustris*, Ps. 16: 3; 2) eminent, noble, e. g. סֵפֶל אַדִּירִים vessel of the great, i.e. splendid vessel. אַדִּירֵי הַצֹּאן the nobles of the sheep, i. e. the shepherds; 3) of physical power and greatness.

אֲדַלְיָא (Persian) p. n. m. perhaps equivalent to עֲדָלִי.

אָדַם (demon. from דָּם) blood-red, to be blood coloured, from the shining red of the corals, (for other objects compare חָמַר, חָמוּץ, אָמֹץ) Pual only part. מְאָדָּם, pl. מְאָדָּמִים red coloured. Hiph. (caus. of Kal) to show a shining red, of the coccus colour. Hith. to become red coloured (the wine), *rutilare.*

אָדָם (without flexion) m. 1) the name of the first man, Ἀδάμ; hence always with the article הָאָדָם, as הָאִשָּׁה of Eve, (compare הַשָּׂטָן, הַבַּעַל) with which may be connected the poetical expression בֶּן־אָדָם or בֶּן־הָאָדָם descendants of Adam, man, mortal being; also in prose, pl. בְּנֵי־א׳ is usually used for men; 2) man or collect. mankind in general, אֶבְיוֹנֵי אָדָם the poor of men = the poorest, Isa. 29: 19; פֶּרֶא אָדָם wild ass of man, i. e. very wild man; זֹבְחֵי אָדָם the sacrificers among men; but especially common, low persons, in contrast to אִישׁ; also in contrast t those already named; 3) man (like אִישׁ) only Ecc. 7 : 28 where אִשָּׁה follows in contrast; 4) p. n. f. name of a city on the Jordan as אֲדָמָה, אַדְמִי.

אָדֹם (from אָדַם) adj. m., אֲדֻמָּה f., pl., אֲדֻמִּים m. glittering red, red, e. g. of blood colour, of the chesnut horse, of the youthful fresh colour of the cheeks, etc., etc.

אֱדוֹם (otherwise עֵשָׂו) 1) p. n. m. twin brother of Jacob, who was oftener called עֵשָׂו; thence as the national name of his descendants, who possessed and governed a mountainous country, full of rocks and clefts, on the south-eastern border of Palestine, hence בַּת, בְּנֵי אֱדוֹם; 2) p. n. f. name of the land Idumea שְׂדֵי אֱדוֹם, אֶרֶץ אֱדוֹם. Ἰδουμαία. See שֵׂעִיר.

אֹדֶם (from אָדַם) f. a red precious stone, (Targ. סַמְקָן the red one, which is also the derivation of σάρδιον and carnelian.)

אֲדַמְדָּם (redoubled form) adj. m. אֲדַמְדֶּמֶת f; pl. f. אֲדַמְדַּמּוֹת here and there red, red striped, mixed with red. The Alef of the root disappears in the middle of the reduplication, like ס in סְחַרְחַר.

אֲדָמָה (primitive, not from אָדַם; with suff. אַדְמָתִי, pl. אֲדָמוֹת) f. properly, the firm hard terrestrial body; hence 1) the firm earth or the building ground, arable land; אִישׁ א׳ man of the arable land, i.e. a tiller of the ground; אֹהֵב א׳ one who is devoted to agriculture, hence taken in the sense of fruit of the arable land; 2) arable land, country, region, as אַדְמַת יְיָ הַקֹּדֶשׁ גֶּבֶר hence אֲדָמוֹת (only in Ps. 49: 12,) countries, lands; 3) terrestrial globe, ball of the earth; 4) p. n. f. of a city in the dominion of Naphtali. For the etymology compare the denom. אִדֵּם, (Rab.) to pull down to the ground. הַדָּם Aram. the same; הֲדֹם the ground firmly trodden over, floor.

אַדְמָה p. n. f. (fruit-ground) name of a city in the circuit of Sodom.

אַדְמוֹנִי adj. m. 1) red of the hair; 2) the red flesh, youthful colour of the cheeks.

אֲדָמִי p. n. f. (arable land, arable field,) a city in the dominion of Naphtali.

אֲדוֹמִי (from אֱדוֹם) adj. m., pl. f. אֲדֹמִיּוֹת Edomitish.

אַדְמָתָא (Pers.) p. n. m.

אָדַן (not used) to pierce, impress, to press in, synon. with אוּן; transferred to rule, to manage, forbid, prevent, resist.

אָדֹן a master, see בַּלְאֲדָן.

אַדָּן (also אַדּוֹן) p. n. m. perh.= אַדִּי.

אֶדֶן (pl. אֲדָנִים, c. אַדְנֵי) m. fundamental base, the steadfast, strong pedestal; hence base of a column, plates used to be laid under wooden walls, etc. Root אָדַן.

אֲדֹנָי see אֲדוֹנָי.

אֲדֹנִי is found in combination with proper names as a Canaanite title.

אֲדֹנִי־בֶזֶק p. n. m. (ruler of Besek,) see בֶּזֶק.

אֲדֹנִיָּה or אֲדֹנִיָּהוּ p. n. m. (worshipper of Jehovah), אֲדֹנִי the same as אָב. Sometimes substituted by אֲדֹנִיקָם.

אֲדֹנִי־צֶדֶק p. n. m. (worshipper of the planet Jupiter), title of a Canaanite ruler.

אֲדֹנִיקָם p. n. m. (the Lord stands), occurs also for אֲדֹנִיָּהוּ.

אֲדֹנִירָם (see הֲדוֹרָם) p. n. m. (a ruler of high rank.) In contraction, this name appears in אֲדוֹרָם, for which also is substituted הֲדוֹרָם.

אָדַר (not used in Kal) properly to glitter, glimmer; hence 1) to be very bright, magnificent; 2) to be famous, shining far; 3) to be distinguished, noble, mighty, to be great in general. Compare אַדֶּרֶת. Niph. to show oneself grand, brilliant. Hiph. to glorify, to make brilliant, Isa. 42: 21.

אֲדָר m. name of the last month of the ecclesiastical year, (about the month of March), but in the reckoning of the civil year Ellul is the 12th month.

אַדָּר (magnificence), see חֲצַר־אַדָּר (magnificent court), p. n.

אֶדֶר m. 1) ornament, set of jewels, hence אֶ׳ הַיְקָר the valuable ornament; 2) = אַדֶּרֶת full dress, splendid dress, the ornamental, *tunica*.

אִדַּר (def. אִדְּרָא, pl. c. אִדְּרֵי, def. אִדְּרַיָּא) Aram. f. a great open place that is raised and stamped fast, forming in the East a thrashing-floor. Root אֲדַר (not גָּדַר) to make great. (Compare אָדַר 3.)

אֲדַרְגָּזֵר only pl. def. אֲדַרְגָּזְרַיָּא Aram. m. a certain officer or bailiwick in the Babylonian empire, which is not distinguished even by the context. Rashi supposes it to be the name of a nation. Saadia is of opinion that it signifies 'magnates,' but, at all events, the etymology of this noun is as little to be sought for in the Semitic as that of אַדְרַזְדָּא.

אַדְרַזְדָּא Aram. adv. right, correct, exact, just. It is like אָסְפַּרְנָא non-semitic.

אֲדַרְכּוֹן (pl. אֲדַרְכֹּנִים, and also דַּרְכּוֹן) m. a golden Persian royal coin, of the value of a drachm χρυσοῦς (about 13s. 9d. English money,) in contrast to the metal pieces in use with merchants. Derived from *Dara*, a king, and *Kaman*, a bow, because an archer was stamped on it; the מ is sometimes dropped; see דַּרְכְּמוֹן.

אֲדַרְכְּמוֹן the original form yet to be found in MSS.; whence אֲדַרְכֹּן is a contraction. The א is, as above, performative.

אַדְרַמֶּלֶךְ = אַדְרַמֶּלֶךְ p. n. m. (probably the glory of Moloch), 1) a deity of the Sefarvians, who were transplanted as colonists to Samaria; 2) p. n. m. son and murderer of the king Sennacherib of Assyria. Respecting its form, compare אֱלִימֶלֶךְ, עֲנַמֶּלֶךְ.

אֶדְרָע (=דְּרָע) Aram. f. properly, arm: hence power, strength, like the Hebrew זְרוֹעַ. The א is preformative.

אֶדְרֶעִי p. n. f. (a place or field which is sown, a plantation); 1) a city in Batanea (Bashan), LXX. Ἐδραείν, Ἐδραΐν, Eus. Ἀδραά, Ptol. Ἄδρα; 2) city within the dominion of Naphtali. Root זָרַע = דְּרַע to sow, to plant.

אַדֶּרֶת (from the m. אַדִּיר = אֶדֶר with suff. אַדַּרְתּוֹ, אַדַּרְתָּם, f. magnificent, splendid, superior, grand: e. g. גֶּפֶן אַ׳; 2) as a noun, the splendour, superiority, splendid dress, or cloak; e.g. אַ׳ שֵׂעָר, שִׂנְעָר. The root אָדַר is equivalent to הָדַר.

אָדַשׁ (only inf. abs. Isa. 28: 28) to thrash, to tread. Syn. with דּוּשׁ.

אָהַב and אָהֵב (hence אֲהַבְךָ; אָהֲבוּ; אֲהַבְתִּיו; אֲהַבְתָּנוּ; אֹהֵבָה fut. יֶאֱהַב; יֶאֱהָב (1 pers. אֹהַב and אֱהַב; inf. frequently אַהֲבָה) to love, partly physical, equivalent to desire; partly spiritual, equivalent to be fond of; hence to do anything with pleasure. The modifications of this idea appear in the construction:—with the accusative of the person or the object, to love; with לְ to love somebody, to manifest love towards somebody; with בְּ to be attached to, to cleave to, (as דָּבַק); with לְ before the inf. to do something with pleasure; with כִּי in a concluding sentence, to rejoice that—, etc.; part. m. אֹהֵב, f. אֹהֶבֶת, in const. sometimes אֹהֲבֵתִי friend, beloved one, female friend, female beloved, always in a high degree of friendship; hence more than רֵעַ. Niph. (only part.) to be lovely, charming. Pi. (only part. מְאַהֵב paramour) to love passionately.

אַהֲבָה f. 1) the loving, (inf. nom. hence with the accus. of the object or the person); 2) love (abst.); 3) the beloved one, (אַהַב as it were fem.; like מַלְכָּה from מֶלֶךְ) or the object of love.

אֲהַבְהַב (redoubled form) to love greatly, occurs but once (Hos. 4: 18), אֲהַבְהֵבוּ = אָהֲבוּ ,הֵבוּ they love greatly, where, however, the flexible affixes of the person are repeated; compare צִמְּתֻתוּנִי from צָמַת.

אֲהָבִים m. pl. (from אָהַב) intercourse of love, love-affair, never concrete for paramour.

אֲהָבִים m. pl. from אֲהַב Rab.; 1) wooing, love, love-affairs; 2) loveliness, gracefulness.

אָהַד (not used) equivalent to איד to be strong, vigorous.

אֹהַד p. n. m. (the power, for the powerful) from אָהַד.

אֲהָהּ interj. a lament; an exclamation; wo! alas! The א is preformative. See הָהּ.

אֵהוּד (= אֵהוּד like אֵבוּס energy, instead of energetic) p. n. m. name of a Jewish judge, LXX. 'Αώδ, 'Ιούδης, 'Ηούδης. See אֹהַד.

אַהֲוָא p. n. m. (a river-district, river, stream), is a river between Babylon and Jerusalem, where Ezra rested with the Jews that returned from captivity; hence נְהַר אַהֲוָא and הַנָּהָר א' the Ahava river, in which another river (הַנָּהָר) flows, which is not far from כָּסִפְיָא a country on the Caspian mountains north-east of Media. Whether it is to be read אַדְיָא, to signify the river Adiava in Assyria (Ammian, Mar. 23: 20) or whether it is to be taken as a non-Semitic appellation of the Euphrates cannot be substantiated for want of proof. As an appellative אַהֲוָה signifies river (water).

אֱהִי (from הִי and אֱ prosth.) adv. where? where then? (only in Hos.) אֱהִי מַלְכְּךָ אֵפוֹא where now is thy king? the pronominal root is here הִי, and אֱ preformative as in אֶבְל, אֲשֶׁר etc.

אָהַל (= הָל) 1) to be light, clear, glitter, to shine (not used); Hiphil, to spread abroad brightness, light, to give light, only in Job 25: 5: לֹא יַאֲהִיל 'it shineth not,' i. e. is not pure, not spotless.

אֹהֶל (with suff. אָהֳלִי, אָהָלְךָ, in pause אָהֳלֶךָ, also אָהֳלֶךָ, אָהֳלוֹ and אָהֳלֹה; with ה mobile אֹהֱלָה, pl. אֹהָלִים and אֳהָלִים, c. אָהֳלֵי, with suff. אָהֳלֵיכֶם, אֹהָלֶיךָ, אֹהָלָיו m.; 1) tent of Beduins and Nomades, but also the Tabernacle, e.g. א' מוֹעֵד, הָעֵדוּת significations of the tabernacle, for which also הָאֹהֶל (compare הָאָדָם, הַבַּעַל) or

curs. Therefore in the distinction for מִשְׁכָּן the round tent covering, hawning, and also the outside of a tent; so also the poet. אֹהֶל בֵּיתִי the tent covering of my dwelling; 2) dwelling, residence, temple in general, hence also castle; 3) p. n. m. (dwellers in tents, Nomades), from which the denom. verb :—

אָהַל (only in the fut. tense יֶאֱהַל) to pitch a tent, i. e. to erect a tent, or to journey with tents. Piel fut. יַהֵל instead of יְאַהֵל (comp. מַלֵּף for מְאַלֵּף).

אָהֳלָה (fem. form, from אֹהֶל) p. n. f. a symbolic name for Samaria, used for a woman that is not virtuous. See אָהֳלִיבָה.

אָהֳלִיאָב p. n. m.

אָהֳלִיבָה p. n. f. a symbolic name for Jerusalem.

אָהֳלִיבָמָה p. n. f. (a mountain-family, mountain nations); 1) the name of a tribe of the Edomites; 2) name of a female.

אֲהָלוֹת (only pl.) f. aloe-trees, which, on account of their fragrance were planted in magnificent orchards, between spikenards and myrtles, etc., but :—

אֲהָלִים pl. m. aloes-wood, ξυλαλόη (ἀλόη John 19: 40) otherwise ἀγάλ-λοχον; this distinction is not always correct. This wood the Hebrews got from India, where, besides other appellatives, it is also called 'aghil' whence, by omitting the mere vowel instead of the aspirated *g* (אֲהָל) ensued

אַהֲרֹן p. n. m. (the enlightened, as אוּרִי Lucinius), the first high-priest, Aaron, the brother of Moses, as ancestor of the priest-family; by בְּנֵי, בֵּית אַהֲרֹן priests in general are understood. The root אָהַר is = אוּר or זָהַר.

אוֹ (pronominal root) conj. the inclusive and exclusive 'or,' also, *vel* and *aut;* hence probably related to אוּ, וּ, e. g. (מְ־אוּ־מָה) 'and,' as also the Latin *vel* (or) is lengthened from *ve*, 'and.' But, if it only separates two objects, and signifies the free choice between them, without distinguishing one of them, the connecting וּ is still apparent; for instance, in the repetition אוֹ־אוֹ either—or, but where this course is abandoned, the following gradations take place: 1) 'or rather' confirming, as it were, the preceding, e. g. אוֹ־זֶה שָׁנִים 'or rather since many years:' 2) 'or (that)' where this rectification no more extends the preceding, but entirely supersedes it; hence it may be translated 'it be then, that,' and the copulative character becomes partly lost; 3) 'or if,' ellept. for אוֹ כִּי, which signification is, however, not required if the strict connection of sentences is dispensed with.

אִי (pronominal root) conj. when, if, *ei*, *si*, (in אִלּוּ, אִלֵּי), differs from אוֹ, where the disjunctive element prevails, and from אִם which expresses the pure condition, without regard whether the action is imagined as taking place or not, and differs also from לוּ, which is generally used to express hope. Compare לוּ, אִם.

אִי (Ketib Prov. 31 : 4) adv. = אֵי where? compare שָׁם and שׁוּם.

אִיאֵל perhaps a contraction from אֲבִיאֵל (compare אִיעֶזֶר) p. n. m.

אוּב (not used) equivalent to אָבַב to be hollow (in אַבּוּב flute).

אוֹב (pl. אֹבוֹת) m. 1) water-bottle, leather pipes for water; 2) the hollow belly (of the conjurers of the dead) in which the conjuring spirit (πύθων) dwells, and speaks hollow, as if out of the ground; hence translated sometimes the demon, sometimes the conjurer ἐγγαστρίμυθος; 3) necromancer in general, who wakes the dead out of the earth to unveil the future, from which בַּעֲלַת א' magician, wizard (necromancer).

אֹבוֹת p. n. (canals, excavations,) encampment of the Israelites in the Arabian desert.

אוֹבִיל p. n. m. captain of the camels of David.

אוּבַל and אֻבַל stream, river, (only Dan.) Root אָבַל.

אוּד (not used) turning; hence transferred to signify powerful, to be strong, as in חַיִל, קָשֶׁר, etc. synonymous with עוּד. Another signification is found in אֵד.

אוּד (pl. אוּדִים) m. *autabulum*, kitchen-jack, poker, a smoking fire-brand. Root אוּד.

אוֹדוֹת pl. f. coll. causes, reasons, motives, circumstances, occasion, only 2 Sa. 13:16, אַל-אוֹדוֹת there is no cause, etc., otherwise in combination: e.g. עַל אוֹדוֹת on account of, עַל אוֹדוֹתֶיךָ for thy sake, concerning thee, עַל כָּל-אוֹדוֹת-אֲשֶׁר, therefore, because. Root אוּד to turn, as סִבָּה cause, from סָבַב to turn.

I. אָוָה only Piel, to wish sincerely, (vehemently) desire, request, to aspire, (usually joined with נֶפֶשׁ mind, soul). Hith. הִתְאַוָּה; fut. apoc. יִתְאָו to long, to yearn, to show oneself longing, desirous, with לְ for something, with the accus. to lust after some-

abs. to have a desire הִתְאַוָּה תַאֲוָה *cupidinem cupere*, i. e. to be lusting. Root אָוָה is a modification in the sound from אָבָה.

II. אָוָה only Hith. הִתְאַוִּיתֶם you shall measure off, or point out for yourself (see Deut. 34 : 10), where אָוָה ought to be = תָּוָה ; but perhaps it may be a corrupted form for הִתְתַּוִּיתֶם = הִתַּוִּיתֶם ; but by no means is אוֹת token, derived therefrom.

אַוָּה (c. אַוַּת) f. desire, lust, longing, usually joined with נֶפֶשׁ (the inward motion, affection).

אוּזַי p. n. m.

אוּזָל p. n. m. name of a Joktanite, who subsequently became progenitor of the Arabs, in Usal (in the Greek called *Ausar*), at present Sanaa.

אֱוִי p. n. m. (the crier, one that wails, = אֱוִי derived from the interj. אוֹי) of a king's son of Midian.

אוֹי (= הוֹי) interj.; 1) exclamation of wailing or threatening, constructed with the dat. and acc.; comp. the Greek οἴ. 2) noun for wailing, wo.

אוֹיָה the same, and with the dative. The ־ָה is enclitical, hence quiescent, as in the pronominal roots שָׁמָּה, הֵנָּה, הַלְאָה, and in nouns and verbs.

אֱוִיל (pl. אֱוִילִים and אֱוִלִים) m. (chiefly in the Prov.) originally, the slack one, the withered one: hence 1) a fool, like נָבָל, inasmuch as weakness signifies folly, and power signifies virtue (compare חַיִל *virtus*, ἀρετή), connective therewith is the adjective foolish ; 2) wicked, infidel, inasmuch as infidelity is associated with vice.

אֱוִיל מְרֹדַךְ p. n. m. a ruler in Babylon, son and successor of Nebuchadnezzer, who, after two year's rule, (Joseph. 18) was murdered by Neriglesser, his brother-in-law. See etymology under מְרֹאדַךְ.

אָוַל (not used) to be slack, to be withered. Related to אָבַל.

אוּל (poet). m. belly, only Ps. 73 : 4, so called on account of its round form. The root is אוּל = אָהַל and אל in אֵלָה, אַלּוֹן related to אִיל, ἴλλω (εἰλέω, εἰλύω) to turn to roll, hence, to be round bellied, (compare חִיל, גִּיל, עָגַל), to which belong אֵיל, אַיִל, and others, of the same root, inasmuch as the idea of rolling (as חָזַק, חוּל) gradually merges into that of strength. Vide אַיִל.

אֱוִלִי adj. m. foolish (rare), formed from אֱוִיל.

אוּלַי p. n. m. name of a river near Susa in Persia, Greek Εὔλαιος, later Χόασπις (comp. Plin. H.

N. 6, 27), it is now called Kerah. Compare Curt. 5, 2, *delicatam vehens aquam.*

אוּלַי and אֻלַי (compound) adv. from אוֹ = *εἰ*; in its conditional sense, 'or if,' 'if but,' and לִי 'not,' therefore, 'if not;' *εἰ, γέ*; next, 'whether not,' which stands for 'perhaps,' it is therefore applied to fear, doubt, and hope, quite as much as the elements of the composition render it possible.

אוּלִים (only c. אוּלֵי Ketib) pl. m. the mighty, the distinguished, princes. The root is אול in the sense of being strong, in the Keri it is therefore אֵילִים, from אַיִל.

אוּלָם or אֻלָם (for מְאֻלָּם; pl. אֻלַמִּים, c. אֻלַמֵּי) m. that which is arched, the vaulted; hence, a vault, a hall, as אֻ' הָעַמּוּדִים the vaulted pillars, hall of pillars; אֻ' הַמִּשְׁפָּט hall of justice, etc. Hence LXX. frequently *ναός*. The root is אָלַם to bind, from binding, and making fast the roof, (compare אָחַז) as אֲגֻדָּה a vault, from אָגַד to bind; compare אַלְמְנוֹת citadels, likewise from אָלַם.

אוּלָם (comp. like אוּלַי) adv. (adversative), but, however it next merges into: but, not, the less, according as the context demands it. The second part of the composition לָם is from לָמָּה, as שָׁם is from שָׁ־מָּה, and אוּ is in אוּ־לַי.

אוּלָם p. n. m. (the lonely one, from אָלַם to be lonely).

אִוֶּלֶת (with suff. אִוַּלְתִּי) f. slackness, hence: 1) foolishness; 2) infidelity. Root אָוַל.

אוֹמָר p. n. m. (from אָמַר of prominent statue, tall).

און (not used): 1) to breathe, like הָבַל, and then transferred to nothingness and vanity; 2) to effect by work, to take pains, as עָנָה; and from these two principal significations all the deriv. may be explained.

I. אָוֶן and אוֹן (with suff. אוֹנִי, אוֹנָם, and in the pl. אוֹנִים) m. breath, *ἀτμός*; hence 1) nothingness, vanity, (compare הֶבֶל breath, and next, nothingness, vanity). Hence the wicked, the bad, or that which is sinful generally, unworthiness, badness; e. g. אַנְשֵׁי, מְתֵי, פֹּעֲלֵי, אָ'; falseness, deception, hypocrisy, backsliding; e. g. שְׂפַת אָ'; 2) idolatry, comp. הֶבֶל, אֱלִיל, hence בֵּית אָ' (town of idols) not identical with בֵּית־אֵל; בִּקְעַת אָ' (valley of idols), etc., likewise אָוֶן (Ezek. 30: 17) for און (Heliopolis), with the sub-signification: town of idolatry.

II. אָוֶן (pl. אוֹנִים) and און m. the

exerting of power, originally that which is attained by labour and pains; fatigue, trouble, difficulty, strait, (comp. עָמָל); e. g. בֶּן־אוֹנִי son of my affliction, לֶחֶם אוֹנִים (comp. לֶחֶם עֹנִי) bread of affliction; בְּמַחַת א׳ under constraint, comp. עֳנִי. The sense of tribulation and suffering is also concentrated in עָנָה; 2) that which it attained by labour, fruit of labour, compare עָמָל, יָגִין, and of exertion of power (for which אוֹן is used), hence property, strength.

און and אֹן (Egyptian), p. n. f. a town in lower Egypt on the eastern shore of the Nile, which is also called the same in the Coptic. The signification is 'sun' which was worshipped there, hence the Greeks called it Heliopolis; the Hebrews also called it בֵּית שֶׁמֶשׁ, poetically עִיר הַחֶרֶס, the Arabs עין שמש (fountain of the sun).

אוֹנוֹ p. n. f. (the powerful one, the rich one; the termination וֹ, as in שִׁילוֹ, עַכּוֹ, יְרִחוֹ is not a suff., but belongs to the formation of the word for ־וֹן) name of the city.

אוֹנִיּוֹת pl. in Ketib for אֳנִיּוֹת, it seems to be a participle form like הוֹמִיָּה, פּוֹרִיָּה.

אוֹנָם p. n. m. (from אוֹן vigour, with the termination ־ָם).

אוֹנָן p. n. m. (the same, with the termination ־ָן).

אוּפָז p. n. name of a gold region, whence כֶּתֶם (a pure Semitic word) and זָהָב were obtained. If the appellation is Hebrew, it is composed of אוּ = אִי land, coast, and פָּז gold, hence, gold coast; at all events it does not appear identical with אוֹפִיר.

אוֹפִיר (also אֹפִר, אֹפִיר) p. n. of a gold region, like אוּפָז, whence Solomon's ships, conjointly with Phœnician navigators obtained the following products: gold (זָהָב), brazil-wood (almug) Sansc. mocha, pearls (כֶּתֶם); precious stones, (אֶבֶן יְקָרָה); silver (כֶּסֶף); ivory (שֶׁנְהַבִּים); apes (קֹפִים); peacocks (תֻּכִּיִּים); (Joshephat's ships of Tarshish fitted out for an expedition to that country foundered not far from Berenice, the present Açiun עֶצְיוֹן גֶּבֶר). Hence generally כֶּתֶם, זְהַב א׳ Ophir gold, and Ophir pearls; also אוֹפִיר alone. Whether this region is to be sought for in Arabia or India has not yet been ascertained.

אוֹפָן (c. אוֹפַן, pl. אוֹפַנִּים) m. (equiv. to אֹפָן which see).

אוּץ 1) inter. to be crowded together, to be pressed together; 2) trans. and reflec. to crowd, to press;

hence to press one's self, to hasten away, e. g. אָץ בִּדְבָרִים he that hastens in speaking; with מִן to push away, to withdraw. Hiph. to press in somebody, with בְּ.

אוֹצָר (c. אוֹצַר, pl. אוֹצָרוֹת) m. that which encloses (comp. חוֹתָם, עוֹלָם), hence 1) a store, magazine, place for storing silver and gold, (2 Chron. 32 : 27), etc.; 2) that which is treasured up in the magazine: stores, treasure. Root אָצַר.

אוֹר to burn, flame: hence brighten, enlighten, illuminate, intrans. to be light, to become light, e. g. of the eyes, of the morning. אוֹר impers. it grows light. Niph. נָאוֹר, fut. יֵאוֹר, to be made light, to be made enlightened, to be illuminated, לְהֵאוֹר=לֵאוֹר part. illuminated, brightened, effulgent. Hiph. הֵאִיר f. apoc. יָאֵר caus.: 1) to cause a thing to burn, to kindle: e. g. מִזְבֵּחַ; 2) to make light, to make bright: e. g. the eyes, equivalent to revive, to rouse; the countenance, equivalent to make cheerful, of the Deity with or without adding פָּנִים, and with בְּ, עַל, אֶל, אֶת, לְ to look upon one graciously; the understanding, equivalent to instruct, etc.; 3) to spread light.

אוֹר (pl. once only אוֹרִים) m. (f. only Job 36 : 32) col. light: as light of the sun, not however the appellation of an illuminated body (מָאוֹר), hence light of day,—lightning,—sun,—morning; next, for morning, lightning, etc. generally. As a figure of speech, or is applied in א׳ חַיִּים light of life, or א׳ פָּנִים cheerfulness, mildness of countenance, or א׳ יִשְׂרָאֵל, א׳ גּוֹיִם etc., for instructors, benefactors, where אוֹר also frequently occurs alone. Root אוּר.

אוּר m. 1) flame, hence אוּר אֵשׁ flame of fire; 2) fire, hence הִבְעִיר בָּאוּר; 3) = אוֹר only pl. אֻרִים, region of light, orient; 4) figuratively, light of faith, revelation, (LXX. δήλωσις), which name is generally joined with תֻּמִּים revelation and truth, (תֻּמִּים) signifies the personifying figures in the breast-plate (חֹשֶׁן) of the high-priest, see תֻּמִּים. The superior judge in Egypt also wore an outward symbol of truth. 5) p. n. name of a city of the Chaldees in Mesopotamia (see כַּשְׂדִּים) which name a Persian castle yet bore at the time of Ammian.; 6) p. n. m. comp. אוּרִי and the later מֵאִיר, שְׁרָגָא.

אוֹרָה f. equiv. to אוֹר light; fig. fortune, like אוֹר.

אֻוְרוֹת (later אֻרָוֹת) pl. f. penn, stable, from אָרָה.

אוּרִי p. n. m. comp. Φωτινός formed from אוּר through the adjective ending ִי.

אוּרִיאֵל p. n. m. (the enlightened of the Lord). The ִי serves for the connecting of words in many compounds of proper nouns.

אוּרִיָּה p. n. m. (the same).

אוּרִיָּהוּ p. n. m. (the same).

אוֹרֹת and אֹרֹת (only pl.) f. verdant, blooming plants, herbs; טַל א׳ refreshing dew of herbs. From אוּר to shine, transferred to blooming: as נֵץ, זָהָה, אֵב and others; comp. אִיָּר spring month; equiv. to זִו, see אוּר to shine.

אוֹשׁ (אֻשׁ) Aram. אֶת, see אִישׁ, אִית; comp. יֵשׁ.

אוֹשְׁשׁ see אָשַׁשׁ, אִישׁ.

I. אוּת (not used) to engrave, to curb in, related to שׂוּם which is the same. See אוֹת.

אוֹת (pl. אֹתוֹת) m. that which is engraved, a token (a letter); hence transferred, 1) a marking, distinguishing sign, a sign of example, proof, e. g. the Sabbath, circumcision, sacrifices, as tokens of covenants (symbols), mentioned between Jehovah and Israel; 2) field marks of single tribes, standards, trans. to signs of the times (לְאֹתוֹת וּלְמוֹעֲדִים); 3) in the most manifold significations, as a token of remembrance, a warning, omen, of truth, of miracle; next, monument, warning, miracle, (related מוֹפֵת). The root is אוּת. The form אוֹת is like קוֹל and the ת is radical. To the same root belongs also אֵת, pl. אִתִּים (like מֵת) an instrument for engraving, curbing, cutting, a hatchet, a ploughshare, thus: like שֵׁם belongs to שׂוּם, the iron cutting, graving, pencil. See שׂוּם, אֵת.

II. אוּת = אָתָה, אֵת (only fut. יֵאוֹתוּ, נֵאוֹת) with ה, נֵאֹתָה, like יֵבוֹשׁ from בּוֹשׁ), to come, to come together, to come to an agreement; hence to consent, to be unanimous, with ל of the person, to consent to, to agree with somebody. This form אֵת is older than the lengthened אָתָה.

אָז (pron. root) adv. dem. abridged from אָכֵן, originaly *ibi*, related with אֵי *ubi?* next transferred to time, 'then,' as well in reference to the past, 'at that time,' as also in reference to the future, 'then'; but אָז never stands pleonastically, as מִן אָז is = מֵאָז since then, since, and also never causal. מֵאָז, (absolute) from (since that time), like אָז of the past: hence formerly, previous to this before this; next, (relat.) from the starting point of the past, hence succeeded by the n. inf. or inf. verb, which may often be translated 'from—until.'

אֲזָא (part. 2 אָזֵה = אָזֵה, inf. מֵזֵא, with suff. מֵזְיֵהּ, Aram. to kindle, to heat, radically related to אֵשׁ, hence אֵשׁ fire.

אָזַב (not used) equiv. to עָשַׁב the root of which signifies 'to shine,' which is finally transferred to blooming.

אָזְבַּי adj. (from אָזַב)p. n. m. (אָזֻב like אֵזוֹב, the one of shining appearance).

אֲזַד Aram. only part. f. אַזְדָּא, confirmed, concluded, unalterably decided upon, as the talmudical אַזְדָּא לְטַעֲמֵיהּ fixed, framed according to his opinion. The root is אָזַד to fasten; hence entirely distinct from אָזַל.

אֵזוֹב (= אֵזֹב) m. ὕσσωπος, hyssop, a spice root, which tied up in a (אֲגֻדָּה) bundle was used at the sprinklings of purification. The root is אָזַב.

אֵזוֹר (= אֵזֹר) m. 1) band, fetter, 2) tie, girdle; hence the phrases אָסַר = אָזַר, דָּבַק, אָסַר, פִּתַּח אֵ׳.

אָז (pron. root) זִי, Aram. אֱדַיִן, related to אִי, only poet. adv. dem. originally *ibi*, but almost generally transferred to time: 'then'; by retaining of the א, arose אָז, both however connected with זֶה.

אַזְכָּרָה (with suff. אַזְכָּרָתָהּ) f. in speaking of sacrifices: the meat-offering of memorial, μνημόσυνον, *memoriale*, which causes the offerers to be mercifully remembered by God, or which causes the glory of the Deity to be remembered by the offerers. See זָכַר.

אָזַל (poet. fut. תֵּאזְלִי for תֵּזְלִי ,תֵּאזְלִי) to move to and fro, to rock: hence 1) moving one thing through another, spinning; only part. Pu. מְאוּזָּל, that which is twisted, that which is spun. From אָזַל; 2) to remove oneself, to roll away; 3 pers. fut. אָזְלַת = אָזְלָה; transferred, to dry up (of water), vanish (of help), exhaust (means of life), etc.

אֲזַל Aram. imp. אֵזֶל = אֲזַל, אֱזֶל to go, to go away, to go to some place.

אֶזֶל m. the going away, departure; hence p. n. אֶבֶן הָאָזֶל, stone of separation.

אֹזֶן (Dual אָזְנַיִם, p. n. אָזְנוֹת from אָזַן) primitive, f. ear. So in the phrases: שָׂם בְּאָ׳, דִּבֶּר בְּאָ׳; הִכְבִּיד, פָּתַח, כָּרָה, גָּלָה, הִטָּה א׳; הַשְׁמָעוֹת אָזְנַיִם the announcing relating in the ears of somebody. From which the dem. —

הֶאֱזִין Hiph. to listen attentively, originally, to incline the ear, with acc. and dat. of the object, and with אֶל, עַל and עַד of the person. Used of the Deity, signifies to hear, to hearken; of man, to obey. See זוּן Hiph. to which belongs 1 pers. fut. אָזִין, and part. מֵזִין.

אָזַן only Pi. אִזֵּן, to consider, to probe, to weigh, (only Ecc.) The root is אָזַן *pendere, suspendere.* Arab. *wasan.*

אֱזַן Aram. equivalent to זַן. See אָזַן, אֹזֶן.

אָזֵן (only once before suff. אֲזֵנְךָ) m. pointed weapon, vessel, tool; the root is אָזַן equivalent to זוּן, שֵׁן to point.

אֻזֵּן or אֻזֶּן (that which is pointed) p. n. of a place which a daughter of Ephraim, שֶׁאֱרָה, had built.

אַזְנוֹת תָּבוֹר p. n. f. (the ridges of the Tabor), town in the dominion of Naphtali. אַזְנוֹת is formed from אֹזֶן (ear) ridge.

אַזְנָח (as אַכְזָר, אַכְזָב) adj. m. dried up, exhausted, from זָנַח (see the verb), from which is the denom. הֶאֱזְנִיחַ Hiph. to cause to be exhausted, for instance נָהָר.

אָזְנִי (adj. from אֹזֶן) p. n. m. one that hearkens.

אֲזַנְיָה p. n. m. (heard of God) אָזַן likewise from אָזַן.

אֲזִקִּים (from sing. אֵזֶק) pl. m. fetters, bonds, the א is performative. For the root, see under זִקִּים.

אָזַר (fut. יֶאְזֹר, with suff. יַאַזְרֵנִי) equiv. to אָסַר to bind, to tie round: hence gird, with the accus. e. g. חֲלָצַיִם the loins = to equip. Like all verbs signifying dressing, therefore also with the accus. of the garment אֵזוֹר אָזוּר girded with a girdle. Niph. part. נֶאְזָר with בְּ const., to gird oneself, to be girded. Pi. to gird round, armed; with double accus. תְּאַזְּרֵנִי = תְּזָרֵנִי. Hith. to equip oneself, with the accus.

אֶזְרוֹעַ (a rare form for זְרוֹעַ) f. fore part of the arm, arm, the א is preformative; comp. Aram. אֶדְרָע. See זְרֹעַ.

אֶזְרָח (const. אֶזְרַח only sing.) m., 1) native, a denizen, he who springs forth in the place where he exists; transferred hence to a native tree not transplanted from another country (exotic); 2) probably a p. n. m. = זֶרַח, hence אֶזְרָחִי p. n. the descendants of אֶזְרָח, i. e. זֶרַח. Used of Ethan and Heman. The root זָרַח which see.

אָח (const. אֲחִי in proper nouns אַח,

no matter whether of both parents or a step brother; a closer definition is only met with when the degree of relationship is the object, pl. אַחִים, const. אֲחֵי) m. brother, e. g. בֶּן־אָב, בֶּן־אֵם, בֶּן־אִשָּׁה אַחֶרֶת. אָח is transferred to more meanings, like אָב, e.g. to a friend, in reference to mental brotherhood, in more enlarged fraternization to brother of a family, brother of the tribe, brother of the country, equiv. to cousin, relative, of the same tribe, a countryman; in reference to other nations and people: confederate, fellow-man, neighbour, and on the last signification is founded the use with אִישׁ preceding, for *alter—alter*, even of inanimate things, if only mas. e. g. אִישׁ מֵעַל אָחִיו one from the other, i. e. to separate one from another; אִישׁ אֶל־אָחִיו one to another, i. e. approximation from one to another. In reference to the etymology, the noun is primitive, like אָב, אֵם.

אָח (only sing. and rare), f. fire, next, fire-oven, viz. the fire-basin which, in the East, is used for heating the rooms inhabited in winter. The root is אָח to glow, to burn.

אָהּ interj. ah! oh! cry of wailing, const. with the dat. Ezek. 6:11.

אָח (Aram.) pl. m. suff. אֶחָיךְ m. brother = אָח.

אֹחַ (only pl. אֹחִים once), m. owl, screech-owl, derived from אָח ah!

אַחְאָב p. n. m. (father's brother, uncle,) name of one of the kings who reigned in Israel, in 918-897, before the Christian era.

אַחְבָּן p. n. m. (the amiable one), from אָחַב = אָהַב, to love, comp. the harder form as it appears in עָגַב.

אֶחָד (const. אַחַד, pl. אֲחָדִים), numerical, m. 1) one, *unus*; which however in calculations of time is used for 'first' as יוֹם אֶחָד לַחֹדֶשׁ, בְּאֶחָד לַחֹדֶשׁ on the first (day) of the month; if it occur two or three times it expresses either *unus, alter, tertius*; or a division, the—the; the same also as an indefinite article, 'one'; 2) any one, some one, where it stands either absolute, like אֶחָד מֵהַנְּעָרִים, מֵאֶחָיו or constructive אַחַד הָעָם any one of the people, hence אֵין אֶ׳, לֹא אֶ׳ nobody; 3) where the numerical makes one of the mass prominent and distinguished, hence, the same, solely, as also אֲחָדִים. The signification of the pl. is besides: single ones, *aliquot*; seldom, however for the singular only, e. g. הָיוּ לַאֲחָדִים they have become one. With prep. כְּאֶחָד like one = together, like כְּאִישׁ אֶחָד ; further must be noticed לְאַחַד אֶחָד one after the other. Considering its derivation it has no verbal root as a numerical, but is primitive. From this is formed the denom. הִתְאַחֵד (once only) to unite within oneself (in vigour), to concentrate within oneself.

אָחוּ (LXX. ἄχει, αχι, Copt. *piachi*, here only sing.) m. that which grows near the water, in the marsh, grass, reed.

אֵחוּד (= אֶחָיוּד) p. n. m. soleness= the only one, for which also אֵחִי, which see.

I. אַחְוָה (poet. formed as אַזְכָּרָה) f. announcement, declaration. The root is חָוָה *in-qua-m*, to say, which see.

II. אַחֲוָה (poet.) f. fraternization, fraternity, derived from אָח.

אֲחוֹחַ p. n. m. fraternization, also אֲחֹחִי, אֲחִיָּה.

אַחֲוָיָה (Aram.) f. equiv. to אַחְוָה from חֲוָא.

אֲחוּמַי p. n. m. (swarth, sun-burnt, from חוּם).

אָחוֹר (pl. אֲחוֹרִים) m. 1) return, back part, *tergum*, distinguished from the pl. which expresses the collective of such back ground; hence on the back part, (in contrast to פָּנִים, קֶדֶם, front, fore part), behind, or in reply to the question whither? backward, back: e. g. סַב ,שָׁב ,נָסוֹג ,זוּר א'. With prep. לְאָחוֹר retro., or with the face turned away; מֵאָחוֹר *a tergo*, from behind; בְּאָחוֹר like לְאָחוֹר in reply to the question where? 2) transferred to the western side, which the Semitics considered as being in the back, (in contrast to קֶדֶם), hence also adv. towards the west, western; 3) future, e. g. לְאָחוֹר in future, in contrast to קֶדֶם past. Root אָחַר.

אָחוֹת (Aram. אֲחָת; const. אֲחוֹת m. s. אֲחוֹתוֹ; once אֲחוֹתוֹ; pl. אֲחָיוֹת, with suff. אַחְיוֹת) f. sister, likewise in the remotest sense like אָח brother; fig. it is used for relatives, cities, countries, etc. With אִשָּׁה preceeding it, as אִשָּׁה אֶל־אֲחוֹתָהּ it signifies *altera—altera*, as אִישׁ אֶל־אָחִיו *alter—alter*. From אָחוֹת where *o* = AU, as frequently occurs is the feminine termination, with the additional ת, like many nouns terminating with a vowel. See אָח.

אָחַז (fut. יֹאחֵז, seldom יֹחֵז from the rare form יֶאֱחֹז, where ֱ ֶ =

áa, â is changed into ô; fut. 1 pers. with âdem. תֹּאחֵז־יֹאחֵז, אֹחֲזָה; imp. אֱחֹז, אֶחֱזִי, אֱחֹזוּ) originally to seize, hasten after, reach, (comp. מָרְחוֹ); hence 1) apprehend, to seize = lay hold of, (in contrast to הָנִיחַ Ecc. 1: 18), partly with the accus. of the pers. or subject, partly with בְּ before the word signifying the member by which it is seized; but it is always transitive, though it may sometimes be rendered intransitive: e. g. to be seized with shuddering, with pain. Likewise to catch: as, for instance, שֻׁעָלִים, דָּגִים, צִפֳּרִים, or, to detain, with the accus. בְּ, e. g. אֲחוּזֵי חֶרֶב *amplexus gladium*; 2) to comprehend together, connect, to insert: e. g. בַּקִּיר in the wall, hence also vaults, the connecting of beams (comp. אָגַד, אָלַם), and: joined together, close together, close, e. g. דְּלָתוֹת; 3) to take out = seize (by lots), hence with מִן. See חוּז. Niph. נֶאֱחַז to be seized, to be taken prisoner, to be retained, נֹאחֲזוּ is however the denom. of אֲחֻזָּה (that which is taken possession of), to make oneself possessed of. Pi. אִחֵז (only in Job) to enclose, to surround with arches: e. g. פְּנֵי־כִסֵּא. Hof. only part. מֻאֳחָזִים to bind together.

אָחָז p. n. m. (*amplexus sc. gladium*, warrior). LXX. Ἀχάζ, Joseph. Ἀχάζης, a king of Judea, 743-728 before the Christian era.

אֲחֻזָּה (= אֲחוּזָּה) f., orig. seizure, e. g. שָׂדֶה, נַחֲלָה which is often added to it; next possession of moveable or immoveable property. The root is אָחַז.

אַחְזַי p. n. m. (with an adj. ending, with its signification like אָחָז.)

אֲחַזְיָה p. n. m. (the warrior of Jah).

אֲחַזְיָהוּ p. n. m. (the same), LXX. Ὀχοζίας.

אֲחֻזָּם p. n. m. (the warrior; *am* is suffix).

אֲחֻזַּת p. n. m. (*at* is suffix).

אֵחִי p. n. m. (= אֲחִי the fraternal one, the united one).

אֵחִי p. n. m. (the same, ־ִי adj. terminates, formed from אָח).

אֲחִיאָם p. n. m. (uncle, on the maternal side, אָם equivalent to אֵם).

אֲחִידָא (Aram. pl. אֲחִידָן) f. equiv. to the Hebrew חִידָה that which is knotted together, that which is enclosed, a riddle. Root חוּד.

אֲחִיָּה p. n. m. (a friend of Jah, or God-like, for in proper nouns, אָח expresses also similarity).

אֲחִיָּהוּ p. n. m. (the same).

אֲחִיהוּד p. n. m. (comp. אֲבִיהוּד, one who appears blooming, the blooming one).

אַחְיוֹ p. n. m. (the fraternal one, the

ô is abridged from ôn, as in שְׁלֹמֹה).

אֲחִיחוּד p. n. m. (the friend of privacy, faithful to a secret; see חוּד).

אֲחִיטוּב p. n. m. (the good friend, the good one; see טוּב).

אֲחִילוּד p. n. m. (friend of the Lydians; see לוּד).

אֲחִימוֹת p. n. m. (affinity, originally relationship, comp. חָם) in the parallel passages חֶמַת = מָחַת likewise from חָם.

אֲחִימֶלֶךְ p. n. m. (the royal relative).

אֲחִימָן p. n. m. (friend, adorers of מְנִי, Venus, comp. אֲחִיָּה adorer of God), name of a heathen.

אֲחִימַעַץ p. n. m. (friend of anger, the angry one).

אַחְיָן p. n. m. (the brotherly one, formed from אָח).

אֲחִינָדָב p. n. m. (comp. אֲבִינָדָב the friend of honesty, the honest-hearted-one).

אֲחִינֹעַם p. n. f. (comp. אֲבִינֹעַם the one attached to gracefulness, the gracious one). See אָח.

אֲחִיסָמָךְ p. n. m. (friend of support, the supporter).

אֲחִיעֶזֶר p. n. m. (friend of help, the helper; comp. אֲבִיעֶזֶר.

אֲחִיקָם p. n. m. (companion of assistance, the helping friend). See קוּם.

אֲחִירָם p. n. m. (= חִירָם the noble born). Comp. חִירָם, which see.

אֲחִירַע p. n. m. (friend of the unfortunate, comforter).

אֲחִישַׁחַר p. n. m. (companion of the morning-dawn, the beauteous one).

אֲחִישָׁר p. n. m. (companion of commerce). See שׁוּר.

אֲחִיתֹפֶל p. n. m. (companion of duplicity, the dissembler).

אַחְלָב p. n. f. (from חָלָב; fruitful district. Comp. חֶלְבּוֹן, חֶלְבָּה), a place in the territory of Asher. For this adjectival formation, compare אַכְזָב, אַכְזָר, אֵיתָן and others.

אַחְלַי (compound from אָח oh! and לִי related to לוּ) particle expressing a wish, would that! oh that! alone, or with the dative.

אַחֲלַי (from לִי and אָח) the same. For לִי see לוּלֵי.

אַחְלַי p. n. m. (the rich in adornment, from חָלָה to adorn).

אַחְלָמָה (the ה at the end is quiescent, as in לַיְלָה) f. name of a precious stone, LXX. ἀμέθυστος and ἀχάτης. Comp. Apoc. 21:20. If the etymology is Semitic, then אַחְלָם and אַחְלָמָה are adjectiv. formations from חָלַם to be strong, to be hard, like אַכְזָב.

אַחְמְתָא (read 'Achmĕt'â for אַחְמָתָן 'achmât'ân), p. n. f. thus is called the capital of Media. בִּירְתָא

דִּי בְּמָנֵי מְדִינְתָּא and no other is understood by it, as Ἀγβάτανα (m here = β) later, Hamadan, which according to Lassen, signifies, (Ind. Bibl. III. p. 36), *ἱπποστασία.*

אֲחַסְבַּי p. n. m. (the blooming one, shining one, from חָסַב = עָסַב, אָבַב). Comp. אִבִּי.

אָחַר (only fut. 1 pers. אֵאֱחַר = אֹחַר Comp. אֹהַב = אֶאֱהַב, and hence 3 pers. = יֵחַר, יַחַר in Ketib, to hesitate, to linger) Pi. אִחַר 3 pers. אֵחֲרוּ, fut. יְאַחֵר, part. מְאַחֲרִים to keep back, to detain, to postpone, or like Kal, lingering very much. Hip. הוֹחִיר equivalent to הֶאֱחִיר. (Comp. הוֹבִיד equiv. to הֶאֱבִיד), only fut. יוֹחַר (Keri) to linger or delay beyond a time; const. with מִן.

אַחֵר (= אָחֵר, const. אַחַר) m. (pl. אֲחֵרִים and once אָחֳרִין, const. אַחֲרֵי, אַחֶרֶת, f. pl. אֲחֵרוֹת) adj. (A) originally delaying, subsequently, to be too late: hence, 1) succeeding, that which is later; 2) the other, second. (Comp. *secundus* from *sequi*) i. e. what follows: e. g. אֱלֹהִים אֲחֵרִים other Gods. (B.) adv. 1) abs. אָחֵר elsewhere, others = deviating, different. Comp. changing; 2) const. אַחַר (*a*) elsewhere, otherwise, (Gen. 22: 18), thus, of place; (*b*) in other time = subsequently, afterwards, thus of time. In both cases originally adj. elsewhere, otherwise. The const. form frequently appears as a particle form, (C.) prepos. 1) const. אַחַר likewise as the adj. (*a*) of place: behind, hence it expresses after verbs a qualification of sense, as: הָלַךְ, בָּא, רָדַף אַחַר etc., and with prefix, as, מֵאַחַר from behind; (*b*) of time, after, as אַחַר כֵּן after this, here upon; more frequently, however, 2) const. pl. אַחֲרֵי, with suff. אַחֲרָיו, אַחֲרֵי, אַחֲרֶיךָ, and (*a*) in reference to place: behind, hindwards, hence like אַחַר after verbs of motion יָרַד, עָלָה, רָדַף, יָצָא, בָּא, הָלַךְ, אַחֲרֵי, or, also after others like מִלֵּא, זָנָה, קָרָא, etc. (*b*) in reference to time, afterwards, after this, with the inf: hence אַחֲרֵי כֵן after (that) thus, after this = hereupon; later אַחֲרֵי זֹאת, Aram. אַחֲרֵי דְנָה, with pref. and other prep. מֵאַחֲרֵי away from behind, later, מֵאַחֲרֵי לְ, מִן־אַחֲרֵי and then also: behind, or of time מֵאַחֲרֵי כֵן thereupon; אֶל אַחֲרֵי behind, where אֶל signifies the tendency, and א' the position; עַל־אַ' behind, originally at—behind, like עַל לִפְנֵי

at — before; בְּאַחֲרֵי as: הַחֲנִית with the spear from behind. (D.) conj. generally with אֲשֶׁר, אֲשֶׁר, אַחַר and אַחֲרֵי אֲשֶׁר after which also אַחֲרֵי כֵן אֲשֶׁר the same.

אַחֲרוֹן (from אָחַר behind) adj. m. אַחֲרוֹנָה f. the hinder one, the one behind (contrast to קַדְמוֹן from קֶדֶם with all its derivatives) as, 1) *posterus*, דּוֹר, יוֹם א׳, the subsequent, the following, the later day, the generation: hence, אַחֲרֹנִים *posteri;* 2) westward (vide אָחוֹר), e. g. הַיָּם הָאַחֲרוֹן the western sea, i. e. the Mediteranean; the eastern sea is the Dead Sea. As an adv. אַחֲרֹנָה *postea*, the last לְאַחֲרֹנָה, בְּאַחֲרֹנָה at last, finally, *tandem*.

אֲחַרְחֵל p. n. m. (= אַקְרַח; constr. after the form אַכְזָב the baldheaded one. Comp. קָרַח).

אֲחַרְחַל p. n. m. (= אַחַרְחַר the quarrelsome one. Comp. יָרִיב).

אָחֳרִי p. n. m. (Aram. only abs.) f. the result, end, consequence, formed from אַחַר. Comp. אוֹחֲרָן, אָחֳרָן, and others.

אַחֲרֵי, const. אַחֲרִית, f. Aram. the same.

אַחֲרִין (contracted אָחֳרִין, Keri pl. Aram. the ends, only in the form: עַד א׳ to the ends, at last.

אַחֲרִית f. the latter, hence: end of time, futurity (contrast רֵשִׁית) e. g. הַיָּמִים א׳; next, the utmost, as הַיָּם א׳ tranferred as a conc. descendant, originally descendancy, posterity.

אָחֳרָן Aram. adj. m. equiv. to the Hebrew אַחֲרוֹן, abbrev. from אוֹחֲרָן.

אֲחֹרַנִּית (originally f., from אֲחוֹרַנִּי, comp. קְדֹרַנִּית) adv. backwards, backways; seldom an adverb-form.

אֲחַשְׁדַּרְפְּנִים (const. ־פְּנֵי Pers.) m. pl. only in Esther where it signifies satraps, or statholder. The sing. is: אֲחַשְׁדַּרְפָּן 'a-k'asdar-pa-n = k's'adra-pan, which signifies according to von Bohlen, satrap of the military power; according to De Sacy *custos provinciæ*, also of the ancient Persian *kschetr*, territory, and bân: *custos*. Both interpretations, however, do not agree with the Heb. orthography, since the first member of the composition is אֲחַשׁ (kh'sa), as it is clear from the other compositions with this word: as אֲחַשְׁוֵרוֹשׁ, אֲחַשְׁתְּרָן where *ks'atr* = province, is impossible to be applied. The composition is more correctly from *khs'a* (אֲחַשׁ) ancient Persian *ksahya* for *csaya*, the modern *shah*, king, and *darpan*, ancient Persian, statholder, originally *regiæ aulæ*, hence statholder of the king.

אֲחַשְׁדַּרְפְּנִין (def. ־פְּנַיָּא m. pl.) Aram. (the same).

אֲחַשְׁוֵרוֹשׁ (=אֲחַשְׁ־שְׁוֵרשׁ) once in the Ketib, אֲחַשְׁ־שְׁרֹשׁ=אֲחַשְׁרשׁ p. n. m. title of the Persian kings, like פַּרְעֹה, hence from Ξέρξης, Καμβύσης (Ezr. 4:6) and Astyages (Dan. 9:1); respecting the etymology, the first member of the composition is like in אֲחַשְׁ־דַּרְפַּן above, Kas'a (אֲחַשְׁ)=*csaya*, modern Persian shah, king, which also exists in the Greek Ἀρταξίας (*magnus rex*) names of Armenian princes; the other member of the composition: שְׁוֵרשׁ Ketib שְׁרשׁ agrees orthographically with the name Ξ as found in mumismatics, *ks'hers'e* (=*ks'ehrs'e*) or *ks'wers'e*, where also like here the fluctuation of the *v* (ו), shows itself and since the ancient Persian *k's'* frequently appears like the Greek ξ, Hebrew שׁ, the Greek letter is, at least in the old style of writing, (Ἀρτα-) ξέρξης is quite the same name. What, however: 'serôs' or 'swérôs', *k's'ehrs* or *K's'wers'e*, ξάρης or ξέρξης as an appell. signifies, is more difficult to ascertain than the formal composition.

אֲחַשְׁתְּרשׁ (see אֲחַשְׁוֵרשׁ) only in Ketib.

אֲחַשְׁתָּרִי p. n. m. (adj. from אֲחַשְׁתָּר).

אֲחַשְׁתְּרָן (=אֲחַשְׁ־שְׁתְּרָן; only pl. ־רָנִים) m. an animal to ride on, in connection with רֶכֶשׁ, סוּס, which the Persian riding mails made use of and which is called בִּרְדָּרְמָךְ. According to the rabbis who translate it dromedary it would be from *shutur* (Pers.) camel (comp. *dromades cameli*, Curt. 5:2) and אֲחַשׁ, where ־ָן is the adjective termination, hence *dromades regii*; if it signifies mule, it is astêra açwatara, mule, hence *regii muli*.

אַחַת (from אֲחַדְתְּ in pause אֶחָת), numeral f. one, seldom the first; as usual this numeral can often be translated *unica*, *alia*, *altera*, *aliqua*, *eadem*. By the omission of פַּעַם time, אַחַת becomes an adv.; 1) once, e. g. אַחַת בַּשָּׁנָה once a year, א׳ לְשָׁלֹשׁ שָׁנִים once in three years, א׳ הֵנָּה *semel huc*, *semel illuc*; 2) like the Aram. חדא solely = certainly, especially in short affirmative sentences. See אֶחָד.

אַט (=לָאט, as אֹם, אֻמָּה and לְאֹם) m. concealment, secrecy, hiding, from לָאַט=לָאט (לָט) λάθω, la *teo*, hiding, but only as an adv.: hid, unnoticed, lightly; also in a complete form הָלַךְ לְאַט soft, flow smoothly, of the Siloa; לְאִטִּי, I will lead on softly ...., for which however, לְאַט is once used, comp. בַּלָּט, בְּלָאט, secret, softly. Root לָאַט.

אָטַד (not used) to pierce, to penetrate, to fasten in. Related to יָתֵד which see.

אָטָד m. buck-thorn (*rhaninus paliurus*, Lin.) from יָתֵד = אָ־טַד, גֹּרֶן הָאָטָד p. n. of a place, buck-thorn place. See אָטָד.

אֵטוּן (= אָטוּן after the form כְּתוּב, rare) m. twisted, entwined, hence yarn, thread, as א׳ מִצְרָיִם thread of Egypt.

אִטִּי (= לְאִטִּי adj. from לְאַט Gen. 28: 14) adj. m. only pl. אִטִּים (= לְאִטִּים) the concealing one, the secret one, the mysterious ones; hence sorcerer. Compare לְהָטִים = לָטִים, the mysterious one, the sorcerer.

אָטַם (part. אֹטֵם) well to close, well to lock up, as the mouth, ears, not to speak or not to hear; then used of windows by lattices, e. g. חַלּוֹנִים, חַלּוֹנוֹת אֲטֻמוֹת lattice-windows, Hip. only fut. apoc. יַאְטֵם, as in Kal.

אָטַן (not used) = טָנָא to twist, to bind, to plait, originally to extend. Comp. the Greek ὀθόνη, ὀθόνιον, Lat. *tenuo*.

אָטַר (fut. יֶאְטַר) to enclose, to shut up, with עַל.

אָטֵר p. n. m. (one who encloses, participle form from אָטַר.

אִטֵּר adj. lame, originally bound, as א׳ יַד יְמִינוֹ his right hand was tied.

אִי (pronominal root) adv. interr. where there? related to הִי here, but only interjectional; 1) = when, e. g. nowhere! hence in several compounds as formal negation: אִי־נָקִי unclean = guilty; אִי־כָבוֹד p. n. ἄτιμος; אִיזֶבֶל p. n. ἄλοχος; אִיתָמָר p. n. not high = small. Comp. מָה; 2) already an interj. אִי־לָךְ אֶרֶץ woe to thee, land, properly not for thee, land! when, etc. אִילוֹ (Ecc. 4: 10, if this reading is correct) woe to him! probably not for him!

אֵי (pronom. root) adv. interrog. where? related to הֵ (הָא) but only used before the suff. in this form: as, אֵיוֹ where is he? אַיֶּכָּה where art thou? אַיָּם, or separated אֵיה הֵם, where are they? and in the lengthened form אַיֵּה, אַיֵּן. More frequently occurs the contracted form:—

אֵי adv. interrog. *ubi?* related to הֵי = הָא *ibi*, like the lengthened form : אִין (where there ! = not) related to הֵן here there. This occurs with אֵי never with suff., and has also like the former (Prov. 31 : 4) the signification of *non.* In connection with prons. and advs. it gives them an interrog. power, as אֵי־זֶה or אֵי זֶה which see ; אֵיךְ ; אֵיפֹה ; אֵיכָכָה ; אֵיכֹה ; אֵיכָה.

אִי (pl. אִיִּים, once אִיִּין, const. אִיֵּי) m. 1) coast, coast-land, e. g. of Tyre, Ashdod ; in pl. therefore generally denoting far off coast-countries ; 2) shore-country, e. g. dry inhabited land, in contrast to river and sea : hence הָאִיִּים הָרְחֹקִים the distant shore-lands, partly of the islands of the Mediterranean Sea, and partly of the Indian isles and coasts ; 3) isle, as, אִי כַפְתּוֹר Kaphtor island (Crete) ; etymological אִי probably = נָאִי that which is inhabited, from נָאָה to inhabit, hence, contrasted to יָם. See נָאָה.

איב (not used) to violate = עִיב to asperse, cover with shame.

אֵיב in אֵיבַת f. female enemy, with suff. אֹיְבִי, אֹיִבְךָ, pl. אֹיְבִים const. f. אֹיַבְתִּי, with the accus., constr. as the common particip. אֹיֵב אֶת־דָּוִד entering into hostilities with David.

אָיַב (denom. only once אָיַבְתִּי) to act as an enemy (אֹיֵב).

אֵיבָה (const. אֵיבַת) f. enmity, hatred.

אֵיד (contracted from אֵיִד, as לַיִל, שֵׁישׁ from לַיִל, שֵׁיִשׁ) m. turn of fate, fate, (equivalent to סִבָּה) hence, misfortune. The root is איד to turn, to twist (like סָב) comp. אוֹדוֹת.

אַיָּה f. : 1) name of a bird of prey, unclean for the Israelites, according to LXX. *ἰκτίν*, Vulg. *vultur*, according to others, hawk ; it hardly signifies a single bird, but rather the whole family of the birds of prey. The etymology appears the same as in אִיִּים, taken from the peculiar cry, אִי, אִי ; 2) p. n. m.

אַיֵּה (from אֵי pronominal root) Jer. 37 : 19, Ketib אַיּוֹ, interr. adv. ; 1) where ? where there ? (related to הִנֵּה here there). As with אֵי it generally expresses the negative. אֵי אַיֵּה or where ? אַיֵּה אֵפוֹא where now ? 2) indef. *ubicunque* (Job 15 : 23) everywhere to, but where it closes a sentence. Comp. Neh. 3 : 17.

אִיּוֹב p. n. m. (the greatly afflicted one, after the form שִׁכּוֹר) Job, the renowned hero, after whom the book is called. LXX. Ἰώβ.

אִיזֶבֶל p. n. f. (one that had not cohabited, *ἄλοχος* = chaste, from זָבַל to cohabit, and אִי *non*),

Jezebel, queen of Israel, 917-897 before the Christian Era.

אֵיזֶה (or אֵי־זֶה) 1) adv. interr. where here? where there? generally not written as one word; 2) an adj. of interrogation, which? e. g. אֵי־זֶה הַדֶּרֶךְ which way? 3) indef. which there? in connection with מִן, the word זֶה only is used, as אֵי מִזֶּה from which? See זֶה.

אִיִּים (poetically) m. pl. the jackals, orig. the criers. The form need not be contracted from אָוִי nor אָיִי, but from אִי the cry peculiar to these animals. See אַיֵּה.

אֵיךְ (from אֵי־כָה, pronominal root) adv.; 1) how? the comparative element lies in כ, and אֵי gives the interrogative power; 2) without interrogation: πῶς; 3) like אֵי interject. how! Oh how! 4) ironically, with a secondary idea of negation, hence may be dissolved into a simple negative sentence.

אִי־כָבוֹד p. n. m. (ἄτιμος. See אִי.)

אֵיכָה (pronominal root) adv.: 1) like אֵיךְ how? and without interrogation: alike, with all variations of the same; 2) like אֵי, only: where? but where כָּה expresses pointing to a thing: where there. See כָּה, אֵי.

אֵיכֹה (Keri אֵיכוֹ once) *ubi?* See כֹּה, כּוֹ.

אֵיכָכָה (from אֵי־כָכָה) adv. how? always with the future.

איל (not used) turning, rolling, Greek ἴλλω (εἰλέω, εἰλύω); comp. חִיל, גִּיל transferred from thence to strength, to be girded, to be fortified. (Comp. חַיִל).

אַיָּל (after the form קַטָּל; pl. אַיָּלִים) originally *epic*, later m. properly a graduative noun from אַיִל a ram, (צַיִר־צִיר) therefore: the strong, wild ram; afterwards more defined: stag, buck, hind. For the feminine subsequently was formed אַיָּלָה, אַיֶּלֶת. The root is איל.

אַיִל const. אֵיל, pl. אֵילִים once אֵלִים const. אֵילֵי the strong one, the powerful one, (from איל): hence 1) a mighty one, a distinguished one: e. g. אֵילֵי הָאָרֶץ (Keri) the distinguished of the land. Thus frequently אֵילִים or אֵלִים, אֵילֵי, אֵלֵי; 2) tall, strong tree, (δρῦς, *robur*), hence used of the oak, terebinth, palm, especially in the pl. See אֵילִן, אֵלִים, אֵיל פָּארָן, אֵילַת, אֵלָא, אֵלוֹן, אֵלָה; 3) ram, so called on account of the strength of his horns (*aries*); 4) a technical expression in architecture; either so called from its being formed like a ram, or from its strength and firmness. Aqu. κρίωμα otherwise κριός; hence sometimes: pillar, post, (of the ancients), sometimes frize, ornamental inlaying of a door, generally: prominent part in the front of a building. More correct according to the context: entrance-wall, wall front, so called from its prominence. See אֵילָם.

אֱיָל m. (once) strength, *vis*. From אִיל, as עֲיָם from עִים.

אַיָּלָה (const. אַיֶּלֶת pl. אַיָּלוֹת const. אַיְלוֹת) f. stag, hind, אַיֶּלֶת בַּשָּׂדֶה the hind of the field, the hind on account of her gracefulness is used figuratively of women. See אַיֶּלֶת formed from epic אַיָּל by the fem. termination ָ

אַיָּלוֹן p. n. having stags, territory of stags. A Levitical town in the territory of Dan; 2) in the territory of Zebulun.

אֵילוֹן p. n. (oaken district, from אֵיל): 1) a city in the territory of Dan. LXX. Ἐλών; 2) p. n. m. LXX. Αἰλώμ, Ἐλώμ.

אֵילוֹת see אֵילַת.

אֱיָלוּת (from אֱיָל) f. (once only) *vires*. Distinct from אֱיָל like צֶדֶק *jus*, צְדָקָה *justitia*.

אֵילָם (pl. ־לַמִּים, ־לַמּוֹת and אֻלָם) m. generally connected with אֵילִים a technical expression in architecture, and either a secondary form of אוּלָם, or from אַיִל. The root is אִיל, and âm is the suffix, like ôm in עֵירֹם.

אֵילִם (with ה dem. אֵילִמָה) p. n. place of encampment of the Israelites in the desert.

אִילָן (Aram. def. אִילָנָא) m. tree; comp. אַיִל. The root is אִיל with *an* suffix.

אֵילַת and אֵילוֹת (probably = אֵילוֹת) p. n. an Edumean port-town (sea-gulf) on the eastern inlet of the Arabian gulf, LXX. Αἰλών, Αἰλάθ; Joseph. Αἰλανή.

אַיֶּלֶת הַשַּׁחַר p. n. of an instrument, or of a method of song. It signifies the hind of the morning dawn, symbolical for: morning.

אִים (not used) equivalent to עִים to roar strongly, violently, to be terrific, probably related to הִים to be violently excited, to roar.

אָיֹם adj. m. אֲיֻמָּה f. (poetically) terrible, frightful.

אֵים (like אַיִל; only pl. אֵימִים): 1) terrors, dismay; 2) objects of which one onght to be in terror, idol, comp. מִפְלֶצֶת from פָּלַץ, דַּחְלָא in Targ. from דְּחַל; 3) אֵמִים p. n. m. (the strong ones, giants). The original inhabitants of the shore of the Arnon (the present Mug'ab) in the vicinity of Areopolis (the present Rabba); the Moabites drove them out. They belong to the very ancient tribes of giants of the Canaanites, עֲנָקִים, זַמְזֻמִּים, רְפָאִים.

אֵימָה (const. אֵימַת־ with a dem. אֵמָתָה־ pl. אֵימוֹת־) f. terror, fear, which one imposes, but not that which one feels: e. g. א׳ מֶלֶךְ fear imposed by a king. The root is אִים.

אִין equivalent to אִי where? אִין יֶשׁ־ פֹּה where is here? (only once). The ן is appended to אִי.

אַיִן (equiv. to אַי) 1) where? related to אַיִן = בֵּין here there, only with pref. מֵאַיִן (talmud. מִנַּיִן whence? and also without its being an interrogative, from whence; 2) as the simple forms אִי, אַי only more frequently a negative, where? = nowhere; hence not, אִם־אַיִן if not, and substantively: nothing. It thus stands like אִי to express the idea of negation, and only with nouns where it follows the non-contracted form, e. g. מַיִם, כֹּחַ, גֶּשֶׁם, מוֹתָר אַיִן, i. e. without water, strength, rain, preference = impotent, unpreferred, etc.; see אֵין. It is only once found as a negation before the preterite. (Job 35: 15) אַיִן פָּקַד "his wroth did not extend to him," he visited him not. —With pref. כְּאַיִן (a) as nothing, like לְאַיִן into nothing; (b) for nothing, i.e. nothing short, almost, (= כִּמְעַט) מֵאַיִן besides which as under; 1) (a) without, מֵאֵין כָּמוֹהוּ without anything like it; (b) from nothing, worse than nothing. In connection with particles אַיִן בִּלְתִּי not besides, orig. where besides? אַיִן זוּלָתִי the same.

אֵין (contracted from אַיִן like אֵי from אַי) adv. always negative, originally however, interrogative; 1) absolute, not like אַיִן (Gen. 47: 13); 2) constructive before indefinite nouns, signifying without: אֵין אָב without a father; before the participle signifying, none, no one, not: מַחֲרִיד, נֹתֵן, פּוֹתֵר, אֵין נִסְתָּר; before the inf. signifying without, nobody: אֵין הָבִין, עֲרֹךְ without being understood, without being matched, without comparison, or with לְ before the inf.; 3) with including the verb 'to be' = לֹא יֵשׁ, as a sentence entirely by itself, especially with suff. אֵינֶנִּי I am not, אֵינְךָ, אֵינֵךְ, אֵינָם, אֵינְכֶם, אֵינֶנָּה, אֵינֶנּוּ; poetically אֵינֵמוֹ. The negative of the idea may be translated sometimes not; personally, nobody; sometimes, without, sometimes nothing, hence א׳ אִישׁ nobody; א׳ אֶחָד

no one; אין מְאוּמָה nothing; אין כֹּל nothing at all. It always is of considerable importance with the other particles, as: אין בִּלְתִּי, אין זוּלָתִי besides me, אין עִמָּדִי not with me; it only remains without any signification when joined to other negatives: as מִבְּלִי אין not; with prepos. אין is generally equivalent to אַיִן, only that it precedes the noun to which it gives the idea of negation: as בְּאֵין חוֹמָה without a wall; לְאֵין אוֹנִים to the strengthless; מֵאֵין יוֹשֵׁב uninhabited, without inhabitant, but בְּאֵין also: in as much as was not, here; לְאֵין to whom there is nothing, i. e. with addition of the verb *to be*. All these words אין, אַיִן, אין, אֵי, אַי, אִי, are pronom. roots and have nothing in common with a verb.

אִיעֶזֶר p. n. m. equivalent to אֲבִיעֶזֶר, for which it also stands, patron. אִיעֶזְרִי. It belongs to the rare cases where ב in the orthography vanishes. Comp. אִיאֵל.

אֵיפָה, אֵפָה f. a corn measure, according to Joseph. equivalent *μέδιμνος* 48 *χοίνικες* (= 1 bushel), or equivalent בַּת (*amphora*), the same, a measure for fluids, 10 עֹמֶר and one tenth חֹמֶר or כֹּר. Thus: א׳ רָזוֹן small (meagre), א׳ שְׁלֵמָה full (sound) ephah; א׳ וְאֵיפָה two sorts of ephah.

אֵיפֹה (אֵי־פֹה) adv. interr.; 1) where there? *ποῦ*? 2) how there? in which manner?

אֵיפוֹא adv. dem. so, thus, from אֵי פוֹא, where the ê, as frequently occurs, is the demonstrative element; hence it is not bad orthography to spell the word אֵפוֹא. See אֵפוֹ, פֹּה.

אִישׁ (from אֱנֹשׁ; hence אִשׁ const. in pp. n.n. The pl. later, and poetically אִישִׁים, commonly אֲנָשִׁים, poetically בְּנֵי אִישׁ, const. אַנְשֵׁי) m.; 1) man, entirely nominal, and (*a*) in reference to strength, courage, and valour, *vir*; (*b*) in reference to manly age; (*c*) in reference to the signification of the mas. gender, hence even used of male children, and of husbands; (*d*) human being, man, as far as according to oriental notions, the same manifests itself in man. Thus, man, an individual; collectively, mankind, in contrast to God, and in contrast to beast; hence also, where no reference is made neither to gender, strength, nor age: for instance, of inhabitants, citizens, warriors, inferiors, associates, relatives, where אִישׁ also collectively signifies people, men; לֶחֶם אֲנָשִׁים meal of relatives, mourning meal; (*e*) signifying the possessor, the origin, the descent; hence, in connection with neutral nouns, to replace the want of adjectives; as, אִ׳ תֹּאַר, אִ׳ דְּבָרִים (*formosus, facundus*), אִ׳ מַתָּן, תּוֹכָחוֹת, חֶסֶד, אָוֶן, אֱמֻנִים, תְּבוּנוֹת, שֶׂכֶל, דַּעַת, אֱמֶת, חָמָס, חַיִל, לָשׁוֹן, שְׂפָתַיִם, שֵׂיבָה, אֱמוּנוֹת, תְּרוּמוֹת, רִיב, מְדָנִים, דָּמִים and others; 2) with gradual dropping of its nominal character: (*a*) in contrast to אָח, עָמִית, רֵעַ, e. g. אִישׁ—אִישׁ the one, the other. (*b*) any one, some one, LXX. τίς, seldom as used in this sense אָדָם, אֲנָשִׁים, אֱנוֹשׁ, compare ἄνθρωπος אִישׁ אִישׁ any one, hence also: one, i. e. every one, or every body. (*c*) every one, every man, may be connected with (*b*). The reciprocal form derived from אִישׁ is הִתְאוֹשֵׁשׁ to conduct oneself manly, sensibly, valourous.

אִישׁ־בֹּשֶׁת p. n. m. (idol champion), LXX. Ἰεβοσθέ, Joseph. Ἰέβοσθος, Saul's son, who was also called אֶשְׁבַּעַל.

אִישְׁהוֹד p. n. m. (a man of blooming appearance.) Also: אִישׁ הוֹד, אִישְׁהוֹד.

אִישׁוֹן (dimin. from אִישׁ, like זֵרְעוֹן, (צִוָּרוֹן) m.; 1) the little man, the apple of the eye, the pupil, (comp. κόρη, κοράσιον, κορασίδιον, Latin, *pupa*, *pupula*, *pupilla*), generally in connection with עַיִן, or it is followed by בַּת עַיִן the daughter of the eye; 2) figure of speech, signifying the midst, the deepest, the highest point; as, אִ׳ חשֶׁךְ, לַיְלָה pupil of darkness, night = the middle, the depth, etc.

אִישַׁי p. n. m. the manly one, the valourous), generally יִשַׁי, LXX. Ἰεσσαί.

אִית (Aram.) def. אִיתָא (Talmud.) pl. אִיתַי (the old form) m. being, existence; hence, possession, οὐσία equivalent to יֵשׁ, but always adverb as the copula term 'for being,' it is, it was, etc. With suff. אִיתַי I am. In biblical Aramaism the pl. is always אִיתַי, as לָא אִיתַי, אִיתַי לָךְ, אִיתַי בִּי with suff. אִיתָךְ thou art, אִיתוֹהִי he is, אִיתָנָא we are, אִיתֵיכוֹן you are. Before the part. it paraphrases the verb, like יֵשׁ. The form is like דִּין, as יֵשׁ is after the form גֵּר; the root is אית, Heb. יֵשׁ (יוש) to be. See יוש.

אִיתוֹן (Keri, after the form תִּיכוֹן, חִיצוֹן) adj. m. *ingressus*, appertaining to entrance: hence שַׁעַר הָאִיתוֹן door of entrance, like שַׁעַר

הָרִאשׁוֹן. The Ketib יאתין is not clear, perhaps = יֶאְתוֹן after the form יְשִׁימוֹן. The root is אית.

אִיתַי p. n. m. (adj. from אִית, the being, the living one, the vigorous one). Comp. אִישַׁי.

אִיתִיאֵל p. n. m. (the possession, property of God), from אִית possession in the genitive form.

אִיתָמָר p. n. m. (not high = small). See אִי.

אֵיתָן (from אֵי ,אִיתָן in אֵ contracted, seldom אֵתָן, pl. אֵתָנִים, adj. very extensive, lasting: hence 1) of time, continuous, duration, רִיב אֵיתָן continual strife; stubborn, uninterrupted, of brooks, streams, i. e. always flowing, (in contrast to אַכְזָב) as נַחַל, נְהָרוֹת, אֵיתָן hence figurat. of flowing brooks, pl. יֶרַח הָאֵיתָנִים month of the flowing brooks (perhaps = מַרְחֶשְׁוָן from רָחַשׁ flowing, rolling), November; 2) strong, firm, durable, hence גּוֹי אֵיתָן a strong valourous people, אֵיתָנִים (*a*) the mighty, distinguished ones; (*b*) the rocks: hence נָוֶה אֵיתָן rocky habitation. The root is יָתַן to extend, from which forms itself אֵיתָן like אַכְזָב.

אֵיתָן p. n. m. (the persevering one), poet, singer, and sage in the time of David. LXX. *Αἰθάμ*.

אַךְ (pronominal root) adv.; 1) properly like כִּי, originally, relative conj. *ὅτι*, *quod*, hence preceding sentences which are dependent upon, and governed by others: e. g. 'and I thought that (אַךְ) he was torn to pieces,' (Gen. 44 : 28); 'I thought that (אַךְ) thou wouldst fear me,' (Zeph. 3 : 7); for which reason it remains untranslated, like כִּי preceding a direct speech, or like כִּי stands as an assurance: certainly! yes! indeed! 2) expression of contrast: hence = but, except, however, like כִּי signifying the same, e. g. he said: they are nevertheless (אַךְ) my people; herewith is connected the idea of restriction, *tantum*, only, in the largest acceptation of the term: e. g. before the preterite to which it gives the sense of the pluperfect; before nouns and adjectives, where it must be translated according to the context, just as much, scarcely, *tantum quod*, entirely, as only (אַךְ) this once; only joyful; only (entire) darkness; before imperatives: only be to me = I beg you be to me; only hearken, etc.; 3) equiv. to כִּי as a sign of conclusion: so, then, as for instance, so shall you on the first day remove the leaven (Exod. 12 : 15), (ה־

אַךְ) 'only alone;' properly an emphatic 'only.'

אָכַד (not used) equiv. to אָרַג to bind, to entwine one in another; related to עָקַד.

אַכַּד p. n. (fortress, from אָכַד=אָגַד a town in Babylon.) LXX. Ἀρχάδ (אַרְכַּד which Bochart compares with the river Ἀργάδης in the country Sittacene.) Ephraim the Syrian reads אָכַר (Acre) and explains it Nisibis.

אַכְזָב adj. m. very deceiving, lying, (from כָּזַב after the form אַכְזָר), hence applied to a brook: exhausted, failing, (contrast to אֵיתָן) where אַכְזָב stands for נַחַל אַ'.
See כָּזַב.

אַכְזִיב p. n.; 1) equiv. to כְּזִיב a town in the territory of Judah; 2) maritime town in Galilee, Greek Ἔκδιππα (אַכְדִּיב) Talm. כְּזִיב, now called Zib. The א is preformative.

אַכְזָר adj. m. strong, firm, = girded: 1) valorous, courageous, bold, and in a bad sense, hard; 2) terrific, destructive, also of poison. The root is כָּזַר = קָשַׁר which see.

אַכְזָרִי adj. m. from the preceding אַכְזָר signifying the same, originally, cruel-like.

אַכְזְרִיּוּת f. from אַכְזָרִי savageness, cruel-like, the abstract termination ות is generally formed from adject. (comp. חֲרִיסוּת, בְּרִיתוּת, שְׁלֵץ, חָכָם, קָבַת from עֲלִיצוּת.

אֲכִילָה f. (originally collective) viands.

אָכִישׁ p. n. m. (probably from בּוּשׁ after the form אָסוּף) a Philistine king.

אָכַל (fut. יֹאכַל, יֹאכֵל, once יוֹכְלוּ= יֹאכְלוּ originally to annihilate, to devour, destroy; hence, 1) to eat, with לְ, בְּ, מִן and accus. of the food, with significations of inconsiderable gradations; part. הָאֹכֵל the eater, used of the lion. Figuratively of the sword, fire, famine, plague, all which devour; of idols who devour the sacrifices, etc. Wherewith may be connected the phrases to eat the harvest, i. e. the fruit; to eat bread, i. e. to hold a feast; with a negative, signifies fasting; to eat at somebody's table, i. e. to be maintained by some one; to eat, of God, i. e. to partake of meats of sacrifices; to eat ashes like bread, i. e. to be plunged in grief; to eat his own flesh, i. e. to pine away; to eat the flesh of somebody, i. e. to proceed cruelly against some one, to malign one; to eat words, i. e. eagerly to receive them; to eat the poor, i. e.

to suck them; to eat the judges, i. e. to kill them; to eat the people, i. e. to destroy them; the beams eat (יֹאכְלוּ) used of upper rooms, i. e. they absorb the space; eating used of love, i. e. to abuse it, to be profligate; אָ׳ תֹּאכְלְהוּ בַּטּוֹבָה to enjoy the good. תֹּאכְלְהוּ = תְּאֻכְּלוּ from תֵּאָכֵל Niph. pass. from Kal. Pual to be devoured, by fire, sword. Hiph. הֶאֱכִיל, future יַאֲכִיל inf. once הָכִיל for הַאֲכִיל to cause to be eaten, to cause to be devoured, to give to eat, to enjoy.

אֲכַל (fut. יֵאכֻל) Aram. the same. Respecting אָ׳ קַרְצִין, see קְרַץ.

אֹכֶל (with suff. אָכְלוֹ) m. 1) food, especially of fruits, and of grain, figuratively food of the fire (fuel), of animals; 2) the eating, the action itself: hence לְפִי אָכְלוֹ according to his eating.

אֻכַל or אֻכָּל p. n. m. to pine away, languish, to be eaten up with grief.

אָכְלָה (as עָצְמָה) f. equivalent to אֹכֶל food.

אָכֵן (from כֵּן, with the â dem.) adv. equiv. to Aram. הָכֵי so much, so great as, *tantum*; hence 1) assuring (Targ. בְּקוּשְׁטָא), certainly, only; 2) restricting or qualifying, as *tantum*, but, indeed, however. See כֵּן.

אָכַף to thrust, to smite; hence to drive on, to incite, only Prov. 16:26, כִּי־אָכַף עָלָיו פִּיהוּ 'for his mouth smites at him,' drives him on.

אֶכֶף m. a blow, only Job 33:7; 'my blow (אַכְפִּי) shall not fall heavy upon him.' The LXX. reads כַּפִּי. The root is אָרַךְ which see.

אַכָּר m. Acre, so Ephraim the Syrian reads for אַכַּד. See אַכָּר.

אִכָּר (pl. אִכָּרִים, const. אִכָּרֵי with suff. אִכָּרֵיכֶם), m. one who occupies himself with the plough, a ploughman. It is a noun of gradation from אָכַר = אָכַךְ, ἀγρός, *ager*, acre, (as מַלָּח from מֶלַח sea), and related to כַּר pasture-ground, grass-plot, כַּרְמֶל fruit-land.

אַכְשָׁף p. n. m. a town in the territory of Asher.

אַל const. אַל or אֶל; 1) dem. pron. a slow pointing, and giving prominence to a thing, and weaker than זֶה, may be translated: that one, equiv. to הַל, אֶל, hence the gradation to an article in Arab., and in Heb., only exceptional in אַלְקוּם; אַלְמוֹדָד; אַלְגּוּמִים; אֶלְגָּבִישׁ; אֶלְעָלֵא and others; 2) adv. and conj. of negation, and starting from pointing to a distance (*a*) of the verb: as μή, *ne*, only negative according to the sense of the speaker; hence w—

the imperfect when it is *jussive* or *cohortative*, (לֹא however is equiv. to οὐκ, *non*, more an objective command), e. g. אַל תִּשְׁלַח, יִפֹּל, אַל יֵצֵא always entreating, not commanding, and negating the whole sentence, (*b*) not before the verb, but negating an imaginary or demonstrative sentence: e. g. אַל־נָא not, I pray thee (also, comp. μή = μὴ τοῦτο); שָׂם לְאַל εἰς μηδὲν τιθέναι, to make to nothing; אַל־בְּנוֹתַי not so, my daughters. Seldom forming a nominal sentence אַל־מָוֶת τὸ μὴ θνήσκειν; 'neither dew nor rain (be)' (2 Sam. 1: 21), אַל־אודות not because; 3) equiv. to μή questioning, where a negative answer is expected, only 1 Sam. 27 : 10, 'whither have you made a road to-day?'

אַל Aram. the same.

אֵל (const. אֵל, אֱלִי in p.p. n.n. with suff. אֵלִי, pl. אֵלִים, const. אֵלֵי) m.; 1) equiv. to אַיִל, const. אֵיל the strong one, the vigorous one, hero, e. g. the hero (אֵל) of nations, of Nebuchadnezzar; the strongest (אֵלֵי) of heroes; comp. the comp. אֲבִיאֵל. אֵל is principally used in the signification: God, synony. with יְהוָה, אֱלֹהִים, אֱלוֹהַּ, mostly with epithets: חַי, עוֹלָם, שַׁדַּי, עֶלְיוֹן the living, the highest, the Omnipotent, eternal God, but in poetry also without epithets. Of Jehovah, הָאֵל with the article is used, or אֵל אֱלֹהִים, אֵל אֵלִים, אֵל אֱלֹהֵי יִשְׂרָאֵל, of the deities of other people אֵל is also used, but generally with the addition of זָר, נֵכָר, אַחֵר the strange, or לֹא־אֵל non-god, etc., herewith are connected the figurative symbols: mountains, cedars of God, for: elevated, high, exalted. The pl. אֵילִים also of Jehovah: hence בְּנֵי אֵילִים sons of gods = angels; 2) abst. strength, originally that which is strong, in the phrase אֵין, יֵשׁ לְאֵל יָד I have (not) the power in the hand; comp. אֲבִיאֵל p. n. Etymologically אֵל is derived from אֱלָה = אול. אֵל, complete בֵּית־אֵל p. n. of a town, formerly: לוּז. (LXX. Βαιθήλ, Joseph. Βηθήλα).

אֵל (const. אֵל with ê dem. אֵלֶּה const. אֱלֵי with suff. אֵלַי, אֵלֶיךָ, אֵלָיו, אֵלֵינוּ, אֲלֵיכֶם, אֲלֵיכֶן, אֲלֵיהֶם, אֲלֵהֶם, once אֵלֵיהֶם, poetically אֵלֵימוֹ dem. pron. equiv. to הַל, אֵל, a widely branched out pronom. root, signifying a slow pointing to a thing, like: 1) אֵל with the article הָאֵל this one, that one, only in the pl. and only in the Pentateuch, from whence it is used in Chronicles. The most ancient form appears to be *il* or *ill*, like the plural *il* shows; 2) אֵלֶּה from אֵל with éh, é demonstrative, (comp. הִנֵּה), only in the pl. these, those, but without a suff. for the gender or number; 3) אֶל־ prep. originally joined by *makkef* with the following noun; hence its constructive form. It signifies direction, or pointing in a local sense, *ad*, *πρός*, hence used with verbs of motion שׁוּב אֶל (to), בָּא (in), עָלָה, הָיָה, שָׁלַח, הָלַךְ, נִהְיָה (*accessit*), הוֹצִיא and others, where it may be translated, to, upon, towards, on; with other verbs it has a signification of a spiritual motion and turning; as הִרְבָּה תַּזְנוּת, הִנָּחֵם, בָּכָה, דָּרַשׁ, שָׁר, הִשְׁלִים, זָנָה, הִתְפַּלֵּל אֶל, הִתְעַצֵּב, where always the secondary idea of motion, or inclining to a thing can be traced. With verbs expressing speech, it signifies the person to whom the speech is addressed: e. g. סִפֵּר, אָמַר אֶל, צִוָּה, דִּבֶּר besides it expresses: into; thus שִׁלֵּם אֶל־חֵיק, הִשְׁתַּפֵּךְ נֶפֶשׁ to recompense into the bosom, to breathe the last breath of life; also with verbs signifying similarity, as נִמְשַׁל, דָּמָה, etc., but before nouns: at, to it, on; on heavens; at table; after, according, *secundum*, *ad*, according to the mouth, i. e. command; according to the sound of the viol; in: in thy vessel, ship, house; under, among: among the vessels, among thorns, briars, etc., complete אֶל־בֵּין unto: unto heaven, unto his mouth, etc.—Compounds אֶל־אַחֲרֵי behind, with the accus. after יָצָא, סַב, הֵסַב; אֶל־אֲשֶׁר thereto, whereto אֶל־בֵּין under, with the accus. and equiv. to אֶל־בֵּינוֹת; אֶל־הַחוּץ or הַ־צָה *extrin-secus;* אֶל־חִנָּם, almost in vain, different from חִנָּם; אֶל־מִבַּיִת within to, innermost; אֶל־מוּל towards, thereto, etc.

אֶלָא p. n. m. (the strong one).

אֶלְגָּבִישׁ see נָבִישׁ.

אַלְגּוּמִּים see גּוּמִּים, גּוּם.

אֶלְדָּד p. n. m. (Friend of the Lord).

אֶלְדָּעָה p. n. m. (one who has knowledge of the Lord), דָּעָה for דָּעָה knowing, from דָּעָה = יָדַע.

אלה only in אֱלֹהַּ which see.

אָלָה; 1) equiv. to אול to be strong, hence אַלְיָה which see; 2) denom. from אֵל God, and (*a*) to declare, swear by God; (*b*) to implore God, partly for the destruction of others = curse, partly for mercy = lament. Hiph. fut. apoc. וַיֹּאֶל he caused him to swear, conjured him.

אָלָה with suff. אָלָתִי, pl. אָלוֹת f. the swearing, oath, denunciation, curse, hence; 1) oath, cursing, הֵבִיא ,בָּא ,בָּא אָ׳ to enter into an oath, i. e. to swear, to administer an oath, to cause to swear; הָיָה, נָתַן לְאָ׳ to become a curse, to make a thing a curse: שְׁבֻעַת־אָלָה oath of cursing; 2) that which is attested on oath, as covenant, etc.

אַלָּה (rare) f. oak, originally that which is strong, the root is איל, for אַלָּה is a mere modification of אֵלָה.

אֵלָה f. equiv. to אַלָּה but more frequent, and signifying a terebinth, which resembles an oak, like δρῦς.

אֱלָהּ (def. אֱלָהָא, pl. אֱלָהִין) Aram. m. God, equiv. to the Hebrew אֱלוֹהַּ and also of gods: בַּר־אֱלָהִין son of gods = angel, as in the Hebrew.

אֵלֶּה (pronominal root) see אֵל, from which it is elongated.

אֱלֹהִים see אֱלוֹהַּ.

אֲלוּ (pronominal root) Aram. dem. pron. formed from אֵל, but always interjectional, there! see there! related to אֲרוּ, which is also formed from a demonstrative.

אִלּוּ (later) conj. if, when; contracted from אִם־לוּ combining a wish and a condition.

אֱלוֹהַּ (with prefix לֶאֱלוֹהַּ and לֶאלֹהוּ) m. God, especially of Jehovah, seldom of other gods; figuratively: he carries God in the hand, i. e. the hand is a god to him; his power is his god; the sing. use of it is only introduced later, or poetically, the ancient and original form is the plural אֱלֹהִים, because in ancient times the idea of God was a concentration of unlimited powers, like in the same sense בְּעָלִים, אֲדֹנִים, קְדֹשִׁים form themselves. The plural may also be construed with the singular as a *unity* of this idea; with adjectives, however, more frequently with the plural, but in no case can a plural be formed from this form, if gods are to be designated; hence the use of the word for male or female deities. Of representatives of God, such as judges, priests; but with the article (הָאֱלֹהִים) only of Jehovah. The most important paraphrases are (*a*) the constructive form where אֱ׳ expresses sometimes possession, e. g. God of Jacob; sometimes the ordaining, e. g. God of heaven. (*b*) It follows in certain connections where the manifold relations are expressed, such as, sons of God (angels, kings); servant, spirit of God, man of God (of angels, prophets, saints); prince of God (of Abraham), where, however, in conjunction with נְאֻם, מְשִׁיחַ, the tetragamaton יְהוָֹה always occurs; (c) Divine, e. g. כִּסְאֲךָ אֱלֹהִים = כִּסְאֲךָ כִּסֵּא אֱ׳ thy throne is a throne of God; glorious, great, e. g. mountain, river, fire of God (lightning); (d) לֵאלֹהִים through God, e. g. a city great through God; the root אָלַהּ is denom.

אֱלוּל m. properly, gathering, hence time of ingathering, the gathering month, September; from אָלַל to gather in, to reap harvest = עָלַל; Aram. עֲלַל corn. The form is passive, like קָצִיר, אָסִיף.

אֱלוּל equiv. to אֱלִיל in Ketib.

אֵלוֹן adj. m. the strong one, hence oak. Also used, as with us, to signify a place, e. g. אֵלוֹן מְעוֹנְנִים p. n. oak of sorcerers, אֵ׳ תָּבוֹר p. n. oak of Tabor; אֵלֹנֵי מַמְרֵא oaks of Mamreh, etc.

אַלּוֹן m. 1) the same. It is a secondary form of אֵלוֹן like אַלָּה from אֵלָה, without being of the separate root אָלַל. 2) p. n. m. (the strong one).

אַלּוּף (or אַלֻּף) adj. m. properly signifying continual following, attachment, hence; 1) the friend who attaches himself to one; 2) tame, tender, attaching to, and pending on one, as כֶּבֶשׂ אַלּוּף very domestic lamb, which is much attached to its master; 3) equiv. to אֶלֶף large cattle, originally the very tame one; 4) den. from אֶלֶף (friendship, family, originally attachment), head of a family, chief of a tribe, to whom the members are bound by allegiance, φύλαρχος. See אֶלֶף.

אָלוּשׁ p. n. f. (encampment for wild beasts), לוּשׁ equiv. to לַיִשׁ lion, λῖς, place of encampment of the Israelites in the desert.

אֶלְזָבָד p. n. m. (gift of God Θεόδωρος). Comp. יְזָבָד.

אָלַח (related with דָּ־לַח) originally, to be obscured, to be dirty, but only in Niph. נֶאֱלַח to become withered, destroyed, dirty, also in a moral sense; see דָּ־לַח.

אֶלְחָנָן p. n. m. (bounty of God).

אֱלִיאָב p. n. m. (God the preserver).

אֱלִיאֵל p. n. m. (God the mighty one).

אֱלִיאָתָה p. n. m. (God of consolation), אָתָה equiv. to אָשָׁה.

אֱלִידָד p. n. m. (equiv. to אֶלְדָּד).

אֶלְיָדָע p. n. m. (equiv. to אֶלְדָּעָה). For which also בְּעֶלְיָדָע.

אַלְיָה f. fat-tailed, of eastern sheep, where the tail is used as a sacrifice. The root is אָלָה to be stout, fat.

אֵלִיָּה or אֵלִיָּהוּ p. n. m. (Jehovah is God), a renowned prophet, LXX. Ἡλίας.

אֱלִידָע p. n. m. (the same).

אֱלִיהוּא p. n. m. (the same).

אֶלְיְהוֹעֵינַי p. n. m.

אֶלְיוֹעֵינַי p. n. m.

אֶלְיַחְבָּא p. n. m. (God the protector).

אֱלִיחֹרֶף p. n. m. (God of the age of manhood).

אֱלִיל (once Ketib אֱלוּל; pl. אֱלִילִים) adj. m. null and void, formed from אַל 'nothing,' hence subst. אֱלִילִים the void ones, idols; רֹפְאֵי־אֱלִיל the healer of nothing, i. e. unskilful physician.

אֱלִימֶלֶךְ p. n. m. (God is king).

אִלֵּין, אִלֵּן (pronominal root), Aram. dem. pron. these, from the unusual sing. אֵל, this one, with the plural termination ־ִין as in אִלֵּין, דִּכֵּן, הִנֵּין.

אֶלְיָסָף p. n. m. (God is the multiplier).

אֱלִיעֶזֶר p. n. m. (God is the help).

אֱלִיעֵינַי p. n. m. (equiv. to אֶלְיוֹעֵינַי).

אֱלִיעָם p. n. m. (God of a family union), for which also עַמִּיאֵל.

אֱלִיפַז p. n. m. (God of gold, riches).

אֱלִיפַל p. n. m. (God of strength; פַּל = פִּיל, פּוּל, *elephas*, figure of strength).

אֱלִיפְלֵהוּ p. n. m. (God distinguishes him. See פָּלָה).

אֱלִיפֶלֶט p. n. m. (God of deliverance). For which also אֶלְפֶּלֶט.

אֱלִיצוּר p. n. m. (God the rock).

אֱלִיצָפָן p. n. m. (God the preserver).

אֱלִיקָא p. n. m. (God is the strength; קָא = קַו strength).

אֶלְיָקִים p. n. m. (God the raiser up). For which also, יְהוֹיָקִים.

אֱלִישֶׁבַע p. n. f. (God of the covenant). LXX. Ἐλισάβετ, Elisabeth.

אֱלִישָׁה (Samar. אֱלִישׁ) p. n. of a western tribe, hence also of a country on the coasts of the Mediteranean Sea, from whence purple was obtained, and which tribe is also mentioned as descendant of Javan (Ἰάονες, Ἴωνες), in connection with Tarsis, *citium*, and Ῥόδιοι, therefore probably Elis, or lengthened Hellas, because the purple shell was very abundant in Laconica and other places. See יָוָן.

אֱלִישׁוּעַ p. n. m. (God is the luck).

אֶלְיָשִׁיב p. n. m. (God is the recompenser).

אֱלִישָׁמָע p. n. m. (God is the hearer).

אֱלִישָׁע p. n. m. (God the noble); a prophet in 896—825 before the Christian era.

אֱלִישָׁפָט p. n. m. (God is judge).

אֱלִיָּתוֹ secondary form of אֱלִיָּתָה.

אֵלֶּךְ (pronom. root) dem. pron. equiv. to אֵלֶּין from אֵל; the ךְ is an abbreviation of another pronom. root ךְ, like in אַךְ, etc.

אלל doubled form (from אֱלַאֱל) to lament, bewail, likewise the same root ἀλαλάζω (related to יָלַל).

אַלְלַי interj. alas! ־ַי is a pronominal suffix in many particles.

אלם to bind, (see אֲלֻמָּה), hence (*a*) of the binding and arching of a building, (see אוּלָם), like אָגַד; (*b*) of the binding, tying of the tongue, (אִלֵּם, אֵלֶם); (*c*) of the lame, of the dumb, and of all who are deprived of the maintenance requisite for life = to be isolated, unmarried, widowed; only in the derivatives. Niph. נֶאֱלַם to be tongue-tied. (Comp. δεσμὸς τῆς γλώσσης), hence to be dumb, to be mute, to be silent. Pi. אִלֵּם to bind fast, to tie together; graduation of the Kal.

אֵלֶם (rare) m. 1) to be dumb, to be mute, to be silent; אֵלֶם צֶדֶק to be silent of, to conceal, righteousness, i. e. the mute righteousness; 2) name of a system of chaunting יוֹנַת אֵלֶם רְחֹקִים (lit. the dove who conceals that which is distant), which method of song is no more traceable.

אִלֵּם (pl. אִלְּמִים) to be tongue-tied, dumb, as a bodily incurable effect, hence its intensive form.

אֻלָם secondary form of אוּלָם, which see.

אֵלֹם see אֲלֻמָּה.

אַלְמֻגִּים see מוּגִּים, מגג.

אַלְמוֹדָד see מוֹדָד (p. n.).

אֲלֻמָּה (from אָלַם, pl. ־ִים, ־וֹת f.) that which is bound, hence a bundle of corn, a sheaf, (related to צְבָתִים, עָמִיר).

אַלַּמֶּלֶךְ p. n. f. town in the dominion of Asher, (probably = אֵלַת־מֶלֶךְ royal oak).

אַלְמָן adj. m. אַלְמָנָה f. *viduus, a*, lonely, widowed. אַלְמָנָה always concrete; widow, as also an anarchal state is called on account of its being unprotected like an orphan.

אַלְמֹן m. widowed, widowed-state.

אַלְמָנָה see אַלְמָן.

אַלְמָנוֹת only pl. f. castles, palaces. The root אָלַם to bind, to arch. Comp. אוּלָם hall.

אַלְמָנוּת (with suffix אַלְמְנוּתָהּ, pl. אַלְמְנוּתִים) f. widowed, symbol. of the exiled Jewish nation, it is formed from אַלְמָן.

אַלְמֹנִי adj. m. to be secluded, estranged, only joined with פְּלֹנִי: yonder distant one, anonymous, concealed one. Hence pronominally a certain one, ὁ δεῖνα.

אַלֹּן see אֵלִין.

אֶלְנַעַם p. n. m. (God of grace). נַעַם equivalent to נֹעַם.

אֶלְנָתָן p. n. m. (God the giver) נָתָן after the form חָכָם.

אֶלָּסָר (equiv. to אֶל־אסר) p. n. of an east Asiatic or a Syriac Babylonian country, but which can no more be traced. The Jerusalem Targum paraphrases it תְּלַשָּׂר, תְּלַאשָּׂר (which see), an Assyrian province mentioned elsewhere, so that אֵל (oak), תֵּל (hill), are only additions to the original אֶסָר, אַשָּׂר. In endeavouring therefore to trace the country, we have only to look to the last two words.

אֶלְעָד p. n. m. (God the protector). See עוּד.

אֶלְעָדָה p. n. m. (diadem of God).

אֶלְעוּזַי p. n. m. (hero of God), *ai* is the adj. termination of עוֹז.

אֶלְעָזָר p. n. m. (God the helper), LXX. Ελεάζαρ, later Λαζαρος.

אֶלְעָלֵה see עָלָה.

אֶלְעָשָׂה p. n. m. (God the Creator).

אָלַף fut. יֶאֱלַף to spread over, ἀλείφω; hence 1) to slip over a thing, as frequently in Heb. the ideas of slipping, sliding, and spreading, are inseparably connected; from this signification arises 2) to slip, to glide, to slide, to draw oneself, hence accustoming oneself in learning a thing; learning, in general, attachment to, and of, confidants and friends; of the tame cattle attaching itself to man, etc.—Pi. to teach, with double accus.; to instruct, with accus. of the person; part. מְלַף = מְאַלֵּף. Hiph. see אֶלֶף.

אֶלֶף 1) only pl. אֲלָפִים epic. the tame, trained (cattle), only of the heifer and cow; 2) βοῦς, signifying the highest value, hence round, highest, overwhelming number; next 1000, dual אַלְפַּיִם 2000, pl. אֲלָפִים thousands. The noun follows in sing. number, later, often *vice versa*. Herefrom Hiph. part. מַאֲלִיפוֹת making thousands, i. e. producing much; 3) a juncture of thousands, i. e. of a large number; hence sometimes equiv. to מִשְׁפָּחָה division of family, tribe, nation; 4) p. n. f.; a city in the territory of Benjamin, (perhaps signifying abundance of people = the populous one).

אֲלַף Aram. equiv. to אֶלֶף in Hebrew.

אֶלְפֶּלֶט see אֱלִיפֶ׳ and פֶּלֶט.

אֶלְפַּעַל p. n. m. (God the worker), see פָּעַל.

אָלַץ to press together, only Piel, to press sorely on some one.

אֶלְצָפָן see אֱלִיצָפָן and צָפַן.

אֶלְקוּם see קוּם.

אֶלְקָנָה p. n. m. (God the Creator).

אֶלְקֹשִׁי see קָשִׁי.

אֶלְתּוֹלַד see תּוֹלַד.

אֶלְתְּקֵא, ־קֵה, see תָּקָא.

אֶלְתְּקוֹן see תָּקוֹן.

אָמַם (not used) f. mother, nurse equiv. to אֵם only in p. n. אֲחִיאָם which see.

אֵם (primitive, with suff. אִמִּי, pl. אִמּוֹת) f. is like אָב the first articulation of the child: ĕmm; hence mother. The signification merges into various branches like in אָב; it also signifies stepmother, grandmother, female ancestor, female progenitor; figur. benefactress, possessor, from thence transferred to mother earth, to people, mother-town, i. e. capital, as a mother, maintaining the inhabitants, hence אֶרֶץ, תֵּבֵל, עִיר, עַם, שְׁאוֹל, גַּיְא, תְּהוֹם, קֶבֶר are generally considered feminine. אָב וָאֵם parents; אֵם הַדָּרֶךְ mother of the road, i. e. cross road.

אִם (pronominal root, properly אִי־ם like the Aram. הֲאִים equiv. to אִי, אַיִן); 1) interr. adv. (*a*) *num? an?* like הֲ in the simple question independent of another sentence; (*b*) in the indirect question *si*, whether, if, therefore dependent on a preceding sentence, generally after verbs of questioning, inquiring, doubting, looking on; (*c*) in the disjunctive question, where אִם, carries on the point of interrogation. The opposite, double questioning parts are kept together הֲ־ ,־אִם הֲ־, וְאִם (*sive*), הַאַף—וְאִם, אִם־אִם אִם; if the interrogation continues, the singleness of the pointings, question, and a variety of subjects, we may also use: הֲ—וְאִם—הֲ or joined: הֲ—הֲלֹא—אִם—הֲ. Herewith is connected: 2) the expression of negation which is manifested by this word, especially with declarations and oaths, e. g. never (אִם) will I do this! never (אִם) will I forsake thee! comp. אַיִן, אִי, אֵי, אַי, etc., which also merge from the interrogative signification into that of negation. This explanation of the negation, arising from the interrogation seems the more probable, since the negation often appears where even no connection or oath exists; 3) conjunctive, if, in conditional sentences, אִם־לֹא if not, with the future, but also with the prosth. as *future exactum* of the Latin: אִם עָשִׂיתִי *si fecero*, עַד אִם עָ׳ *donec fecero*, or before the paras *fut. instans.* To this also belongs אִם in describing repeated circumstances where it may be translated, when, as often as when; when—when אִם־אִם *sive—sive.* In circumstantial sentences, where the subject precedes the condition; after a negative sentence where it is joined to כִּי: but if, or without preceding negation: if only, only; in wishes: if only, where it is also joined with נָא, etc.; 4) it appears in the most ancient, demonstrative, and original sense, as its whole formation, and relationship of sense (אִין, אִי) are originally demonstratives and thus it is = אֵן there! e. g. I hope there for hell as for my house, (Authorised Vers. 'If I wait, the grave is in mine house.' Job 17: 13). Compound: אִם לֹא (*a*) *nonne?* (*b*) if not; (*c*) = *εἰ μή*, *nisi*, Aram. אִם לֹא כִּי if not, that; except it be, that.

אָמָה (with suff. אֲמָתִי pl. אֲמָהוֹת, construct אַמְהוֹת, with suff. אַמְהֹתֵיהֶם, f. hand-maid, maid-servant, female-slave, hence בֶּן אָ׳ son of a female slave = slave. It is also used of women to express subjection. The root is elongated from אָמַם which see.

אַמָּה (from אֵם) f.; 1) mother. capital town, *metropolis*, thus in the phrase: 'and David took the edge of the mother town (Metheg-amma) out of the hands of the Philistines,' (2 Sam. 8: 1) i. e. he subjugated the town; 2) mother of a threshold, i. e. foundation basis; 3) mother of the arm, i. e. the lower part of the arm; hence used to designate a measure: ell, cubit; dual אַמָּתַיִם pl. אַמּוֹת, figurat. אַמַּת בִּצְעֵךְ the measure of thy covetousness (Jer. 51: 13); 5) p. n. of a hill (perhaps mother hill, i. e. chief hill).

אַמָּה (pl. ־ִין) Aram. the same.

אֻמָּה equiv. to אֵימָה; see אֵים.

אֻמָּה (from אם, comp. לְאֹם) f. people, originally, union, connection. In pl. ־ִים, ־וֹת; see עַם and אֵם.

אֻמָּה Aram. the same.

אָמוֹן p. n. of an Egyptian deity, Amon, in the ancient Egyptian, *Amn*; complete *Amn-Re*, i. e. the sun of Amon, he was especially worshipped in Thebes, (נֹא־אָמוֹן, Greek *Διόσπολις*). Amon also signifies, according to Champollion: eminence, greatness.

אָמוֹן m.; 1) work-master, work-mistress, hence also used of the wisdom of the creation, as: work-mistress, where it has yet no famimine form; 2) p. n. m.

king of Judea, (641-639 before the Christian era); 3) once only dialect. for הָמוֹן which see.

אֵמֻנִים ,אֱמוּנִים .pl ,אֱמוּן=אֵמֻן) אֵם const. אֱמוּנֵי) m. originally supported, confirmed; hence firmness, support, reliance, truth. לֹא אֵמֻן truthlessness. The plural signifies (*a*) collectively abst. sureness, truth; *b*) concrete: that on which you may rely, you may be sure of.

אֱמוּנָה (from אֱמוּן, pl. אֱמוּנוֹת) f. sureness, firmness, truth, security, e. g. his hands were steady, (i. e. sure). Exod. 17 : 12.

אָמוֹץ p. n. m. (the courageous, valourous one), father of the prophet Isaiah.

אָמִי p. n. m. for which elsewhere stands אָמוֹן which see.

אֵמִי stands for אֵימִים. See אֵים, אֵים.

אֲמִינוֹן p. n. m. for אַמְנוֹן; the interpolation of ־ִי is considered a deminutive form, for which, however, there is no example in Hebrew. See אַמְנוֹן.

אַמִּיץ adj. m. vigorous, strong, אַ׳ כֹּחַ strong in power; קֶשֶׁר אַ׳ very firm connection, conspiracy.

אָמִיר (after the form of פָּקִיד) m. that which is prominently shewing itself, or that which is made prominent, *cacumen*, hence (*a*) summit of the mountain; (*b*) top of a tree, בְּרֹאשׁ אָמִיר above, at the top of the tree. Root אָמַר.

אָמַל to fall together, to wither, to waste, to languish, only particip. מָה אֲמֻלָה לִבָּתֵךְ how languishing (weak) is thy heart, (Ezek. 16 : 30), from passion. Duplicate form passive, אֻמְלַל ,אֻמְלְלוּ, אֻמְלָלָה ,אֻמְלְלָה ,אֻמְלָלוּ, withered, (of plants) wasted away, pining away, to be downcast.

אֲמֵלָל (pl. אֲמֵלָלִים) adj. m. withering away, weak, duplicate form from אָמַל; the ־ֵ becomes harder from the original intrans. sense. See אָמֵל.

אָמַם (not used) to join, to connect. This idea of union is evidently impressed by *emm*, mother, origin. she who unites tribes or families; âma is a lengthened root, and expresses the state of being connected or united, hence אָמָה, she who belongs to or is connected with a family, like שִׁפְחָה, she who is added to a family; hence of the unity of a people, like: אֻמָּה ,אֹם people, etc. See עָמַם, לְאֹם and others.

אֲמָם p. n. f. (place of assembly), city in the territory of Judah. See אָמַם.

אָמַן to make firm, to be firm, hence

1) to found, to prop, to build; or Lat. *sustentare*, to sustain, to nourish, i. e. to support; אֹמֵן part. nurser, cherisher, sustainer, maintainer, f. אֹמֶנֶת; 2) to be founded, confirmed, hence to be sure, true; אָמוּן, the faithful one, which signification may also be conceived transitively, since only the particip. pass. occurs. Niph. (*a*) to be firm, מָקוֹם נֶאֱמָן firm, sure place, (Isa. 22 : 23 and 25), לֹא תֵאָמֵנוּ 'ye shall not be sure, ye shall not be believed,' (Isa. 7 : 9); (*b*) to be durable, firm, constant: בַּיִת נֶאֱמָן an uninterrupted house (generation), 1 Sam. 2 : 35; but it is also used of a lasting sickness, also of an uninterrupted flowing of the water, etc.; (*c*) to be nursed, to be carried, used of a child; (*d*) to be reliable, sure, unfailing, applied to God, a servant, a messenger, a witness, an artificer, etc. Hiph. to maintain firmly, with בְּ to keep to any thing steadily, hence to trust upon something, to believe in something, (בה׳, in God); but also to cause anything to stand still, used of the horse.

אֲמַן Aram. Af. הֵימַן the same as Hiphil.

אָמָן (= מְאֻמָּן) m. properly, to be exercised, skilful, expert, hence work-master, artificer.

אָמֵן adj. m. sure, true, firm; hence (*a*) n. truth, faithfulness; (*b*) adv. surely, truly, certainly, especially occurs as a confirmation, either once or repeated twice at the conclusion of sentences.

אֹמֶן m. surety, truth, faithfulness.

אֲמָנָה f. 1) (from אָמַן) that which is fixed (of reward, wages), firmness (of a covenant); 2) p. n. of the back of the mountain of Anti-Lebanon (Talm. אֲמָנוֹן); hence the name of a river now called Baradi (Gr. Chrysorrhoas), because it flows down from Amana. The Ketib is אֲבָנָה (by interchanging *m* and *b*); the signification is firm ground, strength.

אֹמְנָה (only pl.) f. pillar, post, column, originally part. f. Kal, that which supports, the column which props.

אָמְנָה (from אמן) f. 1) sustenance, nourishment; 2) = אָמְנָם as adv. indeed, in truth, from which it appears in a mutilated form.

אַמְנוֹן p. n. m. (the sure one, one on whom you may rely, from אָמַן); a secondary form is אֲמִינוֹן derived from אָמִין, אָמַן.

אָמְנָם, אֻמְנָם (from אמן) adv. truly, certainly.

אָמֵץ fut. יֶאֱמַץ, imp. אֱמַץ; 1) to be sharp, especially of the sharp, light dazzling colour of the deep scarlet, as ὀξύς is also used, hence אָמֹץ scarlet; 2) the idea of sharpness transferred and applied to the mind, to be sharp, vehement, bold, strong, with מִן to overwhelm somebody. Pi.: 1) to make hard, i. e. stubborn, inflexible, e. g. לֵב the heart; to make hard or firm, applied to a body, e. g. house, heaven; to make courageous, bold, by affording succour; 2) to make firm, select, distinguished, e. g. בֶּן־אָדָם the son of man, with בְּ, selecting from among others. Hiph. to act courageously, bravely, to exercise strength. Hithph. to shew oneself bold, strong, hence of the rash act, of the firm resolution, of encouraging oneself.

אָמוֹץ (pl. אֲמֻצִּים) adj. m. deep red, as the colour of horses: hence LXX. πυῤῥοί. Respecting this form comp. the usual distinction of colours אָדֹם, שָׂרֹק, שָׁחוֹר.

אֹמֶץ (poet.) valour, strength.

אַמְצָה (from אָמֵץ) f. the same, (poet.) The masc. אֹמֶץ occurs in modern Hebrew.

אַמְצִי p. n. m. (the valorous one, formed from אָמֵץ).

אֲמַצְיָה p. n. m. (God is the strength), a king of Judea (840—11 before the Christian era), LXX. Ἀμεσσίας, Ἀμασίας.

אָמַר fut. יֹאמַר, pause יֹאמֵר inf. cons. אֱמֹר, בֶּאֱמֹר, לֵאמֹר (= לֶאֱמֹר); 1) physically, to stare, to shew forth prominently, to extend, only used in the word אָמִיר that which shews forth prominently, top of a tree, summit. Hith. הִתְאַמֵּר to make onself prominent, great, to boast, with which may be compared אֱמֹרִי, אִמֵּר, אוֹמֶר; 2) spiritually, to say, originally to raise the voice, to produce tones, to sound forth from within; it is therefore used of the non-regulated sounds of the horse, Job 39 : 15. Different from דִּבֶּר, to join words together, pre-supposing a combination; hence אָמַר as insufficient in itself, is always succeeded by what is said, which דִּבֶּר does not require, e. g. speak to Israel, and tell them (the following). Thus לֵאמֹר to say = 'namely,' or viz. is used as the form for quoting, where the very words spoken must follow; or the accus. of what is said follows, which, however, often appears to be omitted: e. g. 'Cain said (it),'. Gen. 4 : 8. The signification merges into four branches: (*a*) to say, plainly with לְ; אֶל to say to, or of some one; (*b*) to name, with לְ, hence אָמוּר named; (*c*) to think, properly elliptical for אָמַר בְּלֵב to say in the heart, (comp. *φημί* in Homer), which often follows it; (*d*) various changes in the signification according to the context; to exhort, to predict, to praise, to point out, to command, which, however, all meet in the primary sense. Niph. to be said, לְ, אֶל to somebody; with לְ to be called; קָדוֹשׁ יֵאָמֵר לוֹ 'holy he shall be called.' יֵאָמֵר (impersonal) it is said, it is understood, especially before a quotation.—Hiph. to cause to say, with the accus. e. g. 'thou hast caused it to be said to Jehovah,' i. e. thou hast solemnly dedicated thyself, etc. (Auth. Vers. avouched), Deut. 26 : 17, 18.

אֲמַר fut. יֵאמַר inf. מֵאמַר, מֵמַר. Aram. 1) to say, verbally or in writing; part. pl. אָמְרִין one says, people say; 2) to command. The root is like in Hebrew.

אֹמֶר (with suff. אִמְרִי, pl. אֲמָרִים const. אִמְרֵי) m. equiv. to אֹמֶר, (poet.) 1) speech, word, sentence, אִמְרֵי אֵל the divine sentences; נֹתֵן אִמְרֵי שָׁפֶר 'goodly speech,' (words), Gen. 49 : 21; poetical effusions, i. e. to make a speech, thus: אִמְרֵי שֶׁקֶר, נֹעַם, אֱמֶת, דַּעַת, בִּינָה, יֹשֶׁר, 2) sentence = decision, lot, fate: אִמְרוֹ מֵאֵל, the lot appointed him by God.

אִמַּר pl. (אִמְּרִין) Aram. m. lamb, properly for עַמַּר *laniger*, from עֲמַר wool.

אִמֵּר p. n. m. (high of stature). See אָמֵר.

אֹמֶר (poet.) m. 1) speech, poetical address, song; 2) prediction; 3) equiv. to דָּבָר matter, *res*, hence for: something.

אִמְרָה (const. ־רַת, pl. אֲמָרוֹת) f. speech, poetical address, sentence.

אֶמְרָה f. the same.

אֱמֹרִי p. n. m. (properly the one who inhabits the summit, the top), a Canaanite tribe on that which was subsequently a mountain of Judah. LXX. Ἀμοῤῥαῖοι; their land, according to Joseph. Ἀμωρῖτις, Ἀμορία (var. Ἀμοῤῥαία, Ἀμωραία). Perhaps from אָמַר No. 1, the gigantic, high-stature people. Comp. אֵמִים.

אִמְרִי p. n. m. (from אֵמֶר eloquent.)

אֲמַרְיָה p. n. m. (the boon of God.)

אֲמַרְיָהוּ p. n. m. the same.

אַמְרָפֶל p. n. m. (equiv. to אַרְפֶּל, probably ־ֶל is the diminutive termination, and אִמְרָף equiv. to

אַרְיוֹךְ with מ interpolated; comp. 'Αῤῥαπαχῖτις, territory of the northren Assyrian, and אַרְפַּכְשַׁד as a p. n. of a Semitic), king of Shinear.

אֶמֶשׁ m. originally that which is departed, passed; 1) the night before (Arab yesterday), shortly, but only as an adverb: yesterday, contrast to מָחָר = מְאָחָר, that which is later, that which follows, i. e. tomorrow; 2) night in general, only Job 30: 3. אֶמֶשׁ שׁוֹאָה night, (grey of night), of the wilderness = nightly desert, as Kimchi, Rashi, and Rabb explain this passage. The root is אֶרְמֶשׁ = מוּשׁ to depart, to vanish.

אֱמֶת (with suff. אֲמִתּוֹ, for אֱמֶנֶת) contrac. from אֲמִינָה f. firmness, constancy, from אָמַן to make firm; hence 1) durability, surety, certainty; 2) faithfulness, truth, especially of religious truth; honest, true mind, generally connected with שָׁלוֹם, חֶסֶד. See אָמַן.

אַמְתַּחַת (only const., and with suff. אַמְתַּחְתּוֹ), pl. const. אַמְתְּחוֹת) f. only in Gen., prob. cloth, from מָתַח to extend, like מִטְפַּחַת, kerchief, from טָפַח, but generally sack, joined to שַׂק.

אֲמִתַּי p. n. m. (the honest-minded one).

אַמְתָּן adj. m. אַמְתָּנֵי const. אַמְתָּנִית f. (Aram.) strong, robust, originally, well or strongly loined, from מַתְנַיִן, the loins, because in them was the seat of strength according to the Semitic doctrines.

אָן interrog. adv. where? in Targ. for אֵי contracted from אַיִן; (comp. דִּתָן and דּוּתַיִן), hence מֵאָן wherefrom? עַד־אָן whereto? till when? till where? how long? seldom for אָנָה.

אֹן. See אוֹן.

אֲנָא or אֲנָה (pronom. root) Aram. equiv. to the Hebrew אֲנִי I. In this word like אֲנִי, *an* is additional to אָה; ־ִי (I) I, an addition like most other personal pronouns have.

אָנָּא (pronom. root = אָה־נָא) a word signifying prayer, imploring: O that! in the beginning where the merely enclitic נָא (only, however,) cannot stand. In very pressing requests the syllable נָא may follow.

אָנָה interrog. adv. whereto? (formed from אָן with ־ָה of motion), in double questions, אֵי־מִזֶּה־וְאָנָה, wherefrom and whereto? אָנָה־וּמֵאַיִן whereto and wherefrom? עַד־אָנָה till when, how long? Seldom

אֲנָה for אָנָה, without being an interrogative. אָנָה אָנָה hither and thither, (where?).

אָנָּה equiv. to אָנָּא from אָן with ה of motion at end.

אָנָה I. originally expressive, meant to mourn, to wail; II. probably to turn, only Pi. אִנָּה to turn, to occasion, originally to give a particular turn to an event; to cause something by chance or Divine Providence.—Pu. pass. Hith. to give opportunity, circumstances, occasion (for a certain action): with לְ against somebody. The difference from No. 1. lies in the syllabic root, which there is אָן, and here [illegible], to which is related [illegible] of the turning, returning motion.

אֲנוּ (pronom. root) pers. pron. we, but where אֲ is only preformative, and נוּ the root, only Jer. 42 : 6, Ketib, else generally אֲנַחְנוּ, which see.

אִנּוּן m. אִנִּין f. Aram. pers. pron. they, from הִין, הֵן, and the demons. syllable ־ִן.

אֱנוֹשׁ (Aram. אֱנָשׁ, pl. אֲנָשִׁים, from אֱנָשׁ, const. אֱנָשׁ), m. man; in prose generally collect. of mankind, poetically בֶּן־אֱנוֹשׁ. Sometimes in poetry with the secondary signification of (*a*) great multitude, אֱנוֹשׁ חֶרֶט popular, legible writing; (*b*) low, base man; (*a*) and (*b*) do not belong, however, necessarily to the principal idea: man. The pl. is also used for אִישׁ, which see.

אֱנוֹשׁ p. n. m. (the manly one).

אָנַח only Niph. נֶאֱנַח to sigh, to complain, *ἀδύρεσθαι*, with עַל, מִן of something.

אֲנָחָה (with suff. אַנְחָתִי, pl. אֲנָחוֹת) f. sighing, complaining.

אֲנַחְנָא or אֲנַחְנָה, Aram. the same, like אֲנַחְנוּ, which see.

אֲנַחְנוּ (pronom. root) pers. pron. we, equiv. to אֲנוּ; like in all person. pronouns אן is also here preformative, and נַחְנוּ = אֲנוּ with the hardened prosth. letter like Aram. חֲנַן = אֲנַן; from which נַחְנוּ is abbreviated.

אֲנָחֲרָת p. n. f. a town in the territory of Issachar.

אֲנִי (pronominal root), pause אָנִי, pers. pron. I, from ־ִי (a form yet remaining as a suff. for: I), with אן preformative; see אָנֹכִי.

אֳנִי ship, as a n. of multitude: hence, fleet, and without pl.; very seldom a single ship, אֳנִי שַׁיִט an oar-ship, but otherwise always used in its stead:—

אֳנִיָּה (pl. אֳנִיּוֹת, once Ketib אוניות) f. ship, as a sing. noun: hence the pl. :—

אֲנִיָּה f. moaning, wailing, Greek *ἀνία*. Root אנה.

אֲנִיעָם p. n. m.

אָנַךְ (not used), to be pointed, to be sharp, or whatever else is connected with this idea, related to חָנַךְ, from which חַכָּה hook, harpoon.

אֲנָךְ m. properly, the being pointed, point; as a tool for building: pointed-hook, (measure-hook, square-rule), thorn, nail, used for tearing things asunder, (related to שָׁמִיר); hence the LXX. and Symmach. correctly render it *ἀδάμας* (pointed iron), for the use of engraving. Comp. Aram. אֵינְכָא *ὄνοξ*.—Only in Amos (four times) 'I will set a plumb-line (of devastation) in the midst of my people Israel,' Amos, 7: 8. 'The Lord stood upon a wall made by a plumb-line with a plumb-line in his hand,' Amos, 7: 7.

אָנֹכִי pause אָנֹכִי, (pronominal root) pers. pron. equiv. to אֲנִי I, but only belongs to the ancient period of the language; hence in Ezek. Eccl., and Chron. אֲנִי. According to the etymology it is composed from the usual *an*, demonst. syllable, and the general form ôchi, I, also like the Coptic *anok*, is composed.

אָנַן (אוֹן) equiv. to אָנָה; 1) only Hith. to complain, (related to הִתְנוֹדֵד.)

אָנַס (Aram. אֲנַס) properly to make anything compressed, or to press; only in Esther.

אָנַף fut. יֶאֱנַף, originally, panting, gasping for something, *inhiare*; gasping, snorting with passion; hence to be wroth, with בְּ against somebody. Hith. to put oneself in a passion. The original idea of breathing; whence the secondary one of snorting with passion and lust is developed, lies in אַף, where the נ is interpolated.

אֲנַף (def. אַנְפָּא pl. אַנְפִּין) Aram. m. equiv. to the Hebrew אַף.

אֲנָפָה f. parrot, (after the Arabic translation), so called from its irritibility, the LXX. strand-snipe, (*χαραδριός*). Others class this bird with the eagle-kind, identical with *ἀνοπαῖα* in Homer.

אָנַק to groan, to complain, to wail, of the wounded; comp. Scandiv. *anken*. Niph. to complain, to sigh.

אֲנָקָה (const. אֶנְקַת) f. 1) groaning, complaint, (related to אֲנָחָה); 2) a sound like that of a lizzard, of a moaning nature.

אָנַשׁ (only part. pass. אָנוּשׁ), to be mortal, malignant, injurious, dangerous, of incurable wound of dangerous pain; figuratively of a day of grief. Niph. to become dangerously, fatally ill.

אֱנָשׁ Aram. equiv. to אֱנוֹשׁ.

אֲנָשִׁים see אִישׁ, אֱנוֹשׁ.

אַנְתָּה properly אַנְתָּה (pronominal root), Aram. thou, (from אַן and תָּה, see אַתָּה) from which is abbreviated אַנְתְּ.

אָסָא p. n. m. a king of Judah, 955-914 before the Christian era. LXX. 'Ασά.

אָסוּךְ m. anointing vessel, אָ is here of the same use as the מְ in מָשׁוּךְ from שׁוּךְ; if סוּךְ is the root; probably it is related to אָסַךְ; נָסַךְ, סָךְ is here to be taken as the root.

אָסוֹן m. hurt, disaster, from אָסָה = עָשׁ *laedere*.

אֵסוּר = אֱסוּר, (pl. אֲסוּרִים) m. incarceration, fetter; בֵּית הָאֵסוּר, house of fetters, prison. See אָסַר.

אֱסוּר Aram. m. the same.

אָסִיף m. equiv. to אָלוּל, the being gathered (of fruit), gathering time of fruit = harvest, from אָסַף. Comp. קָצִיר, בָּצִיר, אָבִיב, חָרִיף.

אָסִיר (and אַסִּיר) m. prisoner, one that is fettered; אָסוּר, however more as a participle.

אָסַם (not used) equiv. to שׂוּם, to put, to lay down; אָ is here preformative, like in many verbs.

אָסָם m. place where something is laid down, warehouse, store; (comp. אוֹצָר, מְמְגֻּרָה).

אַסְנָה p. n. m. (hating very much), after the form אַכְזָב, if the etymology is the Hebrew form.

אָסְנַפַּר p. n. m. Assyr. satrap. The Assyrian appel. signification is not clear.

אָסְנַת p. n. f. daughter of the Egyptian priest, Pôt-i-Fera, Joseph's wife; LXX. 'Ασενέθ, 'Ασεννέθ. In the extraction נַת (= נֵית) Neit,—(Pallas) is the only one to be ascribed.

אָסַף fut. יֶאֱסֹף (אֹסֵף, תֹּסֵף, יֹסֵף, with ה אֹסְפָה); to take, draw, join together, hence: 1) to gather (fruit), equiv. to gather in, to lay in store; the people, equiv. assemble; אָ' אֶל, עַל, to gather, or to put in some place, (e. g. in prison); 2) to draw together, or to draw back, e. g. to draw the feet back on the couch; to withdraw the hand; the stars withdraw their brilliancy; 3) to gather in, to receive, e. g. in the town. Hence of leprosy, to take it away, i. e. by which the one cured is received into society. To close a procession; 4) to gather in, of God, i. e. to take away, e. g. 'thou gatherest their life in,' i. e. they die; 'God gathers my shame,' i. e. he takes it away. Niph. inf. הֵאָסֵף; 1) to gather themselves, with אֶל, לְ, to assemble at, or to repair to some place; with עַל to assemble against somebody; 2) to be gathered = to die, in figurative speech; to be gathered to (אֶל) his people; to be gathered to his ancestors, i. e. in the region of death; hence also to cease, to vanish, to perish; 3) to be received, of the leprous; 4) to withdraw oneself, to draw out, of the sword.—Pi. to gather with zeal, to receive (to oneself), to keep the procession together.—Pu. to be gathered, to be taken together.—Hith. to gather themselves together.

אָסָף p. n. m. (gatherer) a bard and poet in the time of David, whose descendants were yet singers in the time of Nehemiah.

אָסֹף (only pl. אֲסֻפִּים const. אֲסֻפֵּי) m. אֲסֻפָּה (pl. אֲסֻפּוֹת) f. to be gathered, בֵּית הָאֲסֻפִּים or בּ׳ אֲס׳ house of provisions gathered; אֲסֻפָּה assembly (of wisdom); בַּעֲלֵי אֲסֻפּוֹת members of assemblies.

אָסִף m. gathering, gathering of fruit. Comp. אָסִיף.

אֲסֵפָה (from אָסַף) f. gathering. A very rare form.

אֲסַפְסֻף m. multitude of people gathered here and there, with the article, the rabble, mob. It is a doubled form, and אֲסַפְסֻף like פְּקַחְקֹם, שְׁחַרְחֹר, פְּתַלְתֹּל.

אָסְפַּרְנָא Aram. adv. zealous, careful, LXX. ἑτοίμως, ἐπιμελῶς, ἐπιδέξιον. The derivation is uncertain.

אַסְפָּתָא (Persian) p. n. m. (comp. Ἀσπαδάτας, Ασπάδας, as a Persian name, Diod. S. II. 33.) i. e. of the horse, an appellation for the heathen deity Behram, in the figure of a horse, from the Persian *esp*, *equis*, and the usual dât, there.

אָסַר (fut. יֶאֱסֹר, יַאְסֹר inf. with לְ; לֶאְסֹר, לֶאֱסֹר, participle pass. הָאֲסוּרִים=הָסוּרִים); 1) to bind together, to fetter, and imprisoning generally; even without fetters; fig. of the fetters of love; אָסוּר prisoner; 2) to tie on; e.g. the fold, the vine; to harness, e.g. calves to the waggon, hence generally: harnessing (a waggon); fig. אָסַר מִלְחָמָה, to entangle in dispute, i. e. to commence it; 3) to bind, to impose a bond upon oneself, to make a vow, in the emphatic form, אָסַר אִסָּר עַל־נֶפֶשׁ, to impose a fetter on the soul, i. e. to enter into an obligation of a vow of abstemiousness, (contrast נָדַר, to vow); comp. Aram. אֲסַר, (to bind), prohibit, אַפִּיר (to solve), to permit.—Niph. pass.—Pual to be taken prisoner.

אֱסָר, אִסָּר m. vowing to abstain, a vow of abstemiousness, from אָסַר.

אֱסָר Aram. m. commandment of prohibition or denial.

אֵסַר־חַדּוֹן p. n. m. (LXX. Eus. 'Ασορδάν, Tob. 1:21, Σαχερδονός, Alex. Σαχερδών, Joseph. 'Ασσαραχόδδας, Ναχορδάς), a king of Assyria after Senacherib.

אֶסְתֵּר (Persian) p. n. f. (= סְתַר, Persian, *sitareh*, Greek *ἀ-στήρ*, star, asterisk; comp. עַשְׁתֹּרֶת), consort of Xerxes (Ahasuerus), who was formerly called הֲדַסָּה, (myrtle). LXX. 'Εσθήρ.

אָע Aram. m. equiv. to Heb. עֵץ, wood, since often in the Aramaic that ע = צ and א = ע.

אַף (pronom. root) prepos. at, on, and the prepos. expression of approximation, either stable or moving; to, thereto, before, hither, since both ideas are interwoven in all languages; hence conjunctive when it signifies the moving to a place or near it, as 1) likewise, also, e. g. אַף אַחֲרָיו, also after him, i. e. near, close to him, differs from גַּם, which has only a tendency of augmenting; 2) besides, e. g. 'besides God will not do wickedly,' (Job 34 : 12); 3) to, (being a prepos.) 'I have let the matter known to thee,' (אַף אָתָּה); 4) and, indeed, expressed with or without gradation, e. g. 'to thee, O Lord, belongs the day, and even the night.' (Ps. 74 : 16). 'Thou art beautiful, my beloved, and even (yea) pleasant.' (Song of Sol. 1 : 16); 'even (yea) thou castest off fear,' etc. (Job, 15 : 4). Compounds : אַף־אָמְנָם, even, truly; in the first part of the sentence : even indeed, אַף־גַּם, besides also, אַף־כִּי besides that, according to the context; how much more, how much less; הַאַף is it now also (true)? אַף כִּי־אָמַר has he said indeed? = הַאַף is it even that?

אַף Aram. the same as in the Hebrew.

אַף (= *anf.* with suff. אַפִּי; dual אַפַּיִם) m. a snorter, hence nose, anger. The dual אַפַּיִם; 1) properly nostrils, but transferred to snorting with anger; hence the form, long or short suffering, i. e. enduring; 2) the whole face, e. g. אַפַּיִם אַרְצָה, the face to the ground, (ellipsis) turned; לְאַפֵּי

דָוִד before the face of David; (comp. קָלְאַפֵּי = קָלְפֵי, Aram. as before the face); 3) like פָּנִים, πρόσωπον, for person; אַפַּיִם, also two persons, מָנָה אַחַת אַפַּיִם one gift for two persons, i. e. double; 4) p. n. m. The root is אָנַף, which see.

אָפַר (fut. יֶאְפֹּר) to bind, to bind round, to gird round.

אֵפֹר (adj. m. only f. אֲפֻדָּה const. אֲפֻדַּת); 1) to be bound round, to be girded round; hence, חֵשֶׁב אֲפֻדָּתוֹ, the girdle bound, or girded on; 2) the tying round the garment thrown over a person. The root is אָפַד, which see.

אֲפֻדָּה see אֵפֹר.

אַפֶּדֶן (later with suff. אַפַּדְנוֹ), m. castle, palace, burgh. The root is probably אָפַד, to bind, to make fast, to arch; (compare אֲגֻדָּה, אוּלָם), and formed after the method of צִפֹּרֶן, from אָפַד.

אָפָה (fut. יֹאפֶה; once וַתֹּפֵהוּ), to bake, with two accus.; אֹפֶה, אֹפֶה m. and f. baker; שַׂר הָאֹפִים chief of the bakers.—Niph. Pass.

אֵפוֹ, אֵפוֹא (pronom. root) demonst. adv.; 1) properly here there, but always in reference to time: now then, ποτέ, then, in the emphatic speech, e. g. 'then do this (אֵפוֹא) my son,' (Gen. 27 : 8), now then, (אֵפוֹ), 'who is he?' (Gen. 27 : 33), what then? (אֵפוֹא); 2) in the original signification similar to כֹּה, e. g. if not, then (אֵפוֹ), strengthened by כֵּן: as אִם כֵּן אֵפוֹא if it be thus then. It is composed from א dem. and פוֹ=פֹּה.

אֵפוֹד (אֵפֹד c. אֵפוֹד), m. 1) to wrap round, dressing, especially of the high priest, or royal garments, ephod, ἐπωμίς, made from purple, blue, or purple, scarlet, and gold fringes, and made like the garments now used by the Catholic Priests at the Mass, chasuble; 2) that which is wrapped up, heathen idols.

אֲפִיחַ p. n. m. from פּוּחַ = אָפַח (the oppressed one, the one who is snubbed at).

אָפִיל adj. m. אֲפִילָה, f. weak in the stem, drooping in the stem, unripe, tender in the stem; derived from אָפַל, which see.

אַפַּיִם p. n. m. (double person, double pieced). See אַף.

אָפִיק adj. m. 1) strong, vigorous, originally to set in motion, to press, to conquer; hence subst. אֲפִקִים, the strong ones; 2) to move, to flow; hence subst. brook, a vale with a brook; next, water-tube, spout, the bed of a river, etc., always derived from running, flowing The root is אָפַק, which see.

אֲפִיק see אָפַק.

אָפַל to fall; hence, 1) to descend, to sink, to set, of the sun, to become dark; 2) to fall, to sink oneself, to sink the stem; hence to be tender, weak in the stem, to be pliable, always proceeding from its original signification.

אָפֵל adj. m. dark, without sun, of days, (related to חָשׁוּךְ).

אֹפֶל m. setting of the sun, sun-set, darkness; fig. of misfortunes, reverse.

אֲפֵלָה (from אָפַל) f. the same, however more collective.

אֶפְלָל p. n. m. (very tender, weak, redoubled form from אָפַל).

אָפַן (not used) to turn in a circuit, to twist.

אֹפֶן (pl. אֳפַנִּים and אֹפָן, const. אֹפַן, pl. אֹפַנֵּי) m. circumference; hence a wheel; אֹפַן מַרְכְּבֹתָיו, 'wheel of his chariots;' יְדוֹת הָאֹפַנִּים, axle of the wheels; fig. of a speech moving in its own sphere, דָּבָר דָּבֻר עַל־אָפְנָיו a speech spoken in its sphere, i. e. measured.

אֹפָן see אֹפֶן.

אָפֵס equiv. to פַּס, vanish, cease; (comp. פַּס).

אֶפֶס (dual אַפְסַיִם; const. אַפְסֵי) m. the vanishing; hence: end, אַפְסֵי־אֶרֶץ i. e. remote lands; אָפְסַיִם, the two ends of the feet, pair of soles, מֵי אָפְסַיִם water that reaches up to the soles, i. e. shallow; (comp. מֵי מָתְנַיִם, בִּרְכַּיִם); 2) adv. and conj. not, besides, except, originally nothing, e. g. all their princes are nothing (אֶפֶס); ' is any one else, or besides, with thee? and he said, no one (אָפֶס) none;' not, e. g. not (אֶפֶס); from me, except: nothing further except (אֶפֶס) God; hence בְּלֹא=בְּאֶפֶס without; הַאֶפֶס, *an non?* מֵאֶפֶס from nothing = like a nothing, next to תֹּהוּ; עַד אֶפֶס till then, that not; אֶפֶס כִּי, except that; hence also, only that, but, however; אַפְסִי = אֶפֶס, formed like בִּלְתִּי, זוּלָתִי.

פַּס דַּמִּים see אֶפֶס דַּמִּים.

אָפַע (not used) to breathe, to blow, related to פָּעָה, פָּאָה, פָּא. From which אֶפַע, אֶפְעֶה.

אֶפַע (pause אָפַע) m. equiv. to הֶבֶל, a breath; hence מֵאָיִן = מֵאָפַע, from a breath, from nothing. The root is אָפַע, which see.

אֶפְעֶה generally f., originally the breathing one, the hissing one; hence, venemous serpent, from אָפַע, to breathe, to hiss. The termination ĕ is shortened from ā.

Comp. זֶרֶה, עָלְפָּה and others.

אָפַן (poetically) to circumferate, to turn, to twist, related to סָבַב; hence to surround, to encompass, with acc. Ps. 18 : 14, and with עַל Ps. 40 : 13.

אָפֵק (not used); 1) to move, to flow, hence אָפִיק brook. The root is אָרְפַס related to פָּק, סָרְפַק to weigh; 2) trans. to set in motion, to push, to press, to conquer, hence אָפִיק strong, powerful. Only Hith. 1) to force oneself, to make oneself courageous, daring, וָאֶתְאַפַּק וָאַעֲלֶה הָעֹלָה 'I forced myself, therefore, and offered a burnt-offering,' (1 Sam. 13 : 12); 2) to force oneself to take courage, to refrain from something, to curb oneself, e. g. 'the sounding of thy bowels and of thy mercies, are they restrained ?' (Isa. 63 : 15).

אֲפֵק and אָפִיק p. n. f. (city of a canal) name of a town. See אָפַק.

אֲפֵקָה p. n. f. (the same) name of a town. See אָפַק.

אָפַר (not used); 1) equiv. to פָּר פָּרַר, crumbled, to be broken in pieces; 2) equiv. to עָפַר to cover, where ע is softened into א.

אֵפֶר m. 1) dust, originally, to scatter into dust. Comp. דַּק dust, from דָּק to be beaten small, to pulverise; hence מִשְׁלֵי־אֵפֶר 'proverbs or songs like dust,' i. e. vain songs (Job 13 : 12); רֹעֶה אֵפֶר 'he who feedeth on ashes,' i. e. 'who hunts after vanity,' (Isa. 44 : 20); עָפָר וָאֵפֶר 'earth and dust,' figure of transientness (Gen. 18 : 27); 2) ashes from wood, different from דֶּשֶׁן ashes of the sacrifices.

אֲפֵר m. covering, especially covering of the head; (comp. Aram. עֲפַר the same; מַעֲפְרָא turban). The root is אָפַר = עָפַר which see.

אֶפְרֹחַ (pl. ־חִים) m. a young brood, from פָּרַח which see. The א is preformative.

אַפִּרְיוֹן (only Canticles) m. equiv. to פִּרְיוֹן, sedan, φορεῖον, *ferculum*, chariot, from פָּרָה = פָּר which see. The termination יוֹן, is only to be met with in roots ending with vowels (ל״ה), like הֵרָיוֹן ,רַעְיוֹן, hence the root of this word is פָּרָה.

אֶפְרַיִם 1) p. n. m. (from a noun in the sing. אֶפְרִי or פְּרִי from פָּרָה with אֶ preformative) name of the second son of Joseph, Ephraim, and subsequently head of a tribe. After the division of the empire, there was for a long time an Ephramitic dynasty at the head of the Israelitish portion: hence Ephraim = Israel; 2) p. n. f.

name of the territory of Ephraim called so after the head of the tribe; 3) mountain of Ephraim, extending from the plain of Jesrael to the mountain of Judah; 4) Forest of Ephraim, the correct etymology is from פָּרָה, and therefore there is no dual form.

אֲפָרְסָי (Aram.; pl. ־סָיֵא) m. an inhabitant of a town in Syria, perhaps from Prusias (Cellar. ad Plin. ep. 10, 85), or Pyrisa bora (Amm. I, 23, p. 286). Uncertain because the extension of the Syrian dynasty is not clearly ascertained, the terminating ־ָיֵא is contracted from ־ָיֵא which is common in Syriac.

אֲפָרְסְכָי and אֲפָרְסַתְכָי (Aram. pl. ־כָיֵא) p. n. of a people of whom no particulars are ascertained.

אֶפְרָת with the â indicating motion אֶפְרָתָה; 1) p. n. m. equiv. to אֶפְרַיִם (פֹּרֶת a sprout, a sproutling), hence אֶפְרָתִי Ephratite, from Ephraim; 2) p. n. f. a name for Bethlehem, (i. e. a fruit territory).

אַפְּתֹם (Aram.) adv. finally, perhaps equiv. to אַפְּסֹם from אֶפֶס = אָפְסָה with the adverbial termination ôm like שִׁלְשֹׁם (שָׁלֹשׁ) הֲלֹם (הל), פִּתְאֹם (פֶּתַע). Others derive it from Persian *fdam*, which is not unlikely in the Aram. biblical passages. See אֶפֶס.

אֶצְבֹּן p. n. m. (from צֶעֶב = אָצַב beautifully formed) once in its stead אֲבִיהוּד (ornamentally formed).

אֶצְבַּע (with suff. אֶצְבָּעִי, pl. ־עוֹת) f. finger, forefinger, transferred to measure, the breadth of a finger. The finger of God: a token or sign that God is the director: with רַגְלַיִם toe. The א is preformative, and the root is צָבַע which see.

אֶצְבַּע (Aram.) the same, but elsewhere עֶרְבַּע, in the Talmud we find the denominative אִצְבַּע derived from it, signifying to stretch out the fingers for giving a sign.

אָצִיל m. properly to lean on, to be joined to, connected with; hence 1) the noble (joining to his ancestors) descending from the ancient stem; 2) support to lean upon; אֲצִילִים the (supports of the earth), utmost points of support. 'Thou whom I have taken from the ends of the earth' (Isa. 41: 9), similar to קְצוֹת.

אַצִּיל (pl. אַצִּילוֹת, const. אַצִּילֵי), m. properly to lean firmly, to be closely joined; hence, joint, shoulder, elbow, from אָצַל in the intensive form.

אָצַל (not used) to lean, to bend, towards, from which אֵצֶל ,אֲצִיל, אָצִיל. The root is אָדַל, related to עָדַל.

אֵצֶל (with suff. אֶצְלִי), m. support, to lean upon, aside, only prepos. leaning upon, near, close by, מֵאֵצֶל, from near by; French *de chez.* (Comp. מִלִּפְנֵי), from which denom. אָצַל, to put aside, to separate, to select, to distinguish, with מִן and לְ, to select for somebody.—Niph. pass.—Hiph. fut. וַיָּאצֶל, to separate, to distinguish, perhaps אָצַל is in this sense primitive, and related to נָצַל.

אָצֵל 1) p. n. m. (nobly, of noble extraction), in pause אָצַל; 2) p. n. of a place, a cliff, from which must be distinguished בֵּית אָצֵל, p. n. of a place.

אֲצַלְיָהוּ p. n. m. (distinguished, or selected by God).

אֹצֶם p. n. m. (equiv. to עֹצֶם, strength.)

אֶצְעָדָה (equiv. to צְעָדָה), f. 1) ornament of the feet, or of the instep, a small chain round the instep, from צָעַד; compare Lat. *pedica,* ornament of the foot; *manica,* ornament of the hand; *tunica,* ornament of the waist; 2) bracelet, from its similarity with the ornament of the instep.

אָצַר to keep together, to accumulate.—Niph. pass.—Hiph. fut.—first pers. אוֹצְרָה denom. from אוֹצָר, to appoint somebody over the treasury, with עַל.

אֵצֶר p. n. m. (accumulation, heaping up).

אֶקְדָּח (rare) originally adj. m. very glowing, sparkling, dazzling colour; hence subst. אַבְנֵי אֶקְדָּח, high-coloured stones, (Authorised Version: 'pleasant stones'), Isa. 54:12. The root is קָדַח, to burn, to glow.

אַקּוֹ (rare) epic. roe, *caprea,* others *capra;* at all events the root is אַק, to which וֹן = וֹ is added as a suffix, and here like in עָז later, *n* is interpolated.

אר see אוֹר.

אָרָא (not used) to be strong, vigorous, courageous, related to בָּרַר, overwhelm; comp. Greek ἄρω, to make strong; Ἄρη-ς, the powerful one, Mars; ἄρειος, brave, valourous; from which is אָרָא p. n. אַרְאֵל, אַרְאֵלִי p. n. אַרְיֵה, אֲרָה, אֲרִיאֵל.

אָרָא p. n. m. (from אָרָא, properly strength; next, the strong one).

אֶרְאֵל (only with suff. אֶרְאֶלָּם) m. the strong one, the powerful one, hero, collectively, heroism, heroes, from אָרָא (אָרָא) and the termination formed therefore after אֵל, also אֲרִאֵל, (after the form כַּרְמֶל) which is indicated by the doubling of the ל. According to others it is a compound of אֲרִי אֵל lion of God, but in that case would be inexplicable, (*a*) the abbreviation of אֲרִי into אֲר ; (*b*) the doubling of the ל in אֵל for אֵל, only once אֲרִיאֵל for אֲרִאֵל occurs, for as it appears from a false signification by the punctuators, unless a noun formed from אָרָא is the foundation. The root is אָרָא.

אַרְאֵלִי p. n. m. (the heroic-minded) formed from אַרְאֵל.

אָרַב (fut. יֶאֱרֹב) to bind up, to tie, to twine, to knot; here only figuratively *κακὰ ῥάπ-τειν*, to weave or to spin deceit, to lie in wait with לְ, עַל, and accus.; part. אֹרֵב also collective, the plotting one, i. e. the ambush, if not אֹרֵב = אֹרֵב, like אֹבֵד = אֹבֵד.— Pi. part. only מְאָרְבִים, those lying in wait, or ambush, with עַל.— Hiph. fut. only וַיָּאֶרֶב = וַיָּרֶב, to cause laying in ambush.

אֲרָב p. n. f. (joining of houses, n. gent. אַרְבִּי) name of a town.

אֶרֶב m. 1) ambush; 2) place of ambush where beasts are encamped; (comp. מִסְתָּר, מַאֲרָב).

אֹרֶב (with suff. אָרְבּוֹ, אָרְבָּם) m. to concoct, to spin cunning, lying in wait.

אַרְבֵּאל (complete בֵּית אַרְבֵּאל) p. n. of a town, probably Arbêla in Galilee.

אַרְבֶּה m. locust, especially those that appear in swarms, (*gryllus gregarius*) from אָרַב, properly therefore, band, troop, swarm. See גָּזָם.

אָרְבָּה (from אָרַב, only pl. const. אָרְבּוֹת) f. properly snare; hence concoction of deceit, e. g. 'and he shall bring down their pride together with the spoils (אָרְבּוֹת) of his hands,' i. e. that which his hands have woven or concocted, (Isa. 25 : 11).

אֲרֻבָּה (from אָרַב ; pl. אֲרֻבּוֹת), f. properly that which is railed in, hence generally, rail, window, e. g. window of Heaven, from whence the rain comes, dove-cot, smoke-hole, or chimney, etc. R. אָרַב.

אֲרֻבּוֹת p. n. f. a place in the territory of Judah. See אָרַב.

אַרְבַּע m. (for רְבַע, f. אַרְבָּעָה, const. אַרְבַּעַת) ; 1) four ; also the fourth, in regulation of time; with suffix אַרְבַּעְתָּם, four of them; dual אַרְבַּעְתַּיִם, fourfold ; pl. אַרְבָּעִים, forty, often for a round number. See רֶבַע, רְבִיעִי, רֹבַע. 2) p. n. See קִרְיָה.

אַרְבַּע Aram. the same.

אָרַג (fut. יֶאֱרֹג; 2 pers. תֶּאֶרְגִּי); 1) to plait, e. g. the hair in curls; 2) to weave, part. אֹרֵג, אֹרְגָה weaver, masc. and fem.

אֶרֶג m. 1) tress, plait (of the hair); 2) the weaver's shuttle, originally the motion to and fro.

אַרְגֹּב p. n. f. name of a territory of Bashan, the other side of Jordan, with sixty towns. רָגָב in the Mishna, and רִיגוֹבָאָה in the Samaritan translation is generally assimilated to it. The signification is (from רֶגֶב): that which is cloddy, i. e. fruitful, (ἐρίβωλος).

אַרְגְּוָן (Aram.) equiv. to אַרְגָּמָן, which see. Probably from אֲרַג, to weave, with the termination vân; (comp. נִשְׁתְּוָן, מַרְחֶשְׁוָן), therefore originally that which is woven.

אַרְגַּז m. box, chest, derivation obscure. Probably *arg-as* is from אָרַג, i. e. אַרְגְּ, Lat. *arc-a*, with the termination ־ַז *as.* See the letter שׁ.

אַרְגָּמָן m. originally, stuff of various tints, from רָגַם = רָקַם, chequered colouring; hence generally that which is dyed purple,—purple. The form אַרְגְּוָן may be softened from the above word.

אָרַד (not used) probably equiv. to יָרַד to descend, to come down, to be afflicted, אַרְדְּ p. n., אַרְדּוֹן p. n., אֲרוֹד, p. n.

אַרְדְּ p. n. m. equiv. to אֶרֶד, misery (the unhappy one), patr. n. אַרְדִּי.

אַרְדּוֹן p. n. m. (*afflictus*).

אָרָה divides into three entirely unconnected significations; 1) not used = to אָרָא, to be strong, vigorous, from which אֲרִי, אַרְיֵה; 2) poetically, to pluck, to pluck out, to gather, also to gather the grapes (from the vine). From which אֻרְוָה, אַרְיֵה; 3) (not used) equiv. to אוּר, to burn; (comp. עָר, חָרָה, Lat. *are-o*, *ar-d-eo;* *uro*, etc., from which אֲרִיאֵל; all the three significations exist therefore only in the non-primitive words, but have throughout a grammatical analogy.

אֲרוּ (pronom. root) Aram. behold! see! there! but also conjunctive in אֲרוּם.

אֲרוֹד p. n. m. (sadness, affliction), also אֲרוֹדִי.

אַרְוַד p. n. f. a Phœnician insular town on the Phœnician coast, north of Tripoli, now called Ruad, hence gent. n. אַרְוָדִי.

אֻרְוָה (pl. אֻרְוֹת, const. אֻרְוֹת), f. a stable; hence generally the rack of a horse in the stable. From אָרָה to lug, to pluck.

אָרוּז (only pl. אֲרֻזִים), adj. m. to be made firm like a cedar, from אָרַז.

אֲרוּבָה see אֲרֻבָּה.

אֲרוּמָה p. n. f. (a rising ground), town in the territory of Shechem, according to Eus., later it was called Remphin, not far from Diospolis.

אֲרוֹמִים Ketib, once for the Keri אֲדוֹמִים.

אָרוֹן (const. אֲרוֹן) m. f. 1) ark, chest, a box, specially the holy ark of the tablets of the law, called אֲ' אֱלֹהִים, אֲ' הָעֵדוּת, אֲ' הַבְּרִית; 2) case for mummies, coffin. The etymology is uncertain.

אָרַז (not used) originally to be compressed, firm.

אֶרֶז m. cedar, (originally firm-rooted), cedar of Lebanon, in the Arab. several of the *genus pinus.*

אַרְזָה (from אֶרֶז), f. cedar-work, wainscoating; (compare עֵצָה). The root is אָרַז.

אָרַח (without fut.); 1) to go, to wander. The root is אָרַח, related to the Greek *ἔρχ-ο-μαι,* to go.—Part. אֹרֵחַ, wanderer, derivat. אֹרַח, אֹרְחָה; 2) (not used) to fix, to appoint, originally to direct, (*tendere*), to aim at.

אָרַח p. n. m. (equiv. to אֹרֵחַ, wanderer).

אֹרַח (pl. אֳרָחוֹת, const. אָרְחוֹת, with suff. אָרְחֹתָם, but also אֹרְחֹתָם, אֹרְחֹתֶיךָ); com. 1) way, equiv. to דֶּרֶךְ, but in this sense only poetical; figuratively walk of life, conduct, manner: as way of Jehovah, i. e. to walk with God, etc.; poetical, for wanderer, equiv. to אֹרְחָה; 2) certain (i. e. always returning) time, e. g. אֹרַח כַּנָּשִׁים the certain (monthly) time of women. See אָרַח, אָרַךְ.

אֹרַח (pl. אָרְחָן), Aram. the same. In Targum אוֹרַח.

אֹרְחָה (from אֹרֵחַ), f. originally wandering, pilgrimage, but also troop of persons, caravan.

אֲרֻחָה (אֹרַח), f. that which is fixed, measured, (of viands) portion, dish, from אָרַח. 2.

אֲרִי (pl. אֲרָיִים), epic. lion, originally the courageous, mighty one, *ἄρεί-ος,* from אָרָה = אָרָא, after the form טְלִי; (comp. לַיִשׁ, לָבִיא, לְבִי).

אֲרִיאֵל m. (the altar of God), fire-shrine of God, a poetical signification of the altar for burning-sacrifices, from אֲרִי, fire-hearth, and אֵל; hence also of Jerusalem, being the city of this sacred fire-hearth.

אֲרִידַי (Persian) p. n. m. yielding something worthy.

אֲרִידָתָא (Persian) p. n. m. the same.

אַרְיֵה (from אֲרִי ; for אַרְיָה, pl. אֲרָיוֹת), epic. lion. The fem. form has no influence on the genus. The root is אָרָה. 1.

אַרְיֵה (pl. אֲרָיוֹת) equiv. to אַרְנֶה.

אַרְיוֹךְ (Assyr.) p. n. m. the Arian or that which is Ariac, which name has been extended to the Persians, Medes, and Assyrians, אֲרִי is the known syllable, Ἀρι̛ο, in Persian names *ok* is the adj. termination. See the letter כ.

אֲרִיסַי (Persian) p. n. m.

אָרַךְ 1) (not used) to be equalised, appropriate, suitable, from which אֲרֻכָה ; 2) אָרַךְ, fut. יֶאֱרַךְ to extend, *tendere*, to be long, where the root is אָרַךְ, related to אָרַח, to reach, to extend.—Hiph. to extend forward (the tongue), to make long, to lengthen (the days), also without יָמִים; hence to make the days long, to live long, to endure; to postpone, to delay (the anger, the wrath), i. e. to be long-suffering; to extend, i. e. stay.

אֲרַךְ Aram. (like אָרַךְ 1), part. pass. אֲרִיךְ, *conveniens*, suitable.

אֹרֶךְ m. 1) length, extension, e. g. אֹרֶךְ רוּחַ, length of spirit, i. e. long-suffering, אֹרֶךְ הָאֵבֶר, length of the covering of the wing, i. e. long-winged; 2) delay, e. g. אֹרֶךְ אַפַּיִם, delaying the wrath, i. e. long-suffering, 'take me not away (do not destroy me) in thy long-suffering,' (Jer. 15 : 15), i. e. by delaying thy wrath against the enemies; 3) p. n. of a town, Areca, Arecca, (according to Ptolm.) on the Tiger, on the border between Suzana and Babylon, from which n. gent. אַרְכְּוָיֵא ; 4) p. n. of a city in Palestine, from which n. g. אַרְכִּי.

אָרֹךְ m. אֲרֻכָּה, f. adj. long, lasting, enduring, the usual adj. form.

אֶרֶךְ m. length, with יָמִים: length of life, with אַפַּיִם, patience. See אֹרֶךְ.

אַרְכָה (from אֹרֶךְ), Aram. f. length of time, length.

אֲרֻכָה and אֲרוּכָה, f. suitableness, equalisation; hence healing, amendment, salvation, generally joined to עָלָה, צָמַח. See אָרַךְ.

אַרְכֻּבָא (with suff. אַרְכֻּבָתֵהּ) Aram. f. equiv. to רְכֻבָא, knee.

אַרְכְּוָי gent. n. from אֹרֶךְ. 3.

אַרְכִּי gent. n. from אֹרֶךְ 4.

אָרַם (not used) equiv. to רָם, to be high, from which אֲרָם, אַרְמוֹן.

אֲרָם const. אֲרַם, p. n. (high land) Aramia in the farthest extension of the term, but especially Syria; as a national name Aram is mentioned for the son of Shem, Gen.

10 : 22; according to the Greeks it is situated in Ἄριμοι, Ἀραμαῖοι, according to the Hebrews it is only applied to Syrians, constructed with sing. pl. m. and f. The several territories of Aramea bear the names of: אֲ' צוֹבָה, אֲ' מַעֲכָה ; אֲ' נַהֲרַיִם ; אֲ' דַּמֶּשֶׂק פַּדַּן אֲרָם ; אֲרַם בֵּית רְחוֹב.

אֲרָם p. n. m. (the high one).

אַרְמוֹן (pl. const. אַרְמְנוֹת, the ô is dropped), m. palace, castle, citadel, generally comprising several buildings; hence next to בַּיִת, palace. The derivation is obscure, if not, אָרַם is taken for the root.

אֲרַמִּי m. gent. אֲרַמִּיָּה and אֲרַמִּית, f. (also as an adv.) אֲרַמִּים, pl. Aramites, Syrians, Mesopotamians. אֲרָמִית in Aramaic, i. e. in Aramaic language.

אַרְמֹנִי p. n. m. (probably = עַרְמֹנִי, the plane-tree, slender).

אֲרָן p. n. m. (the slender one; אָרַן, according to the Arab. to be slender, slim, related to אָרַם).

אֹרֶן m. 1) kind of cedar, (originally the slender one), from which masts are made. See אֹרֶן, אָרַן. 2) p. n. m.

אַרְנֶבֶת epic. hare, originally plucking, used of the plucking, mowing of grass. The root is רָנַב, which see.

אַרְנוֹן p. n. m. (the murmuring, rushing one, from רָנַן), name of a river and valley (נַחַל) between the countries of Albelka and Karrak, the present Mug'eb.

אַרְנָן p. n. m. (the slender one).

אֲרַוְנָה p. n. m. (the same), Ketib אֲרַנְיָה, Keri אֲרַוְנָה, and אוֹרְנָה, the same.

אֲרַע (def. אַרְעָא Aram.) m. the earth, equiv. to אֶרֶץ; as an adv. below, beneath.

אַרְעִי (Aram.) adj. m. the lower one; formed from אֲרַע.

אַרְעִי (const. אַרְעִית, Aram.) f. soil, floor; this termination is an abstract form.

אַרְפָּד (Syr. רְפָד) p. n. f. (couch, from רָפַד), Syr. a town not far from Epiphania, (חֲמָת), on the Orontes.

אַרְפַּכְשַׁד p. n. of Semitic tribe, whose territory bore the same name; hence the province Ἀῤῥαπαχῖτις in northern Assyria is taken for it. It is said that the Chaldees descend from this Semitic tribe, which, however, the syllable כֶּשֶׂד does not indicate (they are called כֶּשֶׂד).

אֶרֶץ (with the article הָאָרֶץ, with â of motion, אַרְצָה, pl. אֲרָצוֹת), f. (rarely m.) 1) the earth as a continent in contrast to sea; circle of the earth in contrast to Heaven;

next, land generally (אֲדָמָה, תֵּבֵל, אֶ׳ יַבָּשָׁה), fatherland, especially with the Hebrews, Jewish land; earth for soil, *humus;* אַרְצָה, unto earth, *humi;* earth as an element, clod of earth; 2) inhabitants of the earth, signifying everything that moves or creeps on the earth. The pl. signifies countries, especially heathen countries. The word is primitive.

אַרְצָא p. n. m.

אֲרַע (Aram.) equiv. to אֶרֶץ (ע=*gh*, changed into ק=*q*).

אָרַר (1 pers. pret. אָרֹתִי, fut. יָאֹר), to execrate, with the accus. אֹרְרֵי יוֹם those that curse the day, sorcerers; imperat. אֹר and אָרָה, (ôra) before Makkaf, cursers; (comp. קָבַב, נָקַב, קִלֵּל).—Niph. only part. pl. נֵאָרִים, pass.—Pi. denouncing vehemently; הַמַּיִם הַמְאָרְרִים the curse-causing waters.—Hoph. pass.

אֲרָרָט p. n. of a country in Armenia, which is called so to this day, between the Araxes and Ormia, then also for Armenia in general; comp. מִנִּי, תּוֹגַרְמָה. The Targ. renders קַרְדּוּ, קַרְדוֹן, קַרְדּוּנְיָא, i. e. the mountain Gudi, south-west of the sea Van, in the Pashalic Seherezu, which belongs to the Kurdish mountain.

אֲרָרִי p. n. m. (equiv. to הֲרָרִי).

אָרַשׂ (not used) originally to seize, (אָחַז), to take, (נָשָׂא) to take something up, to raise something; only Pi. אֵרַשׂ, generally with accus. אִשָּׁה, to betroth, properly to take a wife for oneself, (לוֹ), quite like נָשָׂא in use and signification. The price for which she was betrothed, with בְּ.—Pu. 3 pers. f. אֹרָשָׂה, part. מְאֹרָשָׂה, pass. (of the girl to be betrothed. See יָרַשׁ.

אָרַשׁ (not used) to seek after something, to desire, to request. The root is אָרַשׁ, related to דָּרַשׁ, from which אֲרֶשֶׁת.

אֲרֶשֶׁת f. the seeking, desiring, requesting.

אַרְתַּחְשַׁשְׂתָּא, אַרְתַּחְשַׁסְתְּא, אַרְתַּחְשַׁשְׂתְּא, (Persian) p. n. m. Arterxerses, a Persian king, which name Pseudo-Smerds and Arterxerses Longimamus bore; the orthography appears to be similar to that found in an inscription by Nakshi, Rustum, and on several Pellevie medals: *Artha-shedz;* if not another derivation is to be adopted, viz. from *Arta*—(אַרְתָּ) *K'sha*—(חְשָׁא) *Sadeh*—(סְתָּא) i. e. son of the great king, on account of the Heb. orthog.

אֲשַׂרְאֵל p. n. m.

אֶשְׂרִיאֵל p. n. m. patron. אַשְׂרִיאֵלִי.

אֵשׁ (with suff. אִשִּׁי, אֶשְׁכֶם), f. (rare, m.) fire in manifold applications; fire of God, for lightning; of the heat of the sun, of brightness, shining, glimmering, of the flame or wrath of war, etc. The root is אָשַׁשׁ 1.

אִשׁ (equiv. to אֵשׁ = יֵשׁ) he is, it is there; (comp. Aram. אִית), originally part. from אִישׁ, Aram. אית to be. See אִית.

אשׁ (pl. אֻשִּׁין, Aram.) m. foundation-ground, from אָשַׁשׁ; see אָשַׁשׁ. II.

אֶשְׁבֵּל p. n. m. (equiv. to אֶשְׁבַּעַל), patron. ־לִי. The component parts are בֵּל, *belus*, and אִשׁ, man, since the form אִשׁ־אִישׁ; (comp. אֵל, אַל in אֵל) is abbrev. to אִשׁ, אֵשׁ in p. n. m. Compare in a Phœnecian inscription, אשכתי = אַשְׁכְּתִּי man of Kition, Cyprian.

אֶשְׁבָּן p. n. m. the man of understanding; אִישׁ־בֵּן, see אֶשְׁבֵּל.

אֶשְׁבֵּעַ p. n. m. (the passionate, violent one; בֵּעַ, part. form from בּוּעַ = בָּעָה, which see. See אֶשְׁבֵּל).

אֶשְׁבַּעַל p. n. m. otherwise אִישׁ־בֹּשֶׁת בַּעַל and אִישׁ · בֹּשֶׁת and אִשׁ are equal.

אָשַׁר (not used) to pour out, to moisten, to irrigate. The root is אָשַׁר; (comp. שַׁד breast, with the original idea to moisten.) Herefrom אֶשֶׁד, אֲשֵׁדָה.

אֶשֶׁד m. pouring out, emptying (of rivers and brooks); hence the place into which the rivers or brooks empty themselves.

אֲשֵׁדָה (pl. אַשְׁדּוֹת), f. the same; hence foot of a mountain where such discharge takes place.

אַשְׁדּוֹד p. n. (fortress, from שָׁדַד), a town of a Philistine principality, (*Ἄζωτος*) now called Ashdod.—Patron. ־ִי, f. ־ִית.

אָשָׁה (not used) equiv. to אָשַׁשׁ, to be encamped, spread out easy, to be firm in foundation.

אִשָּׁה f. fire, only Ketib אִשָּׁתָם, their fire, Keri אֵשׁ תָּם; from which אֶשְׁתָּאוֹל. p. n.

אִשָּׁה (with suff. אִשְׁתִּי, אִשְׁתְּךָ, once אִשְׁתֵּךְ, pl. נָשִׁים, const. נְשֵׁי rare אִשּׁוֹת), f. woman, married or single; hence of a bride, a concubine; next, generally signifying the fem. gender (of animals), also an epithet of reproach for cowards; with emphasis, a woman as she ought to be, i. e. virtuous; with רְעוּת, אָחוֹת in two opposite sentences, the one—the other. The form is derived from the ancient אִשׁ, from which even

אִישׁ is elongated. (See אֶשְׁת), the pl. somewhat changed from the complete form אֲנָשִׁים,. (See אִישׁ, אֱנוֹשׁ.)

אִשֶּׁה (const. אִשֵּׁה, pl. const. אִשֵּׁי) m. fire of sacrifices, flame on the altar; hence generally sacrifice, offering, even that which is not to be burnt. See אֵשׁ. The ê termination is for â, but the fem. gender is here suppressed.

אֻשְׁיָה (only אָשְׁוֹיֹתֶיהָ in the Keri), f. pillar, from אָשָׁה, for which the Ketib אָשְׁיֹתֶיהָ, which see.

אִישׁוֹן m. only Keri, from אִישׁ, c. from אִישׁ, formed with the diminutive termination וֹן; that אִישׁ may be thus abridged, is proved from the pp. nn. composed therefrom. (See אֶשְׁבָּל). The signification does not vary from אִישׁוֹן, as the Ketib has really אִישׁוֹן.

אַשּׁוּר (not אָשׁוּר, pl. אֲשֻׁרִים) f. 1) step, walk, *gressus*, hence fig. 'my foot hath held his (God's) steps' (Job. 23 : 11) i. e. I have followed his steps. The root is אָשַׁר, equiv. to שׁוּר, which see); 2) only pl. אֲשֻׁרִים, from תְּאַשּׁוּר =אַשּׁוּר a kind of cedar; hence שֵׁן בַּת־אֲשֻׁרִים, ivory, daughter of the cedar of Sherbin, i. e. set in such kind of wood; comp. אָשַׁר, from which אָשׁוּר is a pass. form.

אַשּׁוּר f. 1) equiv. to אָשׁוּר, which form need not be considered as a fault in the punctuation; 2) p. n. Assyria, complete אֶרֶץ אַשּׁוּר,(rare אֶרֶץ נִמְרוֹד) origin. only a small province in the capital of Nineveh, (Kurdistan), where the cities רְחֹבוֹת עִיר, כֶּלַח, רֶסֶן are separately named, later, however, signifying Assyria in its largest extension, so that even the ruins thereof (Babylonia and Persia) were called so. Ptolemy, 'Ἀσσυρία, Strabo, 'Ἀτουρία (אַתּוּר Aram.) The appell. signification is obscure.

אַשּׁוּרִים p. n. m. Arabian national tribe.

אַשְׁחוּר p. n. m. (אַשׁ equiv. to אִישׁ, a free man). Root חוּר.

אֻשְׁיָה f. support, foundation, fortress, only Keri; in Ketib, however, אָשְׁוִיָּה both forms of אָשָׁה.

אֲשִׁימָא p. n. of a deity in Syria; comp. Zendic Eshem; Adêw, or Persian *Eshmeni*, (devil) the special signification is obscure.

אֲשֵׁרָה see אֲשֵׁירָה.

אָשִׁישׁ (only pl. const. אֲשִׁישֵׁי), m. founding, fortress, foundation-pillars; next, ruin, originally a piece of the foundation of the for-trees. The root is אָשַׁשׁ II. comp. also אָשָׁה.

אֲשִׁישָׁה (pl. ־ִים, ־וֹת) f. cake, originally stretched out, spread out, like צַפִּיחִית, πλακόεις, from stretching out, spreading out; hence raisin-cake: אֲשִׁישֵׁי עֲנָבִים; cake of sacrifice, etc. The root is אָשַׁשׁ II.

אָשַׁךְ (not used) probably to bind, to bind together, to tie up. The root is אַ־שַׁךְ Rab. Pu. אֻשַּׁךְ with the original idea of tying, from which אֶשֶׁךְ, אֶשְׁכֹּל.

אֶשֶׁךְ m. that which is tied together, cord; only: cord of the testicles, regularly formed from אָשַׁךְ, to tie up, to bind up.

אֶשְׁכֹּל (pl. with suff. אַשְׁכְּ׳, אַשְׁכְּלוֹת from אָשַׁךְ, with ־ל as a diminutive termination), m. tender binding, joining; of grapes, berries: cluster of grapes, (Aram. סְגֹל) from סָג in the same sense; next, generally grape, of the date and vine; of the cyprus flower; comp. Talm. אֶשְׁכֹּל־שֶׁל־בֵּיצִים, a string of eggs.

אַשְׁכְּנַז p. n. of a people of Japheth, which is connected with the Crimeans (גֹּמֶר), and with the Armenians, it signifies Askania in Phrygia, the Arabs use it to signify slaves, the Jews to signify *Germania*, Germans, all resting on the hypothesis as to the descent of these people.

אֶשְׁכָּר (with suff. אֶשְׁכָּרֵךְ), m. originally greatly rewarding, making presents; hence donation, present, from שָׂכַר.

אֵשֶׁל m. tamaric, according to others for אֵלֶשׁ, Greek, ἄλσ-ος, grove; the etymology is obscure.

אָשֵׁם, אָשַׁם fut. יֶאְשַׁם, pl. יֶאְשְׁמוּ; 1) to be desolate, waste, lonely, e. g. מִזְבֵּחַ of the altar, related to שָׁם, יָשַׁם; 2) figur. to be desolate, i. e. to be damned, to be mentally destroyed, e. g. 'Samaria shall be desolate (damned), for she has rebelled against her God,' (Hos. 13 : 16); 3) to be guilty, to commit a trespass, with לְ of the person, and לְ, בְּ of the subject, by which one becomes guilty, inasmuch as guilt, destruction, desolation, and isolation are associated in the same idea.

אָשָׁם (pl. אֲשָׁמִים) m. 1) guilt, guiltiness; 2) the subject of guiltiness, that which a person appropriates unjustly to himself; 3) the sacrifice for atoning such guilt, trespass-offering, (different from חַטָּאת).

אָשֵׁם adj. m. guilty, i. e. either

*lo*aded with the guilt, or bound to atone for the guilt.

אָשָׁם (const. ־ַת), m. originally inf. Kal; hence לְאַשְׁמָה בָהּ, to commit trespass therein, but generally a subst.: 1) trespass-offering, atoning by the trespass-offering; 2) damnation, 'for whereas the damnation of the Lord is already upon us,' (Auth. Version, 'we have offended against the Lord already,'); 2 Chron. 28: 13; 3) idol, e. g. הַנִּשְׁבָּעִים בְּאַשְׁמַת שֹׁמְרוֹן they that swear by the godhead (perhaps אֲשִׁימַת is the reading) of Samaria.

אַשְׁמָן (from אָשַׁם, only pl. אַשְׁמַנִּים) m. a desert, solitude, wilderness, equiv. to צַלְמָוֶת, (צַלְמוּת) region of shadows; hence בָּאַשְׁמַנִּים כַּמֵּתִים, 'we are in desolate places as dead *men*,' (Isa. 59:10) the tradition renders it correctly, darkness. Root אָשַׁם, to be desolate; the termination ־ָן doubles the nasal sound.

אַשְׁמֻרָה (pl. אַשְׁמֻרוֹת), f. night-watch, the third division of the night, *vigilia*, Φυλακή; the second is called: אַשְׁמֹרֶת הַתִּיכוֹנָה; the first: רֹאשׁ אַשְׁמֻרוֹת; the last: אַשְׁמֹרֶת הַבֹּקֶר. Root שָׁמַר.

אַשְׁמֹרֶת f. the same, formed from אַשְׁמֻרָה.

אֶשְׁנָב (with suff. אֶשְׁנַבִּי), m. trellis, originally the fitting of one thing into another, = אֶשְׁלָב; (see שָׁלַב; comp. חָרַךְ, שְׂבָךְ, אֲרֻבָּה). Root שָׁנַב, equiv. to שָׁלַב.

אַשְׁנָה p. n. m. shining brightly! The root is שָׁנָה.

אֶשְׁעָן p. n. of a town, (to lean strongly), from שָׁעַן.

אָשַׁף (not used) probably only branched out from כָּשַׁף, the root of which is שָׁף, moving of the lips, murmuring, and generally seems to have signified secret movement.

אַשָּׁף (from אָשַׁף, pl. אַשָּׁפִים), m. magician, but different from כַּשָּׁף, others connect it with σοφός.

אָשַׁף Aram. the same, but the pl. אָשְׁפִין, def. אָשְׁפַיָּא.

אַשְׁפָּה f. quiver, originally sack, from שָׁפָה, related to שָׁפַח, to spread out; compare אַמְתַּחַת; בְּנֵי אַשְׁפָּה, sons of the quiver, arrows.

אַשְׁפְּנַז (Aram.) p. n. m. perhaps equivalent to אַשְׁכְּנַז.

אֶשְׁפָּר m. measure, portion, from שָׁפַר; the ancients translate it a piece, from שָׁפַר = שָׁבַר.

אַשְׁפֹּת (only pl. אַשְׁפַּתּוֹת), f. heap, dung-hill, originally that which is heaped together, piled up, from סָפָה = שָׁפָה, to heap up.

אַשְׁפֹּת (from אַשְׁפָּה), pl. manure-hill, heap of dirt, (from שָׁפָה = קָפָה), rubbish; hence שַׁעַר הָאַשְׁפֹּת (abbreviated הַשְׁפֹּת), the gate of rubbish.

אַשְׁקְלוֹן p. n. a Philistine prince-town between Gaza and Jamnia, (LXX. Ἀσκάλων, 1 Macc. Ἀσκαλώνιον); hence also the appellation *Ascaloniæ. Escalotes, Shallotts.* Gent. n. ־לוֹנִי, the deriv. is obscure.

אָשַׁר (not used); 1) equiv. to שׁר to walk; hence אָשׁוּר, walk, step; 2) equiv. to יָשַׁר, to be straight, rising above; hence of the straight and erect position; (compare תְּאַשּׁוּר, אֲשֶׁר), figurat. of the straightforward right conduct in undertakings; hence to walk successfully.—Pi. (from 2) to make straight, aright, to conduct (the steps), e. g. 'Enter not into the path (do not conduct your steps) of the wicked,' etc. (Prov. 4 : 14); figuratively to call one blessed, happy, from אָשַׁר, to be happy.—Pu. to be conducted, to be led straightforward, made happy.

אֲשֶׁר 1) relat. pron. demonst. without reference to gender or number, explaining a preceding noun: he, who, etc. As the most important particle, however, in compound sentences, it stands: 1) where it signifies in the power of a noun at the beginning of a sentence the relation thereof, and being a kind of particle is completed by the pronoun or suffix according to its connection with the subject or object, e. g. 'every moving thing (אֲשֶׁר הוּא) which liveth,' (Gen. 9 : 3), where הוּא gives to the relative אֲשֶׁר the signification of the subject: which (m. f. and neuter) אֲשֶׁר כְּלָאוֹ, 'whom he had shut up,' (Jer 32 : 3), where ־וֹ gives to אֲשֶׁר the signification of object. This completion is necessary when אֲשֶׁר relates to a subordinate idea, e. g. אֲשֶׁר—וֹ, whose (son spoke); אֲשֶׁר־לוֹ, to whom (he said), where אֲשֶׁר expresses neither the idea of subject or object; otherwise the completion may be omitted, as it is omitted with אֲשֶׁר when it relates to nouns that express place, time, manner, and mode. Since אֲשֶׁר without completion has merely a relative signification, different, therefore, from the relat. prons. of other languages which are of a pure pronominal character, it may be connected in various manners, e. g. אֲשֶׁר שָׁם where, אֲשֶׁר מִשָּׁם wherefrom, or from whence,

אֲשֶׁר שָׁמָּה whereto or whither; or with the pronoun of the 1st and 2d person, (אֲשֶׁר הוֹצֵאתִיךָ, אֲשֶׁר בָּרִיתִי); in other languages, however, it is only possible with the 3d person. The absence of the pronominal completion often makes אֲשֶׁר an independent relative word, and as such it stands: (*a*) to describe minutely a noun named, e. g. man that (אֲשֶׁר) (were) with him, but as such a descriptive sentence may be easily replaced by a fit adjective apposition, the relative particle is often omitted, e. g. in a land, (that) not theirs, a land (that) he knew, etc., by which an abbreviation of the sentence occurs; (*b*) introducing a new noun not yet mentioned in the preceding sentence, e. g. 'he who (אֲשֶׁר was over the household,' (2 Kings 18: 18); know what (אֶת־אֲשֶׁר) will occur, etc., which, however, is omitted by poets; (*c*) if it gives a general idea of cause and effect, e. g. כָּל־הַיָּמִים אֲשֶׁר הָיָה הוּא שָׁאוּל לַיְיָ ' as long as he liveth (all the days) he shall be lent to the Lord,' (1 Sam. 1: 28); 2) as relative conjunction, *quod*, like כִּי, שֶׁ, but not so distinct and frequent e. g. עוֹד אֲשֶׁר, yet is it that; בַּאֲשֶׁר, inasmuch, where; כַּאֲשֶׁר, as much, like as; עַל־אֲשֶׁר therefore that; אַחֲרֵי אֲשֶׁר, after that, or after intrans. verbs where אֲשֶׁר points out the object, e. g. he shewed that (אֲשֶׁר) he was a Jew; more frequently instead of it אֶת־אֲשֶׁר, or after the const. state of a noun, or after prepositions, e. g. day that, i. e. which day, *quando*.

אָשֵׁר p. n. m. happy one.

אשר (with suff. אָשְׁרִי) m. happiness, from אָשַׁר, 2.

אֲשַׂרְאֵלָה p. n. m. equiv. to אֲשַׂרְאֵל, happiness from God.

אֲשֵׁרָה (rare אֲשֵׁירָה, pl. ־ִים, ־וֹת), f. originally luck or star of fortune (Venus), herefrom is the name of the Syrian divinity, (otherwise עַשְׁתֹּרֶת), connected with בַּעַל; the pl. however, signifies images, statues of this goddess, (connected with פְּסִילִים, מַצֵּבוֹת). The root is אָשַׁר.

אֲשָׁרִים (only const. אַשְׁרֵי, with suff. אַשְׁרֵיךָ, אַשְׁרֶיךָ, אַשְׁרָיו, m. happiness, salvation; interj. hail! happy he! the form of the const. state remains even before the short suff. because the word only occurs in the pl.

אֻשַּׁרְנָא (Aram.) m. wall, of uncertain derivation.

I. אָשַׁשׁ (not used) equiv. to אָתַת, אָזָא, to burn, to glow.

II. אָשַׁשׁ (Aram. אֲשַׁשׁ,) equiv. to אִשָּׁה, which see.

אֵשֶׁת f. wife, secondary form of אִשָּׁה, but not a const. of the same; hence also absolute, formed from the ancient form אִשׁ, man; (hence lengthened אִישׁ), const. אֵשֶׁת (in pp. nn.)

אֶשְׁתָּאֹל p. n. a town (LXX. 'Εσθαόλ Ασταώλ, Eus. 'Εσθαούλ) in the territory of Dan, 10 miles from Eleutheropolis; gent. n. ־אֻלִי.

אֶשְׁתַּדּוּר (Aram.) m. sedition, meeting, from שְׁדַר.

אֶשְׁתּוֹן p. n. m. (the fiery one).

אֶשְׁתְּמֹהַ and אֶשְׁתְּמוֹעַ, p. n. of a town of priests.

אָת (Aram.) m. equiv. to Heb. אוֹת. The root is אוּת, as in the Hebrew.

אַתְּ equiv. to Heb. אַתָּה, m. thou, which see.

אַתְּ pause אָתְּ, person. pron. f. thou, equiv. to אַתִּי; the latter form is contracted, and abbreviated from אַנְתִּי, like אַתָּה from אַנְתָּה, and seldom אַתְּ is contracted from the masc. אַנְתָּה.

אֵת (with suff. אִתּוֹ, pl. אִתִּים), m. hatchet, ploughshare, hoe, originally the instrument which cuts through and digs in, from אוּת, to make incisions, to engrave. See אוּת, אוֹת. Irregularly also occurs the form אִתִּים, אֶתִּיכֶם.

אֵת (before Makkeph ־אֶת, alone אֵת), refl. pron. the same, ipse, formed from a demonst. pron. (comp. αὐτός). The pronom. root is used: 1) joined with suff. in order to replace the omitted accus. of the pers. pron.; since the suffix cannot stand alone, hence always את occurs, e. g. 'I had slain thee,' (אֹתְךָ) Numb. 22 : 33; where the emphasis require the accus. of the person. pron. Likewise when the verb in the person. pronoun has two objects, whilst the suffix of the verb can only express one, where it is with the suff. is expressed by אֹתוֹ him; אֹתָהּ her; אֹתְךָ thee; אֹתָךְ irregular; אֶתְכֶם (rare אֹתְכֶם), אֶתְהֶן, אֶתְכֶן, (אֹתְהֶן) 2) before nouns, generally when they occur at the beginning or are fixed, or personal, e. g. whom? (אֶת־מִי); that which (אֶת־אֲשֶׁר); this (אֶת־זֶה); all this (אֶת־כֹּל), etc., but it always expresses the accus. which the active connection generally calls forth; hence the necessity of translating the verbs carefully, e. g. 'let this land be given,' (Numb.

32: 5) (יָפֶן). 'Let not this thing displease thee,' (2 Sam. 11: 25) (אַל יֵרַע), etc., where traces of the old demonst. signification are yet found dispersed here and there, like as in the Bulgaro Aramaic.

אֶת־,אֵת (sign of the accus.) see under where it belongs.

אֵת, אֶת־ (pronom. root, with suff. אִתִּי) prep. with, generally expressing association and accompaniment; hence also, by, at, with, e. g. שָׁכַב אֶת־, to lie with; עָמַד־אֶת־, to stand by; לִין אֶת־, to tarry over night with, יָשַׁר אֶת־ to sit with, עָרַךְ מִלְחָמָה אֶת־, רִיב, הִשְׁלִים, כָּרַת בְּרִית, הִתְחַתֵּן, to make war, to combat, to make peace, to enter into a covenant, to intermarry with, etc. Otherwise it has the quality of עִם, a possession in the soul or mind, to will, or physically to appoint, and all similar secondary significations may be traced back to the original with, by, at, even where it seems to signify near, next to. מֵאֵת from by, from with, i. e. away from that with whom it was (like מֵעִם) *de chez quelqu'un*, after verbs signifying going away, sending, receiving, buying, requesting, etc., etc.

אֶתְבַּעַל p. n. m. (possession of Baal) אֶת const. from אִית = יֵשׁ possession, Joseph. Ἰθόβαλος, Εἰθώβαλος, (אִיתְבַּעַל).

אֲתָא (Aram.) the same as the Heb. אָתָה, (3 pers. pl. אֲתוֹ, inf. מֵתָא, imp. pl. אֱתוֹ. Af. הַיְתִי, inf. הַיְתָיָה. Pass. perf. third pers. f. הֵיתָיִת, pl. הֵיתָיוּ).

אָתָה, אָתָא (pl. אָתָנוּ, fut. יֶאֱתֶה, תֵּאת, יֵתֵא, pl. יֶאֱתָיוּ, with suff. יֶאֱתָיֵנִי, part. pl. f. אֹתִיּוֹת, imper. אֵתָיוּ); 1) to come, with עַד, לְ of the person to which one comes; 2) like בּוֹא, to occur, to befall, with the accus.; 3) to pass by.—Hiph. הֵתָיוּ imperat. bring. This root is secondary from אִית, hence i. e. אֵת, which see.

אַתָּה (אַתְּה from אַנְתָּה, as the Aram. and Arab. have it), p. אָתָּה, pers. pron. m. thou, also written אַתְּ, seldom entirely abbreviated אַתְּ, the essential root-syllable is תָּה, next to an ancient form תּוּ, (analogous to הוּ, like fem. ת tĕ, next to the ancient form תִּי, (analogous הִי), אַן is a preformative demonst. syllable, like in אָנִי, אָנֹכִי, etc.

אָתוֹן (pl. אֲתֹנֹת), f. she-ass; the Arab. root *atana* is a deriv., for in אָתוֹן the וֹן is suff. and אַת is the root.

אַתּוּן (Aram.) m. oven, chimney, origin. fire, from אתּ = אֵשׁ, to burn, Gr. αἴθ-ειν, with the suff. ־וּן.

אַתּוּק (in the Ketib for אַתִּיק, which see), m. settle, applied to galleries and buildings.—Targ. זִיז, περίστυλον. Root אָרַתק.

אַתִּי (only in Ketib); i. e. אַתְּ from אַנְתִּי pers. pron. f. thou, like אַתְּ which is abbrev. from it.

אַתַּי, אִיתַי p. n. m. the possessor. See אִית.

אַתִּיק (Aram. עַתִּיק. The root is אָרַתק, which see), m. settle, of buildings and galleries, equiv. to אַתּוּק.

אַתֶּם (abbreviated from אַתּוּם), pers. pron. 2 pers. pl. m. ye. The old form תּוּם, (*an* is added) is yet found in תוּ of suffix.

אֵתָם p. n. m. an Egyptian place, LXX. 'Οθώμ.

אֶתְמוֹל (= אֶת־מוֹל, like אֶל־מוֹל), אֶתְמוֹל, אִתְּמוֹל adv. yesterday, long since. See מוֹל and תְּמוֹל, abbrev. from אֶתְמוֹל.

אַתָּן bad orthography for אֵיתָן, which see.

אַתֵּן, אַתֵּנָה or אַתֵּנָה, pers. pron. 2 pers. pl. fem. ye, the reading אַתֵּן might perhaps be derived therefrom.

אֶתְנָה m. present, reward wages of a prostitute, from תָּנָה, originally an adj.

אֶתְנִי p. n. m. (equiv. to אֶתְנִי, to be generous, liberal in giving.

אֶתְנַן (pl. אֶתְנַנִּים), m. gift, present, generally a present to a prostitute. The ground form תְּנַן is for תְּנַן, from תָּנָה.

אָתַק (not used) to move away, to make a settle, used of the building of a terrace, to move forward, to move away, to move aside, related to רָתַק, עָתַק which in their original signification meet together.

אֲתַר (Aram.) def. אַתְרָא, m. place; hence אֲתַר דִּי, equiv. to Heb. מְקוֹם אֲשֶׁר, to the place where = where; hence בָּאתַר, i. e. בְּאַתַר, after; אַלְתַּר (Talmud.) equiv. to אַל אֲתַר, on the spot, soon. The signification of the root is obscure.

אֲתָרִים p. n. m. (places, neighbourhood, countries).

אֲתַת (Aram.) equiv. to אָשַׁשׁ, to burn, to glow, from which אַתּוּן, which see.

ב

ב called *bet*, beth, בֵּית (= בַּיִת pl. בֵּיתִין and בָּתּוֹת), signifies house, like א taken from the ancient form of letters, when hard, *b*, when soft, *v*, and as a numerical 2.

By the close relationship of the labials, *beth* interchanges with פ, ו, מ, *i. e.* p, f, w, m, e. g. בָּרֶקֶת, Sanscr. *marakata*, פֶּצֶל ; בָּצַל, פֶּצַע ; בָּצַע, בָּנַר ; פָּנַר, פַּחַת ; בַּחַת, מָרָא ; בָּרָא, זְמַן ; זְבַן, בָּרַח ; דִּימוֹן, דִּיבוֹן ; צָבַת, צָפַד, Sanscrit *wrig*, and others.

ב A) insep. prepos. is the general grammatical preposition for expressing approximation, and the various significations proceeding from this original meaning develop themselves as follows: 1) the purely local, temporal, or circumstantial nearness; hence (*a*) on, by, at, (from the question where) as בָּעַיִן at the well; בַּשָּׁמַיִם, on heaven; בַּשַּׁעַר, at the gate; בַּמִּקְדָּשׁ, at the sanctuary; and the phrases עַיִן בְּעַיִן, eye to eye; חֹדֶשׁ בְּחֹדֶשׁ, שָׁנָה בְּשָׁנָה, פַּעַם בְּפַעַם, שַׁבָּת בְּשַׁבָּת, יוֹם בְּיוֹם, etc., in this sense many verbs are construed with it, when the immediate approximation is to be expressed, e. g. קָרָא בְ, to call upon; נִגַּשׁ בְּ, to approach to some one; also the verbs of attachment and adherence, דָּבַק בְּ, to cleave to one; אָחַז בְּ, הֶחֱזִיק בְּ to hold to one; נָגַע בְּ, to touch a thing; פָּגַע בְּ, to fall or attack a thing; also the verbs of confidence and faith, as holding fast to any thing, although signifying those of the contrary, e. g. חָסָה, בָּטַח, הֶאֱמִין, נִזְהַר, בָּגַד בְּ, מָעַל, פָּשַׁע, חָטָא, כִּחֵשׁ, מָרַד בְּ, also the verbs of asking, or seeking the deity, e. g. שָׁאַל בְּ, דָּרַשׁ בְּ ; also the verbs of taking pleasure in anything, or of the contrary, e. g. אָהַב, רָצָה, בָּחַר, גָּעַל, מָאַס ; עָלַץ, עָלַז, גִּיל, שָׂמַח, קָט, נָשַׁר בְּ ; also the verbs of resting of the senses upon something, e. g. חָזָה, רָאָה בְּ, to look, to see upon; שָׁמַע בְּ, to hearken to; הֵרִיחַ בְּ, to smell at; likewise the verbs of the spiritual resting upon something in thought or in speech, e. g. שִׂיחַ בְּ, the thought or speech to rest upon something; עָנָה הֵעִיד, הָגָה, דִּבֶּר בְּ where it may be rendered on or upon; (*b*) the expression of accompaniment, or attendance: with, originally near something, or instrumental by something; which may be rendered, by, through; as בַּחִצִּים ; בִּנְצָחָה, בִּתְרוּעָה ; hence the great number of advbs. and adjs. formed by such בְּ ; if placed before nouns, e. g. בְּכֹחַ with strength, i e. strong, thus also בְּשָׁלִי, בְּפֶרֶךְ, בְּקֶרִי, בְּלָט, בְּתוֹם, בִּתְבוּנָה, בְּגֵאוּת, etc. In this sense ²⁴ stands after verbs, which, by the assistance of the בְּ, express the the idea of accompaniment: e. g. הִתְנַבֵּא בְ (through) קִדֵּם, פָּקַד, יָרַד, בָּא, etc.; hence עָבַד בְּ, to serve with somebody; נָשָׁה בְּ, to take usury through somebody, i. e. to lend; נִשְׁבַּע בְּ, to swear by somebody; (*c*) by, at, in reference to objects where it may be translated either within, e. g. of walls, of gates; or upon, if we speak of tall subjects; 2) the moving approximation, signifying as it were a continuous touching; hence (*a*) towards, thereon, thereto, but distinct from אֶל where moving is expressed without approximation. In this sense many verbs of motion are construed with בְּ, when the motion connected with aiming remains within the limits of the movement, e. g. נָתַן בְּ, to give—in; דָּרַךְ בְּ, to tread—in; also the verbs of ruling and prevailing: עָצַר בְּ, to stop, to impede; מָשַׁל בְּ, רָדָה, verbs signifying a hostile attack directed against the mind: as צָחַק, קִלֵּל, דִּבֶּר, רִיב, נִלְחַם, קִנֵּא, חָרָה, קָצַף, הֵחֵל בְּ where in Latin *in* is used in this sense; (*b*) *in* (with accus. or abl.) since approximation is not only expressed by penetrating into a thing, but also by prevailing on space: e. g. בַּבַּיִת in the house; בָּעִיר, בָּאָרֶץ, in the town, in the land; thus, בְּפָנֵי, בְּאָזְנֵי, בְּעֵינֵי for certain forms. Figuratively to signify the mode and manner, e. g. בְּדֶרֶךְ, in or after the manner; בְּדָבָר, according to the command; בְּעֵצָה, according to the counsel; (*c*) in, equiv. to within, among, amongst, thus only a part of the whole; e. g. בַּקֹּשְׁרִים, among the conspirators = a conspirator; בְּכֹל, among all; God is (בְּעֹזְרָי) 'among my helpers = my helper,' (Ps. 118: 7); and in this sense also verbs the action of which refers only to a part of the whole, as הִכָּה בְּ, to smite (many); הִכָּה אֶת־, to smite (entirely); thus also אָכַל, שָׁתָה, הָרַג בְּ; (*d*) in, at, on, as shortly comprehending the whole according to its contents: בָּעוֹף, בַּבְּהֵמָה, (in) of fowl and cattle; figuratively to express the essence of which a thing consists, i. e. the existence of the subject comprehended in one quality, e. g. God is (בְּאֶחָד) in the unity, i. e. he is comprehended in the unity, is not conceivable without it, though the subordinate idea is only an adopted one.

Respecting the etymology of this prepos. it is neither abbreviated from בַּיִת (house), nor from בֵּין (between), nor to be derived from any noun, but it is, in its short form בְּ universally grammatical, as confirmed by analogy. With suff. בִּי, (which see); בְּךָ, בָּכָה, pause בָּךְ, בְּךָ, בּוֹ, בָּהּ, בָּנוּ, בָּהֶם, בָּכֶם, בָּכֶן, and בָּם, בָּהֵמָּה, בָּהֵן, and בָּהֶן, compounds, בְּעַד, בְּעוֹד, etc.—B.) It appears 1) as an abbrev. from בֵּן (son), in some pp. nn.: as, בְּקָהָל, בִּשְׁלָם, equiv. to בֶּן־קָהָל, בֶּן־שָׁלֵם, still more frequent in Arab.; 2) as an abbrev. from בֵּית in names of places, e.g. בְּעֶשְׁתְּרָה = בֵּית־עַ׳, but in both cases this abbreviation must not be extended too far.

בְּ see בְּעַד.

בָּא see בּוֹא.

בִּאָה (for בִּיאָה), f. (rare) entrance; (comp. אִיתוֹן), after the form קִימָה. Root בּוֹא.

בְּאִישָׁה (Aram.) f. wickedness, from בְּאֵשׁ. This form is made from the intensitive conj.

בָּאַר (not used) equiv. to בּוּר, *orare*, to bore, to dig, (related to בָּאַר), as generally with many verbs with the second radical א, are identical with verbs having the second radical ו (ע״ו); from which Piel בֵּאֵר; 1) to bore in, to dig in, to engrave (on tablets); 2) to dig out (the sense), to explain, (related to פָּתַר).

בְּאֵר with ä of motion בְּאֵרָה, with suff. בְּאֵרְךָ pl. בְּאֵרֹת, const. בְּאֵרֹת), f.; 1) pit, equiv. to בּוֹר; 2) well, complete בְּאֵר מַיִם חַיִּים, ‘fountain of living waters;’ 3) p. n. an encampment of the Israelites in the desert, complete בְּאֵר אֵילִים, (well of heroes); 4) p. n. of a place in the territory of Judah; 5) בַּעֲלַת בְּאֵר, also בַּעַל only, p. n. a place in the territory of Simeon.

בְּאֵר אֵלִים see בְּאֵר.

בְּאֵר לַחַי רֹאִי p. n. of the well of Agar, (well of beholding the living God), if not to read בְּאֵר לְחִי רֹאִי a well of the rock of beholding; (see לְחִי), since ל may thus be better explained.

בְּאֵר שֶׁבַע p. n. of a place in the territory of Simeon, (well of oath, well of covenant), Βηρσαβεέ (Βηρσουβεί).

בֹּאר (originally בְּאֵר Ketib for בּוֹר) f. water-pit, cistern, pl. בֹּארוֹת, several instances בֹּרֹת; see בּוֹר, בְּאֵר.

בְּאֵרָא p. n. m. (the explainer); see בְּאֵר.

בְּאֵרָה p. n. f.

בְּאֵרוֹת p. n. a town in the territory of Benjamin, Eus. Βηρώθ, gent. n. בְּאֵרֹתִי and בֵּרֹתִי.

בְּאֵרוֹת בְּנֵי־יַעֲקָן p. n. of an encampment of the Israelites in the desert, also בְּנֵי יַעֲקָן alone, which see.

בְּאֵרִי p. n. m. the illustrator.

בָּאַשׁ (only fut. יִבְאַשׁ) originally bad, odious, (*bos*) to be odious, to be bad, (see Hiph.) Aram. בְּאֵשׁ; hence to smell bad, odious, as bad quality is commonly expressed in the East by bad odour.—Niph. נִבְאַשׁ to shew oneself, bad or base, to make oneself hateful with somebody, with בְּ, אֶת i. e. to stand in bad odour with somebody.—Hiph. הִבְאִישׁ; 1) originally to make base, to act basely; hence to cast odium; hence to bring in evil repute, to make hateful, generally carrying out this figure אֶת־רֵיחַ, to make the savour to be abhorred, (Exod. 5 : 21); 2) to excite, to spread bad odour, (i. e. to become hateful, odious).—Hith. to make oneself hateful, only הִתְבָּאֲשׁוּ, with עִם with, etc.

בְּאֵשׁ (Aram.) the same, with עַל, (in contrast to בְּסַם); see בָּאַשׁ.

בְּאשׁ (with suff. בָּאְשׁוֹ), m. bad odour, stink; (comp. צַחֲנָה). The form is for בְּאֹשׁ, after the ancient and Aram. manner.

בְּאֻשׁ (only pl. בְּאֻשִׁים), originally adj. bad, evil, unripe, of עֲנָבִים, but also as a noun, bad, wild grapes.

בָּאְשָׁה (rare) f. bad, thorny growth, weed; f. form from בְּאֹשׁ.

בָּאתַר (Aram.) see בָּתַר and אֲתַר.

בָּב see בוב.

בָּבָה (only const. בָּבַת), f. originally hollowness, cavity, opening, gate, only בָּבַת עַיִן, gate of the eye, i. e. pupil of the eye, from בוב; (comp. בֵּיב, Talm. cave, pit; בָּבָא Aram. gate). According to others, the little man; (comp. אִישׁוֹן בַּת עַיִן, κόρη, a figure to represent the pupil of the eye; comp. בָּבוּאָה, Talm. little image).

בֵּבַי p. n. m. (comp. Talmud, בָּבָא p. n. probably fatherly, from *bab* father).

בָּבֶל (with ה of motion, בָּבֶלָה), p. n. the principal tribe of Babylonia; next, also the empire of that name, next to אֶרֶץ כַּשְׂדִּים, אֶרֶץ שִׁנְעָר, שִׁנְעָר, which at the time of the Persian dynasty also signified Persia. Scripture also furnishes grammatical explanation for בַּלְבֵּל, division of language, originally confusion; without regard to tradition, it might be equiv. to בָּב בָּל, gate of Balus, or בִּרְבָל, castle of Balus; (comp. בֵּל).

בַּבְלִי, (pl. def. בַּבְלָיֵא), Aram. adj. Babylonian, from בָּבֶל.

בַּג (only Ketib) m. food, it must, however, be read בַּג; (comp. פַּתְבַּג), if the Keri reading בַּז is not correct. The root is בגג.

בָּגַד (fut. יִבְגֹּד, יִבְגַּד); 1) (not used) to cover, to cover up, from which בֶּגֶד, clothing; 2) figur. to cover, to conceal, to hide; hence to act clandestinely, to deceive, (comp. לָבַשׁ, מָעַל), either absolute or with בְּ, rarely with מִן, or accus. of the person which one deceives or treacherously abandons, e. g. wife, friend, God, בֹּגְדִים, the faithless, the treacherous; הַיַּיִן בּוֹגֵד, the wine (drunkard) is treacherous.

בֶּגֶד (with suff. בִּגְדִי, pl. בְּגָדִים, בִּגְדוֹת, const. בִּגְדֵי), m. (once f.) covering, clothing; hence, 1) especially over-covering, (related to מְעִיל), next, cover, sheet; 2) wrapping, deceit, treachery, injustice. The root is בָּגַד, which see.

בֹּגְדוֹת pl. clandestineness, deceit, as to the pl. termination, compare עֲשֻׁקִים, oppression, always with the sing. signification.

בָּגוֹד adj. m. only בָּגוֹדָה, adj. f. female hypocrite, traitor, the first vowel ָ is retained, like in בָּחוֹן, עָשׁוֹק. The root is בָּגַד.

בִּגְוַי p. n. m. (the fortunate one, *felix*); comp. Βαγαῖος, Her.; Βαγώας, Ael. It might also be formed from the Persian bâgh, *hortus, paradisus*.

בָּגְלַל see גָּלַל.

בִּגְתָא (Pers.) p. n. m. (probably equiv. to בִּגְתָן), which see.

בִּגְתָן, בִּגְתָנָא (Pers.) p. n. m. beautifully formed, Persian *beh*, בַּה, good, handsome, and *ten* person, body.

בַּד (pl. בַּדִּים) m, isolation, separation, from בָּדַד, to be secluded, lonely; hence, 1) separate part; בַּד בְּבַד, part by part, which also may be rendered everything by itself; (compare the adv. לְבַד, formed therefrom; alone, separately); בַּדֵּי שְׁאֹל תֵּרַדְנָה, 'they (the hopes) shall go down into the loneliness of the pit,' (Auth. Vers. 'to the bars of the pit,' Job 17:16); where בַּדִּים loneliness, is used in the singular signification; 2) originally string, thread, cord, from בָּדַד, to bind; hence (*a*) collectively thread, linen, e. g. מִכְנְסֵי בַד, breeches of white linen, pl. בַּדִּים, absolute, linen garments; (*b*) branches boughs, so called on account of their being entwined or connected; hence only plural בַּדִּים; next, bars, poles for carrying or for lifting, distinct, therefore, from מַטֶּה; (c) pl. בַּדִּים, joints of the body, originally branches of the body; complete, בַּדֵּי עוֹר, branches of the body; hence figurat. the nobles of the people, as the moving members of the body of the nation; 3) pl. בַּדִּים, talk, gossip; next personally, gossiper, talker, from בָּדַד 3, related to בָּטָא, בָּדָא, which see.

בָּדָא originally to form; hence to invent, to imagine; part. with suff. בּוֹדָאם, for אַתָּה בֹוְדָאם 'thou feignest them (out of thine own heart,') Neh. 6:8. Comp. בָּטָא.

בָּדַד 1) to be separated, forsaken, isolated, lonely. The root is בַּד, to be separated, estranged · בּוֹדֵד, lonely; 2) to bind, related to אָפַד, from which בַּד בַּדִּים; 3) (not used) to talk, (related to בָּטָא).

בָּדָד m. loneliness, separation, solitude; hence also as an adv. lonely, alone; next to לְבָדָד.

בְּדַד p. n. m.

בֵּדְיָה see בֵּדְיָה.

בְּדָיָה. p. n. m.

בְּדִיל pl. בְּדִילִים) m. name of a metal that is mentioned in connection with gold, silver, iron, lead, brass, and by which is understood a kind of tin, (κασσίτερος; Aram. קַסְטִירָא) the pl. בְּדִילִים, (Is. 1:25) signifies several mixtures of tin which are separated as dross from the pure metal. The root is בָּדַל.

בָּדַל 1) (not used) to flow along. The root is בַּד־ל, Βδάλλω, from which בְּדֹלַח, which see; 2) only Niph. נִבְדַּל, to separate oneself, to make oneself lonely, to make onself solitary, with מִן from something; hence figuratively to depart, or altogether to be separated or excluded. With לְ, אֶל, it denotes to be selected, instead of for or to something; hence to be counted with, or selected for something.—Hiph. (caus.) to make something solitary, i. e. to separate, to divide, to partition off; (comp. הִזִּיר, הִפְלָה, הִתִּיק, הִפְרִיד) figuratively to divide, to distinguish, generally connected with בֵּין־בֵּין, בֵּין לְבֵין, בֵּין, but in the signification of connecting joined with מִן, to exclude, with מֵעַל; to select for something, with לְ, and like in Niph. without case.

בָּדָל (only const. בְּדַל), m. part,

division, בְּדַל־אֹזֶן, lap of the ear, (see תְּנוּךְ). The root is בָּדַל.

בְּדֹלַח m. Βδολ-χὸν, Βδέλλ-ιον, originally fragrant resin, or the gum-drops of an Indian tree; hence afterwards used of the form of a drop, pearl, whose whiteness is compared to the grains of manna, and figures in connection with the ruby (שֹׁהַם) and the gold as an important and valuable product of India, (חֲוִילָה, Targum) 1 Chron. 1 : 22, אֲתַר מַפְּקָנוּת מַרְגָּלִיתָא. The etymology is very appropriate from בָּדַל, like the Greek form from Βδάλλω. The original form is here like there, בְּדֹל, Βδολ, Βδελλ, the termination ־ַח appears to be the well-known Semitic adj. termination *ak*.

בְּדָן p. n. m. (=בֶּן־דָּן Danite; hence Targ. Samson), name of a judge of Israel.

בָּדַק (not used) to be out of repair, decaying.

בֶּדֶק (with suff. בִּדְקֵךְ), m. that which is out of repair, delapidated, crazy (of a building), from which denom. בָּדַק, (only in Chron). to be occupied with something out of repair, to repair the same; perhaps בָּדַק signifies there like in Aram. to investigate, to examine.

בִּדְקַר p. n. m. (equiv. to בֶּן־דֶּקֶר, lancer).

בְּדַר (Aram.) equiv. to Heb. בָּזַר.

בָּהָה (not used) equiv. to בָּהַם, which is formed therefrom, to be dumb, mute, to be amazed, to be benumbed.

בֹּהוּ (for בְּהוּ like פְּרִי), m. desolation, voidness, terror, related to תֹּהוּ; see אֶבֶן; the root is בָּהָה.

בַּהַט m. (only Esther) a kind of marble, LXX. σμαραγδίτης, of uncertain derivation.

בְּהִילוּ (Aram. const. בְּהִילוּת), f. eagerness, hurriedness, from בְּהַל.

בָּהִיר adj. m. bright, shining, from בָּהַר.

בָּהַל only Niph.; 1) originally to thrust oneself, to press oneself, to rage against oneself; hence generally to be frightened, terrified, to lose courage; 2) figuratively, to be frightened, to do something timidly, e. g. to fly, to flee, to hasten away, to imagine something, always with לְ the secondary sense of suddenness; hence also suddenly to perish.—Pi. בִּהֵל fut. יְבַהֵל, to rage against something, to frighten, alarm somebody, figuratively, to accelerate, to hasten.—Pu. pass. e. g. 'an inheritance gotten hastily,' (נַחֲלָה מְבֹהֶלֶת, Prov. 20 : 21).—

Hiph. similar to Pi. but also to frighten away.

בְּהַל (Aram.) the same.—Pa. like Pi. Heb.—Ithpa. pass.—Ithpe. inf. הִתְבְּהָלָה, rashness, haste.

בֶּהָלָה f. terror, destruction; from בָּהַל; see בַּלָּהָה.

בָּהַם (not used) is only the lengthened form from בָּהָה, to be dumb, applied to beast, which lack speech; hence אִלֵּם in modern Heb. signifies the animal kingdom, as מְדַבֵּר signifies mankind, the human kingdom.

בְּהֵמָה (c. בֶּהֱמַת, like שְׁאֶלֶת, from שְׁאֵלָה, with suffix, בְּהֶמְתְּךָ, בְּהֶמְתֵּנוּ, pl. בְּהֵמוֹת, const. בַּהֲמוֹת), f. cattle, as a collective noun, especially domestic animals, (in contrast to חַיָּה, wild beast); it is, therefore, used of sheep, goats, bullocks, beasts of burden, never of wild beasts; poetically with the addition of שָׂדַי, יַעַר, הַשָּׂדֶה, הָאָרֶץ, it is also used of tame cattle. The root is בָּהַם, lengthened from בָּהָה.

בְּהֵמוֹת (sing.) m. the Nile-horse; only Job 40 : 15; origin. water-horse, (Coptic *p-ehe-moot*, comp. Italian *bomarino*), a name adopted from a foreign language.

בֹּהֶן (pl. בְּהוֹנוֹת), f. the thumb, (with יָד); the large toe, (with רֶגֶל), probably equiv. to בֹּהֶם, like in Arab.

בֹּהַן p. n. m. (dwarf, a little man), from which the name of a place, אֶבֶן בֹּהַן.

בָּהַק (not used) to shine, to brighten; next, to be white.

בֹּהַק m. an eruption of the skin not of a dangerous tendency, and of a white, pale appearance, (Auth. Vers. 'freckled spot.' Lev. 13 : 49). LXX. ἀλφός, (white).

בָּהַר (not used) equiv. to בָּהַק, where ר, like the ק in the latter word, is additional.

בַּהֶרֶת (pl. בֶּהָרוֹת), f. white freckle in the skin, from בָּהַר.

בּוֹא (fut. יָבֹא); 1) to enter, (in contrast to יָצָא) with אֶל, לְ of the place which one enters, or with הָ of motion; poet. with the accus. (comp. *ingredi urbem*, *intrare domum*), also with אֶל of the person; with בְּ it expresses penetrating. In this most extensive sense it is applied in manifold relations, like בָּא אֶל (עַל) אִשָּׁה 'go in unto a woman.' (Deut. 23 : 13); (comp. βαίνειν, *inire*, used of the coupling of animals) first joining the husband, (of a virgin); to go in and out (יָצָא וּבָא), i. e. to conduct oneself; with לִפְנֵי הָעָם (before the people), to lead the people, to be at their head, which addition is sometimes dropped; to enter, i. e. to engage in a covenant, (בְּרִית), in an oath (אָלָה); to be involved, e.g. in dispute, debt; to enter into office; to obtain admission; to enter into the days, i. e. to get old; to go in (of the sun), i. e. to return to his home, to set, (contrast יָצָא); to enter with the ancestors, i. e. to die, (related to אָסַף); to be gathered in, of the corn; to come in, of revenues, etc. but the original and ancient signification is: to go, in cases where the goal of arrival is added, and the goer is considered at the starting-point of the road: אָנָה אֲנִי־בָא whither shall I go; figur. to live, to walk; with עִם, אֶת to associate with somebody, (like הָלַךְ); 2) to come, i. e. to meet at some place, (contrast to הָלַךְ), with אֶל, עַל, עַד, לְ, and accus. of the pers. or of the place; (comp. אָתָה, Gr. ἔρχομαι, to go and to come); hence with בְּ to come with something, i. e. to bring; figuratively to mention, to quote; originally to come forward with something, e. g. 'I will mention (אָבוֹא בְּ) (go in) the strength of the Lord,' (Ps. 71 : 16) (related to אַזְכִּיר); i. e. I will praise them; with אֶל, עַד, to equal some one; of inanimate things: to arrive at something, (also with לִפְנֵי)—בָּא עַל, to come over some one, to attack, to make desolate, of enemies, also of poverty which overtakes one, in this sense poet. with the accus. and לְ to befall, (related to מָצָא, which see); to occur, to realise a wish, a request, to be fulfilled, (something in the future). The forms which especially should be noticed are: 3 pers. f. with suff. בָּאַתְנוּ 2 pers. f. בָּאת and בָּאתְ, 3 pers. pl. בָּאוּ, once בֹּאוּ, 1 pers. pl. בָּאנוּ, בָּנוּ inf. בֹּא, with suff. בֹּאֲךָ, בֹּאֲכָה, pl. בֹּאֲךָ, בֹּאָן, בֹּאָנָה, imp. בֹּא, בֹּאָה; imperf. יָבֹא, תָּבֹא, תָּבֹאָה, with suff, תְּבֹאֶךָּ, תְּבֹאָתְךָ and others.—Hiph. הֵבִיא fut. יָבִיא, apoc. יָבֵא; generally causative; hence: 1) to carry in, (the thrashing-floor), to bear, to put the hand in the bosom, to enter in the grave, to introduce the bride (into the house), etc.; 2) to lead to, with לְ, אֶל, to bring, to bring away, to offer (presents); to bring about (misfortune), with עַל אֶל, לְ to cause to come, (things which have been predicted or desired); 3) to carry-

e. g. he who carries God in his hand, (Auth. Ver. 'whose hand God bringeth *abundantly*,' Job 12 : 6); to carry back, to carry away, to obtain. The forms are: הֵבִיא, הֵבִיתִי, הֲבִיאֹתִי, with suff. הֲבִיאֹתִי, 2 pers. pl. הֲבִיאֹתֶם; part. מֵבִיא and מֵבִי, inf. with prep. לָבִיא, (for לְהָבִיא), imp. הָבִיא, הָבָא, הָבִי, fut. 1 pers. sing. אָבִי.—Hoph. pass. 3 pers. fut. הֻבָאת.

בוּב (not used) to excavate, *cavare*, (related to אֶרֶב; hence Aram. אַבּוּב, flute; Lat. *ambubaja*, female player of the flute, the *m* in this word is interpolated, like the *n* in Arab).

בוּג (not used, see בַּג, בָּג in פַּת־בָּג) to eat, to cook.

בוּז (fut. יָבוּז); 1) to trample upon, with the feet; hence to despise, with the accus.; but with לְ to manifest contempt towards somebody; 2) to treat with indifference, pass with impunity, with לְ.

בּוּז m.; 1) contempt; 2) p. n. m. 3) p. n. of an Arabian tribe; gent. n. בּוּזִי.

בּוּזָה f. object of contempt.

בּוּזִי p. n. m.

בּוּטָה see בֹּטָה.

בַּוַּי p. n. m.

בּוּךְ not used, equiv. to אָרַךְ, related to רָבַךְ, סָרַךְ), only Hiph. נָבֹךְ, to be entangled, confused, to confound oneself. From which מְבוּכָה.

בּוּל (not used); 1) to flow, to bubble. From which בּוּל, מַבּוּל; 2) to flow in, to gather in, to cause to enter in, from which בּוּל, 2.—3.) to flow down, of branches, the idea of which is borrowed from the flowing of waves; (comp. פֵּל, בַּל, זָל, סַל), hence בּוּל. 3.

בּוּל m.; 1) streaming, flowing; hence the name of the rainy month in the East, (November); comp. Aram. מַרְחֶשְׁוָן, from רָחַשׁ, to overflow; 2) that which is gathered in, harvesting product, (related to תְּבוּאָה); 3) bough, branch, properly that which hangs down; hence בּוּל עֵץ, branch of a tree; next, log of wood generally. See בּוּל.

בּוּם (not used) to be high, probably בָּמָה is the root, equiv. to בָּנָה, to raise up, build. From which בָּמָה.

בּוּן (2 pers. sing. בַּנְתָּ part. pl. בָּנִים), without inf. and fut.; 1) to be distinct, clear, (Arab. bân), hence to observe, with בְּ, לְ, and accus.; to perceive by the senses, also by a motion; 2) to guard, to take notice of something, with אֶל, לְ, עַל, בְּ, and the accus.; 3) to perceive mentally, as a relative verb כִּי following it; to know, to recognise, with the accus. and לְ: 'thou knowest my thoughts,' (לְרֵעִי), Ps. 119: 2; without case, to have insight, consideration.—Niph. (1 sing. נְבֻנוֹתִי, part. נָבוֹן), to shew oneself sensible, knowing, to understand; נְבוֹן דָּבָר, eloquent of speech.—Piel בּוֹנֵן, fut. 3 pers. sing. with suff. יְבוֹנְנֵהוּ, closely to watch something.—Hith. הִתְבּוֹנֵן, originally to be attentive within himself; hence to direct attention to something, with אֶל, עַל, עַד, בְּ and accus.; next, generally to conceive, to comprehend, to understand properly, to shew oneself of understanding.—Hiph. הֵבִין, (2 pers. pl. הֲבִינוֹתֶם; part. מֵבִין; fut. יָבִין; apoc. יָבֵן; inf. הָבִין; with suff. הֲבִינְךָ; imp. הָבִין, הָבֵן); 1) caus. of Kal: to make one understand, to teach, to interpret, to instruct (the people), with 1 and 2 accus. or לְ of the pers. and accus. of the object, generally blended with the signification of Kal; 2) intrans. to take notice, etc., with בְּ of something; hence participle מֵבִין, experienced, conversant, learned in writing: from the Hiph. form a new Kal form ensues by dropping the ה caus. as is common in verbs having a vowel for the second radical, the signification remaining the same as in Hiph. thus: בִּינֹתִי, (equiv. to הֲבִינֹתִי); inf. בִּין (הָבִין), imp. בִּין, בִּינוּ; but no quiescent י in in the middle of a verb must be taken as a radical on account of this word having one.

בִּינָה p. n. m. (insight, knowledge, the man of knowledge).

בֻּנִּי see בּוּנִי.

בּוּס (fut. יָבוּס, יָבֹס), to tread (with feet), equiv. to בּוּז: hence also figuratively; 1) to tread to the ground, to trample upon (enemies); 2) to despise, (equiv. to בּוּז): e. g. food; part. בּוֹסִים, (for בָּזִים).—Pi. בּוֹסֵס, once בּוֹשֵׁס, to tread violently, used of the hostile treading on holy ground.—Hoph. pass. participle מוּבָס.—Hith. הִתְבּוֹסֵס, only Ezek. 16: 6, 22. מִתְבּוֹסֶסֶת בְּדָם, 'polluted in thy blood,' from בּוֹסֵס, to defile, (by treading down).

בּוּעַ (not used) to swell up, to spout, related to בָּעָה, נָבַע, compare Aram. בַּעְבַּע, to spout forth; from which אֲבַעְבֻּעֹת.

בּוּץ (not used) to be white, bright,

related to רָבַץ, Aram. בְּצַץ, עֲבַץ, אֲבַץ.

בּוּץ (later) m. fine, white cotton, Βύσσος, sometimes also for linen, (somewhat different from שֵׁשׁ, חוּר), so called on account of its whiteness; comp. Aram. בּוֹצִין, lamp, from בּוּץ.

בּוֹצֵץ p. n. m. of a rock, (shining).

בּוּק (not used) emptying, pouring out, related to בָּק, which subsequently seems to have merged into the idea of moving, tottering. From which בּוּקָה, מְבוּקָה.

בּוּקָה (rare) f. waste, voidness, from בּוּק.

בּוֹקֵר m. a shepherd (רֹעֶה), originally formed from בָּקָר, herd.

בּוּר (only inf. בּוּר), equiv. to בָּאַר; 1) to bore, *for-are* to dig, (see בּוֹר); 2) to dig out, to explore, to explain, Ecc. 9 : 1.

בּוֹר (with ה of motion בֹּרָה, pl. בֹּרוֹת, בּארוֹת) m. 1) a pit, a hole; hence prison, complete בֵּית הַבּוֹר; next, grave; e. g. עַד־בּוֹר even to the grave; יוֹרְדֵי־בוֹר they that go down into the pit, the dead; אַבְנֵי־בוֹר stones of the grave, i. e. graves built of stone; יַרְכְּתֵי־בוֹר the hindmost sides of the grave, the depths; 2) cisterns, wells.

בּוֹשׁ (בֹּשׁ, בֹּשָׁה, בֹּשְׁתְּ, בֹּשְׁתָּ, בֹּשְׁתִּי, בֹּשְׁתֶּם, בּוֹשׁוּ, fut. יֵבוֹשׁ): 1) to shine, equiv. to בּוּץ, of the sun; 2) to discolour, to blush, (with shame), to be ashamed; turning pale, or blushing, as an indication of shame (comp. חָוַר, כָּסַף, Talm. הִלְבִּין), generally with מִן of the cause of shame. This verb is applied (*a*) to the being deceived, being disappointed, (fading) of hopes, or in the result of an undertaking to become ashamed, to become embarrassed, disappointed, with מִן: hence עַד־בּוֹשׁ until being disappointed, i. e. long; (*b*) of inanimate things, e. g. his source will be ashamed, i. e. dried up. Pi. בּוֹשֵׁשׁ to cause embarrassment, to keep one waiting, to linger, (comp. עַד־בּוֹשׁ). Hiph. הֵבִישׁ and הוֹבִישׁ, exchanging the forms with יָבֵשׁ, fut. יוֹבִישׁ; 1) to make ashamed, to deceive (hopes), or to cause embarrassment or shame to some one; 2) to disappoint, put to the blush, to put to shame, to act basely, hence מֵבִישׁ acting basely (contrast to מַשְׂכִּיל). Hith. הִתְבּשֵׁשׁ to feel oneself ashamed.

בּוּשָׁה f. shame, making ashamed, from בּוֹשׁ.

בּוּת (Aram.) to house (dwell, to make a dwelling, to move into a house, a verb derived from בַּיִת.

בַּז (with suff. בִּזִּי) m. spoil, booty, generally with נָתַן, הָיָה לְ. The root is בָּזַז.

בָּזָא (only 3 pers. pl. בָּזְאוּ): to trample down, to destroy, e. g. 'whose lands the rivers (swarms of enemies) have spoiled,' or rather, 'trodden down,' (Isa. 18 : 3).

בָּזָה (part. בֹּזֶה; fut. apoc. וַיִּבֶז) equiv. to בּוּז to tread with the feet, hence to despise, with the accus. לְ, עַל; וַיִּבֶז בְּעֵינָיו 'and he thought scorn,' (and he despised in his eyes, literally) Esth. 3 : 6; also to be indifferent, e. g. דְּרָכָיו to his walk in life. Niph. only participle, נִבְזֶה, pl. נִבְזִים despised. Hiph. only inf. הַבְזוֹת to cause to be despised, in the eyes of somebody, etc.

בְּזֹה (const. בְּזוֹה) adj. m. despised; בְּזֹה־נֶפֶשׁ of (all) persons despised.

בִּזָּה f. equiv. to בַּז, booty, often next to שָׁלָל, שְׁבִי.

בָּזַז (pl. בָּזְזוּ, בַּזּוֹנוּ or בָּזָזוּ, fut. יָבֹז, inf. בֹּז, imp. pl. בֹּזּוּ); 1) to despise (Zac. 4 : 10) equiv. to בּוּז; 2) בָּזַז equiv. to בָּזַר, origin. to withdraw, to take away, to deprive, to cut off, hence to plunder, to despoil. (Aram. and Arab. to rob) with the accus. of the person, or place which is plundered. Niph. נָבֹז (pl. נָבֹזּוּ, inf. הִבּוֹז, fut. יִבּוֹז) pass. Pu. the same.

בִּזָּיוֹן (later) m. contempt, from בָּזָה.

בִּזְיוֹתְיָה p. n. a place in the territory if Judah.

בָּזַל (not used) probably to be hard, firm, comp *βασάλ-της* iron-marble, of which Pliny says: *invenit Aegyptus in Æthiopia, quem vocant basalten, ferrei coloris atque duritici, unde et nomen ei dedit.* From which בַּרְזֶל.

בָּזַק (not used) to shine upon, to be lustrous, bright.

בָּזָק (only Ezek.) m. splendour, ray, of light, from בָּזַק.

בֶּזֶק p. n. of a town (LXX. Βεζέκ) not far from *Scythopolis*, from בָּזַק.

בָּזַר (fut. יְבַזֵּר) to strew. Pi. to disperse. The root בָּ־זַר is related to פְּ־זַר Aram. retained in בִּזְרָא seed = זֶרַע.

בִּזְּתָא (Persian) p. n.

בָּחוֹן m. prover (of metal); from בָּחַן.

בַּחוּן (rare) m. watch-tower, originally a watch-state, only Keri, from בָּחַן.

בָּחוּר (for בָּחוֹר, hence pl. בַּחוּרִים, const. בַּחוּרֵי) m. originally, the mature one, hence youth, applied to a young man, in the state of manhood (but unmarried) able to serve in war. The root is בָּחַר, II.

בְּחוּרוֹת f. pl. the same as בַּחוּרִים.

בְּחוּרִים m. pl. youth, youthful age; from בָּחַר, II.

בחין equiv. to בָּחוֹן only Ketib.

בָּחִיר (const. בְּחִיר) adj. m. chosen, selected, subst. the chosen one, from בָּחַר I., which see.

בָּהַל (rare); 1) equiv. to בָּעַל to look down upon something, with בְּ to despise; 2) only Pual part. מְבֹהֶלֶת in Ketib, either from מְבֹהֶלֶת Keri, or בָּהַל = בָּהַל as hastily, quickly joined together.

בָּחַן (fut. יִבְחַן) equiv. to בָּחַר; 1) to prove (metal in fire), originally to make glow, (related to צָרַף: hence purifying (by fire): e. g. 'when he hath tried me (purified me from the dross), I shall come forth as gold,' (Job 23 : 10); 2) proving, generally, e. g. the hearts and the loins; 3) not used, to spy; originally to prove, to search.—Niph. pass.—Pu. only בֹּחַן it is proved.

בֹּחַן m. watch-tower, spy tower; from בָּחַן.

בֹּחַן m. trial, proof, e. g. אֶבֶן בֹּחַן corner stone of trial.

I. בָּחַר (fut. יִבְחַר) equiv. to בָּחַן; 1) originally to make low, e. g. metal by fire; hence figuratively, 'בְּחַרְתִּיךָ בְּכוּר עֹנִי I have proved (chosen) thee in the furnace of affliction,' Isa. 48 : 10. The root is בָּחַר related to חָר to glow, חָרָה to burn; 2) to prove, investigate; hence 2 Ch. 34 : 6 (Ketib) בָּחַר בָּתֵּיהֶם he searched there (the idolators' houses); 3) to select, to choose, with accus. בְּ, עַל.—בָּחַר לוֹ to choose unto himself; with מִן to choose rather than; part. בָּחוּר (pl. const. בְּחוּרֵי) select, distinguished; 4) to take pleasure in, to be pleased with (comp. *diligere*, *delectari*), origi. to select, with accus. בְּ, לְ, עַל.—Niph. נִבְחַר to be chosen, with מִן to be preferable to: pass. נִבְחָר, with מִן excellent, eminent, with לְ of the person to be pleasing to some one.—Pu. only once Ketib יְבֻחַר to be selected, to be chosen.

II. בָּחַר (not used) equiv. to בָּכַר Talm. בָּגַר to mature, ripen; from which probably בָּחוּר = בְּחוּר.

בַּחֻרִים p. n. a town in the territory of Benjamin, hence n. genti. בַּרְחֻמִי, בַּחֲרוּמִי, once בַּרְחֻמִי.

בָּטָא, בָּטָה (not used) to speak (comp. *βαττολογεῖν*, related to בַּד, בָּדָא) hence Pi. בִּטֵּא to make speech, to speak without thought, to gossip, origin. to speak much.

בִּטָּה (only *plene* בּוּטָּה) m. speech, talk, in contrast to לְשׁוֹן חֲכָמִים moderation in speaking.

I. בָּטַח (fut. יִבְטַח); 1) originally

to lean upon something (like אָלַף), hence to depend upon; figur. to trust upon, with עַל, אֶל, בְּ and sometimes also with לְ *sibi*; part. בָּטוּחַ dependent upon (בְּ), i. e. to be trusted; 2) to live peaceably, quietly (comp. מָשַׁךְ) e. g. 'the fool rageth and is confident,' (בּוֹטֵחַ); also of carelessness, and indifference, considering himself secure either in a good or in a bad sense. Hiph. הִבְטִיחַ to cause one to be sure, quiet, to inspire with trust, confidence, with עַל, אֶל.

II. בָּטַח (not used) from which אֲבַטִּחִים; but the derivation is uncertain.

בֶּטַח m. 1) confidence, safety: לָבֶטַח adv. trustful, sorrowless, safe, sure, for which also בֶּטַח stands especially with the verbs שָׁכַן, יָשַׁב; 2) p. n. a Syrian city (LXX. Μετεβάκ, Ματαβέθ) which the chronicler renders, טִבְחַת (*Thapsacus?*)

בִּטְחָה f. safety; from בָּטַח 1.

בִּטָּחוֹן m. great confidence, hopes, from בָּטַח I.

בַּטֻּחוֹת pl. f. quiet life, happiness, duration. The pl. signifies here the collective.

בָּטַל (only וּבָטְלוּ, later) to rest, to cease from work, to be unfettered, unbound, to cease.

בְּטֵל (Aram.) the same. Pa. בַּטֵּל (pl. בַּטִּלוּ, inf. בַּטָּלָא) to separate somebody from something, to divide, to prevent, to hinder.

בָּטַן (not used) 1) probably to extend, stretch out. Even the sense to keep (*ten-ere*) proceeds from stretching, extending; comp. *pertinere*; from which בֶּטֶן; 2) to extend, to rise, and generally of extension, either in length or breadth. From which בָּטְנִים, בָּטְנִים.

בֶּטֶן (with suff. בִּטְנִי) f. belly, body, generally; 1) of the external part, womb; generally followed by אֵם, e. g. מִבֶּטֶן אִמִּי, from the womb of my mother, from infancy פְּרִי בֶטֶן, the fruit of the body, children; בֶּטֶן אִמִּי = בִּטְנִי, בְּנֵי בִטְנִי, sons of my mother's body (brothers), but בַּר בִּטְנִי, son of my body; 2) figur. the innermost heart; e. g. חַדְרֵי בֶטֶן chambers of the heart; בֶּטֶן שְׁאוֹל the innermost (κοιλία) of the grave; comp. קֶרֶב; 3) a techical term in architecture: belly of the pillars, a kind of raising; 4) p. n. of a city in the territory of Asher, (Eues. and Hier. בֵּית־בֶּטֶן).

בָּטְנִים m. pl. (Tal. sing בָּטְנָה) *pistacchio*, so called on account of its resemblance to the form of the belly, from בֶּטֶן.

בְּטֹנִים p. n. a town in the territory of Gad.

בִּי particle, upon me (hear)! pray! always with אֲדֹנִי, my Lord! according to others = בְּעִי; (comp. Aram. בְּבָעוּ), pray! from בָּעָה. Perhaps בִּי is originally a prep. = by; therefore בִּי אֲדֹנִי, form of a request, prayer; compare Talmudical בֵּי, on, in, by, at; אַבֵּי, in, at, by.

בִּין see בּוּן.

בֵּין (const. from בַּיִן); 1) m. origin. division, separation; hence בֵּינַיִם, space intervening between two armies (τὰ μεταίχμια), אִישׁ הַבֵּנַיִם middle-man, (single-handed combatants between two armies); 2) בֵּין (pl. בֵּינוֹת, const. בֵּינֵי, with suff. בֵּינִי, בֵּינְךָ, pause בֵּינֶךָ, בֵּינוֹ, pl. בֵּינֵי, בֵּינֵינוּ, בֵּינֵיכֶם, בֵּינֵיהֶם; suff. of the pl. בֵּינוֹת, בֵּינוֹתֵינוּ, בֵּינוֹתָם) prep. between, under; e. g. בֵּין אַחִים, ־יָדַיִם, ־שׁוּרֹת, ־שִׂיחִים, ־הָעֵינַיִם, between brothers, between trees, the eyes, i. e. on the forehead; beneath the walls, etc., for between the one thing and the other stands בֵּין־לְ, בֵּין־וּבֵין, בֵּין־לְ; בֵּין־לְבֵין; hence the verbs that express such separation (e. g. שָׁפַט, יָדַע, הֶעֱרִיךְ; שָׂר, נָתַן, גָּבַל, הִפְלָה, הִבְדִּיל; רָאָה; הֵבִין; הוֹרָה) generally make use of the repetition, and it is but seldom it has the signification of *sive—sive* which is only a modification of between—between. The pl. בֵּינוֹת, const. בֵּינֵי, only occur when the suff. has a plural sense. Compounds אֶל־בֵּין, אֶל־בֵּינוֹת between—there, עַל־בֵּין, on between, to between, מִבֵּין, from between (something); hence ־רַגְלַיִם originally for where *ex utero;* רַגְלַיִם (= מֵעַיִם) expresses gender and root; מִבֵּין, מִבֵּין from between—between, מִבֵּינוֹת לְ from between—away; (comp. מֵעַל לְ; מִתַּחַת לְ, בְּבֵין. Isa. 44: 4) meanwhile, equiv. to כְּבֵין. See בּוּן.

בֵּין (Aram). the same.

בִּינָה f. understanding, knowledge, wisdom, הִתְבּוֹנֵן, יָדַע בִּינָה, to obtain understanding, לָעִתִּים, knowledge of times, a chronologist, equiv. to יָדַע עִתִּים, the Rabbis distinguish it from חָכְמָה, by בֵּן דָּבָר מִתּוֹךְ דָּבָר to conclude, to infer, to deduce. See בּוּן.

בִּינָה (Aram. the same).

בֵּיצָה (only pl. בֵּיצִים), f. egg, so called on account of its whiteness: בֵּ׳ עֲזֻבוֹת (בּוּץ) 'eggs that are left,' (Isa. 10: 14).

בֵּיר (only Jer. 6 : 7 Keri) m. well, from בֹּר.

בִּירָה (later) f. ; 1) castle, fort, e. g. the fort Shushan, (שׁוּשָׁן), castle of the Lord, i. e. the temple ; 2) capital, metropolis, e. g. of Shushan. Comp. בִּירָנִית.

בִּירָה (Aram.) f. the same, (def. בִּירְתָא), the residence Eckbathana.

בִּירָנִיָּה (only pl. בִּירָנִיּוֹת) f. burgh, castle, ־ָנִית is the termination : it is also formed from בִּירָה.

בַּיִת (with ה mobile : בַּיְתָה const. בֵּית, with ה mobile : בֵּיתָה, with suff. בֵּיתִךָ, בֵּיתוֹ, pl. בָּתִּים for בּוֹתִים, const. (בָּתֵּי), m. ; 1) house, in the widest sense, as, pavilion, hut, burgh, palace, temple, for all these things were plainly called house. So also יְלִיד בַּיִת, בֶּן בַּיִת a slave born in the house, (*verna*) בֵּית עוֹלָם, the house of eternity, i. e. the grave. Later בַּיִת was also taken for part of the house or palace, like בֵּית מִשְׁתֵּה הַיַּיִן drinking-hall, בֵּית הַנָּשִׁים haram : 2) in the remotest extension : (*a*) place of staying, dwelling, e. g. for man, animals, or a recluse ; hence for the lower regions, cave, nest, cobweb ; (*b*) a place where a thing is found : a room, cover, case, בָּתֵּי נֶפֶשׁ, scent-boxes, בָּתִּים לְבַדִּים ' the places for the staves,' (Exod. 37 : 14) ; (*c*) of the space in which anything is found, e.g. בֵּית סָאתַיִם a space containing two measures (*seah*) of seed ; בֵּ' אֲבָנִים a place containing stones ; בֵּית־קְבָרוֹת place of graves, burial-ground; בֵּ' צְלָעוֹת ' place of the side chambers,' (Ezek. 41 : 9) : בֵּ' נְתִיבוֹת ' places of the paths,' (Prov. 8 : 2) ; (*d*) expressing generally the innermost, enclosed in a circle, (in contrast to חוּץ), and used as an adv. : e. g. בַּיְתָה within ; מִבַּיְתָה, מִבַּיִת, from within ; מִבֵּית, לְמִבֵּית, בֵּית לְ, inward of ; אֶל מִבֵּית לְ, towards the inward of ; 3) house in the ideal sense, that which morally belongs to a house : as a wife, children, people, servants, who collectively constitute a tribe, family, people, etc. e. g house (people) of Israel ; house (family) of David ; house, (tribe) of Levi ; בֵּית אָב, father of a family, of a house, ancestry, division of a tribe, (distinct from מִשְׁפָּחָה), pl. בֵּית אָבוֹת, ancestoral houses, where, however, בֵּ' is often omitted, when רֹאשׁ, שַׂר, נְשִׂיא, (head or chief) preceeds it : hence figuratively עָשָׂה, בָּנָה בַּיִת, to make, to produce progeny. בַּיִת is also used, though rarely for household property, possession; 4) characteristic of many cities and places: as בֵּית־אָוֶן, (house of idols), town in the territory of Benjamin; בֵּית־אֵל, (house of God), formerly לוּז, a town on a hill between Sechem and Jerusalem; gent. n. בֵּית־הָאֱלִי, בֵּית־אֵצֶל, (house of Ezel), city in Samaria; בֵּית־אַרְבֵּאל (house of Arbel) Arbela in Galilee; בֵּ׳ בַּעַל־מְעוֹן town in the territory of Reuben; בֵּ׳ בִּרְאִי town in the territory of Simeon; בֵּ׳ בָּרָה (house of transition), town of the Jordan; בֵּית גָּדֵר, (house of wall) protected place, town in the territory of Judah; בֵּ׳ גִּלְגָּל (district-house) town between Jericho and the Jordan בֵּ׳ גָּמוּל (camel-house) town in Moab; בֵּ׳ דִּבְלָתַיִם (place of fig-cakes), town in Moab; בֵּ׳ דָּגוֹן (the temple of Dagon), town in the territory of Judah and Asher; בֵּ׳ הַיְשִׁימוֹת (place of desolation), town in the territory of Reuben; בֵּ׳ הָעֵקֶד (house of union), town near Samaria; בֵּ׳ הָרָם (house of pyramids) town in the territory of Gad), (Livias); בֵּ׳ הָרָן (house of mountains) in the same territory; בֵּ׳ חָגְלָה town in territory of Benjamin; בֵּ׳ חָנָן (house of grace) town in the territory of Judah and Dan; בֵּית חוֹרֹן (house of caves), name of two towns in the territory of Ephraim; בֵּ׳ כָּר house of meadows) a Philistine town in the territory of Judah; בֵּ׳ כֶּרֶם (house of vineyards) town in the territory of Judah; בֵּ׳ לְבָאוֹת (house of lions) town in the territory of Simeon; בֵּ׳ לֶחֶם (house of bread or contention) town in the territory of Judah; בֵּ׳ לְעַפְרָה (house of Gazelles) town in the territory of Benjamin; בֵּ׳ מִלּוֹא (house of rampart) name of a castle in Sechem; בֵּ׳ מְעוֹן (place of sojourning) town in Moab; בֵּ׳ מַעֲכָה (lower house) a town at the foot of Hermon; בֵּ׳ מַרְכָּבוֹת (house of chariots) town in the territory of Simeon; בֵּ׳ נִמְרָה (house of panthers) a town in Moab; בֵּ׳ עֶדֶן (house of delight) royal residence of Syrian kings on the Lebanon; בֵּ׳ עַזְמָוֶת town in the territory of Judah; בֵּ׳ עֵמֶק (house of the vale) town in the territory of Asher; בֵּ׳ עֲנוֹת (house of furrows) town in the ter. of Judah; בֵּ׳ עֲנָת (the same) town in the territory of Naphtali; בֵּ׳ עָפְרָה (house of roes) town in the territory of Menasseh; בֵּ׳ עֵקֶד הָרֹעִים (meeting-house of the shepherds) like בֵּ׳ עֲרָבָה, בֵּית הָעֵקֶד (house of deserts) a border town between Judah and Benjamin; בֵּ׳ פֶּלֶט (house of escape) town in the southern vale of Judea; בֵּ׳ פְּעוֹר (house of Peor) a town in Moab; בֵּ׳ פַּצֵּץ (house of destruction) town in the territory of Issachar; בֵּ׳ צוּר (house of cliffs) town on the mountain of Judah: בֵּ׳ רְחוֹב (house of streets) town in the territory of Asher; בֵּ׳ שְׁאָן (house of fortune) also בֵּ׳ שָׁן, בֵּ׳ שְׁן, town in the territory of Manasseh; בֵּ׳ שִׁטָּה (house of accacias) town on the Jordan; בֵּ׳ שֶׁמֶשׁ (house of the sun) town in the territory of Judah, (gent. בֵּ׳ הַשִּׁמְשִׁי), בֵּ׳ תַּפּוּחַ (house of fruit-trees) town in the territory of Judah. In reference to the derivations בַּיִת and בָּתִּים, abbreviated from בּוֹתִים indicate a root, the second radical of which is a vowel, the nominal root בוית, however, appears originally to have signified room, like in 2.

בֵּית (def. בֵּיתָא, בַּיְתָא) Aram. m. the same, from which בֵּית גִּנְזַיָּא treasury-house, בֵּית סִפְרַיָּא manuscript-vault, archive.

בִּיתָן (const. בִּיתַן rare) m. palace, formed from בַּיִת = בֵּית; it is improbable to be derived from the Persian Bâtân, though it only appears in Esther, and only joined to גִּנָּה whose name it appears to be.

בָּכָא (not used) equiv. to בָּכָה. From which:—

בָּכָא and בָּכָה m. 1) the weeping (originally, flowing); hence probably עֵמֶק הַבָּכָא valley of weeping; 2) p. n. of a tree, similar to the balm tree (originally dropping of gum), pl. בְּכָאִים.

בָּכָה (fut. יִבְכֶּה, apoc. יֵבְךְּ) originally, to flow; next, to weep, to wail; in cases of disaster, or in penitence, with accus. to weep for, to beweep; with עַל, אֶל, לְ to weep over something; where, however, עַל over, is also taken in the sense of against, on account of, or locally over some one. Pi. with accus. to beweep; see בְּכִית, בֹּכִים.

בְּכוֹר (pl. בְּכוֹרוֹת) m. originally the maturing, ripening: hence first-birth (abstract) of man and beast, (hence בְּכֹרוֹת pl.) from which: the first-born; figuratively precursor, the first, as בְּכוֹר מָוֶת precursor of death, i. e. sickness; בְּכוֹרֵי דַלִּים the first of the poor, i. e. the poorest. From which verb denom. Pi. בִּכֵּר to make one a בְּכוֹר, to invest with the right of a first-born.

בִּכּוּרָה, בִּכּוּרָה, בַּכֻּרָה (pl. בִּכּוּרוֹת) f. early fig (Spanish *albacora*) originally an adj. to complete תְּאֵנָה, as is proved in תְּאֵנֵי בִּכֻּרוֹת; see בָּכַר.

בִּכּוּרִים pl. m. the firstlings (of fruit, corn), בִּכּוּרֵי עֲנָבִים firstlings of grapes, early grapes; לֶחֶם הַבִּכּוּרִים firstling of bread, used of fresh corn; יוֹם הַבִּכּוּרִים festival of the first fruits, otherwise, feast of weeks. The sing. בִּכּוּר appears only in the Masoretic reading Isa. 28 : 4. Root בָּכַר.

בְּכוֹרַת p. n. m. (first-birth).

בָּכוּת f. weeping, mourning, from בָּכָה.

בָּכִי (paus. בֶּכִי, with suff. בִּכְיִי) m. originally to drop: hence 1) of the water-drops in the shafts, pits (thus δάκρυον); 2) to weep, בָּכָה בְכִי *fletum flere*, where, however גָּדוֹל (violent) and תַּמְרוּרִים bitterness, (i. e. bitterly), is added. Root בָּכָה.

בֹּכִים p. n. of a place.

בְּכִירָה (from בָּכִיר) adj. first-born, subst. eldest. The root is בָּכַר.

בְּכִית f. equiv. to בָּכוּת.

בָּכַר (Kal not used) to break forth, to press forward: hence ripening, maturing. Pi. to make ripe, to mature, לֶחֳדָשִׁים the new fruit. Pu. to be born first. Hiph. to bear the first. But Pu. and Hiph. may also be denominative.

בֵּכֶר (only const. pl. בִּכְרֵי) m. a young camel, therefore different from גָּמָל.

בֶּכֶר p. n. m. (youth), gent. n. בַּכְרִי.

בִּכְרָה (from בֵּכֶר) f. a young she-camel.

בְּכֹרָה f. first-birth, from בָּכַר.

בְּכֹרַת p. n. m. (first-birth, or youth).

בִּכְרִי p. n. m. (adj. from בֶּכֶר, young).

בַּל (in compounds בַּל) adv. negative, not (only poetical), especially before verbs generally = לֹא and interchanging with the same. Before the future it often signifies: that not, sometimes, scarcely, i. e. not yet, but the primitive signification does not differ from בְּלֹא (e. g. בְּלֹא יוּבְלוּ) with which it appears to be related, and hence often for לֹא. No derivation from a verb is necessary if בַּל, בְּלֹא, בְּלִי, בִּלְתִּי, בַּל־עֲדֵי, בִּלְעֲדֵי, אֲבָל are taken as a group. With other prepositions בַּל עַל, אַף בַּל, בַּל עִם.

בַּל (Aram.) m. heart, originally, courage, strength.

בֵּל (from בֵּעַל = בַּעַל, also בֵּל from בַּעַל), m. Bel, Belus, a Babylonian deity, (answering to the planet Jupiter, hence Jupiter Belus, with the Sabians בֵּיל, the planet

Jupiter, to whom the Babylonian tower was dedicated). See גַּד, מְנִי, בָּבֶל. The signification is the strong, mighty one. Compare Phryg. Βαλὴν, mighty one. Compounds with בֵּל, בַּל are found in pp. nn.

בְּלָא (Pael, fut. יְבַלֵּא), Aram. with לְ to speak against somebody, (= מַלֵּל לְ with which it is parallel) originally to bully, bluster, at some one, according to others equiv. to Heb. בָּלָה, which, however, is not at all appropriate.

בַּלְאֲדָן p. n. m. (ruler of Belus), from בַּל, eq. to בַּעַל and אָדֹן ruler, father of King Merodak, Bal-adan.

בָּלַג (not used) to glimmer, to throw light on something, in Arab. used of the shining, of the brightness of the morning-dawn, only Hiph. הִבְלִיג, fut. יַבְלִיג, part. מַבְלִיג, to shine, to lighten, i. e. to throw out light, to remain serene, cheerful, as (Job 9 : 27) 'I will leave off my heaviness and comfort myself,' (look cheerful), so also in (Ps. 39 : 13), 'O spare me that I may recover strength,' (look cheerful); figur. with עַל, to cause to shine upon, or illumine something, as Amos 5 : 9, 'That strengtheneth the spoiler,' (that causeth destruction to pour forth over the strong one, i. e. misfortune overwhelms him). From which בִּלְגַּי, p. n. בִּלְגָּה, p. n. מַבְלִיגִית.

בִּלְגָּה (from בָּלַג) p. n. (cheering, strengthening, illumining). See בָּלַג.

בִּלְגַּי (from בָּלַג) p. n. m. (the shining one, the beautiful one), it stands once for בִּלְגָּה

בִּלְדַּד p. n. m.

בָּלָה (fut יִבְלֶה, 1) to be decaying, to be withered, worn out, used of garments, (related to παλαι-ός), with מֵעַל, to be worn out in something, i. e. on the body (of raiments), figur. of the wearing out or decaying of heaven and earth, which are to fall to pieces like the worn-out clothing ; 2) of the human body, to fall off, to decay, through care or disease.— Pi. to wear out, i. e. to use up, enjoy, figur. to reduce (a people), only 1 Chron. לְבַלֹּתוֹ, if not to read לְכַלֹּתוֹ. From which בָּלֶה, תַּבְלִית, בְּלוֹי, בְּלִי, בְּלוֹ.

בָּלֶה adj. m. בָּלָה, f. worn out (of garments), from בָּלָה, an old part. form.

בַּלָּהָה see בַּעֲלָה and בִּלְהָה.

בָּלַהּ (only once Ketib) equiv. to בָּהַל, from which it is transposed. Herefrom.—

בַּלָּהָה (sing. rare pl. בַּלָּהוֹת, const. בַּלְהוֹת), f. equiv. to בֶּהָלָה, terror, destruction, as terror of darkness: thus, Job 18 : 14, 'and it shall bring him to the king of terrors,' i. e. it drives him on like a king of terrors, 'they are utterly consumed with terrors.' (מִן־בַּלָּהוֹת), Ps. 78 : 19; also Ezek. 26 : 21, 'I will make thee a terror (I will deliver thee up to terror), and thou shalt be no more.' Root בָּלַהּ.

בִּלְהָה 1) p. n. f. (equiv. to בְּלָנָה, beauty) mother of Dan and Naphtali; 2) a place in the territory of Simeon, also בַּעֲלָה and בָּלָה.

בִּלְהָן p. n. m. (equiv. to בִּלְנָן, the beautiful one).

בְּלוֹ (Aram. for בְּלִי), f. tax, perquisites, contribution, from בָּלָה in the sense of that which falls off.

בְּלוֹי (only pl. const. בְּלוֹאֵי and בְּלוֹיֵ) m. the being decayed, worn out; concrete: worn-out garments, rags, generally connected with מְלָחִים, סְחָבוֹת, from בָּלָה. The form is rare.

בֵּלְטְשַׁאצַּר p. n. m. applied to Daniel at the Babylonian Court. See בֵּלְשַׁאצַּר.

בְּלִי m. corruption, from בָּלָה, only Isa. 38 : 17; חָשַׁקְתָּ נַפְשִׁי מִשַּׁחַת בְּלִי, 'but thou hast in love to my soul delivered it from the pit of corruption,' i. e. thou guardest, protectest it, if not מִשַּׁחַת בְּלִי is only to be taken as a poetical transposition for מִבְּלִי שַׁחַת, i. e. so that there was no grave.

בְּלִי (pronom. root) adv. equiv. to בְּלֹא; 1) without, un—, —less: as, בְּלִי־שֵׁם fameless, without calling; בְּלִי־מַיִם (בְּלֹא in the first sentence), without water, waterless; בְּלִי־מָקוֹם, without (empty) place, roomless; בְּלִי־מָשִׁיחַ, unanointed; בְּלִי־הֲפוּכָה, unturned, and thus frequently before a noun; 2) like בְּלֹא also before the verb, before the preterite and fut. e. g. בְּלִי חָשָׂךְ, תָּקוּם where it signifies: without, not. In compounds the same, as בִּבְלִי־דַעַת, unawares, unintentional; לִבְלִי after verbs of motion or purpose; as, לִבְלִי־חֹק; לִבְלִי־חַת, etc.; מִבְּלִי from—without = because not, since not (is); see בַּל, לֹא; compounds בְּלִימָה בְּלִיַּעַל.

בְּלִיל m. provender, grass for fodder, (*farrago*), fodder of mangel wurzel, (related to מִסְפּוֹא), from בָּלַל mixing; from which denom. Kal, fut. only יָבֹל, to provide with provender.

בְּלִימָה (for בְּלִי־מָה), subst. originally, not=what, i.e. nothing, a noun created in poetry.

בְּלִיַּעַל (from בְּלִי־יַעַל) m. 1) not high, hence, depths: נַחֲלֵי בְלִיַּעַל floods of the depths (Auth.Vers. "floods of ungodly men." 2 Sa. 22:5), i.e. deep floods (יַעַל subst. m. יַעַל=עָלָה); 2) figuratively, spoiling, corruption; as, matter, (דְּבַר) of corruption; man (אִישׁ); woman (בַּת); a witness (עֵד) of corruption, i.e. corruptible. See יַעַל.

בָּלַל (fut. יָבֹל) 1) to flow, to stream (comp. שָׁבַל, אָבַל, יָבַל, בּוּל), to overflow, poet. pass. בָּלוּל overflown, i.e. poured over.—2) figur. to pour together, i.e. to mix (comp. *confundo*, συγχέω), to confound (the language), i.e. to split them into various families, נָבְלָה (1 pers. plur. fut. Kal, from נָבוֹל, like יָזֹמּוּ from יָזֹם), let us divide (the languages); from which later, to speak confusedly (unjustly), to stammer.—Hith. הִתְבּוֹלֵל to mix oneself up, to enter into connexion with some body. From which תֶּבֶל, בָּבֶל, בְּלִיל, p.n.

בָּלַם (only inf. בָּלוֹם) to tie up, to fasten, (a bit) to bridle, to curb. The root is בָּלַם, related to אָלַם to bind, where לם is the chief syllable.

בֹּלֵס m. (denom. from בָּלַס a fig, which is yet found in the Arabic, comp. בּוֹקֵר from בָּקָר in the same verse) with שִׁקְמִים "a gatherer of sycamore fruit," or one that nips them in order to assist them in ripening (Hos. 7:14); probably the subordinary occupation of a shepherd (בֹּקֵר).

בָּלַע (fut. יִבְלַע)—1) to swallow, to swallow up, to swallow down eagerly (for man, beast, hell, earth); figur. to annihilate altogether. Proverbially: עַד־בִּלְעִי רֻקִּי till I swallow down my spittle (Job 7:19), i.e. in a moment; inf. Pi. כְּבַלַּע (where spittle is omitted) like the swallowing down of spittle, i.e. in a moment.—Niph. נִבְלַע to be swallowed up (of enemies), i.e. to be conquered; of the wine (מִן־הַיַּיִן), to be swallowed up, i.e. to become intoxicated (comp. הֲלוּמֵי יַיִן—Pi. בִּלַּע (inf. כְּבַלַּע, see Kal) fut. יְבַלַּע; pause, אֲבַלֵּעַ, בִּלֵּעוּ.—1) to swallow entirely, but only figuratively; to swallow injustice, i.e. to exercise it in abundance; 2) like Kal, to destroy, to annihilate.—Pu. pass. to be brought into destruction, to be carried to destruction, e.g. "lest the king be swallowed up, and all the people that are with him" (2 Sa. 17:16) יְבֻלַּע.—Hith. to destroy oneself.

בֶּלַע (with suffix בִּלְעוֹ, בַּלְעִי m. 1) originally the state of being swallowed up, but as concrete, that which is swallowed up; 2) destruction; 3) p.n. m. of persons (patron. בַּלְעִי) and places.

בִּלְעֲדֵי (בִּלְעֲדֵי with מִן) from עַד and בַּל, בַּל (compounded from a pron. root), prep. originally, not till then, not till, only with suff. pl. בִּלְעָדַי, pause עָדָי— not to me, i.e. besides me, nothing (come) to me, it concerns not me; thus, בִּלְעָדֶיךָ without thee; and in the sense of except, without, is suitable to most passages. מִבַּלְעָדַי without me. More frequent, however, is the pl. const. occurring in many prepositions; מִבַּלְעֲדֵי, בִּלְעֲדֵי except, without being accompanied by a noun or verb. See עַד.

בִּלְעָם 1) p.n. m. (from בֶּלַע, formed with the termination עָם— a curser, a denouncer), a heathen prophet (LXX. Βαλαάμ, Jos. Βάλαμος); 2) p.n. of a place, otherwise יִבְלְעָם.

בָּלַק (Kal only part. with suff. וּבוֹלְקָהּ equiv. to בָּקַק to empty (a country), to devastate.—Pu. (only part. f. מְבֻלָּקָה) pass.

בָּלָק p.n. m. (desolator, conqueror), from בָּלַק, which see.

בֵּלְשַׁאצַּר, once בֵּלְאשַׁצַּר (Babylon.), p.n. masc. of the last king of the Chaldeans. The derivation is obscure.

בִּלְשָׁן p.n. m. (enquirer), from בְּלַשׁ, Aram. to enquire. ָן— is the suffix.

בִּלְתִּ (only before suff. בִּלְתִּי, בִּלְתְּךָ), prep. equiv. to בַּל, בְּלִי, בַּל, not, without; בִּלְתִּי without me; hence also, except; the form is derived from בַּל, by adding the termination ת—ֶ.

בִּלְתִּי adv. not=בְּלִי; next prep. without, except; it becomes conjunctive when it stands as an abbreviation for בִּלְתִּי אֲשֶׁר, בִּלְתִּי אִם. It is distinguished from זוּלָתִי, which generally occurs before a single word, and also for אֶפֶס, אַפְסִי, which occurs in parenthetical sentences, by its position before a complete sentence, and there it may be translated "except," but also except that, if; in that case it expresses next to the negation, the condition. Before nouns: not, without, un——, like בְּלִי, בְּלֹא, closely connected with the nouns: as, בִּ׳ טָהוֹר unclean; בִּ׳ סָרָה without ceasing, unremitting; and before inf. with לְ (where לֹא never stands), סוּר, שְׁתוֹת, בֹּא, לְבִלְתִּי עֲשׂוֹת, שְׁמֹעַ, הָבִיא not to—act,—come,—drink,—turn away, etc.; but more rarely before the finite verb: as,

בִּ׳חֶרְפָּתוֹ יָשִׁיב לוֹ "without his own reproach he shall cause it to turn upon him" (Dan. 11:17); בִּ׳ כָרַע־תַּחַת אַסִּיר "not to be bowed down among prisoners, but they will fall among the slain" (Isa. 10:4; Auth. Vers. "Without me they shall bow down under the prisoners, and they shall fall under the slain," which rendering is very obscure). כָּרַע־תַּחַת is like נָפַל־תַּחַת one idea; likewise לְבִלְתִּי; compounds are לְבִלְתִּי (once לְבִלְתִּי) before the inf. not to; before the finite verb, so that not, without that; מִבִּלְתִּי from that not, because not; עַד־בִּלְתִּי till not (before verbs and nouns); בִּלְתִּי אִם not if=*nisi*, it be then, etc.— The form בִּלְתִּי is from בִּלְתְּ, through the old gen. form ־ִי; like זוּלָתִי, מִנִּי, אַפְסִי, and בִּלְתְּ is lengthened from בַּל, בֶּל.

בָּמָה (with ה of motion בָּמָתָה; pl. בָּמוֹת; const. בָּמוֹת and בָּמֳתֵי, from the Ketib בָּמוֹתֵי; comp. בָּתִּים for בָּתִּים; with suff. בָּמוֹתַי, בָּמֹתָיו, בָּמֹתֶיךָ) f. originally, equiv. to *Βωμ-ός*, elevated place, in Heb. signifying: 1) high place, especially sacred heights, high places for altars; the holy chapels there were called בָּתֵּי הַבָּמוֹת; the priest כֹּהֲנֵי הַבָּמוֹת; sometimes בָּמָה for בֵּית הַבָּ׳, to denote the unlawful worship in the cities, on the mountains of Judah, and in the valley of Hinnom. Many of these sacred places were made like tents of canvas, which were called בָּמוֹת טְלֻאוֹת; 2) castle, fortress: hence figuratively, to place on castles, i.e. to secure; to ride on the high places of the earth, i. e. to possess them; of God, to tread on the high places of the earth, i.e. to rule them; also, of the high places of the sea, of the clouds, which God rules. The root is בּוּם, which see. בֹּמֶת is not the basis of this word.

בִּמְהָל p.n. m. (=בֶּן־מְהָל) a circumcised one, a Hebrew).

בְּמוֹ see מוֹ.

בָּמוֹת p.n. of a place; complete, בָּמוֹת בַּעַל heights of Baal.

בֵּן (const. בֶּן־, rare בֵּן, בְּנִי, בְּנוֹ; with suff. בְּנוֹ, בִּנְךָ; plur. בָּנִים, const. בְּנֵי) m. son (a male child in contrast to בַּת); complete בֶּן־זָכָר; also, a king's son, prince; complete בֶּן־מֶלֶךְ; pl. generally, children. Figuratively, sons of my father, or of my mother, i.e. brother on father or mother's side; son of the Ionians, i.e. Greeks; sons of the poor, i.e. the poor. The application of בֵּן, like אָב father, אָח brother, etc., is ver-manifold; since the ancient figurative expression of the name taken from family circles symbolised many circumstances. It stands therefore for—(a) boy, youth, like παῖς, contrast to בַּת; (b) grandchild (as later בַּר), especially בָּנִים (complete בְּנֵי בָנִים; (c) descendants, progeny; hence, the nations: as, בְּ׳ עַמּוֹן ,בְּ׳ יְהוּדָה ,בְּנֵי יִשְׂרָאֵל, Amonites, Israelites, Judeans; as inhabitants of a province, city, country: בְּנֵי הַמְּדִינָה ,נֹף ,קֶדֶם, צִיּוֹן, etc.; as a community: hence, plur. e.g. בְּנֵי כֻשִׁיִּים ,הַיְּוָנִים, Greeks, Ethiopians; (d) pupil, disciple, protegee, favorite; comp. παῖς, *filius*, e.g. children of God, children of my people, i.e. protected by God, favorites of the people: also, figuratively, son of the house, i.e. slave bred in the house; sons of Bashan, i.e. rams, bred at the meadows (of Bashan); sons of the quiver, i.e. arrows. (e) of animals; the young one, בֶּן־אֲתֹנוֹת ,־בָּקָר ,־עֹרֵב ,־יוֹנָה; even of plants: בֶּן־פֹּרָת; (f) purely symbolical, expressing a certain dependence, as, for instance, of time in describing the age, son of so many years, i.e. so old; son of a year, i.e. one year old; son of a night, i.e. arisen in one night; but son of old age, i.e. born in old age of the parent; of the quality: son of abjectness (בְּלִיַּעַל), of affliction, i.e. abject, miserable; of inheritance, of fatness, of anointment; but the qualification may be often differently expressed: e.g. בֶּן־הַכּוֹת worthy to be beaten, בֶּן־מָוֶת guilty of death, etc. Of בֵּן or בָּן a denom. verb is found in the Niph. (only fut. אִבָּנֶה), signifying to obtain sons. The noun בֵּן, plur. בָּן, appears like אָב ,אָח ,אֵם, primitive and ancient, softened from בֵּן=בַּר; the grammatical analogy is similar.

בֶּן־אוֹנִי p.n. m. (son of affliction) so Rachel called Benjamin.

בֶּן־הֲדַד p.n. m. (הֲדַד name of a deity), a king of Damascus. See הֲדַדְעֶזֶר.

בֶּן־חַיִל p.n. m. (the valiant one).

בֶּן־חָנָן p.n. m. (the benevolent one).

בֶּן־יָמִין p.n. m. (son of fortune), once also Ketib for בִּנְיָמִין.

בָּנָה (fut. יִבְנֶה ,וַיִּבֶן, rare וַיִּבְנֶה, inf. abs. בָּנֹה, const. בְּנוֹת, with suff. בְּנוֹתֵךְ), 1) to build (house, city, altar); with accus. of the object (seldom לְ) and the material (seldom בְּ), to found; with accus. of the place, to build upon; with בְּ, to build near some place; with עַל, to build over, to block up. Also, to rebuild, desolate places, waste grounds; figuratively, to build the fortune of the house, i.e. the descendants; of nations, to procure them happiness, prosperity. Niph. pass. is of another signification; see בֵּן. From which תַּבְנִית, מִבְנֶה, בִּנְיָן, בְּנָיָה, יַבְנֶה, p.n., מְבֻנַּי p.n. and others.

בְּנָה. בְּנָא (Aram.), the same; part. בְּנֵה pass.; inf. מִבְנֵא, מִבְנְיָה. Hith. pass.

בִּנּוּי p.n. masc. (family association). Also בָּנִי.

בָּנַט (not used), to bind. From which אַבְנֵט.

בָּנִי see בִּנּוּי.

בֻּנִּי p.n. m.

בְּנֵי־בְרַק p.n. of a town in the territory of Dan.

בְּנֵי־יַעֲקָן see בְּאֵרוֹת ב׳ י׳.

בְּנָיָה p.n. m. (made happy by God), equiv. to בְּנָיָהוּ.

בִּנְיָה f. equiv. to בִּנְיָן building. The root is בָּנָה.

בְּנָיָהוּ p.n. m. (equiv. to בְּנָיָה).

בֵּינַיִם see בֵּין.

בִּנְיָמִין p.n. m. (son of happiness); Israelitish ancestor; gent. noun. בֶּן־יְמִינִי, or only יְמִינִי.

בִּנְיָן m. equiv. to בִּנְיָה building, from בָּנָה, after the form קִנְיָן.

בִּנִינוּ p.n. m. (perhaps, posterity, from בָּנָה, with נוּ terminating).

בְּנַס (Aram.), to be wrath, originally to snort, to foam (syn. with אָנַף to snort).

בִּנְעָה p.n. m.

בְּסוֹדְיָה p.n. m. (i.e. בְּסוֹד־יָה).

בֵּסַי p.n. f. (related to בֵּצַי).

בָּסַס see בּוּס, as such a verb does not exist.

בָּסַר (not used), originally, to look sourly on a thing, to make sour, to produce acidity, i.e. to be sour; of fruits, unripe. The root is בָּ־סַר, related to סִיר, שְׂאֹר to make sour, whose further analogy see under סִיר, from which בֹּסֶר, בֶּסֶר.

בֹּסֶר masc. place for collecting sour grapes, i.e. unripe (בְּאֻשִׁים bad grapes), from בָּ־סַר.

בֶּסֶר m. the same, only varying in the form.

בְּעַד and בַּעַד (pronom. root; with suff. בַּעֲדִי, בַּעֲדֵנִי, בַּעַדְךָ, pause בַּעֲדֶךָ; בַּעֲדֵךְ, בַּעֲדוֹ, בַּעֲדָהּ, בַּעֲדֵנוּ, בַּעֲדְכֶם, בַּעֲדָם) a compound prep. from עַד (which see), and בְּ *bĕ*, or בַּ (significations of approximity), like *apud*, from *ape—ad*, therefore originally expressing: to—there—near—over. The following are the gradations: 1) by, near something (like *apud*): as, בְּעַד יַד הַשַּׁעַר near by the place (יָד) of the gate, for which in other places אֶל־יַד stands; 2) behind, different from אַחַר, which expresses behind, as keeping back; so the form סָגַר בְּעַד to close behind something, near to it, e.g. in going out, closing the door behind oneself, or closing the door immediately after admitting another; figuratively, סָגַר בְּעַד רֶחֶם "closed up (behind) the womb," i.e. to make unfruitful; so also (Judg.3:22), "and the fat closed upon (behind) the blade," בְּ׳ הַלַּהַב; i.e. the haft almost penetrated; "if he cut off and shut up בְּ׳ עֲרָפֶל behind the cloud of night" (Job 11:10); 3) signifying moving approximity, as, towards, that place, or under, near that place, as, בְּעַד מְעָרוֹת towards caves, i.e. under caves; בְּעַד הַשֶּׁלַח "fall upon (or by) the sword" (Joel 2:8); בְּעַד הַחַלּוֹן by, through the window (Judg. 5:28); 4) approximity and circumference, different from סָבִיב, which only expresses surrounding, without consideration of approximity; especially in the verbs גָּדַר, סָגַר, חָתַם, גֵּן, שׂוּךְ surrounding, closing in, fencing round, covering, etc.; figuratively, for the sake of, especially in the verbs, interceding, inquiring, atoning, standing in the breach, for, etc. (כִּפֶּר, הִתְפַּלֵּל, עָמַד, נָשָׂא, דָּרַשׁ, הִתְחַנֵּן, פָּרַץ); — מִבַּעַד — behind — from, with לְ: as, מִבַּעַד לְצַמָּתֵךְ "from behind thy veil" (Auth.Vers., within thy locks), Cant. 4:1.

בְּעֹד see עוֹד.

בָּעָה (fut. יִבְעֶה, 2 pl. תִּבְעָיוּן, imp. plur. בְּעָיוּ), equiv. to בּוּעַ to swell up, to flow along (related to נָבַע), hence of the bubbling of water on the fire; figuratively, to desire, pray, ask, inquire vehemently. The forms ־יוּן, ־יוּ, are Aram., and proceed from the closing vowel ־ֵי. Compare יִרְבְּיֻן, etc. Niph. to be thrust forward, figuratively, drawn forward, sought for, from which בְּ׳.

בְּעָא, בְּעָה (Aram.) 1) to desire, to pray; e.g. בָּעוּתֵהּ his prayer, construed with מִן, קֳדָם, and מִן־קֳדָם; 2) to seek, to seek forth. From which בָּעוּ.

בָּעוּ (Aram.), fem. prayer, request; originally, the vehement longing, from בְּעָא.

בְּעוֹן see בְּעֹן.

בְּעוֹר p.n. m. (probably, a shepherd, from בְּעִיר cattle, herd).

בִּעוּתִים (with suff. בִּעוּתֶיךָ), m. pl. terrors, from בְּעַת.

בֹּעַז p.n. of a pillar on the left in front of the temple (probably the strong one), part. from בָּ־עַז, related to עַז; comp. יָכִין, name of the other pillar, from כּוּן; 2) p.n. m.

בָּעַט (fut. יִבְעַט) 1) originally, to tread, press forward; hence, to tread (with the feet); with בְּ, figuratively, to despise, abhor; 2) to tread away, to kick behind (of the bull); figuratively, of rebellion, disobedience.

בְּעִי see עִי.

בְּעִיר m. collectively, cattle (related to בְּהֵמָה), field cattle, grazing cattle, from בַּעַר=בָּר field; comp. Aram. בְּעִיר=בּוֹר rough, wild. See בַּעַר.

בַּעַל (in pp. nn. בְּעַל, בָּעַל, Aram. בְּעֵל, hence Heb. בֵּל, with suff. בַּעְלִי, בַּעְלָהּ; pl. בְּעָלִים, const. בַּעֲלֵי; בְּעָלָיו, בְּעָלֶיהָ, בַּעֲלֵיהֶן; primitive) m. lord, originally, the mighty one. The signification, master, is applied—1) to possession and power: e.g. בַּעַל הַשּׁוֹר, הַבַּיִת, proprietor of the ox, —the house; בַּעַל הָאִשָּׁה possessor of a woman, husband; בַּעַל נְעוּרִים the husband of a youthful wife; בַּעֲלֵי גוֹיִם the mighty (warriors) of the people; hence, in connection with nouns to signify possession, as possessor of horns, wings, double edges, dreams, arrows, i.e. the horned one, the winged one, the double-edged one, the dreamer, etc. בַּעַל דְּבָרִים busy one, having law disputes. Seldom of the property due to some one but not in his possession; 2) belonging to a thing, especially before names of cities, to denote inhabitants and citizens; 3) with the article: p.n. of a Phœnician deity (Belus), probably the planet Jupiter, which the Grecians always expressed by Ἡρακλῆς; see בֵּל. בַּעַל is often found in Punic inscriptions; as, Hannibal (חַנִּיבַעַל), Hasdrubal (עַזְרוּבַעַל), Adherbal (אַדִּירְבַּעַל), Abibal (אֲבִיבַעַל), etc.; and gradually we find it in Hebrew surnames: בַּעַל בְּרִית (for which also אֵל בְּרִית the Baal of the covenant, comp. Ζεὺς ὅρκιος); בַּעַל זְבוּב the Baal of flies (see זְבוּב); בַּעַל פְּעוֹר see פְּעוֹר; 4) denoting the possession of things not personal: hence, places (like בֵּית), if it is represented to signify possession, and joined to a noun, בַּעַל הָמוֹן, גָּד, צְפוֹן, פְּרָצִים, מְעוֹן, חֶרְמוֹן, חָצוֹר, תָּמָר, שָׁלִשָׁה, which see; 5) p.n. m. pl. הַבְּעָלִים the statues of Baal (compare עַשְׁתָּרוֹת); from which, בַּעַל, בְּעָלִים, בַּעֲלַת, בְּעָלוֹת, בֵּל.

בְּעֵל Aram., the same.

בָּעַל (fut. יִבְעַל, denom. from בַּעַל); 1) to become master, possessor, to govern, with לְ; hence, בָּעַל אִשָּׁה to become the possessor of a wife, to marry (as in Arabic *malaka*); בֹּעֵל husband, בְּעוּלָה and בְּעֻלַת

בָּעַל the one that is ruled over, married; 2) figuratively, to make something subordinate, despise, with בָּחַל=בְּ.—Niph. to be taken as a wife.

בַּעֲלָה f. 1) female possessor, e. g. of the house, of sorcery (witch), used in the same sense as בַּעַל; 2) figuratively, denoting territory, city, especially as a p. n.; (a) city in the north in the dominion of Judah, otherwise also קִרְיַת יְעָרִים, קִרְיַת בַּעַל; (b) in the south of that territory, otherwise also בָּלָה, בִּלְהָה; (c) p.n. of a mountain.

בְּעָלוֹת p.n. of a city in the south of the territory of Judah.

בַּעַל־חָנָן p.n. m. (gracious ruler).

בְּעֶלְיָדָע p.n. m. (adorer, or worshipper of Baal) for which also אֶלְיָדָע (worshipper of God).

בְּעַלְיָה p.n. m. (the mighty one of the Lord).

בַּעֲלִים p.n. m. (probably, more correct with Josephus and 16 MSS. בַּעֲלִים), however, see שׁ.

בַּעֲלָת p.n. of a city in the territory of Dan (Joseph. Βαλίθ).

בְּעֹן p.n. of a place (Βαιάν), probably equivalent to (בַּעַל מְעוֹן) מְעוֹן.

בַּעֲנָא p.n. m.

בַּעֲנָה p.n. m.

בַּעַר (not used) m. probably: 1) equivalent to בָּר a field, meadow, or forest, which is not cultivated. From which בְּעִיר. 2) figuratively, wild, rough (Aram. בּוּר), uncultivated; אִישׁ־בַּעַר a rough, uncultivated man (boor), from which denomin. בָּעַר (fut. יִבְעַר) to be rough, uncultivated, insensible, uncouth; בֹּעַר of no understanding (always next to כְּסִיל, כָּסַל).—Niph. נִבְעַר pass., see בְּעִיר, בָּר. The transition from roughness, wildness, etc., to wickedness, is here like in all other languages.

בָּעַר (fut. יִבְעַר): 1) to kindle, to set on fire (originally to inflame, to fire) as כְּאֵשׁ תִּבְעַר יַעַר „as the fire burneth a wood" (Ps. 83:14). וַתִּבְעַר בַּצֹּאן וּבַנְּעָרִים „The fire of God is fallen from heaven, and hath burnt up the sheep and the youths" (Job. 1:16).—2) intrans. to burn away, especially of combustibles; זֶפֶת בֹּעֵרָה burning pitch. Pi. בִּעֵר (fut. יְבַעֵר, inf. בַּעֵר); 1) to kindle (wood), to make burn (fire), to burn off (flaming arrows); hence, 2) figuratively, to remove, to clear away, to sweep away, with מִן, away from something; with אַחֲרֵי, to clear away after some one, to sweep away everything; רוּחַ בָּעֵר spirit of removing, sweeping; 3) to pasture, to graze. Pual to be

בָּצִיר harvest, cutting of fruit, of berries; comp. אָבִיב, אָסִיף, זָמִיר; 2) adj. Ketib for בָּצוּר.

בָּצַל (not used) to be peeling, peelable. The root is בָּצַל, comp. Greek σκύλ-ον, σκυλ-όω; Germ. Schale, schäl-en, to peel; comp. also פָּ־צַל to peel.—Piel, to peel off, שָׁחַל; hence שְׁחֵלֶת peel; שַׁל, Gr. σκυλ-εύω, the taking off the clothing (the armour); σύλ-ον= שָׁלָל, συλέω=שַׁל; תָּבָל: hence תְּבֵלֶת; Aram חֲ־צַל to cover over, from which מַחְצֶלֶת an over-covering; בָ־צַל, אָ־צַל, etc., where שׁ, ס, ז, צ interchange without any alteration in the principal signification.

בָּצָל (pl. בְּצָלִים), masc. bulbs, hence, onions, on account of the peelableness of the substance; from בָּ־צַל.

בְּצַלְאֵל p.n. m. (claimed by God).

בַּצְלוּת p.n. m. (covering, clothing), for which also בַּצְלִית occurs.

בָּצַע (fut. יִבְצַע; imp. בְּצַע, with suff. בְּצָעָם, with quiescent suff.), to tear, to break, to cut; hence, to rob, to plunder (of enemies); to heap up money=to make profit; next, to wound, with בְּ (comp. פָּצַע, Aram. בְּזַע, related to פָּקַע, בָּקַע), originally to break (Tal. to break the bread); intrans. to be broken

kindled.—Hiph. (caus), like Pi. in all three significations.

בַּעְרָא p. n. m.

בְּעֵרָה f. brand (that which is burnt)

בַּעֲשֵׂיָא p.n. m.

בַּעְשָׁא p.n. m. of a king of Israel (953—930 B.C.E.), LXX. Βαασά, Joseph. Βασάνης.

בְּעֶשְׁתְּרָה p.n. of a Levitical town (contracted from בֵּית עֶשְׁתְּרָה) otherwise עַשְׁתָּרוֹת; LXX. Βοσόρα, Vulg. Bosra; see עַשְׁתָּרוֹת.

בָּעַת (Kal not used) Niph. נִבְעַת (נִבְעַתִּי for נִבְעַתְתִּי) to be affrighted, terrified, in terror, with מִפְּנֵי and מִלִּפְנֵי, of some one (comp. יָרֵא, נִחַת, פָּחַד, עָרַץ).—Pi. בִּעֵת (3 pers. sing. f. with suff. בִּעֲתַתּוּ, בִּעֲתָתְנִי for בִּעֲתַתְהוּ, part. f. מְבַעִתֶּךָ from מְבַעֶתֶת for מְבַעַת; fut. יְבַעֵת), to set in terror, to attack suddenly.

בְּעָתָה f. fear, terror (compare אֵימָה, פַּלָּצוּת, רְתֵת, רֶטֶט, בַּלָּהָה), from בָּעַת.

בִּץ m. a quagmire, a bog, from בָּצַץ to swell.

בִּצָּה (pl. with suff. בִּצֹּאתָיו), f. quagmire, from בָּצַץ, in the Talmud בִּצְבֵּץ.

בֵּצַי p. n. m. (the brilliant one), see בֵּסַי.

בָּצִיר m. 1) time of cutting the grapes, vintage; originally like

open, to be wounded; inf. with suff. בִּצְעֵךְ, as, בָּא קִצֵּךְ אַמַּת בִּצְעֵךְ "thy end is come, and the measure of thy covetousness" (Jer. 51:13), i.e. of thy being cut off. Pi. בִּצַּע (fut. יְבַצַּע) to cut off (חַיִּים) to deprive, to make profit; figuratively, to bring something to its end; hence, to fulfil a word, to accomplish something.

בֶּצַע (with suff. בִּצְעָם) m.; 1) plunder, originally, that which is torn away, or, in an active sense, the tearing away; hence, figuratively, gain, profit, and the phrase (בּוֹ) מַה־בֶּצַע what profit is there (therein)? 2) equiv. to קֵץ end, originally, cutting off, ceasing.

בָּצַץ (not used) equivalent to בָּקַק to swell forth, or swell up; Aram. בִּצְבֵּץ to protrude; the relationship of צ and ק manifests itself in several roots, by tracing which the lexical analysis is rendered easier.

בָּצֵק (only בָּצֵקָה, בָּצֵקוּ) to swell (of the feet), but in other words used also of swelling of a mass; originally, to rise up.

בָּצֵק m., that which swells up; hence, the dough that swells and ferments; next, dough in general.

בָּצְקַת p.n. of a place (height).

בָּצַר (fut. יִבְצֹר); 1) to cut off (grapes); originally, to prune, with the accus. of the vineyard; hence בָּצִיר a vintage (comp. קָצִיר harvest of corn or fruit); בֹּצֵר vintner; figuratively, of the cutting down of the enemy; 2) to hedge off, to mark a boundary, to separate; hence, the fortifying (of walls and cities); בָּצוּר (Ketib בָּצִיר) fortified, entrenched; figur. he limits (יִבְצֹר) the courage of princes. בְּצֻרוֹת that which is inclosed, i.e. incomprehensible. The sense of confining, limiting, and condensing is then, as usual, transferred to clipping, shortening.—Niph. pass. (from No. 2) but only figuratively, to be fortified, i. e. to become inaccessible (מְזִמָּה plan) with מִן of the person.—Pi. בִּצֵּר (fut. יְבַצֵּר, inf. בַּצֵּר) to fortify (wall, fortress).

בֶּצֶר (pause בָּצֶר, pl. בְּצָרִים) masc.; 1) brittle metal (separated from the mine), quarry stone, from בָּצַר to break; 2) p.n. (a metal district) name of town in the territory of Reuben (LXX. Βοσόρ).

בָּצְרָה f., originally, hedging in, surrounding; hence, a pen (comp. מִכְלָא); 2) p. n. of a town (originally, a place walled in, comp. Phœnician גָּדֵר Cadiz in Spain), in Idumea, probably the present

Bessira in Gebael. Another city is *Βόσρα*, Bosara in the dominions of Hauran, which Jeremiah (in 48:24) designates as a Moabite town.

בִּצָּרוֹן (from בָּצַר firm, fortified), m. fortress, castle.

בַּצֹּרֶת (pl. בַּצָּרוֹת) f. want of rain, dearth; from בָּצַר 1. (comp. עָצַר).

בַּקְבֻּק m. 1) flask, leather bottle, so called from the sound *bak*, *bak*, (comp. בָּקַק, בָּק; 2) p.n. (from בָּק to spread out, e.g. the number of a family).

בַּקְבֻּקְיָה p.n. m. (to be extended by God).

בַּקְבַּקַּר p.n. m.

בֻּקִּי p. n. m. (from בּוּק seclusion).

בֻּקִּיָּהוּ p.n. m. (destroyed by God).

בָּקִיעַ m., breach, rend; especially of the breach in the wall; from בָּקַע (comp. בָּצַע, Aram. בְּזַע).

בָּקַע (fut. יִבְקַע; inf. with suff. בִּקְעָם) equiv. to בָּצַע to cut up (bowels of a woman), to split up (the womb), to cleave (wood), to divide (the sea); hence, of the breaking forth of a fountain; figur. to break in (a camp, a town), to conquer; to split eggs, i. e. to hatch them.—Niph. נִבְקַע to split itself, to burst; hence, to open themselves (of fountains), to break forth (of water, light), figur. to be conquered (of a city), to break forth (from the egg) = to be hatched.—Pi. *intens.* from Kal; and only rarely causative.—Pu. pass. from Kal.—Hiph. to cause to break (a town), to raze; with אֶל against somebody, to break through.—Hoph. to be conquered.—Hith. to split, rend, itself asunder.

בֶּקַע m. splitting, hence, the half, but only the half of a shekel, about two drachms.

בִּקְעָא Aram. equiv. to Heb. בִּקְעָה, which see.

בִּקְעָה const. בִּקְעַת, pl. בְּקָעוֹת) f. fall of earth, marshy plain, valley (originally, a ground that splits itself, or has cracks); בִּקְעַת הַלְּבָנוֹן a marshy plain between Anti-Lebanon and the Hermon.

בָּקַק (1st pret. בַּקֹּתִי equiv. to בּוּק to pour forth, to pour out (a root of sound like בַּק, hence, intrans. Rab. to spread itself, used of the voluptuous vine); trans. to pour around, to empty; figur. to despoil (a people), to depopulate (a country).—Niph. נָבַק (נָבְקָה like נָבְלָה) fut. יִבּוֹק (infin. הִבּוֹק) pass. to be emptied out, to vanish (רוּחַ).—Pi. redoubled form בּוֹקֵק equiv. to Kal. From which בַּקְבֻּק, בַּקְבֻּקְיָה p.n., בֻּקִּי p.n., בֻּקִּיָּהוּ p.n., יָבֹק.

בָּקַר (Kal not used) 1) to dig, to break, to plough (the ground);

hence, בָּקָר cattle for ploughing, like *armentum, f. aramentum* ; fig. to break forth (of light), hence, בֹּקֶר (of the day), dawn, early, light of morning; 2) to break asunder, to judge (judging being connected with the idea of dissecting), only Pi. בִּקֵּר (fut. יְבַקֵּר) to decide, to distinguish between בֵּין־לְ ; with לְ to judge, to contemplate; with בְּ to direct, contemplation for the purpose of judging a matter, to contemplate with pleasure; with the accus., to investigate a matter perseveringly, either to protect or punish it; figur. to consider, to reflect.

בְּקַר (Aram.) equiv. to בָּקַר only Pa. בַּקַּר to inquire into, to search.—The derivation is as in the Hebrew.

בָּקָר (pl. בְּקָרִים) com. (a collective noun), origin., cattle for ploughing, *armentum* (=Aram.), cattle or herd for the use of working in the field, the sing. noun is שׁוֹר (comp. צִפּוֹר, עוֹף ; שֶׂה, צֹאן) in the application, however, it signifies, the larger cattle, for which also בְּקָרִים is found. בֶּן־בָּקָר young cattle; פַּר בֶּן־בָּקָר a young heifer; עֵגֶל בֶּן־בָּקָר a young calf; constructed with the fem., cow; as בָּקָר עָלוֹת suckling cows, which denom. בּוֹקֵר herdsmen, shepherd.

בֹּקֶר (pl. בְּקָרִים) masc., originally, to break forth (early dawn), hence, early morning, dawning, from בָּקַר (if בָּקַר is not equivalent to בָּהַר); מִבֹּקֶר עַד עֶרֶב from morning until evening; אַשְׁמֹרֶת הַבֹּקֶר early watch of the night; hence, if בֹּקֶר is mentioned in the day, it generally signifies the next morning. As an adv. בֹּקֶר, בַּבֹּקֶר (in the accusative), לַבֹּקֶר (poetically) of the morning לַבֹּקֶר לַבֹּקֶר, בַּבֹּקֶר בַּבֹּקֶר, לִבְקָרִים, לַבְּקָרִים every morning; seldom בֹּקֶר has the signification of "soon," for which, however, לַבֹּקֶר occurs.

בַּקָּרָה f. protection, from בָּקַר, which see.

בִּקֹּרֶת fem., investigation, inquiry for punishment, from בָּקַר, which see.

בָּקַשׁ (Kal not used), to seek, to seek after something, to desire, to wish; next, to seek out, to select. The root is בָּ־קַשׁ, Aram. בְּ־חַשׁ, with the general idea of investigating, seeking.—Only Piel בִּקֵּשׁ, fut. יְבַקֵּשׁ ; 1) to seek (perseveringly), abs. and with accus. Very frequently for, to visit; hence the phrases, to seek the countenance of the king, i. e. to visit him, to court his favor; to seek God, i.e. to apply to him, to pray to him; 2) seeking for, striving after, meditating for, e.g. רָעָה נֶפֶשׁ after the misfortune, after the life, either to take it away, or to preserve it; 3) to seek=to demand, to desire, with מִן, מִיַּד of somebody; 4) to seek=to request, with מִן, מִלִּפְנֵי of somebody; with עַל for something; 5) to ask, with מִן, Pu. pass.

בַּקָּשָׁה (later) f. desire; comp. אֲרֶשֶׁת, אַוָּה, רְעוּת).

בַּר (poetically, with suff. בְּרִי) masc., son, Aram. From which also, בְּרַת daughter. This word בַּר is primitive; the supposition of a verbal root is therefore wrong.

בָּר and בַּר m. 1) field, arable land, Aram. בַּר, def. בָּרָא the same, in contrast to towns; originally, open, free place; 2) fruit of the field, corn, whilst yet in the sheaf (therefore not of winnowed corn) transferred also to every kind of corn. Comp. Talm. בְּרִיּוֹן, בְּרִיֹנִי rough, uneducated; בָּרַיְתָא the outer (law), i.e. not Mishnaic; בּוֹר the uneducated one (Hebrew בַּעַר).

בַּר adj. m. בָּרָה fem. (from בָּרַר); 1) proven, proved; בַּר לֵבָב of a pious heart; chosen, select; figur. clean, also in a moral sense; 2) clear=void; from בָּרַר.

בֹּר m. 1) cleanliness (כַּפַּיִם; יָדַיִם) of the hands; as a figure of innocence; 2) equivalent to בֹּרִית which see.

בָּרָא (fut, יִבְרָא) 1) to create, to form, originally, to cut out, model. The root is בָּרָא to cut, comp. חָרַב. Used of God's creating objects of nature; בָּרָא לַעֲשׂוֹת he made it in a creating manner, i.e. he created it anew; comp. הִגְדִּיל לַעֲשׂוֹת; 2) not used, to nourish, to feed. —Niph. pass. from Kal to be created, to be originated; עָם נִבְרָא the people being created, rising.—Pi. בֵּרֵא to cut off, to fell, to hew down (a forest), originally, to cut in deeply; to furrow, to pierce, e.g. בְּחֶרֶב to cut in, inscribe.—Hiph. caus. from Kal from signification 2) to give nourishment, to feed.

בְּרֹאדַךְ an orthographical variation for מְרֹאדַךְ, which see.

בְּרָאיָה p.n. m. (son, adorer of God).

בַּרְבֻּר (after the form חַרְחֻר, בַּקְבּוּק) m. name of a bird (not well defined); probably this word is imitating some idea by sound.

בָּרַד equiv. to פָּרַד to strew; hence, figur. to hail. Comp. בָּרָד, בָּרֹד, בֶּרֶד p.n.

בָּרָד m., grain, hail stones. Comp. פְּרֻדוֹת grains of seed, from פָּרַד to strew.

בָּרֹד adj. masc. (pl. בְּרֻדִּים) dispersed (of colors), checquered, spotted.

בֶּרֶד p.n. of a place (probably, place of seed, from בָּרַד to strew, to sow).

בָּרָה 1) equiv. to בָּרָא (not used), to cut; hence בְּרִית; 2) to feed, to feed oneself, to eat; 3) to choose =בָּרַר.—Hiph. הִבְרָה to give to eat, to let eat.

בָּרוּךְ p.n. m. (blessed; *Benedictus*).

בְּרוֹם (only pl. בְּרוֹמִים) m. a colored checquered stuff; גִּנְזֵי בְּרוֹמִים "in chests of rich apparel" (chests of colored stuffs), Ezek. 27:24, probably damask, from בָּרַם, which see.

בְּרוֹשׁ (or Aram. form בְּרוֹת) m.; 1) tree of the fir kind, the wood of which is used for various purposes, e.g. for floors, musical instruments, lances, etc.; the derivation is to be looked for in בַּר, for וֹשׁ- is an ancient termination. The particulars will be found under שׁ.

בְּרוֹת see בְּרוֹשׁ (Aram. pl. בְּרָן from בְּרוֹ).

בָּרוֹת fem. equiv. to בָּרוּת, nourishment, sustenance, from בָּרָה which see.

בָּרוּת food, nourishment, from בָּרָה 2.

בֵּרוֹתָה (probably equiv. to בְּרוֹתָה from בְּרוֹת) p.n. of an Aramaic-Sobaic town (signifying cypress-place), according to some a maritime town. Βηρυτός (later, Felix Julia).

בֵּרֹתַי p.n. (the same).

בִּרְזוֹת (Ketib) בִּרְזָיִת (Keri) p.n. m. (from בַּר son, and זַיִת, זוֹת olive; originally, splendour, i.e. the beautiful one); see זַיִת, זוֹת.

בַּרְזֶל (with suff. בַּרְזִלִּי) m., equiv. to בַּזֶל βασάλ-της with ר interpolated, hard stuff, marble-iron, generally, iron, but only in reference to its hardness; hence, figuratively, hard, strong, e.g., iron sceptre, iron land, i.e. rigorous, severe government, unfruitful land. Comp. Aram. בַּרְזִיל severe commander. Next transferred to fetter, iron instrument. The root is בָּזַל to be hard, close, firm.

בַּרְזִלַּי p.n. m. (the strong, iron one).

בָּרַח (fut. יִבְרַח) 1) to go away, to depart, to hurry away, to flee, with מִן, מִלִּפְנֵי, מִפְּנֵי of the person, from whom one hastens away, escapes; with מִיַּד out of the power of some one; with מֵאֵת to hasten away from the proximity; with אֶל, לְ, accusative of the place whither one flees; with מִן of the place from which one flees; with אַחֲרֵי to flee after, to follow after; 2) figuratively, with בְּתוֹךְ to go away through something=to bolt through, originally denom. from בְּרִיחַ.—Hiph. הִבְרִיחַ (caus.); 1) to make fugitive, to put to flight, to drive away; 2) denom. from בְּרִיחַ; to cause to be bolted.

בְּרִחַ see בָּרִיחַ.

בְּרִי (only in Job) m. serenity, regularly formed from בָּרָה; after the forms חֲצִי, צְבִי, פְּרִי. See בָּרָה.

בֵּרִי (equiv. to בְּאֵרִי) p.n. mas. (*fontanus*).

בָּרִיא adj. m., בְּרִיאָה f. (fattened, of beast and man), fat (of food), from בָּרָא 2.

בְּרִיאָה f. the created, the new one not heard of; from בָּרָא 1.

בִּרְיָה f. 1) food, nourishment (comp. בָּרוּת, בָּרוֹת); 2) part. pass. f. Kal. (after the Aram. form)=בָּרוּי fattened, fat (comp. the form עֲרָיָה), for which, however, some read בְּרִיאָה, from בָּרִיא.

בָּרִחַ, בָּרִיחַ (pl. בְּרִיחִים) adj. m. fugitive; of a serpent, stretching itself, slipping away, quickly; also where נָחָשׁ signifies a planetary figure.

בְּרִיחַ m. 1) the same; hence בְּרִיחֶיהָ her fugitive ones; 2) figuratively, wood stretched forth, a bolt, orig., a bar, e.g. for the closing of gates; the bolts of the earth, i.e. that obstruct the egress. From בָּרַח pass. form.

בְּרִיעָה p.n. m. etymologically equiv. to בְּרָעָה=בְּרִיעָה the unfortunate one), patron. בְּרִיעִי.

בְּרִית fem. originally, the cutting of animals of sacrifices, trans. to covenant, treaty, on account of the custom to pass between two rows of animals cut for sacrifices. Root בָּרָה. In a wider sense, בְּרִית naturally implies all covenants (between nations, friends, and married couples), especially of the covenant of God with the patriarchs, and later, with Israel; hence, sometimes equiv. to promise, ordinance, as part of the covenant; as, אֶרֶץ הַבְּרִית land of the covenant; i.e. Palestine; מַלְאַךְ הַבְּרִית the messenger of the covenant, i.e. the Messiah; לֻחוֹת הַבְּרִית tablets of the law, etc., בְּרִית is sometimes used as a concrete for mediator of the covenant, token of the covenant, circumcision, or people of the covenant. The conclusion of a covenant is expressed by הֵקִים, כָּרַת, בָּא, עָבַר, שָׂם, נָתַן בְּ׳; the dissolving of a covenant is expressed by שִׁקֵּר, חִלֵּל, עָזַב, הֵפִיר בְּ׳.

בַּעַל בְּרִית p.n. of a deity of Sechem (Baal of the covenant; comp. Ζεὺς ὅρκιος, *deus fidius*.)

בֹּרִית f. for which also בֹּר means of cleansing, generally occurs in conjunction with נֶתֶר *νίτρ-ον*, where the latter signifies a mineral, the former, a vegetable kali (alkaline salt extracted) from fullers' earth. The root is בָּרַר.

בָּרַךְ (fut. יִבְרַךְ) 1) to bow, to bend oneself (*inflectere, curvare*), בָּרַךְ עַל־בִּרְכַּיִם kneel; 2) to bend the knees, equiv. to worship, to pray (before God), to obtain by prayer; hence, to bless, only part. pass. בָּרוּךְ blessed, specially in the form of salutation: בָּרוּךְ יְיָ, בָּרוּךְ לַיְיָ to praise.—Niph. נִבְרַךְ see Hith. —Pi. בֵּרֵךְ (with suff. וּבֵרַכְךָ; fut. יְבָרֵךְ; inf. בָּרֵךְ, בָּרֹךְ); 1) to worship (adore, through praise, lauding, invocations), originally, bending the knee, with the accus. of the obj. sometimes with the addition of בְּשֵׁם adoration of the Divine name by calling on it in prayer: בָּרֵךְ אֱלֹהִים וָמֻת (only) pray to God, and die (nevertheless); 2) to implore something from God, either blessing: hence, of the blessing of the priest, the prophet, or of dying parents; or imploring destruction=to curse; hence generally, to bless, with the accusative; sometimes לְ with double accus., blessing with something; also with בְּ of the object; likewise of God, to bless, to felicitate, of the pronouncing of a blessing, or of the effecting of a blessing; to greet (an arriver), to wish luck (to a departer), etc.; to curse.—Pu. pass. —Hiph. הִבְרִיךְ to cause to kneel down (camels), to rest.—Hith. and Niph. to bless oneself; with בְּ of the object whose luck one wishes to assimilate to himself, or whom one implores for a blessing. From which בָּרוּךְ, אַבְרֵךְ, בֶּרֶכְיָהוּ, בָּרֶךְ p. n., יְבֶרֶכְיָהוּ p. n.

בְּרַךְ (Aram.) the same.—Pael בָּרֵךְ equiv. to Hebrew בֵּרֵךְ.

בֶּרֶךְ (dual בִּרְכַּיִם) f. knee, originally, bent, often in use like the Greek *τὰ γούνατα*, from בָּרַךְ, which see.

בְּרַךְ (Aram.) f. the same, otherwise also אַרְכּוּבָא, which see.

בָּרַכְאֵל p. n. m. (the worshipper of God, בָּרֵךְ part. for בָּרֵךְ).

בְּרָכָה (with the interrog. הַ, הַבְּרָכָה, cons. בִּרְכַּת; pl. בְּרָכוֹת, c. בִּרְכוֹת), f. 1) blessing, whether it be as the result of a blessing=present from God, benefit, or as the wish or imploring of a blessing; e. g. נֶפֶשׁ בְּרָכָה blessed (benevolent) soul; עֲשׂוּ אִתִּי בְרָכָה "act salutary (for you) towards me," etc., (Author. Ver. "Make an agreement for me," etc.), 2 Kings 18:31; 2) p. n. of a valley near Tekoa; 3) p. n. m

בְּרֵכָה (const. בְּרֵכַת, pl. בְּרֵכוֹת) fem. originally, bowing, bending, winding, with מַיִם winding of waters, but when standing alone, signifies a pond, similar to that which formed the pool of Siloah (Neh. 3:15), from בָּרַךְ.

בֶּרֶכְיָה p. n. masc. (blessing of God), בְּרָכָה=בֶּרֶךְ, LXX. *Βαραχιας*.

בֶּרֶכְיָהוּ p.n. m. (the same).

בָּרַם (not used) colored, checkered. Arab., in the intensive form, to make colored. From which בְּרוֹם.

בְּרַם Aram. adv. but, however, in Targ. assuring: truly, certainly.

בֶּרַע p.n. m. (probably =בֶּן־רַע).

בָּרַק (not used) 1) to brighten, to lighten; hence בַּרְקוֹס ,בָּרֶקֶת ,בָּרָק p.n.; 2) equiv. to בָּרַךְ to break, to bruise, to shatter; comp. Lat. *fra(n)g-ere*, to break. From which בַּרְקָן.

בָּרָק (pl. בְּרָקִים) masc. 1) lightning, orig., brilliancy; hence בְּרַק חֶרֶב the brilliancy of the sword, i.e. glittering sword; also בָּרָק alone indicates the same; 2) p. n. m. (the brilliant one).

בַּרְקוֹס p.n. masc. (from בָּרָק, see שׁ; comp. the Punic *Bar-cas*.).

בַּרְקָן (only plur. בַּרְקָנִים) masc. the breaker to pieces, the bruiser to pieces (after the form אַלְמָן) according to some, the thrashing machine, according to others, certain thorny plants, from בָּרַק 2.

בָּרֶקֶת f. emerald, so called from its brilliancy. See בָּרַק 1.

בָּרְקַת f. the same.

בָּרַר (בָּרוֹתִי, inf. בָּר, like שַׁךְ, רַד) 1) to elect, to choose, to select, e.g. מֹרְדִים to purge out the rebels; part. בָּרוּר selected, chosen (related to בָּחַר ,בָּרָה); 2) in the physical and moral sense, particip. distinguished, eminent, able; hence, pure, שָׂפָה בְרוּרָה pure language; 3) not used, clean; transferred to emptiness.—Niph. נָבַר (imp. הִבָּרוּ, part. נָבָר) to cleanse oneself (morally) Pi. intensitive from Kal signification 2.—Hiph. (caus.) to make clean (grain), to purify, e.g. the arrow from the rust, i.e. to sharpen.—Hith. to shew, conduct oneself clean, pure (pious); תִּתָּבָר for תִּתְבָּרֵר. From which, בֹּר ,בַּר, בֹּרִית.

בִּרְשַׁע p.n. m. (son of victory, victor, from רֶשַׁע and בֵּן).

בְּשׂוֹר (always, with the article) p.n. a brook, LXX. *Βόσορ*, Joseph. *Βάσελος*, now El-Scheria.

בְּשֹׂרָה see בְּשׂוֹרָה.

בָּשַׁל probably transposed =שָׁבַל to swell, to boil, to seethe; figur. to ripen, originally, to be boiled (by the sun); comp. *πέπτω*, *coqui*.

Aram. שְׁלַק in this double sense. Pi. בִּשֵּׁל to boil (trans.) =מְבַשֵּׁל cook.—Pu. pass.—Hiph. to make ripe (originally, to boil.)

בָּשֵׁל adj. m. בְּשֵׁלָה f. equiv. to בָּשִׁיל cooked, prepared, subst. that which is boiled.

בִּשְׁלָם p.n. m. (=בֶּן־שְׁלָם).

בָּשַׂם (not used) to smell well, to diffuse fragrance. The root is בָּ־שָׂם equivalent to סַם, hence סַם sweet odour; comp. Aram. בְּסַם; Pa. בַּסֵּם and בְּלָסָם, from which Βάλσαμος. From which בֶּשֶׂם, בָּשָׂם, בֹּשֶׂם, בָּשְׂמַת, p. n., יִבְשָׂם p. n., מִבְשָׂם p.n.

בָּשָׂם m. balsam-shrub.

בֶּשֶׂם (plur. בְּשָׂמִים) balsam-odour, sweet odour; רֹאשׁ בְּשָׂמִים precious spices; נָזַל בָּשָׂם the flowing out of spices, i.e. diffusion of fragrance.

בֹּשֶׂם masc. odour of spice, spice; hence קִנְּמָן־בֶּשֶׂם sweet cinnamon, (קִנָּמוֹן, Gr. κίνναμον) קְנֵה־בֹשֶׂם sweet calamus; רָאשׁ כָּל־בֹּשֶׂם the principal spices, עֲרוּגוֹת־הַבֹּשֶׂם, beds or furrows of spices.

בָּשְׂמַת p.n. f. one that is fragrant of balm.

בשן (only with ה affix בָּשְׁנָה f. from בּשׁ shame; ־ָן is a suffix, as probably like in אָזֶן, אָזְנַן, צִפֹּרֶן.

בָּשָׁן p.n. a country the other side of the Jordan, celebrated for its oak forest, and for its cattle pasturage; Samaritan בְּתָנִין, LXX. Βασάν, Eus. Βασανῖτις, Joseph. Βαταναία, Batanæa, now called el-Bottin.

בָּשָׁם; בֹּשֶׂם; see בּוּס.

בִּשֵּׂר (only Pi. בִּשֵּׂר, fut. יְבַשֵּׂר) 1) to announce, relate, whether good or evil; hence, with the addition בִּשֵּׂר טוֹב to announce good; בִּשֵּׂר תְּהִלָּה יְשׁוּעָה to announce praise, help; even to announce a defeat (1 Sam. 4:17); 2) to announce something good, joyful, with the accus. of the person, but it never signifies, cheering.—Hith. only יִתְבַּשֵּׂר origin., it announces itself, it is announced.

בָּשָׂר (pl. בְּשָׂרִים) m. 1) flesh (of the bodies of man and beast); hence, body in general, יְגִעַת בָּשָׂר bodily exertion; 2) figur. (*a*) =σάρξ, hence, man, mortal, in general; זְרוֹעַ בָּשָׂר human arm (i.e. mortal, weak), (*b*) relations of consanguinity (related to שְׁאֵר) properly of the same flesh (of the same kind). Sometimes by way of omission =בְּשַׂר עֶרְוָה nakedness. It is not connected with the verbal root בָּשַׂר.

בְּשַׂר (def. בִּשְׂרָא) Aram. the same.

בֹּשֶׁת (with suff. בָּשְׁתְּךָ) f. 1) shame;

complete, בֹּשֶׁת פָּנִים paleness of face (Auth. Vers. "confusion of face." Dan. 9:7, 8), blushing, disgrace. עָטָה לָבַשׁ בּ' to be covered with shame; figuratively, parts of the body concealed: as, עֶרְיַת בֹּשֶׁת uncovering of the shame, for which also occurs עֶרְיָה־בֹשֶׁת. 2) expression of contempt for an idol. Root בּוֹשׁ.

בַּת (contracted from בֶּנֶת; with suff. בִּתִּי; plur. בָּנוֹת; const. בְּנוֹת; formed from בֵּן) f. daughter, but also granddaughter, female progeny, foster daughter, girl, virgin, female pupil, female inhabitant of a town, etc.; the same gradations as found in בֵּן. בַּת is also used (a) in connection with names of cities and countries, or עַם for inhabitants in general; hence also with the addition בְּתוּלָה (virgin), and even as a surname to cities, like בַּת צִיּוֹן, בַּת בָּבֶל. (b) to signify the age of the f. kind: daughter of one, two, ten years, i.e. so old; (c) in poet. figures, e.g. daughter of the tree, i.e. branch; daughter of the song, i.e. cantatrice; daughter of the eye, i.e. pupil of the eye; daughter of the town, i.e. adjacent premises; see בֵּן.

בַּת (pl. בַּתִּים) m. measure for fluids; originally, *receptaculum*. Comp. בַּיִת.

בַּת (בַּתִּין) Aram. the same.

בַּת רַבִּים p.n. of a gate.

בַּת שֶׁבַע p.n. f. (one that respects, or honors an oath).

בָּתָה (not used) equiv. to בַּת=פַּת, to break, to destroy.

בָּתָה f. destruction, equiv. to בַּתָּה.

בַּתָּה (only plur. בַּתּוֹת) f. the same; נַחֲלֵי הַבַּתּוֹת valleys of destruction, i.e. desolated valleys. Root בָּתַת.

בְּתוּאֵל 1) p.n. m. (habitation of God); 2) p.n. of a place, where בְּתוּל stands once for the above.

בְּתוּלָה (pl. בְּתוּלוֹת) f. virgin; originally, the separated one, the modest one, from בָּתַל; also applied to the betrothed virgin; figur. of cities, countries, and nations, especially of cities never conquered. Probably בְּתוּל is a noun originating from בַּת little, young girl, the וּל being the diminutive termination.

בְּתוּלִים m. pl. virginity, state of virginity (compare זְקֻנִים, עֲלוּמִים, נְעוּרִים); figuratively, tokens of virginity.

בִּתְיָה p.n. m. (=מַתְיָה).

בָּתִּים see בַּיִת.

בָּתַל (not used) equiv. to בָּדַל to be separated, divided: hence of the secluded life of the Eastern virgin. See בְּתוּלָה.

בָּתַק, only Pi. בִּתֵּק to pierce, to thrust down.

בָּתַר, Pi. בִּתֵּר to cut up, to split, related to פָּתַר.

בָּתַר (Aram.) and **בָּאתַר**, equiv. to בְּאַתַר after the place, i.e. hereupon, after.

בֶּתֶר (with suff. בִּתְרוֹ) m. piece, part, from which הָרֵי בָתֶר intersected mountains, i.e. rugged mountains.

בִּתְרוֹן p.n. a clift on the eastern bank of the Jordan.

בָּתַת (not used) equiv. to בָּתָה. From which בַּתָּה.

ג

ג, called *gimel*, גָּמֶל (pl. גְּמָלִין), signifies as much as גָּמָל camel, perhaps from the original similarity of the letter in shape to the neck of a camel; the sound is like *g* (only in Arab. lately grown to a syllable, even without being hardened by the dagesh), and, as a numeral, signifies 3. By the near relationship of the palatives it interchanges with כ, ק; e.g. גָּבַב, כָּפַף; גָּבַל, כָּבַל; גָּבַן, כָּפַן; גָּדַד, קָדַד; אָנַךְ, עָקַר; גָּמַץ, קָמַץ, but also with the palative gutturals ע, ח, e.g. גָּרַם, חָרַם; גָּרַשׁ, עָרַם, seldom with *yod*, which is a modulated palatine.

גֵּא (for גֵּאֶה) m. pride, haughtiness. The const. pl. גֵּאֵי is found only in the Keri (Ps. 123:4).

גָּאָה (fut. יִגְאֶה, inf. abs. גָּאֹה to rise above) of plants. Comp. שָׂגָה, שָׂגָא to swell (of water); figur. to be elevated, majestic (of glory, splendour); and, in the derivations, also in a bad sense.

גֵּאֶה (plur. גֵּאִים) adj. m., גֵּאָה f. 1) high, elevated, eminent; next also in a bad sense, haughty, proud, overbearing; 2) subst. pride, haughtiness.

גְּאוּאֵל p.n. m. (ornament of God).

גַּאֲוָה f. elevation, pride; in a good sense, majesty, highness; in a bad sense, pride, haughtiness: עֹשֵׂה גַאֲוָה doing proudly; עֲנָקָה גַאֲוָה one that embraces haughtiness, with accus. of the person. גַּאֲוָה Job 41:6, is equiv. to גֵּוָה ibid. 20:25, body, back.

גְּאוּלִים (only pl.) m. redemption, deliverance. The pl. is only used in an abstract form.

גָּאוֹן (pl. גְּאוֹנִים, with sing. signification, Ezek. 16:56) m. rising, swelling (of waves), trans. to—1) pride, haughtiness; 2) highness, eminence, glory; גְּאוֹן יַעֲקֹב the glory of Jacob, the holy land, ג׳ הַיַּרְדֵּן the pride, the splendour of the Jordan, its magnificent shore.

גֵּאוּת (with fixed *Tsere*) f. 1) rising

upwards, e.g. of the smoke (עָשָׁן); 2) pride, haughtiness: עָשָׂה גֵאוּת to exercise excellence; 3) swelling, e.g. of the sea (גֵ' הַיָּם); 4) splendour, glory.

גַּאֲיוֹן (only Ketib, plur. גַּאֲיוֹנִים) m. the proud one, the haughty one. The form is like אֶבְיוֹן, עֶלְיוֹן.

גַּאֲיוֹת see גַּי.

גָּאַל (fut. יִגְאַל) 1) trans. to redeem, to loosen that which is bound; to loosen from the enemy, i.e. to save, to liberate; also, to save from servitude, imprisonment, dangers, etc. To loosen a slave, i.e. to set him at liberty; to loosen something vowed or sacred, i.e. to liberate him from the bands preventing certain gratifications; to redeem something sold, i.e. to loosen it from the possessor: hence Job 3:5, "Darkness and the shadow of death shall reclaim him," i.e. again possess him as before the creation (Gen. 1:2). To redeem the blood of the slave, i.e. to avenge; hence גֹּאֵל or גֹּאֵל הַדָּם avenger of blood. The right of redemption and avenging of blood were possessed by the relative only: hence relative; 2) intrans. to be loose, free, i.e. unfettered, profane, because the Hebrew considers that which is sacred inaccessible to the uninitiated, and, as it were, in fetters for him (comp. the modern מֻתָּר loosened, i.e. permitted; אָסוּר bound, i.e. prohibited); hence generally to be rejected, profaned. The same double signification is found in חֹל (חָלַל), which is only a graduation from it, like גָּעַל arose, from גָּאַל. Niph. to be re-bought, to be redeemed; 2) to be profaned, to be polluted, e.g. by sin, blood. Pi. גֵּאֵל to defile. Pu. pass. to be rejected (of the priesthood). Niph. and Pu. מְגֹאָל like Niph. 2. Hiph. to make a garment unholy by blood, only pret. 1st pers. אֶגְאָלְתִּי for הִגְאַלְתִּי. Hith. to defile oneself, to make oneself unclean.

גֹּאַל (const. pl. גָּאֳלֵי) m. desecration, profanation, from גָּאַל 2.

גְּאֻלָּה f. 1) redemption, redeeming of the sold ground, trans. to the right of repurchasing, ground repurchased, price of repurchasing; 2) relationship, having the right of redemption; אִישׁ גְּאֻלָּה relative.

גַּב (from גָּבַב, which see, with suff. גַּבִּי, pl. גַּבִּים, גַּבּוֹת, with double signification), m. that which is hilly, vaulted, hunched; hence, 1) hill, back, something elevated; back of the altar, i.e. the upper part, hence, of the back of man and beasts, hunched-backed, also of the shield (the thick bosses of his bucklers, Job 15:26), a mound, etc., חָרַשׁ עַל גַּב to plough on the back, i.e. to wound; 2) vault, arch, arched booth; hence, dwelling of harlots, so called because they used to sit on these arched or vaulted booths; arches of the wheels (1 Kings 7:33), arches of the eyes, brows, in which, however, only the fem. pl. is used.

גַּב (with suff. גַּבִּי, גַּבֵּיהּ, etc.), Aram. m. back, as in Hebrew, but generally a prepos. עַל גַּב upon, over, near, by.

גָּב part. from גוב which see.

גֵּב (only pl. גֵּבִים) m. that which is cut, a piece, hence, 1) a piece of wood, board, from גוב to cut; 2) cistern, from גוב; equiv. to גּוֹב locusts, from גוב to group together.

גֹּב (def. גֻּבָּא, pl. גֻּבִּין) Aram. m. cistern, pit; equiv. to גֵּב 2 in Hebrew.

גָּבָא (not used) equiv. to גוב either to gather, to put together, or to dig; to both significations the noun derived therefrom suits.

גֶּבֶא (pl. גְּבָאִים) masc. cistern, pit; from גָּבָא, which see.

גָּבַב (not used) to be hilly, vaulted, humped, bent, equiv. to כָּפַף.

גָּבַב (not used) Aram. equiv. to גוב to dig, to deepen, from which גֹּב.

גָּבַהּ (3 pret. f. גָּבְהָא Ezek. 31:5; inf. גָּבְהוּת, fut. יִגְבַּהּ; 3 plur. fut. תִּגְבְּהֶינָה irreg., to rise, to shoot up; hence, 1) to be high of stature; 2) to be elevated, courageous; 3) to be proud, haughty, presumptuous; comp. גָּבַח.—Hiph. הִגְבִּיהַּ to make high, to elevate, generally, caus. from Kal. Related to גָּבַב.

גֹּבַהּ (with suff. גָּבְהוֹ; plur. const. גָּבְהֵי) m. 1) height; 2) highness, majesty; 3) pride, haughtiness; ג׳ לֵב pride of the heart; ג׳ רוּחַ presumption of the mind; ג׳ אַף carrying the nose high, i.e. pride.

גָּבֹהַּ (const. גְּבֹהַּ and also גְּבַהּ, like גָּדֵל from גָּדוֹל) adj. m. גְּבֹהָה f.; 1) high, of objects of nature; next, presumptuous, proud; 2) subst. height; גְּבֹהִים the proud ones; גְּבֹהָה pride.

גַּבְהוּת f. haughtiness, pride.

גְּבוּל (also גְּבֻל; pl. גְּבוּלִים coll.) m. measure for boundaries, cord for measuring landmarks (origin. that which is entwined, twisted) from which 1) border in general (comp. *finis—funis*) hedge, marking off; 2) territory which is hedged off, from which גָּבַל denom. to limit, to draw a boundary, with בְּ to adjoin. Hiph. to border round; see גָּבַל.

גְּבוּלָה (poet.) f. encompassing.—The pl. ־לוֹת like גְּבוּל.

גִּבּוֹר (also גִּבֹּר) 1) adj. m. valorous, strong, valiant, powerful, heroical; transferred to active, able, honest; 2) subst. strong one, hero, warrior, (גִּבּוֹר חַיִל) leader, transferred to tyrant, perpetrator of violence: חֶרֶב גִּבּוֹר sword of a hero; see גָּבַל.

גְּבוּרָא (Aram.) f. valour, power, omnipotence.

גְּבוּרָה fem. strength, power, valour, courage; figur., power of war, power of action (of God), victory, conquest.

גָּבַח (not used) to be high of forehead; related to גָּבַהּ.

גִּבֵּחַ adj. m. to be high of forehead, as an indication of baldness, different from קֵרֵחַ, which signifies baldness of the back of the head.

גַּבַּחַת (the feminine form from גִּבֵּחַ) f. bald, fore part of the head, transferred to bald place of the garment on the furthermost side.

גַּבַּי p. n. m. collector of taxes.

גֵּבִים p.n. masc. a place not far from Jerusalem (cisterns, pits).

גְּבִינָה f. cheese. See גָּבַן.

גָּבִיעַ (not גָּבִיעַ) m. cup, transferred to a calyx, from גָּבַע equiv. to גָּבַהּ, גָּבַב to be arched.

גְּבִיר adj. m. גְּבִירָה f. ruling, leading, vigorous, but also as a substan., lord, master, governor, mistress, lady.

גָּבִישׁ masc. petrified, frozen; hence, ice; figur. crystal, so called from its similarity in appearance. For the etymology, see גָּבַשׁ.

גָּבַל (not used) equiv. to חָבַל, כָּבַל to turn, to twine, to plait, to plait a cord, from which גְּבוּל, which see.

גְּבַל p.n. of a Phœnician city, now called Dschobail, formerly, Byblus (a mountain district, from גָּבַל, equiv. to גָּבַע).

גְּבָל p.n. of a mountainous region, southerly of the Dead Sea (mountain district) now called Dschebâl.

גְּבֻל, גְּבָל, see גְּבוּל.

גַּבְלֻת f. that which is twined, turned, twisted, plaited; hence, wreathen work: שַׁרְשְׁרֹת גַּבְלֻת a little chain resembling cords joined together.

גָּבַן (not used) equiv. to כָּפַן to bend, to cringe, to bow, from which גִּבֵּן crooked-back, hunch, גַּבְנֹן humped mountain, i. e. rugged, גְּבִינָה cheese, probably from its shape.

גִּבֵּן adj. m. humpy, subst. crooked back, hunched-backed.

גַּבְנֹן (only pl. ־נִּים) m. back of a hill, crooked mountain; modern Heb. גַּבְנוּנִית summit.

גָּבַע (not used) 1) to be vaulted,

rounded, arched; hence, 2) to be high, hilly, with the secondary idea of being arched, vaulted. It appears, however, on comparing this root with kindred roots, that the sense of deepening out was also included.

גֶּבַע p.n. (hill-city) a city in the territory of Benjamin; hence, also, גֶּבַע בִּנְיָמִין (the hill of Benjamin).

גִּבְעָא (for גִּבְעָאִי) p.n. m. (dweller on hills).

גִּבְעָה (pl. גְּבָעוֹת) fem. 1) hill; also, hill of ancient times (Prov. 8:25), otherwise, also, called גִּבְעַת עוֹלָם; Zion is called, hill of God (גִּ' יְיָ), like Bethel was formerly called גִּ' הָאֱלֹהִים; sometimes it is used for בָּמָה (Jer. 3:23); 2) p. n. of many cities situate on hills, and (a) a city in the territory of Benjamin, which being the birth-place of Saul was also called גִּבְעַת שָׁאוּל; gent. גִּבְעָתִי; (b) city in the territory of Judah.

גִּבְעוֹן p.n. (hill-territory) a city in the territory of Benjamin; gent. גִּבְעֹנִי.

גִּבְעֹל m. small cup, cup of blossoms, e.g. the flax was bolled, i.e. blossomed (Exod. 9:31); the form is from גֶּבַע with the diminutive עֹל.

גִּבְעַת p.n. (place of a hill), a city in the territory of Benjamin; גִּ' הָאֱלֹהִים a place in Kirjat-Jearim, where, in the dwelling of Abinadab, the ark of the Lord was deposited; גִּ' אַמָּה (the metropolitan hill, not far from גִּיחַ in the territory of Benjamin; גִּ' גָּרֵב (hill of the freebooters) a place in the west of Jerusalem; גִּ' הַחֲכִילָה (beautiful hill) in the south of the desert Siv; גִּ' הַמּוֹרֶה (hill of the archers) a place not far from Gilgal; גִּ' פִּנְחָס (hill of Phineas) town in Ephraim.

גָּבַר (from גָּבֵר, hence, 3 pers. pl. in pause גָּבֵרוּ; fut. יִגְבַּר); to be strong, vigorous, able to defend oneself (related to כָּבַר, אָבַר); hence, to conquer, גָּבַר חַיִל to be strong, rich in property גָּבַר מִן, עַל to be stronger than; the waters were strong, i. e. they increased. —Pi. to make strong, powerful; חֲיָלִים to increase in strength, to sharpen, to enlarge. — Hiph. to exercise strength, to confirm (בְּרִית לָשׁוֹן).—Hith. to shew oneself strong over (עַל) the enemy, i. e. to conquer him; to conduct oneself haughtily, presumptuously (אֶל) to God.

גֶּבֶר (const. גְּבַר Ps. 18:26, where תָּמִים stands as a substantive) m. 1) valourous one, man, warrior, but also like זָכָר of the mas. gender; hence, husband, and also masc. child; in contrast to God, however, equivalent to man, since woman is scarcely esteemed in the east; לִגְבָרִים man for man; 2) like אִישׁ pronom. every one; 3) p.n. masc. (warrior, hero).

גְּבַר (pl. גֻּבְרִין, from גּוּבַר) Aram. m. the same.

גֶּבֶר p.n. m. (not the name of a place: hero).

גִּבָּר (Aram.) m. hero, strong one.

גַּבְרִיאֵל pr. name (hero of God), an angel.

גְּבֶרֶת (originally f. from גְּבִיר, with suff. גְּבִרְתִּי) fem. lady, mistress: גְּ׳ מַמְלָכוֹת mistress over kingdoms.

גָּבַשׁ (not used) to freeze (according to Arab. analogy; since גַּב, however, has the same fundamental signification, viz. to be crowded, merged together, גָּבִישׁ may be derived therefrom, as ־ִישׁ is sometimes only a suffix.

גִּבְּתוֹן p.n. (rising ground). Town in the territory of Dan; in the Talmud it is also called גִּבַּת.

גָּג (with ה at the end גַּגָּה, with suff. גַּגִּי, pl. גַּגּוֹת) m. roof, that which covers, shelters; figur. roof of the altar, i.e. surface. There is, however, no root in Hebrew of which the first and last syllable are alike, except it is reduplicated; hence, the root גָּא, reduplicated גָּאגָא, signifying, to cover. Comp. טִיט, סוּס, לוּל, דַּד, and others.

גַּד m. 1) coriander from גָּדַד to cut in, on account of the small cuts in the grains; 2) luck, originally, that which is allotted, measured to one. With the article, deity of fortune, i.e. *Bel*.

גָּד m. 1) good fortune, בְּגָד (after the Ketib) Gen. 20:11, *ἐν τύχῃ*, with fortune; 2) p.n. (fortunate one); נַחַל גָּד brook of Gad, i.e. Jabok; gent. n. גָּדִי.

גְּדָבָר (only def. pl. גְּדָבְרַיָּא) Aram. m. master of the treasury; see גִּזְבָּר.

גֻּדְגֹּד (with ה at the end ־דָה) p. n. of a place in the desert (incision, rent).

I. גָּדַד (fut. יָגֹד, 3 per. pl. יָגוֹדּוּ, probably also יָגוּד, with dagesh dissolved in a long vowel) equiv. to חָדַד or קָדַד to make an incision, a scratch; hence, figur. to press on (עַל) somebody, almost; to make an incision. In the derivatives, the signification of meting out (of the fate) has been formed from the sense of cutting.—Hithpael הִתְגּוֹדֵד 1) to make incisions in one's own body (as a sign of mourning, idolatry); next, to press oneself into something, or to press together somewhere.

II. גָּדַד (not used) to combine, to connect, to assemble in hosts; from which גְּדוּד troop.

גְּדַד (imp. גֹּדּוּ) Aram. to cut off, to hew down.

I. גָּדָה (not used) to encompass, to make a border round, to enclose (related to גָּדַד 2).

II. גָּדָה (not used) to collect in hosts; see גְּדִי.

גָּדָה (pl. const. גְּדוֹת) f. banks which surround the water.

גְּדוּד (pl. —דִים, once —דוֹת) m. 1) incision (in the skin or in the earth), furrow; from גָּדַד 1; 2) troop, warriors, host; poetically, בַּת גְּדוּד, בְּנֵי הַגְּדוּד, where בַּת signifies the people.

גָּדוֹל (const. גְּדוֹל and also גְּדָל־) adj. m., גְּדוֹלָה fem., great; in the most manifold gradations, e.g. great in mass, in size, in weight (weighty, important), in vehemence (violent); in quantity (much); in property and wealth (rich); in dignity (authority); in eminence (distinguished). The great priest, i.e. the high priest. The day is yet great, i.e. high; as a subst. it signifies the same, but also, the elder one. The pl. f. is often used as an abstract noun, and signifies great actions, wonders; proud speaking, presumptuousness; see גָּדַל.

גְּדוּלָּה (also גְּדֻלָּה, ־לָּה) f. greatness, majesty, glory, concr. also great deeds.

גִּדּוּף (pl. ־פִים, ־פוֹת) masc. offence, scorn, blasphemy; see גָּדַף.

גִּדּוּפָה (f. the same).

גַּדִּי p.n. m. (the fortunate one).

גָּדִי p.n. m. (the same).

גְּדִי (pl. גְּדָיִים, const. גְּדָיֵי) masc. kid, kid of the goat, from גָּדָה II.=גָּדַע to cut off, to pluck off.

גַּדִּיאֵל p.n. m. (the fortune of God).

גְּדִיָּה (only pl. גְּדִיּוֹת) f. from גְּדִי kid, young goat.

גִּדְיָה (pl. c. גִּדְיוֹת only Ketib), fem. bank, after the form דְּוָיָה.

גְּדִיל (only pl. גְּדִילִים) m. that which is entwined, twisted; hence, string, tassel, from their being entwined or twisted. Figur. for the festoons of the capitals of pillars.

גָּדִישׁ m. heap, heap of sheaves, from גָּדַשׁ to heap together; figur. tomb-hill, from its similarity to the piling up of earth for a hill.

גָּדַל (from גָּדֵל, hence גְּדַלְנִי; fut. יִגְדַּל) to twine, to twist (compare גְּדִיל), e.g. the hair; hence, to be strong, firm, after the usual transfer of all verbs signifying binding; but generally, to be or become great, distinguished, powerful, rich, high, important; to grow up, i.e. to become great,—God has great, i.e. exalted. Pi. גִּדֵּל (at the close of a sentence גִּדֵּל) to let become great (plants, hair), distinguished (name), to make powerful, to bring up; figur. to praise. Pu. to be bred (of children). Hiph. to make great (the mercy), to make high, i.e. to elevate; הִגְדִּיל לַעֲשׂוֹת to do great things, but also, to be presumptuous; to make the mouth great (with עַל of the person) to speak haughtily. Hith. to conduct oneself haughtily, proudly (with עַל of the person).

גדל גָּדֵל (pl. const. גִּדְלֵי) adj. masc. great, growing; בָּשָׂר in flesh, i.e. to be large of limb.

גדל גִּדֵּל p.n. m. (the gigantic one).

גדל גֹּדֶל (with suff. גָּדְלוֹ, גָּדְלוֹ) m. greatness; figur. honor, majesty; or in a bad sense, haughtiness, joined to לֵבָב.

גדל גָּדֹל see גָּדוֹל.

גדלה גְּדֻלָּה see גְּדוּלָּה.

גדליה גְּדַלְיָה p. n. m. (one exalted by God), for which also גְּדַלְיָהוּ.

גְּדַלְיָהוּ p.n. m. (the same).

גִּדַּלְתִּי p.n. m. (one rich in glory).

גדע גָּדַע (fut. יִגְדַּע) to cut off (the beard), to hew (a tree); figur. to blot out (men); to destroy (a city); to break (a staff); to break the arm, i.e. to destroy the power. Niph. to be felled (trees), to be blotted out (nations), to be broken down (altars). Pi. a higher gradation of the Kal. Pu. to be felled (of trees); related to this word is גָּזַע, קָצַע, see also גָּדָה II.

גִּדְעוֹן p.n. m. destroyer, feller.

גִּדְעֹם p.n. m. (the same).

גִּדְעֹנִי p.n. m. destroyer.

גדף גָּדַף (Kal, not used) to provoke, to hurt, to offend (related to גָּדַף), from which Pi. גִּדֵּף to blaspheme, e. g. God.

גדר גָּדַר (fut. יִגְדֹּר) to surround, enclose, hedge in, to encompass (related to חָדַר); hence, to wall in, to block up, e.g. פֶּרֶץ breach in the wall; גּ׳ אֹרַח, דֶּרֶךְ to block up the road; גּ׳ בַּעַד to wall in, to enclose; גּ׳ גָּדֵר אֶל to make a wall round some one, i.e. to protect some one; גֹּדֵר one that makes a wall.

גדר גָּדֵר (const. גְּדֵר, comp. עָרֵךְ, עָרֵל, גָּדֵל, כָּבֵד, from עָרֵל, etc., const. 1) that which hedges in, wall (of a vineyard, court, city); פָּרַץ גָּדֵר to break down the wall; בָּנָה ג׳ to build up the wall. Transferred to the place itself which is walled in; 2) p.n. of city (hedge), gent. גְּדֵרִי, 1 Chron. 27:28.

גְּדוֹר (a) p.n. m. one who makes a wall; (b) p.n. of a city.

גדר גְּדֵר see גָּדֵר.

גדרה גְּדֵרָה (const. גֶּדֶרֶת, const. pl. גִּדְרוֹת,

with suff. גְּדֵרֹתָיו) f. 1) wall, like גָּדֵר, but generally of places hedged in for pasture, especially גִּדְרוֹת צֹאן; 2) p.n. of a place in the territory of Judah; gent. גְּדֵרָתִי.

גְּדֵרוֹת p.n. of a town in Judah (pasture land).

גְּדֵרוֹתַיִם p.n., a town in Judah (double pasture).

גְּדֵרִי see גָּדֵר.

גְּדֶרֶת see גְּדֵרָה.

גָּדַשׁ (not used) to heap up, accumulate. From which גָּדִישׁ.

גֵּה (Ezek. 43:13) for זֶה; it is, however, uncertain whether this is a known grammatical interchange.

גָּהָה (fut. יִגְהֶה) to separate, to remove (a disease), i.e. to cure it. The root is accordingly related to דָּנָה, הָגָה.

גֵּהָה fem. driving away (a disease), curing; הֵטִיב גֵּהָה curing well.

גָּהַר (fut. יִגְהַר) to bend down over (עַל) somebody. According to others, to pour forth, sneeze, from זָהַר to shine, pour forth rays.

גַּו (with suff. גֵּוְךָ, גֵּוָם) m. equiv. to גֵּו, only this is derived from גָּוָה = גָּוָה.

גַּו (const. גֹּו, גּוֹא, with suff. גַּוֵּהּ, גַּוַּהּ) Aram. m. equiv. to the Hebrew גֵּו, i.e. back, hump, body in general; but generally transferred to middle, innermost; for which prepositional: in, בְּגוֹ equiv. to בְּתוֹךְ, לְגוֹא, equiv. to לְתוֹךְ, מִן־גּוֹא, equiv. to מִתּוֹךְ.

גֵּו (with suff. גֵּוִי, probably pl. גֵּוִים) m. 1) back, probably also body in general; 2) middle, prep. in; hence מִן־גֵּו (Job 31:5), like Aram. מִן גּוֹא. The root is גָּוָה.

גּוֹא see גַּו (Aram.).

I. גּוּב (not used) to cut through, to dig through; hence, to plough, but also to cut off, to deepen out, to excavate. Related to this is כָּב, קָב.

II. גּוּב (not used), to heap up, to gather in troops, to crowd together. Related to this is חָגָב.

גּוֹב m. 1) troop of locusts, from גּוּב II. Like אַרְבֶּה locust, from אָרַב to join together; חָגָב locust, from חָגַב to troop together. 2) p.n. of a place (a pit, a cistern).

גּוֹבַי m. collective, troop, host of locusts; the suff. ־ַי is the ancient adj. form, like in חַלּוֹנֵי, חֲשׂוּפַי, חוֹרַי.

גּוֹג p.n. m. (Caucasian); see מָגוֹג.

I. גּוּד equiv. to גָּדַד to make an incision, to penetrate. It is possible, however, that the form יְגוּד is only a dissolved one from יָגֹד, so that this root cannot be at all adopted.

II. גּוּד (not used) to bind, to tie, to

fatten; related to עָקַר, אָגַר, from which גִּיד.

גָּוָה (not used), 1) equiv. to גָּבַב, גָּבָה hilly, bellied, to be arched; hence גֵּו, גַּו; 2) like גּוּב II. to troop together, to join, which signification, however, is yet uncertain. See גּוֹי.

גֵּוָה (an Aramaism) f. 1) body, originally, back), formed from גֵּו; 2) abbreviated from גַּאֲוָה = גְּאָוָה, pride, haughtiness, sin; from גָּאָה.

גֵּוָה (Aram.) f. pride, like the Hebrew גֵּוָה 2.

גּוּז 1) to flee, to hasten away, also, to seek refuge; perhaps this is the signification in Numb. 11:31, only that there שַׂלְוִים is construed with the singular; 2) to fly, to hover, from which גּוֹזָל.

גּוֹז (with suff. גּוֹזִי) masc. refuge, the place or the person to which one hastens for succour.

גּוֹזָל (with suff. pl. גּוֹזָלָיו) m. a young bird, especially a young pigeon; formed from גּוֹז with the diminutive termination ־ָל.

גּוֹזָן (refuge), p.n. of a place, in the Talmud גִּנְזַק, the ancient Gazaca, a summer residence of the kings of Media, especially, גִּנְזַק שֶׁל מָדַי.

גּוֹחַ see גּוּחַ.

גּוּחַ (Kal imp. גֹּחִי for גּוּחִי) to break, to push, to press, forth (of a stream, child); hence, to be in labour with child, to bear. Hiph. הֵגִיחַ (part. מֵגִיחַ, future יָגִיחַ, infin. בְּגִיחוֹ for בְּהָגִיחוֹ) to break forth (of an ambush), to bubble (of a river), Related to גָּ־נַח.

גּוּחַ (Aram.) to thrust, to push. Only in affix אַגַּח.

גּוֹי (with suff. גּוֹיִי, pl. גּוֹיִם, גּוֹיִים) m. (contracted from גְּוִי, from which the fem. form גְּוִיָּה) body, being (like גֵּו), person (also of the individual, Gen. 20:4, perhaps also the same signification, 25:23), but especially, corporation, people; next also, of beasts. The plural generally of a heathen people (Gentiles). The root is גָּוָה 1, but if גֵּוָה 2 is the root, גּוֹי is etymologically of the same signification as עַם.

גְּוִיָּה (from גְּוִי) f. body, sometimes of dead bodies.

גּוֹיִם (heathen people, Gentiles) p.n. of a nation.

גּוּל (fut. יָגוּל Ketib) equiv. to חוּל, to whirl, turn round; hence, 1) to triumph (to dance in a circle before the enemy); next, to rejoice; 2) to tremble (from fear); hence, also, to revere, adore.

גּוֹלָה (seldom גֹּלָה) f. emigration, exile; e.g. הָלַךְ, יָצָא בַּגּ׳, to wander in exile; כְּלֵי הַגּ׳ vessels of exile.

sometimes גּוֹלָה stands also for those that have returned from exile.

גּוֹלָן (place of emigration), p.n. a town in the dominion of Manasseh, which gave the name to the province Gaulanitis.

גּוּמָּץ (later), m. a pit; see גֻּמָּץ.

גּוּן (not used), equiv. to גָּנַן to protect, to shelter.

גּוּנִי p.n. m. (the protected, shielded one) gent. n. in the same form.

גָּוַע (future יִגְוַע) equiv. to גָּוָה 2, to gather, to draw together, like נֶאֱסַף, hence, figur. of dying (to withdraw), frequently joined with מוּת.

גּוּף (Kal not used) to encircle, to enclose; hence, to be bellied, arched, from which גּוּפָה. Hiph. to close up, e.g. דֶּלֶת door, proceeding from the original idea of clothing.

גּוּפָה f. body, of its bellied form, in modern Hebrew גּוּף; in ancient Heb., however, like גְּוִיָּה dead body.

גּוֹר see גּוּר.

I. גּוּר (fut. יָגוּר) to gather, to gather together, e.g. Psalm 56:7; 59:4; hence, to conspire together against (עַל), and hence, figur. like אָסַף to turn into a house, to sojourn, to stay, to dwell: גָּר בַּיִת inmate of the house, f. גָּרַת בַּיִת, the place where one stays is joined with בְּ; and the person with whom one dwells, with עִם, בְּ, אֵת, poetically with the accusative of the person and the place. To dwell in the tent of God, i.e. to meditate often of God, related to אָגַר. Hith. as far as related to גּוּר to gather themselves together, to assemble, to sojourn somewhere.

II. גּוּר equiv. to יָגֹר to fear (without excluding the fear of God) of somebody (מִפְּנֵי, מִן) poet. also with the accus. and with לְ to be afraid of somebody.

III. גּוּר (not used) equiv. to עוּר to give to drink, to suckle, from גּוּר. See עוּר.

IV. גּוּר (not used) to hiss, to neigh, to roar; from which גֵּר.

V. גּוּר (not used) equiv. to גָּרַר to roll, of round things; hence גּוֹר in גּוֹרָל the small round stones that roll; comp. גֵּרָה.

גּוּר (const. pl. גּוּרֵי, גֻּרוֹת), m. a young lion, from גּוּר III.

גּוּר (pl. גּוּרִים, גּוּרוֹת) m. 1) young animal, as it is a suckling, especially of a young lion; complete גּוּר אַרְיֵה and only, Lam. 4:3, of young jackalls; see כְּפִיר; 2) p.n. of a city (place of the young lions).

גּוּר בַּעַל (dwelling of Baal), p.n. of a city in Arabia.

גּוֹרָל (pl. גּוֹרָלוֹת) m. a small round

stone for casting lots, from גּוֹר small round stone (see גּוֹר V.), with the diminutive termination ־ָל (comp. גּוֹזָל); next—1) lot. To cast the lot הִשְׁלִיךְ, יָדָה, יָרָה, נָתַן, הֵטִיל, הִפִּיל הַג׳ the lot is cast, נָפַל ג׳; the lot falls on somebody, עָלָה ג׳ עַל or יָצָא לְ; the object, however, for which the lot is cast, constr. with עַל. 2) the inheritance acquired (by lot); next, heritage in general; the fate that meets one.

גּוֹרֶן (Ketib) see גֹּרֶן.

גּוּשׁ (not used), to heap together, related to the root כָּבַשׁ which see; herefrom—

גּוּשׁ m. heap, clod, especially of a clod of earth; hence Job 7:5, "My flesh is clothed with worms, and clods of dust."

גֵּז (plur. const. גִּזֵּי) m. that which is cut off, shorn off, shearing (of sheep, of meadows), "the king's mowings" (Amos 7:1) were probably the first.

גִּזְבָּר (plur. גִּזְבָּרִין, sing. probably גְּזַבָּר; in modern Heb., however, the pl. is גִּזְבָּרִין), Heb. and Aram. m. master of the funds, a manager of the treasury. The word is derived from the Persian, though גֵּז treasure, is also Semitic; בָּר is a Persian formative syllable.

גָּזָה (not used) equiv. to גָּזַז to cut, to hew, to allot, from which גָּזִית. For גּוֹזִי (Ps. 71:6), see גּוּז.

גִּזָּה f. formed from גֵּז shearing.

גִּזֹה (like שִׁילֹה, or probably גִּזּוֹן quarry), p. n. of a place.

גָּזַז (fut. יָגֹז, apoc. וַיָּגָז, inf. גֹּז, גְּזוֹז) to cut off (wool), to shear off, to shave (the hair); but also, generally, to cut off, to sever.—Niph. to be cut off, annihilated.

גָּזֵז p. n. m. (shearer).

גָּזִית fem. the hewing (of stones), אַבְנֵי ג׳ hewing stones, free stone; later also גָּזִית alone, signifying the same.

גָּזַל (fut. יִגְזֹל) to take off the skin, to flay (related to נָצַל, אָצַל, חָסַל, שָׁל), to tear away (snatch something out of one's hand; a child from the mother's breast), to take away; transferred to: to rob, e.g. בַּיִת a house, שָׂדוֹת fields, מִשְׁפָּט judgment; with accus. of the person, to despoil. Niph. pass., e.g. שְׁנָה the sleep.

גָּזֵל (const. גְּזֶל) m. robbery, piracy.

גְּזֵלָה f. (the same).

גָּזַם (not used) equiv. to כָּסַם, and probably קָדַם (in קַרְדֹּם) to cut, to cut off: hence, eating off (used of beasts grazing), like כָּסַם.

גָּזָם m. locust, caterpillar, on accoun. of its devouring.

גָּזָם p.n. m. (devourer).

גָּזַע (not used) equiv. to גָּדַע to hew down.

גֶּזַע (with suff. גִּזְעוֹ) m. stock, roots the branches of which are all hewn down; hence, stem generally.

גָּזַר (fut. יִגְזֹר, יִגְזֹר) equiv. to קָצַר to cut: hence—1) to cut off, to fell (wood); 2) to slaughter, to murder; 3) to divide (יָם, יֶלֶד); 4) to decide (comp. חָתַךְ), with fut. יִגְזַר to separate the sheep from the flock, i.e. to remove them. Niph. pass. of all significations; נִגְזַרְתִּי I am cut off (from the land of the living).

גְּזַר Aram. (like in the Heb.; part. pl. גָּזְרִין to determine, to decree; גָּזְרִין sorcerers, one that casts nativities. Hith. אִתְגְּזַר to tear oneself away; 3 pers. fem. אִתְגְּזֶרֶת, הִתְגְּ׳).

גֶּזֶר (pl. גְּזָרִים) m. 1) piece, portion, a division (of the sea); 2) p.n. of a town on the western border of Ephraim (declivity).

גְּזֵרָא (not גְּזֵרָה, const. גְּזֵרַת) Aram. f. resolution, decision (of fate); transferred to that which is decided, decreed.

גְּזֵרָה adj. f. from גָּזַר divided, burst (from heat); hence אֶרֶץ גְּזֵרָה a land bursting from dearth, viz. desert.

גִּזְרָה f. 1) cut (of the body); hence, sketch, form, shape (comp. קֶצֶב); 2) a parted hall in the temple, from גָּזַר.

גִּזְרִי (that which is cut off, severed) p.n. of a people (Ketib גִּרְזִי).

גָּחוֹן (const. גְּחוֹן) m. that which is bent, crooked: hence, belly, only of creeping animals.

גַּחֲזִי (also גֵּי־) p.n. m. (one who diminishes, negates; גָּחַז equiv. to כָּחַשׁ).

גָּחַל (not used), to glow, to burn, related to קָלָה.

גַּחֶלֶת (pl. גֶּחָלִים, const. גַּחֲלֵי), fem. burning, glowing coals, figuratively for lightning (Ps.18:8); חָתָה גֶּ׳ עַל־רֹאשׁ to heap burning coals upon the head, i.e. mortify deeply (Proverbs 25:22). To extinguish burning coals, i.e. to destroy the last vestige.

גָּחַם (not used), equiv. to גָּחַל to glow.

גַּחַם p.n. m. (glow, he that glows).

גָּחַן (not used), to bow, to cringe; hence, to be bent, crooked; from which גָּחוֹן.

גָּחַר (not used), probably equiv. to גָּחַל to glow, to burn.

גַּחַר p.n. m. glow, the glowing one, equiv. to גַּחַם.

גַּי (also גֵּיא; Zech.14:4, גֵּיא; Isa. 40:4, גַּיְא; const. גֵּיא, גֵּי, plur. גֵּאָיוֹת, גֵּיאוֹת), com. originally—

1) earth, γῆ; next, transferred to lowness, valley; 2) with the article, הַגַּיְא p.n. of an encampment in the Moabite territory. גַּי is often used to signify places; as, גַּי (בְּנֵי) בֶּן־הִנֹּם (גֵּיא) valley of Hinnom, also called הַגַּיְא, גֵּי הִנֹּם; ג' מֶלַח valley of salt, on the Red Sea; גֵּי חֲרָשִׁים valley of carpenters, p.n. of a valley; ג' הַצְּבֹעִים (valley of game).

גִּיד m. band, hoop, cord, sinew, from גוד to bind; "thy neck is an iron sinew" (Isa. 48:4), i. e. stubborn.

גִּיחַ see גּוּחַ.

גִּיחַ (Aram.) see גּוּחַ.

גִּיחַ (a place of wells), p.n. of a place near Hebron.

גִּיחוֹן (whirlpool, stream), p. n. of rivers.

גֵּיחֲזִי see גֵּחֲזִי.

גִּיל (verb) see גּוּל.

גִּיל m. 1) whirling; hence, rolling time, age, period of time; next, like דּוֹר generation; 2) triumph, joy; originally, the whirling motion of the dance.

גִּילָה f. (the same).

גִּילֹנִי see גִּלֹה.

גִּינַת p.n. m. (protection, protector).

גִּיר (verb), see גּוּר IV.

גִּיר (גִּר) m. lime, from its bubbling when mixed.

גִּיר (Aram.) the same.

גֵּיר see גֵּר.

גִּישׁ see גּוּשׁ.

גֵּישָׁן p.n. m. (the dirty one).

גַּל (pl. גַּלִּים) m. 1) ruin, a heap of stones; 2) a spring, from its rolling. Root גָּלַל.

גֹּל m. oil-bottle, that which contains oil, probably from גָּלַל, equiv. to חָלַל to deepen out, to excavate.

גְּלָא (גְּלָה), part. act. גָּלֵא, ־ֵה, pause pass. (גְּלִי, גְּלִי) Aram. to uncover, to reveal. Aph. the same; see גָּלָה.

גָּלַב (not used), to shear off, to shave off (the beard), equiv. to חָלַף, which see.

גַּלָּב m. one that shaves off the beard (barber).

גִּלְבֹּעַ p.n. of a mountain in the territory of Issachar; prominent heap.

גַּלְגַּל (pl. גַּלְגַּלִּים) m. 1) wheel, especially a wheel for drawing water; 2) whirl, from גָּלַל to whirl, to turn round.

גַּלְגַּל Aram. the same.

גִּלְגָּל m. 1) a wheel, of a carriage; 2) p. n. of a place (rolling away) and בֵּית הַגִּלְגָּל is the same.

גֻּלְגֹּלֶת f. skull (hence גֻּלְגָּלְתָּא Γολγοθᾶ, situation of the skull), head; figur. for an individual; so called on account of the round form of the body (belly).

גָּלַד (not used) to crust, to cover round, to enclose (comp. חָלַד).

גֶּלֶד (with suff. גִּלְדִּי) m. originally, peel, but only used in the signification of skin.

I. גָּלָה (fut. יִגְלֶה, ap. יִגֶל) equiv. to גָּלַח to make bare, naked, bald, to uncover, e.g. the nakedness; hence, figur. to lay a thing open, naked; to communicate something without reserve, to reveal; to uncover the ear of some one, i.e. to communicate to somebody; generally, to manifest; to uncover a secret, i.e. to reveal, to pronounce; to uncover a book, i.e. to throw it open. Niph. pass. to be uncovered, to uncover oneself; and figur. to manifest itself; to appear publicly. Pi. גִּלָּה (fut. apoc. יְגַל to uncover nakedness, a covering), to open (the eyes), generally, to reveal, to uncover (something hidden); to lay bare the guilt (with עַל). Pu. to be uncovered. Hith. 1) to uncover oneself; 2) to reveal oneself.

II. גָּלָה equiv. to קָלַע, גָּלַע to fling, to drive, to chase away; hence, to drive into exile (comp. טִלְטֵל, modern Hebrew טִלְטוּל exile). But especially intransitive: "The mirth of the land is gone," Isa. 24:11 (banished); "Until the day of the captivity of the land" (Judg. 18:30). Niph. (only Isa. 38:12) to be driven away. Hiph. to cause to go into exile. Hoph. pass. I. and II. are therefore etymologically not connected.

גֻּלָּה see גֻּלָּא.

גִּלֹה (district) p.n. of a town on the mountain of Judah; gent. גִּילֹנִי.

גֹּלָה see גּוֹלָא.

גֻּלָּה fem. 1) equiv. to גַּל well; 2) a capital in the form of a basin, dome of the capital of pillars, from גָּלַל to roll; 3) a stone bottle for containing oil=to גַּל, from גָּלַל = חָלַל to deepen out.

גִּלּוּל (only pl. ־לִים) m. roller, round log; figur. idol. Perhaps identical with גֵּלֶל.

גְּלוֹם (const. pl. גְּלוֹמֵי) m. garment for wrapping up, cloak.

גֻּלָּן (Keri) see גּוֹלָן.

גָּלוּת f. exile, captivity; sometimes concrete for exiles.

גָּלוּת Aram. f. like in Heb. בְּנֵי ג׳ exiles.

גָּלַח Kal not used) to be bare, bald see גָּלָה). From which Pi. גִּלַּח to make bald, to shave (the head, beard), to shave off (hair of a man), figur. to devastate (the land). Pu. pass. Hith. to shave one's own hair.

גִּלָּיוֹן (pl. גִּלְיֹנִים) masc. 1) a smooth tablet (for writing), from גָּלָה I., especially, of metal; 2) metal plate for a mirror.

גָּלִיל adj. m., גְּלִילָה fem., pl. —לִים, —לוֹת rolling, turning; as a subst. 1) a swinging door; 2) socket (Cant. 5:15 and Esther 1:6); 3) circle, circumference, district.

גַּלִּים (ruins, fragments) p.n. of a place north of Jerusalem.

גָּלְיַת p. n. masc. (captivity, captor).

I. **גָּלַל** (גַּלּוֹתִי, pl. גָּלְלוּ; imp. גֹּל, גַּל (גּוֹל to roll); ג' מֵעַל to roll away (reproach); ג' עַל, אֶל to roll up, to burthen with (affairs). Niph. נָגֹל fut. יִגַּל pass.; 1) to be rolled together, like a book; 2) to roll oneself away. Pu. to be rolled away. Hith. to roll oneself over (עַל) some one (enemy), to attack; גִּלְגֵּל to roll. Hiph. הֵגֵל, like Kal, to roll.

II. **גָּלַל** (not used) to excavate, to deepen out, related to חָלַל, from which גֻּלָּה, גֹּל.

גְּלָל (Aram.) masc. a roller, a stone which one rolls; hence, complete, אֶבֶן גְּלָל free-stone.

גָּלָל (const. גְּלַל) m. 1) a heap (=to גַּל); hence, heap of dung; 2) turning, circumstance, affair, but only connected with בְּ, and as a prep. (with suff. בִּגְלָלְךָ, בִּגְלַלְכֶם) for the sake of, like אוֹדוֹת; the modern, בִּשְׁבִיל …; 3) p.n. m.

גֵּלֶל (with suff. גֶּלְלוֹ, pl. גְּלָלִים, const. גֶּלְלֵי) m. equiv. to גָּלָל dung-hill.

גִּלֲלַי p.n. m. (the moveable one).

גָּלַם (future יִגְלֹם) to roll together; hence, to wrap up.

גֹּלֶם (with suff. גָּלְמִי) m. that which is rolled together, a lump; hence, something in embryo.

גָּלְמַד (not used) sterile, unfruitful.

גַּלְמוּד (f. —דָה) adj. m. originally, hard (of a rocky soil); figur. unfruitful (of woman), lonely, solitary, unhappy, etc.

גָּלַע (Kal not used) to push, to drive, to crowd. Hith. to push one another, to crowd (in strife); next, to excite oneself.

גָּלְעַד (not used) to be hard, rough.

גִּלְעָד 1) p.n. m. (the hard, the rough one), patron. —דִי; 2) p.n. of a town, and district between the Jabok and Arnon.

גַּלְעֵד p.n. of a hill (hill of testimony).

גָּלַשׁ (once) to descend (from a mountain).

גַּם a particle, signifying addition (*cum, com*), not traceable to a verbal root; 1) also, even: "Even a child is known by his doings" (Prov. 20:11); emph. with a repetition of the pronoun; e.g. הִיא גַם הִוא "she, even she herself" (Gen. 20:5); בָּרְכֵנִי גַם אָנִי "Bless me, even me also" (Gen. 27:34); or connected with כִּי as, כִּי גַם, גַּם כִּי even though.

although; or adversative, even so =yet; 2) together, e. g. גַּם שְׁנֵיהֶם *ambo*, שְׁנַיִם *duo*.

גָּמָא (Kal not used) to sip, to imbibe (comp. Aram. גְּמַע. Talm. גְּאַם).

גֹּמֶא m. papyrus, from which also reeds are made, so called from its imbibing water (גָּמָא).

גָּמַד (not used) equivalent to גָּדַם to shorten, to cut off; hence, synom. with מָדַד to measure.

גֹּמֶד m. that which is cut off; hence, a stave; used as a measure, a yard.

גָּמָד (pl. ־דִים) m. equiv. to אִישׁ מִדָּה a tall man, a giant. According to others, from גָּמַד short one, dwarf.

גָּמָה see גָּמַם.

גָּמוּל p. n. m. (the mature one, the one grown up).

גְּמוּל (pl. ־לִים) m. 1) award, recompense, complete גְּ׳ יָדַיִם recompense, in a good and bad sense, הֵשִׁיב, שִׁלֵּם, גָּמַל לְ, עַל to reward some one for his deeds; 2) reward generally.

גְּמוּלָה f. (the same).

גִּמְזוֹ (for גִּמְזוֹן sycamore-plant, from עָמַז probably only a transposition from שִׁקְמָה sycamore) p. n. a town in the territory of Judah (Talm. אִישׁ גִּמְזוֹ a Gimsonite).

I. גָּמַל (fut. יִגְמֹל) 1) to carry (a load), from which גָּמָל; 2) to award, generally constructed with לְ and עַל, figur. to reward, benefit, to recompense good or evil. The root is only a secondary form from עָמַל and חָמַל 2.

II. גָּמַל (fut. יִגְמֹל) 1) intrans. to ripen (of fruits), to become mature (of a child); complete גְּ׳ מֵחָלָב to become ripe, in reference to dispensing with the mother's milk; 2) trans. to make ripe (fruit); to wean (the child being then considered as mature).

גָּמָל (plur. גְּמַלִּים) com. that which bears burden, i. e. beast of burden, camel.

גְּמַלִּי p. n. m. (a camel-driver).

גַּמְלִיאֵל (goodness of God).

גָּמַם (not used) to gather, to heap up, to connect, from which מְגַמָּה, which see. Perhaps the root is גָּמָא=גָּמָה, as the ancients explain it.

גָּמַץ (not used), after the Aramaic, to dig, probably it is equiv. to קָבַץ to gather, so that גּוּמָּץ signifies a place of gathering, like מִקְוֶה.

גָּמַר (fut. יִגְמֹר) 1) intrans. to cease, to end; 2) to conclude, גְּ׳ עַל, בְּעַד to finish a thing for some one; i.e. to lead his cause.

גְּמַר (part. pass. גְּמִיר) Aram. to make complete, to finish.

גֹּמֶר 1) p.n. of a people; 2) p.n. f. (perfection).

גְּמַרְיָה p.n. m. (perfection of God).

גְּמַרְיָהוּ p.n. m. (the same).

גַּן (with suff. גַּנִּי, plur. גַּנִּים) com. a hedged place, garden, orchard; גַּן אֱלֹהִים ,יְיָ of Eden; גַּ׳ הַיָּרָק kitchen garden. Root גָּנַן.

גָּנַב (part. pass., גְּנֻבְתִי with ׳ parag., fut. יִגְנֹב) denom. from גַּב; hence, to put aside, to steal; figur. to deceive; to steal the heart of some one, i.e. to deceive sorely. Niph. pass. Pi. to deceive frequently. Pu. (inf. abl. גֻּנֹּב) pass. with אֶל to come to some one secretly, clandestinely.

גַּנָּב (plur. גַּנָּבִים) m. a thief; חַבְרֵי גַנָּבִים gangs of thieves.

גְּנֵבָה f. that which is stolen, theft.

גְּנֻבַת p.n. m. he that is stolen.

גַּנָּה (pl. גַּנּוֹת) f. equiv. to גַּן.

גִּנָּה (later) f. garden.

גָּנַז (not used) to gather, to heap, equiv. to כָּנַס.

גֶּנֶז (const. pl. גִּנְזֵי) that which is gathered, collected, treasure; trans. also to a chest for preserving or keeping things in.

גְּנַז (plur. גִּנְזִין) Aram. m. the same; בֵּית גִּנְזַיָּא treasury.

גַּנְזַךְ (formed from גֶּנֶז) m. treasury.

גָּנַן (1 pers. pret. גַּנּוֹתִי, inf. abs. גָּנוֹן) to cover, veil, shelter (comp. עָנַן), constr. with עַל. Hiph. (fut. יָגֵן) to shelter; const. with עַל and בְּעַד.

גְּנַף (not used), Aram. to cover, to veil (related to the Heb. כָּנַף, צָנַף, חָנַף, from which גַּף wing, from גַּנְף (גְּנַף), like בַּת according to some from בְּנֶת.

גִּנְּתוֹי p.n. m. (builder of gardens).

גִּנְּתוֹן p.n. m. (the same).

גָּעָה to bellow (crying of the bull).

גֹּעָה (place of bullocks) p.n. of a place.

גָּעַל (fut. יִגְעַל) to defile, to desecrate (comp. חָלַל, גָּאַל); hence, to pollute; figur. to abhor, to despise, reject. Niph. to be defiled, e.g. "for there the shield of the mighty is vilely cast away," i.e. defiled by disgraceful flight (2 Sam. 1:21). Hiph. to reject (to fail in bearing, applied to animals, Job 21:10).

גַּעַל p.n. m. desecration, pollution, a defiler.

גֹּעַל m. abhorrence, disgust.

גָּעַר (fut. יִגְעַר) to cry (comp. עָנַר); hence, to rebuke, to cry against, with בְּ of the person, to scold, to deny, to ward off; with the accus. גָּ׳ בָּאֹכֵל rebuke the devourer, i.e. to ward off the vermin (Mal. 3:11); גָּ׳ הַזֶּרַע to corrupt the seed (Mal. 2:3); גָּ׳ בַּיָּם rebuked the sea, that it dried up (Ps. 106:9).

גְּעָרָה (const. גַּעֲרַת) f. threat, rebuke, reproof.

גָּעַשׁ (fut. יִגְעַשׁ) to be pushed to and fro, to be violently moved, used of an earthquake (comp. גָּרַשׁ). Pu. גֹּעַשׁ pass., of the tottering of nations. Hith. of the shaking of the earth, of the waves, of the reeling of a drunkard.

גַּעַשׁ (quaking, shaking), p.n. of a part of the mountain of Ephraim.

גַּעְתָּם p.n. masc. (probably equiv. to גַּאֲוָתָם haughty one).

גַּף (plur. const. גַּפֵּי) m. equiv. to גַּב back; hence, the high point; figur. person, the body in general; בְּגַפּוֹ with his person, i.e. alone.

גַּף (pl. גַּפִּין) Aram. m. wing; comp. אֲגַף. The root is גָּנַף.

גָּפַן (not used) bent, crooked, equiv. to גָּבַן, which see.

גֶּפֶן (with suff. גַּפְנִי) com. branch of vine: גֶּ׳ שָׂדֶה wild grape, especially vine; complete גֶּ׳ הַיַּיִן.

גָּפַף (not used) equiv. to גָּבַב to be arched, hilly, from which גַּף. Probably the root is גָּנַף, equiv. to כָּנַף.

גָּפַר (not used) equiv. to כָּבַר, גָּבַר to be strong, hard, especially of a tree.

גֹּפֶר m. hard tree, used for ships, and from which also flows a kind of gum. The species of the tree is not known.

גָּפְרִית (formed from גֹּפֶר) f. a gum of the gopher tree; a kind of pitch, generally translated brimstone.

גָּר (participle) m. גָּרָה f. dwelling, sojourning. Root גּוּר.

גֵּר (גֵּיר) m. dweller (in a land), i.e. he who only sojourns in a country, but is not born therein; hence, foreigner, stranger; figur. guest, pilgrim. Comp. אֶזְרָח, תּוֹשָׁב.

גֵּר see גֵּיר.

גֹּר equiv. to גּוּר a young beast.

גֵּרָא p.n. m. (stranger, foreigner).

גָּרַב (not used) to pluck, to scratch, to scrape (comp. גָּרַף).

גָּרָב masc. scurvy, so called from scratching.

גָּרֵב p.n. m. despoiler, plucker.

גַּרְגַּר (pl. const. ־גְּרִים) m. berry, later grain; from גָּלַל=גָּרַר to be round.

גַּרְגֶּרֶת (pl. גַּרְגְּרוֹת, const. ־גְּרוֹת), f. gurgle, throat; from גָּרַר to gurgle, to swallow.

גִּרְגָּשׁ p.n. of a territory (marshy ground), from which gent. גִּרְגָּשִׁי.

גָּרַד (Kal not used) equiv. to חָרַת to engrave; next, scraping, scratching in general. Hith. to scratch oneself, with בְּ of the instrument used for it.

I. גָּרָה (Kal not used) equiv. to חָרָה to glow, to burn, to be angry; hence, Pi. גֵּרָה to excite passion, strife (מָדוֹן). Hith. to put oneself in a passion, (בְּ) with somebody; hence, to dispute, to enter into strife.

II. גָּרָה (not used) equiv. to גָּרַר to swallow, to gurgle.

גֵּרָה (after the form סְפָה) f. 1) that which is swallowed down, from גָּרַר to swallow; הֶעֱלָה גֵרָה or גָּרַר גֵ׳ to chew the cud; 2) germ, grain, bean (of the carob), used as the smallest weight, from גָּלַל=גָּרַר to be round.

גָּרוֹן (const. גְּרוֹן) m. neck, throat; to cry with the throat, i.e. loudly; to walk with a stretched out neck, i.e. proudly. Root גָּרָה.

גֵּרוּת f. a lodging, inn, from גּוּר.

גָּרַז (Kal not used), to divide, to part; hence, Niph. to be separated, i.e. to be destroyed.

גֶּרֶז p.n. of a desolate tract of land; hence, גִּרְזִי or גִּרְזִי a people inhabiting that place.

גְּרִזִים p.n. of a mountain, seat of the Gerezites.

גַּרְזֶן m. axe, hatchet, from גָּרַז, equiv. to גָּזַר.

גָּרַט (not used), equiv. to חָרַט to deepen out, to hollow out (to receive something); from which אֲגַרְטָל, which see.

גְּרָל belongs to גּוֹרָל, see גּוֹרָל, and גְּרָל Prov. 19:19. Ketib; probably גְּרָל stands here for גְּדָל.

גֶּרֶם (pl. גְּרָמִים) masc. skin, covering (comp. Talmudical קְרוּם); transferred to body, bone, and next, like עֶצֶם for self; from which

גָּרַם denom. to flay. Pi. to take the skin off the bones, figur. to suck the sherds.

גְּרַם Aram. bone. Pl. גַּרְמִין.

גַּרְמִי p.n. m. (bony one, strong one).

גָּרַן (not used) to make smooth.

גֹּרֶן (with suff. גָּרְנִי, pl. גֳּרָנוֹת, const. גָּרְנוֹת) fém. threshing-floor, barn; originally, a smooth place, בֶּן־גָּרְנִי son of my thrashing floor, i.e. my crushed people.

גָּרַס equiv. to עָרַס to break, to crush. Hiph. to break to pieces, to dash out (the teeth).

גָּרַע (fut. יִגְרַע) to diminish; hence, to withdraw (the eyes), i.e. to turn away; עַיִן is elliptic. Transferred, to take the beard off; to keep to oneself (אֶל), e.g. wisdom, i.e. to cut it off from others. Niph. to be diminished, withdrawn, reduced. Hiph. to cause to diminish, — to fail.

גָּרַף to pluck off; (comp. חָרַף) to scrape away, earth.

I. גָּרַר (fut. יָגֹר) to draw (in a net), to draw up (food), i.e. to chew the cud; related to which is נָגַר to flow, and to which belongs the part. Niph. נִגָּרוֹת. Hith. הִתְגּוֹרֵר (1 Kings 17:20) belongs to גּוּר like that in Hosea 7:14, but the one in Jer. 30:23 belongs to גָּרַר equiv. to גָּלַל to roll along.

II. גָּרַר (not used) a secondary form from גָּלַל to roll; hence, to be round; comp. כָּרַר.

III. גָּרַר (not used) to swallow, to gurgle.

IV. גָּרַר (Kal not used) to saw to pieces; hence Pual, to be sawn to pieces.

גְּרָר (a circle, from גָּרַר II.) p.n. of a town in Philistia.

גָּרַשׁ (not used) equivalent to גָּרַס to pound, especially of grain.

גֶּרֶשׂ (גְּרָשָׂהּ) masc. that which is pounded.

גָּרַשׁ (fut. יִגְרֹשׁ) 1) to drive away, comp. יָרַשׁ; next, to drive out, to send away (a wife), to clear out (slime), to plunder (the possession, מִגְרָשׁ); figur. to drive out (compare גֶּרֶשׁ), produce, fruit; 2) equiv. to יָרַשׁ to possess; hence מִגְרָשׁ.

גֶּרֶשׁ masc. the driving out, producing fruit, production (of the month).

גְּרֻשָׁה (pl. ־שׁוֹת), fem. driving out, concr. those that are driven out.

גֵּרְשׁוֹן p.n. m. (he that is driven out); patron. ־שֻׁנִּי.

גֵּרְשֹׁם p.n. m. (a stranger there).

גְּשׁוּר (bridge), p.n. of a Syrian province; gent. גְּשׁוּרִי a people at the foot of the Hermon, but also in southern Palestine.

גָּשַׁם (Kal not used) hissing, raining. Hiph. to cause to rain.

גֶּשֶׁם (pl. גְּשָׁמִים, const. גִּשְׁמֵי) m. 1) rain, pouring down; גֶּשֶׁם מָטָר and מְטַר גֶּשֶׁם are only emphatic terms; 2) p.n. m. (*corpus*, body); (see גֶּשֶׁם Aram.) for which also גַּשְׁמוּ.

גֹּשֶׁם (with suff. גֻּשְׁמָהּ) m. equiv. to גֶּשֶׁם.

גֶּשֶׁם (with suffix גִּשְׁמֵהּ, גִּשְׁמְהוֹן, Aram.) m. body, the root is not connected with גֶּשֶׁם.

גַּשְׁמוּ p.n. m. (physical, bodily).

גֹּשֶׁן p.n. of a territory in Egypt, and also the name of a country in the mountain of Judah.

גָּשַׁף (not used) to flatter, probably equiv. to כָּשַׁף.

גִּשְׁפָּא p.n. m. (the flatterer).

גָּשַׁר (not used) equiv. to קָשַׁר to bind; hence, to throw a bridge, from which גְּשׁוּר.

גָּשַׁשׁ (only Pi.) to seek after something, to grope; related with the root in בָּקַשׁ.

גַּת (pl. גִּתּוֹת) f. 1) hole, from נָתַת, not from יָגַן; the wine-press, or the cavity where the grapes are pressed; hence, דָּרַךְ גַּת; 2) p.n. of a Philistine city formed like a cave; gent. גִּתִּי; גַּת חֵפֶר well of a wine-press, p.n. of a city in the territory of Zebulun; (גַּת רִמּוֹן wine-press of Rimmon), p.n. of a town in the territory of Dan.

גִּתִּית f. an instrument in the form of a cave; according to others it stands for נְגִנְתִּית, from נָגַן, which, however, is improbable.

גִּתַּיִם (double wine-press) p.n. a town in the territory of Benjamin.

גֶּתֶר (=גֶּשֶׁר bridge) p.n. of a district in Aramea.

גָּתַת (not used) to deepen out, to receive something; from which גַּת.

ד

ד, called *Dalet* דָּלֶת (pl. דַּלְתִּין). It signifies nearly the same as דֶּלֶת door, from the old shape of this letter; as a numeral, it signifies 4. It interchanges with letters of the same organ of speech, and also with ז.

דָּא dem. pron. fem. (from the m. דֵּן this; דָּא לְדָא one to the other).

דָּאַב (inf. דַּאֲבָה), equiv. to אָרַב to languish, especially of the eye (עַיִן), and of the soul (נֶפֶשׁ).

דְּאָבָה f. the languishing, perishing (with anguish).

דְּאָבוֹן (formed from דָּאַב m. from דְּאָבָה, like רְעָבוֹן from רָעֵב; const. דַּאֲבוֹן), masc. languishing of the soul (נֶפֶשׁ).

דָּאַג (fut. יִדְאַג) to fear, to be sorrowful, const. with accusative and מִן, also with לְ of the person for which one is sorrowing, and with מִן of the object of which one is in fear.

דָּאג a secondary form, from דָּג, which see.

דֹּאֵג p.n. m. (the one that sorrows).

דְּאָגָה f. grief, care, affliction, after the form דְּאָבָה.

דָּאָה (fut. יִדְאֶה, apoc. יֵדֶא), to fly swiftly, to soar, applied to the Deity, that soars (עַל) on the wings the wind; but also used of birds of prey, or eagles.

דָּאָה f. a swiftly flying bird, bird of prey. See דַּיָּה and רָאָה.

דָּאַל (not used) equiv. to דָּלַל to be reduced, poor.

דֹּאר see דּוֹר.

דֹּב (plur. דֻּבִּים) epic, a bear, a she-bear; דֹּב שַׁכּוּל a she-bear robbed of her young. The root is דָּבַב.

דֹּב (Aram.) the same.

דָּבָא (not used) to flow, to flow in, related to זָב, which see.

דֹּבֶא (with suff. דָּבְאֶךָ) masc. influx, fulness; hence, Deut. 33:25, "And as thy days, so shall thy strength (thy prosperity) endure," i.e. for life.

דָּבַב to go sneaking, to slander; properly, tripping, but this signification is probably only a denom.

from דִּבָּה. The original signification is to speak; next, to bespeak, to make speak: "Causing the lips of those that are asleep to speak," Cant. 7:9, i.e. according to the Talm., quoting the sayings of departed authors.

דִּבָּה f. talk, gossip; especially, slander, evil report.

דָּבָה (not used) to cause to flow out, to empty (the body).

דְּבוֹרָה (pl. דְּבֹרִים) fem. 1) a bee, a wasp, from דָּבַר to seize; 2) p.n. f.

דְּבַח (Aram.) equiv. to the Heb. זָבַח to offer, to sacrifice; origin. to slaughter.

דְּבַח (pl. דִּבְחִין) Aram. m. offering, sacrifice, equiv. to the Heb. זֶבַח.

דִּבְיוֹן (only plur. דִּבְיוֹנִים) m. efflux (from the body), dung.

דְּבִיר m. 1) the back part (of the temple), western hall, from דָּבַר to be behind (comp. דֹּבֶר modern Heb., back). 2) p.n. of a city in the dominion of Judah.

דָּבַךְ (not used) equiv. to דָּבַק to join together, to connect, from which נִדְבָּךְ.

דָּבַל (not used) to press tightly together; also, to make a circuit; comp. בָּ־בַל, הָ־בַל, גָּ־בַל.

דְּבֵלָה (const. דְּבֶלֶת, pl. דְּבֵלִים), fem. a mass pressed together, fig-cake; sometimes with the addition of תְּאֵנִים.

דִּבְלָה (a circle, a round) p.n. of a town; Ezek. 6:4, from the Arabian desert until Dibla. In the Syriac דְּבֶלֶת is the name of Antiochus.

דִּבְלַיִם p.n. m. (double circle).

דִּבְלָתַיִם (with ה finis דִּבְלָתָיְמָה) p.n. of a Moabite town (double circle), for which also בֵּית ד׳.

דָּבַק (for דָּבֵק as it appears in pause, fut. יִדְבַּק, inf. דָּבְקָה to cleave to, the tongue to (לְ, אֶל) the roof; to be attached to, with בְּ and לְ; to strive after, in order to join with an object, with אַחֲרֵי; hence transferred, to pursue, to chase, with the accus. בְּ and אַחֲרֵי in order to detain the one pursued; hence also, to overtake. Pual, closely to be attached. Hiph. to cause something to be pursued, attached, chased, with אַחֲרֵי and accus. and then like in Kal, to overtake, to apprehend. Hoph. to be made to cleave (the tongue), const. with the accusative.

דְּבַק (part. pl. דָּבְקִין Aram.) the same.

דָּבֵק m. adj. attached, faithful, const. like the verb with בְּ.

דֶּבֶק (pl. דְּבָקִים) m. attachment.

I. דָּבַר to arrange, to regulate, to string together, e.g. words, i.e.

to speak, *verba serere*. Niph. נִדְבַּר to converse mutually, const. with בְּ and עַל. Pi. דִּבֶּר (in pause דִּבֵּר); 1) to speak, where that which is spoken need not follow like after אָמַר, and may, therefore, stand quite absolute. The person spoken to with אֶל, לְ, עִם, עַל, אֵת (אֹת). Addressing oneself to somebody, constructed with בְּ, seldom with the accus.; speaking of somebody, with אֶל, עַל, בְּ, and accus.; speaking against somebody, with עַל and בְּ; 2) to promise, with accus. and עַל of the person; to command, to exhort, to sing (a poem), according to the context. To address a girl (with בְּ, לְ), i.e. to woo her; דִּבֶּר עַל לֵב to persuade, to console; but when לֵב is joined with the suff. of the person speaking, to speak inwardly; דִּבֶּר טוֹב עַל to vouchsafe good to some one.; דִּ׳ רָעָה עַל to predict evil; דִּ׳ טוֹבוֹת אֶת, אֶל־ to speak friendly; דִּ׳ שָׁלוֹם עִם to speak peaceably with some one; but with אֶל־ and אֵת to predict; with בְּ to wish blessings, and with לְ to speak in favor; דִּ׳ מִשְׁפָּט אֵת to pronounce sentence of punishment on some one. Pu. to be spoken to; figur. to be wooed. Hith. (particip. מִדַּבֵּר) to have mutual conversation.

II. דָּבַר (Kal not used), to drive (cattle), to drive home (a herd); next, to drive (of a raft), also to drive away, to snatch (of pestilence); to destroy. Hiph. הִדְבִּיר to drive, to carry, with תַּחַת under the dominion of some one, i.e. to subject.

דָּבָר (const. דְּבַר, pl. דְּבָרִים) m. 1) speech, origin. the stringing together of words; hence נְבוֹן דָּ׳ an orator; figur. command, ordinance, sentence of God, or of a king, whose words are commands; עֲשֶׂרֶת הַדְּבָרִים the ten commandments, decalogue; next, promise, prediction, oracle, revelation, sentence, advice, proposal, report, intelligence, etc.: הָיָה דְּבַר ה׳ עַל the word of God comes upon some one; with אֶל, addressed to some one; 2) contents, subject-matter (also מִלָּה, פִּתְגָּם; comp. *res*, from *ῥέω*): e. g. הַדָּבָר הַזֶּה this mattter, i. e. this event (דִּבְרֵי) the events or acts of Solomon; the events of days, i. e. history; concern, business, affair; the affair (דְּבַר) of justice, i. e. cause. also, reason, cause of: עַל דְּבַר, דִּבְרֵי something, anything; דְּבַר יוֹם the daily concern, i.e. the daily want; בַּעַל דְּבָרִים one who has דְּבַר מִשְׁפָּט, i.e. lawsuits; אֵין דָּבָר it is nothing, i.e. no matter. Root דָּבַר I.

דֶּבֶר (plur., Hos. 13:14) m. carrying away (from life), snatching away; hence, destruction, pestilence, from דָּבַר II. The plur. signifies the various kinds of death, the most horrible of which is בְּכוֹר מָוֶת, Job 18:13.

דֹּבֶר (with suff. דָּבְרָם ,דָּבְרוֹ) m. 1) driving,—cattle, כְּדָבְרָם as they are generally driven, leading to the pasture; 2) pasture. Root דָּבַר II.

דִּבֵּר m. a sentence, a word.

דִּבְרָא (only const. דִּבְרַת) Aram. f. equiv. to the Heb. דִּבְרָה, which see.

דַּבָּרָה (only pl. דַּבָּרוֹת) f. sentence, word; נָשָׂא מִן דַּ׳ "to receive of the words," (sentences of God) Deut. 33:3.

דִּבְרָה (not דִּבְרָה, formed from דָּבָר, only constr. דִּבְרַת ,דִּבְרָתִי) fem. equiv. to דָּבָר II., matter, cause, kind; עַל־דִּבְרַת on account of, in order to.

דֹּבְרֶת (only pl. דֹּבְרוֹת) f. that which drives, i.e. a raft.

דָּבַשׁ (not used) to be moist, fat, equiv. to טָפַשׁ.

דְּבַשׁ (pause דְּבָשׁ, with suff. דִּבְשִׁי) masc. that which is tender, soft; hence, honey either from bees or berries.

דַּבֶּשֶׁת f. 1) lump of fat, equiv. to טַפֶּשֶׁת figur. the hump of a camel, which is like a lump of fat; 2) p.n. of a place (fruit district).

דָּג (plur. דָּגִים, const. דְּגֵי) m. fish; originally, the swimmer, who drives through the water. See דּוּג.

דָּגָה (constr. דְּגַת) f. the same, but collective.

דָּגָה (fut. יִדְגֶּה) denom. from דָּג to multiply like fish.

דָּגוֹן p.n. of an idol, in the form of a fish (from דָּג). In the mythology the fem. is called דַּגְתָּא *Derceto*, a fish-deity in the form of a woman.

דָּגַל (not used) according to some equiv. to גָּדַל to be great, a transposition of the same; according to others, like נָסַס stands to נֵס, to shine; according to others, to cover, for which, however, there is no analogy in the language.

דֶּגֶל (with suff. דִּגְלִי, pl. דְּגָלִים, const. דִּגְלֵי) m. standard, banner, which is perceived from a distance.

דָּגַל (fut. יִדְגֹּל, part. pass. דָּגוּל), denom. from דֶּגֶל to erect a standard; hence, figur. to distinguish. Niph. נִדְגַּל to furnish oneself with a banner, i.e. to arm oneself; hence, particip. נִדְגָּלוֹת those that have a standard, i.e. the hosts of warriors.

דָּגַן (not used) to sprout, to drive

forth fruit (especially of the sprouting of ears of corn).

דָּגָן (const. דְּגַן) m. fruit of ears, corn, wheat, barley, rye; but it also signifies bread which is prepared from דָּגָן.

דָּגַר according to Targ. and LXX., to gather, to collect, e.g. to gather the young, to shelter, and to warm them, applied to the great owl and to the partridge: hence, Jer. 17: 11, "As the partridge sitteth on eggs, and hatcheth them not, so he that getteth riches," etc.

דֹּד see דּוֹד.

דַּד (dual דַּדַּיִם, const. דַּדֵּי) f. breast (of woman), to suckle, equiv. to שַׁד.

דָּדָה (Kal not used) to drive away, a redoubled form, from the root דָּה.—Hith. הִדַּדָּה, from הִתְדַּדָּה to drive oneself away; hence, אֶדַּדֶּה כָּל שְׁנוֹתַי I shall drag all my years along (Auth. Vers., Isa. 38:15, "I shall go softly"); אֶדַּדֵּם עַד בֵּית אֱלֹהִים Ps. 42:5, "I made a pilgrimage to the house of God, and caused the multitude (הָמוֹן חוֹגֵג) to go with me."—Pi. אֲדַדֶּה, and Hith. אֶדַּדֶּה.—In the Talm. דָּדָה signifies to drive, to cause to run; related to the root דָּה is סָא, which see.

דְּדָן (with ה finis דְּדָנֶה) 1) p. n. of a people and district on the Persian Gulf; 2) p. n. of a people and district in North Arabia. Gent. דְּדָנִים.

דֹּדָנִים p. n. of a people, who derive their origin from Javan. See רֹדָנִים.

דָּהַב (not used) to glisten, to sparkle, equiv. to זָהַב. See מַדְהֵבָה.

דְּהַב (not used) Aram. the same.

דְּהַב (def. דַּהֲבָא, ־בָה) Aram. m. gold. Heb. זָהָב.

דֶּהָי (patron. from דֶּה, def. pl. דֶּהָיֵא) an inhabitant of Dahistan, or of the village דֶּה.

דָּהַם (Kal not used) to be astounded, to stare. Niph. to be horrified.

דָּהַר 1) to run, to trot (of the horse; 2) figur. to continue its course, i.e. to endure, to be uninterruptedly vigorous. See דּוּר.

דַּהֲרָה (pl. const. דַּהֲרוֹת) f. course, trotting, running.

דּוֹב see דֹּב.

דּוּב (only Hiph. הֵדִיב, equiv. to הֶאֱדִיב, from אָדַב, and identical with דָּאַב to dissolve.

דּוּג (Kal not used) equiv. to דּוּחַ, only intrans. to push oneself along, i.e. to swim; from which Hiph. in abbrev. form דִּיג for הֵדִיג to drive along. If the Hiph. is not a a denom. from דָּג in the signification of, fishing.

דַּוָּג (Ketib) m. fisherman.

דּוּגָה f. the fishing, fishery.

I. דּוּד (not used), equiv. to יָדַד to love, to compose love-songs: From which דּוֹד and דָּוִד.

II. דּוּד (not used) to receive, to adopt, to comprehend, to contain, used of a vessel deepened out.

דּוֹד (דֹּד, plur. דּוֹדִים) masc. 1) love, friendship, an amorous song, caressing; the pl. is especially used in this manner: רָוָה דוֹדִים to be intoxicated with love; עֵת ד׳ time of love; 2) concrete, friend, lover; especially uncle, father's brother, sometimes דּוֹד stands for בֶּן דּוֹד. Root דּוּד I.

דּוּד (pl. דּוּדִים and דְּוָדִים) m. basket (comp. modern Heb. בַּלְבָּלָה, from בּוּל), which receives something poured into it; next, kettle, pot, etc. Root דּוּד.

דָּוִד (according to later orthographists, דָּוִיד), p.n. m. (formed from דּוֹד beloved). Comp. the classical proper names: Agapetus, Philomenus, Φιλήτης, Φιλήμων, Ἐραστος, Erasmus, Carus, and others.

דּוֹדָה (formed from דּוֹד) fem. aunt, origin. female friend, father's sister.

דּוֹדוֹ p.n. m. (the beloved one).

דּוֹדָוָהוּ p.n. m. (for דּוֹדְיָהוּ the beloved of God).

דּוֹדַי p.n. m. (the beloved one).

דּוּדַי (pl. דּוּדָאִים, comp. לוּלַי, plur. לוּלָאוֹת) adj. m. in the form of a basket or kettle; next, as a noun: 1) a vessel in the form of a basket to receive figs; 2) name of a herb (a mandrake) or apple, which either has blossoms in the form of a kettle, or which itself resembles a kettle in shape.

I. דָּוָה (inf. const. דְּוֹת) 1) to be sickly, especially of the sickness of women during their menstruations: hence, נִדַּת דְּוֹתָהּ separation for her infirmity; 2) to be sad, down cast.

II. דָּוָה (not used), to clothe, induere, from which מַדְוֶה.

דָּוֶה adj. m., דָּוָה f.; 1) infirm, sick, especially of a woman during the time of her periodical purification. Hence, Isa. 30:22, something unclean in general; 2) sad, mournful, miserable, i.e. sick at heart.

דּוּחַ (Kal not used) equiv. to דָּחָה, נָדַח to drive, push, cast away; hence, Hiph. הֵדִיחַ to reject; figur. to wash away (guilt of blood); hence, to purify.

דְּוַי (after the form שְׁלַו, צְבִי, const. דְּוַי) adj. m. but as a noun. 1) sickness: hence, עֶרֶשׂ דְּוָי the sick bed; 2) that which is loathsome, unclean (of food); hence, דְּוֵי לַחְמִי "sorrowful meat," Job 6:7.

דַּוָּי (a form in a higher degree from דְּוַי) adj. m. sick, morbid (of the heart), i.e. melancholy.

דָּוִיד see דָּוִד.

דוך equiv. to דָּכָא to push, to pound (in a mortar).

דּוּכִיפַת f. name of a bird, according to some, the lapwing; according others, the whoop, or wood-cock; the name arose either from כֵּיפָה stone, and דּוּ lord, i.e. inhabitant of rocks; or from דּוּךְ cock, and כֵּיפַת. The former is the most probable.

דום (not used) equiv. to דָּמַם to be silent, mute; trans. to rest.

דּוּמָה f. 1) stillness, noiselessness; hence, figuratively for the grave, the region of the dead; 2) p.n. of a place in Arabia; 3) p.n. m.

דּוּמִיָּה adj. f. (formed from דּוּמִי) 1) silent, still; hence, figur. submissive, confiding; 2) as a noun, submission, rest, ease; probably it has been formed from דְּמָמָה after the form of בּוּקִיָּה, and the ו interchanged with the ה.

דּוּמָם (from דּוּם with the adverbial termination ָם), adv. still, mute, noiseless, submissive; as a noun, however, it may be derived from דָּמַם, and signifies stillness, muteness.

דּוּמֶּשֶׂק p.n. of the well-known city of Damascus, and is only the rare form for דַּמֶּשֶׂק.

דון (not דִּין; part. דָּן, fut. יָדוֹן for יָדִין) 1) to tread under the feet (like כָּבַשׁ), to subject, related to אָדוֹן; hence, to rule, as in Gen. 6:3, "My spirit shall not always rule with man" (Auth. Version, "strive with man"); 2) to judge, to decide, which, in the East, is identical with ruling; but in this sense it only occurs in the abbreviated form דִּין. Niph. נָדוֹן judging one another, i.e. to dispute, to strive; the same as נִשְׁפַּט. Hiph. הֵדִין, but only in the abbreviated form דִּין, fut. יָדִין 1) to rule over; 2) to judge, of God and man and every relation, e.g. to procure justice, to punish, to carry through a legal proceeding, etc.; and with עִם is almost like Niph.

דון (part. pl. דָּאֲנִין) Aram. the same.

דּוֹן (only Keri) m. judgment. Ketib דִּין.

דּוֹנַג (דֹּנַג) m. wax, from דָּנַג to be soft. The radical of which is found in עָנֹג and תַּנְג.

דוץ (fut. יָדוּץ) to hop, to dance; hence generally to rejoice.

דוק (not used) to observe, to look about; especially, proving and searching.

דּוּק (Aram.) belongs to דְּקַק and דְּקַק.

. דּוּר (not used) to tear, to prick (of thorns), related to עָדַר in the radical; to cut into with the hatchet, from which דַּרְדַּר.

I. דּוּר to make a circuit, to turn; next, figur. to continue, to endure, like all verbs signifying encircling, making a circuit; trans. to inhabit, to dwell; originally, to move somewhere.

דּוּר (Aram.) the same, especially in the signification of dwelling; part. pl. דָּיְרִין, דָּאְרִין.

דּוֹר (דֹּר; pl. דּוֹרִים, דֹּרוֹת) m. circle of time, period, from דּוּר II.; next, period of the human age, generation; דּוֹר וָדוֹר from generation to generation, i.e. for ever; also, מִדֹּר דֹּר, לְדֹר וָדֹר, לְדוֹר דֹּר. In the signification of generation, the pl. is always דֹּרוֹת, but דּוֹרִים is used only in the phrase דֹּר דּוֹרִים and in the sense of eternity.

III. דּוּר (not used) to arrange, to string together, equivalent to תּוּר, and is to be found in the syllabic root from סֵדֶר.

דּוּר m. a pile of wood, something that is generally properly arranged; comp. מְדוּרָה.

דּוֹר (also דֹּאר) p.n. of a city not far from Carmel (circuit).

דּוּרָא p.n. of a plain in Babel (circuit).

I. דּוּשׁ (fut. יָדוּשׁ, inf. abs. according to some אָדוֹשׁ for דּוֹשׁ) the stamping (of the bull), to thresh, to lead the threshing bull. Niph. נָדוֹשׁ; inf. const. הִדּוּשׁ pass. from Kal to be trodden down. Hiph. דִּישׁ for הֵדִישׁ like often with the ע״ו; the signification is like Kal. Hoph. pass. from Hiph.

II. דּוּשׁ (not used) equiv. to דּוּץ to spring, to hop; from which דִּישׁוֹן, which see.

דּוּשׁ (Aram.), like דּוּשׁ I. in Heb.

דָּחָה to push, to drive away, to reject, equiv. to דָּחַח, נָדַח. Niph. נִדְחָה (fut. once יִדַּחוּ for יִדָּחוּ) pass. from Kal; the same as Pual דֹּחָה.

דַּחֲוָה (only pl. דַּחֲוָן), Aram. fem. a table, from דְּחָא, equivalent to מְתָא to spread out; like שֻׁלְחָן is from שָׁלַח; hence figuratively, food.

דֶּחִי (pause דֶּחִי) m. overthrow, fall. Root דָּחָה.

דְּחַל (part. דָּחֵל, pass. דְּחִיל) Aram. to fear; דְּחִיל fearfully. Pi. to frighten, to terrify.

דֹּחַן m. millet, gremil. The derivation is obscure.

דָּחַף to push, to beat, to drive; fig. driving on, to hurry; hence דָּחוּף driven on, hurrying. Niph. נִדְחַף to hurry oneself.

דָּחַק (fut. יִדְחַק) to press, to oppress.

דּוֹחֵק oppressor.

דַּי (const. דֵּי, with suff. דַּיִּי; after the form שְׁמִי ,מִי) m. sufficiency; next as an adj., sufficient; with suff. דַּיֶּךָ sufficient for thee, דַּיָּם their requirement. Hence כְּדֵי as is sufficient; figur. according to measure, בְּדֵי for the want, i.e. for: e.g. בְּדֵי אֵשׁ for the fire; בְּדֵי רִיק for nothing, but also like כְּדֵי so often; מִדֵּי almost like בְּדֵי. The root is דָּיָה to suffice, δέειν, like מָוָה to flow, related to מַיִ water.

דִּי (Aram.) origin. like זֶה demonst., but in use it is; 1) a relat. pron. for sing. and pl., which; but also at the slightest relation, where in Heb. the mere genit. or no relation is expressed at all externally; e.g. the temple in Jerusalem (דִּי בִירוּשְׁלֶם) a stream of fire, נְהַר דִּי נוּר; 2) a relative conj. that, so that, because; it is used in this manner like אֲשֶׁר and כִּי; sometimes also where a whole sentence is introduced relatively, כְּדִי as, since, equiv. to כַּאֲשֶׁר; מִן דִּי from the time, when.

דִּי זָהָב (gold region, gold district) p.n. of a place in the desert.

דִּיבוֹן (marshy district) 1) p.n. of a Moabite city, for which also דִּימוֹן as an allusion to דָּם; 2) a city in the territory of Judah, for which also דִּימוֹנָה.

דִּיג see דּוּג.

דַּיָּג masc. a fisherman, in Ketib for which דַּוָּג.

דָּיָה (not used) to be black, for which דַּיָּה and דְּיוֹ, but the derivation is obscure.

דְּיוֹ (after the Aram. form צְלוֹ; plur. modern Heb. דְּיוֹאוֹת) f. ink, probably not even black, since, according to Josephus, the Hebrews used several colors for writing.

דִּימוֹן see דִּיבוֹן.

דִּימוֹנָה see דִּיבוֹן.

דִּין verb, see דּוּן.

דִּין (Aram.) see דּוּן.

דִּין m. the judging (originally infin. Hiph. from דּוּן); next, trans. 1) the judgment, also when it signifies the assembly of judges; 2) cause of justice, legal punishment, sometimes strife in general. דָּן דִּין, עָשָׂה to carry on legal process; כִּסֵּא דִין judgment-seat; הִשְׁמִיעַ דִּין to proclaim judgment.

דִּין (def. דִּינָא) Aram. m. the same.

דַּיָּן (formed from דִּין, const. דַּיַּן) m. judge.

דַּיָּן (Aram.) the same.

דִּינָה p.n. f. (justice).

דִּינָי gent. n. from דִּין an Assyrian province, the population of which was transplanted to Samaria. The *def.* pl. is דִּינָיֵא, according to the Syriac form.

דִּיפַת see רִיפַת.

דָּיֵק (ancient particip. form, from דּוּק) m. a watch-tower, fort; בָּנָה, נָתַן דָּ׳ עַל to erect a place of observation upon the walls.

דִּישׁ see דּוּשׁ.

דַּיִשׁ m. origin. the threshing; next, time of threshing. Root דּוּשׁ I.

דִּישׁוֹן m. 1) a species of mountain goat, from דּוּשׁ II. 2) p.n. masc. (an antelope, the springer).

דִּישָׁן p.n. m. (the same).

דָּךְ (Aram.) dem. pron. m. דָּךְ f. this, formed from דִּי and כָּא.

דַּךְ (in pause דָּךְ) adj. m. oppressed, humbled, miserable; next, also as a subst. The root is דָּכָה, and formed therefrom like יַד, קַו from קָוָה, יָדָה.

דָּכָא (Kal not used) equiv. to דּוּךְ to beat down, to bruise; figur. to humble, to oppress. Niph. pass. in the figur. sense. Pi. דִּכֵּא (inf. with suff. דַּכְּאוֹ) to bruise, to trample upon; and also, figur. to oppress. Pu. pass. in both senses; as also the Hithpa. הִדַּכָּא, with dagesh replacing the ת.

דַּכָּא (pl. const. דַּכְּאֵי) adj. m. ground, pounded; next, figur. pressed down, contrite, e.g. in mind (רוּחַ); but also as a subst., that which is ground down, dust; הֵשִׁיב עַד דַּכָּא to turn back to dust (Auth. Vers. "Thou turnest man to destruction." Ps. 90:3).

דָּכָה (fut. יִדְכֶּה Kal) equiv. to דָּכָא to bruise, to beat down. Pi. to beat into pieces, e.g. עֲצָמוֹת bones, Niph. to be beaten, in a figur. sense.

דַּכָּה fem. bruising (of the testicles); hence, פְּצוּעַ דַּכָּה wounded by bruising.

דֳּכִי (only with suff. דָּכְיָם) m. the beating (of the waves), breaking of the waves.

דַּכָּן (after the form עֲנָו, only that it appears in the intensive form), adj. m. the humbled, miserable, unfortunate one.

דִּכֵּן dem. pron. pl. דָּךְ and דָּךְ these, but also const. with the sing.

דְּכַר (not used) Aram. to penetrate, to bore (of a spit), equiv. to דָּקַר; hence, figur. to impress (on the memory), to think, to retain.

דְּכַר (only pl. דִּכְרִין) Aram. m. origin. equiv. to זָכָר m. but also specially the masc. of a sheep, a ram, ἄρσης, aries.

דִּכְרָן (def. דִּכְרָנָה) Aram. m. worthy of being remembered, memorable.

דָּכְרָן (def. pl. דָּכְרָנַיָּא) m. equiv. to דִּכְרָן; hence, סְפַר דָּ׳ book of record, chronicle.

דַּל (pause דָּל, plur. דַּלִּים) adj. masc. 1) to move to and fro, to totter, from weakness; hence, weak, poor, unhappy, humble, and, like all adjs. used also as subst. Root דָּלַל. 2) subst. equiv. to דֶּלֶת gate, door (from דָּלָה), or elevation, as the ancients explain it.

דָּלַג to hop, to spring, with עַל to leap over. Piel דִּלֵּג to hop, to spring; also, to leap over, with accus. or עַל, without varying the sense.

דָּלָה (fut. יִדְלֶה) 1) to move to and fro, to hover, equiv. to דָּלַל; 2) trans. to raise, to lift up, to draw up. Pi. דִּלָּה to elevate, to save.

דַּלּוּ see דָּלַל.

דַּלָּה fem. 1) thread-work, thrum, so called from the moving of the threads; hence, figur. a lock of hair (comp. תַּלְתַּלִּים); 2) poverty, neediness; transf. from the first sense; next, also concrete, the poor, the humble; pl. דַּלּוֹת הָעָם the humble amongst the people.

דָּלַח (fut. יִדְלַח) intrans. to be muddy, dirty, equiv. to the root in אָרַח; next, also trans. to cause mud by stirring with the feet.

דְּלִי (with suff. דָּלְיוֹ, as from דֹּלִי) m. vessel for drawing water up, pail. Root דָּלָה.

דְּלָיָה p.n. m. (reared by God).

דְּלָיָהוּ p.n. m. (the same).

דְּלִילָה p.n. fem. unhappy, miserable one, or tender, weak one.

דָּלִית (pl. דָּלִיּוֹת) fem. branch, bough, from its moving to and fro.

דָּלַל (1 pers. דַּלּוֹתִי, 3 pl. דַּלּוּ, דָּלְלוּ, for which occurs once דַּלְיוּ; 1) to move to and fro, to hover, thus equiv. to דָּלַל; hence, to suspend, from (מִן) something; e.g. שֹׁקַיִם the legs; 2) tottering, i.e. to be weak, unhappy, low; figur. of the water, shallow; of the eyes, languishing. Niph. pass. of signification 2).

דִּלְעָן (gourd-place, from דְּלַעַת) p.n. of a place in the territory of Judah.

דָּלַף (fut. יִדְלֹף) to slide along; hence fig. to flow along, to pour down (of the rain): יִדְלֹף הַבָּיִת "the house droppeth through" (of rain); to drop tears (from the eyes); to melt, to flow (of the mind).

דֶּלֶף m. a gutter, a gutter from the roof; in Talm. דַּלְפָן bleared-eyed.

דַּלְפוֹן p. n. m. (the swift-one).

דָּלַק (fut. יִדְלַק) to glow, to burn, to kindle, with בְּ; figur. of arrows, the lips; next transf. to hotly pursuing, with אַחֲרֵי or the accus. Hiph. to kindle (fire), to become hot (e.g. with wine).

דְּלַק (Aram.) the same.

דַּלֶּקֶת (originally inf. Pi.) fem. fever (burning).

דֶּלֶת (dual דְּלָתַיִם, const. דַּלְתֵי, pl. דְּלָתוֹת, const. דַּלְתוֹת), fem. gate, door, the dual signifies a folding-door, double door, but also a gate consisting of two parts; figur. wing of a door (פֶּתַח); side or column of a scroll resembling a door. The root is דָּלָה in the signification of pending, as the door hangs on its hinges.

דָּם (const. דַּם, with suff. דָּמוֹ, דִּמְכֶם, pl. דָּמִים) masc. 1) blood; אָכַל עַל־דָּם to eat with the blood; דָּם נָקִי innocent blood; next also, guiltiness of blood, murder; the pl. especially is used so: e.g. עִיר, בַּיִת, אִישׁ דָּמִים town, house, man, of blood, i.e. of murder. The noun appears to be primitive, and the verb אָדַם derived therefrom; 2) juice, of grapes; figur. (only Ezek. 19:10, בְּדָמְךָ), sap, freshness of life; if the reading is not בְּרִמְךָ.

I. דָּמָה (fut. יִדְמֶה, imp. דְּמֵה) to be placed in relation to something; next, to be similar, alike, always const. with לְ and אֶל; therefore, דָּמִיתִי Jer. 6:2, does not appear to belong to this root. Niph. to be compared, to become alike; const. with the accus. or כְּ. Pi. דִּמָּה to compare, with לְ and אֶל to recite in parables (related to מָשַׁל) to contemplate something (evil) against somebody with לְ. Hith. הִדַּמָּה to compare oneself, with לְ somebody. The root is דָּמַת.

II. דָּמָה equiv. to דָּמַם to cut off, hence to annihilate, to make an end of; figur. to cease; e.g. my eye weepeth and ceaseth not וְלֹא תִדְמֶה. Niph. (only pret. and inf.) pass. to be destroyed, of nations, towns, and countries.

דְּמָה (Aram.) equiv. to דָּמָה I.

דֻּמָּה (for דוּמָה from דּוּם) fem. a hermitage, seclusion, a place of deathlike stillness. Comp. דּוּמָה above.

דְּמוּת f. likeness, similarity; hence, image, figure, pattern; adv. like, as.

דֳּמִי and דְּמִי masc. stillness, quiet; אַל דֳּמִי לָךְ "be not still" (Ps. 83:1)? דְּמִי יָמַי rest of days, i.e. best days.

דִּמְיוֹן masc. equiv. to דְּמוּת image, likeness.

דָּמַם 3 pers. pl. דַּמּוּ, fut. יִדֹּם, יִדַּם, pl. יִדְּמוּ, יִדַּמּוּ, which may be also the fut. forms of the Niph.; 1) to be quiet, to be silent, either from horror and amazement, from pain and grief, or from quiet submission; with לְ to appear silent before somebody; next, like דָּמָה, to cease; 2) equiv. to דָּמָה II., to destroy, to annihilate, generally

דָּמַם only in Niph. Niph. נָדַם (fut. יִדֹּם, יִדַּם, pass. of signification 2; נִדְמָה stands for נִדְּמָה. Pi. דּוֹמֵם to make silent, to appease. Hiph. הֵדַם to destroy.

דְּמָמָה f. stillness, קוֹל דְּ׳ or דְּ׳ וָקוֹל voice of stillness, stillness in voice, i.e. a soft voice.

דָּמַן (not used) to manure, probably secondary from דֹּמֶן.

דֹּמֶן m. manure, dung. The root is of uncertain extraction.

דִּמְנָה (place of manure), p.n. of a city in the territory of *Zebulun*.

דָּמַע (future יִדְמַע) origin. to flow, to run; hence, to weep, to shed tears.

דֶּמַע m. tear, only from the juice of olives and grapes.

דִּמְעָה (pl. דְּמָעוֹת) fem. tear; collect. tears.

דָּמַר belongs to תַּדְמֹר, see under תַּדְמֹר.

דַּמֶּשֶׂק (also with the dagesh analysed דַּרְמֶשֶׂק) p. n. of the city of Damascus, capital of Syria. According to the Arab. place of industry, from דָּמַשְׁק to be industrious; once דּוּמֶשֶׂק occurs for דַּמֶּשֶׂק. דַּמַּשְׂקִי a native of Damascus.

דְּמֶשֶׁק m. damask, silk stuff, so called from דַּמֶּשֶׂק the place where it was manufactured.

דָּן 1) p. n. m. (judge); 2) p.n. of a city, formerly לַיִשׁ so called by the Danites.

דֵּן (Aram.) demonst. pron. m., דְּנָה f. this one; כִּדְנָה equiv. to כְּזֹאת so, thus, origin. like this: עַל דְּנָה like עַל זֹאת for this; אַחֲרֵי דְנָה like אַ׳ זֹאת upon this.

דָּנִאֵל see דָּנִיֵּאל.

דָּנַג (not used) to be soft; the syllabic root is also to be traced in פַּנַּג.

דַּנָּה (lowliness) p.n. of a city in the territory of Judah. The root is דָּנַן to be lowly.

דִּנְהָבָה (place of spoil), p.n. of a city in Idumæa; equiv. to דִּי־נְהָבָה, from נָהַב to despoil.

דִּנָה יַעַן (habitation of the ostrich), p.n. of a town in the territory of Judah.

דָּנִיֵּאל p.n. m. (God is judge). For דָּנִיֵּאל occurs also דָּנִאֵל.

דֵּעַ (origin. inf. plur. דֵּעִים) masc. the knowing, knowledge. The root is יָדַע. תְּמִים דֵּעִים one perfect in knowledge.

דֵּעָה (inf. f. from דֵּעַ), knowledge.

דְּעָה imper. from יָדַע which see.

דְּעוּאֵל p.n. m. (confidence of God), once רְעוּאֵל occurs for it, which is the same.

דָּעַךְ (fut. יִדְעַךְ) originally lengthened from דָּךְ to tread down; transf. to extinguish (of a light). Niph. figur. of the drying up of water. Pu. דֹּעֲכוּ

figur. to be extinguished, destroyed. See זָעַךְ.

דָּעוּאֵל see דְּעוּאֵל.

דַּעַת (inf. from יָדַע, therefore sometimes const. with the accus.), fem. knowledge, insight, wisdom; יָדַע דַּעַת to possess knowledge; בִּבְלִי דַעַת unintentional, unawares.

דָּפָה (not used) to provoke, mock, blaspheme, the root is to be traced in נִדְּפִי.

דֹּפִי (pause דֹּפִי) m. mockery, blasphemy.

דָּפַק to push, to drive, to press, e.g. to drive violently (cattle); to knock violently at (עַל) the door; the root is found also דָּבַק, טָפַק, אָפַק, פָּקַק, רָפַק. Hith. to push oneself against (עַל) the door.

דָּפְקָה (a drove of cattle), p.n. of a city in the desert, now called El-Tobbacha.

דַּק adj. m. דַּקָּה fem. to be bruised, pounded (in small particles); hence, fine (of dust), or dust itself; figur. tender, thin, consumptive, soft, etc., in contrast to fat, strong, and full. Root דָּקַק, which see.

דֹּק m. thinness, concr. that which is thin, a veil, a thin covering.

דִּקְלָה (place of palms), p.n. of a district in Arabia.

דָּקַק (fut. יָדֹק equivalent to יִדַּק); 1) transf. to pound, to beat in pieces, to bruise; 2) to be bruised. Hiph. הֵדַק (inf. הָדֵק and הָדַק) fut., with suff. אֲדִקֵּם stands for אֲדֻקֵּם to pound, to bruise; inf. הָדֵק used as an adv. thin, fine. Hoph. pass.

דְּקַק (3 pers. pret. plur. דָּקוּ for דַּקּוּ) Aram. equiv. to דָּקַק in Heb.; Af. הַדֵּק (3 pers. fem. הַדֶּקֶת; 3 pers. plur. הַדִּקוּ, fut. יַדִּק) to pound, to bruise.

דָּקַר (fut. יִדְקֹר) to pierce, to bore through, to stab. Niph. to be pierced. Pu. דֻּקַּר the same; figur. also of death from hunger. The root is also in דָּקַר, נָקַר, חָקַר.

דֶּקֶר p.n. m. (equiv. to בֶּן דֶּקֶר) lance-bearer.

דַּר masc. pearl, so called from its brightness. See דָּרַר.

דָּר (Aram.) masc. equiv. to דּוֹר in Hebrew.

דֹּר see דּוֹר.

דָּרָא (not used) equiv. to דּוּר found under דַּרְדַּר to tear to pieces; figur. the heart, to rend the mind with pain.

דֵּרָאוֹן (const. דִּרְאוֹן) m. destruction, pain, grief.

דָּרַב (not used) to pierce (with a pointed instrument), to plough up (arable land), related to עָרַב, which see.

דָּרְבָן (pl. דָּרְבֹנוֹת) m. goads (a pointed instrument for driving on the cattle).

דָּרַג (not used) equiv. to דָּרַךְ to pace, to tread; from which, מַדְרֵגָה a step, stairs, degree.

דַּרְדַּע p.n. m. (pearl of knowledge), for which once the contraction דָּרַע.

דָּרוֹם m. south, meridional country. The derivation is obscure. Probably the root is דָּרַם, equiv. to Aram. *daram*, to glow, to seeth, to burn.

דְּרוֹר m. the running, hovering about; hence—1) wild, roving, bird; 2) freedom, unshackled; מָר־דְּרוֹר myrrh of freedom, i.e. myrrh flowing by itself. See דָּרַר.

דָּרְיָוֶשׁ p.n. m. (Daros, king Darius.)

דָּרְיוֹשׁ see דָּרְיָוֶשׁ.

דָּרַךְ (fut. יִדְרֹךְ), equiv. to דָּרַג to pace, to ascend; next, to tread; with בְּ to tread upon; with מִן to tread forth; with עַל to tread forward; sometimes also, to tread to pieces. To tread the bow, i.e. bend the bow; for which also sometimes דָּרַךְ חִצִּים; with יַיִן, גַּת, יֶקֶב, זַיִת, פּוּרָה, and דָּרַךְ only, to press. Hiph. הִדְרִיךְ 1) to cause to tread; with בְּ, to lead; but also with the accus.; to tread the tongue, i.e. to let it run. 2) to overtake, to reach, according to the Aram. use.

דֶּרֶךְ (dual דְּרָכַיִם, pl. דְּרָכִים, const. דַּרְכֵי) com. walk, way (as action, like: עָשָׂה, הָלַךְ דֶּרֶךְ to take a walk, to go a way; next, concrete, the road which one treads upon, e.g. דֶּרֶךְ הַמֶּלֶךְ the king's road, i.e. the high way. To go the way of all flesh, i.e. to die; figur. 1) manner, mode, way, walk of life; 2) path appointed for some one, i.e. fate, destiny.

דַּרְכְּמוֹן (only plur. דַּרְכְּמֹנִים) masc. a drachm, a Persian gold coin.

דָּרַם see under דָּרוֹם, where the verb is already explained.

דַּרְמֶשֶׂק is the complete form for דַּמֶּשֶׂק, which see.

דְּרָע (plur. with suff. דְּרָעוֹהִי) Aram. com. equiv. to the Hebrew זְרוֹעַ arm. See אֶזְרוֹעַ.

דָּרַע p. n. m. a secondary form of דַּרְדַּע.

דַּרְקוֹן p. n. m. (bearer), from דָּרַק, equiv. to דָּרַע to bear.

דָּרַר (not used) only found in the derivations דַּר and דְּרוֹר. 1) to glimmer, to shine, which root may be traced in אָדִּיר, הָדַר. From which דַּר. 2) to rove about, like דּוּר and דָּהַר, which words have the same signification. From which דְּרוֹר, which see.

דָּרַשׁ (fut. יִדְרֹשׁ) origin. to tread down, related to דָּרַס Aram.; or, to cut in, to cut through, related to the root in חָרַשׁ: hence—1) to penetrate into a matter, to press on somebody, to request, to search (comp. the etymology of חָקַר to study); 2) to seek, to search, to enquire, to ascertain, and generally to concern oneself about something. The construction is manifold: דָּ׳ אֶל to seek out (a place), to enquire after (at somebody's), to enquire of (oracles and idols); דָּ׳ לְ to press on some one with a request; דָּ׳ אֶת to visit; דָּ׳ אַחַר to seek after; דָּ׳ עַל to request, to enquire; מֵעִם to ask through or from some one, etc. Niph. pass. to be sought, searched; or, reflexive, to be entreated. Pi. only inf. דַּרְיוֹשׁ for דְּרוֹשׁ.

דָּשָׁא originally, to be fresh (comp. the root in חָרַשׁ; next, to sprout. Hiph. הִדְשִׁיא to cause to spring forth, vegetate.

דֶּשֶׁא m. grass, green, verdure.

דָּשֵׁן to become fat. Pi. to make fat; hence, of sacrifices to be considered acceptable; figur. to anoint. Pu. to become fattened, satiated. Hothp. הֻדַּשֵּׁן to become fat, satiated, of the sword. See דֶּשֶׁן.

דָּשֵׁן (pl. דְּשֵׁנִים) adj. m. fat, full of sap, vigorous.

דֶּשֶׁן (with suff. דִּשְׁנִי) m. 1) fatness, nutriment; 2) ashes from the fat of the animals of sacrifices, or from carcases; hence different from אֵפֶר.

דִּשֵּׁן Pi. denom. from דֶּשֶׁן; 1) to turn into ashes, or become ashes; 2) to clear ashes away. The denom. Pi. forms may receive both significations.

דָּת (const. pl. דָּתֵי) fem. law, edict; the etymology is uncertain.

דָּת (def. דָּתָא) Aram. the same.

דֶּתֶא (def. דִּתְאָה) Aram. m. grass, herb, equiv. to דֶּשֶׁא.

דְּתָבַר (def. plur. דְּתָבְרַיָּא) Aram. m. teacher of the law, judge; formed from דָּת.

דֹּתַיִן (also דֹּתָן) p. n. of a place in Northern Samaria (double well).

דָּתָן p.n. m. (Fontanus).

ה

ה called הֵא *he*, as a numeral 5; but thus ה̈ 5000. As a guttural it interchanges with א, ח, ע, e. g. אֶדֶר-הָדָר, עָנַן-הָנַן, אֶבֶן-הָבְ, חָלַם-הָלַם, אָדָם-הָדָם, but while it interchanges with ח and ע, it corresponds also with נ, כ, and י: e. g. יָדָה-הָדָה, עָנַן-הָנַן, מַהְמֹר—מַכְמֹר, and since like א in the beginning of words it is only as an aspirate, it interchanges with the vowel-letters.

הָ— enclytic particle, the most frequent and common to denote direction. Its use is twofold: (*a*) in nouns, and non-personal objects it is mute: e.g. שֹׁמְרֹנָה towards Samaria; הָהָרָה towards the mountain. If the terminating vowel of the noun is quiescent, it vanishes altogether by the addition of this particle, e.g. אַרְצָה, קֵדְמָה, בַּיְתָה, מָוְתָה, from אֶרֶץ, קֶדֶם, בַּיִת, מָוֶת, sometimes the nominal vowel of the root is abridged, like הָרָה from הַר, or contracted, like שְׁכֶמָה from שְׁכֶם, or loses the accent; like in צֹעֲרָה, אֹהֱלָה; it is joined to constructive as well as to absolute nouns; e.g. מִדְבָּרָה, פַּדֶּנָה from the constructives מִדְבַּר, פַּדַּן; also to nouns fem. by adding ת: as מִרְתָה from מָרָה. In nouns terminating ־ָה this enclytic particle is joined after the dropping of the terminating letter: e.g. מַטָּה downwards, from מַטֶּה declining; מַעְלָה upwards, from מַעֲלֶה rising: (*b*) in verbs to denote the purpose, hence only in the fut. and the imper., and even there in the short forms: e.g. אֶזְמְרָה (אֶזְמֹר), אִמְרָה (אֱמֹר), תְּבוֹאָה (third pers.), נָבְלָה (from נָבַל), and in the imperatives אָסְפָה, גְּשָׁה, שְׁכָה, עִרְכָה, הָבָה, קָבָה־, אָרָה־. Like in the nouns, the ־ָה is not used in roots terminating with a vowel, and only exceptionally occurs in the forms אֶהֱמָיֶה (from אֶהֱמֶה = אֶהֱמָי), נִשְׁתָּעָה (from נִשְׁתַּע), צֵאָה (from צֵא).

הַ abbrev. from הַל is closely connected with the noun, and is originally a demonst., but generally used as an article. The original ל, which never appears, is replaced by the *dagesh forte*; e. g. הַנַּעַר, הַמִּדְבָּר, or it entirely vanishes when the first letter has no vowel; e. g. הַמְבַקֵּשׁ, הַצְפַרְדֵּעַ, or when it is a guttural; e. g. הַחַיִל, הָעִים, sometimes before gutturals we find הָ or הֶ; e. g. הָעָם, הֶרָחוֹק, הָאָרֶץ, הֶעָפָר, הֶחָכָם.

הֲ interr. pron. introduces a question equiv. to εἰ, whether direct or indirect, whether an affirmative or a negative answer is expected. Preceding gutturals, it sounds הַ; e.g. הַאֵלֵךְ (or הֶ; e.g. הֶחָכָם): also before י, like הַיִיטַב, and where the first letter has no vowel, e.g. הַמְשֹׁל. Before א, it has sometimes ־ָ, e. g. הָאַתֶּם.

הָ, הֶ, see הַ, הֲ.

הָא Aram. interj. behold! origin. demonst.

הֵא interjection, here! i. e. behold! See הָא.

הֵא (Aram.) the same הָא כְּדִי see, like as.

הֶאָח (compounded from אָח and הָה) interj. ah! ah! exclamation of joy, or triumphant shout.

הַב see יָהַב.

הַבְהַב (pl. only הַבְהָבַי) m. an offering, a burnt offering; comp. אִשֶּׁה. Root הוּב.

הָבַל (fut. יֶהְבַּל) to breathe, to wave (in the Talm. to steam); fig. to be vain; orig. like a transient breath, or also to act vainly, to hope vainly, to pursue idolatry. Hiph. to make vain, to incite to idolatry.

הֶבֶל (const. הֲבֵל after the form זֶרַע, with suff. הֶבְלִי, pl. הֲבָלִים, const. הַבְלֵי) m. 1) breath, but also a vapour; next as a figure of transientness, nothingness, vanity; and in this sense also, idols, and idolatry; 2) adv. vainly, in vain, i. e. the subst. is used as an adv.; 3) p. n. m. (transientness).

הֲבֵל see הֶבֶל.

הָבַן (not used) to be hard, equiv. אֶבֶן, which see.

הָבְנִי (only pl. הָבְנִים) adj. (from הוֹבֶן) stony, hence pl. ebony, so called from its hardness.

הָבַר (rare) to divide, to cut to pieces, especially to divide into parts; hence הֹבְרֵי שָׁמַיִם, to divide the heavens into certain departments, according to the system of astrologers.

הֵגֵא p. n. m.

הָגַג (not used) equiv. to הָגָה, to speak, to pronounce softly, to whisper; next also of the soft language of the heart. The same root is traced in לְהַג.

I. הָגָה (fut. יֶהְגֶּה) 1) to murmur, to sound dull; e. g. of the plaintive sound of the harp, of the cooing of the dove, of the sighing of lament, of the whispering sorcerer, of the rolling thunder; 2) to speak, to sing, of audible intelligible sounds; 3) of the soft tones of the heart; to think, to contemplate, especially if it is done with inward vivacity. Poel הוֹגָה, but only inf. הֹגוֹ, if this inf. is not to be derived from II. הָגָה or יָגָה. Hiph. only particip. מַהְגִּים, to murmur, to whisper (of a sorceret).

II. הָגָה (inf. הָגוֹ) equiv. to יָגָה, II. to divide, to separate dross; next, figur. to remove (the violent tempest). Po. (according to some) only inf. הֹגוֹ, to separate.

הֶגֶה masc. murmuring, whispering; hence lament, complaint; next the rolling sound of thunder, inward emotions of the heart, quite like the verb

הָגוּת f. soliloquy of the heart, thought.

חַגַּי p. n. m.

הָגִיג (with suff. הֲגִיגִי) m. equiv. to הָגָה, inward lament, emotion (of the heart).

הִגָּיוֹן (const. הֶגְיוֹן) m. 1) the dull sound, especially the soft motion of the harp; (synom. זִמְרָה), hence a kind of music, either subsiding tones as a pause, or a particular kind of music; 2) like the verb, meditation, contemplation, thought.

הָגִין adj. m., הֲגִינָה f., suitable, appropriate, fitting. See הָגַן.

הָגַן (not used) equiv. to שָׁגַן, to surround closely: hence figur. to fit exactly.

הָגַר (not used) to flee, after the Arab.

הָגָר 1) p. n. f., flight, fugitive; 2) p. n. of a district on the Persian Gulf, from which the gent. noun הַגְרִי, pl. הַגְרִיִּים, הַגְרִיאִים, הַגְרִים (from הַגְרִיִּים) the people of that district. הָגָר Arab. Heg'r, as was formerly called the present province Bahrein.

הֵד m. equiv. to הֵידָד, shout of triumph, cry, from הָדַד to sound, which see.

הַדָּבָר (only pl. הַדָּבְרִין) Aram. m. royal council, council of state; probably also a priest appointed over the state papers, after the Persian *Dibir*.

הָדַד (not used) equivalent to הוּד, to raise the voice loudly, to sing, and related to יָדָה. Comp. קָלַל.

הֲדַד p. n. of a Syrian deity, then also a masc. name in general.

הֲדַדְעֶזֶר p. n. masc. (Hadad is the help).

הֲדַדְרִמּוֹן p. n. after the Targum, contraction from הֲדַד בֶּן טַבְרִמּוֹן; according to others, the p. n. of a place.

הָדָה to seize, to lay hold of, to stretch out (the hand) for seizing, just as יָדָה is to יָד; comp. hand and *pre-hend-ere*.

הֹדּוּ (for הֹנְדוּ, הִנְדוּ) p. n. of a country, India.

הֲדוֹרָם p. n. of an Arabian population, the Aramites, between the Himjarites and the Sachalites.

הֹדַי p. n. m. (the joyful one), shouting with rejoicing, in a parallel passage הוֹדְוָה.

הָדַךְ equiv. to דָּכָה to trample upon, with תַּחַת to tread down.

הָדַם (not used) equiv. to אָדַם (under אֲדָמָה), to stamp down, to stamp down with the feet.

הֲדֹם (only const. הֲדֹם) m., origin. something that is stamped down; hence הֲדֹם רַגְלַיִם that which is trodden upon with the feet, i. e, footstool, steps; compare Aram. כִּבְשָׁא stool, from כָּבַשׁ to tread.

הָדַם (Peal not used) to cut asunder. Pa. הַדֵּם to cut to pieces.

הַדָּם (only pl. הַדָּמִין) Aram. m. piece, ruin.

הֲדַס (pl. הֲדַסִּים) m. myrtle. The etymology is obscure.

הֲדַסָּה p.n. fem. (myrtle), the former name of Esther.

הָדַף (inf. יֶהְדֹּף) to push away, to push back, to eject.

הָדַר (fut. יֶהְדַּר) origin. to shine; next figur., to be magnificent; transf. to honor, to decorate, to glorify; comp. דָּדַר. Niph. נֶהְדַּר to be honored, glorified. Hith. to shew oneself glorious.

הֲדַר (Aram) the same. Pa. to honor, to glorify.

הָדָר (pl. הֲדָרִים) m. brightness, ornament, highness; hence, of God, majesty, glory.

הָדָר (later) masc. ornament. הֲדַר מַלְכוּת ornament of the empire, equiv. to אֶרֶץ הַצְּבִי land of beauty.

הֲדַר p.n. m. (majesty, glory).

הֲדָרָה (fem. from הָדָר, const. הַדְרַת) fem. the same, especially of the splendour of a feast.

הֲדַרְעֶזֶר p.n. m. (is another reading for הֲדַדְעֶ׳).

הָהּ interjec. woe, from which אֲהָהּ arose.

הוֹ see הוֹי.

הוּא (pl. הֵם, הֵמָּה) person. pron. he, and the plur. they, origin. it is a demonst., especially God is so called; with the article הַהוּא it signifies that one, after the noun or pronoun it is either translated "self," or it remains untranslated and strengthens the preceding pron., sometimes it stands for the copula "is"; the pl. הֵם is abbrev. from הוּם, like אֹתָם from אתּוּם which is seen in the Aram. That הוּא was originally a gen. com. and is also used for the later הִיא is known by the grammar.

הוּא (Aram.) the same.

הָוָא (imper. הֱוֵא, fut. יְהוּא, contr. from יֶהֱוֶא) equiv. to הָיָה. 1) to thrust down (according to the Arab.), as the most modern explain; but better is the original signification, to wave: hence, הֱוֵא אֶרֶץ wave down upon the earth; 2) to be, originally to breathe, to live.

הֲוָא (also הֲוָה; fut. יֶהֱוֵא=לֶהֱוֵא; pl. לֶהֱוֹן m., לֶהֶוְיָן f.) Aram. to be, like the Heb. הָיָה.

הוּב (not used) to roast, to burn. In the Aram. Pa. הַבְהֵב to roast. See הַבְהַב.

הוּד (not used) 1) equiv. to הָדַד to sound, to sing; hence, to praise, to exalt; 2) like הָלַל to shine; hence, to bloom.

הוֹד m. 1) shouting, with joy; as, הוֹד קוֹל rejoicing of the voice; 2) brightness, glory, ornament; figur. transf. to bloom, freshness of youth; 3) p. n. m. youthful appearance. Comp. אֲחִיהוּד, אֲבִיהוּד.

הוֹדַוְיָה p.n. m. (fame of God), from הוֹדוּיָה.

הוֹדַוְיָהוּ p.n. m. (the same).

הוֹדִיָּה p.n. m. (glory of God).

הוֹדִיָּה p.n. m. (majesty of God).

הָוָה (part. הוֹוֶה, imper. הֱוֵה) equiv. to הָיָה, origin. to blow, to breathe, aspirate (like נָשַׁם); hence—1) figur. to live, to be, to exist; 2) to desire, to pant for something, *adspirare ad aliquid*, if not in this sense, a secondary form of אָוָה; 3) to breathe the last, expiring; hence, to perish, to die.

הַוָּה (pl. הַוּוֹת) f. 1) desire, lust (from הָוָה 2); 2) perishing, death; hence figur. perishableness.

הֹוָה f. equiv. to הַוָּה 2, destruction.

הוֹהָם p.n. m. (God of the multitude).

הוֹי interj. woe! equiv. to אוֹי exclamation of sadness, threat, and exhortation; once הוֹ occurs for it.

הוּךְ (only fut. יְהָךְ, inf. מְהָךְ), Aram. to go; it is not connected with הָלַךְ.

הוֹלֵלָה (only pl. הוֹלֵלוֹת) f. folly, madness. The termination וֹת— appears only to be a secondary form from וּת—, and is, therefore, the sing., just as חַכְמוֹת, עוֹלֵלוֹת.

הוֹלֵלוּת f. the same.

הוֹלָם see חָלַם.

הוּם equiv. to הָמָה, הָמַם to roar, to make a noise, to throw things into confusion (by uproar, alarm).—Niph. (fut. יֵהוֹם) to get into confusion, uproar. Hiph. to cause a noise, an uproar; from Kal only the pret. occurs; from Niph. and Hiph. the fut. only.

הוֹמָם p.n. m. (confusion), from which also הֵימָם.

הוּן (Kal not used) 1) equiv. to און 1. to blow, to breathe; hence, like in הָבַל figur. to be vain; in Hiph. הֵהִין to make vain, to act foolishly; 2) equiv. to און 2 and עָנָה to earn, to gain—in this sense it is only a secondary form of און.

הוֹן (pl. הוֹנִים) masc. equiv. to אוֹן wealth, riches; hence value: e.g. בְּלֹא הוֹן without value; or sufficient property, sufficiency in general.

הוּץ (not used) equiv. to חוּץ to cut to pieces, to divide; from which הֹצֶן a weapon.

הוֹר (pl. const. הוֹרֵי) m. 1) equiv. to הַר mountain; hence הוֹרֵי עַד (according to some readings) the everlasting mountains; like גִּבְעוֹת עוֹלָם 2) p.n. of two mountains.

הוֹשָׁמָע p.n. m. (knowledge of God).

הוֹשֵׁעַ p.n. m. (salvation, help).

הוֹשַׁעְיָה p.n. m. (salvation of God).

הות (Kal not used) to persecute, to hate. Pi. הוֹתֵת to hate violently, to rush upon somebody in a persecuting spirit; const. with עַל.

הוֹתִיר p.n. m. (the saved one).

הָזָה (rare) to gape, gaping (an intoxicating sleep.)

הִי interj. like הוֹי woe! next also as a subst.

הִיא (pl. הֵן, הֵנָּה) pers. pron. f. she, sometimes also a neuter, it; as manifold in its use as הוּא. The pl. הֵן arises from הֵנָּה.

הֵידָד mas. (shout of joy or victory) from הָדַד which see.

הֻיְּדוֹת (only pl. הֻיְּדוֹת) f. a choir, a choir of singers. The form is without analogy.

הָיָה (fut. יִהְיֶה, apoc. יְהִי, inf. הֱיוֹת, הֱיוֹת, later הֲוָה) orig. to breathe, but commonly: 1) to be, either signifying to exist, live, or to be located somewhere; or to be, connecting the subject with the predicate. With לְ of the person: to belong to, to serve for something; with עִם to take one's part; connected with the inf. of another verb, it signifies to be, in order to do something, it must, or one intends to do; 2) to be called into existence, to arise, to become (with לְ or accus.) הָיָה לְאִישׁ to become a man, i.e. to conduct oneself as a man, sometimes to be allotted to a man, to be married; 3) to happen, occur. Niph. נִהְיָה happened, the wish has occurred, i.e. fulfilled; to be done for, e.g. "I was done for (נִהְיֵיתִי) and I became sick" (Dan. 8:27); "the sleep was gone (נִהְיְתָה) from him." (Dan. 2:1.)

הַיָּה (Keri for הַוָּה) f. destruction, death (from הָיָה equiv. to הָוָה 3.)

הֵיךְ conj. equiv. אֵיךְ how, especially in modern writings.

הֵיכָל (const. הֵיכַל, pl. הֵיכָלִים, ־וֹת) com. a palace, a temple, sometimes only the superior part of the temple, a castle; poet. of heaven as being the palace of the world. Root הָכַל.

הֵיכַל (def. הֵיכְלָא) Aram. com. the same, especially royal palace.

הֵילֵל m. splendour; next, bright star, the morning star. Root הָלַל. Another form הֵילִיל belongs to יָלַל and is the imper. of the Hiphil, which see.

הֵם see הוּם.

הֵימָם p. n. m. (destruction).

הֵימָן p. n. m. (faithful one), equiv. to מְהֵימָן particip. of אֲמַן.

הִין m. name of a measure for fluids. The root הוּן or הִין is only a secondary from of אָכְנָה or אָכַי, which see, and signifies to contain.

הָכַל (not used) to contain, to receive; equiv. to כּוּל, יָכֹל; Aram. עֲכַל, from which הֵיכָל.

הָכַר only occurs once in the form תַּהְכְּרוּ, which stands for תַּהְכִּירוּ, probably extended from תַּכִּירוּ= תַּכִּירוּ and belongs to נָכַר, which in Hiph., with לְ, signifies to decide upon something.

הַכָּרָה f. recognising, distinguishing, e.g. פָּנִים, of the person, partiality in judgment.

הַל 1) demonst. particle, forming the foundation to אֵלֶּה, and for the article; from which arose הָלְאָה, the verb נַהֲלָא, and the adv. הֲלֹם. The original signification is: there, yonder, far off; 2) the Heb. art. for which see הַ; 3) the interrog. particle, which always changes into הֲ, and once (Deut. 32:6) occurs in its complete form.

הָלְאָה formed from הַל, but only with the ה of motion, הָלְאָה to yonder side, further off, used of place as well as of time. מִשָּׁם וָהָלְאָה, from thence, and further; מֵהָלְאָה לְ, from the other side of. From which the Niph. נַהֲלָא, to be distant; the particip. of which is נַהֲלָאָה, distant.

הִלּוּל (only pl. הִלּוּלִים) m. rejoicing, song, feast of joy (of the vintners), origin. praise.

הַלָּז demon. pron. com. this. The complete form is :—

הַלָּזֶה m., הַלֵּזוּ f., this; both, however, pointing to something at a distance; comp. from הַל, לְ, זֶה, זוּ, where לְ indicates the distance.

הֵלֶךְ (pl. הֲלִיכִים) m. step, walk, pace.

הֲלִיכָה (formed from הֵלֶךְ) f. 1) walk, march; 2) manner, system; 3) caravan.

הָלַךְ (fut. יַהֲלֹךְ, but יֵלֵךְ belongs to יָלַךְ; inf. הָלוֹךְ 1) to go, in the most versatile applications, and also of inanimate objects; e.g. of the spreading of a report, of the stretching of territory, of driving, of a vessel, flowing, streaming, etc.; also of the continuation of action. In this last sense הָלַךְ is connected with the word expressing the action continued: as הוֹלֵךְ וְקוֹטֵל, הָלַךְ הָלוֹךְ וְקוֹטֵל, or קָטַל הָלוֹךְ וְקָטוֹל; 2) either to walk, i.e. to live, to follow; with בְּ or the accus., of the way which one walks, or in the sense of going away, disappearing, dying. In the first sense, the place to which one is going is const. with אֶל, לְ, and accus., seldom with עַל; with בְּ it signifies to enter, with accus. it signifies also to march through; with בְּ to go with something; with עִם, אֵת, to have intercourse with somebody; הָ׳ אַחֲרֵי, to follow. Niph. נֶהֱלַךְ, to vanish. Pi. הִלֵּךְ, to walk along, *grassari*. Hiph. (only part. מַהְלְכִים) to lead, otherwise, however, only formed from יָלַךְ. Hith. הִתְהַלֵּךְ, to walk by oneself, sauntering (hence מִתְהַלֵּךְ, wanderer); next to live, to conduct oneself, especially of walking before God (a pious life).

הֲלַךְ Aram. the same. Pa. הַלֵּךְ, like הִלֵּךְ. Af. אַהְלֵךְ, like Hiph.

הֵלֶךְ masc. 1) walk, procession; 2) concr. a traveller.

הֲלָךְ Aram. m. money to pay for the road, toll.

הָלַל (fut. יָהֹל, inf. הַל, with suff. הִלּוֹ) 1) to shine; hence also fig. to boast. In this sense the part. הוֹלֵל boaster, bragger, a fool, if it does not stand for מְהוֹלֵל, and derived from Poel; 2) to echo, to sound (related to צָלַל). Pi. הִלֵּל to sing, especially praises, to laud, to praise, with accus. or with לְ, בְּ. Pu. pass. to be praised, to be sung; particip. מְהֻלָּל worthy of praise (of God). Poel הוֹלֵל to make a fool of (comp. Kal 1). Poel pass. hence particip. מְהוֹלָל one acting foolishly. Hiph. to diffuse light, i.e. to shine. Hith. to prove oneself worthy of praise, to boast of (בְּ or עִם), a subject. Hithpoel to feign folly, the two principal significations of the root are closely connected, inasmuch as the latter is the figurative idea of the former.

הִלֵּל p. n. m. (the praiseworthy one).

I. הָלַם originally to beat down; next, to strike, to push, to pound, to bruise; figur. to be beaten down by wine, i.e. to be drunk; of the dispersion of an army, etc.

II. הָלַם (not used) equiv. to חָלַם to be hard. From which יַהֲלֹם, which see.

הֹלֶם (הוֹלֶם) m. a blow, a push.

הֵלֶם p.n. masc. (*Malleolus*, one that strikes on the anvil).

הֲלֹם (formed from הֲל with the termination ־ֹם) adv. of place: hither, עַד הֲ׳ unto, hither, or without sense of motion, here.

הַלְמוּת f. orig. abstract, the striking, but also concrete, a hammer.

הָם p.n. of a place (multitude, wealth, comp. *Turba* in Spain, and *Copia* in Italy).

I. הָם (after the form שֵׁם, only pl. with suff. הֲמֹהֶם for הֲמִיהֶם) m. tumult, noise, assembly of people.

II. הֵם (with ה parag. הֵמָּה) pl. from הוּא they, and is used like the sing., sometimes even for the fem., or also for the verb subst.

הָמָה (fut. יֶהֱמֶה, part. f. הוֹמָה and הוֹמִיָּה) to hum, to break forth in sound, e.g. of the growling of the bear, the snarling of the dog, the cooing of the dove, sighing of man, the clang of instruments, the splashing of rain, the rolling of a carriage, the buzzing of a mob, moaning of the heart (from anguish, etc.); הוֹמִיָּה the noisy one, i.e. the street; הוֹמֶה שֵׁכָר the intoxicating drink confuses; figur. staggering, to be giddy, to reel.

הֵמָּה see הֵם.

הֵם see הָמוֹן.

הָמוֹן (const. הֲמוֹן, with suff. once הֲמָנְכֶם where the ֻ is shortened, pl. הֲמֹנִים) com. 1) noise, tumult, multitude, in the same manifold significations as the verb; 2) p.n. from אָמוֹן which see.

הִמּוֹ (also הִמּוֹן) Aram. person. pron. pl. they, like the Heb. הֵם.

הֲמוֹן ג p. n. masc. (dominion of Amon).

הֲמוֹנָה p. n. of a city in the vicinity of גֵּי הֲמוֹן גּוֹג so called in the prophetic vision.

הֶמְיָה f. the noise of the viol.

הָמַל (not used) to associate, to assemble, the Root may again be traced in כָּ־מֶל: next, to accumulate.

הֲמֻלָּה (also הֲמוּלָּה) fem. multitude, troop; hence קוֹל הֲמֻלָּה noise of a multitude.

הָמַם (in the pret. only once הַמֹּתִי; fut. יָהֹם) to confuse, to set in motion (by fright), i.e. in confusion, or without the secondary idea of confusion, e.g. to set the wheel of a waggon in motion הָמַם גַּלְגַּל עֶגְלָה. Fig. to destroy, to uproot, origin. to rout through confusion.

הָמָן p. n. of a Persian.

הֲמָנִיךְ (according to the Ketib הַמְנוּךְ) Aram. m. bracelet, μανιάκης, but the Greek origin cannot be proved.

הָמַס (not used, and only supposed to be connected with the following הָמַם) to break, to crush.

הָמָס (only pl. הֲמָסִים) m. something broken off, the branches of a tree. The Targ., LXX., etc., have analysed the pl. in הֵמַּס יָם.

הָמַר (not used) equivalent to כָּמַר to twist, to plait, from which it is a softened form. Herefrom מַהֲמֹר=מִכְמֹר.

I. הֵן plur. from הִיא, also הֵנָּה and joined with בכ״לם, the original form appears, e.g. בָּהֵן, לָהֵן, כָּהֵן, מֵהֵן, where the connection with ל forms an exception, since לָהֵן differs from לָהֶן so that the former is only a prepos., on account of, therefore, equiv. to לָכֵן.

II. הֵן (with makkaph הֶן־) a demonst.

particle this, these; hence also, 1) interjec. there! behold! lo! for which, however, the lengthened form הִנֵּה generally occurs; 2) subjunctive particle, if; for which, however, אִם commonly stands; 3) interr. particle, whether.

הֵן (Aram.) like הֵן II. in Hebrew, but only in the signification, 1 & 2.

הֵנָּה 1) the pl. from הִיא they, f.pl. with the article הָהֵנָּה even they, like the shorter form הֵן it is joined with the prepos. בבכ״לם; 2) adv. here, hither, hitherto; הֵנָּה—הֵנָּה here—there; הֵנָּה—וָהֵנָּה hither and thither.

הִנֵּה (seldom הִנָּה) interjec. Behold! see there! (pointing), lengthened from הֵן; with suffix it includes the verb subst., e.g. הִנְנִי (pause הִנֵּנִי, הִנֶּנִּי) behold here I am, etc., joined with the participle it generally points to the future tense.

הֲנָחָה (from נוּחַ) f. granting of rest, e.g. remission of a tax.

הִנֹּם p.n. m. to whom formerly belonged the valley on the south-eastern side of Jerusalem, where later children were sacrificed to Moloch; hence גֵּי בֶן־הִנֹּם, גֵּי־הִנֹּם, גֵּי בְנֵי הִנֹּם the valley (of the son, of the sons) of Hinnom, whose western portion was subsequently called חֲקַל דְּמָא (field of blood).

הֵנַע n. pl. of a town in Mesopotamia.

הַנְגָּפָה inf. Hiph. from נגף, which see.

הָסָה (Kal not used) to rest, to be silent, equiv. to חָשָׁה. Pi. only imp. הַס, הַסּוּ to be quite mute. The imp. is used as an interj. or an adv. Hiph. (fut. apoc. וַיַּהַס) to silence, to appease.

הֲפֻגָה f. origin. fatigue, ceasing, interruption. Root פוג.

הָפַךְ (fut. יַהֲפֹךְ) to turn (the hand), to turn round (the neck), to turn back (to flee), to turn a thing into (accus. or לְ) something else; figur. to destroy (a town, a city), to pervert (words), or of a moral perversion, e.g. הַפְכְּכֶם your perversion. Niph. נֶהְפַּךְ to turn oneself, to be turned into (לְ, עַל) something, e.g. "her pains turned upon her" (עָלֶיהָ), 1 Sam. 4:19; to turn against (בְּ) something, to turn into (לְ or accus.) something, i.e. to be destroyed, to turn with his tongue, i.e. to use the tongue skilfully. Hoph. to turn oneself against (עַל) somebody. Hith. to turn itself (of the drawn, glittering sword), to change into, to roll along. The root הָפַךְ is related to אָפַךְ, which see.

הֶפֶךְ m. contrary, opposite, origin. turned round.

הֵפֶךְ m. the same.

הֹפֵךְ connected with הַפֶּכְכֶם is an inf. from הָפַךְ.

הֲפֵכָה fem. upsetting, destruction, devastation, the same as מַהְפֵּכָה.

הֲפַכְפַּךְ (a redoubled form from הָפַךְ) adj. masc. very crooked, perverse, equiv. to עֲקַלְקַל.

הַצָּלָה f. deliverance. Root נָצַל.

הָצַן (not used) supposed to be connected with חֹצֶן; according to some, to be entrenched, or equivalent to צָנַן to shield, from which צִנָּה.

הֹצֶן m. weapon, from הוּץ, equiv. to חוּץ (to cut to pieces); this termination ־ֶן is also found in אֹזֶן, אֹמֶן, בֹּטֶן, זוֹקֶן and others.

הַר (with the article הָהָר, with ה of motion הָרָה, with the article added thereto הָהָרָה, with suffix, however, הַרְרִי, הֲרָרִי; pl. הָרִים, const. הָרֵי, but also הַרְרֵי; with suff. הָרָיו, but also הֲרָרֶיהָ) masc. mountain, mountainous region, sometimes used for Zion, Sinai, etc., הַר is often joined with proper nouns.

הָרָא mountainous country, p.n. for *Media Magna*, great Media, Arian, hence in a parallel passage, 2 Kings 17:6, it is expressed by מָדָי, but especially the mountainous district of Media.

הַרְאֵל m. equiv. to אֲרִיאֵל, אֲרִאֵל, burnt offering altar, from אָרָא, to burn.

הָרַג (fut. יַהֲרֹג) to slay, to murder, to kill, to destroy; of men, of beasts, and plants, with the accus. and לְ; with בְּ, to slay among others. Niph. and Pu. pass. The original signification is to overwhelm, and is related to the root רְדַג in Aram.

הֶרֶג m. murder, strangling.

הֲרֵגָה f. slaying, strangling, slaughtering; hence, גֵּיא הַה׳ valley of slaying, צֹאן הֲרֵגָה sheep for slaughter.

הָרָה (part. הוֹרָה, plur. הוֹרִים) 1) to conceive, to be pregnant, origin. equivalent to the Aram. בְּטַן, and therefore connected with הַר hill; הוֹרִים parents; 2) figur. to conceive in mind, to brood (mischief). Pual (הֹרָה, infin. הוֹרוֹ) to become pregnant.

הָרָה (origin. part.) adj. m. הָרָה f. (const הָרַת, but the pl. הָרוֹת and הֲרִיּוֹת; comp. פּוֹרִיָּה, בּוֹכִיָּה for פּוֹרָה, בּוֹכָה), to be with child: the m., as a matter of course, does not occur.

הַרְהֵר (the Pa. form) Aram., to perceive, to hear, to conceive, in mind.

הַרְהוֹר (Aram.) m. perception, thought; pl. of the cogitations in a dream.

הֵרוֹן from הֵרָיוֹן which see.

הֹרִיָּה from הָרָה which see.

הֵרָיוֹן masc. conception, pregnancy, with suff. once הֵרוֹנֵךְ for הֵרָיוֹנֵךְ.

הֲרִיסָה f. pulling down; concr. ruin. Root הָרַס.

הֲרִיסוּת f. destruction.

הָרַם (not used) to raise oneself, equiv. to אָרַם and רוּם.

הֹרָם p.n. m. (the exalted one).

הָרָם p.n. m (the same).

הַרְמוֹן p.n. masc. abbrev. in popular language from הֲדַדְרִמּוֹן. According to some it is a p.n. for Armenia, as the Targum renders it.

הָרָן p. n. m. (an inhabitant of mountains).

הָרַס (fut. יֶהֱרֹס) to pull down (cities, walls, posts), to pull out (teeth), figur. to destroy, to do something violently. Niph. pass. Pi. is only a stronger form of Kal, to destroy something from the foundation.

הֶרֶס m. destruction, but in one passage הֶרֶס is rendered sun, or הֶרֶס is to be taken as a softened form from חֶרֶס.

הָרַר (not used) to raise oneself, to be exalted, from which הַר.

הֲרָרִי (also הֲרָרִי) adj. m. (from הַר, inhabitant of a mountain).

הָשֵׁם p.n. m. (the brilliant one, equiv. to חָשֻׁם), in a parallel passage יָשֵׁן (equiv. to חָשֻׁן).

הַשְׁמָעוּת (inf. Hiph.) f. announcement, proclamation. Root שָׁמַע.

הִשְׁמָעָה p. n. m. (announcement).

הִתּוּךְ (inf. Hiph.) m. melting.

הֲתָךְ (Persian) p. n. m.

הָתַל (a secondary verb formed from the Hiph. of תָּלַל), only Pi. הֵתֵל, (fut. יְהָתֵל) to mock, to scorn, to despise). Root תָּלַל II.

הָתֹל (pl. only הֲתֻלִּים) m. mocking, scorning.

הָתַת see הוּת.

ו

ו *vav* (וָו), signifies hook; the shape of the letter is taken from the signification of the word. As a numeral it signifies 6. As a consonant ו interchanges with all labials; e.g. אָבַל—אָוַל, גַּו—גַּף, as a vowel, with א, ה, י. Where ו appears in the root, the beginning, middle, and end, must be distinguished: 1st, in the beginning of the root the ו is omitted, and replaced by a י. The language has, however, made a distinction between those roots originally commencing with ו and those originally commencing with י, and the following roots may be placed under ו, since they only appear with ו at the beginning: וָאַל I. (only נוֹאַל) וָאַל II. (הוֹאִיל) וָנָה (הוֹנָה), וָדָה (הוֹדָה),

(הוֹעִיל) וָעַל, (נוֹלָד) וָלַד, (נוֹכַח) וֹכַח where the *yod* substitute never occurs. 2) in the middle of the roots, the ו only appears as a consonant, אָוַל, חָוַר but the ע״ו are according to historical and analytical inquiry, generally but monosyllabic roots, with ־ intermediate vowel, which the conjugation and the analogy confirm. 3) At the end of roots, where the ו has always the power of a consonant.

וְ (but וּ before sheva and a labial, וָ, if the accent immediately follows it), conj.: and, to connect words and sentences; sometimes as an expletive: and indeed; sometimes contrasting: and yet; it is altogether of very manifold significations, according to its position before causal, consequent, and objective sentences.

וַ (with dagesh following) is the copulative ו of the fut., in the pret. it is וְ, the action is thereby placed in a certain contingency; this ו, therefore, does not change the tense, but further develops it; hence, the unfitness of the name ו conversive.

וְדָן p.n. of a district having two rivers in Arabia, not far from Gabla.

וָהֵב p.n. of a place in the territory of Moab.

וָו (pl. וָוִים) m. nail, hook.

וַיְזָתָא p.n. m. (the pure one).

וָלָד (and also וָלֶד) m. descendant, progeny.

וַנְיָה p.n. m. (tameness).

וָפְסִי p.n. m.

וַשְׁנִי p.n. m.

וַשְׁתִּי p.n. f. (the beautiful one).

ז

ז Zain (זַיִן) signifies weapon, and takes its shape from the signification of the name of the letter. As a numeral it signifies 7. It interchanges with the dentals: שֶׂה—זֶה; דָּבַל—זָבַל; טָבַח—זָבַח; זָהַר; צָהַר, סָהַר—זָהַר; צָהַב—זָהַב; זִלְזֵל; דָּכַר—זָכַר; סוּר—זוּר; טָהַר—זָנַב; צָמַם—זָמַם; תַּלְתַּל, סַלְסַל; זָעַק; דָּעַךְ—זָעַךְ; צָנַח—זָנַח; סָנַף—צָעַק; צָעַר—זָעַר.

זָאַב (not used) equiv. to זָעַף to be furious, grim, from which זְאֵב.

זְאֵב (pl. זְאֵבִים, const. זְאֵבֵי) masc. 1) a wolf. The form is a participle equiv. to זָאֵב. 2) p.n. m.

זֹאת dem. pron. f. this one, or this, neut. The form arose from זֹא = זָא, Aram. דָּא, with the addition of ת, and appears once lengthened in זֹאתָה. Respecting its manifold applications, comp. זֶה.

זָבַב (not used) to be dispersed, scattered, hovering about. From which זְבוּב.

זָבַד (rare) to present, to give.

זֶבֶד m. gift.

זָבָד p.n. m. (the giver, donor).

זַבְדִּי p.n. m. (donor).

זַבְדִּיאֵל p.n. masc. (the present from God).

זְבַדְיָה p.n. m. (the same).

זְבַדְיָהוּ p.n. m. (the same).

זְבוּב (pl. const. זְבוּבֵי) m. origin. a little swarming insect, especially the fly, the gad-fly: זְ׳ מָוֶת mortal fly; בַּעַל זְבוּב the Baal who kills flies, i.e. a deity protecting from vermin.

זַבּוּד p.n. masc. (the presented, the given one).

זַבּוּד p.n. m. (the giver).

זְבוּדָּה p.n. fem. (the gift), in Ketib זְבִידָה (the same).

זְבוּל (with ה mobile, זְבֻלָה) masc. 1) surounded place, habitation, dwelling. In the Talmud, זְבִיל veiling. 2) p.n. m. (the weak one), originally, wrapped, like עֲטוּף.

זָבַח (fut. יִזְבַּח) to slaughter, σφαγ, to sacrifice to some one (לְ or לִפְנֵי). Piel זִבַּח to sacrifice frequently.

זֶבַח (pl. זְבָחִים, זִבְחוֹת) m. 1) offering of sacrifice, every offering which is slaughtered; next, offering (sin, trespass, or thank offering), feast for offering, e.g. זֶ׳ הַיָּמִים annual feast of offering; next, feast (of that which is slaughtered), meal in general; 2) p.n. m. (offering, offerer).

זַבַּי p.n. m. (one roving about).

זְבִידָה see זְבוּדָּה.

זְבִינָא p.n. m. (one that is bought).

זָבַל (fut. יִזְבְּלֵ) 1) (not used) to roll, to heap together, equiv. to זָבַל; hence, modern Heb. זֶבֶל hill (of dung); 2) to encircle, encompass; figur. conjugal cohabitation.

זְבֻלוּן (also זְבוּלֻן, זְבוּלוּן) p.n. m. (the presented one). Gent. זְבוּלֹנִי.

זְבַן (Aram.) to purchase, to acquire, to gain; זְ׳ עִדָּנָא to gain time.

זָג m. skin of the grape, husk, from זוג to enclose.

זֵד (origin. a particip. form, pl. זֵדִים) m. haughty, barefaced, presumptuous, one. Root זוד.

זָדוֹן (const. זְדוֹן) masc. presumption, haughtiness, from

זֶה 1) demonst. pronoun masc., this one, this, always pointing to the present, and seldom connected with a fem. noun. It generally follows the noun (הַיּוֹם הַזֶּה), but if it precedes the noun, it includes the verb-subst., e.g. זֶה הַיּוֹם this is the day. It often stands alone, זֶה—זֶה, this, that; זֶה אֶל זֶה one to another; מִי זֶה, who (is) this one; 2) relat. pronoun, he who, that which, e.g. the place which (זֶה) thou hast founded; but this signification of זֶה is confined to the poetic books of scripture; 3) as a demonst. particle, here, there, e.g. מִזֶּה, from hence; זֶה הַיָּם, this (is) the sea; מִזֶּה וּמִזֶּה, from hence and thence, but also of time, now, at present, e.g. עַתָּה זֶה, just now; זֶה כַּמֶּה שָׁנִים, now so many years since, and in these significations it often strengthens the interrog. particles, e.g. מַה־זֶּה, why then; לָמָּה זֶה, wherefore then; 4) connected with prepositions in demonst. relations, e.g. בָּזֶה, here, then; כָּזֶה, as such; כָּזֹה וְכָזֶה, so and so, this as well as that: the manifold significations of זֹאת are similar to those of זֶה.

זֹה (the original and usual form of the fem. equiv. to זוֹ in זֹאת), pron. demonst., this one, only used in modern writings, but always in connection כָּזֹה וְכָזֶה.

זֶה (only 1 Sam. 17:34) a secondary form from שֶׂה, a lamb.

זָהַב (not used) equiv. to צָהַב, to shine, to glitter, especially of the yellow colour.

זָהָב (const. after vav וּזְהַב) m. gold, glitter of gold, transf. to the gold shekel if preceded by numbers.

זָהַם (Kal not used) to be dirty, unclean; related to טָמֵא. Piel, To make loathsome, disgusting.

זַהַם p.n.m. (loathsomeness, concrete: unclean one).

זָהַר (Kal not used) equiv. to צָהַר, סָהַר, טָהַר, to shine, to illumine, from which Hiph. הִזְהִיר, to diffuse light (of the skies), but often in a morally metaphorical sense, to enlighten, to illustrate, to instruct (with double accus.), to clear up, to warn against (מִן) something. Niph. to be cleared up in (בְּ) something; to be warned of (מִן) something.

זְהַר (Aram.) the same part. pass. זְהִיר, cautious, warned, watchful.

זֹהַר m. brightness (of the sky).

זִו (also זִיו) m. splendour, blossom: hence name of the month of blossoms; complete זִיו נִצָּנַיָּא in Aram. The root is זו (ע"ו) related to זָהַב to shine, to glitter.

זוֹ only a secondary form from זֹה.

זוּ demonst. pron. comm. stands also for זֶה and זֹאת.

זוּב (fut. יָזוּב) equiv. זוּף to flow (of the monthly courses of women, or of the discharge by man), overflowing (of blood, milk), dissolving, i.e. languishing, pining.

זוֹב m. the flowing, whether of the monthly courses of women, or of the discharge from man.

זוג (not used) to enclose, from זָג husk.

זוד origin. to seethe (comp. נָזִיד); hence figur. the rising (of passion), to be presumptuous against (אֶל, עַל) somebody. Hiph. הֵזִיד (fut. יָזִיד) to boil, to prepare (e.g. נָזִיד pottage), figur. to act presumptuously, wickedly against (עַל) somebody.

זוּד (Aram.) the same. Af. inf. הֲזָדָה, like the Hiph. in Heb.

זָוָה (not used) equiv. to זִו to glitter, to sparkle, from which זָוִית and מָזוֹן which see; but in זִיו the root is not זָוָה, but זִו. See זִו.

I. זוּז (not used) to produce in fulness, plentifully, especially of the productions of the field. (The form זוּז is doubled from זו, also for זוּזו). From which זִיז.

II. זוּז (not used) to be prominent, origin. to shine, to excel; hence to be conspicuous. Comp. נֶכֶס, קֶרֶן, פִּנָּה, נֵס. (The form is redoubled from זִו, From which מְזוּזָה. Aram. זִיז).

III. זוּז (not used) to move to and fro (redoubled from זָא, equiv. to זָע). From which זִיז.

זוּזִים p.n. of the ancestry of Amon. (probably the prominent ones, giants).

זוֹחֵת p.n. m. (removing, remover), from זוּחַ.

זָוִית (only pl. זָוִיּוֹת) f. corner (which is prominent), from זָוָה, like פִּנָּה, from פָּנָה in the same sense, corner stone.

זוּל equiv. to זָלַל, to throw—to squander away, related to אָזַל, which see. Hiph. הַזִּיל (Aram. form for הֵזִיל) to throw away, to despise, e.g. מְכַבְּדִים, those that honour one.

זוּלָה f. removal, but only const. זוּלַת; and with suff. as a prep. and conj., besides, otherwise; except.

I. זוּן (Kal not used) to nourish, to maintain. Hoph. הוּזַן to be nourished, to become strong. See אָזַן.

זוּן (Aram.) the same. Hithpa. אִתְּזִין pass.

II. זוּן (not used) to sharpen, to point, Related to שָׁנַן.

זוֹנָה f. 1) harlot, whore, part. f. from זָנָה. 2) weapon, orig. that which is pointed, from זוּן II. only 1 Kings 22:38.

I. זוּעַ (fut. יָזוּעַ) to move, figur. to tremble. Pi. reduplicate זַעְזַע to make tremble, to shake.

II. זוּעַ (not used) to drip, perspire, equiv. to יָזַע, from which זֵעָה.

זוּעַ (part. pl. זָאעִין in the Keri, זָיְעִין in the Ketib) Aram. like זוּעַ I. in Hebrew.

זְוָעָה f. unstableness, shaking, fright, the Keri has always זַעֲוָה.

זוף (not used) 1) equiv. to זוב to melt, to flow; 2) according to the Aram. to borrow; from which זִיף, זֶפֶת.

I. **זור** to be estranged, to turn away (from God, or relatives), hence the particip. זָר stranger, foreigner; figur. heathen, barbarian, sinner, etc., inasmuch as the alienation was considered an evil: רוּחִי זָרָה לְאִשְׁתִּי "my breath is strange to my wife," (Job 19:17) i.e. disagreeable; related to סוּר. Niph. only Isa. 1:6, to estrange oneself from God. Hophal, to become estranged. part. מוּזָר.

II. **זור** (fut. יָזוּר, apoc. (וַיָּזַר) 1) to tie fast, to gird; זֹרוּ Isa. see זֶרֶת. זוּרֶה part. pass. for זוּרָה. From which זֵר, זַרְזִיר, and מָזוֹר; 2) to press together (בֵּיצָה an egg), to squeeze (וַיָּזַר) by pressing together; related to צָרַר.

זות (not used) to be agreeable, lovely, especially of lovely fragrance. From which זַיִת.

זָחַח (Kal not used) to move; hence Niph. (fut. יִזַּח) to move oneself away. The root is also in כָּסַג.

זָחַל to crawl (of serpents); figur. to sneak, to be afraid. Comp. דָּחַל.

זֹחֶלֶת (אֶבֶן) p.n. of a place near Jerusalem (stone of terror).

זִיד see זוד.

זֵידוֹן (after the form עֵירֹם, from עור) adj. m., tossing (of the waves), swelling with pride.

זִיו (Aram.) m. splendour, serenity (origin. brightness of the countenance). See זִו.

זִיז m. 1) fulness, plenty, superfluity, from זוז I., only Isa. 66:2, fulness of glory, it stands parallel with שֹׁד breast. It is possible, however, that זִיז is here only a softer form for צִיץ; 2) according to Kimchi and Abulwalid) animal, game, from זוז III.

זִיזָא p.n. m. (the shining one, the brilliant one).

זִיזָה p.n. m. (splendour, ornament).

זִינָא p.n. m. the same.

זִיעַ p.n. (the terrified one).

זִיף 1) (melting-place) p.n. of a district in the territory of Judah; gent. זִיפִי; 2) p.n. m. (like שָׁאוּל the one lent).

זִיקוֹת see זֵק, from which it is the pl.

זַיִת (pl. זֵיתִים, from זות, after the form בַּיִת from בות) m. olive-oil, complete שֶׁמֶן זַיִת, זֵית; also, olive-tree, complete עֵץ הַזַּיִת; especially the fruit; hence, דָּרַךְ ז׳ to press olives. The root is זות and not זָהָה.

זֵיתָם p. n. m. equiv. to (זֵיתָן).

זֵיתָן p.n. m. (planter of olives).

זַךְ (pause זָךְ) adj. m. זַכָּה f. purified, figur. also in a moral sense.

זְכָא (not used) Aram. purified; hence figur. to be morally pure.

זָכָה (fut. יִזְכֶּה) equiv. to זְכָא, זָכַךְ, זָקַק to be purified; hence morally, to be pure, pious. Piel זִכָּה to cleanse (the heart). Hith. הִזַּכָּה to cleanse oneself.

זָכוּ (const. זָכוּת, def. זָכוּתָא) Aram. f. cleanliness; moral purity.

זְכוּכִית f. origin. that which is purified, transparent; especially, crystal, glass. Root זָכַךְ.

זְכוּר masculine, equivalent to זָכָר male.

זַכּוּר p.n. m. (man).

זַכַּי p.n. m. (pure, innocent, pious one).

זָכַךְ (3 pl. pret. זַכּוּ) to sieve; hence, figur. (intrans.) to be pure, clean, pious. Compare זָכָה. Hiphil, to cleanse, to wash clean.

זָכַר (fut. יִזְכֹּר) origin. to penetrate (comp. זָכָר); hence, to impress, to remember (with accus. or לְ, בְּ), to retain in, or to recall to, the memory. Niph. to be considered (of somebody, or of some subject), to be mentioned to (אֶל) somebody. Hiph. to call to memory, to mention, especially, in favor; hence, to praise, to bring an offering of remembrance or of thanks, to record annals, etc.). Sometimes like Kal. Comp. זֵכֶר.

זָכָר m. origin. the male-kind (that which penetrates, comp. נְקֵבָה); next, the male (of man and beast), from which denom. Niph. נִזְכַּר to be born a male.

זֵכֶר (sometimes זֶכֶר) masc. memory, remembrance, memorial, name, mark of distinction; figur. fame.

זֶכֶר p.n. m. (glory, the famous one).

זִכָּרוֹן (const. זִכְרוֹן, pl. זִכְרֹנִים, ־נוֹת) m. equiv. to זֵכֶר; hence, אֶבֶן ז׳ stone of remembrance; מִנְחַת זִכָּרוֹן offering of remembrance; but also figur. noting down something for memory, remark; סֵפֶר זִכָּרוֹן the book of memory; also, day, feast, sentence of memory, etc.

זִכְרִי p. n. m. (the celebrated one).

זְכַרְיָה p.n. m. (fame of God).

זְכַרְיָהוּ p.n. m. (the same).

זָלַג (not used) to drop, to flow in drops; from which perhaps מַזְלֵג.

זֻלּוּת fem., baseness, vileness, only Ps. 12:9, "when the vilest of men are exalted." Root זָלַל.

זַלְזַל (only pl. זַלְזַלִּים) m. equiv. to סַלְסַל, תַּלְתַּל; bough, branch, especially of the vine. Root זָלַל.

זָלַל (part. זוֹלֵל) origin. to move to and fro, especially of the shaking of branches (compare זַלְזַל) from which זַלְזַל; hence figur. to strew about, to squander; זוֹלֵל spend-thrift; זוֹלֵל בָּשָׂר squanderer of the body, i. e. profligate. Squandering being considered bad, an evil, זָלַל signifies also to be bad, base. Niph. נָזֹל to be strewed about.

זַלְעָפָה (pl. זַלְעָפוֹת, constr. זַלְעֲפוֹת); glow, heat, e. g. of the wind (simoom), of famine. The root appears to be formed from זָעַף and לָעַף.

זָלַף (not used) to drip, to fall in drops; related to דָּלַף.

זִלְפָּה p.n. f. (juice of myrrh, fragrance).

זִמָּה f. 1) spinning of deceit; hence, an abominable deed, vice; next, shame, for whoredom; 2) spinning of thoughts, plan, design. Root זָמַם I; 3) p.n. m. concoction.

זַמָּה f. thinking, thought, only plur. זַמּוֹתַי for ־תַי, according to others it is the inf. of Pi. almost in the same sense; or the 3 pers. pret. for זַמּוֹתִי.

זְמוֹרָה (pl. but with suff. זְמֹרֵיהֶם) f. the shaking branch, bough.

זַמְזֹם (only pl. זַמְזֻמִּים) p.n. of a race of giants (swarm).

זָמִיר (const. זְמִיר) m. after the form קָצִיר, אָבִיב, אָסִיף tune of the feast (song) of vintage, or harvest; next, triumphal songs generally.

זְמִירָה (only pl. זְמִירוֹת) fem. 1) song, song of praise, triumphal song; 2) p.n. masc. vintage, cutting of grapes.

I. זָמַם (1 pers. pret. זָמַמְתִּי and זַמּוֹתִי; fut. יָזֹם; pl. יָזֹמּוּ for יִזְמוּ) origin. equiv. to צָמַם to bind, to plait, to spin; hence, to spin plans, to devise good or evil. Pi. (inf. זַמּוֹת according to some, like שַׁמּוֹת, חַנּוֹת the same.

II. זָמַם (not used) to roar, to bawl. From which זַמְזֹם.

זָמָם m. equiv. to זִמָּה plan.

זָמַן (Kal not used), to number, to measure; hence Piel, to arrange, determine something. Pu. pass. (מְזֻמָּנִים) appointed times. Related to מָנָה.

זְמָן of a modern date (pl. זְמַנִּים) m. time, fixed, appointed time.

זְמַן (Aram.) like זְמָן in Heb. Hith. הִזְדַּמַּן to make mutual appointment; but only in Keri, the Ketib has af. הַזְמַן in the same sense.

זְמָן (def. זִמְנָא, pl. זִמְנִין) Aram. equiv. to זְמָן time, period, but like מוֹעֵד also of a holy period, or time, festival. The plur. is used as an adv., times, e.g. three times.

I. זָמַר (fut. יִזְמֹר) to prune (the vine), but also, cutting off in general; e.g. trimming the light; hence מְזַמֶּרֶת (related to זָמַר). Niph. pass. from Kal, to be pruned.

II. זָמַר (Kal not used) to clatter, to tune; hence Pi. to sing (with the voice), to tune (by string-instruments).

זְמַר (def. זְמָרָא) Aram. m. the tuning of instruments, playing.

זַמָּר (plur. זַמָּרִין) masc. a player on stringed instruments, a singer.

זֶמֶר m. name of a gazelle, the wild goat, or the giraffe.

זִמְרָה (const. זִמְרַת) f. song, sound (of the harp), figur. praise; i.e. the best part (of the country).

זְמֹרָה see זְמוֹרָה.

זִמְרָה see זְמִירָה.

זִמְרִי p. n. m. (vintner), but this form is also patron. from זִמְרָן.

זִמְרָן p. n. m. (the celebrated one).

זִמְרָת f. equiv. to זִמְרָה song, fame, praise.

זַן (pl. זְנִים) m. form; next, kind, manner, way. Root זוּן.

זַן (Aram.) the same.

זָנַב (not used) equiv. to סָנַף (in סַנְפִּיר) wagging, moving to and fro.

זָנָב (pl. זְנָבוֹת, const. זַנְבוֹת), m. a tail; next, anything that drags behind.

זִנֵּב (Pi. denom. from זָנָב) to remove, destroy that which drags behind.

זָנָה (fut. apoc. יִזֶן) whoring, also committing adultery, with the accus. אֶל, בְּ of the person with whom it is carried on; with אַחֲרֵי to follow some one with the object of whoredom; with מִן, מֵאַחֲרֵי, מֵעַל, מִתַּחַת, to desert the person whom one followed in whoredom; Particip. זוֹנָה (or אִשָּׁה זוֹנָה) a harlot. Figur. apostatising from God, of intercourse with idolatrous nations. Pual זוּנָּה pass. Hiph. הִזְנָה (fut. apoc. יֶזֶן) to cause, to seduce to, profligacy.

זָנוֹחַ (marshy ground), p. n. two places in the territory of Judah.

זְנוּנִים (from זְנוּ equiv. to זְנוּת) m. plur. whoredom; figur. apostasy (from God), intercourse with idolaters.

זְנוּת (pl. זְנוּתִים) f. the same.

זָנַח (fut. יִזְנַח) 1) trans. to push away, to desert, to reject (עַל, מִטּוֹב, מִזְבֵּחַ) with accus. זָנַח מִן to forsake some one; 2) (not used) to remove; hence, to decrease, to dry up (of the water) related to צָנַח (see אֶזְנָח). Hiph. הִזְנִיחַ to reject, to banish from (מִן) something. The Hiph. הֶאֱזְנִיחַ, see under אָזְנָח.

זְנִין belongs to זַן see זוּן.

זָנַק (Kal not used) to hasten away. Pi. זִנֵּק to spring forth, with מִן of the place.

זֵעָה f. perspiration, from זוּעַ.

זַעֲוָה f. Keri, equiv. to זְוָעָה Ketib, shaking, fright. Root זוּעַ.

זַעֲוָן p. n. m. (the affrighted one).

זְעֵיר m. a little, a trifle, but also as an adv. small, little.

זְעֵיר (Aram.) adj. m. זְעֵירָה f. small, little, formed from זְעֵיר.

זָעַךְ equiv. to דָּעַךְ to quench, to extinguish; figur. to vanish. Niph. to vanish.

זָעַם (fut. יִזְעֹם, יִזְעַם imper. זָעֲמָה for זְעָמָה) to snort, to foam; figur. to be wroth, especially when the anger indicates punishment, with the accus. or עַל; hence, also to denounce, to curse. Niph. to be wroth, to be vexed; פָּנִים נִזְעָמִים angry countenance.

זַעַם (with suff. זַעְמִי) m. anger, especially the anger of God, punishment; anger of the tongue, i. e. chastising language.

זָעַף (fut. יִזְעַף) to seethe, to snort, to foam; i.e. to be wroth, const. with עַל and עִם; or look sad, to appear sad or melancholy, origin. to be violently moved.

זָעֵף adj. m. angry, snorting.

זַעַף m. anger, the foaming (of the sea).

זָעַק (fut. יִזְעַק, inf. זְעֹק, זַעֲק) equiv. to צָעַק, which appears later, to cry (from pain); to call, with אֶל upon some one; also with לְ and accus.; the object for which one cries, with עַל, לְ and מִלִּפְנֵי. Niph. to be called together, to assemble. Hiph. to cry, to call (with the accus.) to assemble together, to assemble.

זְעַק (pl. זְעִיקוּ in the Targ.) Aram. the same.

זַעַק m. lament, outcry, like זְעָקָה.

זְעָקָה f. equiv. to צְעָקָה cry, lament, tremulous cry.

זָעַר (not used) equiv. to the old form צָעַר, origin. to compress; hence, to be little, small, to be straitened. Aram. זְעַר.

זִפְרוֹן (sweet of odour) p. n. of a northern border town in Palestine, which in the Targum is rendered קרן זכותא.

זֶפֶת (from זוּף, like נֹפֶת from נוּף; קֶשֶׁת from קוּשׁ; נַחַת from נוּחַ) f. pitch.

זֵק (only pl. זִקִּים) m. 1) flame, spark, especially the flaming arrow, from זָקַק I. 2) fetter, bond, from זָקַק 2.

זָקָן (const. זְקַן) m. chin, beard. The root is זָקֵן to sprout, to germinate, perhaps connected in its root with זָקֵן.

זָקֵן (fut. יִזְקַן) grey, white hair, to be old, but only used of man. Hiph. הִזְקִין (like הִלְבִּין) to have grey hair, to be white; also of inanimate nature.

זָקֵן (const. זְקַן, plur. זְקֵנִים) m. age, hoary-man; hence also elder, signifying some one distinguished.

זֹקֶן m. hoary age.

זִקְנָה f. the same.

זְקֻנִים m. pl. the same. בֶּן־זְ׳ a son got in old age.

זָקַף equiv. to שָׁגַב and תָּקַף to fasten, to support; next, to raise (the humble one).

זְקַף (Aram.) the same, to hang up; origin. to raise a piece of wood.

זָקַק (fut. יָזֹק) 1) equiv. to זָכַךְ to sieve, to purify; next also in a moral sense, to cleanse: 2) to burn, to flame, to glow, related to עָשַׁן, from which זִק: 3) to bind, to tie; fig. (Talm.) to compel. Pi. זִקֵּק to refine (gold). Pu. pass. to be purified (of metals or wine.)

זָר (part. from זוּר) m. a stranger; see זוּר I.

זֵר m. that which encompasses an object; hence clasp (of a table), border, from זוּר II.

זָרָא f. equiv. to זָרָה (from זָר) strange, bad, disgusting; hence הָיָה לְזָרָא becoming loathsome.

זָרַב equiv. to צָרַב, שָׂרַף to glow, to burn. Pual זֹרַב to dry up (of rivers).

זְרֻבָּבֶל p. n. m. (scattered to Babel, equiv. to זְרוּעַ־בָּבֶל).

זֶרֶד p.n. of a valley and river, now called Wadi El-ahsa.

I. זָרָה to strew, to scatter about; hence, winnowing. Niph. to be scattered about. Pi. to scatter about (a people), to winnow. Pu. pass. the part. זֹרֶה is for מְזֹרֶה.

II. זָרָה only Pi. in Ps. 139:3, equiv. to זוּר to encompass, to encircle, to hedge in (אֹרַח), i.e. to watch closely.

זְרוֹעַ see זְרֹעַ.

זֵרוּעַ see זֶרַע.

זַרְזִיף (from זָרַף) masc. a shower of rain, the form is contracted from זַרְזְרִיף.

זַרְזִיר (from זוּר equiv. to אָזַר) masc. girded (of the loins); hence, name of the war-horse, or, probably, of a warrior in general. See זוּר II.

זָרַח (fut. יִזְרַח) to shine forth, e.g. of the morning sun, of the light, or of the majesty of God, transf. to the sprouting of plants, of the coming forth of the child (from the mother's womb), of the break-out of leprosy.

זֶרַח m. 1) shining forth, the rising of the sun; 2) p. n. masc. rising; patron. זַרְחִי.

זְרַחְיָה p. n. masc. (arisen through God).

זֶרֶם (after the form נְאֻמִים, עֲרִיץ) m. shower of rain, equiv. to זֶרֶם but only in Isa. 1:7.

זָרַם equiv. to זָרַף, זָרַב to flow, to carry away by a flood; to flow away, e.g. Ps. 90:5, "thou carriest them away as with a flood." Pu. to stream forth.

זֶרֶם m. shower of rain, flood (water, hail, etc.); זֶרֶם קִיר flood against the wall.

זִרְמָה f. flow of semen, of the stallion.

I. זָרַע (fut. יִזְרַע) equiv. to זָרָה I. to strew, to scatter about; hence, to sow (also for plants), to spread the seed (with double accus.) to fertilize; next, figur. to sow, i. e. spread justice, meekness, vanity, happiness. Niph. pass. from Kal, to be sown, fertilize. Pu. the same. Hiph. to beget (by sowing, fertilising), to produce seed, i.e. to have offspring (of a woman).

II. זָרַע (not used) to carry, to bear Aram. דְּרַע, from which זְרֹעַ.

זֶרַע (const. once זְרַע) m. 1) concr. seed of trees, of corn, and of men; but also that which arises from the seed, like plants, corn, fruit; and of man, children, descendants, family in general, generation, tribe; 2) abstr. the sowing, planting; hence also, the seed-time.

זְרַע (Aram.) the same.

זְרֹעַ (also זְרוֹעַ; pl. ־עִים, ־עוֹת) com. the limb adapted for lifting and carrying of burdens, the arm; hence, also power, strength, might, e. g. זְ׳ בָּשָׂר human might; זְ׳ יָד strength of the hand; זְ׳ נְבָא, גָּדַע זְ׳, שָׁבַר זְ׳ to destroy the power, power and strength are used either in a good sense, for help, support, or for violence.

זֵרוּעַ (pl. זֵרוּעִים; but also זֵרוּעַ plur. זֵרוּעִים) m. that which is sown, vegetable.

זֵרָעֹן (only pl. זֵרְעֹנִים) m. vegetable, and the food prepared therefrom.

זָרַף (not used) equiv. to זָרַב (זָרַם) to flow, to stream; from which זַרְזִיף.

זָרַק (fut. יִזְרֹק) to sprinkle, to moisten; hence, to sprinkle water or blood, but it is also used of dry things, to strew, and figur. of the increase of grey hair (שֵׂיבָה). Pu. pass.

זָרַר (only Po. זוֹרֵר) equiv. to זָרָה, זָרַע to scatter about; hence Pa. זוֹרֵר to throw out (phlegm), also, to sneeze. In Latin and Greek, *sternuo*, *πταρνύω*, proceed from the same idea.

זֶרֶשׁ (Persian) p.n. f. (origin. golden) Zendic, *zairish* from *zair*.

זֶרֶת fem. the little finger, contracted from זְעֶרֶת; see זְעֵר.

זַתּוּא p.n. m. (a sprout, from זָתָא = דִּשְׁאָ).

זֵתָם (equiv. to זֵיתָם) p. n. m. (olive-planter).

זֵתַר (Persian) p.n. m. (offerer) Zendic *zaôtar*.

ח

ח cheth (חֵיט=חֵית) signifies, hedge, wall, so called on account of its position and shape. ח is the eighth letter, and as a numeral signifies 8. It interchanges with ג, כ, ק; e.g. חָבָא with כָּפָה; חָבַל with כָּבַל and גָּבַל; חָפַר with קָבַר; חָבַשׁ with כָּבַשׁ; חָדַר with גָּדַר; but as a guttural ח often interchanges with א, ה, and ע: e.g. חָמַר with עָמַר; חוּשׁ with עוּשׁ, etc.

חֹב (with suff. חֻבִּי) m. concealed, hidden place, bosom, lap; Aram. hence also עֻטֵּף.

חָבָא (Kal, not used) to conceal, to hide; related to חָפָה and כָּפָה. Niph. (in the inf. נֶחְבָּה and הֵחָבֵה ה stands for א), to hide, secrete oneself. Pu. the same. Hiph. הֶחְבִּיא (3 pret. f. has הֶחְבְּאַתָה for הֶחְבִּיאָה) to conceal, to secrete. Hoph. pass. Hith. like Niph.

חָבַב (only part. חוֹבֵב) equivalent to חָבָא, origin. to cover, to shelter (hence חֹב bosom), transf. to love, origin. to protect.

חֹבָב p. n. m. (the beloved one) the second name of Jethro.

חָבָה equiv. to חָבָא, but found only in the imper. חֲבִי (equiv. to חֲבָה) and in חֶבְיוֹן.

חֲבוּלָה (Aram.) f. hurt (in a moral sense) fault. See חָבַל.

חָבוֹר p. n. of a stream in Assyria (Arab. *chabur*), the mouth of which is Yakuti in the Tigris, and distinct from כְּבָר in Mesopotamia, which discharges itself in the Euphrates. As an Assyrian province, the Talmud takes it for the whole territory of Adiabene (הַדְיָב). See כְּבָר.

חַבּוּרָה f. a stripe, only Isa. 53:5.

חַבֻּרָה f. the same; see חָבַר.

חָבַט (fut. יַחְבֹּט) to strike; transf. to knock off, fruit; to beat out grain from the ears, also of the striking of water against something. Niph. pass.

חֲבַיָּה p.n. m. (protection from God).

חֶבְיוֹן m. cover, veil, from חָבָה=חָבָא.

חֲבִית (but only pl. חֲבִתִּים for חֲבִיתִּים) m. a pan which is deepened out and encloses the contents. Compare in modern Heb. חָבִית cask, from חָבָה.

I. חָבַל (fut. יַחְבֹּל, יַחֲבֹל) 1) to bind, related to כָּבַל, גָּבַל, hence חֶבֶל sail, cord (see חֶבֶל); 2) figur. to pledge. In this signification חָבַל is constr. with double accus. 3) to act perversely, comp. עָקַשׁ, עָוַל, עָוַת. Pi. to wince (from pain), hence to travail: comp. חוּל.

II. חָבַל equiv. to חָבַר to wound, to hurt. Niph. to hurt, wound oneself. Pi. to destroy, to ruin. Pu. pass.

חֲבַל (only Pa. חַבֵּל) Aram. equiv. to חִבֵּל Heb. under חָבַל II. to hurt, to destroy, to annihilate. Hithp. pass.

חֵבֶל (pl. חֲבָלִים, const. חֶבְלֵי) m. pain, pang, throes (of a woman in labor); next, pain generally. בָּא חֵבֶל לְ some one being attacked with pain; שִׁלַּח חֲבָלִים to cast out pain (Job 39:3), i.e. to bear young with pain; according to others, to be delivered from pain.

חֶבֶל (with suff. חֶבְלִי, pl. חֲבָלִים, const. חַבְלֵי and חֶבְלֵי) com. 1) band, cord, from חָבַל to bind; next, measuring line, or that which is measured with a line: hence, portion of inheritance; next, territory, land, and district generally. 2) snare. 3) band, troop, clique. All significations proceeding from the original sense, to bind. See חָבַל I.

חֲבַל (def. חַבְלָא) Aram. m. wound, hurt, injury.

חֲבֹל m. pledge, הֵשִׁיב חֲ׳ to return the pledge, חָבַל חֲ׳ to take in a pledge.

חִבֵּל m. according to some a denom. from חֶבֶל (cord), i.e. ship's sails; probably however, חִבֵּל, חֹבֵל, תַּחְבֻּלָה descend from חָבַל in the sense of יָבַל to lead, hence חִבֵּל rudder, helm.

חֹבֵל m. steersman, pilot, man at the helm, captain, from חָבַל to lead. See חִבֵּל.

חֲבֹלָה f. equiv. to חֲבֹל pledge.

חָבַץ (not used) equiv. to חָמַץ to be sharp, e.g. of the smell; hence, to smell strong; of colour, hence, to be of a light dazzling colour.

חֲבַצֶּלֶת f. a light coloured or strong smelling flower, about the name of which the biblical interpreters disagree. As to the form, it originates from חֲבַצֶּל, a masc. form changed into a fem. one, by the termin. ־ֶת. In חֲבַצֶּל the dimin. form ־ֶל is affixed to the root חָבַץ.

חֲבַצִּנְיָה p. n. m. (Divine assembly, from חָבַץ after the Aram. to assemble; comp. קְמוּאֵל).

חָבַק (inf. חֲבֹק) equiv. to אָבַק II., to clasp, embrace (a child). Pi. the same, to embrace closely. חִבֵּק יָדַיִם to fold the hands (of the sluggard), but only with a subst.

חִבֻּק m. the folding (of hands).

חֲבַקּוּק (a double form, from חָבַק) p. n. m. folder of the hands.

I. חָבַר to be joined, fraternised, e.g. of the union of nations, of the joining of two subjects; transf. to spell-bind by sorcery. Pi. to join (two subjects); with עִם to enter into a covenant with some one. Pu. חֻבַּר pass., e.g. of a city with which the neighbouring towns are united: הַיְחָבְרְךָ (Ps. 94:20) "Shall — have fellowship with thee?" which stands for הַיִתְחַבֶּרְךָ. Hiph. to act prudently, which signification also חָבַר has. Hithp. to unite oneself.

II. חָבַר (Kal, not used) to cut in. Hiph. הֶחְבִּיר to make an incision, fig. to penetrate, to hurt by speaking (בְּמִלִּים).

חָבֵר (contracted from חָבִיר) adj. m. חֲבֵרָה (c. חֲבֶרֶת) f. joined, fraternized; also a subst. associate, colleague, friend.

חֲבַר (Aram.) m. the same.

חֶבֶר (pl. חֲבָרִים m. 1) association, union; e.g. כֹּהֲנִים, of priests; 2) the spell of sorcery; 3) p. n. m. (for which also occurs חֵבֶר). a sorcerer; patr. חֶבְרִי.

חַבָּר m. (pl.) associates in business, who negotiate on something (כָּרָה עַל), or who dig pits (comp. Job 6:27) to ensnare something; perhaps from חָבַר II., to cut, to pierce, and יִכְרוּ עָלָיו חַבָּרִים "shall the piercers (who conquer the leviathan) pierce him?" (Job 41:6, author. version, "shall thy companions make a banquet of him?"

חַבְרְתָא (Aram.) f. female associate, female companion, equiv. to חֲבֵרָה in Heb.

חֲבַרְבֻּרָה (pl. ־רוֹת) f. stripes (of a leopard) from חָבַר II.

חֶבְרָה f. association, society, company.

חֶבְרוֹן (court) p. n. of an ancient city in the territory of Judah, now called by the Arabs El-Khalil.

חֹבֶרֶת f. juncture, place of joining.

חֹבֶרֶת see חֲבֵרָה under חָבֵר.

חָבַשׁ (fut. יַחֲבֹשׁ and יַחְבֹּשׁ) to bind, to tie round (the root is related to לָבַשׁ) with a turban (פְּאֵר, מִגְבָּעָה), and like all these kinds of verbs with double accusative; but seldom with לְ of the person (Jonah 2:6) and בְּ of the object (Ezekiel 16:10 and Job 40:13). Transf. to bind, equiv. to hold fast, to rule (syn. עָצַר), to bind up, equiv. to saddle; to bind round, equiv. to heal, etc. Pi. 1) to bind up, to heal; 2) to prevent (the streams נְהָרוֹת from running). Pu. to be bound up (of a wound).

חָבַת (not used) equiv. to כָּפַת to enclose, to conceal, related to חָפָה, equiv. to כָּפָה, חָפָה, from which the root is only extended. Comp. Talm. כּוּפְתָא basket.

חַג (const. חַג; pl. חַגִּים) m. celebration of the feast (by circuits) feast, generally, or festival-offerings. עָשָׂה חַג. חָגַג to celebrate a festival, especially the feast of Tabernacles. Root חָגַג.

חָגָּא (for חָגְגָה from חָגַג) f. fear, terror; trembling; from חָגַג to totter, to reel.

חָגַב (not used) to pluck off, to cut off (like קָצַב) related to עֲרִיקָא in the rabbinical; or the root is only an extension from גָּב, above, from which גּוֹב.

חָגָב (pl. חֲגָבִים) masc. 1) locust, like גֹּבַי so called from "nibbling." The Samaritan name חַרְגְּבָה is the same with the ר interpolated; 2) p.n. m.

חֲגָבָה p.n. m.

חָגַג to make a circuit (comp. חוּג) to proceed in a circuit; hence, in a good sense, to dance; in a bad sense, to reel (of a drunkard), fig. to go in procession, or on a pilgrimage.

חָגָה (not used) equiv. to חָקָה, to cut in, syn. with נָקַר, פָּרַץ, נָקַק.

חָגוּ (after the form קָשׂוּ, קָצוּ, מָדוּ; pl. const. חַגְוֵי) m. cleft of a rock, gulf, equiv. to נִקְרַת הַצּוּר, נָקִיק, סֶלַע and others; next, refuge, since these cliffs served as a place of refuge. Root חָגָה.

חָגוּר (const. pl. חֲגוּרֵי) adj. m. (after the form קָדוֹשׁ) to be girded, with the accus. of the object.

חֲגוֹר (after the form שָׁחוֹר, חֲלוֹם) m. girdle; it is the masc. of:—

חֲגוֹרָה f. girdle. See חָגַר.

חַגַּי p.n. m. (festive one, *festivus*).

חַגִּי p.n. m. (the same).

חַגִּיָּה p.n. m. (feast of God).

חַגִּית p.n. f. (the festive one).

חָגַל (not used) to hop, to spring, after the Arabic.

חָגְלָה p.n. f. partridge.

חָגַר (fut. יַחְגֹּר) to gird round with double accus. of the limb and the garment, seldom with בְּ of the garment. Transf. to gird oneself with victory, joy, &c.

I. חַד (only once in Heb.) Aram. a numeral adj. m. חֲדָא (חֲדָה) f. one answering to the Hebrew אֶחָד and אַחַת. The masc. חַד before cardinal numbers multiplies, e. g. חַד שִׁבְעָה sevenfold, the fem. חֲדָה following as a gen. is a substitute for the ordinal number. חֲדָה is also used as an adverb.

II. חַד adj. masc. חַדָּה f. sharp (of a sword). עֵין חַדָּה p.n. of a place; see עַיִן.

חָדַד (fut. יַחַד for יָחֹד after the form יָצַר, יָקַל, יָמַר) to be sharp, pointed (related to קָדַד, גָּדַד) transf. to be rash, vehement. Hiph. (fut. יָחֵד

for יָחַד) to sharpen, to point (iron), transf. fo sharpen the sight. Hoph. pass.

חָדַד p.n. m. (sharpsighted one).

חָדָה (fut. apoc. יִחַדְּ) to rejoice, to be cheerful. Pi. to cheer, to gladden. The original signification is, to shine, related to חָזָה, and next, to be bright, adding the idea of joyfulness.

חַדּוּד m. sting, thorn, point; from חָדַד.

חֶדְוָה f. joy, cheerfulness, from חָדָה. In Aram. the same.

חֲדִי (only in the pl. חֲדִין, with suff. חֲדוֹהִי) Aram. m. breast, equiv. to חָזֶה in the Heb.

חָדִיד point, top of a mountain, p.n. of a mountainous city of the Benjaminites.

חָדַל (also חָדֵל; fut. יֶחְדַּל) to cease, to vanish, to abate; hence in the Targum פְּסַק to desist from something; with מִן to forsake. Hiph. to forsake.

חָדֵל (const. חֲדַל) adj. masc. 1) forsaken, joyless; 2) omitting.

חֶדֶל (pause חָדֶל) m. place of desertion, rest; figur. grave. Compare דּוּמִיָּה.

חַדְלָי p.n. masc. lazy one, or resting one.

חָדַס (not used) to pierce, to cut in, related to חָתַךְ; but the root is חָדַק, which is found again in סָדַק and בָּדַק.

חֵדֶק m. pointed pricking thorn, from חָדַק, comp. קוֹץ.

חֵדֶק m. the same.

חִדֶּקֶל (from an origin. form חֵדֶק with ־ֶל termination) p.n. of the river Tigris (origin. the rapid stream.)

חָדַר equivalent to גָּדַר to enclose, to hedge in, comp. כָּתַר; next, to encircle (of a sword).

חֶדֶר (const. חֲדַר with ה mobile חַדְרָה, pause חָדֶר; plur. חֲדָרִים) masc. room, chamber, so called from enclosing. חֶדֶר is used of a sleeping-room, bridal-chamber, provision-room, chamber of the heart, etc.; the chambers of the south, i.e. the planetary position of the southerly winds.

חַדְרָךְ p.n. of a town not far from Damascus.

חָדַשׁ (Kal not used) to be fresh, new, young (the root is found again in רֵישָׁא). Piel, to renew, to erect anew (ruins of altars, cities), fig. to renew life, the spirit, etc. Hithp. to renew one's youth.

חֹדֶשׁ (pl. חֳדָשִׁים) com. 1) the new moon, time of the new moon, which was celebrated; next, month in general, ח׳ יָמִים a month of time, בֶּן ח׳ a month old: 2) p.n. f. born on the new moon.

חָדָשׁ adj. m., חֲדָשָׁה f. new, young, fresh, and thus in the most various significations: חֲדָשָׁה something new; חֲדָשׁוֹת news.

חֲדָשָׁה (the newly built one) p. n. of a city of Judah.

חֲדָשִׁי p. n. of a city beyond the Jordan.

חֲדַת (Aram.) equiv. to חָדָשׁ in Heb.

חֲדַת (Aram.) adj. m. equiv. to Heb. חָדָשׁ.

חֲוָא (in Pi. rare) Aram. to say, to relate; origin. to pronounce; hence, Pa. חַוִּא to denote, to announce, with the accus. and לְ of the pers.: Af. to denote, to signify, like Pa. with לְ and acc. Instead of א at the end a ה occurs sometimes in the biblical Aram. as usual.

חוּב (Kal, not used) to owe, either a debt of money or goods, or a moral debt. Pi. חַיֵּב to burden one with a debt, to make one indebted.

חוֹב m. a debt, debt of money, חֲבוֹלַת ח׳ a pledge for a debt.

חוֹבָה (formed like a lap) p. n. of a place.

חוּג equiv. to עוּג to encircle, to encompass.

חוּג m. circle, arch, especially of the heavenly arch, or of the circle of the earth.

חוּד (fut. יָחוּד) to be tied up, intricate, the root is related to אָגַד, אָסַר, עָשַׁר; hence, to deliver intricate speeches, riddles. According to others, the origin. signif. is to be sharp, pointed, related to חַד; hence, to make sharp, pointed speeches.

I. חָוָה (not used) equiv. to חָיָה to live, to be, to exist; comp. the relationship between חָיָה and חָוָה.

II. חָוָה (only Pi. חִוָּה, comp. the Aram. חֲוָא) to say, to relate. Pi. to denote, signify, announce, proclaim.

III. חָוָה (not used) to bend, to curve (comp. Aram. חִוְיָא serpent); hence to enclose, to encircle.

חַוָּה fem. 1) life, from חָוָה I.; hence, p. n. of the first woman, producing life; 2) round tent, circle of a tent, village of tents, from חָוָה III.

חוּן (not used) equiv. to חָזָה to look forward, especially of the longing look; hence, מָחוֹן prospect.

חוּק (not used) to cut in, to inscribe, related to חָקָה, חָקַק.

חוֹחַ (pl. חֹחִים, חֲוָחִים) m. 1) pointed hooks, comp. חָח; 2) thorn, brier.

חוּט (not used in Heb.) Aram. to bind, to tie, to hoop. Af. of the re-erecting of a wall pulled down.

חוּט masc. thread, cord, from חוּט to bind.

חִוִּי (inhabitant of a village) p.n. of a tribe.

חֲוִילָה p. n. of a district: 1) on the Persian Gulf, being the eastern border of the Ishmaelites; 2) in Southern Arabia, on the Abyssinian coast; 3) stands for India and Arabia.

חול (fut. יָחוּל, apoc. יָחֹל, יָחֵל, יָחִיל) equiv. to עוּל, to turn, to make a a circuit, like חוּג: hence, 1) to dance; 2) to wince, from pain and anguish, especially of the throes of a woman in labor (comp. עוּל); next, to tremble, const. with עַל; 3) to roll along, of a storm, of the destructive sword, etc.; 4) to be strong, firm (comp. קָוָה, קָשַׁר). Hiph. הֵחִיל (fut. יָחִיל) to cause to tremble. Hoph. הוּחַל to be born. Po. חוֹלֵל the intensive of Kal in all significations. Pu. חוֹלַל pass. Hithp. I. הִתְחוֹלֵל 1) to wince from pain; 2) the rolling of a tempest; 3) to wait, hope. Hithp. II. הִתְחַלְחֵל to be affrighted.

חוֹל district, department: 1) p. n. of an Aram. country on the borders of the Jordan; 2) name of a bird, accord. to tradition, phœnix, called in the Talmud אוּרְשִׁינָא. Others read it in the biblical passage, חוֹל sand.

חוֹל m. sand, from חוּל to heap up, to accumulate, equiv. to גָּלַל.

חוּם (not used) to heat through, to burn black; related to חָמַם (comp. כָּמַר, Aram. אֻכַּם).

חוּם adj. m. burnt black, dark coloured.

חוֹמָה (dual חוֹמֹתַיִם; pl. חוֹמוֹת) f. a wall round about the town, from חָמָה I. to encircle, to enclose.

חוּס (fut. יָחוּס, יָחֹס) to cover, to shelter, to protect: חָס is related to כָּסָה: hence, to spare, to protect some one by countenancing, therefore const. with עַל.

חוֹף see חֹף.

חוּפָם p. n. m. (the protected one) patron. חוּפָמִי.

חוּץ (not used) to separate, to divide (comp. חוֹצֵץ, to separate, in the Talmud), equiv. to חָצָה, to divide.

חוּץ (pl. חוּצוֹת) m. 1) partition wall, equiv. to חַיִץ, transf. to outside; hence, pl. חוּצוֹת, fields, commons, deserts, heaths; 2) adv. without, with ה mobile חוּצָה, outwards; מִחוּץ, from without, outside; מִחוּץ לְ, outward; אֶל מִחוּץ לְ, outward of; חוּץ מִן, except.

חוּק (not used) to conceal, to enclose, to encompass.

חוֹק Ketib for חֵיק, see חֵיק.

חָוַר (fut. יֶחֱוַר) to become white, grey; hence, to turn pale (of the colour of the face), related to עָפַר, to be grey, in עָפֶרֶת.

I. חוּר (not used) the same, from חָוַר.

II. חוּר (not used) equiv. to עוּר, בּוּר, to dig, to excavate. It is not connected with חור from חָוַר.

חוּר (pl. חוּרִים) m. 1) white linen, related to בּוּץ and שֵׁשׁ; from חוּר I.; 2) cave, hole, cave in a dungeon, from חור II.; 3) p.n.m. (noble one, free man) from חָרַר=חוּר.

חוֹר m. hole, cavity (of the eye, the window, the mountain), from חוּר II.

חִוָּר adj. m. (Aram.) white. See חָוַר.

חוֹרַי see חֹרִי.

חוּרִי see חֹרִי.

חוּרַי p.n.m. (linen weaver.)

חוּרִי p.n.m. (noble one; freeman.)

חוֹרִים see חֹרִים.

חוּרָם p.n.m. (one of noble extraction).

חוּרָם אָבִי p.n.m. (one of noble ancestry); for which also חוּרָם אָבִיו.

חַוְרָן (district of caves) p.n. of an Aram. landscape, Hauran.

חוּשׁ (fut. יָחוּשׁ, 3 pers. f. תָּחִשׁ for תָּחוּשׁ). 1) to flee, to hasten away, equiv. to נוּס, עוּף, עוּשׁ; next, to hasten generally. Past pass. חוּשִׁים, the swift one; 2) of the inward motion: The passage in Eccles. 2:25, וּמִי יָחוּשׁ, "or who can hasten thereunto," from חוּשׁ I. Hiph. to hasten, to forward, to flee (sometimes similar to Kal).

חוּשָׁה p.n.m. (haste) part. חוּשָׁתִי.

חוּשַׁי p.n.m. (swift one).

חוּשִׁים p.n.m. (swiftness).

חוּשָׁם p.n.m. (swift one).

חוּת see חָתַת.

חוֹתָם m. 1) originally that which is sealed; next, seal-ring; 2) p.n.m. one that seals.

חֲזָאֵל (vision of God) p.n. of the king of Syria; hence, בֵּית חֲ׳, Damascus.

I. חָזָה (fut. יֶחֱזֶה, apoc. יַחַז) to see, to behold, to see in the mind; next, to look generally, with בְּ; to select, to see into the matter, to experience; transf. to visit, with one's presence, i.e. to inspect; next to get sight of, to find, etc.

II. חָזָה (not used) equiv. to חָצָה, to point, to cut.

חֲזָה (Aram.) equiv. to חָזָה I.

חָזֶה (const. חֲזֵה, pl. חֲזוֹת) m. the prominent part of the body, breast (of cattle), from חָזָה, to be prominent, to appear.

חֹזֶה m. 1) part. from חָזָה, a seer, a prophet; 2) covenant, from חָזָה II. Comp. בְּרִית from בָּרָה.

חֲזוֹ p.n.m. (exhibition, exhibitor).

חֵזוּ (=חָזוּ; def. חֶזְוָא, const. pl. חֶזְוֵי) Aram. f. vision, appearance, form.

חָזוֹן (const. חֲזוֹן) m. vision, revelation; next, also, subject of revelation.

חָזוּת (a secondary form from חָזוֹת, const. חָזוּת) f. revelation.

חֲזוֹת (Aram.), f. look, sight.

חָזוּת f. 1) vision (prophetic), revelation; 2) point, e.g. קֶרֶן חָ׳ pointed horn, from חָזָה II.=חָזַז, according to others, considerableness, dignity, from חָזָה I.

חָזַז (not used) to point, according to some related to חָזָה II. חָצַץ, to cut in, to bore.

חֲזִיאֵל p.n. m. (vision of God).

חֲזָיָה p.n. m. (the same).

חֶזְיוֹן p.n. m. (vision).

חִזָּיוֹן (const. חֶזְיוֹן, pl. חֶזְיֹנוֹת) m. prophetic vision, revelation, prediction.

חָזִיז (c. חֲזִיז, pl. חֲזִיזִים) m. that which is pointed, arrow, wedge; transf. to thunder bolt.

חֲזִיר m. swine, boar, so called from its strength; also *aper*, from strength (see חָזַר). חֲזִיר מִיַּעַר boar of the forest, wild boar.

חֵזִיר p.n. m. (powerful, strong one).

חָזַק fut. יֶחֱזַק to fasten, to support, to maintain; also intrans. to keep fast to, with בְּ, to persevere (לְ) in doing something. Next, to be strong, courageous, to prevail (with עַל) to press on (עַל or acc.) some one. Pi. 1) to gird fast, אַבְנֵט with a girdle, מָתְנַיִם the loins, (with double acc.) to fasten, (קִירוֹת, בֶּדֶק) (to rebuild a ruin); חִ׳ לֵב to harden the heart; חִ׳ פָּנִים to make bold, audacious, חִ׳ יָד, זְרוֹעַ to strengthen the hand (to encourage); חִ׳ בְּיַד to support; חִ׳ דְּבַר רָע to strengthen the bad cause. Hiph. to hold fast (עַל, לְ, בְּ) to something; to seize something (with בְּ acc.), e.g. שָׂפָה, צָרָה, רֶטֶט, חִיל; to exercise power, dominion (מַלְכוּת), to conquer; to afford strength, to support, as manifold as the Kal. Hithpael הִתְחַזֵּק to strengthen, encourage oneself; to show oneself strong before (לִפְנֵי) some one; but also in the original signification, to unite with some one, with עִם and בְּ.

חָזָק (pl. חֲזָקִים, const. חִזְקֵי) adj. m. חֲזָקָה, fem. strong, violent (of a storm, war, disease), hard (of the forehead, i.e. barefaced), hardened (i.e. of the heart, stubborn), audacious (מֵצַח, פָּנִים), etc.

חָזֵק (an old particip. form) adj. m. strong, violent.

חֵזֶק (only with suff. חִזְקִי) m. might, strength, help, protection.

חֹזֶק (with suff. חָזְקִי) m. strength (of the hand), power, boldness.

חֶזְקָה fem. strength (of the wealthy), invigorating; בְּחֶזְקַת הַיָּד by the strength of the hand of God.

חָזְקָה f. 1) erection, fortification; 2) power, strength, hardness, violence.

חִזְקִי p. n. m. (strong one).

חִזְקִיָּה p.n. m. (the strength of God).

חִזְקִיָּהוּ p.n. m. (the same).

חָזַר (not used) equiv. to קָשַׁר to be robust, strong (physically); related to אָזַר.

חָח (with suff. חַחִי, pl. חַחִים for חָחִי, חָחִים) m. 1) hook, harpoon drawn through the nostrils of animals to lead them thereby; 2) buckle, lace (female ornament). The root is חָחַח, which see.

חָחִי (only pl. חָחִיִּים adj. m. from חָחַח, pointed; next, subst. that which is pointed, hook.

חָטָא (fut. יֶחֱטָא) originally, to take away, to diminish, related to the roots חָתָה and פָּחַת; hence, חָטָא מִן הַקֹּדֶשׁ he has taken away from the holy; 1) to miss, to fail (contr. to תָּמַם to be perfect); 2) to miss the aim (God), contr. to מָצָא to find; hence, 3) to fail in a moral sense; to miss the aim, the precept; next, to sin against (לְ) some one, (בְּ, עַל accus.) somebody, or something. Pi. חִטֵּא denom. from חֵטְא, which see. Hiph. to miss the target (of the archer); 2) to seduce to sin; to declare as sinful (before the tribunal). Hithp. to miss oneself, to lose oneself (unable to restrain oneself in terror). In another signification it is a denom. from חֵטְא which see.

חֵטְא (contracted from חֲטָא; with suff. חֶטְאִי, plur. חֲטָאִים, const. חֲטָאֵי) m. fault, sin, trespass; 2) punishment, or expiation of sin. Comp. אָשָׁם guilt and punishment of guilt; from which חִטֵּא denom. 1) to expiate, to remove חֵטְא (the sin); comp. סִקֵּל to clear the stones away (from סָקַל stone); 2) to bring a sin-offering, or to remove the sin by an offering. Hithp. הִתְחַטֵּא to cleanse oneself from sin.

חַטָּא (pl. חַטָּאִים) adj. m. חַטָּאָה fem. 1) sinner (male or female), sinful; 2) the penitent one. This double signification is also found in חֵטְא, חֲטָאָה.

חֲטָאָה f. 1) sin, trespass; 2) expiation of sin, offering. It is the fem. of חֵטְא.

חַטָּאָה fem. equiv. to חֲטָאָה sin and expiation of sin, punishment, sin-offering.

חַטָּאָה (Aram.) the same. The Ketib has חַטָּיָה.

חַטָּאת (once חַטָּאת, const. חַטַּאת, with suff. חַטָּאתִי, חַטֹּאתֵכֶם, pl. חַטָּאוֹת) f. the same; מֵי ח׳ water of the sin-offering.

חָטַב (fut. יַחְטֹב) 1) equiv. to חָצַב, קָצַב, to hew, to cut (wood), to fell. 2) to make stripes, to make a thing of checquered colors; hence חָטוּב

striped, chequered. The idea of making stripes proceeds from that of cutting in. Pu. pass. equiv. to be hewed out.

חִטָּה (primitive, pl. חִטִּים, חִטִּין) fem. wheat, חֵלֶב חִ׳ fat, marrow of the wheat. The plural is used of wheat in the grain.

חַטּוּשׁ p.n. m. (assembled one).

חָטַט (not used) to dig, to search, to explore, like חָקַר.

חֲטִי (with suff. חֲטָיָךְ) Aram. masc., equiv. to חַטָּאָה, חַטָּיָה.

חַטָּיָה see חַטָּאָה.

חֲטִיטָא p.n. m. (the searcher).

חַטִּיל p.n. m. (the trembling one).

חֲטִיפָא p.n. m. (the spoiled one).

חָטַל (not used) to totter, to tremble, perhaps related to חָשַׁל, so that חַטִּיל signifies the weak one.

חָטַם (fut. יַחְטֹם) to close the anger (אַף) against (לְ) some one, only Isa.48:9, where וּתְהִלָּתִי is to be rendered as וּלְמַעַן תְּ׳.

חָטַף (fut. יַחְטֹף) to snatch away, to rob, to despoil.

חָטַר (not used) to support; like שֵׁבֶט, perhaps connected with עָזַר.

חֹטֶר m. stave, stock, staff, like שֵׁבֶט, staff, so called from supporting.

חָטַשׁ (not used) to assemble (after the Arab.), perhaps equivalent to כָּנַשׁ to disperse, to scatter (the enemy); from which חַטּוּשׁ.

חַטָּאת see חַטָּאָה.

חַי (const. חֵי, comp. מֵי, דֵּי, שֵׁי, from מַי, דַּי, שַׁי, only Levit.25:36, חֵי stands in the absolute; pl. חַיִּים) 1) adj. m., חַיָּה (const. חַיַּת, poet. חַיְתוֹ, pl. חַיּוֹת) f. living, alive, חַיִּים the living; 2) subst. living, alive; חַיִּים the living ones; also חַיָּה living, alive; e.g. הַצִּפּוֹר הַחַיָּה, צִפֳּרִים חַיּוֹת, the living bird, living birds, but generally a subst. living thing, espec. beast, coll. beasts, for which also sometimes the pl. חַיּוֹת, and then only it is distinguished from בְּהֵמָה cattle; 3) abst. life, as also the sing. חַי and חַיָּה, more frequently however, חַיִּים and חַיִּין. The idea of life, is transf. to sustenance, refreshening, quickening, happiness, etc. Also in sing. I. strong, vigorous, fresh, raw, etc. חַיַּת יָד renewal of strength; מִלֵּא חַיָּה to fulfil the wants of life.

חַי (def. חַיָּא, pl. חַיִּין) Aram. adj. m. living, alive; pl. life.

חִיאֵל p.n. m. (life of God).

חִידָה f. entangled, intricate speech; hence, riddle, poetry; next, equiv. to מָשָׁל proverb, axiom, metaphor, oracle, riddle. The root is חוּד, which see.

חָיָה (for which once occurs חָי, 3 pers. f., once חָיְיָה) equiv. to חָוָה to live, to be, to exist, related to הָיָה:

next, to live well, to be strong, joyful, youth-like, to recover from (מִן) sickness, to live by something; e g. by the profession of warrior (עַל חֶרֶב). Pi. חִיָּה to give life, to revive, to maintain, to call into life; fig. to rebuild a falling town. Hiph. almost like Pi. to call into life.

חֲיָה (imper. חֱיִי) Aram. the same. Af. אַחְיָא (for אַחְיִיא, part. מַחֵא), to preserve alive.

חָיֶה adj. m. חָיָה (pl. חָיוֹת) f. vigorous, healthy.

חַיָּה only a secondary form of חֶדֶר (which see); round tent, circle of a tent; hence, camp.

חֵיוָא (def. חֵיוְתָא, חַיְתָא, const. חֵיוַת, pl. חֵיוָן) Aram. f. beast, equiv. to חַיָּה. חַיַּת בָּרָא beast of the field.

חַיּוּת f. life. אַלְמְנוּת חַ׳ widowhood during the life of the husband, i.e. absence of the husband.

חַיֵּי see חָיָה.

חִיל see חוּל.

חֵיל (const. חֵיל, only occurs twice for the absolute, 2 Kings 18:17, and Isa. 36:2; pl. חֲיָלִים, with suff. חֵילֵיהֶם) m. 1) power, strength, valor; next, like כֹּחַ in reference to the physical power. עָשָׂה חַיִל to exercise valor: 2) strength, power, transf. to wealth, property, where עָשָׂה חַיִל signifies to acquire property: 3) power, strength of an army; hence, warriors: 4) valor, virtue; hence, אִישׁ חַיִל a virtuous man, אֵשֶׁת חַיִל a virtuous woman. All these significations are derived from חוּל IV.

חַיִל (const. חֵיל, with suff. חֵילָהּ) Aram. the same.

חֵיל see חֵל.

חִיל m. trembling, from חוּל II., especially of the throes of a woman in labor.

חִילָה f. the same.

חֵילָה f. equiv. to חֵל, moat, rampart, or ditch round a rampart.

חֵילָם (also חֵלָאם) p.n. of a city not far from the Euphrates (place of wealth).

חִילֵן p. n. of a city of priests in the territory of Judah.

חִין (extended from חֵן) m. beauty, grace; see חָנַן and חֵן.

חַיִץ m. wall, partition, equiv. to חוּץ. From which is formed:—

חִיצוֹן (after the form תִּיכוֹן) adj. m. חִיצוֹנָה f. the outer one, e.g. the outside building, etc. לַחִיצוֹן from without.

חֵיק (seldom חֵק) m. bosom, lap, from חוּק. שָׁכַב בְּחֵיק to lie at the bosom; אֵשֶׁת חֵ׳ wife, i.e. she who rests on thy bosom; שִׁלֵּם אֶל חֵ׳ to pay in the bosom, i.e. to recompense, likewise הֵשִׁיב אֶל חֵ׳. Lap of the garment, i.e. pocket;

lap of the carriage, i.e. a folding in the same; lap of the altar, i.e. deepening for containing the fire.

חִירָה p. n. m. dignity, nobility.

חִירָם (also חִירוֹם) p. n. m. the same.

חִישׁ swiftness, haste; next, adv. swift, hasty: see חוּשׁ.

חֵךְ (after the form צֵל, חֵל; with suff. חִכִּי) m. palate, comp. מַלְקוֹחַיִם; next, mouth, as organ of speech and taste: see חָנַךְ.

חָכָה (part. חוֹכֶה) to depend on; hence, to trust in, related to בָּטַח, in the original sense. Pi. to trust confidently, to hope (with accus. and לְ), to wait for. Inf. חַכֵּי (for חַכּוֹת) is like חֲיָיה for חֲיוֹת (Ezek. 21:15), רְאֵה (Job 10:15), for רְאוֹת. The root is connected with חָנַךְ.

חַכָּה f. angle, fishing-hook, from חָכַךְ, to catch; מָשַׁךְ בְּחַכָּה, to draw up by the fishing hook.

חֲכִילָה (beauty) p.n. of a hill in the desert of Sif.

חַכִּים (Aram.) adj. wise, prudent one, especially Magicians, after the form of זַקִּיף, אַלִּים, etc.

חָכַךְ (not used), to seize, to catch according to Aram., related to לָקַח, from which חֵךְ.

חָכַל (not used) to paint the face, especially of the red rouge. The root is transposed from כָּחַל.

חֲכַלְיָה p.n. m. ornament of God.

חַכְלִיל (const. חַכְלִילֵי) m. painting, colouring, especially of the eyes; hence, in the Targum, סְמַק.

חַכְלִלוּת f. painting, colouring.

חָכַם (fut. יֶחְכַּם) origin. to know; next, to be wise, to gain wisdom. Pi. to make wise, to instruct. Pu. to become wise, shrewd (of sorcerers). Hiph. to make wise, discreet, to give instruction. Hithp. to boast of wisdom, to conduct oneself cunningly toward (לְ) some one.

חָכָם (const. חֲכַם, pl. חֲכָמִים) adj. m. חֲכָמָה (pl. חֲכָמוֹת) f. wise, sensible, experienced, understanding; but generally as a subst., a wise, prudent, experienced one, etc. Among the branches of prudence and experience (חָכְמָה) is also (like in the verb), cunning and shrewdness inseparable from the sense of wisdom.

חָכְמָה f. wisdom, understanding, experience; modern Hebrew, also knowledge.

חָכְמָה (def. חָכְמְתָא) Aram. f. the same.

חָכְמוֹת or חַכְמוֹת (secondary form from ־מוּת) f. wisdom.

חֵל (seldom חֵיל) m. wall, rampart, moat round a rampart or a town, from חוּל.

חֵלֶד (not used) 1) to hide, to conceal, like עָלַם; next, to cover with rust, like חָלָא, 2) to dig, excavate, from which חֹלֶד.

חֶלֶד p.n. m. concealment.

חֶלֶד (with suff. חֶלְדִּי) m. the dark, covered, unlimited time; hence, 1) futurity; 2) world, worldliness. Similar in etymology and signif. to עוֹלָם.

חֹלֶד m. mole, from חָלַד II.; comp. חֲפַרְפֵּר, which signifies the same animal, from חָפַר.

חָלָה (fut. יֶחֱלֶא, apoc. יָחַל, inf. חֲלוֹת) to suffer, to be oppressed, to be weak; hence, to be sick, with the acc. of the limb from which one suffers; with עַל to grieve at something; 2) to adorn, to embellish, perhaps related to כָּלַל; 3) to flatter, to show tenderness toward some one. The connection of these three significations cannot be traced. Niph. to become ill, weak, to grieve at (עַל) something; מַכָּה נַחְלָה, a morbid wound. Pi. to flatter, to implore, humbly to demand something; 2) to make sick, to weaken. Pu. pass. to become weak. Hiph. to cause illness or grief. Hoph. pass. Hithp. to fret oneself, to feign sickness.

חֶלְדַּי p.n. m. (the covered one, stout one).

חֹל (after the form חֹק) m. that which is profane, not sacred, unfettered, accessible to every one, whilst that which is holy is not accessible to all. The root is חָלַל, loose, free, unfettered, loosened, i.e. not sacred.

חָלָא (not used) to be covered with dirt, to rust, to be covered with rust; חָלָא, to be sick; see under חָלָה.

חֶלְאָה (after the form חֶמְאָה) f. covering of dirt, rust.

חֲלָאִים see חֳלִי.

חָלַב (not used) 1) to draw toward something, to be attached to; related to לֵב, and the roots in יָלַף, אָלַף, etc.; 2) to be white, related to עָלַב, but not connected with signif. I.

חָלָב (with suff. חֲלָבִי) m. milk, quite different from חֶמְאָה, so called from its whiteness, and not from its fatness.

חֵלֶב (only const. חֲלֵב) m. the same.

חֵלֶב (const. חֵלֶב, with suff. חֶלְבּוֹ, pl. חֲלָבִים, const. חֶלְבֵי) m. 1) fatness, fat, stoutness; fig. the best, excellence, the heart; 2) p.n. (stout one).

חֶלְבָּה (fertility, fatness) p.n. of a city in the teritory of Asher.

חֶלְבּוֹן (the same) p.n. of a city in Syria, Aleppo.

חֶלְבְּנָה f. galbanum, perhaps so called from the place, Aleppo.

חֻלְדָּה p. n. f. weasel, mole.

חַלָּה (const. חַלַּת, pl. חַלּוֹת) f. cake, from its round shape, like כִּכָּר. The root is חָלַל to round.

חֲלוֹם (pl. חֲלֹמוֹת), m. dream; figur. folly. Root חָלַם.

חַלּוֹן (pl. חַלֹּנִים, ־נוֹת) com. a window, origin. hole, opening, from חָלַל to bore, to excavate.

חֹלוֹן (place teeming with caves); secondary form from (חִילֵן) p. n. of a city in Moab, and of one in Judah.

חַלּוֹנֵי m. window-work; the form is origin. an adjective one.

חֲלוֹף m. forsaking, vanishing, perishing, from חָלַף to pass away, to vanish.

חֲלוּשָׁה f. defeat, being conquered; see חָלַשׁ.

חֲלַח p.n. of an Assyrian country, to which the ten tribes were sent into exile; in the Talmud called חלזון.

חַלְחוּל p.n. a town in the territory of Judah (earthquake).

חַלְחָלָה f. terror, trembling, anguish, redoubled form from חול; comp. Hithp. II. of חול.

חָלַט (Kal not used) to pull off (equiv. to חָלַץ) to uncover, figur. to do something absolutely, i.e. plainly, uncovered. Hiphil, to explain something exactly, specially, absolutely. In modern Hebrew this form is very common (לחלוטין).

חֲלִי (plur. חֲלָאִים; comp. צְבִי, plur. צְבָאִים; פְּתִי pl. פְּתָאִים) masc. 1) ornament, decoration, from חָלָה II.; 2) (ornament) p.n. of a city in the territory of Asher.

חֳלִי (pause חֹלִי, with suff. חָלְיוֹ, plur. חֳלָיִים) masc. sickness, grief, pain, dejection, evil, and as manifold in signification as the verb; חֳלִי רָע an evil disease, חֳלִי לְאֵין מַרְפֵּא an incurable disease.

חֶלְיָה f. ornament, decoration.

חָלִיל (plur. חֲלִלִים) m. 1) flute, from חָלַל to make hollow; compare נְחִילָה and אַבּוּב in the modern Heb., also נָחַל and אָבַב to hollow out; denom. חָלַל, which see. 2) that which is unfettered, not sacred, profane; next also, that which is defiled; hence with ה mobile, חָלִילָה as an exclamation: "far be it from me" (i.e. it would be a profanation), connected with the dat. of the person and מִן with infin. following; or מִן follows in reference to him, from whom it be far; e.g. מֵה' in reference to God, or אִם follows with the future. See חָלַל II.

חֲלִיפָה f. 1) change (of garments); hence חֲלִיפוֹת בְּגָדִים change of suits, i. e. different suits; sometimes בְּגָדִים is omitted; 2) interchange of friendship, mutual truce;

3) change (of a military post), figur. of being relieved from difficulties; 4) the plur. חֲלִיפוֹת as adv. changing. See חָלַף I.

חֲלִיצָה f. clothing, equipping, arming, garment; from חָלַץ I. to clothe.

חָלַךְ (not used) equivalent to הָלַךְ to walk, to travel. The ה changed into ח.

חֵלֶךְ (with ה of motion חֵלְכָה, like קֵדְמָה in pause חֵלֶכָה m. equiv. to הֵלֶךְ wandering, next concr., wanderer, traveller, and like הֵלֶךְ transferred to, a poor, unhappy one.

חֵלְכִי (for חֵלְכָּי, formed from חֵלֶךְ, plur. חֵלְכָּאִים) adj. masc., which changed into a noun, has the same signification as חֵלֶךְ.

I. חָלַל to bore, to hollow out; comp. חוּל and the derivatives חָלִיל, חַלּוֹן and מְחִלָּה; transf. to pierce, to wound, to hurt, to murder, or in a spiritual sense, e.g לִבִּי חָלַל my heart is wounded. Pi. parallel with הָרַג to slay, to kill. Po. חוֹלֵל to kill (the dragon). Pu. חֻלַּל to be pierced (by the sword). Poal חוֹלַל to be wounded, slain.

II. חָלַל (Kal not used) to become loose (that which was fettered), to be free (that which was restricted, prohibited, inaccessible to us as holy); transf. to be unfettered, free, loosened, accessible, profane, for that which is holy is bound (אָסוּר) for us, whilst the profane is loose (מֻתָּר); next, generally, to be profane. Pi. to loosen (a tie), to redeem (the otherwise holy vineyard); to expose, e.g. a daughter to prostitution; a plantation, i.e to loosen it from the bands of holiness; fig. to profane (a priest, the temple, the sabbath, the name of God), to defile (יָצוּעַ the conjugal bed); חִלֵּל לָאָרֶץ to defile deeply, to disgrace; comp. חֹל, חָלִיל, חָלָל. Hiph. (fut. יָחֵל, אַחֵל) to absolve (from a pledge), to defile (the sacred name). Niph. נִחַל (like נָחַל) fut. יֵחַל, infin. הֵחַל pass. from Pi. to be defiled. Pu. the same.

III. חָלַל (Kal not used) to begin, origin. to open; compare Aram. שְׁרָא to begin, and to absolve. Hiph. הֵחֵל (fut. יָחֵל spec. יָחֵל, rare יָחֵל, as from חוּל) to begin, with inf. following. וַיָּחֵלּוּ Hos. 8:10 stands for וַיּוֹחִילוּ "they shall wait for (Author. Vers. "sorrow for") מִמַּשָּׂא the burden;" תָּחֵל Lev. 21:9 is like תֵּחַל. Hoph. הוּחַל to be commenced; from which תְּחִלָּה beginning.

IV. חָלַל to make a circuit, to move in a circuit (comp. חוּל); hence, to tremble, to bear (children), to roll along, like חוּל; from which חָלָה.

V. חָלַל denom. from חָלִיל (flute); hence part. חוֹלֵל player on the flute. Po. חוֹלֵל the same; hence מְחוֹלְלוֹת female players on the flute. Pi. the same, מְחַלֵּל he who plays on the חָלִיל flute.

חָלָל (const. חֲלַל, pl. חֲלָלִים) m. 1) subst. one that is pierced, wounded, slain (either by hunger or by the sword); 2) adj. m. חֲלָלָה f. defiled, unclean; next, subst. the one who is defiled, dishonoured.

חָלַם (fut. יַחֲלֹם) 1) to be strong, firm, (comp. חָלַם, אָלַם); hence, figur. to be healthy, vigorous, cheerful; 2) to be dumb, to be fettered, fig. to sleep, to dream, to be inactive (comp. אָלַם). The contr. is הֵקִיץ. Hiph. to cause to dream, to make healthy, strong.

חֵלֶם (def. חֶלְמָא, pl. חֶלְמִין) Aram. m. a dream, a vision in a dream.

חֵלֶם p. n. m. (strong one).

חַלָּמוּת f. white of an egg (from חָלַב=חָלַם), or the purslain according to the Syriac.

חַלָּמִישׁ (const. חַלְמִישׁ) m. hard stone, rock, formed from חָלַם with the termination ־ִישׁ.

I. חָלַף (fut. יַחֲלֹף) 1) to withdraw, pass away, slide away (comp. שָׁלַף, אָלַף, סָלַף), e.g. of a flower that withers, of a ship that moves along, of a storm that passeth by: 2) to put aside, e.g. the law; to polish iron (by drawing it through the fire); also, to change, of plants, to grow, sprout again (of renewed courage). Pi. to change (garments), to pull off (a garment, to change it). Hiph. to change the wages (see Kal), to renew strength (כֹּחַ), youth, etc.

II. חָלַף (not used) equiv. to גָּלַב to cut off, to shave off, from מַחֲלָף, which see.

חָלַף (not used) equiv. to כָּלַב to plait (the hair), from which מַחְלָפֹת.

חֲלַף (Aram.) to pass away.

חֵלֶף m. 1) change, as an adv. instead; comp. Aram. חֲלַף, and in Talmud and modern Hebrew תְּמוּר: 2) p. n. of a town in the territory of Naphtali.

חָלַץ (fut. יַחֲלֹץ) 1) to cover, to clothe (comp. חָלַד Aram. חֲלַן), from which חֲלִיצָה cover, garment, and מַחֲלָצָה; transf. to arm, equip, gird: hence, חָלוּץ armed, חֲלָצַיִם the loins; 2) denom. from חֲלִיצָה to take off the arms. Pi. to remove (stones), to deliver (from danger), to take the arms (from the enemy). Niph. to be delivered (from danger); also, to equip oneself. Hiph. to equip others, to arm.

חָלַץ (only dual חֲלָצַיִם) f. the loins, comp. מָתְנַיִם according to a similar etymology, to gird the loins, to equip; to proceed from the loins, i.e. to be begotten.

חֶלֶץ (or חֵלֶץ) p.n. m. (armed one, strong one).

חָלַק (fut. יַחֲלֹק) 1) to be smooth, polished, related to לָקַק, לָשַׁף, יָלַק, from which, 2) to pluck off, cut off (comp. יָלַק); next, to tear off, cut off, to split, to divide. Niph. to be divided, separated (from a whole), to be distributed (either by lot or not). Pi. to divide (booty, inheritance). Pu. pass. Hiph. 1) causative from Kal, to make smooth, to polish (a work of art), words, to smooth the tongue, i.e. to flatter; 2) to distribute, to receive a portion. Hithp. to divide among themselves.

חָלָק adj. m. חֲלָקָה (pl. חֲלָקוֹת) f. 1) physically: smooth, bald, of a man without hair, of a mountain without foliage: 2) fig. flattering, deceitful, smooth; the pl. חֲלָקוֹת is also used in an abstr. sense: 3) p. n. of a mountain (bald mountain).

חֵלֶק (with suff. חֶלְקִי, pl. חֲלָקִים, const. חֶלְקֵי, once חַלְקֵי) m. 1) smoothness, baldness (of a valley, without foliage), fig. flattery: 2) part, portion, booty; next also, that which is allotted, property hence also, acre, land which is allotted to one as property: 3) lot (proceeding from signif. 2, if not taken from the idea of smoothness, or smooth stone, by which the lots were cast, comp. גּוֹרָל): 4) p. n. m., patr. חֶלְקִי.

חֲלָק (with suff. חֲלָקֵהּ) Aram. m. part, portion, equiv. to the Heb. חֵלֶק.

חַלֻּק (const. pl. חַלֻּקֵי) adj. m., smooth. of stones: חַלֻּקֵי אֲבָנִים smooth, stones, origin. the smooth among the stones.

חֲלַקְלַקָּה (only pl. חֲלַקְלַקּוֹת) f. flattery, hypocrisy. The form is derived from חָלָק, like קְטַנָּה from קָטָן.

חֶלְקָה (pl. חֲלָקוֹת) f. 1) smoothness (of the neck), baldness (of the rock), flattery (smoothness of the tongue, lips); hence, plur. חֲלָקוֹת flattery, similar to the plural of חֲלָקָה: 2) piece of land, acre, field, origin. that which is allotted; hence, more frequent with the addition שָׂדֶה.

חֲלֻקָּה f. division, distribution.

חֶלְקַי p.n. m. (the allotted one).

חִלְקִיָּה p.n. m. (portion from God).

חִלְקִיָּהוּ p.n. m. (the same).

חֲלַקְלַק (after the form עֲקַלְקַל, חֲפַכְפַּךְ, יְרַקְרַק) adj. m. חֲלַקְלַקָּה (pl. —קּוֹת) f. smooth, slippery (of localities), smoothness (of the tongue), flattery. The form is redoubled from חָלָק.

חֶלְקַת (plough-field) p.n. of a city in the territory of Asher.

חֶלְקַת הַצֻּרִים (baldness of the rocks) p.n. of a place.

חָלַשׁ (fut. יַחֲלֹשׁ and יַחֲלֹשׁ) 1) to thrust down, to overwhelm, to conquer; with עַל, to triumph over some one; fut. יַחֲלֹשׁ, 2) intr. (יֶחֱלַשׁ) to stretch down, to encamp, equiv. to פָּלַשׁ; hence, to be weak, sickly.

חַלָּשׁ m. one stretched down, weak, from חָלַשׁ II.

I. חָם (with suff. חָמִי, חָמִיהָ) m. father-in-law, from חָמָה III., to be united, related by marriage.

II. חָם 1) p.n. m. (black one); 2) p.n. of a whole district (southern country); 3) p.n. of Egypt, used by the natives (country of the blacks). Root חָמַם.

חָם (pl. חַמִּים) adj. m. hot, warm, from חָמַם. The fem. of which is חַמָּה, which see.

חֹם (with suff. חֻמּוֹ) m. glow, heat, warmth; orig. inf. of חָמַם, hence often translated as the inf.

חָמָא (not used) probably a transposition from מָחָא, to be fat; orig. to anoint. Comp. מָשַׁח, and Aram. מְשַׁח, oil. See מָחָא.

חֵמָא see חֵמָה.

חֱמָא (Aram.) f. glow, anger, from חָמָא; in Heb. חֵמָה is used for it, from חָמָה.

חֶמְאָה (after the form חֶלְאָה, חֶבְאָה) f. fat milk (see חָמָא). That it signifies a fluid, is evident from the passage נַהֲרֵי חֶמְאָה; and that it signifies fat milk, is evident from מַחֲמָאֹת.

חָמַד (fut. יַחְמֹד and יַחְמֹד) 1) to strive, to seek after, to desire; with acc. 2) to take pleasure in something; fut. יַחְמֹד: חָמוּד, that which is desired, beloved; fig. idol. Niph. to be lovely, agreeable, desirable. Pi. to desire vehemently; according to others, to be delighted.

חֶמֶד m. desirableness, delight, precious thing.

חֶמְדָּה fem. 1) desire, wish; בְּלֹא חֶ׳, without being desired; 2) delight, preciousness; 3) object of desire in a good sense, but also in a bad sense, lust; hence, חֶמְדַּת נָשִׁים (lust of women), name of a female deity, *Anaitis*.

חֲמֻדוֹת (rare חֲמוּדוֹת) f. pl. preciousness, loveliness, delightfulness, desirableness.

חֶמְדָּן p.n. m. (lovely one).

I. חָמָה (not used) to enclose, encompass, hedge in, like גָּדַר. Probably the root of חוֹמָה is חוּם.

but the root of חֵמָה is חָמָה.

II. חָמָה (not used) equiv. to חָמַם, to be warm, to glow.

III. חָמָה (not used) to join, to connect oneself by marriage; related to גַּם, עִם, etc., from which חָם and חָמוֹת.

חַמָּה f. a glow, warmth, poetically for the sun, otherwise שֶׁמֶשׁ; orign. fem. of חַם.

חֵמָה (once חֵמָא) f. glow, wrath, fig. poison, on account of its burning in the body.

חֵמָה Job 29:6, contracted from חֶמְאָה; see חֶמְאָה.

חֲמוּאֵל p.n. m. (joined to God).

חֲמוּטַל p.n. f. (combining freshness of life).

חָמוּל p.n. m. (one who is spared).

חַמּוֹן (seat of a tower) p.n. of a city in the territory of Asher, and another in the territory of Naphtali, for which also חַמַּת.

חָמוֹץ (after the form קָדוֹשׁ) m. perpetrator of violence, robber, and אַשְּׁרוּ preceding it (Isaiah 1:17) signifies, lead on the right path.

חַמּוּק after the form (אַלּוּף, שַׁבּוּל) m. encompassing, enclosing, i. e. girdle. See חָמַק.

חֲמוֹר (pl. חֲמוֹרִים) m. 1) he ass, from חָמַר, to be red, on account of the reddish colour of the skin of the ass in the south; 2) burden of an ass, heap, comp. חֹמֶר; 3) p.n. (ass, comp. *Asellus, Asinius*, in Latin).

חֲמוֹרָה, f. burden of an ass, heap, like חֲמוֹר II., and חֹמֶר, only used to play upon the words.

חָמוֹת (after the form חָזוֹת) f. from חָם, mother-in-law. Root חָמָה III., to join, to connect oneself by marriage.

חֹמֶט (not used) to coil, to lie on the ground; according to the Aram. of the Targum, for עָרַע.

חֹמֶט m. a species of lizard.

חֻמְטָה (fortress) p.n. of a city in the territory of Judah.

חָמִיץ adj. m. salt, hence בְּלִיל ח׳, salt provender, i.e. salt herb, like מַלּוּחַ.

חֲמִישִׁי (seldom חֲמִשִּׁי) adj. m. ־שִׁית (pl. ־שִׁיּוֹת) f. formed from חָמֵשׁ, the fifth; subst., fifth part.

I. חָמַל (fut. יַחְמוֹל, inf. חֶמְלָה) to be benign, tender-hearted, ἀμαλός, *molle*, to be compassionate on (עַל) some one, to have forbearance with (אֶל) some one, of things to spare (with אֶל, עַל).

II. חָמַל (not used) only a secondary form from עָמַל, orig. to bear.

חֶמְלָה f. sparing, compassion; from חָמַל I.

חָמַם (1 pers. חַמּוֹתִי, inf. חֹם, const. חֲמֹם, fut. יָחֹם, apoc. יֵחַם, and the intrans. form יֵחַם, יָחֻם; compare (יִצֶּר ,יִדֹּן) to be warm, hot, to glow; figur. of the heat of passion, anger and lust; אֵין גַּחֶלֶת לַחְמָם there is no coal to warm one (חֲמֹם inf.); but לָחֹם Hag.1:6 is trans. Niph. to glow (of the breast, passion) with בְּ, to which belong several forms of the like יֵחַם, future. Pi. חִמֵּם to warm, to brood, to hatch (eggs). Hithp. to warm oneself; comp. חום and חָמָה.

חַמָּן (only plur. חַמָּנִים) m. pillar of the sun, dedicated to the "God of the sun," בַּעַל חַמָּן.

חָמַס (יַחְמֹס) origin. 1) to be sharp, related to חָמֵץ; transf. to be bold, violent; transf. to perpetrate violence, to violate (נֶפֶשׁ the life, תּוֹרָה the law), חָמַס מְזִמּוֹת to sharpen plans against (עַל) some one; 2) to rob, to thrust down, e.g. בֹּסֶר, שֹׁד. Niph. to be robbed, spoiled, i.e. to be stripped.

חָמָס (with suff. חֲמָסִי, pl. חֲמָסִים) m. 1) violence, robbery; 2) property gotten by violence and robbery. 3) audaciousness, e.g. עֵד חָמָס audacious, lying witness.

חָמֵץ (fut. יֶחְמַץ, inf. חִמְצָה) equiv. to חָמַס originally, to be sharp of taste, countenance and mind; hence, 1) to be sour, tough, salt, from which חֹמֶץ, חָמִיץ; 2) of a sharp colour, i.e. scarlet, חֲמוּץ בְּגָדִים scarlet garments or purple; 3) to be of a violent temper, to perpetrate violence. Hiphil, to make sour, to produce fermentation. Hithp. to turn bitter.

חָמֵץ (contracted from חָמִיץ) masc. leaven, sorrel (syn. שְׂאֹר).

חֹמֶץ masc. vinegar, of wine or any other drink.

חָמַק origin. to enclose, encompass, equiv. to סָבַב, as is evident from חַמּוּק; hence, like סָבַב to turn (in order to depart). Hithp. to turn oneself, to rove about.

חָמַר (fut. יַחְמֹר) equiv. to כָּמַר to glow, to burn, from which (like in חום transf. to colour): 1) to be of a burning red colour, to be ruddy, from which חֲמוֹר, יַחְמוּר, חֵמָר and חֹמֶר; 2) to glow, transf. to seethe, foam, ferment in consequence of heat. Pu. חֳמַרְמַר 1) to ferment, to foam (of inward motion), to glow, to burn (of the face).

חֲמֹר see חֲמוֹר.

חֵמָר (after the form נֵכָר, עֵנָב) m. a species of gum (or pitch), perhaps so called from its red-like colour; from which חָמַר denom. to smear with gum.

חֶמֶר m. fermented drink, wine, see חָמַר 2.

חֲמַר (def. חַמְרָא) Aram. m.

חֹמֶר (pl. חֳמָרִים) masc. 1) a kind of earth, potter's earth, so called from its red-like colour; root חָמַר 1; 2) the foaming, roaring (of the sea), from חָמַר 2; 3) denomin. from חֲמוֹר the burden of an ass; hence, heap in general, transf. to measure of a certain lot, measure of dry things.

חַמְרָן p. n. m. (the red one).

חָמַשׁ (not used) equiv. to חָמַץ, חָמַם to be strong, bold, courageous; from which חֹמֶשׁ and the denom. חָמַשׁ are derived therefrom.

חֹמֶשׁ masc. loin, body, as the seat of strength (compare חָלָץ, מֹתֶן of similar extraction); from which:—

חָמַשׁ denom. to gird the loins, to arm generally; hence, part. pass. חָמוּשׁ armed (parallel with חָלוּץ) as the Targum also renders it זְרִיז.

חָמֵשׁ (const. חֲמֵשׁ, pl. חֲמִשִּׁים, with suff. חֲמִשָּׁיו) (cardinal number, m. חֲמִשָּׁה, const. חֲמֵשֶׁת) f. five, the plur. fifty; שַׂר חֲמִשִּׁים captain over fifty.

חִמֵּשׁ Pi. denom. from חָמֵשׁ, to give the fifth part for a levy.

חֹמֶשׁ m. the fifth, a tax of the fifth part, like the present tithe.

חֲמִישִׁי see חֲמִשִּׁי.

חָמַת (not used) according to some, to become rank, decomposed, but this does not agree with the noun; more correctly it is, therefore, to contain, to comprise; equiv. to חָבַת (from which חָבֵת and מַחֲבַת), i. e. to be deepened out for receiving something, from which:—

חֵמֶת (const. חֵמֶת after another reading also חֵמַת Hos. 7:4, Job 21:20) fem. bottle (of leather) so called from its hollowness to receive something; רוּקְבָא, as the Targum renders it, has a similar etymology, for רָקַב is related to קָבַב, נָקַב. That this derivation is the only correct one, is evidenced by its use in the Talmud for bag pipe, flask of the shepherd, on account of the hollowness.

חֲמָת (burgh, fortress) p.n. of a city in Syria on the Orontes, Hamat, later Epiphania, next also, to signify the whole district: complete ח׳ צוֹבָה, ח׳ רַבָּה.

חֵן (with suff. חִנִּי) m. 1) inclination, favor, grace; נָשָׂא, מָצָא חֵ׳ to find, favor, grace; נָתַן חֵ׳ to procure favor; 2) loveliness, grace, e.g. יַעֲלַת חֵ׳, a pleasant roe; אֶבֶן חֵ׳ precious stone; רוּחַ חֵן a gracious spirit; 3) p.n m. (grace, beauty).

חֵנָדָד p.n. m. (grace of Hadad).

חָנָה (fut. יַחֲנֶה, apoc. יִחַן) to incline, to bend (synon. with פָּנָה and related to כָּנַע); hence, to encamp, with עַל, to be hostile against somebody; with לְ, to encamp round something to protect it; to dwell: חֲנוֹת הַיּוֹם equiv. to פְּנוֹת הַיּוֹם which see.

חַנָּה (pl. חַנּוֹת) f. 1) grace, mercy, pl. חַנּוֹת Ps. 77:10, if it is not the inf. from חָנַן: 2) object of compassion, picture of distress, Job 19:17, וְחַנּוֹתִי "and I am a picture of distress:" the pronom. suff. is often used so: 3) p. n. f. grace, beauty.

חֲנוֹךְ 1) p. n. m. (initiated one), patron, חֲנֹכִי; 2) p. n. of a city.

חָנוּן p. n. m. (the presented one).

חַנּוּן adj. m. gracious, merciful, after the form רַחוּם.

חָנוּת (pl. חֲנֻיוֹת) f. place of residence, tent, hut; later also warehouse for the sale of goods, or prison, from חָנָה.

חָנַח erroneously considered by some as belonging to חוּחַ, which see.

חָנַט (fut. יַחֲנֹט) 1) to preserve, and to season things generally (unripe figs): 2) to embalm with spice.

חִנְטָא (for חִטָּא, where the dagesh is analysed by the insertion of נ) Aram. f. equiv. to חִטָּה Heb. wheat.

חֲנֻטִים m. pl. abstract, embalming, mummifying.

חַנִּיאֵל p. n. m. (grace of God).

חָנִיךְ (pl. חֲנִיכִים) m. the initiated one, i.e. experienced one: see חָנַךְ.

חֲנִינָה f. grace, mercy, from חָנַן.

חֲנִית (pl. חֲנִיתִים and חֲנִיתוֹת) f. spear, lance. The root is חָנָה equiv. to קָנָה (קנן), to point.

חָנַךְ (fut. יַחֲנֹךְ) denom. from חֵךְ originally to pass something through the throat, to give the palate something to taste; hence, 1) fig. to instruct, to teach, to instil: 2) to initiate, which idea is taken from 1.

חֲנֻכָּה f. 1) dedication, ἐγκαίνια (of a house, an altar, or a wall): 2) the offering of dedication.

חֲנֻכָּה (Aram) f. the same.

חִנָּם (from חֵן formed with the suff. ָם; comp. יוֹמָם, רֵיקָם) adv. gratuitously (חֵן), i.e. without recompense or reward; hence next, in vain, for nothing, for which also אֶל חִנָּם stands; also, without cause, guiltless: דְּמֵי ח' innocent blood.

חָנַם (not used) to be hard, firm, related to קָנַם and צָנַם, where the same signification is found.

חֲנַמְאֵל p. n. m. (equiv. to חֲנַנְאֵל, grace of God).

חֲנָמַל (in pause חֲנָמָל) masc. origin. stone; next however, hail-stone which breaks the sycamore trees, formed from חָנַם, with the well known termination ַל. Root חָנַם. Kimchi also says מִין מִמִּינֵי הַבָּרָד.

חָנַן (fut. trans. יָחֹן, intr. יֶחֱנַן; with suff. from יָחֹן: יְחָנְּךָ, וַיְחֻנֵּנִי; inf.

חָנַן and (חַנּוֹתִי) origin. equiv. to חָנָה to incline; next morally, to incline favourably, to be gracious. Niph. נֵחַן (comp. נֵחַר) to be worthy of compassion (2 pers. pret. נֵחַנְתְּ). Pi. חִנֵּן to make lovely (the voice), comp. חֵן, חִנָּה. Pi. 1) to have mercy, with the accus. 2) to implore (comp. Hith.), with the accus. Hoph. הֻחַן to be compassionated. Hith. to implore for mercy; with לִפְנֵי. Possibly the sense to implore proceeds from the original idea, to incline, like the Aram. צַלִּי.

חֲנַן (inf. מֵחַן) Aram. the same. Hith. מִתְחַנַּן to implore, to pray.

חָנָן p.n. m. (the gracious one).

חֲנַנְאֵל p.n. m. (grace of God), see חֲנַמְאֵל.

חֲנָנִי p.n. m. (the merciful one).

חֲנַנְיָה p.n. m. (equiv. to חֲנַנְאֵל).

חָנֵס p.n. of a town in central Egypt, so called by the Greeks.

חָנֵף (fut. יֶחֱנַף) origin. to cover, to conceal; hence, transf. to flatter, (comp. מָעַל, בָּגַד); next generally, to lie, to defile, to dishonour, comp. צָנַף. Hiph. to flatter, to defile, to disgrace, to lead to hypocrisy, to pollute.

חָנֵף adj. masc. (origin. part.), but next a substantive, a flatterer, a sinner.

חֹנֶף masc. hypocrisy, dissimulation wickedness.

חֲנֻפָּה f. hypocrisy, next wickedness in general.

חָנַק (Kal not used) to be tight, oppressed, ἄγχω, *ango*, in Aram. שְׁנַק, but it is not connected with עָנַק. Niph. to strangle oneself. Pi. to strangle, to draw tight.

חַנָּתֹן (graceful one) p.n. of a city in the territory of Zebulun.

I. חָסַד (Kal not used) orig. to be intimate (with some one), to be friendly, sociable (related to סוּד, סוֹד); hence, Hith. to show oneself friendly, kind: from which חָסֵד, חָסִיד, חֲסִידָה.

II. חָסַד (only Pi.) equiv. to חָשַׁד to molest, asperse, disgrace, and is not connected with חָסַד I.

חֶסֶד (pl. חֲסָדִים) m. 1) favour, kindness, love, friendship; next, mercy, benevolence, transf. to piety; 2) shame, molestation, dishonour; 3) p.n. m.

חֲסַדְיָה p.n. masculine, (goodness of God).

חָסָה (3 pers. pl. also חָסָיוּ, fut. יֶחֱסֶה, pl. יֶחֱסָיוּן, יֶחֱסוּ) to seek refuge, protection; const. with בְּ or accus., or without any case. The usual forms are חָ' בְּצֵל כְּנָף, תַּחַת כְּנָף, בְּסֵתֶר כְּנָף.

חֹסָה p.n. m. (refuge in God).

חָסוֹן adj. m. strong, mighty, wealthy. See חָסַן.

חָסוּת f. refuge, protection, security.

חָסִיד (pl. חֲסִידִים) 1) adj. m. kind, pious, lovely, gracious; perhaps חֲסִידָה, Job 39:13, is a fem. form of this adj. pious, benevolent; 2) subst. the kind, pious one, sometimes אִישׁ חָ׳; hence pl. חֲסִידֵי ה׳, the pious of God, i.e. his pious adorers.

חֲסִידָה f. the kind, affectionate bird; name of the stork, on account of her affectionate treatment of the young.

חָסִיל m. origin. one that nibbles off; hence, the name of a species of locust. The form is extended from חָסַל, like פְּלִים from פָּלַם.

חָסִין (const. חֲסִין) m. mighty, strong one, from חָסַן.

חַסִּיר (Aram.) adj. m. defective, equiv. to חָסֵר. in Heb.

חָסַל (fut. יַחְסֹל) to nibble, eat off, origin. to tear off, related to גָּזַל, אָצַל, קָצַל, and others.

חָסַם (fut. יַחְסֹם) equiv. to חָתַם, חָטַם, to close, to shut (the mouth of the threshing ox), to hinder (the passer by) from going on.

חָסַן (not used) to be strong, mighty, transf. to be wealthy, rich.

חֲסַן (Aram.) the same. Only Af. הַחְסֵן, to possess.

חֵסֶן (def. חִסְנָא) m. might, strength.

חֹסֶן m. possession, strength, might, treasure; ח׳ יְשׁוּעוֹת, richness in salvation, i.e. abundance of salvation. From which denom. Niph. to be treasured up.

חָסַף (Kal not used) to peel off; comp. קָצַף, from which Pi. חִסְפֵּס (shortened from the double form חספסף). Part. pass. מְחֻסְפָּס, to be pealed, scaled.

חֲסַף (def. חַסְפָּא) Aram. m. sherd, origin. the peel of anything; next, generally a piece, fragment.

חָסֵר (fut. יֶחְסַר, but the pl. יַחְסְרוּ) equiv. to גָּזַר, to cut off; hence, next, to be wanting, deficient; next, to suffer want. Comp. בָּצַר, פָּחַת, and גָּרַע. Pi. to cut off, to diminish. Hiph. to cause want, also to be deficient, wanting.

חָסֵר (const. חֲסַר after the form זָקֵן) adj. m. wanting, deficient, e.g. לֵב, לֶחֶם, bread, understanding.

חֶסֶר m. deficiency, want, need, necessity.

חֹסֶר m. (the same).

חַסְרָה p.n. m. (deficiency).

חֶסְרוֹן m. want, fault.

חַף (after the form קַל) adj. m. polished, rubbed off, from חָפַף; hence, Targ. שְׁזִיג, washed off; generally, however, in a moral sense, pure, innocent.

חָפָא (Kal not used) equiv. to חָפָה, חָבָה, to cover, to veil, to conceal, from which the Pi. חִפֵּא, to cover (עַל) something; ח׳ דְּבָרִים עַל, to speak secretly against some one.

חָפָה equiv. to חָפָא, to cover, to veil, to wrap up (פָּנִים, רֹאשׁ) as an indication of mourning. Pi. to cover over, to wrap up (to overlay with gold or wood) wainscoating. Niph. pass. from Pi. חֻפָּה, is not a Pu. but a noun.

חֻפָּה f. 1) cover, canopy, from חָפַף; 2) p.n. cover, shelter.

חָפַז (fut. יַחְפֹּז) 1) to tremble, related to פָּזַז; 2) to move hastily, to flee. Niph. נֶחְפַּז, to hasten away in fear.

חִפָּזוֹן m. haste, swiftness, flight.

חֻפִּים p.n. m. cover, protection.

חֹפֶן (dual חָפְנַיִם) m. hollow of the hand, also fist; dual, the palms of the hand; what can be taken in the hollow of the hand; hence מְלֹא חֹפֶן, handful; מְלֹא ח׳, to fill a hand. The Root חֹפֶן with the ן terminating, like in אֹפֶן, אֹזֶן, בֹּשֶׁן.

חָפְנִי p.n. m. (the protected one).

I. **חָפַף** (comp. רָחַף) to cover; hence, with עַל, like כָּסָה and חָפָה, to protect, to shelter; from which חֹף not from חָפַף II.

II. **חָפַף** (not used) to rub off, to clean; comp. סָחַף, יָחַף, שָׁחַף, from which חֹף.

חָפֵץ (fut. יַחְפֹּץ) origin. to long, to desire; hence, to take pleasure in something with בְּ; to love something, with accus., to desire.

חָפֵץ (fut. יַחְפֹּץ) only a secondary form from חָפַז, to move to and fro, i.e. the tail (Job 40:17).

חָפֵץ (pl. חֲפֵצִים, const. חֲפֵצֵי) adj. m. חֲפֵצָה, f. desiring, willing, longing.

חֵפֶץ (with suff. חֶפְצִי, pl. חֲפָצִים, with suff. חֲפָצֵיהֶם) m. 1) desire, longing, wish; hence, 2) that for which one desires, precious thing, e.g. אֶרֶץ חֵ׳, precious land; אֶבֶן חֵ׳, precious stone; 3) desirableness, loveliness, e.g. acceptable words; דִּבְרֵי חֵפֶץ; 4) object for which one strives, i.e. affair, subject, matter; next, generally like דָּבָר and עִנְיָן.

חֶפְצִי־בָהּ p.n. f. (my desire is in her).

חָפַר (fut. יַחְפֹּר) 1) to cut in, to dig (a well, a pit), hence also to penetrate, e.g. of the hoofs of the bold horse that penetrate the earth; 2) to dig for something, i.e. to explore, to search. Comp. חָקַר, חָבַר II.

חָפֵר (fut. יֶחְפַּר, pl. יֶחְפָּרוּ) to become red from shame, different from בּוֹשׁ, which signifies to become pale from shame but both as changing the natural colour as an indication of shame. Hiph. to blush with shame, but also to act shamefully; comp. הֶבְאִישׁ equiv. to הוֹבִישׁ from בּוֹשׁ, to cause (בּוֹשָׁה) disgrace. Related to כָּפַר II.

חֵפֶר 1) p.n. m. (shaming) patron. חֶפְרִי; 2) (well) p.n. of several cities.

חֲפָרַיִם (double well) p.n. of a city in the territory of Issachar.

חָפְרַע p.n. m. (priest of the sun).

חֲפַרְפֶּרֶת (pl. חֲפַרְפָּרוֹת) f. an animal that digs up the ground, the exact name of which has not been specified by the commentators.

חָפַשׁ (Kal not used) equiv. to פּוּשׁ, 1) unfettered, to be free; hence, to be stretched out, as indicating freedom; figur. to be free, to move freely; 2) to be stretched down, fig. to be sick. Pu. חֻפַּשׁ, to be liberated, to be freed.

חָפַשׂ (fut. יַחְפֹּשׂ, pl. יַחְפְּשׂוּ) origin. to dig; hence, next, to search, to dive into, almost like חָפַר and חָקַר. Niph. to be searched. Pi. to search for some one; figur. to investigate, morally. Pu. to be searched; hence, חֵפֶשׂ מְחֻפָּשׂ, the investigation which has been made, i.e. searching enquiry; to be sought (from concealment). Hith. to conceal oneself; hence, figur. to make oneself unknown by disguise.

חֵפֶשׂ m. search, inquiry.

חֹפֶשׁ (with suff. חָפְשִׁי) extension, stretching out (of bolsters and mattresses); hence, cover, bolster, generally; perhaps also freedom; 2) couch, e.g. בַּמֵּתִים חָפְשִׁי, my couch, or resting place, is among the dead.

חֻפְשָׁה (from חֹפֶשׁ) f. liberty, freedom.

חָפְשׁוּת f. sickliness, illness, origin. sick bed.

חָפְשִׁי (from חֹפֶשׁ) adj. m. (pl. חָפְשִׁים) to be free, whether in contrast to slavery, imprisonment, or to being tributary, burdened with taxes.

חָפְשִׁית f. the same, like חָפְשׁוּת.

חֵץ (with suff. חִצִּי, pl. חִצִּים) m. 1) an arrow, from חָצַץ, to point, to cut out; hence, בַּעֲלֵי חִצִּים, shooters of arrows, archers; יָרָה חֵץ, to shoot off an arrow; חָמַל אֶל חֵץ, to spare an arrow. Applied to God, חֵץ signifies lightning, next punishment; 2) a shaft, only a secondary form from עֵץ, like in the Keri; אָנוּשׁ חִצִּי, destructive, i.e. poisoned, is my arrow, from which denom. חִצֵּץ, to shoot off arrows, hence particip. מְחַצְצִים, archer.

I. חָצַב (fut. יַחְצֹב) equiv. to קָצַב,

חָצַב, to hew, to hew out (of stone or wood), to dig out (קֶבֶר, אֶבֶן), to spread flames, figur. to destroy, to kill. Niph. to be hewn out on a rock (for a remembrance). Pu. to be hewn out (of a stone), i.e. to originate. Hiph. to destroy, to fell.

II. חָצַב (not used) equiv. to חָשַׁב, to tie, to bind (comp. חָשַׁב) from which חַרְצֹב for חֲצֹב.

חָצָה (fut. יֶחֱצֶה, apoc. יַחַץ) 1) to cut off, to cleave, to part, comp. גָּזָה, קָצָה; hence, 2) to divide in two parts, to halve; חָצָה עַד צַוָּאר (of a river), to divide up to the neck (man), i.e. to reach up to the neck. Niph. to divide oneself in parts.

חֲצוֹצְרָה (יהות) f. trumpet, from חָצַר, to sound; from which the denom. חִצֵּר, חַצְצַר; Pu. חֻצְצַר; Hiph. הֶחְצִיר, to trumpet.

חָצוֹר (a court) p.n. of a place in Palestine, and a district in Arabia.

חָצוֹת (const. חֲצוֹת) f. middle (of two parts), e.g. in the middle of the night.

חֲצִי (pause חֵצִי, with suff. חֶצְיוֹ) m. 1) the middle, equiv. to חָצוֹת, where something separates into two parts; 2) half.

חִצִּי m. equiv. to חֵץ, an arrow.

חֲצִי הַמְּנֻחוֹת p. n. m. (middle of the resting places), patronymic חֲצִי הַמְּנַחְתִּי.

I. חָצִיר (only a lengthened Arabic form from חָצֵר) m. an enclosed place, dwelling, court.

II. חָצִיר (const. חֲצִיר) m. grass, leek, from חָצַר to vegetate, to bloom.

חֹצֶן (with suff. חָצְנִי) m. origin. an incision, an inlet, from חצן equiv. to חזז (in מַחוֹז) to cut; hence, figur. bosom, lap. חָפַן is not to be adopted as the root.

חֵצֶן (with suff. חִצְנוֹ) m. the same.

חֲצַף (Aram.) equiv. to קָצַף Heb. to rage; hence, affix הַחְצֵף to press violently, to rage.

חָצַץ equiv. to גָּזַז to cut, to divide; hence, fig. to be divided in hosts, particip. חֹצֵץ. Perhaps a noun in the sense of a line, row. Pi. only particip. מְחַצְצִים they that divide (the spoil); if this word is not a denom. from חָצָץ. Pu. to be shortened, e.g. the number of the month.

חָצָץ (pl. with suffix חֲצָצֶיךָ) m. 1) small particles, figur. small stone, gravel: 2) lightning, orig. an arrow; next, from 2 denom. Pi. חִצֵּץ to shoot arrows, if it is not formed directly from חֵץ.

חַצְצוֹן־תָּמָר (also חֲצַר) p. n. of a city in the territory of Judah (row of palms).

חֲצוֹצְרָה see חֲצֹצַר.

חֲצוֹצְרָה see חֲצֹצְרָה

חָצַר (not used) to hedge in, to inclose; related to עָצַר: from which חָצֵר and חָצִיר I.

חָצַר (not used) to cry, to scream, it signifies also, like צָלַל and הָלַל, to bloom, to vegetate.

חָצֵר (const. חֲצַר, pl. חֲצֵרִים, חֲצֵרוֹת) com. an enclosed place, court, village, locality, and all that is enclosed as a place of abode, moveable tents are also called so if they are placed like a court. The geographical compounds are חֲצַר אַדָּר (court of magnificence), חֲ׳ גַּדָּה (court of happiness), חֲ׳ סוּסָה (court of horses), חֲ׳ סוּסִים (the same), חֲ׳ עֵינוֹן (court of fountain), חֲ׳ עֵינָן (the same), חֲ׳ שׁוּעָל (court of foxes), חֲ׳ תִּיכוֹן (middle court).

חֶצְרוֹן p. n. m. (the blooming one, from חָצַר).

חֲצֵרוֹת (courts) p. n. of a place.

חֶצְרַי (Keri חֶצְרוֹ) p. n. m. (the blooming one).

חֲצֵרִים p. n. of a place.

חֲצַרְמָוֶת (court of death) p. n. of a province in Arabia, Hadramaut.

חֵק see חֵיק.

חֹק (before makkaph חָק־, with suff. חֻקִּי, חֻקְּךָ, pl. חֻקִּים) m. 1) origin. that which is inscribed, hence that which is appointed (לֶחֶם) measured, fixed, allotted, the appointed time, the fixed aim; 2) law (of God), revelation, divine sentence, edict, the law engraven or appointed. Root חָקַק.

חִקְקֵי (not חֻקֵּי; pl. const. but חִקְקֵי, with the dagesh analysed; the same as צִלְלֵי is from צֵל, עַמְמֵי from עַם) m. conclusion, decree.

חָקָה (Kal not used) equiv. to חָקַק to engrave. Pu. to be inscribed on (עַל) the wall, or painting on something. Hith. to make appointments upon (עַל) something, to draw the boundaries of anything, e. g. to limit the boundaries of the soles of the foot (שָׁרְשֵׁי רַגְלַי).

חֻקָּה (pl. חֻקּוֹת) f. a law, a precept, equiv. to חֹק.

חֲקוּפָא p.n. m. (the bent one) from חָקַף to bend, to coil.

חָקַק (inf. with suff. חֻקּוֹ, חֻקוֹ, imper. with suff. חֻקָּהּ) to engrave (on a rock), to inscribe ("decree unrighteous decrees"), to fix (laws), to draw ("a compass over the depths"), to draw upon (עַל) something, e.g. a town, but especially to inscribe in (עַל) a book. חֹקֵק a law-giver, a leader. Po. חֹקֵק. Part. מְחֹקֵק, fut. יְחֹקֵק, to engrave, to inscribe (laws), to rule, to lead; hence, מְחֹקֵק a law-giver, a leader, equiv. to שֵׁבֶט staff, the leader.

Pu. pass. hence מְחֻקָּק that which is inscribed, the law. Hoph. הֻחַק like Pu. to be inscribed בְּסֵפֶר.

חֻקֹּק (a ditch) p.n. of a city.

חָקַר (fut. יַחְקֹר) orig. to dig; hence, to inquire, to search (with accus. of the person.). The root is related to בָּקַר, בִּקֵּר, etc. Niph. to be searched, searchable. Pi. to explore, to fathom.

חֵקֶר (pl. const. חִקְרֵי) m. 1) search, inquiry, fathoming, e.g. of the heart: 2) that which is searched, i.e. the innermost, the secret of of a thing, e.g. חֵקֶר, חֵ׳ אֱלוֹהַּ, תְּהוֹם, and others.

חֹר see חוֹר.

חָר see חוּר.

חָרָא (or חָרָה, not used) to purge, especially the bowels; hence in the Talm. חֲרָא to sweep away. The derivs. are only in Ketib.

חָרָא (pl. חֲרָאִים, const. חַרְאֵי) masc. refuse, dung, from חָרָא.

חָרַב (Kal not used) equiv. to חָרַף to cut, to be sharp, comp. חוּרְפָּא (Aram), a knife; hence, Niph. to combat. Hoph. like Niph.

חָרֵב (fut. יֶחֱרַב) 1) to dry, to wither, related to קָרַב, צָרַב; hence, to be desolate, destroyed; 2) to be amazed, to stare; comp. שָׁמַם and שָׁעַר. Niph. to become desolate, devastated. Pu. to be dried up. Hiph. to dry up (the sea), next, to devastate (אֶרֶץ, חוּצוֹת, עָרִים).

חָרֵב adj. masc. חֲרֵבָה (plur. with the article הֶחֳרֵבוֹת for הֶחֳ׳) f. dried up. figur. devastated.

חֲרַב (Aram.) only Hoph. to be destroyed, like חָרֵב in Heb.

חֶרֶב (with suff. חַרְבִּי, plur. חֲרָבוֹת, const. חַרְבוֹת) fem. 1) edge, next, the sword, הִכָּה, הָרַג, בַּחֶ׳ to slay by the sword; נָפַל, מֵת בַּחֶרֶב to fall by the sword, transf. to other instruments similar to a sword. Root חָרַב; 2) dearth, from חָרֵב, which see.

חֹרֵב (deserted hill), p.n. of a height on the mountain Sinai.

חֹרֶב m. dearth, transf. to desolation.

חָרְבָּה (from חֹרֶב, pl. חֳרָבוֹת, const. חָרְבוֹת) f. desolation, hence, ruins, desolated places, from חָרֵב.

חָרָבָה fem. dryness, dry land, from חָרֵב.

חֲרָבוֹן (const. חַרְבוֹן, plur. const. חַרְבוֹנֵי) m. dryness, heat.

חַרְבוֹנָא (Persian) p.n. m. (driver of an ass).

חָרַג (fut. pl. יַחְרְגוּ) to tremble; hence, to flee with trembling.

חַרְגֹּל (from חָרַג; formed with the termination ־ֹל) m. a kind of hopping locust.

חָרַד (fut. יֶחֱרַד) 1) to tremble, to be frightened at (לְ) something, for something to be uneasy; 2) to hasten away from (מִן) a place, to hasten toward (לִקְרַאת) some one. Related to רָעַד, רָטַט. Hiph. to terrify.

חָרֵד (pl. חֲרֵדִים) adj. masc. anxious, frightened for (עַל) something; pious.

חֲרָדָה (const. חֶרְדַּת, pl חֲרָדוֹת) fem. 1) fright, fear, anxiety; 2) (place of terror) p.n. of a place.

חָרָה (fut. יֶחֱרֶה) to glow, to burn, namely, of the kindling of wrath, e.g. חָרָה לוֹ his wrath was kindled, more frequently with אַף and the person with whom one is angry, const. with אֶל or עַל and בְּ, sometimes חָרָה בְּעֵינֵי פ׳. Niph. does not occur, for the form נֶחֱרוּ, נֶחֱרִים are derived from חָרַר which see. Hiph. 1) הֶחֱרָה (fut. apoc. יַחַר) to cause the anger to be kindled, with עַל; to do something with ardour, zeal. Hiph. 2) תַּחֲרָה the ה is changed into ת; hence particip. מְתַחֲרֶה, fut. תְּתַחֲרֶה to dispute, to vie with (אֶת, בְּ) somebody. Hith. הִתְחָרָה, fut. apoc. יִתְחַר) to enrage oneself against (בְּ) some one. Comp. חָרַד.

חֲרוֹד (place of terror; fountain of terror) p.n. of a place and a fountain; complete עֵין חֲ׳. gent. חֲרֹדִי.

חָרוּז (only pl. חֲרוּזִים) m. a string (of coral or pearls), origin. that which is strong, from חָרַז to string.

חָרוּל (pl. חֲרֻלִּים) masc. thorn, thorn-bush. Root חָרַר, ל is the termination.

חָרוֹן (const. חֲרוֹן, pl. חֲרֹנִים) m. glow, glowing of anger; hence, generally, complete חֲרוֹן אַף; especially the anger of God.

חָרוּץ (without pl.) m. 1) ditch of a fortress, from חָרַץ 1, equiv. to חָרַת to cut in; 2) legal decision, punishment by law, from חָרַץ 2, to decide; hence עֵמֶק הֶחָרוּץ valley of judgment; 3) gold, a poetical expression, from חָרַץ to glitter, related to חֶרֶס.

חָרוּץ (pl. חֲרוּצִים) adj. m. (for חָרִיץ) 1) robust, active, diligent, from חָרַץ 3; 2) to be pointed, sharp, e.g. מוֹרַג חָ׳ pointed threshing-roller, abridged also חָרוּץ alone, (Isaiah 28:27) transf. to pointed stone; 3) p.n. m. the diligent one.

חֲרוּצָה (only pl. ־צוֹת) f. a pointed, sharp, threshing, cart-wheel, equiv. to חָרוּץ.

חָרַז (not used) to string, to string together (on a cord), from which חָרוּז, which see.

חַרְחַס p.n. m. (the shining one), from redoubled form of חֶרֶס.

חַרְחֻר (from חָרַר) masc. 1) kindling; 2) p.n. m. (noble; free one).

חֶרֶט (not used) equiv. to חָרַת, גָּרַט to hollow, deepen out, or engrave.

חֶרֶט m. a pencil, a chisel with which things are cut or engraved; figur. style.

חַרְטֹם (formed from חֶרֶט, with the termination ־ֹם, like קַרְדֹּם from קֶרֶד: plur. חַרְטֻמִּים like קַרְדֻּמִּים) m. he that understands to draw with the pencil, hieroglyphist; hence also, signifying a class of priests.

חַרְטֹם (pl. חַרְטֻמִּין, def. חַרְטֻמַּיָּא) Aram. m. the same.

חֳרִי masculine, glow of anger, always joined with אַף, from חָרָה which see.

חֹרִי (from חוּר after the form חֹק, with adj. termination ־ִי) adj. m. but already as a subst. that which is dried, baked, compare Aram. חֲרָא, חֲרִיתָא; hence, cake. The root is חָרַר not חוּר.

חֹרִי as a p.n. see חוֹרִי.

חֹרִי (in pause חֹרָי) adj. mas. but already as a subst. *byssus*, linen, fine linen, from חָרַר which has also the signification of חָוַר.

חֲרִיּוֹן (from חָרָא=חָרָה, after the form עֶלְיוֹן, אֶבְיוֹן; pl. חֶרְיוֹנִים) masc. refuse, dung, only in the Ketib.

חָרִיט (pl. חֲרִיטִים) masc. origin. that which is deepened out to contain something, a pocket.

חֹרִים m. pl. 1) holes; 2) the noble ones.

חָרִיף p.n. m. (harvest-time); patron. חֲרִיפִי, Keri חֲרוּפִי.

חָרִיץ (pl. const. חֲרִיצֵי) m. 1) something that is cut off, a piece; חֲרִצֵי הֶחָלָב a slice of cheese: 2) equiv. to חָרוּץ 2, point, or that which is pointed.

חָרִישׁ m. 1) the ploughing; 2) like קָצִיר, אָבִיב, אָסִיף, time of ploughing. Root חָרַשׁ.

חֲרִישִׁי adj. m., but only חֲרִישִׁית f. is used, to be taciturn, quiet. Root חָרַשׁ.

חָרַךְ (not used) 1) equiv. to עָרַךְ to enclose, to enclose together; 2) to seize, to lay hold of, like אָחַז proceeding from the idea of grasping.

חֲרַךְ (Peal not used) Aram. to singe, to burn; hence, Hith. to singe oneself, to be singed.

חָרָךְ (only pl. חֲרַכִּים, comp. קְטַנִּים, גְּמַלִּים, עֲצַבִּים from עָצָב, etc.) m. window-lattices comp. אֲרֻבָּה.

חָרַל a root erroneously adopted as belonging to חָרוּל, which see.

I. חָרַם (Kal not used) to be lonely, forsaken; hence, like אָשַׁם, to be desolate; from which Hiph. to separate, to select for God, i.e. to consecrate, or desolate; next, to tame. Hoph. pass. from Hiph.

II. חָרַם to cut off, to shorten; hence

particip. pass. חָרוּם especially used flatness of the nose.

חֳרֵם (devoted city) p.n. of a place in the territory of Naphtali.

חָרִם p.n. m. (the flat-nosed one).

חֵרֶם (once חֶרֶם, with suff. חֶרְמִי, pl. חֲרָמִים) m. 1) origin. taming; next, a net by which something is tamed, also to decoy generally; 2) desolation, desertion, a ban; sometimes the subject which is devoted, consecrated.

חָרְמָה (ridge of a mountain) p.n. of a Canaanite royal town, formerly צְפַת.

חֶרְמוֹן (ridge of a mountain) p.n. of a mountain of Anti-Lebanon. It is called חֶרְמֹנִים on account of the many ridges on the mount.

חֶרְמֵשׁ (for חֶרְמִישׁ after the form עַכָּבִישׁ, חַלָּמִישׁ, where ־ִישׁ is the termination) masc. sickle, from חָרַם, to cut off.

חָרָן 1) p.n. m. (the noble one); 2) heath, p.n. of a town in Mesopotamia, Karrhæ.

חֹרֹנַיִם (double cave) p.n. of a Moabite city; gent. חֹרֹנִי.

חַרְנֶפֶר p.n. m. (the snoring one).

חָרַס (not used) to break to pieces; comp. רָצַץ, רָסַס; next, to rub, to scrape.

חָרַס (not used) to glitter, to shine, related to חָרַץ which see; from which חֶרֶס 2, and perhaps also חֲרְסוּת.

חֶרֶס masc. 1) scurvy, from חָרַס to scratch, to rub; 2) with ה mobile חַרְסָה sun, origin. glitter, light, from חָרַס to glitter.

חַרְסוּת f. pottery; according to others the rising of the sun; from חָרַס or חָרַס.

חַרְסִית only in the Ketib for חַרְסוּת.

חָרַע (not used) to be cunning, subtle, from which תַּחְרָע.

חָרַף (fut. יֶחֱרַף) 1) origin. to pluck; hence figur. to mock, to scorn, to blaspheme, comp. קָרַץ, אֱכַל: 2) intrans. to be plucked off, to be bare, naked, disgraced. Pi. חֵרֵף (fut. יְחָרֵף) 1) to blaspheme, with לְ and accus.: 2) to lay bare, to expose, e.g. נֶפֶשׁ the life. Niph. to be delivered up (of a woman to a husband). With this root חָרַף, גָּרַף and טָרַף.

חָרֵף p.n. m. (one who has reached the autumn of life).

חֹרֶף (with suff. חָרְפִּי) m. 1) time for plucking off the fruit, harvest: 2) figur. the autumnal age of man. From which denom. חָרַף to stay somewhere during the autumn (חֹרֶף), comp. קִיץ to spend the summer somewhere (קַיִץ).

חֶרְפָּה f. 1) shame, disgrace, which rests upon some one, scorn, transf.

to the secret parts of the body, from חָרַף 2: 2) object of blasphemy, disgrace, scorn, also pl. חֲרָפוֹת.

חָרַץ (fut. יֶחֱרַץ) 1) to cut in, hence to wound, related to חָרַת, to engrave; 2) figur. to decide, to fix (a sentence), to conclude; comp. גָּזַר; 3) to point (comp. חָרוּץ), hence of the moving (pointing) of the tongue by a dog; 4) to arm, to gird; hence, to be active. In this last sense, חָרַץ is a secondary form of חָלַץ, which see. Comp. the Aram. חֲרַץ, loin, Heb. חָלָץ. Niph. to be decided, resolved.

חֲרַץ (def. חַרְצָא, with suff. חַרְצֵהּ, Aram. m. loin, equiv. to the Heb. חָלָץ, from חֲרַץ, to arm, to gird; comp. חָרַץ 4.

חָרַץ (not used) equiv. to חָרַם, glittering, dazzling, of the gold colour; from which חָרוּץ.

חַרְצֹב (from חָצַב, with analysed dagesh by the insertion of ר; pl. חַרְצֻבּוֹת, m. band, knot, transf. to torment, pain, like חֶבֶל. Root חָצַב 2.

חַרְצָן (only pl. חַרְצַנִּים) m. according to tradition, grape-stone; according to others, unripe, sour grapes, from חָרַץ, equiv. to חָמַץ.

חָרַק (fut. יַחֲרֹק) to gnash (the teeth), with the accus. or בְּ of שִׁנַּיִם.

חָרַר (3 pers. f. חָרָה, fut. יֵחַר, after the form יֵקַל) 1) to glow, to burn, to be devoured by flame; related to חָרָה, from which: 2) only in derivatives, to be purified, cleansed, spotless; hence, free, noble, distinguished. Niph. נָחַר (like נָמַס, נָסַב), also נִחַר; (another Niph. form, e.g. נִחַל, נִחַת, hence pl. נִחֲרוּ, pause נִחָרוּ), to be burnt, to be dried up, to excite oneself against בְּ some one. Pi. חִרְחֵר, to kindle (חָ׳ רִיב dispute); from which also חָרוּל.

חָרֵר (only pl. חֲרֵרִים) m. land parched by the sun. Comp. צִיָּה.

חֶרֶשׂ (pl. חֲרָשִׂים) m. 1) earthen, a vessel made of clay, hence כְּלִי חָ׳ earthen vessel, without indicating fragility; יוֹצֵר חָ׳ potter; 2) sherds of an earthen vessel. Root חָרַשׂ, related probably to אָרַץ, hence אֶרֶץ lime-earth, in contrast to אֲדָמָה mould.

חָרַשׁ (fut. יַחֲרֹשׁ) equiv. to חָרַץ, 1) to cut in (wood, metal, or stone); hence, transf. to plough; 2) to plough, in a figur. sense, i.e. to devise good or evil. Niph. to be ploughed, שָׂדֶה a field. Hiph. to devise against some one (עַל), the same signification also occurs in Kal, const. with עַל.

חָרַשׁ (fut. יֶחֱרַשׁ) 1) to be silent, to speak in a whisper, next to be

חֲרֶשֶׁת p.n., see קִיר.

חֹרֶת p.n. of a forest, probably equiv. to חֹרֶשׁ.

חָרַת to engrave on (עַל) a tablet, hence, equiv. to חָרַשׁ.

חָשַׁב (fut. יַחְשֹׁב before makkaph יַחְשָׁב־) equiv. to חָצַב II., to knit, to tie, to bind (comp. חֵשֶׁב, girdle), hence figur. to think, to plan, like in מַחֲשָׁבוֹת, זָמַם, חָ׳, to devise plans against (עַל, אֶל) some one; חָ׳ רָעָה to devise evil, with לְ, for some one; next, to count, to consider, to reckon, with לְ or accus. of the person.; חֹשֵׁב weaver, from the primitive signification. Niph. to be considered like (כְּ, עִם, לְ) something, to be counted to (לְ, עַל) something. Pi. to calculate. Hith. to count oneself among (בְּ) some one.

חֲשַׁב (part. pass. חֲשִׁיב, Aram. the same, to deem, to reckon.

חֵשֶׁב m. girdle, from חָשַׁב to bind.

חַשְׁבַּדָּנָה p.n. m.

חֲשֻׁבָה p.n. m. (understanding).

חֶשְׁבּוֹן m. 1) combination, reckoning, invention; 2) p.n. of the capital of the Amorites.

חִשָּׁבוֹן (only pl. חִשְּׁבֹנוֹת) m. 1) cunning, invention, art; 2) instruments of war

חֲשַׁבְיָה p.n. m. (esteemed by God).

חֲשַׁבְיָהוּ p.n. m. (the same).

inactive; in Targum, to bewitch, of the whispering language of the sorcerers; 2) to be deaf, e.g. אָזְנֵיהֶם תֶּחֱרַשְׁנָה, their ears are silent, i.e. deaf. Hiph. to be silent to (לְ) something, before מִן, אֶל somebody; to pass in silence (with accus.), to be submissive, also to silence. Hith. הִתְחָרֵשׁ, to conduct oneself silently.

חָרָשׁ (const. חָרַשׁ, pl. חָרָשִׁים, const. חָרָשֵׁי) m. artificer, one who cuts in wood, stone, or metal; hence, אֶבֶן, עֵצִים, בַּרְזֶל, figur. one who devises, plans, something, e.g. מַשְׁחִית destruction.

חֶרֶשׁ (pl. חֲרָשִׁים) m. art, artifice, masonry, carpentry; hence, גֵּי חֲרָשִׁים, valley of carpentry; 2) figur. art of sorcery, from חָרַשׁ, also חֲכַם חֲרָשִׁים, equiv. to נְבוֹן לַחַשׁ, hence, secrecy. As an adv., חֶרֶשׁ stands for בַּחֶ׳, secretly, quietly; 3) p.n. m. working man.

חֹרֶשׁ see חָרַשׁ.

חֵרֵשׁ (pl. חֵרְשִׁים) m. (the deaf one), origin. root חָרַשׁ.

חֹרֶשׁ (with ה of motion, חֹרְשָׁה, pl. חֳרָשִׁים) m. a grove, a bush, a small forest. The deriv. is obscure.

חַרְשָׁא p.n. m. (worker).

חֲרֹשֶׁת f. 1) artificial work, or work in wood and stone; 2) (carpentry), p.n. of a place.

חֲשַׁבְנָה p.n. masc. (probably from חֲשַׁבְיָה).

חֲשַׁבְנְיָה p.n. m. (the same).

חָשָׁה (fut. יֶחֱשֶׁה to be silent, to rest (comp. חָרַשׁ) hence, to be mute, dumb. Hiph. הֶחֱשָׁה to observe silence; but also causative, to silence some one (לְ); comp. חָסָה.

חָשׁוּב p.n. m. (thinker, calculator).

חֲשׁוֹךְ (def. חֲשׁוֹכָא) Aram. masc. darkness.

חֲשׂוּפָא p.n. m. (uncovered, naked one).

חֲשׁוּקִים see חָשַׁק.

חֲשַׁח (Aram.) to be necessary, useful, wanted; an abridged form from חֲשַׁחְשׁ.

חַשְׁחוּ (const. חַשְׁחוּת) Aram. f. want, requirement.

חֲשֵׁיכָה see חֲשֵׁכָה.

חֻשִׁים p.n. m. (swiftness, the swift one). See חוּשָׁם.

חָשִׂיף see חָשַׂף.

חָשַׁךְ (fut. יֶחְשַׁךְ) to be or to become obscure, dark, e. g. of the eyes (הָרֹאוֹת, עֵינַיִם), of the sun, the day, the stars, the earth (which is covered by locusts). Hiph. to darken; figur. to darken a counsel, to diffuse darkness.

חָשַׂךְ (fut. יַחְשֹׂךְ to withhold from (מִן) some one; hence, to deny, to deny oneself something; figur. to save, origin. to withhold from (מִן) danger; to spare, to save. Niph. to be spared, saved.

חָשֹׁךְ (only plur. חֲשֻׁכִּים) adj. masc. obscure (of position), i.e. to be low.

חֹשֶׁךְ (with suff. חָשְׁכִּי) m. darkness, obscurity; hence figur. of hell, a dungeon, a subterranean treasure; next, calamity, destruction, dark ness of death, mournfulness; transf. to darkness of spirit, like in most modern languages.

חֲשֵׁכָה (from חֹשֶׁךְ) f. the same.

חֲשֵׁכָה (once חֲשֵׁיכָה; const. חֶשְׁכַת. pl. חֲשֵׁכִים) f. darkness, obscurity.

חָשַׁל (Kal not used) a softer form of כָּשַׁל; hence, to be weak, staggering, lean, thin; the verb חָלַשׁ is only a transposition of חָשַׁל, the latter being the original. Niph. to be weakened, fatigued.

חֲשַׁל (Aram.) to cause to decay, to destroy.

חָשַׁם (not used), equiv. to כָּתַם to glitter; Aram. חֲשַׁם to be noble, distinguished.

חָשֻׁם p. n. m. (noble, distinguished, rich, one).

חֶשְׁמוֹן (riches), p.n. of a city in the territory of Judah.

חַשְׁמֹנָה (the same) p.n.

חַשְׁמַל (formed from חָשַׁם with the diminutive termination ־ַל, like in כַּרְמֶל, חֲנָמַל; with ה of motion

חַשְׁמַלָה (pl. in the Talm. חַשְׁמַלִּים) glittering metal, quartz; later, illustrious being, an angel. Root חָשַׁם.

חַשְׁמַן (from חָשַׁם, formed with the termination ־ַן, compare אַשְׁמַן, חַרְצַן; plur. חַשְׁמַנִּים) m. noble, distinguished one, origin. shining one.

חָשַׁן (not used) equiv. to חָשַׁם to shine; hence, to be adorned, beautified.

חֹשֶׁן m. decoration, so called from its brilliancy, especially the brilliant breast-plate of the high-priest.

חָשַׂף (fut. יֶחֱשֹׂף) equiv. to חָסַף; 1) to peel off (of a tree); hence, to uncover, to expose; 2) to take away, to withdraw (water).

חָשִׂף (pl. const. חֲשִׂפֵי) masc. something separated, divided, division, herds (of goats).

חָשַׁק to attach (related to the root in נָשַׁק to kiss, and נָקַק); hence, generally, to attach oneself to something (from love); next, to have a desire; origin. an attachment. Pi. to attach, connect something. Pu. the pass. of Piel.

חֵשֶׁק (with suff. חִשְׁקִי) masc. desire, pleasure.

חָשֻׁק (pl. חֲשֻׁקִים or חֲשׁוּקִים) m. that which is attached; hence, the fillets connecting the pillars of the temple.

חִשֻּׁק (pl. חִשֻּׁקִים) m. spoke, which connects the nave with the circle.

חָשַׁר (not used) equiv. to קָשַׁר to bind, to tie up, to collect: from which—

חִשֻּׁר (pl. ־ִרִים) m. nave of the wheel that joins all the spokes.

חַשְׁרָה (const. חַשְׁרַת) f. close connexion (of the clouds) thick clouds.

חָשַׁשׁ (not used) equiv. to קָשַׁשׁ (connected with קַשׁ), to be hard, dry, sapless.

חֲשַׁשׁ m. straw, stubble. See קַשׁ. The form חֲשַׁשׁ is analysed from חַשׁ=קַשׁ.

חַת (after the form עַם) in pause חָת; the analysed form is חָתַת; with suff. (חִתְּכֶם) m. fear, terror.

חַת (pl. חַתִּים) adj. m. terrified, affrighted.

חֵת p.n. (fright). From which חִתִּי, which see.

חָתָה (fut. יַחְתֶּה) to seize, lay hold of, e.g. fire from (מִן) the hearth); hence, חָתָה עַל to take and lay upon something.

חִתָּה (after the form סִבָּה) f. fright, fear. Root חָתַת.

חִתּוּל m. bandage of a wound.

חַתְחַת (pl. חַתְחַתִּים) m. fright, terror. Root חָתַת.

חִתִּי (pl. חִתִּים) patron. from חֵת,

name of a tribe dwelling in the vicinity of Hebron.

חִתִּית f. terror, only a secondary form from חִתָּה.

חָתַךְ (Kal not used) to cut, to part, equiv. to גָּזַר, and like it, transf. to decide, appoint. Niph. to be appointed, determined, decreed on (עַל) some one.

חָתַל (Kal not used) to fold, to bind. Pu. and Hoph. to be folded.

חֲתֻלָּה f. covering.

חֶתְלוֹן covered place, haunt, p.n. of a city in Syria.

חָתַם (fut. יַחְתֹּם) equiv. to חָסַם, to close up, hence חָ' בְּעַד, equiv. to סָגַר בְּעַד, to enclose something; transf. to seal up, sometimes with ב, of that which is sealed up, or with which it is sealed; figur. to do something under seal, secretly, or to accomplish, fulfil (by seal). Niph. to be sealed up. Pi. to close up, enclose. Hiph. to shut up, to prevent.

חֲתַם Aram. the same, to seal.

חוֹתָם m. seal, seal-ring. See חוֹתָם.

חוֹתָם after the form שֹׁרֶשׁ) m. perfection, completion. Root חָתַם.

חוֹתֶמֶת f. seal-ring, signet.

חָתַן 1) to join in marriage, hence, חוֹתֵן, father-in-law, i.e. father of the wife; חוֹתֶנֶת, mother-in-law. Hith. to intermarry, const. with אֶת, בְּ, לְ; 2) (not used) to circumcise, i.e. to fulfil the covenant of God by circumcision.

חָתָן (const. חֲתַן, with suff. חֲתָנוֹ, pl. חֲתָנִים m. bridegroom; חֲתַן דָּמִים, a husband of blood, signifies the newly circumcised child. See חָתַן II.

חֲתֻנָּה f. espousing, marriage, origin. connection, union.

חֶתֶף masc. spoil, robbery, concrete, robber.

חָתַף (fut. יַחְתֹּף) to rob, to snatch away, related to קָטַף, חָטַף.

חָתַר (fut. יַחְתֹּר) to break through (a wall), to break into (a house); (with accus.), to break through the waves, to row. The root is found again in בָּ־תַר, פָּ־תַר.

חָתַת (part. חַת, pl. חַתִּים, see adj.; fut. יֵחַת, pause יֵחָת, אֵחַת, with ה, אֵחַתָּה, to fear, to tremble, but always intrans. Pi. חִתַּת, to frighten, to terrify, but also to be in fear, terror. Hiph. הֵחַת (fut. יָחֵת); for הַחִתֹּתִי occurs also (הַחְתַּתִּי), to terrify, to frighten, to humble. The form יְחִיתַן, Hab. 2:17, is supposed to stand for יְחִתֵּן, so that the ן is a suffix.

חֲתַת see חַת.

ט

ט is the ninth letter of the alphabet, hence, as a numeral, it signifies 9. The signification of the name seems to be a serpent, in reference to the shape. This consonant interchanges 1) with the other letters sounding *t*, e.g. טָבַל II. and דָּבַל; טָבַר and תָּבַר; טְנָא and דְּנָא; טוּר and דּוּר; טָעָה and תָּעָה; 2) with the dentals, especially ז, צ, and שׁ; e.g. טָבַח and זָבַח; טָבַל and שָׁבַל; טָבַע and צָבַע; טָעַן and צָעַן; נָטַר and נָצַר; טָפַח and צָפַח; טָהַר and זָהַר, צָהַר.

טָא (Kal not used) to drive, to push away (related to סָא), from which טְאטֵא, and זָע, from which זַעֲזַע, herefrom טֵאטֵא to sweep away, reduplicated from the simple form טָא.

טְאֵב Aram. equiv. to טוֹב, Heb. origin. to shine, next to be joyful over (עַל) something.

טֵאטֵא see טָא.

טַב adj. (Aram.) good, right, agreeable.

טָבְאֵל p.n. m. (approved of God).

טְבוּל (pl. טְבוּלִים) m. turban, a tie, from טָבַל II., to tie, wind round.

טַבּוּר height, mountain, from טָבַר, to be hilly, high; hence, טַבּוּר הָאָרֶץ, height of the earth. See טָבַר.

טָבַח equiv. to זָבַח 1) to slaughter (cattle), especially for no holy purpose, but only for eating. For the former, זָבַח is used; 2) to kill (man).

טֶבַח (with suff. טִבְחָהּ), masc. 1) the slaughtering (of cattle and of man); figur. a meal prepared from that which is slaughtered; 2) p.n. m.

טַבָּח m. 1) cook, origin. a slaughterer of cattle; 2) executioner.

טַבָּח (Aram.) the same, like טַבָּח 2, Heb.

טַבָּחָה fem. cook-maid, formed from טַבָּח.

טִבְחָה f. 1) slaughter; 2) banquet. See טָבַח.

טִבְחַת (equiv. to טִפְחַת, spreading) p.n. of a city in Aram. Compare טָפַח.

I. **טָבַל** (fut. יִטְבֹּל) to wet, to pour over; hence, to dive, to bathe, related to שָׁבַל. Niph. pass.

II. **טָבַל** (not used) to wind, wind round, wrap round; related to דָּבַל, or the root is in דְּ־בַל, נְ־בַל, from which טְבוּל.

טְבַלְיָהוּ p.n. masc. (one crowned by God).

טָבַע (fut. יִטְבַּע) 1) to impress, like טָבַע in the Talmud; 2) equiv. to

צָבַע, to sink, to dive. Pu. to be sunk. Hoph. the same.

טַבָּעוֹת p.n. (impressions).

טַבַּעַת (pl. טַבָּעוֹת, const. טַבְּעוֹת) f. that which makes an impression; hence, seal, seal-ring; transf. to ring generally.

טָבַר (not used) to be raised, hilly, elevated; related to תָּבַר under תָּבוֹר; from which טַבּוּר. A later signification of טַבּוּר, rising of the belly, navel, proceeds from the same idea.

טַבְרִמּוֹן p.n. masc. (the goodness of Rimmon, a Syrian deity).

טַבַּת (probably from טַבְּחַת, extension) p.n. of a city in the territory of Ephraim.

טֵבֵת m. name of the tenth month of the Jewish lunar year. According to modern researches, Tebet is identical with the Indian month *Tapas*, and signifies winter month.

טָהוֹר (const. טְהוֹר, before makkaph, טְהָר) adj. m. טְהוֹרָה, fem. clean, cleanly, in a physical sense, but also in a ritual and a moral sense; subst. cleanliness. The original signification is bright.

טָהֵר (pause טָהֵר; fut. יִטְהַר) equiv. to צָהַר, to shine, to glitter; transf. to be pure, clean, in a physical, ritual, and moral sense. Pi. to cleanse, to pronounce as clean ritually and morally. Pu. pass. Hith. הִטַּהֵר and הִטְּהַר, to cleanse oneself (ritually).

טֹהַר (with suff. טָהֳרוֹ, טְהָרוֹ, masc. brightness, cleanliness, purification; הִשְׁבַּתָּ מִטְּהָרוֹ thou hast diminished his splendour.

טָהֳרָה (formed from טֹהַר) f. cleanliness, purification; דְּמֵי ט׳, blood of purification (of woman in childbed).

טוּא belongs to טֵאטֵא. See טָא.

טָוָא (not used) Aram. equiv. to דָּוָא, to suffer, to be sickly, to fast; from which טְוָת.

טוֹב (pret. טֹב, pl. טֹבוּ; fut. only formed from יָטַב) originally to be bright, like שָׁפַר; hence, to be serene, agreeable, lovely, cheerful. Hiph. הֵטִיב, stands for הֵיטִיב, and belongs to יָטַב.

טוֹב adj. m., טוֹבָה f. 1) good (according to the most manifold modifications as a verb), agreeable, kind, blooming, fresh, useful, abundant, great, benevolent, true, happy, etc., according to the context; 2) subst. the good, happiness, kindness, in which sense the m. as well as the f. is used; 3) p.n. of country beyond the Jordan (fame).

טוֹב אֲדֹנִיָּה p.n. masc. (fame of Adonijahu).

טוּב masc. 1) goodness (of matter), good condition, beauty, excellence, joyfulness, happiness, etc.; 2) concrete, property, riches.

טוֹבִיָּה p.n. m.(the goodness of God).

טוֹבִיָּהוּ p.n. m. (the same).

טָוָה to weave, to spin; origin. to knit, related to צָוָה; from which מַטְוֶה.

טוּחַ (3 person pret. טַח for טָח) to plaister, to wash over. Niph. (inf. הִטּוֹחַ) pass. related to טָחָה, and the root in בְּ־טַח.

טוּחוֹת see טֻחוֹת.

טוֹטֶפֶת (only pl. טוֹטָפוֹת) f. a band, a band on the forehead or round the arm, generally only that on the forehead; next, ornament generally. The form is contracted from טַפְטֶפֶת, and re-duplicated from טוּף.

טוּל (Kal not used) 1) to shake, to move about, to rock, from which טַלְטֵל; 2) to lift up, to lift away. Hiph. הֵטִיל, to carry, throw away, but also to lead, to send away, always proceeding from the original idea to lift. Comp. נָשָׂא. Pi. (reduplicated) טִלְטֵל to shake, to throw about. See טַלְטֵלָה.

טוּן (not used) Aram. to be muddy, soft (similar to סוּן Hebrew, from which סִין); from which טִין.

טוּף (not used) to tie, to wrap round, related to דָּוָה 2, and the root in עָ־טַף, from which טוֹטֶפֶת.

טוּר 1) (not used) to wait, hope for; comp. the root is in כָּ־טַר: 2) to surround for the purpose of protecting, probably from the same original signification as in נָטַר to watch: 3) to arrange, to string together, as a secondary form of תּוּר, שׁוּר.

טוּר (pl. טוּרִים, const. טוּרֵי) m. 1) wall, from טוּר 2, to protect,: 2) row, from טוּר 3.

טוּר (def. טוּרָא) Aram. m. mountain, hill. The root is טְבַר, and טוּר arose from טְבַר=טְוַר (Heb. טַבּוּר, תָּבוֹר, comp. שְׁלָם, Heb. שָׁלוֹם), for which in Targum טְוָר (Heb. טַבּוּר) occurs.

טוּשׁ (fut. יָטוּשׁ) to flee away. Aram. טוּס.

טְוָת (from טְוָא, like קְצָת, כְּנָת, מְנָת, from קְצָא, כְּנָא, מְנָא) Aram. f. the fasting, adv. fasting, during fast.

טָחָה (Kal not used) to push away, to shoot forward, to drive out, related to דָּחָה, but probably only equiv. to טוּחַ; next, to draw, to strain, synon. with מָשַׁךְ. Piel טִחֲוָה to shoot, from טָחָה with the ו interpolated for טִחָה or for טוֹחָה (Poel); hence, part. pl. const. מְטַחֲוֵי. Comp. שָׁחָה in Hithp.

מְחָה (pl. מְחוֹת) fem. kidney, seat of contemplation, from מוּחַ, because the kidneys are covered with fat.

מְחוֹן a mill.

מְחוֹר see מְחֹר.

מְחוֹת see מְחָה.

מְחַח see מוּחַ.

מָחַן (fut. יִמְחַן) to grind (with a hand-mill); to grind the faces of the poor, i.e. to put them to shame, to degrade; to make the woman grind, i.e. to reduce her to work at the mill; מֹחֲנוֹת the grinding ones, i.e. the teeth.

מַחֲנָה f. mill, see מְחוֹן.

מָחַר (not used) to burn, to heat oneself, related to חָרַר, especially of the burning in the posteriors.

מְחֹר (pl. מְחֹרִים, const. מְחֹרֵי) masc. inflammation and swelling in the posteriors; hence, fig. the shape which the diseased part assumes (hæmorrhoids). The Ketib has עֳפָלִים. See מָחַר.

מִיחַ mas. rough-cast, plaster; from מוּחַ.

מִיט masc. clay, lime; the noun has arisen from the reduplicated form of מָא.

מִין (def. מִינָא) Aram. m. clay. See מוּן.

מִירָה (pl. מִירוֹת) f. 1) burgh, fortress, castle, orig. that which protects; hence, also a village of the nomades, or also a wall round the town; from מוּר 2.

טַל (pause טָל, with suff. טַלִּי) masc. dew, from טָלַל to moisten, to bedew.

טַל (Aram.) the same.

טָלָא 1) to be torn in pieces, to hang down in tatters (comp. דַּל, זַל) from which to patch; 2) to be spotted, to be patched together.

טְלָאִים see טְלִי.

טָלָה (not used) equiv. to טָרָה to be young, fresh, blooming. Greek θάλλ-ειν.

טָלֶה (const. טְלֵה, origin. part. from טָלָה) m. young, tender, transf. to a lamb.

טַלְטֵל see טוּל.

טַלְטֵלָה wandering, unstableness, from טִלְטֵל under טוּל.

טְלִי (plur. טְלָאִים for טְלָיִים, comp. צְבִי, pl. צְבָאִים) masc. equiv. to טָלֶה a lamb, from טָלָה.

I. טָלַל (not used) to bedew, to moisten; next, to fall in drops, comp. טָלַה to be full of sap, to be young.

II. טָלַל (Kal not used) to shadow, to cover, to shelter. Comp. צָלַל, from which it is formed. Pi. טִלֵּל to cover, to raft (like קָרָה).

טְלַל (Aram.) the same; hence, Aph. אַטְלֵל to be shadowed.

טָלַם (not used) to press, to oppress.

טֶלֶם place of lambs, arose from טל

of טָלָה with ־ָם as termination; hence, also for which טְלָאִים p.n. of a city in the territory of Judah.

טַלְמוֹן p. n. m. (the oppressor).

טָמֵא (fut. יִטְמָא, inf. טָמְאָה) origin. to be obscure (in contrast to טָהַר to be bright); hence, to be dirty, in this sense related to זָהַם; next, transf. to be defiled, polluted: טָמֵא בְּ to become unclean through something. Niph. 2 pers. plur. נִטְמֵתֶם for ־מֵאתֶם to make oneself unclean, by (בְּ) something (idolatry, adultery). Pi. to defile, to disgrace, to dishonour, to declare as unclean (ritually). Pual pass. Hith. הִטַּמֵּא to defile oneself by (בְּ, לְ) something. Hoph. הֻטַּמָּא pass.

טָמֵא (pl. טְמֵאִים, adj. masc. טְמֵאָה const. טְמֵאַת) f. unclean, morally or ritually, polluted.

טֻמְאָה f. uncleanliness, defiling, anything unclean.

טֻמְאָה f. the same.

טָמָה (Kal, not used) obdurate, stubborn; hence, to be stupid, related to אָ־טַם. Niph. to be considered stupid.

טָמַן (fut. יִטְמֹן) to conceal, to hide; hence, to lay down something secretly (a net, a snare), with לְ, to conceal, to hide, from somebody. Niph. to hide oneself. Hiph. to preserve.

טָנָא (not used) to tie, to plait, twist, related to אָ־טַן. From which:—

טֶנֶא (with suff. טַנְאֲךָ) masc. basket, from טָנָא to twist. Comp. סַל after a similar etymology.

טָנַף (Kal, not used) to be covered with dirt, origin. to cover, wrap up. Pi. to soil, to begrime. The root is related to צָ־נַף.

טָעָה (Kal, not used) equiv. to תָּעָה to err about. Hiph. to lead astray.

טָעַם (יִטְעַם) to taste, to enjoy, transf. to feel, conceive; next also, to recognise, understand, as proved by the nouns מַטְעָם, טַעַם.

טְעַם (Aram.) the same; hence, Po. to give to taste, or to eat.

טַעַם (with suff. טַעְמוֹ) m. 1) taste, from טָעַם in its original signification; 2) in a moral sense, conception, understanding, insight; transf. to royal decree.

טַעַם (Arab.) the same as in Hebrew in signification 2.

טְעֵם (def. טַעְמָא) Aram. m. 1) taste; 2) insight, understanding, prudence, transf. to royal edict; שׂוּם טְעֵם to issue an edict; בְּעֵל טְעֵם stadtholder, administrator of the royal commands.

I. טָעַן (Kal, not used) to thrust down (comp. the root דן, א־דן and תן,

signifying terror), hence Pu. טֹעַן be laid prostrate, with accus. of the instrument used.

II. טָעַן to load, to burden. Comp. צָעַן.

טַף (with suff. טַפִּי) m. collectively, those that trip in their walk, children, family, from טָפַף; טְפַל in Aram. is an extension of this root.

טָפַח (Kal, not used) equiv. to צָפַח to extend, to spread (related to פָּח); hence, Pi. 1) to spread out, to expand (the heavens like a tent); 2) to spread the hands over children, i.e. to swaddle. See טִפֻּח under טָפַח.

טֶפַח (plur. טְפָחוֹת) masc. 1) hand's breadth, span, especially as a measure; טְפָחוֹת as an adv. a few spans, i.e. short, from which according to some טִפַּח to carry on the hands, to rear; 2) corbel (in architecture) on which the beams rest.

טֹפַח m. hand's breadth, as a measure.

טִפֻּחִים masc. pl. the nursing, rearing of children.

טָפַל (fut. יִטְפֹּל) to attach, to plaister; hence, to cover with something (with עַל), related to תָּפַל, from which תָּפֵל plaister.

טִפְסַר (pl. טִפְסְרִים) m. an officer in the army, a colonel; the word is of foreign extraction.

טָפַף origin. equiv. to דָּבַב, to trip, hence, to walk slowly, used of the coquettish gait of a woman.

טָפַר (not used) Aram. equiv. to צָפַר Heb. to be pointed, or transf. to point, to pierce. The root is also found in דָּפַר.

טְפַר (pl. טִפְרִין) Aram. masc. point, prickle, transf. to a nail; comp. צִפֹּרֶן.

טָפַשׁ to be stout, strong, related to פָּשַׁר, פָּתַר, transf. to be fat, later also transf. to be stupid, foolish, stubborn. Compare also דָּבַשׁ.

טָפַת p.n. f. (from נָטַף=טוּף, hence pearl).

טָרַד to push, to drive on; hence, transf. to the continuation of an action.

טְרַד (part. active plur. טָרְדִין, part. pass. טְרִיד) Aram. to push, drive away.

טָרָה (not used) equiv. to טָלָה to be young, fresh, blooming, sapful.

טְרוֹם (Ketib for טֶרֶם Ruth 3:14) equiv. to טֶרֶם which see.

טָרַח (Kal, not used) to take pains, to trouble oneself; hence, Hiph. הִטְרִיחַ to burden, with something heavy, Job 37:11, "also by watering he wearieth the thick cloud."

טֹרַח (with suff. טָרְחִי) masc. burden, trouble, painstaking.

טְרִי (after the form עָנִי) adj. masc. טְרִיָּה f. fresh, moist, from טָרָה.

טֶרֶם see טָרַם.

טֶרֶם (formed from טר with the termination ־ֶם, comp. עֵרֹם, צֶלֶם, תֶּלֶם, from עָר, צֵל, תֵּל) m. origin. hope, from טור I., next as an adv. expecting; hence, generally connected with the future: often connected with prepositions, like בְּטֶרֶם, מִטֶּ, etc. Sometimes טֶרֶם is connected with the pret. For טֶרֶם once in Ketib stands טְרוֹם.

טָרַף (fut. יִטְרֹף, once יִטְרַף) to tear to pieces; e.g. of the tearing to pieces (by a wild beast), of the tearing off of a leaf; comp. the root in חָרַף. Niph. pass. to be torn to pieces. Pu. the same; comp. also דָּרַב and δρεπ-ειν.

טָרַף (Kal not used) to satiate oneself; hence Hiph. to feed, to sustain; comp. τρέφ-ειν.

טֶרֶף (with suff. טַרְפִּי; const. plur. טַרְפֵּי) m. 1) that which is torn, broken off; hence, a leaf (after its being torn off); next, booty, spoil; e.g. הַרְרֵי טֶרֶף mountains of spoil, when there are beasts of prey; 2) food, nourishment, from טָרַף not connected with signification 1).

טָרָף adj. masc. to be fresh, sapful, young; from טָרַף. More likely טָרָף, Gen. 8:11, stands for מְטֹרָף, comp. אָמֻן for מְאֻמָּן.

טְרֵפָה f. that which is torn (by wild beasts) of cattle (generally connected with נְבֵלָה.

טַרְפְּלָא p.n. of an Assyrian district where the Jews were exiled to, seat of Ταρπῆτες on the Maeotic gulf (Strabo I.7:57); hence gent. noun pl. טַרְפְּלָיֵא.

י

י Jod (יוֹד) is the tenth letter of the Alphabet, and its name as well as shape corresponds with its character; as a numeral it counts 10; at the beginning of a root, י is often a substitute for ו. It interchanges 1) with נ as a demivowel, e.g. יָאַר and נָהַר to stream; יָאָה and נָאָה to be appropriate; 2) with the palatines; e.g. יָשִׁישׁ and קָשִׁישׁ; יָשַׁר and כָּשַׁר; 3) with the gutturals. יד=יוד hand.

יָאַב to long for, to desire (לְ) something; related to אָבָה and the root in תָּאַב.

יָאָה equiv. to נָאָה to be proper, suitable, with לְ of the person. See נָאָה.

יְאוֹר see יְאֹר.

יַאֲזַנְיָה p. n. m. (heard by God).

יַאֲזַנְיָהוּ p.n. m. (the same).

יָאִיר p.n. masc. (the beautiful one), patron. יָאִירִי.

I. יָאַל (וְאַל ; Kal not used) origin. to be weary, faint; hence transf. to be foolish, stupified; the root is also found in אֱוִיל. Niph. to appear foolish, to be stubborn.

II. יָאַל (וְאַל ; Kal, not used) to will, desire, to wish: hence Hiph. to strive after something, to begin, to attempt, to undertake, to consent, etc., according to the context.

יָאַר (not used) equivalent to נָהַר to stream, flow along (with the idea of swiftness), origin. to shine, like in the Samaritan.

יְאֹר (with the ה of motion יְאֹרָה, pl. יְאֹרִים, once בְּאֹר for (כִּיְאֹר) m. river, stream, equiv. to נָהָר, especially of the Nile, the pl. used of the arms, branches, of the Nile. Root יָאַר if the name is not Egyptian.

יָאַשׁ (Kal not used) to give up something, to abandon, desist from something. Niph. נוֹאַשׁ to desist from (מִן) something, i.e. to give up; part. נוֹאָשׁ despairing. Pi. to despair of something. The original signification is as in חָדַל.

יֹאשִׁיָּה p. n. m.

יֹאשִׁיָּהוּ p.n. m.

יְאָתְרַי p.n. m. (equiv. to יַעְתְּרַי the rich one).

יָבָא belongs to מוּבָא ; see (מָבוֹא).

יָבַב (Kal not used) to rejoice, to exult; hence, to sound afar off; perhaps related to אָבַב in modern Hebrew, from which אַבּוּב flute; perhaps also, to lament, to howl. Pi. יִבֵּב to call out aloud, to shout.

יְבוּל m. produce, origin. that which is gathered into the house; perhaps from בּוּל, equivalent to יָבַל transf. to wealth, property.

יְבוּס firm soil, trodden down soil, (from בּוּס). Formerly a p.n. of Jerusalem; hence gent. יְבוּסִי the Jebusite, which stands sometimes for עִיר הַיְבוּסִי.

יִבְחָר p.n. m. (the chosen one).

יָבִין p.n. masc. (the one of understanding).

יָבֵישׁ 1) p. n. masc. (deceiver, from בּוּשׁ); 2) source dried up, p.n. of a city in Gilead, on Wadi-Jabes (from בּוּשׁ).

יָבַל (Kal not used) to flow, to wave, to moisten (comp. (יָבָל) related to אָבַל, בּוּל, בָּלַל ; figur. to proceed along; comp. נָזַל and אָזַל. Pi. (not used), to dissolve, to run out (of the matter of a wound). Hiph. הוֹבִיל, equivalent to הֵבִיא, הוֹלִיךְ to bring, to lead, to cause to go in solemn procession, to deliver presents. Hoph. הוּבַל pass. to be led, carried along.

יְבַל (Peal not used), Aram. the same; hence Af. הֵיבֵל, like in the Heb. הוֹבִיל to lead, to bring.

יָבַל (not used) to exult, to shout; related to יָבַב (יב).

יָבָל (pl. const. יִבְלֵי) m. 1) stream, river; 2) p.n. m. (wanderer, nomade).

יִבְלְעָם (devourer of people) p.n. of a city in the territory of Manasseh.

יַבֶּלֶת f. swelling (of cattle), wen, a wound that runs, formed from Piel.

יָבַם (not used) of uncertain derivation; יִבֵּם is only a denom. from יָבָם.

יָבָם (with suff. יְבָמִי) m. brother-in-law, brother of the husband, from which יִבֵּם, to perform the duty of a husband's brother, i.e. to marry his widow.

יְבֵמֶת (probably also יְבֶמֶת, formed from the m. יָבָם) f. sister-in-law.

יַבְנְאֵל (erected by God) p.n. of a city.

יַבְנֶה (the same) p.n. of a Philistine city.

יִבְנְיָה p.n. m. (erected by God).

יִבְנִיָּה p.n. m. (the same).

יָבַץ (not used) equiv. to בּוּץ, to shine, to excel; from which, p.n. תֵּבֵץ, which see.

יַבֹּק (discharging of a river, from בָּקַק; or for יֵאָבֵק, from אָבַק, river of combat) p.n. of the present Wadi Serka, in the vicinity of the mountain of Gilead.

יְבֶרֶכְיָהוּ p.n. m. (blessed of God).

יָבֵשׁ p.n.; see יָבֵישׁ.

יָבֵשׁ (fut. יִיבַשׁ, יָבַשׁ, pl. יָבְשׁוּ, inf. const. יְבשׁ and יְבֹשֶׁת) to be dry, parched, withered, seared. Pi. יִבֵּשׁ to make dry. Hiph. הוֹבִישׁ, to cause to wither (of fruit, plants), but always trans. Another Hiph. form הוֹבִישׁ, is derived from בּוֹשׁ, according to the Aram. and signifies to be ashamed, to look pale; comp. הִלְבִּין.

יָבֵשׁ 1) adj. masc. יְבֵשָׁה, fem. dry, withered; 2) p.n. of a city (see יָבֵישׁ), with ה mobile יָבֵישָׁה.

יַבָּשָׁה f. the dry (land), in contrast to to the sea; hence also, dryness.

יִבְשָׂם p. n. masc. (the agreeable one).

יַבֶּשֶׁת f. the same, as יַבָּשָׁה. Both formed from the intensitive form.

יַבֶּשֶׁת (def. יַבֶּשְׁתָּא) Aram. fem. the same.

יִגְאָל p.n. m. (redeemer, avenger).

יָגַב (only part. יֹגֵב) equiv. to גּוּב, to dig, to plough; hence יֹגֵב, ploughman.

יָגֵב (for יָגִיב, comp. פָּלֶט, יָגֵעַ, for יָגִיעַ, פָּלִיט) masc. that which is ploughed (arable land).

יָגְבְּהָה (with ה mobile יָגְבְּהָה) p.n. of

a place in the territory of Gad (high place).

יְגַדַּלְיָהוּ p.n. m. (reared by God).

יָגָה (Kal not used) to grieve, to weary oneself, related to יָגַע, from which, next, to be mournful, sad. Niph. נוּגָה, to be afflicted; particip. נוּגָה f. (pl. נוּגוֹת, pl. const. m. נוּגֵי) for נוֹגָה (comp. מוּסָר for מוֹסָר); hence, Zeph. 3:18 "they that are sorrowful for (absent from) the solemn assembly." Pi. יִגָּה (fut. וַיֹּגֶה) to afflict, to sadden. Hiph. הוֹגָה, to cause grief. הֹגָה 2 Samuel 20:13, belongs to הָגָה.

יָגוֹן (with suff. יְגוֹנָם) masc. grief, affliction.

יָגוּר (dwelling place) p.n. of a place in the territory of Judah.

יְגִיעַ 1) adj. masc. wearied, but also as subst. the wearied one; 2) exertion, fatigue (only const. יְגִיעַ); hence, that which is got by labour, e.g. a work, possession, wealth.

יְגִיעָה f. exertion, fatigue, labour.

יָגְלִי p.n. m. (the exiled).

יָגַן belongs to נָגַן. See נָתַת.

יָגַע (fut. יִיגַע) origin. equiv. to יָגָה; hence, transf. to labour for (בְּ) something, to be wearied of (בְּ) a matter, to work indefatigably. Pi. to weary, to tire out. Hiph. to trouble, weary some one.

יְגָע m. that which is got by work, property, wealth.

יָגֵעַ (secondary form from יָגִיעַ) adj. m. tired, fatigued, troublesome.

יָגַר (not used) Aram. to accumulate, to heap up; related to אָגַר, Aram. זְגַר.

יְגַר (Aram.) m. heap, hill, heap of stones.

יָגֹר to fear; with מִפְּנֵי or the accus. that of which one is in fear; comp. גּוּר.

יָגֹר (יָגוֹר) adj. m. fearing.

יָד (const. יַד, with suff. יָדִי, יֶדְכֶם) com. 1) origin. the limb which seizes, the hand; from יָדָה, equiv. to הָדַד to lay hold of, the dual יָדַיִם of the hands of the human body; the pl. יָדוֹת artificial hands, tenons, stays (of a throne), axletrees; 2) transf. to power, might, help (by force), force, blow, punishment; 3) side (origin. hand) of a subject, e.g. side of a river; hence with prepositions לְיַד at the side, near by, also בְּעַד יַד, עַל־יְדֵי, עַל־יַד, אֶל־יַד; hence also יָדַיִם both sides, e.g. רַחַב יָדַיִם large on both sides; 4) place; dual, places; 5) hand-ful; hence, portion, part, especially, יָדוֹת transf. to times, e.g. so many times, as an adv.; 6) monument, origin. guide. The most manifold forms and phrases are joined with יָד, and must be rendered according to context, e.g. the hand is against (בְּ some one), i.e. to punish him; but also for some one to assist; the hand is heavy, i.e. rests heavily upon (אֶל) the hand of God is (i.e. rests) upon (עַל) some one; to turn the hand (עַל, אֶל) upon (הֵשִׁיב) some one; נָתַן יָד תַּחַת to give the hand, i.e. to conclude a matter by giving the hand; to subject oneself; יָד לְיָד from hand to hand, i.e. from generation to generation; בְּיַד through, by, with, before, at hand, etc.; כְּיַד according to the power, dignity; בֵּין יָדַיִם on the breast, comp. בֵּין עֵינַיִם, on the forehead; other forms will be found in verbs

יַד (def. יְדָא, with suff. יְדָךְ, יְדְהֹם, dual יְדַיִן) Aram. com. the same in the most manifold applications.

יְדָא (Peal not used) Aram. origin. to name, to pronounce, related to בְּטָא, hence transf. to 1) to pronounce, declare, confess; 2) to praise. Af. הוֹדָא, partic. מְהוֹדֵא but also מוֹדֵא to praise, to thank.

יִדְאֲלָה (the exalted one), p.n. of a city in the territory of Zebulun.

יִדְבָּשׁ p.n. m. (the sweet, agreeable one).

יָדַד (not used) orig. to join some one, to befriend, or to be connected with some one, to love; related to דּוֹד; יְדוֹ belongs to יָדָה.

I. יָדָה (imp. יִדּוּ) to thrust down; more frequently in Pi. יִדָּה (inf. יַדּוֹת) of the casting of lots, of the casting out of the horns of the Gentiles.

II. יָדָה (Kal not used) origin. to name, to pronounce; hence Hiph. הוֹדָה 1) to declare, confess, with עַל to make a confession of something; 2) to praise, i.e. the name of some one, or to proclaim loudly; hence to praise God, שֵׁם יי״, הוֹדָה בְּשֵׁם, also construed with לְ. Hithp. הִתְוַדָּה 1) to confess of oneself, to repent, the object construed with the accus. or with עַל; 2) to praise, joined with לְ.

יִדּוֹ p.n. m. (the loving one).

יָדוֹן p.n. m. (the judge).

יַדּוּעַ p.n. m. (the reputed one).

יְדוּתוּן p.n. masc. (the praised one); For which occurs also יְדֻתוּן and יְדִיתוּן.

יַדַּי (Keri) p.n. masc. (the beloved one).

יָדִיד (const. יְדִיד) adj. m. יְדִידָה (pl. יְדִידוֹת) f. lovely, agreeable, orig. to be joined, from which subst. friend; the fem. pl. that which is beloved, loveliness.

יְדִידָה p.n. fem. (the beloved one)

יְדִידוּת f. love, friendship (transf. to the object of love).

יְדִידְיָה p n. m. (beloved of God).

יְדָיָה p.n. m. (nominated by God).

יְדִיעֲאֵל p.n.m. (distinguished by God).

יְדִיתוּן see יְדוּתוּן.

יִדְלָף p.n. m. the poor one.

יָדַע (fut. יֵדַע, once יִידַע, for יִידַע) comp. in the Hiph. יֵילִיל ,יֵיטִיב; inf. abs. יָדֹעַ, (const. דַּעַת) orig. to perceive by the sight, to see; hence, to recognise, like שָׁמַע to perceive by hearing; טָעַם to perceive by tasting, but all three words are mostly applied to mental perceptions, without reference to the physical one. The significations in use are manifold: 1) to perceive (by seeing, touching, hearing); hence, to suppose, suspect, experience, to feel, to augur, to know, in consequence of physical perception, with בְּ to know by something; transf. to recognize one, also of conjugal cohabitation either of man or woman; 2) to distinguish, יָדַע בְּשֵׁם to point out by name, יֹדֵעַ acquaintance, friend; יְדוּעַ confidant; 3) to understand, to be wise, prudent; hence יוֹדֵעַ equiv. to חָכָם; from which, next, to know of, about something, with בְּ, עַל, also to search, inquire. Niph. נוֹדַע pass. to be or become known by physical means; hence, to feel, to experience, to suffer. Pi. to appoint. Pu. to be known; hence, מְיֻדָּע acquaintance. Po. to make known, to appoint. Hiph. הוֹדִיעַ (imp. הוֹדַע) to make known, with double accus.; to announce, with לְ of the person, to instruct, to reprove, to punish (i.e. to make some one know or feel, always causative from Kal). Hoph. to become known. Hithp. הִתְוַדַּע to make oneself known, to reveal oneself (אֶל) to some one.

יָדָע p.n. m. (one possessing knowledge).

יְדַע (fut. יִנְדַּע) Aram. the same; Af. הוֹדַע (fut. יְהוֹדַע) to make known, to announce.

יְדַעְיָה p.n. masc. one who possesses knowledge of God.

יִדְּעֹנִי (plur. יִדְּעֹנִים) m. 1) spirit of oracle, origin. the knowing one; 2) he who possesses the spirit of oracles. The form is from יָדַע, with the termination וֹן—.

יָהּ the poetic abbreviated name of יְהוָֹה, with the same signification as יְהוָֹה God, sometimes joined to יְהֹ or אֱלֹהִים; in proper nouns the form changes into יוֹ ,יְהוֹ, etc.

יָהַב (imp. הַב, with the ה of motion הָבָה, f. הָבִי, pl. הָבוּ where the accent, on account of the ה, remains on the first syllable) to give, equiv. to נָתַן, from which next, to set, to lay, to impart, to set up, all proceeding from the sense of to give. Respecting הָבוּ see הוּב.

יְהַב (part. pass. יְהִיב which is conjugated יְהִיבָה, יְהִיבוּ) Aram. to give, to expose (the life), transf. to lay a foundation, to set down something, like in Heb. Hithp. אִתְיְהֵב to be given, delivered up.

יָהַד (Kal, not used) denom. from יְהוּדָה or from the abbreviated form יְהוּד, but only Hith. הִתְיַהֵד to declare oneself a Jew, to become a Jew, to confess to Judaism. Similar formations occur in modern Hebrew.

יְהְדַּי p.n. m. (one that seizes).

יֵהוּא p.n. m. (the living one, from הָוָא).

יְהוֹאָחָז p.n.m. (God is the supporter).

יְהוֹאָשׁ p.n. m. (God is the donor).

יְהוּד Aram. 1) equiv. to יְהוּדָה, Judæa, the land of Judah; 2) like יְהוּדָה also as a designation of the Jewish people.

יְהוּדָה 1) p.n. m. (the praised one), hence the tribe so called after him, and later, the whole Jewish people: 2) designation of the territory which belonged to this tribe; hence, עִיר יְה׳ Jerusalem; later including the territory of the tribe of Benjamin, and ultimately used for the whole of Palestine.

יְהוּדִי gent. n. m. from יְהוּדָה, plur. יְהוּדִים and יְהוּדִיִּים, f. יְהוּדִיָּה and יְהוּדִית, Jew, Jewess, i.e. citizen of the empire of Judæa: later, Jew, Hebrew, Israelite, as the general name of the people. יְהוּדִית also as an adv. signifies: in Hebrew, i.e. in the Hebrew language.

יְהוּדַי (pl. יְהוּדָאִין, def. pl. יְהוּדָאֵי, יְהוּדָיֵא) Aram. the same.

יְהוּדִית p.n. f. (Jewess).

יְהֹוָה p.n. of the mighty God of the Hebrews. This name is formed from the fut. הָוָה to be, from which so many proper nouns are formed, and therefore signifies: the ever existing one, as God calls himself אֶהְיֶה אֲשֶׁר אֶהְיֶה in the 1st person. Properly the word should be pointed יַהְוֶה, but as this name was not allowed to be pronounced by the Jews on account of its sanctity, they pronounced instead of it אֲדֹנָי Lord, from which they took the vowel-points. With prefixes this name is sounded בַּיהוָֹה, מֵיהוָֹה, לַיהוָֹה, as if אֲדֹנָי stood; but if אֲדֹנָי follows, יהוה assumes the vowels of אֱלֹהִים, and is then pointed יֱהוִֹה.

יְהוֹזָבָד p.n. m. (presented by God).

יְהוֹחָנָן p.n. m. (graced by God).

יְהוֹיָדָע p.n. m. (beloved of God).

יְהוֹיָכִין p.n. m. (appointed by God).

יְהוֹיָקִים p.n. m. (established by God).

יְהוֹיָרִיב p.n. m. (God leads the cause).

יְהוּכַל p.n. m. (able one).

יְהוֹנָדָב p.n. m. (God is benevolent).

יְהוֹנָתָן p.n. m. (God is the giver).

יְהוֹסֵף p.n. m. (the multiplier).

יְהוֹעַדָּה p.n. masc. (God is his ornament).

יְהוֹעַדָּן p.n. m. (God is his diadem). The Keri has יְהוֹעַדִּין, which is the same.

יְהוֹצָדָק p.n. m. (God is just).

יְהוֹרָם p.n. m. (God is exalted).

יְהוֹשֶׁבַע p.n. m. (God is the covenant), for which also יְהוֹשַׁבְעַת, which signifies the same.

יְהוֹשׁוּעַ p.n. m. (God is the help).

יְהוֹשֻׁעַ p.n. m. (the same).

יְהוֹשָׁפָט p.n. m. (God is the judge).

יָהִיר adj. m. proud, haughty, overbearing. See יָהַר.

יְהַלֶּלְאֵל p.n. masc. (one who praises God).

יַהֲלֹם m. name of a precious stone, so called on account of its hardness. Root הָלַם equiv. to חָלַם to be hard, strong.

יָהַץ (not used) to tread down, to stamp down with the feet; from which—

יַהַץ (with the ה of motion יַהְצָה, p.n. of a Moabite city (place), trodden down.

יָהַר (not used) equiv. to הָרָה, הָדַר, to be high; hence, Aram. Ithpe. אִתְיְהַר to exalt oneself, to be proud.

יוֹאָב p.n. m. (God is Father).

יוֹאָח p.n. m. (God is the helper).

יוֹאָחָז p.n. m. (God is the supporter).

יוֹאֵל p.n. m. (one strong in will).

יוֹאָשׁ p.n. m. (God is the donor).

יוֹב p.n. m. (one who returns, from אוב=יוב).

יוֹבָב p.n. m. and the name of an Arabian people (one who rejoices, or dweller in the desert, after the Arab.).

יוֹבֵל (also יֹבֵל; pl. יוֹבְלִים) masc. 1) jubilation, shouting with joy, from יָבַל, to jubilate, to exult, in connection with קֶרֶן or שׁוֹפָר; horn or trumpet of shouting מְשֹׁךְ בְּקֶרֶן הַיּוֹבֵל, or also מְשֹׁךְ הַיּוֹבֵל (where קֶרֶן is omitted), to blow the horn of rejoicing; 2) horn of the jubilee, omitting קֶרֶן or שׁוֹפָר; hence שְׁנַת הַיּוֹבֵל the year of the jubilee horn, the fiftieth year, which was announced to the people by the jubilee horn. Sometimes יוֹבֵל alone stands for it, without שְׁנַת, and without קֶרֶן.

יוּבָל p.n. masc. (the rejoicer or the

player on the timbrel, from יָבַל) stands for יְבָל, and is formed like גּוּמָץ and others.

יוּבַל m. equiv. to יָבָל, stream, river, from יָבַל. The form is Aramaic.

יוֹזָבָד p.n. m. (God is the donor).

יוֹזָכָר p.n. m. (God excels in fame).

יוֹחָא p.n. m. (revived by God) perhaps an abbreviation from יוֹחָנָן.

יוֹחָנָן p.n. m. (God is gracious).

יוֹיָדָע p.n. m. (God is his friend).

יוֹיָכִין p.n. m. (appointed by God).

יוֹיָקִים p.n. m. (established by God).

יוֹיָרִיב p.n. m. (God leads his cause).

יוֹכֶבֶד p.n. f. (God is her fame).

יוּכַל p.n. m. (the able one)

יוֹם (pl. יָמִים, as from יָם, const. יְמֵי, seldom יָמִין, poetically יְמוֹת, dual יוֹמַיִם) com. day, either including the night, or in contrast to night; יוֹם is applied to signify a special day, e.g. day of fortune or misfortune, birth, festival, coronation, battle, judgment-day, or of any appointed time. As an adverb (origin. accus.) by day, יוֹם יוֹם, יוֹם וָיוֹם, בְּכָל יוֹם וָיוֹם, כָּל הַיּוֹם, יוֹם בְּיוֹם, לְיוֹם בְּיוֹם, day by day, daily; כְּיוֹם בְּיוֹם, as daily. With the def. article הַ, הַיּוֹם, it is almost an adverb, and signifies, to day, by day, at this time, at that time; בַּיּוֹם, on the day, immediately, recently; כַּיּוֹם now, this day; כַּיּוֹם הַזֶּה as now, as at this time, also, at this time; מִיּוֹם from the time, when, since. The plur. יָמִים, rare after the Aram. manner יָמִין is used to express "some." יָמִים indef. signifies, days, or also time indefinitely; also a year, e.g. זֶבַח הַיָּמִים the yearly offering; מִיָּמִים יָמִימָה from year to year. As to the derivation יוֹם or יָם it is primitive, without any verbal root.

יוֹם (def. יוֹמָא, pl. יוֹמִין, const. יוֹמָת, יְמֵי, def. יוֹמַיָּא) Aram. the same.

יוֹמָם (from יוֹם, with the termination ־ָם, comp. רֵיקָם) adv. by day, daily, the whole day.

יון (not used) to ferment; hence, יָוֵן from יון, after the form בַּיִת from בּוּת.

יָוֵן (const. יְוַן) masc. mire, a slough, pool; hence, יְ׳ מְצוּלָה deep mire; טִיט הַיָּ׳ miry clay, formed from יון, on account of the rising of the pool. Comp. טִיט.

יָוָן 1) p.n. m. (the young one), next, the name of a people and country, Ionia, Greece; an Ionian, a Greek, e.g. מֶלֶךְ יָוָן, of Alexander. The Hebrews called the Greeks, Ionians; 2) name of a city in Arabia.

יוֹנָדָב p.n. m. (God is munificent).

יוֹנָה (pl. יוֹנִים) f. 1) a dove; בְּנֵי י׳,

a young dove; יוֹנָתִי, my young dove, term of caressing. Another יוֹנָה, see under יָנָה; 2) p. n. of a well-known prophet.

יְוָנִי patron. from יָוָן, pl. יְוָנִים Greeks, Ionians; בְּנֵי הַיְּוָנִים the Greeks.

יוֹנֵק (origin. part.) m. 1) suckling; 2) young branch, as being a suckling offspring of the tree.

יוֹנֶקֶת fem. offspring, sprout, young branch.

יוֹנָתָן p. n. m. (God is the giver).

יוֹסֵף p. n. masc. (multiplier) בֵּית י׳, בְּנֵי י׳, also יוֹסֵף alone for Ephraim and Manasseh, as the progeny of Joseph, and later for the ten tribes, and also for the whole of Israel.

יוֹסִפְיָה p. n. m. (God is the multiplier).

יוֹעֵאלָה p. n. m. (the useful one).

יוֹעֵד p. n. m. (God is the witness).

יוֹעֶזֶר p. n. m. (God is the help).

יוֹעָשׁ p. n. m. (God is the assembler).

יוֹצָדָק p. n. m. (God is just).

יוֹצֵר (origin. a part.) m. origin. one that forms things generally; next, 1) potter, collect. the potters, כְּלִי הַיּוֹצֵר potter's vessel. But it is also applied to one who works at stones to form something; 2) creator, as being the former of things. See יָצַר.

יוֹקִים p. n. m. (God is the reviver).

יוֹרֶה (for מוֹרֶה) m. 1) the fertilizing rain, from הוֹרָה, in contrast to מַלְקוֹשׁ; 2) יוֹרָה p. n. m. one born in autumn, otherwise חָרִיף.

יוֹרַי p. n. m. (the same as יוֹרָה).

יוֹרָם (God is exalted).

יוּשַׁב חֶסֶד p. n. m. (one to whom homage is paid).

יוֹשִׁבְיָה p. n. m. (one who dwells with God).

יוֹשָׁה p. n. m. (able one).

יוֹשַׁוְיָה p. n. m. (God is sufficient).

יוֹשָׁפָט p. n. m. (God is judge).

יוֹתָם p. n. m. (God is perfect).

יוֹתֵר (also יֹתֵר after the form שׁוֹרֵק) m. the superfluous, the remainder (from the necessary supply); hence, gain, advantage, preference; as an adv. more; י׳ מִן more than, besides (see יֶתֶר); יוֹתֵר שֶׁ besides that.

יוֹתֶרֶת f. that which remained, hanging over; generally, with the addition מִן הַכָּבֵד, הַכָּבֵד, עַל הַכָּבֵד to signify the flap which hangs over the liver or the midriff.

יָזָה (not used) to assemble, after the Arab.

יְזִיאֵל p. n. m. (God is the assembler).

יִזִּיָּה for (יְזִיָּה) p. n. m. (the same).

יָזִיז p. n. masc. the prominent one, from זוּז.

יִזְלִיאָה p. n. m.

יְזַנְיָה p. n. m. (God hearkens).

יְזַנְיָהוּ p. n. m. (the same).

יָוֵם see יָמַם.

יָוֶן see יוּן, אָוֶן.

יָזַע (not used) equivalent to זוּעַ, to run, to drip, to drop; from which:—

יֶזַע m. the sweat running from the body; יֶזַע may have been formed from זוּעַ and equiv. to זֵעָה, so that the root יָזַע is dropped.

יִזְרָח p.n. m. (native one, denizen).

יִזְרַחְיָה p.n. m. (he who dwells with God).

יִזְרְעֶאל (also —עֶא) 1) p.n. masc. (God is the planter); 2) p.n. of a city where Ahab resided, in the vicinity of which there was a valley called עֵמֶק יִזְרְעֶאל. Gent. —עֵאלִי, f. —עֵלִית, or —עֵאלִית.

יָחַד (fut. יֵחַד) equiv. to אָחַד to join, to be united, origin. to be like one, with (אֵת, בְּ) somebody. Pi. יִחֵד to join, to unite oneself. The original idea lies in אֶחָד, as יָחִיד shews.

יַחַד m. union, connection; hence as an adv. together, in common with, jointly; or of time, simultaneously, with סָבִיב around altogether.

יַחְדָּו (also יַחְדָּיו) adverb for יַחְדּוֹ, formed from יַחַד, in the same manner as לְבַדּוֹ, כֻּלּוֹ. In reference to its signification it is used as an adverb, like יַחַד together, altogether, at the same time, at the same place.

יַחְדּוֹ (for יַחְדּוֹן) p.n. m. (the united one).

יַחְדִּיאֵל p. n. m. (rejoiced by God).

יֶחְדְּיָהוּ p.n. m. (the same).

יַחֲזִאֵל p.n. m. (revived by God).

יַחֲזִיאֵל p.n. m. (seer of God).

יַחְזְיָה p.n. m. (the same).

יְחֶזְקֵאל p.n. masc. (strengthened by God); comp. יְחִזְקִיָּה.

יְחִזְקִיָּה p.n. m. (the same).

יְחִזְקִיָּהוּ p.n. m. (the same).

יַחְזֵרָה p.n. m. (the returner).

יְחִיאֵל p. n. m. (he who lives in God), patron. יְחִיאֵלִי.

יָחִיד (pl. יְחִידִים) adj. m. יְחִידָה fem. only one, single one, without an associate or fellow, e.g. of an only son, an only daughter; pl. יְחִידִים single ones, scattered ones; יְחִידָה the only one, life.

יָחִיל adj. m. (a lengthened form of יָחֵל) waiting, hoping.

יָחַל (Kal not used) equiv. to חוּל to wait, to hope; hence, Pi. 1) to long, to hope for (אֶל, לְ) some one, to trust in some one; 2) to give hope. Hiph. הוֹחִיל to long, to wait for (לְ) something, to have hopes, expectations. Niph. נוֹחַל (fut. יִיָּחֵל) to expect, to abide.

יַחְלְאֵל p.n. masc. (waiting upon the Lord), patron. —לְאֵלִי.

יָחַם an extended form from חַם to be warm, glowing, figur. to become ardent, to conceive; hence, the form יֶחֱמַתְנִי from יָחֶמָה, and the pl. יֶחֱמוּ. Pi. to conceive. See חָמַם.

יַחְמוּר m. (a species of stag or hart, of a reddish colour). Root חָמַר.

יַחְמַי p.n. m. (protector).

יָחַף (not used) to be bare, naked; related to חָף, transf. to bare-footed.

יָחֵף adj. m. bare-footed.

יַחְצְאֵל (allotted by God) patronym. יַחְצְאֵלִי.

יַחֲצִיאֵל p.n. m. (the same).

יָחַר see אָחַר.

יָחַשׂ (not used) to sprout, to originate, formed from וָחַשׂ. Hith. הִתְיַחֵשׂ, see under יַחַשׂ.

יַחַשׂ m. tribe, family, generation, from יָחַשׂ to sprout; hence, סֵפֶר הַיַּ׳ book of generations, genealogical registry. From which denom. הִתְיַחֵשׂ to inscribe oneself in the genealogical books, and from which the inf. noun is הִתְיַחֵשׂ inscription in such registers; or as an adv. according to genealogical register.

יַחַת (from יַחֶדֶת) p.n. m. (union).

יָטַב (only fut. יִיטַב ,יֵטַב, once תֵּיטְבִי, the pret. is taken from טוֹב) equiv. to טוֹב to be bright, to be beautiful; hence, transf. to be joyful, with לֵב; comp. צָהַל, שָׂמַח to be pure, good, especially to be morally good, יִיטַב לִי it will be well with me; וַיִּיטַב בְּעֵין פ׳ it pleased some one; seldom const. with לִפְנֵי, or לְ. Hiph. הֵיטִיב (fut. יֵיטִיב ,יֵטִיב, once יְיֵטִיב) to make beautiful, pleasant, good, right, also in a moral sense. The inf. הֵיטֵב is used as an adverb, good, proper, careful, etc.

יְטַב (fut. יִיטַב) Aram. the same; with עַל, to be kind to some one.

יָטְבָה (beautiful town) p.n. of a place.

יָטְבָתָה (the same, comp. Agathopolis) p.n. of a place in the desert, which abounded in brooks.

יֻטָּה (also יוּטָה, probably =יוּטְבָה equiv. to יָטְבָה) p.n. of a place in the territory of Judah.

יְטוּר (Nomade village) p.n. m.; next, designation of a tribe of the people of the Itureans; their territory, Iturea, was on the lake Tiberias.

יַיִן (const. יֵין) masc. wine, בֵּית הַיַּיִן wine-house. If יון "to ferment," is the root, יַיִן bears analogy to חֶמֶר; but it is probable that the primitive form (וין) is not of a Semitic derivation.

יַךְ once for יַד, which see.

יָכַח (Kal, not used) to be strong, firm (in Arab. transf. to make firm).

From which Hiph. הוֹכִיחַ 1) to confirm, figur. to prove, to justify; 2) to arbitrate, to decide, in a court of justice; 3) to punish, to reprove, and many other modifications, according to the context. Hoph. to be reproved, punished. Niph. נוֹכַח 1) parties respectively attempting to prove their cause; 2) to be punished, נוֹכַחַתְּ 2 pers. pret. thou art punished, judged. Hith. הִתְוַכַּח respectively to plead a cause; different to נָכַח, from which נֹכַח and נָכוֹחַ.

יְכִילְיָה (Ketib) p.n. m. (rendered able by God).

יָכִין p.n.m. (firm, strong one), patron. יָכִינִי.

יָכֹל (also יָכוֹל; fut. from Hoph. יוּכַל, inf. יָכוֹל, const. יְכֹלֶת) to contain, to comprise, to endure, to be able, equiv. to כּוּל, הָכַל Aram. כְּהַל; hence, to be able (with the accus. or the inf. following, with or without לְ), physically or morally; hence also, to conquer, to prevail over (לְ) some one.

יְכֵל, יְכִל (fut. יִכֻּל and יוּכַל) equiv. to יָכֹל to be able, to prevail.

יְכָלְיָה p.n. f. (enabled by God).

יְכָלְיָהוּ p.n. f. (the same).

יְכָנְיָה p.n. m. (appointed by God).

יְכָנְיָהוּ p.n. m. (the same).

יָלַד (fut. יֵלֵד, inf. יְלֹד, const. לֶדֶת and לֵדָה, once לְדֹת) to bear, to bring forth, to beget (of man and beast); hence, figur. to create, to form, to nominate, also to lay eggs: יוֹלֵדָה she that bears, i.e. a mother. Niph. נוֹלַד to be born, with אֶת before the object. יִלֵּד to assist in bearing, of the midwife. Pu. יֻלַּד (יוּלַּד) to be born. Hiph. הוֹלִיד 1) once, to cause to be born, i.e. to fructify; 2) to beget (of the father). Hoph. like Pu.; hence, הֻלֶּדֶת or יוֹם הֻלֶּדֶת birth-day. Hith. הִתְיַלֵּד origin. a denom. from (סֵפֶר) תּוֹלְדוֹת to inscribe oneself in the genealogical register. Comp. הִתְיַחֵשׂ.

יֶלֶד (plur. יְלָדִים, const. יַלְדֵי, and יִלְדֵי) masc. that which is born; hence, a child; of beasts, the young; יַלְדֵי נָכְרִים strangers' children; next, youth, generally.

יַלְדָּה (from יֶלֶד) fem. origin. *nata*; hence girl.

יַלְדוּת fem. age of יֶלֶד youthful age, boyhood; concrete, youth, generally.

יִלּוֹד (after the form שִׁכּוֹר, גִּבּוֹר, יִסּוֹר) m. one that is born.

יָלוֹן p.n. masc. he that tarries over night.

יָלִיד (const. יְלִיד, const. pl. יְלִידֵי) m. one that is born, בַּיִת יְ׳ *οἰκογενής*, one born in the house, a slave;

but also, son, like יֶלֶד descendent, progeny.

יָלַךְ (only fut. יֵלֵךְ, imp. לֵךְ, inf. לֶכֶת, but pret. of Kal, Niph., Pi., and Hith. belong to הָלַךְ) equiv. to הָלַךְ to go, which see. Hiph. הוֹלִיךְ and הֵילִיךְ to cause to go, to lead; of things, to carry away; figuratively, to destroy, of the water, to become shallow. See הָלַךְ.

יָלַל (Kal not used) equiv. to אָלַל to wail, to lament; hence, Hiph. הֵילִיל (fut. יְיֵלִיל, יְהֵילִיל) to attune lamentations. The noun תּוֹלָל belongs to תָּלַל II., הוֹלֵלוֹת under הָלַל, שׁוֹלָל under שָׁלַל.

יְלֵל m. howling (of beasts); hence, of the howling in the desert.

יְלָלָה (const. יִלְלַת) f. lament, wailing.

יָלַע (rare) to pronounce incautiously, equiv. to לָעָה, which see.

יָלַף (not used), to attach; transf. to cling, to adhere firmly; comp. לָוָה, אָלַף.

יַלֶּפֶת f. a scab.

יָלַק (not used), equiv. to לָקַק to lick off, to eat off.

יֶלֶק m. a species of locust, originally that which nibbles off. Perhaps יֶלֶק is formed direct from לָקַק.

יָם (from יָמַם; const. יָם and יַם, with ה mobile יָמָּה, pl. יַמִּים) m. the sea, the ocean; next, generally, great rivers, as the Nile and the Euphrates; transferred to the West, on account of the Mediterranean being west of Palestine; hence, רוּחַ יָם west wind; פְּאַת יָם west side; יָמָּה towards the west; מִיָּם from the west; the compounds of יָם, with pp. nn. of certain seas and oceans, see under סוּף, עֲרָבָה, פְּלִשְׁתִּים, מֶלַח, כִּנֶּרֶת, מִצְרַיִם; besides this occurs also הַיָּם הַגָּדוֹל הָאַחֲרוֹן the great, uttermost sea, i. e. the Mediterranean; הַיָּם הַקַּדְמֹנִי the Eastern sea, i. e. the Dead Sea; comp. also נְחֹשֶׁת.

יָם (def. יַמָּא) Aram. the same.

יָם belongs to יָמִים, יָמוֹת, see יוֹם.

יֵם (only pl. יֵמִים) masc. a hot well, from יוֹם, equiv. to חוֹם, so that יֵמִים is synom. with חַמִּים Therma, hot wells being found in this district, (the Author. Version renders it "mules.").

יְמוּאֵל p. n. m. (light of God, from יָם, equiv. to יוֹם).

יְמִימָה p. n. f. (dove, after the Arab. fcrm.)

יָמִין (const. יְמִין) masc. 1) the right side (from יָמַן, origin. to be firm, strong, which see), e. g. שׁוֹק יָמִין, עַיִן—, יָרֵךְ—, יָד— right shank, eye, thigh, hand, especially, the right hand, transf. to, on the right, i. e. the south, מִימִין southern; 2) transf. to fortune, as the right side is the sign of luck; if not, יָמַן, in this sense, equiv. to מָנָה, signifies, to make happy; 3) p.n. m. the happy one, patron. יָמִינִי; from which denom. Hiph. הֵימִין הֶאֱמִין, הֵמִין to turn (the face) to the right, particip. מֵימִין in contrast to הַשְׂמְאִיל.

יְמִינִי (formed from יָמִין) origin. adj. m. right, fortunate, mostly in the derivation of the gen. from בִּנְיָמִין, where יָמִין generally is separated from בֵּן, or בֵּן is entirely omitted, e.g. בֶּן־הַיְמִינִי, בֶּן־יְמִינִי.

יִמְלָא p.n. m. (one that fulfils).

יִמְלָה p.n. m. (the same).

יַמְלֵךְ p.n. m. (ruler).

יָמַם (not used) 1) equiv. to הָמַם to roar, of the roaring waves, from which יָם, which see; 2) equiv. to חָמַם, from which יְמִימָה.

יָמַן (not used) 1) equiv. to אָמַן to support, to make firm, or to be firm, strong; 2) equiv. to מָנָה to make happy; for the denom. הֵמִין, see under יָמִין.

יִמְנָה p.n. m. (the fortunate one).

יְמָנִי (from the old form יָמָן) adj. m. יְמָנִית f. on the right, in contrast to the left.

יִמְנָע p.n. m. (the reserved one).

יָמַר (Kal not used) equiv. to מוּר to change, to exchange: hence, Hiph. הֵימִיר to exchange, if הֵימִיר does not stand for הֵמִיר.—Hith. הִתְיַמֵּר to exchange oneself with somebody, (בְּ) to take some one's place; if in בִּכְבוֹדָם תִּתְיַמָּרוּ (Isa. 61:6) "in their glory you shall supersede them," does not stand for הִתְאַמֵּר (Ps. 94:4).

יִמְרָה p.n. masc. (the rebellious one).

יָמַשׁ (Kal not used) to feel, to grope, only Hiph. (Ketib) הֵימִישׁ to cause to grope. See מָשַׁשׁ.

יָנָה (fut. יִינֶה, part. f. יוֹנָה) to oppress, to exact, synom. with חָמַס, עָשַׁק, שָׁדַד, it is also the active of עָנָה II. inasmuch as י is connected with the palatines ח, ע, ג; hence, הָעִיר הַיּוֹנָה the oppressive city; חֶרֶב הַיּוֹנָה the oppressive sword, and with the omission of חֶרֶב; e.g. חֲרוֹן (מֵחֶרֶב) הַיּוֹנָה; נִינָם יַחַד we will oppress them altogether. Hiph. הוֹנָה (fut. יוֹנֶה) to press hard, transf. (like עָשַׁק) to cheat, to deceive. יוֹנָה as a noun, belongs to יוֹן.

יָנוֹחַ (place of repose) p.n. of a place on the borders of the tribes of Ephraim and Manasseh.

יָנוּם (probably for יָנוּן propagation, transplanting) p.n. of a place in the territory of Judah.

יָנוּם (place of refuge), p.n. of a

place; it stands for יָנוּם in the Keri.

יָנַ belongs to הֵנִּיחַ, see נוּחַ.

יְנִיקָה f. sprout, branch. See יוֹנֶקֶת.

יָנַק (fut. יִינַק) to suck (at the breast); origin. to moisten (comp. נָקָה to drink); transf. to enjoy, e.g. שֶׁפַע יַמִּים of the abundance of the seas; יוֹנֵק suckling. Hiph. הֵינִיק to suckle; hence particip. f. מֵינֶקֶת (with suffix מֵינִקְתִּי) wet-nurse, nurse; but also to cause to enjoy, causative from Kal.

יַנְשׁוּף (־שׁוּף) m. according to tradition, night-bird, the owl; according to others, a bittern, from נָשַׁף to blow.

יָסַד (fut. יִסַּד for יִיסַד, infin. יְסוֹד) origin. to set; comp. the intrans. סוּד to sit; transferred to found. Niph. נוֹסַד; 1) to sit down (in order to consult); comp. סוֹד seat (for consultation); hence generally, to take counsel; 2) to be founded. Pi. יִסַּד to found, also with accusative of the material of which the foundation is laid; fig. to arrange, to appoint. Pu. to be founded. Hoph. הוּסַד the same; hence the infin. the founding; מוּסָד מוּסָּד that which is perfectly founded. See סוּד.

יְסַד m. foundation (of a thing), beginning.

יְסֹדוֹת see יְסוֹד.

יְסוֹד (pl. ־דִים, ־דוֹת) m. foundation, e.g. of the altar, house, world, fortification; fig. the distinguished one.

יְסוּדָה f. foundation, origin.

יִסּוֹר (after the form יִלּוֹד, גִּבּוֹר) m. master, instructor, guide; according to others, יִסּוֹר is the fut. of Kal, from יָסַר, which see.

יָסוּר (plur. with suff. יְסוּרַי Ketib, formed from סוּר) masc. one that turns away, revolts.

יָסַךְ (only fut. יִיסַךְ, which only stands for יוּסַךְ), see סוּךְ and נָסַךְ.

יִסְכָּה p.n. f. (one that watches, observes).

יִסְמַכְיָהוּ p.n. m. (God is the supporter).

יָסַף (only pret., probably the imp. סְפוּ and inf. סְפוֹת, with a fem. termination as in זְמוֹרת, חֲנוֹת, שְׁמוֹת) equiv. to אָסַף to gather; hence, to add, to multiply, with עַל or אֶל and לְ, with inf. following, to repeat, to continue. Niph. נוֹסַף to increase, to add, with עַל; נוֹסָפוֹת additions. Hiph. הוֹסִיף (fut. יוֹסִיף apoc. יוֹסֵף) like Kal. The forms יֹאסֵף, יֹאסִף, יֹאסִיף, are the same as יוֹסִיף, and arose from the original identification with the root אָסַף.

יְסַף (Aram.) the same; hence Hoph.

(after the Hebrew form) הוּסַף to be added.

יָסַר (part. יֹסֵר, fut. יִסֹּר for יִיסֹר, like יִסֹּד for יִיסֹד; hence 1 pers. אֶסֹּר for אִיסֹר, with suff. אֶסֳּרֵם Hos. 10:10) to chastise, to punish, origin. to bind, related to אָסַר; figur. to instruct. Niph. נוֹסַר to be chastised, next figur. to be instructed, to take instruction. Pi. יִסֵּר (fut. יְיַסֵּר, inf. also יַסֹּר and יַסְּרָה) to punish, to chastise, to exhort, to reprove, to instruct; יִסֵּר מִן to warn off. Hiph. הֵיסִיר (comp. הֵיְשִׁיר), fut. אַיְסִיר like the Pi. Nithp. נִוַּסֵּר to allow oneself to be admonished, a mixed form of Niph. and Hith.

יָסַת belongs to הֵסִּית, see סוּת.

יָע (pl. יָעִים) m. shovel, used to remove the ashes from the altar, from יָעָה.

יַעְבֵּץ 1) p.n masc. (one that causes grief), according to 1 Chronicles 4:9, 10; 2) name of a place in Judah.

יָעַד (fut. יִיעַד) to appoint (of time or place), to pronounce (sentence of punishment); transf. to choose for a wife, see עוּד. Niph. נוֹעַד mutually to appoint; hence to meet with (לְ, אֶל) some one, to meet (somewhere) against some one (עַל), of conspirators. Hiph. הוֹעִיד to appoint some one, summon before a court of justice. Hoph. to be appointed, judged.

יֶעְדּוֹ p.n. masc. (a free-booter, an enemy). In the Ketib for which stands—

יֶעְדִּי p.n. m. (the same).

יָעָה origin. to sweep together, thus like אָסַף used to express, to take away. From which יָע.

יְעוּאֵל p.n. m. (removed by God).

יְעוּץ p.n. m. (adviser, admonisher); comp. Εὔβουλος.

יָעוֹר (pl. יְעוֹרִים, only in the Ketib) m. equiv. to יַעַר forest.

יָעוּר p.n. m. (a dweller in the forest).

יְעוּשׁ p.n. m. (gatherer). See יְעִישׁ.

יָעַז (only נוֹעָז part. Niph.) belongs, according to Rashi, to לָעַז, equiv. to לָעַז; נוֹעָז is according to him a noun for לוֹעֵז; but more correctly, according to Kimchi and Targ. for נֶעֱז; from עָזַז, which see.

יַעֲזִיאֵל p.n. m. (comforted by God), for which also עֲזִיאֵל.

יַעֲזִיָּה p.n. m. (the same).

יַעְזֵר (also יַעְזֵר hedge) p.n. of a city of Gad, on the border of the Ammonites.

יָעַט equiv. to עָטָה to wrap up, to clothe, only יְעָטָנִי Isa. 61:10, if this is not a mixed form of the pret. and fut. from עָטָה.

יְעַט (Aram.) equiv. to יָעַץ Hebrew,

origin. to impress, to confirm; hence, to resolve, to take counsel. יָעֵם part. counsellor, royal officer. Ithpa. אִתְיָעַם to take counsel mutually, to resolve upon something in common.

יַעֲשִׂיאֵל p.n. m. (removed by God).

יַעְיר p.n.m. (inhabitant of the forest), in Ketib יָעוּר.

יְעִישׁ p.n. m. (assembler), in Ketib, for Keri יְעוּשׁ.

יַעְכָּן p.n. m. (the sad one).

יַעַל (in בְּלִיַּעַל, contracted from בְּלִי יַעַל) height. See בְּלִיַּעַל.

יָעַל (not used) equiv. to עָלָה to rise, to ascend, to climb up, from which יָעֵל and יַעֲלָה, יַעַל, if these are not formed from עָלָה: 2) to be high, valuable, useful; hence Hiph. of הוֹעִיל II. to be useful, to render valuable; with לְ of the person or object, to make profit.

יָעֵל (only pl. יְעֵלִים, const. יַעֲלֵי) m. 1) originally the climber up; hence chamois, wild goat; 2) p.n. f. (wild goat).

יַעֲלָה (const. יַעֲלַת) f. 1) wild goat, chamois; next, a designation of womanly grace: 2) p.n. m. also יַעֲלָא (climber).

יַעְלָם p.n. m. (concealer).

יָעַן (not used) equiv. to עָנָה to wail, lament, especially of the wailing of the ostrich (also נְעַם Aram. related to נָאַם, origin. to wail; hence, נַעֲמָא ostrich), from which יַעֲנָה, יָעֵן.

יַעַן (from עָנָה) m. origin. sentence (equiv. to מַעַן, also from עָנָה), plan, object, purpose; but generally as a prep. and conjunct. on account, because, proceeding from the original idea: view, purpose.

יָעֵן (after the form יָעֵל, plur. יְעֵנִים) epic. ostrich, so called from his wailing cry in the desert.

יַעֲנָה f. (the same, generally בַּת הַיַּעֲנָה, pl. בְּנוֹת הַיַּ׳) to designate the female ostrich.

יַעְנַי p.n. m. (wailer, crier).

יָעֵף (fut. יִיעַף) 1) to be faint, wearied, tired, equiv. to עוּף, from which עֵיֵף. 2) transposed from יָפַע to shine, only in תּוֹעָפֹת and perhaps also in מֻעָף בִּיעָף. Hoph. הוּעָף to be wearied, perhaps also from signif. II. to be illumined, to be shone upon.

יָעֵף (pl. יְעֵפִים) adj. m. faint, wearied, fatigued, tired.

יְעָף m. weariness, wearying (or swift) flight, only Dan. 9:21, if the orig. signification "lustre" is not to be preferred.

יָעַץ (fut. יִיעַץ) origin. to confirm, to resolve; hence 1) to fix (the eyes) upon (עַל) something firmly, to resolve (a plan, device) against עַל.

אֶל) some one; 2) to advise, to counsel, to exhort. יוֹעֵץ adviser counsellor, also as royal attendant. Niph. נוֹעַץ to take counsel mutually, with עִם, אֶת, אֶל, next also of a single individual. Hithp. הִתְיָעֵץ like Niph. The root יָעַץ is related to עוּץ and עֵצָה.

יַעֲקֹב (he who laid hold of the heel, deceptive one) p.n. m. of the ancestor of the Israelites; hence, also used for the Israelitish people generally, or for the Israelitish empire especially.

יַעֲקֹבָה p.n. m. (deceptive one).

יַעְקָן p.n. masc. (one who perverts justice).

יַעַר (not used) equiv. to עָרָה I. to vegetate, to grow; only in the derivatives יַעַר, יָעוֹר and יַעְרָה, if they are not formed from עָרָה.

יַעַר (pl. יְעָרִים and יְעָרוֹת) masc. 1) thicket, so called from growing, comp. Talmud אֶבָּא forest, from אָבַב; hence, forest generally (in Aram. reed-bank), fig. numerous enemies; בֵּית הַיַּ׳ house of the forest, a blockhouse or armoury of Solomon's in the Lebanon: 2) reed-bank, a resort of the wood-bees; hence, transferred to honey-comb, in the Targ. קַנְיָא from קָן.

יַעְרָה p.n. m. (a dweller in the forest), probably for יַעְרָא and יַעְרַאי.

יַעְרָה f. honey comb, origin. honey-thicket, so called perhaps from its form.

יַעְרֵי אֹרְגִים p.n. m. (forests or bushes of the weavers), also יָעִיר.

יַעֲרֶשְׁיָה p.n. masc. (God is the sustainer).

יַעְשַׂי p.n. m. in the Keri for יַעְשׂוּ.

יַעֲשַׂי p.n. m. (worker, acquirer).

יַעֲשִׂיאֵל p.n.m. (God has wrought it).

יִפְדְיָה p.n. m. (God is the redeemer).

יָפָה (fut. יִיפֶה, apoc. יִיף) equiv. to יָפַע origin. to shine; hence, transf. to be beautiful. Pi. יִפָּה to beautify, to decorate. Pu. (redoubled form) יָפְיָפָה to be very beautiful. Hithp. הִתְיַפָּה to adorn, beautify oneself.

יָפֶה (const. יְפֵה) adj. m., יָפָה (const. יְפַת, pl. יָפוֹת) f. beautiful, in the most extensive relations; hence also, excellent, appropriate, generally with the addition of מַרְאֶה when applied to man.

יְפֵה־פִיָּה adj. f. exceedingly beautiful, a redoubled form from יָפָה.

יָפוֹ (beautiful, famous city) p.n. of a city in Dan on the Mediterranean sea, now called Jaffa, Jafa; Greek Ἰόππη.

יָפוֹא the same.

יָפַח (Kal not used) to blow, to breathe, equiv. to נָפַח, פּוּחַ; hence Hith. הִתְיַפֵּחַ to sob, to moan originally, to breathe heavily, to moan.

יָפֵחַ (const. יְפֵחַ) adj. masc. snorting (for something), hasty, pressing; hence syn. with שׁוֹאֵף Eccles. 1:5.

יֳפִי masc. lustre, beauty, fame, from יָפָה.

יֹפִי (pause יֹפִי, with suff. יָפְיִי) masc. lustre, beauty, fame.

יָפִיעַ 1) p.n. of a place in the territory of Zebulun (beauteous city); 2) p.n. m. (the lustrous, beautiful one).

יַפְלֵט p.n. m. (protector, deliverer).

יְפֻנֶּה p.n. m. (the dexterous one).

יָפַע (Kal, not used) equiv. to יָפָה to shine; hence, Hiph. הוֹפִיעַ to cause to shine, to shed lustre, to appear lustrous. The noun תּוֹעָפוֹת is transposed from תּוֹפָעוֹת.

יִפְעָה f. lustre, beauty.

יֶפֶת p.n. masc. (one who extends far).

יִפְתָּח 1) p.n. m. (the opening one); 2) open place, p.n. of a place in Judah.

יִפְתַּח־אֵל (opened by God) p.n. of a valley in the territories of Zebulun and Asher.

יָצָא (fut. יֵצֵא, imp. צֵא, inf. abs. יָצֹא, const. צֵאת, part. f. once יֹצֵאת for יֹצְאָה, and יֹצֵת for יוֹצֵאת) to go out, to go forth from (מִן) some place, through (בְּ) the gate, or with the accus., e.g. אֶת הָעִיר from the town; פְּרָצִים through ruins, transf. to go forth (to combat, war, business, freedom), to emigrate, proceed, i.e. originate, to escape, i.e. to go forth unmolested, to rise (of the sun), to sprout, to grow (out of the earth), to flow (of a river), to run out (extent of the border), to expend (money), to issue (an edict), to end, etc. Hiph. הוֹצִיא (imp. also הַיְצֵא) to cause to go out, i.e. to lead forward, to fetch, to draw forward; hence, transf. to bring forth (of the earth, of man, e.g. a work of art), to spread (a doctrine, a report), to impose an expense upon some one; with עַל, to let go (the wife by divorce). Hoph. pass. to be brought forth.

יְצָא belongs to שֵׁיצָא, see שֵׁצָא.

יָצַב (Kal, not used) equiv. to נָצַב to support, found, establish, or intrans. to stand firmly; hence, Hith. הִתְיַצֵּב to stand firmly, to represent oneself; with לִפְנֵי, to appear before some one, to attend as servant; with עַל, to stand up against some one, to stand by some one, to assist, with לִפְנֵי and לְ. It is not unlikely that the Hiph. הִצִּיב and Hoph. הֻצַּב are derived from יָצַב and not from נָצַב, but in the

Niph. נִצַּב must be taken for the root.

יְצַב (Aram.) to be established, certain; hence, Pa. to make true, firm, certain, to confirm.

יָצַג (Kal, not used) to stand firmly, equiv. to יָצַק; hence, Hiph. הִצִּיג 1) to cause some one to stand before another, to lay down or to take a firm standing; 2) to cause to stand, or to let stand. Hoph. הֻצַּג to be made to stand.

יִצְהָר m. 1) that which shines or gives light, oil; hence, בֶּן הַיִּצְהָר son of the oil, i.e. the anointed one, the high priest; 2) p.n. m. (the beautiful one), patr. יִצְהָרִי.

יָצוּעַ (pl. const. יְצוּעֵי) m. 1) couch, connubial bed, from יָצַע to spread; 2) f. floor, story, chamber, see יָצִיעַ.

יִצְחָק p.n. m. (one that mocks), for which also once יִשְׂחָק.

יִצְחָר p.n. m. (equiv. to יִצְהָר).

יָצִיא (const. pl. יְצִיאֵי Keri) m. he that comes forth, child, orig. an adj.

יַצִּיב (Aram.) adj. m. certain, true, sure, orig. established, from יְצַב.

יָצִיעַ f. floor, story, chamber.

יָצַע (Kal, not used) equiv. to יָצַג to place firmly, to establish, or intr. to stand firmly; hence, הִצִּיעַ to cause to couch, to spread out. Hoph. הֻצַּע pass. to be spread out for a couch

יָצַק (fut. trans. יִצֹק, intrans. יִצַּק, imp. צַק and יְצֹק, inf. צֶקֶת) 1) equiv. to יָצַג, in Kal only יָצוּק, to be placed firmly, posted, stationed. Hiph. הִצִּיק and הוֹצִיק to place, to set, to put, equiv. to הִצִּיג. Hoph. only particip. מֻצָּק to be firmly set; 2) related with זָקַק to pour (a fluid), to melt (metals); יָצַק לְמוּצָק growing into hardness (for casting); יָצוּק partic. pass. to be cast. Pi. only particip. (Ketib) מְיַצֶּקֶת pouring out, casting; the Keri has מוּצֶקֶת from the Hiph.

יְצֻקָה f. the cast, origin. that which is cast, or that which is poured out,

I. יָצַר (only fut. יֵצֶר, יֵצַר, hence, as often is the case in such forms of the fut., they belong to different roots, e.g. יִיטַב to טוֹב, these belong to צָרַר, which like טוֹב again appear in the preterite), origin. to compress, but generally intrans. to be straitened, confined; transf. to be in trouble, anguish; with לְ to oppress some one; comp. צָרַר and צוּר.

II. יָצַר (fut. apoc. יִיצֶר, יָצַר, but also יִצֹּר, after the manner of the פ״נ; part. יוֹצֵר, which also stands once for אוֹצֵר) to form, origin. to cut, equiv. to גָּזַר; hence next, to form (of the potter) from clay, to work out (of the smith); figur. to design, to form (in the mind); with עַל, against somebody; to form (of God), with לְ, into something. יוֹצֵר potter, former, creator; but in Zech. 11:13, for אוֹצָר. Niph. נוֹצַר to be formed. Pu. to be formed, born; figur. of the birth of days. Hoph. הוּצַר, like Niph.

יֵצֶר (with suff. יִצְרוֹ) m. 1) abstract, the imagination, formation of thought (in the heart); hence generally, thought, formation of ideas; 2) concrete, image, idol; 3) p.n. m. (former), patron. יִצְרִי.

יָצֻר (only pl. יְצֻרִים) m. that which is formed, form of the body.

יִצְרִי p.n. m. (he that forms).

יָצַת (fut. יִצַּת, pl. יִצְּתוּ for יִצְּתוּ) to burn, to blaze; בְּסִבְכֵי הַיַּעַר in the thicket of the forest; to burn away בָּאֵשׁ in fire; in Kal never transitive. Niph. to be kindled (בְּ) with something, with wrath; to be burnt through (בְּ) fire. Hiph. הִצִּית (fut. apoc. יַצֵּת, once in Ketib הוֹצִית for הִצִּית to kindle, to set fire (בְּ or עַל) to something. אֵשׁ is sometimes omitted.

יָקַב (not used) equiv. to נָקַב to hollow, deepen out; from which יֶקֶב.

יֶקֶב (with suff. יִקְבֶךָ, pl. יְקָבִים, const. יִקְבֵי) m. the hollow in which the pressed wine flows, wine press; next, a press in general. The root is יָקַב.

יְקַבְצְאֵל (divine assembly), p.n. of a city in Judah.

יָקַד (fut. יֵקַד and יִיקַד, inf. יְקוֹד) to glow, to burn, to blaze, to be kindled; יְקוֹד is a noun, which see. Hoph. הוּקַד (only fut.) to be kindled, to be set on fire, with בּ of the material, by which, and with עַל of the place where it is kindled.

יְקַד (part. f. def. יָקִדְתָּא) Aram. the same.

יְקֵדָא (יְדָת) Aram. f. brand.

יָקְדְעָם (public place for burning) p.n. of a city in the mountain of Judah.

יָקָה (not used), to be pious, after the Arab.

יָקֶה p.n. m. (the pious one).

יָקַהּ (not used) to obey, to be obedient.

יְקָהָה (const. יִקְּהַת) fem. obedience. The dagesh in the ק is euphonic.

יְקוֹד m. origin. that which is kindled; next, brand.

יְקוֹד m. brand.

יְקוּם masc. that which exists, being; from קוּם.

יָקוֹשׁ (also יָקוּשׁ; pl. יְקוּשִׁים) masc. (origin. adj.) one who lays a snare, a bird-catcher, a fowler.

יְקוּתִיאֵל p.n. m. (worship of God).

יָקְטָן p.n. m. (little one), ancestor of many tribes of Yemen.

יָקִים p.n. m. (establisher).

יָקִיר adj. m. dear, precious, valuable.

יַקִּיר (Aram.) the same.

יְקַמְיָה p.n. m. (God is the assembler).

יְקַמְעָם p.n. m. (assembler of people).

יָקְמְעָם (place of public assembly) p.n. of a city in Ephraim, for which also קִבְצַיִם.

יָקְנְעָם (possession of the people) p.n. of a city in Zebulun.

יָקַע (fut. יֵקַע) 1) to move away; hence, to get out of joint; figur. of the mind, which is alienated from (מִן, מֵעַל) some one; 2) equiv. to תָּקַע to fix, to pitch a tent; hence Hiph. הוֹקִיעַ to fix to, or to hang on, a pole. Hoph. הוּקַע pass.

יָקַץ (fut. יִיקַץ, יִקַץ, יִקָּץ, יֵיקַץ, יָקֵץ) to awake, to be awake; for the pret. the Hiph. הֵקִיץ is generally used.

יָקַר (fut. יֵקַר, יֵיקַר, יִיקַר) to be heavy, weighty (synom. with כָּבֵד); hence transf. to be dear, valuable, important, honored, dignified, the same as כָּבֵד is transf. to. יָקַר מֵעַל to be esteemed by some one. Hiph. הוֹקִיר to make important, valuable, rare.

יָקָר adj. m. יְקָרָה f. 1) weighty, important; hence, precious, noble, dear, dignified, excellent, rare, select; subst. magnificence, preciousness; 2) in Keri for קַר fresh, bright, calm, from קָרַר.

יְקָר m. 1) worth, preciousness, magnificence; e. g. כְּלִי יְ׳, אוֹר יְ׳; 2) honor, dignity.

יְקָר (Aram.) m. the same.

יָקֹשׁ (1st pers. יָקֹשְׁתִּי, the future is formed from קוּשׁ) to lay a net, a snare, יוֹקֵשׁ partic. a bird-catcher, he who lays a snare. Niph. נוֹקַשׁ to be caught in a net, or to be ensnared by something. Pu. the same, where, however, the partic. יוּקָשִׁים stands for מְיוּקָשִׁים.

יָקְשָׁן p.n. m. (the one who ensnares, the enticer).

יָקְתְאֵל (subjected by God) p.n. of a city in Judah, and surname of the conquered town, Selah.

יָרֵא (2 pers. pl. יְרֵאתֶם and יְרֵאתֶם; fut. יִירָא and יִרָא; imp. יְרָא, inf. יְרֹא and יִרְאָה, with לְ as well as לְיִרְאָה לְרֹא) 1) to be afraid of (מִן, מִפְּנֵי) some one or something, to fear (אֶת) something, to fear for (לְ) some one, to fear lest (פֶּן) something happen; 2) to revere (God), to be pious. Niph. נוֹרָא (fut. יִוָּרֵא) to be feared; hence part., fearful, awful, amazing, grand, glorious, and נוֹרָאוֹת remarkable, amazing things. Pi. יֵרֵא to frighten, to terrify. According to some, Hith. הִתְרָאָה for הִתְיָרֵא.

יָרֵא (const. יְרֵא, plur. יְרֵאִים) adj. m. יְרֵאָה (const. יִרְאַת) fem. fearing, revering.

יִרְאָה f., origin. inf. to fear; hence, fear, veneration, reverence, piety.

יִרְאוֹן (town of terror), p.n. of a city in Naphtali.

יְרִאִיָּה p.n. m. (the God-fearing one).

יָרֵם p.n. m. (warrior).

יְרֻבַּעַל p.n. m. (a combatant with or for Baal).

יָרָבְעָם p.n. m. (multiplier of people).

יָרַד (fut. יֵרֵד, apoc. יֵרֶד, pause יֵרַד; imp. רֵד, רְדָה, יְרַד; inf. יְרֹד, const. רֶדֶת, רְדָה) to go down, to descend; to (אֶל or accus.) a place, from a high to a low place; also used of inanimate things, e.g. a river that flows downwards, a road that inclines downwards, the day that declines, the tears that flow down, the felling of the trees of a forest, the reduction of affluence, or falling and perishing generally. Hiph. הוֹרִיד causing to go down, letting, bringing, taking, thrusting, carrying, pushing, fetching, hanging down. Hoph. הוּרַד pass. from Hiph.

יֶרֶד p.n. m. (one that has been reduced).

יַרְדֵּן (that which flows down) p.n. of a river which flowed down from the Anti-Lebanon, Jordan; כִּכַּר י׳ אֶרֶץ the country and plain on the Jordan; גְּאוֹן הַיּ׳ pride, i.e. magnificence, of the Jordan, i.e. the banks of the Jordan.

יָרָה (fut. יִירֶה, inf. יְרֹה, יָרוֹת, יְרוֹא, imp. יְרֵה) 1) to cast (lots), to fling (arrows); hence יוֹרֶה an archer; to throw down, to lay down (a foundation), to erect (a monument); 2) perhaps. equiv. to רָוָה to flow down; hence, to wet, to to pour down, particip. יוֹרֶה former rain; 3) יָרָה perhaps equiv. to אוֹר to shine, see Hiph. Niph. only fut. יִיָּרֶה to be shot by an arrow. Hiph. הוֹרָה (fut. יוֹרֶה, apoc. יוֹר; 1) to throw, to fling; hence part. pl. מוֹרְאִים for מוֹרִים archers; 2) to wet; hence מוֹרֶה former rain; 3) to thrust down, from יָרָה in the first sense; 4) to instruct (from יָרָה 3) with double accus. or with בְּ, אֶל of the object, or with לְ of the person and accus. of the object.

יָרַה (fut. יִרְהַה) equiv. to יָרֵא to tremble, if תִּרְהוּ (Isa. 44:8) does not stand for תִּירְאוּ.

יְרוּאֵל (contracted from יְרוּא־אֵל fear of God) p.n. of a desert.

יָרוֹחַ p.n. m. (one born on the new moon).

יָרוֹק m. the verdure, equiv. to יֶרֶק.

יְרוּשָׁא (also יְרוּשָׁה) p.n. m. (possession, property).

יְרוּשָׁלַםִ (later ־לַיִם) orig. יְרוּשׁ־שָׁלֵם (abode of peace), p.n. of the capital of Palestine, Jerusalem. The dual form is in reference to the division of the town into two parts.

יְרוּשְׁלֶם (־לֵם) Aram. the same.

יָרַח (not used) equiv. to אָרַח to walk, to wander, to make a circuit.

יָרֵחַ m. the moon, origin. a wanderer, (comp. יָרֵחַ יָקָר הֹלֵךְ Job 31:26), so called from its circular revolution: לִפְנֵי יָ׳ in the face of the moon, i.e. as long as the moon will shine, i.e. for ever.

יֶרַח (pl. יְרָחִים, const. יַרְחֵי) m. 1) denom. from יָרֵחַ time of the circuit of the moon, a month, a lunar month; hence synon. with חֹדֶשׁ: 2) p.n. of an Arabian tribe in the vicinity of Hadramaut.

יְרַח (Aram.) the same, a month.

יְרֵחוֹ (also יְרִיחוֹ, יְרִיחֹה) p.n. of a city in Benjamin, Jericho. As an appell. it signifies, a city fragrant with balm, from רוּחַ.

יְרֹחָם p.n. masc. (the beloved one, favorite).

יְרַחְמְאֵל p.n. m. (lover of God).

יַרְחָע p.n. m.

יָרַט (fut. יִרַט, יִירַט) to thrust in the hand (עַל יְדֵי) of some one, with נֶגֶד against some one; related to רָהַט to run.

יְרִיאֵל p.n.m.(from יְרֵא אֵל=יְרִיא־אֵל the God-fearing one).

יָרִיב m. 1) adversary, enemy, antagonist; 2) p.n. m. (the querulous one).

יְרִיבַי p.n. m. (one that is in strife).

יְרִיָּה p.n. m. (for יְרִיא יָהּ the God-fearing one).

יְרִיָּהוּ p.n. m. (the same).

יְרִיחוֹ see יְרֵחוֹ.

יְרִימוֹת see יְרֵמוֹת.

יְרֵימוֹת see יְרֵמוֹת.

יְרִיעָה fem. a curtain, canvass of the tent; from יָרַע to move, to waive.

יְרִיעוֹת p.n. f. (timidity).

יָרַךְ (not used) equiv. to רָכַךְ to be soft, especially of the soft flesh of the loins.

יָרֵךְ (const. יֶרֶךְ, comp. עָרֵל, const. עֲרַל, with suff. יְרֵכִי, dual יְרֵכַיִם) f. 1) loin; hence, of the upper fleshy part of the loin, whilst מָתְנַיִם signifies the lower part of the back; יָצָא יָרֵךְ to proceed from the loins, i.e. to come forth, to be begotten; of animals it signifies, leg: 2) transf. to inanimate objects, side, of a candlestick where the shaft joins the basis.

יַרְכָה (dual יַרְכָּתַיִם, const. יַרְכְּתֵי) f. equiv. to יָרֵךְ 2, i.e. in transferring to inanimate objects, side, hinder part; hence, western side of the temple, the hindermost or innermost part of a house, ship, grave, forest, mountain, or cave, the remote country, e.g. יַרְכְּתֵי צָפוֹן the remote parts of the north; יַ׳ אֶרֶץ the remote parts of the earth, equiv. to כַּנְפוֹת הָאָרֶץ; respecting the transf. of the names of the limbs of the body to inanimate objects, comp. כָּתֵף, שְׁכֶם, כָּנָף, and many more.

יַרְכָא f. (Aram.) loin, side of an image.

יָרַם (not used) probably equiv. to חָרַם (in חֶרְמוֹן) to be high, hilly, prominent; related in this sense to אָרַם and רוּם.

יַרְמוּת (hill, ridge of a mountain) p.n. of a city in Judah.

יְרֵמוֹת (also יְרֵימוֹת, יְרִימוֹת) p.n. m. (haughtiness, pride); for which in the Keri occurs once רָמוֹת.

יְרֵמַי p.n. m. (dweller on a height).

יִרְמְיָה p.n. m. (raised by God), from רָמָה=רוּם.

יִרְמְיָהוּ p.n. m. (the same).

יָרַע from which יָרְעָה Isa. 15:4, "his life shall be grievous unto him," and belongs to רָעַע, like the fut. יֵרַע.

יִרְפְּאֵל (restored place of God) p.n. of a place in Benjamin.

יָרַק (inf. יְרֹק) to spit. The future is formed from רָקַק.

יָרַק (not used) to be green, fresh; related to דָּשָׁא.

יָרָק (const. יְרַק) adj. masc. green, fresh, of plants; as a noun, that which is green, cabbage, vegetable, גַּן הַיָּרָק kitchen garden, אֲרֻחַת יָ׳ a dish, a meal of vegetables.

יֶרֶק m. that which is green, fresh; hence, connected with עֵשֶׂב; but also vegetable, cabbage, as well as the green of the tree.

יֵרָקוֹן m. 1) yellow-green colour of vegetables; hence, withering, fallowing: 2) the yellow-green colour of the face as an indication of disease.

יְרַקְרַק adj. m. (יְרַקְרַקּוֹת pl. f.) greenlike, yellow-green; next, of the yellow colour of the gold.

יָרַשׁ (and also יָרֵשׁ, hence יְרִשְׁתֶּם, fut. יִירַשׁ, imp. רֵשׁ, רַשׁ, pause רָשׁ, with ה, רְשָׁה, inf. רֶשֶׁת) 1) to seize, to lay hold of; hence, to take possession of, transf. to inherit; יוֹרֵשׁ the heir. With accus. of the pers. to inherit; 2) to put oneself in possession of others' property; hence figur. to impoverish. Niph. נוֹרַשׁ (fut. יִוָּרֵשׁ) to become poor. Pi only fut. יְיָרֵשׁ to deprive, to strip. Hiph. הוֹרִישׁ (fut. יוֹרִישׁ) to cause to possess, with double accus. (lands, cities, mountains), "to make to possess the iniquities" (Job 13:26), i.e. to make bear the punishment for ever; 3) to take away the possession, i.e. to drive out; next, to destroy generally, which sense is already found in Kal.

יְרֻשָּׁה f. possession, but commonly the form is:—

יְרֻשָּׁה fem. possession, inheritance; אֶרֶץ יְרֻשָּׁה land of heritage.

יֵשׁ (before makkaph יֶשׁ־) m. 1) the being, existence; next, transf. to property, wealth; 2) taking the place of verbs substantives, in contrast to אַיִן, where יֵשׁ is joined with the suff., e.g. יֶשְׁנוֹ it is, he is, (there is), יֶשְׁךָ thou art, יֶשְׁנוֹ he is, etc., often joined with the particip. to paraphrase the finite verb. יֵשׁ אֲשֶׁר there are some who, etc.

יָשַׁב (fut. יֵשֵׁב, inf. יָשׁוֹב, const. שֶׁבֶת, imp. שֵׁב, שְׁבָה) origin. to draw the legs together, to couch, as also origin. קָפַץ; next com. 1) to sit down, with לְ of the place, often with the reciprocal dat. e.g. יָשַׁב לוֹ to set himself down; 2) to sit, with בְּ, עַל (poet. accus.) of the place; with לְ, of the person; to sit watching against some one; with עִם, to sit with some one, i.e. to have intercourse with him, to throne; hence יוֹשֵׁב תְּהִלּוֹת thou who inhabitest the praises; 3) to occupy (a place); 4) to abide, with the pleon. dative, with לְ of the person, to expect some one; transf. to dwell, with בְּ or עַל of the place, and with accus. to inhabit. Niph. נוֹשַׁב to be inhabited. Pi. יִשֵּׁב to set, to erect (a tent). Hiph. הוֹשִׁיב to cause to sit, to dwell, to set (with בְּ of the place), to cause a woman to dwell, i.e. to take a wife. Hoph. to be caused to dwell.

יֶשֶׁבְאָב p.n. m. (paternal seat).

יֹשֵׁב בַּשֶּׁבֶת p.n. m. (he that dwells in peace).

יִשְׁבָּח p.n. m. (he that praises).

יָשָׁבִי לֶחֶם p.n. m. (he that returns from the combat).

יִשְׁבּוֹ בְנֹב p.n. m. (he that resides in Nob). In the Keri for which stands:—

יִשְׁבִּי בְנֹב p.n. m. (seat in Nob).

יָשָׁבְעָם p.n. m. (dweller among the people).

יִשְׁבָּק p.n. m. (he that forsakes).

יָשְׁבְּקָשָׁה p.n. m.

יָשָׁה (not used) to be, to exist, to live. From which יֵשׁ and תּוּשִׁיָּה.

יָשׁוּב p.n. m. (he that returns), patr. יָשֻׁבִי.

יִשְׁוָה p.n. m. (the moderate one).

יְשׁוֹחָיָה p.n. m. (humbled by God).

יִשְׁוִי p.n. m. (the temperate one).

יֵשׁוּעַ (contract. of יְהוֹשֻׁעַ) p.n. masc. (the helper).

יְשׁוּעָה f. 1) help, deliverance, victory, salvation, happiness: the plural יְשׁוּעוֹת is sometimes used in the same manner, comp. נְכוֹחוֹת, בִּינוֹת; 2) concrete, deliverance, for that which is delivered.

יָשַׁח (not used) to be empty, of the stomach, belly, after the Arabic, from which:—

יֶשַׁח masc. emptiness (of the belly). Probably however, יְשָׁחֲךָ fut. is from שָׁחָה after the form יִפְרְךָ, and must be rendered, "and he will humble thee in the very midst of thee" (Mic. 6:14, "and thy casting down shall be in the midst of thee," Author. Version); or it is a subst. from שָׁחָה.

יִשְׂחָק a rare reading for יִצְחָק, which see.

יָשַׁט only Hiph. הוֹשִׁיט to stretch out, with לְ of the person, to reach something to some one.

יִשַׁי p.n. m. (the living one, formed from יֵשׁ). See אִישַׁי.

יִשִּׁיָּה p.n. m. (the one blessed by God with hoary age, from יָשַׁשׁ).

יִשִּׁיָּהוּ p.n. m. (the same).

יְשִׂימִאֵל p.n. m. (God is the establisher).

יְשִׁימָה (only pl. ־מוֹת) f. 1) horror, destruction (after the Ketib); 2) p.n. of a place. See בֵּית הַיְשִׁימוֹת.

יְשִׁימוֹן m. desert, waste, from יָשַׁם, equiv. to אָשַׁם, שָׁמֵם.

יָשִׁישׁ m. hoary man, from יָשַׁשׁ to become white, to be grey.

יְשִׁישַׁי p.n. masc. (hoary one, grey-headed one).

יָשַׁם (only fut. תֵּשַׁם) equiv. to שָׁמֵם to be desolate, waste, if תֵּשַׁם, תִּישַׁמְנָה do not belong to שָׁמֵם.

יָשֹׂם (only in the fut. Ketib אִישָׂם, יִישָׂם) equiv. to שׂוּם (which see) to sit, to put down.

יִשְׁמָא p.n. m. (the high one, from שָׁמָה=שָׁמָא).

יִשְׁמָעֵאל p.n. masc. (heard by God), patron. יִשְׁמְעֵאלִי, pl. ־לִים, Ishmaelite.

יִשְׁמַעְיָה p.n. m. (heard by God).

יִשְׁמַעְיָהוּ p.n. m. (the same).

יִשְׁמְרַי p.n. m. (the watcher, keeper).

יָשֵׁן (fut. יִישַׁן, inf. יְשׁוֹן) 1) to sleep, to be inactive, weary; hence, of the sleep of death; 2) to wither, to become sapless, old, in contrast to חָדָשׁ fresh. Niph. נוֹשַׁן to be old, sapless; hence, that of former years (of the corn), to get old (of the leprosy), to become old, i.e. to remain long (in a country). Pi. to cause one to fall asleep.

יָשָׁן adj. m. (יְשָׁנָה f.) old, of former years (of the corn), old (of a gate, or a brook).

יָשֵׁן (const. pl. יְשֵׁנֵי) 1) adj. masc. (יְשֵׁנָה f.) sleeping, יְשֵׁנֵי אַדְמַת עָפָר "they that are sleeping in dust," the dead; 2) p.n. m. (the inactive one).

יְשָׁנָה (old town, comp. Palæopolis) p.n. of a city in Judah.

יָשַׁע (Kal, not used) equiv. to שׁוּעַ to be large, spacious (synon. with רָוַח), hence, to be rich, happy. Hiph. הוֹשִׁיעַ (fut. יוֹשִׁיעַ, with the ה retained יְהוֹשִׁיעַ, apoc. יוֹשַׁע) to help, to save, with מִן, from the grasp of some one, e.g. מִיַּד, מִכַּף, מֵחֶרֶב, מִצָּרָה; הוֹשִׁיעַ מֵרָחוֹק to deliver from a distant land (from captivity); with בְּ, to deliver through some one; transf. to make victorious. Niph. נוֹשַׁע to be saved, delivered, supported, also constr. with מִן. Particip. נוֹשָׁע victorious.

יֵשַׁע (with suff. יִשְׁעִי, יִשְׁעֲךָ, יִשְׁעֶךָ) m. deliverance, victory, salvation, happiness, also constr. with the accus.

יֶשַׁע m. the same.

יִשְׁעִי p.n. m. (conqueror, happy one).

יְשַׁעְיָה p.n. m. (salvation of God).

יְשַׁעְיָהוּ p.n. m. (the same).

יָשַׁף (not used) to shine, from which:—

יָשְׁפֵה (־פֶה) m. jasper, perhaps from a non-semitic verbal root.

יִשְׁפָּה p.n. m. (the bald one, from שָׁפָה).

יִשְׁפָּן p.n. m. (the same).

יָשַׁר (fut. יִישַׁר, once יִשַּׁר) equiv. to אָשַׁר, כָּשַׁר to be straight, just, in a physical sense; e.g. of the paths that are straight; next, also figur. just, equitable, agreeable, often joined to בְּעֵינֵי פ׳; 2) to be even, (in contrast to עָקֹל) of the soul, i.e. to be calm. Pi. 1) to make straight (the path), i.e. to walk or to lead in a straight course through life; of God, to make happy; transf. to deem just; 2) to make a road straight for (לְ) somebody. Pu. יֻשַּׁר to be made plain; of gold, to be flattened, fitted. Hiph. הַיְשִׁיר (for הֵישִׁיר) and הוֹשִׁיר (imp. הַיְשַׁר Ketib) to make the road even, to direct the eye straight.

יָשָׁר (pl. יְשָׁרִים, const. יִשְׁרֵי) adj. m. יְשָׁרָה (const. יִשְׁרַת, pl. יְשָׁרוֹת) f. straight, subst. the straight (in contrast to the crooked), right, agreeable; figur. happy, good, just, pious, e.g. יְשַׁר לֵב of an upright heart, יְשַׁר דֶּרֶךְ of an even road, which significations are also taken substantively; e.g. סֵפֶר הַיָּשָׁר book of righteousness, in which the righteous and valorous are sung. יְשָׁרִים signifies also, arbitrations; Dan. 11:17.

יָשָׁר p.n. m. (the upright one).

יֹשֶׁר (with suff. יָשְׁרוֹ) m. uprightness, right, probity.

יִשְׂרָאֵל the second p. n. of Jacob,

(prevailer over angels); later, name of his descendants, the people of Israel. The ten tribes bore the name of the empire of Israel, and their kings מַלְכֵי יִשְׂרָאֵל; after the exile, however, יִשְׂרָאֵל was used for the Jews as a body; gent. m. יִשְׂרְאֵלִי, f. —לִית.

יְשַׂרְאֵלָה p.n. masc. (acceptable unto God).

יְשָׁרָה (const. יִשְׁרַת) fem. see under יָשָׁר, יְשָׁרָה, to which it belongs.

יְשֻׁרוּן m. a surname for Israel, signifying the upright one; perhaps contracted from יִשְׂרְאֵלוּן, if it is not derived from יָשָׁר=יָשַׁר.

יָשַׁשׁ (not used) equiv. to שׁוּשׁ to be white, shining; transf. to grey hair.

יָשֵׁשׁ adj. masc. equiv. to יָשִׁישׁ old, ancient.

יִשָּׂשכָר p.n. m. (one who brings a reward; also יִשָּׂא שָׂכָר as the reading in the Ketib).

יָת (Aram.) equiv. to אֵת (accus.) Heb.

יְתֵב (Aram.) equiv. to the Heb. יָשַׁב to sit, to abide, to dwell; af. הוֹתֵב to cause to dwell.

יָתַד (not used) to pierce, related to אָשַׁד.

יָתֵד (const. יְתַד, pl. יְתֵדוֹת, const. יִתְדוֹת) f. 1) a nail or peg which is stuck in the wall, or a spade which is stuck into the earth; יְתַד הָאֶרֶץ the pin by which the web is fastened to the wall; figur. something fixed, sure; 2) transf. to a prince, leader of a people, to whom all are attached, or on whom they rely for security.

יָתוֹם (pl. יְתוֹמִים) m. orphan, figur. one who is deserted generally. Root יָתַם.

יְתוּר m. superfluity, wealth, abundance (of the mountains), from יָתַר; perhaps יְתוּר stands for יָתוּר, and is a fut. of תּוּר.

יָתַח (not used) to beat, strike, from which תּוֹתָח; probably, however, the root is תּוּחַ, which see.

יַתִּיר (the rich, great city) p.n. of a city of the priests in Judah.

יַתִּיר (Aram.) adj. m. (יַתִּירָא f.) great, eminent, preferable. יַתִּירָא is also used as an adv.

יִתְלָה (a place situated on an eminence) p.n. of a district in Dan.

יָתַם (not used) bereaved, deprived, to be solitary; from which יָתוֹם.

יִתְמָה p.n. m. (solitude).

יָתַן (not used) origin. to stretch, to extend; hence, to endure, to last long; of a river which continually flows. See אֵיתָן.

יַתְנִיאֵל p.n. m. (he that praises God).

יִתְנָן (track) p.n. of a city in Judah.

יָתַר (Kal, not used) to be preferable, to excel, to be abundant, to be superabundant, to be left over; all proceeding from the original sense of excess over the usual quantity, measure, or condition; 2) equiv. to קָשַׁר, קָטַר to bind; from which יֶתֶר, מֵיתָר. Niph. נוֹתַר (fut. יִוָּתֵר) to be left over, or to be preferred; in both significations the excess over the common standard is the original idea. Hiph. הוֹתִיר to leave over, to obtain a preference, to give in abundance to (accus. in בְּ) something.

יֹתֵר see under יוֹתֵר.

יֶתֶר (with suff. יִתְרִי, pl. יְתָרִים) m. 1) the remainder, rest of a thing; 2) preference, excellence, dignity; as an adv. יֶתֶר signifies: especially, very, besides (compare יָתִּיר); 3) cord, gut, bridle, from יָתַר to bind; hence נָסַע יֶתֶר to tear the cord, פִּתַּח יֶתֶר to loosen the bridle; 4) p. n. m. the excellent one; patron. יִתְרִי.

יִתְרָא p. n. m. (preference).

יִתְרָה f. that which is left from the necessary supply; hence, treasure; עָשָׂה י׳ to acquire treasures; in contrast to חֶסְרָה the want.

יִתְרוֹ (from יִתְרוֹן) p. n. m. (the excellent one).

יִתְרוֹן masc. preference, abundance, profit, advantage; only used in modern Hebrew.

יִתְרָן p. n. m. (the excellent one).

יִתְרְעָם p. n. masc. (abundance of the people).

יְתֵת (contracted from יְתֶדֶת) p. n. m. prince, ruler; comp. יָתֵד.

כ

כ (כַּף hand) the eleventh letter of the alphabet; as a numeral it counts 20; as a palatine it interchanges with ג and ק, rarely with י; but as the gutturals ח and ע are in some relations similar to the palatines, we find כ interchanging also with ע and ח.

ךְ־ a non-semetic adj. termination; hence found mostly in non-semetic words of the Bible; e. g. גִּנְזַךְ, כַּרְכֹּךְ, מְרֹאדַךְ and others.

כְּ (before monosyllabic words, or before suffixes כָּ; e. g. כָּהֶם, כָּכֶם) a particle used in manifold instances to express the degree of a quality, whether as an adv. or as a prep. according to the context; 1) to express similarity: like, as; e. g. a feast like a feast (כְּמִשְׁתֵּה) of the king. This similarity may be in reference to size, shape, time, or fate; either entirely alike, or an indefinite similarity, somewhat like; e. g. (כְּמַרְאֵה־אִישׁ) somewhat like a man, about like this (כָּזֶה); hence after words signifying number, measure, or time, to be rendered, *about*, e.g. about ten (כְּעֶשֶׂר) years; כַּחֲצוֹת הַלַּיְלָה about midnight, being a modification of the כַּף הַדִּמְיוֹן (כ *similitudinis*). In these cases, כְּ is: (*a*) an adv. of quality, like כֵּן so, like as, or a relative verb like אֵיךְ; e.g. (כַּחַטָּאת) as the sin-offering, (כָּאָשָׁם) so the trespass-offering; (*b*) where the similarity is not complete, and is only to direct, it must be: according, or accordingly, pursuant to; e.g. (כִּדְמוּתֵנוּ) according to our likeness; as the four winds; 2) similarity not with a real object mentioned, but with an ideal one; e.g. כְּאִישׁ אֱמֶת like a true man, i.e. like a true man should be, כְּמַחֲרִישׁ he conducted himself like a man who was silent, i.e. only like a silent man could conduct himself. In this sense is also כְּעֹמְיָה, כְּמִתְאֹנְנִים, כְּהֶחָכָם, כְּשֹׁד, כַּמָּוֶת, כְּנֹשֶׁה, כִּמְעַט, i.e. as a wise man, as murmurers, as one that is faint of heart, as little (as possible), as a usurer, as death, as the destructive tempest. In this signification, כְּ stands before participles, adjectives, substantives, and adverbs; and the ancient grammarians called it כַּף הָעֶצֶם הַשִּׁוּוּם, because it generally signifies the superlative degree of a quality; 3) the comparison of one action with another, to signify that one is done while the other is going forward, e.g. when I lifted up my voice (כַּהֲרִימִי) he left the garment (וַיַּעֲזֹב). In this sense it occurs generally before infinitives, but also before the verbal noun, and before the participle. As to the derivation, כְּ is connected with the pronominal root כִּי and not abbreviated from כֵּן. See כְּמוֹ, כָּכָה, כַּמָּה, כַּמָּה, כִּי, כְּעֶנֶת, כְּעַן.

כְּ (Aram.) the same, in its most manifold significations, e.g. כְּדִי equiv. to כַּאֲשֶׁר.

כָּאַב (fut. יִכְאַב) originally, to pierce (comp. Aram. כגב); next, to feel pain, to suffer. Hiph. to cause pain or suffering, with accus. of the person; of inanimate things, to destroy.

כְּאֵב (const. כְּאֵב) m. pain, suffering, of the body or mind; כְּ׳ לֵב sorrow of the heart.

כָּאָה (Kal, not used) equiv. to כָּהָה to be faint, weak, sad; hence, to be contrite, humbled. Niph. נִכְאָה to be humbled; hence נִכְאֵה לֵבָב of a contrite heart; according to some נִכְאוּ (Job. 30:8, with euphonic dagesh, they were driven out of the land; Auth. Version, "they were viler than the earth"), belongs to this root, it is possible, however, it belongs to נָכָא, which see. Hiph. to cause (לֵב) faint-heartedness. See כָּהָה.

כָּאֶה (origin. particip.) only plur. in the Keri כָּאִים faint-hearted, unhappy, humbled ones.

I. כָּאַר (not used) equiv. to כָּאוֹר in modern Heb. to be soiled, dirty; some consider that כָּשְׁר Amos 8:8, belongs to this root, and signifies dirty; probably, however, כָּאֹר stands for כַּיְאֹר.

II. כָּאַר (only 3 pers. plur. כָּאֲרוּ) to enclose, to fetter; only Ps. 22:17.

כָּבַב (not used) to be round, form of a ball, from which כּוֹכָב for כָּבְכָּב, compare טוֹטֶפֶת for טַפְטֶפֶת; according to others, the original idea is to shine.

כָּבֵד (once כָּבַד; fut. יִכְבַּד) origin. to be heavy, weighty (in contrast to קָלַל to be light); 1) to be cumbersome, burdensome, with עַל to some one: כָּבְדָה יָד עַל, אֶל, the power rests heavily upon some one; hence, of the burden of sins, or punishment, which bears heavily upon some one: "as a heavy burden they (the iniquities) are too heavy for me" (Ps. 38:4); 2) to be mighty, overwhelming (of the battle, iniquity, labour), not quite in a bad sense; 3) only in a good sense, to be weighty, important, considerable, honorable, numerous, wealthy, in contrast to קָלַל; 4) to be heavy, in reference to the use of the limbs; hence, to be dim-sighted, hard of hearing, slow in movement, to be obdurate, as יָקַר is used in Syriac and Arabic. Niph. נִכְבַּד; 1) to be or become honored, respected, comp. Kal 3; hence particip. pl. f. נִכְבָּדוֹת as a subst. that which is reputable, honorable. In this sense also, to be rich, e.g. נִכְבַּדִּים the wealthy, the rich sources (of water); 2) to manifest oneself great, glorious, towards (בְּ) some one. Pi. 1) to honor, to esteem, to laud, with accus. and לְ of the person; and also in reference to the original signification, with double accus.; with בְּ to honor, through, or in, something; 2) to harden, to make obdurate (the heart). Pu. pass. to be honored. Hiph. הִכְבִּיד 1) to make heavy, oppressive (the yoke); hence, with עַל to oppress; to make obdurate, unwieldy; 2) to make one honored, respected, to award praise. Hith. 1) to honor oneself, to dig-nify oneself, to boast; 2) to make themselves numerous, multiply.

כָּבֵד (const. כְּבַד and כָּבֵד, pl. כְּבֵדִים, const. כִּבְדֵי) adj. m. origin. heavy, burdensome, weighty (of a burden, yoke, rock; hence, 1) the burden, oppression, of sin, famine; כָּבֵד מִן heavier than; also, violent, strong; 2) heavy, as an indication of defect, e.g. heavy of tongue, mouth, lips, i.e. slow of speech; heavy, of a business, i.e. difficult to carry out; 3) rich, great, numerous, mighty, and heavy, generally in a good sense.

כָּבֵד (with suff. כְּבֵדִי) m. liver, either from כָּבֵד to be heavy, because the liver is the most dense part of the entrails, or the noblest, the best; hence figur. used for the heart, the innermost part.

כָּבֹד adj. masc. but only fem. כְּבֻדָּה (כְּבוּדָּה) glorious, magnificent; as a noun fem. glory, magnificence, wealth; respecting the form, comp. אֲדָמָה from אָדֹם.

כָּבֹד as a noun, see כָּבוֹד.

כֹּבֶד m. 1) heaviness, weight, burden, transf. to violence, of war, of fire; 2) multitude, from כָּבֵד to be numerous..

כְּבֵדוּת f. difficulty, heaviness.

כָּבָה (fut. יִכְבֶּה) origin. equiv. to חָבָה to cover, to conceal, to hide, but generally, to quench (fire), to extinguish (a light); transf. to suppress anger, wrath; intrans. to expire. Pi. to extinguish (a light); figur. to extinguish the glory of a people, i.e. to destroy.

כָּבוֹד (const. כְּבוֹד, with suff. כְּבֹדִי) m. 1) honor, fame, joined with עֹשֶׁר and נְכָסִים, it signifies, fortune; and also in a higher sense. Of God, it expresses glory, magnificence, majesty; of the Lebanon, beauty, splendour. Poetically, the noble one, i.e. the heart, the soul, in which signification it is sometimes fem.; 2) superabundance, wealth, like the verb כָּבֵד 3.

כְּבוּדָּה see כָּבֹד.

כָּבוּל (border district) p.n. of a city in Asher, and a whole district of twenty cities in Gallilee. The root כָּבַל is equiv. to גָּבַל.

כַּבּוֹן (border point) p.n. of a place in Judah. The root is כָּבַן, equiv. to כָּבַל.

כַּבִּיר (pl. כַּבִּירִים) adj. m. 1) strong, great, mighty, e.g. mighty water, strong wind, rich in days, i.e. of a high age; 2) famous, glorious, distinguished, mighty; see כָּבַר; 3) adv. much, many.

כְּבִיר masc. mat or mattress spread over something, from כָּבַר to stretch; comp. שֻׁלְחָן.

כָּבַל (not used) to tie round, to enclose, to wrap round, equiv. to גָּבַל to border round. Pi. כִּרְבֵּל (with ר interpolated) for כִּבֵּל to gird round, to wrap round. Pu. part. מְכֻרְבָּל wrapped up; from which כָּבוּל and others.

כֶּבֶל (const. pl. כַּבְלֵי) m. irons or fetters with which the feet are bound.

כָּבַן (not used) equiv. to כָּבַל to bind, to fasten, to bind together; hence מַכְבֵּנָא, מַכְבַּנֵּי, כַּבּוֹן.

כָּבַס (only part. כֹּבֵס) origin. to tread, (with the feet); hence to wash, which used to be done by treading, different, therefore, from רָחַץ, which signifies to wash the body; כֹּבֵס washer, fuller. Pi. כִּבֵּס (in pause כִּבֵּס) to wash, to cleanse; figur. of the cleansing of the heart. Pual pass. Hophal הֻכַּבֵּס (for הֻתְכַּבֵּס) of the wound of leprosy being scraped and cleansed; comp. כָּבַשׁ.

כָּבַע (not used) equiv. to גָּבַע, קָבַע to be high, hilly, or in the form of a hill; hence כּוֹבַע high cap, turban.

I. כָּבַר (not used) equiv. to גָּבַר to be strong, mighty, vigorous, great; hence transf. to be strong in abundance, greatness, or in durability, i.e. to be numerous, durable, multitudinous. Hiph. הִכְבִּיר to make many words; hence part. מַכְבִּיר fulness, abundance; with לְ, לְמַכְבִּיר, adverb, abundant, much, many.

II. כָּבַר (not used) to twist, to wrap up, to tie, to bind up; related to חָבַל, חָבַר, כָּבַן, כָּבַל, כָּמַר, and others.

כְּבָר 1) m. length, track; hence, adv. in reference to time, long ago, long since, already; 2) (great river) p.n. of a river in Mesopotamia, Chaboras, otherwise חָבוֹר.

כְּבָרָה fem. sieve, from כָּבַר to twist, to plait, to twine.

כִּבְרָה (only const. כִּבְרַת) f. length, track; hence in connection with אֶרֶץ, to define a measure of miles, which measure cannot, however, any more be stated with certainty. According to the Septuagint it is a horse course, i.e. as far as a horse can run till he is fatigued, viz. three parasangs.

כָּבַשׁ (fut. יִכְבּשׁ) equiv. to כָּבַס to tread (under the feet); hence transf. to suppress (the sins), to subject (as slaves), to vanquish (a woman), to conquer, to subdue (the sling stones, to prevent their doing harm); all proceeding from the original signif. "to tread under the feet." Pi. to subject. Niph.

pass. from Kal. Hiph. to subject, to subjugate (only in Ketib).

כָּבַשׁ (not used) to glow, to burn; not connected with כָּבַשׁ to tread; from which כִּבְשָׁן.

כֶּבֶשׁ m. footstool, upon which one treads.

כָּבַשׂ (not used) according to some, to multiply oneself, i.e. of the multiplication of sheep, but the signification is uncertain.

כֶּבֶשׂ masc. lamb, sheep up to three years of age; sometimes sheep generally.

כִּבְשָׂה (also כַּ׳) fem. from כֶּבֶשׂ; the female, ewe lamb. Comp. also the transposed nouns כֶּשֶׂב and כִּשְׂבָּה.

כִּבְשָׁן m. lime or melting oven, furnace (different from תַּנּוּר), from כָּבַשׁ to glow.

כַּד (pl. כַּדִּים) com. a vessel for carring water, pitcher. The noun appears to be primitive.

כְּדַב (Aram.) equiv. to כָּזַב to lie, but generally Pa. כַּדֵּב.

כְּדַב (Aram.) adj. m. (כִּדְבָה f.) lying, the fem. as a subst. lie.

כָּדַד (not used) equiv. to יָקַד to burn, to shine, to illuminate, to sparkle.

כַּדַּי see דַּי.

כְּדֵי see דַּי.

כַּדְכֹּד m. a sparkling, precious stone, carbuncle, as explained by Judah ben Karisch.

כָּדַר (not used) equiv. to כָּתַר, עָטַר, to enclose, to surround, to encircle; from which כִּידוֹר and כַּדּוּר.

כְּדָרְלָעֹמֶר p. n. m., as a name of the king of Elam it is probably ancient Persian.

כֹּה adv. so, thus; either referring to the preceding sentence as a comparison, or, and more frequently, to the succeeding sentence; hence, in the form of an oath: "God do so and more also;" or to quote the words of another. Besides this, כֹּה is used: 1) as a particle of time: now, at present, e.g. עַד כֹּה till now; redoubled, till now and then, i.e. meanwhile; 2) as a particle of locality: here, there, yonder, עַד כֹּה hither or thither, כֹּה וָכֹה hither and thither; 3) as a particle of the *modus:* in this manner, in that manner, e.g. כָּכָה—כָּכָה in this way—in that way. In all three significations the demonstrative and original sense is paramount. As to the derivatives, כֹּה is not an abbreviation from כָּהוּא, but belongs to the pronominal roots of כְּ, כִּי and others.

כָּה (Aram.) the same as the Heb. כֹּה.

כָּהָה (fut. יִכְהֶה, apoc. יֵכַהּ, inf. כָּהֹה) equiv. to כָּאָה, faint, weak, timid, shy, negligent; hence, of the weariness of the body, of being worn out by age, of the dulness of grief, of the dimness of the eyes, of faintheartedness. Pi. כִּהָה, only trans. to make sad, fainthearted; with בְּ, to sadden some one by reproof. The form כֵּהָה is adj. and does not belong hereto.

כֵּהָה 1) adj. f. from כֵּהֶה m. dim, extinguishing (of a lamp), faint (of the mind, discouraged), pale, dull (of the colour of a stain), dim (of the eyes), occurs especially as an adj. to נֶגַע plague; 2) subst. softening, soothing the pangs from a wound. The form is in accordance with nouns derived from the Piel.

כְּהַל (only particip. כָּהֵל) Aram. equiv. to כּוּל, יָכֹל in Heb. to be able.

כָּהַן (in Kal, only part. כֹּהֵן) probably equiv. to כּוּן, but trans. to arrange, to prepare; hence:—

כֹּהֵן origin. one who prepares, servant (of God), synonymous with מְשָׁרֵת יְיָ; next, priest, כ׳ הָרֹאשׁ, כ׳ הַמָּשִׁיחַ, הַכ׳ הַגָּדוֹל the high priest, anointed priest, כ׳ הַמִּשְׁנֶה priest of second rank, i.e. after the high priest; also counsellor, as the priests in the time of the ancient Hebrews were the advisers of the king. Pi. כִּהֵן 1) to officiate as priest, to serve, to administer the priesthood; 2) to put on the decorations of the priesthood, i.e. to decorate oneself magnificently.

כָּהֵן (def. כָּהֲנָא, pl. כָּהֲנִין) Aram. m. priest, equiv. to כֹּהֵן Heb.

כְּהֻנָּה f. the priestly office, priesthood, pl. כְּהֻנּוֹת the sacerdotal offices.

כַּו (pl. כַּוִּין) Aram. masc. a window, origin. a hole, from כָּוָה equiv. to קָבַב to be hollow, perforated.

כּוּב p. n. of a country, in conjunction with Egypt and Kush, probably נוּב Nubia.

כּוֹבַע (pause כּוֹבָע, const. כּוֹבַע, pl. כּוֹבָעִים) m. helmet, from קָבַע to be formed like a hill. As to the derivation, it appears to be a mixed one from קֹבַע and כּוֹבַע.

כּוּד (not used) to pierce, to wound with a pointed instrument; transf. to hurt, to injure; from which כִּיד and כִּידוֹן.

כָּוָה (Kal, not used) to brand, to burn a mark in the skin. Niph. נִכְוָה (fut. יִכָּוֶה) to brand oneself, to burn oneself (by fire).

כּוֹחַ see כֹּחַ.

כְּוִיָּה f. burning, mark of burning; origin. abstract formed from כְּוִי the burning in, branding.

כּוֹכָב (from כְּבַכְבַּב, const. כּוֹכַב, pl.

כּוֹכָבִים) m. a star, figur. the distinguished one, the great one who is prominent above all others. The root is כָּבַב, which see.

כּוּל see כֹּל.

כּוּל to measure, origin. to contain, equiv. to כָּלָה, כָּלַל. Pi. (redoubled) כִּלְכֵּל; 1) to contain, to hold (of a vessel); 2) figur. to endure, to bear, e.g. illness; 3) to maintain (by provision of food), to nourish and to support generally. Pu. כָּלְכַּל pass. to be maintained, provided for. Hiph. הֵכִיל to contain, to hold, similar to Pi.; figur. to endure; מַרְבָּה לְהָכִיל containing much; once הֵכִיל for הַאֲכִיל, see אָכַל.

כּוּם (not used), to heap up, *cumulare*; כָּם is related with גַּם, עָם, in the same sense; to gather, to garner; from which כִּימָה.

כּוּמָז (after the form עוּגָב) m. origin. that which is closed up, from כָּמַז; equiv. to כָּמַם to conceal, to lock up; hence, a kind of golden ornament.

כּוּן (Kal only particip. כָּן, as a subst. and particle, the fut. יְכוּנֶנּוּ Job 31:15, belongs to כּוֹנֵן, and stands for יְכוֹנְנֶנּוּ), equiv. to כָּנַן to stand upright, to be, to exist. Pi. כּוֹנֵן 1) to place something (e.g. a chair); 2) to confirm, to uphold (that which is sinking), to found (a city); next generally, to prepare; 3) to direct, e.g. an arrow towards (עַל) a mark, to direct the heart. Pu. כּוֹנַן to be directed, to be firm (of the step). Hiph. הֵכִין almost like Pi., to erect a (seat), to appoint, to prepare, to found, to direct against some one (לְ) the shot, to direct the way, the heart, and the idea of preparing in the widest sense. Hoph. pass. Niph. נָכוֹן to stand high (of the day; hence נְכוֹן הַיּוֹם full noon; 2) to be founded, to stand firmly; 3) in a moral sense, upright, proper, firm in mind, fearless; hence, נְכוֹנָה (particip. fem.) uprightness; 4) to be prepared, הִכּוֹן (imp.) prepare thyself; with לְ to be prepared for some one, or for something. Hithp. הִתְכּוֹנֵן to prepare, arm oneself, but also pass. to be founded, established.

כּוּן (place, stead) p. n. of a Phœnician city, formerly called Berota (Berytus, Beirut), perhaps כּוּן arose from כִּיּוּן, city of Saturn.

כַּוָּן (pl. כַּוָּנִים) m. a cake, especially the cake of offering, from כָּנַן to prepare; according to others, images, figures; also from כָּנַן to prepare, to form.

כּוּס (not used), to preserve, to conceal; from which כּוֹס and כִּיס; related thereto is כּוּת, wherefrom is נְכוֹת.

כּוֹס (pl. כּוֹסוֹת) fem. 1) cup, goblet; origin. that which contains, receives something, *receptaculum*; figur. the lot of fate whether good or bad; 2) name of a bird, pelican, so called on account of its throat resembling a cup or bag.

כּוּר (not used) to pierce, to perforate, to dig through; related to כָּרָה, from which כּוּר, כִּיר, כִּיּוֹר, כָּר, כֹּר.

כּוּר m. melting-oven or crucible (so called from its hollow form), where iron, gold, and silver is melted; figur. place of trial.

כּוֹר see כֹּר.

כּוּר עָשָׁן (the smoking melting-oven) p.n. of a city.

כּוּשׁ 1) p.n. of Ethiopia, which is mentioned in connexion with Egypt and Lybia, and which Saadias renders Abyssinnia; gent. כּוּשִׁי m., כּוּשִׁית f., pl. m. כּוּשִׁים, כּוּשִׁיִּים, Æthiopians; 2) p.n. m. Æthiopian.

כּוּשִׁי p.n. m. (formed from כּוּשׁ).

כּוּשָׁן p.n. m. identical with כּוּשׁ, from which it is formed, like לוֹטָן from לוֹט Gen. 36:29.

כּוּשַׁן רִשְׁעָתַיִם p.n. m.

כּוֹשָׁרָה (a modern word) only plur. כּוֹשָׁרוֹת f. happiness, prosperity, freedom; from כָּשֵׁר, which see.

כּוּת (Kal, not used), to conceal, to preserve; hence, part. Niph. נְכוֹת (after the form נְלוֹז) that which is preserved, the treasure; hence בֵּית נְכוֹת treasury, with suff. נְכֹתֹה for נְכוֹתוֹ.

כּוּת p.n. of an unknown province, from whence the Assyrian king sent colonists to Israel.

כּוֹתֶרֶת see כֹּתֶרֶת.

כָּזַב (only particip. כֹּזֵב) origin. to spin, to bind something together, equiv. to חָשַׁב, חָצַב, comp. זָמַם; hence transf. to concoct, to lie, to flatter, כֹּזֵב liar. Pi. כִּזֵּב to lie, with לְ and בְּ of the person, to belie some one, i.e. to deceive him; figur. to dry up (of water). Hiph. to convict some one of a lie. Niph. to be convicted as a liar.

כָּזָב (plur. כְּזָבִים) m. lie, deceit, hypocrisy; transf. to idolatry, oracle of the idols.

כֹּזֵבָא (drying up of the water), p.n. of a place, identical with כְּזִיב, אַכְזִיב, which see.

כָּזְבִּי (probably abbreviated from כָּזְבִית) p.n. fem. (the lying one). The Samaritan has כזבית.

כְּזִיב (deceiving river) compare נַחַל אַכְזָב, in contrast to נַחַל אֵיתָן, p.n. of a place in Judah, and also equivalent to אַכְזִיב Ekdippe, the present Daib, Zib.

כָּוַר (not used), origin. equiv. to נָזַר to cut, to break in pieces, transf. to be bold, brave, courageous.

כֹּחַ (only once כּוֹחַ, with suff. כֹּחִי) masc. 1) power, strength; hence לֹא־כֹחַ weakness, עָצַר כֹּחַ to retain strength; hence also, ability, and in a bad sense, violence; figur. strength of the earth, i.e. produce, fruit; property, wealth; 2) a species of lizard; origin. the slimy one; see כָּחַח.

כָּחַד (Kal, not used) origin. to keep off; hence Pi. כִּחֵד (fut. יְכַחֵד) to deny; next, to conceal a thing (with לְ or accus.) from (מִן) some-one. Hiph. to make a thing disappear, either by concealment or destruction; hence also, to destroy. Niph. 1) to be concealed from (מִן) some one; 2) to be destroyed, with the addition: from the earth.

כָּחַח (not used) origin. to be moist, fresh, vigorous; especially of the strength of the sap and marrow of life; comp. כֹּחַ 2.

כָּחַל origin. to smear over, but especially to paint the inner part of the eyelids with rouge (alcohol); see חָבַל.

כָּחַשׁ to decrease, to diminish; hence בְּשָׂרִי כָּחַשׁ מִשָּׁמֶן "my flesh faileth of fatness," and in this sense especially in modern Hebrew; hence Pi. כִּחֵשׁ figur. 1) to deny; next, to lie, generally; 2) to simulate, to flatter; e.g. to the conqueror by simulating humility; 3) to deceive, of material objects, i.e. to decrease. Niph. and Hithp. to submit to the conqueror, to flatter him, like Pi. 2.

כַּחַשׁ (with suff. כַּחֲשִׁי) m. 1) leanness, meagreness; 2) lie, hypocrisy, deceit. See כָּחַשׁ.

כֶּחָשׁ (for כַּחַשׁ) m. liar; perhaps it is only an adj. lying.

I. כִּי (contracted from כְּוִי) m. burning, mark of branding, from כָּוָה. From the orig. form כְּוִי, the above form כְּוִיָּה is formed, but the masc. form is seldom preserved in the original; comp. גוי and גְּוִיָּה.

II. כִּי relative conj. but in the most extended significations; 1) that, to connect two sentences; e.g. "and God saw that it was good," but also in a quotation of the words spoken (as in Ruth 1:10), where in modern languages the particle *that* is not used; also after נִשְׁבַּע, and forms of an oath; likewise after adverbs and interjections, prepositions, and other particles; e.g. after אַף, הֵן, תַּחַת, אָמְנָם, עֵקֶב, עַד, עַל, יַעַן, אֶפֶס, הֲלֹא, הִנֵּה; 2) as a relative particle of time, when; e.g. "when

Israel was young I loved her," or וַיְהִי כִּי it came to pass when, etc. In this sense it is often used as a consequence of the preceding sentence, and must be rendered *then*, either after the conditional particles, יַעַן אֲשֶׁר, אֲשֶׁר, אוּלַי, לוּלֵא, לוּ, אִם, לֹא אִם, or after an abstract noun; e.g. Gen. 18:20, "as to the cry of Sodom and Gomorrah, (כִּי) it is great;" 3) as a causal particle: because, therefore, or then. If several causes are assigned, כִּי—כִּי, or כִּי—וְכִי; sometimes it signifies, wherefore; as Gen. 40:15, "wherefore they should put me in the dungeon;" 4) to signify a contrast or negation; but however, but yet, but indeed, but still, etc.

כִּי אִם unite the peculiarities of כִּי and אִם, where, however, one or the other remains untranslated. The significations are: 1) except (כִּי) if אִם, it be then (כִּי) that, only (then) if, but if, except it be (Isaiah 42:19); except only, e.g. Isaiah 55:10, "but watereth the earth;" "but his delight is in the law" (Ps. 1:2); 2) where it is contracted into one word, so that one sense is dropped; it then signifies: only, as only, but, that (after the forms of an oath), for, if, where the proper expression must depend on the context, and כִּי remains in most cases untranslated. In the form כִּי עַל כֵּן the motive or reason of the preceding sentence is expressed, and must be rendered: because; the same as אֲשֶׁר עַל כֵּן.

כִּיד m. hurt, injury, from כּוּד; transf. to destruction, calamity.

כִּידֹד (plur. const. כִּידֹדֵי) m. darting flakes or sparks, flames, from כָּדַד to burn, to glow. The form is for כִּדֹּד.

כִּידוֹן m. 1) spear, lance, from כּוּד to pierce; comp. modern Heb. דָּקָר, from דָּקַר; 2) p.n. of a district; complete, גֹּרֶן כִּידוֹן threshing-floor of the spear; for which נָכוֹן stands in a parallel.

כִּידוֹר (for כִּדּוֹר with the dagesh analysed), m. circle, circle of warriors, next, army in general; probably from כָּדַר, like חַיִל from חוּל.

כִּיּוּן p.n. of a deity (Saturn) whom Israel worshipped in the desert. The derivation is uncertain, but if derived from כּוּן it signifies: image.

כִּיּוֹר (and כִּיֹּר, pl. כִּיּוֹרִים and כִּיּוֹרוֹת) m. basin, on account of its hollow, deepened form, from כּוּר, which see; either a basin for collecting fire, or for washing; figur. a pedestal in the form of a basin.

כִּילַי m. miser, origin. one that seizes, holds fast, from כּוּל *retinuit*, but not from נָכַל. The termination ־ַי is primitive. See כֵּלַי.

כֵּילָף (after the form הֵיכָל, plur. כֵּילַפּוֹת) m. sledge-hammer, axe, club, from כָּלַף, which see.

כִּימָה (from כּוּם) fem. group (heap, group of stars, i.e. the Pleiades, that form a group of stars; hence, Job 38:31, "canst thou bind the fetters (Author. Vers. sweet influences) of Pleiades?"

כִּיס masc. 1) a bag, purse, in which money is carried, or a girdle in which stones used for weighing things in the course of business are carried; hence אַבְנֵי כִיס; 2) equiv. to כּוֹס in Ketib, Prov. 23:31, cup or goblet; as to the form, it is neither from כָּנַס, nor from נָכִים, but from כּוֹס, regularly like רִיב, חִיל, דִּין.

כִּיר (only dual כִּירַיִם) m. hearth, the dual form on account of the hearth consisting of two rows of stones. The root is כּוּר; perhaps כִּירַיִם may be a softened form of קִירַיִם.

כִּישׁוֹר (equiv. to כִּשׁוֹר) m. spindle, distaff, from כָּשַׁר to be straight, stiff; comp. Aram. כָּשׁוֹר beam.

כָּכָה (contracted from כָּה—כָּה equiv. to כֹּה—כֹּה) a relative particle of comparison expressing similarity; in a stronger degreee כֹּה, thus (and) thus, from which אֵיכָכָה, which see.

כִּכָּר (contracted from כִּרְכָּר, const. כִּכַּר, pl. כִּכָּרִים, const. כִּכְּרֵי and in another sense כִּכָּרוֹת, const. כִּכְּרוֹת) com. 1) circle, circuit, circumference, הַכִּכָּר, the circumference of the Jordan especially, now called Elgaur; 2) something of a round shape, round cake, in which sense the plur. is כִּכָּרוֹת; 3) a weight, so called from its round form, generally, a talent, consisting of 3,000 holy shekels. In this sense the pl. m. is כִּכָּרִים and the dual כִּכְּרַיִם. The root is כָּרַר, which see.

כִּכַּר (pl. כַּכְּרִין) Aram. the same as כִּכָּר 3 in Heb.

כֹּל (with makkaph כָּל־) m. the whole, total, equiv. to כָּלִיל, derived from כָּלַל, but generally, when preceding a noun with the article, translated like an adj., e.g. כָּל הָעָם the whole people; it may also follow as a genitive, e.g. חָזוּת הַכֹּל the vision of the whole, or it is used with suff., e.g. מִצְרַיִם כֻּלָּהּ the whole of Egypt; 2) all, everything; joined to the plur., e.g. כָּל הַיָּמִים all the days, כָּל הַנִּפְלָאוֹת all the wonders; the same when connected with a collective noun, e.g. כָּל הַחַיָּה all the beasts; or when joined with a suff. pl., e.g. כֻּלָּנוּ all of us, כֻּלָּם all of them; or with suff. sing., when a collective is understood, e.g. כֻּלּוֹ all of them (Is.1:23), absolute, it signifies everything; with the article הַכֹּל all, i.e. all men, etc., בַּכֹּל against all, poetically, even without the article. If the succeeding noun has no article, it signifies: 1) every one, e.g. כָּל פֶּה every mouth; sometimes the genitive is separated by the noun intervening, e.g. כָּל תִּשָּׂא עָוֹן = כָּל עָוֹן תִּשָּׂא (Hosea 14:3); 2) any one, anything, e.g. כָּל דָּבָר any matter; in connection with a negative, as לֹא, אַל, אֵין it signifies, none, none at all, nothing, e.g. אֵין כָּל חָדָשׁ there is nothing new; 3) all kinds, e.g. כָּל מֶכֶר all kinds of sale, or sale of all kinds; sometimes it stands as an adv., signifying altogether, just so, entirely so, e.g., כָּל הֶבֶל (Ps. 49:6) it is altogether vanity, כָּל עוֹד as long altogether (as), כָּל עֻמַּת־שֶׁ just as much, etc.

כֹּל (with makkaph כָּל־, def. כֹּלָּא, with suff. כָּלְהוֹן) Aram. the same in the most manifold applications; כָּל־קֳבֵל דִּי, just because = because.

כָּלָא (1 pers. pret. כָּלָאתִי for כָּלִאתִי, fut. יִכְלָא) 1) to close up, shut up, to incarcerate; 2) to keep back, to impede, to keep off from (מִן) something, to prevent from, to deny, to hinder. The orignal signification is to separate; comp. כָּלָא. Niph. to be prevented from, to be hindered; hence, to cease. Several forms are from כָּלָה, equiv. to כָּלָא.

כֶּלֶא (with suff. כִּלְאוֹ, pl. כְּלָאִים) m 1) originally, separation; hence, prison, but more frequently joined to בַּיִת; 2) that which is separated, solitary, different from others. Dual כִּלְאַיִם two separated, mutually different things, Author. Vers. divers kinds.

כִּלְאָב p. n. m. (probably equiv. to כָּלֵב crier, yelper).

כָּלַב (not used), to twine, to twist; thus equiv. to חָלַף; from which כְּלוּב.

כָּלַב (not used) to howl, to bark, to yelp (the verb to yelp and the German klaffen approximate in sound to the word כָּלַב), from which:—

כָּלֵב p. n. m. (crier), patron. כָּלִבִּי.

כֶּלֶב m. 1) a dog, originally, the one that barks, transf. as a reproachful term; especially, a hound, dog's head; 2) fornicator, especially of male fornication; hence מְחִיר כֶּלֶב wages of male fornication, which are not allowed as an offering.

כָּלֵב אֶפְרָתָה p.n. of a place.

I. כָּלָה equiv. to כָּלָא, only in the forms יִכְלֶה, כְּלִתִּנִי, כְּלוֹ, but otherwise כָּלָא.

II. כָּלָה (fut. יִכְלֶה, once יִכְלָה after the manner of ל״א) 1) to be finished, at an end, completed; it is used like כָּלַל, e.g. "and the rod of his anger is complete;" also, concluded, determined by (מֵעִם, מֵאֵת) some one; to be fulfilled (of a prophesy); 2) to be destroyed, devoured, routed; also, of the vanishing, languishing, and perishing of a matter; in which sense, כָּלָה is joined with נֶפֶשׁ, רוּחַ, עַיִן, כָּלְיוֹת, signifying, the non-realization or vanishing of hope. Pi. (1st pers. כִּלִּיתִי, כִּלֵּיתִי, inf. abs. כַּלֵּה and כַּלֵּא, c. כַּלּוֹת) 1) to conclude (of a prophesy), i.e. to fulfil, (of a speech) i.e. to cease speaking; and in this sense כִּלָּה occurs before other verbs to signify the concluding of the action; 2) causative of Kal, to cause to vanish or to perish, to use up, to destroy, to rout; figur. to eat off (the branch). Pu. כֻּלָּה and also כֻּלְּלוּ to be completed, ended. See כָּלַל.

כָּלֶה adj. m., כָּלָה f. (origin. particip.) languishing, of the eye. See כָּלָה 2.

כָּלָה (origin. adj. f. which has become an abstr.) f. conclusion, completion; hence as an adv., wholly, entirely; transf. (as in the verb) destruction, annihilation; hence, עָשָׂה כָ׳, with בְּ or אֵת to make an end of some one, to destroy him; without pers. to destroy.

כַּלָּה (from כָּלַל, pl. כַּלּוֹת) f. 1) bride, from כָּלַל to adorn, to wreath, encircle as a garland; 2) daughter-in-law, i.e. the כַּלָּה of the son; comp. כְּלוּלוֹת.

כְּלוּא m. that which is closed or shut up, prison. In the Ketib כְּלִיא.

כְּלוּב m. 1) that which is entwined, from כָּלַב to entwine, plaid, twist; hence, basket to gather fruits in; cage, of entwined branches; 2) p.n. m. (perhaps related to כָּלֵב).

כְּלוּבַי patron., from כָּלֵב=כְּלוּב.

כְּלוּהוּ (Keri) p.n. m.

כְּלוּהַי (Ketib) p.n. m.

כְּלוּלוֹת (denom. from כַּלָּה) fem. pl. espousals, state of being a bride.

כָּלַח (not used) equivalent to קָלַח in Aram., to be straight, stiff, firm; synon. with קָנָה Heb.

כֶּלַח (from כָּלַח) m. 1) equiv. to קֶלַח Aram., stock, stem; hence figur.

firmness, health; as, תָּבוֹא בְכֶלַח אֱלֵי קָבֶר thou shalt come to thy grave in a firm age, i.e. without being weakened by age; אָבַד כָּלַח the firmness (vigour) has vanished; 2) p. n. of an Assyrian town or country (identical with חֲלַח) whither the Ten Tribes were exiled.

כְּלִי (pause כֶּלִי, pl. כֵּלִים, const. כְּלֵי) m. from כָּלָה to complete, to finish, to get ready, thus signifying something that has been completed, i. e. a vessel; hence, 1) any vessel or utensil; e.g. כְּלִי חֶרֶשׂ, זָהָב, כֶּסֶף in reference to the material; כְּלֵי מִזְבֵּחַ, כְּ׳ הָאֹהֶל, הַקֹּדֶשׁ, יְיָ in reference to the use of the same; 2) armour, weapon; hence, נֹשֵׂא כֵלִים arms-bearer, בֵּית כֵּלִים armoury; but complete, כְּלֵי מִלְחָמָה, כְּלֵי מָוֶת; 3) an instrument, a tool, e.g. כְּלִי נֶבֶל, כְּ׳ שִׁיר; figur. כְּלֵי זַעַם; 4) vessel, bark, boat; 5) garments, clothes.

כֵּלַי (from כּוּל) m. miser, equiv. to כִּילַי, which see.

כְּלִיא (Ketib) m. prison.

כִּלְיָה (from the mas. כְּלִי, compare אַרְיֵה from אֲרִי, pl. כְּלָיוֹת, const. כִּלְיוֹת) m. origin. vessel; transf. to a vessel in a medical sense, the innermost, the kidneys, the reins, generally used in pl.; also, the fat of the kidneys; figur. the fat (the best) of wheat, used of the full, ample wheat.

כִּלָּיוֹן (const. כִּלְיוֹן, from כָּלָה) m. 1) the languishing (of the eyes); 2) destruction.

כִּלְיוֹן p.n. m. the languishing one.

כָּלִיל (const. כְּלִיל) 1) adj. m. כְּלִילָה (const. —לַת f.), entire, complete; hence, כְּלִיל יֹפִי perfect in beauty, as also the fem. כְּלִילַת יֹפִי, and as adv., altogether, or as a neuter, the whole; 2) subst. equiv. to עֹלָה כָלִיל, i.e. an offering burnt entirely; hence also, as apposition to עֹלָה.

כַּלְכֹּל p. n. m. maintainer, supporter; orig. abstract.

כָּלַל (3 pers. plur. כָּלְלוּ) 1) equiv. to כָּלָה to complete (the beauty), to conclude; 2) equiv. to חוּל to encircle; next, to adorn =חָלָה to decorate; from which כַּלָּה, כְּלוּלוֹת.

כְּלַל (Aram.) the same, to complete, especially in this sense, שַׁכְלֵל and the pass. אִשְׁתַּכְלַל to conclude, to bring to an end.

כְּלָל p. n. m. completion, perfection.

כָּלַם (Kal, not used), origin. to wound, to hurt; synon. with גִּדֵּף; hence, Hiph. הִכְלִים and הֶכְלִים to put to shame, to blaspheme, to hurt, אֵין מַכְלִים no one make ashamed; hence also, to offend; likewise, of

larity, e.g. כְּמוֹ אֶבֶן as a stone, with suff. כָּמוֹנִי, כָּמוֹהוּ like me, like him; 2) as a conj. as, when, then, entirely like כַּאֲשֶׁר; 3) as an adv. thus, e.g. אֲסַפְּרָה כְמוֹ I shall speak thus like (the wicked speak).

כַּמּוֹן see כַּמֹּן.

כְּמוֹשׁ p.n. of a Moabite and Ammonite deity; hence, Moab is also called עַם כְּמוֹשׁ. See כָּמַשׁ.

כָּמַז (not used, equiv. to כָּמַת) to close up, to conceal; comp. כָּמַס. From which כּוּמָז, which see.

כָּמַן (not used) 1) to conceal, to preserve; 2) to season, to spread over with spice, to cover.

כַּמֹּן m. origin. spice, but specially, cinnamon, *cuminum*, with which something is seasoned.

כָּמַס (part. pass. כָּמֻס) equiv. to כָּמַת, כָּמַז, גָּנַז, כָּנַס to hide, to conceal, to treasure up.

כָּמַר (Kal, not used) to burn, to glow, equiv. to חָמַר; hence like חוּם, transf. to the dark, black colour, to be burnt. Niph. נִכְמַר to be burnt, singed, blackened (of the skin); next, figur. of the burning love towards (עַל, אֶל) some one, i.e. the exciting of love or compassion towards some one.

כָּמַר (not used) to entwine; comp. חָמַר; from which מִכְמָר, and others.

being ashamed of, or disappointed in his hopes. Niph. either pass. to be put to shame, maligned, or reflective, to be ashamed of (מִן) something, to feel shame.

כִּלְמַד p.n. of a place so called, near Assyria; according to the Targ., a country in Media, which, however, is not defined.

כְּלִמָּה (pl. —מּוֹת) f. shame, disgrace, נָשָׂא כְ׳ to bear, endure shame; figur. also כְּ׳ כִּסְּתָה פָּנִים, לָבַשׁ כְּ׳ shame clothes or covereth the face.

כְּלִמּוּת f. shame, disgrace.

כַּלְנֵה (also —נֶה, נוֹ) p.n. of an Assyrian city, which the ancients render Ktesiphon.

כַּלְנוֹ see כַּלְנֵה.

כָּלַף (not used) to strike, to push, to hammer; from which, כֵּילַף, which see.

כַּמָּה see מָה.

כָּמַהּ to long for, desire something; comp. κάμω, κάμνω.

כִּמְהָם (equiv. to כִּמְהָן) p.n. m. (the desirer, demander); once כְּמוֹהָם stands in the Ketib, which has the same signification.

כִּמְהָן p.n. m. (the same).

כְּמוֹ (before suff. also כָּמוֹ) as a prep. like כְּ, which is only lengthened with the indef. מָה=מוֹ; hence, 1) equiv. to כְּ, denoting a simi-

כֹּמֶר (only pl. כְּמָרִים), m. a priest of idols, from כָּמַר, so called either from his burning sacrifices, or from his being dressed in black.

כִּמְרִיר (const. pl. כִּמְרִירֵי) m. sadness, grief, darkness. The form is after שַׁפְרִיר, only that ִ stands instead of ַ, which is a common change; according to the ancients, כְּ is a prep., the noun being מְרִיר.

כָּמַשׁ (not used) equiv. to כָּבַשׁ to subdue, subjugate; from which כְּמוֹשׁ, which see.

כָּמַת (not used) equiv. to כָּמַס to hide, to conceal; from which מִכְמֹתֶת, which see.

כֵּן (origin. a particip. from כּוּן, with makkaph כֶּן־) 1) adj. m. (like all particles, are at the same time adj.), right, upright, firm; hence figur. honest; subst. honesty, לֹא־כֵן vanity, folly; 2) subst. כֵּן place, basis, foundation, e.g. כֵּן־תֹּרֶן the base of the mast, also pedestal of the basin in the court of the temple; foot of a pillar; hence מַעֲשֵׂה־כֵן the work of the base; in this sense, כֵּן is derived from כָּנַן, as is evident when it appears before suffixes, כַּנּוֹ, כַּנִּי, to distinguish it from the adj.; 3) particle (derived from the adj.) generally adv., rightly, correctly. It is also used to denote a comparison; as, so, thus, like as; in this sense, it stands sometimes in a relative position to כְּ, כַּאֲשֶׁר, כְּמוֹ, e.g. כְּ—כֵן like—so, כַּאֲשֶׁר־כֵּן, כֵּן־כְּמוֹ, כֵּן־כַּאֲשֶׁר; also, to compare the quality, such; or to compare the time, so long, so often. Different, however, is the signification when it is joined to prepositions, as אַחֲרֵי, אַחַר כֵּן after that, hereupon; בְּכֵן inasmuch; לָכֵן therefore, because; but also in an adversative sense, yet, nevertheless; עַל־כֵּן therefore; עַד־כֵּן till now. The singular of כַּנִּים is not כֵּן, but כִּנָּה.

כֵּן (Aram.) as an adv. the same.

I. כָּנָה (not used) to name, origin. to recognise, to distinguish; hence Piel כִּנָּה; 1) to name, to pronounce בְּשֵׁם by the name; 2) to give one a flattering surname, to flatter; hence, to circumscribe.

II. כָּנָה (not used) equiv. to כָּנַם to sting; from which כִּנָּה.

כַּנֵּה p.n. of an Assyrian city, probably a contraction from כַּלְנֵה.

כַּנָּה f. sprout, sprig, from כָּנַן; according to others, it is the imp. protect thou, from כָּנַן.

כִּנָּה (pl. כִּנִּים) f. gnat, vermin; from כָּנָה, equiv. to כָּנַם, to prickle, to sting.

כְּנָוֹת see כְּנָת.

כְּנָת see כְּנָן.

כִּנּוֹר (pl. ־רִים, ־רוֹת), m. guitar or harp, κινύρα, a stringed instrument of the Hebrews, celebrated by David playing thereon. Root כָּנַר to rustle, from the rustling sound of the strings. See also כִּנֶּרֶת.

כָּנְיָהוּ see יְהוֹיָכִין.

כָּנַם (not used) equiv. to כָּנָה II. to sting, to prick; compare Greek κνά-ω, κνίπ-ω; from which

כִּנָּם (from כָּנַם after the form אִפָּר) fem. collectively, gnats, vermin; origin. that which stings.

כְּנֵמָא (Aram.) adv. thus, in this manner; origin. as we say, composed of כְּ and נֵימָא, equiv. to נֵימַר, either referring to the preceding or to the succeeding sentence; if, however, it is derived from כְּנָא, with the suffix מָא, it signifies, namely, or by name, from כְּנָא to name.

כָּנַן (not used) equiv. to כּוּן to put or set down; from which כַּנָּה; but כֵּן is from כּוּן, and כַּנָּה from כָּנָה.

כְּנָנִי p. n. m. (protector).

כְּנַנְיָהוּ (and ־כְּ) p.n. m. (protected by God).

כָּנַס to gather (stones, treasures), to assemble (men). The original signification is as in כָּנַס to conceal, to preserve, to save. Pi. כִּנֵּס to gather, to collect. Hithpael, הִתְכַּנֵּס to wrap oneself, to hide oneself, from כָּנַס=כָּנַס.

כָּנַע (Kal, not used) 1) to kneel, to bend; related to חָנָה, חָנַן, to bend, to incline; but especially to כָּרַע, ר having been changed into נ; 2) transf. to put together, to pack; 3) intrans. to bend, to stoop, to be humble, downcast. Hiph. הִכְנִיעַ to humble, to subdue (the enemy). Niph. נִכְנַע humbled, conquered, or to humble oneself before (לִפְנֵי, מִפְּנֵי) some one.

כִּנְעָה (with suff. כִּנְעָתֵךְ) f. ware, trade, originally, bundle (of goods), from כָּנַע II. Probably, however, it is derived from כְּנַעַן and hence signifies goods, wares.

כְּנַעַן (probably from כְּנַעֲנִי, comp. שִׁמְעוֹן from שְׁמַעְנָה) 1) p.n. m. of the ancestor of the Canaanites or Phœnicians; 2) nether-land p.n. of the people and of the land of Canaan or Phœnicia, complete אֶרֶץ כְּ׳; hence also the Hebrew language, which the Hebrews adopted from the Canaanites, called שְׂפַת כְּנַעַן; אִישׁ כְּנַעַן a Canaanite, shortened כְּנַעַן; 3) merchant, trader, אִישׁ כְּ׳, but oftener the shorter form כְּנַעַן; hence with suff. plur. כִּנְעָנֶיהָ her merchants, traffickers.

כְּנַעֲנָה p.n. m. (traffic, trade).

כְּנַעֲנִי (pl. כְּנַעֲנִים) gent. m. כְּנַעֲנִית f. a Canaanite, a Phœnician, formed from כְּנַעַן; hence אֶרֶץ הַכְּנַעֲנִי, מְקוֹם הַכְּנַעֲנִי; 2) trading man or merchant.

כָּנַף (Kal not used) to wrap up, to to hide, to veil; hence Niph. to wrap oneself up, to hide oneself.

כָּנָף (const. כְּנַף, dual כְּנָפַיִם, const. כַּנְפֵי, pl. כְּנָפוֹת, const. כַּנְפוֹת) f. 1) wing, origin. that which protects, covers; hence בַּעַל כָּנָף or בַּעַל כְּנָפַיִם, poetically for bird; sometimes also כָּנָף winged animals; figur. the wings of the wind, of the morning dawn, or also for protection, and in a military sense, wing of the army; 2) that which resembles a wing; as, skirt, either with or without the addition of בֶּגֶד garment; skirt of the bed or cover; hem or seam, corner (of the earth), also in plur. כַּנְפוֹת הָאָרֶץ corners of the earth; top, summit (of the temple), e. g. כְּנַף שִׁקּוּצִים overspreading or covering of the temple of the idolaters. The dual form is also used in the plur. in the sense of wings, but in signification 2 the pl. is כְּנָפוֹת.

כָּנַר (not used), to rustle, to sound, to clatter, onomatopoetically; from which כִּנּוֹר and—

כִּנֶּרֶת (also the plur. כִּנְּרוֹת, כִּנֲּרוֹת; the rushing of a waterfall) p.n. of a city on the sea of Galilee, which received on that account the name יָם כִּנֶּרֶת.

כְּנַשׁ (Aram.) equiv. to the Heb. כָּנַס to gather, to collect, to assemble. Ithp. to gather themselves together.

כְּנָת (from כְּנָאת of the form כְּנָה, comp. קְצָת, מְנָת; only pl. with suff. כְּנָוֹתָיו, like כְּנָוֹת stands for כְּנָאוֹת, comp. מְנָאוֹת from מְנָת), f. nomination, title, transf. to namesake, one of a like title, i.e. fellow-officer; also generally, the titled one, officer; origin. however, abstr., entitling.

כְּנָת (pl. with suff. כְּנָוָתֵהּ, כְּנָוָתְהוֹן) Aram. the same.

כֵּס m. generally taken as an abbreviation from כִּסֵּא throne (which see), if the reading is not נֵס.

כָּסָא (also כָּסָה, not used) equiv. to כָּסַס to number, to define, to appoint; hence of the appointment of a festival; comp. יָעַד, from which מוֹעֵד.

כֶּסֶא (also כֶּסֶה), masc. a festival, a holyday; synon. with מוֹעֵד, likewise from יָעַד, whether it signifies a new or full moon depends upon the festival. In the Talmud, the feast of the new moon of Tishri (beginning of the year); hence the ten days intervening the 1st Tishri, or New Year's Day, and the Day of Atonement (10th Tishri) are generally called בֵּין כֶּסֶא לֶעָשׂוֹר.

כִּסֵּא (also כִּסֵּה, with suff. כִּסְאִי, pl. כִּסְאוֹת) m. chair, throne (of the high-priest, king, or judge); seat, generally, of the throne כִּ׳ הַמַּלְכוּת, כִּסֵּא הַמַּמְלָכָה; figur. seat of judgment, tribunal, seat of honor. The root is neither כָּסָא nor כָּסָה to cover, but כָּרַס to be elevated.

כַּסְדַּי (Aram.) adj. m. a Chaldean, otherwise כַּשְׂדַּי.

כָּסָה (only particip. כֹּסֶה, and particip. pass. כָּסוּי) to cover. Pi. כִּסָּה 1) to cover, with the accus. לְ or עַל of the person or matter covered; and with accus. or בְּ, of the material with which one covers: figur. of the covering, i.e. pardoning of sin, of the secreting and concealing of a matter; כִּסָּה מִפְּנֵי to conceal from some one; 2) to dress, to put on (sackcloth). Pu. to be covered, with (accus. בְּ) something. Niph. like Pual. Hith. to cover oneself, to wrap oneself, to clothe oneself, with (accus. or בְּ) something.

כִּסֵּה see כִּסֵּא.

כְּסוּחָה see סוּחָה; the root is not כָּסַח.

כְּסוּי (const. כְּסוּי) m. cover (of skins).

כְּסוּת fem. 1) covering, from כָּסָה; hence כְּסוּת עֵינַיִם covering of the eyes, i.e. gift to appease (Gen. 20:16); 2) garment, dress.

כָּסַח equiv. to קָצַח to cut off, especially the thorns; but the noun כְּסוּחָה is not derived from it.

כְּסִיל (pl. —לִים) m. 1) a fool, in opposition to חָכָם, sometimes including the idea of infidelity; 2) name of a constellation, origin. the infidel, i.e. the wicked giant fettered to heaven, Orion; the plur. is used for other and similar constellations; 2) p.n. of a place in Judea (comp. כִּסְלוֹן fruitful territory).

כְּסִילוּת f. folly.

I. כָּסַל (only fut. יִכְסָל) to be foolish, origin. probably equiv. to כָּשַׁל to totter, to stagger, to be indolent. According to others it is connected with כָּסַל III. in the sense of having confidence, illusion, vanity.

II. כָּסַל (not used) to be fat, fleshy, from which כֶּסֶל; transf. to be fruitful, moist, of the soil.

III. כָּסַל (not used) to hope, to confide, probably only transposed from שָׂכַל=סָכַל to look forward with confidence. Comp. מַבָּט from נָבַט.

כֶּסֶל (belongs to כָּסַל I., pl. כְּסָלִים)

m. 1) loins, muscles of the loins close to the kidneys, from כָּסַל II., transf. to the innermost of the heart, like קֶרֶב; 2) folly, from כָּסַל I.; 3) confidence.

כִּסְלָה fem. 1) hopes, confidence; 2) folly. The form is from כֶּסֶל.

כִּסְלֵו m. name of the ninth month of the Jewish year. If the name is Semitic, it stands for כִּסְלוֹ, which signifies in Aram. a dunghill, probably in allusion to its being the month for manuring the soil.

כְּסָלוֹן (fruit territory) p. n. of a place in Judah,

כִּסְלוֹן p. n. m. (the strong one).

כְּסֻלּוֹת (fruit districts) p. n. of a place.

כִּסְלֹת־תָּבוֹר loins of the Tabor, i. e. the fortified points; p. n. of a place in Zebulun.

כַּסְלֻחַ p. n. of a people, which is named as a colony of the Egyptians, and supposed to be the Colchians; it occurs only in the pl. ־ִים.

כָּסַם (fut. יִכְסֹם) equiv. to גָּזַם to shear, to cut off, to shave (the head).

כֻּסֶּמֶת (pl. כֻּסְּמִים) f. spelt, so called on account of the ears being cut (Auth. Vers. rye).

כָּסַס (fut. יָכֹס) to count, related to which is כָּסָא.

כָּסַף (fut. יִכְסֹף) 1) to be pale, white; 2) to long for (לְ) something, to desire, wish for something, origin. to languish, which is indicated by paleness. Niph. 1) to turn pale (from shame), to feel ashamed; hence particip. נִכְסָף ashamed, לֹא־נ׳ shameless; 2) to long, languish, for something.

כֶּסֶף (pl. כְּסָפִים) m. 1) silver, from its white color, transf. to a silver shekel; 2) money generally, plur. pieces of money.

כְּסַף (def. כַּסְפָּא) Aram. the same.

כָּסִפְיָא p. n. of a district, on the road from Babel to Jerusalem, which however cannot be the *pylæ Caspiæ*.

כֶּסֶת (pl. כְּסָתוֹת), f. a pillow, from כָּסָה. The form is like קֶשֶׁת, קֶרֶת, from קָרָה, קָשָׁה, and others.

כְּעַל see עַל.

כְּעַן (Aram.) adv. now, at present, origin. at this time, also equiv. to עַתָּה from עֵת; it is from עֶנָא, from which עֶנֶת (*Bereshith Rabba* 5 : 11, *Midrash Koheleth* 11 : 1, *Jalk. Berachoth* 6 : 1), the time, so that עַן is the masc. form; it belongs therefore to עַן.

כְּעֶנֶת (Aram.) adv. (from עֶנֶת time, and כְּ, like כְּעַן, from עַן time, and כְּ) only וּכְעֶנֶת and so forth, i.e. and yet, further, for a length of time; עַת in Heb. has already the same signification: long, *diu*, Hos. 13 : 13, כְּעֶנֶת is contracted in כֶּעֶת in the same sense. See עֶנֶת.

כָּעַס (fut. יִכְעַס) to be angry, vexed. Pi. כִּעֵס caus. to vex. Hiph. to make some one wroth, vexed; in a stronger sense, הִכְעִיס פְּ׳ כַּעַס to vex some one greatly.

כַּעַס (pl. כְּעָסִים) m. vexation, anger, grief. The plural signifies provocation to anger.

כַּעַשׂ m. the same.

כַּף (with suff. כַּפִּי, dual כַּפַּיִם, plur. כַּפּוֹת) f. origin. that which is bent, curved, hollowed; hence, 1) the hollow of the hand; of animals, the paw; next, hands generally. To save from the hand of some one, i.e. from somebody; to put the life in the hand, i.e. to risk it. Pl. כַּפַּיִם, but כַּפּוֹת signifies either handles (compare יָדוֹת) or hands when cut off. Phrases: יְגִיעַ, נְקִי, פֹּעַל כַּפַּיִם; 2) the sole, like רֶגֶל the sole of the foot, in the same signification the plur. כַּפּוֹת, and with animals also כַּפַּיִם; מְקוֹם כַּפּוֹת רֶגֶל foot-stool; 3) pan, dish, on account of its resembling the hollow of the hand, e.g. כַּף הַקֶּלַע the hollow (the middle) of a sling; כַּף הַיָּרֵךְ the hollow of the thigh, in which sense, however, the pl. is כַּפּוֹת; 4) the bent branches of the palm-tree, but as in this sense only the pl. כַּפּוֹת is found, it is possible that the singular is כִּפָּה=כַּפָּה and therefore not belonging to כַּף.

כֵּף (only pl. כֵּפִים) m. top of a rock, from כּוּף to be pointed.

כָּפָה (fut. יִכְפֶּה) origin. equiv. to כָּבָה to cover up, to smother, to extinguish; hence כָּפָה אַף to extinguish (pacify) the anger, as the Targ. דְּעַךְ. The same as כָּבָה, Jer. 7:20.

כִּפָּה f. palm-branch, especially the branch at the top of the tall palm-tree, which bends with the weight of its leaves in the form of an arch; hence used in contrast to the reeds which grow in marshes; figur. the honored one, in contr. to אַגְמוֹן the lowly one. The root is כָּפַף, and כַּף is probably its masc. form.

כְּפוֹר m. 1) dish, especially the one used for sprinkling, equiv. to מִזְרָק, from כָּפַר to make atonement, or from כָּפַר in the sense of spreading, equiv. to אָפַר; 2) hoar-frost, so called from its being spread over the earth.

כָּפִיס m. a rafter which runs through the roof, like a stone in the wall; according to the LXX. a beetle or insect found in wood, like חִפּוּשִׁית in the Talmud.

כְּפִיר (pl. —רִים) m. 1) a young lion; figur. of enemies, from כָּפַר to be strong, bold; 2) equiv. to כָּפָר village, court, from כָּפַר to unite. See כָּפָר.

כְּפִירָה (village district), p.n. of a city in Benjamin.

כָּפַל to fold together, to double up; hence כָּפוּל doubled. Niph. to be doubled, i. e. to be repeated.

כֶּפֶל (dual כִּפְלַיִם) m. double; hence כֶּפֶל רֶסֶן double bridle, כִּפְלַיִם origin. the double one; next, two-fold; often also, manifold.

כָּפַן to languish, pant for something; hence, to desire for something (עַל), from hunger or thirst.

כָּפָן m. hunger.

כָּפַס (not used) probably, to pierce, to thrust; but the etymology is uncertain.

כָּפַף (inf. כֹּף, but in the pret. and particip. the analysed form) 1) to bend, to cringe, כְּפוּפִים those that are bent down; 2) in derivatives, to form like an arch, to make hollow, related to גַּו, גַּב, קָב. Niph. (fut. אִכַּף) to bend, to humble oneself before (לְ) some one. From which כַּף, כִּפָּה.

כָּפַר (Kal, not used, and only denom. from כֹּפֶר) 1) to cover; hence transf. to cover (the sin), to atone, especially in Pi., Pu., Hith., Nithp.; 2) equiv. to גָּבַר to be strong, vigorous, courageous (only in derivatives); hence, כְּפִיר; 3) equiv. to חָבַר to join, to unite (only in derivatives); hence כְּפִיר and כָּפָר; 4) equiv. to חָמַר to be red (only in derivatives); hence, כֹּפֶר; 5) equiv. to פָּרַר to break to pieces (only in Pu.), the sense must be taken according to the verb from which it is formed; hence its numerous significations: Pi. כִּפֶּר (fut. יְכַפֵּר) from כָּפַר; 1) to cover the guilt (comp. כָּסָה); hence, to pardon, to atone a (accus. עַל or לְ) sin; with לְ or בְּעַד of the person, to make atonement for some one (בְּעַד, עַל), to cleanse from sin; to atone through (בְּ) an offering; figur. to conciliate, to appease, to ward off. Pu. 1) from כָּפַר 1, to be atoned for, cleansed from sin; 2) from כָּפַר 5, to be destroyed, frustrated, of a a covenant. Hith. and Nithp. הִתְכַּפֵּר and נִכַּפֵּר to be atoned for, to be cleansed from (accus.) a trespass. The application of כָּפַר in Kal belongs to כֹּפֶר which see.

כָּפָר (pl. כְּפָרִים) masc. village, from כָּפַר 3; comp. חַוָּה.

כְּפַר הָעַמּוֹנִי (Ammonite village) p.n. of a place in Benjamin.

כֹּפֶר (pl. כְּפָרִים in signification 3) m. 1) equiv. to כָּפָר village; 2) pitch, with which something is covered, therefore from כָּפַר, if it is not a secondary form of גֹּפֶר; 3) cypress, so called on account of its red colour, thus from כָּפַר 4; in this sense the pl. כְּפָרִים is used; 4) ransom, money given as ransom (with suff. כָּפְרְךָ) from כָּפַר 1, כֹּ׳ נֶפֶשׁ ransom-money for life.

כִּפֻּר (pl. ־רִים) m. atonement, but only in the plur. חַטַּאת, אֵיל, יוֹם הַכִּפֻּרִים day of atonement, etc.

כַּפֹּרֶת f. covering of the ark, mercy-seat; hence Kimchi מִכְסֶה לָאָרוֹן; transf. to the ark, even the holy of holies; hence בֵּית הַכַּפֹּרֶת place of the ark, the holy of holies, in Targ. for דְּבִיר.

כָּפַשׁ (Kal, not used), equiv. to כָּבַשׁ to subdue; hence Hiph. הִכְפִּישׁ to press down, e.g. in the ashes (בָּאֵפֶר), hence in Targ. כְּבַע.

כָּפַת (not used) to make round, in the form of a ball, to encircle, to crown; related to צָפַת; hence generally, to adorn, like עָטַר, כָּתַר. From which כַּפְתֹּר, which see.

כְּפַת (Aram.) to bind, to fetter; hence pl. pass. כְּפִתוּ they were fettered. Pa. כַּפֵּת (inf. כַּפָּתָה) the same.

כַּפְתֹּר (pl. ־רִים) m. 1) formed from כָּפַת (equiv. to צָפַת) with the old nominal termination ־ֹר, a knop, chapiter, so called on account of its round form resembling a crown; 2) p. n. of a district, probably Cyprus; hence אִי כַּפְתֹּר, though for Cyprus there is another name, כִּתִּים. From which 3) כַּפְתֹּרִים the inhabitants of Caphtor.

כַּר (pl. כָּרִים) m. 1) lamb, mentioned in connection with rams and goats (Gr. *καρ*); it, therefore, appears to have no verbal root; 2) meadow, pasture-place, or field, from כָּרַר, equiv. to אָכַר to plough, if not connected with כִּכָּר; 3) only pl. כָּרִים, from כּר (the verb is כּוּר to bore, to break through), a kind of war instrument for battering walls; 4) pillow, saddle, mattress put under a seat for riding; hence כַּר הַגָּמָל saddle of the camel. The root is כָּרַר, in the sense of stretching, which see.

כָּר belongs to כָּרִי. See כָּרִי.

כֹּר (probably from כּוּר) m. name of a measure for fluids and solids, containing ten ephahs, origin. a vessel deepened out; comp. כִּיּוֹר.

כְּרָא (or כְּרִי) Aram. to be overcast, equiv. to עֲכַר, transf. to sadness, dejectedness of the mind, hence, Hithp. to harm oneself.

כרב (not used) equivalent to קָרַב (in עָרַב ,(עִקְרַב (in שָׂרוֹב) to seize, to lay hold of, to gripe; the same as גָּרַף (in אֶגְרֹף) to hold fast. From which כְּרוּב, which see.

כַּרְבֵּל see under כָּבַל.

כַּרְבְּלָא (Aram.) f. a mantle. See כָּבַל.

I. כָּרָה (יִכְרֶה) equiv. to כּוּר to dig (a pit or well), figur. to lie in wait for some one (עַל), to dig evil, i. e. to prepare mischief; to dig the ears, i.e. to make to hear easily. Niph. to be dug (a pit).

II. כָּרָה (fut. יִכְרֶה) equiv. to קָנָה to buy.

III. כָּרָה to prepare a meal, to attend hospitably.

כָּרָה (after the form שָׁנָה; pl. const. כְּרֹת f. a pit, a cistern (of shepherds).

כֵּרָה f. feast, meal.

כְּרוּב (plur. כְּרוּבִים) m. a symbolical form composed of four figures, of a man, a lion, a bull, and an eagle, which was considered as a symbol of power and strength, as the keeper of paradise; as leading the chariot of God, a cherub: hence רֹכֵב עַל כְּרוּב, יוֹשֵׁב הַכְּרוּבִים the original signification is to hold, on account of its holding the divine chariot. See כָּרַב.

כָּרוֹז (def. כָּרוֹזָא) Aram. m. a crier, a herald.

כְּרַז Aram. to cry, to proclaim; related to קְרָא.

כָּרִי (particip. from כּוּר with the adj. termination ־ִי) m. coll. (comp. כְּנַעֲנִי also coll.) equiv. to כְּרֵתִי executioner, and next, the designation of a kind of body-guard of kings, and occurs always with הָרָצִים, after the Ketib also with פְּלֵתִי.

כְּרִית (a pit) p. n. of a brook where Elijah stayed.

כְּרִיתוּת (also ־ֻתת) f. separation of marriage, divorce; סֵפֶר כְּרִיתוּת bill of divorce.

כָּרַךְ (not used), arisen from the reduplicated form כַּרְכַּר; 1) to wrap up, to enshroud; hence תַּכְרִיךְ; 2) to enclose, to surround; hence כְּרַךְ (כַּרְכְּמִישׁ) enclosed town, fortress, castle.

כִּרְכֵּב (not used), arisen from כִּבֵּב, with the interpolation of the ר, and this has arisen from כִּבְכֵּב to enclose. From which:—

כַּרְכֹּב (with suff. כַּרְכֻּבּוֹ) m. border, compass, so called from its enclosing.

כַּרְכֹּם masc. *curcuma*, Indian saffron. This word is foreign.

כַּרְכְּמִישׁ p.n. of a city on the Euphrates, and probably the place now called Kirissia. The word is compounded from כְּרַךְ fortress, and כְּמוֹשׁ=כְּמִישׁ.

כַּרְכַּס (Persian) p.n. m. eunuch (Sanscrit *karkasa*, strong).

כִּרְכָּרָה (־רוֹת) fem. a female runner, formed from כִּרְכֵּר; see כָּרַר; hence the swift-running female camel, dromedary.

כָּרָם probably only belongs to כֶּרֶם, which see.

כֶּרֶם (with suff. כַּרְמִי, plur. כְּרָמִים, const. כַּרְמֵי) com. formed from כַּר meadow, by the termination ־ֶם, like חֵלֶם, from חֵל; hence origin. pasture, fruit, cultivated, land; e.g. דֶּרֶךְ כְּרָמִים; next, garden plantation כֶּרֶם זַיִת olive garden, but especially a plantation of vine, vineyard, complete כֶּ׳ חֶמֶר.

כֹּרֵם (denom. from כֶּרֶם) m. vintner; comp. שֹׁעֵר, סֹפֵר, בֹּקֵר.

כַּרְמִי p.n. m. (vintner).

כַּרְמִיל m. crimson colour, or the material receiving the colour; formerly שָׁנִי and תּוֹלַעַת were used for it. If it is Semitic, the word arose from כָּרַם (כָּרֹם) warm, with the termination ־ִיל and it would only be a later form of תּוֹלַעַת; but if it is Persian, ־ִיל has also a signification, which is: red, bright.

כַּרְמֶל (formed from כֶּרֶם with the termination ־ֶל; with suff. כַּרְמִלּוֹ) m. 1) plantation, garden, a plough-field (in contrast to desert); hence יַעַר כַּרְמֶל fruitful wood, i.e. a a forest which looks like a plantation; 2) transf. to the fruit of the plantation or of the garden; i.e. good fruit of the garden; e.g. גֶּרֶשׂ כַּ׳ corn beaten out of the full ears, i.e. of the early and best grown; 3) p.n. of a fruitful promontory on a mediterranean sea in Asia, generally used with the article, הַכַּרְמֶל, and on account of its appellative signification by poets, it denotes that which is fruitful, or of thick foliage; 4) p.n. of a mining town on the Dead Sea, with ה finis כַּרְמֶלָה; gent. כַּרְמְלִי m., כַּרְמְלִית f.

כְּרָן p.n. m.

כָּרַס (not used) equiv. to כָּרֵשׂ, קָרַס, to be crooked, hilly, bellied. From which כִּסֵּא and—

כָּרְסֵא (with suff. כָּרְסְיֵהּ, pl. כָּרְסָוָן, as if from כָּרְסוֹ) Aram. fem. a chair, throne. See כִּסֵּא.

כִּרְסֵם (from כָּסַם with interpolation of ר, like כִּבֵּב=כִּרְכֵּב, חֵרְצֹב=חֵצֹב, שַׁבִּים=שַׁרְבִּים to nibble off, gnaw, used of the wild boar; see כָּסַם.

כָּרַע fut. (יִכְרַע) only a secondary form of כָּנַע to bend, to kneel, e.g. עַל בִּרְכַּיִם on the knees, with לְ or לִפְנֵי of the person, of kneeling with reverence, synon. with הִשְׁתַּחֲוָה. It is also used in the following senses: (*a*) of the bending of a woman in labour; (*b*) to stretch over (עַל) a woman, i.e. to lie with to root out, to destroy (living things), etc. To make a covenant with (אֶת, עִם) some one; but with (לְ dat.) the form כָּרַת בְּרִית denotes the dictating of the covenant by the mightier party, but if done by the weaker party, it signifies promise, submission, and in this case, either בְּרִית is omitted, or אֲמָנָה and דָּבָר used for it in later writings. Niph. pass. to be hewn down, destroyed, to perish; of the water, to be divided. Pu. כֹּרַת and כָּרַת pass. like Niph. —Hiph. to uproot, to destroy (families, nations), to separate, with מֵעִם of the person. Hoph. pass. related to it is חָרַת, חָרַט.

כְּרֻתוֹת (origin. particip.) f. pl. beams cut out.

כְּרֵתִי (formed from כָּרַת, like כְּרִיתוּת from כָּרַת) masc. 1) executioner; hence the appell. of a kind of body-guard of kings, connected with פְּלֵתִי a runner, the same as כָּרִי with רָצִים; 2) gent. from כְּרֵת Crete (according to the Septuagint); hence כְּרֵתִים, כְּרֵתִי Cretians, as a surname of the Philistines, who are said to descend from the former.

כֶּשֶׂב m. lamb, from which כֶּבֶשׂ is a transposition.

כִּשְׂבָּה f. like כַּבְשָׂה which is transposed from it; see above.

her; (c) to bend in knees, to totter from fatigue. Hiph. to cause some one to sink (of enemies in war), to humble some one, i.e. to sadden him.

כֶּרַע only dual כְּרָעַיִם fem. the lower part of the thighs or calves; used of the springing power of the legs of the locust.

כַּרְפַּס masc. origin. cotton (Sanscrit *karpasa*), but also white linen, occurring in connection with חוּר.

כָּרַר (Kal, not used) 1) *curro*, to run, which as in דָּהַר is connected with running in a circle; 2) equiv. to אָכַר to plough; next, cultivating land generally, to make a field arable; hence כַּר originally in contrast to desert; 3) to stretch oneself, proceeding from the sense of running; comp. דּוּר. Pi. reduplicated כִּרְכֵּר to run in a circle, to dance; see כִּרְכָּרָה.

כֹּרֶשׁ p.n. of a king of Persia, Cyrus. The word is abbreviated from כּוּרְשִׁיד (ray of the sun).

כָּרַשׁ (not used) equiv. to כָּרַם to be hilly, round; from which:—

כָּרֵשׂ (later) m. belly.

כַּרְשְׁנָא (Persian) p.n. m.

כָּרַת (fut. יִכְרֹת) to cut off (a branch, a skirt), to hew off, to fell (trees), to hew down (idols); to cut off (the foreskin, privy member שָׁפְכָה),

כֶּשֶׂד p.n. of Abraham's brother's son, perhaps the ancestor of the כַּשְׂדִּים, which see.

כַּשְׂדִּי gent. m. from כֶּשֶׂד, but always as the plur. כַּשְׂדִּים (Ketib once כַּשְׂדִּיִּים); 1) Chaldees, the Chaldee inhabitants of Babel; hence לְשׁוֹן, מַלְכוּת כַּשְׂדִּים whence also Babel is called תִּפְאֶרֶת, גְּאוֹן כ׳; 2) Chaldea, the country; complete אֶרֶץ כ׳ but also without אֶרֶץ, and the f. with ה finis כַּשְׂדִּימָה towards Chaldea; בַּת כַּשְׂדִּים inhabitants of Chaldea, for Chaldea itself; sometimes it is not only used of the district on the Chaboras, but also of Babel generally; 3) astrologer, interpreter of the stars, Chaldea having been the cradle of astrology.

כַּשְׂדַּי (def. כַּשְׂדָּאָה, כַּשְׂדָּיָא, plur. כַּשְׂדָּיֵא and כַּשְׂדָּאֵי const. כַּשְׂדָּאִין) Aram. the same, especially in the sense of an astrologer, in connection with אַשָּׁף, גָּזַר חַרְטֹם.

כָּשָׂה probably equiv. to כָּסָה, but especially, to be covered with fat, to become fat.

כַּשִּׁיל m. an axe, a hatchet, from the Pi. כִּשֵּׁל to fell.

כָּשַׁל (fut. יִכְשֹׁל Ketib) origin. to totter, especially of the tottering from feebleness and weariness; hence כֹּשֵׁל the weary one, i. e. the tottering; transf. to stumbling, falling, over (בְּ) something. Niph. נִכְשַׁל (fut. יִכָּשֵׁל) to stumble, to fall; figur. to be plunged (in distress). Pi. to cause to stumble, where the Keri is always שִׁכֵּל. Hiph. to cause to fall, to stumble, to fell. Hoph. to be felled, to which is related כָּסַל, but not קָסַל in כַּרְסֹל, this being derived from כֶּרֶם.

כִּשָּׁלוֹן m. stumbling, a fall.

כָּשַׁף (Kal, not used) origin. to pay close attention, to listen, equiv. to קָשַׁב hence next, to speak softly, appearing more as listening than speaking; transf. to praying softly, to be occupied in whispering (used of the theosophs), etc. Pi. to use magic, particip. מְכַשֵּׁף masc., מְכַשֵּׁפָה fem.

כֶּשֶׁף (only pl. כְּשָׁפִים) m. sorcery.

כַּשָּׁף m. a magician; compare also אַכְשָׁף place of magicians.

כָּשֵׁר (fut. יִכְשַׁר) equiv. to יָשַׁר, אָשַׁר to be straight, right in a physical sense, i.e. to be stiff (comp. כִּישׁוֹר); transf. to be correct, to please, to prosper. Hiph. (inf. abs. הַכְשֵׁיר) to cause to prosper or to succeed; to prepare happiness.

כִּשְׁרוֹן m. prosperity, success; hence also, fortune, profit, advantage.

כָּתַב (fut. יִכְתֹּב) origin. to engrave, to carve (on a wooden tablet) related to חָצַב, חָטַב but next generally, to write something (accus.) upon (עַל, אֶל, בְּ sometimes accus.) something; כָּתַב סֵפֶר to write a letter to (אֶל, עַל) some one; כָּ׳ לְ, כָּתַב עַל, אֶל to proscribe to some one; to inscribe, to register; figur. equiv. to conclude, i.e. to write down a resolution (a decree). Niph. to be written. Pi. to write repeatedly (decrees).

כְּתַב (fut. יִכְתֻּב) Aram. the same.

כְּתָב m. writing, כְּ׳ הַדָּת writing of an edict; also (like in the verb, registry) sometimes a book or even a kind of letter or type, in which sense it only occurs in modern works.

כְּתָב (Aram.) m. the same, but also, prescription, command; hence, דִּי לָא כְ׳ without prescription, i.e. free, according to pleasure; כְּתָב סֵפֶר מֹשֶׁה the Pentateuch.

כְּתֹבֶת f. engraving, inscription, only used of the marks branded in the skin.

כִּתִּי 1) masc. gent. for the city כִּתִּי *Κίττι-ον* in Cyprus; but in the Old Testament only the pl. כִּתִּים, כִּתִּיִּים occurs; next, Cyprians generally; 2) the inhabitants of the land, hence Cyprians; next also, in the widest sense, like אִיִּים of the isles and coasts on the Mediterranean Sea.

כָּתִית adj. m. bruised, pounded, זַיִת is omitted; hence, שֶׁמֶן כָּ׳ oil of olives pounded in a mortar, which makes the oil of a better quality than when the process of pressing is used.

כָּתַל (not used) to separate, to part, synon. with חוּץ, from which is חַיִץ, related to חָצַל, חָסַל to cut off, to separate; from which:—

כֹּתֶל (with suff. כָּתְלֵי, plur. modern Hebrew כְּתָלִים) m. a wall, origin. a partition, for the separating of a space; the same as חַיִץ which see.

כְּתַל (def. plur. כֻּתְלַיָּא, from כּוּתַל) Aram. m. the same.

כִּתְלִישׁ either from כָּתַל wall, separation, partition, with the termination ־ִישׁ, or joined from כָּתַל אִישׁ p. n. of a place in Judah.

כָּתַם (Kal, not used) 1) equiv. to חָתַם to impress, to engrave, to inscribe; 2) to seal, to close up, to preserve. Niph. נִכְתַּם to be sealed up, to be marked of sin; comp. טָמַן, שָׁמַר, צָפַן also applied to עָוֹן. See also מִכְתָּם.

כֶּתֶם m. equiv. to סָגוּר, סְגוֹר that which is closed up, hidden, i.e. that which is precious; hence, poetically for gold, jewels; comp. טָמוּן, צָפוּן Deut. 33:19.

כָּתַן (not used) probably equiv. to תָּנַן to stretch, to expand; hence, to spin; comp. the same in אָמַן.

כֻּתֹּנֶת (with suff. כֻּתָּנְתִּי, pl. כֻּתֳּנוֹת, with suff. כָּתְנוֹתָם f. garment, especially the under-garment made of cotton, worn on the naked body.

כְּתֹנֶת (pl. כָּתְנוֹת) f. the same.

כָּתַף (not used) to carry (a burden); hence

כָּתֵף (const. כָּתֵף, dual כְּתֵפַיִם, hence with suff. כְּתֵפָיו, pl. כְּתֵפוֹת, const. כִּתְפוֹת) f. 1) the shoulder, on which one carries; different from שְׁכֶם origin. neck, back: כָּתֵף סוֹרֶרֶת rebellious shoulder, i.e. that which refuses to carry; בֵּין כְּתֵפַיִם between the shoulders, i.e. the back, transf. to beasts of burden; the pl. is used of parts of inanimate things resembling the shoulder, e.g. of the shoulder-parts of the ephod, of the shoulders of the axle, etc.; 2) side, flank, of a building, of the sea, of a town, a district; in the pl. the spaces at the sides: עוּף בְּכָתֵף to fly on the shoulder of some one (to pounce upon something like a bird of prey).

כָּתַר (Kal, not used) equiv. to עָטַר to surround, to encompass; hence כֶּתֶר. Pi. 1) to encompass, to surround, in a hostile sense; 2) to wait; comp. נָטַר. Hiph. to surround, in a friendly sense, to crown, with the double accus. like לָבַשׁ.

כֶּתֶר m. a diadem, a crown, so called from its encircling.

כֹּתֶרֶת (pl. כֹּתָרוֹת) fem. chapiter of a pillar.

כָּתַשׁ (fut. יִכְתּשׁ) equiv. to כָּתַת to pound, to bruise.

כָּתַת (fut. יַכֹּת, imp. plur. כֹּתּוּ) 1) equiv. to כָּתַשׁ to pound, to beat; hence of the dashing to pieces of a vessel, of the destruction of an enemy; 2) to beat a sword round; כָּתוּת one who is crushed (in the testicles). Pi. an intense signification of Kal; figur. to devastate (a country). Pu. to be pushed (one nation against the other) of a war. Hiph. to destroy (the enemy). Hoph. to be destroyed.

ל

ל Lamed (לָמֶד) is the 12th letter of the Alphabet. Its name, which signifies ox-goad, corresponds with its shape. As a numeral, it counts 30. It interchanges with ם, נ, ר, as being a liquid semi-vowel, and with ד and ת, as being a lingual, e.g. נִשְׁכָּה for לִשְׁכָּה, מַזָּרוֹת for מַזָּלוֹת, רָעַד for רָעַל, &c. As *litera liquida*, ל is sometimes interpolated, instead of the doubling of another letter, e.g. in זַלְעָפָה. As an ancient diminutive suffix, lost in the later ages of the lan guage, ל appears with the most manifold vowels preceding; but in most words the diminutive element is now entirely lost; thus, for instance, the termination ֶל, as כַּרְמֶל, נֵבֶל, סֵפֶל, רֶגֶל; termination ֹל in קַרְסֹל, אֶשְׁכֹּל; the termination ִיל in כַּרְמִיל, פְּתִיגִיל; the termination וּל in חָרוּל, etc.

לְ (sometimes לָ, with suff. לְכָה, לְךָ, לִי, pause לָךְ, לוֹ, לָכֶם, and others) preformative prep., orig. equiv. to אֶל, from which it is abridged, and hence its signification of motion. Its renderings altogether are: A 1) the purely local motion, e.g. after verbs expressing direction or motion, as קָרֵב לְ approaching to some one, בּוֹא לְ coming to some place, like אֶל; thus, הָלַךְ, נוּס, שׁוּב, יָרַד לְ, etc., always on the question, whither? sometimes with verbs expressing a motion or direction mentally, e.g. חִכָּה־, קִוָּה־ לְ, כָּלְתָה־נֶפֶשׁ, חָפֵץ, הֶאֱזִין, שָׁמַע, where לְ denotes the spiritual direction, and to which belong the particles of motion in reference to space, as לְאָחוֹר backward, לְמַעְלָה upward, לְמַטָּה downward, לִקְרַאת toward; also where the motion is continued to the highest point, like עַד *usque*, e.g. לְמוֹתָם unto or until their death, לְשִׁבְעָה to the full; בֵּין—לְ, orig. the intervening space, until, to; מִן—לְ from—till; לְ—וָעֵד until—further. 2) motion transferred to direction towards a person or matter; hence *a*) as dative; thus in verbs signifying giving, awarding, presenting, bringing, etc.; as, עָזַר לְ, הִצְדִּיק, הוֹשִׁיעַ־, עָזַב־, הִנִּיחַ־, יָלַד־, וְמַל, הֵשִׁיב־, סִפֵּר, הִגִּיד־, אָמַר־, הֵבִיא־, נָשָׂא, הֶחֱיָה־, שׂוּם־, נָתַן. *b*) in the most manifold significations, since in Hebrew לְ is not only used for the dative case, but also where in modern languages the relation is expressed by prepositions, e.g. by *for*, רִיב לְ plead for some one; גְּדוֹלָה לֵאלֹהִים, great *by* God, יוֹם לַיי a day of judgment *by* God, and others where the dative signifies belonging to; as יֵשׁ לִי I have, אֵין לִי I have not; *c*) as a sign of the genitive case; also in the sense of belonging to, e.g. בֵּן לְיִשַׁי a son of Jesse, or belonging to Jesse: this mode of signifying the genitive case is used in statements of numbers, e. g. בְּאֶחָד לַחֹדֶשׁ in the first of the month, אַחַת לָהֶם one of them; also where several genitives refer to one noun, e.g. פֶּתַח הַבַּיִת לֶאֱלִישָׁע; likewise with compound particles, e.g. מִחוּץ, מִקֶּדֶם, מִתַּחַת, sometimes after a simple one, as after סָבִיב; *d*) as a sign of the accusative case, and therefore later superseding אֶת; in this sense are שָׁלַח, הָרַג, עָזַב, אָכַל, לָקַח, חָבַק, הִצִּיל לְ; 3) transition from one state to another; hence, to become something, to turn into something, e.g. שׂוּם, הָפַךְ, הָיָה, עָשָׂה, נָתַן לְ; it extends still further where adverbs arise thereby, e.g. לָבֶטַח in safety, safely, לָרֹב in multitude, numerously, לִרְקָמוֹת in raiment of needlework; with plurals, it signifies individuality, e.g. לַבְּקָרִים every morning, לְמֵאוֹת every hundred. B) like לְ in the demonstrative particles, signifying resting; after the question, when? where? etc.; 1) the local resting, e.g. לִימִין on the right, לְיַד at the side, לַפֶּתַח at the door, לִפְנֵי in the presence, לְחוֹף on the coast, לַמִּצְפָּה at Mizpah, לְפִי קֶרֶת at the entrance of the city: 2) the temporal resting, the time of the action, e.g. לַבֹּקֶר in the morning, לָעֶרֶב in the evening, לָאוֹר by light; 3) the resting or abiding in a certain state, e.g. לְאֵל in power, לְבַד in solitude, alone, לָבֶטַח in tranquility, tranquil; לְ is also used before the infin. constr. e.g. לִפְתֹּחַ to open, *ad aperiendum*, לְצֵאתָם of their going out, לֹא לַעֲשׂוֹת not to be done, not a proper time for doing it; the translations of לְ in this case are very manifold: to, until, till that, so that, because, as if, since, inasmuch, as, etc.; לְ also signifies: after such rule, similar or according to, e.g. לְמִינוֹ after his kind.

לְ (Aram.) the same, and in the same double form as in Heb., only לְ appears here peculiarly in its use before the 3 pers. fut., to give it an optative conjunctive character, which by some is considered a secondary form of the preformative י.

לֹא (35 times לוֹא, seldom לוֹ) adv. of unconditional negation, not, whilst אַל is conditional. לֹא is used 1) as a negative reply to a question, and as a refusal; 2) as part of a compound to negative a nominal idea, noun or adj., e.g. לֹא אֵל that which is no God, לֹא בָנִים childless, לֹא דֶרֶךְ where there is no way, לֹא אִישׁ uninhabited, לֹא חָכָם unwise, לֹא עָם no people, i.e. a wretched people, לֹא כֹחַ powerless, לֹא מְעַט not little, much; 3) it signifies a prohibition or a command if it precedes the fut., whilst אַל is only a warning; 4) interrogative sentences, connected with a former sentence, where an affirmative answer is expected. בְּלֹא arises from לֹא being joined to the prep. בְּ, and the significations are guided by the influence of the בְּ, which are: 1) בְּ signifying in בְּלֹא not in (a time), i.e. without, before (the time): e.g. בְּלֹא יוֹם before the day, בְּלֹא עֵת beyond the time; 2) not with (something), i. e. without, e. g. בְּלֹא לֵב without heart, בְּלֹא כַכָּתוּב without being according to the law; 3) not by, e.g. בְּלֹא חַמָּה not by the sun; 4) not for, e.g. בְּלֹא כֶסֶף not for money. From לֹא connected with an interr. (הֲ) arises הֲלֹא in which case an affirmative answer is expected; likewise as pointing to something that is known, where the sense of interrogation becomes lost, e. g. הֲלֹא הֵם כְּתֻבִים are they not written, i. e. they are written; hence sometimes for הִנֵּה. A less significant influence לְ or כְּ have when connected with לֹא.

לָא (once לָה) Aram. the same, with הֲ of interrogation הֲלָא.

לֹא דְבָר (of no matter) p.n of a district in Gilead.

לֹא עַמִּי symbolical p.n.(not my people)

לֹא רֻחָמָה symbolical p.n. (not comforted).

לָאַב (not used) equiv. to לָהַב to burn, transferred to languishing; comp. צָחָה, and others.

לָאָה (fut. יִלְאֶה, apoc. יֵלֶא) equiv. to לָהָה to be weary, fatigued, powerless; transf. to be fruitless. Niph. to become wearied, faint; transf. to weary oneself fruitlessly, to despair. Hiph. הֶלְאָה to wear out, to exhaust, to tire the patience of some one.

לֵאָה p.n. f. (weariness, neglect, exhaustedness).

לָאַם see לַט under לוּט.

לָאַט equiv. to לוּט to hide to wrap up.

לָאַט Job 15:11, see אַט.

לְאַט see אַט.

לָאַךְ (not used) 1) to send, *legare*, compare שָׁלַח; 2) to arrange or transact business; next, to be active generally; as to the connection of the two significations, see מְלָאכָה.

לָאֵל p.n. m.

לָאַם (not used) either a formation from אַם, or from the original root לָא; ם not belonging to the root.

לְאֹם (with suff. לְאֻמִּי, pl. לְאֻמִּים) m. 1) people, equiv. to אֹם, אֻמִּים possibly ־ִם is only a suff. of nouns; 2) as a pl. p. n. of an Arabian people that cannot be defined.

לֵב (before makkaph לֶב־, with suff. לִבִּי, pl. לִבּוֹת, from לָבַב) m. the heart, as the seat of life; also equiv. to נֶפֶשׁ life, soul (comp. as a contrast בָּשָׂר), e.g. "it reacheth unto thine heart," i.e. life (Jer. 4:18), for which otherwise נֶפֶשׁ; hence the forms: the heart lives, to support the heart, the heart is sick, always signifying the soul; the following manifold significations of לֵב must be enumerated: 1) heart, as the seat of physical emotions, viz. love, confidence, joy, sadness, contempt, disinclination, pain, contrition, bitterness, despair, fear, trembling, fearlessness, courage, etc.; hence so many phrases in which the heart is considered the abode of such emotions; for which reason also, shouting, wailing, moaning, deriding, are attributed thereto; 2) as the seat of thought, of character, and of moral emotions; hence, it is spoken of as a pure, true, just, pervert, stubborn, deep, and wicked heart, with which are sometimes used the verbs הִקְשָׁה, חִזֵּק (to harden), etc.; לֵב וָלֵב duplicity. The dimensions of לֵב, as גֹּבַהּ, רֹחַב, גָּדֵל are used as moral standards to denote either haughtiness or timidity, narrow-mindedness or liberality; 3) as the seat of will and resolution; hence, to devise plans, to take counsel, to resolve, to consent, to wish, to resist, to refuse, are ascribed to the heart; next, knowledge, as identical with understanding; in this sense must be taken the forms חֲסַר לֵב, כַּבִּיר לֵב, אִישׁ לֵב, חֲכַם לֵב always in allusion to the understanding; 4) figur. to denote the midst of a thing, e.g. the heart of the sea, the heavens, and the oak, i.e. the midst.

לֵב (with suff. לִבִּי) Aram. the same.

לָבָא (not used) to roar, from which לְבִיא, לָבִי.

לְבָאוֹת as pl. to לָבִי see in *loco*.

לְבָאוֹת (complete בֵּית לְ lion-place) p.n. of a city in the territory of Simeon.

לְבָאִים as pl. to לָבִי which see.

לְבָאִים equiv. to לֹהֲבִים. Ps. 57:5.

לָבַב (Kal not used) to be fat, related to חָלַב, from which לֵב heart, origin. a fat human body. Niph. is denom. from לֵבָב, which see. Pi. לִבֵּב 1) to fatten, to bake or boil in fat, which may also be a denom. from לְבִיבָה. 2) as denom. from לֵבָב, which see under לָבַב.

לְבַב (Aram.) equiv. to לֵבָב Heb. With suff. לִבְבָךְ, לִבְבֵהּ; see also לֵב.

לֵבָב (const. לְבַב, with suff. לְבָבִי, לְבַבְכֶם, once לְבַבְהֶן, pl. לְבָבוֹת),

m. equiv. to לֵב from which it is analysed, heart. The root is לָבַב. From which denom. לִבֵּב to take the heart away, dishearten. Niph. נִלְבַּב to be deprived of the heart.

לָבַד see בַּד.

לַבָּה (from לֶהָבָה), f. flame. It is possible that the root is לָבָה to inflame.

לִבָּה (pl. לִבּוֹת), f. from לֵב heart.

לְבוֹנָה see לְבֹנָה.

לְבוּשׁ (also לְבֻשׁ) m. 1) garment, clothing, often poetical for בֶּגֶד, e.g. לְבוּשׁ שַׂק a garment of sack-cloth (mourning), sometimes, dress of splendour, e.g. and they stand כְּמוֹ לְבוּשׁ as a magnificent garment (Job 38:14); hence also of the scaly covering (garment) of the crocodile (Job 41:13); 2) transf. to husband, wife, perhaps on account of their being as near each other as garments are to the body.

לְבוּשׁ (Aram.) the same.

לָבַט (Kal, not used) to thrust to the ground, orgin. to beat down, related to חָבַט; hence, Niph. to be thrust down, to fall, or to plunge (oneself).

לָבִי (1st plur. לְבָאִים, comp. צְבָאִים, from צְבִי, 2 pl. לְבָאוֹת), com. a lion, a lioness, hence the double pl. according to the gender. See לָבִא.

לָבִיא com. a lion, a lioness; it is sometimes connected with אַרְיֵה and לַיִשׁ.

לְבִיָּא f. from לָבִי a form which has only latterly arisen.

לְבִיבָה (pl. —בוֹת) f. fat-cake, origin. that which is boiled in fat; from which the denom. לִבֵּב to prepare cakes with fat.

לְבָּים see לוּבִי.

לָבַן (Kal not used) to be white. The root is לָב, and is found in חָלָב milk, and in עָלַב. Hence, Hiph. הִלְבִּין either intrans. to be of a white colour, or trans. to make white; figur. to cleanse, to purify. Hith. to purify oneself, only in a moral sense.

לָבָן p.n. m. (the white, fair one).

לָבָן adj. m. לְבָנָה f. white. See especially לָבָן and לְבָנָה as nouns.

לָבָן (const. לְבַן) adj. m. equiv. to לָבָן white.

לַבֵּן see עַלְמוּת.

לְבָנָה f. the moon, origin. the white one.

לְבֵנָה (pl. לְבֵנִים) f. brick, origin. the white one, on account of its being made of white clay; it is therefore not a denom. from לְבָנָה. From which denom. לָבַן to make bricks.

לִבְנֶה m. poplar, probably on account of the white sap which issues on cutting through the bark.

לִבְנָה em. 1) whiteness, clearness,

brightness, transparency of the sapphire (סַפִּיר); 2) p.n. of a town in Judah, perhaps, origin. poplar district; 3) p.n. of an encampment in the wilderness.

לְבֹנָה (לְבוֹנָה) f. 1) frankincense, especially the white, and valuable sort, the best quality of which is called לְבֹנָה זַכָּה; the balm-plants are termed עֲצֵי לְבֹנָה, hence also גִּבְעַת הַלְּבוֹנָה; 2) p.n. of a town near Shiloh.

לְבָנוֹן (white mountain, alp), p.n. of a high mountain chain, between Syria and Palestine, with the article הַלְּבָנוֹן. "The valley of Lebanon," is the valley situate between the chain of mountains of the Lebanon. The Lebanon, forming the northern border of the dominions of the ten tribes; these dominions are called אֶרֶץ לְבָנוֹן.

לִבְנִי p.n. m. (the white, fair one).

לִבְנָה (occurs in the name of the river שִׁיחוֹר לִבְנָת), glass; see שִׁיחוֹר.

לָבַשׁ (in pause or with accent לָבֵשׁ, imp. לְבַשׁ, fut. יִלְבַּשׁ), m. to clothe, to dress, origin. to tie round, related to חָבַשׁ. It has a double accus., like all verbs signifying wrapping round, but it is also found with בְּ of the garment, though the particip. pass. has always the accus.; it is transf. also to clothing, in a moral sense, i.e. the being surrounded or penetrated mentally. Pual, to be dressed in official garments. Hiph. to clothe some one, with double accus.; with עַל, to put on a dress over something. The Hiph., like the Kal, is used also in a figurative sense.

לְבַשׁ (fut. יִלְבַּשׁ), Aram. the same. Af. הַלְבִּישׁ, like the Hiph. in Heb., but with לְ of the person.

לְבֻשׁ see לְבוּשׁ.

לֹג (also לוֹג), m. name of a measure for fluids, and, according to tradition, the twelfth part of a *hin*. The root is לוּג to be hollow, deepened out.

לָגַג see לֹג and לוּג.

לֹד (place of strife), p.n. of a place in Benjamin, later known as Lydda.

לָדַד (root of לֹד, not used), to quarrel, to combat, after the Arab.

לֹה once Ketib for לֹא.

לָה see לָא.

לָהַב (not used), to burn, to flame, related to לָאַב, comp. also שַׁלְהֵב.

לַהַב (pl. לְהָבִים, const. לַהֲבֵי), m.—1) a flame: פְּנֵי לְהָבִים flaming face, i.e. glowing with redness; 2) the glittering part of the sword, the blade; also used of the spear.

לֶהָבָה (const. לַהֲבַת, plur. לְהָבוֹת,

const. לַהֲבוֹת), fem. flame, often connected with אֵשׁ, but also blade, quite like לַהַב; from this probably arose לֶבָה.

לְהָבִים p.n. pl. of a people, probably equiv. to לוּבִים Lybians. So called on account of their living in the desert.

לָהַג (not used), extended from הָגָה; hence sometimes to meditate, to reflect, to study; sometimes, to speak.

לַהַג m. thinking, studying; later, speaking, talking.

לָהַד (not used), probably equiv. to לָהַט to burn, to flame.

לַהַד p.n. m. flame.

לָהָה (fut. apoc. וַתֵּלַהּ), equiv. to לָאָה to be wearied, exhausted, which the Targ. renders לְאָה. Comp. חָלָא the origin. signification is probably, to languish, languish with thirst.

לָהַהּ, only Hith. הִתְלַהְלֵהַּ to be mad, confused, insane; hence, in the particip. form, a madman, he who does things without considering.

I. לָהַט to burn, to flame; hence אֵשׁ לֹהֵט, figur. לְהָטִים flames darting forth, used of the tongue of man which burns, i.e. slanders. Pi. לִהֵט 1) to kindle, burn away; 2) to fan, to produce a flame.

II. לָהַט (not used), only an extended form, from לוּט to hide, to wrap up; next, to practice necromancy; similar to which is לָאַט.

לַהַט m. 1) a flame, transf. to the blade of a sword; 2) pl. sorcery, origin. concealment, masking.

לָהַם (Kal, not used), equiv. to לָחַם to eat, origin. to swallow eagerly; but more correct, equiv. to נָהַם to murmur, to whisper; hence, Hith. particip. מִתְלַהֵם whispering, murmuring, i. e. speaking softly.

לָהֵן see הֵן.

לָהֵן (Aram.) therefore, because, אֱלָהֵן דִּי because why, but, except.

לָהַק (not used), equiv. to קָהַל to assemble.

לַהֲקָה f. equiv. to קְהִלָּה assemblage, congregation.

לֹו for לֹא; see לֹא.

לוּ (or לוּא) a particle for expressing a wish, *ὡς*, *utinam*, would that! O that! joined to the imperf. or fut. if a fut. event is in question, and with the preterite if a past occurrence is in question; in all cases, however, the subject of the wish or of the condition is considered as not fulfilled, and in a certain degree of doubt; e. g. לוּ חָכְמוּ O that they were wise, that they understood this; לוּ יְחִיֶה O that he may live; לוּ

שְׁמָעֵנִי O hearken to me! it is natural that this wish passes into an interj., though we have no reason for considering this signification as primitive. See לוּלֵא.

לוּב (a desert, comp. צִי), p.n. of a country. From which gent. לוּבִי, which see.

לוּב (not used), probably equiv. to לָהַב to burn, to flame; compare also לָאַב.

לוּבִי (but only pl. לוּבִים, once also לֻבִּים), gent. plur. the Lybians, hence in connection with Egyptians and Æthiopians; לְהָבִים is the same.

לוּג (not used), to be hollow, to be deepened out. See לוּחַ.

לוּד (probably from לָחוּד, consequently from לָהַד, which see), p.n. m. (a dweller in the desert), from which gent. לוּדִי Lydian, name of a people.

לוֹ דְבָר see לֹא דְבָר.

לוּדִים p.n. of a people of Africa or Egypt; different from לוּד.

לָוָה (fut. יִלְוֶה) 1) to join some one, hence to accompany or dwell with some one. In this origin. signification לָוָה is connected with יָלַף, חָלַב, אָלַף. 2) to be under an obligation to some one; hence, to borrow from some one, the debitor being under an obligation to the creditor. The same is *nexum esse* in Latin. Niph. to join some one, with אֶל, עַל, or עִם, without distinction of purpose. Hiph. caus. of Kal in the second sense: to place some one under an obligation to oneself, to lend; hence, מַלְוֶה he that lends, but לֹוֶה he that borrows, debitor. In reference to the original signification הִלְוָה is construed with the accus.

לוּז (fut. יָלוּז), to deviate, to turn away, מֵעֵינֶיךָ from the looks. Niph. נָלוֹז to be perverted; hence נָלוֹז equiv. to עִקֵּשׁ the perverted one, as a pers. noun, or the perversion itself as a neuter. Hiph. (fut. יַלִּיז after the Aram.) to remove.

לוּז (from נוּז) m. 1) an almond or nut tree, but different from אֱגוֹז; 2) p.n. of a city, afterwards called Beth-El; with ה finis לוּזָה.

לוּחַ (not used), according to some, to shine; hence, to be polished, from which לוּחַ; according to others, the original signification is to engrave: thus, לוּחַ tablet for engraving.

לוּחַ (plur. לוּחוֹת, dual לֻחֹתַיִם) m. a tablet, usually of stone, on which something is engraven, but also of wood; hence —תַיִם tablet-work. The tablets of the law were called

לֻ׳ הָעֵדוּת, לוּחוֹת הַבְּרִית; figur. the tablet of the heart.

לוּחִית (probably tablet-work, or engraving), p.n. of a Moabite city.

לוֹחֵשׁ p.n. m. (the silent one, or the whisperer), generally with the article הַלּוֹחֵשׁ; see לָחַשׁ.

לוּט equiv. to לָאַט 1) to wrap up, to conceal, particip. לוּט pass., f. לוּטָה. The particip. form לוּט is used to distinguish it from לָט in the sense of secretly. 2) to be secreted, hidden, from which לָט particip. secreting, especially בַּלָּט, בַּלָּאט. 3) to practice sorcery, necromancy, from which the part. pl. לָטִים or לְהָטִים. Hiph. הֵלִיט (fut. apoc. וַיָּלֶט) to wrap up פָּנִים the face in (בְּ) something.

לוֹט 1) m. veil; 2) p.n. m. (mourner, or necromancer).

לוֹטָן p.n. m. (one that conceals).

לֵוִי p.n. m. (one that is encircled, from לָוָה to encircle); next also patron. for לֵוִיִּי, plur. לְוִיִּם Levites, a portion of the tribe of Levi.

לֵוִי (plur. לֵוָיֵא), Aram. the same.

לִוְיָה f. wreath, from לָוָה to encircle.

לִוְיָתָן (formed from לִוְיָה), m. origin. an animal which winds itself; hence, serpent, rattle-snake; next, transf. to crocodile or large winding sea animals.

לוּל (not used) reduplicated from the single root לו, in the sense of winding, circling.

לוּל (pl. לוּלִים) m. a spiral staircase, on account of its winding.

לוּלֵא (also לוּלֵי conditional conjunction, if not composed from לֹא=לֵא and לוּ, hence its distinction from אִם לֹא like אִם differs from לוּ.

לוּלֵי (from לוּל by adding the old adj. termination; pl. לֻאוֹת, const. לֻלְאוֹת) f. (in the pl.) loops, from לוּל to wind. The plur. form is from the sing. form לוּלָאָה, and the latter is from the m. לוּלֵי.

I. לוּן (hence pret. לָן, 3 f. לָנָה=לָנָה, 1 pl. לַנּוּ, inf. לָלוּן, לָלוּן, particip. לָנִים) to tarry over night, probably from לוּל (from which לַיִל); next, to stay or tarry generally, and also used of inanimate beings. Hiph. to allow to tarry; more frequently the abridged form לִין for הָלִין, fut. יָלִין, imp. לִין; but the causative element becomes gradually lost. Hith. הִתְלוֹנֵן to tarry over night.

II. לוּן (Kal not used) to revolt, to murmur, origin. equiv. to לָעַן to curse; hence Niph. with עַל to murmur against some one. Hiph. (also after the Aram. תַּלִּינוּ, יַלִּינוּ, part. מַלִּינִים) to murmur against (עַל) some one, almost like Niph.

לוּעַ to sip, to swallow, connected

with שָׁתָה. To which belongs also the redoubled form לַעֲלַע, which is abbreviated in עֲלַע; see עָלַע.

לוץ to scorn, to mock, to laugh at, to deride. לֵץ a scoffer, a scorner. Hiph. הֵלִיץ (fut. יָלִיץ) 1) to scorn, to deride, with the accus. and dat. 2) to interpret, hence מֵלִיץ interpreter. Pi. לוֹצֵץ (particip. pl. מְלִ=לוֹצְצִים) to scoff, to scorn. Hith. הִתְלוֹצֵץ to conduct oneself as a scoffer, i. e. as a perverted one, a sinner. In reference to signification 2 of Hiph., see מְלִיצָה.

לוּשׁ 1) to knead, connected with דּוּשׁ to press; 2) not used, to lick, from which לָשׁוֹן; 3) to be strong, from which לַיִשׁ.

לוּשׁ once Ketib for לַיִשׁ, which see.

לְוָת (formed from לְוָאת, from לְוָא) Aram. f. binding, joining, but only as a prep. by, at, מִן לְוָת equiv. to מֵעִם in Hebrew.

לָז see זֶה, הַלָּז.

לָזָה (not used) to deviate from something, equiv. to לוּז.

לָזֶה see זֶה, הַלָּזֶה.

לָזוּ see הַלָּזוּ, זוּ.

לָזוּת f. perverseness, from לָזָה.

לַח (pl. לַחִים) adj. m. moist, sapful; hence, fresh, young, transf. to new, unused. The root is לָחַח, which see.

לֵחַ m. freshness, cheerfulness, from לָחַח.

לָחָה (not used) probably equiv. to לָחַח to look fresh.

לְחוּם (with suff. לְחֻמִי, לְחֻמָם) m. 1) origin. equiv. to לֶחֶם food, used of the fire and brimstone which the Lord caused to rain down as food for the wicked; 2) the flesh, the body, connected with signification 1.

לָחַח (not used) fresh, sapful; hence, to be young, in the vigour of life, new, related to לָחָה, and perhaps also to לָחַם.

לְחִי (in pause לֶחִי, with suff. לֶחֱיוֹ, pl. לְחָיַיִם, const. לְחָיֵי, with suff. לְחָיֶיךָ, לְחָיֵהֶם) f. 1) jaw, cheek, so called from its freshness (as in other languages); to strike on the cheek, i. e. to humble; 2) chin; 3) p.n. of a district, complete רָמַת לְחִי hill of jaws of rocks, i. e. pointed cliffs. The name is illustrated in the history of Sampson.

לָחַךְ equiv. to לָקַק to lick, to nibble off. Pi. to lick up; figur. to lick the dust, i. e. to prostrate oneself unto the dust.

לָחַם (fut. יִלְחַם) 1) to partake of food, to eat, comp. לְגַם Aram. (the root-syllable is לח, extended by ם); hence equiv. to אָכַל with the accus.; with בְּ, however, to eat of something, to enjoy something, to delight in something; לְחֻם רֶשֶׁף devoured by the flame; 2) to combat, to battle, with אֶת and לְ, origin. to devour the enemy, אָכַל is used similarly when speaking of the sword (Isa. 1:20; Ezek. 21:33). Niph. נִלְחַם (inf. absolute נִלְחֹם) mutually combating, origin. devouring one another. The person against whom one makes war stands in the accus., or construed with בְּ, עִם, אֶל and עַל, but also with לְ, עַל it signifies to make war for some one; to besiege a town, const. with בְּ, עַל, עִם.

לָחֶם (const. לְחֶם) m. combat, siege (of the gates), the constructive form לְחֶם is put for לָחֶם.

לֶחֶם (with suff. לַחְמְךָ) com. food, nourishment, bread, bread-cake, also corn. The food from the tree, i.e. its fruit; the bread of God, i.e. sacrifice; אָכַל לֶ׳ to partake of a feast; עָשָׂה לֶ׳ to prepare a meal; אִישׁ לַחְמִי my associate, he that partakes of my bread.

לְחֶם (Aram.) the same.

לַחְמִי under בֵּית הַלַּחְמִי, see under בֵּית לֶחֶם, but also as a p.n. m.; the meaning, however, cannot be defined.

לַחְמָס p.n. of a place in Judah.

לְחֵן (not used) Aram. to cohabit, to copulate.

לְחֵנָא (with suff. לְחֵנָתָהּ, formed from the m. לְחֵן) f. a concubine.

לָחַץ (fut. יִלְחַץ) equiv. to נָחַץ to press (comp. the changes between נָחַשׁ and לָחַשׁ, לוּן and נוּן). Niph. to press oneself forward against (אֶל) something.

לַחַץ (with suff. לַחֲצֵנוּ) m. oppression, affliction, לֶחֶם לַחַץ, מַיִם לַ׳ bread or water of tribulation.

לָחַשׁ (Kal, not used) equiv. to נָחַשׁ to hiss, to whisper, or speaking with a soft hissing sound. Pi. of the whispering of conjurors, hence to conjure, to practice necromancy. Hith. הִתְלַחֵשׁ mutual whispering, conversing secretly; with עַל to hiss at some one.

לַחַשׁ (pl. לְחָשִׁים) m. origin. whisper; hence, as in the verb, conjuring of sorcerers; concrete, amulet, transf. to prayer, which is read softly.

לָט see לוּט.

לֹט m. a kind of odoriferous medicine, perhaps *laudanum* (Auth. Vers. myrrh). The root is uncertain.

לָטָא (not used) according to some equiv. to לוּט to conceal, to hide, like לְטָא Aram.

לְטָאָה f. a species of lizard, so called from its hiding itself.

לְטוּשִׁים p.n. of a people in Arabia.

לְמִים see לוּט.

לָטַשׁ (fut. יִלְטֹשׁ to sharpen, to point, especially of the sharp looks of man; of the sharpening of iron, or of the ploughshare, transf. to hammer. Pu. לֻטַּשׁ to be pointed, sharpened.

לִיָה (for לִוְיָה, from the masc. לִוְי, pl. לִיּוֹת) f. wreath, garland, festoon, equiv. to לִוְיָה.

לַיִל (const. לֵיל, with ה paragogic לַיְלָה, plur. לֵילוֹת) m. night, and also as an adv. nightly, in opposition to יוֹמָם, figur. calamity, like חֹשֶׁךְ. Root לוּל.

לֵילְיָא (Aram.) the same.

לִילִית fem. nightmare, a spectre; in Cabala, a p.n.f. supposed to be the mother of devils, formed from לַיִל by the termination ־ִית.

לִין see לוּן.

לִישׁ see לוּשׁ 3.

לַיִשׁ m. 1) a lion, from לוּשׁ to be strong; 2) p.n. of a border town in Palestine, later called Dan; 3) p.n.m.

לָכַד (fut. יִלְכֹּד) origin. to draw the net in (comp. the root in אָגַד, עָקַד), next, generally to catch, to gather in (water), to conquer (a town) by siege, to take (by lot); figur. to catch some one by artifice. Niph. pass. to be caught, to be conquered. Hith. to join, to connect oneself, to adhere together, e.g. of the water by the frost, of the scales of the crocodile.

לֶכֶד m. catching, either by an enemy, or in a snare.

לְכָה as an imp. from יָלַךְ; see יָלַךְ.

לְכָה for לְךָ unto thee. See לְ.

לֵכָה p.n. of a place in Judah.

לָכִישׁ (the invincible one), p.n. of a city in Judah.

לָכֵן see כֵּן.

לָכַשׁ (not used) to be invincible (after the Arab.), from which לָכִישׁ.

לְלָאוֹת see לוּלֵי.

לָמַד (fut. יִלְמַד) origin. to meditate, to learn. From to learn, לָמַד is transf. to train; hence, לְמוּד מִלְחָמָה trained to war; generally with (אֶל) to train to something. Pi. to instruct, to teach, with accus. of the person, and with dat. בְּ, מִן of the subject. Pu. to be trained, of beasts, soldiers, or songsters.

לָמָּה, לָמָה, לְמָה; see מָה.

לְמוֹ see מוֹ.

לְמוּאֵל and לְמוֹאֵל p.n. m. (consecrated to God).

לִמּוּד (לִמֻּד, pl. לִמּוּדִים) adj. m. (after the forms שִׁבּוֹל, קִשּׁוּב) 1) learned, trained, practised, the tongue of the learned, i.e. a practised tongue; 2) subst. a practised one, a pupil, a disciple.

לָמַךְ (not used) after the Arab. to taste.

לֶמֶךְ p. n. m.

לָמָן see מָן.

לְמַעַן see מַעַן.

לֹעַ m. throat, neck, from לוּעַ.

לָעַב (Kal, not used) to be pale, white, transf. like כָּסַף and בּוֹשׁ to be ashamed. Hiph. הִלְעִיב to shame, figur. to scorn, to deride; comp. עָלַב in עַלְבוֹן.

לָעַג origin. to stutter, to stammer, like עָלַג transf. to speak unintelligibly, outlandish, to scorn, to deride (origin. to mock the stammering of some one). Niph. to stammer; hence נִלְעָג a stammerer, an unintelligible one. Hiph. to scorn, to mock, to deride; constr. with לְ, בְּ and עַל, with אַחֲרֵי to mock some one speaking.

לַעַג m. scorn, scoffing, mocking; also used as the cause of scorn.

לָעֵג adj. m. scorning, speaking outlandish, לַעֲגֵי מָעוֹג (Author. Vers. mockers in feasts), slanderer.

לָעַר (not used) after the Arab. to put in order.

לַעְדָּה p.n. m. (order).

לַעְדָּן p.n.m. (one that puts in order).

לָעָה 1) to speak, to relate, not in a bad sense; hence לָעוּת speech; 2) to stammer, equiv. to לָעַג; לָעוּ (Job 6:3) is, according to some, in the same sense with the accent ante-penultimate on account of the pause.

לָעוּת (only Isa. 50:4) f. speech.

לָעַז equivalent to לָעַג to stammer, or to speak outlandishly; hence עַם לֹעֵז.

לָעַט (Kal, not used) origin. to eat, to taste; hence in Hiph. הִלְעִיט to cause to eat, to give to eat, always with the sub-signification of eagerness.

לָעַן (not used) equiv. to לוּן 2, to denounce, to curse, from which:—

לַעֲנָה f. wormwood, poisonous herb.

לָעַף only in שַׁלְהֶבֶת־וְלַעַף; hence= לָהַב according to some; possibly, however, the ל is interpolated.

לָפַד (not used) to flame, to burn; the radical is לף, related to לב, if the ד in לַפִּיד is not merely the suffix of a noun (—יד) without belonging to the verb.

לַפִּיד (pl. ־דִים) m. flame, לַ׳ בּוּז despised torch, i.e. torch cast away; flame, לַ׳ אֵשׁ flame of fire.

לַפִּידוֹת p.n. m. (flames, torches).

לִפְנֵי see פָּנֶה.

לָפַת (fut. יִלְפֹּת) to bend, to curve; hence, to cause something that is straight to bend or to fall; related to לָבַט. Niph. 1) to cringe, to turn round for the purpose of looking; 2) to curve, i.e. to take an indirect way.

לָצוֹן m. scorn, scoffing, אִישׁ לָצוֹן, i.e. לֵץ.

לָצַץ belongs to לוֹצְצִים; see לִוּץ.

לָצַר (not used), probably equiv. to נָצַר, to guard, to watch, to keep; hence, to superintend; from which probably מֶלְצַר, which see.

לַקּוּם p.n. of a place in Naphtali.

לָקַח (fut. יִקַּח, imp. קַח, seldom לְקַח, with ה finis קְחָה, inf. לָקוֹחַ, const. קַחַת) to seize, to lay hold of by (בְּ) the hand; next, to take, generally; this, the general signification, is used in the most manifold applications, e.g. to take a wife, i.e. to marry; to take a wife for (לְ) some one; to take away, to take off; to accept, to receive, to take under protection; to take in, i.e. to insinuate oneself in some one's favor (by looks or by manner); to conquer (in a hostile sense); to fetch away, to bring away, to take away, to offer as a present; to take possession of, and other verbs in which the sense of "taking" is predominant. Niph. to be taken away, to be taken as booty, to be removed, etc.; more frequently, however, occur as passive, Pu. לֻקַּח in pret. and Hoph. יֻקַּח in fut. Hithp. הִתְלַקֵּחַ to adhere together, used of the fire which flames up; comp. הִתְלַכֵּד.

לֶקַח (with suff. לִקְחִי) m. 1) the taking in or possessing by enticing; prepossession; 2) that which one receives, adopts: doctrine, knowledge, wisdom.

לִקְחִי p.n. m. (one rich in knowledge, or one who prepossesses people in his favour).

לָקַט (fut. יִלְקֹט) to gather, to gather up (ears of corn, manna, flowers, stones, etc.), proceeding from the original signification of "taking up," equiv. to נְקַט in Aram. Pi. to gather up often. Pu. to be gathered (one to another, Isaiah 27:12). Hithp. to gather themselves, to assemble at (אֶל) a place.

לֶקֶט m. the gathering (of ears of corn, grapes), after-gathering, gleaning.

לָקֻם see לַקּוּם.

לָקַק (3 pers. pl. לָקְקוּ, fut. יָלֹק) to lick, especially to drink in a licking or sipping way, applied to man as well as to dogs. Pi. לִקֵּק the same.

לָקַשׁ (Kal, not used), origin. to be hard, sapless, transf. to be late in season (of fruit). Pi. לִקֵּשׁ (is denom. from לֶקֶשׁ fruit late in season), to gather the fruit late in season. See לָקַשׁ, קַשׁ.

לֶקֶשׁ m. 1) grass in late season, math; 2) fruit late in season, from which לִקֵּשׁ; to gather the לֶקֶשׁ.

לָשַׁר (not used) to suck, to sip the

juice; the root is לָשַׁר equiv. to שַׁר, זָת (זַיִת), and others.

לְשַׁר (after the form קָטָן, with suff. לְשַׁדִּי) m. 1) sap, juice, transf. to sweet, juicy things (of cakes); hence לְ׳ הַשָּׁמֶן oil-cake; 2) vigour, sap of life.

לָשׁוֹן (const. לְשׁוֹן, pl. לְשֹׁנוֹת) com. tongue, proceeding from the idea of licking (formed from לוּשׁ, לָשׁ, with the termination וֹן—); but next, tongue generally, as the organ of speech; hence, upon, under the tongue, of speech; אִישׁ לָשׁוֹן a man of tongue, i.e. a slanderer; בַּעַל הַלָּשׁוֹן a babbler, a mountebank; hence, generally speech, language, and in the latter sense used for people with a distinct language. לָשׁוֹן is also transf. to inanimate subjects, e.g. golden tongue, i.e. a bar of gold; fire-tongue, i.e. flame; tongue of the sea, i.e. a gulph, for which לָשׁוֹן alone is sometimes used.

לָשַׁךְ (not used) to lay, to lay down, to abate; the same is שָׁךְ in reference to anger, tide, storm.

לִשְׁכָּה (pl. לְשָׁכוֹת, const. לִשְׁכוֹת) f. assembly-room, dwelling-room, from לָשַׁךְ, like λέσχη, λέχος, from λέγω, *cubiculum* from *cubare*; especially used of the chamber of the priesthood. See נִשְׁכָּה.

לָשַׁם (not used) probably to shine, for which some analogies are found. From which:—

לֶשֶׁם m. 1) name of a precious stone, opal or ligure; 2) p.n. of a city, which was formerly called לַיִשׁ or דָּן.

לָשַׁן denom. from לָשׁוֹן, but only Po. לוֹשֵׁן to use the tongue, i.e. to slander; hence Part. מְלוֹשְׁנִי in Keri, מְלָשְׁנִי from Pi. Hiph. the same.

לִשָּׁן (def. pl. לִשָּׁנַיָּא) Aram. equiv. to לָשׁוֹן Heb. the tongue, speech, people, etc.

לָשַׁע (not used) after the Arab. to cleave, to split.

לֶשַׁע (split of the earth) p.n. of a city on the east of the Dead Sea, having warm baths. The Targum has קַלְדָהִי Callirrhoe.

לָתַח (not used) to extend, to expand, to spread out, especially of a garment or mat; hence related with מָתַח (in אַמְתַּחַת), comp. מִטְפַּחַת in טָפַח. From which מֶלְתָּחָה, which see.

לָתַךְ (not used) to receive, to take up, to hold, probably related to לָקַט or לָשַׁךְ, or לָתַךְ is equiv. to תּוּךְ, since ל in many verbs of מ״ל is not of the root.

לֶתֶךְ m. name of a corn measure, the half of a *cor*. See the verb.

לָתַע (not used) equiv. to נָתַק to tear off, to break off (comp. נָתַח, נָתַץ). Niph. נִלְתַּע=נִתַּע to be broken, dashed to pieces (of the teeth); see מַלְתָּעָה.

מ

מ Mēm (מֵים), the thirteenth letter of the alphabet, and as a numeral counts 40. The signification of the name is: a well, water, not unlike the shape of the letter. It interchanges with ב and פ as a labial, sometimes also with the weak labial ו, e.g. דִּיבוֹן, דִּימוֹן, פִּלְטֵר, מֶלֶט, תָּמַהּ, Aram. תְּוַהּ. As a liquid מ interchanges with ל, ר, נ, as will be seen in the course of this letter. מ is used—1) as extending the form of some short roots, e.g. דָּרַם; 2) in the formation of the quadriliterals; 3) as nominal affix to form long nouns from short ones, e.g. ־ָם in כָּרֶם, כָּחָם, עֵלָם, עֶצֶם, גֶּשֶׁם, חֶלֶם, פֶּרֶם and others; ־ָם as סֻלָּעָם, יוֹמָם, ־ֹם as אָמְנָם, רֵיקָם, חַרְטֹם, חֲלֹם, מְתֹם, פִּרְיֹם.

מַ (i.e. followed by *dag. forte*); see מָה.

מִ see מִן.

מָא (Aram.) interr. pron. what? and also without being an interrog., something. like מָה in Hebrew. מָא דִי that which.

מַאֲבוּס m. place for feeding or fattening cattle, stable; or place where the fodder is kept, magazine. Root אָבַס.

מְאֹד masc. power, strength, might; hence בְּכָל־מְאֹד with all might; frequently as an adv. בִּמְאֹד מְאֹד with great might, i.e. very; likewise, עַד לִמְאֹד, עַד מְאֹד the same, מְאֹד very, entirely, swiftly, soon, according to the context. The root is אוּד.

מָאָה (not used) to measure, to fix limits, comp. מְעָא Aram., similar to מָא in מָאן a vessel, utensil, etc.

מֵאָה (const. מְאַת, dual מָאתַיִם, pl. מֵאוֹת) fem. origin. a quantity, a number; next, a fixed number; 1) a hundred, after the analogy of אֶלֶף and רִבּוֹ which also assumed the signification of a definite number from an indefinite one. The pl. מֵאוֹת sounds in Ketib מֵאְיוֹת, as being from the sing. מֵאְיָה. Ecclesias. 8:12, מְאַת stands for מ׳ פְּעָמִים or מ׳ שָׁנִים. 2) one from a hundred (monthly), a per centage as interest; 3) p.n. of a tower in Jerusalem.

מְאָה (dual מָאתַיִן) Aram. the same.

מַאֲוַי (only pl.) m. desire, longing. Root אָוָה.

מְאוּם (contracted מוּם) m. a fault, blemish, quite like חֶסֶר used either of a physical or moral defect. See מָאַם.

מְאוּמָה adv. (contracted from מָה וּמָה) 1) anything; after the negations of לֹא, אַיִן not anything, nothing; 2) any how. It is not connected with מוּם or with מְאוּם, nor is it the fem. of these words.

מָאוֹר (const. מְאוֹר, pl. —רִים, —רוֹת) m. light, an object giving light; hence of the sun, the moon, candlestick, whilst אוֹר denotes the light itself that shines. מְנוֹרַת הַמָּאוֹר the candlestick (that diffuses light), figur. מְאוֹר עֵינַיִם the light, or the cheerful look of the eyes.

מְאוּרָה f. from מָאוֹר brilliancy, i. e. the brilliant eyeball of the basilisk. The feminine termination often serves to express a metaphor, as in מִצְחָה, כְּנָפוֹת, קְרָנוֹת. According to others, it is equivalent to מְעָרָה, מְעוּרָה.

מֹאזֶן (only dual מֹאזְנַיִם) f. balances, the dual on account of the two scales. The root is אָזַן to weigh.

מֹאזְנַיִן (Aram.) dual, the same.

מְאָיוֹת see מֵאָה.

מַאֲכָל m. that which is eaten, that which serves for food; hence, food, corn, fruit, עֵץ מַאֲכָל fruit-tree, צֹאן מַ׳ sheep for slaughter.

מַאֲכֹלֶת fem. the same, in a figur. sense, the devouring; מַ׳ אֵשׁ food of the fire.

מַאֲכֶלֶת (pl. מַאֲכָלוֹת) fem. a knife, origin. that with which one eats (part. Hiph.)

מָאֵל p.n. of an Arabian people, designated the descendants of Yoktan, whose first ancestor was אֲבִימָאֵל, which see.

מָאַם (not used) to lack, to want, in contrast to תָּם to be perfect. The form is abridged from מְאַמֵא, which is reduplicated from מָא to diminish, to take away. Comp. מָאַן; from which מְאוּם and מוּם.

מַאֲמָץ (plur. מַאֲמַצִּים) m. strength (origin. subject of strength), with כֹּחַ strong in power, also in wealth; hence, treasure.

מַאֲמָר m. word, command, origin. that which is said or commanded.

מֵאמַר (Aram.) the same.

מָאן Aram. (def. מָאנָא, plur. מָאנַיִן, const. מָאנֵי) m. a vessel, origin. size, measure, from מָא equiv. to מֵאָה Heb.; comp. also כְּלִי. —ן is the formative syllable, as in לָשׁוֹן.

מָאֵן (Kal, not used) not being, wanting, formed from מָא, and the same as מָה (see below). Pi. מֵאֵן (fut. יְמָאֵן) to negative, refuse. Comp. also מָאַם.

מָאֵן (origin. particip.) adj. m. to negative, refuse.

מָאֵן (pl. מֵאֲנִים) adj. m. the same.

מָאַס (fut. יִמְאַס) to despise, disdain, reject, constr. with accusative and בְּ. Niph. 1) to be despised; 2) formed from מָסַס: to melt, to be dissolved, to vanish.

מַאֲפֶה m. that which is baked, from אָפָה.

מַאֲפֵל m. darkness, from אָפַל.

מַאְפֵּלְיָה f. the darkness from God; יָה is here like יָה in שַׁלְהֶבֶתְיָה; according to others, —לְיָה is an adj. termination from —לִי, and hence fem. for —לִיָּה.

מָאַר (Kal, not used) to stab, pierce, origin. to hurt, either equiv. to מָרַר or אָרַר. Hence, Hiph. to cause pain, to wound, to hurt, סִלּוֹן מַמְאִיר piercing thorn, צָרַעַת מַמְאֶרֶת a fretting leprosy.

מַאֲרָב m. 1) place of watching, ambush; 2) the act of watching; concr. for abstract, they that lie in ambush.

מְאֵרָה (from מָאַר, after the form יְרֵשָׁה) f. imprecation, curse.

מֵאֵת=מִן, see אֵת.

מִבְדָּלֹת f. separated place.

מָבוֹא (מְבוֹאִים, ־אוֹת) masc. 1) entrance, avenue (to a gate, to the sea), from בּוֹא to come in; 2) descent, of the sun, origin. its going to set; hence also, the west, western parts.

מְבוּכָה fem. confusion, confoundedness, from בּוּךְ.

מַבּוּל (from יָבַל) masc. flood, especially of the great deluge.

מְבוֹנִים (Ketib) m. plur. formed from מָבוֹן (root בּוּן) insight, prudence, wisdom; transf. to wise doctrines, abs. for concr.

מְבוּסָה f. treading down (with the feet), destruction. Root בּוּס.

מַבּוּעַ (pl. ־עִים) m. a spring, from נָבַע.

מְבוּקָה (for מְבֻקָּה) fem. emptiness, void, waste; from בָּקַק.

מָבוּשׁ (only plur. מְבוּשִׁים) m. privy part; from בּוּשׁ.

מִבְזָה f. contempt, disdain; hence נִמְבְזָה, which see.

מִבְחוֹר m. selection, choice; concr. that which is chosen.

מִבְחָר m. 1) the same; 2) p. n. m.

מַבָּט (with suff. מַבָּטָהּ) m. prospect, hopes, object of hopes; from נָבַט.

מִבְטָא m. connected with שְׂפָתַיִם pronunciation, speech. See בָּטָא.

מִבְטָח (with suff. מִבְטַחִי, plural מִבְטַחִים) m. confidence, object of confidence, safety; from בָּטַח.

מַבְלִגִית f. brightness, cheerfulness. See בָּלַג.

מִבְנֶה m. a building, from בָּנָה.

מִבְצָר (const. —צַר, pl. —צָרִים, —רוֹת) m. 1) fortress, fortification, with or without עִיר; עִיר מִבְצָרוֹת for עָרֵי מִבְצָרוֹת castles, burghs; 2) p.n. masc. (fortification, or rather fortifier).

מִבְרָח masc. flight, concr. fugitive. See בָּרַח.

מְבֻשִׁים see מָבוֹשׁ.

מִבְשָׂם p.n. m. (fragrance).

מְבַשְּׁלֹת (plur. —שְּׁלוֹת) f. hearth, on which the cooking is prepared.

מָג m. a magi, a priest (among the Persians); hence רַב מָג head-magi.

מַגְבִּישׁ p.n. of a place.

מִגְבָּלֹת f. cord, string; from גָּבַל = חָבַל.

מִגְבָּעָה fem. a turban, from its hill-like appearance; different from מִצְנֶפֶת.

מָגַד (not used) to be distinguished, precious, excellent. From which:

מֶגֶד (pl. מְגָדִים) m. that which is noble, precious things, e.g. of heaven, i.e. fruit; also joined with פְּרִי precious fruit.

מְגִדּוֹ (also —דּוֹן origin. that which is noble, adorned, rich in fruit) p.n. of a city in the territory of Manasseh; hence, בִּקְעַת מְגִדּוֹ, מֵי valley, water near Megiddo, i.e. the valley and the brook of Kishon.

מַגְדִּיאֵל p.n. m. gift of God.

מִגְדּוֹל (a tower) p. n. of a city in Egypt.

מִגְדָּל (plur. מִגְדָּלִים, —לוֹת) m. 1) a tower (of castles), or a small one in a vineyard; 2) anything of elevated position, as a scaffold, stage, balcony; figur. eminence, greatness; concr. the great. 3) in several proper names of places, e.g. מִגְדַּל אֵל (the Tower of God) p.n. of a city in Naphtali; מִגְדַּל גָּד (Tower of Gad) p. n. of a city in Judah; מִגְדַּל עֵדֶר (Tower of herds) p.n. of a place near Bethlehem.

מִגְדָּנָה f. preciousness, nobleness, only pl., precious gifts.

מָגוֹג p.n. of a northern people, whose king was called גּוֹג; this people is, according to Josephus, of Scythian origin.

מָגוֹר (pl. מְגוּרִים) m. 1) fear, from יָגֹר = גּוּר. 2) from גּוּר (to dwell) abode, sojourning (as a stranger); hence, pilgrimage, itineracy, in the biblical sense.

מְגוּרָה f. 1) from מָגוֹר 1, fear, terror, like מְגֹרָה of which the plur. occurs in this sense; 2) store, magazine, from גּוּר to assemble, to collect.

מַגְזֵרָה f. an axe, from גָּזַר.

מַגָּל m. a sickle, from נָגַל.

מְגִלָּה f. something rolled together, roll of manuscript; complete, מְגִלַּת סֵפֶר, especially of the scroll of the Law.

מְגַמָּה (const. —מַּת) f. according to some, multitude, host, from גָּמַם;

but the more correct derivation is from נָמַר, so that מְנָמַּת is a contraction from מְנָמֶּרֶת, signifying, end, aim, goal; compare קֵץ.

מָגַן (Kal, not used) to be enabled; hence מִגֵּן 1) to deliver into the power of some one, to surrender (the enemy) into the hand of some one (בְּיַד); 2) denom. from מָגֵן to protect, to shield, to surround (of a crown).

מָגֵן (with suff. מָגִנִּי, pl. מָגִנִּים, const. —נֵּי) com. a shield, from גָּנַן to shield, to protect; hence אִישׁ מָגֵן an armed man (a robber); transf. to God, as Protector; the princes also are called, the shields of the earth.

מְגִנָּה (formed from מָגֵן) f. a cover, which protects; figur. מְ׳ לֵב the cover of the heart, i.e. stubbornness, obduracy.

מִגְעֶרֶת f. threatening (of God), reproof, curse.

מַגֵּפָה f. a blow, a plague, through war or pestilence; next, the perishing of multitudes.

מַגְפִּיעָשׁ p.n. m.

מָגַר equiv. to נָגַר to flow along, to pour forth; also, trans. מָגוּר to be poured forth, to be delivered up to (אֶל) the sword. But generally in this sense only in Pi. מִגֵּר to deliver up forcibly; also הִגִּיר, from נָגַר.

מְגַר (Aram.) the same. Pi. to thrust, overthrow.

מְגֵרָה f. a saw, from גָּרַר.

מִגְרוֹן (thrust), p.n. of a city in Benjamin.

מִגְרָעוֹת fem. diminishing, deduction, from גָּרַע, only used in pl.

מֶגְרָפָה fem. clod, lump, from גָּרַף, which see.

מִגְרָשׁ (pl. ־שִׁים, ־שׁוֹת) m. 1) origin. liberties which belong to the possession of the town; hence also, the open place round a building, place of pasture. 2) district belonging to the town, עִיר מְ׳ town having a suburb. See גָּרַשׁ II.

מַד (with suff. מַדִּי and מִדּוֹ, plur. מַדִּים and מִדִּין)—1) garment, which is worn on the body, from מָדַד. מִדּוֹ בַד (like חַיְתוֹ אֶרֶץ) linen garment. 2) tract, extent; hence, מִדָּהּ her extent; 3) measure, מְנָת מַד the portion meted out.

מַדְבַּח (Aram.) masc. an altar for sacrifices.

מִדְבָּר m. 1) a place to which cattle are driven, meadow, common, plain (not cultivated), steppe, but always where there is pasture for cattle; hence, יִרְעֲפוּ נְאוֹת מִ׳. 2) a desert, a waste, either from a natural cause or from the power of man; complete, מ׳ שְׁמָמָה. הַמִּדְבָּר the Arabian desert, of which פָּארָן, סִינַי, סִין, צִין, are only parts. Figur. deserted, i.e. naked and bare, stripped of ornament. 3) speech, address, from דִּבֵּר to speak, which is more correct than, "organ of speech," as translated by some.

מָדַד (in the pret., more frequently the analysed form; fut. יָמֹד, inf. מֹד) 1) to measure, to mete out; hence, figur. to recompense. 2) to stretch, to extend, probably the original idea of signification I. Niph. to be measured, meted out. Pi. with the double signification of Kal. Po. מוֹדֵד to measure. Hithp. הִתְמוֹדֵד to stretch oneself out, to spread oneself.

מִדַּד m. according to some = מְנֻדַּד, flight, departure (of sleep); according to others, 3 pers. pret. Pi. from מָדַד; thus מִדַּד עָרֶב (Job 7:4) the night stretches, i.e. lasts too long for me; Author. Vers. however, "and the night be gone."

מָדָה belongs to מָדוֹן; see מוּר,

מָדָה belongs to מָדוֹ; see דָּוָה.

מָדָה (not used) to be in the midst; hence מָדַי p.n.

מִדָּה (from the masc. מַד) f. 1) extent, size, stature, אִישׁ מ׳ a man of high stature; the same is the pl. מִדּוֹת; hence אַנְשֵׁי מִדּוֹת, and transf. to space and time: מִדַּת יָמִים duration of life, בֵּית מִדּוֹת spacious house; 2) measure, measurement; hence קַו מ׳, חֶבֶל מִדָּה, קְנֵה מ׳ cord for measuring, a measuring reed; figur. tribute, origin. quantum, measure; 3) equiv. to מַד garment, thus the plur. מִדּוֹת, פִּי מִדּוֹת hem of the garment or garments.

מִדָּה (also מִנְדָּה, const. מִנְדַּת) Aram. f. tax, tribute; origin. appointed tax; the same as מִדָּה in Heb.

מַדְהֵבָה f. surname or poetic term for Babel, she who exacts gold, or takes gold for booty; from דְּהַב Aram. = זָהָב, or, seat of gold, wealthy one; according to some, the reading is מַרְהֵבָה, which see.

מַדְוֶה (in signification 1, only plur., with suff. מַדְוֵיהֶם) m. 1) garment, raiment, from דָּוָה II.; 2) sickness, from דָּוָה I.

מַדּוּחַ m. seduction, from נָדַח.

I. מָדוֹן (pl. מְדָוְנִים in the Keri often for מִדְיָנִים m. 1) strife, quarrel, contention, or concr. object of contention; 2) p.n. of a Phœnician city.

II. מָדוֹן masc. length, size; hence אִישׁ מִדָּה = אִישׁ מָדוֹן. The Ketib reads מָדִין.

מַדּוּעַ (compounded of מָה יָדוּעַ) adv.

holdership, country; מִשְׁמַנֵּי מְ׳ the fat country, i.e. Palestine; see דּוּן.

מְדֹכָה f. mortar, stamper, from דּוּךְ.

מַדְמֵן place of manure, p.n. of a Moabite city. Root דָּמַן.

מַדְמֵנָה fem. 1) dung-hill; equiv. to דֹּמֶן; 2) (dunghill) p.n. of a city not far from Jerusalem; 3) p.n. of a city in Judah.

מְדָן (from דּוּן, like מְצָד from צוּד) m. 1) strife, contention; only pl. 2) p.n.m. quarrelsome one; gent. מְדָנִים for מִדְיָנִים.

מַדָּע (plur. מַדָּעִים) masc. knowledge, science, from יָדַע; the י is replaced by dagesh.

מֹדָע see מוֹדָע.

מַדְקָרָה f. piercing, from דָּקַר

מְדָר (Aram.) masc. equiv. to מְדוֹר dwelling; see דּוּר.

מַדְרֵגָה f. steps, stair, stile, terrace, from דָּרַג to step up; also, degree.

מִדְרָךְ m. step, also place on which one steps.

מִדְרָשׁ m. origin. research, investigation, expounding; next, every exposition of a text; hence מִדְרַשׁ סֵפֶר הַמְּלָכִים a complete history of the book of Kings; see דָּרַשׁ.

מְדָתָא (generally הַמְּ׳, הַ supposed to be the article) p.n.m.; more correctly however הַמְּ׳, see under ה׳, הַ not being the article.

מָה (in the closer connexion of words of interrogation, why? wherefore? origin. on what grounds? different from לָמָּה for what purpose?

מְדוֹר (Aram.) masc. dwelling, abode, from דּוּר.

מְדוּרָה f. wood-pile, stake, funeral-pile, from דּוּר.

מְדוּשָׁה f. the threshing, concr. that which is threshed; hence figur. מְדֻשָׁתִי my threshed (oppressed) people.

מִדְחֶה m. thrust, fall, from דָּחָה.

מַדְחֵפָה f. thrust, fall, destruction, from דָּחַף to push.

מָדַי middle country, p.n.f. of a country, Media; used also as the name of the people; gent. מָדִי a Mede.

מָדַי (Aram.) the same; gent. מָדָי, def. מָדָאָה (Ketib מָדָיָא) Median.

מַדַּי (contracted from מַה־דַּי) sufficient, that which suffices; therefore belongs to דַּי.

מִדֵּי see under דַּי.

מִדְיָן (pl. מִדְיָנִים, which stands also in the Keri for מְדוֹנִים, from מָדוֹן) m. 1) strife, from דּוּן; 2) p.n. of an Arabian national tribe on the East of the Ælanitic Gulf; gent. —נִי.

מִדִּין track, p.n. of a city in the desert of Judah.

מְדִינָא (Aram.) equiv. to מְדִינָה, a province, a country, from דּוּן.

מְדִינָה f. district of a certain jurisdiction; hence, province, district, stad-

מָה; else מַה, which is joined by makkaph to the succeeding word, and is also followed by dagesh forte; preceding gutturals, מָה is used, e.g. before א and ר, sometimes מֶה; before ה, ח, ע, מַה or מֶה with few exceptions) interr. pron. what? of inanimate things (see מִי) used of a direct or indirect question, mostly in the beginning of the sentence, and without distinction of gender and number, as in some languages. מָה is applied: 1) as a subst., hence also, as second part of state of const., e.g. חָכְמַת מָה whose wisdom; in this sense, or where the sentence is suddenly interrupted by a question, as וְנַחְנוּ מָה (Ex. 16:7, "and what are we?") מָה follows at the end; 2) what? of what kind? especially when referring to persons, e.g. מָה אֵלֶּה of what kind are these? 3) what! as reproaching, censuring, rejecting; hence equiv. to why? how? this mode of question sometimes turns into a negation, e.g. מַה־טֹּבוּ how goodly! מַה־נּוֹרָא how awful! מַה־תְּרִיבוּן why chide ye with me? מַה־יַּהֲלֹךְ what goes away? (nothing goes away); 4) as an indefinite, somewhere, something, in which case it follows at the end, e.g. וִיהִי מָה whatever it be; with שׁ succeeding; hence, that which, where the relative שֶׁ or אֲשֶׁר is sometimes omitted. The following compositions ensue from connection with prepositions: 1) בַּמָּה, בַּמֶּה wherein? whereat? whereby? wherefore? according to the signification of בְּ in the context; 2) כַּמָּה about what? as what? i. e. in what condition? how large? how much? how often? how long? where כְּ is used as a comparison, and מָה what, to be taken in a suitable relation. Sometimes less as an interrogative than as an exclamation, e.g. עַד־כַּמֶּה פְעָמִים how many times! זֶה כַּמֶּה שָׁנִים O how many years! later even indefinite; 3) לָמָּה (where the connection is so close that מָה has lost the accent; the forms לָמָה Job 7:20, לָמָה Ps. 42:10, 43:2, are exceptions) why? what for? לָמָּה זֶּה why then? later: that not, lest; comp. מָה. The orig. form לָמָה is used before gutturals only; לְמָה on which account, because, is only found later. Prepositions less closely connected with מָה are: עַד־מָה how long; עַל־מָה upon what? why? מָה is sometimes entirely joined to the succeeding word, e.g. מַדּוּעַ, מַזֶּה, מַלָּכֶם,

מַה־לָּכֶם ,מַה־זֶּה ,מַה־דִּי ;מַה־תְּלָאָה ,מַדּוּעַ ,מַתְּלָאָה compounded of מַה־יָּדוּעַ. See also מְאוּמָה.

מָה (Aram.) the same, otherwise מָא; מָה דִּי that which, כְּמָה like that, as, לְמָה that not, lest; likewise דִּי לְמָה.

מָה (not used) to flow, to run, from which מַי (pl. מַיִם). In like manner the roots נָה, דָּה are formed, from which arose דַּי, נַי.

מָה (Kal, not used) to refuse, to negative; comp. the root מָא in מָאֵן. From which Hithp. of the reduplicated form הִתְמַהְמַהּ to hesitate, to linger.

מְהוּמָה (const. ־מַת) f. noise, alarm, rage, roaring, transf. to confusion, from הוּם.

מְהוּמָן (Pers.) p.n. m.

מְהֵיטַבְאֵל p.n. m. (God is the Benefactor).

מָהִיר (const. מְהִיר) adj. masc. swift, hasty; hence, expert, ready, skilful (e.g. in writing).

מָהַל origin. to cut off, enervate, to deprive some one of power; hence figur. of the wine, to weaken it by mixing; related to מוּל to circumcise.

מַהֲלָךְ m. either abstr. walking, walk, or concr. journey, road; מַהְלְכִים particip. plur. Hiph. they that accompany.

מַהֲלָל m. praising, exalting, approval; therefore used as a subs. verb.

מַהֲלַלְאֵל p. n. m. (praise of God).

מַהֲלֻם (only pl. מַהֲלֻמוֹת) m. blow, stroke, from הָלַם.

מַהֲמֹרֶת (only pl. ־מֹרוֹת) f. equiv. to מִכְמֹרֶת, from which it is a softened form, a net, from כָּמַר=הָמַר.

מַהְפֵּכָה (const. מַהְפֵּכַת) fem. overthrowing, destruction, from הָפַךְ to overthrow.

מַהְפֶּכֶת f. according to some, turning, changing, improving; hence, בֵּית הַמַּ׳ house of correction, of amendment; according to others, from הָפַךְ to turn, to bend; a house whose inmates are put in the stocks.

מָהַר (Kal, not used, and Psa. 16:4, uncertain) to hasten, run away; the origin. signification is, to flow, transf. to swift walking or running; comp. הָלַךְ, יָבַל, רָהַט, (אָזַל) נָזַל, hence related to מָרַר. Niph. נִמְהַר to over hurry, act precipitately; hence, figur. to be inconsiderate, impetuous (of the enemy), לֵב to be over hasty in daring, not persevering in courage. Pi. מִהֵר to hasten, despatch, to prepare to take flight; figur. to do something readily, skilfully. The infin. מַהֵר is also used as an adv. quickly, swiftly.

מָהַר (fut. יִמְהַר) origin. to barter, change, equiv. to מוּר, since purchasing formerly consisted in bartering; also, to buy, to purchase, especially of the bartering for idols, and of the purchase of a wife by a dowry (to endow).

מֹהַר m. enlistment money, purchasing price of a wife, i. e. the dowry which she brings the husband.

מַהֵר (origin. infin. Pi.) adv. swiftly, quickly, probably also an adj. m.

מְהֵרָה fem. (after the form יְרֵשָׁה, הֲרֵגָה) hurry, haste, quickness; frequently, however, only as an adv., swiftly, quickly, like מַהֵר, especially with prepositions.

מַהֲרַי p. n. m. (swift one).

מַהֲתַלָּה f. scorning, deception, deceit; see הָתַל.

מוֹ equiv. to מָה, and only used in connection with the prepositions בְּ, כְּ, לְ; see כְּמוֹ.

מוֹאָב 1) p.n. m. (the desirable one, מוֹאָב=מוֹאָב from יָאַב) from this the name of a national tribe, whose ancestor was called Moab; 2) p.n. of the country (hence fem.), Moab, on the east side of the Dead Sea; gent. מוֹאָבִי m., —בִיָּה and —בִית f.

מואל read מוֹאָל; see מוּל.

מוֹבָא m. entrance, equiv. to מָבוֹא; comp. מוֹצָא.

מוּג masc. red sandal-wood (Kimchi renders it brazil-wood); but frequently with the article אַלְמוּג.

מוּג (fut. יָמוּג) to flow; hence fig. to be disheartened; origin. the courage melting from fear, dissolving. Niph. נָמוֹג to be melted, dissolved, figur. of the dissolution of a host of people from timidity and fear. Piel מוֹגֵג to cause to melt or dissolve, to dishearten; of the earth, to soften it by rain. Hithp. הִתְמוֹגֵג the heart melting away or dissolving from fear.

מוּד (not used) to stretch, to extend, to expand; hence, of time, to last.

מוֹדֵד belongs to מָדַד; from which תָּמִיד and מָדוֹן.

מוֹדָע (—דַּע) m. knowledge, from יָדַע to know; hence conc. an acquaintance.

מוֹדַעַת fem. the same, formed from מוֹדָע.

מוֹט (fut. יָמוּט) to stagger, to totter, of the foot, of mountains, countries, empires; מָטָה יָד the hand, riches or wealth, sink, are reduced. Niph. to totter, tremble, of the steps. Hiph. to cause to totter, to sink, to be reduced. Hithp. הִתְמוֹטֵט to shake, to tremble, of the earth.

מוֹט m. 1) the tottering, staggering; hence, fall; 2) carrying-pole or litter, consisting of several poles or bars, so called from its moving to and fro; see מוט; 3) yoke, especially the bent pole of the yoke which rests on the neck of the bull.

מוֹטָה f. equiv. to מוט in signif. 2 and 3, if it is not connected with מַטֶּה.

מ (fut. יָמוּג) equiv. to מוג to melt away; figur. to become reduced, impoverished.

מ (fut. apoc. וַיָּמָל) origin. equiv. to מָלַל and מָהַל (see the latter), but generally in the sense of circumcising, with the accus. of the person, to cut off the foreskin; figur. of the foreskin of the heart. Niph. נָמוֹל (inf. and imp. הִמּוֹל, fut. יִמּוֹל) to circumcise oneself, to be circumcised; also in a moral sense. Other forms of Niphal and Kal comp. under מָלַל. Pi. מוֹלֵל, see מָלַל as well as הִתְמוֹלֵל. Hiph. הֵמִיל to destroy, to annihilate (a people).

מ (once מול and מואל, read מוֹאל) prep. before, e. g. before the sons of Ammon, before God; hence also, over against, e. g. of the window, מול over against to the (אֶל) window; origin. contracted from מוּאָל. Connected with other prepositions, e. g. אֶל־מוּל towards (something), in front of; succeeding verbs of motion or rest, מִמּוּל away from before something, from opposite; hence, מִמֻּלִי from before me, i. e. near me. See also אֶתְמוֹל.

מוֹלָדָה (birth-place) p. n. of a city in Judah, ceded to Simeon.

מוֹלֶדֶת fem. 1) birth, אֶרֶץ מוֹל׳ land of birth, fatherland; מוֹלְדוֹת descendencies; 2) concr. they that are born, children, descendants, family, people. See יָלַד.

מוּלָה (after the form דּוּגָה) f. circumcision.

מוֹלִיד p. n. m. progenitor.

מוּם (arose from מְאוּם) m. origin. want, fault; hence, blemish, stain, defect, also in a moral sense.

מוּן (not used) to think, to reflect, to contemplate, and hence like זָמַם transf. to lie, to speak falsely; from which מִין and תְּמוּנָה.

מוּסַב (from סָבַב) m. circle, circumference of a house.

מוֹסָד (pl. —סָדוֹת, const. —סְדוֹת, but also מוֹסְדֵי) m. 1) to be founded, e. g. of the earth; 2) ground, foundation, fundament of a thing. Root יָסַד.

מוּסָד m. founding, foundation מוּסָד מוּסָּד founded foundation, i. e. the firm one, the proved one.

מוּסָדָה f. foundation, arrangement, hence מַטֵּה מ׳ the staff (chastising rod) of the decree.

מוּסָךְ (from סָכַךְ) m. covered walk, Ketib מֵיסַךְ.

מוֹסֵר (for מַאֲסֵר, from אָסַר, plur. —רוֹת, —רִים) m. 1) bonds, fetters; 2) p.n. of a place in the desert.

מוּסָר (from יָסַר) m. 1) chastisement, discipline, שֵׁבֶט מ׳ rod of chastisement; next, discipline, force; thus similar to מוֹסֵר; hence, פִּתַּח מ׳ to loosen the bond or release the force; 2) instruction, reproving, warning, exhorting; hence, repentance, recognition, insight, prudence.

מוֹסֵרוֹת equiv. to מוֹסֵר 2.

מוֹעֵד (plur. מוֹעֲדִים, const. —דֵי) m. 1) appointed time, future time; such only as is fixed, festival, complete יוֹם מוֹעֵד; festival offering, like חַג; next, year, space of time; in all these significations the idea of "appointed time" is the basis; 2) appointed sign, signal; 3) assembly, meeting (from יָעַד to appoint a place for assembling), especially of festival meetings; hence, אֹהֶל מוֹעֵד; also place of assembly, e.g. מוֹעֲדֵי־אֵל the places of assembling on the festivals of the Lord. Root יָעַד.

מוֹעָד (pl. מוֹעָדִים) m. host, assembly that meets on the מוֹעֵד festival.

מוֹעָדָה f. festival, from יָעַד.

מוּעָדָה f. appointed place, place of refuge; hence, joined to עִיר, city of refuge, asylum.

מוֹעֲדֵי Job 12:5; see under מָעַד.

מְמוּעֶדֶת=מוּעֶדֶת; see מָעַד.

מוּעָף m. obscuring, darkening, from יָעַף or עוּף; the same is מָעוּף.

מֹעֵצָה (only pl. מוֹעֵצוֹת) f. counsel, resolution, determination, from יָעַץ.

מוּעָקָה (from עוּק) fem. oppression, oppressive burden.

מוֹפֵת (contracted from מוֹפְאֵת, pl. מוֹפְתִים) f. origin. excellent, brilliant deed; hence, 1) wonder, especially of divine miracles, and often joined to אוֹת; נָתַן, שׂוּם מ׳ to work, to do wonders; 2) token, sign, which is sometimes the object of a miracle; hence, proof, token of truth, type, prognostic, אִישׁ מוֹפֵת a man of proof, proven, Author. Vers. "man of wonder" (Zech. 3:8).

מוּץ 1) to press out, like מָצַץ; 2) to separate, e.g. the chaff from the corn; but מֵץ is probably a noun from מָצַץ.

מוֹץ (also מֹץ defective) masc. chaff; origin. that which is separated from the corn.

מוֹצָא (pl. מוֹצָאִים) m. 1) outgoing; of the sun, rising; of God, revealing, manifesting; 2) gate, place whence one goes out; מוֹצָא מַיִם, place whence water flows; hence also, place where the sun rises, the east; מוֹצָאֵי בֹקֶר וָעֶרֶב place of the rising and setting of the sun; place where metals are found; 3) that which proceeds from the lips, sentence; origin, descent, extraction; 4) p.n.m. (origin, descent).

מוֹצָאָה fem. 1) descent, origin, like מוֹצָא; 2) sewer; compare צֹאָה dung, from יָצָא.

מוּצָק masc. cast work, that which is cast, from יָצַק.

מוּצָק (origin. particip. Hoph. from צוּק) m. strait, straitened, רֹחַב מַיִם בְּמוּצָק the breadth of the water is straitened (Job 37:10); figur. affliction; pressure, in the transferred sense.

מוּצָקָה fem. vessel for pouring, from יָצַק to pour.

מוּק (only Hiph. הֵמִיק) to jest, to mock; hence Hiphil, scorning, laughing at, deriding.

מוֹקֵד m. 1) glowing, burning; 2) material for burning, wood, faggot, from יָקַד to burn.

מוֹקְדָה f. place of burning, especially where the sacrifices were burnt, from יָקַד.

מוֹקֵשׁ (pl. מוֹקְשִׁים, —וֹת, const. —שֵׁי) m. a snare, cord used for a trap, מֹ׳ מָוֶת snare of death; fig. one who entraps people as with a snare, decoyer, seducer, destroyer. Root יָקֹשׁ.

מֹר see מֹר.

מוּר (Kal, not used) to barter, to change, equiv. to מָהַר; hence Hiph. הֵמִיר, once הֵימִיר, changing, exchanging something for (בְּ) something else; to change an oath, a covenant, i.e. to break it; figur. of the changing of the earth. Niph. נָמַר for נָמוֹר to be changed, altered. Hithp. הִתְיַמֵּר, after a strange formation of the Hithp. of ע״י, to place oneself in the stead of another, to change, as it were, with another. See also יָמַר.

מוֹרָא (with suff. מוֹרַאֲכֶם, pl. מוֹרָאִים) m. either abstr. fear, terror, or concr. subject of fear or reverence; hence also, wonder, from יָרֵא.

מוֹרָג (pl. —רַגִּים and —רִינִים) masc. a threshing wheel, threshing roller, from מָרַג to roll, to turn, which see.

מוֹרָד (from יָרַד) masc. a slope, declivity; fig. festoon, as a piece of work hanging down.

מוֹרֶה (origin. part. Hiph., from יָרָה) m. 1) shooter, from יָרָה to throw; hence, archer; transf. to early or former rain, from its shooting down; 2) teacher, instructor, also from יָרָה but in the sense of enlightening; hence also, 3) p.n.m. (teacher, instructor), from which an oak in the vicinity of Sichem received the name אֵלוֹן מוֹרֶה.

I. מוֹרָה m. a razor, from מָרָה=מָרַח to strop, which see.

II. מוֹרָה (from יָרָה) f. guidance, instruction, only Ps. 9:21; hence, equiv. to תּוֹרָה, and שִׁית מוֹרָה is almost the same as שִׁית חֹק. On the similarity between מ and ת preformative, compare מוֹצָא and תּוֹצָא, מַחְלוּי and תַּחְלוּי, מְבוּסָה and תְּבוּסָה, מְשׁוּבָה and תְּשׁוּבָה and others.

מוֹרָט (origin. particip. Pu. for מְמוֹרָט, comp. מְמֻשָּׁךְ to which it is joined) adj. origin. to be pointed, sharp; hence like חַד vehement, rash, and in connection with גּוֹי violent, rash nation. Author. vers. "pealed."

מוֹרִיָּה see מֹרִיָּה.

מוֹרָשׁ (pl. const. מוֹרָשֵׁי) m. possession of the heart, i.e. thoughts, hopes.

מוֹרָשָׁה f. the same, from יָרַשׁ.

מוֹרֶשֶׁת גַּת (possession near Gath) p.n. of a place near Eleutheropolis; gent. מוֹרַשְׁתִּי, where גַּת is omitted.

מוּשׁ (fut. יָמוּשׁ) to move, to move back; comp. אָמַשׁ, but the form וּמַשְׁתִּי (Zech. 3:9) stands for הֲמִשׁתִּי, and is abridged from the Hiph., which often occurs with the ע״ו in that conjugation. Hiph. to cause to move back, to withdraw, to release; hence, to cause to cease, to vanish.

מוּשׁ in the signification of מָשַׁשׁ, see under מָשַׁשׁ.

מוֹשָׁב m. 1) seat, chair, a place upon which one sits; 2) dwelling, place, where one stays or sits; hence, בֵּית מוֹשָׁב dwelling-house; 3) time of dwelling; 4) the inhabitants, abstr. for concr.

מוּשִׁי p. n. masc., as also מֻשִׁי; the patron. is of the same formation.

מוֹשָׁכָה (only pl. const. מוֹשְׁכוֹת) f. a cord, rope, from מָשַׁךְ to stretch, to extend.

מוֹשָׁעוֹת (only pl.) f. salvation, help, release, saving, from יָשַׁע, which see.

מוּת (pret. מֵת, 1 pers. מַתִּי) to die, naturally or violently, with בְּ, מִפְּנֵי to die of something. As in other languages, the idea of dying is transferred in Hebrew to other subjects, e.g. to the dying of plants, to the withering of the heart and perishing of states. Part. מֵת a dying one, but also a dead one, a corpse; the idols are figur. called מֵתִים. Pi. מוֹתֵת to kill, to murder. Hiph. to kill or to decree death; hence, especially used of God; מְמִיתִים they who kill, the angels of death. Hoph. pass. to be killed. As to the orig. form מֵת, according to some, arose from מָוֶת, which opinion is favoured by the analogy of languages: according to others, from מָתָה to be struck down, to die.

מָוֶת (const. מוֹת, with ה finis מָוְתָה, plur. מוֹתִים) masc. 1) natural or violent death; hence בֶּן מָ׳, אִישׁ מָ׳ one guilty of death; but also, deadly sickness, the plague, also as in modern languages, the figure "sleeping" is used, as יָשֵׁן הַמָּוֶת to sleep (the sleep of) death; 2) personified; as, region of death, joined to gates (שַׁעֲרִים) and chambers (חַדְרִים); hence equiv. to lower regions, hell; 3) figur. calamity, destruction. The plural, as in חַיִּים, is translated in the singular.

מוֹת (Aram.) m. the same.

מוֹתָר (from יָתַר) m. superfluity, preference, excellence, according to the context.

מִזְבֵּחַ (const. מִזְבַּח, pl. מִזְבְּחוֹת) m. an altar, especially the altar of God in the temple; also, in connection with הָעוֹלָה, הַנְּחשֶׁת, הַזָּהָב, הַקְּטֹרֶת, to designate the different kinds of altars for the use of offerings; transf. also to the altar of idols.

מָזַג (not used) equiv. to מָסַךְ to mix, to spice (wine); from which:—

מֶזֶג m. equiv. to מֶסֶךְ mixed, spiced, seasoned wine.

מָזָה equiv. to מָצָה to suck out; hence מָזֶה (after the forms יָפֶה, קָצֶה) an old form of the particip. active, const. pl. מְזֵי (after the form יְפֵי) sucking; with רָעָב to gnaw from hunger, Author. Vers. burnt with hunger (Deut. 32:24).

מִזָּה see מזה.

מִזָּה p. n. masc. (disheartening, from מָזַז).

מָזוּ (only pl. מְזָוִים; origin. for מִזְוֶה, from זָוָה) masc. magazine, storehouse. See זָוָה.

מְזוּזָה f. door-post, from זוז, which see.

מָזוֹן m. sustenance, food, from זון.

מָזוֹן (Aram.) the same.

מָזוֹר m. bandage (of a wound), from זור to bind round; hence fig. for healing; 2) fetter, net; also from זור in the signif. of binding.

מָזַז (not used) to flow, melt away, to be disheartened.

מָזַח (not used) a verb from the derivatives מֵזַח, מְזִיחַ, which, however, belong to זָחַח, equiv. to זָקַק.

מֵזַח (after the forms מֵצַר, מֵסַב, מֵמַר) m. a girdle, bonds, fetters, from זָחַח to bind.

מְזִיחַ (for מֵזַח, since *sere* may be lengthened into *chirik*) masc. the same.

מַזָּל (only pl. מַזָּלוֹת) m. originally, wanderer; hence, a wandering star, a planet, from נָזַל, equiv. to אָזַל, which see.

מַזְלֵג (but pl. מִזְלָגוֹת) m. fork, from זָלַג, which see.

מְזִמָּה f. origin. thinking, reflecting; hence, 1) thought. i.e. that which has occupied the mind; 2) concoction of artfulness, trickery, wickedness, crime, destructive plans—all in a bad sense; 3) cunning, shrewdness, dexterity, prudence, in a good sense. The root is זָמַם which see.

מִזְמוֹר m. a song, hymn, from זָמַר.

מַזְמֵרָה f. pruning-hook used by the vintner, from זָמַר.

מְזַמֶּרֶת (only pl. מְזַמְּרוֹת) f. an instrument for cutting off, from זָמַר, especially a kind of scissors for candles, snuffers.

מִזְעָר masc. littleness, trifle; also of time. As an adv. little.

מָזַר (not used) to mix, from which מַמְזֵר. Similar to מָצַר, from which מִצְרַיִם.

מַזָּר (only pl. מַזָּרוֹת) m. probably the same as מַזָּל, through the interchanging of ר and ל. If מָזַר, however, is the root, it signifies the northern group of stars, from מָזַר, to mix, to join.

מְזָר (only pl. מְזָרִים) masc. probably equiv. to מַזָּר, thus the northern group of stars; and next, northern countries, or point generally.

מִזְרֶה m. vessel for winnowing, winnowing shovel. Author. Vers. "fan."

מִזְרָח (const. ־רַח, with ה finis מִזְרָחָה, מִזְרָחָה) m. the east, eastern point; origin. the point where the sun rises; complete מִזְרַח שֶׁמֶשׁ. With proper nouns, on the east of, e. g. מִזְרַח יְרִיחוֹ.

מִזְרָע (const. מִזְרַע) m. seed, מִ׳ יְאוֹר seed on the Nile, from זָרַע.

מִזְרָק (from זָרַק; pl. ־קִים, ־קוֹת) m. origin. vessel for sprinkling (of the blood of sacrifices); next, basin, generally; transf. to bottle, in which the wine was tempered before it was put in the cup; thus origin. vessel for pouring out. See זָרַק.

מֵחַ (pl. מֵחִים, from מָחַח) m. something that is fat, especially a fat sheep or ram.

מֹחַ m. marrow (of bones), from מָחַח, which see.

מָחָא (fut. יִמְחָא) to strike (the hand); with accus. to shake hands as a sign of friendship; thus = הִכָּה כַּף. Pi. the same. Comp. *μάχομαι*.

מְחָא (Aram.) the same: hence, 3 pret. f. מְחָת. Pa. מַחָא to prevent; joined to יַד, origin. to push the hand back. Ithp. to be fastened, to be knocked on, to be nailed on, used of one who is hanged.

מַחֲבָא m. concealment, hiding place, from חָבָא.

מַחֲבֹא (only pl.) m. the same.

מַחְבֶּרֶת fem. place of joining two things, junction, from חָבַר.

מְחַבְּרוֹת pl. —בְּרוֹת, fem. origin. that which joins, cramp-iron, beams which join.

מַחֲבַת fem. pan, from חָבַת, which see.

מַחֲגֹרֶת fem. putting on (mourning clothes), girding round. Root חָגַר.

מָחָה (fut. יִמְחֶה) 1) origin. to pass over something softly, to stroke; hence, to wipe (the mouth), to wipe off (tears, writing, sin=to forget); with עַל, to push towards or against something; to strike out, to blot out, to destroy (a city, country, a name, the memory); 2) to be fat, full of marrow, proceeding from the origin. signif. to pass over softly. In this sense, מָחָה occurs only in Pu. and is equal to מָחַח; 3) (not used) to strike, equiv. to מָחָא, which, however, is not connected with signif. 1 and 2. Niph. (fut. apoc. יִמָּח=יִמַּח, from יִמָּחֶה) to be wiped off, to be blotted out (a tribe, name, deed, disgrace, book, mankind). Pu. to be full of marrow, of fat viands (שְׁמָנִים) or to be strong. Hiph. (fut. apoc. תֶּמַח; infin. with ל, לְמְחוֹת) to destroy.

מְחוּגָה fem. a compass, origin. an instrument by which circles are defined, from חוּג.

מָחוֹז (const. מְחוֹז) m. haven, from חוּז, which see.

מְחוּיָאֵל p. n. m. (smitten by God).

מַחֲוִים gent. n. of an unknown מַחֲוֵי.

מָחוֹל m. 1) dance, especially a dance in a circle, from חוּל; 2) p. n. m. of an ancient and celebrated singer, whose descendants were called בְּנֵי מָחוֹל.

מְחוֹלָה (also מְחֹלָה) f. 1) dance, from חוּל; 2) p. n. m. in אָבֵל מְחוֹלָה.

מַחֲזֶה masc. vision, appearance in a vision, from חָזָה.

מֶחֱזָה f. window, from חָזָה.

מַחֲזִיאוֹת p. n. m. (visions).

מָחַח (not used) to be fat, full of marrow, probably related to מָקַק; to be soft, or with מָחָה, to stroke over.

מְחִי masc. a blow, a stroke, from מָחָא=מָחָה.

מְחִידָא p. n. m. (one who joins.)

מִחְיָה f. 1) maintenance, sustenance of life, means of living, from חָיָה; 2) blow, mark, token; hence, מִחְיַת הַמִּכְוָה, mark of the burning wound (Author. Vers. the "quick flesh that burneth," Lev. 13:20). It is formed from the m. מְחִי.

מְחִיָּיאֵל p. n. m. (smitten by God).

מְחִיר (pl. מְחִירִים) m. 1) purchasing price; בִּמְ׳ for money; לֹא בִמְ׳ without reward or recompense, for nothing; 2) p.n. m. (the purchased one).

מְחֹלָה see מְח.לָה.

מַחֲלָה m. sickness, from חָלָה.

מַחֲלָה fem. 1) sickness; 2) p.n. fem. (sickness, the sick one).[4]

מְחִלָּה f. cavern, from חָלַל.

מַחֲלוּי (only pl. ־לֻיִים) m. equiv. to תַּחֲלוּי, sickness.

מַחְלוֹן (formed from מַחֲלָה) p. n. m. (the sick one).

מַחְלִי p.n. m. (the same) from חָלָה.

מַחֲלָף (from חָלַף = גָּלַב) m. a knife, a knife of sacrifice.

מַחְלָפֶת (pl. ־לְפוֹת) f. hair-plaid, hair-locks, from חָלַף.

מַחֲלָצָה (pl. ־לָצוֹת) fem. festival or official garment, origin. dress. See חָלַץ.

מַחֲלֹקֶת with suff. מַחֲלֻקְתּוֹ, plur. מַחְלְקוֹת fem. 1) division, used of the divisions of the Levites and priests; 2) defilement, from חָלַק, to separate, which see.

מַחְלְקָה (pl. מַחְלְקָן) Aram. f. the same.

מַחֲלַת m. name of a melody (not an instrument) to which Ps. 53 and 88 were sung; hence, עַל מַחֲלַת לְעַנּוֹת to sing according to Machalath. Probably the burden of an old melody, like יוֹנַת אֵלֶם רְחֹקִים, שׁוּשַׁן, שׁוֹשַׁנִּים עֵדוּת, שֹׁשַׁנִּים אֶל, עֲלָמוֹת לַבֵּן, נְחִילוֹת, עֵדוּת תַּשְׁחֵת, and others.

מַחֲלַת p.n. f.

מְחֹלָתִי gent. from אָבֵל מְחוֹלָה, which see.

מַחֲמָאֹת (pl. מַחֲמָאוֹת) fem. denom. from חֶמְאָה, softness, smoothness; hence, flattery, hypocrisy; but if the reading is מֶחֱמָאוֹת, the sing. is חֶמְאָה.

מַחְמָד (pl. ־מַדִּים, const. ־מַדֵּי) m. that which one desires, or which is desirable, dear, precious; hence also, desire, loveliness, preciousness, from חָמַד.

מַחְמֹד (only pl. מַחֲמֻדִּים) m. preciousness, beauty.

מַחְמָל (const. ־מַל) m. the carrying, lifting up (of the heart) towards something; hence, wish, desire; with נֶפֶשׁ, equiv. to מַשָּׂא נֶפֶשׁ. See חָמַל.

מַחְמֶצֶת f. leaven, that which ferments, from חָמֵץ.

מַחֲנֶה (const. ־נֵה, dual מַחֲנַיִם; pl. מַחֲנִים; hence with suff. מַחֲנֶיךָ, מַחֲנוֹת) com. 1) a camp, from חָנָה to encamp, used of the camps of nomades and armies; next, generally, crowd, army, host (of angels), used even of locusts; 2) place of encampment, especially of the priests in the courts of the temple.

מָחַק to pierce through, to cut through, equiv. to חָקַק; hence, of the splitting of the head.

מֶחְקָר m. depth, the innermost, from חָקַר to be deep, to fetch from the depth.

מָחַר (not used) equiv. to מָכַר to sell, also, to buy, origin. to exchange. See מָכַר.

מָחָר (contracted from מַאֲחָר, that which is later, the latter) origin. that which follows, or the sucession (see אָחַר in this sense); transf. to the morrow, the following day; complete יוֹם מ׳; לְמָחָר for to-morrow; כָּעֵת מָחָר or מָחָר כָּעֵת הַזֹּאת at this time to-morrow; by adding שְׁלִישִׁי it signifies, the day after to-morrow.

מַחֲרָאָה fem. sewer, sink, from חָרָא, which see.

מַחֲרֵשָׁה (pl. ־שׁוֹת) f. ploughshare, from חָרַשׁ.

מַחֲרֶשֶׁת (with suff. ־רַשְׁתּוֹ) f. ploughknife, ploughshare.

מָחֳרָת (const. מָחֳרַת) f. formed from מָחָר, with the same signif.; complete יוֹם מָחֳרָת the morrow following; with prep. לְמָ׳, מִמָּ׳ on the following day.

מָחֳרָתָם adv. to-morrow; ־ָם is an adverbial termination, like יוֹמָם, חִנָּם, רֵיקָם.

מַחֲשָׁבָה (pl. ־שָׁבוֹת, const. ־שְׁבוֹת)

מַחֲנֵה־דָן (the camp of Dan) p.n. of a place in Judah.

מַחֲנַיִם (double host) p.n. of a city beyond the Jordan.

מַחֲנָק m. strangling, death, from חָנַק.

מַחְסֶה (מַחֲסֶה) from חָסָה, with suff. מַחְסִי), m. refuge, place of refuge.

מַחְסוֹם m. muzzle, origin. closing up, closing of the mouth, from חָסַם.

מַחְסוֹר (pl. with suff. מַחְסוֹרֶיךָ) m. want, deficiency, indigence; hence אִישׁ מַ׳ an indigent man, from חָסֵר, which see.

מַחְסֵיָה p.n. m. refuge in God.

מָחַץ (fut. יִמְחַץ) to cleave, to split, to crush, equiv. to חָצָה, חוּץ; hence, of the wounding of the head, the loins, the temple (of the head); also absolute, to bruise; וְחִצָּיו יִמְחַץ and he shall split them (Author. Vers. pierce them through), with his arrows, where בְּ is omitted; fig. also, the beating of the raging sea; מָחַץ רֶגֶל בְּדָם to bruise the foot against blood (corpses), Author. Vers. "to dip the foot in the blood."

מַחַץ m. wound, bruise, origin. that which is struck.

מַחְצֵב masc. the hewing (of stones), from חָצַב; hence, אַבְנֵי מַ׳ hewn stones.

מֶחֱצָה f. the half, from חָצָה.

מַחֲצִית f. the middle, half, from חָצָה.

f. 1) thought (like מְזִמָּה); next, motive, object, plan, design, device, and like מְזִמָּה in a bad sense, even without adding רָעָה; 2) artificial work. The root is חָשַׁב to bind, to tie.

מַחְשָׁךְ (pl. מַחֲשַׁכִּים, const. —שַׁכֵּי) m. darkness, obscurity; the pl. is used of dark places, hiding, lurking holes, and of the dreary regions of the שְׁאוֹל pit or hell.

מַחְשֹׂף m. uncovering, laying bare, peeling, from חָשַׂף.

מַחַת p n. m.

מַחְתָּה f. pan, from חָתָה, especially for the collecting of cinders; hence, fire-basin, but also, tongs or shovel, by which the cinders are removed.

מְחִתָּה f. fright, terror, despondency, from חָתַת; transf. to destruction.

מַחְתֶּרֶת f. breaking-in, burglary, from חָתַר.

מַט the original form of מַטָּה.

מְטָא (3 f. מְטָת, 3 pl. מְטוֹ, fut. יִמְטֵא) Aram. origin. equiv. to מָצָא Heb. next, to enter, to come in, to arrive at, to come, and figur. to reach unto.

מַטְאֲטֵא masc. a besom, that which sweeps away. See טֵאטֵא.

מַטְבֵּחַ masc. the slaughtering, the defeat; from טָבַח.

מַטֶּה (pl. מַטּוֹת and also מַטִּים; hence, with suff. מַטָּיו) com. from נָטָה to stretch out; hence, that which spreads easily, which is slender, slim: as, branch, staff, stick (to lean on): מַטֵּה לֶחֶם the staff, i.e. stay of bread, sustenance, to break which signifies to cause famine; rod or cane (for chastisement), rod of the back, i.e. which hits on the back; sceptre (of the king); also, rule; spear, used for piercing; fig. tribe (of a people), similar to שֵׁבֶט; רָאשֵׁי הַמַּטּוֹת the heads of the tribes.

מַטָּה adv. (from מַט or מַטֶּה in another signif. to that previously given, formed with ה finis) to incline downward, to decline; from נָטָה to bend; sometimes joined to לְמַטָּה down, מִן לְמַטָּה under, less, מִלְמַטָּה from below, from under. See נָטָה.

מִטָּה f. couch, bed, pillow, sofa, on which one inclines; also, death-bed, litter.

מֻטָּה (pl. מֻטּוֹת) f. origin. that which is extended, the spreading (of the wings), from נָטָה.

מֻטֶּה m. the bending, inclining, perverting of justice, from נָטָה to bend.

מַטְוֶה m. that which is spun, from טָוָה to spin.

מְטִיל (const. מְטִיל) m. iron bar, from טִל. No similar masc. formation occurs from this form, but only the fem. formation, e.g. מְרִיבָה, מְדִינָה, and others.

מְטַל belongs to מָטִיל. See טול.

מַטְמֹן (pl. מַטְמֹנִים) m. place of keeping and preserving things, from טָמַן; hence, store, treasury, transf. to the treasure itself.

מַטָּע m. plant, from נָטַע.

מַטְעַם (only pl. מַטְעַמִּים) masc. that which is tasteful, dainty (Author. Vers. savoury meat), from טָעַם to taste, especially of eating tasty things.

מַטְעַמָּה (only pl. מַטְעַמּוֹת) fem. the same, savoury meat.

מִטְפַּחַת (pl. מִטְפָּחוֹת) f. a wide upper garment, Author. Vers. veil, from טָפַח to spread out.

מָטַר (Kal, not used) to rain. Hiph. הִמְטִיר to cause to rain, to pour down, also of hail, manna, and lightning. Niph. to be rained upon. The root is מָרַר and origin. signifies to flow, to run.

מָטָר (pl. מְטָרוֹת, const. מִטְרוֹת) m. rain, in connection with טַל, זֶרֶם, קוֹל, בָּרָד, different to גֶּשֶׁם, with which מָטָר is once joined in the state of const.

מַטְרֵד p. n. f. exile, banishment.

מַטָּרָה f. 1) place of keeping, from נָטַר; 2) aim, target, likewise from נָטַר.

מַטְרִי p. n. m. (probably = מַצְרִי the expectant one).

מֵי see מַיִם.

מִי inter. pron. who? generally of persons, but also of inanimate objects. This pronoun not being restricted to any particular gender or number, is joined with the plur. as אֵלֶּה, as well as with the fem. מִי זֹאת; in the plur., however, מִי וָמִי is also used. מִי is applied: 1) as the second part of the const. state, succeeding the noun, e.g. בַּת מִי whose daughter? 2) מִי always retains its personal relation, though it may stand before an inanimate object, whilst מָה, though used of persons only, inquires after the matter, e.g. מִי הַמַּחֲנֶה who is that host? i.e. who are the persons composing the host? 3) connected with הוּא, to give emphasis, e.g. who is he that? and with זֶה, still closer connected with the object; 4) מִי often takes a negative turn, like מָה, expressing astonishment, e.g. מִי יוֹדֵעַ who knows? i.e. nobody knows; 5) מִי is often translated in the sense of how? e.g. מִי יָקוּם יַעֲקֹב who will stand like Jacob? (Author. Vers. by whom shall Jacob arise?) but the subst. verb has to be supplied after מִי; 6) indefinite.

מֵידְבָא p. n. of a Moabite city, formerly belonging to Reuben.

מֵידָד p. n. m. (love).

מֵיטָב (const. מֵיטַב—) m. the good, best (of sheep, of the vineyard, the field, the land), from יָטַב.

מִיכָא p. n. m. (who is like unto God).

מִיכָאֵל p. n. m. (the same).

מִיכָה p. n. m. (the same).

מִיכָהוּ p. n. m. (the same).

מִיכָיָה p. n. m. (the same).

מִיכָיָהוּ p. n. m. (the same).

מִיכָיְהוּ p. n. m. (the same).

מִיכַל (const. מִיכַל—) 1) m. cistern, ditch, from כּוּל=יָכַל to hold, to contain; 2) p. n. f. small brook, rivulet.

מַיִם (const. מֵי, reduplicated form מֵימֵי, with suff. מֵימָיו, מֵימֶיךָ, etc., with ה finis מַיְמָה) pl. m. from the sing. מַי (from מָה) origin. that which flows; hence, pl. water, for drinking; connected with names of places it signifies, well, fountain, brook, rivulet, pond, sea, etc.; connected with רֹאשׁ it signifies juice; with רַגְלַיִם urine; fig. מַיִם is used as indicating danger, as a symbol of the melting or desponding heart; as denoting superabundance; and water boiling over, to represent overbearing, frivolity. Besides מֵי being joined to proper nouns, where it really signifies water, fountain, well, e. g. מֵי מְרִיבָה, מֵי מְגִדּוֹ, מֵי נִמְרִים, it is also joined to the following proper nouns:—

מֵי הַיַּרְקוֹן (clear water) p. n. of a place in Dan.

מֵי זָהָב p. n. m. (water bright as gold).

מֵי נֶפְתּוֹחַ (opening spring) p. n. of a spring in the vicinity of the valley of Hinnom.

מִיָּמִין and מִנְיָמִין p. n. m. (a corrupted form from בִּנְיָמִין).

מִין (from מוּן) masc. origin. image, form, transf. to that which is after a certain class, i. e. kind; thus לְמִינוֹ after its kind.

מֵינֶקֶת f. a nurse (origin. particip. f. Hiph. יָנַק).

מֵיסַךְ (from מָסַךְ, Ketib for מוּסַךְ) m. covered walk.

מֵיפַעַת (also מֵפַעַת, and once in Ketib מוֹפַעַת; beauty, from יָפַע) p. n. of a Levitical city beyond the Jordan.

מִיץ m. that which is pressed out, from מוּץ.

מִישָׁא p. n. m. (refuge), from מוּשׁ.

מִישָׁאֵל p. n. m. (who is like unto God?) comp. מִיכָאֵל.

מִישׁוֹר m. 1) a plain, from יָשַׁר to be even, especially the name of a plain near Medba; 2) honesty, probity, from יָשַׁר, as an adv. justly.

מֵישַׁךְ (from מִישׁ and שָׁךְ modern Persian, guest of the king) p. n. m.

מֵישַׁע p. n. m. (salvation), from יָשַׁע.

מֵישָׁע (p. n. m. (the same).

מֵישָׁר (only plur. מֵישָׁרִים) masc. 1) straightness, uprightness, probity, justice; with בְּ and לְ, right, just; 2) עָשָׂה מֵישָׁרִים to act equitably.

מֵיתָר (only pl.) m. string (of a bow), cord (of a tent), from יָתַר: comp. יֶתֶר.

מַכְאֹב (plur. —בִים, —בוֹת) m. pain, affliction, from כָּאַב.

מַכְאוֹב see מַכְאֹב.

מַכְבִּיר (after the form מַשְׁחִית) m. fulness (origin. part. Hith. from כָּבַר).

מַכְבֵּנָא (connection) p.n. of a place.

מַכְבַּנַּי p.n. m. (one that connects).

מַכְבֵּר m. mat, plaid-work, from כָּבַר, which see.

מִכְבָּר (const. —בַּר) m. lattice work, from כָּבַר.

מַכָּה (pl. מַכּוֹת, twice מַכִּים, as from מַכֶּה) f. 1) a stroke, a wound, a plague, a defeat, as a concrete; 2) the defeating, e.g. מַכַּת אֹיֵב, חֶרֶב. מַכּוֹת 2 Chron. 2:9, see under מַכֹּלֶת.

מִכְוָה f. part of the skin in which there is a brand or burn, from כָּוָה.

מָכוֹן m. a place on which something stands, a stead; hence also, foundation, basis of a foundation, dwelling place, from כּוּן to stand.

מְכוֹנָה (with suff. מְכֻנָתָהּ) f. 1) equiv. to מָכוֹן, also signifies a pedestal to something; 2) foundation, p.n. of a city in Judah. מְכֹנָה is the same.

מְכוֹרָה equiv. to מְכוּרָה.

מְכוּרָה f. place of origin; of men, extraction, ancestry, from כּוּר to dig out.

מָכִיר p.n. m. (origin, extraction) from כּוּר, patron. מָכִירִי.

מָכַךְ (3 pl. fut. יָמֹכּוּ) equiv. to מָקַק, מוּךְ to sink, to fall off, to become reduced, to perish. Niph. נָמַךְ (fut. יִמַּךְ) to sink, used of a beam or arch. Hoph. הֻמַּךְ (3 pers. pl. הֻמְּכוּ for הֻמַּכּוּ) to fall in, to sink.

מְכַל belongs to מִיכָל; see יָכַל.

מִכְלָה f. 1) perfection, but only pl. מִכְלוֹת זָהָב perfect gold, i.e. pure, unalloyed gold; comp. כָּלָה in this signification; 2) equiv. to מִכְלָא (from כָּלָא) herd, from its being penned up, pl. מִכְלָאוֹת.

מִכְלוֹל m. (from כָּלַל) perfection (of beauty), לְבֻשֵׁי מִכְלוֹל they who are in full dress.

מִכְלָל m. the same.

מַכְלֻל (only pl. —לִים) m. the same; hence, beautiful garments.

מַכֹּלֶת (contracted from מַאֲכֹלֶת) f. food. The form מַכֹּלֶת is in Chronicles again contracted into מַכּוֹת; hence חִטִּים מַכּוֹת לַעֲבָדֶיךָ wheat as food for thy servants (Author. Vers. "beaten wheat," 2 Chron. 2:13). The parallel passage corroborating our view is in הַחִטִּים מַכֹּלֶת לְבֵיתוֹ 1 Kings 5:11

"wheat for food to his household."

מִכְמָן (only pl. **-נִּים**) m. a treasure, from **כָּמַן** to hide.

מִכְמָס p.n. of a place in the tribe of Benjamin.

מִכְמָר m. a net, from **כָּבַר=כָּמַר**.

מַכְמֹר masc. the same, from which **מַחְמוֹר** is a softened form.

מִכְמֶרֶת f. a net, from **כָּמַר**.

מִכְמֹרֶת f. the same.

מִכְמָשׁ (**-מַשׁ**) p.n. the same as **מִכְמָס**.

מִכְמְתָת p.n. of a place between Ephraim and Manasseh.

מַכְנַדְבַי p.n. m.

מִכְנָס (only dual **מִכְנָסַיִם**, const. **מִכְנְסֵי**) m. a kind of breeches worn by the priests, so called from **כָּנַס**, in the sense of: hiding, covering, wrapping up.

מֶכֶס m. census, tax, origin. number, from **כָּסַס** to count.

מִכְסָה f. (formed from **מֶכֶס**) number, amount, sum, from **כָּסַס**. In modern Heb. the verb **מָכַס** arose from it.

מִכְסֶה m. covering, cover, from **כָּסָה**.

מְכַסֶּה m. the same; transferred to the network covering the entrails, from **כִּסָּה**.

מַכְפֵּלָה (double cavern or double grave), p.n. of a place where the patriarchs were buried.

מָכַר (fut. **יִמְכֹּר**) to sell for (**בְּ**) a price, i.e. to barter, to exchange (related to **כָּרָה**); hence, for a price (**מֹהַר**) to sell the daughter, i.e. to marry her; of God, to sell the people, i.e. to deliver them up. Niph. pass. of Kal, to be sold, delivered up; 2) reflective, to sell oneself. Hith. like Niph., but also figur. to sell oneself to a subject, i.e. to give oneself up to something, e.g. **לַעֲשׂוֹת הָרַע** to evil-doing.

מֶכֶר (with suff. **מִכְרִי**) masc. 1) that which is saleable (property) or that which is exposed for sale; 2) value or purchasing price.

מַכָּר (from **נָכַר**) m. an acquaintance, a friend.

מִכְרֶה m. a pit, from **כָּרָה**.

מְכֵרָה (pl. **מְכֵרוֹת**) f. 1) sword, origin. an instrument for piercing, from **כּוּר**, which see; 2) p.n. of an undefined place.

מִכְרִי p.n. m. (the saleable one).

מְכֵרָתִי gent. from **מְכֵרָה**.

מִכְשׁוֹל m. stumbling-block, as being the subject which causes stumbling; also in a figurative sense, stumbling, seduction, vexation, cause of falling, etc.; **מִכְשׁוֹל לֵב** stumbling of the heart, i.e. conscientious scruples.

מַכְשֵׁלָה f. 1) vexation, subject of seduction; hence, **מַכְשֵׁלוֹת**; figur. the idols; 2) fall (of the state).

מִכְתָּב m. a writing, a letter; next generally, that which is written, a song.

מְכִתָּה f. a piece of something that is broken, from כָּתַת.

מִכְתָּם m. according to some equiv. to מִכְתָּב, writing, song; according to others, from כָּתַם to conceal, thus similar to *απόκρυφον*; and according to a third opinion, related to כֶּתֶם, golden or precious song. See כָּתַם.

מַכְתֵּשׁ m. 1) a mortar, from כָּתַשׁ to pound, to bruise; 2) of the shape of the same, the deep seat of the the teeth; 3) p. n. of a valley round Jerusalem.

מָלֵא (once מָלָא, 1st pret., once מָלְתִי, 3 pl. once מָלוּ, inf. מְלֹאת, מְלֹאות, fut. יִמְלָא) origin. to overflow, from which, 1) trans. to fill (a space); with double accus., viz. the accus. of the space and of the material, the latter is sometimes joined with מִן. The following phrases must be noticed: מִלְאוּ הַשְּׁלָטִים gather the shields, i.e. surround yourselves by them (comp. מִלֵּא הַקֶּשֶׁת); to fill the hand for God, i.e. with offerings; מָלֵא לֵב לַעֲשׂוֹת to fill the heart to do something, i.e. to venture, to undertake a task; but generally it is 2) intrans. to be or become full, with accus. or מִן of the matter by which something is full or being filled; in this sense מָלֵא is applied (*a*) to denote the lapse or expiring of time, e.g. the days to be delivered are fulfilled (מָלְאוּ); (*b*) with נֶפֶשׁ, the filling or satisfying the mind. Niph. pass. of Kal, and also of the expiring of time; hence equiv. to die, e.g. Job 15:32, "shall be accomplished before its time" (תִּמָּלֵא), i.e. it dies before its time. Pi. מִלֵּא (sometimes מִלָּא), inf. מַלֵּא, מַלֹּאות, fut. יְמַלֵּא (—לֶּה) to fill, to fill up; מִלֵּא יַד פ׳ to fill the hand of some one, i.e. to appoint him to the office of priest; to fill the hand for God, i.e. to approach him with offerings; to fill the bow, i.e. to draw it up; to fill the soul (נֶפֶשׁ, חַיָּה), i.e. to still the hunger; to fill a number, i.e. to complete it; to fill the word, i.e. to finish the word commenced; to fill a time, i.e. to let it expire, to endure it; to fulfil a prophecy, a request, a promise; to fill in, pour in, e.g. a drink-offering; to fill precious stones, i.e. to set them; to fill the hand with the bow, i.e. to seize it; to fill with wisdom (with double accus. sometimes with מִן of the object), etc. In connexion with other verbs it assumes an adverbial significa-tion, e.g קְרָא מְלָא be called fully, i.e. in a strong voice, מִלֵּא לָלֶכֶת אַחֲרֵי יי״, מִלֵּא אַחֲרֵי יי״ he followed God fully, i.e. perfectly. Pu. to be filled up, used of the setting of precious stones, with בְּ something. Hith. to fill, in an assembly, to assemble; comp. מְלֹא a host.

מְלָא (Aram.) to fulfil. Ith. pass.

מָלֵא adj. m. מְלֵאָה f.; 1) full, מְלֵא יָמִים full of days, i.e. aged; a full wind, i.e. violent one; 2) fulfilling, filling out; 3) subst. fulness, orig. neuter, e.g. מֵי מָלֵא full water, water in fulness; 4) adverb, completely, loudly, fully.

מְלֹא (also מְלוֹא, מְלֹ, with suff. מְלוֹאָהּ) m. fulness, origin. that which fills; hence, multitude, host, crowd. It is often in the const. state to that which is full, e.g. מְלֹא חָפְנַיִם the hands full, מְ׳ ־ סֵפֶל the dish full, מְ׳ הַקָּנֶה a full reed (the length of a measuring rod), etc.; מְ׳ בַּיִת a house full, מְ׳ עֹמֶר, בֶּגֶד, הַחֶבֶל, etc.

מְלֵאָה f. fulness, superabundance of corn or wine; figur. the tenth part or tithe, which is considered as an offering of the superfluous.

מִלֻּאָה f. setting precious stones, see מִלֵּא.

מִלֻּאִים m. plur. 1) the initiation or consecration of a priest, from מִלֵּא in this sense; transf. to the consecration offering; 2) setting of precious stones, like מִלֻּאָה.

מַלְאָךְ (const. ־אַךְ, plur. ־אָכִים) m. origin. abstract, sending, mission, but next also concr. messenger; as messenger of God, angel, priest, and symbolically, the Jewish nation. Root לָאַךְ.

מְלָאכָה (from מַלְאָכָה, const. מְלֶאכֶת, with suffix מְלַאכְתְּךָ, const. plur. מַלְאֲכוֹת) fem. 1) origin. mission, transaction, business; hence, work (of the artist or mechanic), occupation, management, service, and in pl. of the works of God; 2) that which is got by work, i.e. property, wealth, etc.

מַלְאָכוּת (const. מַלְאֲכוּת) f. message, mission, from לָאַךְ.

מַלְאָכִי p. n. m. (messenger).

מִלֵּאת f. origin. מְלֵאת fulness, especially rich fountain; according to others, setting (of precious stones).

מַלְבּוּשׁ masc. garment, dress, from לָבַשׁ.

מַלְבֵּן (denom. from לְבֵנָה) m. furnace for making bricks.

מִלָּה (pl. מִלִּים and מִלִּין) f. of manifold significations, like דָּבָר word, speech, conversation, transf. to a thing, matter, from מָלַל.

מִלָּה (def. מִלְּתָא, pl. מִלִּין) Aram. f. the same.

מְלוֹ see מְלֹא.

מְלוֹא see מְלֹא.

מְלוֹא masc. rampart, origin. a place filled with rubbish; hence also, 1) name of a part of fortifications, and from this sense; 2) name of a castle in Sichem. According to some מְלֵאוֹת is the same in a figurative sense.

מְלוּאִים see מִלֻּאִים.

מַלּוּחַ m. a kind of briny plant, which was the food of the poor.

מַלּוּךְ p. n. m. (a counsellor).

מְלוּכָה f. kingdom, dominion, עִיר הַמְּ׳ king's town, metropolis; עָשָׂה מְ׳ to exercise rule or dominion. Root מָלַךְ.

מַלּוּכִי equiv. to מַלּוּךְ.

מָלוֹן (from לוּן) m. place for staying over night, inn.

מְלוּנָה (from מָלוֹן) f. m. a lodge for the watchman in gardens and vineyards.

מָלַח (Kal, not used) to flow, to flood, equiv. to פָּלַג; hence, Niph. נִמְלַח to dissolve, to which sense the verbs signifying flowing are commonly transferred; figur. of the dissolving and vanishing of the heavens.

מֶלַח masc. origin. a salt flood, a sea, from מָלַח to flow; next, salt generally; יָם הַמֶּלַח salt sea, גֵּי מֶ׳ salt valley, בְּרִית מֶלַח a covenant of salt, i. e. everlasting; from which denom. מָלַח to salt. Pu. pass. to be seasoned, salted. Hoph. הָמְלַח to be bathed in salt water (of new-born children). Inf. abs. הָמְלֵחַ.

מְלַח (Aram.) the same, salt, from which denom. מְלַח to eat salt.

מֶלַח (only pl. מְלָחִים) m. a torn garment, tatters, from מָלַח.

מַלָּח (pl. מַלָּחִים) masc. denom. from מֶלַח salt-flood; hence, one whose calling is on the water, a skipper, a pilot.

מְלֵחָה f. origin. saltness, barrenness of a country; hence, transf. to a desolate, unfruitful country.

מִלְחָמָה (with suff. מִלְחַמְתִּי, plur. מִלְחָמוֹת) f. 1) war, combat, battle; hence, אִישׁ, כְּלֵי מִ׳: to carry on war עָשָׂה מִלְ׳, construed with אֵת (אֶת), and עִם.

מָלַט (Kal, not used) to pass over softly, to stroke over; hence, fig. to slide away, slip off, to escape, related to פָּלַט. Pi. מִלֵּט, in pause מִלֵּט to let escape, נַפְשׁוֹ his life, i. e. to save, transf. to lay eggs; (origin. to cause to escape). Hiph. like Pi. to save, transf. to bear, deliver. Niph. to be saved; also reflective, to save oneself, to escape from (מִן) danger; also, to pass along quickly, to hasten. Hith. to escape.

מֶלֶט m. mortar, lime, from מָלַט to stroke over.

מְלַטְיָה p. n. m. (saved by God).

מְלִיכוּ equiv. to מַלּוּךְ.

מְלִילָה f. the ear of corn that is cut or plucked off, from מָלַל.

מְלִיצָה fem. 1) a song, origin. poesy, from לוּץ which see; hence also, 2) doctrine, brief reflection (gnome).

מָלַךְ (fut. יִמְלֹךְ) to rule, to reign over (עַל, בְּ) something, to be appointed king; the original signification is not to counsel (this being only the secondary one), but probably, to excel; next, to be king; and lastly, to counsel. Niph. to take counsel, after the Aram. Hiph. to appoint as king, with acc., rarely with dat. Hoph. to be appointed as king.

מֶלֶךְ (with suff. מַלְכִּי, plur. מְלָכִים, once מְלָאכִים, and מְלָכִין) m. 1) a king, הַמֶּלֶךְ the king of the country; the Lord is called מֶ׳ יִשְׂרָאֵל, מֶלֶךְ יַעֲקֹב; the Babylonian kings assumed the title of מֶלֶךְ מְלָכִים, the Assyrian king מֶלֶךְ הַגָּדוֹל; 2) p. n. m. sometimes the word is found with the article as a p. n.

מֶלֶךְ (def. מַלְכָּא, pl. מַלְכִין, —כִים, def. מַלְכַיָּא) Aram. m. the same, מֶלֶךְ מַלְכַיָּא king of kings, of the kings of Babylon and Persia.

מְלַךְ (with suff. מִלְכִּי) Aram. masc. counsel.

מֹלֶךְ (king) p. n. of an Ammonite idol, to whom the Israelites sometimes sacrificed human beings, Moloch. Always with the article הַמֹּלֶךְ.

מַלְכֹּדֶת f. net, snare, catchrope, from לָכַד.

מַלְכָּה (from מֶלֶךְ, pl. מְלָכוֹת) fem. queen, pl. princesses, who descend from kings.

מַלְכָּה (Aram.) f. the same.

מִלְכָּה p. n. f. (counsel, device).

מִלְכָּה see מְלוּכָה.

מַלְכוּ (const. —כוּת, def. —כוּתָא, const. pl. מַלְכְוָת, def. pl. מַלְכְוָתָא) fem. Aram. rule, reign, dominion, kingdom.

מַלְכוּת (pl. מַלְכֻיוֹת) f. kingdom, dominion, empire; also, the ruling.

מַלְכִּיאֵל p. n. masc. (a king is God), patron. —אֵלִי.

מַלְכִּיָּה p. n. m. (the same).

מַלְכִּיָּהוּ p. n. m. (the same).

מַלְכִּי־צֶדֶק p. n. m. (king of righteousness), king of Salem.

מַלְכִּירָם p. n. m. (king of eminence).

מַלְכִּישׁוּעַ p. n. m. (king of salvation).

מַלְכָּם 1) p. n. of an Ammonite idol, equiv. to מֹלֶךְ; 2) p. n. m.

מִלְכֹּם p. n. the same.

מְלֶכֶת f. origin. queen, formed from the Aram. מַלְכָּה, but complete מְ׳ הַשָּׁמַיִם queen of the skies, as the name of Venus, which was worshipped as an idol.

מַלְכֶת p.n. f. (female ruler) with the article.

I. מָלַל to speak, a rare term for דִּבֶּר, origin. to utter forth, part. מוֹלֵל. Pi. מִלֵּל to speak, to express (the deeds of God), with לְ to speak to some one, to tell.

II. מָלַל transf. to cut off, to circumcise (of the foreskin). Niph. נָמַל (2 pers. pl. נְמַלְתֶּם for נְמַלֹּתֶם, fut. יִמַּל) to be cut off, to be plucked off, used of flowers, ears of corn, grass, etc. Po. מוֹלֵל (fut. יְמוֹלֵל) to cut off (flowers); probably also, Prov. 6:13, to scrape with the feet, as this word is used in modern Hebrew (Author. Vers. "he speaketh").

מְלַל (Aram.) only Pa. to speak.

מִלְלַי p. n. m. (the eloquent one).

מַלְמָד (const. מַלְמַד) m. instrument for driving the cattle, ox-goad, from לָמַד, only with the addition of הַבָּקָר.

מָלַץ (Kal, not used) according to some, equivalent to מָלַט, to slide along; transf. to flatter; hence Niph. נִמְלַץ to be smooth-tongued, insinuating; according to others, נִמְלַץ is only denom. from the noun מְלִיצָה (interpretation), and therefore signifies, to be distinct, clear, intelligible.

מֶלְצַר m. origin. abstract, overseeing, from לָצַר; next concrete, overseer; probably, however, it is not a Hebrew but a Persian word.

מָלַק to pinch off, to pluck off, perhaps related to פָּרַק, at all events, with the later מָלַג.

מַלְקוֹחַ (dual מַלְקוֹחַיִם) m. 1) that which is taken away, booty, spoil, either of living beasts, or of prisoners generally, but never of inanimate things; 2) only dual, jaws, origin. they that lay hold of something (the upper and lower jaws).

מַלְקוֹשׁ m. denom. from לָקַשׁ latter rain, harvest-rain; in contrast to יוֹרֶה and מוֹרֶה, which see.

מֶלְקָח (only dual ־קָחַיִם) m. instrument used in taking up something, tongs; also applied to snuffers, and only used in the dual form, owing to its twofold form.

מֶלְתָּחָה fem. wardrobe, from לָתַח = מָתַח, which see.

מַלֹּתִי p. n. m.

מַלְתָּעָה (pl. ־עוֹת, const. ־תְּעוֹת) f. tooth (Author. Vers. jaw); originally, that which bites, from לָתַע. מְתַלְּעָה is the same.

מַמְּגֻרָה f. denom. from מְגוּרָה store-house, from גּוּר, which see. The dagesh in the מ is euphonic.

מֵמַד (only pl. מְמַדִּים) m. from מָדַד, measure, extent, space; after the form מֵצַר.

מָמוּכָן (Persian) pn. m.

מָמוֹת (only pl. מְמוֹתִים) m. death, once in Keri for מוּמָתִים, they that are killed.

מַמְזֵר m. one of mixed birth, whose father is an Israelite, and whose mother is a Philistine; next generally, bastard, who is the issue of adultery, from מָזַר to mix, in reference to sex; comp. תֶּבֶל.

מִמְכָּר m. 1) sale; 2) concr. subject of sale, that which is for sale, saleable.

מִמְכֶּרֶת f. the same.

מַמְלָכָה (const. מַמְלֶכֶת, with suff. מַמְלַכְתִּי, pl. מַמְלָכוֹת) f. dominion, kingdom, equiv. to מְלוּכָה; hence עִיר הַ_מ׳ royal residence.

מַמְלְכוּת (const. ־לְכוּת) f. the same.

מִמָּן see מִן.

מִמְסָךְ m. mixed wine, from מָסַךְ to mix.

מֶמֶר m. vexation, from מָרַר.

מַמְרֵא p.n. m. (corpulent one), and from which אֵלוֹנֵי מַמְרֵא the oaks of Mamre, for which also מַמְרֵא stands alone.

מַמְרוֹר (only pl. מַמְרוֹרִים) m, bitterness, from מָרַר.

מִמְשַׁח masc. extension, spreading; cherub of spreading, i. e. with spread wings, from מָשַׁח.

מִמְשָׁל (pl. ־לִים) m. ruling, dominion, pl. heads of the people.

מֶמְשָׁלָה (const. ־שֶׁלֶת, with suff. ־שַׁלְתּוֹ, const. pl. מֶמְשְׁלוֹת, מֶמְ׳) fem. 1) rule, empire, dominion; transf. to chief.

מִמְשָׁק (const. ־שַׁק) m. possession, from מָשַׁק.

מַמְתָּק (pl. מַמְתַּקִּים) m. sweetness, loveliness, from מָתַק.

מָן (with suff. מַנְךָ) m. the Arabian manna, a kind of sweet gum flowing from certain trees. The orig. signification is, according to some, gift, present, from מָנָה to award, to allot.

מָן (before makkaph מַן) Aram. inter. pron. who? what? equiv. to the Heb. מִי: מַן דִּי every one who.

מֵן (const. מִן, only in connection with מִן, and with suff. מִמֶּנּוּ, מִמֶּנִּי, const. pl. מְנֵי) m. a part; hence מִמֶּנִּי from me, on my part, so that מִן is only added to strengthen the sense, but the state of const. loses entirely the character of the noun.

מִן (or מִי, i.e. with compensating dagesh forte, before gutturals מֵ, seldom מִ) prep. from, out of; as a particle of motion, from or out of a thing, in contrast to אֶל motion *to* or *towards* a thing. The significations may be thus classified; 1) local removal from a subject, after the verbs to proceed, to emigrate, to carry, bring, draw, rend, deliver, help forth, etc; also after to fear, to conceal, to shut out, to guard, secrete oneself, etc., from or against anything, in which the idea of local removal is predominant.—To this belong also בּוֹשׁ מִן to be ashamed of some one, נוּחַ, שָׁבַת מִן to rest from something, בָּגַד מִן to apostatise from some one, אָבַד מִן to be lost from some one, כָּלָה מִן to desist from, רָשַׁע מִן to degenerate from, חָלִילָה לִּי מִן far be it from; מִן also signifies without, e.g. מִפַּחַד Job 21:9, מִמֶּלֶךְ 1 Sam. 15:23; מִמּוּם; comp. חָפְשִׁי, צֵל מֵחֹרֶב, רַב מַעֲלוֹת, מֵאֲדֹנָיו; it also signifies a comparison, in which case it is rendered, more than, which is called by the grammarians מֵם הַיִּתְרוֹן, e.g. טוֹבָה חָכְמָה מֵחָרוּץ wisdom is better than fine gold, hence רַב, נָקַל, עָמַד, נָפַל, הִשְׁחִית, גָּבַהּ, עָקֹב מִן, בָּחַר מִן, עָצַם, אָמֵץ; it also signifies the separation of part of a whole, which the grammarians call מֵם קְצָצִית, and follows the verbs to go, to give, to take, to receive, to leave over, to eat, to drink, to fall (in battle), especially after numbers, always to separate a part from the whole: in some phrases מִן is rendered, part of some of, several of, e.g. מִיָּמַי one of my days, מִנְּשִׁיקוֹת some kisses, מִן שָׂרָיו one of his princes, מִן הָעָם some of the people, מִדָּם some of the blood, מֵאַחַד אַחֶיךָ of any one of thy brothers; also with negatives, where the מִן is scarcely translateable in a modern language, e.g. מֵאַיִן, מֵאֶפֶס, it can only be rendered: nothing at all, nothing whatever, nought; also מִמַּעַל from above, מִתַּחַת from under, מִבַּיִת from within, מִחוּץ from without, מִשְּׂמֹאל, מִיָּמִין, מִסָּבִיב, מִיָּם, מִמּוּל, מֵרָחוֹק, מִקֶּדֶם round about (from all sides), מִפְּנֵי, etc.; 2) removal (in reference to time), as מִנְּעֻרַי from my youth, מִבֶּטֶן אֵם from the mother's womb, מִיּוֹם since there has been day, מִשְּׁנַת הַיֹּבֵל from the beginning of the year of the jubilee, מִיֹּמַיִם from two days, i.e. immediately after two days; like a dream מֵהָקִיץ immediately after waking, מֵרֶחֶם on leaving the womb, מִקֵּץ at the end (of a time), מִיָּמִים after days, מִשְּׁלֹשׁ חֳדָשִׁים after three months, likewise in מֵאָז, מֵעוֹלָם from olden times, from days of yore, מִטֶּרֶם since, not yet, ere, מִמָּחֳרָת on the following day; 3) the local motion transf. to designate the cause, the means, the instrument or occasion of the action, whether physical or mental, e.g. מִיַּיִן from wine, מֵאֹפֶה kindled by the baker, מִבִּינָתְךָ through thy understanding, מֵחֶזְיֹנוֹת through visions, מֵרֹב through the multitude (of thy sins); in many phrases מִן must be rendered, on account of, e.g. מִפְּשָׁעֵינוּ on account of, or owing to, our transgressions, מִקּוֹל הַקּוֹרֵא owing to the voice of him that cries; in this sense are found several particles joined to מִן, e.g. מִבְּלִי, מִבִּלְתִּי, because, not, etc.; when the cause is a preventive, מִן is translated, from or on account of, e.g. they could not drink the water מִמָּרָה from bitterness; מִן also signifies, according, e.g. מִפִּי according to order. Thus several verbs are construed with מִן to signify the cause, e.g. שָׂמַח מִן he rejoiced of, i. e. on account of, something; in some places, because, e.g. מֵאַהֲבַת because of love. As to the joining of מִן with particles, or as to the various shades of its signification, the context must decide. With suffix, the above-mentioned noun מֵן is added to מִן; hence, מִמֶּנִּי (rare and poetical are the forms מִנִּי, מֶנִּי), מִמְּךָ, מִמֶּנּוּ (poetically מִנְהוּ, מֶנְהוּ); only with הֵם, הֵן, כֵּם, כֵּן, מִן retains its simple form, see also לְמַן.

מִן (with suff. מִנְהוֹן, מִנֵּהּ, מִנָּךְ, מִנִּי) Aram. equiv. to מִן Heb. from, out of, etc.; hence, מִן־יַצִּיב from firmness, certain, מִן־קְשֹׁט according to truth, truly, מִן לְוָת on the part of some one, מִן קֳדָם from before (some one), מִן אֱדַיִן from the time, since, מִן־דִּי from the time that, etc.

מֵן belongs to מִנִּים. See מִנִּים.

מְנָא (Aram.) equiv. to the Heb. מָנָה to number; hence, the Lord hath numbered thy kingdom, i. e. the years of thy reign; part. pass. מְנֵא numbered. Po. to appoint to an office.

מְנָאוֹת see מָנָת.

מַנְגִּינָה f. equiv. to נְגִינָה in the sense of, a song of derision. Root נָגַן.

מִנְדָּה (Aram.) see מִדָּה.

מַנְדַּע (Aram.) masc. equiv. to Heb. מַדָּע knowledge, understanding. The נ is the letter replaced by the dagesh forte.

מָנָה 1) origin. to part, to separate, related to בָּן (בּוּן) to distinguish; next, to divide; transf. to number, which properly is a division in parts, as in סָפַר; 2) to determine, as expressed by all verbs signifying splitting, e.g. חָרַץ, חָתַךְ,

נִמְנָה. Niph. to be numbered, determined, with אֶת (אֵת) to be counted to. Pi. מִנָּה (fut. apoc. יְמַן, imp. מַן) to appoint, to prepare, to allot, to award, to arrange. Pu. pass; hence part. מְמֻנֶּה one who is appointed over (עַל) something.

מָנֶה (pl. מָנִים) m. origin. a number, weight; of a certain number, shekel, maneh.

מָנָה (pl. מָנוֹת) f. gift, part, portion; origin. a portion awarded; then transf. like חֵלֶק, to the lot awarded.

מֹנֶה (only pl. מֹנִים) m. portion, gift, but only as an adv. time; comp. יָד in the same sense.

מִנְהָג masc. the driving or carrying along, from נָהַג. In modern Heb. custom, usage.

מִנְהָרָה f. a channel, a ditch, a cleft, formed from נָהָר.

מָנוֹד (const. מְנוֹד) m. the shaking of the head; also, the subject of the shaking of the head or of astonishment.

מָנוֹחַ (pl. מְנוּחִים) m. 1) rest, tranquillity, state of quietude; 2) resting place; 3) p.n. m.

מְנוּחָה f. (formed from מָנוֹחַ) equiv. to מָנוֹחַ rest, quietness, tranquil dwelling.

מָנוֹן m. denom. from נִין; progeny, dynasty, child. See נוּן.

מָנוֹס (with suff. מְנוּסִי) m. refuge, where protection is found; or, flight. See נוּס.

מְנוּסָה f. of the above, and signifies the same.

מָנוֹר (const. מְנוֹר) masc. a coulter; transf. to a weaver's beam (Kimchi יְתַר הָאֶרֶג). Compare נִיר.

מְנוֹרָה f. candlestick, from נוּר.

מִנְּזָר (with euphonic dagesh in the נ, pl. מִנְּזָרִים) m. origin. crowning; hence, the crowned one, monarch. According to others, from נָזַר, one who is distinguished from the people.

מָנַח (not used) to present, probably from מָנָה, with the origin. signification of: to award.

מִנְחָה (pl. מְנָחוֹת, const. מִנְחוֹת) f. 1) gift, present, especially offering of sacrifices, meat or drink-offering; hence its connection with זֶבַח; 2) tax, tribute.

מִנְחָה (pl. with suff. מִנְחָתְהוֹן) Aram. f. the same.

מְנַחֵם p. n. m. (comforter).

מָנַחַת 1) p. n. m. (rest); 2) resting-place, p. n. of a place.

מְנִי p. n. of a deity (Venus) which the Jews in Babylon idolatrously worshipped; its signification is, probably, fate, destiny, from מָנָה to award.

מִנִּי p. n. of an Armenian district, similar to אֲרָרָט.

מְנִי poetical form for the state of const. מִן, which see.

מִנֵּי state of const. pl. from מֵן, after the manner of אֱלֵי and others.

מְנָיוֹת see מְנָת.

מִנִּים (for מִנְעִים, hence a sing.) m. name of a musical instrument, so called from its lovely tone, like עוּגָב (from עָגַב) thus from נָעֵם; according to others, as a plur. from מֵן a string, from מָנַן to split, to sever, as supported by analogy.

מִיָּמִין see מְנְיָמִין.

מִנְיָן (Aram.) m. a number, from מְנָא, in modern Heb. signifies ten, the quorum for a congregation for religious worship.

מִנִּית (allotment) p. n. of an Ammonite place.

מִנְלֶה (with suff. מִנְלָם) m. property, wealth, riches, see נָלָה; מִנְלָם is probably equiv. to מִן־לָהֶם that which, or some of that which belongs to them, i. e. their property; comp. אֶרְאֶלָּם Isa. 33:7, which ancient commentators analyse in אֶרְאֶה לָּם. The contraction of לָהֶם in לָם is quite regular, as בָּם for בָּהֶם.

מָנַן (not used) to divide, to award, from which מִן (מִנִּי) מֵן (מָן), מְנָת, and, according to some, also מָנוֹן.

מָנַע (fut. יִמְנַע) to withhold, to prevent, to refuse, with מִן and לְ of the person to whom one refuses something; related to מֵאֵן. Niph. pass. to be withheld, refused; or reflective, to withdraw (oneself), to refuse.

מַנְעוּל m. a bolt, from נָעַל.

מִנְעָל m. the same.

מַנְעַם (only plur. —עַמִּים) m. dainty food, from נָעֵם.

מְנַעַנֵעַ (only pl. מְנַעַנְעִים) m. an instrument in the temple music, cornet, or sistron, so called from the rushing of the iron staves, from נוּעַ.

מְנַקִּית (only plur. מְנַקִּיּוֹת) f. vessel, used for libation, bowls of offerings, from נָקָה, which see.

מֵינֶקֶת see מֵנֶקֶת.

מְנַשֶּׁה 1) p. n. m. (he who causes forgetfulness of the native country) a son of Joseph, but also one of the twelve tribes; 2) subsequently the name of the territory of the tribe.

מְנָת (pl. מְנָאוֹת and מְנָיוֹת; it arose from מְנָאת f. the portion allotted, the part, the lot awarded; מְנָת כּוֹס portion of the cup, fate.

I. מָס m. the desponding one, the despairing one, from מָסַס, after the form עַם.

II. מַס (plur. מִסִּים) m. origin. gift, reward, present; of the irregular and undefined tribute, different from מָכַס, the definite one; מַס עֹבֵד tribute of service or serving under tribute; judging from the fem. מִסָּה the origin. signif. is to measure; hence the noun, that which is meted out, allotted, gift. The phrases in connection with מַס are: שׂוּם לָמַס, נָתַן לָמַס, שׂוּם מַס עַל to impose a tribute upon some one; שַׂר הַמַּס officer of the tribute.

מֵסַב (from סָבַב, plur. מְסִבּוֹת and const. pl. מְסִבֵּי) m. a circle, a circular seat, round of a table, from which, as an adverb, round about; plur. the same; hence, הִתְהַפֵּךְ מְסִבּוֹת to turn round, to turn in a circle, מְסִבֵּי יְרוּשָׁלִַם round about Jerusalem.

מַסְגֵּר (origin. particip. Hiph.) masc. locksmith; 2) prison, origin. that which shuts up or encloses.

מִסְגֶּרֶת (sing. Exod. 25:25) f. 1) that which encloses; hence, a border, a frame, and as in מַסְגֵּר transf. to enclosure, prison; 2) the border of the brazen basin in the temple, a kind of ornament.

מַסַּד (from יָסַד) m. foundation, fundament, basis.

מִסְדְּרוֹן (with ה finis —רוֹנָה) masc. denom. from סֵדֶר, a row of pillars, portico.

מָסָה (Kal not used) equiv. to מָסַס to dissolve, to melt, related to מָאַס; hence Hiph. 3rd pers. pl. הִמְסִיו the Aram. form for הִמְסוּ; (fut. apoc. יָמַס) to cause to dissolve in tears, to melt the heart, i.e. to affright it.

מַסָּה (plur. מַסּוֹת) f. 1) temptation, trial, the trial of the people, i. e. to test their confidence; tempting God, i.e. to murmur against him; fig. the sufferings by which God tries man; 2) p.n. of a place in the wilderness.

מִסָּה (const. מִסַּת) fem. formed from מַס, measuring, numbering, something that is measured, meted out; hence as a prepos. in the const. state to the succeeding noun: according to the standard; origin. according to measure, accordingly. See מַס.

מַסְוֶה m. cover, veil, from סָוָה, which see; comp. סוּת.

מְסוּכָה f. a thorn-hedge, from סךְ = שׂוּךְ. See סָאָה.

מַסָּח (from נָסַח) masc. relieving a (מִשְׁמֶרֶת) guard; origin. removing, removing of the sentinel or outpost.

מִסְחָר m. origin. travelling, trafficking, trading, trade, from סָחַר.

מָסַךְ equiv. to מָזַג to mix, temper (the wine); hence, in connection with יַיִן and שֵׁכָר, transf. to confuse, confound.

מֶסֶךְ m. mixed wine, equiv. to מֶזֶג.

מָסָךְ (const. מָסַךְ, from סָכַךְ) m. a covering, a curtain. See סָכַךְ.

מְסֻכָּה (from the masc. מָסוֹךְ) fem. a covering, a covering over, from סָכַךְ.

I. מַסֵּכָה f. the same, from נָסַךְ 2.

II. מַסֵּכָה (pl. מַסֵּכוֹת) f. 1) a mould; hence עֵגֶל מ׳, אֱלֹהֵי מ׳ a molten god, a molten calf, i.e. a cast idol (different from פֶּסֶל a graven idol), a cast calf; 2) the pouring out, libation; transf. to a covenant sanctioned by libation.

מִסְכֵּן m. a poor man, an indigent man, from סָכַן, which see.

מִסְכֵּנוּת f. poverty, neediness, from סָכַן, which see.

מִסְכְּנֶת (only plur. מִסְכְּנוֹת) f. storehouse, magazine, treasury, from סָכַן, which see. Its origin, of מִכְנֶסֶת from כָּנַס, cannot, however, be defined.

מַסֶּכֶת f. thread-work, weaving, from נָסַךְ to weave, to twist; comp. מַסֵּכָה in the same sense.

מְסִלָּה (pl. —לּוֹת) f. 1) a raised, i.e. a beaten road, highway, high road; transf. to wandering, pilgrimage; 2) walk, course of life, comp. דֶּרֶךְ; 3) equiv. to סֻלָּם ladder, staircase, rising step. See סָלַל.

מַסְלוּל (from סָלַל) m. a path, a pathway.

מַסְמֵר (only pl. מַסְמְרִים and מִסְמְרִים) m. a nail, a peg, from סָמַר (to be pointed), which see.

מַסְמֶרֶת (only pl. const. מַסְמְרוֹת and מַסְ׳) f. the same.

מָסַס (inf. const. מֹסֹס) to melt, dissolve; figur. of the perishing of one in sickness. Niph. נָמֵס (pause נָמָס, 3 pl. נָמַסּוּ, inf. const. הִמֵּס, fut. יִמַּס, pl. יִמַּסּוּ, but also with the dagesh analysed, יִמָּאֵס, יִמְאֲסוּ) 1) to melt away, to dissolve, physically, but transf. also to the dissolving of the fetters; to be disheartened, to be affrighted, with the addition of לֵב; and of inanimate nature, to vanish, to perish. Hiph. הֵמֵס to cause to be disheartened.

מַסָּע (from נָסַע) m. 1) stone quarry; hence, whole (uncut) stones אֶבֶן מַסָּע from the quarry; 2) journey, march, departure; next, travelling station, and in this sense is the pl. מַסָּעִים. In signif. 1 the root is סוּעַ=נָסַע.

מִסְעָד m. support, stay, baluster, on which one leans, from סָעַד.

מִסְפֵּד (const. —פַּד, with suff. מִסְפְּדִי) m. mourning, lament, cry of woe, from סָפַד.

מִסְפּוֹא m. fodder, provender, from סָפָא, which see.

I. מִסְפַּחַת f. equiv. to סַפַּחַת scurf,

origin. that which sticks, a scab. See סָפַח.

II. מִסְפַּחַת (only pl. מִסְפָּחוֹת) f. a covering, a mat, from סָפַח, equiv. to צָפַח, טָפַח, which see.

מִסְפָּר (const. —פַּר) m. 1) number, amount; also, after numerals, e.g. twenty-four in number; לְאֵין מ׳, אֵין, עַד אֵין without number, innumerable; 2) numerable; next, that which can be counted, few, e.g. men (אַנְשֵׁי, מְתֵי) of number, i. e. a few; 3) narrative, tale, from סִפֵּר; 4) p. n. m.

מִסְפֶּרֶת p. n. m. (narrative).

מָסַר (inf. const. before makkaph לִמְסָר־) to deliver up, to transmit, transf. to commit oneself, to commit a trespass against God, in a parallel passage לִמְעֹל מַעַל. Niph. to be removed, to be delivered up. The origin. signification is, to take away, to remove, for the purpose of delivering up. In this sense is the signification of committing an act of treachery or fraud by abstracting or removing something.

מֹסֵר (=מוּסָר) m. admonition, chastisement, instruction, from יָסַר.

מֹסֵרָה (contracted from מַאֲסֹרֶת) f. a fetter, from אָסַר.

מִסְתּוֹר (from סָתַר) m. lurking hole, where people hide themselves.

מִסְתָּר m. the same.

מֵעֶה (only pl. מֵעִים, const. מְעֵי and מֵעוֹרֵת, const. מְעוֹרֵת, after the form שֵׁם) m. 1) the inner part, entrail, bowels, used as the seat of propagation, of the mind, of the disposition, etc.; hence the forms יָצָא מִמְּעֵי פ׳ to descend (by birth) from some one, עוֹד בָּנִים בְּמֵעִים yet to bear children, children being called צֶאֱצָאֵי מֵעִים; 2) offsprings (of the sea), i. e. fishes, but in this sense only the form מֵעוֹת is used; complete צֶאֱצָאֵי מֵעוֹת; hence, כִּמְעֹתָיו like its (the sea's) fishes.

מְעֵה (pl. with suff. מְעוֹהִי) Aram. the same.

מַעְבָּד m. deed, the doing, from עָבַד.

מַעֲבֶה m. thickness, density, from עָבָה.

מַעֲבָר m. 1) abstract, the passing by, going along; 2) place of passage, pass, ford.

מַעְבָּרָה f. point of transition, ford.

מַעְבֶּרֶת (only plur. מַעְבָּרוֹת, const. מַעְבְּרוֹת) f. the same.

מַעְגָּל (pl. —לִים, const. מַעְגְּלֵי, —לוֹת) m. denom. from עֲגָלָה a waggon, a chariot; hence, 1) waggon track, road on which the waggon rolls along, transf. to a road, way, path, course of action (comp. נְתִיבָה, דֶּרֶךְ); 2) castle of chariots. See עָגַל.

מָעַד (fut. יִמְעַד) equiv. to מוּט to

totter; מוֹעֲדֵי רֶגֶל they whose feet are tottering. Pual מֻעַד, hence part. with omission of ם, מֻעֶדֶת to totter. Hiph. to shake.

מַעֲדַי (an adj. form from מַעֲדָה an ornament) p. n. m.

מַעַדְיָה p. n. m. (the diadem of God).

מַעֲדָן (only pl. מַעֲדַנִּים, מַעֲדַנּוֹת) m. delight, loveliness, joy; fig. dainty things.

מַעֲדַנָּה (only pl. —נּוֹת) f. a fetter, a bond, from עָדַן, equiv. to עָנַד to fetter, to bind.

מַעְדֵּר m. an instrument for digging vineyards or ploughing fields, a mattock. See עָדַר.

מָעָה (not used) according to some, to be soft, tender, related to מָהָה to flow, or מוּג to melt away.

מָעוֹג m. a cake, equiv. to עֻגָה. According to Aruch (under ענא) ענא signifies scorn, jest, לְשׁוֹן עֲנָא, i.e. it is used satirically (not *sermo placentae*) לַעֲגֵי מָעוֹג "mockers in feast," i. e. sycophants. The root is in עוּג.

מָעוֹז (מָעֹז, with suffix מָעוּזִי, מָעֻזִּי, pl. מָעֻזִּים) masc. strong place, a fortress; hence עָרֵי מָ׳. Tyre was called מָעֹז הַיָּם sea fortress, and a Syrian deity was called אֱלֹהֵי מָעֻזִּים god of the strong ones, fig. defence, asylum, refuge. The form מָעֻזְנֶיהָ (Is. 23:11) is instead of מָעֻזֶּיהָ with dagesh analysed.

מָעוֹם see מְעָמָה.

מָעוֹךְ p. n. m. (the needy one) from מָעַךְ equiv. to מוּךְ.

מָעוֹן (pl. מְעוֹנִים) masc. 1) dwelling, from עוּן; accus. in the dwelling, like בֵּית in the house; 2) cities of refuge; 3) p. n. of a city in Judah, near which there was a desert; 4) p. n. of a people.

בֵּית מְעוֹן, בַּעַל מְעוֹן, בֵּית see מְעוֹן בַּעַל מְעוֹן.

מְעוֹנָה fem. equiv. to מָעוֹן dwelling, habitation.

מְעוֹנִים 1) gent. from מָעוֹן, a dweller of Maon; 2) p. n. m.

מְעוֹנֹתַי p. n. m. (my cities of dwelling).

מָעוּף masc. darkness, origin. veiling, covering, from עוּף.

מָעוֹר (only pl. מְעוֹרִים) m. the privy parts, orig. uncovering, from עוּר.

מָעֹז see מָעוֹז.

מַעַזְיָה p. n. m. (strength of God).

מַעַזְיָהוּ p. n. m. (the same).

I. מָעַט (inf. const. מְעֹט, fut. יִמְעַט) 1) (not used) equiv. to מָחַץ to split, to cleave, to break off, transf. to diminish, comp. פָּחַת; 2) intr. to be little, trifling (in contrast to רָבָה), e. g. as regards number, value, character or position; also to become little, few. Pi. מִעֵט to do little. Hiph. הִמְעִיט (fut. יַמְעִט) to diminish, to lessen, to do something by little or feebly. That

subject, to prophesy in the name of something; בַּבַּעַל, בְּשֵׁם יי, בַּשֶּׁקֶר; transf. to the inspired song. Hithp. הִתְנַבֵּא and הִנַּבָּא (2 pers. הִתְנַבֵּיתָ, inf. הִתְנַבּוֹת, after the manner of the ל״ה) 1) to prophesy, construed entirely like Niphal; 2) to speak convulsively, frantic; hence, in connection with שָׁגַע to be mad. The reflective form is always used to express prophesying, because it is an emotion of the mind, and implies both passiveness and activity.

נְבָא (Aram.) the same, but only הִתְנַבִּי to prophesy.

נָבַב to bore, to hollow out; hence, particip. pass. נָבוּב hollow, נְבוּב לֻחוֹת hollow (made) of tablets, fig. hollow-headed. To express the idea of hollowing out, the following roots, which must be distinguished from one another, have been formed in the language: קָב, כַּב, נַב, אֵב, אַב, בֹּא, בַּו; which, however, are evidently connected with each other.

נָבָה (not used) to rise, to arch, to become prominent, comp. נָפָה and נוּף, and probably also נוּב.

נָבָה see נב.

נְבוֹ 1) p. n. of a Moabite mountain, and also the name of a city in its vicinity; 2) p. n. of a city in Judah; 3) p. n. of the Chaldean Mercury, who was worshipped idolatrously, similar to Hermes and Anubis in Egypt. In signif. 1 and 2, נְבוֹ denotes hill, hilly place; in signif. 3, it probably stands for נָבִיא=נְבוֹא the interpreter, נְבוֹ being the mythological secretary of heaven. נְבוֹ 3 frequently occurs in compound Babylonian and Syrian proper nouns.

נְבוּאָה prophecy, prophetic writings.

נְבוּאָה (Aram.) the same.

נְבוּזַרְאֲדָן p. n. of a Babylonian field-marshal (נְבוּ=נְבוֹ 3, זַר=שַׂר, אֲדָן=אָדוֹן; thus, the great prince of Mercury). זַרְאֲדָן is found in the p. n. זַרְאַרְדְּפַל Sardanapalus, the great ruler of power. For פַּל comp. פְּלֶאֶסֶר, פּוּל.

נְבוּכַדְנֶאצַּר (also —רֶאצַּר, —נֶצַּר, —רֶאצּוֹר) p. n. of the Babylonian king Nebuchadnezzar, who led the Jews into captivity. (The signif. is, the great king of Mercury.)

נְבוּשַׁזְבָּן p. n. of a Babylonian field-marshal (worshipper of Nebo). שַׁזְבָּן=*Achespan*, Persian.

נָבוֹת p. n. m. (the prominent one).

נְבִזְבָּה (pl. נְבִזְבְּיָן) Aram. f. a gift, a present, from בָּזְבַּז to lavish, to squander, with נ=מ as a copulative, probably to avoid the clashing with the ב.

נָבַח to bark, of dogs.

נֹבַח p. n. m. and from which, the p. n. of a city.

נִבְחַז p. n. of an idol of the Avians, of uncertain derivation

נָבַט (Kal, not used) to look, to behold, to view, the root is בָּ֫יַט, but only in Niph. נִבַּט to look, לָאָרֶץ to the earth, most frequently Hiph. הִבִּיט to look after something (לְ, עַל, אֶל), to look from somewhere (מִן), to view something (acc.), to look at something with pleasure (בְּ), to look after some one, with אַחֲרֵי; but הִבִּיט מֵאַחֲרֵי to look (from) behind some one; figur. to regard something (accus. לְ, אֶל), to look hopefully upon (אֶל) something.

נְבָט p. n. masc. (aspect, view; more correct, however, agriculture or increase, from נָבַט, Talmud, to grow).

נָבִיא (const. נְבִיא, plur. נְבִיאִים) m. 1) a prophet, generally of the Lord, but also of Baal, Astarte; the disciples of the prophets were called בְּנֵי הַנְּבִיאִים; 2) speaker, interpreter, orator; which, however, is not the original signification; transf. to a friend or faithful servant of God.

נְבִיא (def. נְבִיָּא or נְבִיאָה, def. plur. נְבִיַּיָּא, נְבִיאַיָּא) Aram. the same.

נְבִיאָה f. 1) a prophetess, transf. to songstress, poetess; 2) wife of a prophet, e.g. wife of Isaiah.

נְבָיוֹת (pl. from נְבָת, which see) 1) p. n. of a son of Ishmael, brother of Kedar; hence, 2) name of an Arabian people, like קֵדָר, who derive their origin from the son of Ishmael, the Nabatians; as to the locality of the residence of the Nabatians, there exists a variety of opinions; it appears that most of the agricultural and trafficking Saracens were so called, in contrast to the nomades.

נָבַךְ (not used) to overflow, to gush forth, related to נָבַע, the ground-syllable is also found in בָּכָה.

נֵבֶךְ (const. pl. נִבְכֵי) m. a spring-place; according to others, a whirlpool.

נָבֵל (fut. יִבֹּל; נָבֵל is the reading in Isa. 64:5) to wither, to drop off (of leaves, flowers), transf. to be decaying, wearied, worn out, and according to the frequent transfer of sluggishness to folly, it signifies also to act foolishly, badly. Piel נִבֵּל to despise, to dishonor, to outrage, causative of the signification as transferred.

נָבָל (pl. נְבָלִים) m. a fool; next, according to general mode of transferring, as in אֱוִיל, infidel, sinner, wicked one; Ps. 14:1, who says "there is no God."

נֶבֶל (also נֵבֶל, pl. נְבָלִים, const. נִבְלֵי, with suff. נִבְלֵיהֶם) m. 1) leather-bottle (from נָבַב to be hollow, or to hollow out, with the usual termination ־ֶל; comp. סֵפֶל a dish, from סַף basin (from סָפַף) used for wine; next, utensils or vessels resembling a leather bottle, as an earthen bottle, נ׳ חֶרֶשׂ, יוֹצֵר; 2) a musical instrument, somewhat in in the shape of a bottle, psaltery. The root is נָבַב.

נְבָלָה f. folly; next, wickedness, sin, hideous crime, especially, the vice of lewdness; synon. with זִמָּה; Job 42:8, "Lest I deal with you after your folly."

נְבֵלָה (const. נִבְלַת, with suff. נִבְלָתוֹ, only 1st pers. נְבֵלָתִי forms an exception) f. origin. that which is fallen down; hence, corpse; of beasts, a carcase; figur. of the prostrate idols, which are also called מֵתִים.

נַבְלוּת (with suff. —לֻתָהּ) f. shame, in the sense of nakedness; hence, privy parts.

נְבַלָּט p.n. of a city in Benjamin.

נָבַע equiv. to נָבַךְ to spring forth, to gush forth; comp. נָבָא, בּוּעַ, and others. Hiph. הִבִּיעַ, 1) to pour forth, to cause to flow (song of praise, words, evil, the spirit); next, generally, to announce, to make known; 2) to swell, to cause perspiration or an unpleasant odour.

נֶבֶק belongs to נִבְקָה, see בָּקַק.

נְבַר (not used) Aram. equiv. to בָּהַר, to shine, to glitter, not formed from נוּר.

נֶבְרְשָׁא (from a masc. נֶבְרַשׁ, def. נֶבְרַשְׁתָּא) f. a candlestick, formed from נְבַר Aram.

נִבְשָׁן (fat soil) p.n. of a city in Judah.

נְבָת (after the form קְצָת, מְנָת, בְּנָת, a very old Aramaic form; hence pl. נְבָיוֹת; Samaritan נְבָאוֹת, like מְנָיוֹת, etc.) equiv. to נָבַט; the signification of נְבַט=נְבָת cannot be defined; נָבַט in the Talmud signifies to sprout, to grow; but according to the history of the נְבָיוֹת, the signification is rather to cultivate the ground, like פָּלַח. See נְבָיוֹת.

נָגַב (not used) to be dried up, from which:—

נֶגֶב (with ה finis נֶגְבָּה) m. the region of the south, or noon, called dryness on account of the heat of the sun; especially, the name for south Palestine; נֶגְבָּה לְ southerly of, מִן נֶגְבָּה the same; בַּנֶּגֶ׳, לַנֶּגֶ׳, in the country towards the south.

נָגַד (Kal, not used), in front, before

the face, to be manifest; hence, Hiph. הִגִּיד to declare, to shew (synon. with הֶרְאָה), thus Isa. 3:9, "they declared their sin;" from this original signification the following secondary significations branch out: to announce, to notify, to give information, intelligence upon (עַל) something; to relate, to denounce, to accuse, to predict, to confess, to promulgate; next also, to sing praises, etc. Hoph. הֻגַּד (fut. יֻגַּד) pass.

נְגַד (Aram.) to draw along, to flow on; probably not at all connected with נָגַד Hebrew.

נֶגֶד (with suff. נֶגְדִּי) m. the front, that which is present, visible; but used only as a prep. before, over against, opposite, towards, e. g. נֶ׳ אֱלֹהִים before God, נֶ׳ הָהָר opposite the mountain. נֶגֶד is used with prepositions in the following manner: 1) כְּנֶגֶד corresponding with, or resembling, another thing; Gen. 2:18, "meet for him," כְּנֶגְדּוֹ; 2) לְנֶגֶד in the presence of, generally לְנֶגֶד עֵינֵי פ׳; also, against, in a hostile sense, e. g. לְנֶגֶד הַבּוֹנִים against, i. e. in opposition to, the builders; also used like כְּנֶגֶד in comparisons; 3) מִנֶּגֶד away from something, from the opposite side, especially after verbs signifying removal or concealment; also as an adv., off something, from off, however, yet, on the contrary; more frequently, in connection with nouns, מִנֶּגֶד לְ occurs.

נֶגֶד (Aram.) the same, but also in the direction towards, נֶ׳ יְרוּשְׁלֶם towards Jerusalem.

נָגַהּ (fut. יִגַּהּ) to radiate, to beam, to shine, in Aram. נְגַהּ. Hiph. הִגִּיהַּ to cause to shine, illumine, to light.

נֹגַהּ (with suff. נָגְהָם) f. 1) brightness, brilliancy (of fire, the candle; of the sword, of the sun, and others); 2) p. n. m.

נֹגַהּ (def. נָגְהָא) Aram. f. the same.

נְגֹהָה (pl. ־הוֹת) f. brightness of light.

נָגַח (fut. יִגַּח) to push, to gore, used of horned cattle. Pi. to push repeatedly; transf. to the pushing of enemies, i. e. to thrust them down. Hith. to push one another; hence, to carry on war, which signification is the most frequent in Aramaic.

נַגָּח adj. m. goring, butting (of cattle).

נָגִיד (const. נְגִיד, plur. נְגִידִים) m. origin. leader; hence, principal officer (of the temple, of the palace, of the war); next, prince, generally, as מְשִׁיחַ נָגִיד anointed prince, נְגִיד בְּרִית prince of the covenant (confederacy); transf. in the pl. נְגִידִים that which is noble, excellent, as abstract.

נְגִינָה (pl. —נוֹת) f. playing on a stringed instrument, song of derision; but whether it is at the same time a kind of instrument, as it would appear from the heading of some of the Psalms, has not been defined.

נָגַל (not used) equiv. to חָלַל, נָחַל to pierce through, to wound, origin. to make an incision; from which מַגָּל.

נָגַן to sound; next, generally, to play; hence נוֹגְנִים players on stringed instruments. Pi. to play on the strings, e.g. to play the כִּנּוֹר harp. The noun גַּת does not belong to נָגַן, but to גָּתַת, which see.

נָגַע (fut. יִגַּע, inf. const. נְגֹעַ and גַּעַת) origin. to strike against (בְּ) something; hence נָגוּעַ one who is smitten =מֻכֵּה אֱלֹהִים; next, to touch upon (בְּ) something, to bear hard upon (עַל) something, to carry to (אֶל) something, to reach unto (עַד) something, according to the local destination of the touching; transf. to hurt, to injure, to meet, to arrive, to attain; each of these significations being construed with either אֶל, עַל, or בְּ, according to the context. Niph. pass. from Kal, to be struck (so that one flees). Piel, to smite (of divine punishment), comp. נָכָה, נָגַף. Pu. pass. from Piel. Hiph. הִגִּיעַ to cause something to be touched, i.e. to bring near to, e.g. הִגִּיעַ עַל פִּי he has laid (the stone) close upon (עַל) my mouth; to join house to (בְּ) house, to lay a building in (עַד, לְ) the dust, to cause to attain to (לְ) rule, etc.; in all significations of the Kal and causative. Related are נָגַח and נָכָה, but not נָגַף, נָקַף, נָגַן, נָגַשׁ, as considered by some.

נֶגַע (with suff. נִגְעִי, pl. נְגָעִים, const. נִגְעֵי) m. 1) blow, stroke, especially of the plagues sent by God; 2) a plague, leprosy, but generally a spot or mark.

נָגַף (fut. יִגֹּף) to push, to strike (related to it is נָקַף, and the root is also found in אָ־כַף, דָּ־חַף), as for instance, of the goring of horned cattle, and of stumbling; also, of the divine punishments, either sickness, pestilence, disease, or war. Niph. to be smitten (by the Lord) before (לִפְנֵי) some one, i.e. in his presence, or by him. Hith. to push the foot against something, i.e. to stumble.

נֶגֶף m. 1) a plague, punishment; 2) stumbling, אֶבֶן נ׳ stone of stumbling.

נָגַר (Kal, not used) origin. to draw along; hence, to flow, to run. Niph. נִגַּר to be poured out, אַרְצָה to the earth, יָדִי לַיְלָה נִגְּרָה וְלֹא תָפוּג my place, i.e. my bed (comp. יָד Isaiah 57:8, Numb. 2:17, Deut. 23:13) overflows (with tears) the whole night without intermission. Hiph. הִגִּיר to pour out (Ps. 75:9), transf. to throw (stones), to pour away, to deliver up עַל יְדֵי חֶרֶב into the hands of the sword; comp. הֶעֱרָה in this sense. Hoph. to be poured down (of the water). See נִגָּר.

נָגַשׁ (pret. Kal, not used; fut. יִגַּשׁ, imp. גַּשׁ, גְּשָׁה, גֶּשׁ־, plur. pause גֹּשׁוּ, inf. גֶּשֶׁת, with suff. גִּשְׁתִּי) to approach (בְּ) something, to move, to come, to step, towards (אֶל, לְ) some one, to go to some one (עַד), to arrive at (בְּ, עַל) somewhere or something, to meet, to alight (acc.) somewhere, to join, to connect oneself; to approach the wife, i.e. to embrace her connubially; to approach God, i.e. to adhere to Him; גֶּשׁ הָלְאָה to move away. Niph. the same. Hiph. causative from Kal, to lead to, to bring to, to move to, to bring an offering, to cause to approach. Hoph. הֻגַּשׁ pass. from Hiphil. Hithp. to approach.

נָגַשׂ (fut. יִגֹּשׂ, once יִנְגּוֹשׂ) to press (the creditor), to drive on (to work); hence נֹגֵשׂ taskmaster, oppressor, collector of taxes; next, ruler, tyrant. Niph. to be pressed hard (by the enemy), to push oneself forward, to be driven, i.e. to be wearied, to be oppressed. נָחַץ is related.

נֵד (from נוּד II., not from נָדַד) m. 1) heap, syn. with עֲרֵמָה; hence, נֵד קָצִיר heap of the harvest, i.e. heap of sheaves; 2) a dam, a dike, wall, from נוּד to heap up.

נָדָא (Kal, not used) equiv. to נָדַח; hence, Hiph. הִדִּיא equiv. to הִדִּיחַ to remove, to drive away.

נָדַב (fut. יִדֹּב) to incite, to stimulate, נָדַב לֵב the heart urges some one (acc.) to do something voluntarily, i.e. from impulse; more frequently, however, occurs the Hithp. to urge oneself to something, to volunteer, to give freely, willingly, to present.

נְדַב (Aram.) the same, but only in Hithp. הִתְנַדַּב, from which the nominal verb הִתְנַדָּבוּ.

נָדָב p. n. m. (liberal in gifts, noble one), comp. אֲבִינָדָב.

נְדָבָה (plur. נְדָבוֹת, const. נִדְבוֹת) f. 1) free-will, readiness, liberality; hence, בִּנְ׳ voluntarily, freely; thy people are ready, i.e. willing; rain of benevolence, i.e. plentiful; 2) voluntary gift, liberal gift, from נָדַב.

נְדַבְיָה p. n. m. (ennobled by God).

נִדְבָּךְ (Aram.) m. cemented bricks, a wall. See דְּבַק.

נָדַד (the pret. has only the analysed form, infin. נְדֹד, fut. יִדֹּד, יִדַּד) equiv. to נוּד, נוּט, to move to and fro, to wander about, to flee; hence, נוֹדֵד fugitive. Po. נוֹדֵד to escape, to disappear (of the sun). Hiph. הֵנֵד (only fut. with suff. יְנִדֻּהוּ) to chase away, to cause flight. Hoph. הֻנַּד (fut. יֻדַּד) to be driven, to be cast away. Hith. הִתְנוֹדֵד to flee.

נְדַד (Aram.) the same (3 pret. fem. נַדַּת).

נְדֹד (plur. נְדֻדִים) m. erring, casting about, wandering.

I. נָדָה (Kal, not used) to hate, to despise, to abhor, origin. to exclude; hence, Piel נִדָּה to keep something at a distance, to despise, to exclude.

II. נָדָה (not used) to give, to present; which, however, is not connected with נָדַב.

נֵדֶה or נֵדָה (after the form הֶגֶה, קֵצָה) m. a gift; namely, the gift as wages of a harlot.

נִדָּה (from נָדַד, after the form מִלָּה) f. origin. abstract, removing, separation; next, conc. that which is removed, separated, rejected; hence, of the state of woman during the time of her separation, of the abomination of idolatry, and of consanguine connection: מֵי הַנִּ׳ water for purifying the unclean. Probably the root is נָדָה, which see.

נָדַח (fut. יִדַּח) to push, to push away, related to דָּחָה. Niph. נִדַּח to be cast, driven away; hence, particip. נִדָּח an outcast, a fugitive. But נִדַּח is also pass. from Hiph. הִדִּיחַ, hence, to be enticed; נִדְּחָה יָד בַגַּרְזֶן the hand is pushed by the axe, i.e. the balancing of the axe carries the hand with it, so that the hand loses its power over the axe. Hiph. הִדִּיחַ to push away, to drive away, to thrust, to disperse, to cause to wander about, to entice. Pu. to be pushed, driven away. Hoph. the same.

נָדִיב (const. נְדִיב, pl. ־בִים) adj. m., נְדִיבָה (pl. נְדִיבוֹת) f. voluntarily, readily, willingly, especially of giving, spending; transf. to noble-minded, distinguished; but both m. and f. are changed into substantives of concrete signification; hence, m. a noble one, liberal one, distinguished one, prince; fem. nobility, distinction.

I. נָדַן (not used) to be hollow, deepened out for containing something.

II. נָדַן (not used) equiv. to נָתַן to give, to present.

נָדָן (with suff. נְדָנָהּ) m. 1) sheath of a sword, from נָדַן I.; 2) a gift, a gift to a harlot, generally a present, from נָדַן II., which see.

נִדְנֶה (after the form לִבְנֶה) Aram. m. the same, transf. to the body, being the sheath of the soul. Probably נְדָנָהּ is the proper reading, so that נְדַן is the absolute state.

נָדַף (fut. יִנְדֹּף and יִדֹּף) to drive away, to disperse (of chaff, smoke), transf. to drive the enemy to flight, to conquer. Niph. (inf. const. הִנְדֹּף for הִנָּדֵף) pass.; hence קַשׁ, עָלֶה, הֶבֶל נִדָּף. Related to which is הָדַף and דָּפָה.

נָדַר (fut. יִדֹּר and יִדַּר) origin. =*spondere*, i.e. to distribute in benevolence (comp. דָּרַר to pour forth); hence, to resolve upon an act of benevolence, to vow doing something (in contrast to אָסַר binding oneself *not* to do something); compare *despondere*, to promise; *sponsus*, betrothed; *sponsio*, promise, vow; נָדַר נֶדֶר to vow a vow.

נְדַר belongs to the Aram. אַדַּר. See אֲדַר.

נֶדֶר and נֵדֶר (with suff. נִדְרִי, plur. נְדָרִים, const. נִדְרֵי) masc. a vow, שִׁלֵּם, עָשָׂה נְדָרִים to fulfil a vow; 2) an offering of a vow, בַּר נְדָרַי the son of my vows, i.e. the son entreated of God by a vow.

נֹהַּ m. the beautiful, the excellent, from נוּהַּ; according to others, from נָהָה to desire, to wish; hence, נֹהַּ that which is desired, desirable.

נָהַג (fut. יִנְהַג) to drive, to move along, to move away; hence, of the driving a herd of cattle, of the driving of horses, of the driving of a carriage, of the carrying into exile, of the leading of an army, e. g. he hath led me and brought me into darkness; transf. to be occupied with something, to act, to do, to conduct. Pi. to set in motion (a carriage or waggon).

נָהַג (Kal, not used) only Pi. נִהֵג to wail, to sigh; related to נָהַג.

נָהַד a verb erroneously considered as belonging to הוֹד, which see.

נָהָה to wail, to moan, related to הָהּ, or with נה, equiv. to אָ־נָה. Niph. to assemble; comp. זָעַק.

נְהוֹר (def. נְהוֹרָא) Aram. fem. light. See נְהַר.

נְהִי (pause נֶהִי) m. song of lament.

נִהְיָה fem. a cry of lament, formed from נְהִי.

נְהִיר Ketib for נְהוֹר, which see.

נַהִירוּ (Aram.) f. enlightenment, wisdom, from נְהַר Aram.

נָהַל (Kal, not used) to flow on (comp.

(אָזַל, נָזַל); hence, to proceed, to walk. Pi. נֵהֵל (fut. יְנַהֵל) to lead on, to drive, to accompany, and from the leading of the cattle to the meadow, transf. to protect carefully. Hith. to proceed along, to walk.

נַהֲלָל m. 1) a meadow, from נָהַל, 2) p.n. of a city in Zebulun.

נַהֲלֹל p.n. of a city, the same as נַהֲלָל.

נָהַם (fut. יִנְהֹם) roaring (of the lion), raging (of the sea), moaning (of the sick); comp. הָמָה, which is the original form.

נַהַם m. the roaring (of the lion).

נְהָמָה (const. נַהֲמַת) f. raging (of the sea), moaning.

נָהַק (fut. יִנְהַק) crying, braying (of the ass), figur. of the hungry mob; related to נָאַק.

נָהַר (fut. יִנְהַר) 1) to flow; figur. to wander, to pilgrimise; 2) to glitter, to shine; hence (like צָהַל, אוֹר) to be cheerful, merry. The connection of these two significations cannot be defined.

נָהָר (const. נְהַר, plur. נְהָרִים, const. נַהֲרֵי and נְהָרוֹת, const. נַהֲרוֹת) m. 1) nominal verb, streaming; next, concrete, river, stream; the river of Egypt, i.e. the Nile; the river of Goshen, i.e. the Chaboras; the rivers of Ethiopia, i.e. the Nile, and the Astaboras; the rivers of Babel, i.e. the Euphrates with its branches, sometimes הַנָּהָר alone is used for the Euphrates. The dual, נַהֲרַיִם the two rivers is only used in connection with אֲרָם, and signifies the Euphrates and the Tigris.

נְהַר (def. נַהֲרָא) Aram. m. the same.

נְהָרָה f. light, daylight, from נָהַר 2.

I. נוּא (fut. יָנוּא Ketib) to refuse, to negative; hence the Hiph. הֵנִיא (fut. יָנִיא) to disallow; next, like הֵפִיר to frustrate; Ps. 141:5, "it shall be an excellent oil which shall not break my head" (i.e. not make my head recoil).

II. נוּא (not used) to be raw; from which נָא, which see.

נוּב m. Ketib for נִיב, which see.

נוּב (fut. יָנוּב) to sprout, to grow; hence, to increase in prosperity, in strength and riches, to flourish. Po. נוֹבֵב to cause to sprout, to increase, to prosper.

I. נוּד (fut. יָנוּד, sometimes יָנֹד) 1) to wander about, to rove about, to flee, to be fugitive; related to נָדַד, and according to some נֵד קָצִיר Isa. 11:17, is from this root; 2) to shake the head, as an indication of regret or compassion; next, generally, to mourn, to bewail. Hiph. 1) to drive away; 2) to move the head to and fro as a sign of derision.

Hith. הִתְנוֹדֵד, 1) to totter to and fro; 2) to shake the head either in derision or in grief.

נוּד (Aram.) the same, to flee, fut. יְנֻד.

II. נוּד (not used) to join, to heap up; hence נֵד, which see.

נוֹד m. 1) flight; 2) p.n. of a district.

נוֹדָב p.n. m. (equiv. to נָדָב).

נוּהַּ (not used) after the Arab., to be magnificent, splendid; related to נָאָה.

נָוָה (fut. יִנְוֶה) 1) equiv. to נָאָה, to stay, abide, dwell; וְלֹא יִנְוֶה and he remains not dwelling (in the land, Auth. Vers. "neither keepeth at home"); 2) to be proper, fit, beautiful; comp. נָאָה. Hiph. to glorify, to exalt, from נָוָה in the sense of being beautiful.

נָוֶה (const. נְוֵה, with suff. נָוֵהוּ, נָוְךָ, נְוֵהֶם) m. dwelling, habitation, and in the Nomadic language it signifies a meadow.

נָוָה f. the same as נָוֶה.

נָוֶה adj. m. נָוָה (const. נְוַת) fem. 1) dwelling, inhabiting; hence the term housewife נְוַת בַּיִת; 2) beautiful, proper.

נוּחַ (fut. יָנוּחַ) origin. to incline; hence, to lie down, to rest; next, to enjoy tranquillity, to be silent. Hiph. 1) הֵנִיחַ to lay down, to let down, הֵ' חֵמָה בְּ to vent his rage on something; next, to cause to rest, to afford rest, to lead to rest; 2) הִנִּיחַ to set down, to lay down; with בְּ and אֶל of the place, to allow rest, to appease, to throw down, to let rest; hence, generally, to allow, to afford, to leave over, to leave, to leave behind; with מִן to forbear from something: the various significations must be used according to the context. Hoph. 1) הוּנַח to be allowed to rest; 2) הֻנַּח (הֻנִּיחַ) to be set down; particip. מֻנָּח to be left over, left empty; comp. also חָנָה.

נוֹחַ (also נֹחַ, with suff. נוֹחֶךָ) m. 1) rest; 2) p.n. m. Noah.

נוֹחָה p.n. m. (rest).

נוּט (fut. יָנוּט) equiv. to מוּט to totter, of the earth; related to נוּד.

I. נוּךְ (not used) to point; from which תְּנוּךְ, which see.

II. נוּךְ (only particip. נָךְ, plur. נָכִים, after the form מֵת) to jest, to carry on foolery, to be insensate; hence נָךְ a fool.

נְוַל (Aram.) equiv. to נָבַל, to drop off, to wither; and hence Pa. נַוֵּל to lower, to debase.

נְוָלוּ (Aram.) f. debasement; transf. to ruin.

נְוָלִי (Aram.) f. the same.

נוּם (fut. יָנוּם) to slumber.

נוּמָה f. slumber; comp. תְּנוּמָה.

נוּן belongs to נִין and מָנוֹן. See נִין.

נוּס (fut. יָנוּס) origin. equiv. to נוּץ to flee, to fly; hence also, like in נוּץ to dart, of the darting motion (comp. פָּרַח); generally, to flee (of the shadow), to hasten away. Pi. נוֹסֵס to urge, drive (of the Divine Spirit); according to others, to shine, or to flourish. Hiph. הֵנִיס to drive to flight, or to save by flight; הִתְנוֹסֵס belongs to נָסַס, and signifies to unfold or plant (נֵס) a standard.

נוּעַ (fut. יָנוּעַ, inf. const. נוֹעַ and נוּעַ) to totter, to stagger (of the blind), to reel (of the drunkard), to tremble (with fear), to hang down and reel (of the miners; Author. Vers. Job 28:4, renders it "they (the waters) are gone away from man"), to hover over (עַל) something, i.e. to rule, etc., but also like נוּד, נָדַד to wander about. Niph. pass. to be moved, shaken. Hiph. הֵנִיעַ to shake (the head), either in triumph or derision; likewise בְּרֹאשׁ, or to shake (a hand, a sieve); next, generally, to cause tottering or dropping of the knee, or after the manifold and extensive significations of the Kal.

נוֹעַדְיָה p.n. m. and f. (appointed by God).

נוּף (Kal, not used) 1) to move, to shake; hence Hiph. הֵנִיף to swing, e.g. a saw, i.e. to use it, to draw it; a staff, a rod, i.e to rule; to swing the sickle, over (עַל) something; of the moving to and fro of the joints (of the animals) for the sacrifices, and the leading to and fro of live cattle; to shake, e.g. a sieve, the hand, either to make a sign or as an indication of threatening, with עַל. Hoph. הוּנַף pass. Pi. נוֹפֵף to shake the hand against something as a threat; 2) (Kal, not used) to flow; hence Hiph. הֵנִיף to wet, to moisten, to sprinkle; once the abridged form נַפְתִּי occurs; 3) (not used) to be elevated, arched, or to raise oneself; related to נָבָה; 4) to cover, from which some derive נוֹף, this signification is, however, uncertain.

נוֹף m. an elevation, i.e. a hill, from נוּף 3; according to others, from נוּף 4, in the signification of the top of a tree.

נוּץ (Kal, not used) equiv. to נָצַץ to glitter, to shine; hence also, after the general mode of transferring (comp. זִיז and פָּרַח) to bloom, to flourish, and next also, to fly, to flee, and in the last sense perhaps, Lam. 4:15, נָצוּ גַּם נָעוּ "they fled away and wandered." Hiph. הֵנֵץ (but 3 pl. הֵנֵצוּ for הֵנִיצוּ; fut. יָנֵאץ, according to some) to bloom.

נוֹצָה (after the form קוֹמָה) f. 1) flag, feather, from נוץ; 2) for נוֹצָא from יָצָא, excrement of the crop (of a fowl), comp. צֵאָה and צוֹאָה.

נוק see יָנַק, to which also belongs וַתְּנִיקֵהוּ.

נור (not used) 1) to burn, to shine; comp. נָהַר; 2) to till, to plough, to cut through the soil; hence נִיר, מָנוֹר.

נור (def. נוּרָא) Aram. f. fire.

נוש (fut. יָנוּשׁ) to be sick, ill; related to אָנַשׁ, and partly to עָנַשׁ.

נָזָה (fut. יִזֶּה, apoc. יִזְ, יִז, comp. יִם) equiv. to נָצָה (Arab. נצח) and probably also נָסַךְ: to sprinkle, e. g. blood upon a garment or upon the wall, with עַל and אֶל; 1) Hiph. to sprinkle upon (אֶל, עַל) something, especially of the sprinkling for cleansing from sin; 2) Kal (not used), equiv. to יָזָה to assemble; hence, Hiph. הִזָּה (only fut. יַזֶּה) to cause to assemble; hence, Isaiah 52:15, כֵּן יַזֶּה גוֹיִם רַבִּים "thus will he assemble many people." From נָזָה in signif. 2, are to be derived the proper nouns יִזִּיָּה, equiv. to יְזִיאֵל, and יִסְמַכְיָהוּ.

נָזִיד masc. boiled pottage, from זוד: But the form being without analogy, the root is perhaps נָזַד, in the signif. of זִיד (זוד).

נָזִיר (const. נְזִיר, pl. נְזִירִים) m. 1) the separated, consecrated one, from נָזַר (equiv. to זור but not equiv. to נָדַר), a Nazarite; hence also, prince, as being consecrated to God, or as being distinguished from the people; 2) the consecrated, uncut and untouched vine, resembling the Nazarite, who durst not have his hair cut; if it is not equiv. to נֵזֶר ornament, decoration.

נָזַל (fut. יִזַּל) 1) to flow, to run, of water, tears, which flow; to overflow; figur. of the flow of speech, of the spreading of odour; 2) (not used) to wander, to walk, related to אָזַל, which is from the same root, and transferred in a similar manner, from which מַזָּל, which see. Hiph. הִזִּיל to cause to flow. נָזְלוּ see under זָלַל, the same הִזִּיל.

נָזַם (not used) equiv. to זָם to tie round, to enclose, but not to pierce.

נֶזֶם (pl. נְזָמִים, const. נִזְמֵי) m. an ornament of the ear or of the nose, in the form of a ring, so called from its enclosing; from נָזַם.

נְזַק (particip. נָזֵק=נְזִק) Aram. to suffer injury; hence, Af. הַנְזֵק to cause injury, inf. הַנְזָקָא.

נֵזֶק m. injury, loss.

נָזַק equiv. to נָזַק, which see. The root is in בָּזַק.

נָזַר (Kal, not used) to separate, to exclude, related to סוּר, זוּר; hence, to consecrate, to select. Niph. נָזַר (imp. הִנָּזֵר) 1) to separate oneself, to depart, e.g. from following the Lord, מֵאַחֲרֵי י״י; hence, transf. to separate oneself from (מִן) something; 2) to devote or consecrate oneself to (לְ) something. Hiph. הִזִּיר 1) to remove some one, to cause some one to depart; 2) to consecrate some one (לְ). הִזִּיר must be taken as denom. from נָזִיר, having an intrans. signif. i.e. to live as a Nazarite.

נֵזֶר (with suff. נִזְרוֹ) m. 1) equiv. to זֵר, a crown, a wreath; hence, a jewel, a diadem (of the king or priest), אַבְנֵי נ׳ stones of a diadem, i.e. precious stones; 2) separation, distinction, consecration, transf. to the consecrated head, i.e. the unshaven head.

נַחְבִּי prop. noun masc. (the hidden one).

נָחָה to lead, to conduct, with בְּ, of the place. Hiph. הִנְחָה (fut. יַנְחֶה) to lead, with acc., to some one (אֶל), to some place (עַד), before some one (אֶת פְּנֵי, לִפְנֵי), to lead away (מִן), often of leading in a moral sense.

נַחוּם p.n. m. (comforter).

נָחוּם see רָחוּם.

נִחוּם (only pl. נִחוּמִים) m. comfort, compassion, from נָחַם.

נָחוֹר p. n. m. (the snorting one).

נָחוּשׁ (from נְחֹשֶׁת) adj. m., נְחוּשָׁה f. brazen, the f. is used as a subst. equiv. to נְחֹשֶׁת.

נְחוּשָׁה see נָחוּשׁ.

נְחִילָה name of a musical instrument, from נָחַל, to hollow out.

נְחִיר (only dual נְחִירַיִם) m. nostrils, from נָחַר to snort.

I. נָחַל (fut. יִנְחַל, inf. const. נְחֹל) 1) intrans. to take possession of as one's property, or as one's inheritance. The root נ־חַל is connected with חָלַל to redeem. Pi. נִחַל to take possession of, with acc. and לְ, of the person. Hiph. הִנְחִיל to cause to possess, to divide the inheritance or the possession. Hoph. to be made to possess, especially of something not unpleasant. Hith. to put oneself in possession of something.

II. נָחַל (not used) equiv. to חָלַל, to pierce, to hollow out; not at all connected with נָחַל I.

נַחַל (with ה finis נַחְלָה, dual נַחֲלַיִם, pl. נְחָלִים, const. נַחֲלֵי) masc. 1) a ditch, pit; hence, transf. to a shaft; 2) a valley, especially one with a brook, transf. to a brook, brooks being generally found in valleys. Several names of brooks in Palestine are thus compounded with נַחַל, and many names of valleys. The root is נָחַל II.

נַחֲלָה see נַחַל.

נַחֲלָה (const. ־לַת, pl. נְחָלוֹת) f. the taking possession; next concrete, possession, property, inheritance, transf. to that which is allotted to some one, lot, destiny, fate; comp. חֵלֶק. Root נָחַל I.

נַחֲלִיאֵל (valley or possession of God) p. n. of a place in the desert.

נֶחֱלָם p. n. m. (the strong one) from which the patron. נֶחֱלָמִי.

נַחֲלַת f. equiv. to נַחֲלָה, possession, portion, lot.

נָחַם (Kal, not used) to moan, to groan, related to נָהַם; hence Niph. נִחַם (inf. הִנָּחֵם, fut. יִנָּחֵם) 1) to sigh, to grieve, to repent, to have compassion, to regret something, with עַל, אֶל, לְ, sometimes מִן; 2) to comfort oneself at (עַל, אַחֲרֵי) a loss; 3) to revenge oneself, orig. to vent one's wrath, constr. with מִן, related to נָקַם. Pi. to comfort, to manifest compassion, with acc. of the person, and with מִן and עַל, of the subject on which one condoles. Hith. הִתְנַחֵם (once הִנַּחֵם) in significations as various as in the Niph. and construed as the same.

נַחַם p. n. m. (comfort).

נֹחַם m. repentance.

נֶחָמָה f. comfort, consolation.

נְחֶמְיָה p. n. m. (comfort of God).

נַחֲמָנִי p. n. m. (the repentant one).

נַחְנוּ pers. pron. pl. we, abbreviated from אֲנַחְנוּ, which see.

נָחַם belongs to פִּינְחָם, which see.

נָחַץ equiv. to לָחַץ, to urge, to press, to drive on; נָחוּץ pressed, hasty, urgent.

נָחַר (not used) to snort, from which נָחִיר.

נַחַר m. the snorting.

נַחֲרָה f. the same.

נַחְרַי (נַחֲרַי) p. n. m. (snorter).

I. נָחַשׁ (Kal, not used) equiv. to לָחַשׁ, חָשָׁה, to hiss, to whisper, to speak softly; hence Pi. נִחֵשׁ to whisper, to divine, to carry on necromancy; transf. to an omen, to forbode, to have a presentiment. It is also possible, that the Piel form is only a denom. from נָחָשׁ, and that the original signification is from נָחַשׁ, equiv. to רָחַשׁ to move along softly, to creep.

II. נָחַשׁ (not used) to shine, to flame; related to חַשׁ, belonging to חָשַׁן; from which נָחוּשׁ and נְחֹשֶׁת.

נַחַשׁ m. a spell, an omen, foreboding, sorcery.

נָחָשׁ (pl. נְחָשִׁים) m. 1) serpent, either from נָחַשׁ in the signification of hissing, or in the signification of creeping, so that it is equiv. to

זְחֵל עָפָר; transf. to the dragon, as a constellation; 2) (brass-mine) p.n. of a town; 3) p.n. m. (magician, sorcerer).

נְחָשׁ (Aram.) m. copper, brass, especially Cyprian brass, so called on account of its light red colour.

נַחְשׁוֹן p.n. m. sorcerer.

נְחֹשֶׁת (with suffix נְחֻשְׁתְּךָ, dual נְחֻשְׁתַּיִם) com. 1) brass, copper, (on account of the red colour, and having been in ancient times steel-polished, the word was used as a figure of strength; 2) brazen fetters, only dual, to denote the fetters both on hands and feet; 3) money, origin. that which is made of brass.

נְחֻשְׁתָּא p. n. f. brass.

נְחֻשְׁתָּן (formed from נְחֹשֶׁת) m. brazen serpent, which was worshipped as a symbol.

נָחַת (fut. יִנְחַת, תִּנְחַת, but also יֵחַת, תֵּחַת for יִחַת; but יֵחַתּוּ belongs to חָתַת) to descend, to go down to (עַל) some one; hence, in a hostile sense, to meet some one, to come down upon some one, to press deeply in (בְּ) some one; תֵּחַת גְּעָרָה בְּמֵבִין "a reproof enters into (penetrates) a wise man." Niph. נִחַת to press forward against something. Pi. נִחַת to press down (the bow), i.e. to strain it, to set it, to flood (the furrows) by plentiful rain. Hiph. הַנְחִית (imp. הַנְחַת) to thrust down; comp. חוּת.

נְחַת (particip. נָחֵת) Aram. to descend; Af. אַחֵת (fut. יַחֵת, imp. אַחֵת) to bring down, to carry down, to lay down, to preserve. Hoph. הָנְחַת to be thrust down.

נַחַת 1) m. (from נָחַת, related to חַת, חוּת, but not from נוּחַ) sinking, letting down (the arms), fall, defeat; 2) f. from נוּחַ, like שַׁחַת from שׁוּחַ, rest, quiet, appeasing, calming, soothing, refreshing, thus almost opposite to נַחַת I.; 3) p.n. m.

נָחֵת (only pl. נְחִתִּים) adj. m. descending, going down; according to the form the root is חָתַת, not נָחַת.

נָטָה (fut. יִטֶּה, apoc. יֵט, before makkaph יַט־) 1) origin. to extend, to stretch; hence, to stretch out (the hand, the lance), to stretch out the rule for measuring, to stretch the neck, to go down (of the shadow), to spread out (a tent, the heavens); figur. נָטָה רָעָה עַל to spread evil over some one; שָׁלֹשׁ אֲנִי נֹטֶה עָלֶיךָ three things I extend over thee, Author. Vers. offer unto thee; 2) to incline, to sink, e.g. to the earth (Job 15:29), of the declining day, of the shadow of the sun dial, of inclining to fall; 3) to turn towards some one, or to turn away from (מֵעִם, מִן) some one, נָטָה אַחֲרֵי to turn after some one, i.e. to devote oneself to him or to his party; but also, generally, to go away, or trans. to turn towards, to conduct. Niph. נִטָּה pass. to be stretched out, extended (of the shade, of brooks). Hiph. הִטָּה (fut. יַטֶּה, apoc. יַט, imp. הַט) to extend, to spread out, to expand, to incline (the ear to some one), to turn, to lead; הִטָּה חֶסֶד עַל to extend mercy unto some one, to turn away, to decline, to dismiss; especially in the sense of perverting the judgment (in a court of justice), sometimes omitting the word מִשְׁפָּט, e.g. in the form נָטָה אַחֲרֵי רַבִּים לְהַטּוֹת to incline after the many to wrest judgment. Hoph. only in the nouns מַטֶּה, מִטָּה. As to the root, it is related to מָ־תַח and לָ־תַח, as well as to טָחָה and מוּחַ (מָח).

נָטִיל adj. m. laden, burdened (with acc. כֶּסֶף, with money); origin. to carry, standing for נָטַל.

נָטִיעַ (only pl. נְטִעִים) m. plant; orig. that which is planted.

נְטִיפָה (only pl. ־פוֹת) f. origin. a small drop; next, an ornament of the ear, ear-drops; so called from the shape; according to others, a pearl, as pearls resemble drops.

נְטִישָׁה f. branch, bough, from נָטַשׁ.

נָטַל (fut. יִטּוֹל) to lift up, to take up, to take away; with עַל, to lay upon; כַּדַּק יִטּוֹל "He taketh up the isles as a very little thing" (as a little dust). Pi. to lift up, to carry, to bear; related to טוּל, דָּלָה.

נְטַל (1 pers. נִטְלֵת) Aram. the same.

נֵטֶל m. burden, heaviness; comp. מָטִיל from טוּל.

נָטַע (fut. יִטַּע, inf. נְטוֹעַ and טַעַת) 1) to set up, to set, to put in, to plant; fig. to plant a people, i.e. to give them a settled residence; 2) to drive in (a nail, the pegs of a tent); hence, to pitch a tent, to erect an idol image; transf. to plant the heavens as a tent. Niph. pass. The radical syllable is נָ־טַע, related to תָּח (תּוּחַ).

נֶטַע (const. נְטַע, comp. סַחַר, חֶדֶר, זֶרַע, with suff. נִטְעִי, pl. נְטָעִים, m. either as a verbal noun of the planting, or as conc. coll. the plantation, or especially, that which is planted, plant.

נְטָעִים (plantations) p.n. of a place.

נְטִעִים see נָטִיעַ.

נָטַף (fut. יִטֹּף) to drop, to drip, to flow, to flow down (of rain, water, myrrh, wine); related to צוּף, זוּב,

הִטִּיף. Hiph. to cause to drop down (new wine), to cause to stream down; transf. to cause the speech to flow, to prophesy.

נָטָף (const. pl. נִטְפֵי) masc. drops; transf. to a species of gum or balm, so called from its issuing in drops.

נְטֹפָה (dripping of the resin) p.n. of a city in Judæa; gent. נְטוֹפָתִי.

נָטַר (fut. יִטֹּר, and only once יִנְטוֹר) origin. to look at something attentively, to observe; related to נָצַר, hence מַטָּרָה; 2) to guard, to keep, to preserve, to watch, especially the anger אַף, i. e. to be wrathful, or to bear a grudge (but אַף is always omitted) with לְ and אֶת of the person.

נְטַר (1 pers. נִטְרֵת) Aram. the same.

נָטַשׁ (fut. יִטֹּשׁ) 1) to stretch, to extend, of branches; hence, נְטִישָׁה, equiv. to שְׁלֻחָה, branch, bough; hence, to be dispersed, עַל פְּנֵי הָאָרֶץ; of the battle becoming general; but also transf. to extend, to spread about, to scatter (into the desert, into foreign lands), to shed blood; 2) to scatter away, to abandon, to eject (synonymous with הִשְׁלִיךְ); and generally to let lie still the ploughfield, to desist (from a contest), to remit (a debt), to admit, to allow; 3) to stir, to palpitate, equiv. to לָטַשׁ, which in the origin. signif. is probably like the root in נָטַשׁ. Niph. to extend oneself, to spread, to be suspended (of pillars, columns), to be stretched along (of branches), to spread itself (of an army), to lay down outstretched. Pu. to be abandoned, forsaken.

נִי (only Ezek. 27:32 בְּנִיהֶם) masc. wailing, lament, for נְהִי, but eleven manuscripts read בְּנִיהֶם, which is more suitable to the context.

ניא see נוא.

ניב (from נוב) m. fruit, fig. נִיב שְׂפָתַיִם fruit of the lips, i. e. song of thanksgiving, praise, prayer.

נֵיבַי p.n. m. (the fertile one).

נִיד m. comfort, consolation, commiseration, from נוד.

נִידָה f. equiv. to נִדָּה, disdain, exile, wandering, from נָדַד or נוד.

נְיוֹת (habitations). Keri for נָוִית, which see.

נִיחֹחַ (after the form נִיצֹץ, from the Pi. נוֹחֵחַ, with suff. נִיחֹחֲכֶם, pl. נִיחֹחִים) m. pleasantness, acceptableness, taking pleasure, delight at something; origin. gratification, but only used in connexion with רֵיחַ, to express a sweet odour of sacrifices acceptable unto God. Root נוח.

נִיחֹחַ (Aram.) m. the same, but with the omission of רֵיחַ.

נִין (with suff. נִינִי) masc. a sprig, sprout; hence, transf. to that which sprouts anew. The root נוּן, is originally a redoubled form, and signifies to be new, fresh young. From the denom. נוּן, to have descendants. Niph. fut. יִנּוֹן, to beget descendants, to continue growing, endure (of fame).

נִינְוֵה p.n. of the capital of Assyria, Nineveh; probably of non-Semitic origin.

נִים (Ketib for נָם) adj. m. fugitive; next, the fugitive.

נִיסָן m. Nisan, the first month of the Hebrew year, called also חֹדֶשׁ הָאָבִיב. The etymology is non-Semitic.

נִיצוֹץ masc. a spark, from נָצַץ, to spark, sparkle.

נֵיר equiv. to נֵר, a lamp.

נִיר an abbreviated form of the Hiph. from הֵנִיר, to plough, to make the soil arable; belongs to נור 2.

נִיר m. 1) light, lamp, equiv. to נֵר; figur. the continuance of the progeny; 2) modern Heb. land made arable. The form נַנִּירָם is 1 pl. fut. Kal from יָרָה, with suff. ־ָם.

נָכָא (Kal, not used) equiv. to נָכָה, to strike; hence, the Niph. נִכָּא, with מִן, of the part struck, to be chased out of a country. From which נָכָא, which see.

נָכָא adj. m., נְכֵאָה f. to be cast down, to be humbled in mind, from נָכָא, but in a spiritual sense.

נְכֹאָה (only pl. נְכֹאוֹת, but always contracted נְכֹאת) f. name of a spice, probably gum tragacanth (after the Arab.)

נְכָאִים see נָכָה.

נָכַד (not used) to sprout, to grow.

נֶכֶד (with suff. נֶכְדִּי) m. descendant, sprig, offspring.

נָכָה (Kal, not used) to be hurt, wounded, or trans. to strike, to smite, to hurt; hence, Niph. נִכָּה, to be smitten, slain. Pu. to be struck (of the standing corn), Hiph. הִכָּה (fut. יַכֶּה, apoc. יַךְ, imp. הַכֵּה, apoc. הַךְ) to strike, in the most extensive sense; hence, also of God, to punish; of inanimate things, to overturn, to destroy, to conquer (a town), to blow (with a horn), to hit (with an arrow), to dash to pieces, to destroy (of the hail); next, to slay, to kill, sometimes with the addition of נֶפֶשׁ life, to accomplish a defeat; הִכָּה לֵב אֶת־פל׳ the heart of some one beats, strikes him; הִכָּה בַסַּנְוֵרִים to smite, or to strike with blindness; to take root, to sprout. Hoph. pass.

נָכֶה (const. נְכֵה, pl. נְכָאִים, comp. (רָפֶה, טְלָאִים from טָלֶה, רְפָאִים) adj. masc. origin. hurt, wounded, struck; hence, נְ׳ רַגְלַיִם struck in the feet, i.e. lame; נְ׳ רוּחַ of contrite spirit; the plur. is used as an abstract.

נְכֹה (also נְכוֹ) p. n. Necho, king of Egypt, son of Psammetichus.

נָכוֹן 1) particip. Niph. from כּוּן; 2) p. n. of a threshing-floor, in the parallel passage כִּידוֹן.

נָכַח (not used) probably equiv. to יָכַח, if it is not an original root, in the sense of, to be near, to approach.

נֹכַח m. proximity, synon. with עִמָּה, אֵצֶל, in its use only as a prep.: near, by, before; as נֹכַח י״י before God, =לִפְנֵי י״י, but נֹכַח לְ opposite. שׂוּם נֹכַח פָּנִים before the face, i.e. to set down (something) before oneself; אֶל־נֹכַח towards something; לְנֹכַח straight before oneself; and after the verbs of request it signifies: for, עַד־נֹכַח till opposite a place.

נֶכַח (only with suff. נִכְחוֹ) masc. the same, opposite.

נָכֹחַ (with suff. נְכֹחוֹ, pl. נְכֹחִים) adj. m., נְכֹחָה (pl. נְכֹחוֹת) f. straight on, straight along before one; הֹלֵךְ נְכֹחוֹ he who goes his straight way; hence, just, correct, honest, especially in this sense fem. sing., plur. masc. and fem.

נָכַל origin. to conceal, to hide, transf. to act clandestinely, to deceive, synon. with מָעַל, בָּגַד. Pi. to act deceitfully, artfully, against (לְ) some one. Hith. to devise deceitful, artful, plans against (acc. and בְּ) some one. The root is כָּלַל.

נֵכֶל (only pl. with suff. נִכְלֵיהֶם) m. artfulness, deception.

נָכַס (not used) to conceal, to preserve (of treasures); hence, to gather; from which כָּנַס is a transposition.

נֶכֶס (only plur. נְכָסִים) m. property, goods, wealth, from נָכַס

נְכַס (pl. נִכְסִין) Aram. the same.

נָכַר (Kal, not used) to be strange, foreign, origin. to be marked, distinguished from others, from כָּרַר, related to זָכַר to notice; כּוּר to make a mark. Pi. 1) to estrange, next, to forsake, to eject: 2) related to מָכַר to deliver. Hiph. הִכִּיר 1) to recognise, to penetrate into a matter; 2) to be enabled, to know, to understand, all proceeding from the original signification of penetration; 3) to see, to have an insight, to recognise. Niph. to feign being a stranger, and generally passive, to be known, recognised. Hith. is quite like the Niph. i.e. reflective and passive.

נֵכָר (const. נֵכַר) masc. that which is strange, the strange place, בֶּן־נ׳ a stranger, אֵל נ׳ a strange god, i.e. idols from a strange land.

נֶכֶר m. strange-like, that which one rejects, ill fate, or anything which is unpleasant.

נֹכֶר (with suff. נָכְרוֹ) m. the same.

נָכְרִי (formed from נֹכֶר, plur. נָכְרִים) adj. m., נָכְרִיָּה (pl. נָכְרִיּוֹת) f. one from a foreign country, always in a hostile sense, transf. to strange-like, unheard-of, hostile, repulsive. Synon. with זָר.

נְכֹתֹה Ketib, נְכֹתוֹ Keri, precious things; בֵּית נ׳ treasury.

נָלָה (Kal, not used) to arrive at a certain object; hence, to obtain, to acquire. Hiph. הִנְלָה (only in the form כַּנְּלֹתְךָ inf.) to accomplish, to complete something: but it may be read כְּכַלֹּתְךָ, so that the root entirely vanishes. The same is the case with the noun מִנְלָה (supposed to be derived therefrom) in מִנְלָם, it may be read מִכְלָם their herds.

נְמִבְזָה adj. fem. despised, bad, mean, probably compounded from נִבְזָה and מִבְזָה.

נְמוּאֵל p. n. m. (probably equiv. to יְמוּאֵל), patron. נְמוּאֵלִי.

נָסַךְ appears to belong to the root הֵסֵךְ ,יָסֵךְ, see סָכַךְ.

נָמַל equiv. to מָלַל to cut off, to cut off; hence, probably from which נְמָלָה. The forms יִמַּל ,נְמַלְתֶּם, belong to מָלַל, and נִמּוֹל belongs to מוּל.

נְמָלָה (pl. נְמָלִים) f. an ant, probably from נָמַל.

נָמַר (not used) to flow, to run; next, to be clear as water, to be clear, related to מָרַר to flow; from which נִמְרִים ,נִמְרָה.

נָמַר (not used) to be striped, spotted, the root נ־מר is related to that in חָ־בַר.

נָמֵר (pl. נְמֵרִים) m. panther, also including the tiger.

נְמַר (Aram.) m. the same.

נִמְרֹד p. n. of the founder of the Babylonian empire; hence, אֶרֶץ נ׳ Babylon.

נִמְרָה ,נִמְרִים, see under בֵּית.

נִמְשִׁי p. n. m. (one who is drawn out).

נֵס (with suffix נִסִּי) masc. equiv. to תּוֹפָעָה that which is elevated as a signal to be seen at a distance, as a flag, a standard, a banner, a high pole for a signal, transf. to a mark of caution. The root is נָסַס II., which see.

נְסִבָּה fem. turn, fate, destiny, from סָבַב, origin. particip. Niph.

נָסַג (fut. יִסַּג, inf. abs. נָסוֹג) equiv. to נָסַח, זוּחַ to move away, to turn back. Hiph. הִסִּיג to remove something, to move something back (a landmark.) Once with שׂ instead of ס. Hoph. הֻסַּג to be moved back, to turn back.

נָסָה (Kal, not used) to test, try, prove. Pi. נִסָּה to put to the test, to try, by scepticism or infidelity: different from בָּחַן, which signifies to try by the medium of the senses.

נָסַח (fut. יִסַּח) equiv. to נָסַע to tear away, to tear out, to tear off, e.g. from a house, to expel (from a country), to pull down (a house). Niph. to be driven away, ejected.

נְסַח (Aram.) the same. Ithp. pass.

נָסִיךְ (with suff. נְסִיכָם, pl. with suff. נְסִיכֵיהֶם) masc. 1) that which is poured out, drink-offering; 2) molten image, equiv. to מַסֵּכָה; 3) poetically, the anointed one, king, ruler, all three significations from נָסַךְ I.

I. נָסַךְ (fut. יִסְּכוּ, inf. נְסֹךְ) equiv. to סוּךְ to pour, to pour out (the spirit of deep sleep) over some one, wine-offering, to worship a deity; transf. to close a covenant, libations having been used on such occasions; 2) to manufacture casting-work, i.e. to cast metals; 3) to anoint. Niph. to be anointed, i.e. to be appointed a ruler. Pi. to spend, to pour a libation before God. Hiph. the same. Hoph. pass.

II. נָסַךְ 1) to tie, to weave, to entwine, only in מַסֶּכֶת; 2) to cover, to wrap up, from which is מַסֵּכָה 2. Related is סָכַךְ, סָג, and others.

נְסַךְ (Aram.) the same; hence, Pa. voluntary offering; transf. also to the bringing of an offering.

נֶסֶךְ (and נֵסֶךְ, with suff. נִסְכִּי, pl. נְסָכִים, const. נִסְכֵּי) m. 1) drink-offering; 2) molten image, equiv. to מַסֵּכָה.

נְסַךְ (def. נִסְכָּא) Aram. m. the same.

נִסְמָן masc. appointed, fixed, marked place, from סָמַן.

I. נָסַס to be sick, ill (equiv. to נוּשׁ); origin. to decrease, to become lean, meagre, to decline; נֹסֵס, the sick one.

II. נָסַס to shine, of the spirit of God, that enlightens man. Hith. הִתְנוֹסֵס to shine forth, to be exalted, placed in an eminent position, so as to shine far off.

נָסַע (fut. יִסַּע, inf. נְסֹעַ, imp. סְעוּ) to move away, to push away, to break away (comp. נָסַח, סָא, זָעַע, זוּז) to break off (door posts or pegs of a tent), to break off (a tent), to break up a horde of nomades, of an army, or a tempest, i.e. to draw off, to depart. Niph. to be broken up (of a tent). Hiph. to break up, to cause to depart, to remove, to break off, to break out (stones).

נָסַק (fut. יִסַּק) to ascend, to rise; but as no pret. occurs, יִסַּק may stand for יִסְלַק, from סָלַק.

נְסַק (Aram.) the same; hence, Af. הַסֵּק (inf. הַנְסָקָה), to cause to ascend, rise. Hoph. הֻסַּק pass.

נִסְרֹךְ p.n. of a Ninevite idol; the etymology is obscure.

נָסַת belongs to הֵסִית. See סוּת.

נֵעָה (trembling) p.n. of a place in Zebulun.

נֹעָה p.n.f. (the wandering, fugitive one).

נְעוּרוֹת (denom. from נַעַר) fem. pl. youth, youthful age; figur. the youth of a people.

נְעוּרִים m. pl. the same.

נְעִיאֵל (probably = נְאִיאֵל dwelling-place of God) p.n. of a place in Naphtali.

נָעִים (const. נְעִים, pl. נְעִימִים, adj. m. נְעִימָה (pl. נְעִימוֹת) fem. pleasant, lovely, kind, graceful. The pl. m. and f. is also used as an abstract subs. in the sense of joys, pleasant or lovely scenes of country.

נָעַל (fut. יִנְעַל) to bolt, to shut up, to close; transf. to the fastening of the the sandals to the feet. Hiph. same.

נַעַל (dual נַעֲלַיִם, pl. נְעָלִים and נְעָלוֹת) fem. a sandal, a shoe: שׂוּם נַעַל בְּרַגְלַיִם to put a shoe on, חָלַץ נַעַל מֵעַל רַגְלַיִם to pull a shoe off; the same is נָשַׁל and שָׁלַף to cast the shoe upon something, i. e. to take possession of something; חֲלוּץ הַנָּעַל one who has given up his possession; transf. to, something trivial, mean, especially in the dual and pl.

נָעֵם (fut. יִנְעַם) to be pleasant, agreeable, kind, lovely; origin. to accept (not connected with לָחַם).

נַעַם p.n. m. (loveliness).

נֹעַם m. propriety, grace, loveliness, delight; kindness, grace (of God).

נַעֲמָה 1) p.n. fem. (loveliness, lovely one); 2) p. n. of a city in Judah; gent. נַעֲמָתִי.

נַעֲמִי see נַעֲמָן.

נָעֳמִי (for נַעֲמִית) p.n. f. (the graceful one).

נַעֲמָן (pl. נַעֲמָנִים) masc. 1) loveliness, gracefulness; 2) p.n.m. (the graceful one), patron. נַעֲמִי for נַעֲמָנִי.

נָעַץ (not used) to sting, to prick, as in the Aram.

נַעֲצוּץ m. thorn-bush, thorn-hedge, after the form נַאֲפוּף.

נַעַר (primitive, pl. נְעָרִים) m. 1) youth, lad, boy; in the ancient period of language, also girl. In reference to age, it signifies the new-born child, as well as the youth of twenty years. In reference to position, it signifies one's own child, as well as youth, lad, boy, attendant; also, the common soldier. From which is derived נְעוּרוֹת, נַעֲרָה, נֹעַר, נְעָרִים; 2) (from נָעַר II.) that which is dispersed; only Zech. 11:16, but even in that passage it may be rendered the young one, which, on account of its littleness, escapes the shepherd.

נָעַר to roar, of the young lion. The form נָעוֹר belongs to עוּר.

I. נָעַר to move to and fro, to shake (the hand), to shake off (leaves), orig. to stir, equiv. to עוּר. Niph. 1) to release oneself (from bonds), to shake off; 2) to be driven away. Pi. to throw into (בְּ) something, e. g. into the sea. Hithp. to shake oneself from (מִן) something, e. g. from the dust.

נַעֲרָה (pl. נְעָרוֹת) f. 1) a damsel, a maid-servant, maid, as also a young married woman; 2) p. n. of a city in Ephraim; 3) p. n. f.

נַעֲרַי p. n. m. (the youthful one).

נְעַרְיָה p. n. m. (godly youth).

נַעֲרָן p. n. of a city.

נְעֹרֶת f. tow, origin. that which is thrown out of the flax, from נָעַר 2.

נָעֵשׁ according to some, the root belongs to עָשַׁשׁ, which see.

נֹף p. n. Memphis, see מֹף.

נָפַג (not used) to grow, to sprout; compare the Aram. נְבַג; from which:—

נֶפֶג p. n. m. sprout.

נָפָה as a root. See נוּף.

נָפָה (from נוּף) f. 1) a height, a hill, from which the p. n. נָפַת דּוֹר the hill of Dor, or the plur. נָפוֹת ד׳; 2) sieve, from נוּף to move to and fro.

נְפוּסִים (Keri) p. n. m. (extension, increase). The Ketib has נְפִיסִים, which see.

נָפַח (fut. יִפַּח, inf. פַּחַת), equiv. to פּוּחַ; 1) to fan, to breathe, to blow (the fire), with and without בְּ, to blow away, to puff away, also with בְּ; to breathe the last (breath of life); with acc. to cause to breathe over (עַל) something, to breathe into (בְּ) something. Pu. to be fanned, blown. Hiph. 1) to blow away, to puff away; i. e. to despise, slight, disregard; 2) to exhale, to breathe the last.

נֹפַח (fragrance, place of fragrance) p. n. of a Moabite city.

נְפִיל (only pl. נְפִילִים) m. equiv. to פִּיל the strong one; next, a giant. The root is נָפַל 2.

נְפִיסִים equiv. to נְפוּסִים, which see.

נָפִישׁ p. n. m. (the recovered one).

נְפִישְׁסִים a mixed form, from נְפִיסִים and נְפִישִׁים.

נָפַךְ (not used) to paint, to be of various colours, related to פּוּךְ.

נֹפֶךְ m. name of a precious stone (Author. Vers. an emerald).

I. נָפַל (fut. יִפֹּל, inf. נְפֹל, with suff. נָפְלוֹ) to fall down, to sink (down from something מֵעַל), to fall into (בְּ, אֶל) something, to fall off (מִן) something, to fall upon (עַל) something, but also absolute, to lie, in a state of trance, dream-like; נָפַל is used to denote falling in battle (often with the addition בַּחֶרֶב), by the hand (בְּיַד) of another, or by the enemy; to fall upon (לְ) the bed of sickness; to be born (in the derivative used of a premature birth); transf. to arise, to revive, to fall off in the body, i.e. to become lean, or to fall off in spirit, i.e. to lose courage; next, generally, to fall into trouble, to go to ruin, of men and empires; to fall, of the lot; hence, to be allotted to some one; in comparison to another, לִפְנֵי מִן to fall off, i.e. to be inferior; to fall to the ground, i.e. to remain unfulfilled, of a promise; to result; to elapse; to fall upon something; to befall, with עַל (of sleep or terror); to descend (of a revelation), to be revealed; to throw oneself down, to let oneself down; to rush on the sword; to alight, to encamp, dwell, settle, somewhere; to lay down (submit) a supplication (לִפְנֵי) before some one. Hiph. הִפִּיל (inf. with לְ, לְהַפִּיל) causing something to fall, to throw, to cast down, to cast (into the fire), to slay (by the sword); to cast lots, to allot; to cast, in the sense of to bear; to fell, to hew down; to cause to fall (the face of some one), i.e. to vex some one; to lay a request before some one; to drop, to desist from something, etc. Hithp. to throw oneself down; with עַל, to throw oneself upon some one, to attack him. Pilpel נִפְלֵל to precipitate suddenly, violently.

II. נָפַל (not used) to be strong, vigorous; comp. פול and בָּעַל, from which נְפִיל.

נְפַל (fut. יִפֵּל) Aram. the same.

נֵפֶל m. origin. birth, but generally premature, i.e. miscarriage, from נָפַל in the sense of to bring forth.

נִפְלַל see נָפַל.

נָפַס (not used) to extend, to spread out; from which נְפִיסִים, נְפוּסִים.

נָפַץ (imp. and fut. is taken from פוּץ) equiv. to פוּץ; 1) to reduce to dust, *fundere*, to be scattered about; hence, to be dispersed, scattered, of a people, of a flock; reflective, to extend oneself, to disperse oneself; 2) to dash to pieces, to shatter. Pi. to break to pieces (earthen vessels); but also like Kal, to scatter, to disperse; hence נֶפֶץ

(inf.) scattering (of the Jewish nation). Pu. pass. to be scattered, dispersed.

נֶפֶץ masc. shower of rain, from its violent pouring on all sides.

נְפַק (3 fem. נִפְקַת, 3 plur. נְפַקוּ and נְפַקָה, imp. פּוּק) Aram. to go away, to go out, quite like יָצָא in Heb. transf. to the issuing of an edict. Af. הַנְפֵּק, הַנְפִּיק to bring out, to carry out; comp. אַפֵּק.

נִפְקָא (def. —קְתָא) Aram. f. expense, outlay; comp. modern Hebrew הוֹצָאָה.

נָפַשׁ (Kal, not used) to breathe, to draw breath, to inhale; hence, to live, transf. to exhale. Niph. נִפַּשׁ to recreate, refresh oneself (after labor), orig. to draw breath; next, to refresh oneself, to recover. The root נ־פשׁ, is related to נ־פר־ת, which see.

נֶפֶשׁ (with suff. נַפְשִׁי, pl. נְפָשׁוֹת, once נְפָשִׁים) com. 1) breath (of life); next, life, strength of life, soul (as animating the body); next, soul, as in modern language, person; שׁוּב, יָצָא נֶפֶשׁ, life returns, life departs; קִוָּה נֶפֶשׁ to hope for the death of some one, i.e. or the departure of life: but always in reference to the animal life; hence, speaking of the soul, we say, to live, to die, to kill it, to require it, to cast it away, to save it; and in many phrases נֶפֶשׁ is used for mind, heart, as the seat of emotions. Its use for person, living thing, man, or slave, is as in some modern languages, but joined to מֵת it signifies carcass, or dead person; sometimes, even without the word מֵת, e.g. טָמֵא לָנֶפֶשׁ or טָמֵא נֶפֶשׁ to become unclean by a dead body; 2) with suff. נֶפֶשׁ is used for self, in the sense of a reflective pronoun; 3) fragrance; hence, בָּתֵּי נֶפֶשׁ scent-boxes.

נָפַת (Kal, not used) related to נָפַשׁ; hence, to exhale, to diffuse fragrance, or probably connected with נ־פט in modern Heb. in the sense of, to flow.

נֶפֶת fem. equiv. to נָפָה I., height, elevated place, according to others, a circle, from נוּף to encircle.

נֹפֶת m. that which flows, the sweet of the sugar-cane (סוּף=צוּף), or honey-comb; hence, נֹפֶת צוּפִים liquid of the cane, i.e. sugar; according to others, honey-comb.

נַפְתּוּל (only pl. —לִים) m. a combat, struggle, from פָּתַל in Niphil, to wrest, to wrestle.

נַפְתֻּחַ p. n. of an Egyptian district; hence, patron. —חִים.

נַפְתָּלִי (for נַפְתָּלִים) p. n. m. (a wrestling); hence, LXX. Νεφθαλείμ.

נֵץ (from נָצַץ) m. 1) a flower, the same as the f. נִצָּה; 2) a hawk, sparrow-hawk, so called from its swift flight. For both significations, comp. נָצַץ.

נָצָא (inf. abs. נָצֹא) equiv. to נָצָה 1, to fly, to fly away, to fly off; hence, the paranomasia נָצֹא תֵּצֵא flying off, i.e. thou departedst swiftly, Auth. Vers. "that it may flee and go away" (Jer. 48:9).

נָצַב (Kal, not used) equiv. to יָצַב, to put, to place, to set, or to cause to stand. Niph. נִצַּב 1) to be placed, appointed over (עַל) something; hence, נִצָּב manager, director; 2) to stand, to stand firmly (of animate and inanimate objects); next, to stand erect, to be sound, נִצָּבָה the sound cattle; 3) to place before oneself (לְ), to step toward (לְ) some one. Hiph. הִצִּיב to cause something to stand, to erect (a monument), to heap up (stones), to set up (gates), transf. to הִצִּיב יָד to erect a power, הִצִּיב דָּרְבָן to sharpen the goad, and generally, to fix, to appoint. Hoph. הֻצַּב to be erected, planted, also to be appointed, part. מֻצָּב.

נִצָּב m. the hilt (of a dagger), a handle, from נָצַב.

נִצְבָּא (def. נִצְבְּתָא) Aram. f. firmness, hardness (of the iron) or stem, i.e. nature of iron.

נָצַג see יָצַג.

נָצָה 1) equiv. to נָצָא, נָצַץ, to fly, to flee; hence, נָצוּ גַּם נָעוּ when they fled away and wandered; 2) (Kal, not used) to pluck out, to contend. Hiph. הִצָּה to make strife against (עַל) some one, to carry on war with (אֵת) some one. Niph. 1) נִצָּה to contend, quarrel mutually; 2) to be waste, desolate, עָרַיִךְ תִּצֶּינָה thy cities shall be laid waste; 3) to become desolate, גַּלִּים נִצִּים ruinous heaps. The connection of significations 2 and 3, with signification 1, is obscure.

נִצָּה f. a flower, equiv. to נֵץ from נָצַץ.

נֹצָה f. 1) equiv. to נוֹצָה a wing, a pinion, a plume; 2) for נוֹצָא (from יָצָא) excrement (of the crop).

I. **נָצַח** (Kal, not used) origin. 1) to shine, to glitter, from נָ־צַח (comp. צַח, מָ־צַח), figur. to excel, either by deeds or in position, to be great, mighty, distinguished; comp. a similar mode of transferring in חָרַד; 2) clean, figur. to be faithful; comp. טָהַר, origin. to shine; 3) to last, to be constant, origin. to be strong, firm, to excel in power. Pi. נִצַּח to excel above all, to superintend a matter (לְ), to be appointed over (עַל) something; hence מְנַצֵּחַ, often used in the language of the temple service to denote the director of the temple music. The proper use of the verb and of לַמְנַצֵּחַ is obvious from the phrase לְנַצֵּחַ עַל־מְלֶאכֶת בֵּית י״י. Niph. to be lasting, constant; hence particip. fem. נִצַּחַת enduring, lasting, persevering.

II. נָצַח (not used) equiv. to נָזָה to sprinkle, orig. to wet, to moisten.

נְצַח (Aram.) the same as נָצַח I; hence Ithp. to be victorious over (עַל) something, origin. to excel over something.

נֶצַח (seldom נֵצַח, with suff. נִצְחִי, plur. נְצָחִים) 1) brightness, lustre, fame; hence, victory; 2) fidelity, purity, faith, confidence, e.g. my strength and my hope is perished; judgment is not pronounced faithfully (Auth. Vers. "judgment doth *never* go forth," Hab. 1:14); 3) endurance; hence, eternity, especially in the forms לָנֶצַח, נֶצַח, לְנֵצַח נְצָחִים, עַד־נֶצַח eternal, eternally, unto eternity, for ever; transf. to entirely, altogether, pure, e.g. ruins altogether (Auth. Vers. "destructions are come to a perpetual end," Ps. 9:6).

נֵצַח (from נָצַח II.) m. juice (of the pressed grape), blood of grapes.

נְצִיב m. 1) the appointed one, officer, director, equiv. to נִצָּב, but also a post, situation; 2) a post, a pillar, a column; hence נְצִיב מֶלַח a pillar of salt; 3) p.n. of a town in Judah.

נְצִיחַ p.n. m. one who excels.

נָצִיר (Ketib) m. the preserved, saved one, thus equiv. to נָצוּר.

נָצַל (Kal, not used) to pull off, to draw off, to tear out (related to נָשַׁל and שָׁלַל) figur. to extricate from danger, to save. Niph. נִצַּל 1) to be saved, delivered, from מִן, מִכַּף, מִיַּד; 2) to save oneself, to escape, from before some one (מִפְּנֵי), to some one (אֶל). Pi. to extricate (accus.) from danger, to snatch something away, to rob, to plunder. Hiph. הִצִּיל to separate (contending parties), to snatch away from (מִן) some one, to withdraw; generally, to save, to release some one (accus. seldom לְ) from some one (מִן, מִיַּד, מִכַּף). Hoph. הֻצַּל to be pulled out, to be delivered (from the fire). Hith. to take off something from oneself, e.g. the ornament.

נְצַל (Aram.) the same. Af. הַצֵּל, like the Heb. Hiph.

נִצָּן m. a flower, formed from נֵץ.

נָצַע see יָצַע.

נָצַץ equiv. to נוּץ; 1) to glitter, to shine, to sparkle; hence נֹצְצִים shining, sparking; 2) to bloom, to flourish; comp. נָזַח; 3) to fly-comp. the same mode of transferring in פֶּרַח.

נָצַץ see יָצַע.

נָצַר (fut. יִצֹּר, seldom יִנְצֹר, imp. נְצֹר, נִצְּרָה, with suff. נִצְּרָהּ with euphonic dagesh) origin. to shine, to glitter (comp. חָצַר); hence, 1) to look at, to see (comp. שָׁזַף), transf. to (*a*) to watch by inspection, to guard, to keep; נֹצֵר watcher, keeper; מִגְדַּל נֹצְרִים watch-tower; to keep from (מִן) something; (*b*) to preserve, to hide; hence נְצוּרוֹת those who are hidden, unknown; נְצוּרִים those who are saved; also, hiding-place; figur. of the secret, stubborn heart; (*c*) to lie in wait, to besiege (a town); hence נֹצְרִים besiegers; עִיר נְצוּרָה a besieged town; 2) (not used) to bloom, to flourish, as generally (see נָצַץ) proceeding from the sense of shining.

נֵצֶר m. sprout, twig, sprig, offspring; from נָצַר 2.

נָצַת see יָצַת.

נְקָא (Aram.) to be clean; comp. Heb. נָקָה; hence particip. נְקֵא clean.

נָקַב (fut. יִקֹּב, seldom יִנְקֹב) 1) to hollow out, to bore through (the head), to perforate, to make holes (in a bag); 2) to cut asunder, to sever, to part, to distinguish, to nominate, to define, to name; hence נְקֻבִים, equiv. to אַנְשֵׁי נְקֻבוּ בְשֵׁמוֹת, or אַנְשֵׁי שֵׁם, i. e. they that are named, the distinguished; the same mode of transferring is found in קָצַב, נָזַר; 3) equiv. to קָבַב, to defame, blaspheme, curse, origin. to cut something through (comp. חָרַף). In connection with שֵׁם יי״ some render it according to signification 2, to pronounce; others, according to signification 3, to curse. Niph. pass. of signif. 2, to be named, nominated.

נֶקֶב m. 1) box for containing precious stones, from נָקַב; 2) with the article, p.n. of a place in Naphtali, orig. hollowing out, cavity.

נְקֵבָה f. female, only in reference to the genitals, from נָקַב, like its contrast זָכָר, which see; comp. the abbreviation קֵבָה.

נָקַד (not used) 1) origin. to stick into something, to indent; hence, to mark with points or dots, to note, to denote; next, generally, to point, punctuate; 2) to distinguish some of the flock by a point or mark; next, generally, to occcupy oneself with a superior flock.

נָקֹד (pl. נְקֻדִּים) adj. m. pointed, dotted, spotted, sprinkled.

נֹקֵד m. shepherd of a choice flock, or the possessor of such a flock, Author. Vers. sheep-master.

נֶקֶר m. 1) crumb, origin. the bread fallen to crumbs; 2) a kind of small cake.

נְקֻדָּה f. (origin. from נָקֹד) the point, studs of silver (of the neck-chain).

נָקָה (only inf. נָקֹה) to be clean, to be free or bare from something. Niph. נִקָּה to be free from guilt, construed with מִן; to be free from punishment, from an oath, from an obligation; next, generally, to be or become vacant, empty, desolate, lonely; also of persons, if in this sense, נִקָּה is not equiv. to נִבָּה. Pi. נִקָּה (fut. יְנַקֶּה) to make free, to free from debt (equiv. to הִצְדִּיק) to allow to go free, without punishment; נִקָּה דָם to cleanse the blood, i. e. to avenge. The signification of to spend, or pour out, is not found in the Hebrew form of the word.

נְקוֹדָא p. n. m. (owner of cattle).

נָקַח see לָקַח.

נָקַט see קָטַט.

נָקִי (const. נְקִי, pl. נְקִיִּים) adj. masc. clean, innocent, not guilty, exempt from punishment; next generally, free from something (responsibility, obligation, military service); as a subs. the innocent.

נָקִיא the same, with א appended.

נִקָּיוֹן (const. נִקְיוֹן) masc. cleanliness, cleanness of teeth (a scriptural phrase for famine); נ׳ כַּף cleanliness of the hands, a figure of innocence; transf. to moral purity.

נָקִיק (const. נְקִיק, pl. const. נְקִיקֵי) masc. cleft, crack, ridge, from נָקַק.

נָקַם (fut. יִקֹּם, inf. נְקוֹם) origin. equiv. to נָחַם, נָהַם, to snort, to breathe revenge, to have revenge, to avenge some one (acc. עַל), or something (acc.) The person or the thing on which one revenges oneself stands with מִן, מֵאֵת, מִיַּד, לְ, and acc. Niph. נִקַּם (fut. יִנָּקֵם) to revenge oneself, or to be revenged on (בְּ or מִן) some one. Pi. נִקֵּם to avenge something. Hoph. הֻקַּם (fut. יֻקַּם) to be avenged (a deed), i.e. the deed shall be punished. Hiph. to be penetrated with revenge, to be vindictive.

נָקָם m. revenge, נָקַם נ׳ to take revenge, עָשָׂה נ׳, לָקַח נ׳, הֵשִׁיב נ׳ לְ to exercise revenge.

נְקָמָה (const. נִקְמַת, with suff. נִקְמָתִי, pl. נְקָמוֹת) fem. 1) revenge; with gen. following, to take revenge for something; otherwise with the same forms, as in נָקַם; 2) vindictiveness, בִּנְקָמָה with vindictiveness.

נָקַע erroneously supposed to belong to נָקְעָה, which, however, like נָבְקָה, (from בָּקַק), belongs to קָעַע, as well as the fut. יָקַע, belonging to the same. See also קוּעַ, יָקַע.

נָקַף (fut. יִנְקֹף) 1) equiv. to נָגַף to strike, to knock, to knock off, to knock to pieces; 2) to make a circuit (on festivals), from נָקַף, equiv. to קוּף, from which תְּקוּפָה. Pi. נִקֵּף to hew (a forest), to destroy (the skin, the body), if נִקְּפוּ, Job 19:26, is not to be taken in another sense. Hiph. הִקִּיף (may be formed from קוּף, after the Aram.) to proceed in a circuit, to make a shaven crown (baldness of the head); next generally, to surround, to encompass, with the accus. and עַל, sometimes with אֶל. Inf. הַקֵּף round, used as an adv.

נֹקֶף m. knocking off, shaking off (of the olives from the tree).

נִקְפָּה (formed from the m. נָקַף) f. a cord, a bond, by which one is led to prison, from נָקַף equiv. to קוּף to encompass.

נָקַק (not used) to make an incision, to bore, related to נָקַר, but more correctly, to sharpen; hence, נָקִיק point, ridge, and נְקִיק הַסֶּלַע is equiv. to שֵׁן הַסֶּלַע, as it is rendered in the Targ. שְׁקִיף; related to which is נוּק 1.

נָקַר (fut. יִקֹּר, pl. יִקְּרוּ, inf. const. נְקוֹר) to bore, to put out the eyes, fig. to pierce the bones with pain. Pi. נִקֵּר, the same. Pu. to be dug out (from a shaft), fig. to originate from.

נְקָרָה (const. נִקְרַת, pl. const. נִקְרוֹת) f. cavity of a rock.

נָקַשׁ origin. to tie fast, to make a snare, to lay a snare, to catch. Comp. יָקַשׁ and the root רָכַס. Niph. (fut. יִנָּקֵשׁ) to be ensnared. Pi. נִקֵּשׁ to lay a snare, a trap; next, to catch generally. Hith. to waylay, with בְּ, or perhaps to design cunning, craft, against some one.

נְקַשׁ (particip. f. pl. נָקְשָׁן) Aram. to strike, to push.

נֵר (pl. נֵרוֹת) m. 1) a lamp, a light, a taper, a candle, from נוּר, to shine, figur. the golden (glorious) age of a nation; next, as a figure of prosperity, e.g. the candle of the wicked is put out, i.e. their prosperity vanishes; 2) p.n. m. prosperity.

נִר m. the same. Comp. נִיר.

נָרַג (not used), to babble, to chatter, to gossip, origin. to trumpet forth, from גָּרַג, equiv. to גָּהַג, but the root is not connected with מֶרַג.

נֵרְגַל (from נָרַג, with the termination ־ַל) p.n. of a Cuthic deity, probably Mars.

נֵרְגַל שַׁרְאֶצֶר (Aram.) p.n. of a chief of the Magii. See שַׁרְאֶצֶר.

נִרְגָּן (from **נָרַג**) m. a babbler, a slanderer, formed from **נָרַג**, after the form **כִּבְשָׁן**.

נֵרְדְּ (with suff. **נִרְדִּי**, pl. **נְרָדִים**) m. a kind of fragrant herb (spikenard, Author. Ver.), from the Indian, signifying a stork.

נֵרִיָּה p.n. m. (the lamp of God).

I. **נָשָׁא** (Kal, not used, inf. **נָשֹׁא**, but it is from **נָשָׁה**) to err; hence, Hiph. **הִשִּׁיא** (fut. **יַשִּׁיא**) to entice, to mislead, to deceive; const. with the accus. and dat. Niph. to be deceived. The root is not connected with **נָסַע**.

II. **נָשָׁא** (particip. **נֹשֶׁא**=**נֹשֶׁה**) to lend upon usury, to carry on usury; the original signification is probably equiv. to **נָשַׁךְ**: **נֹשֶׁא**, the creditor. Hiph. **הִשִּׁיא** to press as creditor, const. with **בְּ**.

נָשָׂא (fut. **יִשָּׂא**, inf. abs. **נָשׂוֹא**, const. **נְשֹׂא**, **שׂוֹא**, **שְׂאֵת** and **שְׂאת**, with suff. **נָשְׂאִי** and **שְׂאֵתִי**; imp. **נְשָׂא** and **שָׂא**; particip. pass. **נָשׂוּא**, once **נָשׂוּי**, as if the root were **נָשָׂה**) 1) to lift, lift up, raise, e. g. (*a*) the head, i.e. to be cheerful, to become powerful; to lift up the head of some one in prison, i.e. to release him; (*b*) to lift up the face, i.e. to be conscious of innocence, even with omitting **פָּנִים**; **נָשָׂא פָּנִים אֶל** to look upon some one, with confidence; (*c*) to lift up the eyes, i.e. to look toward, upon, or for (**אֶל**) something; (*d*) to lift up the hand, i.e. to swear with **לְ**, also to beckon, to implore, or to lift up the hand against (**בְּ**) some one; (*e*) to lift up the voice, i.e. to weep, to call, to cry, to shout, or to commence a parable, attune a song; next generally, to pronounce (the name of God, or a blasphemy); (*f*) to lift up the heart, the mind, the soul, after (**לְ**, **אֶל**) something, i.e. to wish, to long for something; to lead or elevate the mind for something; all proceeding from the sense of lifting, but in a spiritual sense. In a physical sense it signifies: (*a*) to lay, to lift upon something; (*b*) to weigh; 2) to carry (a child, garments), fig. to bear the guilt, the sin, i.e. to expiate; 3) to lift, carry away, i.e. to remove, e.g. **נָשָׂא רֹאשׁ מֵעַל** to take the head off some one, to take away the sin, i.e. to forgive: with dative of the person, **נְשׂוּא עָוֹן** one whose sin is forgiven, sin being considered as a burden; **נָשָׂא נֶפֶשׁ** to take one's life; 4) to take, (*a*) **נָ׳ אִשָּׁה** to take a wife, sometimes **אִשָּׁה** is omitted; (*b*) **נָ׳ פָּנִים** to regard persons (to take reward), i.e. to be partial to some one, or in a good sense, to esteem a person, נְשׂוּא פָנִים respected, esteemed; (*c*) to take up, i.e. to number, generally with רֹאשׁ or מִסְפָּר; (*d*) to accept: 5) to lift, raise, exalt oneself. Niph. נִשָּׂא 1) to raise oneself, or to be raised, elevated (a valley); 2) to be carried; 3) to be carried away. Pi. נִשֵּׂא and נַשֵּׂא 1) to lift up some one, or something, נִשֵּׂא נֶפֶשׁ לְ to lift up the heart for some one, i.e. to long for him; 2) to support, assist some one (with presents); 3) to carry or lead away. Hiph. הִשִּׂיא 1) to cause some one to bear (a guilt); 2) to put on something (a cord). Hithp. הִתְנַשֵּׂא and הִנַּשֵּׂא to lift oneself up, to exalt oneself over (לְ) some one, to boast over (עַל) some one.

נְשָׂא (imp. שָׂא) Aram. the same, partly in the signification, to take, and partly in the signification of, to snatch away. Ithp. to raise himself over (עַל) some one.

נְשֵׂאת fem. a present, from נָשָׂא, according to some it is derived from Pi. after the form מְלֵאת, according to others, as a second form of the inf. Niph. =נִבְכּוֹף, but it may be particip. Niph.

נָשַׁב (a softened form for נָשַׁף) to breathe, to blow; שָׁאַף is also related to it. Hiph. הִשִּׁיב (fut. יַשִּׁיב, apoc. יַשֵּׁב) to puff away, to chase away.

נָשַׂג (only in the Hiph. הִשִּׂיג) equiv. to נָסַג; 1) to remove, related to סוּג, זוּחַ; 2) to hold, to seize, related to the root in חָזַק. Hiph. 1) to remove (a landmark); 2) to bring near something, to attain, to reach, to acquire property, to reach or overtake some one, to meet, to happen, to befall, some one; always proceeding from the original idea of seizing.

נְשׂוּאָה fem. that which is carried, a burthen.

I. נָשָׁה (inf. irregular נְשֹׁא) to forget, to forsake, the original signification is to remove, forgetting being the removal from memory. Niph. (fut. יִנָּשֶׁה) to be forgotten, תִּנָּשֵׁנִי equiv. to תִּ' מִמֶּנִּי. Pi. to cause to forget; hence, נַשַּׁנִי he has made me forget, for נִשַּׁנִי. Hiph. הִשָּׁה to cause to be forgotten (sins), i.e. to disregard. The form תַּשִּׁי belongs to שָׁיָה.

II. נָשָׁה to lend, also to borrow, according to the context, often with בְּ of the person, or of the price given. נֹשֶׁה creditor, but also usurer; the original signification is probably equiv. to נָשַׁךְ.

נָשֶׁה m. a thigh, the part of the tendon, origin. the contracting nerve, from נָשָׁה, in the sense of contracting.

נְשִׁי m. debt, from נָשָׁה II.

נְשִׁיָּה (from an obsolete masc. form נְשִׁי) fem. oblivion; hence, אֶרֶץ נְ׳ the region of the dead, syn. with שְׁאוֹל and אֲבַדּוֹן.

נָשִׁים see אִשָּׁה.

נְשִׁיקָה f. a kiss, from נָשַׁק.

I. נָשַׁךְ (fut. יִשֹּׁךְ and יִשַּׁךְ) origin. to cut; next, to bite, fig. to torment, to take usury, a similar mode of transferring is found in the Aram. נְכַת. Pi. to bite (of the serpent). Hiph. הִשִּׁיךְ orig. to cause something to be bitten; hence, to take usury: לַנָּכְרִי תַשִּׁיךְ thou mayest *give* interest to the stranger.

II. נָשַׁךְ (not used) to lay down, to lie down, to set down, from which נִשְׁכָּה, comp. also לִשְׁכָּה.

נֶשֶׁךְ m. interest, usury, שׂוּם נֶ׳ עַל to lay usury upon some one, נָתַן נֶ׳ to give interest, לָקַח נֶ׳ to take interest, הִשִּׁיךְ נֶ׳ to give interest.

נִשְׁכָּה (pl. נִשְׁכוֹת) fem. origin. seat, couch, from נָשַׁךְ II.; hence next, room, chamber, comp. לִשְׁכָּה.

נָשַׁל (fut. יִשַּׁל in the intrans. signif., imp. שַׁל) 1) to pull off (the shoe), to send away, to drive away (a people), the head (the iron) slippeth from the wood (the helve). 2) intrans. to fall down, to drop. Pi. to drive out from (עַל) something. Related to שָׁלַל, שָׁלָה but also נָצַל.

נָשַׁם (not used, the fut. אֶשֹּׁם belongs to שָׁמַם) to breathe, related to נָשַׁב, נָשַׁף, and the transposed נָפַשׁ.

נִשְׁמָא (Aram.) f. breath of life.

נְשָׁמָה (const. נִשְׁמַת, plur. נְשָׁמוֹת) f. 1) breath; hence, like נֶפֶשׁ, the essence of life in the human body, the soul; next, especially the soul of understanding; 2) the breath, the wrath of God.

נָשַׁף equiv. to נָשַׁב, to breathe, to wave, with בְּ, to blow upon, to fan.

נֶשֶׁף (with suff. נִשְׁפּוֹ) m. twilight, dawn, so called from the cool evening breezes, transf. to darkness.

נָשַׁק (fut. יִשַּׁק and יִשֹּׁק) origin. to join, to attach; hence, 1) to join the mouth to something, i.e. to kiss; with לְ, of the person, or with the acc. to kiss some one; 2) to put on armour, to arm oneself; hence, נֹשֵׁק קֶשֶׁת to strain the bow or to hold it firmly; 3) to join, עַל פִּיךָ יִשַּׁק כָּל־עַמִּי by thy command shall all the people be joined, i.e. obey (Auth. Vers. according unto thy word shall all my people be ruled), likewise in Psalm 85:11, righteousness and peace shall join (Author. Vers. have kissed each other). Piel, like Kal I., to kiss. Hiph. הִשִּׁיק to cause to join, to connect together, with אֶל, synon. with חָבַר. The root is נָשַׁק and זָקַק, related to the root in חֵשֶׁק.

נֶשֶׁק (after the massorah) m. armoury, weapon, especially armoury worn on the body; נֶ׳ בֵּית הַיַּעַר armoury of the house in the forest, where the arms were hung up.

נָשַׂק (Kal, not used) to glow, to burn; hence Niph. נִשַּׂק to become ignited. Hiph. הִשִּׂיק to kindle. The root is נָשַׂק, and related to צַח, זִק.

נָשַׁר (not used) probably, to fly, though the tracing of the etymology to נֶשֶׁר eagle is obscure.

נֶשֶׁר (pl. נְשָׁרִים, const. נִשְׁרֵי) m. an eagle.

נְשַׁר (pl. נִשְׁרִין) Aram. the same.

נָשַׁר (not used) to saw through, cut through; hence מַשּׂוֹר; the root, however, may be שׂוּר.

נָשַׁת belongs to נִשְּׁתוּ, נָשַׁתָּה, see שָׁתַת.

נִשְׁתְּוָן (Aram. def. נִשְׁתְּוָנָא) m. writing, copy, written document.

נָתַב (not used) to tread down, to stamp with the feet; from which נָתִיב.

נְתוּנִים Ketib for נְתִינִים, which see.

נָתַח only Pi. נִתַּח, to cut in pieces; related to נָשַׁךְ or נָסַח, as נָתַךְ is only a secondary form from נָסַךְ; נָתַע from נָסַע.

נֵתַח (pl. נְתָחִים) m. piece cut off.

נָתִיב (const. נְתִיב) m. trodden path, path, foot-path; sometimes נָתִיב is adj.; hence נְתִיבָה adj. f. trodden (of a path or road).

נְתִיבָה f. the same.

נָתִין (only pl. נְתִינִים) m. one who is given, i. e. consecrated (to the temple service); next, servant in the temple, generally used of the subjugated Canaanites.

נְתִין (def. pl. —נַיָּא) Aram. the same.

נָתַךְ (fut. יִתַּךְ) equiv. to נָסַךְ to pour out, of the pouring forth of anger, a curse, of water, of rain. Niph. נִתַּךְ to pour forth (of water, rain, also, figuratively, of anger), but also, to dissolve, to melt away. Hiph. הִתִּיךְ to pour out, to melt; inf. c. הַנְתִּיךְ. Hoph. הֻתַּךְ pass. related to נָסַךְ and סוּךְ.

נָתַל (not used) equiv. to נָתַן to give; from which תִּילוֹן (for נְתִ׳) p. n. m. (the given or presented one).

נָתַן (2 pers. נָתַתָּ and נָתַתָּה, with the *nun* dropped; 1 pl. נָתַנּוּ, with the compensated *nun*; infin. const. נְתוֹן, before makkaph נְתָן־, but generally תֵּת, with suff. תִּתִּי; imp. תֵּן, תְּנָה, תֶּן־, fut. יִתֵּן, יִתֶּן־, 1 pers. before makkaph (נֶתֶּן־) to give, to hand (comp. נָדַן); sometimes with acc. of the person, to give for (בְּ) something (at a price), to give to (אֶל) something, i.e. to add. Sometimes נָתַן is used impersonally, as, here exists, there arises. The interrog. form מִי יִתֵּן is used sometimes as a wish, who would give! would that! and sometimes as a negation, which, however, arises more from the question than from the verb. The applications of נָתַן and the forms with which it is joined are manifold, and the context only can decide as to the correct translation. The principal applications are: 1) to give, in the widest sense, e.g. (*a*) to hand over, בְּיַד פּ׳; to deliver, give up to, with לְ; but in a good sense as נ׳ עַל יַד to give into the care of some one, נ׳ עַל to deliver up to some one (a kingdom); (*b*) to bring, to bear (fruit), origin. to bring forth; (*c*) to turn (the back, the face), orig. to direct; (*d*) to grant (favour, mercy, justice); (*e*) to send forth (a voice קוֹל, בְּקוֹל, odour, a miracle, etc.); (*f*) to sell (contrast to לָקַח); (*g*) to teach, communicate knowledge; 2) to set, to put, to lay, remove, e.g. to put, to place, to establish, to erect something in (בְּ or acc.); to put something in, to put something upon (עַל), e.g. to pour out, to shed, to attach to (בְּ) something, נ׳ לִפְנֵי to submit, to lay before, נ׳ לֵב עַל equiv. to נָתַן לֵב לְ or שׂוּם לֵב עַל to direct the mind or the heart to something, נָתַן דָּבָר אֶל לֵב to put something in the mind of some one, also abbbreviated נָתַן אֶל־לֵב; 3) almost like שׂוּם and שׁוּת to set, to do, e.g. נ׳ מוּם בְּ to cause a blemish in something; to turn into something, either with double accus. or with לְ before the predicate, נָתַן דָּבָר בְּ to assimilate one thing to another; נ׳ לִפְנֵי to take, consider, for something. Niph. נִתַּן 1) to be given to some one לְ, to be delivered unto (בְּיַד) some one; 2) to be set, to be put, to be placed; 3) to be made, with acc. to be assimilated to something. Hoph. like Niph.

נְתַן (inf. מִנְתַּן, but not מִתַּן, fut. יִנְתֵּן and יִתֵּן, before makkaph יִנְתֶּן־) Aram. the same. This verb is sometimes replaced by יְהַב.

נָתָן p. n. m. (gift, i.e. of God).

נְתַנְאֵל p. n. m. (the same).

נְתַנְיָה p. n. m. (the same).

נְתַנְיָהוּ p. n. m. (the same).

נְתַן־מֶלֶךְ p. n. masc. (present of the king).

נָתַס equiv. to נָתַץ, נָתַשׁ to dash to pieces, to shatter, to tread down.

נָתַע (Kal, not used) equiv. to נָסַע, to tear away; hence Niph. נִתַּע to be torn away from its place, to be knocked out (of the teeth).

נָתַץ (fut. יִתֹּץ) to destroy, to pull down a (house, altar, castle, wall), but also applied to persons. Pi. to destroy totally, annihilate, uproot. Niph. Pu. Hoph. pass. The original root is נָ־תַשׁ, נָ־תַץ.

נָתַק (fut. אֶתֹּק, with suff. אֶתְּקֶנְךָּ with dagesh lene in ךּ, and נ interpolated before the suffix; in the pret. occurs נְתַקְּנוּהוּ with the euphonic dagesh in קּ, to move away, to push away, to tear away, related to אָתַק and עָתַק; hence of the breaking of the testicles, נָתוּק castrate; of the breaking up of a camp, of the ejecting from (מִן) a place. Niph. pass. to be torn off (a string, a cord, or a sail), rooted out, of the tabernacle, to be banished from a place, to be cut off. Pi. to rend asunder (fetters), to tear up (roots), to rip up (the breasts). Hiph. to draw out the enemy (from the city), to pull out (sheep for slaughter). Hoph. like Niph. The root is נָ־תַק.

נֶתֶק m. a scall, scurf (on the head or the beard), transf. to the scabby one. The root appears to be נָתַק to cover, to overlay.

I. נָתַר (fut. יִתַּר) to tremble, to shiver, as the Targ. renders it טְפַז; hence, to tremble from (מִן) its place (of the heart). Pi. to hop, to spring (of the locusts). Hiph. to make tremble (nations).

II. נָתַר (Kal, not used) to break off, to loosen, from נָ־תַר, equiv. to שְׁרָה; hence, Hiphil הִתִּיר to loosen, to untie the girdle, the bonds; of the hand, to stretch out. וַיַּתֵּר, 2 Sam. 22:33, see תּוּר.

נְתַר (equiv. to נְשַׁר) Aram. to fall off, to drop off, of the fruit or leaves of a tree; hence, Af. אַתַּר to throw off, to drop (the leaves).

נֶתֶר m. a kind of mineral salt, alkali, potash (Auth. Vers. nitre), different from בֹּרִית, which is a vegetable alkali. The etymology is obscure.

נָתַשׁ (fut. יִתּשׁ, inf. נְתוֹשׁ) origin. to pull down, like נָתַץ, but most frequently in contrast to נָטַע (to plant), i. e. to uproot (the plants), to destroy, devastate (cities), to pull down (idol images), to banish (from a country); the root is נָ־תַשׁ, related to כָּתַשׁ, מוּשׁ. Niph. pass. 1) to be destroyed (the kingdom); 2) of the water, to be dried up, to fail, but in this sense נָתַשׁ cannot be connected with נָשַׁת, the latter root not existing. Hoph. הֻתַּשׁ to be torn out, pulled out.

ס

ס *samech* (סָמֶךְ), the fifteenth letter of the alphabet, as a numeral it counts 60. Its name signifies, support, or arm chair; the name of the letter arises from its shape. It interchanges most frequently with the letters of a hissing sound: as עָלַז—עָלַס, צָפַן—סָפַן, נָתַץ—נָתַס, רָמַשׂ—רָמַס, בּוֹשֵׁשׁ—בּוֹשֵׁס; but also with ת, which sometimes also has a hissing sound. The difference between ס and שׂ however indistinct in the present pronunciation, is strictly maintained in the orthography, and they but rarely change one for the other; like מְסוּכָה and מְשׂוּכָה and others.

סָאָה (not used) to split, to divide, transf. to measure, comp. שְׁעָא in Aram., from which שְׁעָא a division of time, an hour.

סְאָה (dual סָאתַיִם, pl. סְאִים, comp. שָׁנִים from שָׁנָה) fem. measure, especially a corn measure, a third of an ephah.

סְאוֹן (after the form שְׁחוֹר, שְׁכוֹל) m. weapon, orig. that which is pointed, sharpened, from סָאַן, equiv. to שָׁנַן, זוּן.

סָאַן equiv. to זָן, שָׁן, to point, to sharpen, to pierce, transferred, to wound; according to some, to be dirty, miry, for which nothing definite can be traced in the Heb.

סַאסְּאָה f. according to some contracted from סְאָה סְאָה, i. e. to be of complete measure; more correct, however, is the opinion that it is an inf. from סַאסְּאָ (see סוא) and not a noun.

סָבָא origin. to inhale, to imbibe, to suck; hence, to drink to an excess; it is thus related partly with שָׁאַב, and partly with שָׂבַע, perhaps also with צָבַע; סֹבֵא a drunkard; סָבוּא the intoxicated one.

סָבָא (only pl. סְבָאִים in the Keri) m. a drunkard; the Ketib has סוֹבְאִים.

סְבָא 1) p. n. m. the first-born of Kush, i. e. the first commercial settlers of the Ethiopians; next, 2) a p. n. for Meroe, where the ancient commerce of Ethiopia flourished. Gent. noun סְבָאִים, who are described as being of high stature (אַנְשֵׁי מִדָּה).

סֹבֶא (with suff. סָבְאָם) m. drink, a drinking-bout.

סָבַב (in the pret. sometimes the analysed and sometimes the contracted form, inf. סֹב, but with לְ, לָסֹב; fut. יָסֹב, but not יִסֹּב) 1) to surround, to encompass; transf. to surround a town, to besiege it; to surround a table, to partake of a meal; 2) to turn into something, i. e. change into something, to become like something; 3) to turn, to induce, to occasion, to cause something. The signification to turn oneself, which some ascribe to Kal, belongs to Niph.; the forms derived from סָבַב, according to the three principal significations, are easily understood by the context. Niph. נָסַב (3 f. נָסְבָה for נָסַבָּה; fut. יִסֹּב, pl. יִסַּבּוּ) 1) to turn, of the door which turns upon its hinges; to turn round to do something, to oneself, to (אֶל; עַל) some one, or from (מִן, מֵעַל) some one; to turn to follow some one (אֶל־אַחֲרֵי), without case, to step forward or to turn back, and of inanimate beings, to be turned, brought to some one (לְ); 2) like Kal joined with the accus. to surround; with עַל, in a hostile sense. Pi. סִבֵּב to turn, in the sense of changing. Po. סוֹבֵב to turn about in a place (בְּ, עַל, and accus.), to surround, with accus. especially by way of protection; hence, Jer. 31:22, "a woman shall encompass a man." Hiph. הֵסֵב (fut. יָסֵב, יַסֵּב) to cause some one to turn to, toward (אֶל) something, to bring, to procure, to lead something round, to change (the name). Hoph. הוּסַב (fut. יוּסַב) to turn itself (of the flaps of the door, of the wheels of the thrashing waggon); next generally, to be turned (the face), to be surrounded, to be fitted in, to be changed. The root סָבַב is origin. equiv. to אָסַף to enclose.

סִבָּה (after the form חִתָּה, מִלָּה) fem. turning, fate, destiny (of God מֵעִם יי); later, נְסִבָּה is used for it.

סָבִיב (const. סְבִיב, pl. סְבִיבִים, and f. סְבִיבוֹת) m. 1) circle, circumference; hence, the m. pl. סְבִיבִים the circumference, the environs, sometimes applied to persons, surrounding company; the same is the f. pl. סְבִיבוֹת: but frequently 2) as an adv. round, round about; סָבִיב סָבִיב round and round; סָבִיב לְ (prep.) round about something; מִסָּבִיב round about on all sides; מִסָּבִיב לְ round away (of something); the same is the pl. with suff. round about, e. g. סְבִיבָיו round about him; סְבִיבוֹתַי round about me, or the state of const. as סְבִיבוֹת הָאֹהֶל round about the tent; 3) circuitous course, especially the f. pl. סְבִיבוֹת.

סָבַךְ origin. to bind, to make intricate, to entwine, of the entwining of the branches. Pu. סֻבַּךְ to be entwined one in another (of the roots).

סְבָךְ (the const. also סְבָךְ; with בְּ,

סְבָךְ; const. pl. (סִבְכֵי) masc. a thicket, bush; origin. entwining.

סְבָךְ (with suff. סֻבְּכוֹ, according to Kimchi) m. the same.

סַבְּכָא (Aram.) f. sambuca, an instrument something like a harp, origin. something like a net (שבכה).

סִבְּכַי p. n. m. (man of the thicket).

סָבַל (fut. יִסְבֹּל) to drag, carry, to bear (a heavy burden); transf. to the bearing of pain, punishment, sin, in the sense of burden. The root is סָ־בַל, similar to the Aram. יְ־בַל, from which מוּבָלָא burden. According to others, equiv. to שָׁבַל to drag. Pu. to be with young (of cattle), origin. to be heavily laden. Hithp. הִסְתַּבֵּל to become burthensome.

סְבַל (Aram.) the same; in the transferred sense, to lift (a burden); next, to lift up, to raise. Poal סוֹבַל to be raised, erected.

סַבָּל (pl. ־לִים) masc. 1) carrier of a burden; 2) heavy burden, equiv. to סֵבֶל.

סֵבֶל (not סֶבֶל) m. burden.

סֹבֶל (with suff. סֻבֳּלוֹ) masc. the same; עֹל ס׳ the burthensome yoke.

סִבְלָה (only pl. const. סִבְלוֹת, and with suff.) f. burthensome labour, soccage.

סִבֹּלֶת see שִׁבֹּלֶת.

סְבַר (fut. יִסְבַּר) equiv. to the Heb. שָׂבַר to hope, to wish, to trust; it is not connected with סָבַל to drag.

סִבְרַיִם (from סָבַר) double hope, p. n. of a city in Syria.

סַבְתָּא (and ־תָּה) p. n. of a Cushite tribe, adjacent to the present Artico, and also the name of a district.

סַבְתְּכָא p.n. of a Cushite district.

סַג belongs to סִגִים. See סִיג.

סָגַד (fut. יִסְגֹּד) to bow, bow down, to prostrate oneself (for worship) before (לְ) some one, but only used in the worshipping of idols.

סְגִד (fut. יִסְגֻּד) Aram. the same; to fall down before idols. The root is related to קַד.

סְגוֹר m. 1) enclosure (of the heart), i.e. the breast, in which the דֹּב שַׁכּוּל a bear robbed of her whelps first fixes her paws; 2) equiv. to זָהָב סָגוּר, which is explained under סָגַר, which see. For the explanation of סְגוֹר, Ps. 35:3, see under סְגֹר.

סָגַל (not used) to enclose; transf. to own, acquire, as possession, related to סָגַל. The root is סָ־גַל, and related to כָּלָא to enclose.

סְגֻלָּה f. property, possession (Author. Vers. a peculiar treasure), thus equiv. to נַחֲלָה.

סָגַן (not used) equiv. to סָכַן (comp.

סָכַר and סָגַר), to gain, to profit; next, to manage, to superintend, i. e. to gain by management. See סָגַן.

סָגָן (only pl. סְגָנִים) m. manager, superintendent; next, stadtholder, and generally, the noble one, from סָגַן. According to others, it is a foreign word, without Hebrew etymology.

סְגַן (pl. סִגְנִין, def. ־נַיָּא) Aram. the same.

I. סָגַר (fut. יִסְגֹּר) 1) to shut up, to close up; with בְּעַד, to shut in; with עַל, to close over some one, to enclose; 2) to close together, to fasten; hence, זָהָב סָגוּר dense, pure gold. The root is סָ־גַר, related to סָכַר, which is found also in חָ־גַר. Niph. נִסְגַּר to be closed, of gates and doors; to be shut in, of persons, or reflective, to shut oneself in (the house). Pu. to be closed. Hiph. הִסְגִּיר to close, to shut up; as to the significations, to deliver, to give up, they probably only belong to סָגַר II.

II. סָגַר (Kal, not used) to flow, to flow down, to rain, related to נָגַר; hence Pi. to pour out; next, transf. to deliver, to give up; the same is Hiph. הִסְגִּיר. Comp. הֶעֱרָה, הִגִּיר.

סְגַר (Aram.) the same.

סַגְרִיר (from סָגַר II., after the form חַכְלִיל, שַׁפְרִיר) m. rain.

סַד masc. stocks in which the feet were confined, from:—

סָדַד (not used) to enclose, to encompass.

סָדַם (not used) according to some, equiv. to שָׂרַם to burn, to burn away, equiv. to שָׂרַם 1, which see.

סְדֹם (conflagration) p. n. of a city in in the valley of Siddim.

סָדִין (pl. סְדִינִים) masc. linen undergarment worn on the naked body. Author. Vers. sheet.

סָדַן (not used) of uncertain etymology.

סָדַר (not used) to put in order, regulate, to arrange, related to דַּר, עָדַר.

סֵדֶר (only pl. סְדָרִים) m. row, range, order; לֹא סְדָרִים disorder, i. e. chaos.

סָהַר (not used) to be round, of a circular form, related to סָחַר to surround, to enclose, from which:—

סַהַר m. roundness (of a basin).

סֹהַר masc. a tower, castle, from its round form, from which בֵּית הַסֹּהַר prison, from סָהַר to be round.

סוא only Pi. סַאסֵא to drive, to drive away, comp. סַאסְאָא, זַעְזַע; hence the infin. with suff. בְּסַאסְאָה in driving them away. According to others בְּסַאסְּאָה, it is a noun; thus the Author. Vers. renders it "in measure."

ס p. n. of an Egyptian king, and probably the last at Mantheo, who was called Σεθως, Ζητ. סוֹא is thus for סוֹת, comp. זוֹ and זֹאת.

סוּג (fut. יָסוּג) to give way, to retire, to withdraw (from God), סוּג לֵב a heart turning from, i.e. forgetting God. Niph. נָסוֹג (inf. abs. נָסוֹג, fut. יִסּוֹג) to move back, turn back, joined with אָחוֹר or מֵאַחֲרֵי, backsliding (from God), but also absolute. Hiph. הִסִּיג (for הֵסִיג after the Aram.) to remove, to move away. Hoph. הֻסַּג pass.

. סוּג equiv. to שׂוּךְ, to hedge round.

ס m. (Ketib) equiv. to סִיג, which see.

סוּגַ m. cage or den of the lion.

סו (not used) 1) to sit, for which יָסַד is generally used; 2) to set, to found, to erect, related to שׁוּת.

סו (from סוּד, after the form קוֹל, but not abbreviated from יְסוֹד) m. seat, origin. bolster, pillow, transf. to sitting, a circle composed of members sitting; next, council, confidence, and that which is communicated in confidence, secret.

סוֹ p. n. m. (confidant).

סָוָ (not used) to veil, to wind round, to tie; next, to wrap up, to veil generally, from which מַסְוֶה and סוּת.

סוּ (not used) probably equiv. to סָחָה, to wipe off, to remove, from which:—

סוּחַ p. n. m.

סוּחָה (from סָחָה) f. equiv. to סְחִי, sweepings, excrement.

סוּט (not used) equiv. to שָׂטָה, to turn away, to deviate, from which :—

סוּטַי p. n. m. (the backslider).

סוּךְ (fut. יָסוּךְ) to rub (with oil), e. g. the body, garments; next, to anoint. The form יִיסַךְ belongs to יָסַךְ. Hiph. (fut. apoc. וַיָּסֶךְ) to rub in, omitting the matter used for rubbing in; but the part. מֵסִיךְ stands for מֵסֵךְ, and belongs to סָכַךְ.

סוּמְפֹּנְיָה (sometimes with מ omitted in the Ketib סִיפֹּנְיָה) Aram. f. generally bagpipe; it is difficult, however, to ascertain whether the word has a Semitic origin.

סְוֵנֵה p. n. the southern border town of Egypt, Syene.

סוּס (a verb not used, and uncertain) according to some, to rejoice, orig. to spring with triumph; hence, to gallop.

סוּס (pl. סוּסִים) masc. 1) a horse, a courser, from סוּס, probably so called from its breeding country, Susa (comp. פָּרָשׁ); 2) (Ketib) name of a bird of passage, crane, or swallow, or some similar bird, the derivation being uncertain.

סוּסָה f. a mare.

סוּסִי p. n. m. (rider, horseman).

סוּעַ (not used) related to זוּעַ, סוּא, to drive, to drive away, comp. נָסַע. From which מַסָּע and סִיעָה.

סוּף (fut. יָסוּף) to cease, to end, to finish, comp. סָפָה, but it is not connected with אָסַף. Hiph. הֵסִיף (fut. יָסִיף, with suff. אֲסִיפֵם) to make an end, to take, snatch away. The Hiph. is joined to אָסַף (which, in a transferred sense, has a similar signification) by way of paranomasia. The noun סוּפְּרָה arose from סְעוּפָה, and belongs to סָעַף.

סוּף (3 fem. סָפַת) Aram. the same. Af. to destroy, to make an end of.

סוּף m. 1) reed, rush, bulrush, seaweed, reed of the Nile, origin. a sword, as in Aram. and in modern Heb. סַיִף; hence, sword-grass, so called from its shape; 2) p. n. of a place.

סוֹף masc. an end, where something ceases; hence, also, the last in a procession, rearward.

סוֹף (def. סוֹפָא) Aram. m. the same.

סוּפָה (with ה finis סוּפָתָה, plur. סוּפוֹת) fem. storm, tempest, gale, whirlwind, contracted from סְעוּפָה from סָעַף, equiv. to נָעַף, which see.

I. סוּר (fut. יָסוּר, apoc. יָסַר) equiv. to זוּר, 1) to go away, to turn away (from the road), to deviate, depart from (מִן, מֵעַל, מֵעִם, מֵאַחֲרֵי) the way of God, to move away from (מִן) something, to forsake something (with acc.), to leave off from (מִן) something; it is applied to the spirit of God, of strength, of dominion, of sense which departs from some one. The prepositions and cases are used according to the qualified significations, e. g. סוּר, without any case, to apostatise, to degenerate; with מִן, to deviate, to depart; with accus., to forsake, to transgress, to remove, etc.; 2) to turn toward something for the purpose of looking, also with עַל; to turn in at (אֶל) some one's place, to have access to (אֶל), the origin. signif. being like *cedere*. Hiph. הֵסִיר (fut. יָסִיר, apoc. יָסֵר), to cause some one to depart, move from a place; hence, to put off, to put away (clothes, intoxication, etc.), to take off (the ring, ornament), to take the head off, i. e. to execute, generally to remove, clear away, turn away, take back, always proceeding from the origin. signif. of moving; from signif. 2 of the Kal, is formed the signif. of Hiph. הֵסִיר אֵלָיו causing something to be brought to himself. Hoph. הוּסַר to be removed, turned away. Pi. סוֹרֵר to cause to depart (from the road), i. e. to seduce, to lead astray. See סָרַר.

II. סור (not used) equiv. to שׁוּר, belonging to מְשׁוּרָה to hollow out, to deepen out; hence, to pierce, to stick in; from which סִיר, סוּר.

סוּר adj. m. (origin. particip. pass.), סוּרָה fem. wandered, departed; וְסוּרַי those that have departed from me, in Keri; but the Ketib has יְסוּרַי, which belongs to יָסַר, or it may be taken as a noun יָסוּר, from סוּר.

סוּר (only pl. const. סוּרֵי) m. 1) equiv. to סִיר thorn, wild plant; it belongs to סוּר II.; 2) p. n. of a gate of the temple, for which, in a parallel passage, stands שַׁעַר הַיְסוֹד.

סות (Kal, not used) to speak, to talk; hence Hiph. הֵסִית, and after the Aramaic manner הִסִּית (fut. יָסִית and יַסִּית, apoc. יָסֶת) to persuade, to entice, especially to something bad; with בְּ of the person, to entice against some one; with מִן, to dissuade from something, to decoy. In the signification of to mislead, to seduce, is also to be taken הֲסִיתְךָ, Job 36:16; in the same sense, יְסִיתְךָ verse 18 in the same chapter.

סוּת (for סְוּוּת from סָוָה) f. covering, wrapper, garment, from סָוָה to wrap up, to clothe; comp. מַסְוֶה.

סָחַב (fut. יִסְחַב, inf. const. סְחוֹב) to pull, to drag, to tear about; hence, to tear to pieces (of ferocious dogs); also, of the rending of a garment; related to סָחָה.

סְחָבָה (only plur. סְחָבוֹת) f. origin. tearing to pieces; but next torn garments, rags.

סָחָה (Kal, not used) to pull, to tear; hence Pi. סִחָה to remove, to tear up (the earth from a place), equiv. to סָחַב and סָחַף, or perhaps synon. with the root in נָסַח.

סְחִי m. dragging about, wandering about, according to Eben Ezra; according to others, that which is thrown away, sweepings.

סָחִישׁ m. after-sprout, after the third year of sowing, a dry sapless plant, from סָחַשׁ.

סָחַף to drive away, to sweep away, to wash away, or like סָחַב in the sense of to drag about, to fling about; hence, מָטָר סֹחֵף a sweeping rain, one accompanied by a tempest. Niph. נִסְחַף to be dragged or swept away, of the mighty ones of the earth, as Divine punishment.

סָחַר (fut. יִסְחַר) to travel, to journey, to traffic, especially to trade, syn. is תּוּר; סֹחֵר a travelling merchant,

f. סֹחֶרֶת she who has mercantile intercourse with others. Pi. סְחַרְחַר, probably in the sense of חַרְחַר to glow, to burn, applied to the heart.

סָחַר (c. סְחַר) m. trading-place, trade; next, that which is got by trade.

סַחַר (with suff. סַחְרָהּ) m. property acquired by trade.

סְחֹרָה (with suff. סֹחַרְתֵּךְ) f. trade, סְחֹרַת יָדֵךְ trade of thy hand, i.e. industry.

סֹחֵרָה (from סָחַר, in the signif. of to surround, to enclose) f. a shield (a round one); hence Targ. עֲגִילָא.

סֹחֶרֶת f. a species of precious marble for paving; but as red marble was formerly used for paving, סֹחֶרֶת may stand for סֹמֶרֶת, at least, in the same signification.

סָחַשׁ (not used) probably equiv. to חַשׁ, קַשׁ to be sapless, dry, like stubble or straw, used of the dry after-growth.

סֵט see שֵׂט, from שׂוּט.

סִיג (pl. סִיגִים, frequently in manuscripts סִגִּים) masc. that which is thrown out, dross; hence כֶּסֶף סִיגִים, silver not yet purified from dross; transf. to the inferior metals generally. See סוּג.

סִיוָן m. name of the third month of Heb. year; after a Semitic etymology, spring month, but probably the name is foreign.

סִיחוֹן p.n. m. (the conqueror).

סִין 1) p.n. of the eastern border-city of Egypt; according to Heb. etymology, it signifies, in the opinion of some, town of manure; 2) p.n. of a desert adjacent to Mount Sinai.

סִינַי (the ridged one) p.n. of the granite Mount Sinai, celebrated by the Divine revelation having been given to Moses on it; complete הַר סִי׳, מִדְבַּר סִי׳.

סִינִי p.n. of a Canaanite people or tribe. In the district of Lebanon there is actually found a city called Sinna (according to Strabo).

סִינִים (complete אֶרֶץ ס׳) p.n. of a country far distant from Palestine, probably the name stands for Sina (China), this name might have been the more current among the Hebrews, since it was used only by foreigners, not Chinese.

סִיס masc. a swallow, a crane. See סוּס 2.

סִיסְרָא p.n. m. (battle array).

סִיעָא p.n. m. (assembly).

סִיעֲהָא p.n. m. (the same), from סִיעָה and סִיעָא.

סִיפֹּנְיָה see סוּמְפֹּנְיָה.

סִיר as a verb to the noun סִיר. See סוּר II.

סִיר plur. סִירִים and סִירוֹת) com. 1) something deepened out, pot, ba-

סָכַךְ (2 pers. סַכֹּתָה, סַכֹּתָ, fut. יָסֹךְ) 1) to cover, with עַל (upon or over), something; hence, to protect, to shield; סֹכֵךְ that which covers, protects, shelters. Comp. נָסַךְ II. סַכּוֹתָ בֶעָנָן לָךְ thou hast covered thyself with a cloud, Lam. 3:44; 2) to entwine, to interweave, to hedge round; transf. to the interweaving (Author. Vers. covering) of the embryo in the mother's womb. Hiph. הֵסֵךְ to hedge round; with בְּעַד, to shield, to cover; with לְ or עַל, to cover the feet, i.e. to go to stool. Hoph. to be covered. Pi. סִכְסֵךְ generally rendered, to provoke, to stir up; more probably, however, it is to arm, equip, from the origin. signif. of covering.

סְכָכָה (hedging) p.n. of a place in the desert of Judah.

סָכַל (Kal, not used) to be foolish, only a transposition from כָּסַל, which is the original form. Niph. to act foolishly, to sin. Pi. to turn counsel or wisdom into folly, i.e. to frustrate. Hiph. to make foolish, in connection with עָשָׂה to act foolishly.

סָכָל m. a fool, in opposition to חָכָם.

סֶכֶל m. folly.

סִכְלוּת fem. folly, for which once שִׂכְלוּת.

sin, kettle, סִיר רַחַץ washing-basin, סִיר נָפוּחַ seething-pot; in this sense the pl. is סִירִים, sometimes סִירוֹת; 2) thorn, from סוּר to stick in; hence also, a sharpened hook.

סָךְ (probably a shortened form from סֹךְ) m. dense crowd, from סָכַךְ to entwine; according to others, a mass, a sum; origin. complex, of the same root.

סֹךְ (with suff. סֻכּוֹ, סֻכֹּה) m. a hut covered with foliage, tabernacle, thicket; transf. to tent, dwelling, den of beasts.

סָכָה (not used) equiv. to שָׂכָה to look at, inspect; from which יִסְכָּה.

סֻכָּה (from סֹךְ, plur. סֻכּוֹת) f. a hut covered with foliage, from סָכַךְ to hedge round, or to cover with foliage; transf. to a house like a hut, a small abode, a shelter, or hedge, thicket, like סֹךְ.

סֻכּוֹת (tents, tabernacles) 1) p.n. of a Gadite city; 2) p.n. of an encampment of the Israelites in the desert; 3) סֻכּוֹת בְּנוֹת huts of the daughters, p. n. of a subject of idolatrous worship; perhaps it may be read סֻכּוֹת בָּמוֹת.

סִכּוּת f. name of a tent carried about by the Israelites in the desert, for the worship of Moloch, from סָכַךְ.

סֻכִּי (only pl. סֻכִּיִּים), p.n. of an African people dwelling in tents.

I. סָכַן (fut. יִסְכֹּן) to procure or yield profit, gain; לֹא יִסְכֹּן it is profitless; next, to manage, oversee, i.e. to preserve something, to nourish it, to benefit it; סֹכֵן treasurer, chancellor; סֹכֶנֶת a nurse, next generally, to serve some one, to become useful to some one. Hiph. to superintend something, to manage an affair, to nourish something, also to be used or accustomed to do something; but the sense of "confidant" is not found in the verb.

II. סָכַן (Kal, not used) to make an incision, to wound, to hurt; next, to endanger. Niph. to be cut, wounded, endangered. Pu. סֻכַּן, the same: transf. to be oppressed, reduced, needy, necessitous.

סָכַר (Kal, not used) equiv. to סָגַר to close, to shut; hence, Niph. to be shut up, to be closed in. Pi. equiv. to הִסְגִּיר to give up, to deliver up; also in the sense of to purchase, to hire. See under שָׂכַר.

סָכַת (Kal; not used) equiv. to שָׁקַט to be silent, quiet; hence Hiph. הִסְכִּית to listen silently.

סַל (pl. סַלִּים) masc. basket, wicker-basket, from סָלַל to entwine, not from סָלַל to shake.

סִלָּא (path) p.n. of a place in the neighbourhood of Jerusalem.

סָלָא (Kal, not used) equiv. to סָלָה, סָלַל, to lift up, to weigh, origin. to rock or shake something to and fro; hence, Pu. to be weighed, valued, compared.

סַלָּא see סַלּוּא.

סָלַד only Pi. to triumph, to spring with joy. In modern Heb. סָלַד signifies 1) to request vehemently, e.g. מְסַלְּדִים in the festival Piyutim; hence, סֶלֶד supplication, in connection with רֹן, but also, to praise, exalt; 2) to rejoice, shout in triumph, from which סֶלֶד joy.

סֶלֶד p.n. m. (joy).

סָלָה equiv. to סָלָא 1) to lift up, to weigh, from which 2) to lift away, to remove; the mode of transferring the sense is as in זָלַל to despise, which see. Pi. to despise. Pual to be weighed, balanced, to be valued, compared with (בְּ) something. Comp. סָלָא.

סֶלָה (from סָלָה, after the form אֶחָד, only with the difference that the accent is on the last syllable) m. raising of the voice, attuning of the instrument, or from סָלָה in the sense of, to be silent; hence, a pause. All the explanations of this word are insufficient; it is certain, however, that the form cannot be an imperative.

סַ (for סַלּוּת) p.n. m. exaltation.
סַלּוּ p.n. m. (the exalted one).
סַלּוּ p.n. m. (the eminent one).
סִ (but the pl. סַלּוֹנִים) m. thorn, from סָלַל, to tear, to prickle, which root is also found in חָ־סַל.
סָ (fut. יִסְלַח, once אֶסְלוֹחַ Ketib) to forgive, to pardon; with לְ, of the person who is pardoned, and also with לְ before חַטָּאת and עָוֹן (the sin or iniquity which is forgiven). The origin. signif. is to lift away, or to remove the sin, from סָלָה, סָלָא=סָלָה. Comp. נָשָׂא. Niph. נִסְלַח to be forgiven (of the sin).
סַ m. he that forgives, pardons.
ס p. n. m. (the exalted one).
סְלִי f. forgiveness, pardon.
סָ (not used) equiv. to הָלַךְ to go.
סַלְ (for סַלָּכָה walk, wandering) p.n. of a city in Bashan.
סָ (particip. pass. f. סְלוּלָה, imp. סָלּוּ, before suff. סָלּוּ, fut. יָסֹל 1) equiv. to תָּלַל, to raise, to heighten, related to כָּ־סַל, טוּל, סָלָה, סָלָא, תַּל, תָּלָה, דָּלָה, where the original sense of heightening predominates; transf. 2) to pave the way, to raise it (by throwing up earth); next generally, to heap up; 3) to lift up high, i. e. either to esteem, or to extol, praise. Pi. סִלְסֵל to exalt (wisdom), i.e. to value it, syn. with רוֹמֵם. Hithp. 1) הִסְתּוֹלֵל to exalt oneself, to conduct oneself haughtily, boastingly towards (בְּ) some one; 2) to shake, to move to and fro, origin. to swing up, similar to דַּל, זַל, תַּל, but this signification is found only in the derivatives where the orig. signif. is, to entwine; 3) (belongs to סִלּוֹן) equiv. to the root in חָ־סַל, to tear, to tear off; hence, סִלּוֹן a thorn.

סֹלְלָה (pl. סֹלְלוֹת) f. a heap of earth or stones; hence, wall, rampart, שָׁפַךְ ס׳ to cast up a bank, נָתַץ אֶל־הַס׳ to pull down houses and turn them into bulwarks (Author. Vers. thrown down by the mounts.)

סֻלָּם m. ladder, either from סָלַל or from סָלַם, related to שָׁלַב to join together (of the steps).

סַלְסַל (only pl. סַלְסִלּוֹת) m. a basket, redoubled form from סַל.

סָלַע (not used) 1) equiv. to סָלָא, in the sense of, to be weighty, heavy, comp. שָׁקַל to weigh, origin. to be heavy; 2) to devour, to swallow, related to לוּעַ and to the root in בָּ־לַע.

סֶלַע (with suff. סַלְעִי, pl. סְלָעִים) m. 1) a rock, origin. burden, weight, stone, so called on account of its heaviness; 2) p. n. of the Edomite capital, Petra, sometimes with the article, הַסֶּלַע.

סָלְעָם (for סָלְעָם, from סָלַע 2) m. a species of locust.

סָלַף (Kal, not used) equiv. to שָׁלַב to be fitted in one another, entwined, twisted together, syn. with עָוָה, עָוַת, עָבַת, עָבַט, עָקַל, which have a similar original signification; hence, Pi. סִלֵּף to turn, to pervert דִּבְרֵי צַדִּיקִים the words of the righteous; to pervert the way, i.e. to lead on the wrong way, equiv. to עִוָּה נָתִיב, transf. like הָפַךְ to overthrow, to destroy, etc. The verb is not connected with אָלַף.

סֶלֶף m. perverseness, perverse conduct.

סְלַק (3 pl. סְלִקוּ) Aram. to step up, similar to נְסַק, to step out from (מִן) something: whether it is connected with סָלַע, cannot be defined.

סָלַת (not used) belongs to סֹלֶת, of uncertain origin, if the root is not סוּל, סַל, or סָלָה. The Aram. סְמַד appears to be synonymous.

סֹלֶת (with suff. סָלְתָּהּ) com. fine flower, different from קֶמַח meal of wheat or barley.

סַם (only pl. סַמִּים) masc. spice, fragrance, odour, from סָמַם, which see; קְטֹרֶת סַמִּים sweet incense.

סַמְגַּר נְבוֹ p. n. of a chief of a Chaldean army (origin. warrior of Nebo).

סְמָדַר masc. blossom, vine blossom, formed from סָמַד, with ר affixed.

סָמַךְ (fut. יִסְמֹךְ) 1) to lean, to rest, upon something, origin. to press upon something (related to מָכַךְ), ס׳ יָד עַל to lay the hand upon something; hence, עָלַי סָמְכָה חֲמָתֶךָ thy wrath lieth hard upon me; 2) to support, to strengthen, to invigorate, either by nourishment or help, generally with double acc.; hence סָמוּךְ to be assisted, supported, strong, comp. תָּמַךְ; 3) to approach some one (אֶל), a signif. very common in modern Hebrew. Niph. to lean for support upon (עַל) some one. Pi. to support, but only like סָעַד, transf. to refresh.

סְמַכְיָהוּ p. n. m. (support from God).

סָמַל (not used) according to some equiv. to צָלַם, according to others equiv. to מָשַׁל, but both opinions are improbable as appears from the noun.

סֶמֶל (also סֵמֶל) m. a drawing, design of a figure; figur. פֶּסֶל הַסֶּמֶל an image hewn out; the noun arose from סַם (from סוּם) drawing, with the nominal termination ־ֶל, as in כַּפֶּל; and סַם which is only found again in the secondary form שֵׁם appears as a verb in Heb. only in the lengthened form סָמַן.

סָמַם (not used) origin. to breathe out, to exhale (of fragrance), to diffuse fragrance, to season.

סָמַן (Kal, not used; a lengthened root from סוּם) to draw, to design, to appoint, to assign; hence, Niph. to be set apart, to be marked, appointed, especially of a field parted off.

סָמַר to stand up, to bristle (of the hair), also with the omission of שַׂעֲרָה. Pi. the same. Comp. אָמַר, תָּמַר.

סָמָר adj. masc. bristling up, standing up (of the hair), hairy, rough, used as an attribute to יֶלֶק caterpillars.

סָנָא (not used) to sting, to prickle, transf. to hate, origin. to hurt, from which:—

סְנָאָה (thorn-hedge) p. n. of a city in Judah.

סַנְבַלַּט (foreign) p. n. m. (overseer of the army).

סָנָה (not used) equiv. to שָׁנַן (comp. שָׂנֵא, אָרַן, זָן) to sting, to prickle, to stick, to scratch, from which:—

סְנֶה (const. סְנֶה) a thorn, a thorn-bush, thorn-shrub, so called from its pricking.

סֶנֶּה (point of a rock) p. n. of a rock opposite Michmash.

סַנָּה (in קִרְיַת סַ׳) p. n. of a city (thicket).

סְנוּאָה p. n. fem. (the one who is injured), with the article.

סַנְוֵר (only pl. סַנְוֵרִים) m. blindness, from a Pi. form סַנְוֵר, from סָנַר, which see.

סַנְחֵרִיב (foreign) p. n. m. (conqueror of armies).

סָנַן (not used) equiv. to טָנָא to entwine; comp. סָלַל in the same signif. From which:—

סַנְסִן (only pl. סַנְסִנִּים) m. branch, entwining of branches.

סַנְסַנָּה (thicket) p. n. of a city in Judah.

סָנַף (not used) equiv. to זָנַב, to wag, to swing to and fro, from which:—

סְנַפִּיר (from סָנַף, with the nominal termination ־ִיר) m. fin, so called from its tail-like motion.

סָנַר (not used) to bore, to hollow out, related to צָנַר, from which צִנּוֹר a canal, from which Pi. (not used) סַנְוֵר to put the eyes out, to blind, with the ו interpolated, as in שַׁחֲוָה, from which the noun סַנְוֵר.

סָס m. a moth, an insect that destroys the garments, the etymology is obscure.

סִסְמַי p. n. m.

סָעַד (fut. יִסְעַד, imp. סְעַד, סַעֲדָה) to support, comp. עַד; hence, to assist, to help, סָ׳ לֵב to strengthen, to revive the heart, sometimes with the omission of לֵב.

סְעַד (Aram.) the same; hence Pa. to support, to help (לְ) some one.

סָעָה (only particip. f.) to tear away, to drive away; hence רוּחַ סֹעָה windy storm, tempest.

סְעִיף (const. סְעִיף, pl. סְעִפִּים, dagesh for quiescent *yod*, pl. const. סְעִפֵּי) com. 1) a cleft, abyss; hence סְ׳ סֶלַע cleft of a rock, the same Targ. שְׁקִיף crack; 2) separation, party, only in the plur.; hence to halt between (עַל) two branches (parties); 3) branch, bough, from סָעַף.

סָעַף (not used) to bloom, to flourish; related to עָפָה, from which עֳפִי branch; from which סְעִיף 3. Pi. סֵעֵף (denom. from סְעִיף) to branch off; the denominatives have often the privative significations, like סִקֵּל, זִנֵּב.

I. סָעַף (not used) to split, to divide; related to which is the root in שְׁ־סַף and שֵׁב; from which סְעִיף and סֵעֵף.

II. סָעַף (not used) equiv. to זָעַף to rage, to storm; from which סוּפָה for סְעוּפָה.

סֵעֵף (pl. סֵעֲפִים) sceptic (Author. Vers. "vain thoughts"); from סָעַף I.

סְעַפָּה (from the m. סָעַף, thus after the form קְמַנָּה) f. branch, from סָעַף; see סַרְעַפָּה.

סָעַר (fut. יִסְעַר) 1) to storm, to rage, of the raging of the sea, of the enemy; 2) to be tossed about. Niph. pass. to be tossed about. Pi. (fut. אֲסָעֵר for אֲסַעֵר) to scatter with a whirlwind. Pu. סֹעַר, (only fut. יְסֹעַר for יְסֹעַר) to be driven with the whirlwind; related to which is שָׂעַר.

סַעַר (with suff. סַעַרְךָ) m. a storm, a tempest, a whirlwind.

סְעָרָה (pl. סְעָרוֹת, const. סַעֲרוֹת) fem. a storm, whirlwind; sometimes joined to רוּחַ.

סַף (with suff. סִפִּי, pl. סִפִּים, סִפּוֹת, סִפּוֹת) m. 1) basin, so called from its containing something (comp. כְּלִי from כָּלָה), from סָפַף, which see; 2) place of entrance, where the comers in are received, thus not only the door-post, but the vestibule; 3 p.n.; for which also stands סִפַּי. See סָפַף.

סָפָא (not used) according to Abulwalid and Kimchi, to eat, to feed; according to others, and more correctly, to gather, to heap up; related to אָ־סַף, which is more suitable to the noun, fodder, provender. See מִסְפּוֹא.

סָפַד (fut. יִסְפֹּד) to knock, to push against something; transferred, to knock against the breast as a sign of anguish; סָפַד עַל, לְ to mourn, to wail, for some one; sometimes construed with לִפְנֵי. The original signification is obvious from the phrase עַל שָׂרִים סְפֻרִים similar to מְתוֹפְפוֹת עַל לִבְבֵיהֶן. Niph. to be lamented, mourned for.

סָפָה (inf. const. סְפוֹת, fut. יִסְפֶּה) 1) equiv. to אָסַף and יָסַף to gather, to add to something, to increase, const. with עַל; 2) equiv. to סוּף to cease, to end; but also transitive, to make an end of, to destroy. Niph. 1) to be gathered in his house, i.e. to keep at home; 2) to be destroyed, to perish (in battle). Hiph. to heap up, with עַל to heap something upon some one.

סְפֻן see סְפוּן.

I. סָפַח (imp. with suff. סְפָחֵנִי) to join, to annex oneself; also trans. to join, to annex some one to אֶל something. Niph. to be joined, annexed, to cleave to (עַל) something. Pu. to be gathered, or to gather themselves somewhere. Hith. to join, to unite oneself with (בְּ) something; related to סָפָה in this sense.

II. סָפַח (not used) to spread out, to stretch out; related to טָפַח and צָפַח; from which מִסְפַּחַת, סַפַּחַת, צַפַּחַת, מִסְפָּחָה, and probably סָפִיחַ.

III. סָפַח (Kal, not used) equiv. to שָׁפַךְ and שָׁפַח to pour out. Pi. סִפֵּחַ to pour forth (wrath), or to pour in.

סַפַּחַת fem. a scab, from סָפַח II. so called from its spreading nature.

סַפַּי p. n. m. (doorkeeper).

סָפִיחַ (const. סְפִיחַ, pl. סְפִיחִים) m. 1) after-growth, that which grows after the harvest (Author. Vers. such things as grow of themselves); origin. the additional growth, from סָפַח I.; 2) flood, from סָפַח III. to pour forth, but not to overflow, which is only found in תִּשְׁטֹף.

סְפִינָה f. a ship, origin. that which is arched or cooped, tub-like, from סָפַן.

סַפִּיר (pl. ־רִים) masc. a sapphire, a sparkling precious stone, from סָפַר, equiv. to שָׁפַר to shine.

סֵפֶל (from סַף basin, formed with the nominal termination ־ֶל) m. a dish, small basin.

סָפַן (fut. יִסְפֹּן) 1) to arch, to vault; 2) equiv. to צָפַן to hide, conceal, store up, hoard; חֶלְקַת מְחוֹקֵק (Deut. 33:21) to treasure up the portion allotted by the lawgiver; but in this passage also the signif. may be to be surrounded, like סָפַן I., and as in the Auth. Vers. "was he seated."

סָפַף (not used) equiv. to שָׁפָה to take in, to hold, synonymous with כּוּל, כָּלָה to contain. The Hithpael הִסְתּוֹפֵף belongs to סַף, from which it is the denom. It signifies to stand at the threshold, Auth. Vers. to be a doorkeeper.

I. סָפַק (fut. יִסְפֹּק) to press or knock together, to push, to strike; related to דָּפַק; hence סָ׳ אֶת כַּפַּיִם to clap the hands (with indignation), and the same, with עַל, over some one, i.e. to scorn some one; sometimes without כַּפַּיִם; סָ׳ עַל יָרֵךְ to knock, smite upon the thigh, as a sign of mourning or indignation; 2) to chastise, punish; see שָׂפַק; 3) to stagger, to reel, of a drunkard.

II. סָפַק (not used) to flow, to overflow; comp. אָפַק, to overflow, overstream.

סֵפֶק (with suff. סִפְקוֹ) m. abundance, fulness, sufficiency.

סָפַר (fut. יִסְפֹּר) 1) to cut in, to engrave, to inscribe; transf. to write. The same mode of transferring is found in כָּתַב (equiv. to חָצַב, קָצַב, חָטַב), and with the same root צָפַר (in צִפֹּרֶן) is related; 2) to number, origin. to mark, to make incisions, from which מִסְפָּר, סְפֹרָה, to relate; 3) to declare, orig. to mark the sense by different words or sounds. In this sense it occurs in Pi. and Pu. only. Niph. to be numbered. Pi. 1) to number, count; 2) to relate, also to converse; next, to declare, praise. In the sense of narrating, it stands with accus. of the object, and לְ of the person; or with אֶל and בְּאָזְנֵי of the person, and עַל of the subject; sometimes also with אֶל of the subject. סִפֵּר כְּמוֹ to declare thus or as follows. Pu. to be related, declared, with לְ, of the person, and also with לְ, of the subject.

סֹפֵר (origin. a denom. from סֵפֶר) m. a scribe; קֶסֶת הַסֹּ׳ writing materials, inkstand, inkhorn; ס׳ הַמֶּלֶךְ the king's scribe, secretary of state; also without מֶלֶךְ, in a military sense, the general, who superintends the enlisting and reviewing, leader of the army. In modern Heb. scriptural scholar, teacher of the law, and learned one generally.

סָפֵר (Aram.) m. the same.

סֵפֶר (with suff. סִפְרִי, pl. סְפָרִים, סִפְרֵי) m. 1) writing, character of writing; hence, יֹדֵעַ סֵפֶר one who is learned; 2) that which is written, writ, e.g. a bill of purchase or sale, an action, a bill of divorce, and a letter generally; 3) book, especially of the book of the law; hence, הַסְּפָרִים in Daniel, the holy writ; also used of post-biblical profane writings, as עֲשׂוֹת סְפָרִים is used of polygraphy.

סְפַר (pl. סִפְרִין) Aram. m. the same.

סְפָר (after the form כְּתָב) masc. 1) numbering; 2) p. n. of an Arabian city which still exists under the name of Isfôr, between Merbat and cape Sagir.

סְפָרַד p.n. of a country to which the citizens of Jerusalem were exiled; according to an ancient tradition of Hieronymus, it is the Bosphorus, the present peninsular of Tauris, which was actually called *Sparad*, as perceived by a cuniform inscription. According to another tradition, it is Spain, for which there is no etymological proof.

סִפְרָה f. equiv. to סֵפֶר a book.

סְפֹרָה (pl. ־רוֹת) f. border, demarcation. See סָפַר 2.

סְפַרְוַיִם p.n. of an Assyrian city, from whence colonists were sent to Samaria, probably the Sipparenon of Eusebius, on the Euphrates. Gent. סְפַרְוִים, in Ketib סְפָרִים.

סֹפֶרֶת p.n. m. (office of secretary).

סָקַל (fut. יִסְקֹל) to stone, to throw (with stones), formed from סֶקֶל stone, as a denom. The root סָקַל signifies, like שָׁקַל, to be heavy, weighty. Niph. to be stoned to death. Pi. 1) to throw stones on some one, or at some one לְעֻמַּת פ'; 2) to remove the stones, to clear a place of the stones מֵאֶבֶן. Pu. to be stoned to death.

סַר adj. m., סָרָה f. to look wrath, sad, grieved. See סָרַר.

סָרַב (not used) to resist, to be refractory, rebellious; origin. to contend against something. Compare רָב.

סָרָב (only pl. סָרָבִים) m. the refractory one, the rebellious one; being connected with סָרַב, סַלּוֹנִים is according to some, in that passage equiv. to סָרָף and חָרוּל=סָרָב.

סַרְבָּל a quadriliteral, supposed to belong to סַרְבָּל, which opinion, however is not correct.

סַרְבָּל (pl. סַרְבָּלִין) m. a kind of dress, a kind of garment, either long and wide breeches, or a capacious cloak; no etymological proof can be given for either.

סַרְגּוֹן p. n. of an Assyrian king.

סָרַד (not used) equiv. to שָׂרַד to flee, from which:—

סֶרֶד p.n. m. (flight) patron. סַרְדִּי.

סָרָה (after the form קָמָה) fem. 1) turning away (comp. סוּר) from the law, apostasy, backsliding, sin, offence; 2) forsaking, abandoning, cessation, omission.

סִרָה (סִירָה) gushing of water, p. n. of a cistern, a well.

I. סָרַח (fut. יִסְרַח) to be stretched along, spread out, עַל עֶרֶשׂ upon the bed; גֶּפֶן סֹרַחַת a spreading vine; to reach beyond something, or to be suspended, of the turbans (Author. Ver. "attire upon the head").

II. סָרַח only the Niph. נִסְרַח to be bad, of bad smell, figur. like בָּאַשׁ, used of bad reputation, or disrepute.

סֶרַח masc. that which hangs over, reaches over (Author. Version, "remnant").

סִרְיוֹן m. equiv. to שִׁרְיוֹן coat of mail.

סָרִיס (const. סְרִיס, pl. סָרִיסִים, const. סָרִיסֵי and סְרִיסֵי) masc. eunuch, a castrate, keeper of the harem; figur. an officer, or courtier generally. See סָרַס.

סָרֵךְ (only pl. סָרְכִין, def. pl. סָרְכַיָּא) Aram a chief, probably of foreign origin.

סֶרֶן (pl. סְרָנִים, const. סַרְנֵי) m. 1) an axle, probably from צִיר=סַר, formed with the nominal termination ָן; 2) figur. a prince, origin. an axle, a mode of transferring common in the Arab.

סָרַס (not used) equiv. to שָׁרַשׁ to castrate; if it is not equiv. to שָׁרַת to serve, especially as in the derivatives and in the Aram. the sense of serving is predominant.

סַרְעַפָּה f. equiv. to סְעַפָּה, a branch, with the ר interpolated.

סָרַף (Kal, not used) equiv. to שָׂרַף, to burn, to burn away (a dead body); hence, particip. Pi. מְסָרֵף the one that burns it, i.e. the nearest relative.

סִרְפַּד (from סָפַד, with ר interpolated; comp. בַּרְזֶל, from בָּזַל) m. thorn, nettle, from סָפַד.

סָרַר only used in the analysed form; 1) to be refractory, rebellious, dissolute, used of man and beast; to shew a rebellious shoulder, i.e. to throw the yoke off; סָרֵי סוֹרְרִים (superlative) they that are thoroughly rebellious; 2) to be sad, only in the derivative סַר.

סָתָה (not used) to stand, to be stagnant, of the ponds in the rainy season, i.e. winter; the sense of wintering in this word is denom.

סְתָו (Keri סְתָיו) m. time of rain, rainy season, winter.

סְתוּר p. n. m. the hidden one.

סָתַם (fut. יִסְתֹּם to stop up, to shut up, to enclose; hence figur. to secrete; סָתוּם the secret; related are the roots in אָטַם and חָתַם. Niph. to be stopped of a breach. Pi. to stop (a well).

סָתַר (fut. יִסְתֹּר) to hide, to conceal, orig. to cover, to veil; Niph. 1) to be hidden מִן from something, or with מִנֶּגֶד, מִלִּפְנֵי, מִפְּנֵי; נִסְתָּרוֹת hidden, secret things (used of sins etc.); 2) to hide oneself from (מִן, מִפְּנֵי) some one. Pi. to hide. Pu. to be hidden. Hiph. הִסְתִּיר 1) to conceal from the eyes (מֵעֵינֵי) of some one; הִס׳ פָּנִים to hide the face from (מִן) some one; applied to God it signifies the withdrawal of Divine providence, the wrath of God against something; 2) to conceal, to secrete something from (מִפְּנֵי, מִן) some one; 3) to shield, to protect, מַסְתֵּר Isa. 53:3 is a verbal substantive; see מַסְתֵּר. Hith. הִסְתַּתֵּר to hide oneself.

סְתַר Aram. to throw into confusion, to destroy.

סֵתֶר (with suff. סִתְרִי, pl. סְתָרִים) m. 1) enclosure, a veil, a wrapper; transf. to shelter, protection; 2) that which is hidden, secret, hidden place.

סִתְרָה f. shelter, protection, shield.

סִתְרִי p. n. m. the protected one.

ע

ע *Ain* (עַיִן) is the 16th letter of the alphabet, and as a numeral counts 70. The name signifies an eye, and hence the round shape in the ancient character. Its peculiar sound was partly soft and mild, like the vowel *ah*, and partly strong, approaching the *gn*. This double pronunciation is yet found in the Greek translation of the bible, and gives many a clue for explaining and comparing of roots. The softer ע interchanges with the softer gutturals א and ה; the harder ע interchanges with ג, כ, ק, as will be seen from numerous examples by comparisons in the language. The ע is as a soft sound often thrown out; e.g. in שְׁמוּאֵל equivalent to שְׁמוּעַ־אֵל, זְרֻבָּבֶל from זְרוּעַ־בָּבֶל, בֵּל from בַּעַל, מְנִים from מְעָנִים, מוּם from מְעוּם, זֶרֶת from זֶעֶרֶת, סוּפָה from סְעוּפָה. Sometimes it is used as a vowel.

עָב (const. עַב, pl. עָבִים and עָבוֹת) com. 1) darkness, darkness of the cloud, cloud, wrapped in a cloud, from עוּב to wrap, to cover; 2) a thicket, thickness of the forest, from עוּב, in the sense of, to be covered, thick, dense; 3) a cornice, a doorpost, or entablature over a post, from the signif. of covering.

עֹב see עוּב.

עָבַב belongs to עָב and עֹב. See עוּב.

עָבַד (fut. יַעֲבֹד) 1) to do, to make; next, to work, to labour (in a vineyard), to plough a field, to pull flax, where sometimes the object "field" is omitted; עָבַד הָעִיר to build up the town, origin. to work at the town; עָבַד בְּ to impose work upon some one; 2) to serve one, to work for some one, with לִפְנֵי to serve before some one, but also with עִם and לְ of the person; transf. to serve God, absolute and with accus. and לְ, and with double accus., to serve God by something, e.g. by sacrifices. Niph. 1) to be worked, cultivated (of a plough-field; 2) to be adored (of a king). Pu. to be worked; עֻבַּד בְּ work to be imposed upon some one. Hiph. 1) to make some one work, to weary him (syn. with הוֹגִיעַ); 2) to cause some one to serve (either God or man). Hoph. to allow oneself to be made to serve, especially to the service of idols.

עֲבַד (Aram.) like עָבַד in Heb. and stands also for עָשָׂה; עֲבַד קְרָב to carry on war; with בְּ, עִם, to deal with some one. Ithp. to be made, to be done.

עֶבֶד (with suff. עַבְדִּי, pl. עֲבָדִים) m. 1) a slave, servant, origin. abstract, service; עֶבֶד עֲבָדִים a servant of servants, i. e. of the lowest degree; also servant of the king, vassal, courtier, sometimes applied to denote devotion to a superior. The prophets, Divine messengers, and the pious, were called servants of God; 2) p.n.m. (servant).

עֲבֵד (def. עַבְדָּא, pl. ־דִין) m. (servant, adorer of God).

עֲבָד (only pl. with suff. עֲבָדֵיהֶם; after the form כְּתָב) masc. work, deed, action.

עֹבֵד p. n. m. adorer, disciple.

עַבְדָּא p. n. m. (servant).

עֹבֵד אֱדֹם p. n. masc. (subject of the Edomites).

עַבְדְּאֵל p. n. m. (servant of God).

עֲבֹדָה f. 1) work (of the servant); מְלֶאכֶת עֲבֹדָה a business of work, i. e. a business connected with work; next generally, work, service, business; hence the peculiar form עָבַד עֲבֹדַת עֲבֹדָה to do the business of the service; also, cultivation, agriculture, or any kind of work, according to the context; 2) that which belongs to work, such as tools, utensils, etc.; 3) effect, produce of work; hence, עֲבֹדַת הַצְּדָקָה the work, product, or effect of righteousness.

עֲבֻדָּה (from the m. עָבֹד) f. domestic servants, household.

עַבְדּוֹן 1) p. n. of a city in Asher; 2) p. n. m. (subject).

עַבְדוּת f. servitude, slavery, bondage.

עַבְדִּי p. n. m. (subject).

עַבְדִּיאֵל p. n. m. (servant of God).

עֹבַדְיָה p. n. m. (the same).

עֹבַדְיָהוּ p. n. m. (the same).

עֶבֶד מֶלֶךְ p. n. m. (the king's servant).

(גְּנוֹא) עֶבֶד נְגוֹ p.n. m. (adorer of the planet Venus, נֹגַהּ=נְגוֹ).

עָבָה to be fat, thick, well fed; also used of inanimate things, to be thick, dense, transf. to be respectable, related to עוּב.

עֲבוֹט (after the form עֲבוֹת) masc. a pledge. See עָבַט.

עָבוּר (const. עֲבוּר) m. equiv. to the Aram. עֲבוּר that which is begotten by the earth, i.e. corn.

עֲבוּר (after the form זְבוּל, גְּמוּל) the passing over, but only in connection with בְּ, viz. בַּעֲבוּר, and only as a preposition or conjunction, over, therefore, thereof, thereupon; 1) referring to a person, for some one's sake, on account of some one, בַּעֲבוּרֶךָ for thy sake, on account of thee; 2) referring to a matter, for the sake of, or on account of something, signifying the cause; 3) for, as the price at which something passes from one to another, e.g. בַּעֲבוּר נַעֲלַיִם for shoes; 4) because, in order that, while, whilst (i.e. so long as), used instead of the complete form בַּעֲבוּר אֲשֶׁר.

עָבַט (fut. יַעֲבֹט) equiv. to עָבַת, עָוַת, to exchange, barter (comp. עָרַב), in Kal signifies, to borrow upon a pledge, in the sense of exchanging. Pi. to exchange, to change the road, i.e. to take another road. Hiph. to lend some one (accus.) upon (accus.) a pledge.

עַבְטִיט (after the form שַׁפְרִיר, סַגְרִיר) m. burden or obligation of debt, orig. a mass of pledges, from עָבַט.

עֳבִי m. thickness, density, from עָבָה.

עֲבִי (with suff. עָבְיוֹ) m. thickness, from עָבָה.

עֲבִידָא (const. —דַת, def. עֲבִידְתָּא) fem. Aram. like the Heb. עֲבוֹדָה labor, work, management.

עָבַל (not used) to be bare, leafless, of an unfruitful country: from which עֵיבָל.

עָבַץ (not used) transposed from עָצַב, to be grieved, from which יַעְבֵּץ.

עָבַר (fut. יַעֲבֹר) 1) to pass over something, to cross (acc. seldom בְּ or בְּתוֹךְ) a river or stream (נָהָר), the sea (יָם); sometimes omitting the word river, and only naming the destination, with acc. or אֶל; to pass over something, e.g. a road, or the back of some one; fig. of the razor which passes over the beard, or of the wind which sweeps over (בְּ) something; 2) to pass through a place, (acc.) through something (בְּ), between (בֵּין) something, through the midst (בְּקֶרֶב, בְּתוֹךְ) of persons or a thing; כֶּסֶף עֹבֵר לַסֹּחֵר money passable (current) among merchants, or abridged כֶּסֶף עֹבֵר or rent money; 3) to pass beyond something, without case, or with the accus. e. g. beyond the quarries (אֶת־הַפְּסִילִים), transf. to overtake (with עַל) some one; next generally, to pass by, also const. with עָבַר עַל, לִפְנֵי, עַל־פְּנֵי, מֵעַל; דֶּרֶךְ to pass the way; hence, עֹבֵר דֶּרֶךְ the passer by; עָ׳ תַּחַת הַשֵּׁבֶט to pass under the rod (of the shepherd), i. e. to be numbered; of time, which elapses; of the sin, i. e. to forgive; of the chaff, which flies away; 4) to go from (מִן) one place to (לְ) another, to go away, to go on (without case), to go on (בְּ) a journey, to walk upon (עַל) a place, to walk to and fro עָבַר וָשָׁב; to go towards a place (with accus. or אֶל); to turn into (בְּ) a town, a gate; figur. to enter into a covenant, an oath, or enter into something generally; עָבַר בַּשֶּׁלַח to pass through the sword, i. e. to fall by it, עָבַר בַּשַּׁחַת to go down to the grave, עָ׳ לִפְנֵי to pass on before, עָ׳ אַחֲרֵי to pass on behind, עָ׳ מֵאֵת, מִן to go away from something, to forsake something, seldom with מֵעַל; עָבַר עַל to pass from one way to another, also to lay or bring upon some one; 5) something to befall, עָבַר עַל to overflow, to over-stream, to be victorious over some one, to conquer something, מֹר עֹבֵר flowing myrrh. Niph. to be crossed (a river). Pi. 1) causing something to pass through; hence, to bolt, to lock; 2) to fertilize, to engender (Job 21:10). Hiph. הֶעֱבִיר, caus. of Kal, 1) to lead through (acc. or בְּ) a river, to pass a razor over (עַל) something, to lead from one town into (לְ) the other, to transfer an heritage (לְ) to some one; 2) to cause to resound (a voice) through (בְּ) the camp; in the same sense הֶעֱבִיר שׁוֹפָר; 3) to cause something to be passed over, to forgive the sin; 4) to bring (syn. with הֵבִיא), to offer, to consecrate, e. g. לַמֹּלֶךְ to Moloch; according to others, to pass through (בָּאֵשׁ) the fire, i. e. in honor of Moloch, only בָּאֵשׁ is sometimes omitted; הֶעֱבִיר בַּמַּלְבֵּן to pass through the red hot oven; 5) to carry away, to take away, to do away, to sweep away, to remove. Hith. to overflow, but only figur.; to go to excess in passion, origin. to transgress the limits, to burst forth in passion against (בְּ, עִם, עַל) some one, to be overbearing.

עֵבֶר (with suff. עֶבְרוֹ, plur. עֲבָרִים, const. עֶבְרֵי) m. 1) a district beyond the river, עֵבֶר הַיָּם a district beyond the sea; עֵבֶר הַיַּרְדֵּן country beyond the Jordan, the country understood by עֵבֶר הַיַּרְדֵּן depends upon the local position of the historian; hence, sometimes the eastern, and sometimes the western country of the Jordan; the same עֵבֶר הַנָּהָר sometimes the eastern, and sometimes the western country of the Euphrates; 2) side, opposite another side, and separated from it by space: thus, מִכָּל עֲבָרִים on all sides, עָבַר הָעֵבֶר to pass to the opposite side, אֶל־עֵבֶר opposite, towards the country, אֶל עֵבֶר פָּנָיו straight along before one, the same לְעֵבֶר; עַל עֵבֶר פָּנָיו straight before, מֵעֵבֶר on the other side of, or beyond something; 3) p. n. m. also the name of the ancestor of the Hebrews; hence, בְּנֵי עֵבֶר and עֵבֶר the Hebrews.

עֲבַר (Aram.) m. equiv. to עֵבֶר 1 in Heb.; hence עֲבַר נַהֲרָא the country west of the Euphrates, orig. the other side of the river.

עֲבָרָה (pl. const. עַבְרוֹת in Ketib, for which more correctly the Keri עַבְרוֹת) f. a ford, a ferry.

עֶבְרָה (with suff. עֶבְרָתִי, pl. עֲבָרוֹת, const. עֶבְרוֹת and עַבְ׳) fem. orig. transgressing, especially of passion; next, generally, passion, anger, transf. to Divine punishment; also, haughtiness, presumption; comp. the Hith. הִתְעַבֵּר.

עַבְרוֹן p. n. f. of a city in Asher, otherwise עַבְדּוֹן.

עַבְרֹנָה (passage), p. n. of a place not far from Ezion Geber, on the coast of the Red Sea.

עִבְרִי (gent. m. from עֵבֶר, pl. עִבְרִים or עִבְרִיִּים, f. עִבְרִיָּה, pl. עִבְרִיּוֹת) originally, descendant of Heber, a Hebrew.

עֲבָרִים (the countries beyond) p.n. of a mountain on the other side of the Jordan; complete הַר־הָעֲבָרִים or הָרֵי־הָעֲ׳. From עִיֵּי הָעֲ׳ it is evident it was originally the name of a country.

עָבַשׁ (rare) to rot, to become decomposed (by heat), of bodies under the ground; the root is compared by some with יָבֵשׁ, and by others with בָּאַשׁ.

עָבַת (Kal, not used) to entwine, to bind; related to עָוַת, עָבַט. Pi. to twist, to entangle.

עָבֹת adj. m., עֲבֻתָּה fem. tightly entwined, entangled (of the branches of a tree).

עֲבֹת (pl. עֲבֹתִים and עֲבֹתוֹת) com. origin. that which is entwined; hence cord or hurdle-work, entwining of branches, from עָבַת; comp. סְבַךְ.

עָגַב (fut. יַעְגַּב) to love, to dote upon.

especially used of the unchaste love, construed with the accus. and עַל; עֹגֵב lover. Related to חָבַב, אָהַב.

עָגָב see עוּגָב.

עֶגֶב (only pl. עֲגָבִים) m. loveliness, pleasantness; hence שִׁיר עֲ׳ love-song.

עֲגָבָה (only with suff. עַגְבָתָהּ) f. love, only of the unchaste.

עֻגָה (also עֻגָה, pl. עֻגוֹת or עֻגּוֹת) f. a round cake, from עוּג to round, עֻגַת רְצָפִים a cake baked upon hot stone.

עָגוּר m. the shrieking (עָגוּר) bird, from עָגַר to shriek; according to some, the crane; according to others, the swallow.

עָגִיל (pl. —לִים) m. a hoop, a ring, especially of the ear-ring, from עָגַל.

עָגַל (not used) to turn round, to roll; related to גָּלַל; similar is חָלַל, קָלַל, and others.

עָגֹל adj. m. עֲגֻלָּה (pl. —לּוֹת) f. round, rounded.

עֵגֶל (with suff. עֶגְלְךָ, pl. עֲגָלִים, const. עֶגְלֵי) m. orig. that which is rolled together, a mass, a lump; but also like גֹּלֶם to which it is related; in embryo, transf. to the young of beasts, *pullus*, but used only for a calf; עֵ׳ מַרְבֵּק fattened calf, עֵ׳ מַסֵּכָה molten calf. Nations were called figuratively calves, as the princes were called bulls.

עֶגְלָה f. 1) a calf, עֶ׳ מְלֻמָּדָה a heifer that is taught, trained; עֶ׳ שְׁלִשִׁיָּה, עֶ׳ מְשֻׁלֶּשֶׁת a calf three years old; 2) p.n. f.

עֲגָלָה (from עָגַל to roll, with suff. עֶגְלָתוֹ, pl. עֲגָלוֹת, const. עֶגְלוֹת) f. a waggon, for driving and carrying; but also, chariot of war and threshing cart.

עֶגְלוֹן 1) p.n. m.; 2) p.n. of a city in Judah.

עָגַם origin. to sigh, to moan; next, to be sad; related to אָגַם, נָמָה. Particip. עָגֵם, pl. const. עֲגֻמֵי, for which stands אַגְמֵי.

עָגַן (Kal, not used) to enclose, to surround; the root is עָ־גַן, related to גָּנַן. Niph. to shut oneself up for (לְ) some one, i.e. a woman secluding herself in expectation of being married to a certain man, Author. Vers. "stay for them for having husbands."

עָגַר (not used) to cry, related to נָשַׁר and קָרָא; according to others (Gesenius, etc.), equiv. to עָגַל to roll, to turn round.

עַד (joined with the copulative וְ, וָעֶד) masc. 1) orig. the veiled, hidden time; next, eternity; a similar mode of transferring the sense is found in עוֹלָם, חֶלֶד; the root is either עֲדָה, equiv. to עָטָה, or עָדַד in the same sense; לָעַד equiv. to לְעוֹלָם for ever, עֲדֵי עַד unto eternity; more emphatic, לְעוֹלָם וָעֶד for ever and ever; אֲבִי עַד eternal father; 2) booty, spoil, like מַלְקֹחַ that which is seized, from עָדָה = הָדָה, which see.

עַד (poetically עֲדֵי, with suff. עָדַי, עָדֶיךָ, עָדָיו, עֲדֵיכֶם, once עַד־הֵם for עֲדֵיהֶם) prepos. and conj.; 1) unto, *ad*, unto something (of space), to express direction to a certain end, e.g. עַד קְצֵה הָאָרֶץ to the end of the earth, עַד־הֲלֹם, עַד הֵנָּה till here, hither; עַד is sometimes joined with מִן in double sentences, as, מִן עַד־וְעַד, מִן וְעַד, מִן עַד; more emphatic is עַד לְ, עַד אֶל; in this sense many verbs are construed with עַד to express partly the direction towards an end, partly the arrival at, and attaining of, the end, e.g. בּוֹא עַד to arrive at a place, נָגַע עַד to touch some one, הִתְבּוֹנֵן עַד to consider something, הֶאֱזִין עַד to hearken to something; 2) direction to an end, including the idea of gradation, e.g. עַד(לְ)מְאֹד very much, עַד־מְהֵרָה very hurriedly, עַד־לְמַעְלָה to the highest point, very high; עַד in this sense does not, however, signify the highest point, but often only a gradation, e.g. עַד־כַּמֶּה פְעָמִים how many times, עַד הַגֶּפֶן even the vine; sometimes it is used for comparison, e.g. עַד סִירִים like briars; 3) direction in reference to time; as, עַד הַבֹּקֶר until the morning; hence its frequent use to form adverbs, e.g. עַד־בְּלִי, עַד־כֹּה, עַד־מָתַי, etc. As a conj. עַד is used: 1) in reference to time, till, *donec*, complete עַד אֲשֶׁר, עַד־שֶׁ; עַד כִּי till that, עַד אִם till when, עַד־אֲשֶׁר־אִם till that when, connected with the pret. and fut.; 2) till that, so that; to denote the degree, where עַד stands for עַד אֲשֶׁר, e.g. "so that he shall acccomplish, like an hireling, his days" (Job 14:6), "so that thou didst not lay these things to thy heart" (Is. 47:7); 3) whilst, for עַד אֲשֶׁר, עַד שֶׁ, so long as, and as a negation עַד־לֹא for עַד אֲשֶׁר לֹא. As to the etymology, עַד cannot be derived from a verbal root, but is probably an original pronominal root.

עַד (Aram.) as in the Heb.; hence, as a prep. of space and time; עַד כְּעַן until now, עַד דִּבְרַת דִּי for the purpose that. As a conj. עַד דִּי whilst that, till that; עַד אָחֳרֵין till at last.

עֹד see עוֹד.

I. עֵד (pl. עֵדִים) masc. 1) a witness (from עוּד), origin. confirmer; also fig. supporter, sustainer; 2) abst. evidence, equiv. to עֵדוּת; עָנָה עֵד בְּ to give evidence against some one.

II. עֵד (thus is the sing. in the Talm., pl. עִדִּים) m. monthly time (of women), hence בֶּגֶד עִדִּים.

עָדַד (not used) to number, to count, to reckon (comp. מָנָה, סָפַר, כָּסַס, כָּסָא); transf. to appoint (comp. יָעַד). The Pi. עוֹדֵד belongs to עוּד, which see.

I. עָדָה (fut. יַעְדֶּה, apoc. יַעַד) equiv. to עָטָה to wrap, to wrap up, to cover, syn. with לָבַשׁ; fig. to clothe or adorn oneself with something (acc.), e.g. with majesty, with glory; next generally, to adorn. Hiph. 1) to adorn some one with something (double accus.); 2) privative, to put off the garment, if it does not belong to עָדָה II.

II. עָדָה equiv. to עָטָה II., to pass along something (=עָבַר), over (עַל) something. Hiph. to pull off, to take off, equiv. to הֶעֱבִיר to put off בֶּגֶד a garment. See עָדָה I.

III. עָדָה (not used) equiv. to הָרָה to seize, to lay hold of; from which the derivative עַד booty.

עֲדָה (fut. יֶעְדֵּא) Aram. equiv. to עָדָה II. in Heb., to pass by (בְּ) something, to pass away from (מִן) something; figur. like עֲבַר to pass away, to depart, of a law, of a kingdom. Af. to cause to pass away, to remove (kings).

עָדָה p.n. f. (ornament, beauty, or the ornamented one).

עִדָּה belongs to עִדִּים. See עֵד.

I. עֵדָה (const. עֲדַת, formed from יָעַד, comp. (שָׁנָה) f. an assembly, a congregation, especially of Israel, but also the members of a family, or house; also, host or mob that join for a certain purpose; figur. swarm (of bees). See יָעַד.

II. עֵדָה (from עוּד, pl. עֵדוֹת) fem. formed from the m. עֵד; hence, female witness, transf. like עֵד, to evidence, confirmation of a covenant, or precept, law, decree. Comp. עֵדוּת.

עִדּוֹ p.n. m. (one born on a festival).

עִדּוֹא p.n. m. (the same).

עֵדוּת (pl. עֵדְוֹת after an Aramaic declension) fem. that which is appointed, fixed testimony; hence parallel with מִשְׁפָּט, חֹק, תּוֹרָה law, statute, judgment; next, that which is revealed, songs of revelation, אֹהֶל הָעֵ׳ tabernacle of the testimony, אֲרוֹן הָעֵ׳ ark of the testimony, לֻחוֹת הָעֵ׳ tablets of the law, testimony, etc.

עֲדִי (in pause עֲדִי, with suff. עֶדְיִי,

plur. (עֲדָיִים) m. 1) an ornament (from עָדָה I.), עֲ זָהָב a golden ornament, עֲדִי עֲדָיִים the highest ornament; 2) the noblest; hence equiv. to כָּבוֹד, and like כָּבוֹד, poet. for heart, soul (Ps. 103:5).

עֲדִיאֵל p.n. m. (ornament from God).

עֲדָיָה p.n. m. (the same).

עֲדָיָהוּ p.n. m. (the same).

עָדִין adj. m. עֲדִינָה, f. 1) tender, soft, delicate, given to pleasure, sensual; 2) p.n.m. the pampered one.

עֲדִינָא p.n. masc. (the sensual one) name of one of the chiefs of king David's army.

עֲדִינוֹ (for עֲדִינוֹן) like עֲדִינָא p.n.m. of one of the chiefs of king David's army, with the surname הָעֶצְנִי, i.e. from the family called עֵצֶן.

עֲדִיתַיִם (double ornament) p.n. of a city in Judah.

עָדַל (not used) to be just, to be noble, after the Arab.

עַדְלַי p.n. m. (the just one).

עֲדֻלָּם (contracted from עָדַל עַם) p.n. of a city in Judah; gent עֲדֻלָּמִי.

עָדַן (Kal, not used) origin. to live well, to refresh oneself; next, to be tender, delicate. Hith. הִתְעַדֵּן to delight, enjoy oneself; עֵדֶן is probably related with the root in עָדַן.

עֵדֶן (pl. עֲדָנִים) m. 1) joy, delight; 2) p.n. of a country where the garden (or paradise) of the first man was situated; hence גַּן עֵ, עֲצֵי־, etc. Root עָדַן.

עֵדֶן (pleasant country) 1) p.n. of a place in Mesopotamia; 2) complete בֵּית עֵדֶן, which see under בַּיִת.

עֲדֶן (contracted from עַד הֵן) a particle, until here, hitherto.

עִדָּן (pl. עִדָּנִין, def. עִדָּנַיָּא) Aram. m. time, in prophetic speech, a year; comp. מוֹעֵד and יָמִים. The root is עֲדַד.

עַדְנָא p.n. m. (joy, delight).

עַדְנָה p.n. m. (the same).

עֶדְנָה f. sensuality, pleasure of procreation.

עֲדֶנָּה (compounded from עַד־הֵנָּה) a particle, until here, hither.

עַדְעָדָה (border) p.n. of a city in Judah.

עָדַף 1) to overspread, overstrain, to overhang, origin. to overflow, related to טָפָא, especially of the overhanging of a curtain; 2) to remain over. Hiph. to leave over.

עָדַר (Kal, not used) to leave off, to leave out, to leave behind, to go away; hence, Niph. נֶעְדַּר to be left behind, to be missing, or to be wanting. Pi. עִדֵּר to cause to fail.

I. עָדַר equiv. to סָדַר, to order, regulate, arrange, עָ מַעֲרָכָה to array a battle.

II. עָדַר (Kal, not used) to cut in, to engrave. Niph. נֶעְדַּר to be dug, ploughed.

עֵדֶר (with suff. עֶדְרוֹ, pl. עֲדָרִים) m. 1) herd, flock, origin. a row; hence, figur. עֵדֶר י״י flock of the Lord (Israel); 2) p. n. of a city in Judah; 3) p. n. m.

עֶדֶר p. n. m. (herd).

עַדְרִיאֵל p. n. m. (flock of God).

עָדַשׁ (not used) to be round.

עֲדָשָׁה (pl. —שִׁים) f. lentil.

עַוָּא see עִוָּה.

עוּב (Kal, not used) 1) to veil, to cover, equiv. to כָּפָה, חָפָא, חָבָא; from which Hiph. הֵעִיב to wrap in darkness, to darken; 2) equiv. to עָבָה to be thick, stout.

עוּב (only pl. עֻבִּים) m. a kind of door-post or entablature, origin. that which covers over.

עוֹבָל p. n. of a district in Arabia, also the name of a people there.

עוּג (not used) equiv. to חוּג to round, to encircle; the form עוּג used is denom. from עוּגָה II.

עוֹג p. n. m. (from עֲנָק=עֹנֶג a giant).

עוּגָב (also עֻגָב) m. a flute, so called from its delightful tone.

עוּד (fut. יָעוּד in the Ketib) 1) equiv. to אוּד to turn, to encircle; Pi. עִוֵּד to enclose, surround; 2) transf. like all verbs signifying encircling, to be firm, strong (comp. חוּל). Pi. עִוֵּד to encompass (comp. חָזַק). Hiph. הֵעִיד (fut. יָעִיד) to confirm, to affirm, to corroborate, to attest, to declare; next generally, to bear witness, to give evidence (בְּ) against some one, to give evidence in favor of some one, to praise, also, to declare to some one; also, to resolve, to order, to prescribe, to admonish (with עַל, בְּ, and acc.), to warn, etc. Hoph. הוּעַד to be attested, appointed, warned. Po. עוֹדֵד to confirm, to erect. Hith. to prove strong, firm, i. e. to maintain its existence.

עוֹד (after the form קוֹל, with suffix עוֹדְךָ, עוֹדִי) m. origin. strength, power; hence, transf. to time, duration, space of time, but only as an adv., continually or repeatedly, again, once more, always anew, further, yet; אֵין עוֹד no more, none further, כָּל עוֹד only so long yet, עוֹדֶנִּי I am yet, עוֹדֶנָּה she is yet, עוֹד הֵם for עוֹדָם: joined with prefixes עוֹד has several significations; as, בְּעוֹד whilst (it is) yet, in contrast to בְּטֶרֶם; hence, בְּעוֹדִי whilst I am, i. e. so long as I exist, מֵעוֹד since, מֵעוֹדִי since my being, existence.

עוֹדֵד p. n. m. (establisher).

עָוָה to bend, to pervert (the walk, the way); hence, to act perversely, to sin against (עַל) some one. Niph. נַעֲוָה to be crooked (morally perverse), or to be bowed down (with anguish or pain), part. נַעֲוֵה־לֵב of a crooked or perverse mind, נַעֲוַת הַמַּרְדּוּת perverse, rebellious woman. Pi. to overthrow the face of the earth, i.e. to devastate it; to upset the path, i.e. to destroy it. Hiph. הֶעֱוָה to overthrow, to pervert (the walk, the way, the conduct), i.e. to act wickedly, perversely; related is חָוָה III.

עַוָּא and עִוָּא (destruction) p. n. of a city, from whence Assyrian colonists were sent to Samaria. The inhabitants were called עַוִּים, from a masc. form עַוָּה.

עַוָּה fem. destruction, heap of ruins, ruin, from עָוָה.

עוֹן see עָוֹן.

עוֹז see עֹז.

עוּז (Kal, not used) equiv. to חוּשׁ,עוּשׁ, to flee, to escape; according to some, לָעוֹז (Is.30:2) is in the Kal of this root, but מָעוֹז leads us to suppose that the root is עָזַז. Hiph. הֵעִיז (equiv. to הִבְרִיחַ, הֵנִיס) to afford a refuge, to lead into safety; hence, to gather.

עוּט (not used) to pierce, to etch, to engrave, similar to אוּת, etc.: from which עַט, עֵיט.

עַוִּי (pl. עַוִּים) gent. m. from עַוָּה.

עַוְיָא (עֲוָיָא, plur. with suff. עֲוָיָתָךְ) Aram. fem. perverseness, crookedness.

עֲוִיל (only pl. עֲוִילִים) masc. equiv. to עוּל, a suckling, a child; next, a youth. The form is lengthened from עוּל.

עֲוִיל m. the pervert one, the unjust one, from עָוַל.

עַוִּים (generally with the article, ruins) p. n. of a place in Benjamin.

עֲוִית (ruin) p. n. of a city in Edom.

עָוַל (Kal, not used) equiv. to אָוַל to be sluggish, transf. like אֱוִל, to be sinful, wicked (comp. סָכַל and כָּסַל). Pi. עִוֵּל to act unjustly, sinfully, wickedly.

עַוָּל m. the unjust one, wicked, fool.

עָוֶל (an old form for עָוֶל, const. עֶוֶל, with suffix עַוְלוֹ) m. injustice, dishonesty, wickedness.

עוּל (only particip. fem. pl. עָלוֹת) to suckle, but also to suck, used of beasts, עָלוֹת the young ones, פָּרוֹת עָלוֹת young heifers. Pi. עִלַּע (for עִלְעֵל) to drink, to sip.

עוּל m. a suckling, a child, complete עוּל יָמִים young in days.

עַוְלָה (or contracted עוֹלָה, pl. עוֹלוֹת) fem., formed from עָוֶל, injustice, iniquity, בְּנֵי עַ׳ the unjust, the wicked; with ה finis, עַוְלָתָה and עֹלָתָה.

עוֹלָה f. an offering. See עֹלָה.

עֹלֵל (pl. עֹלָלִים, from מְעוֹלֵל, as עוֹדֵר is from מְעוֹדֵר) m. a child, a youth, equiv. to עוּל; עול is also the root. See מְעוֹלֵל.

עוֹלֵל (pl. עוֹלָלִים) m. the same.

עוֹלֵלוֹת see עֹלֵלוֹת.

עוֹלָם (pl. עוֹלָמִים) m. 1) that which is hidden, veiled, the distant time; hence, fig. eternity, time of yore, unlimited futurity; also as an adv., always, ever, eternally; pl. עוֹלָמִים eternities, and as an adv. eternally; 2) in modern Hebrew, world, universe, origin. eternity. See עֵילוֹם.

I. עוּן (not used) to dwell, abide, related to חָנָה. Hiph. (according to some) to dwell; hence מַעְיָנַי (Ps. 87:7), for which they read מְעִינַי the dwellers. (Author. Vers. "my springs.")

II. עוּן (not used) to flow, to spring forth, from which עַיִן; the verb עָיַן is a denom. from עַיִן.

עוֹן see עַיִן.

עָוֺן (from עָוָה, seldom עָווֹן, const. עֲוֹן, pl. עֲוֹנִים and עֲוֹנוֹת) m. perverseness; transf. to sin, guilt, crime, iniquity; also, the punishment of crime, i.e. calamity, unhappiness; עֲוֹן קֵץ iniquity leading to an untimely end (Auth. Ver. "the iniquity has an end"); עֲ׳ חֶרֶב iniquity leading to the sword (Auth. Ver. "the punishment of the sword"); עֲ׳ פְּלִילִים an iniquity to be punished by the judges: שְׁתֵּי עֹוֹנֹתָם, Hosea 10:10, (Keri) their two iniquities, i. e. the two golden calves.

עוֹנָה fem. cohabitation, from עוּן I.; some explain it according to the Talmud, time, period, then as a euphemism, cohabitation.

עִוְעָה (only pl. עִוְעִים for עִוְעֲיִם) m. perverseness, from עָוָה.

עוּף (fut. יָעוּף, apoc. יָעֹף, יָעַף, יָעֶף) 1) to fly, of birds; fig. the darting of an arrow, of an army, of a fleet; also, of the transientness of a dream; 2) to cover, to veil, to wrap in darkness and obscurity; 3) equiv. to יָעֵף, עָיֵף, to be fatigued, to faint, similar to the mode of transferring the sense in עָלַף, עָטַף. Pi. עוֹפֵף 1) to fly repeatedly; 2) to cause something to fly, to brandish (the sword). Hiph. (only Keri) to cause to fly. Hith. to fly away, to vanish (the glory).

עוֹף (without pl.) m. origin. a wing, i.e. the limb of flying, but generally, collective, winged animals, equiv. to בַּעַל כָּנָף, fowl, bird.

עוֹף m. (Aram.) the same.

I. עוּץ (only imp. עֻצוּ) equiv. to יָעַץ to advise, to counsel. See יָעַץ.

II. עוּץ (not used) to penetrate, to

impress, especially in soft ground; from which עוּץ p.n.

עוּץ soft, fruitful soil; 1) p.n. of a people and country that belonged to Aram; 2) p.n. of a people and country in Edom.

עוּק (Kal, not used) equiv. to צוּק, to be pressed, oppressed. Hiph. הֵעִיק to oppress, to press hard; הֵעִ֫יק תַּחַת to press down (Author. Vers. "to be pressed under").

I. עוּר (Kal, not used) equiv. to כּוּר, קוּר, חוּר, to bore, to hollow out, to excavate. Pi. עִוֵּר (comp. עוּד, Pi. עִוֵּד) to put out the eyes (comp. נִקֵּר), to blind; transf. in a moral sense; from which מְעָרָה, עִוֵּר, עִוָּרוֹן, עַוֶּרֶת.

II. עוּר (not used) equiv. to כָּרָה, כּוּר (from which קִרְיָה) to surround, to enclose, to encompass, from which עִיר an enclosed place, a town, city.

III. עוּר (fut. יָעוּר in the Keri, particip. עֵר) m. 1) to be awake, stirring, contrast to יָשֵׁן; next generally, to watch, hence עֵר watcher; עֵר וְעֹנֶה watcher and replier (Auth. Ver. "the master and the scholar?"); proverbial expression for every living one, originating from the watch in the temple, where one called out and another answered; 2) to wake up, to stir up (from sleep). Niph. נֵעוֹר (fut. יֵעוֹר) 1) passive from Hiph., to be awoke, stirred up; 2) reflective, to awake oneself, to rouse oneself, to stir up, of a nation, of God, etc. Pi. עוֹרֵר 1) to awake (from sleep), to stir up, to incite against some one, to stir up tranquil palaces (Auth. Ver. "to set up palaces"); 2) to lift up, to swing, e.g. a spear, a scourge. Hiph. like Pi. to awake, to stir, to set in motion, to urge, to keep watch over (עַל) something. Hith. הִתְעוֹרֵר to rouse oneself, to set oneself in motion against (עַל) some one; also, to jump, to spring with joy. Another Pi. form is עִרְעֵר, which is sometimes abbreviated in עוֹעֵר; it signifies, to urge, to incite, to excite. Hithp. הִתְעַרְעֵר to be utterly broken. Comp. עוּר IV.

IV. עוּר (Kal, not used) to be bare, naked, comp. עָרָה and עָרַע; hence Niph. נֵעוֹר (fut. יֵעוֹר) to be uncovered (of the bow); Author. Ver. "I shook my lap," Neh. 5:13. Pi. עוֹרֵר to destroy, to lay bare, to lay in ruins; the same sense has, according to some, the reduplicate form עִרְעֵר, and the Hithp. הִתְעַרְעֵר. See עוּר III.

V. עוּר equiv. to צוּר, to straighten, to harass; hence, particip. עָר

an enemy. Comp. צַר, and עַיִר, anguish.

עוּר (Aram.) m. chaff, origin. husk; related to עוֹר, which see.

עוֹר (with suff. עוֹרוֹ, pl. עוֹרוֹת) masc. skin, covering (of the body); hence also, leather, next especially the skin; עוֹר שִׁנָּיִם the flesh which covers the teeth, the gums; עוֹר בְּעַד עוֹר skin for skin, i.e. life for life; transf. to life, body. The root is עוּר, in the sense of, to enwrap, to enclose, for which there are several analogies in the language.

עִוָּרוֹן masc. blindness, formed from עִוֵּר. See עור 1.

עֲוָרִים Ketib, for the Keri עֲיָרִים, which see.

עַוֶּרֶת f. blindness.

I. עוּשׁ equiv. to חוּשׁ, to hasten.

II. עוּשׁ (not used) belongs to עַיִשׁ, עָשׁ, which see.

עָוַת (Kal, not used) to be crooked, bent; related to עָבַת, עָבַט. Pi. עִוֵּת to bend, to pervert, e.g. of the perverting of justice, of the perverting of the road, i.e. to lead astray; next, generally, to falsify something. Pu. only particip. מְעֻוָּת that which is crooked, bad. Hith. to bend, to bow oneself.

עוּת (only inf. with ל, לָעוּת) equiv. to עוּשׁ to hasten (for the purpose of assisting); next, generally, to support, to assist, with double acc.; from which עוּתַי, which see.

עַוָּתָה (after the form כַּפָּרָה) f. tribulation, oppression; origin. erring about; comp. עַוַּת דֶּרֶךְ.

עוּתַי p. n. m. (supporter).

עַז (pause עָז, pl. עַזִּים, from עָזַז) adj. m. עַזָּה (pl. עַזּוֹת) fem. strong (of man), firm (of things); solid, vigorous; transf. to hard, cruel, barefaced, bold, audacious, insolent. As a subst. עַז strength, power; the pl. עַזּוֹת audacity, insolence.

עֵז (pl. עִזִּים) f. a goat, גְּדִי עִזִּים a kid of the goat. The pl. is used of the hair of goats. The root is not עָנַז, but עָזַז.

עֵז (pl. עִזִּין) Aram. the same.

עֹז (rarely עוֹז, before makkaph עָז, with suff. עֻזִּי, עָזִּי, and עוּזִּי) m. 1) strength, power, of living things; but also, firmness, strength, of a castle, tower, mountain; 2) the consequence of strength, victory; hence also, glory, majesty, magnificence; thus of the glory and majesty of God, equiv. to כְּבוֹד יי׳, and in this sense כְּלֵי עֹז, to denote instruments serving to the glory of God; 3) hardness (in a moral sense), obduracy; hence עֹז פָּנִים insolence, overbearing. See עָזַז.

עֻזָּא p.n. m. (strength, power).

עֲזָאזֵל masc. according to Rashi and Saadiah, name of a huge high mountain-ridge, contracted from עָזַז אֵל; according to Kimchi, the goat which was sent away as an atonement שְׂעִיר הַמִּשְׁתַּלֵּחַ, thus composed from עֵז אָזַל; according to Aben Ezra, it is the name of a demon, to appease whom an offering was sent—this explanation is confirmed in Pirke Rabbi Eliezer (Section 46) and in the Book of Enoch; according to this rendering, it is composed from עֲזָז אֵל insolence towards God.

I. **עָזַב** (fut. יַעֲזֹב) 1) to leave, to loosen (something bound, e.g. a girdle); hence עָזֹב תַּעֲזֹב עִמּוֹ thou shalt untie, or release (the ass) with him (the owner), i.e. thou shalt help him to untie; עָזוּב that which is loosened, released, free, in contrast to עָצוּר a slave; עָ׳ שִׂיחַ to give free course, vent, to lamenting; 2) to bequeath (something for somebody), to leave behind, to leave something to some one; construed with עַל, לְ, אֶל; עֲזוּבָה desolation, orig. abandonment; 3) to cease from, to forbear (from anger, or from some action). Niph. to be forsaken, abandoned, נֶעֱזַב לְ to be abandoned to some one. Pu. עֻזַּב to be forsaken. The original signification is to sever the bonds (related to חָצַב) to loosen, synon. with פָּתַח.

II. **עָזַב** (fut. יַעֲזֹב) to tie, to bind; related to קָזַב in the same original sense; figur. of the breaches in the wall, like חוּם; hence וַיַּעַזְבוּ Neh. 3:8, "they repaired" or "fortified;" in this sense, according to some עֻזָּב Jer. 49:25. From עָזַב II. is to be derived:—

עִזָּבוֹן (only pl. עִזְבוֹנִים with suff.) m. 1) exchange, barter, traffic, from עָזַב II., comp. מַעֲרָב from עָרַב; 2) place for carrying on such traffic, emporium; 3) that which is acquired by trafficking, wares (comp. סַחַר).

עַזְבּוּק p.n. m. (strong in devastation).

עַזְגָּד p.n. m. (strong in fortune).

עָזָה (not used) to comfort, from which the pr. names מַעַזְיָה, יַעֲזִיָּה, יַעֲזִיאֵל.

עַזָּה (the fortress) p.n. of a city on the south border of Palestine, Gaza, gent. עַזָּתִי.

עֲזוּבָה p.n. f. (the forsaken one). In the signification of desolation, see עָזַב I.

עִזּוּז adj. m. strong, mighty, of God; subst. the strong one, hero, from עָזַז.

עֱזוּז m. might, strength.

עַזּוּר see עַזֻּר.

עָזַז inf. const. עֱזוֹז and עֹז, עוֹז; imp.

עֹזְּזָה, fut. יָעֹז, apoc. (יָעֹז) to be or become strong, firm, e. g. to strengthen themselves in the strength of Pharaoh (Isa. 30:2); "when he strengthened the fountains of the deep" (Prov. 8:28); figur. mighty, barefaced, insolent, audacious; or in a good sense, to become bold, courageous, victorious, with עַל, over something; to rule mightily. Niph. נֶעֱז (only particip. נוֹעָז from נֶעֱז) to be insolent; comp. Hiph. הֵעֵז to harden (the countenance), i.e. to act audaciously, הֵעֵז בְּפָנִים to be insolent against some one.

עָזָן p. n. m. (the powerful one).

עֻזִּיָּהוּ p.n. m. (strong through God).

עֻזִּי p.n. m. (the mighty one).

עֲזִיאֵל p.n. masc. comforted through God). See יַעֲזִיאֵל.

עֻזִּיאֵל p. n. m. (God is the mighty one), patron. עָזִּיאֵלִי.

עֻזִּיָּה p. n. m. (the same).

עֻזִּיָּהוּ p.n. m. (the same).

עֲזִיזָא p.n. m. (the strong one).

עָזַל (not used; from which, according to some, (עֲזָאזֵל) related is אָזַל, only in the active signification, to remove. The root is not known in Hebrew.

עַזְמָוֶת p.n. m. (courageous in death).

עָזַן (equiv. to אָזַן) to be sharp, of the sight. From which:—

עָזְנִיָּה f. a species of eagle (from (עָזַן); Author. Vers. "osprey," so called from its sharp sight, if עָזְנִיָּה is not derived from עָזִיָּה, and the name from עָזַז, to be strong (comp. the Aram. (עָזְיָא).

עָזַק (Kal, not used) to dig, to cut in the ground; hence, Pi. עִזֵּק to dig round, to make arable (a field), to cultivate (a vineyard).

עִזְקָא (with suff. (עִזְקְתֵהּ) Aram. f. a seal-ring, a signet, from עֲזַק to engrave; compare טַבַּעַת, from טָבַע.

עֲזֵקָה (novale) p.n. of a city in Judah.

עָזַר (fut. יַעֲזֹר, pl. (יַעְזְרוּ) origin. to enclose, as indicated by the relative roots עָצַר and אָזַר, and by the noun עֲזָרָה; next transf. to protect (comp. (סָכַךְ, גָּנַן), to help, to support; עָזַר עִם to assist; עָזַר אַחֲרֵי to follow in support, with לְ of the subject, to help to something; עֹזֵר supporter, friend; hence עֹזְרֵי מִלְחָמָה comrades of war; עָזֻר the protected one. Niph. to be supported (by some one); נֶעְזַר עַל to be supported against some one. Hiph. (particip. pl. מַעְזְרִים, inf. (לַעְזִיר) to help, to support.

עֵזֶר (with suff. (עֶזְרִי) m. 1) help, support; הָיָה עֵ׳ מִן to help some one from another. Concr. helper, supporter, applied also to a wife, helpmate; 2) p.n. (help).

עֵ p.n. m. (help).

עֵ p.n. m. (helper, supporter).

עֶזְרָ p.n. m. (help) the well-known name of the priest, who, 458 years before the Christian era, led a colony of Jews from exile to Jerusalem.

עֶזְרָא p.n. m. (the help of God).

עֶזְרָה f. 1) help; 2) p.n. masc., for which also עֵזֶר.

עֲזָרָה fem. enclosed place, syn. with חָצֵר in its origin, court in the Temple.

עֶזְרִי p.n. m. (one who affords help).

עַזְרִיאֵל p.n. m. (the help of God), comp. עֲזְרוּבַעַל in the Punic.

עֲזַרְיָה p.n. m. (the same).

עֲזַרְיָהוּ p.n. m. (the same).

עַזְרִיקָם p.n. m. (help is at hand).

עֶזְרָתָ fem. help; the form is like זִמְרָת, and only poetically for עֶזְרָה.

עֵט m. pencil, origin. that which engraves, etches; עֵט סוֹפֵר the pen of a writer. See עוּט.

עֵטָא (Aram.) f. equiv. to עֵצָה Heb. advice, counsel, understanding, from יְעַט=יָעַץ.

. עָטָה (fut. יַעְטֶה) 1) to cover, to veil, to wrap up (over עַל) something; thus as a trans. verb; 2) to cover oneself, to clothe oneself, i. e. to put on something, with the accus.; 3) to wrap up, to roll up, to put round (to overturn a country) like a mantle; also reflective, to wrap oneself up, i.e. to shrink, to pine away (comp. עָלַף, עָטַף), to hide the beard, i.e. to mourn; particip. f. עֹטְיָה she who wraps a mantle round her, i.e. the shepherdess; comp. כַּאֲשֶׁר יַעְטֶה הָרֹעֶה אֶת־בִּגְדוֹ Jer. 43:12. Hiph. הֶעֱטָה to cover, with double accus. or עַל of the subject; יַעְטֶה מוֹרֶה, Ps. 84:7, belongs to Kal; מְעֻטָּה Ezekiel 21:20, belongs to Pu. The form יַעְטֵנִי is a mixed one, from the pret. and fut. of Kal.

II. עָטָה (Kal, not used) to rush upon something, a secondary form from עָדָה. Hiph. הֶעֱטָה (fut. יַעַט) to fly upon (אֶל) something; to attack, with בְּ.

עָטִין (only pl. עֲטִינִים) m. an artery, sinew, tendon, nerve; עֲטִינָיו מָלְאוּ חָלָב his nerves are full of milk, i.e. sap, marrow (Author. Vers. "his breasts"). The root is עָטַן.

עֲטִישָׁה f. sneezing, from עָטַשׁ.

עֲטַלֵּף m. according to Eben Ezra, a bat; the root appears to belong to טָלַף.

עָטַן (not used) equiv. to אָטַן to tie, to knot, from which עָטִין artery, sinew, nerve, like גִּיד from גּוּד,

עֲטָרוֹת בֵּית יוֹאָב p. n. of a city in Judah.

עַטְרוֹת שׁוֹפָן p.n. of a city in Gad.

עָטַשׁ (not used) to sneeze, probably related to נָטַשׁ to strew, scatter, from which עֲטִישָׁה.

עַי (heap, ruin) p. n. of a city on the east of Beth-El.

עִי (pl. עִיִּין and עִיִּים) m. a heap, a ruin. In proper names, the sense of heap is often transferred to hill (comp. עִיבַעַל hill of Baal, p.n. of a town; Punic). The same sense appears to predominate in עִיֵּי הָעֲבָרִים hill of Abarim.

עַיָּא p.n. of a city in Benjamin, probably identical with עַי.

עִיב see עוּב.

עֵיבָל (unfruitful) p.n. of a mountain point in the territory of Ephraim.

עַיָּה p. n. identical with עַי.

עִיּוֹן (ruin) p. n. of a city in Naphtali.

עַיּוּת Ketib for עַוִּית, which see.

עִיט see עוּט and עָטָה.

עַיִט (after the form בַּיִת) m. bird of prey, and in a collective sense, birds of prey, figur. the surname of Cyrus, on account of his rapidity as a conqueror and a destroyer.

עֵיטָם (haunt of beasts of prey) p. n. of a city in Judah.

עִיִּים see עִי.

עֵילוֹם m. equiv. to עוֹלָם eternity.

to tie, bind, and מֵיתָר, from יָתַר, in the same signification.

עָטַף (fut. יַעֲטֹף and יַעְטֹף) 1) to cover, to clothe, to wrap up, from טוּף=עָ־טַף; 2) intrans. to be covered, clothed, e.g. the pastures are clothed with flocks, Psalm 65:13; next, to be veiled, hidden; יַעְטֹף יָמִין he hides himon the right, i.e. in the south; 3) like עָטָה to languish, to pine away, especially with לֵב; next generally, to be weak, feeble; עָטוּף languishing; עֲטוּפִים the feeble sheep. Niph. (only inf. with ב) בֵּעָטֵף to pine away. Hiph. to cast feeble lambs (used of sheep). Hith. to pine away; הִתְעַטְּפָה נֶפֶשׁ בְּ the soul pines away in some one. In the same sense is בְּהִתְעַטֵּף עָלַי רוּחִי.

עָטַר equiv. to אָטַר, כָּתַר, כָּדַר, to surround, encircle, either in a hostile sense, or to protect. Pi. to crown, to wreathe, with double accus. or with dative of the person. Hiph. to crown, to distribute crowns.

עֲטָרָה (const. עֲטֶרֶת, pl. עֲטָרוֹת) f. a crown, a wreath, transf. to an ornament, a diadem; 2) p.n. fem. (ornament).

עֲטָרוֹת (circles, circus) p. n. of a city in Gad.

עַטְרוֹת אַדָּר p.n. of a city in Ephraim.

עִילַי p. n. m. (chief, =עִלִּי).

עֵילָם p. n. of a province in the kingdom of Persia, the later Kusistan, Koordistan.

עָיֵם m. only in connection with בַּעְיָם רוּחוֹ, it signifies violence, might, from אַיֵם=עָיֵם, if the reading is not בְּעֹצֶם.

עין as the root to עַיִן, see עוּן II.

עַיִן (const. עֵין, with suff. עֵינִי, dual עֵינַיִם, const. עֵינֵי; in the second signification plur. עֵינוֹת, const. עֵינוֹת) f. 1) eye, as the fountain from whence tears flow, and as the organ of sight; in the following forms עַיִן is used figuratively, in עֵינַיִם רָמוֹת high, proud looks, i.e. pride, in contrast to שַׁח עֵינַיִם downcast looks, i. e. modesty: to enlighten the eyes, i.e. to cheer; of clean eyes, i.e. to turn away from evil; an evil eye, i.e. envy; גְּלוּי עֵינַיִם of open eyes, i.e. seeing visions. Many verbs are construed with לְעֵינֵי, מֵעֵינֵי, בְּעֵינֵי פ׳, to express in the presence of, before: שׂוּם עַיִן עַל to direct the eye upon some one, either for good or for evil, sometimes the verb is omitted. עַיִן is transf. to signify, (*a*) face, countenance, the eye being considered the seat of expression of the whole countenance; (*b*) seer, prophet, as being the eye of the people; (*c*) the visible part of an object, surface, e.g. עֵין הָאָרֶץ, or appearance, figure; 2) well, fountain, spring, עֵין מַיִם spring of water, עַיְנָה unto the well: in this sense the pl. עֵינוֹת, const. עֵינוֹת, to distinguish also signification 1 and 2 in the form (comp. יָדוֹת from יָד). Many names of cities are formed with עֵין, on account of being situated near wells, some with עַיִן only; as, 1) p. n. of a city in Simeon; 2) in northern Palestine. Compounds are, עֵין גֶּדִי (well of kids) p. n. of a city in the desert of Judah, the former name of which was חַצְצוֹן־תָּמָר; עֵין־גַּנִּים (garden well) (*a*) p. n. of a city in Judah; (*b*) a Levitical city in Issachar; עֵין דֹּאר or עֵין דּוֹר (well of habitation) p. n. of a city in Manasseh; עֵין חַדָּה (rapid well) p. n. of a city in Issachar; עֵין חָצוֹר (grass well) p. n. of a city in Naphtali; עֵין חֲרוֹד (well of terror) p. n. of a city otherwise unknown; עֵין מִשְׁפָּט (well of judgment) p. n. for קָדֵשׁ; עֵין עֶגְלַיִם (well of the two calves) p. n. of a city north of the Dead Sea; עֵין שֶׁמֶשׁ (sun-well) p. n. of a town on the borders of Judah and Benjamin; עֵין is also used in the names of wells, e. g. עֵין רֹגֵל (fuller's well) p. n. of a w...

near Jerusalem; עֵין הַתַּנִּים (dragons' well) also near Jerusalem. From עַיִן is derived:—

עַיִן (denom.) origin. to look at, or upon, but only in an envious sense; hence poetically, עֹיֵן to eye, for which in Ketib עוֹיֵן from עָוַן from עוּן.

עַיִן (Aram.) the same as עַיִן in Heb.

עֹיֵן see עַיִן.

עֵינַיִם (double fountain) p. n. of a city in Judah.

עֵינָם p. n. (the same). The suff. ־ָם is the old dual form of termination.

עֵינָן p. n. masc. (abundant in wells). Comp. חֲצַר עֵינָן under חָצֵר.

עִיֵף equiv. to יָעֵף and עוּף to be weary, fatigued, faint.

עָיֵף (pl. עֲיֵפִים) adj. m., עֲיֵפָה fem. weary, fatigued, languishing (with hunger or thirst); אֶרֶץ עֲיֵפָה parched land; נֶפֶשׁ עֲיֵפָה one that languishes; עֲיֵפָה substantive, the wearied (cattle).

עֵיפָה (with ה finis עֵפָתָה) f. 1) thickness, density, darkness, from עוּף; 2) p. n. of a Midianite country, and also of the people inhabiting it; 3) p. n. m.; 4) p. n. f.

עֵיפַי p. n. masc. (the languishing, wearied one).

עַיִר (with suff. עִירֹה, pl. עֲיָרִים) m. a young ass, from עוּר=גּוּר (from which also the noun גּוּר) in the sense of suckling; עַ׳ פֶּרֶא young ass of the forest, a wild ass; עַיִר is also frequently used of the grown ass.

עִיר as a verb see עוּר in the five significations.

I. עִיר (a rare sing. עָר, pl. עָרִים from עָר, once עֲיָרִים) fem. 1) enclosed place, city, town; hence also, a fortified camp, a watch-tower, e.g. עִיר נְצוּרָה, עִיר מִבְצָר of the enclosed and fortified towers; Jerusalem is called עַ׳ אֱלֹהִים, עַ׳ הַקֹּדֶשׁ, עַ׳ י״י or also הָעִיר and עִיר. עִיר signifies sometimes the native city, as, עַ׳ נָחוֹר, עַ׳ סִיחוֹן, the birthplace of Sihon (i. e. Heshbon), of Nehor (Haran). עִיר also signifies a part of a city only, e.g. עִיר הַמַּיִם part of the town of Rabah; likewise עִיר דָּוִד; עִיר בֵּית הַבַּעַל of Zion; sometimes the inhabitants of a town, like אֶרֶץ the inhabitants of a country; 2) p. n. of towns in which עִיר forms part of the composition of the name, as עַ׳ הַמֶּלַח (salt city) p. n. of a town in Judah, near the Salt Sea; עִיר נָחָשׁ (serpent town) p. n. of a town otherwise unknown; עִיר שֶׁמֶשׁ (sun town) p. n. of a city in Dan; עַ׳ הַתְּמָרִים (palm city) name for Jericho; עִיר הַהֶרֶס see הֶרֶס; 3) p. n. for עִירִי.

II. עִיר masc. generally excitement of wrath, from עוּר III., to stir up, Hos. 7:4, 11:9, Ps. 73:20, in all these passages, however, עִיר may also be rendered city.

III. עִיר m. anguish, fear, equiv. to צִיר, from עוּר V.

עִיר (pl. עִירִין) Aram. m. watcher, as the name of an angel.

עִירָא p. n. m. (citizen).

עִירָד p. n. m. (courser).

עִירוּ (for עִירוֹן) p. n. m. (citizen).

עִירִי p.n. m. (the same). See עִיר.

עִירָם p.n. m. (the same).

עֵירֹם (עֵרֹם, pl. עֵירֻמִּים) masc. bareness, nakedness, in connection with עֶרְיָה. It is after the form מְתֹם, i.e. from עֵר with the termination ־ֹם; the same as עָרֹם from עֵר with the termination ־ֹם, and even מַעֲרֹם is only a secondary form from מָעוֹר. The מ׳ was, however, considered in all these forms as a radical.

עַיִשׁ m. name of a constellation; according to some, the Great Bear; according to others, *cupillæ*; Author. Vers. Arcturus; related to עָשׁ.

עַיָּת (heap of ruins, or hill) p.n. equiv. to עַי.

I. עָכַב (not used) equiv. to עָקַב, חָנַב to weave, to knot; related to which is קָוָה, from which קַו; from which עַכָּבִישׁ, which see.

II. עָכַב (not used) to gnaw, to bite; related is the root in נָקַף, חָף, and many others.

עַכְבּוֹר (the gnawing one) p.n. m.

עַכָּבִישׁ masc. spider, בֵּית ע׳ spider-house, cobweb, קוּרֵי ע׳ spider's web. The noun arose from עָכַב (spinner), with the ancient termination ־ִישׁ; as in חַלָּמִישׁ, which see.

עַכְבָּר (const. pl. עַכְבְּרֵי) m. origin. a gnawing insect, a mouse, from עָכַב II., with the termination ־ָר, like סְמָדַר, from סָמַד.

עַכּוֹ p.n. of a port town in Asher, and yet known by the name of Acca or Acre.

עָכוֹר (trouble, grief) p.n. of a valley not far from Jericho.

עָכַךְ (not used) to be hot, of a soil heated by the sun, after the Arabic; from which עַכּוֹ.

עָכַן (not used) equiv. to עָכַר to sadden, to trouble, from which יַעְכָּן, and:—

עָכָן (equiv. to עָכָר) p.n. m. (one who troubles).

עָכַס (not used) to bind, to fetter, from עָכַס; related is רָכַס, רָקַשׁ; next, in modern Heb. to roll up, to shrink together (of the serpent).

עֶכֶס (pl. עֲכָסִים) m. bonds of the feet, stocks; also, bracelets of silver, gold, ivory, which the women used to wear round the ancles; וּכְעֶכֶס אֶל־מוּסַר אֱוִיל, and as with the stocks (for וּכְבְעֶכֶס), i. e. slowly, the fool is led to instruction (Author. Vers. or as a fool goeth to the correction of the stocks); from which denom. עִכֵּס to make a tinkling with the feet (or with the chains on the feet.)

עַכְסָה p.n. f. (fettering).

עָכַר (fut. יַעְכֹּר) to trouble, to grieve, i.e. to plunge into misfortune, orig. to stir (the water), to provoke, comp. כְּרִי Aram. Niph. נֶעְכַּר to be roused (from pain), to be shaken up, to be rattled up; part. נֶעְכֶּרֶת distracted.

עָכָר p.n. m. the troubled one, or one who troubles.

עָכְרָן p.n. m. trouble, grief.

עָכַשׁ (not used) equiv. to עָכַס to wrap oneself up, to shrink together, of a serpent.

עַכְשׁוּב m. adder, serpent, probably from עָכַשׁ serpent, formed with the termination ־וּב; comp. שַׁעֲלַב.

עַל (עָל) m. 1) height; concrete, the High One, the Most High, i. e. God; לֹא־עָל the non-high, i.e. the low one, an idol; 2) adj. high, eminent, הֻקַּם עָל to be raised up on high; מֵעָל from above, above. The root is עָלָה.

עַל (from עָלָה, const. pl. עֲלֵי, and pl. with suff. עָלַי, עָלֶיךָ, etc.; it is possible, however, that the plural form is only in appearance, and that the *yod* originates in the ה being the third radical) 1) prep. upon, in the most extensive applications, which may be classified as follows: (*a*) on, upon, over, one subject being over or upon another, e.g. to sit upon a chair, to stand on the legs, to lie on the bed, the child on his mother (Ps. 131:2); of speech עַל לָשׁוֹן, עַל פֶּה the mouth and the tongue being the seat of speech; עַל בַּיִת upon the house, i.e. upon the ruins thereof, and generally in reply to the question—where, expressing the resting upon a place; hence α) in, e.g. עַל אֲדָמָה in the land, עֲלֵי אֲדָמוֹת in the lands, עַל מַמְלָכָה in the kingdom; β) on, of the clothes on the body, e. g. the coat of many colours which he had on (אֲשֶׁר עָלָיו) or from the wearing of a shield or a coat of mail; γ) of a burden resting upon some one, either physically or as an obligation or duty; hence after the words הָיָה לְמַשָּׂא, הָיָה לְטֹרַח, כָּבֵד which are construed with עַל, like הֵקַל with מֵעַל; hence עָלַי it is incumbent upon me; δ) to signify the means of support, e. g. חָיָה עַל

לֶחֶם to live on the bread, חָיָה עַל חֶרֶב to live by the sword; ε) of the time, in which, or the manner after which, something is done, e. g. עַל דִּבְרָתִי according to the manner, עַל־כָּכָה in such a way, עַל־שֵׁם after the name, נִקְרָא עַל to be called after some one; also instruments or melodies with which hymns are to be chaunted; (*b*) of a movement towards the surface of something, especially, *α*) something coming from a higher position, in which sense כָּתַב, נָתַן, הִשְׁלִיךְ are construed with עַל; also with the verbs to command, to charge, to transfer (דִּבֶּר, אָמַר, כָּתַב, צִוָּה, פָּקַד), or such as to denote the befalling of misfortune (בּוֹא עַל); *β*) of the upward movement, e. g. עָלָה עַל הַר to go up the mountain, הֶעֱלָה עַל to bring up, תָּלָה עַל to hang upon, עָלָה עַל לֵב to enter the mind; *γ*) to denote addition, as יָסַף עַל to add to, נֶחֱשַׁב עַל to be counted to; hence the phrases, trouble upon (עַל) trouble, day upon (עַל) year; (*c*) over, where one subject does not touch the other, e. g. עֲלֵי רֹאשִׁי over my head; in this sense עַל is applied *α*) to the verbs signifying ruling הִפְקִיד, מָשַׁל, מָלַךְ עַל; *β*) to the verbs covering or protecting, as הָיָה חוֹמָה, עָטָה, סָכַךְ, פָּסַח, גָּנַן, and in the same sense also נִלְחַם הִתְפַּלֵּל, כִּפֶּר, עָמַד, עַל; *γ*) to denote beyond something, e. g. עַל־נִדָּתָהּ beyond her time of purification; *δ*) to denote the reason or cause of something, e. g. עַל זֹאת, עַל זֶה, עַל כֵּן therefore, עַל מָה wherefore; in this sense, after the verbs of, to rejoice, to mourn, to laugh, to weep, to lament, to be wroth, to have compassion, to console, at or over something; or after the verbs to relate, to speak, to swear, to confess, to behold (a vision), to prophesy; or also to signify the wages or the price of anything; (*d*) to express nearness, approximation, as עַל־הָעַיִן by the well, עַל־הַמַּיִם by the water; עַל הַיָּם by the sea, עַל פִּי יְאֹר on the mouth of the river; sometimes, over, e. g. אֵם עַל־בָּנִים the mother over the children; also, near at hand, at the side of some one, as עַל־יַד at hand, עֲלֵי קֶרֶת near the town; in this sense נִצַּב עַל to stand by something; sometimes to denote accompanying, with, next, by, e. g. the men with the women, עֲלֵי אוֹר by the light of the sun; עַל is likewise sometimes transf. to the significa-

of עִם and אֵת to denote the seat, especially of emotions, e. g. תִּשְׁתּוֹחַ עָלַי נַפְשִׁי, נֶהְפַּךְ עָלַי לִבִּי, עָלַי לִבִּי דַוָּי; likewise for the formation of adverbs, e. g. עַל־שֶׁקֶר falsely, עַל נְקַלָּה lightly, עַל רָצוֹן acceptably, עַל־יֶתֶר richly; (e) where עַל signifies the motion towards or upon something, like אֶל, and hence often interchanging with it—in this sense שָׁלַךְ and נָתַן, כָּתַב, נָפַל, שָׁלַח are construed with עַל, often interchanging with אֶל, and sometimes with עַד, and in this signif. עַל may be used in a friendly or in a hostile sense; 2) conjunc. for עַל אֲשֶׁר although, though, however, nevertheless, because, or for עַל כִּי; it also occurs with the following prepositions: (a) כְּעַל according, suitable to; (b) מֵעַל α) from upon, away from, e. g. מֵעַל הַכִּסֵּא from upon the throne—in this sense of removal many verbs (like הִרְחִיק, נָשָׂא) are construed with מֵעַל; β) from near, e. g. מֵעַל אֹהֶל from near the tent—in this sense many verbs (like סוּר, זָנָה, עָלָה, עָבַר) are construed with מֵעַל; γ) from above, with לְ joined to the following noun, in contrast to מִתַּחַת לְ, and in this sense מֵעַל signifies sometimes: on, near, and sometimes, over, at, in answer to the question whither or where? e. g. גָּבֹהַּ מֵעַל גָּבֹהַּ a high one above a high one. As to the derivation of עַל, it is from עָלָה; but the form עֲלֵי is not constructive as is generally supposed, but belongs to the formation of the preposition.

עַל (with suff. עֲלוֹהִי, עֲלֵיהוֹן, etc.) Aram. the same, only with the peculiarity that it is often substituted for אֶל and sometimes for לְ.

עֹל (seldom עוֹל, with suff. עֻלּוֹ) masc. yoke, which is laid on the neck of beasts, origin. something round, rolling, from עָלַל in the signif. of גָּלַל, which see; hence, to bear a yoke is a figure of subjection or suffering; to break a yoke is a figure of release from oppression.

עֵל (def. עִלָּא) Aram. m. equiv. to מֵעַל in Heb., height, or that which is uppermost; generally as a prep. with מִן over or above something.

עֻלָּא p. n. m. (yoke).

עָלַב (not used) to be ashamed, orig. to be white, pale, like לָבַן; hence עַלְבוֹן in the p. n. אֲבִי־עַלְבוֹן.

עָלַג (not used) to stammer, equiv. to לָעַג, which see.

עִלֵּג adj. m. stammering, formed from the Pi.

עָלָה (fut. יַעֲלֶה) 1) to be high, elevated; next, to rise, e. g. of the shooting up of plants; עוֹלָה poet. the growth; of the rising of the smoke, of the dawn of the morning. etc.; 2) to ascend upon (עַל) something, towards (לְ ,אֶל) something, along (בְּ) something, to ascend something (with accus.); next, to journey from a low to a high country, e.g. from Egypt, Assyria, Babel, or even from the kingdom of Israel, to Judea, to go up to the sanctuary, transf. to the rising of a road or a country; of the lot which comes up (from the urn); figur. to rise in a mental sense, i.e. to rise in opulence, to get stronger (in power), with עַל, to surpass something; 3) to be put over, or at something, e.g. of a garment, a bandage, a razor; of being entered upon or inscribed on tablets; to be carried away, removed. Niph. נַעֲלָה (fut. יֵעָלֶה) 1) to be carried up, or carried away; 2) to raise oneself; 3) to be exalted. Hiph. 1) to bring up, to carry up; transf. to bring a host of people upon some one, to bring an offering on the altar, and generally, to offer, to light (candles); 2) to put on an over garment, to enter on a tablet; 3) to take away, to destroy. Hophal הֹעֲלָה (for הָעֳלָה) passive, from Hiph. Hithp. to exalt oneself, to boast.

עָלֶה (const. עֲלֵה, with suff. עָלֵהוּ, pl. const. עֲלֵי) masc. a leaf (from עָלָה, in the signification of shooting up); hence, עָ׳ נִדָּף a shaken leaf (by the wind), עֲלֵה זַיִת an olive leaf.

עִלָּה (const. עִלַּת, def. עִלְּתָא, pl. עִלָּן) Aram. fem. motive, pretext, from עֲלַל to cause, to occasion, like סִבָּה in Heb.

עֹלָה (rare עוֹלָה, pl. עֹלוֹת) f. 1) that which is brought up (on the altar), i.e. offering, especially of the burnt offering, which was entirely burnt; 2) rise, step, comp. מַעֲלָה. For the term עֹלָה or עוֹלָה, which is contracted from עַוְלָה see under עַוְלָה.

עֲלוּ (pl. עֲלָוָן) Aram. f. burnt-offering.

עַלְוָה f. 1) a transposition from עַוְלָה, which see; 2) p.n. of an Edomite tribe.

עֲלוּמִים (after the form בְּתוּלִים, זְקוּנִים, and denom. from עֶלֶם) pl. m. youthful age, youth, transf. to youthful vigour.

עַלְוָן p.n. m. (the unjust one), for which also עַלְיָן.

עֲלוּקָה f. orig. leech, horseleech, from עָלַק, equiv. to לָקַק to suck, to lick, transf. to a legendary monster that sucked blood.

עָלַז (fut. יַעֲלֹז) equiv. to עָלַץ, עָלַם, orig. to shine, to illumine; next, transf. as in שָׂמַח to be glad, to rejoice, to exult; to rejoice, triumph over (בְּ) something.

עָלֵז adj. m. joyful, triumphant.

עָלַם (not used) to veil, to wrap up; next, generally, to be obscure, dark, related to לָט.

עֲלָטָה f. darkness, obscurity, mist, fog, from עָלַט.

עֵלִי p. n. m. (the exalted one).

עֱלִי m. a pestle, the instrument with which anything is broken in a mortar, from עָלָה equiv. to גָּלַל, to be round. The pl. according to some עֲלוֹת 2 Chron. 24:14. According to Kimchi, mortar, so called on account of its round shape.

עִלִּי adj. m., but only עִלִּית fem., the uppermost one, e.g. of a well.

עִלָּי (def. עִלָּאָה or עִלָּיָא, plur. עִלָּאִין) Aram. adj. m. the upper one, the high, the highest; hence אֱלָהָא עִלָּאָה the High God, also עִלָּאָה alone.

עַלְיָה see עֲלָוָה.

עֲלִיָּה f. 1) loft, garret, upper chamber, figur. of the chambers of heaven; the heaven is termed עֲלִיּוֹת י״י; 2) equiv. to עֹלָה step, staircase, stairs.

עֶלְיוֹן adj. m., עֶלְיוֹנָה (pl. --נוֹת) fem. the upper one, the high, the highest one, often joined with אֵל, י״י, or אֱלֹהִים, sometimes עֶלְיוֹן alone, the Most High, of God.

עֶלְיוֹן (Aram.) masc. (pl. עֶלְיוֹנִין) the same as in Hebrew.

עַלִּיז (pl. עַלִּיזִים) adj. m., עַלִּיזָה fem. joyful, rejoicing, or boisterous, noisy, in a bad sense.

עֲלִיל (const. עֲלִיל) m. furnace, oven for the melting of metal, orig. like כּוּר that which is hollowed out, from עָלַל, see חָלַל; בַּעֲלִיל לָאָרֶץ in a furnace of earth, i.e. which is in the ground, ל is here, as often in modern Hebrew, a sign of the genitive.

עֲלִילָה (pl. עֲלִילוֹת) f. 1) a deed, work, either in a good or a bad sense, from עָלַל to do, to work, to make; 2) equiv. to עִלָּה (Aram.) pretext, orig. motive, design (in a bad sense), occasion, inducement, cause.

עֲלִילִיָּה (a fem. form of the old form עֲלִילִי) f. deed, work (of God), like עֲלִילָה.

עַלְיָן see עַלְוָן.

עֲלִיצוּת fem. joy, rejoicing, shouting, from עָלַץ.

עִלִּית (Aram.) f. upper chamber. The absolute form is originally עִלִּי.

עָלַל (Kal, not used) equiv. to גָּלַל and חָלַל, hence, 1) to roll, to turn; from which Po. עוֹלֵל to act, to work, to do. The origin. signif. occurs in Job 16:15, עוֹלַלְתִּי בֶעָפָר קַרְנִי I rolled (Author. Vers. defiled) my horn in the dust. Poal עוֹלַל pass. to be done, worked. Hithpo. הִתְעוֹלֵל to do, orig. to turn, to move in a matter. Hithpa. הִתְעַלֵּל to perpetrate or accomplish something on (בְּ) some one, equiv. to הִתְעוֹלֵל בְּ; hence, to revenge oneself; 2) to roll, to turn, in a tropical sense, to repeat (the idea of turning is often transf. in Hebrew to that of duration, continuation), to do again; hence, Po. עוֹלֵל to glean, of the vintage; figur. of a defeat after the chief battle; 3) equiv. to חָלַל to hollow out, deepen out; hence עֲלִיל, melting-oven, furnace.

עֲלַל (3 pret. עַל, f. עַלַּת, עֲלַלַת, pause pl. עַלִּין and עֲלַלִין) Aram. to turn in, to go in, to enter. Af. הַנְעֵל (נ instead of dagesh forte, inf. הַנְעָלָה, imp. with suffix הַעֲלְנִי, infin. const. also הַעָלָה) to bring in, to carry in (a house, to some one).

עֹלֵלוֹת (const. עֹלְלוֹת) f. pl. gleanings, or the fruit to be gleaned, especially of grapes.

עָלַם to hide, to secrete, to conceal; hence עֲלֻמִים hidden sins. Niph. נֶעְלַם to be concealed, hidden from (מֵעֵינֵי, מִן) some one; part. נַעֲלָמִים, hidden people, dissemblers, נַעֲלָמָה wrapt in obscurity, unknown, forgotten. Hiph. הֶעֱלִים 1) to hide, conceal from (מִן) some one, הֶעֱלִים עַיִן מִן to hide or withdraw the eye from some one (either not to help or not to punish him); הֶעֱלִים אֹזֶן to hide or withdraw the ear, i.e. not wishing to hear; 2) from the origin. signif. in Kal, to wrap in darkness; fig. to blame, reproach. Hith. to hide or withdraw oneself from (מִן) something. In the original signif. עָלַם is related to גָּלַם. Of עַלְמָה, עֶלֶם and עֲלוּמִים the root is עוּל.

עָלַם (def. עָלְמָא, pl. עָלְמִין) Aram. m. eternity; sometimes also, the future or the past.

עֶלֶם (denom. from עוּל=עַל, from the root עוּל) m. a youth, orig. freshness of youth; as to the form, comp. חֵלֶם, צֶלֶם from חַל, צַל.

עַלְמָה (pl. עֲלָמוֹת formed from עֶלֶם) f. a girl, a damsel, but extensively used like עֶלֶם. See also עֲלָמוֹת.

עַלְמוֹן (hiding-place) p.n. of a place in Benjamin, for which עָלֶמֶת occurs once.

עַלְמוֹן־דִּבְלָתָיְמָה (place of fig-cakes) p.n. of an encampment of the Israelites in the desert.

עֲלָמוֹת a term of an ancient hymn;

hence עַל עֲ׳ after Alamoth, as denoting a melody in the Psalms.

עֲלָמוֹת f. 1) youthful vigour, as denoting a melody in the Psalms, probably from an ancient hymn; 2) formed from עוֹלָם eternity.

עֵלְמָי (pl. עֵלְמָיֵא) Aram. adj. m. an Elamite, one from Elam.

עַלֶּמֶת (hiding-place) p.n. of a place in Benjamin.

עָלֶמֶת (youthfulness) p. n. m.

עָלַס (fut. יַעֲלֹס) equiv. to עָלַז to be glad, to rejoice, origin. to be cheerful. Niph. to rejoice. Hith. to rejoice mutually at (בְּ) something.

עָלַע belongs to the form יְעַלְעוּ, see under עוּל.

עֲלַע (pl. עִלְעִין) masc. a rib, like the Heb. צֵלָע.

עָלַף (Kal, not used) to wrap up, to cover; transf. to pine away, as in עָטָה and עָטַף. Pual 1) to be veiled, enclosed, set, overlaid (in precious stones); 2) to pine away. Hith. to wrap oneself up (with a veil); to languish, pine away.

עֻלְפֶּה m. mourning, pining away. The form is to be explained like לְבֵנָה, פִּשְׁתָּה.

עָלַץ (fut. יַעֲלֹץ) equiv. to עָלַז to be glad, to rejoice; with בְּ of the subject at which one rejoices; with לְ, to triumph over some one.

עָלַק (not used) to suck, sip, lick; related to לָקַק. From which עֲלוּקָה.

עַם (in pause, and after the article עָם; with suff. עַמִּי, pl. עַמִּים and after the Arab. form עֲמָמִים, const. עַמֵּי, seldom עַמְמֵי, with suff. עַמֶּיךָ, seldom עֲמָמֶיךָ) com. 1) orig. an individual, body, person; hence also, of an individual (comp. Talm. עַם הָאָרֶץ a man from the country, a boor, ignoramus, especially in the proper names עַמִּיאֵל, עַמִּינָדָב, etc.); 2) family-body, people, tribe, family. Israel is called עַם קָדוֹשׁ, עַ׳ יי״, עַ׳ נַחֲלָה; עַמִּים the Israelitish tribes, but also other nations. עָם is also used in contrast to princes; thus, subjects, crowd, or peasants, people of the country; rarely of the whole human race, and still more rarely of beasts.

עַם (def. עַמָּא, def. pl. עַמְמַיָּא) Aram. the same.

עִם (with suff. עִמִּי, עִמּוֹ) m. origin. connection, association, but used only as a prep. "with," e.g. figs with (עִם) pomegranates. עִם is used with verbs signifying assistance, as הָיָה, הִתְחַזֵּק, עָזַר; or association, as חָלַק, כָּרַת בְּרִית, שָׁכַב, דִּבֵּר; or antagonism, as רִיב, נִלְחַם, etc. עִם must therefore be translated according to the verbs with which it is connected, either—against, like as, as long, as great (in comparisons), at, in, under, etc. It differs from אֵת (with), which rather expresses approximation, whilst עִם more expresses association. מֵעִם away from something, signifying a removal from the approximation denoted by עִם; thus, away, out of, from; many verbs expressing departure, removal, dismissing, are therefore construed with מֵעִם. The root is עָמַם.

עִם (Aram.) the same in the most manifold significations.

I. עָמַד (Kal, not used) equiv. to מָעַד to totter, from which Hiph. הֶעֱמִיד to cause to totter or tremble.

II. עָמַד (fut. יַעֲמֹד) origin. to be stretched (comp. מַד and מָתַח); next, to stand erect (neither lying, nor sitting, nor leaning), different from יָצַב, which signifies rather, standing firmly, resting immoveably upon something. עָמַד is used to signify; 1) to stand (לִפְנֵי) before some one; transf. to serve, to attend, hence עָ׳ בְּהֵיכָל as a servant stands before his master; 2) to stand up (equiv. to קוּם), to rise; hence figur. of the arising of war, of standing up against (עַל) some one; 3) to stand still (in contrast to going away); transf. to cease, to leave off from (מִן) something, or, to remain, to stay, to bide; transf. to remain alive, standing, existing; with לִפְנֵי or בִּפְנֵי, to resist some one; with בְּ, to stand, abide by something; fig. to be appointed over something; with עַל (Ezra 10:11), to assist, trust in, depend upon something. Hiph. הֶעֱמִיד caus. of Kal, to erect (a statue, a house), to appoint (to an office), to resolve, to determine, to maintain, to confirm, to excite, etc. Hoph. to be put, placed.

עִמָּד (only with suff. 1 pers. עִמָּדִי) equiv. to עִם with. Probably it arose from עִם, and the dem. דִּ; hence, more emphatic than עִמִּי.

עֹמֶד (only with suff. עָמְדִי) masc. a place where one stands, a stand, a stall; transf. like in עַמּוּד to a stage, a platform.

עֶמְדָּה f. a stand.

עָמָה (not used) to join, to connect oneself; related is עָמַם, חָמָה.

עֻמָּה (only const. עֻמַּת, and with suff. עֻמָּתוֹ, pl. עֻמּוֹת) f. 1) association, connection; hence construed as a prep. near by, near, of the connection with the subject, either by locality or circumstance; also, in the sense of opposite, agair therefore used in comparison, as עַם like as; כָּל־עֻמַּת exactly as, just as; מִלְּעֻמַּת near by; 2) commonality, p.n. of a city in Asher.

עַמּוּד (pl. עַמּוּדִים) m. 1) that which is stretched out, erect, a pillar; 2) a stage, a platform. See עָמַד.

עַמּוֹן (countryman) p.n. masc. also the name of a people; in the latter sense, more frequently בְּנֵי עַמּוֹן. The territory is called אֶרֶץ בְּנֵי עַמּוֹן. Gent. m. עַמּוֹנִי, f. ־נִית.

עָמוֹס p.n.m. (the bearer of a burden).

עָמוֹק p.n. m. (the profound one).

עַמִּיאֵל p.n. m. (man of God).

עַמִּיהוּד p.n. m. (man of beauty).

עַמִּיזָבָד p.n. m. (man of reward).

עַמִּיחוּר p.n. m. (man of nobility).

עַמִּינָדָב p.n. m. (man of liberality).

עֲמִיק (Aram.) adj. masc. עֲמִיקָא (def. ־קְתָא), f. deep, unfathomable.

עָמִיר equiv. to עֹמֶר sheaf; origin. that which is bound together.

עַמִּישַׁדַּי p.n. masc. (man of the Almighty).

עָמִית f. 1) abstract, association, connection; hence גֶּבֶר עֲמִיתִי man of my association, i.e. one near me; 2) concrete, a confederate, neighbour. See עָמָה.

עָמַל (fut. יַעֲמֹל) to labour, to toil, to weary oneself; with בְּ, to labour at something, but especially of hard labour, to carry burthens; עָ׳ עָמָל to do work; עָמַל לְ to labour, to weary oneself for some one. Related is גָּמַל and חָמַל.

עָמָל (const. עֲמַל, with suff. עֲמָלִי) com. 1) trouble, work, in a physical and mental sense; transf. to that which is got or acquired by labour; 2) affliction, calamity, tribulation, misery: מְנַחֲמֵי עָמָל miserable, troublesome comforters; 3) p.n. m. labourer.

עָמֵל (pl. עֲמֵלִים) adj. m. 1) to weary oneself, to labour hard, subst., labourer; 2) sufferer, unhappy, miserable one.

עֲמָלֵק 1) p.n. m.; 2) name of an ancient people (רֵאשִׁית גּוֹיִם Num. 14:20) who dwelt southwest of Palestine. Gent. עֲמָלֵקִי an Amalekite, which is also used collectively.

I. עָמַם (not used) to join, to associate; related to גָּמַם, אָמַם. From which עָמָה.

II. עָמַם to be gloomy, dark, faint; hence figur. to darken, to throw into the back ground; "there is no secret that they can hide from thee" (Ezek. 28:3). Hoph. הוּעַם to be darkened (of splendour).

עֲמָמִים see עַם.

עַמְמִין see עַם Aram.

עִמָּנוּאֵל (God with us) symbolical name of a son of Isaiah.

עָמַס (fut. יַעֲמֹס) to lift up, to carry (a burden); עָ׳ עַל to lift up, to load, to lay a burden; עָמַס לְ to burthen some one. Hiph. הֶעֱמִיס to put a load upon (עַל) something, or to put a yoke upon some one.

עֲמַסְיָה p. n. m. (burthen of God).

עַמְעָד (lasting union) p. n. of a city in Asher.

עָמַק origin. to be sunk, low (comp. מָךְ, מַק); next, to be deep, figur. to be unfathomable. Hiph. to make deep, but generally only in the adverbial construction, e. g. הֶעֱמִיק לָשֶׁבֶת to dwell deeply (in the earth); הֶעֱמִיק לַסְתִּיר to hide deeply; הֶעֱמִיק סָרָה to revolt deeply; הַעֲמֵק שְׁאָלָה ask it from the depths.

עָמֵק (only pl. const. עִמְקֵי) adj. deep, unintelligible (of language).

עָמֹק adj. m. עֲמֻקָּה, f. deep, low, but also figur. unfathomable, unexplorable.

עֵמֶק (with suff. עִמְקִי, pl. עֲמָקִים, const. עִמְקֵי) m. deep place, valley, plain of a valley; הָעֵמֶק the valley, the plain, poetically applied to Jerusalem; עֲמָקִים stands for the inhabitants of the valleys; עֵמֶק stands in proper nouns as the first part of the composition; עֵ׳ הָאֵלָה. (terebinth valley) near Beth-Lehem; עֵ׳ בְּרָכָה (valley of blessing) near En-Geddi; and so עֵ׳ רְפָאִים, עֵ׳ הַמֶּלֶךְ, עֵמֶק הַבָּכָא, עֵ׳ בְּגִבְעוֹן, עֵ׳ קְצִיץ, עֵ׳ שִׂדִּים, עֵ׳ יִזְרְעֶאל, עֵ׳ חֶבְרוֹן, עֵ׳ סֻכּוֹת, עֵ׳ יְהוֹשָׁפָט, עֵ׳ אַיָּלוֹן.

עֹמֶק m. depth.

I. עָמַר (Kal, not used) to bind. Pi. עִמֵּר to bind together (sheaves), related to חָמַר, כָּמַר; hence מְעַמֵּר the binder of sheaves. From which עָמִיר and עֹמֶר.

II. עָמַר (Kal, not used) to serve; hence, Hithpael, הִתְעַמֵּר to make one servile, to treat as a slave, to make merchandise of him, with בְּ.

עָמֵר (not used) to mete out, to measure; hence, עֹמֶר II.

עֲמַר (not used) Aram. equiv. to צָמַר in Heb., to sprout, to spring forth.

עֲמַר (def. עַמְרָא) Aram. masc. wool; see צֶמֶר.

עֹמֶר (pl. עֳמָרִים) m. 1) sheaf, bundle, from עָמַר I.; 2) an omer, measure of corn, from עָמֵר.

עֲמֹרָה (a forest, see עֲמַר) p. n. of a city in the valley of Siddim.

עָמְרִי p. n. m. (the servile one).

עַמְרָם p. n. m. (the exalted one). Patron. —מִי.

עָמַשׂ equiv. to עָמַס, which see.

עַמְשָׂא p.n. m. (burden, load).

עַמְשַׁי p. n. m. (a carrier of a burden).

עַמְשְׁסַי p. n. m. (from עַמְשַׁי and עַמְסַי).

עַמֹּת see עִמָּה.

עֲנָא (Aram.) like עָנָה I., II. and III. in Heb.; 1) to answer; 2) to sing, to attune; 3) to humble oneself, to suffer; עֲנַיִן the afflicted ones.

עָנַב (not used) to be round, hilly (related to נוף) from which עָנָב p. n., and עֵנָב.

עֲנָב (a hill) p. n. of a city in the mountain district of Judah.

עֵנָב (the same) p. n. of a city.

עֵנָב (pl. עֲנָבִים, pl. const. עִנְּבֵי) m. grape, orig. a berry, on account of its round shape.

עָנַג (Kal, not used) to be soft, related to פִּנֵּק; next, to be tender. Pu. to be delicate, pampered. Hith. 1) הִתְעַנֵּג to pamper oneself, through (בְּ) something; 2) to delight oneself, at (מִן or עַל) something, to enjoy a thing, and in a bad sense, to make sport of something.

עָנֹג adj. m., עֲנֻגָּה fem. delicate, pampered, voluptuous.

עֹנֶג masc. enjoyment, delight, voluptuousness.

עָנַד to bind, with עַל, to bind round; from which, through the transposition, מַעֲדַנָּה.

I. עָנָה (fut. יַעֲנֶה, apoc. יַעַן) origin. equiv. to פָּנָה to pronounce, to relate circumspectly; next, 1) to reply, to answer, to instruct, to pronounce openly, e. g. "he gives not open account of all his matters" (Job 33:13), "the Lord will pronounce," i. e. manifest, "the welfare of Pharaoh" (Gen. 41:16). The signif. of answering, is used sometimes as a reply to a question, sometimes as defence against reproach, sometimes as compliance with a request, in which case עָנָה must be rendered "to grant"; with accus. of the person, and בְּ of the subject, to make a present to some one; 2) to pronounce sentence (of a judge), to give evidence, orig. to answer the questions of the judge, to bear witness against (בְּ) some one. Niph. נַעֲנָה pass. from Kal, to be answered, (refuted), to be heard (one's request). Hiph. to hearken to, to grant, only Ecc. 5:19 מַעֲנֶה, which however may be a substantive.

II. עָנָה equiv. to קָן, orig. to sing, but generally to commence, to attune, to open (a speech, a song). Pi. the same.

III. עָנָה (fut. יַעֲנֶה) equiv. כָּנַע, to be humbled, oppressed, afflicted; of a song, to be mute; also to humble oneself before (מִן) something, to weary oneself in (בְּ) something. Niph. to be humbled, oppressed; or reflective, to humble oneself before (מִפְּנֵי) some one. Inf. לַעֲנוֹת for לְהֵעָנוֹת. Pi. to humble, to afflict, to oppress, to sadden, to annoy, to torment, to consume (the strength), to force (a woman), i. e. to commit a rape (comp. עָבַר); to afflict the soul, i. e. to fast; to subdue (the waves). Pu. to be oppressed, afflicted, pass. from Pi. עֻנּוֹתוֹ his affliction, sorrow. Hiph. only 2 Chron. 6:26, to humble. Hith. הִתְעַנָּה to humble, afflict oneself, to suffer from (מִן) something.

עֲנָה (hearing) 1) p. n. m. and from which; 2) name of an Edomite tribe.

עָנָו (pl. עֲנָוִים, const. עַנְוֵי) masc. the humble one, transf. to the afflicted, the sufferer, the helpless one; or in an ascetic sense, the sufferer, the meek one. The form probably arose from the particip. pass. עָנוּ.

עֲנוּב p. n. m. (the ally).

עֲנָוָה f. meekness, humility, modesty; of God, clemency, loving-kindness. With suff. עַנְוָתְךָ and עֲנֹתְךָ.

עַנְוָה f. the same.

עָנוֹק masc. a giant, valiant knight, otherwise עֲנָק.

עֱנוּת (after the form גָּלוּת, const. עֱנוּת for עֱנוּת) f. affliction, suffering, sorrow; according to others, the crying, from עָנָה II.

עָנֵו belongs to עָנָו, which see.

עָנִי (pl. עֲנִיִּים) adj. masc., עֲנִיָּה fem. humbled, suffering, afflicted, transf. to poor, forbearing, meek, peaceable; in all these significations also used as a subst. עֲנָוִים often interchanges with עֲנִיִּים, owing to the similarity in the signif.

עֳנִי (pause עֹנִי, with suff. עָנְיִי) masc. affliction, suffering, oppression; בְּנֵי עֹנִי the afflicted, לֶחֶם עֹנִי bread of affliction, poor bread.

עֻנִּי p. n. m. (the humbled one).

עֲנָיָה p. n. m. (answered by God).

עָנָיו Keri for עָנָו, which see.

עָנִים (wells, contracted from עֲיָנִים) p. n. of a city in Judah.

עִנְיָן (const. עִנְיַן) m. 1) work, travail, affair in which one takes pains, from עָנָה III.; hence, עִ׳ רָע sore travail; 2) like דָּבָר a thing, matter, subject, orig. the calling, or object of a matter, from עָנָה I.

עָנַךְ (not used) probably equiv. to אָנַךְ, which see: from which הָעֲנָךְ.

עֵנָם (double fountain, for עֵינַיִם) p. n. of a city in Issachar.

עֲנָמִים p. n. of a people of Egyptian origin, probably the Blemians.

עֲנַמֶּלֶךְ p. n. of an idol of the Sippharians, probably from עָנָם מֶלֶךְ, the king of flocks, in an astronomical sense.

עָנַן (Kal, not used) equiv. to גָּנַן, to cover, to veil; hence Po. עוֹנֵן (fut. יְעוֹנֵן, particip. מְעוֹנֵן) to carry on sorcery (Author. Vers. an observer of times, from עָנָן cloud), origin. to conceal, to act secretly, covertly. In the particip. form the מ is sometimes omitted, e. g. עוֹנֵן, עוֹנְנָה for מְעוֹנֵן, מְעוֹנְנָה. Another Pi. form עִנֵּן is a denom. from עָנָן, which see.

עָנָן (c. עֲנַן, pl. עֲנָנִים) m. 1) a cloud, so called from its covering the sky; figur. of a multitude of people, which covers everything as a cloud; 2) p.n. m. (equiv. to עוֹנֵן sorcerer). As a denom. from עָנָן occurs the Pi. עִנֵּן the gathering of clouds. Inf. with suff. בְּעַנְנִי, with omission of the dagesh.

עֲנַן (const. pl. עֲנָנֵי) Aram. m. a cloud.

עֲנָנָה f. clouds in a collective sense.

עֲנָנִי p.n. m. (protector).

עֲנָנְיָה 1) p.n. m. (protected by God; 2) p.n. of a place in Benjamin.

עָנַף (not used) to wave, to shake to and fro; hence related to נוּף (comp. זָנַב, סָנַף) or the origin. signif. is to sprout, related to נוּב.

עָנָף (const. עֲנַף, pl. with suff. עֲנָפֶיהָ) m. a branch.

עֲנַף (plur. with suff. עַנְפּוֹהִי) Aram. m. the same.

עֲנַף (with suff. עַנְפְּכֶם) m. the same.

עָנֵף (adj. m. עֲנֵפָה) f. branched, full of branches.

עָנַק (not used) to incline the neck; but the עָנַק and Niph. הֶעֱנִיק, which are used, are merely denom. from עֹנֶק neck, which has become obsolete. See below under עָנַק.

עֲנָק (origin. for עָנַק, comp. אֵפֶר and אֲפֵר; pl. עֲנָקִים) m. one with a long neck, a giant, but only as the p.n. of a giant, the progenitor of a race of giants; hence בְּנֵי יְלִידֵי הָעֲנָק.

עֲנָק (const. עֲנַק, pl. עֲנָקִים and עֲנָקוֹת) m. a necklace, ornament of the neck.

עָנַק (denom. from עֹנֶק), neck, which, however, has become obsolete in the language; fig. of pride, which is manifested in the haughty bearing of the neck. Hiph. הֶעֱנִיק, origin. to load upon the neck or back; next, generally, to load some one (with presents).

עָנֵר 1) p. n. m.; 2) p.n. of a Levitic town in Manasseh.

עָנַשׁ (fut. יַעֲנֹשׁ) to punish, to inflict a fine; with double acc. or לְ of the person; to levy a war-tax; also, of the imposition of a fine to be paid in products. Niph. pass. to be punished, or to expiate, i.e. to suffer punishment.

עֹנֶשׁ m. punishment, penitence, contribution (of a tax).

עֲנָשׁ (Aram.) m. the same.

עֲנָת p. n. m. (hearing), from עָנָה.

עֲנַת (Aram.) time, equivalent. to עֵת Hebrew; hence כְּעֶנֶת, equiv. to כְּעֵת, כְּעַתָּה.

עֲנָתוֹת 1) p.n. of a Levitical city in Benjamin, from which gent. עַנְּתֹתִי; 2) p.n. m.

עַנְתֹתִיָּה p.n. m. (heard by God).

עָסִיס (const. עֲסִיס) m. the juice of grapes, new wine.

עָסַס (not used) 1) to tread, to press (of the pressing of fruit); 2) to tread down, to stamp.

עָעַר belongs to יְעֹעֵרוּ. See עור.

עֵפָה see עֵיפָה.

עָפָה (not used) to bloom, to vegetate; comp. אָבַב.

עֳפִי (plur. עֳפָאִים, compare צְבָאִים, טְלָאִים) m. a green branch.

עֳפִי (with suff. עָפְיֵהּ) Aram. m. the same.

עָפַל (Kal, not used) to rise; transf. to swell up. Pu. עֻפְּלָה to be puffed up, proud, presumptuous. Hiph. הֶעְפִּיל to act presumptously, proudly; synon. with הֵזִיד.

עֹפֶל (pl. עֳפָלִים, const. עָפְלֵי, with suff. עָפְלֵיכֶם) m. 1) an elevated place, height, hill, and in this sense, as p.n. of the height in the eastern part of Zion; 2) swelling, a boil on the fundament, for which in Keri stands טְחוֹרִים emerods.

עָפַן (not used) probably equiv. to כָּפַן, which see.

עָפְנִי (gent. from עֹפֶן) p.n. of a place in Benjamin.

עַפְעַף (dual עַפְעַפַּיִם, only const. ־פֵּי, with suff. ־פָּיו) m. eye-lid, orig. wing of the eye, from עוּף; figur. עַפְעַפֵּי שָׁחַר, equiv. to כַּנְפֵי שָׁחַר of the darting rays of the rising sun.

עָפַר (not used) 1) equiv. to אָפַר, פָּרַר to rub to pieces, to crumble, from which עָפָר; 2) equiv. to כָּפַר, גָּבַר to be vigorous, strong, from which עֹפֶר.

עָפַר (not used) to be of a pale red, related to כָּפַר; or pale grey, related to חָוַר to be white, from which עֹפֶרֶת lead.

עָפָר (const. עֲפַר, with suff. עֲפָרָם, pl. עֲפָרוֹת, const. עַפְרוֹת) masc. dust, powdered earth, from עָפַר 1; transf. to rubbish, lime for walls, earth, soil, clod of earth, in mines; figur. to designate the grave, lowliness or transientness, e.g. dust and ashes; to go down into the dust, i. e. the grave: to put the mouth in the dust, i. e. to be humbled to silence.

עֵפֶר p.n. m. (the strong one).

עֹפֶר (pl. עֳפָרִים) m. young roe, young hart, from עָפַר 2.

עֲפְרָה (gazelle) 1) p. n. of a place in Benjamin, for which also בֵּית לְעַפְרָה; 2) p. n. of a place in Manasseh; 3) p. n. m.

עֶפְרוֹן (a roe) 1) p. n. of a city on the border of Benjamin; 2) p. n. of a mountain; 3) p. n. m.

עֶפְרַיִן (pair of Gazelles) Keri for עֶפְרוֹן, as the name of a city.

עֹפֶרֶת f. lead, so called from its grey colour; אֶבֶן הָעֹפֶרֶת a leaden weight, or the weight of lead, from עֵפֶר.

עֵץ (for which once חֵץ, pl. עֵצִים, const. עֲצֵי) m. 1) origin. a stem, a stock, a shaft, from עָצָה to be hard, firm; next, tree, or collectively, trees; 2) wood as a material, e.g. כְּלִי עֵץ wooden vessel, especially a pillar (a gallows), a block, as an idol; עֵצִים pieces of wood for building (timber), or for burning. See עֵצָה.

עָצַב (Kal, not used) equiv. to חָצַב and קָצַב to cut in, to carve; transf. to form, to shape; a similar mode of transferring is used in קָצַב, חָצַב, etc. Pi. to form, to shape by carving, but also to form generally. Hiph. to form (idols).

עָצַב to suffer, to feel pain, to be sad; עָ׳ רוּחַ to be sad in spirit; seldom transf. to sadden, to grieve. Niph. to weary oneself, to labour hard at (בְּ) something, to grieve at (אֶל, עַל) something. Pi. עִצֵּב to mortify, to sadden, to offend (the spirit of God). Hiph. the same, to sadden. Hith. to grieve, to be sad, to be wroth.

עֲצַב (Aram.) only particip. pass. עֲצִיב sad, downcast, grieved, gloomy (of the voice).

עָצָב (after the form קָטָן, pl. עֲצַבִּים, const. עֲצַבֵּי, like קְטַן) m. carved image, idol, from עָצַב 1; next, any image, molten, or otherwise formed; בֵּית עֲצַבִּים house of idols.

עֶצֶב (pl. עֲצָבִים, with suff. once עַצְּבֵיכֶם) masc. 1) equiv. to עָצָב, something formed, finished; hence, an idol, or a vessel; 2) trouble, labour, pain, grief, sorrow, bitterness, דְּבַר עֶ׳ bitter word; 3) that which is acquired by labour.

עֹצֶב (with suff. עָצְבִּי, עָצְבְּךָ) m. 1) idol, image, from עָצַב 1, parallel with פֶּסֶל and נֶסֶךְ; 2) pain, sorrow, grief, from עָצַב 2.

עִצָּבוֹן (const. עִצְּבוֹן, with suff. ־נֵךְ) m. 1) trouble, labour, exertion; 2) tribulation, pain, grief.

עַצֶּבֶת (const. עַצְּבַת, const. pl. עַצְּבוֹת) f. pain, sorrow, grief, tribulation; next, wound, in a spiritual sense.

עָצַד (not used) to split, to cut, to cleave. Comp. Aram. חֲצַד.

עָצָה 1) to shut closely (the eyes), origin. to press tightly; comp. אָץ, לָחַץ, נָחַץ; 2) (not used) equiv. to עוּץ to be hard, firm. From which עֵצָה, עֵץ, עֵצָה.

עָצֶה masc. back-bone, spine, from עָצָה 2.

עֵצָה (formed from עֵץ) f. collectively, wood, especially wood for building, timber.

I. עֵצָה (from יָעַץ, const. עֲצַת, pl. עֵצוֹת) f. counsel, advice, whether received or given; transf. to a confirmed sentence, decree, prophetic promise, device, design, and counsel, being the result of prudence and deliberation; עֵצָה signifies also, deliberation, prudence; בְּעֵצָה deliberately; אִישׁ עֵצָה either counseller, adviser, or accomplice in a plan.

עָצוּם (pl. עֲצוּמִים) adj. masc. firm, strong; transf. to mighty, distinguished, numerous, powerful, etc., according to the context.

עֲצוּמִים (from עָצוּם) m. pl. 1) power, might, predominance; 2) the mighty, the heroes.

עֶצְיוֹן גֶּבֶר (back-bone of a man, so called from its similarity in shape) p. n. of a port town of Idumea, not far from Elath, from whence Solomon shipped goods to Ophir.

עָצַל (Kal, not used) to be indolent, sluggish. Niph. to linger in doing something, to be lazy.

עָצֵל adj. m. indolent, sluggish, but generally as a subst., sluggard.

עַצְלָה (dual עֲצַלְתַּיִם) f. sluggishness; the dual signifies excessive sluggishness.

עַצְלוּת f. the same.

עָצַם (in pause עָצֵם, fut. יַעֲצֹם) 1) intrans. to be or become firm, strong, mighty; transf. to be numerous; 2) to bind (the eyes): this signification is rare, but it is the original one etymologically, for the roots צַם, אָטַם, are related. Pi. 1) to bind (shut the eyes); 2) denom. from עֶצֶם (bone), to gnaw (a bone). Hiph. to make strong, mighty.

עֶצֶם (pl. עֲצָמִים, עֲצָמוֹת) f. origin. that which is hard, firm, strong; hence, 1) bone; עֶצֶם מֵעֲצָמַי bone of my bones; עֲצָמוֹת used often of bones of the dead (comp. יָדוֹת, תַּבּוֹת); 2) the whole human body, and thus for persons, individuals; 3) self, oneself, inasmuch as it replaces the person; e.g. כְּעֶצֶם הַשָּׁמַיִם like the heaven itself; hence also בְּעֶצֶם in the midst of a thing, origin. in itself, e.g. בְּעֶצֶם תֻּמּוֹ in the midst of of his affluence (Auth. Ver. "in his full strength," Job 21:23);

4) fortress, p. n. of a city in Simeon.

עֹצֶם (with suff. עָצְמִי) m. 1) strength, might; 2) body, being, person, like עֶצֶם.

עָצְמָה f. strength, might; transf. to strength in number, quantity.

עֲצֻמָה (only pl. עֲצֻמוֹת) f. bulwark, defence; figur. argument, proof, refutation.

עַצְמוֹן (strong, firm place) p. n. of a city on the southern border of Palestine.

עָצַן (not used) according to some equiv. to עָצַם. See עֲדִין.

עֶצֶן m. spear. See עֲדִין.

עָצַר (fut. יַעְצֹר, יַעֲצֹר) origin. to enclose, to lock (related to חָצֵר, אָצַר); next 1) to shut up, to close up (accus.) e. g. the heaven, that there be no rain, a woman (not to bear children); עָצַר בְּעַד to shut in, e. g. in a prison, to shut out, from the sight of some one; עָצוּר מִפְּנֵי to be shut up, or shut out, from some one; עָצוּר the incarcerated one, i. e. a slave, in contrast to עָזוּב the free one; 2) in a spiritual sense, to prevent, to impede, with לְ and בְּ of the object; hence, to restrain (the power), to curb (a kingdom), i. e. to rule; 3) to preserve, and generally, to assemble, to gather together. Niph. 1) to be shut up (of the heaven); 2) to be restrained; 3) to be assembled, pass. from Kal.

עֶצֶר masc. dominion, rule, dynasty, comp. עָצַר 2.

עֹצֶר m. 1) shutting up (of the womb), used of barren women; 2) oppression, tribulation, from עֲצַר to press, after the Aram.

עֲצָרָה f. assembly (of people, e. g. of the wicked, but commonly of a festive assembly) and next, generally, festival.

עֲצֶרֶת (pl. with suff. עַצְּרֹתֵיכֶם) fem. the same, especially the festival on the eighth day of the feast of Tabernacles.

עָקַב (fut. יַעְקֹב, with suff. יַעְקְבֵנִי) 1) equiv. to עָבַב I., to weave, to spin; hence fig. to concoct deceit, to deceive (comp. כָּזַב, זָמַם, etc.); 2) to be high, hilly, related to גַּב, גִּב and גִּבְעָ); 3) to linger, hesitate; hence Pi. to keep something back; related to עָכַב in Aram.

עָקֵב (const. עֲקֵב, with suff. עֲקֵבוֹ, pl. const. עִקְּבֵי, עִקְּבֵי and עִקְּבוֹת) m. 1) orig. the hilly part of the foot, heel; of beasts, hoof, from עָקַב II. if it is not derived from עָקַב III. in the sense of the last (comp. אָחַר); 2) trace or track of the steps, orig. step of the heel; 3) the rear, or last part of an army, the army being fig. considered as a human body; 4) the artful one, the deceiver, from עָקֵב I.; denom. עָקַב to lay hold of the heel.

עָקֹב (adj. m. (עֲקֻבָּה) f. 1) deceptive, artful, of the heart; 2) the lower part of a building, i.e. foundation (compare עָקֵב and עָקֵב); hence (קִרְיָה) עֲקֻבָּה מִדָּם a city founded in (Author. Vers. polluted with) blood, i.e. its foundation is laid in guiltiness of blood; 3) hill, height, in contrast to מִישׁוֹר (Auth. Vers. crooked). See עָקֵב.

עֵקֶב m. like עָקֵב in the transf. signification, the end, the last of a thing; hence, consequence or reward of a deed, and as an adverb, at last, to the last, i.e. always; as a prep. for, i.e. for reward, as a reward, especially עַל עֵקֶב; as a conj. for that, orig. for, as עֵקֶב כִּי, עֵ׳ אֲשֶׁר.

עָקְבָה f. artfulness, deceit.

עָקַד (fut. יַעֲקֹד) to bind, to fetter, related to עָנַד, אָגַד.

עָקַד (not used) to cut in, to indent, comp. נָקַד, קָדַד. It is probably connected with עָקַד I.

עָקֹד (pl. עֲקֻדִּים) adj. masc. spotted, striped, of sheep.

עָקָה (not used) to enclose, surround, from which מַעֲקֶה.

עָקָה f. oppression, from עוּק, which see.

עַקּוּב p. n. m. (successor), comp. עָקֵב.

עָקַל (Kal, not used) to turn, to twist, comp. עָגַל and קָלַע; from which Pu. עֻקַּל to be turned, to be perverted (of justice).

עֲקַלְקַל adj. m., עֲקַלְקַלָּה f. crooked winding of a road, even with the addition of אֹרַח.

עֲקַלָּתוֹן (from עֲקַלָּה, with the affix וֹן—) adj. m. crooked, winding serpent.

עָקַן (not used) equiv. to עָקַל, which see.

עָקָן p.n. m. (perversion).

עֲקַר (Aram.) to pull out, to tear out. Ith. אִתְעֲקַר passive.

עָקָר see עֵקֶר.

עֵקֶר m. 1) a root, sprout, or that which shoots up from the root, stem; figur. settlement, naturalization, in a country, orig. to take root; hence עֵקֶר מִשְׁפַּחַת גֵּר the settler, denizen (Authorised Version, the stock) of the stranger's family; 2) p.n. m.

עִקֵּר (denom. from עֵקֶר) to tear out the עֵקֶר (root) to uproot, complete עָקַר נָתוּשׁ. Niph. to be destroyed, of a town. Pi. to cut through the vein (עֵקֶר, similar to the root of a tree); of beasts, to maim them (Author. Vers. hough their horses.

עָקָר adj. m., עֲקָרָה (const. עֲקֶרֶת) f.

unfruitful, barren (orig. defective in the roots, i.e. in the genitals) of man or woman.

עִקַּר (Aram.) m. (const. עִקַּר) stem or stock of the root.

עַקְרָב (pl. עַקְרַבִּים) m. 1) scorpion (origin. a beast powerful by its prickles); 2) a kind of scourge made with hooks resembling the prickles of the scorpion. The root is קָרַב II.

עֶקְרוֹן (naturalization) p.n. of a tribe of Philistines settled in Palestine, and hence their territory; gent. עֶקְרֹנִי.

עָקַשׁ to turn, to pervert, fut. יַעְקְשֵׁנִי of the perversion of justice in the court; the former, however, is fut. of Hiph. Pi. to turn, to pervert (the walk, justice). Niph. to be pervert in (acc.) his walk of life. Hiph. like Pi. The root is עָיַקשׁ, related with the root in רָכַם, יָקַשׁ.

עִקֵּשׁ adj. m. (pl. עִקְּשִׁים, const. עִקְּשֵׁי) 1) crooked, perverse, e.g. דּוֹר עִ׳ a perverse generation; sometimes עִקֵּשׁ succeeds the noun, and sometimes it is used as a substantive, the perverse one; 2) p.n. m. (the perverse, false one).

עִקְּשׁוּת f. perversion, deceit.

עָר 1) equiv. to עִיר a city, from which also the plur. עָרִים is formed, especially the p.n. of the Moabite metropolis, complete עָר מוֹאָב; 2) equiv. to צַר an adversary; comp. עִיר in the same signification.

עָר (Aram.) m. an enemy.

עֵר p.n. m. (the watchful one).

I. עָרַב (fut. יֶעֱרַב) to entwine, to connect, related to אָרַב; next, to mix; hence, 1) to barter, to exchange, to carry on traffic, proceeding from the original signification of connection; 2) to pledge, either in a moral sense in confirmation of something, or from the original signification of exchanging, a mode of transferring the sense as in חָבַל, עָבַט. עָרַב לֵב to pledge the courage, i.e. to pledge oneself to do something; comp. חֵרֵף נֶפֶשׁ; 3) to be surety, or give security for (לְ, לִפְנֵי) some one, to stand surety (acc. עִם) for some one, to defend or protect one; אָנֹכִי אֶעֶרְבֶנּוּ I will be surety for him. Hith. to mix oneself, to interfere in (בְּ) something, to enter into a matter with (אֵת, עִם, לְ, בְּ) some one, either friendly or in a dispute.

II. עָרַב (inf. const. עֲרוֹב) 1) to darken, to be dark, gloomy, related to עָרַף (belongs to עָרִיף and עֲרָפֶל) and probably also to רָפָה (belongs to רְפָאִים shades), namely of the darkness after the setting of the sun; 2) (not used) to be of dark colour, grey, from which עֲרָבָה.

III. עָרַב (not used) to cut in, equiv. to קָרַב, חָרַף; hence, transf. to deepen out, to cut out, or to seize, attack (with prickles), of an animal of the scorpion species; from which עָרֹב.

עֲרַב (Aram.) equiv. to עָרַב I. in Heb.; hence, Pael עָרֵב to intermix. Ith. אִתְעָרַב passive.

I. עָרֵב (not used) to be waste, desolate, barren; related to חָרֵב, which see. From which עֲרָבָה ,עֲרָב.

II. עָרֵב (fut. יֶעֱרַב) to be sweet, agreeable, pleasant, the original signification is probably to suck.

עָרֵב adj. masc. sweet, agreeable, pleasant.

עָרֹב masc. a reptile, resembling the scorpion, which cuts with its prickles; it was one of the Egyptian plagues. Auth. Vers. "flies."

עֲרָב (also עֲרַב, orig. an arid land) p. n. of Arabia; gent. עֲרָבִי an Arabian, also עַרְבִי, pl. עַרְבִים and עֲרְבִיאִים.

עֶרֶב masc. 1) darkness, strangeness, more probably mixture, mob, rabble, like אֲסַפְסֻף, which explains it in the context; 2) the woof of the warp, from עָרַב to mix.

עֶרֶב (dual עַרְבַּיִם, according to some also pl. עֲרָבוֹת) com. 1) darkness, duskiness; hence, evening: בָּעֶרֶב, לָעֶרֶב, לְעֵת עֶרֶב or accus. עֶרֶב on the eve. The dual עַרְבַּיִם is, according to the Karaites, the time between sunset and complete darkness; according to the Rabbinites, from when the sun is about setting till complete darkness. זְאֵבֵי עֶרֶב night wolves, who go out at night for prey; more probably, however, "wolves of the desert," as זְאֵבֵי עֲרָבוֹת shews; 2) desert, arid steppes, thus equiv. to עֲרָבָה, especially the Arabian desert; hence, מַלְכֵי הָעֶרֶב kings of the desert; the pl. עֲרָבִים belongs to עֲרָבָה. As a denom. from עֶרֶב (evening), the Hiph. הֶעֱרִיב is used to do something at evening, in the phrase הַשְׁכֵּם וְהַעֲרֵב.

עֹרֵב (pl. עֹרְבִים) m. 1) a raven, so called from its dark colour, comp. Cant. 5:11, עֹרְבֵי נַחַל ravens of the valley; 2) p. n. of a Midianite tribe.

עֲרָבָה (pl. עֲרָבוֹת and עֲרָבִים) f. 1) darkness, cloud, from עָרַב II., transf. to heavens of clouds, comp. עָרִיף, to which it is related in the Root. רֹכֵב בָּעֲרָבוֹת he that rideth upon the heavens; comp. רֹכֵב בִּשְׁמֵי שְׁמֵי קֶדֶם ,עַל־עָב קַל רֹכֵב; 2) willow, so called from the grey colour of the leaves, from עָרַב II.; in the Bible only the pl. עֲרָבִים, const. עַרְבֵי; in the Mishna the sing. עֲרָבָה: נַחַל הָעֲרָבִים (brook of the willows, comp. (עַרְבֵי נַחַל) name of a brook in Moab, the present Wadi El-Ahsa; 3) arid steppe, desert; הָעֲרָבָה is the name of a lowland on both sides of the Dead Sea and the Jordan, of which lowland one part was called עַרְבוֹת יְרֵחוֹ and the other עַרְבוֹת מוֹאָב; יָם הָעֲרָבָה (sea of the desert) is the same as נַחַל הָעֲרָבָה, a border river between Moab and Edom, though some explain the former as of the Dead Sea, and the latter of the Jordan or Kidron; 4) steppe, p. n. of a city in Benjamin, probably identical with בֵּית הָעֲרָבָה; gent. עַרְבָתִי.

עֲרֻבָּה (with suff. (עֲרֻבָּתָם f. security, surety, pledge; עָרַב עֲ to be surety, לָקַח עֲ to receive a pledge as security, from עָרַב I.

עֵרָבוֹן masc. a pledge, נָתַן, לָקַח עֵ׳ to give or take a pledge, this word was transf. from the Phœnician into ἀῤῥαβών, *Arrhabo.*

עָרַג (fut. (יַעֲרֹג to cry (languishing) for (עַל, אֶל) something; comp. רְנַג in Aram., נָשַׁר in Hebrew.

עָרַג (not used) to arrange, to order, related to עָרַךְ; hence, figur. to stir, to stretch, to extend, in other derivatives of this root.

עָרַד (not used) to roar, to bray, of the wild ass.

עֲרָד (probably for בֵּית עֲ place of wild asses) 1) p.n. of a city in the desert of Judah; 2) p. n. m. (the wild one).

עֲרָד (def. pl. (עֲרָדַיָּא Aram. masc. a wild ass.

I. עָרָה (Kal, not used) to be naked, bare, related is עוּר, עָרַע; hence Pi. עֵרָה (fut. (יְעָרֶה to lay bare, the foundation of a building, i. e. to destroy; to make bare the chest, i. e. to empty it; to discover the secret part of a woman (פֹּת) i.e. to expose it; to lay bare the shield, i. e. to join the combat. Hiph. הֶעֱרָה the same, of the uncovering of the nakedness of woman. Hith. הִתְעָרָה to uncover oneself (of a drunkard).

II. עָרָה (Kal, not used) to flow, to run, related to נָהַר, נָגַר; hence Niph. נֶעֱרָה to be poured forth (comp. Pi.) of the spirit of God. Pi. (fut. apoc. יְעַר to pour out, to empty (a bottle), to pour out the life, i. e. to expose it, to empty out, to despise. Hiph. to pour out the life, i.e. to expose it.

III. עָרָה (Kal, not used) to sprout, to grow, comp. עָרַד, יַעַר; hence

Hithpael, הִתְעָרָה to sprout, to grow.

עֲרוּגָה f. a furrow (an elevated one), from הָרַג to arrange, to put in order.

עָרוֹד m. a wild ass, from עָרַד.

עֶרְוָה (const. עֶרְוַת) f. the nakedness; in the original sense, and transf., to the nakedness of the land, i. e. where it is vulnerable; next generally, something odious, stained, or reproachful, shame, disgrace, dishonour; עֶרְוַת אֵם nakedness of the mother, for shame of the mother; עֶרְוַת אָב nakedness of the father's wife. The root is עָרָה I.

עַרְוָה (Aram.) fem. expenses, loss, orig. nakedness.

עָרוֹם (also עָרֹם, pl. עֲרוּמִּים) adj. m. עֲרֻמָּה f. naked, bare (in reference to clothing), either entirely without clothing, or badly clothed. See עוּר.

עֵרוֹם see עֵירוֹם.

עָרוּם adj. masc. subtle, cunning, shrewd, artful, from עָרַם.

עֲרוֹעֵר (עֲרֹעֵר) masc. 1) only a secondary form of עַרְעָר, which see; 2) p. n. of several cities, e. g. one on the northern coast of the river Arnon, another called Rabbath Ammon. Gent. עֲרֹעֵרִי.

עָרוּץ (const. עֲרוּץ) m. cleft, crevice, only a secondary form of חָרוּץ.

עָרוֹת (a noun sing., like חָזוֹת, רַבּוֹת) f. green lawn, meadow, from עָרָה III. Comp. יַעַר.

עֵרִי p. n. m. (watcher).

עֶרְיָה f. equiv. to עֶרְוָה nakedness, barrenness.

עֲרִיסָה (only pl. ־סוֹת) fem. dough; (according to tradition); also the cake baked from the dough. According to others, a kind of coarse flour, grits.

עָרִיף (only pl. עֲרִיפִים) m. darkness, darkness of the clouds, the heavens, from עָרַף.

עָרִיץ (for עֲרִיץ, pl. עָרִיצִים, const. עָרִיצֵי) adj. m. 1) terrific, terrible, powerful, mighty, either in a good or bad sense; עָרִיצֵי גוֹיִם the terrible of the nations; 2) subst. a tyrant, the violent one.

עֲרִירִי (pl. עֲרִירִים) adj. m. lonesome, solitary, deserted, childless, from עָרַר to be bare.

עָרַךְ (fut. יַעֲרֹךְ) to arrange, regulate, to prepare, to put something in order, e. g. wood on the altar, the table for a meal, to array the battle or the combat against (לִקְרַאת, אֶת) some one; to lay a cause before the justice; to direct words, i. e. to excite them in order against (אֶל) some one, or before (לְ) some one; the word מִלִּים is sometimes omitted: transf. to arm, or prepare for battle, with omission of מִלְחָמָה; to compare with (לְ) something; to value (by comparison); related to עָרַג. Hiph. to value, to appraise. Comp. with the root in אָרַח, אָרַךְ.

עֵרֶךְ (with suff. עֶרְכִּי m. 1) a series, order (in the situation), a suit of apparel, an equipment, a full armour; 2) transf. to valuation, value, comparison of value, equality; hence כְּעֶרְכִּי mine equal.

עָרֵל (const. עֲרַל and עָרֵל, pl. עֲרֵלִים) uncircumcised, having a foreskin; transf. to uncircumcised lips, i.e. heavy of speech; uncircumcised ears, i.e. hard of hearing; uncircumcised heart, i.e. insensible, immoveable. In a Jewish point of view, עָרֵל is a term of reproach. As to the etymology, the original form is most likely עֹרֶל (from which the f. עָרְלָה), as a diminutive form of עוֹר; hence, foreskin.

עָרַל (denom. from עָרְלָה) 1) to have a foreskin, to be uncircumcised; 2) to remove the foreskin, i.e. to remove that which is defective or unclean. Niph. to appear uncircumcised, to be exposed to scorn.

עָרְלָה (pl. עֲרָלוֹת, formed from עֹרֶל) f. foreskin; בְּשַׂר עָרְלָה the member having the foreskin. In a transferred sense, עָרֵל is used of an obdurate heart, of the first fruits of the new tree which are prohibited as unclean. The plural עֲרָלוֹת p.n. of a hill.

עָרַם (inf. עֲרוֹם) 1) (not used) to bind (a sheaf); 2) to concoct deceit; next, to be cunning, artful (comp. גָּנַב, חָשַׁב, צָמַם, זָמַם). Niph. to be heaped up, to accumulate (of water), after the first signification. Hiph. to exhibit cunning, artfulness, subtlety.

עָרַם in the signification of exposing, laying bare. See under עוּר.

עָרֹם naked, bare. See עָרוֹם.

עָרְם (with suff. עָרְמָם) m. artfulness, deceit; also, dexterity, shrewdness, cunning.

עָרְמָה (fem. from עָרְם) f. artfulness, deceit, cunning.

עֲרֵמָה (pl. עֲרֵמִים and ־מוֹת) fem. a heap of sheaves, corn, or rubbish.

עַרְמוֹן (pl. ־נִים) m. (chesnut tree) in Targum דִּלּוּב, from אָרַם=עָרַם to be high.

עֵרָן p.n. m. (the active one, from עוּר).

עָרַס (not used) probably equiv. to חָרַס to dry, to bake; hence עֲרִיסָה dough, equiv. to חֲרָרָה, in the Mishna, cake, from חָרַר to dry.

עֲרֹעֵר p.n. of a Moabite city, which in another place is called עֲרוֹעֵר.

עַרְעָר masc. (the forsaken one, the rejected one) from עָרַר to be naked: transf. to a solitary tree (in the wilderness).

עֲרֹעֵר see עֲרוֹעֵר.

עֲרֹעֵר see עֲרוֹעֵר.

I. עָרַף (fut. יַעֲרֹף) transposed from רָעַף to overflow; comp. רָוָה, especially of the flowing of the rain or of the dew.

II. עָרַף (not used) equiv. to עָרַב to be dark, to be gloomy, from which עֲרִיף, which, however, according to others, is derived from עָרַף I.

עֹרֶף (with suff. עָרְפִּי). m. neck, back, from עָרַף to turn the neck (comp. רָפָה, belonging to רְפָאִים giants, and also the modern Heb. רִפְרֵף); נָתַן עֹרֶף to turn the back, i.e. to turn away; the same פָּנָה עֹרֶף אֶל, otherwise הָפַךְ, פָּנָה ע׳ to flee; to cause the neck to turn, i.e. to cause to flee.

עָרַף (denom. from עֹרֶף) to break the neck of a beast; next, transf. to overthrow (altars).

עָרְפָּה p.n. f. (a transposition from עָפְרָה gazelle).

עֲרָפֶל (from עָרַף, formed with the suffix ־ֶל, comp. כַּרְמֶל, סַפֵּל) m. thin cloud, in a weaker sense than עֲרִיף.

עָרַץ (fut. יַעֲרֹץ) to terrify (enemies); also intrans. to be afraid of (מִפְּנֵי) some one or something; related is רָעַץ, which see. Niph. נַעֲרָץ to be terrible; hence נַעֲרָץ the terrible one, in a stronger sense than נוֹרָא. Hiph. to be terrified, to be in fear of something.

I. עָרַק to flee after (accus.) something. The root is עָרַק, related with אָרַח, בָּרַח; הָעֹרְקִים צִיָּה they who flee into the wilderness.

II. עָרַק (not used) to tie, to bind; related to אָרַג, חָרַךְ. From which:—

עֹרֶק m. sinew, artery; comp. גִּיד and מֵיתָר.

עַרְק p.n. of a city, Arce, in Syria, some miles north of Tripolis; hence gent. עַרְקִי inhabitant of עַרְק.

עַרְקִי see עַרְק.

עָרַר (not used) bare, naked; hence to be solitary, forsaken, childless. The imp. עֹרָה belongs to עוּר, as also עֹרֵר, עַרְעֵר; הִתְעַרְעֵר, but of עֲרִירִי, עַרְעָר and עֲרוֹעֵר, the root appears to be עָרַר.

עָרַשׁ (not used) to nourish, after the Syriac; from which יַעֲרֶשְׁיָה.

עָרַשׂ (not used) origin., to bind, and next like אָגַד to arch; comp. יָרַשׁ in the sense of binding.

עֶרֶשׂ (with suff. עַרְשִׂי, pl. עַרְשׂוֹת) f. an arched bed, i.e. a bed with a tester.

עָשׁ (origin. form, for which next עַיִשׁ) m. 1) a goat, and hence the constellation *Capella* or *Arcturus*, etymologically connected with עָן; 2) a moth, from עָשֵׁשׁ.

עָשַׁב (not used) to shine, to bloom, to grow; related to אָזַב, זָהַב, צָהַב; from which עֵשֶׂב.

עֵשֶׂב (with suff. עֶשְׂבָּם, pl. c. עִשְׂבוֹת) masc. herb, especially for feeding cattle; also collectively, herbage, vegetables.

עֲשַׂב (def. עִשְׂבָּא) Aram. m. the same.

I. עָשָׂה (fut. יַעֲשֶׂה, apoc. יַעַשׂ) 1) to make, to manufacture (clothes, arms, a ship); in this sense also, to form, to create, to shape, with the accus. of the material, from which, and לְ of the object, for which, something is made; comp. בָּנָה, יָצַר, sometimes with בְּ of the material; applied to God, עָשָׂה signifies to create (heaven, earth, man); hence עֹשֶׂה creator; 2) to prepare, e.g. food, a meal, to trim the beard, to anticipate events, to prepare a sacrifice; hence, to sacrifice; עָשָׂה לַה" to offer to God; to appoint to an office, to make into (לְ) something; to make peace or war; 3) to carry out, accomplish (a counsel, a vow, a resolution); to celebrate, the Sabbath, a feast; to spend the time, to live, עָשָׂה טוֹב to enjoy one's-self; 4) to bear, to produce, used of the reproduction of beasts and plants, e.g. the cow makes, i.e. gives milk; the tree makes, i.e. bears fruit; 5) to work, to do, simply expressing the idea of activity; to execute, to practise, to continue; 6) to acquire, by labour (property, slaves, wages). Niph. נַעֲשָׂה (fem. נַעֲשְׂתָה) to be made, to be done, to become; לֹא יֵעָשֶׂה it is not done, not usual. Pi. עִשָּׂה to press (the breasts). Pu. to be made, prepared.

II. עָשָׂה belongs to the p.n. עֵשָׂו, which see.

עֲשָׂהאֵל p.n. m. (God has formed).

עֵשָׂו p.n. m. (the hairy one) son of Isaac; next, the name of a whole tribe or people whose ancestor he was; hence הַר, בֵּית, בְּנֵי עֵשָׂו.

עָשׁוֹק m. oppressor.

עֲשׁוּקִים m. pl. oppression.

עָשׂוֹר masc. a number of ten; either of days, ten days, the tenth day; or of strings, decachord; hence נֵבֶל עָ׳ a harp of ten strings.

עָשׁוֹת (after the form קָדוֹשׁ) adj. m. artificial, בַּרְזֶל עָ׳ artificial iron, i.e. steel.

עַשְׁוָת p.n. m.

עֲשִׂיאֵל p.n. m. (created by God).

עֲשָׂיָה p.n. m. (the same).

עָשִׁיר (pl. עֲשִׁירִים) masc. a rich one, wealthy one, transf. to a noble, distinguished one, and in a bad sense, to a haughty, proud one; hence, sinner, wicked one.

עֲשִׂירִי (formed from עֶשֶׂר) an ordinal number, masc.; עֲשִׂירִית, עֲשִׂרִיָּה, f. the tenth. The fem. is also used to denote the tenth part, tithe.

עָשֵׁן (fut. יֶעְשַׁן) to smoke, to burn; figur. of the wrath of God.

עָשֵׁן (pl. עֲשֵׁנִים) adj. masc. smoking, burning.

עָשָׁן (const. עֲשַׁן and עָשָׁן) masc. 1) smoke, תִּימְרוֹת, עַמּוּד, גֵּאוּת עָ׳ pillar of smoke, fig. of wrath, also of a cloud of dust; 2) p. n. of a city, perhaps identical with כּוּר עָשָׁן.

עָשַׁק (fut. יַעֲשֹׁק) orig. to press, to urge; hence, 1) to oppress (the poor, the helpless), to subjugate (a people), to chastise (said of God), עָשׁוּק violence done to the blood of any one; 2) to cheat, defraud (with the acc. of the person, and also with the acc. of the object of which one is defrauded); figur. of a river which encroaches on, or overflows, its banks; to be proud, haughty. Pu. of violence perpetrated on a virgin.

עָשַׂק (Kal, not used) orig. to touch a matter, to occupy oneself with something, thus equiv. to עָשָׂה. Hith. with עִם, to have to do with some one, i.e. to strive or contend with some one.

עֵשֶׁק p. n. m. (oppression, exaction).

עֹשֶׁק m. 1) violence, oppression; next, property got by oppression, the gain of cheating; 2) trouble, strait, distress.

עֵשֶׂק (strife, contention) p. n. of a well near Gerar.

עָשְׁקָה f. distress, anguish; more correctly, however, to take it as imp. like עָרְבֵנִי, to which it is joined, Isa. 38:14; comp. אָרְחָה־לִּי, but in the sense of חָשַׁק, to be inclined towards (לְ) something.

עָשַׁר (fut. יַעְשַׁר) to be straight, upright, related to אָשַׁר, כָּשַׁר (יָשַׁר), transf. to thrive, to be prosperous, (אָשַׁר) to be rich: the orig. signif. is, according to some, in the Ketib עָשַׂר 1 Kings 22:49, to erect; probably, however, the more correct reading in that passage is עָשָׂה. Hiph. הֶעֱשִׁיר (fut. יַעֲשִׁיר) 1) to present richly (of the fructifying of the soil), to enrich; 2) to gather, get riches. Hith. to appear, or to pretend to be rich. Comp. עָתַר.

עֹשֶׁר (with suff. עָשְׁרִי) masc. riches, wealth, happiness, transf. to pride, wickedness.

עֶשֶׂר a cardinal number, f.; עֲשָׂרָה (const. עֲשֶׂרֶת) masc. ten, always connected with the plur., or like עֲשָׂרָה לֶחֶם collectively. The pl.

עֶשְׂרוֹת signifies, tens. The etymology cannot be traced to any verbal root.

עִשֵּׂר (denom. from עֶשֶׂר, fut. יַעְשֹׂר) to tithe, to impose the tenth as a tax (on צֹאן, כֶּרֶם). Pi. עִשֵּׂר to tithe, to give the tenth to (לְ) some one. Hiph. הֶעְשִׂיר (inf. with לְ, לַעְשֵׂר) the same.

עָשָׂר a cardinal number, m., עֶשְׂרֵה fem. ten, only in connection with units to denote the numbers from 11 to 19. From עֶשְׂרֵה arose the dual עֶשְׂרִים (for עֶשְׂרַיִם) twice 10=20, which is also used as an ordinal number.

עֲשַׂר f., עַשְׂרָא m. Aram. the same, ten; עֶשְׂרִין twenty.

עֶשְׂרֵה see עָשָׂר.

עִשָּׂרוֹן (pl. עֶשְׂרֹנִים) m. a tenth, as a measure for corn or flour; formed from עָשָׂר.

עָשֵׁשׁ (in pause עָשֵׁשָׁה) to decay, to become old, of the sight being consumed.

עָשַׁת (3 pl. עָשְׁתוּ) to glisten (with fatness), comp. עָשַׁשׁ modern Heb. to shine; hence, עֲשָׁשִׁית lantern.

עָשַׁת (Kal, not used) to spin, to weave (comp. שָׁתָה in signif. 2); hence, transf. to reflect, to think, a mode of transferring as in חָשַׁב and זָמַם. Hith. הִתְעַשֵּׁת to consider, to reflect, for (לְ) some one.

עֲשִׁת (Aram.) the same, to reflect upon something.

עֶשֶׁת (contracted from עֶשְׁתֶּת, comp. מְשָׁרֶת for מְשָׁרֶתֶת, to avoid the clashing of the two ת) fem. something artificially designed, work of art, similar to מַחֲשֶׁבֶת, מְלָאכֶת.

עַשְׁתּוּת (after the form עַבְדוּת) f. the consideration, reflection, formed from עָשַׁת.

עַשְׁתֵּי in connection with עָשָׂר and עֶשְׂרֵה eleven; also as an ordinal number, the eleventh. According to Abulwalid it is contracted from עַד שְׁתֵּי or עַל־שְׁתֵּי.

עֶשְׁתֹּנֶת (after the form אַרְמֹנֶת, only pl. with suff. עֶשְׁתֹּנֹתָיו) f. thought, plan, from עָשַׁת.

עַשְׁתֹּרֶת (pl. עַשְׁתָּרוֹת, const. —תְּרוֹת, from a sing. עַשְׁתֶּרֶת) f. 1) Astarte, a Phenician goddess, who was worshipped by licentious rites, and adored in common with בַּעַל, she was a symbol of the planet Venus, hence also the goddess of fortune and love. The plur. signifies the statues of Astarte, comp. בְּעָלִים; 2) figur. the ewes of the flock which yield increase, and thus similar to the goddess Astoreth; 3) p.n. of a city where the worship of Astarte was practised, which city is sometimes called

בְּעַשְׁתְּרָה, i.e. בֵּית עַשְׁתְּרָה, sometimes עַשְׁתְּרוֹת or בֵּית עַשְׁתְּרוֹת קַרְנַיִם (the horned Astarte), gent. עַשְׁתְּרָתִי from עַשְׁתְּרָה.

עֵת (before makkaph עֶת, with suff. עִתִּי, pl. עִתִּים and עִתּוֹת) com. 1) time (from עָנַת). e.g. עֵת הַזָּמִיר, עֵת נְקָמָה, also with the genitive following. מֵעֵת עַד־עֵת, מֵעֵת אֶל־עֵת from time to time. עֵת is joined with prepositions to define the time, as כְּעֵת, לְעֵת, בְּעֵת, בְּעֵת at or about the time; sometimes only acc. עֵת; 2) a special time; (a) time of youth, עִתֵּךְ עֵת דֹּדִים thy time was the time of love (or youth); וִיהִי עִתָּם לְעוֹלָם their time should have endured for ever; (b) the proper, fitting time, e.g. Ps. 1:3, "that bringeth forth his fruit in his season" (בְּעִתּוֹ), the same (אָכְלָם, דָּבָר, מָטָר בְּעִתּוֹ); לֹא עֵת (accus.) not at the proper time, premature; (c) time of the year, e.g. כָּעֵת חַיָּה according to the time of life, at the revival of this time, i.e. in the next spring; הָעֵת גְּשָׁמִים the season is (a season) of rain; (d) a certain time appointed by Providence, time of misfortune, the last time (hour), e.g. Eccles. 3:1, "to everything there is a season;" 9:11, "time and chance happeneth to them all." The pl. עִתִּים 1) times, in reference to chronological calculation; hence יֹדְעֵי בִינָה לָעִתִּים or יֹדְעֵי הָעִתִּים those who understand the times, astrologers; 2) in the sense of fate, destiny, e.g. צוֹק הָעִתִּים, where also עִתּוֹת is used; 3) times, e.g. עִתִּים רַבּוֹת many times.

עַתָּ see עַתָּה.

עֵת קָצִין (with ה finis עִתָּה קָצִין, people of the judge; עֵת being contracted from עָנַת) p.n. of a city in Zebulum.

עָתַד (Kal, not used) to be prepared, ready; hence Pi. עִתֵּד to prepare, to appoint. Hith. to be prepared, appointed for (לְ) something; the original signification is to found; related to יָסַד, שֵׁת.

עָתָה (not used) belongs to עַתָּה, which see.

עַתָּה (in pause עָתָּה, from עֵת with ה finis) adv. now, at present, orig. at this time, in contrast to אָז; עַתָּה זֶה now then, עַד עַתָּה until now, לֹא עַתָּה no further, וְעַתָּה and now? עַתָּה הִנֵּה behold now! אֵיפֹה עַתָּה well now! גַּם עַתָּה thou art now; transf. to the sense of soon, in a short time.

עתוּד (in Ketib for עָתִיד, pl. עֲתוּדוֹת Keri) adj. m. prepared, ready; the plur. signifies property, gotten or prepared, treasures.

עֲתַלְיָה p. n. m. & f. (humbled by God).

עֲתַלְיָהוּ p. n. f. (the same).

עָתַם (Kal, not used; a secondary verb from עָם, עִים, like שָׁתַן from (שָׁן) to glow, to burn; hence Niph. נֶעְתַּם to be burnt, to be set on fire (of a country).

עָתַן (not used; comp. (יָתַן) to be strong, powerful; from which:—

עָתְנִי (formed from עֹתֶן a lion) p. n. m. (lion-hearted one).

עָתְנִיאֵל p. n. m. (lion of God).

עָתַק (fut. (יֶעְתַּק) to remove, e. g. a rock; related to נָתַק, אָתַק. Hiph. to remove from one place to another, i. e. the tent; thus, to journey, to remove mountains, to translate from one writing to another, to copy; to carry together, compile; to move away, to take away words, i. e. to deprive some one of speech; from which עַתִּיק 1.

עָתֵק (intrans.) to get old, aged, in Targ. for בָּלָה; 2) to be stiff; hence, to be strong, firm; transf. to be comely, distinguished.

עָתָק m. that which is strong, bold, daring, insolent, from עָתֵק 2; דִּבֶּר עָתָק to speak hard things, i. e. haughtily.

עָתֵק adj. m. strong, mighty, of property, i. e. that which is available, tangible, durable.

עַתּוּד (plur. (עַתּוּדִים) m. he-goat, a buck, orig. the robust, strong one, from עָתַד; transf. to leaders of the people, who like the buck take the lead of the flock.

עַתַּי p. n. m. (equiv. to עִתִּי born at the proper time).

עִתִּי (formed from עֵת) adj. m. one who is present at the opportune time, or one who is appointed at a certain time.

עָתִיד (pl. (עֲתִידִים) adj. m. עֲתִידָה (pl. (עֲתִידוֹת) f. prepared, appointed, ready, for (לְ) something, practised to do something; עֲתִידוֹת as a subst. riches, treasures, orig. property got or prepared; comp. עֲתוּדוֹת.

עֲתִיד (Aram.) the same.

עֲתָיָה p. n. m. (probably equivalent to (עֲשָׂיָה).

עָתִיק adj. m. comely, beautiful, of a dress, orig. firm, strong; see עָתֵק 2.

עַתִּיק (pl. עַתִּיקִים, const. (עַתִּיקֵי) adj. m. 1) removed (from the breast), i. e. weaned, from עָתַק; 2) old, from עָתֵק.

עַתִּיק (Aram.) adj. m. old (in days).

עָתַךְ (not used) to turn in, to alight, after the Arab; from which:—

עֲתָךְ (an inn), p. n. of a city in Judah.

עָתַל (not used) to act violently, after the Arab. from which:—

עַתְלַי p. n. m. (oppressor).

I. עָתַר (fut. יֶעְתַּר) origin. equiv. to קָטַר to pay homage to deities; transf. to implore, to pray to (לְ, אֶל) God, to worship. Niph. to be entreated (with לְ); hence, to hearken, to grant a request; inf. absolute נַעְתּוֹר. Hiph. to address a prayer to (אֶל) some one, and to pray generally; with לְ or בְּעַד, to pray for or in behalf of some one.

II. עָתַר (Kal, not used) to overflow; related to יָתַר, perhaps only a secondary form from עָשַׁר. Hiph. הֶעְתִּיר to do something in abundance, to increase, to multiply words against (accus.).

עָתָר (const. עֲתַר) m. 1) fragrance, e. g. עֲתַר עֲנַן הַקְּטֹרֶת; 2) after the form חָכָם; adorer, worshipper, from עָתַר I.

עֶתֶר (abundance) p.n. of a city in the tribe of Simeon.

עֲתֶרֶת (formed from עֶתֶר) f. abundance, richness, fulness, from עָתַר II.

עָתַת (not used) equiv. to עָדַד to number, to calculate, from which עֵת, like עִדָּן, from עָדַד.

פ

פ פ׳ ף (פֵּא) is the seventeenth letter of the alphabet; its name (פֵּא=פֶּה mouth) was chosen on account of its shape; as a numeral, it counts 80. At the beginning of a syllable, פּ is pronounced like the letter *p* in English; at the end of a syllable, it is soft, and pronounced like *ph*. It interchanges often with ו, מ, ב, its fellow labials, as חָפַר and קָבַר, פָּזַר and בָּזַר, and others.

פֹּא equiv. to פֹּה here; comp. פֹּה, פּוֹ.

פָּאָה (Kal, not used) to breathe, to blow, comp. פָּרַח, אֶפַע, פָּעָה; hence, Hiph. הִפְאָה (fut. יַפְאֶה) to puff away, to strew, to scatter about.

פֵּאָה (const. פְּאַת, dual פְּאָתַיִם, from which const. פַּאֲתֵי, pl. פֵּאוֹת) f. 1) wind, orig. that which waves (from the masc. פָּאָה); transf. to the region, or side of the wind, part of the world (after the analogy of רוּחַ), e. g. פְּאַת יָם western side; פְּאַת צָפוֹן northern side; 2) territory, country generally, e.g. פַּאֲתֵי מוֹאָב the sides of Moab (the two sides of the country of Moab); 3) corner, side of a thing, e.g. the corner of the beard, field, bed; קְצוּצֵי פֵאָם people whose beards are shorn in the corner, as a name of derision of several nationalities. The root is פָּאָה.

פְּאֵם belongs to פּוּם and פִּימָה. See פּוּם.

פָּאַר (Kal, not used) to shine, to glitter, related to בָּהַר; transf. 1) to bloom, to grow, which ideas in Hebrew always proceed from brightness; comp. זִיו, פָּרַח, יָרַק, etc.; 2) to be distinguished, glorious; comp. אָדַר, הָדַר. Pi. פֵּאֵר to glorify, to decorate, e.g. "to beautify the meek with (בְּ) salvation," תְּפָאֵר Deut. 24:20, is the denom. from פֹּארָה, to which it belongs. Hith. 1) to be glorified; 2) to glorify oneself; in a bad sense, to boast against (עַל) some one, to exalt oneself proudly over (עַל) something.

פָּאַר (not used) to deepen out, to dig, related to בָּאַר, especially of a utensil.

פְּאֵר (pl. פְּאֵרִים, const. פַּאֲרֵי, with suff. פְּאֵרֵיכֶם, פְּאֵרְךָ) m. magnificent decoration; transf. to turban, head-dress, from פֵּאֵר to beautify.

פֹּארָה (from פֻּארָה, comp. שְׁאֵלָה from שְׁאֻלָּה; pl. פֹּארוֹת for פֻּארוֹת, with suff. פֹּארֹתָיו, also פֹּרְאֹתָיו, where the א is transposed) f. beauty of the tree (according to Kimchi), branch, from פָּאַר, in the signification of blooming; from which פֵּאֵר (Pi.) to go over the branch or bough again.

פֻּארָה (for פֹּארָה) f. the same.

פָּארוּר (from פָּארוּר, after the form (נַאֲפוּף, נַעֲצוּץ) masc. brightness, beauty; קִבֵּץ פ׳ to draw in the beauty (Author. Vers. "to gather blackness"); comp. אָסַף נֹגַהּ.

פָּארָן (from פָּאַר cavern-district) p.n. of a steppe between the peninsular of Sinai, Palestine, and Idumea, in the interior of which are הַר פָּארָן, אֵיל פ׳, הַרְרֵי פ׳, etc.

פָּגַג (not used) to be unripe, orig. to be cold; comp. בָּשַׁל to be ripe, orig. to be cooked; hence:—

פַּגָּה (sing. not used, pl. פַּגִּים) fem. unripe figs, those which grow in winter.

פִּגּוּל masc. that which is unclean, loathsome; בְּשַׂר פִּגּוּל abominable flesh; פִּגֻּלִים unclean food.

פָּגַל (not used) to be polluted; hence, to excite disgust; related is בָּחַל, which see.

פָּגַע (fut. יִפְגַּע) orig. to push violently against something; hence, 1) to attack, to fall upon something (to hurt it), to kill; 2) to press out, to urge, entreat, to alight, to meet something or some one, to border on (אֶל, בְּ) something, all in a good sense; 3) to bind, to make a covenant with (accus.) some one. In all these significations, the original idea is to come in contact with something. Hiph. הִפְגִּיעַ 1) to cause some one to be beat violently, or to be hurt generally; 2) to cause some one to pray or request urgently; 3) to cause some one to attack; hence מַפְגִּיעַ an enemy, an attacker.

פֶּגַע masc. occurrence, anything that meets or happens to some one, as lot, fate, event, from פָּגַע to meet.

פַּגְעִיאֵל p.n. m. (destiny from God).

פָּגַר (Kal, not used) to be wearied, slack; hence transf. to be indolent, sluggish. Pi. פִּגֵּר to be exceedingly sluggish, or to forbear, desist from (מִן) something. See פֶּגֶר.

פֶּגֶר (const. pl. פִּגְרֵי) m. corpse, orig. weak, wearied, mass; hence, fig. of the blocks of the idols.

פָּגַשׁ (fut. יִפְגֹּשׁ) orig. to push against something; hence, 1) to cease, to attack, comp. פָּגַע; 2) to meet some one (accus.) after the same gradation of significations as in פָּגַע. Niph. נִפְגַּשׁ mutually to meet. Pi. to meet, with the accus.

פדד belongs to פַּדָּן. See פַּדָּן.

פָּדָה (fut. יִפְדֶּה) orig. to separate, to loosen; transf. to redeem, to release by purchase (from bondage), to liberate, to save. Niph. to be redeemed. Hiph. הֶפְדָּה to cause to be redeemed. Hoph. (inf. הָפְדֵּה) pass.

פְּדָהאֵל p.n. masc. (God is the Redeemer).

פְּדָהצוּר p.n. m. (the same).

פְּדוּיִ (after the form כְּסוּי, pl. פְּדוּיִים) m. redemption, ransom-money, different from the particip. pass., which signifies the redeemed.

פָּדוֹן p.n. m. (redemption).

פְּדוּת f. 1) separation, interval, intervening space, after the original signification פָּדָה; 2) redemption, liberation, release.

פְּדָיָה p.n. m. (God is the redeemer).

פְּדָיָהוּ p.n. m. (the same).

פִּדְיוֹם (after the form חַרְטֹם) masc. redemption, ransom money.

פִּדְיוֹן (the common form) m. the same.

פָּדַן (not used) to stretch along, to extend, related to בָּטַן, from which פַּדָּן, which see.

פַּדָּן (const. פַּדַּן, with ה finis פַּדֶּנָה) m. field, plain, but only in connection with אֲרָם; פ׳ אֲרָם plain of Syria, for which פַּדָּן but seldom stands alone. It signifies the plain of Syria, including the desert.

פָּדַע (only imp. with suff. פְּדָעֵהוּ) equiv. to פָּצַע to cut off, to sever; hence, to liberate, like נָצַל, which see.

פָּדַר (not used) to nourish, to feed, to fatten, from which:—

פֶּדֶר (with suff. פִּדְרוֹ) m. fat, orig. nourishment. See פָּדַר.

פָּה (not used) to breathe, to puff, to blow, related to פָּאָה, אֶפַע and פָּעָה, transf. to speak; from which the original particip. פֶּה, after the form שֶׂה from שָׂה.

פֶּה (const. פִּי, with suff. פִּי, פִּיךָ, פִּיו, פִּיהוּ, פִּיהֶם, poetically פִּימוֹ; pl. פִּים and פִּיוֹת) masc. mouth, from פָּה, which see; also of the bill or beak of birds, or of the mouth or opening of anything, e.g. of a sack; פִּי הָרֹאשׁ opening of a dress for the head, פִּי קֶרֶת entrance to the city, פִּי שְׁאוֹל gate of the pit of hell. פֶּה is used in the following significations: 1) as organ of speech, e.g. כְּבַד פֶּה heavy of speech, פִּי מִרְמָה, פֶּה חָלָק, etc.; hence the phrases, פֶּה אֶל־פֶּה from mouth to mouth, i.e. without medium, likewise פִּיו עִם פִּיו, פִּיהוּ אֶת־פִּיךָ; פֶּה אֶחָד one mouth, i.e. unanimous, שׂוּם, נָתַן בְּפִי פ׳ to put words in one's mouth; מַה בְּפִיו what does he say to it; to be a mouth-piece, i.e. a speaker, a pleader: transf. to sentence, command; hence, עַל־פִּי according to the sentence, command; שׂוּם יָד עַל פֶּה to put the hand upon the mouth, i.e. to be silent, the same יָד לְפֶה; 2) as the organ of tasting and eating; hence, בְּפִיו after his taste; transf. to inanimate objects, to denote that part which eats or devours as a mouth, e.g. פִּי חֶרֶב edge of the sword; לְפִי חֶרֶב (by the edge of the sword) is a phrase joined to הָרַג, הִכָּה, נָפַל, חָלַשׁ, הָמַם, הֶחֱרִים; 3) lip; next, edge, border, the utmost end of a thing, the opening being like the mouth and the border resembling the lips: thus, פֶּה לָפֶה, מִפֶּה אֶל־פֶּה from one end to another; 4) mouthful; hence, portion, part, פִּי שְׁנַיִם a double portion. Joined with prepositions it has the signification of a particle: 1) כְּפִי according to the command, sentence, expression, statement, standard, manner; אֲנִי כְפִיךָ לָאֵל I am like thee ("according to thy wish," Auth. Vers.) in God's stead; כְּפִי אֲשֶׁר after the manner, or according to, אֲשֶׁר is sometimes omitted; 2) לְפִי according to the standard, suitable to, לְפִי רֹב הַשָּׁנִים according to the number of years; 3) עַל־פִּי according to command, order; hence, sometimes like כְּפִי and לְפִי after, according to. The pl. forms, both masc. and fem., signify edges of swords or other instruments, and in reference to פִּיּוֹת, compare פִּיפָה.

פֹּה (co-relative to כֹּה, comp. ποῖος)

adv. 1) here, signifying the place of resting; 2) hither, signifying motion; 3) almost like כֹּה; thus, מִפֹּה from here, hence; see אֵפוֹא, אֵיפֹה.

פוֹ equiv. to פֹּה, which see.

פּוּאָה p. n. m.

פּוּג (fut. יָפוּג, apoc. יָפָג) to be cold, benumbed (of the heart), transf. to be faint, fatigued, wearied, slackened; the law is slacked, i.e. not practised. Niph. נְפוֹג to be without vigour, activity, of life. Comp. פָּגַר.

פּוּגָה fem. orig. weariness, slackness; hence, ceasing; comp. הֲפוּגָה.

פּוּד (not used) equiv. to מוּת to die, more correctly, however, to thrust down.

פּוּחַ (fut. יָפוּחַ) to breathe, to blow, to puff, to fan; hence, to cool oneself; הַיּוֹם יָפוּחַ the day cools. Hiph. הֵפִיחַ (fut. יָפִיחַ) 1) to blow (the fire), to fan (with בְּ and acc.), to cool a garden, to diffuse it with fragrance; הֵפִיחַ קִרְיָה to fan a city, i.e. to set it in commotion; 2) according to the mode of transferring the sense, as in פֶּה, to speak, especially in a bad sense, to speak lies (כְּזָבִים); 3) to snub, to puff at some one, const. with בְּ and לְ, e.g. to snub at the unfortunate one. יָפֵחַ, Hab. 2:3, is an adj. See יָפֵחַ.

פּוּט (not used) to be sad, to sadden, after the Syriac.

פּוּט p. n. of an African people, which some identify with the Lybians, and others with the Mauritanians.

פּוּטִיאֵל p.n. m. (saddened by God).

פּוֹטִיפַר p. n. of an Eliopolitanic priest, father-in-law of Joseph.

פּוֹטִיפֶרַע p. n. m. (the same).

פּוּךְ (not used) to color, to paint (Talmud פּוּחַ), from which:—

פּוּךְ m. paint, rouge; אַבְנֵי פ׳ glittering stones; especially the color with which the eyebrows were painted; hence, שׂוּם עֵינַיִם בַּפּוּךְ to paint the eyebrows.

I. פּוּל (not used) to be round, namely of the roundness of an elevated object. Related in the root to עֹפֶל.

II. פּוּל (not used) to fall; like the root in נָפַל, from which מַפָּל, which see.

III. פּוּל (not used) to be strong, powerful, comp. the second signification above in נָפַל, and the relative root בָּעַל to be strong.

פּוֹל m. a bean, from פּוּל I., so called on account of its round shape.

פּוּל 1) p. n. of a people and country in Africa, in connection with פּוּט and לוּד, from פּוּל III.; 2) p.n. m. (the strong one), probably related with פִּיל an elephant, so called from its strength.

I. פּוּם (not used) Aram. orig. פָּם, a secondary formation from פָּה to breathe; from which פּוּם.

II. פּוּם (not used) to nourish, to feed, the root being lengthened by ם, as in פּוּם I.; from which פִּימָה.

פּוּם (with suff. פּוּמֵהּ for פָּמֵהּ) Aram. m. mouth, like פֶּה; hence also, mouth, opening.

פּוּן (fut. אָפוּן) equiv. to פָּנָה to turn away, to vanish.

פּוּן p.n. m.

פּוּנֶה (the front part) p.n. of a gate in Jerusalem, if not equiv. to פִּנָּה.

פּוּנִי patron. formed from פּוּן.

פּוּנֹן p.n. of an Idumean city between Petra and Zoar, called later Φαίνω, and by the fathers of the church Φίννη.

פּוּעָה (for פּוֹעָה) p.n. f. (the crier), from פָּעָה.

פּוּץ (fut. יָפוּץ) to disperse, scatter, comp. נָפַץ; פּוּצִים the dispersed (i. e. the Israelites); also intrans. to spread, *fundi*. Niph. נָפוֹץ to be scattered, spread (of a people, army, flock). Po. פּוֹצֵץ to shatter to pieces (a rock). Pilpel פִּצְפֵּץ to dash to pieces (a human being). Hiph. הֵפִיץ to scatter, disperse (a people, seed, flock, etc.), to spread, drive about; מֵפִיץ the disperser, the destroyer, the enemy. Hithp. הִתְפּוֹצֵץ to be scattered abroad, destroyed. Respecting the form תְּפוֹצוֹתֵיכֶם see תְּפוּצָה.

פּוּק to totter, to stagger, to stumble; פָּקוּ פְּלִילִיָּה they stumble in judgment. Hiph. הֵפִיק to cause to move, i. e. to deliver, to accomplish, to carry out. Comp. נָפַק.

פּוּקָה fem. stumbling, that which causes one to stagger, orig. abstract, staggering.

I. פּוּר (inf. absolute פּוֹר) equiv. to פָּרַר to break to pieces, to crumble; hence Hiph. הֵפִיר to dissolve, to break (a covenant). The Piel forms פּוֹרֵר, פִּרְפֵּר, and the Hithp. הִתְפּוֹרֵר, may also be brought under this root, but they may also belong to פָּרַר, which see.

II. פּוּר (not used) to hollow out, to dig; comp. פָּאַר and בָּאַר, בּוּר.

פּוּר m. a lot, orig. a piece, a part, which may be derived from פּוּר I; פּוּרִים the name of a Jewish feast.

פּוּרָה f. winepress, orig. the hole or cavity for pressing, from פּוּר II.

פּוֹרָתָא (Persian) p.n. m. (orig. from פּוּרְדָתָא awarded by lot).

פּוּשׁ (2 pl. פִּשְׁתֶּם, fut. יָפוּשׁ) equiv. to פּוּץ to spread, e.g. of the spreading of a host of horsemen; transf. to the frivolous and vicious beasts. Niph. to be spread, scattered about.

פוט see פות.

פּוּר (not used) according to some, to be parted, divided; probably it is equiv. to פָּתָה to be open, or equiv. to בּוּר to be deepened out.

פּוּתִי (formed from פּוּת) p. n. masc. (simplicity) from פָּתָה = פָּת. Comp. פִּיתוֹן.

פָּז 1) adj. m. cleansed (by purging), of gold; 2) a subst. purified gold. Comp. בְּדִיל from בָּדַל. See פָּזַז I.

I. פָּזַז (Kal, not used) to separate (of metals); hence, to cleanse, to purge, related to פָּצַץ, פָּצָה. Hoph. part. מוּפָז purified (joined with זָהָב), for which also מְאוּפָז occurs.

II. פָּזַז (fut. יָפֹז) to move to and fro, to be flexible, pliant; וַיָּפֹזּוּ זְרֹעֵי יָדָיו and the arms of his hands were flexible, pliant (Auth. Ver. "were strong"). Pi. פִּזֵּז to hop, to spring, syn. with רָקַד, כִּרְכֵּר.

פָּזַר equiv. to בָּזַר (comp. זָרַע, זָר) to strew, scatter; שֶׂה פְזוּרָה a scattered sheep. Niph. to be scattered. Pi. פִּזַּר to scatter about, to scatter the ways; fig. to spend liberally, richly.

I. פַּח (pl. פַּחִים) masc. a snare, net, trap; פַּח יוֹקֵשׁ, יָקוּשׁ snare of the fowler; יָקֹשׁ, טָמַן, נָתַן פַּח לְ to lay a snare, or spread a net; fig. destruction, snare. The root is פָּחַח I., to bind, to tie.

II. פַּח (only pl. פַּחִים, const. פַּחֵי) m. that which is spread out, extended, thin plate, from פָּחַח II., to spread out.

פַּחַם belongs to פֶּחָם. See פֶּחָה.

I. פָּחַד (fut. יִפְחַד) to tremble, to fear (related to חַת ,פָּחַז, חָתַת), to be afraid of (מִפְּנֵי, מִן) something; also, to tremble with joy. The orig. signif. is to hasten; hence פָּחַד אֶל to flee trembling to some one. Pi. to be in continual fear or dread of (מִפְּנֵי) something; also absolute, to be thoughtful, intent. Hiph to cause to fear or tremble, to affright.

II. פָּחַד (not used) to tie, to bind, from פַּ־חַד; related is עָ־קַר, from which פַּחַד 2; which see.

פַּחַד (with suff. פַּחְדִּי, plur. פְּחָדִים, with suff. פַּחֲדָיו) m. 1) fear, trembling, terror; transf. to object of fear, i.e. God, from פָּחַד I.; 2) (only pl.) testicle, from פָּחַד II. Comp. אֶשֶׁךְ and גִּיד.

פַּחְדָּה f. terror, fear, fright.

פֶּחָה (const. פַּחַת, with suff. פֶּחָתְךָ, once פֶּחָם for פֶּחָתָם, if פֶּחָה is not the reading; pl. 1 פַּחוֹת, with suff. פַּחוֹתֶיהָ; pl. 2 פַּחֲווֹת, as if the sing. were פַּחוּ) m. pacha, or governor. The original signif. is associate or friend (of the king), according to the etymology of the old Persian.

פֶּחָה (const. פַּחַת, def. pl. פַּחֲוָתָא) Aram. m. the same.

פָּחָה (only Hiph.) denom. from פַּח, to lay a snare, or spread a net, to catch in a snare, only Isaiah 42:22.

פָּחַז equiv. to פָּחַד to move to and fro; hence, equiv. to the transposed חָפַז to hasten, transf. to swerve, to transgress the path, to be frivolous, overbearing. The signif. to boil over, is tropical.

פַּחַז m. haste, swiftness; fig. unstableness, wantonness.

פַּחֲזוּת f. transgression of the limits, frivolity, wantonness.

I. פָּחַח (not used) to tie, to bind: related to בָּךְ, and the roots in אֲ־בָךְ, סְ־בָךְ; hence פַּח a net, and the denom. פָּחָה to spread nets, which see.

II. פָּחַח (not used) to spread out or along; comp. the root in טְ־פַח, סְ־פַח, צְ־פַח; from which פַּח 2.

פֶּחִים (after the form צַדִּיק) m. equiv. to פֶּחָם glowing of fire, live coals; transf. to lightning, from פָּחַם.

פָּחַם (not used) to glow, to burn; related to חַם; transf. to be black as a coal.

פֶּחָם (for פָּחָם) m. a live coal, from פָּחַם, which see; rarely for the dead coal.

פָּחַר (not used) to form, to shape; synon. with יָצַר; from which פֶּחָר. Another signification, to seethe, to boil, is only an extended form of חַר.

פֶּחָר (origin. for פַּחַר) Aram. m. a potter.

פָּחַת (not used) origin. to decrease, diminish (related in the root with חָמָא and חָתָה); hence, to dig out, to deepen out. From which:—

פַּחַת (pl. פְּחָתִים) m. a pit, something deepened out; פִּי־פ' mouth or edge of a pit.

פַּחַת־מוֹאָב (stadtholder of Moab) p.n. m. in the period after the exile.

פְּחֶתֶת f. deepening, especially that which arises from a plague spread in the garment; Author. Vers. "fret inward"

פִּטְדָה fem. a topaz, as generally explained etymologically.

פֶּטֶר m. that which breaks forth in the flower, the bud.

פְּטִיר Ketib instead of פָּטוּר, which see under פָּטַר.

פַּטִּישׁ m. a hammer that shatters the rock; hammer of the earth, i.e. destroyer, devastator.

פַּטִּישׁ (Ketib, pl. פַּטִּישִׁין) m. Aram. overcoat or garment, from פָּטַשׁ to spread over.

פָּטַר (fut. יִפְטַר) origin. to cleave, to break; hence, to break forth (of flowers), to break up (for a journey), to loosen, to let the water take its course, to liberate, to release; hence פְּטוּרִים (Ketib פְּטִירִים) the released (from service); to dismiss, i.e. to liberate; also intrans. to be free from service. Hiph. to divide the mouth, i.e. to open it widely as an indication of scorn. The root in פָּ־טַר is related to that in בָּ־תַר, חָ־תַר, פָּ־תַר, and נָ־תַר.

פֶּטֶר m. origin. breaking through (of the womb), matrix; hence, generally, connected like רֶחֶם; next concr. that which breaks through, the first-born.

פִּטְרָה f. the same.

פָּטַשׁ (not used) to beat something thin, to flatten, to hammer. The root is related to that in נָטַשׁ. From which פַּטִּישׁ.

פִּי const. from פֶּה, which see.

פִּי־בֶסֶת p.n. of a city in Lower Egypt, Bubastis (originally dedicated to Diana, the Diana of the Egyptians being called בֶּסֶת.

פִּיד m. calamity, destruction, from פּוּד, which see.

פָּיָה a root erroneously adopted for פֵּיָה, which see; comp. פֶּה.

פֵּיָה (an extended form from פִּי, which also occurs in the absolute form) f. edge of the sword. The Root is פֶּה, as belonging to פִּי.

פִּי הַחִירוֹת p.n. of a place in Egypt. Etymologically it signifies place of reeds.

פִּיחַ m. ashes, dust, that which is easily blown away, from פּוּחַ.

פִּיכֹל p.n. m. (a colourer, a painter, from פּוּךְ, with the nominal termination ־ֹל).

פִּילֶגֶשׁ see פִּלֶגֶשׁ.

פִּימָה f. fat, corpulence, from פּוּם.

פִּינְחָס p.n. m. (the brazen-mouthed one).

פִּינֹן p.n. of an Idumean chief of a tribe.

פִּיפִיּוֹת f. pl. double-edges, פִּי being doubled. See פֶּה.

פִּיק m. tottering, staggering, trembling, from פּוּק.

פִּישׁוֹן (pouring forth, from פּוּשׁ) p. n. of a river, by which some understand the Indus, and others, the Ganges.

פִּיתוֹן p.n. m adder, serpent.

פַּךְ (from פָּכָה) m. flask, bottle.

פָּכָה (Kal, not used) equiv. to בָּכָה to flow, to pour forth; hence Pi. to flow out.

פָּכַר (not used) to bind, to fetter (after the Syriac). From which:—

פֹּכֶרֶת הַצְּבָיִים p.n.m. net of the rose. The name appears to have arisen from some event occurring there.

פָּלָא (Kal, not used) to divide, to separate, to distinguish; related to פָּלַל. Pi. פִּלֵּא to select something from the mass, to consecrate by a vow, as פִּלֵּא נֶדֶר. Hiph. הִפְלִיא and הִפְלָא (as from פָּלָה) to consecrate (a vow), also, according to the original signification, to make something extraordinary, distinguished, wonderful; inf. לְהַפְלִיא as an adv. wondrously. Niph. נִפְלָא to be separated, select, distinguished, extraordinary, wonderful, immeasurable, difficult, e. g. "three things are too wonderful for me" (נִפְלְאוּ), "is there anything too hard for the Lord" (יִפָּלֵא)? "thy love to me was wonderful" (נִפְלְאַתָה); most frequently occurs the part. נִפְלָאוֹת wonders, which is also used as an adv. wonderfully, or as a subst. דַּבֵּר נִפְלָאוֹת speaking wonderful things. Hith. to shew oneself powerfully against (בְּ) some one, i.e. in punishing him.

פֶּלֶא (with suff. פִּלְאֲךָ, pl. פְּלָאִים and פְּלָאוֹת) m. wonderful, great, extraordinary thing; next, wonder, generally; the masc. plur. is also used as an adverb, wondrously, remarkably.

פִּלְאִי adj. m. from פֶּלֶא; the fem. is פִּלְאִיָּה wonderful. The Keri has פְּלִי and פְּלִיאָה, quite after another formation. See פָּלִיא.

פְּלָאיָה p.n.m. (distinguished by God).

I. פָּלַג (Kal, not used) equiv. to פָּלַח to separate, to split (related to פָּלַח). Hence Niph. נִפְלַג to be divided (of the dispersion of the nations in consequence of the confounding of speech). Pi. to divide (the tongue), i.e. to disunite.

II. פָּלַג (not used) to flow, to spring forth; with which the root in זָלַג is related.

פְּלַג (Aram.) to divide; particip. pass. פְּלִיג.

פֶּלֶג (pl. פְּלָגִים, const. פַּלְגֵי, with suff. פְּלָגָיו) m. 1) a river, a stream, even of the Euphrates; פֶּ׳ אֱלֹהִים mighty-river; פְּלָגִים water streams; 2) p.n. m. (division).

פְּלַג (Aram.) m. a half.

פְּלַגָּה (only pl. פְּלַגּוֹת) f. a division, part of a family, a host; according to others, rivers, brooks, which, however, is less suitable to the context.

פְּלֻגָּה (from a masc. form פְּלֹג) fem. division, class, order of priests.

פְּלֻגָּה (with suff. פְּלֻגָּתְהוֹן) Aram. f. the same.

פִּלֶגֶשׁ (more frequently פִּילֶ׳, plural פִּלַגְשִׁים) epic. orig. a harlot; next, concubine, she that cohabits, and in the same original sense also of man; the syllable שׁ‍ֶ is only the form of termination, the root is פָּלַג II.

פָּלַד (not used) to flame, to shine; thus only a transposition from לַפִּד, from which:—

פְּלָדָה (only pl. פְּלָדוֹת) f. blade of a sword, comp. לַהַט.

פִּלְדָּשׁ p. n. m.

פָּלָה (Kal, not used) to separate, to part off, equiv. to פָּלָא and פָּלַל; next, 1) to select; 2) to distinguish. Niph. to be separated. Hiph. 1) to separate, with בֵּין, to divide between one thing and another; 2) to distinguish, to select.

פַּלּוּא p. n. m. (the distinguished one), patron. פַּלֻּאִי.

פָּלַח equiv. to פָּלַג I. to cut in, to plough, to furrow; hence, to till the earth. Pi. to strike through (the liver), to divide (the womb), i.e. to bring forth young, to cut in pieces (fruit).

פְּלַח (Aram.) orig. to plough, to till the ground; next generally, to work, to serve, transf. to serve God, with accus. and לְ.

פֶּלַח f. that which is cut off, a piece (of fruit), transf. to a stone cut round, especially a mill-stone, the upper one of which is called פֶּלַח רֶכֶב the rider, and the lower פֶּלַח תַּחְתִּית.

פִּלְחָא p. n. m. (birth).

פָּלְחָן (Aram.) m. service, especially divine service, worship.

פָּלַט to escape, related to מָלַט. Pi. 1) to let some one escape, i. e. to save him, construed with מִן; 2) to bear, to bring forth, orig. to be delivered; 3) to drive away (Job 23:7, Auth. Vers. to be delivered). Hiph. to deliver, to afford refuge, and to bring into safety.

פָּלֵט (plur. פְּלֵטִים) adj. masc. flying, fugitive.

פֶּלֶט m. (orig. inf. Pi.) escaping, delivering.

פֶּלֶט p. n. m. (escape).

פַּלְטִי p. n. masc. (abbreviated from פְּלַטְיָה, delivered by God).

פִּלְטַי p.n. m. (the same).

פַּלְטִיאֵל p.n. m. (the same).

פְּלַטְיָה p.n. m. (the same).

פְּלַטְיָהוּ p.n. m. (the same).

פְּלִי see פִּלְאִי.

פֶּלִיא adj. m., פְּלִיאָה f. wondrous; see פִּלְאִי.

פְּלָיָה p. n. m. (equiv. to פְּלָאיָה).

פָּלִיט equiv. to פָּלֵט, m. (orig. adj.) fugitive.

פָּלֵיט equiv. to פָּלֵט.

פְּלֵיטָה (or פְּלֵטָה) f. escape: concrete, that which has escaped, and in this sense also coll. הָיְתָה פְלֵיטָה לְ there is yet escape for some one; the same נָתַן פְּלֵיטָה, נִשְׁאַר פְּ'

to afford escape; הָיָה לְפְ׳ to serve as means of escape.

פָּלִיל (only pl. פְּלִילִים) masc. judge, עָוֹן פְּלִילִים a crime amenable before the judges, orig. adj. m.

פְּלִילָה f. justice, orig. intercession, separation of the parties.

פְּלִילִי adj. m. (from פָּלִיל), פְּלִילִיָּה f. judicial, amenable to the court of justice; fem. also subst. justice, judge.

פָּלַךְ (not used) to turn, transf. to be round, from which :—

פֶּלֶךְ (with suff. פִּלְכּוֹ) m. 1) circuit, district (Author. Vers. half part), like כִּכָּר, גָּלִיל, after a similar etymology; hence, פֶּלֶךְ יְרוּשָׁלַיִם the district of Jerusalem, שַׂר פְּ׳ ruler of a district; 2) a round stick, for walking, transf. to a distaff, or spindle, on account of its round shape.

פָּלַל (Kal, not used) to divide, to part (synon. with גָּזַר); hence, to decide, related to פָּלָה and פָּלָא, from which Pi. פִּלֵּל to judge, i.e. to distinguish between right and wrong, transf. to believe, consider. Hith. הִתְפַּלֵּל to arbitrate, to judge between two parties, transf. to intercede for (לְ, עַל, בְּעַד) some one, to request, pray, implore (לְ, אֶל, לִפְנֵי) some one, for (אֶל) something, generally to pray to God.

פָּלָל p.n. m. (judge).

פְּלַלְיָה p.n. m. (Divine judge).

פָּלַם (not used) to conceal, to close up, comp. בָּלַם; hence, like in אָלַם, to be concealed, closed up, lonely, solitary.

פַּלְמֹנִי (from פַּלְמֹן, like אַלְמֹנִי, from אַלְמֹן) adj. m. a certain one, orig. whose name is not known, or the unknown one, the concealed one, from פָּלַם.

פְּלֹנִי 1) adj. m. (from פָּלוֹן) a certain one whose name is concealed, or any one, from פָּלָה to denote; 2) gent. of a place פָּלוֹן.

פָּלַס (Kal, not used) to be plain, smooth; hence Pi. to pave (a road); next generally, to make a road, a straight way. The signif. to weigh, is denom. from פֶּלֶס, which see.

פֶּלֶס m. weights, scales, by which two things are balanced; from פָּלַס to weigh, fig. to measure exactly.

פָּלַץ (Kal, not used) to tremble, to totter; hence not connected with פָּרַץ, but related with פָּלַשׁ I. Hith. to tremble, to shake.

פַּלָּצוּת fem. terror, trembling, shuddering.

I. פָּלַשׁ only Hith. to roll about, e.g. in ashes (בָּאֵפֶר), in dust (עָפָר). The orig. signif. is to move to and fro, like פָּלַץ.

II. פָּלַשׁ (not used) equiv. to פָּלַט, פָּלַת to flee, to hasten away; hence, to wander, either to migrate to or from a place. From which פְּלֶשֶׁת.

פָּלַשׁ (not used) equivalent to פָּלַט, which see.

פְּלֶשֶׁת (orig. migration to or from a place) p. n. of a tract of land in Palestine (orig. land of migration); later it was used as the name for the whole of Palestine. From which:—

פְּלִשְׁתִּי (pl. ־תִּים or תִּיִּים) gent. from פְּלֶשֶׁת Philistines who had emigrated from כַּפְתֹּר; the Mediterranean sea is therefore called יָם פְּלִשְׁתִּים Philistine sea.

פָּלַת (not used) equiv. to פָּלַט to hasten away, to flee. From which:—

פֶּלֶת p.n. m. (flight, haste).

פְּלֵתִי (formed from פֶּלֶת, like כְּרֵתִי, from כָּרֵת) adj. m., which, however, is used as a subst.; runner, from פָּלַת, in connection with כְּרֵתִי executioner, forming the body-guard of the king. See also כְּרֵתִי.

פֵּן erroneously supposed to belong to פִּנָּה, Prov. 7:8. See פִּנָּה.

פֶּן (with makkaph following, thus from פֵּן; hence, probably from פָּנָה) orig. a subst., removal, but used only as a conjunctive, lest, *ne*, preventing an action the occurrence of which is dreaded. In this sense, פֶּן stands either in the concluding sentence, succeeding the action which is to prevent another, or at the beginning of a sentence of prohibition, admonition, or caution. In the latter case, it must be rendered "if only not."

פָּנַג (not used) equiv. to פָּנַק to be soft, smooth; transf. to be dainty, savoury.

פַּנַּג m. a dainty pasty: if it signifies balm, it is also appropriate to the above etymology under פָּנַג.

פָּנָה (fut. יִפְנֶה, apoc. יִפֶן, otherwise נִפֶן, תֵּפֶן, אֵפֶן) orig. to shine, to be visible; 1) to turn towards some one; 2) to turn generally, either to go away, or to go towards; with אֶל, לְ, accus. and ה of motion, to turn to (אֶל) some one; of the approaching of time, e.g. לִפְנוֹת הַבֹּקֶר towards morning; to turn, in order to look at something; פָּנָה אַחֲרֵי to turn, in order to follow; פָּ' מֵעִם to turn away from some one; פָּ' עֹרֶף to turn the back, i. e. to flee. Pi. פִּנָּה to cause a covered place to be seen, i.e. to clear, to move, to remove; to clear away, i.e. to make a road, with o-without דֶּרֶךְ. Hiph. הִפְנָה (fut. apoc. יֶפֶן) to turn (the back), to direct, sometimes elliptical, to turn the back, i.e. to flee; to turn round, of one who is fleeing; with אֶל, to turn the face to some one. Hoph. to be turned, directed. The orig. signif. is obvious in פָּנִים.

פָּנֶה (only pl. פָּנִים, const. פְּנֵי) com. origin. the visible part of a thing; hence, face, or the sides turned towards some one; hence also the plur. with the sing. signification, which is used as a plur. "faces." פָּנִים is often used in a transferred sense: 1) the face turned toward some one, in especial reference to be favourable toward; in verbs of direction, it signifies as much as looking upon or towards something, e.g. נָתַן, שׂוּם פָּנִים אֶל, with the inf. following, to be intent upon something; hence, intention, direction, purpose, e.g. פָּנָיו לַמִּלְחָמָה his intention is war; 2) פָּנִים in a bad sense, hence, wrath, passion, e.g. נָתַן, שׂוּם פָּנִים בְּ to direct wrath against some one; 3) person, the face being the means of identifying personality; hence, personal presence, e.g. פָּנַי יֵלֵכוּ "my presence shall accompany you;" Gen. 46:30, after having seen you personally; פָּנִים has the same signification in the phrases נָשָׂא, הִכִּיר פָּנִים—the presence of God is especially paraphrased by this word; 4) surface, e.g. פְּנֵי יָם, אֲדָמָה, הָאָרֶץ, כִּסֵּא, תְהוֹם, and this signification appears also to be the basis of עַל־פְּנֵי, אֶל־פְּנֵי; connected with garments (לְבוּשׁ, הַלּוֹט), פָּנִים signifies the outer part which covers; figur. the outward appearance of a thing, of man, of beast; next, mode and manner, inasmuch as such is dististinguishable by appearance; 5) the face or front of a thing, e.g. the front of an army, the part of a pot turned towards a fire, the edge of a sword; hence, פָּנִים adv. before, in contrast to אָחוֹר; and לְפָנִים forward (of a place), formerly or before (of time), מִלְּפָנִים from olden times, מִפָּנִים from the front. In connection with a house פָּנִים signifies the side visible on entering, פְּנִימָה within, inward. In connection with prepositions, פְּ' appears in the state of const. פְּנֵי as a particle, e.g. אֶל־פְּנֵי before the face; and, according to the signification of אֶל, in reply to the question, where or whither? אֶת־פְּנֵי before, the front of the thing, e.g. אֶת־פְּנֵי הָעִיר before the town, אֶת־פְּנֵי י״י before God; מֵאֵת־פְּנֵי away from some one, sometimes corresponding with אֶל־פְּנֵי ; בִּפְנֵי equiv. to לִפְנֵי before, hence the form עָמַד בִּפְנֵי to stand before some one, קוּם בִּפְנֵי to be disgusted with something. לִפְנֵי (with suffix לְפָנַי, ־נֶיךָ, לִפְנֵיכֶם) 1) in the presence of some one or something, e.g. לְ שֶׁמֶשׁ as long as the sun endures, לִפְנֵי יָרֵחַ as long as the moon endures; 2) at, with, e.g. to find favor, pleasure, grace with some one, to be great (גָּדוֹל) with his master; hence, sometimes equiv. with בְּעֵינֵי; 3) before, in reference to time and place, e.g. before the tent of the congregation, before the time of harvest, לִפְנֵי מִזֶּה previous; 4) before, to denote preference, precedence, e.g. לִפְנֵי דָל before thee, i.e. preferable to the poor; 5) against, especially after הִתְיַצֵּב, עָמַד, יָצָא, קוּם, קָרָה, in a hostile sense; 6) like פָּנִים according to the mode and manner, like, as; e.g. לִפְנֵי עָשׁ like the eating of the moth; and in this sense נָתַן לִפְנֵי to give for something. מִלִּפְנֵי from before some one, e.g. מִלִּפְנֵי י״י from before God; hence, after the verbs to flee, to drive away, to fear, to be terrified, to tremble, to be disheartened, to be discouraged, to humble oneself; seldom equiv. to לִפְנֵי before, of time, or equiv. to מִפְּנֵי because of, e.g. to cry because of something. מִפְּנֵי away from something, e.g. מִפְּנֵיהֶם away from them; hence after the verbs to go, to flee, to hide oneself, to save oneself, from some one; to fear, to reverence, to humble oneself, to rise, to be silent (from reverence) before some one; also in the other sense of מִן, denoting the cause, where מִפְּנֵי must be rendered on account of, through, מִפְּנֵי אֲשֶׁר. עַל־פְּנֵי must be translated according to the significations of עַל; hence, 1) before the face, before the eyes, i.e. manifest, עַל־פְּנֵיכֶם manifest before you; 2) on the front side, before, e.g. before the wind, before the expanse, i.e. of the heavens; or in reference to the place, east of; in reference to time, before, previous, and thus according to all the significations of פָּנִים and עַל: generally on the surface, or toward the surface; מֵעַל פְּנֵי away from the surface or presence.

פִּנָּה (from פָּנָה, with suff. once פִּנָּהּ for פִּנָּתָהּ, pl. פִּנּוֹת) fem. corner, orig. that which is prominent, from פָּנָה to shine; comp. קֶרֶן and זָוִית after the same gradation: fig. the heads or princes of the people who were prominent from the masses.

פְּנוּאֵל 1) p. n. m. (countenanced by God); 2) p. n. of a place. Sometimes פְּנִיאֵל.

פְּנִי adj. m. the inner part, joined with לְ, לִפְנֵי.

פְּנִי (only pl. פְּנִיִּים in the Ketib) m. pearl or coral, from פָּנָה to shine. Comp. דַּר.

פְּנִיאֵל p. n. masc. (the same as פְּנוּאֵל).

פָּנִים see פָּנָה.

פְּנִים m. pl. (abbreviated from פָּנִים) the inner part of a house which is visible at entering, only used in a compound; מִלִּפְנִים from within. From which פְּנִימִי.

פְּנִימָה (from פְּנִים with ה finis) orig. towards the inner part, but the signification of the ה has become lost, and signifies in the house, within; לִפְנִימָה לְ, לִפְנִימָה, מִפְּנִימָה innerly, inwardly, from within.

פְּנִימִי (formed from פְּנִים) adj. masc. (pl. פְּנִימִים), פְּנִימִית (pl. פְּנִימִיּוֹת) fem. the inner part, in contrast to חִיצוֹן.

פָּנִין (after the form קָצִין, from קָצָה, only pl. פְּנִינִים) masc. a pearl, equiv. to פְּנִי.

פְּנִנָּה (contracted from פְּנִינָה, and arose from פָּנִין) p. n. f. (pearl or coral).

פָּנַק (Kal, not used) to be soft, tender, equiv. to פָּנַג. The root is found also in עָנַג and דָּנַג, which see. Piel to faddle, fondle, pamper.

פַּס (from פָּסַס, only pl. פַּסִּים) m. orig. the end, the utmost of a thing, somewhat equiv. to אֶפֶס; next, especially extremities, hands and feet, from which כְּתֹנֶת פַּסִּים a coat reaching down to the end of the hands and feet, a stately coat (Author. Vers. "a coat of many colours").

פַּס (def. פַּסָּא) Aram. masc. the extremity of the hand, sometimes for כַּף.

פָּסַג (Kal, not used) to divide; next, to mark off, related to פָּצַע, פָּצָה, פָּשַׂק, פָּשַׂח, from which Pi. to cut through, i. e. to march through, probably related to פָּשַׂע.

פִּסְגָּה (origin. part, piece; hence, ridge of a mountain) p. n. of the top of a mountain in Moab, southerly of Sichon.

פַּס דַּמִּים equiv. to אֶפֶס דַּמִּים, which see.

פָּסָה (not used) equiv. to פָּשָׂה to

spread out; hence, to be in abundance.

פִּסָּה (from פָּסָה, const. פִּסַּת) fem. abundance, orig. spreading out; פִּ׳ בַר abundance of corn.

פָּסַח 1) origin. to remove from an object; next, to pass over, to spring over, and in const. with עַל, equiv. to עָבַר עַל to pass over something; of the destroyer, to spare; 2) to halt, to limp, fig. to be dubious, to be uncertain, of an opinion. Pi. to dance, only used by way of derision, mocking. Niph. to become lame.

פָּסֵחַ p. n. m. (the lame one).

פֶּסַח (pause פָּסַח, pl. פְּסָחִים) masc. orig. passing over (of the sparing of the Israelites in Egypt, at the plague of the first born): it also signifies 1) the sacrifice commemorating this exemption; hence, the forms שָׁחַט, אָכַל, זָבַח, עָשָׂה פֶּסַח, and in this sense the pl. signifies Paschal lambs; 2) the feast of Passover, which commences on the 14th Nissan, about Easter time: complete חַג הַפֶּסַח.

פִּסֵּחַ (plur. פִּסְחִים with the dagesh omitted) adj. m. lame, limping.

פָּסִיל (pl. פְּסִילִים) m. 1) a carved or chiselled image; 2) quarry or place where the stones are dug. Root פָּסַל.

פָּסַךְ (not used) equiv. to פָּסַג to split, to divide. From which:—

פָּסַךְ p. n. m. (equiv. to פָּסַךְ) divider.

פָּסַל (fut. יִפְסֹל) to hew out, to cut out (of stone and wood), especially to make an image; related to פָּצַל.

פֶּסֶל (with suff. פִּסְלִי). m. an image, either carved from wood or chiselled from stone, seldom of a molten image, for the pl. פְּסִילִים is used; פֶּ׳ הָאֲשֵׁרָה image of Astarte.

פְּסַנְתֵּרִין (also —תְּרִין) Aram. m., Gr. *ψαλτήριον*, a stringed instrument resembling the cither; according to some, Psalter: the termination *ιον* generally changes in Aram. into ־ִין.

פָּסַס (3 plur. פַּסּוּ) equiv. to אָפֵס to cease, to vanish, to end; hence parallel with גָּמַר, from which פַּס, the extremities of the hands or feet; but פִּסָּה belongs to פָּסָה.

פִּסְפָּה (contracted from פְּסַפְּסָה, from פָּסָה to spread out) p. n. m. (extension of progeny).

פָּעָה (fut. יִפְעֶה) equiv. to אָפַע and פָּאָה to breathe, like נָהַם in its original signification; next, to gasp, to moan, to groan.

פָּעוּ p. n. of an Idumean city, for which also stands פָּעִי.

פְּעוֹר (orig. uncovering of the nakedness, after the use of the root פָּעַר

in the Mishna and Talmud, equiv. to גִּלּוּי עֶרְוָה; 1) p.n. or rather the surname of the Moabite Baal, called בַּעַל פְּעוֹר, and which was worshipped by maidens offering their virginity; 2) p.n. of a Moabite mountain.

פָּעַל (fut. יִפְעַל, once יִפְעָל, before makkaph יִפְעָל־) poetically for עָשָׂה to make, to do, to act; also to produce, to prepare, to procure, to create, etc.; פֹּעֵל the creator; but פֹּעֵל אָוֶן worker of iniquity, evil-doer; פָּעַל לְ, בְּ, to do some one evil or good.

פֹּעַל (with suff. פָּעָלְךָ, פָּעֳלוֹ, seldom פָּעֳלוֹ; pl. פְּעָלִים) m. 1) a deed of man, good or evil, without defining the quality; 2) that which is done, work, used of Divine punishment, as well as of the beneficent deeds of God; 3) that which is acquired by activity or work, property, wages, etc., like פְּעֻלָּה.

פְּעֻלָּה (from an obsolete masc. form פָּעֻל) f. 1) the doing, acting, working, way of acting; 2) wages.

פְּעֻלְּתַי (probably abbreviated from פְּעֻלְּתְיָה) p.n. m. reward of God.

פָּעַם origin. to strike, to push, but generally urging by the spirit of God. Niph. נִפְעַם to be pushed, urged, troubled. Hith. like Niph.

פַּעַם (pl. פְּעָמִים and פְּעָמוֹת) com., origin. stroke, pushing; hence, 1) foot-step, pace; transf. to the course or wheels of a waggon, foot, pl. פְּעָמוֹת artificial feet (of a table); 2) an anvil, that upon which one strikes; 3) times, stroke, פַּעַם אַחַת once, or as an adverb, at once, but also without אַחַת; פַּעֲמַיִם twice, and so on the plur. פְּעָמִים is used with the numeral fem. gender, thus פְּעָמִים רַבּוֹת many times, פַּעַם חֲמִשִּׁית the fifth time, פַּעַם וּשְׁתַּיִם once and again, הַפַּעַם this time, עַתָּה הַפַּעַם now this time, or once, כְּפַעַם בְּפַעַם one time as the other, i.e. as usual, פַּעַם—פַּעַם now—and then.

פַּעֲמֹן (pl. —מֹנִים) masc. something which strikes to and fro, a bell, from פָּעַם.

פַּעְנֵחַ see צָפְנַת.

פָּעַר to open wide, e.g. פֶּה (once בְּפֶה) the mouth; with עַל to open the mouth against some one, with לְ for something, as an indication of wish or desire. The signification of uncovering or exposing the nakedness is only found in modern Hebrew.

פַּעֲרַי p.n. m., appears to be a corruption of נַעֲרַי, which see.

פָּצָה (fut. יִפְצֶה) equiv. to פָּצַע, to split, to cut to pieces; hence fig. 1) of the opening of the lips, either to swallow, or as a gesture of scorn, with עַל, or to speak rashly; 2) to release, to save, origin. like פָּדָה (to which it is related), to part, to separate.

פצח פָּצַח (fut. יִפְצַח) orig. equiv. to פָּצָה, generally, to break (of bones); fig. to break forth in joy, triumph; hence, generally connected with רִנָּה. Pi. to break the bones.

פְּצִירָה f. incision, cutting in, cleft; 1 Sam. 13:21, "and the mattocks had cracks" (Author. Vers. "and they had a file for the mattocks."

פצל פָּצַל (Kal, not used) to have a shell or peel. Pi. to peel off; transf. to cut in; related to בָּצַל.

פְּצָלָה (pl. פְּצָלוֹת) f. peeling, cutting off the peel.

פצם פָּצַם to cut in, to cleave (the earth). The root is an extension from פָּצָה.

פצע פָּצַע equiv. to בָּצַע to cut to pieces, Arab. to crush, to squash, in Heb. to wound, to bruise; פְּצוּעַ דַּכָּה wounded, crushed (in the testicles).

פֶּצַע (with suff. פִּצְעִי, pl. פְּצָעִים) m. wound, bruise.

פצץ פָּצַץ (not used) to scatter, to disperse, equiv. to פּוּץ.

פִּצֵּץ p. n. m. scattering, dispersion, with the article.

פצר פָּצַר (fut. יִפְצַר) origin. to cut in, comp. בָּצַר; transf. to urge, to press into some one, with בְּ of the person, either by request or by violence; comp. פָּרַץ, גָּדַר. Hiph. to press urgently, to do something intensely, perseveringly, unremittingly; inf. הַפְצַר as a noun, stubbornness, thus like מְרִי in the parallel passage, 1 Sam. 15:23.

פקד פָּקַד (fut. יִפְקֹד) orig. to visit, seek, like בִּקֵּשׁ (with which it seems to be related); hence, 1) פָּקַד לְשָׁלוֹם to seek, enquire after the well-being, like שָׁאַל לְשָׁלוֹם, בִּקֵּשׁ; next, to visit, with בְּ, of that with which one visits; 2) to seek something or some one, i.e. to concern oneself about it, like דָּרַשׁ in this sense; hence, to inspect, either to observe, to investigate, or to muster and number: פ׳ נָוֶה to visit the habitation, i.e. to search it, פְּקוּדִים they that are numbered; 3) in a bad sense, to visit some one in order to attack or punish him, with אֶל, עַל, בְּ, sometimes with the addition בְּדֶרֶךְ; 4) to require, to demand from some one; hence, to charge him with something, to appoint some one over (עַל) something, with אֵת (אֶת) to assist some one in overseeing, פְּקוּדִים overseers, officers; hence, to charge, to command; 5) to deposit something, to give it into some one's charge. Niph. 1) to be desired, wished for (of something missed); 2) to be chastised, punished; 3) to be charged with something, to be appointed overseer. Pi. to muster, to number. Pu. 1) to be mustered, numbered; 2) to be sought for (something missed). Hiph. to appoint over (לְ, בְּ, עַל) something; or absolute, to appoint as overseer or manager; with בְּיַד, עַל־יְדֵי, to deliver something to some one; with אֶת (אֵת), to deposit something with some one, and generally to give something to the charge of some one. Hoph. 1) to be chastised, punished; 2) to be appointed over something; 3) to be deposited. Hith. to be numbered, mustered. Hothpael to cause themselves to be mustered.

פְּקֻדָּה (pl. פְּקֻדּוֹת) f. 1) numbering, mustering: 2) punishment, chastisement, revenge; 3) watching, overseeing; hence, custody, prison, e.g. בֵּית הַפְּקֻדּוֹת: 4) that which is taken care of, property, wealth; 5) that with which some one is charged, office, transaction; conc. officer, overseer.

פִּקָּדוֹן masc. that which is delivered to keep, i.e. to take care of, deposit.

פְּקִדוּת f. overseeing, charge, probably from פָּקִיד.

פְּקוֹד m. 1) overseeing, management, and concrete, overseer, manager, ruler; 2) symbolical name for Babel, orig. visitation, chastisement, punishment.

פִּקּוּד (pl. פִּקּוּדִים) m. charge, command, from פָּקַד in signif. 4.

פָּקַח (fut. יִפְקַח) 1) to open (the eyes), to see; joined with עַיִן; with עַל to look upon something graciously, to open some one's eyes, either to make one (the blind) to see, or to give one something to look at: "the Lord opens His eyes upon something," is a phrase signifying He visits it with punishment; 2) to open something that is fettered or bound, transf. to open the ears, i.e. to cause to hear, and in this sense, to release, i.e. to open the prison. Niph. to be opened, of the eyes, and also in a spiritual sense.

פִּקֵּחַ adj. m. seeing, tropically, prudent, sensible, pl. פִּקְחִים.

פֶּקַח p.n.m. (opening of the eyes, or the beholding of God).

פְּקַחְיָה p.n.m. (the gracious beholding of God).

פְּקַח־קוֹחַ (orig. equiv. to פְּקַחְקֹחַ) m. orig. the opening (of a prison); hence, release, from פָּקַח. The form is after שְׁחַרְחֹר, פְּתַלְתֹּל.

פָּקִיד m. an overseer, officer, of the war, etc.

פָּקַע (not used) equiv. to בָּקַע to cleave, to split, to break forth, and like בָּקַע, may be used of the breaking forth of certain fruit.

פֶּקַע (only pl. פְּקָעִים) m. knop, an architectural ornament in the shape of a wild gourd or cucumber.

פַּקֻּעָה (pl. ־עוֹת) fem. a bitter, wild gourd or cucumber, in the shape of an egg, so called either from its rapid growth, or from its bursting on being touched. See פָּקַע.

פַּר (pause פָּר, pl. פָּרִים for פַּרִּים) a young bullock, heifer; hence שׁוֹר פַּר בֶּן־בָּקָר as explanatory; an ox or bullock; פָּרִים עִם אַבִּירִים young and old bulls (Auth. Ver. "and the bullocks with the bulls"), especially of the bulls for sacrifices. The orig. signif. is either the swift runner, from פָּרָא=פָּרַר, like עֵגֶל from עָגַל, כִּרְכָּרָה from כָּרַר; or from פָּרַר, in the signification of ploughing, a plough-ox.

I. **פָּרָא** (Kal, not used) equiv. to פָּרָה to bear, to bring forth; hence, Hiph. הִפְרִיא to bear (or bring forth) fruit, which is more probable than to take it as a denom. from פֶּרֶא related to פָּרָה 1., which see.

II. **פָּרָא** (not used) to be wild, orig. to rove, thus equiv. to פָּרָה II. Comp. *fer-us*. From which:—

פֶּרֶא (seldom פֶּרֶה, pl. פְּרָאִים) masc. orig. wild, especially the wild ass; transf. פֶּרֶא אָדָם a wild man.

פִּרְאָם p.n.m. (from פֶּרֶא the wild one).

פֹּרֹאת see פֹּארָה.

פַּרְבָּר (Persian, also פַּרְוָר, pl. פַּרְוָרִים) m. an open hall; transf. to suburb, a country seat for the summer.

פָּרַד 1) to strew about, to scatter, equiv. to בָּרַד, which see; hence פְּרֻדָה; 2) to spread out, e.g. the wings, equiv. to פָּרַשׂ, פָּרַץ; 3) to separate, part, divide, equiv. to פָּרַט. Niph. 1) to be dispersed, divided (comp. נָפַץ), from signif. I.; 2) to separate oneself, to part from (מִן, מֵעַל) something; נִפְרָד a singular, strange person. Pi. to go often aside; thus intensitive of Kal. Pu. to be separated, isolated. Hiph. to separate, distinguish between (בֵּין) two objects, to divide, with acc. Hith. to separate oneself, to part from.

פֶּרֶד (with suff. פִּרְדּוֹ, plur. פְּרָדִים, with suff. פִּרְדֵיהֶם) masc. a mule, from פָּרַד to flee, to run, after the Aram.

פִּרְדָּה f. she-mule.

פְּרֻדָה f. corn, grain, grain of seed,

from פָּרַד to strew (comp. זָרַע), or from פָּרַד to part, to specify (comp. פָּרַט).

פַּרְדֵּס (pl. —סִים) m. an orchard, a park, pleasure-garden. The word is of foreign origin, paradise.

פָּרָה to bear, to bring forth (fruit), פֹּרֶה רֹאשׁ a root bearing gall, particip. fem. פֹּרִיָּה and פֹּרָת; next, to be fruitful generally (of the multiplying of man and beast); figur. פָּרָה יֶשַׁע salvation blooms, springs forth. Hiph. הִפְרָה (fut. apoc. וַיֶּפֶר) to make fruitful, to increase, to beget abundant progeny.

פָּרָה (pl. פָּרוֹת) f. 1) young cow, derived from פַּר, also of a cow with calf, or of a cow for the yoke; the cows of Bashan, i.e. the fat cows of Bashan, are used in the Scriptures as symbols of the voluptuous women of Samaria; root פָּרַד; 2) p.n. of a city in Benjamin.

פֻּרָה p. n. m. (wine-press or presser).

פֻּרָה see פָּרָא.

פֵּרָה see חֲפַרְפֵּרֶת.

פְּרוּדָא p. n. m. (the sollitary one, the recluse).

פְּרוֹזִי (only Ketib, pl. פְּרוֹזִים) m. inhabitant of a lower country; next, generally, inhabitant of a small, town, villager.

פָּרוּחַ p.n. m. (the blooming one).

פַּרְוַיִם p.n. of a gold region; according to some, Taprobane; according to Wilford, inhabitant of the East generally.

פַּרְבָּר see פַּרְוָר.

פָּרוּר m. a pot, a kettle, contracted from פָּארוּר.

פָּרַז (not used) equiv. to פָּרַשׂ to be spread out; hence figur. to be independent, sovereign. This derivation is obviously from פְּרָזָה and פְּרָזִי.

פְּרָז (plur. with suff. פְּרָזָו) m. ruler, chief of the war, but not equiv. to שׁוֹפֵט or מְחוֹקֵק.

פְּרָזָה (only pl. פְּרָזוֹת) f. extensive, uninclosed place, plain, flat country, in contrast to a walled, fortified place.

פִּרְזוֹן (with suff. פִּרְזוֹנוֹ) m. ruler, chief of the war, like פְּרָז. The ancients explain it as equiv. to פְּרָזוֹת, which, however, is not suitable to text, Judges 5:11.

פְּרָזִי m. inhabitant of a flat country, villager (pl. פְּרָזִים).

פְּרִזִּי inhabitant of a flat country; gent. from פְּרָז, and name of a Canaanite people.

פַּרְזֶל (def. פַּרְזְלָא) Aram. masc. iron, equiv. to the Heb. בַּרְזֶל.

פָּרַח (fut. יִפְרַח) 1) to sprout, to bloom; transf. to the flourishing condition of man or of a people;

figur. of the breaking forth of leprosy, or of an ulcer; 2) to fly, comp. נָצַץ after the same gradation of ideas. Hiph. to cause to bloom, to bring forth blossom, to bud.

פֶּרַח (with suff. פִּרְחִי) m. a sprout, a flower, a blossom; transf. to the decoration of flowers.

פִּרְחָה fem. fledged brood; transf. to despicable people.

פָּרַט equiv. to פָּרַד, to part, to separate; hence figur. to open the mouth wide for singing, like פָּצַח רִנָּה; e.g. פָּרַט עַל־פִּי הַנָּבֶל to sing to the tune of the harp.

פֶּרֶט masc. that which is separated, single; hence, single berries which drop during the gathering.

פְּרִי (with suff. פִּרְיִי, פֶּרְיְךָ, פִּרְיְכֶם, with quiescent *yod* פִּרְיהֶם) masc. fruit (of the trees, or of the earth); hence, seed, corn; also of the fruit of the womb, descendants, with or without בֶּטֶן; transf. to fruit, i.e. a consequence of something, also of property acquired by labour (of the hands).

פְּרִידָא p.n. m. (equiv. to פְּרוּדָא).

פָּרִיץ (const. פְּרִיץ, but plur. פָּרִיצִים, const. פָּרִיצֵי) adj. m. violent, attacking, hurting, but generally as a subst. the violent one, the robber מְעָרַת פָּרִיצִים cave or den of robbers.

פָּרַךְ (not used) 1) to break to pieces, to crush; equiv. to פָּרַק, related to פָּרַע; hence, 2) to separate, to part, like פָּרַק.

פֶּרֶךְ m. oppression, rigour, severity, harshness.

פָּרֹכֶת (according to Eben Ezra, it is *milrang*) f. origin. partition-wall, curtain of partition, a veil for the ark, partition.

פָּרַם (fut. יִפְרֹם) orig. to split; transf. to tear, to rend (garments).

פַּרְמַשְׁתָּא (Persian) p.n. m. (chief, distinguished one).

פַּרְנָךְ p.n. m.

פָּרַס (fut. יִפְרֹס) to break to pieces, to part, e.g. לֶחֶם bread, transf. to the meals of consolation in mourning, Jer. 16:7 (Auth. Vers. "tear themselves"), with the omission of לֶחֶם. Hiph. הִפְרִיס to divide the hoof.

פְּרַס (Aram.) to divide, to part, particip. pl. פָּרְסִין, those who divide or shall be divided.

פָּרַס (land of horses) p.n. of a country, Persia; from which gent. פַּרְסִי.

פֶּרֶס m. name of a bird, ossifrage.

פַּרְסָה (pl. פְּרָסוֹת, const. פַּרְסוֹת, but also פַּרְסֵיהֶן) f. hoof, claw, especially the divided one, from which denom. הִפְרִיס having strong or large hoofs, being well hoofed.

פַּרְסִי gent. m. a Persian.

פַּרְסִי (def. פַּרְסָאָה, Ketib פַּרְסָיָא) Aram. m. the same.

פָּרַע (fut. יִפְרַע) equiv. to פָּרַץ; 1) to cut in, to break in; hence, to press violently into something, to invade in a hostile sense, בִּפְרֹעַ פְּרָעוֹת בְּיִשְׂרָאֵל and violent attacks broke forth in Israel; 2) to divide, to separate; hence, to destroy, to tear asunder; e.g. of the frustrating of a counsel, of the abandoning of discipline, or righteous course; 3) to rove about wildly, like פָּרַץ; פָּרֻעַ הוּא the people are refractory; to isolate, by division, פְּרָעֹה אַהֲרֹן Aaron has isolated them; 4) to break off, to cease, to remit, לֹא אֶפְרַע I shall not forbear. From this signification the sense of loosening, redeeming, paying, has originated in the Aram. and in the Talmud. Niph. to be divided, split, of a people. Hiph. 1) to cause some to break off something, to hinder from (מִן) a work; 2) to make refractory, reckless; the signification to uncover, see under פָּרַע.

פֶּרַע m. hair, from פָּרַע to part, to split, orig. that which is split, like שֵׂעָר hair, from שָׂעַר equiv. to שָׁעַר; from which denom. פָּרַע to shave off the hair.

פְּרָעָה (only pl. פְּרָעוֹת, const. פִּרְעוֹת) f. equiv. to פִּרְצָה breach, attack, hostility, rent; next, wound, bruise, רֹאשׁ פַּרְעוֹת אוֹיֵב the bruised head of the enemy.

פַּרְעֹה native title of the Egyptian kings, which sometimes precedes the special name, e.g. פַּרְעֹה נְכֹה, פ׳ חָפְרַע. The signif. must be derived from the Egyptian.

פַּרְעֹשׁ (from פָּרַע formed with the suff. ־ֹשׁ) m. 1) a pricking insect, a flea; 2) p. n. m. (the piercing one).

פִּרְעָתוֹן (a rent, breach, bay, formed from פִּרְעָה) p. n. of an Ephraimite city, gent. פִּרְעָתֹנִי.

פַּרְפַּר (mobility) p. n. of a small river in the vicinity of Damascus, now called El-Faiga.

פָּרַץ (fut. יִפְרֹץ) equiv. to פָּרַע to cut in, to tear, rend; hence, 1) to pull down (a wall, fortress, hedge); 2) to press upon or in (בְּ) something, to break into something, (acc.) to penetrate violently, i.e. to make a defeat among (בְּ) something, fig. to press some one by request; 3) only a secondary form of פָּרַשׂ to disperse, spread out, to overflow, and to increase generally. Niph. to be spread, extended (of prophecy). Pual, to be pulled down (of a wall). Hith. to separate, to release oneself, used of slaves who arbitrarily release themselves.

פֶּרֶץ (pl. פְּרָצִים and פְּרָצוֹת) m. 1) a rent, breach, עָמַד בַּפֶּ' to stand forth in the breach, i.e. to ward off danger; 2) attack, defeat, פֶּ' עַל פֶּ' attack upon attack; 3) scattering, pouring out of water; 4) p.n. of a place (defeat), e.g. פֶּ' עֻזָּה (defeat of Ussah); 5) p.n. m. (breach), patron. פַּרְצִי.

פָּרַק (fut. יִפְרֹק) 1) to break, to break off, to tear off, orig. to break the bones; 2) fig. to release from danger, or to break the fetters. Pi. to tear off (the hoofs), to destroy, to shatter (mountains). Hith. 1) to tear oneself away from some one or something, or mutually to plunder themselves; 2) to be destroyed, shattered.

פְּרַק (Aram.) to loosen, redeem, release, comp. Heb. פָּרַק in signification 2.

פָּרָק (const. פְּרַק) m. equiv. to מָרָק, that which is boiled; hence, broth. The root פָּרַק is identical with מָרַק.

פֶּרֶק m. 1) violence, robbery, from פָּרַק to tear away; 2) turn of the road, cross road, from פָּרַק to break off.

פָּרַר (inf. פֹּר=פּוֹר) 1) to crush, to bruise, to pound (related to עָרְפַר, פָּאַר, פָּר, אָרְפַר); hence, 2) to cut in, to plough, from which פַּר. Hiph. הֵפֵר (in pause הֵפַר, infin. הָפֵר, with suff. הֲפִרְכֶם) to break, destroy, of the breaking of a covenant, of the frustrating of a counsel, of the breaking of a vow, etc. Hoph. pass. Po. פּוֹרֵר to split, divide (the sea). Pilpel פִּרְפֵּר to shiver, to shatter. Hith. הִתְפּוֹרֵר to be shattered, shivered to pieces.

פָּרַשׁ (fut. יִפְרֹשׁ) 1) to separate, to part, equiv. to פָּרַד, transf. to define, specify, i.e. to state all the special parts; 2) to spread out. Niph. to be scattered, dispersed. Pu. פֹּרַשׁ to be explained distinctly, expounded, part. מְפֹרָשׁ distinct, exact. Hiph. to pierce, to cut in, equiv. to פָּרַס.

פָּרַשׂ (fut. יִפְרֹשׂ) 1) equiv. to פָּרַס to break (the bread), to divide, and generally to divide into pieces (of food); 2) equiv. to פָּרַץ to spread out (a garment, a net, the canvass of a tent, the hands, the wings), to stretch out (the hands) for prayer, or for giving a present, or for plunder, fig. to diffuse, extend (folly). Niph. to be scattered (e.g. לְכָל רוּחַ). Pi. פֵּרַשׂ (fut. יְפָרֵשׂ) 1) to spread out (the hands), also with בְּ; 2) to scatter about.

פְּרַשׁ (Aram.) the same as פָּרַשׁ. Pa.

to explain distinctly. Part. מְפֹרָשׁ distinct, exact.

פָּרָשׁ (const. פָּרַשׁ, pl. פָּרָשִׁים) m. 1) rider, horseman (from an obsolete word פָּרָשׁ a horse), sometimes it is followed by the expletive רֹכֵב סוּס; צֶמֶד פ׳ a pair of riders, בַּעֲלֵי פָּרָשִׁים masters of horses, riders; 2) horse, but the form has changed with פָּרָשׁ=פָּרָשׁ; hence, pl. פָּרָשִׁים instead of פְּרָשִׁים.

פֶּרֶשׁ (with suff. פִּרְשׁוֹ) m. 1) dung, excrement, orig. that which separates from the body; 2) p. n. m. (separation).

פָּרָשָׁה (const. ־שַׁת) fem. definite statement, a certain sum. In modern Heb. a division of scripture, a part.

פַּרְשֶׁגֶן see פַּתְשֶׁגֶן.

פַּרְשְׁדֹן (with ה, ־דֹנָה, from פַּרְשַׁד with the suff. ־וֹן) m. dung, excrement. The suff. ־ַד is found also in other nouns.

פַּרְשֵׁז a quadriliteral from פָּרַשׂ to spread out or extend over (עַל) something.

פַּרְשַׁנְדָּתָא (Persian) p. n. m. (granted by prayer).

פָּרַת (not used) to be sweet, of water (after the Arab.). Probably equiv. to פָּרַץ.

פְּרָת (sweet water or waterfall) p. n. of a river, the Euphrates, frequently הַנָּהָר פְּ׳, נְהַר פְּ׳; with ה finis פְּרָתָה towards the Euphrates.

פֹּרָת particip. f. from פָּרָה, which see

פַּרְתָּם (pl. פַּרְתְּמִים) masc. the first, the distinguished, noble one (a foreign word).

פַּשׁ only Job 35:15. According to the LXX, an abbreviated form from פֶּשַׁע; according to tradition, however, from פוּשׁ=פָּשַׁשׁ masc. in the signification of multitude (of transgressions).

פָּשָׂה (fut. יִפְשֶׂה) to spread out, of the leprosy; related to פָּשָׂה, פָּשׂ.

פָּשַׁח (Kal, not used) equiv. to פָּסַג, פָּצַח to split, divide, tear asunder, only used in Piel.

פַּשְׁחוּר p. n. masc. (extension, from פָּשַׁח, with the suff. ־וּר).

פָּשַׁט (fut. יִפְשֹׁט, imp. פִּשְׁטָה) to spread out, to spread along, related to פָּשַׂט of the spreading of an army over (עַל) something, to plunder; next generally, to invade, for spoilation, with עַל, בְּ, אֶל, and accus., of the persons over whom the enemy spreads; transf. to the pulling off of a garment. Pi. to plunder (חֲלָלִים), orig. to strip them. Hiph. to cause some one to pull something off, to strip one, with accus. of the person and the subject; also with מֵעַל and מִמּוּל of the person, to strip off his garments, to plunder; transf. to flay (cattle). Hith. to strip, pull off (a garment).

פָּשַׁע (fut. יִפְשַׁע) to revolt from (מִתַּחַת) under whose sway one stood, to trespass against (בְּ or עַל) something, and generally to offend, especially of the rebellion of the people against their ruler. Niph. to offend one another; אָח נִפְשָׁע one brother who has offended the other.

פָּשַׂע (fut. יִפְשַׂע) to stride, to pace, orig. equiv. to פָּשַׂק spread open, with בְּ, to proceed against something.

פֶּשַׁע (with suff. פִּשְׁעִי, pl. פְּשָׁעִים) m. 1) rebellion, transgression, trespass, stronger than חַטָּאת, but like it, generally, sinning against God; 2) punishment for sin, trespass-offering, similarly to חַטָּאת is used.

פֶּשַׂע m. step, stride, pace.

פָּשַׂק to split, to divide, to spread open, e. g. to open the lips wide, to spread the feet wide (for whoredom). Pi. the same of the feet. Comp. פָּשַׂח.

פָּשַׁר (not used) equiv. to פָּתַר, orig. to split, divide; next, to explain, interpret; comp. בָּאַר with the similar gradation of ideas. From which פֵּשֶׁר.

פְּשַׁר (Aram.) the same, to interpret, to expound, inf. מִפְשַׁר. Pa. to interpret (dreams).

פְּשַׁר (def. פִּשְׁרָא, pl. פִּשְׁרִין) Aram. m. interpretation, explanation.

פֵּשֶׁר (later) m. the same.

פָּשַׁת (not used) adopted as the radical to פֵּשֶׁת and פִּשְׁתָּה, in the signif. of carding cotton, or the root is פָּשַׁשׁ, in a similar sense. It appears, however, that the supposed derivatives are of foreign origin.

פֵּשֶׁת (with suff. פִּשְׁתִּי, pl. פִּשְׁתִּים) m. cotton, complete פִּשְׁתֵּי הָעֵץ stalks of flax, signifies also cotton; next generally, linen, flax; hence אֵזוֹר, בֶּגֶד, פְּתִיל פִּשְׁתִּים, as an adj. is rendered linen. Isa. 19:9, שְׂרִיקוֹת, is only in apposition; though the ו is omitted, the word is of Egyptian origin.

פִּשְׁתָּה f. 1) the linen plant; 2) the cotton wick; hence פ׳ כֵּהָה glimmering wick (Auth. Ver. "smoking flax"), sometimes with the omission of כֵּהָה.

פַּת (with suff. פִּתִּי, pl. פִּתִּים) masc. morsel, piece, from פָּתַת to break in pieces, especially of a morsel of bread; hence, most frequently joined with לֶחֶם; pl. פִּתִּים morsels, pieces, crumbs.

פֹּת pl. **פֹּתוֹת**, from **פּוּת**) m. 1) privy part of a woman, orig. an opening; 2) the opening or hinges on which the door hangs. Root **פּוּת**.

פְּתָאִים see **פְּתִי**.

פִּתְאֹם (from **פֶּתַע**, with an adverbial termination **ם—**) adv. suddenly, momentarily, orig. in the twinkling of an eye; also **בְּפִתְאֹם**, or in connection with **פֶּתַע**, as **בְּפֶתַע** **פִּתְאֹם לְפֶתַע**, and **לְפֶתַע פִּ׳, פִּתְאֹם**. See **פֶּתַע**.

פַּתְבַּג (with suff. **פַּתְבָּגוֹ**) m. king's meat, i.e. superior viands. The word is of Persian origin, from **פַּת** lord, and **בַּג** food.

פָּתַג (not used) to state, to pronounce; next generally, to pronounce sentence, only a secondary form of **פְּסַק**; (Aram.) to decide. From which **פִּתְגָם**, which, however, is considered to be of foreign origin.

פָּתַג (not used) equiv. to **מָתַג** to tie, to wrap round; hence, to clothe. See **פְּתִיגִיל**.

פִּתְגָם (Heb. and Aram.) m. sentence, decision, edict; next generally, word, equiv. to **דָּבָר**, and like it, transf. to matter, thing. Root **פָּתַג**, if it is not a mixed form from *pedam* (Pelvi), and *peigham* (Persian), the word.

פָּתָה (fut. **יִפְתֶּה**, apoc. **יִפְתְּ**) 1) transf. to make wide, to spread out; hence, of the lips, to open wide; 2) to be wide, of the heart, to receive impression or enticement; next, to be prone to enticement, or to be enticed; particip. **פֹּתֶה** the simple one, fem. **פּוֹתָה**. Niph. to be enticed to (**עַל**) something. Pi. to entice some one (to something bad), to mislead, to decoy. Pu. pass. Hiph. to make large, spacious, extensive.

פְּתוּאֵל (for **פְּתוּעֲאֵל**) p. n. m. (beholding of God); comp. **שְׁמוּאֵל** for **שְׁמוּעֲאֵל**.

פִּתּוּחַ (pl. **־חִים**) m. engraving, graven work, sculpture; **פִּתַּח פִּ׳** to engrave.

פְּתוֹר (ditch, pit) p. n. of a place in Mesopotamia on the Euphrates.

פְּתוֹת (pl. **פְּתוֹתֵי**) m. piece, crumb.

פָּתַח (fut. **יִפְתַּח**) equiv. to **פָּתָה, פֶּתַע** to open (used of the opening of doors, gates, windows, etc.; to open the mouth, i.e. for speaking, in contrast to not opening the mouth, i.e. to be silent; to open the ear of some one, i.e. to reveal something; to open the hand, i.e. to be liberal; **פָּתַח בַּר** to open the granary, i.e. to sell openly; to open the sword, i.e. to draw it; to open the prisoners, i.e. to release them; to open a song, i.e. to begin it. Niph. to be opened (the gate, the heaven, the mouth), to be loosened (of a girdle), to be released (of a prisoner), to be let loose, or to break forth, i. e. evil. Pi. 1) to open, to loosen, the girdle, bonds; מְפַתֵּחַ he that loosens (the girdle) after the combat; 2) to furrow (the plough-field), to engrave on (precious stones). Pu. pass. to be engraven. Hith. to release oneself, to burst the fetters.

פְּתַח (Aram.) the same, to open.

פֶּתַח (with suff. פִּתְחִי, with ה finis פֶּתְחָה, pl. פְּתָחִים, const. פִּתְחֵי) m. opening, entrance; hence פֶּתַח הַשַּׁעַר entrance of the gate; transf. to door, gate, portal; בְּפֶתַח, פֶּתַח, לְפֶתַח at or before the door; פִּתְחֵי עוֹלָם gates of eternity; fig. פִּתְחֵי פִי the gates, i.e. the opening of the mouth; the signification of פְּתִיחָה is not defined.

פֵּתַח m. openness, distinctness; according to others, beginning.

פִּתְחוֹן (const. פִּתְחוֹן) m. opening of the mouth, to speak; figur. and joined with פֶּה, defence.

פְּתַחְיָה p.n. m. (delivered by God).

פֶּתִי (pause פֶּתִי, pl. פְּתָיִים or פְּתָאִים) m. orig. openness; hence transf. to simplicity, folly, the heart being open to every impression; conc. the simple one, the inexperienced one, easy to be enticed, a fool; sometimes in the sense of the inoffensive one.

פְּתַי (with suff. פְּתָיֵהּ) Aram. m. orig. width; next, breadth; from פְּתָא =Heb. פָּתָה.

פְּתִיגִיל (arisen from פְּתִיג with the termination ־ִיל, like כַּרְמִיל from כֶּרֶם, and the termination ־ִיל) m. a wrapper, a mantle, festive garment, in contrast to מַחֲגֹרֶת שָׂק, thus from פָּתַג to wrap round; hence in the Aram. פִּתְגָּ mantle.

פְּתַיּוּת f. simplicity, concrete, the simple one, from פָּתָה.

פְּתִיחָה (only pl. ־חוֹת) f. origin. an adj. to חֶרֶב drawn (sword), but only subst. sword (the drawn one); פֶּתַח has not this signification.

פָּתִיל (const. פְּתִיל, pl. ־לִים) masc. orig. that which is entwined, spun; next, thread, cord, lace, from פָּתַל to spin, to tie; פָּתִיל, Num. 19:15, stands for פָּתוּל bound, but not a substantive.

פָּתַל (particip. pass. פָּתוּל=פָּתִיל) to tie, to entwine, to spin; the root is also found in גָּדַל, חָתַל. Niph. origin. to be knotty, entwined; hence, 1) to be false, artful, i.e. to act intricately, pervertly, covertly; 2) to wrestle, to wrest; comp. חָבַק=אָבַק in the same sense. Hith. to prove oneself false, artful.

פְּתַלְתֹּל (after the form שְׁחַרְחֹר) adj. m. intricate, insidious, pervert.

פִּתֹם p. n. of a city in Lower Egypt; according to tradition, it is identified with Fajum, a city in Upper Egypt. The etymological meaning in the Egyptian is narrow pass.

פָּתַן (not used) to stretch, to extend; Related to יָתַן, מָתַן.

פֶּתֶן (pl. פְּתָנִים) m. something that stretches itself; hence, adder.

פָּתַע (not used) equiv. to פָּתַח to break forth, to open (the eyes).

פֶּתַע m. origin. opening of the eyes; hence, moment; as an adv. suddenly, momentarily, instantly, unawares; also, unintentionally.

פָּתַר (fut. יִפְתֹּר) origin. to break through; hence, to explain, to interpret (a dream); comp. Aram. פְּשַׁר.

פִּתְרוֹן (with suff. פִּתְרוֹנוֹ) m. interpretation, explanation, exposition.

פַּתְרוֹס p. n. of Upper Egypt, native country of the Egyptians, origin. country of the south; gent. plur. פַּתְרֻסִים.

פַּתְשֶׁגֶן (also פַּרְשֶׁגֶן) m. copy of a mandate, a royal edict; the word is foreign.

פָּתַת (only inf. abs.) to break to pieces, to break off; from which

פַּת, that which is broken off, a piece, a morsel.

צ

צ *Saddê* (צָדֵי) is the eighteenth letter of the Alphabet, and as a numeral counts 90. The peculiarity of the צ is in its being compounded from a hissing (dental) and tongue (lingual) letter. It interchanges, therefore, on comparing the roots, with the linguals ד, ט, ת, as צָהַר and טָהַר, צָבַע and טָבַע, נָצַר and נָטַר, צָבַב and דָּבַב; as well as with the dentals ס, ז, שׂ, as צָלַל and עָלַם, צָבָא and סָפָא, צוּף and סוּף, צוּק and זוּק, etc. It likewise interchanges, on comparing the roots, with ע, ג, כ, ק, from which we may infer that צ arose from a composition of the sounds of *s* and *k*. These interchanges we find in בָּקַע and בָּצַע, צָרַע and גָּרַע, צוּק and עוּק, צָנַע and כָּנַע, צָעַר and כָּעַר, etc.

צֹאָה f. issue from the body, excrement, dung, from צוֹא, equiv. to יָצָא. Comp. צוֹא and צוֹאָה.

צֹאת, צוֹאִי, צֹאִי see צוֹאָה.

צָאַל (not used) equiv. to צָלַל, to overshadow, to cover; comp. מָאַס and מָסַס. See the noun צֶאֱל.

צֶאֱל (pl. צֶאֱלִים) m. probably, shady bush, thus for צֵלֶל; according to others, after the Arabic, lotus shrub.

צָאַן (not used) equiv. to צָפַן to shelter, to guard (comp. צָלַל=צָאַל).

צֹאן (for צְאֹן, with suff. צֹאנִי) com. a herd; collective, orig. that which is kept, guarded; but generally, small cattle, *μῆλα*, especially, sheep. צֹאן, however, is never used of a single sheep.

צַאֲנָן (place of herds) p. n. of a city in Judah.

צֶאֱצָא (—אִים, const. —צְאֱצָאֵי) masc. that which issued (from the mother's womb), sprout, sprig, descendant, issue, child. Root יָצָא.

צָב (pl. צַבִּים) m. 1) a litter, sedan-chair, or slow vehicle, from צָבַב to move softly; 2) a species of lizard, so called from its sliding, sneaking movement (Auth. Ver. "tortoise").

צָבָא (fut. יִצְבָּא) orig. equiv. to סָפָא to gather, to assemble (in large numbers); צָבָא עַל to assemble round some place, to besiege it; also construed with the accus. צָבָא צָבָא a host, or an army, assembles. Hiph. הִצְבִּיא to assemble a host, to levy recruits for war.

צָבָא (const. צְבָא, pl. צְבָאוֹת, const. צִבְאוֹת, but with suff. also צְבָאָיו, as if the pl. were צְבָאִים) masc. (seldom fem.) a troop, a host; שַׂר הַצָּ׳ a general; אִישׁ הַצָּ׳ warrior; יָצָא צ׳, בַּצָּ׳, אִישׁ הַצָּ׳ to go to war, orig. to go in the army; transf. to service of the army, or war, or field, or post, soccage, slavery; the host of heaven, of God, i.e. the host of angels, stars, planets: also called צְבָא הַמָּרוֹם; hence, the Lord is called אֱלֹהֵי, צְבָאוֹת יי׳, sometimes אֱלֹהִים צְבָאוֹת, for which, in the more recent books, אֱלֹהֵי הַשָּׁמַיִם is used.

צְבָא (fut. יִצְבֵּא, inf. with suffix מִצְבְּיֵהּ) Aram. orig. to spring forth, thus equiv. to רָחַשׁ; next, to desire, to wish, to will, after the same mode of transferring the sense as in בָּעָא.

צְבָאוֹת, צְבָאִים in the signification of a gazelle. See צְבִי.

צְבֹאִים (probably equiv. to צְבֹעִים place of the hyenas) p. n. of a place in the valley of Siddim. See צְבֹיִם, צְבֹיִּים.

צָבַב (not used) equiv. to דָּבַב to move along softly, to glide, slide. From which:—

צֹבֵבָה (with the article) p. n. fem. (the sliding one).

צָבָה 1) equiv. to זָהָה to shine; hence, to be beautiful, adorned, from which צְבִי; 2) like צְבָא in Aram. to swell; 3) equiv. to צָבָא to assemble (of an army), to which probably belongs צֹבֶיהָ, Is. 29:7, if it does not stand for צֹבְאֶיהָ.

צָבֶה adj. m., **צָבָה** f. swelling of the belly, from **צָבָה** 2.

צְבוּ (def. צְבוּתָא) Aram. fem. will, desire; hence, like חֵפֶץ, affair, matter, from צְבָא.

צָבוּעַ m. a beast of prey, from צָבַע to seize, attack (Author. Vers. "a speckled bird").

צָבַט (fut. יִצְבֹּט) probably equiv. to צָבַת, to bind, to tie together; צָ׳ קָלִי ears of corn bound up; according to others, to hand, to deliver.

I. **צְבִי** (pause צֶבִי, pl. const. probably צִבְאוֹת גּוֹיִם Jer. 3:19) m. ornament, beauty, glory, glory of kingdoms, i.e. Babel; land of beauty, i.e. the land of Israel, for which also צְבִי alone stands; the glorious, holy mountain, i.e. the mountain of the temple. Root **צָבָה** I.

II. **צְבִי** (pl. צְבָאִים, צְבָיִם, צְבָיִים and צְבָאוֹת) m. a gazelle, probably so called on account of the beauty of its appearance.

צִבְיָא p.n.m. (ornament, beauty).

צְבִיָּה (from צְבִי) fem. the female gazelle.

צִבְיָה p.n.f. (the same as צִבְיָא).

צְבֹיִים for צְבֹאִים and this for צְבֹעִים.

I. **צָבַע** (not used) equiv. to טָבַע, to dive, to dip into; hence next, to paint, to colour, orig. to dip into the paint.

II. **צָבַע** (not used) to seize, to attack; next, to rob, from which צָבוּעַ, beast of prey, hyena, and also אֶצְבַּע.

צְבַע (Aram.) equiv. to צָבַע I., Heb. to dip in, to wet; hence Pa. צַבַּע to wet. Ithpael אִצְטַבַּע to be wetted.

צֶבַע (pl. צְבָעִים) m. origin. that into which something is dipped; next, colour, paint, transf. to coloured garment.

צִבְעוֹן p.n.m. (the wild one, robber), from צָבַע II.

צְבֹעִים (haunt of hyenas) p.n. of a valley and place in Benjamin.

צָבַר (fut. יִצְבֹּר) to heap up, to garner, to gather.

צִבֻּר m. a heap.

צָבַת (not used) to bind, to tie, related to צָפַד. The same is צָמַת and צְוַת in Aram.

צֶבֶת (pl. צְבָתִים) m. a sheaf, bundle (of corn).

צַד (with suff. צִדִּי, with ה finis, צִדָּה, pl. צִדִּים) m. 1) side; hence עַל־צַד, מִצַּד as an adv.; 2) only pl. צִדִּים for צִידִים, from צוּד a net, for catching, according to Ibn Gannach.

צַד (Aram.) the same.

צָדָא (not used) Aram. in Targum only Af. to mock, scorn, from which הַצְדָּא mocking.

צָדַד (not used) equiv. to שָׂטָה to turn away, from which צַד side, orig. turning away.

צְדָד (also צְדָדָה mountain-side) p. n. of a place, north of Palestine.

I. **צָדָה** equiv. to צוּד to waylay, to lay a trap; צ׳ אֶת־נֶפֶשׁ to hunt the soul, i. e. to hunt one's life.

II. **צָדָה** (Kal not used) to destroy, to devastate; hence Niph. נִצְדָּה to be destroyed. The orig. signif. is to cut off, to annihilate.

צֵדָה see צֵידָה.

צָדוֹק p. n. m. (the pious one, the just one).

צְדִיָּה f. hunting, lying in wait, artfulness, from צָדָה I.

צִדִּים (only with the article, mountain side) p. n. of a city in Naphtali.

צַדִּיק m. the just, righteous, upright one; in a matter of law, he that is right; in reference to the moral course of life, he that is honest; hence, synonymous with נָקִי, תָּמִים, יָשָׁר.

צָדַק (fut. יִצְדַּק) to be just, upright; next, to be pious, good, honest, with all secondary significations. Niph. to be justified (before a tribunal); the sanctuary shall be justified, i. e. its honour shall be saved. Pi. to justify, to declare as just. Hiph. to make righteous, i. e. to declare one as righteous before justice, to acquit. Hith. הִצְטַדֵּק to justify oneself, to defend oneself.

צֶדֶק (with suff. צִדְקִי) m. 1) straightness (of the path); next, righteousness, justice; שְׁמַע צ׳, פֹּעַל צ׳, שְׁפַט צ׳, בַּשֵּׂר צ׳; in the genitive, hence, correct, proper, just; as, מֹאזְנֵי צ׳ just balances, זִבְחֵי צ׳ sacrifices of righteousness; in a judicial sense, a just cause, the right which some one has, or is ceded to him; generally, honesty, probity, uprightness, salvation, happiness, etc.

צְדָקָה f. equiv. to צֶדֶק, hence also benevolence, just deed, virtue; מוֹרֶה לִצְדָקָה the former rain in abundance (Author. Vers. moderately).

צִדְקָה (def. צִדְקְתָא) Aram. fem. the same.

צִדְקִיָּה p. n. m. (righteousness of God).

צִדְקִיָּהוּ p. n. m. (the same).

צָהַב (Kal, not used) to shine, to glitter, related to זָהָב. Hoph. to shine as gold, to be of gold color, yellow, gilt; hence, participle, מֻצְהָב glittering.

צָהֹב adj. m. glittering, gold-colored, yellow.

צָהָה as the root to צִי, צִיָּה, צִיִּי, צִיּוֹן, see צִיָּה.

צָהַל (fut. יִצְהַל imp. f. צַהֲלִי) 1) to be bright, to shine; 2) to shout, with joy, to triumph, transf. to neighing, bellowing (of beasts). Hiph. to cause to shine (the face), to cheer, to gladden.

צָהַר (not used) equiv. to טָהַר, but related also with צָהַל to shine, to glitter, to illumine; from which, יִצְהָר (with suffix יִצְהָרְךָ, plur. יִצְהָרִים) orig. that which shines, oil. It is a noun formed from the fut. like יָשָׁר, יָעֵל, יַנְשׁוּף, יֶלֶק, יַחְמוּר, יַלְקוּט, יְקוּם, יָתוֹם, and others; from which the denom. הִצְהִיר, to press oil (יִצְהָר).

צֹהַר (dual צָהֳרַיִם) fem. light, ray, transf. to an opening to admit light, window, like φῶς in Greek, the dual צָהֳרַיִם noon, orig. the point of turning between the increasing and decreasing light, fig. luck, prosperity, i.e. the time when the sun is in his zenith.

צַו (pause צָו, after the form קַו) m. a sign post, a road index, related to צִיּוֹן; הָלַךְ אַחֲרֵי צ׳ to walk after the index of the road (Auth. Vers. commandment), figur. precept, commandment. Root צָוָה.

צוֹא (not used) equiv. to יָצָא, to issue, of excrement, dung; from which:—

צוֹאָה f. excrement, dung, קִיא צוֹאָה vomit and filthiness, or filthy vomit, as a figure of abomination. Root צוֹא.

צוֹאִי adj. m. filthy, of garments.

צַוָּאר (const. צַוַּאר, with suff. צַוָּארִי, but also צַוָּרֵם, pl. צַוָּארִים, const. צַוְּארֵי) m. neck, seldom throat, orig. the narrowest of the upper part of the body, from צוּר to be narrow; בְּצַוָּאר with stretched out neck, the plur. signifies sometimes the front and back part of the neck, and sometimes the rumps, the heads of which being cut off.

צַוָּארֹת (only pl. with suff. צַוְּארֹתֵיכֶם) f. the same.

צוֹבָא (abbreviated from נְצוֹבָא, from נְצַב a post) p. n. of a Syrian state, complete אֲרַם צ׳, later it was used for Nisibis.

צוּד (fut. יָצוּד) equiv. to צָדָה to lie in wait, to waylay (אֵת acc.) some one; hence, to catch, to hunt (for game), צוּד נֶפֶשׁ to hunt the life. Pi. צוֹדֵד the same, with accus. sometimes even omitting נֶפֶשׁ. The Hith. הִצְטַיֵּד is a denom. from צַיִד, which see.

צָוָה (Kal, not used) orig. to fix, to place firmly, related with יָצַב,

צָבָא (comp. the deriv. צִיּוּן for צִוּוּן), from which Pi. צִוָּה to appoint or nominate some one over (עַל) something; next, 1) to command, to charge, with acc., sometimes const. with עַל, אֶל, לְ, and the thing commanded stands then in the accus., the command follows either after לֵאמֹר or indirect in the inf.; 2) to order, with עַל, of the person to whom the order is directed; with אֶל, לְ, of the person in whose behalf the order is given; צַוֵּה לְבֵיתוֹ, אֶל־בֵּיתוֹ to put his house in order, i.e. to make his last will. Pual, to be charged, commanded.

צָוַח (fut. יִצְוַח) to cry, to call; hence, קָרָא in modern Heb. to call, to give a name; related is שָׁבַח.

צְוָחָה (const. צִוְחַת) f. a cry, either for joy or grief.

צוּל (not used) equiv. to צָלַל and צָהַל to roar, to snort (syn. with הוּם), from which מְצוּלָה, and—

צוּלָה f. the roaring precipice, depth, syn. with תְּהוֹם.

צוּם (fut. יָצוּם) origin. equiv. to צָמֵא to languish, to famish; next, to fast; הֲצוֹם צַמְתֻּנִי did ye at all fast for me.

צוֹם (with suff. צֹמְכֶם, pl. צוֹמוֹת) m. the fasting, or concrete, the fast-day.

צוּעַ (not used) equiv. to יָצַע to lay, to stretch, to lay down in rows, from which צַעֲצֻעַ image-work of gold and silver.

צוֹעַר see צֹעַר.

צוּעָר p. n. m. (littleness).

צוּף equiv. to זוּף to overflow, construed with עַל. Hiph. to cause to overflow, to flood.

צוּף (plur. צוּפִים) m. 1) honey-cell, from צוּף to overflow; according to others, honey-comb, in the sense of being round; more correctly, however, equiv. to סוּף; hence, from the sugar-cane, the juice of which (sugar) is called נֹפֶת; 2) p.n. m. for which once in Keri צִיף and צוֹפַי occur.

צוֹפַר p. n. m. the dancing, hopping one.

צוּץ origin. to shine, to glitter; hence transf. to bloom. Hiph. 1) to shine forth, look forth; modern Heb. to look, behold; 2) to break forth in blossom or flower, and generally, in a figurative sense, to flourish.

I. צוּק (Kal, not used) equiv. to זָקַק, זָקַח to enclose, to bind round; hence Hiph. הֵצִיק (part. מֵצִיק) to straiten, to oppress, construed with the dative and accus.; or also, to press in some one, to urge, with accus. or לְ; to straiten a town, i.e.

to besiege it. מְצִיק the oppressor. Hoph. הוּצַק pass.

I. צוק (fut. יָצוּק) equiv. to יָצַק to pour out, to pour forth, to melt; hence, Job 28:2, "and brass is molten out of the stone"; צָקוּן לַחַשׁ they pour out (for צָקוּ) in prayer.

III. צוק (Kal, not used) to put, to place firmly, related to יָצַג; hence Hiph. הֵצִיק to place some one. Hoph. (if it does not belong to צוק II.) to be placed, origin. to be fixed, cast.

צוֹק m. strait, oppression, from צוק I.

צוּקָה f. the same.

צוֹר see צֹר.

צוּר (fut. יָצוּר, apoc. יָצַר) 1) to enclose; next, to besiege (comp. the root in עָצַר, חָצַר, בָּצַר, etc.), construed with עַל, אֶל, and accus.; 2) to straiten, oppress, to persecute, related to צָרַר; 3) equiv. to יָצַר and זָר to tie up (money), to bind together, to tie, comp. צָרַר in this sense; 4) to cut, to form, comp. יָצַר in this sense; from which צוּר sharp edge; 5) (not used) to walk, to go, comp. שׁוּר, תּוּר; 6) to be strong, connected with signif. 3, comp. חוּל. Hiph. 1) to oppress; 2) to have pangs, throes (of a woman in travail), denom. from צִיר, which see

צוּר (pl. צוּרִים and צוּרוֹת m. 1) stone, rock, from צוּר to be firm, strong, hard; צ׳ נְחָלִים the stones of the rocks; צ׳ יִשְׂרָאֵל the Rock of Israel, i. e. God; sometimes צוּר alone; also, to denote the ancestor of a people; in this sense the plur. is צוּרוֹת; 2) sharp edge (of the sword), חַרְבוֹת צוּרִים sharp knives; 3) image, form, shape, from צוּר to form; 4) p. n. m.

צֻוָּר see צַוָּאר.

צוּרָה f. form, shape (of a house or a temple).

צַוְּרֹן (from צַוָּאר formed with the termination ־וֹן, comp. אִישׁוֹן from אִישׁ, זֵרְעוֹן from זֶרַע) m. a little neck.

צוּרִיאֵל p. n. m. (God is the Rock).

צוּרִישַׁדָּי (the Rock is the Almighty).

צות (Kal, not used) to kindle, to burn, to light; hence Niph. נִצַּת (fut. יִצַּת, pl. יִצַּתּוּ) to burn with (בְּ) something, to be heated, to be wroth against (בְּ) some one; also, to be set on fire, to be destroyed. Hiph. הִצִּית (once Ketib הוֹצִית) to kindle, to set fire to (עַל, בְּ) something, the same הִצִּית בָּאֵשׁ.

צַח adj. m., צָחוֹת plur. f. 1) glowing, hot (of the wind); transf. to bright, serene, cheerful, e. g. of the cheering warmth of the sun; 2) shining, glittering, dazzling, of the bright colour of the skin; 3) luminous, brilliant, distinct, clear, in a spiritual sense, of speech. The plur. צְחוֹת stands as an abstract.

צִחָא p.n. m. (brightness, beauty).

צָחָה (not used) origin. to glow, to burn; next, to be dry, parched, related to צָחַח, זָנַק; transf. to languish, to burn with thirst.

צִחֵה (according to Kimchi צָחֶה) m. the languishing one, with (accus.) thirst (after the form עִקֵּשׁ).

צָחַח (3 pl. צָחוּ) to glow, to burn; next, to be dazzling, shining, white. See צָחָה.

צְחִיחַ (const. צְחִיחַ) m. dearth, dryness, צ׳ סֶלַע barren rock.

צְחִיחָה f. waste, dry, parched, country; comp. צִיָּה.

צְחִיחִי (pl. ־ִים— Ketib) adj. m. dry, parched, placed, formed from צְחִיחַ.

צָחַן (not used) equiv. to זָנַח to be filthy; hence, to stink.

צַחֲנָה f. bad odour, stink.

צַחְצָחָה (pl. ־חוֹת—) fem. cheerfulness (of the heart), joy.

צָחַק (fut. יִצְחַק) equiv. to the later שָׂחַק to laugh, to mock at (לְ) some one. The root is צָ־חַק. Pi. 1) to laugh, to mock, repeatedly at (בְּ) some one; 2) to jest, to play, to sport, indicated by laughter, especially of the sport of love.

צְחֹק m. scorn, sport, laughter.

צָחַר (not used) to be dazzling white, to shine, origin. equiv. to צָהַר, which see.

צַחַר m. dazzling white (of wool).

צָחֹר (only pl. f. צְחֹרוֹת) adj. m. shining, white, used of the color of the white ass.

צֹחַר p. n. m. (shining); for which זֶרַח once stands.

צִי (contracted from צְוִי, pl. צִים) m. a ship, a fleet, from צָוָה (related to the root in קָ־צַב, חָ־צַב) to hollow out, origin. that which is hollowed out. The form צִיִּים belongs to צִיִּי; the form צִיּוֹת belongs to צִיָּה, to which also the root צִיּוֹן belongs.

צִיבָא p. n. masc. (a post, as if from נְצִיבָא).

צַיִד (const. צֵיד, with suff. צֵידִי) m. 1) hunting, the chase; 2) concrete, the object of hunting, game, venison; 3) food, meal, provision for a journey.

צַיָּד m. huntsmen, hunter, from צוּד.

צֵידָה (also צֵדָה) f. food, especially provision for a journey.

צִידוֹן (fishing) 1) p. n. of a Phenician city (as such fem.), complete צ׳ רַבָּה the great Sidon having been the celebrated commercial town of Phenicia, hence in the Bible סֹחַר צִידוֹן; the state was called

בַּת צִידוֹן; 2) p. n. of the first-born son of Canaan (hence masc.), and next also, the name of the people. The gent. was called:—

צִידֹנִי (pl. צִידֹנִים, צִידֹנִין) m., צִידֹנִיָּה (pl. צִידֹנִיּוֹת or צִדְנִיּוֹת) fem. the Sidonian.

צָיָה (for צָוָה, not used) 1) to glow, to burn; related is the Aram. טְוָא, not =צָהָה; 2) to hollow out, to deepen (חָצַב=צָרְבָה in the radicals). The two significations are not connected.

צִיָּה (formed from a masc. צִי) f. a dry parched country; hence also, desert, steppe, generally in connection with אֶרֶץ and מִדְבָּר, sometimes alone. The plur. צִיּוֹת is rendered by some, ships. Root צִי.

צָיוֹן m. dry land, parched soil.

צִיּוֹן (a stronger form from צָיוֹן; hence appell. dry place, or probably equiv. to צִיּוּן hill) p. n. of a hill of Jerusalem, on which a castle stood, and which was later the seat of divine glory; hence, צִיּוֹן הַר הַקֹּדֶשׁ. In prophetic language צִיּוֹן was later used for Jerusalem; hence the inhabitants, בְּנֵי צ׳, יוֹשֶׁבֶת צ׳, בַּת צ׳, עַם בְּצ׳. With the gen. it occurs in the phrase צִיּוֹן קְדוֹשׁ יִשְׂרָאֵל Zion of the Holy One of Israel.

צִיּוּן (pl. צִיֻּנִים) masc. a little hill for pointing out the road, road index, transferred, to tomb, monument, probably from צָוָה thus for צִוּוּן.

צִיִּי (only pl. צִיִּים, formed from צִי) adj. m. 1) inhabiting a dry country, inhabitant of the desert, either of man or beast; 2) ship-master, sailor, from צִי ship.

צִין (or צִן, with ה of motion צִנָה) p.n. of a desert south of Palestine, wherein the place קָדֵשׁ בַּרְנֵעַ was situated.

צִינֹק masc. a prison, orig. enclosure, from צָנַק to enclose, to shut up. The form is after כִּידֹד, קִיטֹר, קִימוֹשׁ.

צִיעֹר (littleness) p.n. of a place in Judah.

צִיף equiv. to צוּף.

צִיץ as a verbal root, see צוּץ.

צִיץ (pl. צִצִּים for צִיצִים, with dagesh for the quiescent *yod*) masc. 1) a plate, orig. that which is visible at a distance; comp. צוּץ in the Hiph.; 2) flower, blossom, orig. glittering, after the usual gradation in Hebrew from shining to blooming; 3) wing, after the mode of transferring in פֶּרַח; hence also, fins (of fishes); in the Aram. צִיצִין, equiv. to כַּנְפֵי שַׁחַר; 4) p.n. of a place.

צִיצָה (const. צִיצַת) fem. a flower, צִיצַת נֹבֵל a flower of fading, where

נֹבֶל is a noun after the form שֶׁרֶק; the reading is not צִיץ הַנֹּבֶל.

צִיצִית (צִיצִת) fem. 1) hair or lock in front, so called on account of its wing-like form; 2) fringe of garments, also on account of its wing-like appearance. The Targum כְּרוּסְפְּדִין is the *κράσπεδα* of the LXX.

צִיקְלַג see צִקְלַג.

צִיר as a verbal root see צוּר, but the Hith. הִצְטַיֵּר is only a denom. from צִיר 3.

צִיר (from צוּר, which see) m. 1) pain, pangs, woes; צִירֵי יוֹלֵדָה the pangs of a woman that travaileth, from צוּר writhing; 2) hinge of the door, probably after the same derivation, from צוּר to turn, as is evident from תִּסּוֹב in the context; 3) a messenger, from צוּר to walk, to go; from which denom. הִצְטַיֵּר to repair for wandering, walking; 4) image, figure, from יָצַר=צוּר to form, transf. to idol-image.

צִיָּה see צוּת.

צֵל (with suff. צִלִּי, with analysed dagesh צְלָלוֹ, plur. צְלָלִים, const. צִלְלֵי, but probably also צְאֱלִים) m. (seldom f.) shadow, from צָלַל=טָלַל to cover, to veil; צֵל נָטוּי a shadow that declineth, i.e. towards evening, the same is צִלְלֵי עֶרֶב; צֵל עֹבֵר the passing shadow; hence generally as a figure of transientness, e.g. צֵל יָמֵינוּ the transientness of our days: צֵל is also used as a figure of protection, shelter, and refuge, as צֵל קוֹרָה shadow of the roof, i.e. protection of the house: also as a symbol of nothingness, perishableness, e. g. יְצֻרַי כַּצֵּל my members are like a shadow, i. e. lean, wasted.

צְלָא (Aram.) orig. to incline, to lean, like נָטָה in Hebrew; hence, Pa. to pray, orig. to bend the knee (for prayer). The root appears to be only a secondary form from צָלַע (צְלַע), which see.

צָלָה (fut. יִצְלֶה, inf. צְלוֹת) to roast (meat). The root צָלָה has its analogy in בָּשַׁל.

צִלָּה p. n. fem. (singing, song, from צָלַל).

צְלוּל (Ketib) m. a rattling (according to Kimchi), thus from צָלַל to sound; according to others from גָּלַל=צָלַל, hence equiv. to כִּכָּר, which corresponds with מִתְהַפֵּךְ in the context.

צָלַח (in pause צָלֵחָה, fut. יִצְלַח) 1) (not used) to cut in, to deepen out, from which צַלַּחַת, צְלֹחִית; 2) to cut through (a river), i.e. to wade through it, comp. בָּקַע in the same sense in modern Heb.,

צְ׳ הַיַּרְדֵּן to cross the Jordan; 3) to penetrate, to break forth, e. g. of the spirit of God, which breaks forth over (אֶל, עַל) some one; also of the breaking forth of fire; hence פֶּן יִצְלַח כָּאֵשׁ lest he break out like fire; 4) to thrive, to prosper, orig. to go on prosperously, thus connected with signif. 2; צָלַח לְ to be fit, adapted for something. Hiph. (of signif. 4) to cause to prosper (an undertaking), to carry out something happily, to cause to prosper the way, i. e. equiv. to be successful, used of one who succeeds in everything.

צְלַח (Aram.) equiv. to צָלַח Heb. in the signification of, to go through; hence, הַצְלַח to make one prosperous, and generally of the thriving and prospering of an undertaking.

צְלָחָה (only pl. —וֹת) f. dish, cruse.

צְלֹחִית f. the same.

צַלַּחַת (in pause צַלָּחַת) f. dish, cruse, orig. that which is deepened out, from צָלַח; transf. to the hollow of the bosom, and the lap.

צָלִי (const. צְלִי) m. roast, or meat for roasting.

צְלִיל Keri for Ketib צְלוּל, which see.

צָלַל (3 plur. צָלְלוּ) 1) to sound, to tingle; hence, of the quivering of the lips, related to צָהַל, צוּל; 2) to cover, equiv. to טָלַל; hence, to overshadow (comp. כְּ־צַל); 3) to sink, in which sense it is frequently used in modern Hebrew; 4) equiv. to גָּלַל to roll, to move round: all these significations are found again in the derivatives. See צֵל, צְלָצַל, מְצִלָּה, צְלוּל, and others.

צְלֶלְפּוֹנִי p. n. m.

צָלַם (not used) to shadow, to cover, only an extended form of צָלַל; צֶלֶם, צַלְמָוֶת, are probably formed from צֵל.

צֶלֶם (with suff. צַלְמִי, pl. צְלָמִים) m. orig. shadowing; next, a phantom, or image, figur. idol-image generally; also, of the human figure, which has a resemblance to another: צֶלֶם is probably formed from צֵל, with the termination ־ָם, like חֵלֶם from חֵל, לֶחֶם from לַח, כֶּרֶם from כַּר, טֶרֶם from טַר.

צְלֵם (but also צֶלֶם; def. צַלְמָא) Aram. m. the same, but only in the signification of idol image.

צַלְמוֹן (shadowed mountain) 1) p. n. of a mountain in Samaria; 2) p. n. m.

צַלְמֹנָה (shadowed place) p. n. of an encampment of the Israelites in the desert.

צַלְמָוֶת f. probably equiv. to צַלְמוּת.

formed from צֶלֶם, after the form קַדְרוּת, עַבְדוּת, according to the opinion of Abulwalid and Kimchi; hence, darkness, shade, especially of the shade *Orcus* (Auth. Ver. "shadow of death"); also, land, gates of darkness, syn. with אֹפֶל.

צַלְמֻנָּע p. n. m. (refusal of shelter, i. e. delivering up; מָנַע=מְמֻנָּע).

צָלַע 1) to incline, to lean; comp. the Aram. צְלָא, which root is also found in עָצַל; hence 2) to halt, to limp, a defect shown by inclining on one side. Possibly, however, צָלַע in signif. 2, is only a denom. from צֶלַע.

צֵלָע (const. צֶלַע and צְלַע, with suff. צַלְעִי, pl. צְלָעִים and צְלָעוֹת, const. צַלְעוֹת) f. (but the pl. צְלָעִים m.) 1) side, leaning, from צָלַע; hence שֹׁמֵר צַלְעִ he that watches at the side of some one, i. e. a friend (Author. Vers. "watching for my halting") (?); transf. to the side of inanimate objects, e. g. side of the tabernacle, an anti-chamber of a building, wing of a door; also, side, equiv. to part, in reference to the position; 2) rib, on account of its being inclining, or of its being at the side of the body. The plur. צְלָעוֹת is used besides of ribs, also of the sides of the altar, or any side piece, counter-part, also of the ribs or skeleton of a building, i. e. of the beams, flooring, etc.; 3) p. n. of a Benjaminite city.

צֶלַע masc. the halting, the limping, fall, adversity.

צָלַף to break to pieces; next generally, to strike, to give a blow.

צָלָף p. n. m. (the breaker).

צְלָפְחָד p. n. m. (sharp wound).

צֶלְצַח (shelter against the sun) p. n. of a place in Benjamin.

צְלָצַל (pause צְלָצָל; const. צִלְצַל, pl. צֶלְצְלִים, const. צִלְצְלֵי) masc. 1) a tinkling, clattering instrument; hence pl. basins, cymbals; 2) a kind of chirping insect, cricket (Author. Vers. "locust"); 3) the rustling (of wings), i. e. the tumult of armies, in which sense is probably to be understood צִלְצַל כְּנָפַיִם; 4) fish-hook, from צָלַל to sink deeply.

צָלַק (not used) equiv. to צָלַח to split, to divide.

צֶלֶק p. n. m. (splitting).

צִלְּתַי p. n. m. (the covered, veiled one).

צַם see צֹמִים.

צָמֵא (1 pret. צָמֵתִי, fut. יִצְמָא) to languish, to thirst, figur. to pant (for God, etc.), related to צוּם.

צָמָא m. thirst.

צָמֵא (pl. צְמֵאִים) adj. m., צְמֵאָה f. thirsting, languishing.

צִמְאָה f. thirst, languishing, applied to ardour, fervency.

צִמָּאוֹן (const. צִמְּאוֹן) masc. parched, languishing, country.

צָמַד (Kal, not used) equiv. to עָמַד (in עָמְדִי) and צָפַר to bend, to tie together; hence Niph. to attach oneself to (לְ) something, e. g. to the worship of Baal. Pu. to be tied firmly on (of the sword). Hiph. הִצְמִיד to concoct, to devise artfulness, craftiness.

צֶמֶד (with suff. צִמְדּוֹ, plur. צְמָדִים, const. צִמְדֵי) m. 1) a pair (of oxen, asses), orig. joining, e. g. צֶמֶד בָּקָר a pair of oxen, צֶמֶד חֲמוֹרִים a pair of asses, רוֹכְבִים צְמָדִים horsemen riding in pairs; 2) a yoke, an acre, i. e. a piece of ground, to the ploughing of which a pair of oxen are required, *jugum.*

צַמָּה fem. a veil, from צָמַם to veil round, as Abulwalid renders it מַסְוֶה; according to others, hair-plaids, hair-tails.

צִמּוּק (pl. ־קִים) dried grapes baked to cakes, from צָמַק.

צָמַח (fut. יִצְמַח) to sprout forth, to grow; the root syllable is צָ־מַח: it is applied to the growing of plants, trees, and the hair, fig. of the springing forth of new events. Pi. to grow strongly and prominently (of the hair). Hiph. to cause to sprout forth (with double accus.), fig. to cause to appear or spring forth.

צֶמַח (with suff. צִמְחוֹ) m. the sprouting, growing; טַרְפֵּי צ׳ sprouting leaves, but generally conc., sprout, or a branch, fruit, product (of the earth, field), and synon. with פְּרִי or טוּב הָאָרֶץ; צֶמַח י״י that which God causes to grow, product; sprout of righteousness, applied to the progeny of David, a future king from the house of David.

צָמִיד (pl. צְמִידִים) m. 1) bracelet tied round the arm; 2) cover of a vessel, which is fastened to the vessel.

צַמִּים (after the form פַּטִּישׁ, צַדִּיק) m. snare net, from צָמַם to entwine, to bind; hence יַחֲזֵק עָלָיו צַמִּים the snare (Author. Vers. robber) shall lay hold of him; synon. פַּח, חֶבֶל, מַלְכֹּדֶת, רֶשֶׁת in the same passage; transf. to the one who lays the snare, robber, e. g. וְשָׁאַף צַמִּים חֵילָם and the robber lies in wait for (Auth. Vers. swallows up) their substance.

צְמִיתֻת f. orig. destruction, but only לִצְמִיתֻת, adverbially, equiv. to כָּלָה, i. e. entirely, altogether, for ever.

צָמַם (not used) 1) equiv. to זָמַם (comp-the radical in חָ־סַם) to entwine, to bind, to tie fast (comp. the Aram. צַמְצֵם; 2) to veil round, to wrap round, to cover, probably from signif. 1. See צַמָּה and צַמִּים.

צָ) to shrink together, to dry up, by which something is lessened and becomes lean; hence שָׁדַיִם צֹמְקִים dry breasts; related to the root מַק.

צָ) (not used) equiv. to סָמַר (related to אָמַר and Aram. עֲמַר) to sprout forth, to break forth, to grow, especially of the wool, like סָמַר of the hair, and אָמַר of the foliage.

צֶ) (with suff. צַמְרִי) masc. wool; גִּזַּת צ׳ wool-shearing.

צְמָ p. n. of a Phenician people, whose city, Simyra, was on the western foot of the Lebanon, and the ruins of which are yet to be seen.

צְמָרַ p. n. of a city in the territory of Benjamin, from which הַר צ׳.

צַמֶּ (with suff. צַמַּרְתּוֹ) f. foliage (Author. Vers. highest branch) of the cedar, *coma arboris*, thus connected with צָמַר. Comp. אָמִיר.

צָמַ to destroy (the life), to cut off, to exterminate; related to שָׁמַד, and probably also to נָמַר. Niph. to be destroyed; transf. to dry up, of a river. Pi. צִמֵּת like Kal; צִמְּתֻתוּנִי with the doubling of the last radical signifies they have entirely destroyed me. Hiph. הִצְמִית to destroy, to uproot, to annihilate.

צֵן belongs to צְנִים, see צִנָּה.

צִן see צִין.

צָנָא (not used) equiv. to צָאַן to shelter, to protect, like צָנַן; hence:—

צֹנֶא and צֹנֶה (with suff. צֹנַאֲכֶם) m. herd, flock, so called from their being sheltered. Comp. צֹאן.

צִנָּה (from צָנַן, pl. צִנִּים and צִנּוֹת) f. 1) thorn, prickle, especially in this sense the plur. צִנִּים; 2) a shield which covers the whole body, from צָנַן in the signification of covering, נֹשֵׂא הַצִּ׳ shield-bearer; 3) fish-hook, especially in this sense the plur. צִנּוֹת, if it is not to be rendered a boat, a sculler, from צָנַן in the sense of to bend, to entwine; 4) cooling, cold, from צָנַן to be cold.

צֹנֶה see צֹנֶא.

צָנוֹף, צָנוּף Ketib, see צָנִיף.

צִנּוֹר (pl. צִנּוֹרִים) m. a canal, a water-spout, especially of a pipe; fig. a cloud (Auth. Vers. water-spout), Ps. 42:8. See צַנֵּר.

צָנַח (fut. יִצְנַח) 1) to decline, to remove downwards, to alight from (מֵעַל) something; 2) to penetrate into (בְּ) something, related to נָחַת, נָחַן.

צְנִין (only plur. צְנִינִים) masc. thorn, prickle, from צָנַן to be pointed.

צָנִיף (const. צְנִיף; pl. צְנִיפוֹת) masc. head-dress, turban, either of the head-dress of women, of distinguished persons, or of priests. Once in Ketib צנוף for Keri צָנִיף.

צָנַם to be hard, in modern Heb. of bread, of the withered ears of corn; related is קָנַם in קִנָּמוֹן.

צְנָן see צַאֲנָן.

צָנַן (not used) 1) equiv. to שָׁנַן to be sharp, pointed, from which צָנִין, צִנָּה; 2) equiv. to גָּנַן to shelter, to protect, to cover, from which צִנָּה; 3) equiv. to צָנָא, טָנָא to entwine, to tie; hence צִנָּה boat (made of wicker-work) and צִנְצֶנֶת basket (Author. Vers. pot); 4) equiv. to צָלַל to be shady, cool; hence צִנָּה cold.

צָנַע to decline, to alight, a secondary form of כָּנַע; next, to be humble, meek; צָנוּעַ the humble one, the modest one. Hiph. to walk, i.e. to conduct oneself humbly.

צָנַף (fut. יִצְנֹף, with suff. יִצְנָפְךָ) to wrap round (a turban); next, to conceal: related to כָּנַף.

צְנֵפָה fem. wrapper, veil; hence, Isa. 22:18, "he will surely veil thee round" (Author. Vers. "violently turn and toss thee").

צִנְצֶנֶת fem. basket, from צָנַן to entwine; according to some, vessel generally (Auth. Vers. pot), from צָנַן to protect.

צָנַק (not used) to enclose; related to חָנַק, but not to צוק.

צָנַר (not used) equivalent to סָנַר to hollow out, from the hollowing of pipes.

צָנַת (not used) to be hollow, from which:—

צַנְתָּר (pl. —רוֹת) f. canal, pipe, tube, through which the oil runs in the lamp; the same is *κάνθαρος*, *cantharus*. If the root is צָנַת, ־ָר is the additional syllable to form the termination, like ־ֹר in כַּפְתֹּר from כֶּפֶת, etc.

צָעַד (fut. יִצְעַד) to stride, to pace, hence, 1) to pace (on the plain ground), to stride along, with solemnity, e.g. in procession, to walk with a measured step, to proceed (through a country); of God, who majestically passes (marches) over the earth; 2) to step up, to ascend, e.g. עֲלֵי שׁוּר over the wall (Auth. Vers. to run over). Hiph. to cause some one to proceed, to lead; hence, Job 18:14, and thou leadest him (Auth. Vers. it shall bring him) to the king of terrors.

צַעַד (with suff. צַעֲדִי, pl. צְעָדִים) m. step, walk, הִרְחִיב צ׳, הֵכִין צ׳ to enlarge the steps, to make the steps firm, a figure of good success; in contrast to straitening the steps, a figure of failure. To number the steps of some one, is a figure of designing evil against him.

צְעָדָה (pl. ־דוֹת) f. 1) the marching (proceeding) of God; 2) a kind of ornament worn by the women of the east on the legs, compare אֶצְעָדָה.

צָעָה to incline, to bend, e.g of the holding of a vessel down for emptying it, of the stretching down of a harlot, of the bending or bowing of one that is fettered, צֹעֶה the captive exile; of the throwing back of the head as a gesture of pride. Pi. to bend a vessel to empty it.

צָעוֹר Ketib for צָעִיר, which see.

צָעִיף (with suff. צְעִיפָהּ) m. a veil, a covering or wrapper (round the head).

צָעִיר (once for which צָעוֹר, plur. צְעִירִים) 1) adj. masc., צְעִירָה fem. small, little (in days, years); next, generally the younger one, transf. to inferior in value; 2) p.n. of a place (littleness).

צְעִירָה f. young, of age, abstract; from which מִצְּעִירָה, joined to a noun by מִן and צ; and littleness, in reference to height.

צָעַן (fut. יִצְעַן) to wander (of the nomades), orig. to load the beasts, it being only a secondary form from טָעַן; fig. Is. 33:29, a tabernacle that shall not wander, i. e. not be taken down.

צֹעַן p. n. of an ancient city in Lower Egypt, on the eastern border of the branch of the Nile, otherwise called Tanis, in Egyptian *Dschane*, i. e. the lower.

צַעֲנַנִּים (wanderings) p. n. of a city of the Kenites, in the territory of Naphtali.

צָעַף (not used) to veil, to cover. The form appears to be transposed from עָטַף; from which צָעִיף.

צַעְצֻעַ (only pl. ־עִים) masc. a row, from יָצַע=צוּעַ; hence מַעֲשֵׂה צַעֲצֻעִים trellis-work (Auth. Ver. "image work").

צָעַק (an older form for זָעַק; fut. יִצְעַק) to cry aloud, to call out (for help), to call to some one (with אֶל, לְ of the person); the object for which one cries stands in the accus. Pi. to cry repeatedly. Hiph. to call together, to assemble, like הִזְעִיק. Niph. to be called together.

צְעָקָה f. cry; צַעֲקָתָם the cry over them.

צָעַר fut. יִצְעַר) equiv. to זָעַר to be little, inferior, in reference to ap-

II. צָפַע (not used) equiv. to אָפַע, פָּע to breathe, to blow, to puff; hence of the breathing or hissing of the serpent (comp. אֶפְעֶה); comp. also פָּעָה.

צֶפַע m. adder, viper, from צָפַע to breathe, to hiss.

צִפְעֹנִי (pl. —נִים) masc. formed from צֶפַע species of adder. The form is as in יִדְּעֹנִי.

I. צָפַף (Kal, not used) to hiss, to chirp, to peep, or to bring forth any piping sounds, only in Pi. (in a reduplicate form), צִפְצֵף to peep.

II. צָפַף (not used) to set, to plant; analogous to which is the root in רָצַף, יָצַב.

צַפְצָפָה (from צָפַף II.) f. plant.

I. צָפַר (fut. יִצְפֹּר) to turn, in a circle, from which צְפִירָה.

II. צָפַר (not used) to be hairy; in the radical it is related with פָּרַע; from which צָפִיר.

III. צָפַר (not used) to point, to edge, to cut in (related to חָפַר); from which צִפֹּרֶן.

IV. צָפַר (not used) to chirp.

צְפַר (pl. צִפְּרִין, def. צִפְּרַיָּא, const. צִפְּרֵי) Aram. com. a bird.

צְפַרְדֵּעַ m. (coll. f.) a frog, pl. צְפַרְדְּעִים. The etymology is obscure.

צִפֹּרָה p. n. f. (little bird).

צִפֹּרֶן (pl. with suff. צִפָּרְנֶיהָ) masc. 1) nail of the fingers, orig. the point; 2) point of a pencil; comp. אֲנָךְ. The root is צָפַר III.

צָפַת (not used) equiv. to צָבַת to bind, to tie round; hence transf. to adorn, as in צָפַר; it is also connected with the signification of; to order, to arrange, to lay in rows.

צֶפֶת f. knop, orig. that which surrounds or adorns the head of a pillar.

צְפַת (watch tower) p. n. of a Canaanite city.

צְפָתָה (the same as צְפַת) p. n. of a valley in the territory of Judah.

צִצִּים see צִיץ.

צָקַל (not used) according to some, to bind together, like עָקַל; according to others, to hollow out, to deepen out; from קָלַן.

צִקְלוֹן (only with suff. צִקְלֹנוֹ) masc. sack, pocket, from צָקַל.

צִקְלַג (or צִיק—, in pause לָג) p. n. of a Philistine city.

צַר (with a tonic accent, or the article, צָר; with suff. צָרִי, pl. צָרִים, צָרֵי) 1) adj. m. צָרָה (pl. צָרוֹת), f. narrow, straitened, confined; 2) subst. abstract, strait, trouble, tribulation, and in this sense the masc. form צַר is often used; as צַר לִי I am in a strait, בַּצַּר in trouble, צַר וּמְצוּקָה trouble and anguish; sometimes the f. form צָרָה, lengthened with ה mobile,

עֵת, עִתּוֹת, יוֹם צָרָה, e.g. בְּצָרָתָה time, day of trouble; צָרָה לִי in my trouble; צָרַת נֶפֶשׁ anguish of the soul, as apposition to צוּקָה, תּוֹכֵחָה, מְצוּקָה, חֲשֵׁכָה; 3) conc. צַר m. enemy, adversary, oppressor, persecutor; hence, apposition to אוֹיֵב; צָרָה f. adversary, rival (applied to a wife whose husband has more than one wife); 4) צַר in the sense of צוּר a rock, a stone. See צָרַר and צוּר.

צֵר (strait, confinement) p. n. of a city in Naphtali.

צֹר masc. 1) a rock, a stone, a flint, equiv. to צוּר which see; 2) sharp edge, probably, a knife, from צוּר; 3) equiv. to צוֹר Tyrus. See צוֹר.

צָרַב (Kal, not used) equiv. to זָרַב, סָרַף to glow, to burn. The Niph. נִצְרַב to be burnt, to glow (of the face).

צָרָב adj. m. but only occurs in the fem. צָרֶבֶת burning, glowing, of the glowing fire.

צָרֶבֶת f. burning, burning wound, or inflamed spot on the skin.

צָרַד (not used) to be cool, fresh, from which:—

צְרֵדָה (cooling) p. n. of a city not far from Scythopolis; see also צְרֵרָה and צָרְתָן, which stand for it.

צָרָה (not used) equiv. to צָרַע to cut in something (to wound) burn; 2) to cut in a tree or shrub for the balm to ooze out.

צָרָה as a fem. from צַר, and thus from the root צָרַר, see צַר and צָרַר.

צְרוּיָה p.n. f. (the wounded one): her children were called בְּנֵי צ׳. It is possible that צ׳ is only a secondary form of צְרוּעָה.

צְרוּעָה p. n. f. (the wounded one).

צְרוֹר see צְרֹר.

צָרַח 1) to cry, to cry aloud, related to עָרַג, שָׁרַק; 2) to shine, to glitter, but only in the derivative צְרִיחַ. Hiph. of signif. 1, to let the voice resound afar off, used of the shouting of war.

צֹרִי a Tyrian, gent. from צֹר Tyrus. Another צֹרִי is the form in pause from צְרִי, which see.

צְרִי (with vav copulative וּצְרִי, pause צֹרִי) masc. balsam, a gum which drops from the balsam tree, and belongs to זִמְרַת הָאָרֶץ best fruits of the land (Palestine).

צְרִי gent. for יִצְרִי, see יֵצֶר 3.

צְרִיָה equiv. to צְרוּיָה.

צְרִיחַ (pl. צְרִיחִים) m. tower, watch tower, from צָרַח to be visible at a distance.

צָרַךְ (not used) orig. to desire something; hence, to need, want. The verb is frequently used in the Aram.

צֹרֶךְ (with suff. צָרְכְּךָ) masc. want, need.

צָרַע to wound, to hurt, to strike; hence, צָרוּעַ the wounded one, transf. to the leprous one (comp. נָגַע and נֶגַע). Pu. to become leprous. Only particip. מְצֹרָע (pl. —עִים) fem. מְצֹרַעַת he or she that suffers from leprosy.

צִרְעָה f. hornet, wasp, from צָרַע to sting; according to Saadia, Abulwalid, and Aben Ezra, plague, calamity, disease.

צָרְעָה (for בֵּית צִרְעָה, place of wasps) p. n. of a city in Judah, from which the gent. צָרְעִי and צָרְעָתִי.

צָרַעַת (with suff. צָרַעְתּוֹ) f. leprosy, of man, houses (a sort of corrosion), and garments (a kind of mould), the form is after אַדֶּרֶת, דַּלֶּקֶת, kamets being only substituted for the dagesh.

צָרַף (fut. יִצְרֹף) to smelt (metals) by burning; hence, צוֹרֵף a worker in gold and silver, transf. to cleanse, to purify (from the dross), figur. to try, to cleanse. In a moral sense, צָרוּף pure, tried. Niph. to be tried, purified (in a moral sense). Pi. to melt, cleanse (metals).

צֹרְפִי p.n. m. (worker in gold).

צָרְפַת (smelting-place, with ה of motion צָרְפַתָה, —תָה) p.n. of a Phenician city between Tyrus and Sidon, Sarepta, now Sarfend. According to tradition it is France.

צָרַר (3 pret. צָרַר and צַר, 3 f. צָרָה, 3 pl. צָרְרוּ, with suff. צְרָרוּנִי; the same in the particip., sometimes the contracted, sometimes the analysed form; fut. intrans. יֵצַר, יֵצֵר, trans. יָצֹר) 1) to bind up, e.g. in a garment, or water in a cloud, the sin, the testimony (i.e. it is hidden); to be shut, of women, i.e. not to marry; the root is found again in אָסַר, אָזַר, עָצַר; 2) to oppress, to persecute; hence particip. צַר adversary, persecutor, and particip. f. צָרָה. It is also used impersonally and intrans. with לְ; as, I am in trouble, in a strait, in anguish; with עַל, to be anxious for something; fig. of the mutual jealousy and rivalry of two wives (of one husband): fut. יָצֹר; 3) (not used) to be hard, hence צַר a rock, equiv. to צוּר. Pu. to be bound together, particip. מְצֹרָר. Hiph. הֵצַר (fut. יָצֵר, pl. יָצֵרוּ) to press (the enemy), to besiege, to hurt, to offend; אִשָּׁה מְצֵרָה a woman having throes, i.e. in labour; for signif. 2, comp. צָרַע.

צְרוֹר (also צְרוֹר, pl. צְרוֹרוֹת) masc. 1) bundle, bag, or sack (with gold), and generally something bound up, e.g. a bundle of myrrh;

צְרוֹר נָקוּב a bag with holes, צְרוֹר אֶבֶן a bundle of precious stones, figur. צְרוֹר הַחַיִּים bundle of life; 2) little stone, equiv. to צַר; hence, a grain.

צְרֵדָה p.n. for צְרֵדָה heap.

צֶרֶת p. n. m. (brightness), for צֹהֶרֶת.

צֶרֶת הַשַּׁחַר (brightness of the morning), p.n. of a city in the territory of Reuben.

צָרְתָן (probably formed from צְרֵדָה, for which it stands) p.n. of a city in the tribe of Manasseh.

צָתַת see צות.

ק

ק called Koph (קוֹף, pl. קוֹפִין) signifies the hole of an axe where the handle is put in; the figure arises from the name; as a numeral it signifies 100. It interchanges, 1) with the gutturals, including ע; 2) with ח, as שָׂקָה and שָׁתָה; פָּקַח and פָּתַח and others.

קֵא (with suff. קֵאוֹ) m. that which is spewed out, from קוּא.

קָאַת (const. קְאַת) f. an aquatic and land bird; according to some, a pelican, so called on account of its spitting out the shells which it swallows; thus from קוּא, in the Talmud קָקָא.

קַב m. name of a vessel; hence, a measure for solids, from קָבַב to hollow out, to deepen out; comp. כּוּר.

I. קָבַב (inf. קֹב, imper. קָבָה־, fut. יִקֹּב to blaspheme, to curse (God or man); related is נָקַב and the root in כָּאַב, אֶ־כַף, נֶ־קַף.

II. קָבַב (not used) 1) equiv. to עָקַב, גַּב, קָבַע to be arched, hilly; 2) to hollow out, to arch, or to make something dome-like, from which קַב and קֻבָּה. The words קֵבָה and קֹבָה are from נָקַב.

קֵבָה (for נְקֵבָה that which is hollow) f. the maw of cattle, so called from its hollowness, from קוּב.

קֹבָה (with suff. קֳבָתָהּ) f. the privy part of a woman; thus also from נָקַב or קוּב, and hence equiv. to נְקֵבָה.

קֻבָּה f. arched tent, from קָבַב to arch.

קִבּוּץ (plur. ־צִים) m. heap, mass of idols.

קְבוּרָה f. 1) the burial, the burying; 2) a grave, equiv. to קֶבֶר.

I. קָבַל (Kal, not used) to receive; especially Pi. קִבֵּל to accept something offered; fig. of the receiving of instruction. The origin. signification is to seize, to lay hold of.

II. קָבַל (Kal, not used) to be in front or opposite something; hence Hiph. הִקְבִּיל to stand opposite something.

קְבֵל (Aram.) the same, like קָבַל I.; hence Pa. קַבֵּל to receive, to accept.

קְבֵל and קֳבֵל (Aram.) m. that which is in front or opposite one (synon. with פָּנִים), but only used as a prep., before, opposite, or like מִפְּנֵי because of; כָּל־קֳבֵל־דִּי just because of; the same כָּל־קֳבֵל־דְּנָה; לְקָבְלָךְ before thee.

קֹבֶל (const. and before makkaph קָבָל־, with suff. קָבָלוֹ) masc. the same, but only as a prep., before, opposite; מְחִי קֹבֶל pushing against, signifying the breaker down of the wall (Auth. Vers. "engines of war").

I. קָבַע (not used) to be round, arched; related to כָּבַע and גָּבַע.

II. קָבַע (fut. יִקְבַּע) orig. to spin, to entwine (comp. עָקַב, עָכַב); hence after the usual mode of transferring, to deceive, to cheat, to overreach, to trick; קֹבַע deceiver.

קֻבַּעַת f. cup.; ק׳ כּוֹס cup or chalice for drinking, to distinguish it from the chalice of a flower; according to others, settling of the dregs, from קָבַע in the sense of (especially in modern Heb.) fixing, settling in a place.

קָבַץ (fut. יִקְבֹּץ) orig. to hold together (related to קָמַץ and גָּמַץ); hence, to gather (corn, booty) at (אֶל) a place, עַל־יַד in the possession or for the possession (with לְ of the person) for those for whom the gathering takes place, or also to assemble (men), to (אֶל, עַל) some one's. Niph. to be gathered, of inanimate objects, to assemble at (אֶל, עַל) some one. Pi. to gather the lambs and carry them in one's bosom, i.e. to protect them, or gathering generally (sheaves, water in fish-ponds, wages of a harlot, beasts, people, etc.); to gather in the beauty, i.e. to withdraw it, to cease to shine; but it is especially used of the gathering in of the dispersed of Israel. Pu. pass. Hith. to assemble at (אֶל) some one's.

קַבְצְאֵל (place of Divine assembly) p. n. of a city in Judah. See יְקַבְצְאֵל.

קְבֻצָה f. a collection, heap (of gold and silver).

קִבְצַיִם (double-heap) p. n. of a city in Ephraim.

קָבַר (fut. יִקְבֹּר) origin. equiv. to חָבַר, חָפַר to dig; generally, to dig a pit, bury (a corpse); according to others, the original signification is like in צָבַר. Niph. to be buried. Pi. to bury several or often. Pu. pass.

קֶבֶר (with suff. קִבְרִי, plur. קְבָרִים,

const. קִבְרֵי and קְבָרוֹת, const. קִבְרוֹת) m. a grave; the pl. stands sometimes for a place containing a number of graves, i. e. a burial-ground.

קִבְרוֹת הַתַּאֲוָה (graves of lust) p. n. of a place in the Arabian desert.

קָדַד (not used) to split, to divide, to cut; related to חָדַד, נָדַד, from which קָדְקֹד and קִדָּה; the קָדַד, however, which is used, is only a denom.; according to another explanation of קָדַד, equivalent to חָדַד to be pointed, from which קָדְקֹד, the crown of the head being the top point of the human body.

קִדָּה f. in signification and etymology, equiv. to קְצִיעָה cassia, so called on account of the sticks being divided up the middle.

קָדַד (not used) to possess; hence יָקְדְעָם p.n., which see.

קָדוּם (but only pl. קְדוּמִים, after the form עֲלֻמִים, נְעֻרִים to designate a certain age) m. former time, time of old, time of yore; hence נַחַל (הַרְרֵי קֶדֶם) נַחַל עוֹלָם=קְדוּמִים ancient brook.

קָדוֹשׁ (or קָדֹשׁ, const. קְדוֹשׁ, plur. קְדוֹשִׁים) adj. m. clean (physically or morally); next, holy, i. e. free from sin, or consecrated (of the priest, of the Jewish nation); also, of holy places and days. The Lord especially is called קָדוֹשׁ or קְדוֹשׁ יִשְׂרָאֵל, and in the plur. קְדוֹשִׁים; the last term, however, is also used of angels, the pious, and the Israelites generally.

קָדַח 1) to glow, to burn, e. g. fig. of the burning of the fire in wrath, i. e. of the kindling of wrath; 2) to kindle.

קַדַּחַת f. burning ague, from קָדַח. Comp. דַּלֶּקֶת.

קָדִים (with ה of motion קָדִימָה) m. that which is in front; hence, east; פְּאַת קָ׳ east side, רוּחַ קָדִים east wind, but in both instances also קָדִים alone, and in the last sense fig. for רוּחַ vanity: קָדִימָה signifies either forward or toward the east.

קַדִּישׁ (pl. קַדִּישִׁין) Aram. adj. masc. holy, but as a subst. the holy one, like קָדוֹשׁ, and also used like it of angels and the Israelites.

קָדַם (Kal, not used) to be before, in front; hence Pi. to precede, in reference to time, place, and action, and it is therefore joined with other verbs; קִדֵּם בְּ׳ to anticipate by something, i.e. to meet one with presents. Hiph. הִקְדִּים to precede, to anticipate, to act obligingly by anticipation of some one's wishes.

קֶדֶם (with ה of motion קֵדְמָה, comp. קֵדְשָׁה from קֶרֶשׁ, pl. const. קַדְמֵי) m. front side, that which is before or in front; hence 1) eastern part (in contrast to אָחוֹר), eastern territory; מִקֶּדֶם from the east, in reference to the east; בְּנֵי ק׳ sons of the east, inhabiting the desert of Arabia; הַר הַקֶּדֶם the Arabian mountains; הַרְרֵי קֶדֶם the Mesopotamian mountains, and these countries were called אֶרֶץ קֶדֶם, אֶרֶץ בְּנֵי קֶדֶם; מִקֶּדֶם לְ from the east of; 2) in reference to time, time of yore, eternity; מִקֶּדֶם from ever; מַלְכֵי קֶדֶם kings of ancient times, next as an adv., formerly=לְפָנִים, and as a prep., before, and in this sense also pl. const. קַדְמֵי; 3) practices of the east, witchcraft, only Isaiah 2:6, מִקֶּדֶם, for which some read מִקֶּסֶם; קֵדְמָה eastward.

קֵדֶם belongs to קֵדְמָה. See קֶדֶם.

קֳדָם (or קֳדָם, with suff. pl. קֳדָמַי, קֳדָמוֹהִי, קֳדָמֵיהוֹן, קֳדָמָיךְ) Aram. m. the same, but usually as a preposition, before, either of locality or time; מִן־קֳדָם from before, from opposite.

קַדְמָה (const. —מַת, with suff. —מָתָהּ, pl. suff. קַדְמוֹתֵיכֶם) fem. (formed from קֶדֶם) orig. beginning, former existence; but also as a prep. before, previous, ere, especially the state of const.

קַדְמָה (Aram.) fem. the same, the former time, but only used as a prep. מִקַּדְמַת־דְּנָא or מִן־קֳ׳ דְ׳ previous, prior.

קֵדְמָה p. n. m. (the East).

קִדְמָה (only const. קִדְמַת) fem. the East, but only as a prep. east of.

קַדְמוֹן adj. m., —מוֹנָה fem. easterly, from קֶדֶם.

קְדֵמוֹת (ancient place) p.n. of a city in the tribe of Reuben, and also the name of the neighbouring desert.

קַדְמַי (def. קַדְמָאָה, pl. קַדְמָאִין, but also contracted קַדְמָיֵא) Aram. adj. m., קַדְמָאָה (def. קַדְמֵיתָא or קַדְמָיְתָא, def. pl. קַדְמָיָתָא) f. the first, in reference to succession.

קַדְמִיאֵל p.n. masc. (ancient time of God).

קַדְמֹנִי (pl. קַדְמֹנִים) adj. m., קַדְמֹנִית (pl. —נִיּוֹת) f. 1) the further one, the front one, in reference to locality; hence, easterly; יָם הַקַּדְמֹנִי the East i. e. the Dead Sea; 2) ancient, old, יָמִים קַדְמֹנִים the ancient days, מְשַׁל הַקַּדְמֹנִי the ancient proverb or the proverb of the ancients, קַדְמֹנִיּוֹת ancient, past; 3) (ancient) p. n. of a nation.

קָדְקֹד (with suff. קָדְקֳדוֹ) m. crown of the head, ק׳ שֵׂעָר crown of the hair, orig. division, parting, from קָדַד.

קָדַר to be dark, to be black, e.g. of the darkening of the sun and moon, figur. to mourn, or to go in mourning, black garments; to look dark, gloomy, blackish (of waters). Hiph. to darken, figur. to cause to mourn. Hith. to be darkened (of the heavens).

קֵדָר (the black one) p. n. m. of the ancestor of an Arabian tribe of nomades; hence בְּנֵי קֵדָר later for the Arabs generally.

קִדְרוֹן (the dark brook) p. n. of a brook and valley between Jerusalem and the Mount of Olives; the brook discharges itself in the Dead Sea.

קַדְרוּת f. blackness, darkness, of the heaven.

קְדֹרַנִּית adv. mourning, in mourning, comp. adv. אֲחֹרַנִּית.

קָדַשׁ (once in pause קָדֵשׁוּ, fut. יִקְדַּשׁ) to be clean (physically and morally); related to חָדַשׁ, thus orig. to shine; hence, to consecrate oneself to some one, accus., to be holy; also of inanimate objects to be consecrated. Niph. to be considered, treated as holy, to prove oneself holy towards (בְּ) something, to be sanctified. Pi. קִדֵּשׁ to sanctify, to consecrate (an altar, a building, for the office of priest, for sacrifice, for battle), or to treat or declare as holy, to institute something holy (fast); next, generally, to prepare something, to arm, to select as sacred. Pu. pass. מְקֻדָּשׁ the hallowed, consecrated, prepared one. Hiph. to hallow, to sanctify, to consecrate to God. Hith. to sanctify oneself, i.e. to cleanse oneself (syn. with הִטַּהֵר), or to prove oneself holy; to be kept holy or to be sanctified, of a festival.

קָדֵשׁ (pl. קְדֵשִׁים) adj. m. קְדֵשָׁה (pl. —שׁוֹת) fem. 1) a male or female devotee to the worship of Astarte, where boys and girls sacrificed their chastity (Auth. Ver. "whore, sodomite"). The Aram. form was transferred to the Israelites, with the idolatry of the Arameans; hence, its being used only in this sense; 2) p. n. of a place in the desert: complete קָ׳ בַּרְנֵעַ.

קֶדֶשׁ (with ה of motion קֶדְשָׁה) 1) p. n. of a city in Judah; 2) a city in the tribe of Naphtali; 3) a city in the tribe of Issachar, for which once קִשְׁיוֹן.

קֹדֶשׁ (with suff. קָדְשִׁי, plur. קֳדָשִׁים, const. קָדְשֵׁי) m. 1) holiness, cleanliness; hence, in the genitive following a noun as an adj., e.g.

שֵׁם קֹדֶשׁ holy name, אֶבֶן קֹדֶשׁ holy stone; 2) sanctuary, or consecrated gift. The pl. is used of the holy vessels, or consecrated offerings; קֹדֶשׁ קֳדָשִׁים the holy of holies, i.e. the Most Holy.

קְדֵשָׁה see קָדֵשׁ.

קָהָה (fut. יִקְהֶה) equiv. to כָּהָה to become dark, weak, but only used of the teeth; קֵהָה to be blunt, of iron; see כָּהָה.

קָהַל (Kal not used) equiv. to קוֹל, belonging to קוֹל to call together; hence Niph. to assemble, or to be assembled. Hiph. to convene, to cause to assemble.

קָהָל (const. קְהַל, with suff. קְהָלָם) m. an assembly called together; next, congregation generally, mass of people, like in קְ׳ גּוֹיִם ,קְ׳ יִשְׂרָאֵל, קְהַל ה׳, but also a mass of nations (or an army).

קְהֵלָה (assembly) p. n. of an encampment of the Israelites in the desert.

קְהִלָּה fem. assemblage, congregation.

קֹהֶלֶת p.n. m. Being also an appell. it stands sometimes with the article, and having a fem. form, it is once construed with the fem. The signification is, the gatherer, preacher, etc.

קָהַת (not used) to assemble; hence קְהָת and תִּקְהַת, if יִקָּהָ is not the original.

קְהָת p.n. m. (assemblage), patron. קְהָתִי.

קַו (const. קַו, with suff. קַוָּם) m. 1) cord, string, from קָוָה to wind, to bind, to twist; but generally, (*a*) a cord for measuring, a line; to draw the measuring line over something is a biblical figure for devoting to destruction; (*b*) string of an instrument; hence, sound; (*c*) law, command: thus, line in a figur. sense; 2) strength, power, from קָוָה, which see, only Is. 18:2, and only according to some interpreters.

קוא (3 fem., probably קָאָה *milrang*, imp. קִיוּ for קְאוּ) to spit out, to spew; figur. to spew out a people, i.e. not suffer them. Hiph. (fut. apoc. יָקֵא) to vomit (something eaten or drunk); figur. to cast off.

קוב (not used) to be hollow; related is קָבַב and כָּ־קַב; from which קֻבָּה and קֵבָה.

קוֹבַע (const. קוֹבַע) m. a helmet, orig. that which is arched, from קָבַע I.

קָוָה (particip. קוֹוֶה) equiv. to גָּוָה orig. to bind, or intrans. to join; hence קַו and תִּקְוָה I., and from which, as in חוּל, to be firm, strong, vigorous. The verb is used to signify, to wait, to long, to hope, thus orig. like חול and יָחַל to adhere firmly to something, to trust in something firmly. Niph. to be joined, gathered (of water, nations). Pi. to wait, to hope for, (accus. לְ, אֶל) something; to hope, trust (in God); transf. to await, to lie in wait for some one.

קָוֶךְ (not קָוֶה, only in Ketib, const. קְוֵה after the usual manner) m. cord, string. It is the original form from which קַו arose.

קוֹחַ see פְּקַח־קוֹחַ.

קוּט (pret. קָט, fut. יָקוּט and probably יָקוֹט) 1) equiv. to קוּץ to be disgusted, to be wearied, grieved, with something; hence const. with בְּ, like קוּץ; but also with the accus. in קוּט כֶּסֶל to give up the hopes, if it does not belong to קָטַט; כִּמְעַט קָט but a little he would have been wearied with thee (Author. Vers. "but as if that were a very little thing, thou wast corrupted." Niph. to be weary of (בִּפְנֵי or with בְּ) something. The form נָקֹטָּה for נָקֹטּוּ, נְקֹטָה are as if from Hith. הִתְקוֹטֵט to be weary, disgusted with (בְּ) something.

קוּט (Aram.) equiv. to קוּץ II., to cut off; from which קַיִט.

קוּל (not used) to call, to cry, also to say, to speak. Comp. קָהַל.

קוֹל (pl. קוֹלוֹת) m. a voice (of man), a sound, noise, of inanimate things. In the first instance קוֹל בְּכִי loud weeping; קוֹל עַנּוֹת (or קוֹל alone) singing; קוֹל שִׂמְחָה, רִנָּה shouting (of triumph), or as a voice of one that speaks; if with a loud voice, it is expressed by קוֹל רָם, קוֹל גָּדוֹל; קוֹל אֶחָד in one voice, unanimous, or the noise of a multitude: used of beast, קוֹל signifies the braying, neighing, bellowing, etc., according to the context. Used of inanimate objects, it signifies the sound produced by an instrument, or the sounds on certain occasions; hence, rustling, gushing, rattling, rushing, etc. In poetic language, thunder; נָשָׂא, הֵרִים קוֹל to lift the voice; נָתַן קוֹל to break into a cry, either weeping, or to calling together; שָׁמַע קוֹל פ' to give ear to, to hearken to some one; הֶאֱזִין קוֹל פ'. הֶעֱבִיר קוֹל בְּ, לְקוֹל פ', שָׁמַע קוֹל פ', נָתַן קוֹל בְּ to make something known.

קוֹלָיָה p. n. m. (the voice of God).

קוּם pret. קָם, once קָאם, fut. יָקוּם, apoc. יָקֹם, יָקָם, imp. קוּם & קוּמָה, particip. קָם, but once, 2 Kings 16:7, קוֹם) 1) to stand, to exist, to be (compare יְקוּם); next, to maintain oneself, to remain, to endure, on a certain place; in connection with עַל, to insist upon something, to persevere, or to be confirmed; to be fulfilled, established, of a prediction, a plan, a vow; with לְ, to assist some one; with לִפְנֵי to exist before some one; with עֵינַיִם, to stand still, immoveable, as a description of blindness; 2) to rise from (מֵעַל, מִן) a place, before (מִפְּנֵי) some one, to meet (לִקְרַאת) some one; in connection with other verbs, it signifies, rising to do something, beginning; with עַל, בְּ, לְ, אֶל, לִפְנֵי to rise against some one in a hostile sense; קוּם is used in many other significations, which, however, may be reduced to the two above. Pi. קִיֵּם (fut. אֲקַיֵּם, in the later Scriptures) 1) to confirm, with עַל; to impose a duty upon some one or upon one's-self; קִיֵּם שְׁבוּעָה to fulfil an oath; קִיֵּם דָּבָר to fulfil a thing; 2) to preserve life, from קוּם. Po. קוֹמֵם 1) to build up, to re-establish (ruins); 2) to place oneself in various localities, e.g. לְאֹיֵב יְקוֹמֵם he will rise as an enemy in various places. Hiph. הֵקִים (fut. יָקִים, apoc. יָקֵם) 1) to raise (the fallen one), to incite, to arouse, rebellion; to provoke, arouse, the enemy, against עַל some one, to bring misfortune over עַל some one; 2) to cause to arise, to raise (judges, prophets, kings, a new generation) to cause to spring forth (a plant), to call forth a progeny, to establish a name הֵקִים שֵׁם לְ; 3) to erect (a pillar, a tent, an altar, a monument), to erect anew (something fallen); fig. to restore, re-establish (a people, a covenant), to revive (the dead); 4) to appoint (a king), to confirm. Hoph. pass. to be established, erected, appointed. Hith. הִתְקוֹמֵם to raise oneself against (לְ) some one, מִתְקוֹמֵם an adversary, an opponent.

קוּם (particip. קָאֵם, pl. קָאְמִין, Keri קָיְמִין, fut. יְקוּם) Aram. the same, to stand, to arise, to endure. Pa. קַיֵּם (inf. קַיָּמָה) to establish (a decree). Af. אֲקִים, הֲקִים (pl. הֲקִימוּ, particip. מְהָקִים, fut. יְקִים and יְהָקִים) to erect (a column, a pillar), to nominate (a prince), to appoint over (עַל) something. Hoph. הֳקַם (after the Heb. הֳקִימַת 3 fem.) to be placed, to stand.

קוֹמָה f. height, stature, orig. erect position, e.g. שִׁפְלַת ק׳, גָּבְהָ, also man generally, e.g. כָּל־קוֹמָה every stature, i.e. every man; קוֹמַת אֲרָזִים the height of cedars.

קוֹמְמִיּוּת adv. erectly, with upright body, with great safety.

I. קוֹן (Kal, not used) to sound; next, to wail (comp. נָהָה, הָגָה), from which Pi. קוֹנֵן to attune a song of lament, to lament over (עַל, אֶל) something. The root is related to that in רָנַע.

II. קוֹן (not used) to cut in, to sharpen the point; not related to the preceding root.

קוֹס belongs to קָסַם, which see.

I. קוּעַ a softened form from קוּר, i.e. *ar* (קָר) is softened into *â* (קָע), Similarly בָּצַע and בָּקַע ,בָּצַר and מָעַט ,קָצַע and קָצַר ,בָּקַר ,מָרַט ,קָרַע and קָרַר, origin. to engrave, to dig through, figur. as in זָכַר to spring (of the camel); possibly, however, it is equiv. to קוּץ II.

II. קוּעַ (Kal, not used) equiv. to קוּץ I. to be wearied, disgusted (the interchanging of ע and צ is frequent). Niph. נָקַע (secondary form for נָקוֹעַ 3 pret. f. נָקְעָה) to be wearied of (מֵעַם, מֵעַל) something, to be indignant. Another signif. of the root קָע, see under יָקַע, for which הוֹקִיעַ.

קוֹעַ m. prince, ruler, occurs in connection with שׁוֹעַ and פְּקוֹד, orig. a trained camel, comp. עַתּוּד and others.

קוּף (not used) equiv. to נָקַף to encircle; transf. to be moveable, dexterous, from תְּקוּפָה and קוֹף. See also נָקַף.

קוֹף (pl. קוֹפִים) m. an ape, orig. the dexterous one, from קוּף.

I. קוּץ (fut. יָקוּץ ,יָקֻץ, apoc. יָקֹץ) 1) to be wearied, disgusted (with בְּ) some one, to be in fear (מִפְּנֵי) of some one. For this root קָץ, comp. קוּט and קוּעַ II. and the root in שִׁקֵּץ. Hiph. הֵקִיץ Isa. 7:6, to affright, which, however, according to some, belongs to קוּץ II.; 2) Kal, not used, to be moveable, stirring, =יָקַץ. Hiph. הֵקִיץ to awake, to arouse, from a sleeping or a torpid state.

II. קוּץ (Kal, not used) equiv. to קָצַץ to cut in. Hiph. הֵקִיץ, Isa. 7:6, to hurt, to torment, to cut off (fruit); hence like קָצַר of the reaping of fruit, harvesting.

קוּץ in the signification of, to abide the summer. See under קַיִץ.

קוֹץ (pl. קוֹצִים, const. קוֹצֵי) m. thorn, from קוּץ to sting, to prickle; also coll. thorny plants.

קְוֻצָּה (pl. קְוֻצּוֹת) lock of hair, a curl (synon. with תַּלְתַּל, דַּלָּה).

I. קוּר (1 pret. קַרְתִּי) to dig (for water). Comp. the root בּוּר, and that in כָּרַר ,חָדַר. Pi. (reduplicated) קַרְקַר to dig under, to undermine; transf. to destroy (a wall): probably קַרְקַר is only a denom. from קִיר, or from קוּר, equiv. to עָקַר.

II. קוּר to flow, comp. כָּר, orig. to roll along. Hiph. to cause to flow, to spring forth; figur. to beget (wickedness).

III. קוּר (not used) to bind, to tie; hence, to weave, from which:—

קוּר (only pl. קוּרִים) m. thread, wove, of the web of the spider.

קוֹרֵא see קָרָא.

קוֹרָה (or, also קֹרָה, pl. קֹרוֹת, after the form קוֹמָה) fem. beam, so called from its connecting the building, thus from קוּר III., not from קָרָה; figur. a house, from which only denom. Pi. קֵרָה to lay the beams; fig. to arch, to build (בָּתִּים, עֲלִיּוֹת). Hiph. הִקְרָה to build up (עָרִים).

קוּשׁ (not used) to be bent, crooked; the same is the root in עִקֵּשׁ; the fut. יְקֹשׁוּן belongs to יָקֹשׁ=קָשַׁשׁ, or it is a pret. from יָקֹשׁ, to seize.

קוּשָׁיָהוּ p.n. m. bow of the Lord, i.e. rainbow. Comp. קוֹלָיָה; as a p.n. probably thunder.

קָטַב (not used) equiv. to חָטַב to cut; hence, to destroy. Comp. חָצַב.

קֶטֶב m. 1) destruction; שֹׁעַר קֶ׳ a destroying storm; 2) pestilence, joined with מְרִירִי, bitter pestilence (Auth. Ver. "destruction").

קֹטֶב (with suff. קָטָבְךָ) m. pestilence, destruction.

קְטוֹרָה f. frankincense, from קָטַר I.

קְטוּרָה p.n. f. the girded one, from קָטַר II.

קָטַט (Kal, not used) equiv. to קוּט to be wearied, disgusted; hence, Niph. נָקֹט (3 fem. נָקֹטָה for נָקְטָה, 3 pl. נָקֹטּוּ, 2 pl. נְקֹטֹּתֶם, to be wearied with (בְּ, בִּפְנֵי) something or some one. The form קָט belongs to קוּט, and not to קָטַט.

קָטַל (only poetically, fut. יִקְטֹל) to kill, to slay.

קְטַל (particip. קָטֵל, pass. קְטִיל) Aram. the same. Pa. קַטֵּל to kill, several or many. Ithp. pass.

קֶטֶל m. slaughter, murder.

קָטֹן (1 pret. קָטֹנְתִּי, fut. יִקְטַן) to be little, small (in contrast to גָּדַל to be great) from קָטַן to shorten, to cut off; fig. to be considered little, insignificant, unworthy. Hiph. to make small (a measure).

קָטָן (pl. קְטַנִּים) 1) adj. m. קְטַנָּה (pl. קְטַנּוֹת) f. little, in reference to the size of a person, in contrast to גָּדוֹל, and like it used also of inanimate objects, e.g. עִיר קְטַנָּה a little city, fig. insignificant; of persons, young, tender. Rarely as an abst. littleness, as כְּלֵי הַקָּטָן a vessel of littleness, i.e. a small vessel; יוֹם קְטַנּוֹת a day of small things, i. e. little beginnings; 2) p. n. little one.

קָטֹן (const. קְטֹן) adj. m. the same.

קֹטֶן (with suff. קָטָנִי) m. orig. littleness; hence, little finger: others read קְטַנִּי, as if from קָטֹן.

קָטַף (fut. יִקְטֹף) equiv. to חָטַף to tear off, to pluck off; hence, of the plucking off (of ears of corn, mallows, etc.). Niph. to be plucked off.

I. **קָטַר** (Kal, not used) equiv. to עָתַר to diffuse fragrance (comp. יָתַר and the Aram. עֲטַר). Pi. קִטֵּר to burn frankincense, in honour of a deity, especially of idols; particip. f. מְקַטֶּרֶת altar for frankincense. Pu. מְקֻטֶּרֶת perfumed with myrrh. Hiph. הִקְטִיר to burn (with accus. of the object), orig. to cause to be consumed in smoke, e. g. an offering connected with burning, as חֵלֶב, עוֹלָה, and with the accus. of the place where the offering is burnt; but the deity to whom the offering is made, stands in the dative or with לִפְנֵי. Hoph. pass. מָקְטָר that which is burnt or consumed in smoke.

II. **קָטַר** equiv. to קָשַׁר to bind (so קְטַר Aram.); hence, in architecture, to arch; חֲצֵרוֹת קְטֻרוֹת arched courts, Auth. Vers. joined; according to the tradition קָטַר in this passage (Ezek. 26. 23) is rendered in the sense of קָצַר.

קְטַר (def. קִטְרָא, pl. קִטְרִין, Aram. m. 1) knot, origin. that which is intricate; hence figur. of mystery, riddle; 2) joint, connecting the limbs.

קִטֵּר (after the form שִׁלֵּם) m. burning, consuming in smoke.

קִטְרוֹן (probably, the little one) from קָטַר=קָצַר) p. n. of a city in Zebulun, for which once קַטָּת, i. e. קְטַנַּת stands.

קְטֹרֶת (with suff. קְטָרְתִּי) f. 1) frankincense, e. g. of spices (סַמִּים); מִזְבַּח הַקְ׳ altar of frankincense; 2) that which is burnt (of sacrifices), as קְ׳ אֵילִים.

קַטָּת (the little one, for קְטַנַּת) p. n. of a city in Zebulun, for which also קִטְרוֹן stands, which signifies the same.

קִיא (with suff. קִיאוֹ) masc. spitting, spittle, from קוֹא.

קִיָּה belongs to קִיו, see קוֹא.

קַיִט (def. in the Targ. קַיְטָא) Aram. m. equiv. to קַיִץ Heb. summer.

קִיטוֹר (for קִטּוֹר) masc. smoke (of an oven), נֹאד בְּקִיטוֹר a bottle in the smoke, i. e. shrinking together; transf. to the mist or fog resembling smoke.

קִים (after the form רִיב, with suff. קִימָנוּ) m. the hostile rising against one; hence, enmity; transf. to enemy, adversary.

קְיָם (def. קְיָמָא) Aram. command, edict, from קַיֵּם (synon. with בְּרִית, חֹק).

קַיָּם (Aram.) adj. m., קַיָּמָא fem. firm, constant, lasting.

קִימָה f. the rising, infinitive noun.

קִימוֹשׁ see קִמּוֹשׁ.

קִין see קוּן.

קַיִן (with suff. קֵינוֹ) m. 1) a lance, spear, orig. that which is pointed, from קוּן; 2) p.n. m. (smith; according to the Scripture, he that was gotten); 3) p.n. of a people; hence קֵינִי a Kenite; 4) p.n. of a city in Judah, used with the article.

קִינָה (pl. קִינִים and קִינוֹת) fem. 1) mourning-song, נָשָׂא קִינָה עַל, אֶל, to lift up the voice of lament over some one; 2) (smithy) p.n. of a city in Judah.

קֵינִי (also קֵנִי and קִינִי) gent. m. a a people descending from a certain Cain, and living among the Amalekites.

קֵינָן p.n. m. (smith), equiv. to קַיִן.

קַיִץ (with suff. קֵיצֵךְ) m. 1) orig. the cutting off (of fruit); next, reaping of fruit (comp. קָצִיר); בִּכּוּרָה בְּטֶרֶם קַיִץ a hasty fruit before the summer; next, summer generally; 2) summer-fruit, especially figs. Root קוּץ.

קִיצוֹן (for קִצּוֹן) adj. m., קִיצוֹנָה f. the outmost, the last.

קִיקָיוֹן m. according to Samuel Ibn Chofni, the wonder-tree, *ricinus*; according to others, a kind of gourd (קָרָא) in the shadow of which Jonah the prophet rested.

קִיקָלוֹן (for קְלַקְלוֹן, a double form from the simple קָלוֹן) m. shame, disgrace, equal to קָלוֹן. The word arises from קָלָה and not from קָלַל.

קִיר (also קִר, plur. קִירוֹת) masc. 1) wall; אֶבֶן קִיר stone of a wall; חָרַשׁ קִיר master-mason, קִיר הָעִיר city-wall, מַשְׁתִּין בְּקִיר one that pisseth against the wall, i.e. a dog; מוֹשַׁב הַקִּיר a seat on the wall; זֶרֶם קִיר a storm against the wall, i.e. that which destroys the wall; sometimes only a part, only a side of the wall; hence קִיר הַחוֹמָה; figur. of the sides of the altar, of the walls of the heart, etc.; עֲלִיַּת קִיר קְטַנָּה a little chamber on the wall (קְטַנָּה refers to עֲלִיָּה); 2) a place fortified by a wall, i.e. a castle, fortress, especially in many proper names of places, e.g. קִיר מוֹאָב, קִיר חֶרֶשׂ; 3) p.n. of an Assyrian people and district, formerly inhabited by the Aramæans, probably it is the country round the river Cyprus, now called Cur or Kur.

קִירֹס (also קֵרֹס) p. n. m. (bending, bowing, from קָרַס).

קִישׁ p.n. masc. (catching, from קוּשׁ, which see).

קִישׁוֹן (curve) p.n. of a brook springing from the Tabor, and discharging itself in the gulf Acco (Arab. נהר חיפא, of the city חיפא).

קִישִׁי stands for קוּשָׁיָהוּ, which see.

קִיתָרֹס (so in the Ketib, for which in the Keri קַתְרוֹס) m. *κίθαρος*, coat of mail; next, in the sense of *κίθρις*, *cithern*; the word is of Greek origin, like the name of many musical instruments.

קַל (pl. קַלִּים) adj. m., קַלָּה f. 1) light, swift (in running), sometimes with the addition of בְּרַגְלָיִם; subst. קַל a swift runner, swift horse, courser (Isa. 30:16); next, generally, one who is light of foot; adv. swiftly, quickly, easily, lightly. Root קָלַל.

קָל (Aram.) m. equiv. to קוֹל in Heb. voice.

קֹל (infin. noun from קָלַל) m. shame, disgrace, only Jer. 3:9, thus=קָלוֹן, origin. lightness, in a moral sense.

קָלָה (Kal, not used) equiv. to קָהַל assembly; hence in Niph. וַיִּקָּלֵהוּ, if the word is not misspelled for וַיִּקָּהֲלוּ, in which case, the root קָלָה does not exist at all.

I. קָלָה equiv. to צָלָה to roast by the fire, to dry (ears of corn); hence קָלִי parched corn, like קָלִי; transf. to burn (human beings as a punishment). Niph. pass. but only particip. נִקְלָה burning or inflamed wound.

II. קָלָה (Kal, not used) equiv. to קָלַל to be despicable, insignificant, or transf. to despise; hence Niph. נִקְלָה to seem vile, to be contemned, despised; particip. נִקְלֶה (in contrast to נִכְבָּד) the poor one, the despised one. Hiph. to despise, to esteem low: particip. מַקְלֶה despising, setting light (the parents).

קָלוֹן (const. קְלוֹן, with suff. קְלֹנִי) m. disgrace (in contrast to כָּבוֹד), shame (of face); transf. to shameful deed or speech, דִּין וְקָלוֹן strife and reproach.

קָלַח (not used) probably only a secondary form from צָלַח in the signif. of to deepen out; hence:—

קַלַּחַת f. only a secondary form from צַלַּחַת kettle, dish, orig. something deepened out; according to others, from קָלַח to pour out.

קָלַט 1) to be contracted, to be shrunk together, particip. pass. קָלוּט *contractus*, a dwarf, a cripple (Auth. Vers. "lacking in his parts"), in contrast to שָׂרוּעַ, having anything superfluous; 2) to hold, to contain, to gather (within itself);

hence מְקַלֵּס; the p. n. קְלִיטָא belongs to signification 1.

קָלִי (once קָלִיא) masc. parched corn (when yet in the ear); hence equiv. to the complete phrase אָבִיב קָלוּי בָּאֵשׁ.

קַלַּי p. n. m. (swift runner).

קֵלָיָה p. n. m. (contempt).

קְלִיטָא p. n. m. (dwarf).

קָלַל (2 per. קַלּוֹתָ, 3 pl. קַלּוּ, fut. יֵקַל, pl. יֵקַלּוּ) to drive, to run (comp. *cell-o*, *κέλλ-ω*), like the Pi. קִלְקֵל and the relative קָלַע I. prove; transf. 1) to be swift, flexible, e.g. swifter (קַלּוּ) than the eagles; 2) to be light, i.e. insignificant, diminishing, in reference to quantity, corresponding with חָלָה II.; 3) to be despised, low, in reference to quality. Niph. נָקַל (after the form נָסַב) and נְקַל (after the form נָמֵס; 1 pers. נְקַלֹּתִי, fut. יִקַּלּוּ) to become light, vile (לְ) to some one, to be light, i. e. easy, or to be despised, esteemed low (בְּעֵינֵי) to some one; also, to be light of foot. Pi. קִלֵּל to make light of something, to despise, to curse (comp. כִּבֵּד to esteem as weighty, i. e. to honor), with accus. and לְ, seldom construed with בְּ; ק׳ בְּשֵׁם יי׳ or בֵּאלֹהִים to curse some one by the name of God; קִלֵּל לוֹ to curse oneself. Pu. to be cursed, or to be destroyed by a curse. Hiph. הֵקַל (inf. הָקֵל, fut. יָקֵל) causative of all significations of the Kal; hence, 1) to lighten, to make light (something heavy), to take off (the work) from (מֵעַל, מִן) some one's hands, or to lighten the work; 2) to despise. Pilpel קִלְקֵל 1) to shake (the arrows), i.e. to shoot; 2) to point, to sharpen (פָּנִים) the edge, or to polish, to make bright, equiv. to גָּלַל. Hithpalpel הִתְקַלְקֵל to be shaken.

קָלָל adj. m. polished, bright, used of metal.

קְלָלָה (const. קִלְלַת) f. curse, blasphemy, transf. to one who bears the curse of God, who is sentenced to death.

קָלַס (Kal, not used) orig. to cry, to call aloud; next, to mock, to scorn, קַלֵּס אֶתְנַן to scorn the wages of a harlot, i.e. to feign modesty. In Aram. and modern Heb. to laud, to praise loudly. Hith. to make sport of (בְּ) some one, to mock or laugh at (מִן) some one.

קֶלֶס m, scorn, mockery (synon. with חֶרְפָּה, לַעַג).

קַלָּסָה f. the same.

I. קָלַע equiv. to קָלַל and גָּלַע, to drive, to fling (Aram. קְלַק), to scatter about, קוֹלֵעַ one that flings,

בָּאֶבֶן with stones. Pi. קִלַּע the same.

II. קָלַע to cut in, to deepen, either by carving out or by engraving, also used of sculpture; comp. חָלַל, and the root in צֶ־קֶל.

III. קָלַע (not used) to entwine, to weave, like קָלַע in modern Heb. and קְלַע in Aram., from which קְלָעִים. A fourth signification of קְלָעִים, 1 Kings 6:34, is not to be adopted, as קְלָעִים stands in that passage for צְלָעִים.

קֶלַע (pl. קְלָעִים, const. קַלְעֵי) m. 1) a sling, קַלְעוֹ his sling, אַבְנֵי קֶ׳ stones for slinging, from קָלַע I.; 2) a curtain, covering, from קָלַע III. to weave, to entwine, like מָסָךְ after the same analogy; 3) only 1 Kings 6:34, as a secondary form of צְלָעִים.

קַלָּע a slinger.

קְלֹקֵל adj. m. inferior, bad (of bread). The form stands for קְלַקְל, like עֲרֹעֵר for עֲרַעְר; in a similar manner is צְלָצַל for צְלַצְל, and סְמָדַר for סְמַדְר.

קָלַשׁ (not used) to sting, to prickle. The Aram. קְלַשׁ is only a secondary form from חֲלַשׁ; but possibly equiv. to זָלַג.

קִלְּשׁוֹן masc. a prong, a point, שְׁלֹשׁ קִלְּשׁוֹן a three-pronged instrument, a pitchfork.

קָמָה (not used) probably only an extended form from קָם to assist.

קָמָה f. seed yet in the ears, standing corn, from קוּם.

קְמוּאֵל p. n. m. (assistance from God).

קָמוֹן (a pillar) p. n. of a place in Gilead.

קִמּוֹשׁ (also קִימוֹשׁ, pl. קִמְּשֹׂנִים, as if from a sing. קִמָּשׁוֹן) m. thorn, thistle, and generally prickly plant, from קָמַשׁ to prickle.

קָמַח (not used) to pound, to grind, related to מָחָא, מָחָה, there the root is קִ־מַח. Probably related to מֹחַ to be marrowy.

קֶמַח m. meal.

קָמַט (fut. יִקְמֹט) to press, to hold together, related to קָמַץ, transf. to seize. Pu. קֻמַּט to be imprisoned, fettered. In modern Heb. to shrink together, to have wrinkles.

קָמַל (pause קָמֵלוּ) equiv. to אָמַל, to wither (of plants), to dry up, to perish.

קָמַץ equiv. to קָפַץ, to press together, to close (the hand), to take a handful; in modern Heb. also of the closing of the mouth.

קֶמֶץ (only pl. קְמָצִים) m. a bundle, a heap; hence, לִקְמָצִים in full bundles, i.e. in abundance (used of corn).

קֹמֶץ (with suff. קֻמְצוֹ) m. a handful, generally with the addition of מְלֹא.

קָמַשׁ (not used) to prickle, probably related to קָלַשׁ in קִלְּשׁוֹן. From which קִמּוֹשׁ.

קִמְּשׁוֹן see קִמּוֹשׁ.

קֵן (const. קַן, with suff. קִנּוֹ, pl. קִנִּים) m. 1) a tent, cell, without conveying the idea of being small; 2) a nest, a bird's nest, transf. also to a nestling. The root is קָנַן to erect, to build. As a denom. from קֵן occurs the Pi. קִנֵּן to build a nest, or to dwell in a nest, of the dove and other birds, used even of the cell of a serpent. Pu. to nestle, to dwell.

קָנָא (Kal, not used) to glow, to burn, comp. the root-syllable in שְׁחִין and בֹּחַן; next, to turn red, with passion or jealousy. Pi. 1) to glow with zeal or jealousy, to be jealous of (accus.) a wife, to be envious of (בְּ, accus. לְ) some one, to be zealous for (לְ) some one, to emulate (בְּ) some one, and generally to glow with zeal for a person or a cause; 2) to excite to wrath or to jealousy, almost like Hiphil; קִנֵּא קִנְאָה, קִנֵּא for חֵמָה קִנֵּא to be very zealous or very wroth. Hiph. to excite jealousy, wrath, particip. מַקְנֶה for מַקְנִיא.

קְנָא (Aram.) to buy, equiv. to קָנָה Heb.

קַנָּא adj. m. zealous, jealous, אֵל קַנָּא a jealous, or rather zealous God.

קִנְאָה (pl. קְנָאוֹת) f. jealousy, envy; next, zeal, wrath, for something or some one, emulation, vying, and the same gradation of sense as occurs in the verb; מִנְחַת קְנָאוֹת a meat offering of jealousy, i. e. on account of jealousy; סֶמֶל הַקִּנְאָה the image of jealousy, i. e. which excites the divine jealousy.

I. קָנָה (fut. יִקְנֶה, apoc. יִקֶן) to buy; hence, to get, to acquire, to possess; thus the Lord is called קֹנֵה, i. e. possessor of heaven and earth: also of the getting of a wife; hence קֹנֶה lord, master, owner: most frequently, however, קָנָה is used in the sense of buying at a certain price; hence, sometimes with the addition בְּכֶסֶף. The person of whom one buys is construed with מֵאֵת, מֵעִם, מִיַּד. Niph. to be bought. Hiph. to sell (as a slave). מִקְנֶה belongs to קָנָה. The root is קָנָה=כָּרָה.

II. קָנָה (not used) to stand upright, erect; related to which is כֵּן and קָנַן.

קָנֶה (const. קְנֵה, pl. קָנִים, and in the orig. signif. קְנוֹת) m. a reed, cane, so called from its erect position; hence, 1) bulrush, חַיַּת קָ beast of the bulrush, i.e. crocodile, as a symbol of Egypt; 2) spice reed, sweet reed, e. g. קְנֵה בֹשֶׂם, קָנֶה הַטּוֹב;

3) a stalk of the ears of corn; 4) a measuring reed or rod, complete מִשְׁעֶנֶת קָנֶה, קְנֵה הַמִּדָּה; 5) the beam of a balance; 6) the upper bone of the arm, also branch of a candlestick, in which sense the pl. קָנוֹת; 7) a reed for writing, which signification may be connected with signif. 2.

קָנָה (place of bulrushes) 1) p. n. of a brook in the borders of Ephraim; 2) p.n. of a city in the tribe of Asher.

קַנּוֹא adj. m. equiv. to קַנָּא, zealous, arduous in the defence of some cause.

קָנַז (not used) to hunt (according to the Arab.), to get by hunting; according to some, related to קָנַץ.

קְנַז (the old form for קֵנָז) p. n. masc. (hunter) from which the patron. קְנִזִּי, a descendant from קְנַז. There is, however, another form:—

קְנִזִּי p. n. of a Canaanite people, probably descending from an ancestor called קְנַז.

קֵנִי see קֵינִי.

קִנְיָן (with suff. קִנְיָנָם) m. that which is bought, acquired, got; hence, possession, that which is bought for money (Levit. 22:11), i.e. a slave; מִקְנֶה וְקִנְיָן cattle and possessions, (fig. creatures, as being the possession of God).

קָנַם (not used) equiv. to צָנַם to be hard, hence קִנָּמוֹן; according to others, equiv. to קָנָה II., with reference to the noun קָנֶה. Such an extension of root, however, is uncommon.

קִנָּמוֹן (const. קִנְּמָן, with shortening of the cholem) m. formed from קָנַם (with the termination וֹן—) cinnamon reed or cane; Κίνναμον, *cinnamum*, used for ointments and frankincense, so called from its hardness, or from its reed-like shape.

קָנַן (not used) equiv. to קָנָה, כּוּן, to build, to erect; hence, to prepare. From which קֵן, but Pi. קִנֵּן, and Pu. are only denom. from קֵן.

קִנֵּץ belongs to קִנְצֵי, Job 18:2, which, however, belongs to קֵץ.

קְנָת (possession) p. n. of a city in Hauran.

קָסַם (fut. יִקְסֹם, imp. f. קָסֳמִי) equiv. to גָּזַם, פָּסַם to cut, to divide; hence, as in גָּזַר, transf. to decide, to divine; next, to soothsay (of false prophets and necromancers, similar to נִבָּא of true prophets); קָ׳ קֶסֶם to carry on sorcery; קָ׳ כָּזָב to predict lies; קֹסֵם sorcerer, necromancer.

קֶסֶם (pl. קְסָמִים) m. orig. knowledge of divination, also from the signification of cutting, in קָסַם; decision, sentence, e.g. decision from the lips of the king. Commonly, however, it signifies sorcery, soothsaying; transf. to the wages of sorcery.

קָסַם (Kal, not used) equiv. to קָצַץ to cut off. Po. קוֹסֵם to cut off (fruit).

קָסַת (not used) equiv. to קָשַׁט to divide, to split; transf. to measure, from which קֶסֶת: possibly, however, that the root is קָסָה=קָשָׁה in the sense of to hold, to contain, which is more suitable to the following:—

קֶסֶת f. a cup, a vessel for containing ink, an inkstand; hence, generally joined with הַסֹּפֵר.

קָעַל (not used) probably equiv. to קָלַע, to fortify, to enclose, from which:—

קְעִילָה (burgh, castle) p.n. of a city in Judah (comp. קַלְעָה), in modern Heb. (of the same root) a castle, e.g. קַלְעַת אִיּוֹב Job's castle, Calatajud in ancient Aragonia; קַלְעָה Kale, in the Crimea, etc.

קָעַע (not used) equiv. to קָצַץ to cut in, to etch; hence, in the reduplicated form קַעְקַע, m. modern Heb. to castrate, to uproot, to annihilate.

קַעֲקַע m. a cut (in the skin), or digging in, grafting, e.g. a mark in the skin.

קָעַר (not used) to deepen out; related is כָּרָה, כַּר, קַר, and the roots in בָּשַׁר, חָשַׁר, דָּשַׁר, כָּשַׁר.

קְעָרָה (pl. קְעָרוֹת, const. קַעֲרוֹת, with suff. קַעֲרֹתָיו) f. a vessel deepened out, a dish, a basin, comp. שְׁקַעֲרוּר.

קָפָא to draw in, to shrink, like גָּבָא, or transf. to draw together (the feet, in sitting), to coagluate, to curdle (of whey to cheese), to congeal (of the floods), to settle to the bottom (of the dregs). In Zech. 14:6, the Ketib has יְקִפָּאוּן. Hiph. הִקְפִּיא to curdle. Niph. according to some in the above passage in *Zech.*; יְקָרוֹת יְקִפָּאוּן bright stars shall draw in. The Auth. Vers. renders it according to Keri וְקִפָּאוֹן "the light shall be neither clear nor dark."

קִפָּאוֹן masc. congelation, frost, from קָפָא.

I. קָפַד (Kal, not used) to cut off; hence Pi. קִפֵּד to cut off (a web, wove); transf. to cut off the life, from which a later sig. to shorten, which is found in the Aram.

II. קָפַד (not used) equiv. to צָפַד to join, to be attached, annexed (of the skin), which signification is suitable to קִפֹּד.

קִפֹּד m. the leech, on account of its attaching itself, from קָפַד II.; according to others, on account of its shrinking together, from קָפַד I., Auth.Ver. the bittern, and, according to Gesenius, hedgehog.

קְפָדָה (*Milêl*, hence masc.) destruction). It is possible, however, that קְפָדָה is fem., and that the accent receded on account of its being joined to a monosyllable.

קִפּוֹז m. arrow-snake (Author. Vers. "the great owl"), from קָפַז to spring, so called from its swift springing.

קָפַז (not used) equiv. to קָפַץ to spring, to hop, to hasten away.

קָפַץ (fut. יִקְפֹּץ) equiv. to קָמַץ to close together, to gather, to shut (the hand or mouth); fig. to shut up his tender mercies (of God). Niph. to be taken out of the way, i. e. to be destroyed. Pi. to spring, to leap, comp. קָפַז.

קֵץ (with suff. קִצִּי, plur. const. once קִנְצֵי) m. origin. the point where something is cut off; hence, end, of locality and times; מְלוֹן קִצּוֹ the lodging of the borders, i. e. at the utmost end; also in reference to actions and circumstances, the end, the utmost; hence אֵין קֵץ without end, מִקֵּץ at the end, after, the same as לְקֵץ. Transf. (*a*) downfall, עֲוֹן קֵץ iniquity leading to downfall, קִצִּי my death; (*b*) the end of a prophecy, i.e. its fulfilment; the end of time, i.e. the kingdom of the Messiah; complete קֵץ הַיָּמִים, מוֹעֵד קֵץ, עֵת קֵץ. The plur. Job 18:2, is used only in the sense of the singular, end; hence שׂוּם קִנְצֵי לְמִלִּין to make an end of words.

קָצַב (fut. יִקְצֹב, יִקְצָב־) equiv. to עָצַב to cut off, to hew (wood); figur. to cut, in the sense of forming, shaping, עֵדֶר הַקְּצוּבוֹת a well-formed flock (Auth. Vers. a flock of sheep that are even shorn).

קֶצֶב (pl. const. קִצְבֵי) m. 1) cut, in the sense of form, shape; 2) end, from קָצַב to cut off.

קָצָה (inf. קְצוֹת) equiv. to חָצָה to cut off; hence fig. to destroy (nations). In the derivative, to decide, judge, it is analagous with גָּזַר. Pi. to cut off (the feet), to cut off (one tribe after the other) a community. Hiph. to scrape off (from a wall); comp. קָצַע in this signification.

קָצֶה (const. קְצֵה, plur. with suff. קְצֵיהֶם) orig. adj. m. קָצָה (pl. const. קְצוֹת, with suff. קְצוֹתָם) f. ceasing, ending, but generally only a subst.; 1) the end, uttermost part (of a hill, a river, a camp, a country), קְצֵה גְבוּל the utmost border: מִקָּצֶה from all ends; 2) in reference to time, hence before num-hew מִקְצָה, equiv. to מִקֵּץ; 3) in reference to the mass, i.e. the whole, מִקְצֵה אֶחָיו from the whole number of his brethren. The fem. is used especially to signify the border; hence מִקְצָה at the border; the plur. const. קְצוֹת signifies the utmost extremity of a thing, e.g. קְצוֹת הָאָרֶץ the utmost end of the earth, קְצוֹת דְּרָכִים the extreme parts of ways, works; but also in the sense of a sum total, e.g. מִקְצוֹתָם from the whole of them, מִקְצוֹת הָעָם from the whole of the people.

קָצָה see קָצֶה.

קָצֶה (after the form מִסְפָּר) m. the end.

קֵצוֹ (after the forms מִדּוֹ, מָרוֹ, חֲנוֹ, שַׁלּוֹ, from קָצָה; pl. const. קַצְוֵי) m. end, קַצְוֵי אֶרֶץ the ends of the earth.

קְצָוָה see קָצָה.

קְצָוָה see קָצָה.

קָצַח (not used) equiv. to פָּשַׂח to cut, which, however, does not agree with the succeeding noun in the context, more correct therefore appears to be the original sense, to strew.

קֶצַח masc. black cummin, from קָצַח to strew.

קָצִין (const. קְצִין, plur. const. קְצִינֵי, with suff. קְצִינַיִךְ) m. judge, a cadi, orig. he that decides, formed from קָצָה, equiv. to נָגַד; transf. to leader (in war), the distinguished one, etc.

קְצִיעָה (pl. קְצִיעוֹת) f. rind of cinnamon, cassia, from קָצַע to peel; comp. קִדָּה; 2) p.n. f. (cassia).

קָצִיר (const. קְצִיר, plur. with suff. קְצִירֶיהָ) m. 1) that which is cut off, a bough, a branch, the same in the plur.; 2) abst. reaping, harvest, or concrete the corn reaped. Comp. בָּצִיר, אָסִיף; קְצִיר חִטִּים harvest of wheat, ק׳ שְׂעֹרִים harvest of barley, קְצִיר יְאֹר fruit of the Nile. Seldom for אַנְשֵׁי קָצִיר reapers.

קָצַע (Kal, not used) equiv. to גָּדַע, קָצָה to hew, to cut off; hence Pu. to be cut off, particip. מְקֻצָּעוֹת corners, which, however, is probably a subst. like מִקְצֹעַ. Hiph. to scrape off, especially from the wall. Hoph. only part. מְהֻקְצָעוֹת corners, which, however, is probably a subst.

קָצַף (fut. יִקְצֹף) origin. to snort, to fume, to rage; transf. to be wroth against (אֶל, עַל) some one or something, קָצַף קֶצֶף to be excessively wroth. Hiph. to provoke one to wrath. Hith. to become wroth; related is the Aram. חֲנַף.

קְצַף (Aram.) the same.

קֶצֶף (with suff. קִצְפִּי) m. 1) anger,

wrath; transferred to contention, strife; 2) foaming (of the waters). Comp. אַף=אוּפְיָא in the Talmud.

קְצַף (Aram.) masc. the same, anger, wrath.

קְצָפָה f. destruction, orig. like כַּעַס, חֵמָה that which provokes the Divine wrath; hence parallel with שַׁמָּה.

קָצַץ (2 pers. pret. קַצּוֹתָה) equiv. to קָצַע, to cut off (the hand), to shear off (the beard). Pi. קִצֵּץ and קִצֵּץ to cut off (a cord), to chop off (hands, thumbs), to tear off, to break off, to cut to pieces (string). Pu. pass., particip. מְקֻצָּץ being cut off.

קַצֵּץ (Aram.) the same. Pa. to cut off (branches).

קָצַר (fut. יִקְצֹר) to cut off, to reap, to mow (related to נָזַר), especially fruit, ears of corn, etc. Particip. קוֹצֵר the reaper, but particip. pass. קָצוּר belongs to קָצֵר. Hiph. הִקְצִיר to reap, to mow.

קָצַר (fut. יִקְצַר, once תִּקְצֹרְנָה for תִּקְצַרְנָה) to be short, to be stumpy (from קָצֵר), the hand of some one is short, i.e. he is weak in power; with רוּחַ and נֶפֶשׁ, short of suffering, i.e. impatient, not forbearing; with בְּ, at something; comp. אֶרֶךְ אַפַּיִם; figur. the years, days, are short. Pi. to shorten (the days). Hiph. the same.

קָצֵר (const. קְצַר, pl. const. קִצְרֵי) adj. m. short, קְצַר יָד weak in power, קְצַר יוֹם short lived, קְצַר רוּחַ and קְצַר אַף impatient, not forbearing.

קֹצֶר masc. shortness, with רוּחַ, not forbearing, impatient.

קְצָת (after the form מְנָת, בְּנָת, from קָצָה, with suff. קְצוֹתָם, pl. קְצוֹת, with suff. קְצוֹתָיו, Ketib) f. end, מִקְצָת at the end, pl. the ends (of the earth), the borders (of a thing).

קְצָת (const. קְצָת) Aram. the same, but also in the signification of totality, the whole sum total.

קִר see קִיר.

קֹר m. the cold, from קָרַר.

קַר (pl. קָרִים) adj. m. cold, cool (of water), figur. calm, quiet (רוּחַ) in mind.

I. קָרָא (fut. יִקְרָא) 1) to cry, to lift up the voice loudly (related to נָעַר), to call; hence, קֹרֵא the crier (the partridge), but especially of man, sometimes with the addition of בְּקוֹל גָּדוֹל; לִפְנֵי קָ׳ to call before some one; קָרָא אֶל to call to some one, seldom עַל; אַחֲרֵי קָ׳ to call after some one; קָרָא אֶת to call upon, especially God, with לְ, אֶל, and עַל, of the person; to call upon God in behalf of some one. Also, to proclaim, e.g. קָ׳ צוֹם to proclaim a fast, קָ׳ דְּרוֹר to proclaim liberty, most frequently of the proclaiming of prophecies and predictions; 2) to call one, in the sense of inviting, where the pers. is construed in the acc. and with לְ, and אֶל; קָ׳ אֵלָיו to call to oneself, e.g. שֵׁם a name, i.e. to acquire a name; to invite to a feast, קָרָא עֲצָרָה to call together to a feast, קְרוּאֵי הָעֵדָה they that are called to the assembly, קָרָא לְשָׁלוֹם לְ to invite to peace; to assemble an army, to choose from the mass, to appoint, in this sense קָרָא בְשֵׁם also to praise (the name of God), rarely of idols; 3) to name, complete קָרָא שֵׁם לְ, sometimes with the omission of שֵׁם; hence, קָרָא לְ, followed by the accus., of the name; קָ׳ אֶת־שֵׁם to give a name; 4) to read (loudly), בְּסֵפֶר from a book; בְּאָזְנֵי פ׳ to read to some one. Niph. נִקְרָא 1) to be called with (acc.) שֵׁם a name; בְּשֵׁם פ׳, נ׳ עַל שֵׁם to be called after the name of some one: נ׳ שֵׁם עַל the name is given to something; נ׳ מִן means the same; 2) to be read, recited. Pual, 1) to be called, named; 2) to be appointed, selected for (לְ) something. The 3 fem. pret. קָרָאת for קְרַאת inf. besides קְרֹא also קְרֹאות, fut. with suff. יִקְרָאוּ for יִקְרָאוּ.

II. קָרָא (fut. יִקְרָא) equiv. to קָרָה I. 1) to meet with, to befall, either good or evil; 2) to go towards some one; hence, inf. with לְ, as prep. לִקְרַאת towards, to meet (with suff. לִקְרָאתוֹ, לִקְרַאתְכֶם), but also over against. Niph. נִקְרָא to be met, found, with לִפְנֵי, עַל; next, to happen, by chance. Hiph. to cause to meet, befall (evil, with double accus.).

קְרָא (particip. קָרֵא, pass. קְרֵי, inf. מִקְרָא, fut. יִקְרָא) Aram. like the Heb. קָרָא I. Ith. אִתְקְרִי to be called.

קֹרֵא m. orig. the crier, transf. to a partridge.

קִרְאָה (an infin. noun) f. happening, meeting, but only in a state of const. and with suff. in a prepositional sense, towards, opposite, over against. See קָרָא II.

קָרַב (not used) to attack, to seize; related is חָרַב, כָּרַב, עָרַף, גָּרַף, גָּרַב; from which עַקְרָב scorpion, and קְרָב battle.

קָרֵב (but without being in pause קָרֵב, infin. קְרֹב, with suff. קָרְבְכֶם, and the fem. form קָרְבָה, fut. יִקְרַב) to approach, to draw near, like קָרָה, נָגַע, נָגַשׁ; hence, with אֶל, לְ, rarely with בְּ, עַל; e.g. and the time drew nigh that Israel must die; also construed with לִקְרַאת, מוּל, עַד. In a hostile sense in phrases לַמִּלְחָמָה, אֶל־מִלְחָמָה, עַל־פְּ, אֶל־הָעִיר; and with אֶל alone, signifies connubial intercourse. Niph. to approach, to draw near. Pi. קֵרֵב to bring near, rarely intransitive, to draw near. Hiph. to cause to approach, to bring near, especially of the bringing of offerings, presents; to cause two things to touch each other; הִקְ׳ מִן to cause to draw back, to remove; seldom intrans. like Pi. and Kal.

קְרֵב (Aram.) the same. Pa. קָרֵב to bring near. Aph. הַקְרֵב to bring (gifts and offerings).

קָרֵב (pl. קְרֵבִים) adj. masc. drawing near, approaching, orig. part.

קְרָב (pl. קְרָבוֹת) m. battle, war, from קָרַב to meet. Possibly, however, קְ׳ is from קָרַב, thus from the orig. signif. to seize, to attack.

קְרָב (def. קְרָבָא, pl. קְרָבִין) Aram. the same.

קֶרֶב (with suff. קִרְבִּי, pl. קְרָבִים) m. orig. body, entrails, heart; transf. to the inward part, the middle, as a prep. בְּקֶרֶב in the midst, among, within, e.g. בְּקֶרֶב הָאָרֶץ in the midst of the land. The verbs בִּעֵר, כָּרַת, הֵסִיר, are construed with בְּקֶרֶב, to denote removal from the midst; קֶרֶב is a nominal root, without being connected with the verb קָרַב. Comp. Aram. גְּו body, in a similar mode of transferring the sense.

קִרְבָה (const. קִרְבַת) f. nearness, approach; קִ׳ אֱלֹהִים the nearness of God.

קָרְבָּן (and קֻרְבָּן, const. קָרְבַּן, with suff. קָרְבָּנִי, pl. with suff. קָרְבְּנֵיהֶם) m. an offering, gift of an offering, orig. that which is brought near; hence also, of offerings without blood, oblation. Comp. הִקְרִיב.

קֻרְבָּן (later; const. —בַּן) masc. the same, offering.

קָרַד (not used) equiv. to חָרַת, כָּרַת, חָרַם, גָּרַם to cut, to hew, from which :—

קַרְדֹּם (with suff. קַרְדֻּמּוֹ, pl. קַרְדֻּמִּים and קַרְדֻּמּוֹת, —מּוֹת) m. axe, so called from its hewing; comp. גָּרְזֶן from גָּרַז. The form is as in שִׁלְשֹׁם, פִּתְאֹם, מְתֹם, פִּרְכֹּם, חַרְטֹם, and others, which termination ◌ֹם, has subsequently become an adverbial suffix.

קָרָה f. cold, orig. adj. fem. from קַר, which has become an abstract noun.

I. קָרָה (fut. יִקְרֶה, once יִקְרָה, after the manner of ל״א, apoc. יִקֶר) equiv. to קָרָא II., to meet (some one), but with accus. of the person, to befall some one, either good or evil; also, of the fulfilment of a promise (with accus. of the person); וַיִּקֶר מִקְרֶהָ and her hap was to light on, etc. Niph. to meet, to happen, by chance, with some one (לִקְרַאת, עַל, אֶל), which significations originate all in קָרָא II. Hiph. to cause to meet, to bring something about at the proper time, opportunely.

II. קָרָה (Kal, not used), to join, to connect; hence, Pi. קֵרָה to lay the beams, i.e. to connect the building through the crossing of the beams; next, to build, to erect, through laying beams. Perhaps only a denom. of קוֹרָה.

קָרֶה (c. קְרֵה) m. chance, occurrence, from I. קָרָה; מִקְרֵה לַיְלָה (uncleanness) that chanceth by night; modern Heb. קֶרִי in this sense.

קָרוֹב (after the form רָחוֹק, pl. קְרוֹבִים) adj. m. קְרוֹבָה (pl. —בוֹת) f. near, 1) in a local sense, with לְ, אֶל, seldom אֵצֶל (by) a person or thing; שָׁכֵן קָרוֹב a near neighbour; קְרֹבֵי יי those that are near the Lord (in dignity), of priests and Levites, figur. near, said of God, i.e. easily answering or protecting; the nearness of the name of God, i.e. frequently mentioning the divine name; 2) of time, the day of the Lord is near, i.e. soon to come; בְּקָרוֹב in a short time; מִקָּרוֹב after a short time, or recently; קָרוֹב מִפְּנֵי a little distance from something; 3) in reference to relationship, קְרוֹבַי my relatives, transf. to acquaintance and friendship.

קָרַח (fut. יִקְרַח) to shave off, to make bald, related to גָּלַח and גָּרַע. Niph. a baldness made (לְ) in honour of some one. Hiph. to shave off, to make baldness (לְ) in honour of some one. Hoph. pass.

קֹרַח p. n. m. (the bald-headed one).

קֵרֵחַ (after the form גִּבֵּחַ) m. bald-headed one, at the back of the head, different from גִּבֵּחַ, the fore part of the head.

קֶרַח m. ice, cold, so called from its smoothness; transf. to crystal, on account of its similarity to ice.

קֹרַח (with suff. קָרְחוֹ) m. 1) equiv. to קֶרַח ice, hail; 2) p. n. m. bald head, patron. קָרְחִי.

קָרְחָא see קָרְחָה.

קָרְחָה (—חָא, with suff. קָרְחָתֵךְ) fem. baldness, as an indication of mourning, generally on the forehead, seldom equiv. to גַּבַּחַת; קָרַח קָ׳ בְּרֹאשׁ to make a bald place on the head.

קָרְחִי patron. from קֹרַח, which see.

קָרַחַת (with suff. קָרַחְתּוֹ) f. baldness, transf. to the bald place on a garment.

קְרִי (pause קֶרִי) masc. orig. chance, occurrence, from קָרָה I. (comp. קָרָה); but generally meeting in a hostile sense, resistance; הָלַךְ קְרִי עִם to walk contrary unto one; בְּקֶרִי in a contrary way; בַּחֲמַת קְרִי acting contrary with fury.

קָרִיא (origin. particip. pass.) called, invited.

קִרְיָא (—יָה, def. קִרְיְתָא) Aram. fem. the same, like the Heb. קִרְיָה.

קְרִיאָה f. calling out, proclamation.

קִרְיָה (const. קִרְיַת) f. a city, equiv. to עִיר, but only in the poetical books, from קָרָה to build. So קֶרֶת (Phœnician קַרְת *Kart*; קַר *Kar*; קֹר, קַר *Kor*, *Kur*). In the following proper noun of cities, קִרְיָה is found as a component part.

קִרְיַת אַרְבַּע city of Arba, the Anakite, p. n. of the city, later חֶבְרוֹן; according to some, so called on account of the four giants residing there, and according to others, on account of the four couples of patriarchs buried there.

קִרְיַת בַּעַל (city of Baal) p.n. of a city in Judah, identical with ק׳ יְעָרִים.

קִרְיַת חֻצוֹת (street-town) p.n. of a city in Moab.

קִרְיַת יְעָרִים (contracted קִרְיַת עָרִים, also with the article הַיְּעָרִים; forest-town) p. n. of a city on the border between Judah and Benjamin, seldom קִרְיַת alone.

קִרְיַת סַנָּה (city of the senna plant) p.n. of a city in Judah, for which also:—

קִרְיַת סֵפֶר (town of letters) p.n. of the city formerly called דְּבִיר.

קִרְיַת עָרִים see קִרְיַת יְעָרִים.

קְרִיּוֹת (cities) 1) p.n. of a city in Judah; 2) in Moab; from signif. 1, arose the gentile אִישׁ קְרִיּוֹת Ἰσκαριώτης.

קִרְיַת see קִרְיַת יְעָרִים.

קִרְיָתַיִם (double city) p. n. of a city in the territory of Reuben, later belonging to Moab. Another of the same name was in Naphtali.

קָרַם (fut. יִקְרַם) to crust, to cover (with skin), construed with עַל, frequent in modern Hebrew.

קֶרֶן (with suffix קַרְנוֹ, dual קַרְנַיִם, קְרָנַיִם, const. קַרְנֵי, plur. קְרָנוֹת, const. קַרְנוֹת) f. horn (of a bull or ram), also of artificial horns made of iron, transf. to vessels made of horn, symbolically as a sign of strength, power, in which sense the forms הִצְמִיחַ, רוּם, הֵרִים ק׳, נִגְדַּע ק׳, the figure of power and strength is taken from the bull.—קֶרֶן also signifies, 1) a musical wind instrument, the horn, *cornu*; 2) the tusks of an elephant; hence, קַרְנוֹת שֵׁן, on account of their size; 3) horn of the altar (plur. const. קַרְנוֹת), i.e. the points which protruded like a horn, but not the corner; hence, וְעָשִׂיתָ קַרְנֹתָיו עַל אַרְבַּע פִּנֹּתָיו (Ex. 27:2); 4) top (of a mountain), especially of the peak; 5) rays, in the dual form, of the flashes of lightning or of the rays of the sun, so called from their horn-like shape. The root is קָר (see קוּר) to dig through, and ןָ is only a nominal addition. From which denom.:—

קָרַן to beam forth, to shine (see קֶרֶן 5), of the shining of the countenance. Hiph. הִקְרִין to have large horns; comp. הִפְרִיס under פָּרַס.

קֶרֶן (def. קַרְנָא, dual קַרְנַיִן, def. קַרְנַיָּא) Aram. the same, horn.

קֶרֶן הַפּוּךְ p.n. f. (paint-horn).

קָרַס to bow down; related to כָּרַע, and קָרַץ, according to some.

קֶרֶס (plur. קְרָסִים, const. קַרְסֵי, with suff. קְרָסָיו) m. a hook or pin, so called on account of its bent shape. It is also the original form for קַרְסֹל.

קֵרֹס p.n. m. (for קֵרוֹס, the bent one).

קַרְסֹל (dual קַרְסֻלַּיִם, with suff. קַרְסֻלָּי) masc. origin. ankle, joint; next, knuckles, formed from קֶרֶס, with the diminutive suffix ־ֹל.

קָרַע (fut. יִקְרַע) 1) to tear asunder, to rend, e.g. garments; לִקְרָעִים, קָרַע קְרָעִים to tear in pieces; to tear a book in pieces, fig. to rend the heaven, a nation, a kingdom, with מִן, מִיַּד, מֵעַל, of the person from whom something is torn away; to cut out a window, i.e. to open a hole in the wall; to rend the eyes with paint, i.e. to paint them; 2) to blaspheme, comp. חָרַף. Niph. to be torn (of a garment), figur. to be destroyed (of an altar).

קֶרַע (pl. קְרָעִים) masc. a rent, a tear, concrete that which is torn, torn garments.

קָרַץ (fut. יִקְרֹץ) equiv. to קָרַע (comp. גָּרַס and עָרַס), to tear open, to open wide; hence, the figur. expressions, קָרַץ עֵינַיִם, קָרַץ שְׂפָתַיִם, indicating maliciousness, scorn; according to others the original signification is to pound, to grind, thus קָרַץ joined to עַיִן signifies winking, and with שְׂפָתַיִם biting the lips. Pu. to be nipped off, e.g. of the clay which the potter breaks off from the mass.

קֶרֶץ m. destruction, from קָרַץ in the transf. sense.

קְרַץ (pl. with suff. קַרְצוֹהִי) Aram. m. a piece of meat torn off; hence, figur. אֲכַל קַרְצוֹהִי דִּי פ׳ to eat the pieces of a person, i.e. to slander him.

קַרְקַע m. 1) ground, floor, e.g. of the floor of a house, of the bottom of the sea, of the pavement, the cover or ceiling of a house of several floors, inasmuch as the ceiling of the lower room is the floor of the upper one. The form is contracted from רְקַעְרְקַע; thus from רָקַע, if not from קַרְקַר; 2) p.n. of a place in Judah.

קַרְקֹע (digging) p.n. of a place.

קָרַר (not used) to be cool, cold, transf. to be calm of mind.

קָרַשׁ (not used) equiv. to חָרַשׁ, גָּרַז, to cut to pieces. From which:—

קֶרֶשׁ (with suff. קַרְשְׁךָ, plur. קְרָשִׁים, const. קַרְשֵׁי, with suff. קְרָשָׁיו) m. board, plank, orig. something cut off, collectively boarding.

קֶרֶת (after the form דֶּלֶת, בֶּסֶת, from קָרָה II.) f. equiv. to קִרְיָה a city, מְרוֹמֵי קָרֶת the high points of the city, פִּי קָ׳ the entrance of the city.

קַרְתָּה (city) p.n. of a place in the territory of Zebulun.

קַרְתָּן (dual from קֶרֶת, double city) p.n. of a city in the territory of Naphtali, for which is also the general dual form קִרְיָתַיִם.

קַשׁ (pl. modern Heb. קַשִּׁים) m. straw, stubble קַשׁ נִדָּף, עוֹבֵר driven stubble, stubble that passeth away by the wind; from which denom. קָשַׁשׁ to gather straw; also Po. קוֹשֵׁשׁ to gather straw or wood. In Kal, to be gathered or received (of an outcast, comp. אָסַף). Hith. to gather oneself, to be received again in the congregation, as a sign of cleanliness; thus in both conjugations used only in the transferred sense. The root is קָשַׁשׁ.

קָשָׁא (not used) according to the Talmud equiv. to קָשֶׁה hard, difficult (to digest). From which:—

קִשֻּׁא (pl. קִשֻּׁאִים) m. a melon, cucumber, from קָשָׁא. The modern Heb. קִשּׁוּת, pl. קִשּׁוֹת is contracted from קִשְׁאָה, pl. קִשְׁאוֹת.

קָשַׁב (fut. יִקְשַׁב) probably equiv. to אָשַׁף to be eager for something; hence, to listen, hearken, or equiv. to קָצַב to incline the ears in order to listen; generally in Hiph. joined with אֹזֶן; but also with omission of אֹזֶן, and construed with בְּ, לְ, אֶל, עַל and acc.

קַשָּׁב (after the form סַלָּח) adj. m., קַשֶּׁבֶת fem. attention, listening, hearkening.

קַשֻּׁב adj. m., קַשֻּׁבוֹת f. hearkening, attentive.

קֶשֶׁב m. hearkening, attention, רַב קֶ׳ great attention; הִקְשִׁיב קֶ׳ he hearkened diligently.

קָשָׁה (fut. יִקְשֶׁה, apoc. יִקֶשׁ) 1) to be juiceless, dry, comp. קָשַׁשׁ, חָשַׁשׁ

and the root in לְקֹשׁ; next, to be hard, difficult, cruel (of wrath, violence, request). Niph. to be burdened, oppressed, enervated. Pi. קִשָּׁה to make hard, difficult; קִשָּׁה בְלִדְתָּהּ to have hard labour (of childbirth). Hiph. הִקְשָׁה (fut. apoc. וַיֶּקֶשׁ) to harden (the neck), to be stiffnecked, to harden (the heart), to be stubborn, to make heavy (a yoke); hence, in connection with other verbs, to express importance, difficulty, e.g. הִקְשָׁה לִשְׁאוֹל to ask a hard thing; הִקְשָׁה לְשַׁלַּח hardly let go; 2) (not used) to make firm, hard (a plait or lock of hair); from which מִקְשֶׁה and מִקְשָׁה.

I. קָשָׁה (not used) equiv. to כּוֹס (כּוּס) קָסָה to hold, to contain (of a dish or basin).

II. קָשָׁה (not used) equiv. to כָּסָה, to cover, to protect; hence קַשְׂקֶשֶׂת, which see.

קָשֶׁה (const. קְשֵׁה, pl. קָשִׁים, const. קְשֵׁי) adj. m., קָשָׁה (const. קְשַׁת, pl. קָשׁוֹת) fem. difficult, hard (of words, a yoke, bondage). קְשֵׁה עֹרֶף stiffnecked; with לֵב ,פָּנִים, presumptuous brow, obdurate heart; קְשֵׁה יוֹם one whose day is hard, i.e. the unfortunate one; חָזוּת קָשָׁה hard visions, i.e. prophecy of calamity; קְשַׁת רוּחַ heavy of spirit, i.e. melancholy; always in accordance with the noun to which the adjective is joined; also, mighty, violent, etc. The fem. קָשָׁה is also used in the abstract, that which is hard, unfortunate.

קְשׁוֹט (Aram.) m. firmness; hence, מִן קְ׳ ,קְשֹׁט in truth, truly.

קָשַׁח (Kal, not used) a hardened form from קָשָׁה, comp. צָפָה and צָפַח; from which Hiph. 1) to harden (the heart), to be hardened (used of the ostrich towards its young).

קָשַׁט (not used) probably, to make firm, to confirm; thus synon. with אָמַן belonging to אֱמֶת. The root in קֹשְׁטְ is equiv. to שׁוֹת.

קָשַׁט (not used) to portion, to measure, to mete out. Comp. קֶסֶת.

קֹשֶׁט m. firmness; hence (like אֱמֶת) truth; according to several versions, קֹשֶׁט is equiv. to קֶשֶׁת and הִתְנוֹסֵס מִפְּנֵי קֹ׳ to flee from the archers.

קֹשְׁטְ (origin. form for קֹשֶׁט) masc. truth.

קְשִׁי m. hardness, stubbornness, obduracy.

קִשְׁיוֹן (hardness of soil) p. n. of a place in Issachar, for which קֶדֶשׁ stands once.

קְשִׂיטָה f. something weighed; next, name of a weight for gold and silver, probably of the value of four shekels.

קַשְׂקֶשֶׂת (pl. קַשְׂקְשׂוֹת, and with suff. קַשְׂקְשֹׂתֶיךָ) f. scales, so called on account of its covering things; שִׁרְיוֹן קַ׳ a coat of mail.

קָשַׁר (fut. יִקְשֹׁר) to bind, to tie, to join to (בְּ) something, e.g. "his life is bound up in (בְּ) the lad's life;" to bind (an animal) to (with עַל or without) something; to join, i. e. to conspire against (עַל) some one, complete קָשַׁר קֶשֶׁר עַל. The part. קָשֻׁר is used in the transf. sense, to be strong (of sheep); comp. חָזָק in a similar mode of transferring the sense. Niph. to be attached (to a person), to be joined (of a wall). Pi. to bind round (a girdle). Pu. only part. מְקֻשָּׁרוֹת the strong cattle. Hith. to conspire against (אֶל) some one.

קֶשֶׁר (with suff. קִשְׁרוֹ) masc. 1) conspiracy, קָשַׁר קֶ׳ to make a conspiracy; 2) joining.

קִשֻּׁר (only pl. ־ִים) m. a girdle (of a bride or wife).

קָשַׁשׁ (not used) equiv. to חָשַׁשׁ, to be juiceless, hard, dry; from which קַשׁ and the denom. קֹשֵׁשׁ, which see under קַשׁ.

קֶשֶׁת (with suff. קַשְׁתִּי, plur. קְשָׁתוֹת, c. קַשְׁתוֹת, with suff. קַשְּׁתוֹתֵיהֶם) com. 1) a bow (on account of its bent form, from קוּשׁ) for shooting; קֶ׳ רְמִיָּה a deceitful bow, i. e. to fly and not to shoot, in order to deceive the enemy; בֶּן־קֶ׳ i.e. an arrow; נָחַת, נָשַׁק, דָּרַךְ קֶ׳ to bend the bow; רָמָה, יָרָה קֶ׳ to shoot with the bow; transf. to archer, like קַשָּׁת, for which also אִישׁ קֶשֶׁת, plur. אַנְשֵׁי קֶ׳, once, song of the bow, i.e. David's elegy on Saul, in which the bow is mentioned; figur. strength, power; hence, to break some one's bow, i. e. to destroy his power; my bow is strengthened, i. e. my powers increase; 2) rainbow, complete bow of God. The root is קוּשׁ, from which קֶשֶׁת, after the form of קֹלֶת.

קַשָּׁת m. an archer; this form, signifying a calling or trade, is common in modern Hebrew.

קַשְׂוָה (after the form כַּנָּה, מְנָת, only pl. קְשָׂוֹת, const. קְשׂוֹתָיו) f. dish or basin, so called from its holding or containing things (from קָשָׂה I.).

קָתָה (not used) after the Arab. to serve; from which יְקֻתִיאֵל.

קַתְרוֹס (Ketib קִיתָרוֹס) Aram. m. the cithern, answers to Κίθαρος, and thus orig. coat of mail, from its similarity.

ר

ר *Resh* (plur. רֵישִׁין) is the twentieth letter of the alphabet, and as a numeral counts 200. Its name is owing to its similarity in shape to the head. ר interchanges with several other letters; 1) with ל and נ, e.g. נְגַהּ and רְגַהּ; זְרַח Aram. דְּנַח; נְהַר Aram. נְהַן; אַלְמָנוֹת and אַרְמְנוֹת, מַזָּרוֹת and מַזָּלוֹת; 2) it is softened in ע, only retaining the guttural sound of the ר; בָּקַע, מָעַם and מָרַם, צוּר and צוּעַ and קָצַע, בָּצַר and בָּצַע, בָּקַר and קָצַר; קַרְקַע, Talm. קַרְקַר: ר has some other peculiarities; 1) it is interpolated to dissolve the hardness of a dagesh forte, e.g. סַרְפָּד for סַפָּד (root סָפַד); שַׁרְבִּיט for שַׁבִּיט (root שָׁבַט); בַּרְזֶל for בַּזֶּל (root בָּזַל); חַרְצֹב for חַצֹּב (root חָצַב); כַּרְכֹּב for כַּכֹּב (root כָּבַב); כִּרְסֵם for כִּסֵּם (root כָּסַם); 2) the radical ר is assimilated to the following letter, e.g. כִּסֵּא from כִּרְסֵא (from כָּרַס); hence also, יַבֹּק from יַרְבֹּק, later יַרְמוּךְ; אַכַּד from אַרְכַּד, hence LXX. Ἀρχάδ; 3) the dissolution of ר, or the termination ־ַר in וֹ, as is the case with ־ַל, e.g. חֲצוֹצְרָת for חֲצַרְצֶרֶת, שׁוֹפָר for שְׁמוֹפָר, from שְׁפַרְפָר; דּוֹדָנִים from דְּרְדָנִים, and others. ר occurs at the end of several words only as a nominal suffix, since there is no ר in the original root, e.g. *âr*: סְמָדַר formed from סָמָר, עַכְבָּר from עָכֶב, צַנְתָּר from צֶנֶת; or, כַּפְתֹּר from כֶּפֶת, עַכְבֹּר from עָכָב; *îr*, סְנַפִּיר from סָנָף, and others.

רָאָה (fut. יִרְאֶה, apoc. יֵרֶא, יַרְא, inf. abstract, רָאֹה, רָאוֹ, const. רְאֹה, רְאוֹת, once רְאָוָה) 1) to behold, to see (physically) ὁράω (accus.) something or some one, seldom with לְ or double accus., as אוֹתְךָ רָאִיתִי צַדִּיק. In this signification, רָאָה very often occurs in connection with the following sentence, to explain and complete the former, commencing with כִּי or הִנֵּה, e.g. and the Lord saw that (כִּי) the wickedness of man was great (Gen. 6:5). Sometimes the object is entirely omitted: to see the face of some one, i.e. to be his confidant; of prophets, to see visions, revelations; to see, in the sense of to live, complete, to see the sun; 2) to see (mentally) i.e. discerningly, attentively; hence, to inspect (a city, a boundary), to look at the affliction (בְּ) with compassion, to look (בְּ) among the people, to look at (בְּ) a sport, to look after (בְּ) something attentively, to look upon (בְּ) something with pleasure, gladness; to look down (from an eminence), or fig. with contempt upon (accus.) something; to have care for, or to oversee something (with accus.); to select, choose, to visit, to salute, complete רָאָה אֶת שְׁלוֹם פ׳; to look (hoping for assistance) upon אֶל, עַל, some one; to look at, i.e. to take for something or for some one (with בְּ); to look at, i.e. to learn something from (מִן) some one; to have an eye (i.e. to purpose) upon something; 3) to experience something, either by the understanding, or other senses, e.g. by the hearing, tasting, touching; רָאִיתִי אוּר I felt the heat; also by the emotions, to enjoy, thus רָאָה בְּרָעָה, רָאָה בְּטוֹב to see life, i.e. to enjoy it; to see death, i.e. to die; to learn wisdom, i.e. to adopt it. Niph. 1) to be seen, visible, to shew oneself (of man and inanimate things), construed with לְ and אֶל; with God, to appear in the sanctuary, נִרְאָה אֶת פְּנֵי י״י; 2) to be seen, i.e. to be protected by God. Pu. (3 pl. רֻאוּ, with dagesh in א) to be seen. Hiph. הִרְאָה and הֶרְאָה (fut. יַרְאֶה, apoc. יַרְא, like Kal) 1) to cause to see, to shew, with double accus., of the person and object, rarely with כִּי in the concluding sentence; to reveal in a dream; 2) to cause some one to experience, to enjoy (either good or evil), in which sense it is, as in Kal, construed with בְּ. Hoph. to be shewn something. Hith. mutually to behold, to look at one another, either as an indication of hesitating, or to measure one another for a combat. The derivatives are very numerous and manifold.

רָאֶה (const. רְאֵה), adj. m. seeing, beholding; רְאֵה עָנְיִי seeing affliction.

רָאָה f. name of a bird of prey, Auth. Ver. the glede, so called on account of its sharp sight. Some read דָּאָה, which actually occurs in a parallel passage.

רֹאֶה (pl. רֹאִים) m. 1) a seer, prophet, thus as a noun particip.; 2) vision, as a noun infin.; שָׁגוּ בָרֹאֶה they err in vision.

רְאוּבֵן p.n. m. of the eldest son of Jacob, afterwards the name of the tribe called after him. According to the biblical etymology, it is equiv. to רָאוּ בָעֳנִי they have seen upon the affliction, hence illustrated through רָאָה בְּעָנְיִי; perhaps equiv. to רְאוּת בֵּן beholding of the son.

רַאֲוָה (orig. inf.) f. the seeing, with

בְּ, to look upon something attentively.

רְאוּמָה p. n. fem. (the elevated one) from רוּם=רְאֵם.

רְאוּת f. the seeing, thus the Keri, but the Ketib has רְאִית.

רְאִי masc. a mirror, for which also מַרְאָה.

רֳאִי (pause רֹאִי) m. 1) the seeing, beholding; 2) look, like מַרְאֶה, hence מֵרֹאִי at a view (Author. Ver. "that it cannot be seen"); 3) appearance; טוֹב רֳאִי good-looking; 4) spectacle, example; שׂוּם כְּרֹאִי to make for an example, a warning.

רְאָיָה p. n. m. (God is the beholder) once הָרֹאֶה stands for it.

רְאֵים see רְאֵם.

רְאִישׁוֹן see רִאשׁוֹן.

רְאִית f. the seeing, beholding; Ketib for רְאוּת

רָאַל (not used) equiv. to רָעַל to tremble; from which תַּרְעֵלָה.

I. רָאַם (not used) to be high; equiv. to רוּם, אָרַם, which see.

II. רָאַם (not used) to roar, equiv. to רָעַם, which corresponds better with רְאֵם than with רָאַם I.

רְאֵם (also רְאֵים and רֵים, pl. רְאֵמִים and רֵמִים) m. the wild boar or buffalo, whose horns were considered very dangerous, and at the same time high and prominent; בֶּן רְאֵמִים the young buffalo. Biblical interpreters differ as to the species of רְאֵם; according to some, it is the rhinoceros or unicorn; according to others, a kind of gazelle; the former, however, is more probable.

רָאמוֹת f. pl. 1) heights; fig. things unattainable; 2) p. n. of a city in Gilead, otherwise רָמוֹת; 3) p. n. of a city in the tribe of Issachar; 4) pearl, coral; hence its being mentioned in connection with other precious things.

רָאמַת נֶגֶב (height of the south) p. n. of a city in the territory of the tribe of Simeon, otherwise for which רָמוֹת נֶ'.

רָאשׁ see רֵישׁ.

רֵאשׁ poverty. See רֵישׁ.

רֵאשׁ (pl. רֵאשִׁין, with suff. רֵאשֵׁהוֹם) Aram. m. 1) the head; the visions or views of the head, i.e. fancies, imaginations; 2) transf. to sum, chief, principal, as רֹאשׁ in Heb. See the root:—

רָאַשׁ (not used) equiv. to רָעַשׁ to move to and fro, especially of the head. This root, though existing in all Semitic dialects, has nowhere been preserved in a verb.

רֹאשׁ (origin. contracted from רָאשׁ; pl. רָאשִׁים for רְאָשִׁים, but with suff. once also רֹאשָׁיו) m. 1) head (of man or beast), origin. top, so called from its moving to and fro; נָתַן, הֵשִׁיב, בְּרֹאשׁ פ׳ are phrases to express the making some one to experience something; רָאשֵׁי הֶחָלוּץ bands that were ready armed; לְרֹאשׁ גָּבֶר to every man; next, to signify life, thus בְּרָאשֵׁינוּ to the jeopardy of our heads, synon. with נֶפֶשׁ; ראשׁ is transf. to (*a*) the upper part or top of anything; hence, top of a mountain, tower, throne, pillar; highest point of a country, top part of the bed; personally, chief, leader, etc.; (*b*) sum, mass (like *summa* from *summus*) of physical or spiritual objects, e.g. ראשׁ דְּבָרִים the sum of words; (*c*) beginning, the first; also, as an adverb, before, above; the root is רָאַשׁ; 2) ראשׁ (once רוֹשׁ) m. a kind of poppy-head, the contents of which were bitter and pernicious; מֵי ראשׁ the juice of poppy-heads, a kind of opium; next, poison, venom, generally; it is closely connected with ראשׁ head, and derived from it on account of its similarity in shape; 3) p.n. of a Scythian people, mentioned in connection with מֶשֶׁךְ and תּוּבַל, probably a tribe of the northern Taurus.

רֵאשָׁה (only pl. רֵאשׁוֹת) f. beginning, former time. The form stands for רֵאישָׁה.

ראשָׁה (for רֹאשָׁה) adj. f. the uppermost; אֶבֶן הָר׳ the uppermost stone, i.e. the corner stone; ראשָׁה after the form גְּדוֹלָה; according to others, הָר׳ is a subst. and signifies the foundation stone, because it is laid down the first.

רִאשׁוֹן (formed from רָאשׁ, sometimes רִאישׁוֹן, and once רִישׁוֹן, pl. רִאשֹׁנִים) adj. m., רִאשֹׁנָה (pl. —נוֹת) f. that which is at the head of anything, the foremost, the chief, the first in rank or position, e.g. הָרִאשֹׁנִים לְיַד הַמֶּלֶךְ, and this sense רִשֹׁנָה in this first, highest place, orig. adv. foremost; also in reference to position and order, the first, the foremost, רִשֹׁנָה furthermost, בָּרִאשֹׁנָה at the head; also, in reference to time, e.g. the first day, רִאשׁוֹן אָדָם the first man, —נִים the ancestors, the ancients; especially, in contrast to successors, the last, hence the phrase רִאשׁוֹן וְאַחֲרוֹן the first and the last, in which sense —נִים signifies also former deeds; sometimes it signifies soon, or that which is to follow immediately; hence בָּרִאשׁוֹן *primo tempore*, soon, early, the same בָּרִאשֹׁנָה. In the absolute form the pl. m. signifies ancestors, the ancients, שׁוֹמְמוֹת רִאשֹׁנִים the ruins of ancient times; plur. fem. former deeds, events of old. Joined with prepositions, the significations are in conformity with the peculiarity of the prepositional syllables.

רִאֲשׁוֹת see מְרַאֲשֶׁת.

רֵאשִׁית (also רֵשִׁית, from רֵאשׁ, רֵישׁ, with the formative syllable ־ִית) fem. 1) beginning (in contrast to אַחֲרִית), e.g. of the kingdom, of strife; but also absolute, the beginning of all things; or relative to something later, the former position, the former time, the first of its kind, both in reference to time and value; hence, the firstlings (of fruit, corn, wool-shearing, or birth); transf. to the firstlings of the creation; 2) the highest, chief, e.g. ר׳ שְׁמָנִים chief ointments, ר׳ הַגּוֹיִם the first of nations, ר׳ גְּבוּרָה the chief of might.

רִאשֹׁנִי adj. m. (from רִאשׁוֹן) only רִאשֹׁנִית f. the first.

רַב (pause רָב, pl. רַבִּים) adj. m., רַבָּה (pl. רַבּוֹת) fem. 1) in reference to quantity, much, many, numerous; also of collectives, which consist of many individualities, and are joined to a whole. It not only succeeds the noun as an adjective in the same number and gender as the noun, but it sometimes precedes the noun in the constructive state, independently, and as a substantive, e.g. רַב תְּבוּנָה, רַבָּתִי עָם, רַבַּת אוֹצָרוֹת, רַבַּת בָּנִים; and after this substantive use, רַב and רַבָּה are used as adverbs in the signification of much, enough; seldom in the constructive state רַבַּת; 2) in reference to quality, great, mighty, aged, distinguished, uppermost, etc., according to context; hence, as a subst. abstract, greatness, power; or concrete, chief, leader, master (comp. רַב הַחֹבֵל, רַב טַבָּחִים, רַב בֵּית הַמֶּלֶךְ) the aged one, etc. The rendering of רַבִּים archers, Job 16:13, is unnecessary, as it may be translated the mighty ones, or the warriors.

רַב (def. רַבָּא, but in the plur. only the redoubled form רַבְרְבִין) Aram. adj. masc., רַבָּא (def. רַבְּתָא, plur. רַבְרְבָן) f. as in the Heb. great, e.g. אֱלָהּ רַב the great God, יַמָּא רַבָּא the great sea; especially high dignities are expressed by רַב, e.g. רַב חַרְטֻמַּיָּא, סִגְנִין; מַלִּל רַבְרְבָן to speak great things, i.e. boastingly.

רֹב see רִיב.

רֹב (later also רוֹב, before makkaph רָב־, with suff. רֻבְּכֶם, pl. const.

רִבֵּי) masc. a multitude, many, a great number, the noun following in the pl. or in the sing. with a collective signification; also the sum, total, like רַב; adverbially לָרֹב occurs in multitude, many, or very, מֵרֹב the cause of the multitude, רֻבֵּי תוֹרָה the whole of the law (Auth. Vers. great things of the law).

I. רָבַב (only 3 pl. רַבּוּ, and inf. רֹב) orig. to overflow (comp. רָוָה and the root in יָרַב in Aram.); next, to be or become much, abundant, to increase; also, to be numerous, mighty, powerful. The form מְרֻבָּבוֹת belongs to רְבָבָה, from which it is a denom. The forms רַב and רַבָּה, which are generally considered as adjectives, may also be taken as verbs.

I. רָבַב (3 pret. רַב Ps. 18:15, but 3 pers. רֹבּוּ, from an old form רֹב, like זוֹר) to throw, to fling, ῥιπ-τω; hence, to shoot (arrows, of an archer).

רְבָבָ (only plur. in Keri רִבְבָן, for which the Ketib רִבְוָן, from רִבּוֹ) Aram. f. equiv. to רְבָבָה Heb.

רְבָבָ (pl. —בוֹת, const. רִבֲבוֹת) f. orig. multitude, transf. to a definite high round number, 10,000, pl. myriads; רִבֲבוֹת קֹדֶשׁ myriads of angels or saints.

I. רָבַד equiv. to רָפַד to cover to overspread; ר׳ עֶרֶשׂ to spread out a couch. From which מַרְבַד.

II. רָבַד (not used) to bind, to tie round; comp. רָפַד, and the root in צָ־בַת, אָ־פַד, צָ־פַד. From which רָבִיד.

רָבָה (fut. יִרְבֶּה, apoc. יֶרֶב or יִרֶב) equiv. to רָבַב to increase, to be numerous, with all the sub-significations of the root רָבַב; hence, to be or become great, mighty, numerous, abundant, to grow up (comp. Pi.). Pi. רִבָּה to make numerous, to increase, to acquire much, to bring up, to rear, thus causative from Kal. Hiph. הִרְבָּה (fut. יַרְבֶּה, apoc. יֶרֶב, imp. apoc. הֶרֶב, infin. absolute הַרְבָּה and הַרְבֵּה, const. הַרְבּוֹת) to make much, to increase, to enrich; also, to speak largely, i.e. to boast. With the inf. following, with or without לְ, it paraphrases the adv. numerously, greatly, very; rarely with the verb finite following. The inf. הַרְבֵּה, seldom הַרְבּוֹת, also becomes an adv. much, too much; with מְאֹד very much; לְהַרְבֵּה in multitude. Comp. הֵיטֵב.

רְבָה (orig. רְבָא, 3 fem. רְבָת) Aram. the same, to be or become great, Pa. רַבִּי to make great, to elevate.

רַבָּה (orig. adj. fem. from רַב) f. the

great one; hence, transf. to capital, metropolis; 1) p.n. of the Ammonite capital, complete רַבַּת בְּנֵי עַמּוֹן, later called by *Ptolemy Philadelphos*, Philadelphia; 2) a city in Judah. The root is רָבַב.

רִבּוֹ (from רִבּוֹ=רְבָבוֹ, for which also רִבּוֹא, dual רִבּוֹתַיִם, pl. רִבֹּאוֹת or רִבּוֹאוֹת, רִבּוֹת) f. myriad, =רְבָבָה orig. multitude.

רִבּוֹ (pl. Ketib רִבְּוָן) Aram. the same.

רְבוּ (def. רְבוּתָא) Aram. f. greatness.

רִבּוֹת see רִבּוֹ.

רָבִיב (only pl. רְבִיבִים) m. showers of rain, from רָבַב in the original sense of overflowing, not on account of the multitude of drops.

רָבִיד (const. רְבִד) masc. neck-tie, or chain, from רָבַד II.; next generally necklace or ornament for the neck.

רְבִיעִי (pl. רְבִיעִים) ordinal number m., רְבִיעִית f. the fourth, (formed from רְבַע=אַרְבַּע), בְּנֵי רְבִיעִים sons of the fourth generation; comp. רִבֵּעִים; רְבִיעִית the fourth part of a measure, a fourth.

רְבִיעַי (Aram.) the same, f. רְבִיעָאָה or רְבִיעָיָא (def. pl. רְבִיעָיְתָא).

רַבִּית (capital) p.n. of a city in the territory of Issachar.

רָבַךְ (Kal, not used) to mix, to mingle; hence, Hoph. to be mixed, especially of liquids.

רָבַל (not used) to be fruitful (after the Arab.). From which:—

רִבְלָה (fruit-place) p.n. of a city near Hamath.

I. רָבַע (inf. const. רִבְעָה) equiv. to רָבַץ (through the exchanging of צ with ע) to lie, to couch; with accus. following, of the copulation of beasts. Hiph. to cause copulation.

II. רָבַע is the ground form for אַרְבַּע, which see; and hence the denom. verb רָבַע to be or to make four-cornered, squared, particip. pass. רָבוּעַ (pl. רְבֻעִים), f. רְבֻעָה four-cornered, square. Pu. to be of four sides; particip. מְרֻבָּע, fem. מְרֻבַּעַת (pl. מְרֻבָּעוֹת) almost like רָבוּעַ.

רֶבַע (with suff. רִבְעִי) m. 1) a couch, or couching, from רָבַע I.; 2) the fourth part (of a measure), fourth side of a body; hence עַל אַרְבַּעַת רִבְעֵיהֶן on their four sides; 3) p.n. m.

רֹבַע m. the fourth part of Israel, i.e. the number that encamped under one standard (דֶּגֶל) in the wilderness, where Israel was divided under four standards (דְּגָלִים). According to others, progeny, from רָבַע I. The first explanation is preferable.

רִבֵּעַ (only pl. רִבֵּעִים, after the form

שִׁלֵּשׁ) masc. descendants in the fourth generation, the sons of the grandchildren.

רָבַץ (fut. יִרְבַּץ) to lie, to couch (of four-footed animals); next, to rest, to lie under a burden, of the dragon that lieth in the midst of his rivers, of the dam that sits upon her young, of the wild beast that lies in wait for prey, etc.; fig. of the sin that lies in wait. Hiph. הִרְבִּיץ to cause to lie down (flocks or men), to cause to dwell, fig. to lay or to set (precious stones); related is רָבַע I.

רֵבֶץ (with suff. רִבְצִי) masc. place of lying down, dwelling for man and beast.

רָבַק (not used) to bind, to tie, e. g. to the crib, and generally to bind together; the root is רַ־בַק, which is also found in חָ־בַק, אָ־בַק, דָּ־בַק, and others. According to others, רָבַק signifies to fatten, for which signification there are several analogies in the language.

רִבְקָה p. n. f. (enchanting ring) orig. (fetter) so called from her enchanting beauty.

רַבְרַב (pl. רַבְרְבִין) Aram. adj. masc. רַבְרְבָא (only plur. רַבְרְבָן, def. —בָתָא) fem. great, considerable, like רַב in Hebrew.

רַבְרְבָן (pl. —בָנִין, with suff. רַבְרְבָנוֹהִי) Aram. adj. masc. the great one, magnate.

רַבְשָׁקֵה p. n. of an Assyrian general (chief butler, from רַב and שָׁקָה).

רָגַב (not used) to heap up; the root רַ־גַב is found in חָ־גַב and גּוּבַי, i. e. גֵּב, if it is not to be taken as related to גָּרַף or רָגַם.

רֶגֶב (only pl. רְגָבִים, const. רִגְבֵי) m. a clod or lump of earth; רִ׳ נַחַל the clod of the valley. The original signification may be connected with דָּבַק.

רָגַז (fut. יִרְגַּז) equiv. to רָגַשׁ and רָעַשׁ to quake, to tremble, from wrath, joy, terror, fear, especially to rage, to be furious, to be wroth, to start up. Hiph. to cause to tremble, to shake, to excite wrath Hith. to rage.

רְגַז (Aram.) the same; from which Aph. הַרְגִּז to excite wrath, to provoke.

רְגַז (Aram.) m. anger, wrath.

רֹגֶז (with suff. רָגְזְךָ) m. raging, noise (of horses, thunder), anger, provocation, disquiet.

רַגָּז adj. masc. trembling, quaking, shaking.

רָגְזָה f. quaking, trembling.

רָגַל orig. denom. from רֶגֶל to use the feet, i.e. to go, to walk about, but only in a fig. sense; 1) like רָכַל to go about slandering; hence, the phrase רָגַל עַל־לָשׁוֹן to slander; 2) to stamp with the feet upon clothes for the purpose of washing and fulling; hence רֹגֵל washer, fuller, in עֵין רֹגֵל and רֹגְלִים. Pi. רִגֵּל to go about frequently for slandering, next, slandering generally; transf. to spy (a country); particip. מְרַגֵּל a spy. Hiph. only תִּרְגַּלְתִּי to use one to walk, to lead; where the ת must be considered a substitute for the ה, if not a noun in the form of תִּרְגֶּלֶת is to be adopted for the basis of this word.

רֶגֶל (probably from the root רָג to go (which see), with ancient nominal suffix ־ֶל; comp. נֶבֶל from נָב to be hollow, סֵפֶל from סַף, etc., but not from רָגַל, which is itself only a denom.; with suff. רַגְלִי, dual רַגְלַיִם, which is also used for the pl.; the pl. רְגָלִים is used in a different sense) com. the foot (for walking), of man and beast; hence, the phrases מֵרֹאשׁ וְעַד רֶגֶל, or מִכַּף רֶגֶל וְעַד קָדְקֹד. Individual parts of the foot are described in שֹׁרֶשׁ, בֹּהֶן, אֶצְבַּע רֶגֶל; רֶגֶל is used euphemistically for the privy parts, שַׂעַר, מֵימֵי רַגְלַיִם, and probably also the phrase הֵסֵךְ רַגְלַיִם, which see; מְקוֹם רֶגֶל, הֲדוֹם רֶגֶל, מְקוֹם כַּפּוֹת רַגְלַי place for the resting of the feet; בְּרֶגֶל, בְּרַגְלַיִם (and with suff.) on foot; transf. 1) step, walk, pace; 2) trace, track; hence בְּרַגְלֵי פ׳ in the track of some one, thus also לְרַגְלִי, לְרֶגֶל; 3) retinue, i.e. those that follow on the foot, e.g. בְּרַגְלֶיךָ the whole people which follow thee. To signif. 1 belongs the pl. רְגָלִים, signifying times, orig. like פְּעָמִים paces. In modern Heb. festival, the celebration of which having been connected with a pilgrimage to the temple. In the phrase הִקְשָׁה ר׳, בְּרֶגֶל signifies the treading with the feet, with the assistance of a machine worked with the feet, as was common in the East for watering the ground.

רְגַל (also רֶגֶל, dual רַגְלַיִן, def. רַגְלַיָּא, with suff. רַגְלוֹהִי) Aram. the same.

רַגְלִי (pl. רַגְלִים) adj. m. pedestrian, in a military sense, foot soldiers.

רֹגְלִים (fuller's place) p.n. of a place in Gilead.

I. רָגַם to heap up, to gather, especially stones; hence like סָקַל to stone, with עַל, בְּ, and accus. of the person, complete רָגַם בָּאֶבֶן, אֶבֶן, בָּאֲבָנִים. The root is רָ־גַם, and is again to be found in עַם, כָּם, גַּם; if not a noun, רֶגֶם stone, is to be taken as the basis.

II. רָגַם (not used) equiv. to רָקַם to

embroider, to draw, to write. See תִּרְגֵּם.

רֶגֶם p. n. m. (orig. connection, friendship, from רָגַם I.; hence, friend).

רֶגֶם מֶלֶךְ p. n. m. (friend of the king).

רִגְמָה f. host, assembly, from רָגַם I.

רָגַן to murmur; also, to rage; hence, to be refractory. Niph. to rebel, to murmur; the root is רָ־גַן.

רָגַע 1) origin. equiv. to גָּעַר to rage, threaten, rebuke, e.g. the sea; next, to terrify; 2) equiv. to רָעַע to break asunder, to burst (of the skin); hence, synon. with בָּקַע. The root is רָג־ע, which is also found in חָרַג.

רָגַע (Kal, only particip. רֹגֵעַ, c. pl. רִגְעֵי) to be quiet, still, tranquil; hence רִגְעֵי אֶרֶץ the quiet of the land. Niph. נִרְגַּע to rest, to conduct oneself quietly. Hiph. הִרְגִּיעַ; 1) to give, afford rest, to quiet; הִרְגִּיעַ מִשְׁפָּט to make the judgment to rest, i. e. to establish it; 2) to enjoy rest; another Hiph. הִרְגִּיעַ is a denom. from רֶגַע and does not belong to this root. See רֶגַע.

רֶגַע (pl. רְגָעִים, const. רִגְעֵי) m. 1) a moment, orig. moving, stirring, a twinkling of the eye; thus from רָגַע in the first signification, comp. *momentum* for *movimentum*; רֶ' אֶחָד but one moment; כְּרֶגַע in a moment, i. e. quickly, the same כְּמוֹ רֶגַע, כְּרֶגַע, sometimes רֶ' alone in this sense; לִרְגָעִים every moment, i. e. always; 2) like זְמָן as an adv. time, once; from which denom. הִרְגִּיעַ to pass a moment, to do it in a moment; generally 1 pers. fut. as an adverb, momentarily, if אַרְגִּיעָה itself is not an adverbial form, which like רֶגַע is to be taken in the accusative.

רָגַשׁ equiv. to רָעַשׁ to rage, tumultuate. Related is also רָגַז.

רְגַשׁ (Aram.) the same. Aph. to run to (עַל) some one impetuously.

רֶגֶשׁ m. a bustling multitude; comp. הָמוֹן.

רִגְשָׁה f. a multitude.

רָדַד (particip. רוֹדֵד, inf. רַד) 1) to thrust (to the ground); hence, to rule, to subjugate (nations); the root is related to that in יָרַד; 2) to spread out, expand (synon. with טָפַח) to extend; from which רְדִיד. Hiph. (fut. apoc. וַיָּרֶד) to spread out, to overspread or overlay with metal.

I. רָדָה (fut. יִרְדֶּה, apoc. יֵרְדְּ) to tread, (the wine-press), to tread down, rule, to subject (comp. כָּבַשׁ and רָדַד) in the same mode of transferring the sense; construed with בְּ. The phrase רָדָה עַל־יַד signifies to be active, ready. Pi. רִדָּה (fut. apoc. יֵרְדְּ) to conquer, to subjugate, to tread down (e. g. שְׂרִיד לְאַדִּירִים. the remnant of the mighty ones), if יְרַד (Judg. 5:13) is not an imper. of יָרַד, or an Aramaic form from יָרַד to descend. Hiph. to subjugate.

II. רָדָה to take, to take away, e.g. honey from the carcase, Judg. 14:9; רָ' אֶל־כַּף to take something away in the hand.

רַדַּי p.n. m. (subjugator).

רָדִיד (with suff. רְדִידִי, pl. רְדִידִים) m. a veil; hence Targ. for צָעִיף. The root is רָדַד to spread out, to extend, somewhat like מִטְפַּחַת.

רָדַם (Kal, not used) to sleep deeply, fast. Niph. to fall in a deep sleep, to be stupified, unconscious.

רֹדָנִים gent. pl. of a רוֹדָן, name of a people who are mentioned in connection with כִּתִּים the Cypriots, probably the Rhodians; according to the reading דֹּדָנִים, which after the Medrash דַּרְדָּנִים arose from it, signifies Dardanes or Trojans.

רָדַף (fut. יִרְדֹּף) origin. to drive, to push (comp. the roots in הָדַף, נָדַף, גָּדַף, דָּפַה having the same original signification); next, to pursue; with אַחֲרֵי to follow after or to persecute, also with accus., seldom with אֶל, לְ; also from the following or imitating of something good; to put to flight; רוֹדְפִים the pursuers. Niph. to be pursued; hence, in a spiritual sense, נִרְדָּף that which is pursued, i.e. the uncertain, hypothetical; according to others, that which is fled, passed. Pi. to pursue strongly and frequently, e.g. after justice, words, etc. Pu. pass. Hiph. הִרְדִּיף to pursue, to prosecute; the particip. Hoph. מֻרְדָּף is used as a subst. in the sense of prosecution.

רָהַב (fut. יִרְהַב) to rage, to roar (related to רוּב) of the heart, to tremble; next, with בְּ of the person, to attack some one, parallel with נָגַשׂ to press. Hiph. הִרְהִיב to make impetuous, bold, courageous (the heart).

רַהַב m. 1) rage, impetuosity; hence, pride, boldness, audacity; עֹזְרֵי רַהַב the proud helpers; 2) poetical designation of an impetuous wild sea animal, probably, the crocodile; hence also, the name for Egypt; רַהַב הֵם שָׁבֶת Egyptian is the rest, i.e. will remain tranquil.

רָהָב (pl. רְהָבִים) m. the proud, the haughty one.

רֹהַב (with suff. רָהְבָּם) masc. pride, also that of which one is proud.

רָהַג (not used) to cry (according to the Arab.) From which:—

רָהְגָּה p.n. m. (cry) in Ketib רוֹהֲגָה.

רָהַה (only fut. יִרְהֶה) to tremble, to quiver, to be afraid. Related to רָעַע.

רָהַט (not used) only an Aramaic extended form from רָץ to run; of the water, to flow. Compare also רוּד.

רַהַט (only pl. רְהָטִים) m. 1) a watering trough for cattle, spout; 2) locks, so called from their flowing down.

רָהִיט m. a beam in the shape of a spout: according to others it signifies, gutter of the house.

רָהַם (not used) to rage, tumultuate, synon. with הָמָה, but related to רָעַם; hence the noun רָהָם a bustling multitude (synon. with הָמוֹן), which is found in the name of אַבְרָהָם.

רֵו (contracted from רְאֵו) Aram. fem. look, appearance, from רָאָה.

ריב (not רִיב; hence, pret. רָב, רַבְתָּ, fut. in p.n. יָרוּב, inf. רֹב, particip. רָב) contending with (עִם, אֵת, אֶל, בְּ and acc.), to contend with some one for (לְ) another; next, to defend, to plead the cause of some one before justice, complete רָב אֶת־רִיב פְּ׳. Hiph. הֵרִיב (but in this complete form only part. מֵרִיב, and fut. יָרִיב apoc. יָרֵב, יָרֶב־; otherwise the abridged form הֵרִיב, 2 pers. (הֲ)רִיבוֹתָ, imp. הָרִיב to cause contention, strife; hence, to contend or strive, and altogether like Kal; similar abridged Hiphil forms, לִין, שִׁית, שִׁיר, בִּין, שִׂים, דִּין, etc., the root is identical with that in נָדַב and חָדַף.

רוג (not used) is probably the root to רָגַל in the signif. of, to walk; related to חָדַג.

רוד to rove about; hence, to act violently, unruly; רַדְנוּ we are free (Auth. Vers. "we are lords"), רָד עִם אֵל is frivolous, unruly against God. According to others, it is related to רָדָה in the sense of to rule, to wrest. Hiph. הֵרִיד (fut. יָרִיד) to wander about, to rove about, i.e. unruly, throwing off the yoke, also to wander about in affliction. From which מָרוּד, and according to some, the p.n. אֲרוֹד.

רָוָה (fut. יִרְוֶה, 3 pl. יִרְוְיֻן) to overflow (synon. with שָׂבַע=שָׁפַע); hence, to drink abundantly, to satiety; with accus. and מִן, of that which one drinks; next generally, to be intoxicated (of blood, and lust of love, etc.), or to enjoy in fulness, in abundance. Pi. 1) intensitive, to drink very abundantly; 2) transf. to water richly, to moisten, with double accus.; the form אֲרַיָּוְךָ

appears to stand for אֲרַוֶּךָּ: if not a peculiar Pi. form, רִיָּוָה, mixed from רָוָה and רִיָּה, is to be adopted. Hiph. to dispense something abundantly, e. g. to water the ground abundantly; also used of the fattening of beasts for sacrifices.

רָוֶה (const. רְוֵה) adj. masc., רָוָה fem. watered abundantly (of a garden); the fem. is also used as a subst., the satiated one.

רוז (not used) to secrete, to conceal; comp. the root in חָרַשׁ.

רָוַח as a denom. of רוּחַ, see under the noun רוּחַ.

I. רוּחַ (Kal, not used) to breathe, to blow, to wave, related in the orig. sense with נוּחַ and פּוּחַ. Hiph. הֵרִיחַ to inhale; next generally, to smell; הֵרִיחַ בְּ to delight in something, to have pleasure in something, e. g. בְּיִרְאַת י״י. According to others, he will inspire with the fear of God. Transf. to enjoyment generally, especially of a spiritual kind; hence, to conceive.

II. רוּחַ (not used) to walk, to wander, hence p. n. יָרוֹחַ (wanderer); יָרֵחַ moon, orig. the wanderer (of heaven). Related is אָרַח in the same original sense.

רוּחַ (pl. רוּחוֹת) com. 1) breath, orig. the waving; hence, ר׳ אַף the snorting of the nose, anger, or pride, with the omission of אַף; ר׳ פֶּה, ר׳ חַיִּים, ר׳ שְׂפָתַיִם the breath of the mouth, of life, but רוּחַ alone also means the breath or spirit of life; הֵשִׁיב רוּחַ to draw breath, שָׁאַף רוּחַ to gasp for breath, רוּחַ הַיּוֹם the breath of the day, i. e. the refreshing, cooling wind of the day; most frequently, however, wind, tempest, e. g. רוּחַ כַּבִּיר, קָדִים, קָשָׁה, גְּדוֹלָה, זִלְעָפוֹת, סְעָרָה, צָפוֹן; to strew in the wind לְרוּחַ, לְכָל־רוּחַ, poetically wings of the wind, transf. to, (a) region, part of the world, such being divided according to the winds; hence, אַרְבַּע רוּחוֹת the four parts of the world; (b) vanity, nothingness; hence, דִּבְרֵי רוּחַ vain words, דַּעַת רוּחַ vain knowledge, רְעוּת, רַעְיוֹן רוּחַ hunting after vanity; 2) the animating element of the body, the spirit of life, the animal soul; hence, also, for life generally in many relations, and transf. to the Divine spirit; 3) the spirit of understanding, the mind, the seat of emotions, passions, reflections; hence, the numerous connections with רוּחַ to denote certain motions and passions, e. g. קְצַר רוּחַ

impatience, not forbearing; אֶרֶךְ רוּחַ long-suffering, patience; גֹּבַהּ רוּחַ pride; רוּחַ נָכוֹן a firm mind; רוּחַ זְנוּנִים spirit of whoredom; רוּחַ קִנְאָה spirit of jealousy; transf. to will, resolution, insight, etc.; 4) the spirit of God, in the sense of prophecy, thus in many phrases of prophetic language. From which denom. רָוַח (fut. יִרְוַח) to be large, in reference to space, fig. to find enlargement, relief, comp. the contrast, צַר לִי I am straitened. Pu. רֻוַּח to be airy, large, of a room. See רָוַח and רְוָחָה.

רוּחַ (def. רוּחָא, pl. const. רוּחֵי) Aram. com. the same, wind, spirit, region of the world, etc.

רֶוַח m. enlargement, spaciousness, transf. to relief, release.

רְוָחָה (with suff. רַוְחָתִי) f. enlargement, relief, release.

רְוָיָה fem. overflowing, satiety, abundance, fullness, from רָוָה.

רוּם (fut. יָרוּם, apoc. יָרֹם, יָרָם) 1) to rise (also of inanimate things), to lift oneself up; of the heart, i.e. to be proud; of the eyes, i.e. to despise; of God, to exalt himself in might or in praise; 2) to be high, elevated; transf. to excel others in might or fame; of God, to be high, i.e. to remove himself from man, not to assist him; 3) to be lifted up, raised, e.g. of the road, to be made even; of the hand, to prevail; next, of the lifting up of the head or the horn, as a sign of becoming powerful; in this particip. appears frequently in connection with זְרוֹעַ, יָד, etc. Po. רוֹמֵם to raise (a house), to bring up (children), to cause to grow (plants); fig. to raise a lowly man (from the dust), to cause some one to conquer, to bring some one in safety, i.e. on a high place; or in a spiritual sense, to exalt, to praise. Po. רוֹמַם pass. to be lifted up. Hiph. הֵרִים (inf. הָרִים, imp. הָרֵם, before monosyllabic words הָרֶם) to raise the ground, to make it even; to raise some one, i.e. to place him in safety; to lift up the head, the hand, the horn, as a sign of boldness, courage, power, etc., always causative of Kal in the same connections; to lift up the hand, the right hand to God, i.e. to swear; to lift up the hand or feet, i.e. to move; to lift up the voice, i.e. to call; with לְ, to call to some one, with עַל, against some one. הֵרִים קוֹל is used of the accompanying by an instrument, to play, to blow, etc.; to lift up an offering, i.e. to separate it from the other; to lift up food, i.e. to deck; to lift up presents, gifts, i.e. to bring them into the temple, or to the priests; to raise folly, i.e. to advance it. הֵרִים is often used in the signification of to remove, to take away; hence the phrase הָרֵם לְךָ take thyself away; also, to carry away, e.g. הֵרִים קָלוֹן he carries away shame (Author. Vers. "shame shall be the promotion of fools"). Hoph. to be delivered, to be presented, a gift, an offering. Hith. הִתְרוֹמֵם (fut. once אֶרוֹמָם for אֶתְרוֹמָם to lift oneself up, to look proudly and contemptibly upon something or some one; but also, to exalt oneself, in a good sense. Related with רום is רָמַם I. to which several of the forms above mentioned belong.

רוּם (3 pret. רָם) Aram. the same, to lift oneself up. Palpel רוֹמֵם to exalt, to praise; pass. אִתְרוֹמַם to lift oneself up against (עַל) some one. Af. אֲרִים to raise, from the dust.

רוּם masc. height, lifting up, with עֵינַיִם and לֵב, to signify haughtiness, pride.

רוּם (with suff. רוּמֵהּ) Aram. m. the same, height.

רוֹם (after the form קוֹל) m. the same.

רוֹמָה f. lifting up, pride; הָלַךְ ר׳ to walk about proudly.

רוּמָה a high place, p. n. of a place in the neighbourhood of Neapolis.

רוֹמָם masc. lifting up, exaltation, praise.

רוֹמֵמֻת (with suff. רוֹמְמֻתֶךָ, pl. const. רוֹמְמוֹת) fem. 1) eminence, greatness; 2) exaltation, praise. The pl. is in this sense also rendered as a singular.

רוֹן a mistaken verbal root; יָרֹן stands for יָרֹן, and belongs to רָנַן, to which also הִתְרוֹנֵן is to be taken.

רוּעַ (Kal, not used; the forms רַע, רֹעַ, הֵרַע, רָעַע, as well as the fut. Niph. יֵרוֹעַ, belong to רָעַע) to cry, to break forth with the voice, to cry aloud; comp. ἐρεύγ-ω, rugio. Hiph. הֵרִיעַ (3 pret. pl. once הֵרִעוּ, and 2 pl. הֲרֵעֹתֶם, but otherwise regular) 1) to make a noise, to cry loudly, with עַל, over some one, especially of the shouts of war and rejoicing over (עַל) a conquered enemy, or in the honor of some one: in the first case, תְּרוּעָה is sometimes added; seldom of the cry of lamentation; 2) to blow (the trumpet), with בְּ joined to the instrument, especially for the breaking up of a camp, in which it is distinguished from תְּקַע. Pual (reduplicated) רוֹעַע to be shouted or rejoiced over. Hith. הִתְרוֹעַע to break forth into shouting, to triumph over (עַל) some one (comp. רָעַע).

I. רוּף (Kal, not used) to throw, to toss about (comp. רָבַב and רָפָה); hence Pu. רוֹפַף to tremble, to totter, to shake (of the pillars of heaven). Comp. רַפְרֵף in modern Hebrew.

II. רוּף (not used) to pound, to grind, from which רִיפוֹת.

III. רוּף (not used) equiv. to רָפָא, to heal, from which תְּרוּפָה, if תָּרַף is not to be taken for the root.

רוּץ equiv. to רָהַט to run (of man and beast); with אֶל to run to some place, לִקְרַאת towards some one; רוּץ אַחֲרֵי to run after some one; ר׳ לְרַע to hasten to evil; רוּץ אֹרַח to run a race; with עַל (also acc. and אֶל) to rush upon some one, to assail some one; with בְּ, to seek refuge with some one. Part. רָץ, runner, messenger, courier. Pl. רָצִים, רָצִין, the runners before the royal carriage; hence satellites, state runners among the Persians, who published the royal edicts in the provinces. In the language of weavers, it signifies, tow, a tow-rope. Niph. נָרוֹץ belongs to רָצַץ. Pi. (reduplicated) רוֹצֵץ to run along (of a carriage). Hiph. הֵרִיץ to cause to run or to fetch, bring back quickly (from prison); to cause the hands to hasten, i.e. to hasten with presents.

רוּק (Kal, not used) to pour forth, to flow; hence, related with יָרַק and רָקַק ἐρεύγομαι, *ructo;* from which Hiph. הֵרִיק to empty, to pour out (rain, blessing); to draw the sword, i.e. to empty the sheath; transf. to lead forth (the young warriors); comp. הוֹבִיל from יָבַל, in the same original sense; 2) to to leave empty (נֶפֶשׁ רָעֵב). Hoph. הוּרַק to be emptied (of a vessel); the form תּוּרַק (Canticles 1:3) is probably a noun, as indicated by שֶׁם, with which it is joined.

רוּר to cause slime or phlegm, to emit spittle, semen, etc., with accus.

רוֹשׁ in the signification of poppy, opium, poison. See רֹאשׁ.

רוּשׁ equiv. to יָרַשׁ to seize, to lay hold of; hence, to take alms; comp. אָבָה to desire for charity, from which אֶבְיוֹן. Probably, however, רָשׁ is equiv. to רָשַׁשׁ to be downcast, like רָצַף, synon. with דָּכָא, דַּךְ, from which דַּךְ the poor one; next, to be poor, part. רָשׁ, or *plene* רָאשׁ the poor one.

Po. רוֹשֵׁשׁ to break, to pull down (fortified castles). Hith. הִתְרוֹשֵׁשׁ to pretend to be poor.

רוּת p.n. f. (equiv. to רְעוּת a female friend).

רָז (def. רָזָא, pl. רָזִין, def. רָזַיָּא) Aram. m. a secret, secresy. See רזז.

רָזָה to make thin (comp. רָדַד to beat thin); רָדָה to tread down; hence, to make lean, meagre, to decrease, fig. to destroy (the idols of the land). Niph. נִרְזָה (only fut. יֵרָזֶה) to wax lean (of fatness of the body).

רָזֶה adj. m. רָזָה f. lean (of a lamb), unfruitful (of a plough field).

רָזוֹן m. 1) after the form חָזוֹן leanness (of the body), consumption; transf. to the meagreness, scantiness of a measure; 2) after the form קָדוֹשׁ, a prince; from רָזַן.

רְזוֹן p.n. m. (a prince, distinguished one).

רָזַח (not used) to cry, to call out, probably related to צָרַח, or the root רָזַח is related with זָעַק, צָעַק.

רָזִי (after the forms שְׁנִי, עֳנִי, קָלִי) m. leanness, consumption. Root רָזָה.

רָזַם (3 fut. pl. יִרְזְמוּן) transf. from רָמַז to wink, to blink.

רָזַן (not used) to be important, distinguished; according to others, equiv. to רָסַן to bridle, to curb; next, to rule.

רֹזֵן (pl. רֹזְנִים) m. a prince, a ruler, orig. distinguished, esteemed one. Comp. רָזוֹן 2.

רָחַב (probably a transposition from רָוַח) to be spacious, wide, to widen, to enlarge (of the mouth, heart, a chamber), similar to רָוַח. Niph. to be broad, large (of meadows). Hiph. הִרְחִיב to enlarge, to widen, in reference to size and space; to enlarge some one, i.e. to afford access, or (comp. יֶשַׁע) to release from trouble; to open the mouth largely against (עַל) some one, as a sign of scorn, mocking; הִרְחִיב נֶפֶשׁ to enlarge one's desires, i.e. to open wide one's jaws; to enlarge the boundaries, etc., according to the context.

רָחָב (const. רְחַב, plur. const. רַחֲבֵי) adj. m. רְחָבָה (const. רַחֲבַת) f. 1) wide, spacious, large, extended, broad, of a country, a sea, a city, a wall, etc. Generally, יָדַיִם is added, to signify extension of space, as רְחַב יָדַיִם, רַחֲבַת. Fig. of the mind, or of the heart, or of other spiritual things; 2) רָחָב p.n. f.

רַחַב (pl. const. רַחֲבֵי) masc. a wide, broad place, an extensive space.

רֹחַב (with suff. רָחְבּוֹ) m. breadth, in reference to measure, circumference (of a country); figur. largeness (of the heart), i.e. a comprehensive heart.

רְחֹב (often רְחוֹב, with suff. רְחֹבָהּ, pl. רְחֹבוֹת) f. 1) a broad place, in a city, in a street, also a *forum*, a broad place before the gate, e.g. the open place (רְחוֹב) before the house of God; 2) in proper nouns, of cities. See בֵּית רְחוֹב.

רְחֹבוֹת (open places, streets) 1) p.n. of a well; 2) רְ׳ עִיר (streets of the city) an Assyrian city; 3) רְ׳ הַנָּהָר (streets of the Euphrates) a city not far from Idumea, or one of that name near the Euphrates.

רְחַבְיָהוּ p.n. m. (deliverance by God).

רְחַבְעָם p.n. m. of the son and successor of Solomon, from 975—958 (enlargement of the people).

רָחָה (not used) to pound, to grind; the root is רָחָה, which is also found in מָרַק, מָרַח, but is not connected with that in אָרַח.

רֵחֶה (after the form קָצֶה, only dual רֵחַיִם) m. a millstone, but in the dual, a handmill, consisting of two stones, the one called רֶכֶב, and the other פֶּלַח תַּחְתִּית.

רַחוּם adj. masc. merciful, generally connected with חַנּוּן.

רְחוּם p.n. m. (the merciful one) for which once נְחוּם stands, and transposed חָרִם.

רָחוֹק (pl. —קִים) adj. m. רְחוֹקָה (plur. —קוֹת) f. 1) far, distant (of place), remote, subst. distance; hence לְמֵרָחוֹק, מֵרָחוֹק, בְּרָחוֹק at or from a distance; עַד מֵרָחוֹק until the distance; 2) far (of time), hence מֵרָחוֹק of far time, i. e. future; לְמֵרָחוֹק a long time since, of the past time; עִתִּים רְחֹקִים the remote (future times); 3) distant, in the sense of strange, foreign, incomprehensible, costly, not present (absent) to render assistance, etc.

רָהַט (not used) a transposed form from חָרַט to chisel, to do turnery work; probably, however, in the derivative which occurs, the proper reading is רָהַט.

רָחִיט (only Ketib, for which Keri רָהִיט, pl. רְחִיטִים) m. if the Ketib is correct, turnery-work, masonry; according to the Keri, entablature.

רֵחַיִם see רֵחֶה.

רַחִיק (pl. —קִין) Aram. adj. m. equiv. to the Heb. רָחוֹק.

רָחֵל (not used) an ancient secondary form from רָחַם, in the signification of (to be tender); next, to be lovely, amiable, the original sense of which exists in רָחַם, and the roots connected with it: the interchange of ל and ם is not uncommon in the language. From which:—

רָחֵל (pl. רְחֵלִים, with suff. רְחֵלֶיךָ) f. 1) tender lamb, ewe, orig. the tender, amiable one; 2) p. n. f. the lovely one. Comp. the modern Heb. בְּהֵמָה דַקָּה for sheep.

רָחַם (fut. יִרְחֹם, with suff. יִרְחָמְךָ) 1) intrans. to be tender, lovely, comp. רָחֵל; 2) transf. to love, to have mercy, with accus. of the object.

רָחַם (Kal, not used) to glow inwardly: the root is רָ־חַם, identical with חַם. Pi. רִחַם to glow, or feel warmly for something or some one, to have mercy, compassion; it is construed with the accus., seldom with עַל, to express the love of parents towards children, of God to man, of compassion on the poor and afflicted, and sometimes of things which one is attached to. Pu. to be compassionated, to obtain mercy. Part. רֻחָמָה for מְרֻ׳ one that has obtained mercy from God, but it is not to be taken as a third pret. f.

רֶחֶם (with suff. רַחְמָהּ) m. matrix, womb, orig. seat of glowing, fervency; עֹצֶר, סָגַר ר׳ the unfruitfulness, barrenness; פָּתַח ר׳ to be fruitful; מֵרֶחֶם from the womb, i.e. before thou camest forth out of the womb; פֶּטֶר רֶחֶם the first (opening) of the womb. The same signification has:—

רַחַם (plur. רַחֲמִים) m. 1) the same, the womb; fig. a maid, a woman, from their distinguishing member (comp. in English, *woman*, for *womb-man*). 2) p.n.m. compassion, mercy. The plur. רַחֲמִים signifies originally the bowels as the seat of inward emotion; next, compassion, tender love, mercy, kindness, benevolence, etc.; hence connected with חֶסֶד; נָתַן ר׳ לְ׳, שׂוּם to have compassion towards some one; נָתַן פ׳ לְרַחֲמִים לִפְנֵי, עָשָׂה ר׳ אֶת to procure mercy for some one.

רָחָם (with paragogic ה רָחָמָה) m. name of a bird (Auth. Vers. the gier eagle) so called from its compassion towards its young. Comp. חֲסִידָה.

רַחֲמָה (only dual רַחֲמָתַיִם) f. a damsel, a maid, a woman, comp. רַחַם, only used in poetical language.

רַחֲמִין (Aram.) plur. equiv. to רַחֲמִים in Hebrew.

רַחֲמָנִי adj. m., רַחֲמָנִית (pl. רַחֲמָנִיּוֹת) f. merciful, compassionate.

רָחַן (not used) probably equiv. to רָנַן to murmur, to complain, to rage, from which the p.n. תִּרְחֲנָה.

I. **רָחַף** (Kal, not used) to cover, to shelter; the root is רָ־חַף and identical with that in חָפָה, or רָחַף is only a secondary form of רָחַם. Pi. to hover (protectingly) over something, of the spirit of God, which waved over the chaos, to form and create; of the fluttering of the eagle over its young, to nourish and protect them.

II. רָחַף to totter, to tremble, of the bones. The root רָ־חַף is identical with that in דָּ־חַף.

רָחַץ (fut. יִרְחַץ, inf. רְחֹץ, and the fem. form רָחְצָה) to wash, to cleanse (the body); hence, to bathe, to wash oneself. It never occurs like כָּבַס of the washing of garments. Pu. רֻחַץ to be washed, to be cleansed, from filth. Hith. to bathe, to wash oneself.

רְחַץ (Aram.) to seize, to lay hold of (comp. Heb. רָכַס and the root in אָחַז); but transf. to trust, to confide, to rely firmly upon עַל something, and only Hith. אִתְרְחִץ.

רַחַץ (with suff. רַחְצִי) m. the washing; סִיר רַחַץ the wash-basin or pot.

רַחְצָה fem. bathing-place (for small cattle).

רָחַק (fut. יִרְחַק, inf. רָחֳקָה) 1) to be distant, far, from (מִן) some one, from a day, an object, or purpose; 2) to remove, estrange oneself from (מִן, מֵעַל) some one, or something; to withdraw from something; figur. to loathe something. Niph. only Ketib, to be removed far off. Pi. to remove far off. Hiph. to remove, to drive away (a people) from (מִן, מֵעַל) something; to lead into exile; with the inf. following as an adv. far distant; the same the inf. הַרְחֵק, where לָלֶכֶת is elliptical; the orig. signification is to push away, related to דָּחַק. A relation of פ״ר with פ״ד is found in רָחַף II. and דָּחַף; רָבַק and דָּבַק; רָכַךְ and דָּכַךְ and others.

רָחֵק (only pl. רְחֵקִים) adj. m. to remove oneself; substantive, he who removes himself from God.

רָחַשׁ (rare) to be moved, excited; thus related to רָגַשׁ; according to others, to overflow, to gush (related to רָחַץ); transf. to the overflowing of the heart.

רַחַת (from רוּחַ) f. a winnowing shovel. The form is like נַחַת from נוּחַ.

רָטַב (fut. יִרְטַב) to be wet, soaked through (by rain), to be moist, juicy (of plants). The root is רָ־טַב and related with the root in נָדַב, נָ־טַף. The form רָטֹב does not belong to the verb, but is an adjective.

רָטֹב adj. m. fresh, moist, juicy (of plants).

רָטָה (supposed root to יִרְטֵנִי Job 16:11) probably equiv. to רָדָה to rule, to prevail; hence the construction with עַל יְדֵי; possibly, however, it may be derived from יָרַם, which see.

רָמַם (not used) equiv. to רָתַת to tremble, to quake. Related is the root in חָרַד and רָעַד.

רֶטֶט m. fear, terror.

רָטַן Job 16:11; according to some, the root is connected with that in the signification of to fetter, to bind (comp. the roots אָטַן, טָנָא). See יָרַט.

רָטַף (not used) equiv. to רָטַב to be moist, fresh, from which the quadriliteral רֻטְפַשׁ, and from which only the pass. רֻטֲפַשׁ occurs, signifying to bloom, or to become fresh again.

רָטַשׁ (Kal, not used) to dash to pieces (comp. the root פָּטַשׁ). Pi. to dash, e.g. children against the rock; next, generally, to thrust down (pierced by arrows). Puel pass.

רִי (contracted from רְוִי) m. watering, overflowing.

רִיב as a verb, see רוּב.

רִיב (once רִב, with suff. רִיבִי, plur. רִיבוֹת, const. רִיבֵי) masc. strife, contention, אִישׁ רִ׳ adversary, opponent; cause or matter of contention or dispute, connected with אִישׁ one who has a cause of dispute; proof, evidence in a matter of dispute, e.g. רִיבוֹת שְׂפָתַיִם verbal evidence; transf. to war.

רִיבַי p.n. m. (adversary, opponent), comp. יְרִיבַי.

רִיחַ as a verb, see רוּחַ.

רֵיחַ m. exhalation (of odour); hence, odour, smell, scent, once רֵיחַ אַף; transf. to רֵיחַ מַיִם that which only smells the water, i.e. that which only touches the water.

רֵיחַ (Aram.) m. the same.

רֵים see רְאֵם.

רִיעַ as a verb, see רוּעַ.

רֵיעַ (later) equiv. to רֵעַ, which see.

רִיפוֹת fem. pl. grits or bruised corn, from רוּף to pound.

רִיפַת p.n. of a country and race of the Cimmerians, by which Josephus understands Paphlagonia.

רִיק as a verb, see רוּק.

רִיק m. emptiness, nothingness, כְּלִי רִיק an empty vessel; next, like הֶבֶל vanity, also as an adv. vainly, in vain, especially in this sense בְּדֵי רִיק, לְרִיק, לָרִיק.

רֵיק (also רֵק after the form מֵת, pl. רֵיקִים) adj. m., רֵיקָה (pl. רֵיקוֹת) f. empty, joined with נֶפֶשׁ hungry; transf. to vain (of words), poor, stripped, wanton; as a subst. the wanton, wicked one.

רֵיקָם (formed from רֵיק, with the termination ־ָם, compare אָמְנָם, שִׁלְשֹׁם) adverb, empty (with empty hands), vain, futile, without cause, synon. with חִנָּם.

רִיר m. spittle, from רוּר.

רֵישׁ (also רִישׁ and רֵאשׁ) m. poverty, from רוּשׁ. For this form comp. רֵיק, רִיק.

רִישׁוֹן equiv. to רִאשׁוֹן.

רַךְ (pl. רַכִּים) adj. m., רַכָּה (pl. רַכּוֹת) f. tender, delicate; hence, weak (in reference to strength), bleared or tenderness (of the eyes), soft, smooth, insinuating, timid (of the heart); hence, רַךְ לֵבָב faint-hearted: the pl. fem. רַכּוֹת is used as an abstract to signify flattering words.

רֹךְ m. tenderness, delicateness.

רָכַב (fut. יִרְכַּב) origin. to lie upon something; of God רֹכֵב שָׁמַיִם, רֹכֵב בִּשְׁמֵי שְׁמֵי קֶדֶם to lie upon the heavens, and thus to drive; next, to ride on horseback, to ride in a waggon or carriage, i.e. to drive, construed with עַל, seldom with בְּ and the acc. Hiph. הִרְכִּיב to cause some one to ride or to drive; to cause one to ride upon the heights of the earth, i.e. to make him distinguished; to cause men to ride upon the head of some one, i.e. to make them rulers over some one. The root is identical with that in שָׁ־כַב.

רֶכֶב (with suff. רִכְבִּי, pl. const. רִכְבֵי) masc. 1) waggon, chariot; hence chariot of war, in connection with רוֹכֵב and פָּרָשׁ; רֶכֶב בַּרְזֶל iron chariots used in war, עָרֵי רֶכֶב cities for chariots of war, שָׂרֵי רֶכֶב the officers of the war chariots; sometimes רֶכֶב is used as a collective to signify a row of chariots or chariots and horses together, or the war chariots of the heavenly host; 2) a rider, animals for riding, רֶכֶב אִישׁ a chariot of men, thus according to some עָרֵי הָרֶכֶב; 3) upper millstone, the rider, the lower is called in modern Heb. שֶׁכֶב.

רַכָּב (with suff. רַכָּבוֹ) m. a horseman, a charioteer.

רֵכָב p.n. masc. (charioteer) 1) an ancestor of a nomade tribe, the Rechabites; 2) p.n. of another people.

רִכְבָּה fem. the riding; according to the Targum, a chariot.

רֵכָה p.n. of a place.

רְכוּב m. chariot for driving.

רְכוּשׁ (also רְכֻשׁ, with suff. רְכוּשָׁם) m. substance, goods, possessions, orig. that which is accumulated, brought together; hence, especially moveable goods.

רָכִיל masc. slander; hence, אִישׁ רָ׳ slanderer, הָלַךְ רָ׳ to go about as a tale-bearer; possibly, however,

רָכִיל stands as a particip. form for רָגֵל.

רָכַךְ (3 pers. sing. רַךְ, 3 pl. רַכּוּ, fut. יֵרַךְ after the form יֵמַר) orig. to be ground, thin, related to רָקַק; hence, 1) to be tender, delicate, pampered (of good living), to be smooth (of words); 2) to be timid, faint-hearted. Niph. does not occur; the form יֵרַךְ belonging to Kal. Pu. to be mollified, of a wound which is softened by ointment. Hiph. to make one faint-hearted. See רַךְ.

רָכַל (only particip. Kal) equiv. to רָגַל, for which it only appears to be a secondary form, to travel, to move about; hence, 1) to traffic, comp. סָחַר, origin. to travel about as a merchant.—רֹכֵל merchant, dealer, fem. רֹכֶלֶת; 2) to go about as a tale-bearer, which signification, however, is only found in the derivatives.

רָכָל (mercantile place) p.n. of a city in the territory of Judah.

רְכֻלָּה f. trade, traffic, also that which is acquired by trade, merchandise.

רָכַס (fut. יִרְכֹּס) to bind on, to tie on (related with the root in אֶרְגָּז), e.g. to tie the חֹשֶׁן breastplate to something.

רֶכֶס (plur. רְכָסִים) masc. mountain-chain, a range of mountains connected together and admitting of no pass.

רֹכֶס (pl. const. רֻכְסֵי) m. troop, band, in the sense of wicked people; according to others, conspiracy, somewhat like קֶשֶׁר.

I. רָכַשׁ to gather, accumulate property or substance; next, generally, to acquire, to get.

II. רָכַשׁ (not used) equiv. to רָגַשׁ, רָעַשׁ, to rage, storm; transf. to the furious running of an animal; from which:—

רֶכֶשׁ m. a racer, a swift horse; but as it occurs in connection with סוּס, it seems to signify a peculiar species or noble breed.

רָם 1) adj. m. high, the fem is רָמָה; 2) p.n. m. (the high one).

רָם see רְאֵם.

רְמָא (3 pret. pl. רְמוֹ and רְמִיו, inf. מִרְמֵא) Aram. the same as the Hebrew רָמָה; to throw (into a pit); also, to set up, erect thrones; also, to impose a tax or tribute. Ithpael pass. to be thrown.

רָמָה to throw (like the Aram); hence also, of the shooting of arrows, רֹמֵה קֶשֶׁת an archer. Pi. רִמָּה to cause to fall; transf. to deceive, to cheat. The root in רָמָה seems to be equiv. to רָבָה in this sense.

רָמָה (from רוּם) f. 1) a high place, a height, for idol-worship, syn. with

רָמָה; 2) (height) p.n. of a city in the territory of Benjamin; a city in the mountain of Ephraim, the dwelling-place of Samuel, complete רָמָתַיִם צוֹפִים; a city in the territory of Naphtali; רָמַת הַמִּצְפֶּה (height of the watch-tower), a city in Gilead, otherwise called רָמוֹת and רָאמוֹת; finally, p. n. of a city or a place, complete רָמַת לְחִי. Gent. רָמָתִי.

רִמָּה f. a worm, a reptile, also collectively, reptiles, creeping things. Root רָמַם II.

רִמּוֹן (pl. ־נִים) m. 1) a pomegranate, pomegranate-tree; transf. to artificial pomegranates on pillars, etc.; 2) p.n. of a city on the southern border of Palestine in the territory of Simeon, sometimes joined with עַיִן; also, of a rock near Gibeah; also, of a city in the boundary of Zebulun; רִמּוֹן פֶּרֶץ (granate of the breach) p.n. of an encampment of the Israelites in the desert; 3) p.n. of a Syrian idol, e.g. in טַבְרִמּוֹן, הֲדַדְרִמּוֹן, גַּת רִמּוֹן, where רִמּוֹן probably is to be taken in the sense of עֶלְיוֹן, the upper, from רָמַם, equiv. to רוּם; 4) p.n. m. (the great or proud one).

רָמוֹת (heights) p.n. of a Gileadite city, otherwise רָאמוֹת.

רָמוֹת נֶגֶב (southern heights) p.n. of a city in the tribe of Simeon, for which otherwise רָאמַת נֶ׳.

רָמוּת fem. height, hill, comp. רָמָה; transf. to heaps of corpses, e.g. to fill the valleys with hills of corpses, Ezek. 32:5.

רָמַח (not used) to thrust, to pierce. The root is רָמָה, related with בָּרְחָה.

רֹמַח (pl. רְמָחִים, with suff. רָמְחֵיהֶם) m. a spear, a javelin; from רָמַח (comp. דֶּקֶר modern Heb.) מָרַק ר׳ to sharpen (the point of) the lance.

רַמִּי (for אֲרַמִּי, pl. הָרַמִּים) the Syrian. See אֲרַמִּי.

רַמְיָה p.n. m. (appointed by God).

רְמִיָּה (after the form אֳנִיָּה, קְרִיָּה) f. 1) carelessness, neglect, origin. throwing down; hence כַּף ר׳ a slack hand, נֶפֶשׁ ר׳ an idle soul; also as an adv. indolently, sluggishly, neglectfully; 2) deceit, deception, cheating, artfulness; hence עָשָׂה ר׳ to work deceit, לְשׁוֹן רְמִיָּה a deceitful tongue, קֶשֶׁת רְמִיָּה a deceitful bow, i. e. that does not hit.

רָמַךְ (not used) a verbal root adopted for רַמָּךְ, but the signif. is obscure.

רַמָּךְ (pl. ־כִים) f. a mare (according to the Arab); hence בְּנֵי הָר׳ foals; according to others, studs of (royal) horses (after the Syriac); according to others, concubines.

רָמַל (not used) to adorn, to decorate; from which:—

רְמַלְיָהוּ p.n. m. (adorned by God).

I. רָמַם equiv. to רוּם, from which there are only a few forms, as רֹמּוּ, רָמּוּ, and probably particip. רוֹמֵמָה. Niph. to lift oneself up, to raise oneself, only in the forms יֵרֹמּוּ, הֵרֹמּוּ; but the Hithpael הִתְרוֹמֵם belongs to רוּם.

II. רָמַם (not used) to creep, as וַיָּרֻם, Exod. 16:20, "and it bred worms." From which רִמָּה.

רֹמַמְתִּי־עֶזֶר p.n. m. (height of support).

רָמַס (fut. יִרְמֹס) to tread, with the feet, equiv. to רָפַס to tread down; also, as a sign of pollution, desecration, רֹמֵס the treader down, the tyrant. Niph. pass.

רָמַשׂ denom. from רֶמֶשׂ, which see.

רֶמֶשׂ (from רָם to creep, formed with the termination ־ֶשׂ) m. creeping animals; with אֲדָמָה, that which creepeth on the earth, also of aquatic animals; from which denom. רָמַשׂ to creep (of animals); the earth creeps, i.e. swarms with animals.

רֶמֶת (height, equiv. to רָמָה) p.n. of a city in Issachar.

רֹן (const. pl. רָנֵּי) m. a shout of joy, rejoicing; רָנֵּי־פַלֵּט shouts for deliverance.

רָנָה (only fut. יִרְנֶה) equiv. to רָנַן to sound, to rattle, to whiz, used of the rattling of the arrows in the quiver, or of the whizzing of the arrows shot from the bow.

רִנָּה (with suff. רִנָּתָם) f. 1) shouting, song; also, of the moaning of lamentation; 2) p.n. m. The root is:—

רָנַן (inf. רֹן, imp. רָנִּי, pause רֹנִּי, fut. יָרֹן, once יָרוֹן, pl. יָרֹנּוּ) to raise a shout of joy, or to moan (of one who laments), generally of human beings, sometimes figur. of inanimate things. Pi. רִנֵּן to rejoice often over (בְּ) something or some one; with עַל, to triumph over the downfall of some one; also, to praise, to extol, construed with בְּ, לְ and אֶל. Hiph. 1) to cause some one to rejoice, to shout with joy; 2) to attune songs of praise or joy unto (לְ) some one. Hith. to break out in songs of joy (in intoxication).

רְנָן (so in modern Heb., but in the Bible the pl. is רְנָנִים) m. orig. the whining, whimpering; next, the ostrich, on account of its whining cry (Job 39:19). Some modern commentators render it in this passage, nightingale, which, however, is improbable.

רְנָנָה (pl. רְנָנוֹת) f. shouting, singing,

songs of praise; the pl. רְנָנִים belongs to רְנָן, which see

רִסָּה (heap of ruins) p. n. of an encampment of the Israelites in the desert.

רְסִיס (only pl. רְסִיסִים, const. רְסִיסֵי) m. 1) a drop, from רָסַס I.; 2) breach, crag (parallel with בְּקִיעַ), from רָסַס II.

רָסַן (not used) to bind, to fetter; the orig. signif. is found in רֶסֶן.

רֶסֶן (with suff. רִסְנוֹ) m. 1) a bridle; hence fig. שִׁלַּח רֶסֶן מִפָּנִים to let loose the bridle, i.e. to be unruly in conduct; also, bit, hence כֶּפֶל רִסְנוֹ double bit; 2) p.n. of a Syrian city.

רָסַס (inf. רֹס) to moisten, to wet, e.g. the flour (Author. Vers. "to temper with the flour").

רָסַס (not used) equiv. to רָצַץ to break, to dash to pieces. From which רְסִיסִים.

רַע (from רָעַע, form in pause רָע, and with *Vav* וָרָע, with the article הָרַע and הָרָע, pl. רָעִים) 1) adj. m. רָעָה (pl. רָעוֹת) f. bad, in contrast to טוֹב, and like it, used in manifold significations according to the context, e.g. bad of look, of taste. In reference to physical or moral qualities, base, valueless, unfit for food, unfruitful, hateful, ugly, shameful unrefreshing, malignant, sick, corrupt, sad, etc. רַע בְּעֵינֵי פ׳, רַע לִפְנֵי פ׳ to be evil in the face of some one, i.e. to displease him; בִּעֵר הָרַע מִקֶּרֶב to remove the evil from the community; 2) as a subst., like many adjectives, the evil, badness, unpleasantness, a bad deed, a bad word, baseness, calamity, in as extensive a sense as the adj. In this double character of adj. and subst., both רַע and רָעָה are used; the latter, however, is more frequently used as a subst.

I. רֵעַ (from רוּעַ, with suff. רֵעֹה) m. noise, shouting, cry (either for joy or sorrow), thunder, or the voice of thunder.

II. רֵעַ (from רָעָה, thus for רֵעֶה, with suff. רֵעֵהוּ (seldom רֵעוֹ), רֵעִי, pl. רֵעִים, and with suff. רֵעַי, רֵעֶיךָ and רֵעֵיהֶם) masc. 1) friend, associate, confederate, also transf. to the beloved one (by a wife), also neighbour, fellow-man; hence like אִישׁ, used as a pronoun, the other one, whether אִישׁ precedes or not, e.g. אִישׁ אֶל־רֵעֵהוּ one to another, אִישׁ מֵרֵעֵהוּ one from another; 2) after the Aram. sense of the root, thought, will. Comp. רַעְיוֹן.

רֹעַ (seldom רוֹעַ, from רָעַע) m. badness (of a thing), but also, in a moral sense, baseness, wickedness, sadness, unpleasantness, and in as manifold significations as רַע.

רָעֵב (fut. יִרְעַב) origin. to languish, desire for something; next, to hunger: the root is related to that in חָרֵב. Hiph. to cause one to suffer hunger.

רָעָב (after the form קָהָל, אָשָׁם), with suffix רְעָבָם) m. hunger, famine, מוּת בָּר׳ to die of hunger, ר׳ לַלֶּחֶם to hunger, languish for bread.

רָעֵב (pl. רְעֵבִים) adj. m., רְעֵבָה fem. hungry, suffering hunger.

רְעָבוֹן (const. רַעֲבוֹן) masc. hunger, suffering of hunger, and also that which satisfies the hunger.

רָעַד (fut. יִרְעַד) to shake, to quiver, to tremble (of the earth). For the root, comp. רָטַט, רָתַת, חָרַד, and others. Hiph. to labour under fear, terror, trembling.

רַעַד m. the trembling.

רְעָדָה f. the same.

I. רָעָה (fut. יִרְעֶה, apoc. יֵרַע) 1) to feed a flock, to lead to pasture, with accus., seldom with בְּ, as רֹעֶה בַצֹּאן a shepherd, or feeding of the flock; the particip. רֹעֶה the shepherd, fem. רֹעָה. Fig. to feed, i. e. to lead the people; hence רֹעֶה leader, prince, instructor; 2) to feed, to nourish, e. g. Hos. 9:2, "the floor and the winepress shall not feed them;" 3) to feed on the meadow, construed with בְּ and עַל; next, to eat off (the grass), with accus.; fig. to devour, to sweep away, not connected with רָעַע; 4) to enjoy, delight in something, e. g. רָעָה אִוֶּלֶת to delight in folly, to desire, long for something, e. g. רוּחַ after the wind (vanity): signif. 4 seems to be the basis of the verb, so רָעָה is equiv. to רָצָה. Hiph. to feed, to lead to pasture.

II. רָעָה 1) to tie, to connect, join; hence, like עָשַׁת, זָמַם, חָשַׁב, to think; 2) to join some one, to associate, e.g. רֹעֶה כְסִילִים he who associates with fools; hence, in the parallel passage, הֹלֵךְ אֶת. Pi. to choose for an associate or confederate, or to join some one (לוֹ) to himself. Hith. הִתְרָעָה (fut. apoc. יִתְרַע) to join or connect oneself with (אֵת) some one; the orig. signif. is in רע־ה, which root has some similarity with אָרַג and חָדַק.

רָעָה as an adj. f. from רַע, see רַע.

רֵעֶה (const. רֵעֵה) an acquaintance, associate, companion, friend, orig. a particip. hence:—

רֵעָה (pl. רֵעוֹת) f. a female friend or companion.

רֹעָה inf. fem. from רָעַע, breaking or dashing to pieces.

רֵעִי p.n.m. (friendship, companionship).

רְעוּ (const. רְעוּת) Aram. desire, will, wish.

רְעוּאֵל p.n.m. (befriended by God).

רְעוּת (an abstract form, like רְאוּת, פְּדוּת) f. 1) companionship, friendship; 2) thought, reflection, e.g. רוּחַ after vanity, perhaps also pleasure, favor, from רָעָה I.; 3) concrete, female friend or associate. The basis of all 3 signif. is in רָעָה. The pl. רְעִיוֹת only Ketib.

רְעִי (after the form שְׁבִי) m. pasture or feeding; more correctly, however, as an ancient particip. pass. form, fed; hence, בָּקָר רְעִי fed or fattened cattle.

רֵעִי (formed from רֵעַ) p.n.m. (friend).

רֹעִי (formed from רֹעֶה shepherd) adj. masc. pertaining to shepherds, subst. shepherd, e.g. רֹעִי אֱלִיל bad shepherd.

רַעְיָה (after the form שְׁבִיָּה) f. orig. like רְעוּת friendship, companionship; next, concrete, the beloved one, the friend, of a female.

רַעְיוֹן masc. 1) thinking, reflecting, striving, aspiring, e.g. רוּחַ after vanity; 2) thought, like in Aram.

רַעְיוֹן (Aram.) the same, also of nightly dreams or visions.

רָעַל (Kal, not used) to tremble, to shake; hence, Hoph. הָרְעַל to be terribly shaken (of the fir trees), or to be swung (of lances); probably רָעַל is related with רָעַד.

רַעַל m. shaking to and fro, reeling, staggering. See רָעַל.

רְעָלָה (only pl. רְעָלוֹת) f. a veil, so called from its flowing motion.

רְעֵלָיָה p.n.m. (terror of God), for which once רַעַמְיָה in the same signification.

רָעַם (3 plur. רָעֲמוּ, fut. יִרְעַם) to tremble, to shake, e.g. of the raging of the sea, figur. of the countenance, to be agitated. Hiph. 1) to thunder, to cause thunder; 2) fig. of the provoking to anger, probably רָעַם is only a denom. from:—

רַעַם (רַעַמְךָ) masc. thunder, סֵתֶר רַ׳ clouds containing thunder, transf. to a thundering, raging voice; the form is probably from רַע (from רוּעַ), with nominal termination ־ַם, comp. תֶּלֶם, כֶּרֶם; in the same manner רַעַל appears to arise from רוּעַ with another nominal termination, from which subsequently the verb רָעַל arose.

רַעְמָה fem. 1) trembling mane; according to others, the far-sounding neighing; which, however, is less suitable to the context; 2) p.n. of a Cushite people, and hence the name of a city and country, probably Regma (Ῥέγμα), a city on the Persian Gulf.

רַעְמְסֵס (also רַעַמְסֵס) p. n. of an Egyptian city in Goshen; according to Saadia, Heliopolis; according to others, Heröopolis.

רָעַן (Kal, not used) to be green, verdant, fresh. From which the Pilpel רַעֲנֵן to bloom, to be fresh, to flourish, used as an emblem of prosperity; only f. רַעֲנָנָה, which, however, may be an adj.

רַעֲנָן (pl. —נַנִּים) adj. m. fresh, green.

רַעֲנַן (Aram.) adj. m. the same, figur. prosperous.

I. רָעַע (inf. רַע and רֹעָה, fut. יָרֹעַ, with suff. יְרֹעֵם) to break, to dash in pieces, related is רָצַץ, רָצַץ. Niph. (fut. יֵרוֹעַ) to be broken, dashed to pieces; according to others, the Niph. belongs to רוּעַ. Hiph. (rare) to break, to dash to pieces. Hith. to be violently shaken or ruined (of the earth); comp. Aram. רְעַע.

II. רָעַע (fut. יֵרַע, comp. יֵקַל, יֵצַר, יֵרַךְ, which are of fut. Kal, imp. רֹעַ) to rage, to be wroth, to be evil disposed, in contrast to kindness, which is connected with the idea of calmness; transf. to be injurious, hurtful, pernicious, malignant, envious, sad, grieved, as in רַע. Hiph. הֵרַע and הָרַע (inf. הָרֵעַ, in pause הָרֵעַ, fut. יָרֵעַ, apoc. יָרַע, particip. מֵרַע, pl. מְרֵעִים) to act basely, to do evil, in contrast to הֵטִיב; hence, הֵרַע לַעֲשׂוֹת, הֵרַע מַעֲלָלִים to do evil, מֵרַע evildoer; הֵרַע is construed with לְ, עַל, אֶת, עִם, בְּ, to signify causing evil to some one.

רְעַע (fut. יֵרֹעַ) Aram. to break, to dash in pieces. Pa. רָעַע the same.

רָעַף (fut. יִרְעֲפוּ) to flow, to drop, with accus., seldom עַל. Hiph. to cause to drop. The roots in רָוָה and זָרַב are related.

רָעַץ equiv. to רָצַץ, to shatter, to dash to pieces (the enemy), figur. to oppress a people. Comp. רָעַע I. and עָרַץ.

רָעַשׁ to storm, to snort, to rush, to tremble, to shake, of the heavens, earth, mountains, cities, walls, castles, towers; fig. of the waving of the corn. Niph. to be shaken, to quake, of the earth. Hiph. to shake, to cause to leap (of the locust). The verbs רָגַשׁ and רָגַז are related.

רַעַשׁ m. shaking, trembling, earthquake, tumult, also used of the rattling of a chariot, of the snorting of a horse, of the noise of a mob, etc.

רָפָא (fut. יִרְפָּא) orig. to bind round or bind up, transf. to heal, orig-to bind up the wound, figur. to help, to save, to restore, to rebuild, to support. Niph. to be healed, mended, repaired, restored. Piel, to bind up that which is broken, to restore; next, to heal a wound, a disease, or to procure remedies; fig. to comfort. Hith. to let himself be healed; comp. רָפָה I., in the same sense, from which several forms are derived.

רְפָאָה (plur. ־אוֹת) f. cure, healing, bandage; fig. recovery, soothing.

רִפְאוּת fem. healing, recovery. The form is like סִבְלוּת.

רָפָא belongs to רְפָאִים. See רָפָה (=רָפָא).

רְפָאִי see רָפָה.

רְפָאֵל p.n. m. (God is the healer).

רָפַד (fut. יִרְפַּד) to spread out, to bed, or perhaps only intrans. Pi. to spread a couch; רִפֵּד Cant.2:5, signifies to prepare the couch (Author. Vers. "to comfort me").

רָפָה equiv. to רָפָא to heal, after which are to be explained the forms: הַרְפֵּה, נִרְפָּתָה, תִּרְפֶּינָה, יְרַפּוּ, יֵרָפוּ, which are conjugated according to ל״ה.

I. רָפָה (not used) to darken, to make gloomy; related are the roots in עָרַף and עָרַב, with the same original signification.

II. רָפָה (not used) to shiver, to tremble, figur. to cause fear, terror, thus transitive; with the root רְפָדָה is related רַף (רוּף).

IV. רָפָה (fut. יִרְפֶּה) to hang down, to droop (of the hand), to be bowed down, oppressed (of the spirit); transf. to be slack, idle, to despond, to be dejected; orig. to relax; the day slackens, i.e. evening approaches; the flame slackens (consumes) the chaff; the root רָפָה to be slack, loose, is in contrast to חָזַק to be firm, tied together. Niph. to be sluggish, indolent. Pi. to loosen, to untie, e.g. מְזִיחַ the girdle; transf. to droop the wings, to slacken the hands, i.e. to dishearten. Hiph. to let loose, to forsake, with יָדַיִם or יָד the hand from some one, sometimes יָד is omitted; to forbear, to withdraw. Hith. to behave oneself slackly, remissly, to let one's courage fail.

רָפָה (also רָפָא) p.n. m. ancestor of a race of giants (רְפָאִים), from which רְפָאִים may be derived as a gent. noun. The signification is like רָפָה 2.

רָפָה (after the form נָוֶה, נָכָה, טָלֶה, plur. רְפָאִים, like נְכָאִים, טְלָאִים) subst. m. 1) shadow; hence, of the appearance of night and dark visions, also of the inhabitants of the regions of death, from רָפָה II.; 2) giant, origin. one who causes terror, the fearful one, from רָפָה III. but only used in the plur. רְפָאִים, and as the name of a Canaanite race of giants, from which the giant Og descended, and mentioned in connection with זַמְזֻמִּים, אֵימִים and עֲנָקִים. See רָפָה.

רָפֶה (const. רְפֵה) adj. m., רָפָה (pl. רָפוֹת) f. sluggish, slack (of hands), as a figure of despondency; next, weak, faint, etc. Root רָפָה IV.

רָפוּא p. n. m. (the healing one, physician).

רָפַח (not used) after the Arab. to be rich. From which:—

רֶפַח p.n. m. (riches).

רְפִידָה f. couch, encampment. See רָפַד.

רְפִידִים (places of an encampment) p.n. of an encampment of the Israelites in the desert.

רְפָיָה p.n. m. (God is the healer).

רִפְיוֹן m. slackness, the drooping (of the hand); transf. to fear.

רָפַס (and רָפַשׂ, fut. יִרְפֹּשׂ) equiv. to רָמַס to tread, only in the sense of making water muddy or turbid by treading. Niph. to become troubled or turbid (of a fountain). Hith. הִתְרַפֵּס to let oneself to be trodden on, or to cringe, as a sign of subjugation, e.g. Ps. 68 : 31, "submit himself with pieces of silver;" in a similar sense is to be taken הִתְרַפֵּס Prov. 6 : 3. The root is also to be traced in רָפַס, as in רָמַשׂ.

רְפַס (Aram.) to tread down, to tread in pieces.

רַפְסֹדֹת (formed from a masc. רַפְסֹד, for which in a parallel passage stands דֹּבְרוֹת; pl. רַפְסֹדוֹת) fem. float, raft, from רָפַס to slide along. The last syllable ־ֹד is an ancient nominal suffix, so that the nominal word is orig. רֶפֶס (Arab. *ramat*, Ethiopian *rams*).

רָפַף belongs to רוּפַף. See רוּף.

רָפַק (Kal, not used) to lean, to support oneself. Hith. to lean upon (עַל) some one. The root is רָפַק, and related with that in דָּבַק, חָבַק.

רָפַשׂ (not used) is connected in the root probably with פָּשׂ. From which:—

רֶפֶשׁ m. mire, slime, which the sea casts up, orig. casting out; comp. פִּישׁוֹן from פּוּשׁ proceeding from a similar original signification.

רָפַשׂ see רָפַס.

רָפַת (not used) probably the root for רֶפֶת, which, however, may be connected with רָפַף.

רֶפֶת (pl. רְפָתִים) m. a stable, stall; origin. a rack, a grate.

רֶץ (const. pl. רַצֵּי) m. that which is broken off, a piece; hence, bar (of silver); comp. the modern Hebrew חֲתִיכָה. Root רָצַץ.

רָץ see רוּץ.

רָצָא (only inf. abs. רָצוֹא) equiv. to רוּץ, which see.

רָצַד (Kal, not used) equiv. to רָקַד to totter, to tremble. Pi. intensitive, in the same sense, to leap, only Ps. 68:17, comp. Ps. 29:6; 114:4, 6.

רָצָה (1 pers. רָצִאתִי, fut. יִרְצֶה, apoc. יִרֶץ) equiv. to רָעָה to join some one; with עִם, to have pleasure or to take delight in something, or in some one; with accus. and בְּ of the person or object, to be gracious, kind, willing, or to receive some one kindly; transf. to satisfy; hence, to pay (a creditor), fig. to liquidate a debt, e.g. the earth shall pay off (Author. Vers. "enjoy") her sabbaths. Niph. נִרְצָה to be paid off (of a debt), to be expiated (of sin), to be accepted graciously (of sacrifices and offerings). Pi. to pacify, to satisfy, by the restoration of the property to the owner. Hiph. to pay, to satisfy the creditor. Hith. to make oneself pleasing towards (אֶל) some one. See רָעָה.

רָצוֹן masc. pleasure, grace, favour, delight, acceptance, satisfaction, graciousness, good will; עַל רָ׳ לְךָ acceptable (to or with God), i. e. well pleasing to him; בְּכָל רָצוֹן with all the heart, or good will.

רָצַח (fut. יִרְצַח) to pierce through, to thrust, equiv. to רָצַע; next, to slay, to murder, to kill generally, complete רָצַח נֶפֶשׁ; רֹצֵחַ a murderer. Niph. pass. Pi. to kill repeatedly, or several; transf. to dash in pieces, to destroy. Pu. (only according to Ben Naphtali) pass.

רֶצַח m. 1) a wounding, a slaying, a slaughtering; 2) equiv. to צְרַח cry, from which it is transposed.

רִצְיָא p. n. m. (pleasure, delight).

רְצִין p. n. m. (the strong one).

רָצַע equiv. to רָצַח to pierce, to bore (the ear).

רָצַף origin. to put, to lay, to arrange; related in the root with צָרָה, צָבָא, יָצַב; hence, to lay down stones for pavement. The sense of joining, arranging, putting in order, is conveyed, in modern Heb., by צֵרֵף, which seems to be a transposition from רָצַף.

רָצַף equiv. to רָשַׁף to glow, to burn, from which, according to some, רָצוּף, Cant. 3:10.

רֶצֶף (only pl. רְצָפִים) m. 1) equiv. to

רֶשֶׁף a burning coal, orig. a glowing coal; עֻגַת רְצָפִים a cake baked on glowing coals; according to some, on a hot stone, as used by the Orientalists for roasting; 2) p.n. of an Assyrian city, Resapha (Ῥησοφα), in Palmyrene.

רִצְפָּה (const. רִצְפַּת) f. formed from רֶצֶף 1) paving; hence, pavement, from רָצַף; 2) a burning coal, from רֶצֶף; 3) p.n. f. (glow).

רָצַץ (2 pers. רַצּוֹתָ, particip. pass. רָצוּץ, fut. יָרוּץ for יָרֹץ) equiv. to רָצַע, רָעַץ to break in pieces (a wheel), to dash in pieces (the head), to bruise, to break (a reed); figur. like עָשַׁק, to oppress, treat with violence. Niph. to be broken to pieces (a wheel, a reed). Pi. רִצֵּץ to dash to pieces (the head), fig. to oppress sorely. Po. רוֹצֵץ to oppress. Hiph. (fut. יָרֵץ for יָרֵץ) to dash to pieces (the skull). Hith. הִתְרוֹצֵץ to push one another, to struggle. The root רַץ is also to be traced in חָרַץ, קָרַץ, and others.

רַק 1) adj. m. רַקָּה (pl. רַקּוֹת) f. thin; hence, of the flesh, meagre, lean, dry; 2) only m. as subst., and fig. in the sense of restriction, or negation; hence, as an adv., only, except; sometimes, indeed certainly, surely; רַק רַע only evil; רַק הַיָּשָׁר only the right.

רֵק (and רֵיק) adj. masc. empty, from רוּק. See רֵיק.

רֹק (with suff. רֻקִּי) m. spittle, from רָקַק to flow, to run.

רָקַב (fut. יִרְקַב) to be hollow, worm-eaten, rotten; figur. decayed, inwardly destroyed.

רָקָב (const. רְקַב) masc. rottenness, inward wasting (of the bones), deficient in substance.

רִקָּבוֹן m. rottenness, decadency.

רָקַד (fut. יִרְקֹד) to tremble, to shake, to skip, to leap, to dance. Pi. of the jolting of a swift chariot. Hiph. to cause to skip.

רַקָּה f. the temple (of the head) from רָקַק, in the signification of to beat, on account of the pulsation in that place; transf. to cheek.

רַקּוֹן (coast-district, origin. a place around which the water washes, from רָקַק II.), p.n. of a city in the territory of Dan.

רָקַח (fut. יִרְקַח) to spice, season, to make ointment (by the seasoning of oils); hence רֹקֵחַ one that prepares ointment, an apothecary. Pu. to be seasoned, spiced. Hiph. to season (food); the root appears to be equiv. to רָקַע to beat thin, on account of the pounding of the spices.

רֶקַח m. spice; with יַיִן spiced-wine.

רֹקַח m. ointment, origin. that which is seasoned, spiced.

רַקָּח (pl. —חִים) adj. m., רַקָּחָה (pl. —חוֹת) fem. he or she who spices the ointment.

רִקֻּחַ m. spiced ointment.

רָקִיעַ (const. רְקִיעַ) m. expansion, arching (of the heaven), firmament, complete רְקִיעַ הַשָּׁמַיִם.

רָקִיק (const. רְקִיק, const. pl. רְקִיקֵי) m. thin cake, a wafer, from רָקַק.

רָקַם (only particip. רֹקֵם) orig. equiv. to רָגַם II., to mark (with points), to cut figures into something; transf. to embroider, to work with various colours; hence רֹקֵם the embroiderer, one that works with various colours. Pu. רֻקַּם figur. to be formed, shaped of the embryo in the mother's womb.

רֶקֶם 1) (probably equiv. to רֶגֶם heap of stones) p. n. of a city in the territory of Benjamin; 2) p. n. m. (according to the Arab, equiv. to רֶגֶם a friend).

רִקְמָה (with suff. רִקְמָתָם, dual רִקְמָתַיִם, pl. רְקָמוֹת) f. embroidered garment; transf. to anything that is embroidered, or of various colours; hence, of the variegated feathers of the eagle, and also of many coloured stones.

רָקַע (fut. יִרְקַע) to expand, to spread out; next, to tread something down, for the purpose of spreading out. The various significations may thus be classified; 1) to spread out, e. g. the earth over the waters, Psalm 136:6; 2) to stamp (with the feet), to express indignation or joy; 3) to stamp, tread down. Pi. to hammer, to beat out (metallic plates), but also a denom. from רִקֻּעַ to overlay with tin. Pu. pass. to be beaten out to thin plates. Hiph. (to spread out (the heavens).

רִקֻּעַ m. a thin plate, orig. that which is beaten out, extended.

I. רָקַק (Kal, not used) to be beaten thin. Hiph. (only fut. אֲדִיקֵם) irregular, to stamp, to tread down. The root is probably related to רָקַע.

II. רָקַק (only fut. יָרֹק) orig. to flow, to run (comp. the root רוּק and יָרַק); next, to flow (from the mouth), to spit; with בְּ, to spit at some one; related is רָכַךְ.

רַקַּת (coast territory, from רָקַק) p. n. of a city in Naphtali. In the Talmud (Megilla, 5 *b*) it is maintained by one רַקַּת זוֹ טְבֶרְיָא that Rakath is Tiberius, and by another רַקַּת זוֹ צִפּוֹרִי Rakath is Zephorius.

רָשׁ poor one, see רוּשׁ.

רָשָׁה (not used) probably equiv. to רָשַׁע to exercise power over some one or something; hence, to be able. The modern Heb. Hiph. הִרְשָׁה is quite the same signification as הִשְׁלִיט Ecc. 5:18, to empower or permit some one to do something.

רִשְׁיוֹן masc. grant, permission, empowering.

רֵשִׁית see רֵאשִׁית.

רָשַׁם (only particip. pass. רָשׁוּם) to note (בִּכְתָב) in writing. The root רָשַׁם is found as well in שֵׁם.

רְשַׁם (fut. יִרְשֻׁם) Aram. the same.

רָשַׁע (fut. יִרְשַׁע) origin. to exercise power, to rule (comp. רָשָׁה), from which, to be wicked, to act wickedly; with מִן, to apostatise from some one; to be guilty, liable to punishment. Hiph. 1) to overpower, to act wickedly; 2) to pronounce guilty, to condemn (of a judge).

רָשָׁע (pl. רְשָׁעִים) 1) adj. m., רְשָׁעָה f. wicked, sinful, ungodly; 2) subst. (*a*) the wicked one, a sinner, orig. a violent one, in contrast to עָנָו, עָנִי humble, meek one; generally used in contrast to צַדִּיק the righteous one; (*b*) the guilty one, e.g. רָ׳ לָמוּת guilty of death; (*c*) to have an unjust cause (before a judge).

רֶשַׁע (with suff. רִשְׁעוֹ, pl. רְשָׁעִים) m. violence; also, power, transf. to wickedness, injustice, lie, deceit, pl. wicked deeds.

רִשְׁעָה f. wickedness, wicked deed, lie, deceit, profligacy.

רִשְׁעָתַיִם see כּוּשַׁן.

רָשַׁף (not used) equiv. to רָצַף to glow, to flame, to burn.

רֶשֶׁף (pl. רְשָׁפִים, const. רִשְׁפֵּי, with suff. רְשָׁפֶיהָ) m. glow, flame, e.g. of the ardour of love; next, lightning, orig. the flame of God; the flames of the bow, i.e. arrows; sons of lightning (Job 5:7), i.e. birds of prey darting with the quickness of lightning, according to others, sparks: transf. to burning pestilence.

רָשַׁשׁ (Kal, not used) equiv. to רָצַץ to destroy, to dash in pieces; hence, Po. רוֹשֵׁשׁ to destroy. Pu. pass.

רָשַׁשׁ belongs to תַּרְשִׁישׁ, see under תָּרַשׁ.

רֶשֶׁת (from יָרַשׁ, with suff. רִשְׁתִּי) f. a net, פָּרַשׂ רֶשֶׁת עַל to spread a net over something, מַעֲשֵׂה רֶשֶׁת net work.

רַתּוּק (pl. רַתּוּקוֹת in the Keri) m. a chain, from רָתַק.

רָתַח (Kal, not used) to boil, to seethe. For the root רַ־תַח, comp. רָתַךְ, קָדַח, and others. Pi. to cause to boil or seethe, e.g. רָתַח boiling, seething. Pu. to be heated, like נִכְמַר of the agitation of the heart as an indication of intense emotion. Hiph. like Pi. to cause to boil, to seethe.

רֶתַח (only pl.) m. seething, boiling.

רָתַם (only imp. רְתֹם) orig. to curb, to tame; next, to tie, to yoke or harness. The root ר־תַם is found also in חָ־טַם.

רֹתֶם (pl. רְתָמִים) m. (f. according to the Ketib) a kind of birch or broom, so called from its use for binding; according to others, juniper tree.

רִתְמָה (place of birches or juniper trees) p.n. of an encampment of the Israelites in the desert.

רָתַק (Kal, not used) to bind, to chain, from which Niph. (in Keri) to be bound; since, however, this rendering would make no sense in the context, Ecc. 12:6, and as the Niph. is never used in a privative sense, it must be rendered according to the Ketib יֵרָחֵק removed. Pu. רֻתַּק to be chained, bound.

רַתֻּקָה (pl. ־קוֹת) f. a chain.

רְתֵת m. terror, trembling.

רָתַת (not used) equiv. to רָטַט to tremble. Related is רָעַד and the root in חָרַד.

שׁ, שׂ

שׁ *Shin* (שִׁין), שׂ *Sin* (שִׂין) form originally one letter, the 21st of the alphabet, i.e. the hard *sh* and the soft *s*, were expressed by one and the same character, but latterly grammarians have distinguished one from the other by the diacritic point, which distinction, however, affords no reason for considering them as separate letters in the Lexicon in alphabetical order. The name *shin* was chosen from שֵׁן tooth, to which the form of the letter bears resemblance; as a numeral it signifies 300. It interchanges with the hissing sounds ז, ס, צ, seldom with the sounds in *t*; but also with the aspirates ה and א. Both שׁ and שׂ are often used as nominal suffixes, e.g. חַרְמֵשׁ, רֶמֶשׁ, עַכָּבִישׁ, חַלָּמִישׁ, פִּלֶגֶשׁ, and others.

שֶׁ or שַׁ (with *dagesh forte* following, seldom שְׁ) 1) relative pron. which, who, joined to the following word, whether noun, particle, or verb, and, like אֲשֶׁר, without distinction of gender or number; in modern Heb. it stands for genitive, especially joined with לְ, e.g. מִטָּתוֹ שֶׁלִּשְׁלֹמֹה the bed of Solomon; this afterwards formed itself in

שֶׁל, with suff. שֶׁלִּי, etc., and it is used to strengthen the possessive pronoun, e.g. כַּרְמִי שֶׁלִּי my vineyard; 2) as a relative conj. after certain verbs, that, because; and in this sense, occur the compositions כִּמְעַט שֶׁ scarcely that, עַד־שֶׁ till that, שַׁלָּמָה for why; with other prepositions, בְּשֶׁ־ because, כְּשֶׁ־ like as; or if as a particle of time, when. This pronoun is supposed to be derived by some from שֶׁר (the original root for אֲשֶׁר); by others, from שֶׁל; probably, however, the original form is שֶׁה =זֶה, the relative character having only merged from the demonstrative one.

שָׁא equiv. to סָא (belongs to סַאסְּאָ) סָע to drive, to push, away; hence reduplicated שִׁשֵּׁא (from שִׁאשֵׁא), to drive away, to lead away.

שָׂא (not used) equiv. to נָ־שָׂא to lift up, from which the derivative שִׂיא, שׂוֹא, also שְׂאֵת, שִׂיאוֹן, which see.

שָׁאַב (fut. יִשְׁאַב) to draw, e.g. מַיִם water, orig. connected with שָׁאַף.

שָׁאַג (fut. יִשְׁאַג) equiv. to צָעַק, זָעַק to cry, to call (of man), to roar (of lions), to roll (of thunder), etc.

שְׁאָגָה (const. שַׁאֲגַת) f. cry, roaring.

I. שָׁאָה (Kal, not used) to rage, to make a noise, from which Niph. to rush, to rage, of mighty waters.

II. שָׁאָה to be desolate, waste (of cities). Niph. to be laid waste; with the adverbial addition שְׁמָמָה into desolation. Hiph. (inf. const לְהַשְׁאוֹת, and contracted לְהַשּׁוֹת) to desolate.

III. שָׁאָה (Kal, not used) according to some, equiv. to שָׁעָה, שָׁכָה, to gaze; probably it is, as Rashi and Eben Ezra explain, to be amazed; thus equiv. to שָׁמֵם and connected with שָׁאָה II. Hith. to be amazed, or to gaze at, with לְ.

שַׁאֲוָה (only Ketib, but the Keri for which שׁוֹאָה) f. tempest, storm.

שְׁאוֹל (with ה of motion שְׁאוֹלָה) com. origin. cave, pit, and next, hell, lower regions, where darkness dwells, dwelling of the departed, the Hades of the Hebrews. Root שָׁאַל.

שָׁאוּל p. n. m. (the desired, demanded one), patron. שָׁאוּלִי.

שָׁאוֹן (const. שְׁאוֹן, with suff. שְׁאוֹנָהּ) m. 1) rushing, raging of the sea, noise, tumult (of war, of multitudes of people), בְּנֵי שָׁאוֹן warriors; בּוֹר שָׁאוֹן probably stands for בּוֹר שְׁאוֹן מַיִם; 2) desolation, like שׁוֹאָה.

שָׁאַט (not used) equiv. to שָׁעַט to tread with the feet, to push away: transf. to despise, reject.

שְׁאָט (after the form יְהָב, קְרָב, with

suff. שְׁאָטְךָ) m̄. contempt, rejection, בִּשְׁאָט נֶפֶשׁ with contempt of soul, i.e. with utter contempt.

שְׁאִיָּה f. orig. desolation; next concrete, a ruin.

שָׁאַל (fut. יִשְׁאַל) 1) equiv. to שָׁעַל to hollow out, to dig through, comp. σκάλλ-ω, from which the derivative שְׁאוֹל; 2) after the same graduation of ideas, as in חָקַר; *perscrutari*, to dive, to investigate; next, like דָּרַשׁ to desire, demand; to request, to require, i.e. to dig after something (comp. חָתַר), with accus. of the object one demands, and מִן, מֵאֵת, accus. of the person from whom it is demanded; שָׁאַל נֶפֶשׁ to require the life of some one, i.e. to wish for his death, שָׁאַל אֶת־נַפְשׁוֹ לָמוּת to wish for one's own death; the following are the sub-significations: (*a*) to ask, to beg something from (מֵעִם, מֵאֵת, מִן) some one; שָׁאַל דָּבָר לְ to ask something for some one; (*b*) to ask for a loan, i.e. to borrow; שָׁאוּל to be lent; (*c*) to ask for something as a present; hence, with the sub-signification, to ask for alms; (*d*) to question some one (accus. and לְ), to inquire after (לְ, עַל, accus.) something or some one; to inquire of God (with בְּ) or of the oracle; שָׁאַל לְפ' לְשָׁלוֹם to inquire after the welfare of some one, i.e. to salute; in signification 2, שָׁאַל occurs sometimes as intransitive, hence the forms שְׁאֶלְתֶּם ,שְׁאֵלְתִּיו, as if from שָׁאֵל. Niph. נִשְׁאַל (inf. abs. נִשְׁאֹל) to intreat something from (מִן) some one. Pi. שִׁאֵל 1) to ask for gifts, to beg; 2) to ask frequently. Hiph. 1) to give as a loan; 2) to give as a present asked for, Exod. 12:36.

שְׁאָל p.n. m. (request, desire, demand).

שְׁאֹל see שְׁאוֹל.

שְׁאֵל (1 plur. שְׁאֶלְנָא, particip. שָׁאֵל) Aram. the same as the Heb. שָׁאַל, to ask, to beg, to request, to desire, to demand, to inquire.

שְׁאֵלָא (definite שְׁאֵלְתָא) Aram. f. 1) a wish, a request; 2) like חֵפֶץ Heb. affair, matter, desire, object (Dan. 4:14).

שְׁאֵלָה (with suff. שְׁאֵלָתִי ,שְׁאֶלָתִי, שְׁאֶלְתְּכֶם, once without א, שֵׁלָתֵךְ) f. request, desire, demand, שָׁאַל שׁ' to make a request, נָתַן שׁ' to grant a request, בָּאָה שׁ' the request is fulfilled; transf. to the concrete, the thing or object requested or demanded.

שְׁאַלְתִּיאֵל p.n. m. (entreated of God). for which once שַׁלְתִּיאֵל.

שָׁאַן (Kal, not used) to rest, to be inactive; the original signification is, to be in a leaning position, as a sign of being free from care; related with שָׁקַט and יָשַׁן. Pilpel שַׁאֲנַן to be calm, to be quiet, free from care, tranquil.

שַׁאֲנָן (with suff. שַׁאֲנַנְךָ, pl. שַׁאֲנַנִּים) 1) adj. m., שַׁאֲנַנָּה (pl. —נַנּוֹת) f. quiet, secure, tranquil, undisturbed, prosperous; in a bad sense, proud, overbearing, origin. careless; 2) as a subst. pride, haughtiness, carelessness, or concrete, the proud one.

שְׁאָם see שָׁסַם.

שָׁאַף (fut. יִשְׁאַף) origin. to breathe with open mouth, to snuff up (the air); hence figur. to desire, long, languish, for something; next, to snort; hence, to hasten after a thing, to assail with violence, spoken of wild animals, and metaphorically, of savage enemies. Related to שׁוּף, or to the root in כָּסַף.

שָׁאַר to remain. Niph. to be left (from a mass or a number); sometimes the Niph. signifies only to continue. Hiph. הִשְׁאִיר to let remain, to leave, to leave behind, to keep back.

שָׁאַר (not used) belongs to מִשְׁאֶרֶת, where probably מִשְׁאֶרֶת is the reading, or at least the noun is to be referred back to שָׁאַר.

שָׁאַר (not used) to be sour, acerb, comp. the root בָּסַר; from which שְׂאֹר.

שְׁאָר (after the form כְּתָב) m. rest, remnant, remainder, from שָׁאַר.

שְׁאָר (Aram.) m. the same.

שְׁאֵר (primitive, with suff. שְׁאֵרִי) m. flesh (comp. the root in בָּשָׂר); generally, however, fig. 1) body; hence, crime of murder, e. g. Jer. 51:35, חֲמָסִי וּשְׁאֵרִי the violence done to me and to my flesh; 2) blood relationship, consanguinity, complete שְׁאֵר בְּשָׂר; בָּשָׂר is likewise used in this sense; 3) food; comp. לָחוּם.

שְׂאֹר m. leaven, from שָׁאַר.

שַׁאֲרָה f. blood relationship, consanguinity, conc. kindred by blood.

שֶׁאֱרָה p. n. f. (blood relationship).

שְׁאָר יָשׁוּב a symbolical p. n. of the son of Isaiah (the remnant shall return).

שְׁאֵרִית (once contracted שֵׁרִית, with suff. שְׁאֵרִיתָם) fem. remnant, remainder, especially after a general overthrow, synon. with פְּלֵיטָה, שָׂרִיד; remainder of his wrath (חֵמוֹת), i.e. that which was not yet given vent to, the whole wrath.

שֵׁאת (formed from שָׁאָה, thus for שְׁאֵת) f. 1) noise (tumult of the warriors), thus equiv. to שָׁאוֹן; but in this sense, generally the contracted form שֵׂת; 2) destruction, downfall, origin. desolation, from שָׁאָה.

שְׂאֵת (either formed from שָׂא, or more correctly from נָשָׂא, of which it may be the infin.; with suff. שְׂאֵתִי, once concrete שֵׂתוֹ) fem. 1) lifting up, e.g. of the face, as a sign of cheerfulness; 2) forgiveness, comp. the verb נָשָׂא עָוֹן; 3) sentence or burden (of a prophecy), comp. מַשָּׂא from נָשָׂא to pronounce; 4) rising on the skin, or swelling.

שְׁבָא (according to the Ethiopian, man) p. n. m. sometimes of the grandson of כּוּשׁ, sometimes of the son of Yoktan, and also sometimes of a grandson of Abraham by Keturah; hence, two different ancestors, one of whom became the head of a national tribe in the north, and the other of one in the south of Arabia. Hence, 1) Sheba or Sabenus, a people and country in the south of Arabia, distinguished by commerce and wealth; 2) a people and country in northern Arabia.

I. **שָׁבַב** (not used) to glow, to burn, to flame. With the root שַׁב the roots in רָשַׁף and רָצַף are related.

II. **שָׁבַב** (not used) to cut in pieces (comp. the roots חָצַב, עָצַב, קָצַב). Under this root, Kimchi brings the Po. שׁוֹבֵב, which, however, is not correct.

שָׁבָב (only pl. שְׁבָבִים) m. a splinter, piece, orig. that which is cut or broken off.

שָׁבָה (fut. יִשְׁבֶּה, apoc. יִשְׁבְּ) to drive away, to carry away; hence, either of the driving away of cattle, or of the carrying away of property, but especially of leading people into captivity. Niph. pass.

שְׁבוֹ m. name of a precious stone, achates, according to tradition. The root appears to be שָׁבָה equiv. to שָׁבַב I.; hence, like in אֶקְדָּח, transf. to shining, glittering.

שְׁבוּאֵל p. n. m. (led into captivity by God); for which once שׁוּבָאֵל.

שְׁבוּל in the Ketib once for שְׁבִיל, which see.

שָׁבוּעַ (const. שְׁבֻעַ, dual שְׁבֻעַיִם, pl. שָׁבֻעִים, —עוֹת, const. שְׁבֻעוֹת, with suff. שָׁבוּעוֹתֵיכֶם) m. a number of seven, from שֶׁבַע seven; hence, 1) seven days, a week comprising seven days; Feast of Weeks, i.e. Pentecost, on account of the numbering of seven weeks from Passover to Pentecost, but חַג שָׁבוּעוֹת יָמִים feast of seven days, i. e. Passover, which, according to scripture, lasts seven days; שְׁלֹשָׁה

שָׁבֻעִים יָמִים three weeks long (see יָמִים); 2) a week of years, i. e. seven years.

שְׁבוּעָה fem. 1) an oath, swearing; שְׁ׳ י״י an oath by God; sometimes with the genitive, of the swearer, or of him by whose name the oath is taken; hence בַּעֲלֵי שְׁבוּעָה bound to a person by an oath, allies, confederates; 3) an oath of imprecation, a curse, complete שְׁבוּעַת הָאָלָה.

שְׁבוּת fem. abstract, captivity, from which, conc. the captives; שׁוּב שְׁ׳ to bring back the captives (of a people), which phrase is also used as a figure of restoration to prosperity. Root שָׁבָה.

שָׁבַח (Kal, not used) to lift up the voice, to speak, to call; hence, Pi. 1) to praise, to laud; 2) to appease, to assuage, to check, to quiet (floods, anger); שַׁבֵּחַ Ecc. 4:2, stands for מְשַׁבֵּחַ. Hiph. to appease, quiet (the floods or waves). Hith. to boast or laud oneself (with בְּ of the object, boasting of). The root is related to that in צָוַח.

שְׁבַח (Aram.) the same; hence, Pa. to praise, to commend.

שָׁבַט (not used) according to some, to support, make firm, thus syn. with שָׁגַב, but more probably, to beat; hence, in modern Heb., to beat out, to unfold, thus related with חָבַט.

שֵׁבֶט (pause שָׁבֶט, with suff. שִׁבְטִי, pl. שְׁבָטִים, const. שִׁבְטֵי) com. 1) a staff, a rod, a stick or rod for chastisement; hence, rod of correction, also in a figur. sense; 2) staff for leading or measuring; hence, staff of the shepherd, staff of the ruler, i. e. sceptre; measuring rod, transf. to inheritance of a portion of land allotted by the measuring rod; 3) shaft, stem of a tree, transf. to spear; fig. like מַטֶּה tribe (of a people), e.g. of the tribes of Israel, and frequently of the division of a tribe; 4) only Numb. 23:17, parallel with כּוֹכָב, which like שָׁבִיט in the Mishna, was, even in ancient times, translated "comet;" originally, rod, on account of the form of that planet.

שְׁבַט (Aram.) com. the same as in signification 3 in Hebrew.

שְׁבָט m. name of the eleventh month of the Jewish ecclesiastical year. The etymology is obscure.

שְׁבִי (pause שֶׁבִי, with suff. שִׁבְיוֹ, שִׁבְיְכֶם, שִׁבְיֵךְ) masc. 1) captivity, into which one is led or in which one is; 2) driving away (of the cattle). Both significations are also used as concretes in the sense of prisoner or prisoners; but it is never used as an adj., see שְׁבִיָּה.

שֹׁבַי p.n. m. (captivator).

שֹׁבִי p.n. m. (the same).

שָׁבִיב (const. שְׁבִיב) m. a glow, a flame, from שָׁבַב I.

שְׁבִיב adj. fem. (from a masc. שְׁבִי) female prisoner.

שְׁבִיָּה (Aram.) m. the same.

שִׁבְיָה (formed from שְׁבִי) f. captivity; but also concrete, like שְׁבִי.

שְׁבִיל (once in Ketib שְׁבוּל, pl. const. שְׁבִילֵי) m. way, path. See שָׁבַל.

שְׁבָיִם (only pl. שְׁבִיסִים) caps of network, from שָׁבַץ=שָׁבַם.

שְׁבִיעִי ordinal number m., שְׁבִיעִית f. the seventh; the fem. alone sometimes, the seventh year.

שְׁבִית f. equiv. to שְׁבוּת captivity.

שָׁבַךְ belongs to the p.n. שׁוֹבָךְ, which see.

שָׂבַךְ (not used) to knot, to entwine. Related is סָבַךְ, and the root is also found in בָּךְ, אָרַבָךְ.

שָׂבָךְ (only pl. שְׂבָכִים) masc. lattice work.

שַׂבְּכָא see סַבְּכָא.

שְׂבָכָה (pl. —כוֹת) f. lattice or network, transf. to trap-gate or trapdoor.

שָׁבַל (not used) 1) to roll on, to flow, stream along; 2) to walk, to go, synon. with אָזַל, יָבַל, in the same mode of transferring the sense; 3) to totter, to shake; hence, of the shaking or waving of branches, ears of corn, etc.

שֹׁבֶל m. trail or train of a garment, from שָׁבַל to flow.

שַׁבְּלוּל (after the forms נַאֲצוּץ, נַאֲפוּף) m. snail, so called from the moisture which it imparts whilst moving along, from שָׁבַל to flow.

שִׁבֹּלֶת (pl. שִׁבֳּלִים, but const. שִׁבְּלֵי for שִׁבֳּלֵי) fem. 1) ear of corn, so called from its waving; branch, bough of a tree; 2) streaming, flowing, from שָׁבַל 1.

שָׂבַם (not used) probably only transposed from בָּשַׂם.

שְׂבָם (balsam-place) p. n. of a city in the territory of Reuben.

שִׂבְמָה p. n. (the same).

שָׁבַן (not used) according to the Arab. to be tender.

שְׁבְנָא (also —נָה) p.n. m. (tenderness).

שְׁבַנְיָה p.n. m. It appears a corruption from שְׁכַנְיָה or שְׁכַנְיָהוּ, both of which are sometimes used for it.

שָׁבַם (not used) equiv. to שָׁבַץ (Aram. שְׁבַשׁ) to entwine, to make net work, if the supposition is not to be adopted that שְׁבָיִם is derived from שָׁמַשׁ.

שֶׁבַע (const. שְׁבַע) 1) cardinal number

fem., שִׁבְעָה (const. שִׁבְעַת, with suff. שִׁבְעָתָם) m. (the dual form is שִׁבְעָתַיִם, comp. אַרְבַּעְתַּיִם; the plur. form is שִׁבְעִים) seven, generally before the noun, later, however, after it.—The use of the masculine form for the feminine gender and the feminine form for the masculine gender takes place in all cardinal numbers from 1 to 10, and the same peculiarity manifests itself in their composition from 11 to 20; for שִׁבְעָה עָשָׂר m., שְׁבַע עֶשְׂרֵה f. seventeen, has the same peculiarity. The dual signifies sevenfold, the plur. seventy, both masc. and fem. The use of seven as a sacred number is well known. Sometimes שֶׁבַע stands as an adv.: seven times. 2) שֶׁבַע p. n. m. (covenant); 3) שִׁבְעָה (well of the covenant) p. n. of a well. From which:—

שָׁבַע denom. (from שֶׁבַע) to swear, to testify on oath (of a covenant), either by sacrificing seven offerings or by testifying of seven witnesses, etc.; שְׁבֻעֵי שְׁבֻעוֹת they who have taken an oath; נִשְׁבַּע origin. to bind oneself by seven; next, to swear by (בְּ) a person or an object; to swear by God or by idols, i.e. to worship them; to swear by an unfortunate one, i.e. that if he breaks his word he should become unfortunate like him; נִשְׁבַּע לְ to swear to some one, with accus. of the object, i.e. to pledge oneself sacredly to fulfil something; נִשְׁבַּע מִן followed by an inf. to swear, to refrain from something. Hiph. to cause to swear, to pledge one on oath; also, to conjure, to press on some one.

שָׂבַע (in pause שָׂבָעוּ, fut. יִשְׂבַּע) to overflow, related is שָׂפַע, סָבָא; hence, like רָוָה used of anything done in abundance, as, to be filled, satiated, with drink; hence, of the earth being filled or satiated; to be satisfied with bread, with מִן, בְּ, or לְ, before the inf. Fig. 1) to be full, i.e. tired, weary of, disgusted with, something; שְׂבַע יָמִים to be full of days, weary of life; 2) to be filled with contempt or shame; 3) in the transf. sense of being frivolous, overbearing. Pi. to satisfy, satiate. Hiph. to satisfy with מִן, בְּ, of the object, and also fig.

שָׂבֵעַ (const. שְׂבַע, pl. שְׂבֵעִים) adj. m., שְׂבֵעָה f. orig. overflowing; hence, full, satisfied, and, like the verb, also in a fig. sense, e.g. שְׂבַע רָצוֹן rich in grace of God; שְׂבַע רֹגֶז full of trouble; שְׂבַע יָמִים full of days, i.e. weary of life; in one instance יָמִים is omitted.

שָׂבָע m. abundance, plenty (comp. שֶׁפַע) satiety.

שֹׂבַע (with suff. שָׂבְעֲךָ) m. the same.

שִׂבְעָה see שָׂבָע.

שָׂבְעָה (from שֹׂבַע) f. fulness, abundance, satiety.

שָׂבְעָה f. the same.

שִׁבְעָנָה m. equiv. to שִׁבְעָה, with the additional termination ־ָנָה).

שָׁבַץ (Kal, not used) equiv. to שָׁבַם, to entwine, to knot, especially of net and check-work; hence Pi. שִׁבֵּץ to embroider. Pu. to be woven, worked in, to be set (of precious stones).

שָׁבָץ m. giddiness, perplexity, from שָׁבַץ to entwine; to be intricate, in a figurative sense.

שְׁבַק (inf. מִשְׁבַּק, imp. שְׁבֻק) Aram. to leave, to forsake, abandon. The origin. signif. is like עָזַב. Ithpael, to be left.

שָׁבַר (fut. יִשְׁבֹּר) to break, to shatter; also fig., e.g. the arm, the staff. the support, the bow, i.e. to destroy the power; שָׁבוּר to be broken (of a limb); שָׁבַר is also used variously in a figurative sense, e.g. to break the heart, i.e. to mortify; to break the thirst, i.e. to quench it; also, to set a boundary by cutting off or measuring off; another signif. of שָׁבַר see under שֶׁבֶר, from which it is the denom. Niph. to be broken; of ships, to founder; of men and beasts, to be broken in the limbs, or to be injured, wounded, generally; with לֵב, figur. to be of a broken, contrite, heart; to be routed, of an army; to be reduced, of a city or a state. Pi. to dash in pieces (altars, idols), to shatter (the teeth). Hiph. to open (of the womb), orig. to cause to break through; see שֶׁבֶר. Hoph. pass. to be wounded, hurt (of the heart). The root in שָׁ־בַר is related with the roots in פַּר ,אָ־פַר ,עָ־פַר ,חָ־פַר.

שְׂבַר equiv. to סְבַר (Aram.) to hope, to wish; next, to wait, in the most extensive sense, שֹׂבֵר בְּחוֹמָה to wait or watch on the wall. Pi. שִׂבֵּר to wait, hope, to look hopefully or expectingly for (אֶל, לְ) some one.

שָׁבֵר (not used) orig. to bear, or with reference to the etymology, to nourish, feed, thus transitive, the root being שָׁ־בַר or שָׁ־בֵר, related with בָּר and בָּרָה, and from which is to be derived שֶׁבֶר, in the signification of corn.

I. שֶׁבֶר (three times שֵׁבֶר, with suff. שִׁבְרְךָ, plur. שְׁבָרִים, with suff. שְׁבָרֶיהָ) m. breach, breakage (of a limb, or of a wall); fig. wound, breach (of a state), brokenness of spirit, sadness; solution or interpretation of a dream, ruin (of a state); poetically, terror, especially in the plural.

II. שֶׁבֶר (with suff. שִׁבְרָם) m. origin. fruit, nourishment; hence, corn, related (also etymologically) with בַּר and בָּרִי, שֶׁבֶר רַעֲבוֹן corn for the hunger; שָׁבַר שֶׁבֶר to buy corn. From which:—

שָׁבַר (fut. יִשְׁבֹּר; denom. from שֶׁבֶר II.), to occupy oneself with corn, to buy or sell corn, with or without the adding of שֶׁבֶר or בַּר; fig. also of milk and wine. Hiph. to sell corn.

שֵׂבֶר (with suff. שִׂבְרִי) m. hope, expectation; הוֹבִישׁ מַשְׂ to destroy the hopes.

שִׁבָּרוֹן (const. שִׁבְרוֹן) m. the breaking, e.g. of the loins, as a figure of violent pain; transferred to ruin, destruction.

שְׁבַשׁ (Aram.) to entwine, perplex; thus related with Heb. שָׂבַךְ, שְׂבָכָה; hence Ithpael אִשְׁתַּבְּשִׁין to become confused, perplexed (with reference to the mind).

שָׁבַת (fut. יִשְׁבֹּת and יִשְׁבַּת) 1) to rest, to keep holiday, to cease (מִן) from labour; of land that is not cultivated; of the wayfaring man who ceases wandering; of the elders who rest from the gate, i.e. who visit it no more; 2) to cease, generally, to refrain from (מִן) something; fig. to be at an end, to vanish. Niph. to perish. Hiph. causative of the various significations of Kal: 1) to cause or induce some one to cease from (מִן) a work, where מִן is added either before the inf. or לְבִלְתִּי; to let rest, to assuage; 2) to let rest or cease (war, strife, triumph); to cause some one to miss something; next, to remove, to destroy generally. It is related in the original signif. with יָשַׁב in the sense of resting quietly at a place.

שֶׁבֶת (with suff. שִׁבְתּוֹ) m. abiding, resting, ceasing from labour; also, interruption, loss of time, indolence. In some passages, שֶׁבֶת may be taken as an infin. from יָשַׁב.

שַׁבָּת (appears to be formed from שַׁבֶּתֶת; const. שַׁבַּת, with suffix, שַׁבַּתּוֹ, pl. שַׁבָּתוֹת, const. שַׁבְּתוֹת) com. day of rest, sabbath, not occasioned, but a regularly fixed day (the seventh day of the week), as is expressed by the intensitive form שׁ׳ שַׁבָּת to celebrate the sabbath; שַׁבַּת שַׁבָּת, שַׁבָּת בְּשַׁבַּתּוֹ sabbath after sabbath, i.e. every sabbath; שַׁבַּת שָׁנִים the sabbatical year, or year of release generally; 2) a week.

שַׁבָּתוֹן (formed from שַׁבָּת, with the termination וֹן—) m. great sabbath, a more intense signif. than שַׁבָּת, and, when joined with it, signifies an extraordinary festival.

שַׁבְּתַי p.n. masc. (one born on the sabbath).

שָׂגָא (not used) equiv. to שָׁגָה II., which see; from which שְׁגִיאָה, and:—

שָׂגֵא p.n. m. (the erring one).

שָׂגָא (Kal, only fut. יִשְׂגֶּה, as if from שָׂגָה) to grow, to become great, to be exalted, related to גָּאָה. Hiph. הִשְׂגִּיא (fut. יַשְׂגִּיא) to make great, to increase, fig. to praise.

שְׂגָא (fut. יִשְׂגֵּא) Aram. the same, to laud, to exalt. "May your joy increase" (יִשְׂגֵּא), is a form of saluting.

שָׂגַב 1) transitive, orig. equiv. to זָקַף to raise up; next, to make one high, mighty, to protect; 2) intrans. to be high, elevated, to be protected, firm; שׂ׳ יֵשַׁע to be or become strong in help. Niph. נִשְׂגַּב to be exalted (of God), fig. to be inscrutable, incomprehensible; also, to be protected, secured. Pi. to raise, protect, save; with מִן of the person, from whom one is saved. Pu. pass. Hiph. to manifest greatness or exaltation (of God).

שָׁגַג equiv. to שָׁגָה, שׁוּג to err, to offend or transgress through error or ignorance, in contrast to הֵזִיד. The orig. signif. is to totter, like a person who is confused. Related is שָׁגַע; בְּשַׁגָּם, Gen. 6:3, is rendered by some as the inf. with suff., in their erring; possibly, however, it is an adv., formed from the noun שַׁג with ־ָם).

שָׁגַג belongs to שִׁגְשֵׁג. See שׁוּג.

שְׁגָגָה (with suff. שִׁגְגָתוֹ) f. an error, mistake, transgression from ignorance or error.

I. שָׁגָה (only in the derivative שִׁגָּיוֹן) to call loudly, to sing; the root שָׁג״ח is found also in ר־־ח. The signif. of occupying oneself with something is found only in modern Hebrew.

II. שָׁגָה equiv. to שָׁגַג 1) to wander, to go astray (of sheep), with מִן, to go astray from the path; also, to reel (from intoxication, either of wine, or from love); 2) figur. like שָׁגַג, to err, to offend through ignorance or mistake; with מִן, to go astray (from the law of God, etc.). Hiph. to lead astray, the blind, the pious), to mislead, to seduce. In its orig. signif. related with שָׁגַע. See שָׁגַג.

שָׂגָה equiv. to שָׂגָא to grow, to increase, only fut. יִשְׂגֶּה. Hiph. to increase, make great, rich, abundant. (The signif. in Hiph. is rather uncertain).

שְׂגוּב p. n. m. (the protected one). The Keri has שְׂגִיב.

שָׁגַח (Kal, not used) equiv. to שָׁעָה, שָׂכָה to look upon something attentively; hence, Hiph. הִשְׁגִּיחַ to direct one's attention or care upon (אֶל) some one or something; with מִן, to view from somewhere, e. g. from the window; הַשְׁגָּחָה, in modern Hebrew, providence.

שַׂגִּיא adj. masc., great (in power), mighty, from שָׂגָא.

שַׂגִּיא (Aram.) adj. m., שַׂגִּיאָן f. pl. great, mighty, probably also as an adv. greatly.

שְׁגִיאָה (from שָׁגָא) fem. error, going astray; hence, transgression through error.

שָׁגַל (fut. יִשְׁגַּל) to glow, to be fervent (synon. with יָחַם); transf. to lie with a woman, connubial intercourse in a sensual signif.; hence שָׁכַב being substituted for it in the Keri by the Massorites. Niph. pass. Pu. the same. The root is שָׁגַל, and related to that in קָלָה, גָּחַל.

שֵׁגָל (after the form צֶלַע, עֵנָב) fem. origin. abstract, connubial intercourse; next conc. wife or spouse, even without any obscene secondary sense.

שֵׁגַל (only with suff. שֵׁגְלָתֵהּ, שֵׁגְלָתָךְ) Aram. the same.

שַׁגָּם adv. from שַׁג (from שָׁגַג), formed with the adverbial termination ָם; must be rendered "as to their erring." Some take it as an inf. from שָׁגַג, with suff., which is, however, less probable.

שָׁגַע (Kal, not used) orig. to wander about without any certain object or purpose, thus related with שָׁגָה II.; hence, Pu. to be tossed about, to rave, to be maddened. Hith. to rove about, to rave.

שִׁגָּעוֹן m. madness, raving.

שָׁגַר (not used) to throw down; hence, to send off, send away; transf. to bear or cast (of cattle). Comp. נָפַל, מָלַט.

שֶׁגֶר (const. שְׁגַר, like זֶרַע, סְחַר, from זָרַע, סָחַר) m. that which is cast, the young (of cattle).

שַׁד (pl. שָׁדַיִם, const. שְׁדֵי, with suff. שָׁדַי) m. female breast for suckling (of man and beast), from שָׁדָה to suckle. Comp. the root in לְשַׁד. It is also used to signify the seat of sensuality.

שֵׁד (pl. שֵׁדִים) m. orig. the destroyer, the violent one; transf. to destructive demon, devil; זָבַח לַשֵּׁדִים

to sacrifice to the demons or devils. The root is שׁוּד.

שֹׁד m. 1) from שָׁדַד rigour, oppression, violence, desolation, destruction; hence, robbery, depredation; שֹׁד עֲנִיִּים that which has been exacted from the poor, or that of which they have been robbed; שֹׁד בְּהֵמוֹת desolation by wild beasts; שֹׁד לָהֶם desolation upon them! 2) for שַׁדַּי from שָׁדָה breast, comp. שַׁד.

שֵׂד only pl. שִׂדִּים (plain) p. n. of a valley, the spot where subsequently the Dead Sea was.

שָׁדַד (3 pret. pl. שַׁדּוּ and שָׁדְדוּ, inf. שָׁדוֹד and שְׁדוֹד, fut. יָשׁוּד for יָשֹׁד, but with suffix יְשָׁדֵּם, (יְשָׁדְדֵם) orig. to hurt, to injure; next, to act harshly, violently, cruelly, to exercise violence against some one; שֹׁדֵד a robber; שָׁדוּד overpowered, conquered, slain. Transferred, to desolate, devastate. Niph. to be destroyed, desolated. Pi. to practise violence, to hurt. Pu. שֻׁדַּד and שֻׁדַּד to be desolated, laid waste. Poal like Piel. Hoph. הוּשַׁד to be treated with violence.

שָׂדַד (Kal, not used) orig. to part, separate. Pi. שִׂדֵּד to break (the clods), i.e. to harrow the soil for ploughing; from which שַׂד a harrowed field, i.e. a plain.

I. שָׁדָה (not used) to wet, to moisten; hence, to suckle, from which שַׁד and שֹׁד 2. Related is the root לָשַׁד, which see.

II. שָׁדָה (not used) after the Aram. to throw, cast, fling; from which שְׁדֵיאוּר.

שָׂדָה (not used) equiv. to שָׂדַד to break the clods, to harrow; hence, to make the soil plain, even.

שִׁדָּה (formed from a masc. שֵׁד, pl. שִׁדּוֹת) fem. a princess, a lady, a mistress, a wife, thus from שָׁדַד in the signification of ruling. According to the LXX., which renders it male and female butler, the reading is שִׁדָּה וְשִׁדּוֹת in Ecc. 2:8; according to the Targum, fountain, in the signification of שְׁדָא to pour forth.

שָׂדֶה, שָׂדַי (const. שְׂדֵה, pl. שָׂדוֹת const. שְׂדוֹת and שְׂדֵי, with suff. שְׂדֹתָם, שְׂדוֹתֵיהֶם, but also שְׂדֵי, שָׂדֶיךָ) masc. harrowed soil, arable land, plough-field, in contrast to forest, mountain, garden, and vineyard; transf. to 1) field, as suburb of a town, also village district; 2) in contrast to inhabited districts, e.g. אִישׁ שָׂדֶה, חַיַּת הַשָּׂדֶה, where it must be taken in the sense of a waste; it also signifies a plain, especially in the designation of certain tracts of land, e.g. שְׂדֵה

אֲרָם the plain of Aram, i.e. Mesopotamia; sometimes also continent, in contrast to sea.

שַׁדּוּן (from שַׁד formed with the termination וּן—) m. Keri for שַׁדִּין.

שַׁדַּי (from שַׁד formed with the old adj. termination ַי—) masc. the almighty, all-powerful, omnipotent. It is erroneous to take the word in a plural sense.

שָׂדַי m. equiv. to שָׂדֶה a field; שָׂדַי is the older form, and used in poetic language.

שְׁדֵיאוּר p.n. m. (darting fire).

שִׂדִּים p.n. of a valley, see שַׂד.

שַׁדִּין m. the powerful, mighty one; from שַׁד, with the termination ִין—; only thus according to one reading. See שַׁדּוּן.

שָׁדַם (not used) according to some equiv. to שָׁדַף to singe, to burn, as שְׁדֵמָה once occurs in the signification of שְׁדֵפָה; but this interpretation is not suitable to the general sense of שְׁדֵמָה. See:—

שְׁדֵמָה (pl. שְׁדֵמוֹת, const. שַׁדְמוֹת) f. 1) a field, plantation for corn or vines; שַׁדְמוֹת קִדְרוֹן fields of Kidron, i.e. the surrounding district. Possibly שְׁדֵמָה may be an enlarged form of שָׂדֶה, or the root is שָׁדַם in the sense of cutting or harrowing; 2) by interchanging of מ and פ, *for* שְׁדֵפָה, which see.

שָׁדַף to singe, to burn, to parch, to blast (by the east wind, which parches and blackens the corn). The root is שָׁדַף, and related is that in שַׁב, רָ־צַף, רָ־שַׁף, etc.

שְׁדֵפָה f. burning of corn, blackened or blighted corn.

שִׁדָּפוֹן m. a blackening or blight of the corn, caused by the east wind.

שְׁדַר (Aram.) equiv. to שָׁדַל to strive, to desire, pursue, hunt eagerly, after something. Ithpael אִשְׁתַּדַּר to exert oneself, to make strong efforts, followed by the inf. and לְ.

שָׂדַר (not used) equiv. to סָדַר to put in order, arrange, adjust.

שְׂדֵרָה (only pl. שְׂדֵרוֹת) f. an order, row of soldiers or of chambers; according to Kimchi, also of the rows of cedar beams.

שַׁדְרַךְ (majestic, from *Khsatkra*, with the suff. *Ka*, Sendic) p.n.

שֶׂה (not used) an ancient monosyllable root for שַׁי present, gift, as מָה, נָה, יָה, belong to מִי, נִי, דַּי. The signification is like the root in נָשָׁה to put oneself under an obligation to some one, to be attached to some one, thus like לָוָה, which subsequently was transf. to borrowing.

שָׁה (not used) a monosyllable root to be adopted for שָׁוָה, of which it is evidently a participle form, signifying to arise, to come into existence, to be born (of small cattle, sheep). From which:—

שֶׂה (particip. form, const. שֵׂה, but with suff. שֵׂיו, שֵׂיהוּ, with *yod* for the ה radical on account of *sere*) com. young (orig. equiv. to וָלָד in the Talmud) of sheep or goats; hence the necessity of an additional word to define the kind.

שָׂהַד (not used) orig. equiv. to סָעַד to confirm, transf. to witness, to confirm by evidence. A similar etymology is found in עוּד.

שָׂהֵד (a particip. form but where the *kamets* remains before the suff., with suff. שָׂהֲדִי) m. a witness.

שָׂהֲדוּ (def. שָׂהֲדוּתָא) f. evidence, testimony, from שָׂהַד equiv. to שָׂהֵד.

שָׂהָה (adopted as a root for תְּשִׂי Deut. 33:18, where it stands for תְּשְׂהִי) equiv. to נָשָׂה.

שָׂהַם (not used) to be of a pale green colour, related to שָׁם (שׁוּם), from which שׁוּם leek, on account of its pale green colour.

שֹׂהַם m. leek coloured, pale green precious stone; hence the LXX. *ὁ λίθος ὁ πράσινος*. The commentators are at variance in reference to its speciality; according to some it is the onyx, according to others the sardonyx.

שָׂהַר (not used) equiv. to סָהַר, צָהַר to shine, glitter, from which שַׂהַר the moon, orig. the shining one; from which:—

שַׂהֲרֹן (only pl. שַׂהֲרֹנִים) m. an ornament worn on the neck, and resembling the moon or half-moon, in the shape of a crescent; derived from שַׂהַר.

שׁוּ only once in Ketib for שָׁוְא.

I. שׁוּא (not used) equiv. to שָׁאָה to rage, transf. to be shuddering, amazing, desolate, to lie waste. Similar gradations of the sense are found in שָׁאָה.

II. שׁוּא (not used) orig. to stray, to reel; from which, to fail.

שׁוֹא (only pl. with suff. מִשֹּׁאֵיהֶם) m. terror, trembling, shuddering; hence, ruin, destruction.

שָׁוְא (after the form מָוֶת from מוּת, thus שָׁוְא from שׁוּא, if it is not a transposition from שָׁאוּ) masc. 1) error, mistake; next, vice, sin (through ignorance), and like אָוֶן falsehood, deceit, lie, vanity, nothingness, either as a subst. or an adv.; 2) like שׁוֹא or שׁוֹאָה, destruction, ruin. It is more probable, however, that the origin. signif. of the root is שׁוּא to blow, to storm, somewhat like הָבַל, און (in אָוֶן); hence like אָוֶן, הֶבֶל, breath, i.e. transient, false, perishable; next, sin, and according to another, development of the orig. signif. storm, tempest, destruction, calamity; לַשָּׁוְא in vain. As a p.n. see שָׁרְיָה.

שׁוֹאָה (const. ־אַת) f. orig. shuddering, terror; hence, storm, tempest which bursts forth violently and desolates), ruin, downfall, destruction; also concr. a desolated place, ruin.

שׁוּב (fut. יָשׁוּב, יָשֹׁב, apoc. יָשָׁב, infin. abs. שׁוֹב, imp. שׁוּבָה) origin. to turn, turn round (related to אָף, סָבַב); hence, with מִן, to turn away (from a place), with מֵאַחֲרֵי, from some one previously followed; with אֶל or acc. to turn towards something. From which: 1) to return to (עַל, עַד, בְּ, אֶל, לְ) some one or something, e.g. to God; and without addition, to repent, inasmuch as it is returning to God; figur. with לְ or אֶל, to be restored to the possession of something; 2) of inanimate objects, to be restored to their former state, i.e. of a diseased limb, to be healed; of a command or prophesy, to be recalled; of a thing, to be restored to its owner; שׁוּב אַף the anger is turned away, i. e. is relaxed; with מִן to forbear from being angry with some one; שׁוּב אֶל־עָפָר to turn to dust again; 3) to abandon or desist from (מִן) a resolution; 4) to repeat an action or deed; or used as an adv. again, e.g. וַיָּשָׁב וַיִּשְׁלַח and he sent again; 5) to lead back, as שָׁב שְׁבוּת to lead back the captives. Po. שׁוֹבֵב 1) to lead back the exile, to restore (נְתִיבוֹת) the path; fig. with נֶפֶשׁ, to refresh; 2) to lead away; fig. to lead to rebellion, revolt. Pu. שׁוֹבַב pass. to be returned; figur. be saved, restored. Hiph. הֵשִׁיב (fut. יָשִׁיב, apoc. יָשֵׁב, יָשֶׁב, causative from all the significations of Kal: 1) to lead back (the captives), to withdraw (the hand), to refresh, with נֶפֶשׁ, i.e. to restore, breath, life; 2) to drive back, to keep off, to hinder, to turn away the face from some one, i.e. not to countenance him; to turn away the anger, i.e. to pacify one; 3) fig. to restore, to compensate, requite, with לְ and עַל of the person; to return words, מִלִּין אֲמָרִים, i.e. to reply; with to bring back word, tidings; or in this sense, הֵשִׁיב alone, to answer; 4) to recall, renounce, to compensate, or bring an offering, a tribute. The sense of the verb must be rendered according to the prep. following, e.g. with מִן, מֵעַל to turn away from some one or something; with אֶל, עַל, to turn towards some one or something; הֵשִׁיב יָד עַל, בְּ, to turn the hand against some one; הֵשִׁיב עַל, אֶל לֵב to lay to heart, to consider well, to repent. Hoph. pass. to be led back, restored.

שׂוּב (1 pret. שַׂבְתִּי, part. שָׂב) origin. to be white, especially of the white or grey hair of the aged; hence, to become grey or old; שָׂב the aged, hoary man. The root is found again qualified in כֶּ־סֶף.

שׁוּבָאֵל equiv. to שְׁבוּאֵל.

שׁוֹבָב pl. ־ִים) adj. masc. rebellious, backsliding, orig. a participial form; 2) p.n. m. (the backsliding).

שׁוֹבֵב adj. m., שׁוֹבֵבָה f. the same.

שׁוּבָה f. restoration, reviving, refreshing, comp. הֵשִׁיב נֶפֶשׁ.

שׁוֹבָךְ p.n. m. one that pours forth, (from שָׁפַךְ=שָׁבַךְ). In a parallel passage שׁוֹפָךְ.

שׁוֹבֶךְ equiv. to סְבָךְ, which see.

שׁוֹבָל p.n. m. (wanderer).

שׁוֹבֵק p.n. m. (one that forsakes).

שׁוּג (not used) equiv. to שָׁגָה, to err, to go astray, from which מְשׁוּגָה, which see.

I. **שׂוּג** (Kal, not used) to turn back, equiv. to סוּג; hence Niph. נָשׂוֹג, more frequently נָסוֹג.

II. **שׂוּג** (Kal, not used) equiv. to סוּג to hedge in (comp. שׂוּךְ), from which the reduplicate form שִׂגְשֵׂג to hedge in (a wine-plant).

שׁוֹד as a noun, see שֹׁד.

שׁוּד (fut. יָשׁוּד) 1) to be violent, to hurt, injure, destroy; 2) to prevail, rule, domineer, from which שֵׁד, but שַׁד in שָׁדַיִם belongs to שָׁדָה.

שׁוּד (not used) equiv. to זוּד to seethe, to hiss, from which שִׁיד, and from that again the denom. שׂוּד.

שָׁוָה to be even, smooth, without rising or deepening (comp. שְׁעָה in the Aram.); transf. to be equal, alike in reference to value, merit, profit, gain, in quantity or quality, and may be rendered, suitable, corresponding, sufficient, appropriate, serviceable, similar, etc. שָׁוָה is construed with לְ or בְּ, of the object to which another is like or resembles. It is also used impersonally, e. g. שָׁוָה לִי satisfaction was given to me, i.e. I have been requited according to merit; שָׁוָה לְ it is suitable, agreeable, to some one. Pi. 1) to make even, smooth (a plain), to smooth the soul, i.e. to assuage it; sometimes נֶפֶשׁ is elliptical; 2) to put, to set in order; hence שִׁוָּה עֵזֶר, הָדָר עַל to afford assistance to some one, to bestow beauty; שִׁוָּה פְּרִי to prepare fruit; שִׁוָּה כְּ to make like something. Pu. only once תְּשֻׁוֶּה, probably for תְּשֻׁאֶה, and does not belong to this root. Hiph. to compare, to liken to some one (לְ). Nithpael (a composition from Niph. and Hith.); נִשְׁתַּוָּה to be mutually alike, only Prov. 27:15.

שְׁוָה (Aram.) equiv. to שָׁוָה Heb. to be equal, to be likened, part. pass. שְׁוִי in Ketib. Pael, to liken, to compare with (עִם) something. Ithpael, to be made like or into (accus.) something; comp. Heb. שָׁוָה in signif. 2.

שָׁוֵה (a particip. form) m. a plain; hence in proper nouns, as עֵמֶק שָׁוֵה and שָׁוֵה קִרְיָתַיִם.

שׁוּחַ (fut. יָשׁוּחַ) equiv. to שָׁחַח, שָׁחָה to sink down, to be bowed down, to sink unto death (אֶל מָוֶת), to be bowed down to the dust (לֶעָפָר), the soul is bowed down within me (עָלַי), i.e. dejected. Hiph. like Kal, but only in Keri.

שׁוּחַ p.n. m. (the bowed down one), hence the name of a tribe, patron. שׁוּחִי.

I. שׁוּחַ (not used) equiv. to שָׂגָה to sprout, to grow forth; from which שִׂיחַ shrub.

II. שׂוּחַ (inf. const. שׂוּחַ) origin. to speak, to tell; transf. 1) to lament, implore, pray; 2) to speak in the heart, to give oneself up to religious reflection, to meditate, to think: the same gradation of the sense from speaking to thinking is found in הָגָה. Pilpel שׂוֹחֵחַ to meditate or to speak on (בְּ) something (e.g. the works of God), but if construed with the acc. it signifies the same as שִׂיחַ with the acc. (Ps. 145:5), i.e. to speak, tell, or declare. Hiph. only in the abridged form שִׂיחַ for הֵשִׂיחַ to speak; with לְ, to some one; with בְּ, on some subject, i.e. to make some subject the topic of meditation or conversation; with acc. to converse with, to address some one. Sometimes also in the signification of, to sing, to lament.

שׁוּחָה f. 1) orig. depth; hence, a pit, abyss; 2) p.n. m. (probably for שׁוּחָם).

שׁוּחָם p.n. m. (the bowed down one), for which חֻשִׁים stands in the parallel passage.

I. שׁוּט equiv. to שָׁאַט, שָׁטַט origin. to tread with the feet; hence, to despise. Particip. שָׁאט with quiescent א, like in קָאם. See שׁוּט.

II. שׁוּט (fut. יָשׁוּט) 1) to move to and fro (comp. סוּט in the Talmud), from which to row, i.e. to move a boat by rowing; שָׁטִים the rowers; 2) intr. to rove about, שׁוּט בָּאָרֶץ to go to and fro (wander or rove) on the earth. Piel שׁוֹטֵט to rove about, to run to and fro; with בְּ, of the place; figur. to investigate, to search. Hith. הִתְשׁוֹטֵט to drive about, move about.

שׁוֹט (pl. שׁוֹטִים) masc. a scourge or whip, so called on account of its motion to and fro; the scourge of the tongue, i.e. slander; the overflowing scourge, i.e. an invading army that overruns the country,

שׂוּט equiv. to שָׂטָה to incline, to turn towards something, e.g. כָּזָב lying.

שׂוּךְ (particip. שָׂךְ) 1) equiv. to שָׂכַךְ, orig. to twist, entwine; next, to hedge in, to fence, transf. to protect; with בַּעַד, to make a hedge round one, i.e. to protect him; 2) to enclose, to shut up, to block up the road. Pi. שׂוֹכֵךְ to twist, to weave, e.g. Job 10:11, Thou hast woven me out of bones and sinews; the Auth. Vers. renders it in the sense of signif. 1, "Thou hast fenced me with bones and sinews."

שׂוֹךְ (with suff. שׂוֹכֹה) m. entwining of branches, hedge, fence.

שׂוֹכָה f. the same.

שׂוֹכוֹ (for שׂוֹכוֹן thorn-hedge) p. n. of a city in the territory of Judah.

שׂוּכָתִי gent. noun of a place שׂוּכָה.

שׁוּל (not used) to hang down, and to move to and fro; related to שָׁבַל. The root is also found in נָשַׁל.

שׁוּל (pl. שׁוּלִים) masc. 1) train (of a garment), equiv. to שֹׁבֶל; to turn up the trail is a phrase indicative of the greatest dishonor; 2) the seam or hem of a garment.

שׁוֹלָל (probably for מְשׁוֹלָל) masc. 1) stripped naked, hence in conjunction with עָרוֹם, from שָׁלַל to pull off; 2) bound in chains, from the same root, from which שַׁלְשֶׁלֶת in modern Hebrew; according to others, a prisoner.

שׁוּלַמִּית p. n. fem. (probably formed from שׁוּנֵם=שׁוּלֵם, from which it is a gent. noun).

I. שׂוּם (only 3 pret. שָׂם, Ecc. 3:17) to value, to appraise; with עַל, to test something whether it is good or bad; the verb is very common in modern Hebrew.

II. שׁוּם (not used) to be pale green, of plants; or related with the root in נָשַׁם to exhale, comp. שֹׁהַם. From which:—

שׁוּם (pl. שׁוּמִים) m. leek, garlick, so called either on account of its pale green colour, or on account of its strong smell.

שׂוּם (pret. שָׂם, fut. seldom יָשׂוּם, inf. abs. שׂוֹם, const. שׂוּם) 1) to set, to place, to put, like the root in אָרָם, but in the signif. like שׁוּת, to set a tree, i.e. to plant it; to set a building, i.e. to found it; to set a people, i.e. to form a nation; to set the name of God somewhere, i.e. to erect an edifice for divine worship, thus equiv. to שִׁכֵּן שֵׁם; to beget children; to arrange an army or camp, sometimes with the omission of מַחֲנֶה; to appoint a king or judge over (עַל) something; to determine, to fix; the significations must be determined according to the context; 2) of inanimate objects, to lay; to lay down the wrath, i.e. to heap it up; to take to heart, with אֶל, עַל; to lay before one, or to submit to, with אֶל or בְּאָזְנֵי; שׂוּם לְנֶגֶד to lay something down before one's eyes, i.e. clearly; to impose a burden or a duty, with לְ, עַל, בְּ; to lay the fire, to put on garments, with accus.; 3) to set or to lay, with the sub-signification of direction, in reply to the question whither, e.g. שׂוּם לֵב, פָּנִים, עַיִן to direct the heart, the face, the eye, towards something, construed with לְ, עַל, אֶל, seldom with the omission of לֵב; 4) to make to something, i.e. to change one's circumstances or position; שׂוּם אִלֵּם to make dumb, with acc., לְ, כְּ, of the predicate; next generally, to make, to do, e.g. wonders; followed by לְ of the person, to prepare something for some one, to give, to afford. Hiph. often in the abridged form שִׂים for הֲשִׂים, but entire in the signification of Kal. Hoph. only in the Keri, pass.

שׂוּם (Aram.) the same, שׂוּם שֵׁם to give a name, שׂוּם טְעֵם עַל to regard; שׂוּם בָּל לְ to be concerned for something or some one. Ith. אִתְּשָׂם to be laid in timber (in the wall), to be made into something, to be changed to something.

I. שׁוּן (not used) equiv. to שָׁאַן to be still, to be quiet, from which שׁוּנִי, which see.

II. שׁוּן (not used) to piss, from which שִׁין to piss, and the denom. שָׁתַן, which see.

שׁוּנִי p.n. m. (fortunate one). The patron. has the same form.

שׁוּנֵם (probably contracted from שׁוּנַיִם two resting places) p.n. of a city in the territory of Issachar; gent. m. שׁוּנַמִּי, —מִּית f.

שָׁוַע (Kal, not used) to call, to cry (related to צָוַח), hence Pi. שִׁוַּע to cry for help in trouble, to cry loudly in prayer; hence synon. with הִתְפַּלֵּל, צָעַק and forming a paranomasia with הוֹשִׁיעַ Psalm 18:42.

שׁ (not used) equiv. to יָשַׁע to be wide, broad, spacious; hence equiv. to רָוַח to be enlarged, i.e. happy, rich, powerful, in contrast to צַר to be straitened or in trouble; from which the noun תְּשׁוּעָה, and not from יָשַׁע.

שֶׁ (with suff. שַׁוְעִי) m. cry for help, imploring, prayer.

שׁ m. 1) (the happy, rich, noble one) from שׁוּעַ; 2) equiv. to שֶׁוַע cry for help.

שׁ (with suff. שׁוּעֲךָ) m. 1) abstract: riches, fortune, happiness, from שׁוּעַ; 2) cry for help, from שֶׁוַע; 3) p. n. m. (the rich one), equiv. to שׁוֹעַ.

שׁוּעָא (probably abbreviated from שׁוּעָאִי) p. n. m. the rich one.

שַׁוְעָה call or cry for help, formed from שֶׁוַע.

שׁוּעָל (pl. שׁוּעָלִים and שֻׁ־) m. 1) orig. one that excavates, digs out; hence, a fox, a jackal, or a similar animal, which digs its own cave or hole, from שָׁעַל to hollow out; 2) p.n.m.; 3) complete אֶרֶץ שׁוּעָל (jackal-land), p. n. of a district in the territory of Benjamin; comp. the proper names שַׁעֲלִים and שַׁעַלְבִים.

שׁוֹעֵר (denom. from שַׁעַר gate) masc. gate-keeper.

I. שׁוּף (only fut.) equiv. to שָׁפַף to pierce, to stick into something; hence in the Targum for דְּכָא, construed with accusative; transf. to break to pieces, to bruise, Job. 9:17.

II. שׁוּף to veil, wrap round, to cover; חֹשֶׁךְ יְשׁוּפֵנִי darkness shall cover me.

שׁוֹפָךְ p. n. m. he that throws up the earth for a rampart, otherwise for it שׁוֹבָךְ.

שׁוּפָמִי patron. from שְׁפוּפָם, which see.

שׁוֹפָר (const. שׁוֹפַר, pl. שׁוֹפָרוֹת, const. שׁוֹפְרוֹת, with suff. שׁוֹפְרֹתֵיהֶם) m. trumpet, horn, so called on account of its being hollowed out, like חָלִיל and Aram. אַבּוּב; it is distinguished etymologically from חֲצֹצְרָה, which is so called from its clear tone; תָּקַע שׁ׳ to blow the trumpet; poetically בְּדֵי שׁוֹפָר whenever the trumpet sounds. The root is שָׁפַר in the sense of to hollow out, and the nominal form is like עוֹלָם; from the same root is the modern Heb. שְׁפוֹפֶרֶת for שְׁפַרְפֶּרֶת that which is hollowed out, a tube.

I. שׁוּק (Kal, not used) to join closely, to attach oneself to some one (thus related with the root in חָ־שַׁק, נָ־שַׁק, זִק); next, to desire, wish, long for something. Poel. שׁוֹקֵק to long, yearn for something; also, to have pleasure, delight in something (accus.), from which תְּשׁוּקָה.

II. שׁוּק (Kal, not used) to flow, to run, related with שָׁקָה, from which Poal שׁוֹקֵק, to overflow, to water the soil abundantly. Hiph. הֵשִׁיק to overflow with something. It is construed with accus., like all verbs of plenty, from which שֹׁקֶת water-trough.

שׁוֹק (dual שׁוֹקַיִם, const. שׁוֹקֵי) f. leg or lower thigh (of man or beast); poetically, foot-soldiers or people on foot; comp. רַגְלִי; גִּלָּה שׁ׳ to uncover the thigh, a phrase indicating leading into captivity; הִכָּה אוֹתָם שׁוֹק עַל יָרֵךְ he smote them hip and thigh, i. e. altogether. The general derivation of the noun from שׁוּק to run about is very uncertain.

שׁוּק (pl. שְׁוָקִים, comp. דְּוָדִים for דּוּד) masc. street, market, or market-place. The derivation is uncertain.

I. שׁוּר (generally without a fut.) orig. to sound; next, to sing something (accus.), to sing praises; with לְ, to sing to some one, i. e. to praise; with בְּ, to sing of something; with עַל, to direct a song to some one. Hiph. הֵשִׁיר, or in the abridged form שִׁיר, in the same sense as Kal, by which some grammarians were misled to take שִׁיר for the root. Po. שׁוֹרֵר to attune a song, to praise. Part. מְשׁוֹרֵר male singer, מְשׁוֹרֶרֶת female singer. Hoph. הוּשַׁר to be sung (a song).

II. שׁוּר (fut. יָשׁוּר) to run about, to walk about, to travel, journey (for mercantile purposes); with לְ, to go to some one; בַּשֶּׁמֶן to go to some one with ointment, or with anointed head. From which תְּשׁוּרָה; related is תּוּר.

III. שׁוּר (fut. יָשׁוּר) to look, to view, to behold, to look down, to watch, either for a hostile purpose, or to assist or care for some one; related to תּוּר to spy. Po. שׁוֹרֵר to lie in wait for some one; part. שׁוֹרֵר for מְשׁוֹרֵר one who lies in wait, or watches an enemy.

IV. שׁוּר (not used) to be straight, erect, just; thus related with the root in אָשַׁר, בָּשַׁר, יָשַׁר. According to others, the orig. signif. of the root is to put in order, to arrange, to adjust; from which שׁוּר and שַׂר.

שׁוּר (pl. with suff. שׁוּרַי) m. 1) he that watches or lies in wait, an enemy, from שׁוּר III.; 2) (with the pl. שׁוּרוֹת, with suff. שׁוּרוֹתָם) a wall, from שׁוּר IV.; next, houses, or a row of houses; 3) p.n. of a city on the borders of Egypt and Palestine. There is now a place called Shur, in the vicinity of Suez. מִדְבַּר שׁוּר is the present Dschofar.

שׁוּר (def. שׁוּרָא, ־יָה) Aram. masc. a wall.

שׁוֹר (with suff. שׁוֹרְךָ, pl. שְׁוָרִים) m. a bullock, an ox, epically used for a cow (Job 21:10). Its general signif. is an animal of the ox kind; the collective of it is בָּקָר. The verb שְׁוַר in Aram., is derived from שׁוֹר. See תּוֹר.

I. שׁוּר (only inf. with suff. שׁוּרִי) equiv. to סוּר to turn away from (מִן) some one, to move back, to deviate. The Masora counts this word among those that must be read with ס.

II. שׁוּר (fut. apoc. וַיָּשַׂר) *serrare*, to saw, from which מַשּׂוֹר, for which a root נָשַׂר, has been erroneously adopted.

III. שׂוּר equiv. to שָׂרָה, שָׂרַר to rule, to prevail, fut. apoc. וַיָּשַׂר. The original signif. appears to be, to shine; thus שַׂר, שָׂר, equiv. to סָהַר, from which the sense of greatness, distinction, and next, to rule. Hiph. הֵשִׂיר to cause to rule, to appoint for a ruler.

IV. שׁוּר (not used) to put in order, in a row, arrange (related to דּוּר, תּוּר). From which שׁוּרָה, but מְשׂוּרָה is from שׂוּר II.

שׁוּרָה f. a row, series; as an adv., in rows.

שׁוֹרֵק see שֹׂרֵק.

שׁוּשׁ (not used) to be white or grey, as is evident from the derivatives שׁוֹשַׁנָּה, שׁוֹשָׁן, שׁוּשַׁן, שֵׁשׁ, שַׁיִשׁ, יָשִׁישׁ, יָשֵׁשׁ.

שׂוּשׂ (fut. יָשׂוּשׂ, inf. שׂוֹשׂ, const. שׂוּשׂ) orig. to hop, to spring; next, to rejoice, to be glad; comp. גּוּל (the same signification is, according to some, in סוּס); with עַל or בְּ to rejoice over something, שׂוּשׂ בַּיְיָ to rejoice in the Lord. Hiph. (in the preterite only in the abridged form, שִׂישׂ for הֵשִׂישׂ, fut. יָשִׂישׂ) the same.

שַׁוְשָׁא p.n. m., a corrupted form of שְׂרָיָה, which see.

שׁוּשַׁן m. 1) a lily, origin. the white flower; מַעֲשֵׂה שׁ׳ lily-formed work, as an ornament on the pillars; 2) name of a song or melody, or a musical instrument, but only in connection with עֵדוּת; 3) p.n. of the metropolis of Susiana, where Schusch is now situated, on the river Choaspes. See שׁוֹשָׁן.

שׁוֹשָׁן (only pl. שׁוֹשַׁנִּים) m. 1) lily, like שׁוּשַׁן; 2) lily-formed work on columns; 3) name of an instrument. In all three significations only in the plural.

שׁוֹשַׁנָּה f. lily. The root is שׁוּשׁ.

שׁוּשַׁנְכָיֵא (Aram.) gent. plur. from שׁוּשַׁן, an inhabitant of Susa.

שׁוּשַׁק p. n. Ketib for the Keri שִׁישַׁק.

I. שׁוּת (not שִׁית, hence the pret. שַׁת, שָׁתָה; joined with the affixes תִּי, תָּ, the radical ת is united with them, as שַׁתָּה, שַׁתִּי, inf. abs. שׁוֹת, but in the fut. the Hiph. form is used), to put, to set, to place, to lay; thus synon. with שׂוּם, and like it in the various significations. Hiph. (in the abridged form שִׁית for הֵשִׁית, but only used in the future, imperative, and infin.), like Kal. The significations may be thus classified: 1) to set, to put, to lay; to form an army, even with omission of מַחֲנֶה; to spread a net; to place a watch or sentinel; with עַל, to array oneself against some one; to ordain over something; to add; to appoint to something; with בְּ of the place, to put one somewhere or in another position; to add some one to a number or class; to receive one among (בְּ) others; to give one a place under some one; שׁוּת עִם to place together, to compare; to set or fix a boundary or term; 2) to lay, e.g. under the feet, i.e. to submit, subjugate; to lay the hand upon (עַל) something, i.e. to protect, or of the judge, to decide; שׁוּת יָד עִם to join some one, to have intercourse with him; שׁוּת יָד מִן to withdraw the hand from some one, even with omission of יָד; שׁוּת בְּ to remove something from one place to another; שׁוּת עֲדִי עַל to put on an ornament; שׁוּת לְ to impose upon some one (a burden, a debt); to lay the blame upon some one; 3) to direct, to turn in a certain direction, as שׁוּת לֵב, פָּנִים, עֵינַיִם, to direct the face or the eyes towards somewhere, i.e. to purpose something; to direct the heart towards something, i.e. to regard it, to attend to it, with אֶל, לְ; and in all other gradations of the orig. signif., as in שׂוּם. Hoph. pass. with עַל, to be laid upon, e.g. כֹּפֶר a ransom.

II. שׁוּת (not used) equiv. to שָׁתָה II. to weave, to spin, to mix, to knot, to entwine; from which שִׁית, שֵׁת.

שׁוּתֶלַח p. n. masc. (probably a corruption or an abbreviation from מְתוּשֶׁלַח), patron. שֻׁתַלְחִי.

שְׁזַב (Pael, not used) Aram. to leave (a place); to remove from some one or something; next, to go about freely, without being confined to one place (related to עָזַב in the same sense, as in the phrase עָצוּר וְעָזוּב). Only Pael שֵׁיזֵב or שֵׁיזִיב (fut. יְשֵׁיזֵב, inf. שֵׁיזָבוּ) to release, to let escape; next, generally, to save, construed with מִן.

שָׁזַף equiv. to שָׁקַף to look, to behold; the interchanging of ז and ק to be regarded like that of צ with ק; possibly, however, the orig. signif. is to glow, to burn, related to שָׂרַף, from which the the signification to look forward ardently or fervently may be derived.

שָׁזַר (Kal, not used) to twist the thread. Hoph. past. מָשְׁזָר fine-twined linen, *byssus*. The root lies in שָׂרַר.

שַׁח adj. m. orig. to be bowed down, sunk, of the eyes; hence, dejected.

שֵׂחַ (with suff. שֵׂחוֹ) masc. equiv. to שִׂיחַ thought, reflection.

שָׁחַד (fut. יִשְׁחֹד) origin. to award; hence, to present, to make a gift, especially for bribing, to purchase deliverance from punishment; שָׁחַד בְּעַד to bribe for some one; שׁ׳ אֶת to bribe some one.

שֹׁחַד masc. a present, gift; hence, a bribe; לָקַח שׁ׳ to receive a bribe (of a judge); שָׁפַט בְּשׁ׳ to judge according to a bribe.

שָׁחָה (imp. שְׁחִי) equiv. to שׁוּחַ, שָׁחַח to stoop, bow down, to couch. Hiph. הִשְׁחָה to bring, throw, or press down. Hith. הִשְׁתַּחֲוָה (with interpolation of ו before final ה, as in נַאֲוָה; fut. יִשְׁתַּחוּ, pause —תָּחוּ, plur. יִשְׁתַּחֲווּ) to bow or throw oneself down as a sign of worship and reverence, sometimes with the addition of אַפַּיִם אַרְצָה, and with לִפְנֵי ,עַל, עַל, of the person before whom one bows; to bow down before God, i.e. to worship Him; next, to worship generally. The form מִשְׁתַּחֲוִיתֶם is a form of conjugation from the particip. as in the Aram.

שָׂחָה (inf. const. שְׂחוֹת) to swim, related to סְחָא (Aram.) to bathe. Hiph. to make to swim, bathe, according to the orig. signif.

שָׂחוּ (after the form אָחוּ) f. swimming.

שְׁחוֹחַ masc. bowing down, dejection, humiliation.

שְׂחוֹק see שְׂחֹק.

שָׁחוֹר see שָׁחֹר.

שְׁחוֹר see שִׁיחוֹר.

שַׁחוּר m. blackness, as an abstract noun from שָׁחַר.

שְׁחוּת (after the form גָּלוּת, with suff. שְׁחוּתוֹ) fem. pit, ditch, orig. deepening, from שׁוּחַ=שָׁחָה.

שָׁחַח (3 pret. שַׁח, 1 sing. שַׁחוֹתִי,

3 plur. שַׁחוּ Milrang, but also the analysed form שְׁחָחוּ; fut. יָשַׁח, and probably as an exceptional form יִשְׁחָה) to be bowed down, downcast, e.g. to the dust לֶעָפָר; to destruction אֶל־מָוֶת; of the hills being brought low, of the humbling of pride (רוּם, גַּבְהוּת), etc. שְׁחוֹחַ is a noun but not inf. Kal. Niph. to be bowed down, to be depressed, of the voice of the singer. Hiph. הֵשַׁח to bring or throw down. Hith. הִשְׁתּוֹחֵחַ to be cast down, dejected, humbled.

שָׁחַט 1) orig. to cut in pieces (the root is שָׁחַט, and related with which is (גָּר, קַר); next, to slaughter, beasts for sacrifices, also of human sacrifices; next generally to slay animals, transf. to murder, slay; חֵץ שׁוֹחֵט deadly arrow; the infin. שַׁחֲטָה only Hosea 5:2; 2) probably only a transposition of שָׁטַח to spread out, to expand; hence, זָהָב שָׁחוּט beaten gold, i.e. good gold.

שְׁחַט (fut. יִשְׁחַט) to press out, or squeeze out (grapes), Aram.

שְׁחִיטָה f. the slaughtering (of sacrifices).

שְׁחִין masc. inflammation, a boil, a sore, an ulcer, especially of the elephantiasis or of the boils of leprosy. Root שָׁחַן.

שָׁחִיס see סָחִישׁ, as in the parallel passage.

שְׂחִיף (const. שְׂחִיף) m. something meagre, thin; next, a thin piece of wood.

שְׁחִית (pl. שְׁחִיתוֹת) fem. pit, ditch, deepening, from שָׁחָה.

שְׁחִיתָא see שְׁחַת.

שַׁחַל (not used) to roar, of a lion.

שָׁחַל (not used) to peel off, to separate.

שַׁחַל m. the roarer, lion, from שָׁחַל.

שְׁחֵלֶת f. shells of muscles, which, when burnt, yield a fragrance. The root is שָׁחַל.

שָׁחַן (not used) to glow, to burn, related to קָנָא; next, to be inflamed.

שָׁחַס see סָחַשׁ.

שַׁחַף m. an unclean bird, so called on account of its leanness; according to some, the sea-gull; according to others, the horned or night-owl. From which:—

שָׁחַף (not used) to be thin, lean, diminished, of the body.

שַׁחֶפֶת fem. consumption, origin. decreasing.

שָׁחַץ (not used) to walk proudly, haughtily; the derivation is obscure.

שַׁחַץ m. pride, haughtiness; *also*, majesty; hence בְּנֵי שַׁחַץ the lions, or the great beasts of prey generally.

שַׁחֲצִים (haunt of beasts of prey) p.n. of a place in Issachar. The Ketib has שַׁחֲצוֹם.

שָׁחַק to pound, to bruise, e.g. to pound spices to dust, figur. to scatter the enemy. The root is שָׁחַק, related to חַק (Aram.).

שָׂחַק (fut. יִשְׂחַק) 1) to laugh, to mock; with עַל, at something; with אֶל, to laugh or smile with some one or upon something; with לְ, to deride at something; 2) to joke, to jest, to sport. Pi. שִׂחֵק to play, to sport; שִׂחֵק לִפְנֵי to sport, to have a mock fight before some one; מְשַׂחֵק a player (on an instrument), dancer, etc. Hiph. const. with עַל, to mock, to deride, to scorn.

שַׁחַק (in signif. 2, the plur. שְׁחָקִים) masc. 1) that which is pounded, dust; 2) thinness; hence, thin cloud, thin vapour which obscures the sky; in the pl. heavens, the seat of the clouds.

שְׂחֹק (*plene* שְׂחוֹק) masc. laughing, jesting, scorning, mocking, or concrete, subject of scorn; also in a good sense, cheerfulness, joy, laughter.

I. שָׁחַר 1) origin. to glow, to burn; hence, to shine, to illuminate, from which שַׁחַר; 2) to be black, as in חוּם, a mode of transferring the sense from glowing, burning.

II. שָׁחַר to seek, to search, to inquire after something; the root is related with that in בָּחַר and בָּקַר; hence, to desire, long for something; generally, however, Pi. to seek after something (accus.), or to apply inquiringly to (אֶל) something. The connection of the two roots may be thus explained; the orig. signif. of שָׁחַר II. being to try, search, thus synon. with בָּחַן, and proceeding from the original sense to glow.

שַׁחַר (with suff. שַׁחְרָה) m. the morning light, dawn, from שָׁחַר to brighten up; כַּנְפֵי שַׁחַר the wings of the morning dawn; בֶּן־שַׁ the morning star; עָלָה הַשַּׁחַר the dawn appears; הָיָה שַׁחַר לְ a morning dawns for him; שַׁחַר, בַּשַּׁחַר, are used as adverbs in the sense of, early, in the morning, swift; לֹא יָדַע שַׁחַר not observing the suddenness (of an occurrence).

שָׁחֹר (pl. שְׁחֹרִים) adj. masc., שְׁחוֹרָה (pl. —רוֹת) f. black, of the colour of the face, or of the hair, etc.).

שְׁחוֹר m. blackness. See שְׁחוֹר.

שְׁחוֹר see שִׁיחוֹר.

שַׁחֲרוּת fem. blackness of the hair; thence transf. to the age of black hair, i. e. youth, in contrast to שֵׂיבָה. In the Talmud, שְׁחוֹרֵי הָרֹאשׁ lads, boys.

שְׁחַרְחֹר (after the form פְּתַלְתֹּל) adj. m., שְׁחַרְחֹרֶת f. black, blackish, of colour.

שְׁחַרְיָה p.n. masc. (early visitation of God).

שְׁחֲרַיִם p.n. m. (morning and evening dawn).

שָׁחַת (Kal, not used) to destroy, to corrupt. Niph. to be corrupted or destroyed, physically or morally; transf. to be desolate. Pi. 1) to destroy, devastate (cities or countries); to wound, hurt (men); to slay, uproot (a people); to destroy or cast off compassion; to destroy wisdom, i.e. to neglect it; 2) to act corruptly, to do evil. Hiph. to lay waste (countries, cities, kingdoms); to slay (men); to corrupt the walk, the deed, i. e. to act corruptly; equiv. to הֵרַע; part. מַשְׁחִית destroyer; הַמַּלְאָךְ הַמַּ׳ the destroying angel. The heading of some Psalms אַל תַּשְׁחֵת destroy not, is probably taken from the beginning or burden of the song.

שְׁחַת (Aram.) the same, to destroy; hence particip. pass. שְׁחִית base, corrupt; the fem. שְׁחִיתָה is used also as a subst.

שַׁחַת (formed from שׁוּחַ, like נַחַת from נוּחַ) f. pit, for the preserving of water, for the securing of wild beasts, for the confining of a prisoner, for interring a corpse, etc.; hence, cistern, dungeon, grave. The LXX. renders it sometimes "destructive," as if derived from שָׁחַת.

שֵׂט (pl. שֵׂטִים) he that turns away or deviates (from the good path), the backslider, sinner, wicked one. The form is a participial one.

שָׂטָה (fut. יִשְׂטֶה, apoc. יֵשְׂטְ) to turn away, to deviate from something, e. g. from a way; hence, figur. of a wife that becomes unfaithful; construed with תַּחַת הָאִישׁ.

שִׁטָּה (pl. שִׁטִּים) f. 1) a thorny plant, from שָׁנַט to sting, to prickle; next specially the acacia tree, particularly in pl. in connection with עֵץ; 2) (place of acacias) p. n. of a valley in Moab, on the borders of Palestine.

שָׁטַח (fut. יִשְׁטַח) 1) to spread out, to expand (in space); hence, to make wide, spacious; 2) to scatter about (bones, etc.). Pi. שִׁטַּח to spread out (the arms). The root is שָׁטַח.

שֹׁטֵט m. a scourge, whip, equiv. to שׁוֹט. The form is for מְשֹׁטֵט.

שָׂטַם (fut. יִשְׂטֹם) to hate, to be hostile, persecute, probably related with שָׂטַן which has the same sense originally.

שָׂטַן (particip. שֹׂטֵן) to be hostile, to oppose, to hinder, persecute;

with נֶפֶשׁ, adversary to the soul, i.e. to the life; שֹׂטֵן persecutor.

שָׂטָן m. the hater, adversary, opponent (in war or before justice); לְשָׂטָן לְ as an opponent or hinderer to some one; הַשָּׂטָן the adversary, enemy; in later theology, of an angel of evil, Satan.

שִׂטְנָה f. 1) hatred, enmity, accusation; 2) (well of contention) p. n. of a well.

שָׁטַף (fut. יִשְׁטֹף) to gush or stream out, to flow in abundance (related to the root in נָ־טַף), to pour forth in streams (of rain), to overflow, overwhelm, inundate (with accus. of the object); to wash away (the dust of the earth); to sweep or wash away; figur. of righteousness, to overflow, i. e. to be powerfully practised; transf. to the overrunning of a country by an army; or the plunging of a horse. Niph. pass. Pu. to be washed, rinsed, of a vessel.

שֶׁטֶף (once שֵׁטֶף) m. an overflowing of water, a flood, stream, inundation, and in the transf. signif. like the verb בְּשֶׁטֶף adv. with a flood, i. e. suddenly.

שָׁטַר to inscribe, engrave (comp. חָ־תַר with the same orig. signif.); hence, 1) to write (synon. with כָּתַב), comp. Aram. שְׁטָר written document; 2) to oversee, direct, probably so called from the writing down of law proceedings; hence שֹׁטֵר overseer, officer. It is possible that שָׁטַר, in the orig. sig., is identical with סָדַר to order, arrange, adjust.

שְׁטָר (Aram.) m. a written document; according to some, from שְׁטַר to write; according to others, rule, dominion; more probably, however, it is to be taken as equiv. to סְטַר a side.

שִׁטְרַי p. n. m. (writer).

שַׁי (after the form גַּי, חַי, מַי, דַּי) m. a present, gift, orig. debt, tribute, from שָׁה (comp. נָ־שָׁה): the presents in the East being considered as the liquidation of debts.

שִׁיא belongs to שַׁי. See שָׁה.

שִׂיא m. eminence, greatness, formed from שׂוֹא.

שִׁיאוֹן (desolation, devastation) p. n. of a city in Issachar.

שִׂיאוֹן (top, height) p.n. of the mountain of Hermon.

שִׂיב see שׂוּב.

שֵׂיב (with suff. שֵׂיבוֹ) m. old age.

שֵׂיבָה f. the same, אִישׁ שֵׂ׳ an aged hoary-headed man; sometimes אִישׁ is omitted.

שִׁיבָה f. 1) sitting, abiding, staying, concr. habitation, dwelling, from יָשַׁב; 2) returning, coming home;

returning; concrete, they who return home, from שׁוּב.

שִׁיב m. turning or moving back, from שׁוּג I. = סוּג; hence, departure. According to Kimchi, business, affair, from נָשַׂג to reach, attain.

שִׂיד m. lime, plaister, whitewash, to spread over walls, from שׂוּד.

שִׂיב as a verb see שׂוּד.

שָׁיָה adopted as the root for תֶּשִׁי Deut. 32:18. See under שָׁיָה.

שִׁיָּה see שֶׂה.

שִׁיז (not used) to love ardently; after the Arab.

שִׁיזָא p.n. m. (the beloved one).

שִׁיזָב see שֵׁזָב.

שִׂיחַ as a verb, see שׂוּחַ.

שִׂיחַ (with suff. שִׂיחוֹ, pl. שִׂיחִים) m. 1) a plant, shrub, bush, e.g. שִׂיחַ הַשָּׂדֶה from שׂוּחַ I. to sprout, to shoot up; 2) a saying, speech, word, from שׂוּחַ II.; transf. to song, lamentation, thought, meditation, quite in as manifold significations as the verb.

שִׁיחָה (from שׁוּחַ) f. equiv. to שׁוּחָה pit; only in the Ketib.

שִׂיחָה (fem. equiv. to שִׂיחַ thought, speech, prayer, meditation, devotion.

שִׁיחוֹר also שִׁחוֹר, שִׁחֹר (the black, turbid, river) p.n. of the Nile, according to the Semetic manner, like the Greek *Μέλας*, Latin *Melo*, for which otherwise יְאֹר. It stands also for נַחַל מִצְרַיִם, by which *Rhinocorura* is understood.

שִׁיחוֹר לִבְנָת (the glass-river) p.n. of a river in the territory of Asher, the Belus, from the sand of which glass was first made.

שַׁיִט m. 1) equiv. to שׁוֹט scourge, only Ketib, from שׁוּט; 2) an oar, equiv. to מָשׁוֹט.

שִׁילֹה (resting-place, from שָׁלָה, after the form קִימוֹר) p.n. of a city in Ephraim, where the tabernacle was erected. The gent. שִׁילֹנִי indicates an original form שִׁילוֹן; also שִׁלֹה, שִׁלוֹ, שִׁילוֹ occur for it. In the passage, Gen. 49:10, some take it as a p.n., either of the tabernacle or of the Messiah, and others as a common noun in the above signification.

שֵׁילָל Ketib for שׁוֹלָל, which see.

שִׁילֹנִי 1) gent. from שִׁילֹה, compare גִּלֹנִי from גִּלֹה; 2) for שֵׁלָנִי, where שֵׁלָה is the basis.

שִׂים see שׂוּם.

שִׁימוֹן p.n. m. (the appointed one).

שִׁין as a verb belongs to שָׁיַן. See שׁוּן.

שַׁיִן (only plur. שֵׁינִים) m. urine, the Keri always transcribes this noun.

שִׁישָׁא from שָׁשָׁא, which see.

שִׁיר as a verb, see שׁוּר.

שִׁיר (with suff. שִׁירוֹ, שִׁירָה, plur.

שִׁירִים, with suff. (שִׁירֵיכֶם) m. a song, sometimes also, of the playing of instruments, which are called כְּלֵי שִׁיר; שִׁיר מְצִלְתַּיִם the playing of cymbals. The further applications of שִׁיר, either as a heading of songs, or in special relations, are easily understood from the context.

שִׁירָה f. a song or a parable arranged according to metre.

שַׁיִשׁ masc. marble (white), alabaster, from שׁוּשׁ to be white.

שִׁישָׁא see שְׂרָיָה.

שִׁישַׁק p. n. of a king of Egypt, contemporary with Jeroboam, who, according to Manetho, was called Sesochis.

שִׁית see שׁוּת.

שִׁית m. wrapper, dress, from שׁוּת II.; hence עָטָה שִׁית to be wrapped in a garment, שִׁית זוֹנָה the mask of a harlot.

שַׁיִת (with suff. שֵׁיתוֹ) m. thorn-hedge, from שׁוּת II.; next, collectively, thorns; comp. a similar gradation in סְבָךְ.

שַׁךְ inf. from שָׁכַךְ, which see.

שֵׂךְ (only plur. שִׂכִּים) thorn, from שָׂכַךְ I. in the signification of to prickle, to cut.

שֹׂךְ (with suff. שֻׂכּוֹ) masc. a hedge, fence, from שָׂכַךְ II. to entwine.

I. שָׁכַב (fut. יִשְׁכַּב, inf. שְׁכַב, with suff. שָׁכְבָהּ, but also שְׁכֹב, hence, with suff. שָׁכְבְּךָ) orig. to lie down, especially for sleep, or to lie sleeping, to rest; שָׁכַב is also used in the sense of lying sick, to lie dead, to die, as in the phrase שָׁכַב עִם אֲבוֹתָיו to lie down with his ancestors; with עִם or אֶת to lie by or with some, with accus. to have connubial intercourse. Niph. the same of a woman. Pu. the same. Hiph. to cause to lie down, to cast down. Hoph. to be laid down, also to lie.

II. שָׁכַב probably a transposition from שָׁפַךְ=שָׁבַךְ to pour out, pour forth, which signif. the Kal probably has, in the sense of copulation. Hiph. to empty (a vessel), Job 38 : 17, and also in some derivatives, which, however, is uncertain.

שְׁכָבָה (const. שִׁכְבַת) f. 1) copulation, complete שִׁכְבַת זֶרַע, and to have connubial intercourse שָׁכַב אֶת־אִשָּׁה שִׁכְבַת־זֶרַע; 2) lying down, layer, row; hence, שִׁ׳ הַטַּל the dew lay down.

שְׁכֹבֶת (with suff. שְׁכָבְתּוֹ, after the form כְּתֹבֶת) f. copulation, connubial intercourse, נָתַן שְׁכָבְתּ or נָתַן אֶת־שְׁכָבְתּוֹ לְזֶרַע בְּאִשָּׁה אֶל to copulate, to have connubial intercourse.

שָׂכָה a root adopted for מַשְׂכִּים, Jer. 5:8, which some render in the sense of שָׁגָה to run to and fro; others adopt a verb שָׂכַם for it; more probably, however, מַשְׁכִּים is contracted from מְאַשְׁכִּים, and derived from אֶשֶׁךְ.

שָׂכָה (not used) to look, view, behold, related to שָׁעָה, שָׁגַח, etc. From which שֶׂכְוִי, שְׂכִיָּה and מַשְׂכִּית.

שֻׂכָּה f. a thorn, prickle, transf. to a pointed weapon, from שָׂכַךְ.

שֶׂכוּ (prospect) p. n. of a place near Ramah.

שֶׂכְוִי an extended form of שֶׂכוּ, m. view (of the heart or mind), insight, transf. to the heart, as the seat of reflection. In modern Heb. שֶׂכְוִי signifies the cock, so called on account of his proverbial sagacity in exactly distinguishing day from night.

שְׁכֹל (after the form מְלוֹא) m. childlessness, origin. being deprived, transf. to a forsaken state, like אַלְמֹן.

שַׁכּוּל adj. m., שַׁכֻּלָה (pl. שַׁכֻּלוֹת) f. robbed of the young, or forsaken (speaking of the young).

שִׁכּוֹר (pl. שִׁכּוֹרִים, const. שִׁכּוֹרֵי) adj. m., שִׁכֹּרָה f. (after the form יִלּוֹד, גִּבּוֹר) drunk, intoxicated; frequently used as a subst. the drunken, intoxicated one, drunkard.

I. שָׁכַח (but in pause שָׁכֵחַ, fut. יִשְׁכַּח) to forget something (acc.) or followed by the inf. with מִן, to leave something behind through forgetfulness. Niph. to be, or become forgotten. Piel, to make forget. Hiph. to cause to be forgotten. In the orig. signif. the verb is equal to שָׁגַג in the sense of being removed, forsaken, somewhat like נָשָׁה.

II. שָׁכַח (Kal, not used) to find, as in the Aram.; hence Hith. to be found, to be, exist, extant.

שָׁכֵחַ (pl. שְׁכֵחִים, const. שְׁכֵחֵי) adj. m. forgetting, forgetful.

שְׁכַח (Peal, not used) Aram. to find; hence, Ithp. הִשְׁתְּכַח, with בְּ, of the place where something is found; to be found, i. e. to prove (accus.) pious. Aphal הַשְׁכַּח to find, to find out, obtain. Comp. מְצָא.

שְׂכַנְיָה p. n. m. (appeased with God) from, שׂךְ formed from שָׂכַךְ.

שְׂכִיָּה (only pl. שְׂכִיּוֹת) fem. image-work, a figure or picture made for public view, according to the LXX.; according to some, a sight, appearance.

שַׂכִּין (in modern Heb. the pl. שַׂכִּינִים) m. a knife; the root is שָׂכַךְ to cut, related with כָּסַח and the root in דָּרְשֹׁךְ in the original sense of sticking in, and ־ִין is the nominal suff. as in תַּנִּין, קָצִין, etc.

שָׂכִיר (c. שְׂכִיר, with suff. שְׂכִירְךָ, pl. with suff. שְׂכִירֶיהָ) m. a hireling, a labourer by the day, or any labourer hired for a certain time. Root שָׂכַר.

שְׂכִירָה f. hiring, hired, or as a conc. hired people, hirelings, from שָׂכַר.

שָׁכַךְ (inf. שֹׁךְ) equiv. to שָׁחָה to bow down, to stoop (of a fowler); next generally to sit, lie down, to settle, to subside (of water, wrath). Hiph. הֵשֵׁךְ to still, quiet an uproar or murmuring from or against (מֵעַל) some one. In modern Heb. the Pi. שִׁכֵּךְ is used.

I. שָׂכַךְ (not used) to cut, to stick in, related to כָּסַח, from which שִׂכִּין, which see.

II. שָׂכַךְ (not used) to entwine, to entangle; hence, to hedge in, to fence; from which שֹׂךְ, מְשׂוּכָה.

שָׁכֹל (1 pers. pret. שָׁכֹלְתִּי, pause שָׁכָלְתִּי, fut. יִשְׁכַּל) orig. to cease, to perish (the root is related to כָּלָה), from which to be deprived of a possession, especially to be deprived of children, either being childless or losing the children. Part. pass. שְׁכוּלָה the childless one (of a female). Pi. שִׁכֵּל to make childless by killing the children, or the young of beasts, or through being devoured by wild beasts; hence, fig. of the slaughter of young men in war, making the state childless, as it were; also used of the miscarrying of a woman, both trans. and intrans.; of the vineyard being unfruitful. Hiphil, to slaughter the young warriors; to have a miscarriage, e.g. רֶחֶם מַשְׁכִּיל a barren womb. From which שַׁכּוּל, שְׁכוּל.

שְׁכֹל (pl. with suff. שְׁכֻלַיִךְ) m. childlessness, state of childlessness, or of being forsaken.

שָׂכַל orig. to look at, to behold; next, to look mentally, to have insight, to be prudent, wise; with מִן following, to be wiser than. Pi. שִׂכֵּל (Gen. 48:14) he laid the hands intentionally, if שִׂכֵּל is not to be taken in this passage in the sense of סִכֵּל to pervert. Hiph. 1) to behold, contemplate (some beloved object), to consider, to attend to, have care upon (accus., בְּ, אֶל, עַל) something or some one; 2) to have insight (בְּ) into something, to be or become wise or intelligent, to have understanding; part. מַשְׂכִּיל a wise, intelligent one, transf. to a pious, religious one; in this sense the inf. הַשְׂכֵּל and הַשְׂכִּיל are used as substantives; also trans. to make wise, to instruct; 3) to act prudently, wisely; transf. to be successful, prosperous, considered as a consequence of prudence; also in a transferred sense, to cause one to prosper or thrive, equiv. to הִצְלִיחַ. מַשְׂכִּיל also occurs as a subst. in the heading of Psalms, where it is rendered by some, song, and by others, song of instruction, or moral poem.

שְׂכַל (Aram.) the same; hence, Ithpael אִשְׂתַּכַּל to look upon (בְּ) something, to regard, consider.

שֶׂכֶל and שֵׂכֶל (with suff. שִׂכְלוֹ) m. wisdom, understanding, prudence, cunning. The origin. signif. is view, appearance, equiv. to מַרְאֶה; thus טוֹבַת שֶׂכֶל, not unlike טוֹבַת מַרְאֶה: שׂוּם שֶׂכֶל to give the understanding or sense of any thing. The root is either שָׂכַל, in the sense of beholding, or the noun is formed from שָׂכָה, ־ֶל being a nominal suffix.

שִׂכְלוּת fem. folly, equiv. to סִכְלוּת, from כָּסַל=סָכַל.

שָׂכְלְתָנוּ fem. Aram. wisdom, understanding.

שְׁכֶם (in pause שֶׁכֶם, with ה finis שִׁכְמָה, with suff. שִׁכְמִי) masc. 1) the shoulder, on which burdens are carried; the upper part of the back or the neck; rather different from כָּתֵף: שְׁכֶם is considered as the limb for carrying a burden, yoke, rule; שְׁכֶם אֶחָד with one accord (to serve); מַטֵּה שְׁכֶם the rod for the back; הִפְנָה שְׁכֶם לָלֶכֶת to turn the back to go; שׁוּת שְׁכֶם to make some one turn the back, i.e. to drive to flight (comp. נָתַן עֹרֶף); fig. like כָּתֵף shoulder, i.e. tract of land; 2) (land-tract) p. n. of a Levitical town in Ephraim, Sychem, the present Nablous; שְׁכֶמָה towards Sychem; 3) p. n. m.

שָׁכַם (Kal, not used) denom. from שְׁכֶם, and only Hiph. הִשְׁכִּים, orig. to lay upon the shoulder (a burden), to load; next, in the language of the nomades, to rise up early for journeying with their burdens, in contrast to שָׁרָא to loosen, to unpack, i. e. to return home when the day expires. Later the verb שָׁכַם is used generally for rising early, and in connection with other verbs, as an adverb, early, eagerly, urgently, e.g. הִשְׁכִּים הָלַךְ to pass away early (of the dew; הִשְׁכִּים וְדַבֵּר to speak urgently; הִשְׁכִּים הַשְׁחִית to destroy relentlessly, i. e. to act wickedly; אַשְׁכֵּים Jeremiah 25:3, stands for הַשְׁכֵּם.

שְׁכֶם p. n. m. (shoulder) patron. שִׁכְמִי.

שִׁכְמָה Job 31:22, for שִׁכְמָהּ.

שָׁכַן (but in pause, as in many intrans. verbs, with a *seré* שָׁכֵן, fut. יִשְׁכֹּן, inf. with suff. שָׁכְנוֹ, after the form פָּתְחוֹ) orig. to let itself down, to rest, e. g. of a pillar of fire, cloud; to encamp (of man and beast), to dwell, with בְּ of the place; to inhabit, with accus., especially of the tranquil dwelling; of God, שֹׁכֵן עַד dweller (of heaven) in eternity, fig. to possess; hence שָׁכַן עָרְמָה to possess prudence; שָׁכַן is also used in the sense of being inhabitable, inhabited. Particip. pass. שָׁכוּן inhabitant, originally, domiciled. Pi. 1) to cause to dwell, e. g. the name of God, i. e. to place the residence of His glory somewhere, comp. שׂוּם שָׂם; 2) to pitch or erect a tent. Hiph. הִשְׁכִּין 1) to cause some one to dwell, to lay down, e. g. לֶעָפָר into the dust; 2) to erect a tent.

שְׁכַן (Aram.) the same. Pa. שַׁכֵּן to cause to dwell (the name), to cause the glory of God to dwell somewhere.

שָׁכֵן (origin. particip. const. שְׁכַן, pl. שְׁכֵנִים) adj. m., שְׁכֵנָה (with suff. שְׁכֶנְתָּהּ, pl. שְׁכֵנוֹת) f. only subst. dweller, inhabitant, neighbour, neighbouring state, etc.

שֶׁכֶן (only with suff. שִׁכְנוֹ) m. dwelling-place; probably שִׁכְנוֹ is only an inf. with suff.

שְׁכַנְיָה p. n. m. (faithful servant of God) for which stands, in a parallel passage, שְׁבַנְיָה.

שְׁכַנְיָהוּ p. n. m. (the same).

I. שָׁכַר (not used) to seethe, to boil; next, to brew, comp. חָרָה, חָרַר, etc., from which :—

שֵׁכָר masc. strong drink, intoxicating liquors, of wine or of other prepared beverages, orig. that which is prepared by boiling or brewing, from which denom. :—

שָׁכַר (fut. יִשְׁכַּר) to get drunk (with שֵׁכָר), to be intoxicated, and generally, drinking of anything leading to merriment or intoxication, with accus. or מִן of the beverage; transf. to be senseless, unconscious; שִׁכּוֹרָה the drunken one. Pi. to make drunk, intoxicated; fig. to plunge into ruin. Hiph. the same. Hith. to conduct oneself as being drunk. From which שִׁכָּרוֹן, שִׁכּוֹר.

II. שָׁכַר (not used) equiv. to שָׂכַר to reward, present, from which אֶשְׁכָּר, if it is not equiv. to אֶשְׁפָּר.

שָׂכַר (fut. יִשְׂכֹּר) to barter for wages, to buy (at a price), to hire troops; transf. to buy some one, i. e. to bribe him. Niph. to hire oneself (בְּלֶחֶם for bread). Hith. the same. According to others, to gain or profit by purchase. The root שָׂכַר is related to that in כָּרָה and אָגַר.

שָׂכָר (const. שְׂכַר, with suff. שְׂכָרִי) m. 1) price of hiring or of purchase, wages of a labourer; next generally, reward; 2) p. n. masc. (after the form רֶשַׁע) hireling.

שֶׂכֶר reward; עֹשֶׂה שֶׂכֶר to acquire a reward.

שִׁכָּרוֹן masc. drunkenness, intoxication.

שִׁכְּרוֹן (place of the palm wine) p. n. of a city on the northern border of Judah.

שַׁל (from שָׁלָה after the form יַד from יָדָה) masc. erring, trespass, offence; the same is שָׁלוּ in Aram.

שֶׁל (later) part. to signify a relation, either of one noun to another, thus to denote the genitive case, or of two sentences; generally, however, its use is like that of אֲשֶׁר and שֶׁ (followed by *dagesh forte*), with which it is etymologically connected. In compounds, בְּשֶׁל is equiv. to בַּאֲשֶׁר לְ on account of; בְּשֶׁלְּמִי equivalent to בַּאֲשֶׁר לְמִי on account of whom; בְּשֶׁלִּי on my account or on account of me. בְּשֶׁל אֲשֶׁר which once occurs (if the reading is correct) is equiv. to בִּגְלַל דִּי because of.

שַׁלְאֲנָן (equiv. to שַׁאֲנָן) adj. m. at ease, quiet, tranquil, secure, prosperous. The root is שָׁאַן, with interpolation of לְ, as in זַלְעָפָה.

שָׁלַב (Kal, not used) to entwine, to knot together; hence Pu. שֻׁלַּב, joined, Auth. Vers. "set in order against one another."

שָׁלָב (plur. שְׁלַבִּים, comp. קָמָן, plur. קְמַנִּים) masc. ledge, corner-ledge, from שָׁלַב, as these ledges connected the two sides; modern Heb. sprout.

שָׁלַג (not used) to shine, to glitter, to be white. From which:—

שֶׁלֶג m. snow, origin. that which shines. From which:—

שָׁלַג only Hiph. הִשְׁלִיג to be white as snow, used of the bones of the slain growing pale.

שָׁלָה (Kal, not used) to err, to totter (the root is also found in כָּשַׁל). Niph. to err, to commit oneself. Hiph. to lead astray, to mislead, to deceive. From which שַׁל. In Aram. שְׁלָא signifies the same, from which שָׁלָה and שָׁלוּ.

שָׁלָה (after the form שָׁנָה) Aram. f. error, trespass, sin. Only occurs in Ketib for שָׁלוּ.

שֵׁלָה 1) f. contracted from שְׁאֵלָה,

request; 2) p. n. m. for שֵׁלָה (the erring one); from which patron. שֵׁלָנִי.

שִׁלֹה p.n.m. of a city. See שִׁילֹה.

שָׁלָה (not used) according to some, to be fat (after an Arab. analogy); according to others, equiv. to צָלַל to sound forth; from which שְׂלָו.

שַׁלְהֶבֶת f. flame, from the root לָהַב; in Aram. the verb שַׁלְהֵב is formed therefrom. The form שַׁלְהֶבֶתְיָה is, according to some, fem. from שַׁלְהֶבְתִּי.

שָׁלָו (1 pers. שָׁלַוְתִּי, but the 3 pers. שָׁלֵו for שָׁלַו, 3 fut. יִשְׁלָיוּ, as is sometimes the form in the ל״ה) to be quiet, peaceable, prosperous, syn. with שָׁקַט. The form יִשַׁל is either to be referred back to שָׁלָה =שָׁלַל, or to שָׁאַל, the א being elliptical.

שָׁלֵו (const. pl. שַׁלְוֵי) adj. m., שְׁלֵוָה f. quiet, at ease, contented, prosperous; but also, in a bad sense, careless, inconsiderate, frivolous, wicked, forgetful of God. As a noun, שָׁלֵו signifies: tranquillity, prosperity. The root is שָׁלֵו.

שֶׁלֶו m. quiet, ease, prosperity.

שְׁלֵו (as a verb) Aram. equiv. to שָׁלֵו in Heb.; particip. pass. שְׁלֵה for שְׁלֵו.

שָׁלוּ (Aram.) f. error, trespass, sin from שְׁלָא.

שְׁלוֹ see שִׁילֹה.

שְׂלָו (in pause שְׂלָו and שְׂלָיו, plur. שַׂלְוִים) f. a quail, origin. the fat bird, always collective.

שְׁלֵוָא (with suff. שְׁלֵוְתָךְ) Aram. fem. ease, quiet, prosperity.

שַׁלְוָה (pl. שַׁלְוֹת) fem. 1) ease, tranquillity, prosperity, and in the same sense the plur. בְּשַׁלְוָה suddenly, origin. in the midst of security or prosperity; 2) carelessness, criminal security.

שִׁלּוּחַ (only pl. —חִים) m. origin. abstract, the sending away, dismissal, but generally concr.; 1) bill of divorce; 2) dowry given to a daughter at her marriage; comp. שִׁלַּח; Pi. from שָׁלַח.

שָׁלוֹם (after the form קָדוֹשׁ, pl. שְׁלֹמִים) 1) adj. m. in health, well, prosperous, peaceable, uninjured, safe, complete in number, friendly; in pl. the peaceable ones, the tranquil ones; 2) as a subst. wellbeing, welfare; especially in this sense in the phrases שָׁלוֹם לְ; שָׁאַל לְפ׳ לְשָׁלוֹם; רָאָה, יָדַע, פָּקַד; אֶת־שְׁלוֹם פ׳, הָלַךְ לְשָׁלוֹם, etc.; transf. to salvation, happiness, quiet, ease; 3) peace (in contrast to מִלְחָמָה), e. g. קָרָא לְשָׁלוֹם לְ to offer some one peace; עָנָה שׁ׳ אֶת to answer peaceably; עָשָׂה שׁ׳ לְ to give peace; אִישׁ שׁ׳ a man of peace;

דְּבַר שׁ׳ a word of peace; 4) friendship, concord; אִישׁ שׁ׳ a friend, a confederate; דְּבַר שׁ׳ a friendly word; as a p.n. it is found in אַבְשָׁלוֹם and אֲבִישָׁלוֹם.

שִׁלּוּם see שִׁלֻּם.

שִׁלּוּם (also שִׁלֻּם, pl. ־מִים) m. payment, reward, requiting, retribution, from שִׁלֵּם.

שַׁלּוּן p.n.m. (either equiv. to שִׁלּוּם, or it is derived from שָׁלַל to rob, to plunder.

שָׁלוֹשׁ see שָׁלֹשׁ.

שָׁלוּת equiv. to שָׁלוֹ.

שָׁלַח (fut. יִשְׁלַח, inf. abs. שָׁלֹחַ, const. שְׁלֹחַ and שְׁלַח) 1) to send some one (acc. seldom לְ) to (אֶל, seldom עַל) some one; the acc. of the person is sometimes omitted and replaced by בְּיַד; to send help, a plague (of God); שׁ׳ דְּבָרִים to send a message or order through (בְּיַד) some one; to send word through some one, with or without adding לֵאמֹר; to bid or command some one, in one instance including the sense of calling (2 Sam. 15:12); in the sense of sending word, the message is construed with the acc., and in the sense of charging some one with something, with double acc.; 2) to send off (without reference to any purpose or object), to dismiss, to let go, or let loose (the hand or mouth); hence, שָׁלַח מִן to withdraw, draw back (the hand) from something; 3) to stretch out or forth, e.g. the finger, as an indication of scorn; the staff, the hand; in this sense the form שָׁלַח יָד is variously used according to the prepositions following; with בְּ, to lay hands upon some one (to injure him), to violate some one's property; with עַל, to put forth the hand after something; with אֶל, as with בְּ; with מִן, to put forth the hand somewhere. Particip. pass. שָׁלוּחַ stretched out, slim, slender; שְׁלֻחוֹת sprouts, shoots. Niph. (inf. abs. נִשְׁלוֹחַ) to be sent. Pi. 1) in the intensive form, to send forth plagues, pestilence, punishment (of God), with אֶל, בְּ of the person or subject; to discharge, dismiss (a slave, a prisoner), hence the phrase, to send a daughter away, i.e. to give her away in marriage; to send a wife away, i.e. to divorce her (see שִׁלּוּחִים); to dismiss some one, to deliver him up, generally with the addition of בְּיַד or בְּ of the person into whose power something is given; to cast off something, get rid of it; 2) to throw (arrows), to send forth (fire into a city, to set on fire, for which also the form שְׁלַח בָּאֵשׁ is used), to stretch out (the hand), to spread (the branches); next, to send generally, with עַל, to some one. Pu. to be sent, dismissed, released, forsaken, driven away, as pass. both of Kal and Piel. Hiph. almost like Pi.

שְׁלַח (fut. יִשְׁלַח) Aram. the same, to send, send forth, stretch out (the hand), to lay hands upon (לְ) something, and in as various significations as the Hebrew.

שֶׁלַח (with suff. שִׁלְחוֹ) m. 1) shot, missile, weapons, or a pointed weapon, a spear, dart, sword; from שָׁלַח in the signif. of throwing, עָבַר בַּשֶּׁ׳ to perish by the shot, Author. Vers. by the sword; 2) a sprout, shoot, from שָׁלַח to spread out, to stretch out, comp. שְׁלֻחָה; in this sense only the plur. with suff. שְׁלָחַיִךְ; 3) streaming; next, a stream, probably equiv. to שִׁלֹחַ the well-known pond or spring on the south-west of Jerusalem; 4) p.n. m. (the shooter).

שִׁלֹחַ (for שָׁלוּחַ streaming, comp. גִּיחוֹן a gushing fountain) p.n. of a conduit or pool on the south-west of Jerusalem.

שְׁלֻחָה f. a sprout, shoot, from שָׁלַח to spread out.

שִׁלְחִי p.n. m. (shooter or shot).

שִׁלְחִים (streams), p.n. of a city in Judah.

שֻׁלְחָן (const. שֻׁלְחַן, plur. ־חָנוֹת) m. origin. that which is spread out (from שָׁלַח), a table, אֹכְלֵי שֻׁ׳ those that eat at one's table, friends; the table of God, i.e. the altar; שֻׁ׳ הַפָּנִים the table of shewbread, also called שֻׁ׳ הַמַּעֲרֶכֶת; עָרַךְ שֻׁ׳ to spread or set a table.

שָׁלַט (once שָׁלֵט in a transitive signif., fut. יִשְׁלַט) origin. to lead; next, to rule over, to be master of (בְּ, עַל) something. In the transitive sense, שָׁלֵט signifies, to empower. Hiph. to let rule, give power or permission, synon. with הִתְקִיף (Eccl. 6:10) in the same sense.

שְׁלֵט (fut. יִשְׁלַט) Aram. the same, to rule or have power over (בְּ) something; also, to atack something. Aphal, to cause to rule, to appoint as a ruler.

שָׁלַט (not used) to protect, to shelter, to cover (the root שָׁ־לַט is related to לָאַט, לָט, Aram. שְׁלַד; hence in the Talm. שַׁלְטוֹן covering of the head. From which:—

שֶׁלֶט (only pl. שְׁלָטִים, const. שִׁלְטֵי) m. a shield, origin. that which protects, synon. with מָגֵן of a similar derivation; שִׁלְטֵי הַזָּהָב the golden shields—the שְׁלָטִים (shields) were sometimes hung up on the walls for ornament; to fill the shield, i.e. to arm oneself with them; to fill the hand with the shield, i.e. to lay hold of it.

שִׁלְטוֹן masc. mighty, powerful, e.g. "where the word of the king is, there is power" (Eccles. 8:4); אֵין שִׁ׳ בְּ׳ there is no power over, etc.

שִׁלְטוֹן (const. pl. —טֹנֵי) Aram. m. an officer, a ruler (of a province).

שָׁלְטָן (const. שָׁלְטָן) Aram. m. rule, power, dominion, command. The pl. signifies kingdoms, dominions; also concr. rulers, regents.

שַׁלֶּטֶת fem. from שַׁלִּיט, which see.

שְׁלִי (only pause שֶׁלִי) m. rest, quietness, stillness, from שָׁלָה; בַּשֶּׁלִי adv. softly, quietly, secretly, orig. in the quiet, in secrecy.

שִׁלְיָה (with suff. שִׁלְיָתָהּ) f. the after birth, probably from שָׁלָה in the signification of hanging down, suitable to the explanation by the ancients, bag, in which the child was considered to lie in the mother's womb.

שְׁלָיו and שְׂלָיו equiv. to שְׂלָו, which see.

שַׁלִּיט (pl. שַׁלִּיטִים) adj. m., שַׁלֶּטֶת, (as if from שַׁלֶּט) f. 1) ruling, having power; next, as a subst. the powerful, mighty one; 2) in a bad sense, harsh, violent; also, imperious, shameless, of a harlot.

שַׁלִּיט (pl. שַׁלִּיטִין) Aram. adj. m. 1) mighty, powerful, having power; hence, as a subst. a ruler, high officer; 2) as an abstr. power; hence, with the addition of לְ before the infinitive, it is permitted, allowed to be done.

שָׁלִישׁ (pl. שָׁלִישִׁים) masc. 1) a third part, *triental*, as a corn measure, the third part of an ephah, or a large measure containing three smaller ones, which, however, cannot be defined now; שָׁלִישׁ as an adverb formed in the accus., full in measure or according to measure, e.g. thou givest them tears to drink in great measure (בִּדְמָעוֹת שָׁלִישׁ); 2) a musical instrument, according to Kimchi, consisting of three strings; probably, however, a triangle; 3) a kind of warriors or combatants in chariots, three standing together in the chariot, two of whom served as seconds to the combatant. The ancient commentators explain the word similarly to מִשְׁנֶה the second after the king; thus שָׁלִישׁ the third in rank. רֹאשׁ הַשָּׁלִישִׁים occurs in a sense similar to שַׂר הָרֶכֶב head of the charioteers; rarely in this sense רֹאשׁ הַשָּׁלִישִׁי or הַשָּׁלִשׁ with ם apoc.

שְׁלִישִׁי (pl. שְׁלִשִׁים) adj. m., שְׁלִישִׁיָּה or שְׁלִישִׁית fem. the third, from שָׁלוֹשׁ, e.g. the chamber on the third floor, the third part, the third day; reckoned from the time of speaking; thrice, repeating something three times; the third year, etc.; שְׁלִשִׁתָה adv. a third time; כָּעֵת מָחָר הַשְּׁלִישִׁית about this time the day after to-morrow (Author. Vers. "about to-morrow any time or the third day," which rendering is adopted in consequence of the זָקֵף separating כָּעֵת from מָחָר.

שָׁלַךְ (Kal, not used) orig. equiv. to שָׁלַח to send off, to cast off, but only Hiph. in this sense; הִשְׁלִיךְ עַל to throw upon some one (a missile); also in a spiritual sense, to cast something upon some one, i.e. to commend or entrust it to him; הִשְׁלִיךְ נַפְשׁוֹ מִנֶּגֶד to cast one's life away, i.e. to expose it; הִשְׁ׳ אַחֲרֵי גֵו, אַחֲרָיו to throw something behind one's back, i.e. to disregard it; הִשְׁ׳ מֵעַל פָּנִים (spoken of God) to cast some one away from His countenance, i.e. to withdraw His providence from him. It is used besides in a physical sense in manifold significations. Hoph. הָשְׁלַךְ and הֻשְׁלַךְ pass. and also in the figur. sense הִשְׁלִיךְ עַל to trust in one entirely.

שָׁלָךְ masc. the cormorant or the plungeon, so called from its shooting down, like an arrow, from the high cliffs, and plunging into the water to seize its prey. From שָׁלַךְ.

שַׁלֶּכֶת (Piel-noun) f. 1) the falling (of a tree), or the dropping of the leaves from the tree; 2) p. n. of a gate in the temple.

שָׁלַל (2 pers. שַׁלּוֹתָ, inf. abs. שֹׁל, fut. יָשֹׁל) 1) to pull off, to pull out: 2) to plunder, to rob, especially of booty, to spoil; שָׁלַל שָׁלָל to make booty. The root is related to that in נָשַׁל, אָצַל, נָזַל. Hithpael אֶשְׁתּוֹלֵל (for הִשְׁתּוֹלֵל according to Aram. analogy) to be plundered, spoiled, to become a prey. See שׁוֹלָל.

שָׁלָל (const. שְׁלַל, with suff. שְׁלָלָהּ) m. origin. that which is drawn away from the enemy; next, booty generally; also in a figur. sense, gain, profit, or anything acquired by a struggle.

שָׁלֵם (particip. שָׁלֵם, fut. יִשְׁלַם) orig. to be whole, entire, sound, complete, in contrast to חָסֵר; hence, 1) to be well, affluent, happy, prosperous, peaceable, to live in friendship with others, secure;

particip. שָׁלֵם, equiv. to אִישׁ שָׁלוֹם a friend; particip. pass. שָׁלוּם peaceable; 2) to be completed, finished, e.g. of a building, of a time. Pi. שִׁלֵּם in a trans. sense, 1) to preserve in happiness, prosperity; 2) to make complete, finish, transf. to restore (that which is stolen), to pay (a debt), to discharge (an obligation), to fulfil (an offering, a vow), to recompense, requite, reward, generally with the addition of גְּמוּל. Pu. pass. 1) to be paid, recompensed, requited, rewarded; 2) to be befriended; hence, used of the Hebrew nation מְשֻׁלָּם, equiv. to עֶבֶד יְיָ orig. a friend, or one devoted to God. Hiph. 1) to be peaceable, or to live in peace with (אֶת, עִם) some one, to submit, subject himself to some one; 2) to fulfil, to make an end of, complete something.

שְׁלֵם (particip. pass. שְׁלִים) Aram. the same, but only in the signif. of completing. Af. הַשְׁלֵם 1) to make an end of, complete; 2) to restore, recompense, deliver back.

שְׁלָם (def. שְׁלָמָא, with suff. שְׁלָמְכוֹן) Aram. masc. wellbeing, welfare, prosperity, peace, equiv. to שָׁלוֹם Hebrew.

שָׁלֵם (pl. שְׁלֵמִים) adj. m., שְׁלֵמָה (pl. שְׁלֵמוֹת) fem. 1) whole, uninjured, complete; hence, full, in reference to weight, measure, or number; complete, in numbers or numbering of an army; untouched, or not hewn, of a stone; 2) in a mental sense, peaceable, friendly, devoted; hence שָׁלֵם עִם יְיָ devoted to God, in which sense עִם יְיָ is sometimes omitted; 3) p. n. of the city, later called יְרוּשָׁלַםִ, which name is the basis to the subsequent appellations.

שֶׁלֶם (pl. שְׁלָמִים) m. reward, thanks, recompense, for which generally the plur. in the abstract sense; hence זֶבַח שְׁלָמִים peace or thank-offering, equiv. to זֶבַח תּוֹדָה. Sometimes זֶבַח is omitted, without altering the sense.

שִׁלֵּם (after the form דִּבֵּר, כִּפֵּר) m. 1) recompense (in connection with נָקָם); 2) p. n. m. for which once שַׁלּוּם; patron. שִׁלֵּמִי.

שַׁלֻּם p. n. m. (recompenser). This name is often found.

שָׁלֹם see שָׁלוֹם.

שִׁלֻּמָה (formed from שִׁלּוּם) recompense, retribution (of the sinner).

שְׁלֹמֹה p. n. of the renowned and wise king Solomon. The name is formed from שָׁלוֹם, with the termination ה ֹ = וֹ = וֹן — and signifies the peaceful one.

שַׂלְמָה (const. שַׂלְמַת, with suffix שַׂלְמָתוֹ, plur. שְׂלָמוֹת, with suffix שַׂלְמֹתַי) f. 1) garment, transposed from שִׂמְלָה, which contains the orig. signif., though שַׂלְמָה occurs very frequently; 2) p.n. m.

שַׂלְמוֹן p.n. m. (the clothed one) for which also שַׂלְמָה occurs.

שַׂלְמַי p.n. m. (the same).

שְׁלֹמִי p.n. m. (the peaceable one).

שְׁלֻמִיאֵל p.n. masc. (befriended by God).

שֶׁלֶמְיָהוּ p.n. m. (devoted to God).

שְׁלֹמִית 1) p.n. fem. (the peaceable one); 2) p.n. f. (friendship).

שַׁלְמַן p.n. of a king of Assyria; complete שַׁלְמַנְאֶסֶר.

שַׁלְמֹן (only pl. שַׁלְמֹנִים) m. recompense, reward, also bribe, from שִׁלֵּם to reward.

שָׁלַף (fut. יִשְׁלֹף) to draw (the sword), to pull off (the shoe), to pull out (grass), to draw out an arrow from the body which it has penetrated; most frequently, however, of the drawing of a sword; hence שֹׁלֵף חֶרֶב a warrior, origin. he that draws the sword.

שֶׁלֶף p.n. of a people in Arabia Felix, probably the *Ζαλαπηνοί* of Ptolemy.

שָׁלשׁ (שָׁלוֹשׁ, const. before makkaph שְׁלָשׁ־) cardinal number; f. שְׁלֹשָׁה (const. שְׁלֹשֶׁת, with suff. שְׁלָשְׁתָּם) masc. three, generally before the noun, and but rarely after the noun. The numeral itself, however, is often considered as a noun, and therefore stands in the constructive state when it occurs before a noun; but when it occurs after a noun, it stands in the absolute state; e. g. כְּמִשְׁלֹשׁ חֳדָשִׁים at about after three months; בִּשְׁנַת שָׁלֹשׁ in the third year; joined with עֶשְׂרֵה for the fem., or with עָשָׂר for the masc., it signifies thirteen; the plur. שְׁלֹשִׁים signifies thirty.

שָׁלִשׁ p.n. m. (triune).

שָׁלִשׁ see שָׁלִישׁ.

שִׁלֵּשׁ (Piel, formed from שָׁלֹשׁ) 1) to divide into three parts; 2) to do something on the third day (from the day spoken of); 3) to do something the third time; joined with other verbs, it stands as an adv. taken from the numeral. Pu. to be threefold, or three years old; hence, part. מְשֻׁלָּשׁ.

שִׁלֵּשׁ (after the form שִׁלֵּם) masc. the third (i. e. grandsón) after the son, viz. great-grandson. A son of the שִׁלֵּשׁ is called רִבֵּעַ.

שָׁלִשָׁה p.n. of a district in Ephraim, wherein the city בַּעַל שָׁלִשָׁה (according to Eusebius, בֵּית שָׁ׳) is situate, and, according to the same authority, fifteen Roman miles north of Diospolis.

שלשה p.n. m. (triune).

שלשום (formed from שלש with the adverbial termination ־ֹם) adv. the day before yesterday, orig. three days ago; generally in connection with אתמול, תמול.

שלתיאל see שאלתיאל.

שם (with ה finis שמה) dem. adv. 1) there, of the place, in reply to the question, where? אשר שם relative, in which place, the relative being separated from שם by the insertion of several words; שם—שם yonder—there, משם from thence, אשר—משם from whence; שמה thither, denoting a motion towards a place; 2) there, then, of time, transf. from the sense of locality; 3) there, rather like a demonstrative, and equiv. to, this; also in reference to the material; hence משם out of, from out.

שם (before makkaph ־שם, with suff. שמי, שמכם, plur. שמות, const. שמות) m. 1) sign, mark (by which one is recognised); ביה שמו Yah is His name, i.e. He is identified by that name; next, name generally; בשמות, בשם by name; קרא בשם to call by name; איש שם a man of repute, renown; בלי שם of no repute or distinction; שם is especially used of a good name, or of good report (in contrast to שם רע), or remembrance, good memory (after death); hence, to blot out the name, i.e. to obliterate the memory; sometimes as a concrete, that which perpetuates the remembrance, i.e. monument, memento; applied to God, שם signifies the manifestation of his glory or majesty, etc.; hence the many phrases in this sense, e.g. for the sake of His name, to call upon the name of God, to know the name of God, etc.; 2) p.n. m. Shem, from whom, according to Mosaic analogy, descended the nations of South-western Asia, as the Persians, Assyrians, Syrians, Hebrews, etc., and which nations are called the "Semitic."

שם (with suffix שמה, plur. const. שמהת, and with suff. שמהתהם) Aram. the same.

שמא (equiv. to שמאי, a contracted form from שמעאי) p.n. m. (the celebrated one).

שמאבר (probably of foreign origin) p.n. m.

שמאה (equiv. to שמעה fame) p.n.m.

שמאל see שמאל.

שמאל (sometimes plene שמאול, compounded from שמאל) m. orig.

the obscure or less known part of the world, the north; comp. צָפוֹן in the same sense and of a similar derivation; transf. to the north side, the left side; מִשְּׂמֹאל on or from the left, followed by the genitive or dative; מִשְּׂמֹאל לְ north of. The root is שָׂמַם equiv. to טָמַם, צָמַם, to conceal, hide, from which שְׂמֹאל is formed (with the termination ◌ֹל), like אֶשְׁכֹּל, גִּבְעֹל, חַרְגֹּל, קַרְסֹל. From which denom. הִשְׂמִיל, הִשְׂמְאִיל, הִשְׂמָאִיל, to be at, or to turn to, the left; also to use the left hand.

שְׂמָאלִי adj. m., שְׂמָאלִית f. left, to be on the left; in contrast to יְמָנִי. See שִׂמְלָה.

שַׁמָּא (equiv. to שִׁמְעָא fame) p. n. m. interchanging with שִׁמְאָה.

שַׁמְגַּר p. n. m. (the signification is obscure).

שָׁמַד (Kal, not used) to cut off, to destroy; related with צָמַד and צָמַת, which see. Hiph. הִשְׁמִיד (like הִכְרִית) to destroy, to uproot, to blot out, e.g. people, nations; also of inanimate beings, to desolate, lay waste (cities, altars, etc.); the inf. הַשְׁמֵד is used as a noun, destruction. Niph. to be destroyed, desolated (of places), to be blotted out (of people, nations).

שְׁמַד (Aram.) the same; hence, Af. הַשְׁמֵד like Hiph. in Heb.

שָׁמָה (not used) to be high, elevated, as in the Arab. From which שָׁמַיִם.

שָׁמָּה see שָׁם.

שַׁמָּה (from שָׁמַם, pl. שַׁמּוֹת) fem. 1) desolation, transf. to astonishment, amazement, terror, shuddering; 2) p. n. m. probably contracted from שִׁמְעָה fame, in which also שִׁמְעָה and שִׁמְעָא occur. The forms שַׁמְהוּת and שַׁמּוֹת which occur for it, stand probably for שִׁמְעוּת and שִׁמְעוֹת in the same signif.

שַׁמָּה p. n m. (valuation), only occurs as a patron. שַׁמָּתִי.

שַׁמְהוּת see שַׁמָּה.

שְׁמָהָן (Aram.) pl. from שֻׁם.

שְׁמוּאֵל p. n. masc. (contracted from שְׁמוּעַ־אֵל, heard by God).

שַׁמּוּעַ p. n. m. (the famed one). See שִׁמְעָא.

שְׁמוּעָה (const. שְׁמוּעַת, pl. ־עוֹת) f. 1) concrete, that which is announced, i. e. tidings, news, rumours, report (either good or bad); applied to God, it signifies, a message from, or instruction by, Him, also doctrine; 2) abstract, the announcing, informing. Root שָׁמַע, proceeding from the signif. in Hiph.

שִׂמּוּר Ketib for **שָׁמִיר**, which see.

שָׂמַח (fut. **יִשְׂמַח**) origin. to shine, to be bright (comp. **צָהַל**); next, to be cheerful, glad, to rejoice at (**מִן, עַל, בְּ**) something, or with **כִּי** in the sentence following; with **לִפְנֵי**, to rejoice before some one; but with **לְ**, to rejoice or triumph at the misfortune or hurt of another. Pi. **שִׂמַּח** to rejoice, gladden some one; with **מִן, עַל, לְ**, to cause some one to rejoice or triumph over another's misfortune. Hiph. like Pi.

שָׂמֵחַ (pl. **שְׂמֵחִים**, const. **שִׂמְחֵי**, once **שְׂמֵחֵי**) adj. m., **שְׂמֵחָה** f. rejoicing, being glad, cheerful, at something, with **לְ, אֶל**, etc.

שִׂמְחָה (plur. **שְׂמָחוֹת**) joy, rejoicing, gladness, cheerfulness, merriment; transf. to feast or festival of rejoicing; **שָׂמַח שׂ׳** to rejoice greatly, exceedingly.

שָׁמַט (fut. **יִשְׁמֹט**) 1) to cast, to break loose (of the beasts of burden), to fling (out of the window); the Targum renders it **מְגַר**; the root is **שָׁמַט**, which is found again in **מָט**; 2) to remit, e.g. a debt, to release, e.g. the land, i.e. to let it lie uncultivated; with **מִן**, to cease from something. Niph. to be scattered, to be loosed, to be thrown down, e.g. from a rock. Hiph. to release, remit (a debt). Another **שָׁמַט** in the signif. of **צָמַת**, is found only in modern Hebrew.

שְׁמִטָּה f. remission (of a debt), release (of a land from being cultivated); hence **שְׁנַת הַשְׁ׳** year of release, i.e. every seventh year, when debts were cancelled and agriculture intermitted; **דְּבַר הַשְׁ׳** matter referring to the year of release.

שַׁמַּי p.n. m. (perhaps compounded from **שִׁמְעִי** the famed one).

שְׁמִידָע p.n. m. (famous in knowledge), contracted from **שְׁמִיעַ יָדָע**; patron. **—דָעִי**.

שְׂמִיכָה fem. mattress or bed-cover, from **שָׂמַךְ** to stretch along.

שָׁמַיִם (pl. from a sing. **שָׁמַי**, comp. **מַיִם** from a sing **מַי**; const. **שְׁמֵי**, with **ה** finis **שָׁמַיְמָה**) m. origin. height; transf. to heavens in the remotest sense; often joined with **אֱלֹהִים** and **י״י**; **שְׁמֵי הַשָּׁמַיִם** the heaven of heavens. It is often used for "God," as in many modern languages.

שְׁמַיִן (plur. from **שְׁמַי**, def. **שְׁמַיָּא**) Aram. m. the same.

שְׁמִינִי (formed from **שְׁמֹנָה**) adj. m., also as an ordinal number, **שְׁמִינִית** f. the eighth. The fem. **שְׁמִינִית** signifies also, a musical instrument of eight strings, or, according to some, a certain melody or tone (*ottava*), which, however, cannot be defined.

שָׁמִיר (with suff. שְׁמִירוֹ) m. 1) thorn, thistle, or collectively, thorn-bush; figur. enemies, from שָׁמַר to invade, penetrate, pierce; 2) a diamond, used for engraving, from the same original signif.; 3) p.n. of two cities; 4) p.n. m. for which in the Ketib שָׁמוּר.

שְׁמִירָמוֹת p.n. m. (fame of eminence). In modern Hebrew (Esth. Rabba) Semiramis was so written.

שָׂמַל (not used) but is the basis for שִׂמְלָה) masc. garment, raiment, covering, from שָׂמַם to cover, with the ancient form of termination ־ֶל, as in כַּרְמֶל, גָּבָל, שָׁרָל, etc.; but the fem. form only is used.

שִׂמְלָה (plur. שְׂמָלוֹת, with suffix שִׂמְלוֹתָם) f. a garment, covering, especially the spacious and broad robe in which the orientalists wrap themselves, from which שַׂלְמָה is transposed, with a similar signif.

שַׂמְלַי p.n. m. see שַׁלְמַי.

שְׂמָלִי see שְׂמָאלִי.

שָׁמֵם (Kal used in the dissolved form, imper. שֹׁם, inf. שַׁמּוֹת, fut. trans. יָשֹׁם, but pl. יָשֹׁמּוּ, intrans. יֵשַׁם, after the form יֵקַר ,יֵצַר ,יֵשַׁל ,יֵחַת; in the intrans. signif. the futures of Kal and Niph are blended together, as is the case with קָלַל and דָּמַם) 1) to terrify, to cause amazement; hence, to lay waste, to desolate; שׁוֹמֵם the desolater, ravager, tyrant; שִׁקּוּץ שׁוֹמֵם the abomination (idol) of the desolater; 2) intrans. to shudder, gaze, to be amazed at (עַל) something; transf. to be waste, desolate, ruined, and in this sense שׁוֹמֵם desolate; applied to people, it signifies, languishing, perishing, solitary; pl. שׁוֹמֵמוֹת desolate, waste places, ruins. Niph. נָשַׁם to be amazed, to gaze at (עַל) something; next, as in Kal, waste, desolate, forsaken; of people, to be perishing, lonely, languishing. Hiph. הֵשַׁם (fut. יַשִּׁים, inf. הַשְׁמֵם, particip. מְשִׁמִּים) 1) to amaze, terrify; transf. to lay waste, to desolate; 2) intrans. as in Kal, to be amazed, terrified at (עַל) something. Hoph. הָשַׁם (3 pl. הָשַׁמּוּ) to be amazed; transf. to be laid waste. Hith. הִשְׁתּוֹמֵם (future יִשְׁתּוֹמֵם) to be amazed, stunned, disheartened. The root is identical with that in אָשַׁם and תָּמַהּ.

שְׁמַם (Aram.) the same; hence Ithp. אֶשְׁתּוֹמַם.

שָׁמֵם adj. m., שְׁמֵמָה fem., desolate, waste.

שָׁמַם (not used) origin. to exhale; generally, to diffuse a bad odour; also, to poison; comp. סַמָּם in modern Hebrew.

שְׁמָמָה (pl. c. שִׁמְמוֹת and שְׁמָמוֹת) f. 1) terror, amazement, astonishment, shuddering; 2) desolation, devastating; concr. a waste, a ruin, a wilderness.

שִׁמָמָה f. the same.

שִׁמָּמוֹן m. amazement, astonishment, shuddering, terror.

שְׂמָמִית fem. a species of venomous lizard (Auth. Ver. "the spider."). In several MSS. the reading is שְׁמָמִית.

שָׁמֵן (fut. יִשְׁמַן) to be or become fat, corpulent. Hiph. 1) to make fat (the heart), a scriptural figure indicating stubborness, a heart inaccessible to exhortation; 2) to grow fat. The verb seems to have arisen as a denom. from שֶׁמֶן.

שָׁמֵן adj. m., שְׁמֵנָה f. fat, corpulent; fertile, of a soil; nourishing, of bread.

שֶׁמֶן (with suff. שַׁמְנִי, plur. שְׁמָנִים, with suff. שְׁמָנֶיךָ) m. 1) fat, corpulence, e. g. of the bull (Isaiah 10:27); transf. to fat viands, hence מִשְׁתֵּה שְׁמָנִים a fat or sumptuous feast; fruitfulness, fertility, of a soil; 2) oil, so called on account of its fatness; hence עֵץ שֶׁמֶן oil tree (the wild one), transf. to spiced oil, ointment, either for annointing, or as a means of cure. The root seems to be שם, and ־ֶן is as in חֹצֶן, חֹשֶׁן, חֹפֶן, בֹּשֶׁן, גֹּפֶן, גֹּרֶן, חֹרֶן, סֶרֶן, אֹזֶן, אַפֶּדֶן, אֹפֶן a form of termination.

שֹׁמֶן (after the form קֹמֶן, hence pl. שְׁמַנִּים, after the form קְמַנִּים) m fatness, fruitfulness (of a country district); hence, a fruit district.

שְׁמֹנָה (const. שְׁמֹנַת) cardinal number, fem. שְׁמֹנֶה (const. שְׁמֹנַת) m. eight; the pl. שְׁמֹנִים is common, and signifies eighty. From which שְׁמִינִי.

שָׁמַע (3 pers. pl. in pause שָׁמֵעוּ, fut. יִשְׁמַע) 1) to hearken to, or to hear some one (accus.) speak something (accus.); to listen to, with accus., אֶל, לְ, of the person, or to listen to something (with לְ); 2) to hear or hearken to (applied to God) some one (accus. or אֶל, or אֶל קוֹל, בְּקוֹל, קוֹל פּ׳); 3) to obey, with לְקוֹל, בְּקוֹל פּ׳, לְ, אֶל; 4) to understand, synon. with מֵבִין. Niph. 1) to be heard by (לְ) some one, to be understood, thus pass. of Kal; 2) to shew obedience, from the sense of obeying in Kal. Pi. to call, proclaim, announce. Hiph. 1) to cause some one to hear (his voice or cry), to let some one hear; with omission of קוֹל, to cause to sing, or sound forth: 2) to proclaim, announce. From the Hiph. the noun הַשְׁמָעוּת is formed, which see.

שְׁמַע (Aram.) the same; with עַל, to hear something of or about some one. Ith. to obey, to show obedience, to submit.

שָׁמָע p. n. m. (the obedient one).

שֵׁמַע (in pause שֵׁמָע, with suff. שִׁמְעִי, שִׁמְעָם) m. the hearing; transf. to report, repute, renown, information; also in the sense of a clear sound, and in all significations of the verb.

שֶׁמַע p. n. m. (report).

שְׁמַע (fame) p.n.m. of a city in Judah.

שֹׁמַע (with suff. שָׁמְעוֹ) m. report.

שִׁמְעָא p. n. m. (for שִׁמְעָאִי the renowned one). Sometimes שִׁמְעָה and שִׁמָּה (for שִׁמְעָה) are used for it, which signify the same.

שִׁמְעָה p. n. m. (the same), patron. שִׁמְעָתִי. See שַׁמָּה II.

שְׁמָעָה (with the article) p. n. masc. (the same).

שְׁמוּעָה see שְׁמֻעָה.

שִׁמְעוֹן p.n. m. (the one that is heard or answered), patron. שִׁמְעֹנִי.

שִׁמְעִי p. n. m. (the renowned one).

שְׁמַעְיָה p. n. m. (heard or answered by God).

שְׁמַעְיָהוּ p. n. m. (the same).

שִׁמְעָת p. n. f. (renown, fame).

שֶׁמֶץ (not used) probably only a secondary form from שָׁמַע, by which the following nouns will be easily explained:—

שֶׁמֶץ masc. a short gentle sound, a whispering. Comp. שֵׁמַע.

שִׁמְצָה fem. an evil report, disgrace; comp. שֵׁמַע רָע; also smiting, thrusting, overthrow.

שָׁמַר (fut. יִשְׁמֹר) orig. to penetrate, impress, urge (comp. שָׁמִיר); next, 1) to impress on the memory, to keep (in remembrance), to keep or retain the anger (sometimes אַף or עֶבְרָה are omitted); with accus., to keep a thing in memory concerning some one; 2) to observe, to notice (the way, the walk, a deed), construed with עַל or אֶל of the person; to observe a command, a covenant, a sabbath, or to keep anything promised; to observe, i. e. to besiege a town; 3) to guard, to watch (a flock, a garden, a house), and in a spiritual sense, to protect, maintain, with accus., בְּ, אֶל or עַל of the object; with מִן, to guard or preserve from something. In this sense שֹׁמֵר a keeper, guard, shepherd; transf. to a prophet; 4) almost reflective, like Niph., to guard oneself, to beware from (מִן) something or some one. Niph. 1) pass. to be kept, watched, guarded; 2) reflective, to keep or guard oneself from (מִן, מִפְּנֵי) something, to beware from (also with בְּ) something; frequently with the inf. following, or with (פֶּן) and the fut. in the concluding sentence, and in the imp.; often with the addition of לְנַפְשׁוֹתֵיכֶם, בְּנַפְשׁוֹתֵיכֶם to give emphasis to the caution; 3) to do something attentively, carefully, with לַעֲשׂוֹת following. Po. to keep as an observance. Hith. to guard oneself from (מִן) something, to keep a law, to take heed.

שֶׁמֶר (only pl. שְׁמָרִים) m. 1) origin. the remainder, or that which is retained; hence, the dregs, the sediment at the bottom of a cup or cask, the lees of wine, also used of wine that keeps well; שָׁקַט אֶל שְׁמָרִים, קָפָא עַל שְׁמָרִים "to rest upon one's lees," is a figure, indicating to continue quietly, unconcerned, in one's former condition.

שֶׁמֶר p. n. m. (watch); once שֹׁמֵר (guard) is used for it.

שִׁמֻּר (only pl. שִׁמֻּרִים) m. observance of a festival; according to others, preservation.

שֹׁמֵר 1) p. n. m. (keeper), once for שֶׁמֶר; 2) p. n. f., for which once שִׁמְרִית.

שְׁמֻרָה f. eyelash. The derivation is obscure.

שָׁמְרָה f. watch, guardianship; formed from a masc. form שֹׁמֶר.

שִׁמְרוֹן p. n. m. (guard), patr. שִׁמְרֹנִי.

שֹׁמְרוֹן Samaria (watch mountain), p. n. of a mountain, and also of a city built thereon, which was the metropolis of the kingdom of Israel and the royal residence; later a village called Sebaste, also Shemrun or Shemrin; transf. to the kingdom of Samaria. Gent. שֹׁמְרֹנִי.

שִׁמְרִי p. n. m. (keeper).

שְׁמַרְיָה p.n.m. (guarded by God).

שְׁמַרְיָהוּ p. n. m. (the same).

שָׁמְרַיִן (Aram.) equiv. to שֹׁמְרוֹן in Hebrew.

שִׁמְרִית p. n. f. (female watcher). See שֹׁמֵר.

שִׁמְרָת p. n. m. (guard).

שְׁמַשׁ (Poal, not used) Aram. to serve, to wait, attend upon; also of frequent use in modern Heb. Pael, to serve, especially of divine service; hence in Targum for שֵׁרֵת and כִּהֵן.

שֶׁמֶשׁ (with suff. שִׁמְשִׁי, pl. שְׁמָשׁוֹת, with suff. שִׁמְשֹׁתַיִךְ) com. the sun; under the sun, i. e. on earth;

before the face or under the eyes of the sun, figur. expressions for indicating: publicly, openly; the sun goeth forth, i.e. rises; the sun returns, i.e. sets. The pl. signifies the sun's rays, or anything protruding as rays, e.g. battlements, pinnacles, turrets (on a wall).

שִׁמְשׁוֹן Samson, p.n.m. (the brilliant one), formed from שֶׁמֶשׁ.

שִׁמְשַׁי p.n. m. the same.

שַׁמְשְׁרַי p.n. m. (compounded from שִׁמְשַׁי and שְׁמַרְיָ).

שֻׁמָתִי see שׁוּמָה.

שֵׁן (before makkaph שֶׁן־, with suff. שִׁנּוֹ, dual שִׁנַּיִם) com. 1) origin. point, edge, prong; hence, sharp cliff, point of a rock; next, tooth of a human being, and also of an elephant, ivory, thus בָּתֵּי שֵׁן ivory palaces; the dual form is used on account of the two rows of teeth; to carry the life between the teeth, is a scriptural figure for risking one's life; 2) (edge of a rock) p.n. of a place, perhaps of a rock.

שָׁנֵא a rare form for שָׁנָה, which see.

שְׁנָא (3 plur. שְׁנוֹ, fut. יִשְׁנֵא) Aram. equiv. to שָׁנָה in Heb. to change, to become different, e.g. of the changing of the general colour of the face; especially to change for the worse; with מִן, to be different from something. Pael שַׁנִּי (3 pl. שַׁנִּיו) to change; with מִן, to turn something different from another; to alter the word of the king, i.e. to transgress his command. Ithp. to be altered, changed, disfigured; and also reflective, to alter (oneself). Af. אַשְׁנִי to change (the times); also like Pa. to transgress a royal order.

שֵׁנָא (a secondary form from שֵׁנָה) f. sleep; see יָשֵׁן.

שְׁנָא (Aram.) f. sleep.

שָׂנֵא (fut. יִשְׂנָא, inf. שִׂנְאת) orig. to cut, stick into something (related to סָנָה), transf. to hate; hence, שׂנֵא a hater, an enemy; with suff. שׂנְאוֹ, equiv. to שׂנֵא לוֹ. Niph. pass. to be hated. Pi. to attack violently. Part. מְשַׂנֵּא violent enemy.

שְׂנֵא (particip. pl. שָׂנְאִין) Aram. the same as שָׂנֵא in Heb.

שִׁנְאָב p.n. masc. (the etymology is obscure).

שִׂנְאָה (origin. inf. Kal) fem. 1) the hating; 2) conc. hatred.

שִׁנְאָן (the plur. in modern Hebrew שִׁנְאַנִּים) masc. probably equiv. to מִשְׁנֶה repetition; thousands of repetitions (Ps. 68:18), i.e. many many thousands; according to others, שִׁנְאָן signifies an angel, and they render the passage in the Psalms, thousands of angels.

שֶׁנְאַצַּר p. n. m.

שָׁנַב (not used) to entwine, related to עָנַב in a similar sense, from which אֶשְׁנָב lattice, window. In a similar manner אֲרֻבָּה, חֲרַךְ, and שְׂבָכָה are derived from verbs signifying to entwine.

I. שָׁנָה (fut. יִשְׁנֶה, once יִשְׁנָא, and the א appears also in the derivative שִׁנְאָן) 1) to repeat, to do something a second time; hence, to continue in (בְּ) something, to stir up something (בְּ) anew, as if the verb were a denom. from שְׁנַיִם; 2) to be different from (מִן) something, to differ always, i.e. to be changeable, uncertain; hence, שֹׁנִים the uncertain ones; 3) to alter (for the worse), to be disfigured. Niph. to repeat itself (of a dream). Pi. (once שִׁנֵּא) 1) to change (the dress), to alter (the course of life), to change justice for injustice, i.e. to pervert justice; 2) to disfigure the countenance, fig. in the phrase שַׁנָּה אֶת טַעְמוֹ to disfigure one's understanding, i.e. to pretend to be mad or foolish; 3) to change the place of anything, i.e. to carry it to another. Pu. pass. to be changed, altered. Hith. הִשְׁתַּנָּה to change one's dress, i.e. to disguise oneself.

II. שָׁנָה (not used) to shine, to glitter; after the Arab. From which שָׁנִי, which see.

שָׁנָה (const. שְׁנַת, with suff. שְׁנָתוֹ, dual שְׁנָתַיִם, pl. שָׁנִים const. שְׁנֵי; poetically שָׁנוֹת, const. שְׁנוֹת, with suff. שְׁנוֹתֶיךָ) fem. orig. circuit, return (of time); hence, a year, comp. *annus* a year, orig. a circle; שָׁנָה שָׁנָה, מִדֵּי שָׁנָה בְשָׁנָה, שָׁנָה בְשָׁנָה from year to year, annually; the plur. signifies an uncertain number of years, and transf. to the produce of years. The dual שְׁנָתַיִם is often joined to יָמִים, to denote uninterrupted continuation. Joined with numerals, the latter always succeed שָׁנָה, and sometimes שָׁנָה is again added, following the numerals. The root is שָׁנָה.

שֵׁנָה (from יָשֵׁן) f. sleep; transf. to a dream.

שְׁנָה (pl. שְׁנִין) Aram. f. 1) a year; 2) sleep; in both significations like the Hebrew.

שֶׁנְהַבִּים (formed from a singular שֶׁן־הַבָּה) f. ivory, orig. elephant's teeth.

שָׁנַט (a root adopted for שִׁפָּה) to pierce. See שִׁפָּה.

שָׁנִי (formed after the usual manner from שָׁנָה, const. שְׁנִי, pl. שָׁנִים) m. the crimson colour obtained from the turtle insect, *coccus ilicis*

(תּוֹלַעַת); transf. to materials dyed with this colour; especially the pl. in this sense. The root is שָׁנָה II., to shine; comp. זְהוֹרִי in Aram. According to others, the root is שָׁנָה I., and the origin. signif. is double dyed, which may be etymologically correct; but is not substantiated as a matter of fact.

שֵׁנִי (formed from שְׁנַיִם, pl. שֵׁנִים) ordinal number, m., שֵׁנִית f. the second. The pl. masc. signifies especially, the second row or class, or the rooms in the second story. The fem. sing. signifies a second time.

שָׂנִיא adj. m., שְׂנִיאָה f. hated, hateful.

שְׁנַיִם (const. שְׁנֵי, with suff. שְׁנֵיהֶם) cardinal number, m., שְׁתַּיִם (const. שְׁתֵּי) f. two; שְׁנַיִם שְׁנַיִם two and two, a pair; שְׁנֵיהֶם both of them; the fem. also signifies two kinds, or at a second time; פַּעַם וּשְׁתַּיִם once and again. The form שְׁנַיִם is not a dual one, but is formed from שָׁנָה, after the manner of ל״ה. The f. form שְׁתַּיִם is contracted from שְׁנְתַיִם, from which אֶשְׁתַּיִם, and the א was subsequently dropped. The abridged forms שְׁנֵים, שְׁתֵּים, only occur in connection with עָשָׂר and עֶשְׂרֵה. From which שֵׁנִי; see also עַשְׁתֵּי.

שְׁנִינָה fem. sharp, piercing words, mockery, scorn, derision, from שָׁנַן to sharpen.

שְׂנִיר (coat of mail) p.n. of a ridge of mountains of Hermon (among the Amorites), equiv. to שִׂרְיוֹן (among the Sidonians).

שָׁנַן (denom. from שֵׁן, 1 pers. pret. שַׁנּוֹתִי, plur. שָׁנַנּוּ) to sharpen (the sword); to sharpen the tongue, i.e. for slander; to sharpen or point (the arrows). Pi. to sharpen (in a spiritual sense), to teach diligently, to exhort, to inculcate. Hith. הִשְׁתּוֹנֵן to be penetrated or pierced (with pain).

שָׁנַס (Kal, not used) to pinch, to compress, related to אָנַס; hence Pi. שִׁנֵּס to gird (the loins).

שִׁנְעָר p.n. of the plain before Mesopotamia, or of the territory of Babylon; in the former, the ancient commentators recognise the river and town of Singara. The word is of foreign origin, and signifies the land of lions.

שָׂנַר (not used and only adopted for שְׂנִיר) to enclose; hence שְׂנִיר coat of mail.

שֵׁנָת f. equiv. to שֵׁנָה sleep. The root is יָשֵׁן.

שָׁסָה (particip. pl. שֹׁסִים) equiv. to שָׁסַס orig. to tear off, to snatch; next, to plunder; שֹׁסִים plunderers, robbers. Poel, שׁוֹשָׂה (for שׁוֹסָה) to spoil, to rob.

שָׁסַס (3 plur. with suff. שַׁסּוּהוּ, fut. יָשֹׁס, particip. שֹׁסִים, after the Syriac manner for שֹׁסְסִים) the same, to plunder, spoil, rob. Niph. נָשַׁס (fut. יִשַּׁס) to be plundered.

שָׁסַע to make an incision, to cleave, split; also intrans. שָׁסַע שֶׁסַע to divide the hoof, to have a cloven foot. Pi. to tear in pieces (a lion), to make a rent; figur. to chide, rebuke.

שֶׁסַע m. a cleft, splitting or dividing of the hoofs.

שָׁסַף (Kal, not used) to split, to cut in pieces, to hew. The root is שְׁ־סַף, and related with that in חָ־סַף, סָעַף. Pi. to tear in pieces, to split.

שָׁעָא (only def. שַׁעְתָּא, שַׁעֲתָא) Aram. f. orig. glance, look; next, twinkling of the eye, a moment, equiv. to רֶגַע; transf. to a certain definite time, an hour. In biblical Aram. it signifies, a while, a short time.

I. שָׁעָה (fut. יִשְׁעֶה, apoc. יִשַׁע) to look, behold, related to שָׁבָה, שָׁגַח to look about or forward (for help), to look graciously upon (אֶל) something (spoken of God); to look upon (עַל, אֶל, בְּ) something; to look away from (מֵעַל or מִן) something. Hiph. to look attentively, or to gaze at something; with מִן, to look away. The imp. in the apoc. הָשַׁע. Hith. הִשְׁתָּעָה (fut. apoc. יִשְׁתָּע) to look forward for help, to look at one another, i. e. to measure one another for a combat. From which the Aram. שְׁעָא, which see.

II. שָׁעָה (fut. יִשְׁעֶה) to spread over (with paint), related to שָׁעַע, fig. of the eyes being overspread, i. e. dazzled, closed, blinded; generally to labour under an illusion.

שָׁעָה belongs to מִשְׁעִי, which see.

שָׁעַט (not used) to tread, to pace, to stamp with the feet. From which:—

שַׁעֲטָה (after the form בְּרָכָה, const. שַׁעֲטַת) f. the stamping (of horses' hoofs).

שַׁעַטְנֵז (a foreign word), m. a cloth made of different threads, e. g. of wool and linen. The commentators differ as to its etymology, and orig. signif.

שָׂעִיר (const. שְׂעִיר, pl. שְׂעִירִים) adj. m., שְׂעִירָה (pl. שְׂעִירוֹת) fem. 1) hairy, rough, formed from שֵׂעָר, especially of the hairiness of the body; 2) as a subst., a buck or he-goat, so called on account of his hairiness; שְׂעִיר עִזִּים a kid of the goats; שְׂעִירַת a she-goat, always joined with שָׂעִיר עִזִּים; and the pl. שְׂעִירִים are next used to signify wild men or demons in the form of he-goats, similar to the Grecian satyrs; 3) שְׂעִירִים showers of rain, from שַׂעַר II.

שֵׂעִיר 1) p.n. masc. (the hairy one) synon. with עֵשָׂו; 2) (foliage) p.n. of a mountain-district, extending from the Dead Sea to the Elanitic Gulf. The northern part of that district is now called Djebal, the southern, El Shera.

שְׂעִירָה f. 1) a she-goat, see שָׂעִיר; 2) p.n. of a place in the mountain of Ephraim.

שָׁעַל (not used) equiv. to שָׁאַל to hollow out, to excavate (see שָׁאַל); next, intrans. to be hollow, from which שׁוּעָל, מִשְׁעוֹל and—

שֹׁעַל (with suff. שָׁעֳלוֹ) m. the hollow of the hand, a handful; comp. כַּף with a similar derivation.

שֹׁעַל (pl. שְׁעָלִים, const. שַׁעֲלֵי) masc. handful.

שַׁעַלְבִּים (only pl. שַׁעַלְבִּים and שַׁעַלְבִין) p.n. of a city in the tribe of Dan. As an apell. it signifies the haunt of jackals, equiv. to שׁוּעָל, with addition of ב; gent. שַׁעַלְבֹנִי.

שַׁעֲלִים (jackal district) p.n. of a district in Benjamin.

שָׁעַן (Kal, not used) to lie, to rest, related to שָׁאַן; hence Niph. to lean, to stay, to support oneself upon (עַל) something; עַל יַד to lean on the hand of some one, as oriental monarchs do on the hand of their officers; transf. to the leaning or bordering of one country on another, construed with לְ; fig. to rely upon, to trust in (אֶל, עַל, בְּ) something.

שָׁעַע (i.e. שַׁע, imp. pl. שֹׁעוּ) equiv. to שָׁעָה II. to spread over, to make smooth, or intrans. to be overspread (of the eyes) blinded. Hiph. (imp. הָשַׁע) to overspread, close (the eyes), i.e. they will not see. Pilpel שִׁעֲשַׁע, orig. to smooth, to flatter; next, generally, to delight oneself, to play. Pulpel שֻׁעֲשַׁע to be flattered, caressed. Hithpalpel הִשְׁתַּעֲשַׁע to delight oneself at or with (בְּ) something. As to the reduplicated forms, the original root may correspond with that in יָשַׁע to be enlarged, from which the sense of delighting, rejoicing. See שַׁעֲשֻׁעַ.

שָׁעַף (not used) probably equiv. to שָׁאַף panting or snorting for something, e.g. for revenge. From which:—

שַׁעַף p.n. m. (snorting with revenge).

שָׂעַף (not used) equiv. to סָעַף to split, divide; next, fig. to judge, decide, try, prove; comp. שָׁפַט

with violence, to storm. Niph. to be carried away by a storm; also, to rage, be tempestuous. Pi. to carry away in a storm, to sweep away. Hith. to storm, to rage like a tempest. Comp. סָעַר and שָׂעַר II.

שְׂעִפִּים (only pl. שְׂעִפִּים, const. שְׂעִפֵּי) masc. thoughts or visions (in a dream), orig. the powers of deciding and judging. It is erroneous to adopt סְעִפָּה for the basis of this form.

and בְּשַׂר with a similar origin. signif. From which:—

שַׂעַר (with ה finis שַׂעְרָה, dual שַׂעֲרַיִם, pl. שְׁעָרִים, const. שַׁעֲרֵי, with suff. שְׁעָרֶיךָ) f. 1) origin. cleft, division, a breaking through, from שָׁעַר I.; next, a gate, of a camp, city, castle; and the gate having been formerly the place of public meetings, it signifies also a forum or tribunal of justice, assembly, principal part of the city, and city generally; בַּשַּׁעַר openly, publickly; בִּשְׁעָרֶיךָ within thy gates, i. e. in thy cities. The following are special names of gates of Jerusalem; שַׁעַר הָעַיִן the fountain-gate; שַׁעַר הָאַשְׁפֹּת (contracted שַׁ׳ הַשְׁפֹּת) the dung-gate; שַׁ׳ הַגַּיְא the valley-gate; שַׁ׳ הַפִּנָּה or שַׁ׳ הַפֹּנִים the corner-gate; שַׁ׳ הַיְשָׁנָה שַׁ׳ הָרִאשׁוֹן the old gate; שַׁ׳ הַדָּגִים the eastern gate; שַׁ׳ הַסּוּסִים the fish-gate; שַׁ׳ הַצֹּאן the horse-gate; שַׁ׳ הַמַּיִם the sheep-gate; שַׁ׳ אֶפְרַיִם the water-gate; שַׁ׳ הַמִּפְקָד the gate of Ephraim; the review-gate, or the gate of justice; שַׁ׳ הַחַרְסִית the potter's

I. שָׁעַר origin. to divide, to cut in pieces, to split, related is תָּעַר (from which תַּעַר); hence transf. as in חָתַךְ, גָּזַר to decide, determine, decree, and especially to fix (the price), to value, measure. From which in modern Heb. שִׁעוּר task, שַׁעַר price, etc. From which שַׁעַר.

II. שָׁעַר (not used) equiv. to שָׂעַר to shudder, to be amazed; also, to shower, to storm, to rage; comp. שָׂעַר II.

שָׁעַר (denom. from שַׁעַר) to watch at the gate; hence שֹׁעֵר gatekeeper; comp. סֹפֵר from סֵפֶר, בֹּקֵר from בָּקָר.

I. שָׂעַר (not used) equiv. to שָׁעַר I. to split, to divide, to separate, synon. with פָּרַע, from which פֶּרַע; from which שֵׂעָר, שָׂעִיר, שַׂעֲרָה, שְׂעֹרָה, שְׂעוֹר.

II. שָׂעַר (fut. יִשְׂעַר) 1) to storm, to rage, to shudder or shiver from fear or anguish, to be amazed at (עַל) something; next, generally, to be terrified; 2) trans. to assail

gate; שׁ׳ הַמַּטָּרָה the prison-gate; 2) only pl. שְׁעָרִים measures. See the verb.

שֹׁעָר (only plur. שֹׁעָרִים) adj. m. (the form probably from מְשֹׁעָר) abominable, hateful, vile, detestable, mean, from שָׁעַר II. The plural תְּאֵנִים, with which it is joined in the constructive state, Jer. 29:17, is used as a masc.

שַׂעַר m. 1) equiv. to סַעַר storm; 2) shuddering, shivering, as a const. from שָׂעַר. See שֵׂעָר.

שֵׂעָר (const. שְׂעַר, once שֵׂעַר, with suff. שְׂעָרוֹ) m. origin. that which is split; hence, a hair, generally collective; joined with other nouns it is used as an adj. hairy; בַּעַל שֵׂעָר a man with a hairy garment; compare etymologically פֶּרַע and the Aram. בְּנִית.

שְׂעַר (Aram.) m. the same.

שְׂעֹר (only pl. שְׂעֹרִים) m. only Ruth 3:15, measure, equiv. to שַׁעַר 2.

שְׂעָרָה fem. only another reading for סְעָרָה, storm, tempest.

שַׂעֲרָה (c. שַׂעֲרַת, with suff. שַׂעֲרָתוֹ, const. pl. שַׂעֲרוֹת) f. a hair, whilst שֵׂעָר is a collective; this form, however, is rarely used as a collective.

שְׂעֹרָה (pl. שְׂעֹרִים) f. a kind of rough corn or barley, so called on account of the roughness of its ears, from שָׂעַר rough. The sing. is used of the barley when it is yet in the ear; but the pl. is used of the grain. The same distinction is between חִטָּה and חִטִּים.

שַׁעֲרוּר adj. m., שַׁעֲרוּרָה f. something terrible, horrible, abominable, orig. that which causes shuddering. The fem. is used also as a subst.

שַׁעֲרוּרִי adj. m., שַׁעֲרוּרִיָּה fem. the same.

שַׁעֲרוּרִית f. the same.

שְׁעַרְיָה p.n. m. (decision of God).

שַׁעֲרַיִם (double gate, compare חַלֹּנַיִם double window, דְּלָתַיִם double gates) p.n. of a city in the territory of Judah.

שְׂעֹרִים p.n. m. (hairiness).

שַׁעַשְׁגַז (foreign) p.n. of a Persian eunuch.

שַׁעֲשֻׁעַ (pl. ־עִים) m. subject of joy or delight, comp. שָׁעַע.

I. שָׁפָה (not used, and adopted only for אַשְׁפָּה I.) to hold, contain. The root שָׁפָה is related with סַף in this sense, and also connected with שָׂפָה.

II. שָׁפָה (not used, and adopted only for אַשְׁפָּה II., אַשְׁפֹּת and שְׁפֹת) to heap up, to gather in heaps. Related with the root in אֶרְסָף and סַפָּה.

III. שָׁפָה (Kal, not used) to be plain, even, probably related to שָׁוָה;

hence Niph. נִשְׁפָּה to be bald, naked, without foliage, etc. (of a mountain). Pual, שֻׁפָּה of bones stripped of flesh. From which שְׁפִי.

שָׂפָה belongs to the const. pl. שִׂפְוֹת, see שָׂפָת.

שָׂפָה (not used) to hold, contain, take up; but not, as according to some, equiv. to סָבָא to drink. From which:—

שָׂפָה (dual שְׂפָתַיִם, const. שִׂפְתֵי, with suffix שְׂפָתָיו; the const. שִׂפְתוֹת, which has for a sing. שֶׂפֶת, not used) f. 1) the organ which takes up, the mouth, the lip, comp. מַלְקוֹחַ, transf. to speech, word, language, etc.; the word of the lips, i.e. babbling, idle talk; burning lips, i.e. warm professions of friendship; of deep lips, עִמְקֵי שָׂפָה i.e. of unintelligible language; 2) border of a vessel, border or hem of a garment, border of a river or coast of the sea, border or boundary of a country, etc.

שְׁפוֹ p. n. m. (nakedness, baldness), for which שְׁפִי once stands.

שְׁפוֹט (pl. שְׁפוּטִים) m. chastisement, punishment. See שָׁפַט.

שְׁפוּפָם (probably equiv. to שְׁפִיפוֹן) p. n. m.

שְׁפוּפָן p. n. m. (the same).

שָׁפַח to join, adhere, annex; thus related with סָפַח. From which מִשְׁפָּחָה and שִׁפְחָה.

שָׁפַח belongs to שָׁפַח, which is probably only a denom. of סַפַּחַת, in the signification to scrape, to take off the scurf, or to make bald (the head), to cause the hair to fall off (by sickness).

שִׁפְחָה (־חַת), with suff. שִׁפְחָתִי, pl. שְׁפָחוֹת, const. שִׁפְחוֹת) f. a handmaid, a female servant, orig. one who joins the house, the family.

שָׁפַט (fut. יִשְׁפֹּט) 1) orig. to cut, to split, to part; hence, like most verbs signifying cutting, to decide, to judge; שָׁפַט בֵּין וּבֵין or בֵּין לְ to judge between two parties; שֹׁפֵט a judge; 2) to afford justice, with acc. of the person to whom justice is afforded; to save some one from some one, construed with מִיַּד or מִן; 3) to sentence, to condemn, to punish (the guilty); 4) to judge, with the secondary signif. of ruling, inasmuch as the judgment in the Orient proceeded from the ruler, and among the Israelites the judges were at one time also the rulers. Niph. 1) to contend with (אֵת, אֹת, עִם, לְ) some one, about (עַל, אֹת) some matter, to manifest oneself as judge or ruler of some one; applied to God, it signifies to punish, to exercise punishment; 2) to be judged. Poal (part. מְשׁוֹפֵט) to judge. The root of the verb is שְׁ־פַט, and related with פַּד.

שְׁפַט (particip. pl. שָׁפְטִין) Aram. the same.

שֶׁפֶט (for 1, only the plur. שְׁפָטִים; but for the 2, only in the sing.) m. 1) chastisement, punishment, judgment; עָשָׂה שׁ׳ בְּ to execute judgment on some one; שְׁפָטִים רָעִים calamitous judgments; 2) p.n. m. (judge).

שְׁפַטְיָה p.n. m. (God is the judge).

שְׁפַטְיָהוּ p.n. m. the same.

שִׁפְטָן p.n. m. (judge).

שְׁפִי (after the form צְבִי, גְּדִי, plur. שְׁפָיִים, in many manuscripts, שְׁפָאִים, in pause sing. שֶׁפִי from שָׁפָה) m. 1) origin. a plain, like שָׁוֶה a bald place, i.e. not covered with wood; transf. Job 33:21, in Ketib, to the baldness of bones, i.e. stripped of the flesh; 2) a bald cavern, mountain, or hill, i.e. without wood or foliage, as the hills in a forest; 3) p.n. masc. (baldness for the bald one). See שְׁפוֹ, with which it interchanges.

שְׁפִיב p.n. m. (from שׁוּף I.) piercing, wounding, bruising.

שְׁפִיפֹן m. a kind of serpent, *cerastes*, from שָׁפַף to wound, to bruise.

שָׁפִיר (beauteous city) p.n. of a city otherwise unknown.

שַׁפִּיר (Aram.) adj. m., pleasant, fair.

שָׁפַךְ (fut. יִשְׁפֹּךְ) 1) to pour out, to pour forth, to spill, to shed, e.g. blood, water; to pour out the soul or the heart, i.e. to break forth in tears and lamentations; to pour out the wrath over (עַל) something or some one, i.e. to be very wroth; 2) to pour out or empty (of solid objects); to spend, squander (money), to throw up (a rampart, wall). Niph. 1) to be poured out (of fluids), to be poured like water, i.e. to be powerless, faint; 2) of solids, to be spent, wasted. Pu. to slip, of the steps. Hith. to pour itself out, of the soul, in tears and lamentations, of the wrath, of prayer, etc. The root is related to סָפַח, and that in שָׁפַךְ is found also in פַּכִּים.

שֶׁפֶךְ m. the pouring out (of ashes), but generally concrete, the place of pouring out; hence the rendering in the Targ. בֵּית מְשַׁר קִטְמָא.

שָׁפְכָה (from a masc. form שֹׁפֶךְ) f. the testicles, origin. entwining of testicles, from שָׁפַךְ in the sense of שָׂבַךְ to entwine; or the orig. signif. is channel; comp. שֶׁפֶךְ and שְׁפִיךְ in modern Heb. channel, gutter, spout.

שָׁפֵל (fut. יִשְׁפַּל, inf. שְׁפַל, after the form שְׁכַב) 1) to sink, fall down; also of inanimate objects, e.g. the forest, i.e. the trees are felled; also of a city, but generally of persons; 2) in a spiritual sense, to be low, humbled; to be subdued, of the voice, etc. Hiph. 1) to lower, to make low, to humble (in contrast to הֵרִים); in connection with other verbs it is used as an adv. e.g. הִשְׁפִּיל שֶׁבֶת to set low; also intrans. to be brought low, to be cast down; 2) to thrust down, to cause to fall (the walls).

שְׁפַל or **שְׁפֵל** (Pael, not used) Aram. the same. Aphal הַשְׁפֵּל 1) to subdue, oppress, humble; 2) to throw down (kings from the throne).

שָׁפָל (const. שְׁפַל, pl. שְׁפָלִים) adj. m., **שְׁפָלָה** (const. שִׁפְלַת) f. low, used in as manifold significations as the verb; hence, of a deep mark of leprosy; of the sinking of the earth; of lowness, humbleness, dejection of spirit; of lowness or meanness in reference to position or rank, i.e. contemptible, mean, despised; also, of lowness of stature.

שְׁפַל (Aram.) adj. m. the same.

שֵׁפֶל (with suff. שִׁפְלֵנוּ) m. lowness, low place, low position, condition, rank.

שִׁפְלָה f. lowness, meanness.

שְׁפֵלָה (from a masc. שְׁפֵל, with suff. שְׁפֵלָתוֹ), fem. lowness; with the article, the low country from Joppa to Gaza, and in this sense frequently used.

שִׁפְלוּת f. the letting down or slacking (of the hand); used as a figure of sluggishness, indolence; only used in connection with יָדַיִם.

שָׁפַם (not used) adopted as the root for שְׁפָם, שָׁפָם, שִׁפְמוֹת; this signification is obscure.

שָׁפָם (not used) adopted as a root for שְׁפָם; the signif. is obscure.

שְׁפָם p. n. masc. (the cunning one), from שָׁפָם, equiv. to שָׁפָן.

שְׁפָם (perhaps identical with שְׁפִי) p. n. of a place in Judah; from which the gent. שִׁפְמִי.

שָׂפָם (with suff. שְׂפָמוֹ) masc. beard, especially the beard over the mouth, on the lips; according to some, the whole chin; עָשָׂה שׂ׳ to arrange, trim the beard; עָטָה אֶת, עַל שׂ׳, to wrap up, cover the beard as a sign of mourning.

שִׂפְמוֹת (equiv. to שְׁפָם) p. n. of a place in Judah.

שָׁפַן (not used) according to some, equiv. to סָפַן to conceal or hide oneself, from which שָׁפָן a rabbit, so called on account of its hiding itself in the cave; according to others, to be artful, cunning, after the Arab., which signification is also applicable to the rabbit; more correct, however, is the signif. to hop, to spring, as rendered in the Targum.

שָׁפַן probably equiv. to סָפַן, צָפַן to hide, conceal; שְׂפֻנֵי טְמוּנִים the hidden, i.e. the valuable or precious treasures.

שָׁפָן (pl. שְׁפַנִּים, after the form קָטָן, pl. קְטַנִּים) m. 1) a springing hare, or rabbit, from שָׁפַן to hop, to spring; the Targum renders it טַפְזָא the springer; 2) p.n. masc. springer.

שָׁפַע (not used) to overflow, to stream; related is סָבָא and זָב.

שֶׁפַע masc. overflowing, abundance, wealth; שֶׁ׳ יַמִּים the abundance or wealth of the seas.

שִׁפְעָה (formed from the m. שֶׁפַע) f. overflowing, multitude (of water), a troop (of horses, camels); transf. to a multitude of men, a band, a troop.

שִׁפְעִי p.n. m. (the rich, wealthy one).

שָׁפַף (not used) to pierce, to bruise, wound, like שְׁפַף in Aram.; related is שׁוּף I. above.

I. **שָׂפַק** (fut. יִשְׂפֹּק) equiv. to סָפַק, to clap the hands together, indicating the concluding of a covenant, but also as a sign of wonder and amazement; with עַל, to clap the hands together over some one. Hiph. הִשְׂפִּיק to enter with (בְּ) some one into a covenant by the clapping of hands, or to close an alliance, e.g. בְּיַלְדֵי נָכְרִים with the children of strangers, Author. Version, "and they please themselves."

II. **שָׂפַק** (fut. יִשְׂפֹּק) to overflow, to exist in abundance, fulness; to suffice, to be sufficient; comp. סְפַק in Aram. A similar signification is originally in דַּי to suffice.

שֶׂפֶק (with suff. שִׂפְקוֹ, according to some) m. fulness, abundance, e.g. in the fulness of his sufficiency he shall be in straits (Job 20:22); also, beware lest abundance mislead thee (Job 36:18), from שָׂפַק II. The Author. Vers. renders it in the sense of clapping, striking; "beware lest he take thee away with his stroke," from שָׂפַק I.

שָׁפַר (Kal, not used) orig. to hollow out, to deepen out, for holding something, or for any other use. The root is שָׁדַר, and related to that in חָפַר. From which Pi. שִׁפֵּר to hollow, to arch, of the arched expansion of a tent; fig. of the arched heavens. From this root are the derivatives שׁוֹפָר, שַׁפְרִיר, and אֶשְׁפָּר.

שָׁפַר equiv. to סָפַר to shine, to glimmer (see סַפִּיר); the root lies in שְׁ־פַר, and is found again in חָ־פַר, עָ־פַר, and others. Transf. to be beautiful, fair, lovely, agreeable, pleasant, acceptable; with עַל to be pleasant to some one. Derivative שֶׁפֶר.

שְׁפַר (fut. יִשְׁפַּר) Aram. the same, with קֳדָם or עַל like in Hebrew. From which שַׁפִּיר and שְׁפַרְפַּר.

שֶׁפֶר masc. 1) beauty, brightness, pleasantness; 2) (beautiful mountain) p. n. of a mountain in the Arabian desert.

שִׁפְרָה f. 1) beauty, brightness, lustre, like שֶׁפֶר; thus, according to some, Job 26:13, by his spirit his hand has adorned (Author. Vers. "garnished") the heavens. The word יָדוֹ his hand, which occurs in the parallel passage of that verse, refers back to the first part of the verse; 2) p. n. fem. (beauty).

שַׁפְרִיר (after the form סַגְרִיר, in the Ketib שַׁפְרוּר) m. a tent, probably so called from its arched shape, from שָׁפַר; according to others, "an elegant covering." נָטָה שׁ׳ to spread the tent.

שְׁפַרְפַּר (def. שְׁפַרְפָּרָא) Aram. m. the dawn of morning, *Aurora*, light or brightness of the morning, from שְׁפַר to be bright. In Targum, the word is used for the Hebrew נְהָרָה.

שָׁפַת (fut. יִשְׁפּוֹת) to set, lay, put, place, synon. with שׁוּם, שׁוּת. The root is in שְׁ־פַת, which is also found in רָ־פַד. שׁ׳ הַסִּיר to put or set the kettle on.

שָׁפָת (only pl. שְׁפוֹת) fem. cheese, equiv. to חֲרִיצֵי חָלָב, from שָׁזָה to be heaped up; שְׁפוֹת בָּקָר cow-cheese.

שֶׁפֶת (after the form קָטָן, dual שְׁפַתַּיִם) m. stalls or stables for cattle, consisting of two rows; hence the dual form. If such cattle stalls are in the open field, it signifies a pen, a hurdle. According to others, it also signifies a nail or hook, in the court of the temple, from which the cattle for sacrifices were suspended whilst taking off the skin, which signif. is in accordance with שָׁפַת. See מִשְׁפָּת.

שְׁצָא (Peal, not used) Aram. to make an end of something, to destroy; from which Pael שֵׁיצָא and שֵׁיצִיא to blot out, to annihilate. This rare Pael form is on account of the otherwise clashing of the two dentals ז and שׁ.

שָׁצַף (not used) probably only a secondary form from שָׁטַף in the signification of overflowing, pouring forth. From which:—

שֶׁצֶף m. equiv. to שֶׁטֶף Prov. 27:4, the pouring forth (of anger).

שָׁק (only pl. with suff. שָׁקוֹהִי) Aram. m. thigh, shank, leg.

שַׂק (with suff. שַׂקִּי, pl. שַׂקִּים, with suff. שַׂקֵּיהֶם) m. a sack, a kind of coarse hair-cloth, either for wrapping oneself up in (as a sign of mourning) or to wrap or pack up something in; figur. mourning-garments generally, or the dress of the prophet. The root is שָׂקַק, which see.

שָׁקַד (fut. יִשְׁקֹד) 1) to hasten away, like שְׁקַד in Aram.; 2) the sense of hastening transferred to that of zeal; hence, to be zealous, to watch something zealously, to be eager for or intent upon something, to be awake, vigilant, watchful (of the watchman); to attend carefully, to lie in wait (of the leopard). The part. Pu. מְשֻׁקָּדִים see under שָׁקֵד.

שָׂקַד (Kal, not used) to engrave, to indent, after the Aram.; according to Kimchi, to knot, to tie; related to עָקַד. Niph. to be tied fast; according to the former opinion, to be engrafted, indented.

שָׁקֵד (pl. שְׁקֵדִים) m. 1) almond-tree, so called on account of the earliness of its flowers and fruit; 2) almond (the fruit), from which denom. שִׁקֵּד to be formed like the blossoms of almonds, of ornaments.

שָׁקָה (Kal, not used) according to the ancient interchanging of ק with ת equivalent to שָׁתָה, comp. פָּתַח and פָּקַח; from which Hiph. הִשְׁקָה to cause to drink, i.e. to water (the cattle, the soil); to give to drink (of man), hence מַשְׁקֶה butler; in a fig. sense, to allot or award something to some one. Niph. only Amos. 8:8, where the form וְנִשְׁקָה stands for וְנִשְׁקְעָה. Pu. to become or grow fresh, moistened, sapful (of the marrow of bones).

שִׁקּוּ (for שִׁקּוּי, pl. with suff. שִׁקּוּיָ) m. drink, beverage.

שִׁקּוּי (plur. with suff. שִׁקּוּיַי) m. the same, especially of wine; figur. revival; origin. moistening, refreshing.

שִׁקּוּץ (pl. שִׁקֻּצִים) m. abomination, disgust, detestation; transf. to unclean things in a religious sense, especially to idols, which are frequently designated abominations.

שָׁקַט (fut. יִשְׁקֹט) equiv. to שָׁבַת to be quiet, silent, calm, undisturbed מִמִּלְחָמָה by war; also, to rest, to have repose, to be inactive, applied to God, it signifies, with holding His support. Hiph. to cause to rest, to still, to appease, to silence (the dispute), to afford rest, ease; also, to enjoy rest, to diffuse quietness (of the calmness of the air); infin. הַשְׁקֵט as a subst. rest, quiet.

שֶׁקֶט masc. quiet, ease, tranquillity, rest, peace.

שָׁקַל (fut. יִשְׁקֹל, but with ה, אֶשְׁקְלָה, as if the basis were אֶשְׁקֹל) orig. to shake, related in the root with קַל, קָלַע, גָּלַע, in reference to the shaking of the scales; next and generally, to weigh, to weigh out, to put on the scales; שָׁקַל is construed with לְ, עַל יְדֵי, in the signification of weighing to some one, i. e. paying some one by weight, as formerly payments were made by weighing uncoined gold and silver. Niph. pass. to be weighed, paid out.

שֶׁקֶל (pl. שְׁקָלִים, const. שִׁקְלֵי) masc. origin. weight; a certain weight, consisting of 20 gera, by which gold and silver were weighed. It is supposed to be equal to 240 grains of Troy weight. The shekel of the sanctuary appears to have been different from the king's shekel.

שקם (not used) a verb adopted for the root of שִׁקְמָה.

שִׁקְמָה (the pl. שִׁקְמִים and שִׁקְמוֹת; the first pl. may be explained like the pl. of בִּיצָה, יוֹנָה, בִּנָּה, but there appears to be a m. form שֶׁקֶם as the basis) fem. a sycamore tree, the leaves of which resemble mulberry leaves, and the fruit, figs. The fruit grows out of the trunk and larger branches.

שָׁקַע (fut. יִשְׁקַע) to sink, to sink down (in modern Hebrew, of the sinking or setting of the sun); to sink or fall (of a country); to be overflowed (of the Nile); to burn down (of the fire which sinks). Niph. (only Ketib נִשְׁקְה, Amos 8:8, for the Keri נִשְׁקְעָה) pass. Hiph. הִשְׁקִיעַ to let sink (water), i. e. to cause it to fall; transf. to press down the tongue (Job 39:25) (Auth. Ver. "or his tongue with a cord which thou lettest down").

שְׁקַעֲרוּרָה (only pl. —רוֹת) f. deepening, sinking, cavity, hollow place. The root is קָעַר, but not שָׁקַע; the שׁ is only preformative.

שָׁקַף (not used) to cover, to overlay; transf. to arch, to lay the beams. Related is סְקַף in Aram., from which סְקוּפָא, beams, arches.

שָׁקַף (Kal, not used) to look, to behold, not connected with שָׁקַף. Hiph. הִשְׁקִיף to look upon something or some one, especially to look down from an eminence; construed with accus., אֶל, עַל; with בְּעַד, to look through something, i.e. through the window. Niph. to be visible, to be seen far off, to bend forward for seeing; construed like the Hiph.

שֶׁקֶף m. arch work, roofing; רְבָעִים שֶׁקֶף the square roofing, from שָׁקַף. Comp. שָׁקֻף 2, and מַשְׁקוֹף.

שָׁקֻף (only pl. שְׁקֻפִים) adj. m. 1) looking through (describing the window); חַלּוֹנֵי שְׁקֻפִים equiv. to חַלֹּנִים שְׁקֻפִים windows for looking through, in contrast to חַלּוֹנִים אֲטֻמוֹת blind windows; 2) arched, vaulted, but generally as a subst., arch work, vaulting.

שָׁקַץ (not used) to be wearied of, or disgusted with, something; related with קוּט, קָץ; hence Pi. שִׁקֵּץ to loathe, to abominate, make unclean; to pollute נֶפֶשׁ (the soul), to despise or hate, as an abomination (idols).

שִׁקֻּץ see שִׁקּוּץ.

שֶׁקֶץ m. abomination, that which is unclean, loathsome.

שָׁקַק (fut. יָשֹׁק) origin. to run about, to run to and fro, origin. to flow, to stream along; of the swift running of the locust, of the tramping of the greedy bear, of the eager running of a thirsty person. Hith. הִשְׁתַּקְשֵׁק to rove about (in the streets). The orig. signif. is obviously from the modern Heb., where שִׁקְשֵׁק signifies to give to drink, to water. From which מַשָּׁק, but תְּשׁוּקָה is from שׁוּק.

שָׂקַק (not used) to knot, to tie together. Comp. זָקַק, in the signif. of binding, fettering. From which שַׂק.

שָׁקַר (fut. יִשְׁקֹר) orig. to colour, to paint, related to סְקַר in Aram.; transf. to lie, to speak lies, to deceive; construed with לְ of the person, belied or deceived. Pi. with בְּ, to act as a liar towards some one, or to violate a covenant; to deceive, to break faith.

שָׂקַר (Kal, not used) to twinkle or wink, like סְקַר in Aram. According to others, to paint, use false colours, like שָׁקַר in the orig. signif. Pi. to ogle or wink, indicating coquetry, Auth. Vers. "wanton eyes."

שֶׁקֶר (pl. שְׁקָרִים, with suff. שִׁקְרֵיהֶם) masc. a lie, falsehood, deception; לַשֶּׁקֶר, בַּשֶּׁקֶר adv. falsely, also used as a concrete: deceiver or for אִישׁ שֶׁקֶר liar; שֶׁקֶר or לַשֶּׁקֶר adv. in vain.

שֹׁקֶת (pl. const. שִׁקֲתוֹת, as if the sing. were שִׁקָּת) fem. drinking-trough, from שָׁקָה. It is possible, however, that the root is שׁוּק.

שַׂר (pl. שָׂרִים, const. שָׂרֵי) m. ruler, prince, chief, officer, captain (of the body guard), courtier, etc. In the later epoch of the language, שַׂר שָׂרִים is applied to God; שָׂרֵי קֹדֶשׁ to the priests; and שַׂר to the chief or archangel.

שֹׁר (with suff. שָׁרֵּךְ, with *dagesh* in *resh* according to the Massorah, or according to the dissolved form שָׁרְרֵךְ, for which no other noun can be assumed as the basis; comp. צֵל, הַר, גַּל) m. 1) nerve, sinew, muscle, from שָׁרַר to knot, to tie; next generally, 2) the navel, strictly the navel string.

שְׁרָא (only once שָׁרֵא, particip. plur. שָׁרַיִן, inf. מִשְׁרֵא) Aram. 1) to untie, loosen (a girdle), comp. שָׁרָה Hebrew; next, to go about freely, loosened (from bonds), orig. from the untying of beasts of burden for resting; 2) to dwell, to alight, turn in; orig. to untie the beasts of burden, which, among the nomades, was done on turning in. Pa. שָׁרֵא (3 pl. שָׁרִיו) to dissolve, also to begin, to open, comp. the same gradation of the sense in חָלַל. Ithp. אִשְׁתְּרָא to be dissolved; "the bands of the loins are dissolved," is a figure signifying he can no longer keep erect.

שַׂרְאֶצֶר p.n. masc. (according to the Persian, prince of the fire).

שָׁרַב (not used) to glow, to burn, related with צָרַב, שָׂרַף, זָרַב.

שָׁרָב masc. heat of the sun, transf. equiv. to צִחִיחָה parched ground, waste land, from שָׁרַב to burn.

שֵׁרֵבְיָה p.n. m. (fire of God).

שַׁרְבִיט (orig. for שַׁבִּיט, with ר interpolated, but שַׁבִּיט is then equiv. to שֵׁבֶט) m. sceptre, rod.

שָׂרַג (Kal, not used) to entwine, to knot, interweave; Aram. סְרַג, Heb. שָׂרַךְ, from which Pu. שֹׂרַג to be or become entwined, interwoven. Hith. to be interwoven, fastened, עַל־צַוָּאר round the neck.

I. **שָׂרַד** (not used) to join, sew together (a coat of mail), the same סְרַד in Aram. From which שְׂרָד.

II. **שָׂרַד** (not used) to be red, according to Kimchi; according to others, equiv. to שָׂרַט to make an incision, to cut in, to indent; from which שֶׂרֶד.

III. **שָׂרַד** to flee, escape, hasten away (after a general defeat), from which שָׂרִיד, which see.

שְׂרָד m. a garment in the form of a coat of mail, as the curtains of the tabernacle and the official garments of the priests were wrought. The root is שָׂרַד I.

שֶׂרֶד m. red chalk for drawing, or red

earth, from שָׂרַד II.; according to others, the tool used by workmen to mark out an image on a rough block.

שָׁרָה (fut. יִשְׁרֶה, with suff. יִשְׁרֵהוּ) equiv. to שְׁרָא Aram. to loosen, to let loose, transf. to send off; thus, Job 37:3, He sends it (the thunder) off (Auth. Vers. directeth it) under the whole heaven. Pi. שָׁרָה, only Jer. 15:11, to loosen the bonds, i.e. to release, as rendered by Dunash, and which is suitable to the context.

I. שָׁרָה (not used) to join, to tie together, comp. זָרַד; from which שִׁרְיָה, שִׁרְיוֹן, etc.

שָׁרָה (only pl. שָׁרוֹת) f. a wall, equiv. to שׁוּר, which see.

שָׂרָה to rule, to prevail, to contend, orig. to array for battle.

שָׂרָה orig. f. from שַׂר; 1) princess, mistress, the first in rank; 2) p.n.f. (princess).

שָׁרָה (only pl. שֵׁרוֹת, possibly, however, from a sing. שֵׁר) fem. small chain as an ornament round the arm, from שׁוּר to link together; the other forms שַׁרְשְׁרָה and שַׁרְשָׁה are also derived from שׁוּר in the orig. signif. to link together.

שְׂרוּג p.n. m. (vine-branch, or the interweaver).

שָׁרוּחֶן (שָׁרוּ־חֵן abode of grace) p.n. of a place in the territory of Simeon.

שְׂרוֹךְ m. latch, joined with נַעַל, shoe latch, from שָׂרַךְ to tie, entwine.

שָׁרוֹן (formed from יְשָׁרוֹן, from יָשַׁר in the signification of a plain) p.n. of a district between Joppa and Cæsarea; always with the article. From which שָׁרוֹנִי is the gent.

שְׁרוּקָה (only Ketib) fem. hissing or shrieking. See שְׁרִיקָה.

שְׂרוּקֶּיהָ see שָׂרֹק.

שֵׁרוּת fem. the beginning, from שָׁרָה after the Aram., but the reading of the Keri שֵׁרִיתִךָ is more correct as a Pi. from שָׁרָה. See שָׁרָה.

שֶׂרַח p.n. m. (abundance) probably equiv. to סֶרַח.

שָׂרַט (fut. יִשְׂרֹט) to cut in, to make an incision in the skin. Niph. to tear, hurt or wound oneself (by lifting). Related is סְרַט in Aram. The root is related to that in קָדַד, חָרַת, גָּרַם.

שֶׂרֶט m. cut, incision.

שִׁרְטַי p.n. m. equiv. to שִׁטְרַי (scribe).

שָׂרֶטֶת f. incision, cut.

שָׁרַי p.n. m. (redeemer).

שָׂרַי p.n. m. (princess).

שָׂרִיג (pl. שָׂרִיגִים) m. entwining of vine branches, from שָׂרַג to entwine, interweave.

שָׂרִיד (after the form פָּלִיט, plur. שְׂרִידִים, const. שְׂרִידֵי, with suff.

(שְׂרִידָיו) m. 1) one that escaped or remained; collective, they that escape or are saved; 2) the rest, remnant, syn. with אַחֲרִית.

שִׁרְיָה fem. coat of mail, habergeon, from שָׁרָה to join together, with reference to the scales.

שְׂרָיָה p.n. masc. (God is the ruler). This name is found corrupted in שְׁיָא, שִׁישָׁא, שַׁוְשָׁא, in which, however, the same signification can hardly be assumed.

שִׁרְיוֹן (pl. —נִים, and —נוֹת) m. 1) a coat of mail, habergeon, equiv. to שִׁרְיָה; the same is also סִרְיוֹן; 2) p.n. of the mount שְׂנִיר, among the Sidonians, probably so called on account of the similarity of the ridge of that hill to a coat of mail.

שִׁרְיֹן m. the same.

שָׂרִיק adj. m., שְׂרִיקָה (pl. —קוֹת) f. combed, hatchelled, used as an attribute to פִּשְׁתִּים flax.

שְׁרִיקָה (only pl. —קוֹת) f. 1) hissing, mockery, derision, for which in the Ketib שְׁרוּקוֹת; 2) fifing, piping, of the herdsmen. The root is שָׁרַק, which see.

שָׁרִיר (only const. pl. (שְׁרִירֵי) m. equiv. to שֹׁר sinew, muscle, especially of the muscles and sinews of the body.

שְׁרִירוּת f. origin. that which is entwined, fastened; hence, firmness, transf. to obduracy, stubbornness, joined with לֵב or לֵב רָע; בְּשׁ׳, הָלַךְ אַחֲרֵי שׁ׳ to continue acting stubbornly, obdurately.

שֵׁרִית a rare reading for שְׁאֵרִית.

שָׂרַךְ (Kal, not used) equiv. שָׂרַג to entwine, interweave, to make intricate; hence Pu. שֵׂרֵךְ to run about in various directions, applied to a swift camel that maketh her way intricate, i.e. runs wild with the desire of copulation.

שָׂרַם (not used) to cut in, to plough; related is חָרַם II. in its original sense. From which:—

שְׁרֵמָה (only pl. (שְׁרֵמוֹת) fem. field, plough-field, orig. equiv. to שָׂדֶה, so called from ploughing; another reading for it is שְׁדֵמוֹת, which see.

שַׂרְסְכִים p.n. of a chief of the eunuchs in the army of Nebuchadnezzar.

שָׂרַע to stretch out, to extend; related is סָרַח; hence part. pass. שָׂרוּעַ having a limb preternaturally large, especially of the ear, one who has a long ear. Hith. הִשְׂתָּרַע to stretch oneself out.

שַׂרְעַף (only plur. (שַׂרְעַפִּים) masc. a thought; the ר is interpolated, and the word is identical with שְׂעִפִּים.

שָׂרַף (fut. (יִשְׂרֹף) 1) equiv. to צָרַב,

זָרַב to burn, to burn off, in the widest sense, e.g. of the burning of houses, cities, etc., often with the addition of בָּאֵשׁ in fire; also, of the burning of a dead body and other funeral rites; 2) to burn, in the sense of cementing by burning, e.g. bricks. Niph. pass. Pu. the same. In modern Heb. שָׂרַף has the signif. of sapping or sipping, from which שְׂרָף gum, rosin.

שָׂרַף (not used) to cringe, crawl, for which root there are analogies in other languages. From which:—

שָׂרָף (pl. שְׂרָפִים) m. 1) serpent, comp. the appellation of the serpent זֹחֵל עָפָר; שָׂרָף מְעוֹפֵף is the same as נָחָשׁ מְעוֹפֵף; 2) seraph, a kind of angel, symbolically of the serpent; 3) p.n. m.

שְׂרֵפָה fem. burning, conflagration; hence, a mountain of burning, i.e. a devastated mountain, especially of the burning of dead bodies; to become a burning, i.e. to be burnt away.

שָׁרַץ (fut. יִשְׁרֹץ) to creep, to crawl, to swarm, to increase abundantly; probably the verb is a denom. from:—

שֶׁרֶץ m. equiv. to רֶמֶשׂ a worm, a reptile, creeping things; also, of winged reptiles, e.g. a bat; likewise, small aquatic reptiles, small fishes. The root appears to be in שָׁרַץ, and ־ֶץ is an ancient nominal suffix.

שָׁרַק (fut. יִשְׁרֹק) to help, with לְ, to lure by hissing, e.g. flies, bees, nations; transf. to deride; with עַל, to hiss at some one or something; with מִן, to hiss or hoot one away from his place.

שָׂרַק (not used) to comb, to hatchel (flax); related to סְרַק in Aram. The origin. signif. is probably, to beat in pieces, to bruise. From which שָׂרִיק, which see.

שָׂרַק (not used) origin. to shine; related to זָרַח; transf. to be red, reddish.

שָׂרֹק (only plur. שְׂרֻקִּים, with suff. שְׂרוּקֶּיהָ) adj. m. 1) reddish, of the colour of roses; 2) a kind of branch with red grape. Both significations from שָׂרַק.

שֹׂרֵק m. 1) a kind of wine-branch, choice species of vine, and is to be explained like שָׂרֹק 2; 2) (grape-valley) p.n. of a valley between Gaza and Askalon.

שְׁרֵקָה f. hissing, derision.

שֹׂרֵקָה f. vine-branch.

שָׁרַר (not used) 1) to tie, to bind; the root is שר and is found in קָשַׁר, חָשַׁר; from which שֹׁר, שָׁרִיר and שְׁרִירוּת; 2) to link, to join, from which שָׁרָה, שַׁרְשְׁרָה and שַׁרְשָׁה,

if these forms are not to be derived from שׁוּר related to שָׂרַד. The particip. שׁוֹרֵר in the sense of an enemy belongs to שׁוּר.

שָׂרַר (particip. שׂוֹרֵר; of the fut. יָשַׂר, it is uncertain whether it belongs to this root) to rule, to prevail, to govern. Hith. to make oneself a ruler or governor over (עַל) something or some one. From which probably שַׂר, שָׂרָה.

שָׁרָר p.n. m. (the strong one).

שֹׁרֶר a noun erroneously adopted as the dissolved form of שֹׁר, which see.

שָׁרַשׁ (not used) to grow, to sprout, to take root. From which:—

שֶׁרֶשׁ p.n. m. (taking root, settling).

שֹׁרֶשׁ (with suff. שָׁרְשׁוֹ, const. plur. שָׁרְשֵׁי, with suff. שָׁרָשָׁיו) m. 1) origin. sprout which shoots up; and in a spiritual sense, descendant; 2) a root, as being the first sprout from the seed; transf. to the undermost, i.e. the root of a thing, e.g. the foot of a mountain, the bottom of the sea, the undermost part of the foot; fig. ground for complaint or dispute; settling of a people; from which denom. שֵׁרֵשׁ (in a privative anse), to uproot, to annihilate. Pu. pass. Po. שֹׁרֵשׁ pass. to take deep root. Hiph. הִשְׁרִישׁ to cause to take root; sometimes with the addition of שָׁרָשִׁים to thrive, mature.

שֹׁרֶשׁ (pl. with suff. שָׁרְשׁוֹהִי) Aram. m. the same.

שַׁרְשָׁה (abbreviated from שַׁרְשְׁרָה, const. pl. שַׁרְשׁוֹת) f. small chain, proceeding from the original sense of linking together.

שְׁרשׁוּ (Keri שְׁרשִׁי) Aram. f. uprooting, annihilation, figur. ejection. Comp. שֹׁרֶשׁ in Hebrew.

שַׁרְשְׁרָה f. a chain, redoubled from שָׁרָה.

שָׁרַת (Kal, not used) to serve. Pi. שֵׁרֵת (particip. fem. מְשָׁרֶתֶת for מְשָׁרַתַת, inf. שָׁרֵת) to serve unremittingly, i.e. to do service; to officiate, partly of the higher and voluntary service (different from עָבַד), and partly of the service of the priest, and religious service generally; hence, to serve in the name of God, i.e. to worship Him, call upon His name. The etymology is obscure.

שָׂרַת (not used) and only adopted for the derivative מַשְׂרֵת) to engrave, to indent, to ingraft; related to שָׂרַט to make an incision, and שָׂרַד II. See מַשְׂרֵת.

שָׁרֵת m. service (the holy one) e.g. the vessels for the holy service.

I. שֵׁשׁ a cardinal number, f., שִׁשָּׁה (const. שֵׁשֶׁת) m. six. The plur.

שִׁשִּׁים signifies sixty; from this numeral arose the verb שִׁשָּׁה to divide into six parts, or to give the sixth part.

I. שֵׁשׁ (formed from שׁוּשׁ) masc. 1) white marble, equiv. to שַׁיִשׁ; 2) white (Egyptian) cotton, *byssus*, and next, the cloth made therefrom. The name has also a Heb. etymology.

שִׁשֵּׁאתִיךָ Ezek. 39:2. See שָׁשָׁא.

שֵׁשְׁבַּצַּר (foreign) p. n. masc. (fire-worshipper).

שֵׁשׁוֹ m. see שֵׁשׁ.

שָׁשׁוֹ as a verb see שׁוּשׁ.

שָׂשׂוֹן (const. שְׂשׂוֹן) m. joy, gladness, synon. with שִׂמְחָה; oil of joy signifies that which is used for anointing at festival banquets. Root שׂוּשׂ.

שֵׁשַׁי p.n. m. (commander; see שָׁשָׁא).

שֵׁשַׁי p.n. of a giant (commander).

שִׁשִּׁי a secondary form for שֵׁשׁ, chosen for the sake of a paronomasia with מְשִׁי.

שִׁשִּׁי an ordinal number, m. (from שֵׁשׁ) שִׁשִּׁית f. the sixth; שִׁשִּׁית the sixth part.

שִׁשִּׁים see שֵׁשׁ.

שֵׁשַׁךְ p.n. of a Babylonian province or city. The etymology is obscure.

שָׁשַׁן p.n. m. (lily) comp. שׁוֹשַׁן.

שֵׁשָׁק p.n. m. (desire).

שָׁשַׁר (not used) to be red, probably from the reduplicated form שְׁרַשַׁר, for which the simple root שַׁר is the basis.

שָׁשַׁר (in pause שָׁשָׁר) m. red chalk or red colour, probably red earth for dyeing; ruddle.

שָׁת (pl. שָׁתוֹת) m. a pillar, foundation, from שׁוּת to place; comp. עַמּוּד pillar, from עָמַד; figur. chief of a state, corner stone of a building, support (of the people), the distinguished one, the head.

I. שֵׁת in the sig. of tumult of war, contracted from שְׁאֵת, syn. with שָׁאוֹן. See שְׁאֵת.

II. שֵׁת in signif. 1, the plur. (שָׁתוֹת) m. 1) the posteriors, the buttocks, from שׁוּת to sit; the pl. is as if formed from שָׁתָה; 2) p.n. masc. (orig. sprout, sproutling).

שֵׁת only a contracted form from שְׂאֵת.

שֵׁת, שִׁת (Aram.) equiv. to שֵׁשׁ in Heb. six. The pl. שִׁתִּין sixty.

I. שָׁתָה (fut. יִשְׁתֶּה, apoc. יֵשְׁתְּ, inf. const. שְׁתוֹ) to drink, origin. to quench the thirst, *sedare sitim*, to satisfy the thirst, related with שָׁתַת and שׁוּת; שָׁתָה is construed with the accus. Hiph. מִן, to drink a part of the whole; with בְּ, to drink from a vessel, with the sub-signification of comfort; transf. to banquet, feast, in the signif. of to sit down at the table, figur. to drink iniquity or wrath, i. e. to be full of it. Niph. pass. to be drunk (of a beverage); for the Hiph. הִשְׁקָה is used.

II. שָׁתָה (not used) to spin, to weave, like the root שָׁתַת. From which שְׁתִי 2.

שְׁתָה (3 pl. אִשְׁתִּיו, with א preformative; particip. שָׁתֶה, plur. שָׁתַיִן) Aram. to drink, like שָׁתָה I. in Hebrew. From which מִשְׁתֶּה.

שְׁתוֹת see שֵׁת.

שְׁתִי m. 1) the drinking, transf. to feasting, banqueting; 2) origin. woven, specially the warp, from שָׁתָה II., in contrast to עֵרֶב the woof.

שְׁתִיָּה (formed from שְׁתִי) fem. the drinking, feasting, banqueting.

שָׁתִיל (const. pl. שְׁתִילֵי) m. a plant, sprout, from שָׁתַל to set, to plant.

שְׁתַּיִם see שְׁנַיִם.

שָׁתַל (fut. יִשְׁתֹּל, hence 1 pers. fut. with suff. אֶשְׁתֳּלֶנּוּ) orig. to place firmly, to fix; next, to plant, for which generally נָטַע.

שָׁתַם (like שָׁתַם in modern Heb., e.g. end of *Mishna, Aboda Sara*) to break open, to open (the eyes), in contrast to סָתַם; hence שְׁתֻם הָעַיִן used in parallel with גְּלוּי עֵינַיִם.

שָׁתַם equiv. to סָתַם, which see.

שָׁתַן a form from שִׁין (see שִׁין), from which Hiph. הִשְׁתִּין to make water, to piss; מַשְׁתִּין a pisser; מַשְׁתִּין בְּקִיר he that pisses against the wall, according to some, a little boy, and according to others, a dog.

שָׁתַק (fut. יִשְׁתֹּק) orig. to cease, to rest, to stand still; hence, to be silent from dispute, to be quieted, subdued (of the waves), etc.

שָׁתַר (another reading for שָׁתַר, Kal not used) to break asunder, to break forth, to break out (of a swelling), related with פָּדַר and פָּטַר, having the same original signification in the root. Niph. to break out (of ulcers, boils).

שֵׁתָר (foreign) p. n. m. (star).

שְׁתַר בּוֹזְנַי p. n. m. (luminous star).

שָׁתַת (3 pl. שָׁתוּ) orig. equiv. to שִׁית, שָׁתָה to place, to put; hence, lay down (of a herd of cattle), to set the mouth against something, i.e. to speak against something. Niph. נָשַׁת (3 f. נִשְּׁתָה for נָשְׁתָה, comp. נָבַקָּה for נָבְקָה, in pause נִשָּׁתָה). to which also belongs 3 pl. נִשְּׁתוּ) to cease, to vanish (of power, strength), to fail, dry up (of water), to be immoveable, motionless (of the tongue from thirst).

ת

ת *tav* (תָּו, plur. תָּוִין) is the twenty-second letter of the alphabet, and signifies, as a numeral, 400. The word תָּו signifies a sign, mark. As to the pronunciation of the letter, according to modern researches ת (without *dagesh lene*) is pronounced like *th* in English, תּ (with *dagesh lene*) like ט or *t*. ת interchanges with all other *t* sounds, and also with שׁ. The following are its peculiarities; 1) a considerable number of verbs commencing with *t* sounds harmonise with such as commence with א, e.g. אָוָה and תָּוָה to dwell; תָּרַן and אָרַן to be firm, strong; אָמַר and תָּמַר, אָבַל and תָּבַל, and many more; 2) in many verbs the ת appears to be preformative for the formation of new roots from some already existing and having no ת, e.g. אָבָה and תָּאַב, אָנָה and תָּאַן, גָּרָה and תָּגַר, לָעָה and תָּלַע, אָם and תָּאַם, אַר and תָּאַר, and others; 3) is inserted as a middle consonant in some verbs, according to an old form of conjugation, e.g. שָׁתַן from שָׁן, עָתַם from עָם, etc.

תָּא (pl. תָּאִים, const. תָּאֵי, with suff. תָּאָיו and תָּאוֹת) masc. a room, chamber, from תָּאָה in the signif. of תָּוָה to dwell, corresponding with אָוָה.

I. תָּאַב equiv. to אָבָה, to long, wish, desire after (לְ) something.

II. תָּאַב (Kal, not used) only a secondary form of תָּעַב; hence, Pi. תֵּאֵב to despise, hate, abhor, loathe, abominate.

תַּאֲבָה f. longing, desire, wish, from תָּאַב I.

I. תָּאָה (not used) probably equiv. to תָּעָה to err, rove or wander about; or equiv. to תָּוָה to be waste, desolate. From which תְּאוֹ.

II. תָּאָה (Kal, not used) to mark, to note, make a sign, equiv. to תָּוָה; next, to mark off, to set a landmark, a boundary. Pi. תֵּאָה to denote, mark off, set a limit or boundary.

תַּאֲוָה f. desire, wish, longing; in a bad sense, lust; concrete, the object desired or wished for, the object of lust; in a good sense, that which is desirable, agreeable, lovely, pleasant, delightful, ornamental. Root אָוָה.

תָּאוֹם (only plur. תְּאוֹמִים, once def. תוֹמִם, const. תְּאוֹמֵי) m. twins. See תָּאַם.

תְּאֹן (only pl. תְּאָנִים), masc. labor, toil, trouble, tribulation, hardship, from תָּאָה I. or אָוֶן.

תַּאֲלָה f. a curse, from אָלָה.

תָּאַם orig. to be entwined; next, to be double, twofold, twins; hence, particip. תּוֹאֲמִים twins, double. Hiph. to bring forth twins, if it is not a denom. from תְּאֹם.

תְּאֹם (const. pl. תְּאֹמֵי) masc. twin, from which Hiph. denom. to bring forth or bear twins.

I. תָּאַן (not used, probably the root belongs to תַּאֲנִיָּה, תַּאֲנָה, תֹּאֲנָה, and תְּאוֹן) equiv. to אָנָה, 1) to surround, encompass, also of connubial embrace; likewise to cause, occasion, induce, like סָבַב; 2) to moan, to lament; from which, 3) to weary, fatigue oneself.

II. תָּאַן (not used, belongs to תְּאֵנָה) probably equiv. to תָּנַן to stretch along, to expand, which root is also applied in western languages to the designation of trees.

תַּאֲנָה f. copulation, sexual desire or heat in animals, from תָּאַן or אָנָה; according to others, the gasping for or aspiring at something.

תְּאֵנָה (but the pl. תְּאֵנִים, with suff. תְּאֵנֵיכֶם) f. fig-tree, from תָּאַן to stretch out, to extend; transf. to the fruit, a fig.

תֹּאֲנָה (formed from the masc. תֹּאַן, and stands for תְּאֻנָּה) f. opportunity, occasion. See אָנָה.

תַּאֲנִיָּה fem. mourning, lamentation, grief, sadness. See אָנָה.

תְּאֻנִים see תְּאוֹן.

תַּאֲנַת שִׁלֹה (circumference of Shiloh) p.n. of a place in Ephraim.

תָּאַר origin. to mark out, to make prominent (a plain), to designate (compare תֹּאַר equiv. to מַרְאֶה); next, to mark off a boundary. The Kal is generally used intrans. in the sense of being marked off, as the boundary. Pi. to denote, mark off, describe. Pu. תֹּאַר to extend, in which sense רִמּוֹן הַמְּתֹאָר Jos.19:13.

תֹּאַר (with suff. תָּאֳרוֹ and תֹּאֲרוֹ) m. 1) form (of the body), visage, syn. with מַרְאֶה, used of man or beast; 2) a beautiful form, beauty.

תַּאְרֵעַ p.n. m. (cunning, or the cunning one) equiv. to תַּחְרֵעַ.

תְּאַשּׁוּר masc. sherbin, a species of cedar, from אָשַׁר to be straight, erect; according to other versions, fir, poplar.

תָּבָה (not used) probably to dig out, to deepen (for containing something). Probably related with אָבָה in אֵבֶה especially as אוב occurs in this sense.

תֵּבָה f. chest, box, transf. to a ship, ark, boat, vessel, from תָּבָה.

תְּבוּאָה f. that which is brought in (in the threshing floor or barn), increase, produce, product (of the field, the threshing floor, the wine-press); transf. to any product, profit, or gain; and like פְּרִי, is also used in a spiritual sense.

תְּבוּן m. wisdom, understanding, only with suff. תְּבוּנָם, which, however, may stand for תְּבוּנָתָם. Root בּוּן.

תְּבוּנָה f. wisdom, understanding; in the plur. arguments, proofs, wise speaking. Root בּוּן.

תְּבוּסָה f. treading down, ruin, destruction.

תָּבוֹר (mountain top, equiv. to טַבּוּר) 1) the Tabor, p.n. of a mountain in Galilee; 2) p. n. of a grove of turpentine trees in the tribe of Benjamin; 3) p. n. of a Levitical city in Zebulun.

I. תָּבַל (not used) to flow, to moisten, related with בָּלַל to wet, and שָׁבַל to moisten; transf. to produce, bring forth. From which תֵּבֵל and תְּבַלֻּל.

II. תָּבַל (not used) equiv. to בָּלַל to mix, to mingle, especially in a sexual sense. From which תֶּבֶל and תַּבְלִית.

תֵּבֵל (from תָּבַל I., according to others, from יָבַל) fem. origin. the earth, i. e. the productive one, which produces fruit and plants, syn. with אֶרֶץ; but is also used generally for the globe, the world, the inhabited earth; fig. the inhabitants of the world. Sometimes it is used of a country only.

תֶּבֶל (from תָּבַל II.) m. sexual mixing, carnality; transf. to impurity, pollution, lewdness, sin or wicked deed. According to others, from בָּלַל, after the form תֹּמֶם.

תַּבְלִית f. shameful, wicked deed, thus according to some, identical with תֶּבֶל, which rendering is preferable to that of deriving it from בָּלָה to consume, to waste, destroy. According to others, the reading (Isaiah 10:25) is תַּכְלִית, which is also suitable to the context.

תְּבַלֻּל (formed from תָּבַל) m. origin. running of the eyes, bleareyedness; according to others, having a white spot in the eye (Author. Ver. "one that hath a blemish in his eye").

תָּבַן (not used) probably equiv. to אָבַן to be hard, dry, only used of ears of corn. From which:—

תֶּבֶן m. straw, transf. to fodder for cattle, provender, from תָּבַן. The same etymology has חֲשַׁשׁ and קַשׁ.

תַּבְנִי p.n.m. (model). Comp. תַּבְנִית.

תַּבְנִית f. model, pattern, figure, after which anything is built; transf. to figure, image, or likeness generally. See בָּנָה.

תַּבְעֵרָה (burning-place) p.n. of a place in the Arabian desert.

תֵּבֵץ (bright prospect) p.n. of a place not far from Sichem. The root is יָבַץ to shine.

תָּבַר (Kal, not used) to be pure, clean, innocent; thus equiv. to בָּרַר. Hith. הִתַּבָּר (for הִתְתַּבָּר) to act or conduct oneself purely, innocently.

תְּבַר (Aram.) equiv. to שְׁבַר in Heb., to break, to dash to pieces.

תִּגְלַת פִּלְאֶסֶר p.n. of an Assyrian king. The name is also written תִּלְּגַת פִּלְנְאֶסֶר, תִּגְלַת פְּלֶסֶר.

תַּגְמוּל m. recompense, reward, benefit, from גָּמַל.

תָּגַר (not used) to provoke, to excite strife or contention. Related is גָּרָה, with a similar signif.

תִּגְרָה (const. תִּגְרַת) f. provocation, strife, contention; transferred to threat, rebuke, punishment. Root תָּגַר.

תֹּגַרְמָה (also תּוֹ׳) p.n. of a northern country, probably Armenia, as the Armenians trace their extraction from an ancestor named Torgom.

תִּדְהָר m. name of a tree, either a plane tree or an oak, from דָּהַר to be firm, strong; according to others, beech, pine, cypress, larch, etc.

תְּדִיר (Aram.) adj. m., תְּדִירָא f. continual, constant, the fem. as an adv., e.g. בִּתְדִירָא constantly, continually. The orig. signif. is going round in a circle, from דּוּר.

תַּדְמֹר (palm city) p.n. of one of Solomon's cities, between Damascus and the Euphrates, Palmyra, whose gigantic ruins are yet in existence.

תִּדְעָל p.n. m. (reverence, worship) from דָּעַל equiv. to דָּחַל to fear.

תָּהָה (not used) to be amazed, terrified; next, to be waste, desolate; in Aram., to shudder, to be terrified, confounded, amazed at something. From which:—

תֹּהוּ (after the form קֹדֶשׁ) m. void, desolate, a waste; also as an abst., desolation, destruction, waste; fig. nothingness, emptiness, vanity; תֹּהוּ (as accus.) and לְתֹהוּ, are used as adverbs, in vain, vainly.

תְּהוֹם (plur. תְּהוֹמוֹת) com. origin. roaring, raging (of the waves of the sea); 1) wave, billow, and generally, flood or multitude of waters; 2) abyss, depth of the sea; next, depth generally. The root is הוּם.

תָּהַל (not used) to be slack, sluggish, indolent; related is שׁוּל and שָׁלָה in the original signification.

תְּהִלָּה (pl. תְּהִלּוֹת) f. praise, fame, glory; also, the subject of praise, fame, or boasting, i.e. that which is deserving of praise, glorification, or celebration; transf. to song of praise, extolling. The root is הָלַל.

תָּהֳלָה (formed from a masc. תֹּהַל) f. slackness, sluggishness, indolence; also, fault, folly, error, defect; שׂוּם תָּהֳלָה בְּ׳ to charge one with folly. Root תָּהַל.

תַּהֲלוּכָה fem. procession, company, guard.

תַּהְפּוּכָה (only pl. ־וֹת) f. falsehood, deceit, perverseness, folly.

תָּו (const. pl. תָּוֵי) m. 1) a mark, sign, from תָּוָה to mark, draw, engrave, inscribe; 2) signature of a writing or document.

תּוֹא see תְּאוֹ.

תּוּב (fut. יְתוּב) Aram. equiv. to שׁוּב to return, to come back. Aph. הָתִיב (inf. הֲתָבוּ, fut. יְתִיב) to give or send back; הֲתִיב פִּתְגָם to send word back, to reply; עֵטָא to give advice.

תּוּבַל (also written תֻּבַל) p. n. of a people in Asia Minor, west of Meschech.

תּוּבַל קַיִן p. n. m. of the inventor of brass and iron-work or smithery. As an appellative, it signifies, a smith who purges the iron or brass of dross, or slacks.

תּוּבָנָה Ketib for תְּבוּנָה.

תּוּגָה fem. grief, sorrow, mourning, sadness, from יָגָה.

תּוֹגַרְמָה see תֹּגַר.

תּוֹדָה f. 1) confession; 2) thanksgiving; next, song of praise; 3) thank-offering; complete זֶבַח תּוֹדָה; sometimes also with omission of זֶבַח.

תְּוַהּ (Aram.) equiv. to תְּהָא to be astonished, amazed, to be terrified.

I. תָּוָה (Kal, not used) equiv. to תָּאָה II. to mark off, describe, design. Pi. תִּוָּה to make marks, signs, or etchings, to scribble upon (עַל) something. Hiph. like Pi. to mark. Hith. הִתְאַוָּה for הִתְתַּוָּה to make marks or signs for oneself, to mark off.

II. תָּוָה (Kal, not used) equiv. to תְּוַהּ in Aram. to be amazed at something. Hiph. to astonish, amaze, some one; also, to cause some one to feel grief or remorse, or to repent.

תּוּז (Kal, not used) to cut off. Hiph. הֵתַז (for הֵתִיז) to hew off.

I. תּוּחַ (not used) to cut in pieces, to split; related is תָּחַח in modern Heb. to rub in pieces, to bruise, to cut asunder, to split; from which תּוֹתָח.

II. תּוּחַ (not used) to sink down, to lie down, let oneself down; from which תַּחַת after the form נַחַת (from נוּחַ),

תּוֹחַ p.n. m. (lowness, the low one).

תּוֹחֶלֶת f. hope, expectation, from יָחַל.

תּוּךְ (not used) to divide, split, to cut in pieces; related to תּוּחַ. From which:—

תָּוֶךְ (const. תּוֹךְ, with suff. תּוֹכִי) m. midst, middle, origin. the place where an object is divided into two parts; transf. to the innermost part of anything. The constuctive state is used as a prep. in, through, among; thus, בְּתוֹךְ through the midst, in the midst; מִתּוֹךְ out of the midst; אֶל־תּוֹךְ within, the midst; comp. תִּיכוֹן.

תּוֹךְ in the signification of oppression, see תֹּךְ

תּוֹכֵחָה (from יָכַח) f. rebuke, chastisement, instruction, improvement, punishment.

תּוֹכַחַת (with suff. תּוֹכַחְתִּי, plur. תּוֹכָחוֹת) f. 1) the demonstrating or proving (of a matter), defence, rejoinder, orig. the assertion of a right; 2) rebuke, reproach, blame, chastisement, punishment, exhortation, admonition. The root as in תּוֹכֵחָה, with which it is formally connected.

תּוּכִּיִּים see תֻּכִּי.

תּוֹלַד (begotten) p. n. of a place in Simeon, complete אֶלְתּוֹלַד, probably name of a Phenician deity.

תּוֹלֶדֶת (only plur. תּוֹלְדוֹת) f. origin. birth; transf. to family, generation, especially in a genealogical sense; סֵפֶר תּוֹלְדוֹת book of generations, family register, genealogical history; later also without סֵפֶר, family history or history generally. Root יָלַד.

תּוֹלָל (pl. תּוֹלָלִים) m. a robber, especially who carries away captives, from תָּלַל equiv. to שָׁלַל.

תּוֹלָע (pl. תּוֹלָעִים) masc. a worm, in the widest sense of the word, but especially of the kermez, the turtle insect, and the colour prepared from it; it is used rarely for the crimson dye or crimson garments; figur. as a figure of powerlessness and contempt; 2) p. n. m.; patron. תּוֹלָעִי. The root is תָּלַע or יָלַע.

תּוֹלָעָה (and תּוֹלַעַת) f. the same, but only used in the sing.

תּוֹם belongs to תּוֹמִים. See תְּאֹם תְּאוֹמִים.

תּוֹמָן once Ketib for תֵּימָן, which see.

תּוֹעֵבָה (const. ־עֲבַת, pl. תּוֹעֵבוֹת) f. that which is to be loathed, abhorred, abomination, loathsomeness, from תָּעַב to abhor, abominate; transf. to idols, images, or idol worship, or anything unclean, unlawful to use, disgusting, loathsome, horrible.

תּוֹעָה f. error, apostacy, backsliding (from God), figur. hurt, injury, calamity, inasmuch as such were considered the consequences of apostacy and error.

תּוֹעָפֹת (from יָעַף, equiv. to יָפַע to shine, to glimmer, pl. תּוֹעָפוֹת) f. 1) brightness, lustre, transf. to treasure; 2) swift course, swiftness (of the buffalo or *rehem*), derived from the sense shining, as this gradation of the sense is common in all verbs signifying brightness or shining; 3) weariness, wearisome labour.

תּוּף (not used) to dry up, to parch, burn, of the burning of dead bodies, of the drying of a cake, etc., as will be seen in the derivatives. Related is the root in שָׁדַף. From which תְּפִין ,תֹּפֶת ,תָּפְתֶּה.

תּוֹצָאֹת (only pl. תּוֹצָאוֹת) f. 1) place of going out (from a gate), transf. to a spring, fountain (of life), fig. escape, deliverance, i.e. getting out of danger; 2) end or extent, border, extremity, limit, of a place or country. Root יָצָא.

תּוּר (particip. plur. once אֲתָרִים for תָּרִים; fut. יָתוּר) equiv. to דּוּר to turn in a circuit, to go about, next like רָגַל ,רָכַל to spy,) by going about), or carry on traffic, trade, by journeying through the country; from which the signif. of inquiring, searching, construed with עַל; with אַחֲרֵי to follow after something, to trace something out. Hiph. to spy, search out or through, only Judges 1:23.

I. תּוֹר (with suff. תּוֹרְךָ, plur. תּוֹרִים) m. a turtle-dove, *turtur*, so called from the sound or noise which it makes, fig. of a beloved subject; hence of the Jewish nation as the favourite people of God.

II. תּוֹר masc. a row, a string, from תּוּר equiv. to טוּר to arrange, to string, to link.

תּוֹר (pl. תּוֹרִין) Aram. m. oxen, for the Heb. שׁוֹר

תּוֹרָה (formed from יָרָה in the Hiph. signif., pl. תּוֹרוֹת) f. 1) doctrine, instruction, whether of God or man; 2) concrete, the law, precept, containing instruction (syn. with חֹק ,מִשְׁפָּט), especially the divine law communicated through Moses, the complete name of which is סֵפֶר הַתּוֹרָה, book of the law.

תּוּרָק probably p.n. of a certain province, perhaps of טַרְכוֹן Trachonitis, mentioned in the Targum. Ibn Ezra has also taken it for the name of a place.

תּוּשׁ (not used) probably equiv. to אוּשׁ to be strong, vigorous. The connection of the פ"ת and פ"א is obvious from many verbs. From which תּוּשִׁיָּה.

תּוֹשָׁב (from יָשַׁב) m. a sojourner, a foreigner who has settled in another country (without the right of citizenship).

תּוּשִׁיָּה (formed from יָשָׁה, after the form תַּאֲנִיָּה) f. 1) assistance, support, comfort; 2) that which is essential (either for profit or loss); 3) wisdom, understanding, origin. the real, essential. See יָשָׁה in its various significations.

תּוֹתָח (another reading for תּוֹתָח, after the form טוֹטָף) masc. a club, cudgel, from תּוּחַ or תָּחַח, which see.

תַּזְן see תזן.

תַּזְנוּת (pl. תַּזְנוּתִים) fem. whoredom, fornication; figur. idol worship, idolatry. The plur. is used as an abstract.

תַּחְבּוּלָה (pl. תַּחְבּוּלוֹת) fem. leading, guiding, directing, conducting (of a state), from חֹבֵל a pilot, or "the man at the helm;" next, generally the act of conducting, council, advice; or perhaps orig. equiv. to מְזִמָּה, from חָבַל in the orig. signif., like זָמַם.

תֹּחוּ p.n. m. (the low one) equiv. to תּוֹחַ.

תְּחוֹת (with suff. always in plur., as תְּחוֹתוֹהִי) Aram. prep. under, like תַּחַת in Heb.

תַּחְכְּמוֹנִי p.n. m. (the wise one), retained only in a patron. form —מֹנִי. Comp. חַכְמֹנִי.

תְּחִלָּה f. beginning, commencement, from חָלַל; בַּתְּחִלָּה in the beginning, previously, formerly.

תַּחֲלוּא (pl. —אִים) m. sickness, illness, disease, languishing; from חָלָא, equiv. to חָלָה.

תַּחְמָס m. name of an unclean bird of prey, probably the male ostrich; from חָמַס to rob.

תַּחַן p.n. m. (place of encampment), for תַּחֲנָה; patron. תַּחֲנִי.

תְּחִנָּה f. 1) grace, mercy, compassion; next, supplication, prayer, from חָנַן, which see; 2) p.n. m.

תַּחֲנוּן (pl. —נִים and נוֹת) m. prayer, supplication, likewise from חָנַן.

תַּחֲנוֹת pl. m. place of encampment, where the camp is erected, from חָנָה.

תַּחְפַּנְחֵס (also תְּחַפְנְחֵס) p.n. of a city in Egypt, probably Daphne, not far from Pelusium, a frontier fortress of the Egyptians towards Syria. The Egyptian name signifies "head of the land," capital.

תַּחְפְּנֵיס p. n. of an Egyptian queen.

תַּחְפְּנֵס Ketib for תַּחְפַּנְחֵס.

תָּחַר (not used) to enclose, to lie firm round the body, probably only transf. from תָּרָה. From which:—

תַּחְרָא masc. a linen coat of mail or

habergeon; according to some, preparation for war, from חָרָה.

תַּחֲרָה see חָרָה.

תַּחְרֵעַ p.n.m. (artificer).

תַּחַשׁ (plur. תְּחָשִׁים) m. name of a certain animal, whose skin was variously used. The Biblical interpreters do not agree whether it is *tahash*, dolphin, badger, or seal.

תַּחַת (after the form of נַחַת from נוּחַ, קֶשֶׁת from קוּשׁ, שַׁחַת from שׁוּחַ; with suff. תַּחְתַּי, but also with suff. pl.) f. 1) orig. sinking, depth; next, the lower part, as an adv., under, below; the same is מִתַּחַת; under the tongue, under the lips, are used for: in the mouth; "I tremble under me," i.e. my feet are tottering; many verbs are construed with תַּחַת or מִתַּחַת to signify a downward motion or below something, even in a spiritual sense; with prefixes תַּחַת is used: (*a*) מִתַּחַת from under, signifying a removal from beneath an object; מִתַּחַת לְ beneath something; rarely in this sense לְמִתַּחַת לְ, and only in reply to the question, Whither? (*b*) אֶל תַּחַת under, below, in reply to the question, Where or Whither? 2) in the place of, instead; 3) p.n. of an encampment of the Israelites in the desert (lower place); 4) p.n. m. The root is תּוּחַ.

תְּחוֹת (with suff. תְּחוֹתוֹהִי) Aram. the same; for which also stands תְּחוֹת, which see.

תַּחְתִּי (pl. תַּחְתִּיִּים) adj. m. תַּחְתִּיָּה or תַּחְתִּית (pl. תַּחְתִּיּוֹת) f. the lower, under one, deep one; אֶרֶץ תַּחְתִּיּוֹת the depths of the earth, the lower regions; figur. in the mother's womb; בּוֹר תַּ׳ the deepest pit; תַּחְתִּיִּים the lowest chambers.

תִּיו see תָּו.

תִּיכוֹן (adj. m., תִּיכֹנָה (pl. תִּיכוֹנוֹת) fem. the middle one; fem. plur. the middle parts (of a building). This adj. is derived either from תָּוֶךְ or from another noun תִּיךְ.

תִּילוֹן (from נָתִילוֹן) p.n. m. (present, gift). The Ketib has תּוּלוֹן, with the same signification.

תֵּימָא (also תֵּמָא) p.n. of a country and people in the northern desert of Arabia, probably abbreviated from תֵּימָן.

תֵּימָן (situate in the south) p.n. of an unknown city; from which gent. תֵּימְנִי, which is not to be confounded with תֵּימָנִי.

תֵּימָן masc. (it is fem. only when it stands for רוּחַ תֵּימָן) 1) that which lies to the right, the south, southern district (comp. אָחוֹר), formed from יָמִין=יָמָן; תֵּימָנָה southward;

2) poetically for the south wind, as צָפוֹן for north-wind, in which case it is used as a fem.; 3) p.n. of a people; next, of a country in the east of Idumea (origin. south-country, southern); patron. in this sense is תֵּימָנִי.

תִּימָרָה (only plur. תִּימָרוֹת, but also תִּמָּרוֹת) f. a pillar, or column (of smoke) from תָּמַר, to be prominent. In prose עַמּוּד stands for it. The correct orthography is תִּמָּרָה.

תִּירוֹשׁ (also תִּרשׁ) m. that which is gotten from the fruit, i.e. must, new wine; also of the juice of grapes. The root is יָרַשׁ to gain, to get, to possess.

תִּירְיָא p.n. m. (fear, terror).

תִּירָס p.n. of a national tribe and country. Josephus, Jerome, and the Jerusalem Targum take it for Thrace, as the name also suggests.

תַּיִשׁ (pl. תְּיָשִׁים) a buck, a he-goat, from תּוּשׁ, equiv. to אוּשׁ, to be strong, powerful.

תֹּךְ (seldom *plene*) m. orig. cheating, usury; next, oppression, violence.

תָּכָה (Kal, not used) to lie down, to be encamped; hence Pu. תֻּכָּה (3 pl. תֻּכּוּ) to lie down לְרַגְלֶיךָ at the feet of some one.

תְּכוּנָה f. 1) a place, seat, from כּוּן; 2) arrangement, structure, preparation; 3) costliness, costly apparatus (comp. תַּבְנִית), derived from תָּכַן.

תֻּכִּי (only pl. תֻּכִּיִּים) m. a peacock; according to others, pheasant. The word is foreign.

תָּכַךְ (not used) origin. equiv. to the root in נָשַׁךְ to bite, but generally, to oppress, to spoil, to snatch away. In Aram. תְּכַךְ signifies to punish.

תְּכָכִים (only plur. תְּכָכִים) m. origin. usury; next, spoliage.

תָּכַל (not used) equiv. to שָׁחַל to peal, from which תְּכֵלֶת, which see.

תִּכְלָה (from כָּלָה) f. finishing, completion (of a matter).

תַּכְלִית (from כָּלָה) fem. 1) equiv. to תִּכְלָה completion, finishing: the completion of hatred, i.e. the utmost hostility; 2) the end, where something ceases or ends, the outmost.

תְּכֵלֶת fem. origin. equiv. to שְׁחֵלֶת mussel-shell, from תָּכַל; next, especially, the purple mussel with blue shell, from the juice of which the bluish or violet purple is made; transf. to bluish purple or thread or cloth coloured therewith.

תָּכַן equiv. to תָּקַן to put or place firmly, straight, just (also by weighing); next, to weigh, to prove, try, or test (the spirits, the hearts), Niph. נִתְכַּן to be levelled, made even, smooth (of a road), to be just, good (of actions); לֹא יִתָּכֵן דֶּרֶךְ י״י "the way of the Lord is not right (equal)," Ezek. 33:17, quoted, as said by the wicked. Pi. to establish, to fix; 2) to measure or mete out, to weigh out (synon. with שָׁקַל, מָדַד) to try, prove. Pu. to be weighed out, e.g. הַכֶּסֶף הַמְתֻכָּן the money weighed out.

תֹּכֶן m, 1) a task, a work measured out; next, measure generally, number, or quantity; 2) even place, p.n. of a place in the territory of Simeon.

תָּכְנִית f. 1) a measure, pattern, structure; next, an ornament, beautiful arrangement; 2) perfect in beauty or measure. The word is derived from תֹּכֶן.

תַּכְרִיךְ m. a white garment, a mantle, in modern Heb. תַּכְרִיכִים shrouds; from כָּרַךְ, which see.

תֵּל (with suff. תִּלָּהּ) m. a hill, a heap (either of stones or rubbish), from תָּלַל; תֵּל is used in the following compounds as a proper noun, תֵּל אָבִיב (hill of ripe ears) p.n. of a place in Mesopotamia, on the river Chaboras; תֵּל־חַרְשָׁא (hill of the wood) p.n. of a city in Babylonia; תֵּל־מֶלַח (salt hill) p.n. of a city in Babylonia; it also appears in תְּלַאשַּׂר, תְּלַשַּׂר (hill of Assur) p.n. of a city in Assyria; the same geographical form is also found in the Phenician, e.g. תֵּל בָּר (corn hill) *Tillibari*.

תָּלָא equiv. to תָּלָה to hang, to be suspended, e.g. of the life, i.e. to be in constant danger, fig. to be inclined, attached to something.

תְּלָאָה (from לָאָה) f. labour, trouble, distress; comp. תְּעָלָה from עָלָה.

תַּלְאוּבָה fem. dryness, drought, of a country, dearth; אֶרֶץ תַּל׳ land of dearth.

תְּלַאשַּׂר (also תְּלַשַּׂר the hill of Assur) p.n. of an Assyrian province, but cannot be defined.

תִּלְבֹּשֶׁת f. a garment, clothing. The root is לָבַשׁ.

תְּלַג (Aram.) masc. snow, equiv. to שֶׁלֶג Heb.

תִּגְלַת פּ׳ see **תִּגְלַת פִּלְאֶסֶר**.

תָּלָה to hang, to suspend, e.g. to hang on a tree, death punishment; also of the suspending of a shield, etc. Niphal pass. Piel, of the hanging up on something, construed with בְּ and עַל.

תְּלֻנָּה f. murmurings, from לוּן.

תָּלַח (not used, after the Aram.) to break, to dash to pieces.

תֶּלַח p.n. m. (breach).

תְּלִי (with suff. תֶּלְיְךָ) m. the quiver

or weapon, origin. that which is suspended at the side of the body.

תְּלִיתָי (Aram.) adj. masc. the third, formed from תְּלָת three.

I. תָּלַל to raise or heap up, used of something that is thrown up to make a heap; related is סָלַל.

II. תָּלַל orig. equiv. to סָלַל, זָלַל, to move to and fro, to shake, e.g. of locks of hair; transf. like זָלַל to throw away, to despise, to mock, especially in Hiph. and Hoph. where the ה of the Hiph. was adopted as a radical, and hence the formation of a secondary root הָתַל.

III. תָּלַל (not used) equiv. שָׁלַל to spoil, rob, plunder; from which תְּלָל.

I. תָּלַם adopted for תָּלַם, which, however, is uncertain, as the latter might have been formed from תֵּל.

II. תָּלַם (not used) to be bold, courageous, related to קְלַם in Aram., transf. to be daring, to rob; from which תַּלְמַי p.n.

תֶּלֶם (formed from תֵּל with the nominal formation ־ֶם, pl. תְּלָמִים, const. תַּלְמֵי) m. furrow-hill, the furrow is called גְּדוּד.

תַּלְמַי p.n.m. (the violent one), from תָּלַם II.

תַּלְמִיד (later) m. a disciple, a pupil; from לָמַד.

תָּלַע (not used) 1) equiv. to לָעַע to swallow, to lick off; next, to eat off, to destroy; 2) after the Arab. to stretch the neck out long; from which תּוֹלָע, and from this as a denom. Pu. תֻּלַּע to be clothed in crimson. The p.n. תּוֹלָע is from תָּלַע 2.

תָּלַף (not used) equiv. to לְפַף in Aram. to entwine, to join, to link. From which:—

תַּלְפִּית (only pl. תַּלְפִּיּוֹת) f. terrace, so called from its being in rows; according to others, an armoury where weapons were hung up, as on the turrets and walls of eastern cities.

תְּלַאשַּׁר see תְּלַשַּׂר.

תְּלָת (Aram.) cardinal number, fem., תְּלָתָא, תְּלָתָה m. three, like the Heb. שָׁלוֹשׁ, plur. תְּלָתִין thirty. The form תַּלְתָּא belongs to תַּלְתִּי.

תַּלְתִּי (only def. תַּלְתָּא for תַּלְתָּאָה) Aram. adj. m. the third (in rank) who follows the מִשְׁנֶה; subst. the third in rank.

תְּלִתַי (Aram.) adj. m. the same.

תַּלְתַּל (only pl. תַּלְתַּלִּים) m. lock of hair, so called on account of its motion, origin. waving branch, like זַלְזַל.

תָּם adj. m., תַּמָּה f. orig. complete, finished; next, perfect, just, upright, pious, innocent, blameless, used in both genders as a subst.; as an abstract, innocence. Root תָּמַם.

תַּם (Aram.) equiv. to שָׁם Heb., with ה, תַּמָּה there.

תֹּם (once תּוֹם, before makkaph תָּם־, with suff. תֻּמִּי) m. orig. completion, perfection; כְּתֻמָּם in their fulness, i. e. complete; hence, 1) like שָׁלוֹם, of a similar signif. in the original, happiness, peace, prosperity; בְּעֶצֶם תֻּמּוֹ in the midst of his prosperity; 2) in a moral sense, integrity, innocence, piety, with or without לֵב; הָלַךְ בְּתֹם to walk in innocence; 3) (only pl. תֻּמִּים, connected with אוּרִים) truth, next specially, revelation. The root is תָּמַם.

תֵּמָא see תֵּימָא.

תָּמַהּ (fut. יִתְמַהּ) to wonder, to be astonished, to be amazed at (עַל) something; often, with the subsignification of fear or terror, to gaze at one another with amazement. Hith. הִתַּמַּהּ to wonder, to be astonished.

תְּמַהּ (Aram.) the same. From which:—

תְּמַהּ (pl. תִּמְהִין, def. תִּמְהַיָּא, with suff. תִּמְהוֹהִי) Aram. masc. that which is astonishing, wonder.

תִּמָּהוֹן (const. תִּמְהוֹן) m. fear, terror, from תָּמַהּ.

תַּמּוּז masc. name of a Syrian deity, which was worshipped by mourning women among the Hebrews. It is also the name of the fourth month of the ecclesiastical year of the Jews.

תְּמוֹל (abbreviated from אֶתְמוֹל, —מוֹל, in which the etymology is also to be found) adv. yesterday, connected with שִׁלְשֹׁם; once for אִישׁ תְּמוֹל a man of yesterday.

תְּמוּנָה (derived from מִין) f. a form, figure, likeness, image.

תְּמוּרָה (from מוּר) f. changing, exchange; concrete, that which is changed or exchanged; 2) in a spiritual sense, recompense, restitution, compensation. See מוּר.

תְּמוּתָה f. death; בֶּן תְּ׳ son of death, i. e. one condemned to die. Root מוּת.

תָּמַז (not used) belonging to תַּמּוּז, which see.

תֶּמַח (probably equiv. to שָׂמַח) p. n. masc. (joy).

תָּמִיד m. 1) orig. continuance, constancy, from מוּד to extend (especially of time); אִישׁ תָּמִיד a man of constancy, i.e. hired constantly; continual offering, i.e. every day, morning and evening; continual bread, i.e. the shewbread that was always lying on the table in the temple; 2) adv. continually, constantly, always.

תְּמִים (contracted from תְּאוֹמִים) m. pl. the double ones.

תָּמִים (const. תְּמִים, plur. תְּמִימִים, const. תְּמִימֵי) adj. masc., תְּמִימָה (pl. ־מוֹת) f. in all significations of תָּם, orig. complete, perfect, whole (in reference to extent); next, 1) complete, both physically, i.e. without blemish, sound; and spiritually, i.e. perfect in knowledge, where תְּמִים stands in the state of const. to the following subst.; 2) in a moral sense, i.e. honest, innocent, irreproachable, pious, and as a subst. in this sense, honesty, integrity, truth, e.g. to walk in innocence, in integrity, to give truth, i.e. to utter truth.

תָּמַךְ (particip. תּוֹמֵךְ equiv. to תּוֹמִיךְ, fut. יִתְמֹךְ) to support, to hold, to keep up, often construed with בְּ or the accus.; related to סָמַךְ; transf. to assist, help; next, to hold fast, to seize, with the secondary sense of supporting oneself; to hold together (of two objects), so that the one supports the other. Niph. pass. to hold one another; as to the interchanging of ס and ת, comp. נָתַךְ and נָסַךְ, תָּמַר and סָמַר, חָתַם and חָסַם, רָתַק Talmud, רָסַק, נָגַס and נָכַת and others.

תָּמַל (erroneously taken as belonging to תְּמוֹל) see תְּמוֹל and אֶתְמוֹל.

תָּמַם (3 pers. תַּם, 3 pl. תַּמּוּ, but 1 plur. תַּמְנוּ, inf. תֹּם, before makkaph תָּם־, with suff. תֻּמִּי, fut. יִתֹּם; transf., apoc. יִתַּם, intrans. יֵתַם, seldom יִתַּם) 1) transf. to make something complete, to complete, finish, conclude (a deed), synon. with שָׁלַם, כָּלַל; transf. to bring to an end, to remove entirely, to come to an end, to vanish, in an intransitive sense, as it were; 2) intrans. to be complete, finished, at an end; transf. to be complete, or in full number, to be finished, consumed, to cease, especially of thorough destruction; fig. to be honest, perfect, irreproachable. Hiph. הֵתַם (1 pret. הֲתִמֹּתִי, 3 plur. הֵתַמּוּ, inf. with suff. הֲתִימְךָ for הֲתִמְּךָ, fut. יַתֵּם) 1) to prepare for eating (meat), to do something perfectly, fully, to cause something to cease, to remove it entirely; 2) in a spiritual sense, to carry out a plan, to make one's walk perfect, irreproachable; 3) to count up, to pay off. Comp. שִׁלֵּם in this sense. Hith. הִתַּמֵּם to conduct oneself honestly, innocently towards (עִם) some one.

תֵּימָן see תֵּמָן.

תִּמְנָה (portion, possession, from מָנָה) p.n. of a city in the Philistine territory, assigned to the tribe of Dan; with ה finis תִּמְנָתָה, gent. תִּמְנִי.

תֵּימָנִי see תֵּמָנִי.

תִּמְנִי see תִּמְנָה.

תִּמְנָע 1) p.n. f. (modesty); 2) (the same) p.n. of an Edomite tribe.

תִּמְנָתָה see תִּמְנָה.

תִּמְנַת חֶרֶס (sunny-place) p.n. of a city in the mountain of Ephraim, for which also תִּמְנַת סֶרַח occurs, which may be a transposition from the former.

תֶּמֶס m. dissolving, melting; used of the snail, which in its course throws off a slimy matter. Root מָסַס.

תָּמַר (not used) equiv. to סָמַר to rise prominently, to stare, to stand on end.

תָּמָר (pl. תְּמָרִים) masc. 1) palm, so called on account of its rising like a pillar; height; עִיר הַתְּמָרִים palm city, a designation for Jericho; 2) (palm district) p.n. of a district on the southern boundary of Palestine; 3) in Ketib for תַּדְמֹר; 4) p.n. f. (the slender one).

תֹּמֶר m. 1) palm; 2) pillar.

תִּמֹּר (pl. תִּמֹּרִים) m. equiv. to תִּמֹּרָה.

תִּמֹּרָה (pl. —רוֹת) palm-branch, but only in an architectural sense, i.e. an ornament in the shape of a palm branch.

תַּמְרוּק (pl. תַּמְרֻקִים) m. 1) cleansing, purification, from מָרַק; 2) the ointment for purification; 3) fig. means of cure or improvement.

I. תַּמְרוּר (pl. תַּמְרוּרִים) m. bitterness, as an adv. bitterly, from מָרַר.

II. תַּמְרוּר (pl. תַּמְרוּרִים) a prominent pillar or post, as a guide, from תָּמַר.

תַּמְרִיק m. Ketib for תַּמְרוּק in sig. 3.

תַּן (pl. תַּנִּים, once after the Aram. form תַּנִּין) masc. a kind of jackal, or generally, beast of the desert having a wailing voice, and thus almost equiv. to אִי; according to others, dragon, or a species of serpent; and according to others again, a sea monster; which, however, it is difficult to determine. The root is תָּנַן to stretch along, hence used of a slender, stretching animal.

תָּנָא to dwell, belongs to תַּנּוֹת, see תַּנָּה.

תְּנָא (Aram.) equiv. to שָׁנָה Heb. to repeat.

I. תָּנָה (equiv. to תָּנַן, יָתַן, נָתַן) to hand, to reach, to award, to present, to distribute gifts; only Hosea 8.10, יִתְנוּ. Hiph. almost in the same sense, Hosea 8:9. Probably, however, both forms in Hosea, הִתְנוּ and יִתְנוּ, stand for הִזְנוּ and יִזְנוּ, in the sense of, to follow whoredom, ז and ת interchanging. This signif. is certain in the derivative אֶתְנָה.

II. תָּנָה (Kal, not used) to relate, to recite, comp. שָׁנָה to learn, study (in modern Heb.), and תְּנֵי Aram. Pi. תִּנָּה to praise, to celebrate, construed with acc. and לְ, and somewhat parallel with הִלֵּל.

תַּנָּה (only pl. תַּנּוֹת) fem. dwelling place (in the desert); according to others, a jackal, thus as a fem. form of תַּן. In the first case, it is to be derived from תָּנָא to dwell, or from נָאָה (thus תַּנָּה equiv. to תַּנְאָה); in the second case, it would be only a secondary form from תַּן.

תְּנוּאָה fem. forsaking, withdrawing, enmity; from נוא, which see.

תְּנוּבָה fem. fruit, produce, increase; from נוב.

תְּנוּךְ (const. תְּנוּךְ) masc. the tip (of the ear), not derived from תָּנַךְ but from נוך, which see.

תְּנוּמָה f. sleep, slumber (particularly from laziness or inactivity); from נום.

תְּנוּפָה fem. 1) moving to and fro, waving or shaking of the hand (as a threat), but especially the waving of joints of the animal of sacrifice or other offerings, a ceremonial of consecration; in this sense, הֵנִיף, הֵנִיף תְּנוּפָה; 2) tumult, movement of battle, the orig. signif. being moving to and fro.

תַּנּוּר m. a place where the fire burns, a fire-oven, formed from נור with the preformative תַּ.

תַּנְחוּמִים (only pl. תַּנְחוּמִים) m. consolation, comfort, pity, compassion; from נָחַם.

תַּנְחוּמֶת (in signif. 2, תַּנְחוּמוֹת) 1) p. n. m (comfort); 2) f. comfort, consolation, compassion.

תַּנִּים as a sing. see תַּנִּין.

תַּנִּין (once תַּנִּים, pl. תַּנִּינִים) masc. a serpent, a crocodile, a dragon, whale, shark, so called from its slender, stretching form. It is distinguished from תַּן, the former being a sea animal, whilst the latter is generally a beast of the desert.

תִּנְיָן (def. ־יָנָה) Aram. adj. m. two, from תְּנָה. From which:—

תִּנְיָנוּת (Aram.) adv. a second time.

תָּנַךְ belongs to תְּנוּךְ, see נוך.

תָּנַן (not used) 1) to stretch out, stretch forth, to extend, e.g. of serpents and kindred animals; next, to be slender, thin; 2) to hand, to reach (related to נָתַן,

תִּנָּה ,יִתֵּן, etc.), to deliver; 3) to extend somewhere, i.e. to dwell; 4) to extend (of time), i.e. to endure, last, which signif. is found in יָתַן, to which it is related. A root תָּנַן has been erroneously adopted for אַתּוּן Aram., since the former is to be derived from אֵשׁ=אֶתֶת to burn.

תִּנְשֶׁמֶת fem. 1) a species of lizard; according to some, a chameleon; according to others, a mole, from נָשַׁם to gasp for breath; 2) an aquatic bird, a species of heron or a sea-gull; according to others, the pelican. Root נָשַׁם.

תָּעַב (Kal, not used) to abominate, to abhor, to loathe, comp. תָּאַב in signif. 2. Pi. תִּעֵב to abominate, to loathe, to despise, reject, to make to be abhorred, to pollute (of persons or things); the form מְתָעֵב Isa. 49:7, is an abstract noun in the state of const. instead of מְתָעָב, in the sense of object of abomination (of the nations). Hiph. הִתְעִיב to make abominable or shameful, i.e. their actions, comp. הֵרַע ,הִשְׁחִית. Niph. to be despised, rejected, abominated, in abhorrence. The root in תָּ־עַב is identical with עָב (עוּב).

תָּעָה (fut. יִתְעֶה, apoc. יֵתַע) 1) to err, wander, about (without any definite object), with בְּ, in some place; with acc. to wander through some place; with מִן ,מֵעַל or מֵאַחֲרֵי used in a spiritual sense, to err from the right path, to apostatize or backslide from God; in this sense it is used sometimes as a subst., e.g. תֹּעֵי רוּחַ ,תֹּעֵי לֵבָב those that err in the mind or heart; transf. in this sense to giddiness, the reeling or staggering of the drunkard, תָּ׳ מִן־הַשֵּׁכָר to be giddy, to stagger, or to reel from strong drink; 2) like אָבַד to be forsaken, abandoned, solitary, as a consequence of wandering about. Niph. 1) to err about (of the drunkard); 2) to be in error, deceived; נִתְעָה the deceived, deluded one. Hiph. הִתְעָה, fut. יַתְעֶה, apoc. יַתַע; 1) to mislead, lead astray, seduce or entice (to idolatry), to cause to reel (the drunkard), to cause to go astray from (מִן) something; 2) to go astray, in a spiritual sense; comp. תָּעַע.

תֹּעוּ p.n. m. (the erring one), once for which תֹּעִי (the same).

תְּעוּדָה f. that which is fixed, established and common (see עוּד); hence, custom, manner, habit; next, like תּוֹרָה law, testimony.

תְּעוּפָה (from עוּף, after the form תְּנוּפָה, תְּאוּן ,תְּבוּן from נוּף ,בּוּן ,און;

with ה finis (תְּעוּפָה) masc. dark, gloomy, the same as עֵיפָה. See עוּף.

תְּעוּפָה see תְּעוּף.

תָּעַל (not used) to hollow out, to dig out, related to שָׁעַל and שָׁאַל, from which:—

I. תְּעָלָה (after the form בְּרֵכָה, const. תְּעָלַת, pl. with suff. תְּעָלֹתֶיהָ) f. a trench, a canal, a water-conduit, from תָּעַל, but not from עָלָה.

II. תְּעָלָה f. a bandage, a plaster, for a wound, from עָלָה, comp. הֶעֱלָה אֲרֻכָה in this sense.

תַּעֲלוּל (only pl. —לִים) m. fate, destiny, especially the evil one, from עָלַל to roll, as in modern language, "the wheel of fortune," comp. סִבָּה; hence Isa. 3:4, and ill fate or cruelty, abstr. for concr. the cruel ones (Author. Vers. babes) shall rule over them; according to others, תַּעֲלוּל signifies a babe, a boy.

תַּעֲלֻמָה (pl. —מוֹת) f. that which is hidden, concealed, hidden things, secret, from עָלַם.

תַּעֲנוּג (pl. —גִים and —וֹת) m. origin. pleasure, enjoyment, delight, desire, luxuriousness, "the children of thy delight," i.e. who are thy delight.

תַּעֲנִית f. self-mortification or chastisement, fasting, from עָנָה.

תַּעְנָךְ (also תַּעַנַךְ; sandy soil) p.n. of a city in Manasseh, near Megiddo, on this side of the Jordan.

תָּעַע (Kal, not used) equiv. to תָּעָה to err or wander about; hence Pilpel תִּעְתַּע to stagger, to reel (of the drunkard); according to others, to mock, to deride; also, to deceive. Hith. הִתַּעְתֵּעַ to conduct oneself as a drunkard, to stagger, to reel; also, to act foolishly towards (בְּ) some one; according to others, to mock, deride.

תַּעֲצֻמָה f. strength, might, equiv. to עֹצֶם, See עָצַם.

תָּעַר (not used) equiv. to שָׁעַר to split, divide, cut off. From which:—

תַּעַר (with suff. תַּעְרִי) m. 1) a sharp knife, either for shaving (razor), or the writer's knife תַּעַר הַסֹּפֵר, probably used to sharpen the point of his calamus; 2) sheath (of a sword), from תָּעַר to divide.

תַּעֲרוּבָה f. pledge, security, surety, from עָרַב I.; next abstr. pledging, the sons of pledging, i. e. hostages.

תַּעְתֻּעַ (pl. —עִים) m. erring, deceit; hence figur. idolatry.

תֹּף (pl. תֻּפִּים) m. 1) tabret, timbrel, or kettle-drum, from תָּפַף to push, to strike, to beat; 2) a kind of jewel-casket, so called on account of its similarity to a timbrel.

תִּפְאָרָה but not תִּפְאֶרֶת (with suff.

(תִּפְאַרְתּ) f. 1) beauty, ornament, of vessels, garments, and articles of taste; next, splendour in outward appearance; 2) in a spiritual sense, glory, honor, fame, praise, greatness; transf. as a concrete to the object of glory or praise, the seat of majesty and glory (the ark of the covenant). Root פָּאַר.

תַּפּוּחַ (plur. ־חִים, const. ־חֵי) m. 1) origin. fragrant fruit, from פּוּחַ to be fragrant; next, specially, an apple, including the whole kind, as citrons, peaches, apricots, etc.; תַּפּוּחֵי זָהָב golden apples, oranges or apricots; 2) apple-tree; 3) (orchard) p.n. of several cities.

תְּפוּצָה (plur. ־צוֹת) fem. dispersion, scattering (of a people).

תֻּפִּין (with the nominal formation ־ִין, comp. the same termination in סַכִּין, פָּנִין, קָצִין and others, pl. c. (תֻּפִּינֵי) m. that which is baked or dried, from תּוּף to dry, from which root תֹּפֶת is also to be derived.

תָּפַל (Kal, not used) to overspread with paint, to overlay, from טָפַל in the origin. signif.; next, in a spiritual sense, to deceive. Hith. הִתַּפֵּל to act covertly, falsely, perversely.

תָּפֵל m. lime, whitewash, used for the walls; 2) anything soft, sticky; also, unseasoned, unsavoury; fig. insipidity, absurdity, foolishness, or that which is disgusting, despicable, loathsome.

תֹּפֶל (chalky ground) p. n. of a place in the Arabian desert.

תִּפְלָה f. equiv. to תָּפֵל in a figurative signification, that which is absurd, insipid, foolish.

תְּפִלָּה (pl. ־לּוֹת) fem. 1) intercession, prayer, generally; נָשָׂא תְ׳, הִתְפַּלֵּל תְ׳ to recite prayer = to pray; 2) a peculiar kind of hymn or psalm, the distinctive element of which cannot now be defined. Root פָּלַל.

תִּפְלֶצֶת f. origin. equiv. to מִפְלֶצֶת, fear, terror, from פָּלַץ.

תִּפְסַח (ford) p. n. of a considerable city on the western bank of the Euphrates, Thapsacus. The root is פָּסַח.

תָּפַף (Kal, not used) to smite, to beat, to strike, e. g. the tabret, or any musical instrument; to strike or beat on the breast; hence Po. תּוֹפֵף to beat upon (עַל) the heart or breast. The root is also found in דָּפַק, נָדַף, etc. The Kal תָּפַף to beat the timbrel, from which pl. fem. תּוֹפְפוֹת, is only a denom. from תֹּף.

תָּפַר (fut. יִתְפֹּר) to sew, join together; hence Piel, to sew fast together (garments, coverings).

תָּפַשׂ (fut. יִתְפֹּשׂ) 1) to seize, to lay hold of, construed with בְּ or acc.; hence, to catch, to take prisoners, to conquer (cities); 2) to hold fast or firm, of things not yet possessed; handle, manage, of things already possessed; to handle the bow, the sickle; to keep in possession (a town), to follow (the law); 3) to seize, with the sub-signification of hurting, injuring, e.g. to take the name of God (in vain), i.e. to swear falsely by His name; 4) to set, enchase, e.g. to inlay stones with metal; תָּפוּשׂ זָהָב inlaid or overlaid with gold. Niph. to be taken prisoner, to be conquered, to be caught, captured, seized. Pi. to seize (frequently). In modern Heb. תָּפַס.

תֹּפֶת (formed from תּוּף, after the form בֹּשֶׁת) f. 1) place of burning, stake, funeral pile, partly for burning dead bodies, and partly for carrying children through the fire for the worship of Moloch; 2) with the article, denoting the place, in the valley of Hinnom, where the abominable worship of Moloch took place; 3) fig. terror, abhorrence, loathing, from the name of the place of הַתֹּפֶת, which was a spot of terrible abomination.

תָּפְתֶּה (formed from תֹּפֶת) m. place of burning (dead bodies), stake, funeral pile. The termination is as in בָּשְׁתָּה from בֹּשֶׁת.

תְּפַת (not used) Aram. to decide, judge, related to שָׁפַט. In both words the root is פַּת, פַּט, which has several analogies in the language.

תִּפְתָּי (def. pl. תִּפְתָּיֵא, after the Syriac manner) Aram. masc. judge, arbitrator.

תָּקָא (not used) to fear (after the Arabic), from which אֶלְתְּקֵא.

תָּקְהַת p. n. m. (obedience).

תִּקְוָה (const. תִּקְוַת, with suff. תִּקְוָתִי) f. 1) a cord, thread, string, from קָוָה, in the signif. of binding, tying; 2) hope, expectation, comp. the verb קָוָה; "the prisoners of hope," i.e. the hoping prisoners; 3) p. n. m. (expectation), for which once תָּקְהַת, and Keri תּוֹקְהַת occurs.

תְּקוּמָה fem. standing, existing, from קוּם. According to others, in the passage, Levit. 36:37, withstanding, resistance.

תְּקוֹמֵם m. an enemy, adversary, for מִתְקוֹמֵם, or abbreviated from the same.

תְּקוֹעַ (pitching of a tent or settlement, from תָּקַע to fix, to settle on a certain place) p. n. of a village south-west of Bethlehem.

The desert bordering on it is called מִדְבַּר תְּקוֹעַ.

תְּקוּפָה (pl. ־פוֹת) f. going round, circuit, revolution of the sun, expiration or end of the year, from קוּף, which see.

תַּקִּיף adj. m. strong, mighty; only Ecc. 6:10, if הִתְקִיף is not the reading.

תַּקִּיף (plur. ־פִין) Aram. adj. masc., תַּקִּיפָה f. the same.

תְּקַל (Aram.) to weigh out, equiv. to שָׁקַל Hebrew, particip. pass. תְּקִל weighed, balanced, from which part. a present tense is formed, to be weighed in the balance.

תָּקַן (later inf. const. תְּקֹן) equiv. to תָּכַן to be straight, just, upright. The root is found again in קָנֶה, כֵּן. Pi. תִּקֵּן to make straight or even (that which is crooked), to form, establish, arrange, prepare, adorn, to set in order (proverbs).

תְּקַן (Aram.) the same. Hoph. (after the Heb. manner), to be founded, established, to be re-established or restored (of a kingdom).

תָּקַע (fut. יִתְקַע) origin. to pierce, prickle (from תָּ־קַע, related with קַע, יָקַע, and נָקַע); hence, 1) to strike into something (into the hand), either as a sign of joy, or of derision, or of mutual friendship; next, to pledge oneself for (לְ) some one, even with omission of כַּף; to drive into the wall (a nail), to pitch a tent (by driving in the tent pins), to thrust into the body (a sword or spear), to fling (into the sea); 2) of wind instruments, to blow with great force, either the trumpet or the horn. Niph. 1) to pledge oneself by the shaking or clapping of hands; 2) to be blown, of the trumpet.

תֵּקַע m. blowing (with a trumpet).

תָּקַף (fut. יִתְקֹף) to overpower, to prevail over, or oppress a person. Related is אָכַף, according to the connection of פ״א with פ״ת. See אנשׁ. The Hiph. הִתְקִיף, Eccles. 6:10, is only a denom. from תַּקִּיף, in the sense of being mighty, powerful.

תְּקֵף (Aram.) the same, but in a bad sense, to grow frivolous, haughty. Pa. to make strong, to confirm.

תֹּקֶף (with suff. תָּקְפּוֹ) masc. power, might, strength, authority, respect.

תְּקֹף (def. תָּקְפָּא) Aram. m. the same.

תֹּר a turtle dove. See תּוֹר.

תַּרְאֲלָה p.n. of a city in Benjamin.

תַּרְבּוּת f. increase, offspring, brood; from רָבָה, which see.

תַּרְבִּית f. increase, interest, usury; it is a milder term than נֶשֶׁךְ; according to tradition נֶשֶׁךְ signifies usury on loans of money only, but תַּרְבִּית includes loans of kind, etc.

תִּרְגַּל as a verbal form, see under רָגַל.

תִּרְגֹּלֶת f. leading, conducting, from רָגַל.

תִּרְגֻּם as a verbal form, the same as תְּרַגֵּם, see under רָגַם.

תַּרְדֵּמָה f. a deep sleep, fig. inactivity, indolence, sluggishness, apathy.

תִּרְהָקָה p.n. of one of the kings of Ethiopia and Upper Egypt, which name has been found on inscriptions in Thebes.

תְּרוּמָה (pl. תְּרוּמוֹת) f. 1) that which is brought, delivered, a gift, present, comp. מַשְׂאֵת, from נָשָׂא; hence אִישׁ תְּרוּמוֹת a man of presents, i.e. who receives bribes; 2) especially a gift to the priest and the temple, and all offerings of that kind, in which sense the verb הֵרִים is especially used, signifying "heaving," complete תְּרוּמַת יָד; שְׂדֵי תְּרוּמוֹת fields of heave offerings, or of the first and best fruit; 3) a heave offering, so called from the ceremonial of heaving or lifting it up. The root is רוּם; see Hiph. under that root.

תְּרוּמִיָּה adj. f. formed from תְּרוּמִי that which appertains to a heave offering.

תְּרוּעָה f. a cry of jubilee, shouting, especially of the sounding of a trumpet, a shout for battle; the sounding of the horn or trumpet, and day or feast of sounding the trumpet, are used in scripture to designate the new year of the Hebrews, or the day of memorial.

תְּרוּפָה f. healing, from רוּף, equiv. to רָפָא to heal, which see.

תָּרַז (not used) equiv. to אָרַז, תָּרַשׁ, to be hard, firm. From which:—

תִּרְזָה f. a species of strong tree, the holm oak, scarlet oak, or holly.

תָּרַח (not used) to last, endure (of time), or to appoint a time.

תֶּרַח 1) p.n. m. (endurance); 2) p.n. of an encampment of the Israelites in the desert.

תִּרְחֲנָה p.n. m. (probably security, hostage, from רָחַן, equiv. to רָהַן in modern Heb.).

תְּרֵין (const. תְּרֵי) Aram. a cardinal number, תַּרְתֵּין f. two.

תָּרְמָה fem. a lie, deceit, artfulness, from רָמָה, which see.

תַּרְמִית f. lying, artfulness, deception, cheating, in the Ketib תַּרְמוּת from רִמָּה to deceive, to cheat, or to bring to ruin.

תָּרַן (not used) equiv. to אָרַן to be firm, strong, or to rise prominently. From which:—

תֹּרֶן (with suff. תָּרְנָם) m. 1) the mast

of a ship, so called on account of its resembling a pillar, related is אֹרֶן and of similar etymology; כֵּן הַתֹּרֶן stand, base, or foot of the mast; 2) pole, standard, flag, or banner, used as a signal on the tops of mountains.

תְּרַע (Aram.) m. equiv. to the Heb. שַׁעַר gate, door, port, entrance (of a palace).

תָּרָע (def. pl. תָּרָעַיָּא) Aram. m. door or gatekeeper, porter. The root is common and for תְּרַע. It corresponds with the Hebrew שֹׁעֵר, from שַׁעַר, after the form of מַלָּח.

תִּרְעָה (port, gate) p.n. of an unknown place; from which gent. תִּרְעָתִי, one from תִּרְעָה.

תַּרְעֵלָה f. drunkenness, intoxication, reeling, staggering; hence the prophetic terms, the cup of trembling, the wine of trembling, signifying confusion and calamity.

תִּרְעָתִי see תִּרְעָה.

תָּרַף (not used) equiv. to טָרַף in the signification of feeding, nourishing, to maintain or sustain by provisions. From which:—

תָּרָף (after the form חָכָם, but only in the pl. תְּרָפִים) m. origin. the sustainer, transf. to a kind of penates or household gods, which were looked upon as sustainers of the family, though later they sank to the character of oracle images.

תִּרְצָה (pleasantness, grace, from רָצָה) 1) p.n. f.; 2) p.n. of a city in the kingdom of Israel.

תָּרַשׁ (not used) to be strong, firm, hard. Comp. תֹּרֶן and others.

תֶּרֶשׁ (foreign) p.n. of a eunuch at the Persian court.

תַּרְשִׁישׁ (with ה finis שָׁה—) 1) p.n. of a city and country in Spain, probably Tartessus, the great commercial mart of the Phenicians; the ships of Tarshish are those which carried merchandise to Tartessus; 2) p.n. of a precious stone, probably from Tartessus, if the name is not derived from the root תָּרַשׁ to be hard; the commentators differ as to the speciality of the stone; according to Josephus, it is the chrysolite, the modern topaz; according to others (Auth. Ver.), a beryl; and some render it, amber.

תִּרְשָׁתָא (always with the article) a surname or title of a pacha or stadtholder פֶּחָה, and also that of Nehemiah and Ezra. The word is of Persian origin.

תַּרְתָּן (probably of Persian origin, tall of stature) p.n. of an Assyrian general under the Assyrian kings Sargon and Sennacherib.

תַּרְתָּק p.n. of an idol of the Avites (after a Pehlevian etymology, it signifies prince of darkness).

תְּשֻׁאָה (pl. —אוֹת) f. noise, clamour, raging, crying, shouting; from שׁוּא.

תִּשְׁבֶּה (captivity) p.n. of a city in the territory of Naphtali. From which gent. תִּשְׁבִּי the Tishbite, a surname of Elijah.

תַּשְׁבֵּץ m. cloth worked in cells or checquers, also embroidery; hence, כְּתֹנֶת תַּ׳ a coat of chequered cloth, or embroidery, or braided work.

תְּשׁוּבָה fem. 1) return; 2) answer, reply. In modern Heb. repentance, penitence. See שׁוּב.

תְּשׂוּמֶה (const. —מֶת for —מַת) fem. that which is laid down, deposited, synon. with פִּקָּדוֹן; but it is also possible that תְּשׂוּמֶת stands for תְּשֻׂמֶת, after the form נְחֹשֶׁת.

תְּשׁוּעָה f. help, deliverance, salvation, from שׁוּעַ equiv. to יָשַׁע.

תְּשׁוּקָה f. desire, longing (of a woman after man). The root is שׁוּק, which see.

תְּשׁוּרָה f. present, gift offered, from שׁוּר in the sense of delivering, offering.

תְּשִׁיעִי adj. m. (from תֵּשַׁע), תְּשִׁיעִית f. the ninth.

תֵּשַׁע (const. תְּשַׁע) cardinal number f., תִּשְׁעָה (c. תִּשְׁעַת) m. nine; sometimes, also, for the ordinal number, the ninth; the pl. תִּשְׁעִים signifies ninety. The etymology is not to be traced to a verbal root.

תַּתְּנַי (foreign) p. n. of a Persian governor; according to the Persian it signifies, present.

WERTHEIMER AND CO., PRINTERS, CIRCUS PLACE, FINSBURY CIRCUS.

Printed in the USA
CPSIA information can be obtained
at www.ICGtesting.com
LVHW050346261023
761875LV00030B/30